LAW SCHOOL ADVISORY BOARD

CO-CHAIRS

Howard P. Fink
Isadore & Ida Topper Professor of Law
Ohio State University
College of Law

Stephen A. Saltzburg
Class of 1962 Professor of Law
University of Virginia
School of Law

MEMBERS

Charles B. Craver
Professor of Law
George Washington University
National Law Center

Jane C. Ginsburg
Associate Professor of Law
Columbia University
School of Law

Edward J. Imwinkelried
Professor of Law
University of California at Davis
School of Law

Daniel R. Mandelker
Howard A. Stamper Professor of Law
Washington University
School of Law

Mark V. Tushnet
Professor of Law
Georgetown University
Law Center

MURRAY ON CONTRACTS

MURRAY ON CONTRACTS

Third Edition

JOHN EDWARD MURRAY, JR.

President
Professor of Law
Duquesne University

THE MICHIE COMPANY
Law Publishers
CHARLOTTESVILLE, VIRGINIA

PREFACE

It is difficult to decide the correct moment for a revision of any textbook, particularly a book dealing with contract law. Sixteen years have elapsed since the last edition of this volume. When that edition appeared, the revision of the Restatement of Contracts was underway, but the final version would not appear for several more years. Courts would require more years to begin their assimilation of the Second Restatement. Meanwhile, they continued to struggle with the contract law of the Uniform Commercial Code. A great deal of scholarship in contract law has appeared since the last edition, including my own efforts to contribute more refined analyses to this increasingly complex area. The appearance of the last edition coincided with the publication of what has become a famous little volume entitled *The Death of Contract,* which, itself, inspired a large volume of scholarship questioning the historical, analytical and philosophical bases of what is sometimes captioned neoclassical contract law. That scholarly discussion continues apace and reveals the critical importance of the concept of contract in society. The relation between contract law and economics has resulted in considerable literature and has, itself, been attacked as a model of existing hierarchical structure.

The mountain of new case law and scholarship required much more than a revision of the Second Edition. As those familiar with the Second Edition will quickly discover, the book is completely rewritten in the Third Edition. Hundreds of new cases and citations to new authority are found in this edition, but the increased size of the volume is due principally to the necessity of expanding the analyses of virtually every aspect of modern contract law. The conventional wisdom of 1974 contract law was based upon certain historical and analytical constructs. That wisdom has now become history and must be understood in its historical context if current judicial and scholarly analyses are to be understood. It is not enough to provide a narrative of the new case law and of the Second Restatement or Uniform Commercial Code provisions which have such an overwhelming influence on modern contract doctrine. Critical analyses must be included to provide the student with the insights necessary to gain a comprehensive view of the subject. Statutory modifications of neoclassical contract doctrine beyond the Uniform Commercial Code must also be considered and analyzed critically. Particular attention must be paid to those areas of contract law which have caused the greatest difficulty for courts, scholars and students of contract law. To accomplish these purposes within the confines of even a substantially expanded volume has proven extremely difficult. Whether I have succeeded must await the judgment of those who use this book. My single regret is that the subject is so vast that a single volume or even a multiple volume treatment of the subject necessarily leaves certain matters for another day.

In this edition many of the sections have been divided into captioned subdivisions so that the reader may be more easily directed to topical discussions within the sections. Citation tables to Restatement and Uniform Commercial Code sections as well as a table of cases have been continued along with an even more expansive index. It is the content itself, however, which is designed to provide the user with a modern, comprehensive analysis of the complex tapestry of contract law.

Finally, as this revision was nearing completion, the United Nations Convention on contracts for the International Sale of Goods (CISG) was ratified by eleven nations, including the United States. Eight more nations have since ratified this Convention which governs international contracts for the sale of goods, and it is more than likely that every major and many minor trading nations throughout the world will follow this trend. The inclusion of CISG throughout this volume would have been entirely premature. At the same time, it is essential for any lawyer, judge or other student of contract law to be aware of CISG. To meet that need, an appendix containing the text of the Convention has been included. The final chapter provides an introduction to CISG and compares its key provisions with the Uniform Commercial Code and other principles of American contract law.

Those who have taught me contract law are many indeed. I number among them thousands of judicial opinions and innumerable scholarly efforts that have guided me to a better understanding of this wonderful addiction, contract law. I take this occasion, however, to mention two scholars who have had a pervasive influence on my work, Arthur Linton Corbin and Karl Nickerson Llewellyn. Their insights over the years have proven most valuable to me in my pursuit of the best approximation of truth of which I am capable in this splendid arena. Beyond scholarly assistance, it is important to state another truth, to wit, that none of this would have been possible absent the assistance and support of my wife, Isabelle. Finally, I dedicate this work to my grandchildren, Jonathan, Jennifer, Timothy, Jessica, Katherine, and Kerri Ann, none of whom were born when the last edition of this work appeared.

John E. Murray, Jr.

Pittsburgh
April 1990

SUMMARY TABLE OF CONTENTS

TABLE OF CONTENTS

Chapter 3

THE VALIDATION PROCESS

Chapter 4

THE STATUTE OF FRAUDS

Chapter 5

OPERATIVE EXPRESSIONS OF ASSENT

(Parol Evidence, Interpretation and Mistake)

Chapter 6

ABUSE OF BARGAIN, UNCONSCIONABILITY, GOOD FAITH, AND ILLEGALITY

Chapter 7

CONDITIONS

Chapter 8

RISK ALLOCATION

Chapter 9

REMEDIES FOR BREACH OF CONTRACT

Chapter 10

CONTRACT BENEFICIARIES

Chapter 11

THE ASSIGNMENT OF RIGHTS AND DELEGATION OF DUTIES

Chapter 12

THE DISCHARGE OF CONTRACTS

Chapter 1

INTRODUCTION

§ 1. The Concept of "Contract."

Historically and philosophically, the most fundamental concept of contract is that promises ought to be kept — *pacta sunt servanda*.[1] The concept is at least as old as the covenant between Jehovah and the people of Israel. The failure of the people to adhere to the covenant was a sin, but it was also a breach of contract.[2] Political philosophers who differ markedly in other respects seem compelled to adhere to a social contract theory, or government by the mutual consent of the governed.[3] The Lockian concept of social contract

---

[1] "It is, therefore, a most sacred precept of natural law, and one that governs the grace, manner and reasonableness of all human life, *That every man keep his given word*, that is, carry out his promises and agreements." S. PUFENDORF, DE JURE NATURAE ET GENTIUM, Bk. III, ch. IV, § 2. In the same section, Pufendorf quotes ARISTOTLE, RHETORIC, Bk. I, ch. XV[22]: "If contracts are invalidated, the intercourse of men is abolished."

[2] "When the people of Israel in the wilderness worshipped at the feet of the golden calf, they were guilty of sin, but even worse — as my beloved friend and master, Edwin Patterson would have said — they were guilty of material breach of contract discharging Jehovah from performance of his side of the holy bargain." Jones, *The Jurisprudence of Contracts*, 44 U. CIN. L. REV. 43, 45 (1975).

[3] *See, e.g.,* T. HOBBES, LEVIATHAN XIV; J.J. ROUSSEAU, THE SOCIAL CONTRACT; J. LOCKE, THE SECOND TREATISE OF GOVERNMENT ch. VIII; I. KANT, THE FOUNDATIONS OF THE METAPHYSICS OF MORALS.

1

forms the basis of our constitutional philosophy,[4] and recent elaborations of the same view maintain the concept of social contract as the indispensable element of a just society.[5] Early American judicial thinking is clearly the product of a natural law tradition that regarded contract rights as emanating from immutable principles that preceded human law.[6]

In the late nineteenth century, Sir Henry Maine stated his famous aphorism, "The movement of the progressive societies has hitherto been a movement *from status to contract.*"[7] In these "progressive" societies, the determination of the legal rights and duties of any member of that society no longer depends upon the status into which one was born. The development described by Maine was inevitable because the status society did not reflect the felt needs and desires of its members. Human beings wish to make choices — they seek freedom to elect among alternatives. They have free will. Human beings are also aware of the future, and they are capable of projecting into the future. They wish to plan and to design their futures. They are capable of bringing the future plan into the present and contemplating that plan. They are capable of recognizing the geometric benefits available through reciprocal planning with others.[8] The basic problem of society has been described as that of "establishing, maintaining and perfecting the conditions necessary for community life to perform its role in the complete development of man."[9] If man cannot project his realistic needs, desires, and aspirations into the future and be assured that they will be fulfilled, there is a major deficiency in society that can only be remedied by the social institution of contract.

---

[4]J. LOCKE, THE SECOND TREATISE OF GOVERNMENT ch. VIII, *Of the Beginning of Political Societies.*

[5]"My aim is to present a concept of justice which generalizes and carries to a higher level of abstraction the familiar theory of the social contract as found, say, in Locke, Rousseau, and Kant. In order to do this we are not to think of the original contract as one to enter a particular society or to set up a particular form of government. Rather, the guiding idea is that the principles of justice of the basic structure of society are the object of the original agreement. They are the principles that free and rational persons concerned to further their own interests would accept in an initial position of equality as defining the fundamental terms of their association. These principles are to regulate all further agreements; they specify the kinds of social cooperation that can be entered into and the forms of government that can be established. This way of regarding the principles of justice I shall call justice as fairness." J. RAWLS, A THEORY OF JUSTICE 11 (1971).

[6]"If, on tracing the right to contract, and the obligations created by contract, to their source, we find them to exist anterior to, and independent of society, we may reasonably conclude, that those original and pre-existing principles are, like many other natural rights, brought with man into society; and, *although they may be controlled, are not given by human legislation.*" Chief Justice Marshall in Ogden v. Saunders, 25 U.S. (12 Wheat.) 212, 344 (1827) (emphasis added).

[7]H. MAINE, ANCIENT LAW 141 (New Universal Library ed. 1905).

[8]Professor Ian Macneil identifies the "primal roots" of contract as society, specialization of labor and exchange, choice, and awareness of the future. I. MACNEIL, THE NEW SOCIAL CONTRACT 1-4 (1980).

[9]Snee, *Leviathan at the Bar of Justice,* in GOVERNMENT UNDER LAW (essays prepared for discussion at a conference on the occasion of the two hundredth anniversary of the birth of John Marshall, at the Harvard Law School, September 22-24 (1955)) 47, 52, *as cited in* H. HART, JR. & A. SACKS, THE LEGAL PROCESS: BASIC PROBLEMS IN THE MAKING AND APPLICATION OF LAW (tent. ed. 1958).

§ 2. The Enforcement of Promises — Early History — Covenant, Detinue, and Debt.

One of the central questions of contract law is, which promises should be enforced? Neither the common-law system nor any other legal system has attempted to enforce all promises.[10] However, it is well to remember that "[t]he question, what promises should the law enforce, must not be confused with its cousin, what kinds of promises should people keep."[11] One might subscribe to the axiom *pacta sunt servanda* (promises must be kept) without simultaneously demanding that all promises be enforced by the legal system. A donative (gift) promise that does not result in any measurable injury, though it may result in disappointment, is the kind of promise that a reasonable legal system such as ours may choose not to enforce. A social promise is another example of the kind of promise that a legal system will not enforce. Numerous reasons can be suggested to support this view. The recipient of such a promise (the promisee) should not reasonably regard such promises as legally enforceable. It would be very difficult to measure the injury in terms of money (damages) incurred by the breach of such a promise. The legal system could be overburdened by any attempt to enforce such promises. Notwithstanding the lack of legal sanctions, there may be more effective social or moral sanctions available to deal with those who breach such promises. An unexcused failure to appear at a dinner party may constitute a breach of promise resulting in a form of social ostracism that affects the promise-breaker in a more significant fashion than the payment of damages.[12] Our system of contract law has developed devices for deciding which promises ought to be legally enforceable, i.e., which promises ought to be validated by the legal system. All of these devices and related questions will be explored in a subsequent chapter dealing with the validation process.[13] The central question, which promises should be enforced, is at the heart of the history of the law of contracts. At this point, it is important to sketch that history as a foundation to a basic understanding of the modern law of contracts. Absent such a foundation, it will be impossible to understand how our law developed current devices for the separation of legally enforceable promises from other promises made by the members of our society.

Since all promises will not be enforceable, it is not remarkable that Roman law developed categories of promises which would give rise to legal sanctions.[14] The common law, however, did not build upon the foundations of

---

[10]"Many of us indeed would shudder at the idea of being bound by every promise, no matter how foolish, without any chance of letting increased wisdom undo past foolishness." Cohen, *The Basis of Contract*, 46 Harv. L. Rev. 553, 573 (1933).

[11]Eisenberg, *Donative Promises*, 47 U. Chi. L. Rev. 1 (1979).

[12]*See The Invitation to Dinner Case*, in H. Hart, Jr. & A. Sacks, The Legal Process 477-78 (tent. ed. 1958). The student should consider an important work dealing with the inherent enforceability of promises, C. Fried, Contract as Promise (1981).

[13]*See infra* Chapter 3.

[14]The Roman *stipulatio* was a promise made according to prescribed forms in a ceremony. It bound only one party (the promisor), i.e., it did not depend upon a reciprocal promise from the other party (the promisee). The "real" contract involved the conferring of a benefit under circumstances that bound the other party to perform, *e.g.*, a loan that bound the other party to repay once the loan was made. A "consensual" contract involved an exchange of promises — what would now be called an executory contract with performances promised but unperformed on both sides,

Roman contract law, though there is some evidence of Roman contract law traditions in England. Like Roman law, the common law evolved categories of enforceable promises. To be enforceable, a promise had to fit within one of the procedural categories that are known as common-law writs, i.e., forms of action that were the exclusive classifications providing remedies for claims. Yet, no matter how meritorious the claim, if no writ or form of action existed for that claim, there was no relief at common law.[15]

While the early common-law courts were inhospitable to the enforcement of private agreements, merchant courts developed as part of medieval fairs that were authorized by royal charters. These piepowder courts[16] were willing to deal with the promises of merchants before juries composed of merchants in proceedings that were expeditious, due to the pragmatic necessity of adjudicating disputes between itinerant merchants.[17] Another source of relief not available in the common-law courts was the Chancellor, who, in equity and good conscience, had discretion to provide a remedy. Certainly, canon law was pervasive and breach of a promise was a serious or mortal sin according to those standards. Since private agreements (exchanges of promises) could be enforced elsewhere, the common-law courts ultimately decided to treat the enforcement of promises more seriously.[18] It must be said, however, that this was due, essentially, to the general desire of these courts to expand their jurisdiction rather than any perceived need to enforce promises. Having succeeded in wresting jurisdiction from merchant courts, church courts, and the Chancellor, it was necessary for the common-law courts to develop an effective methodology for distinguishing between enforceable and unenforceable promises. The common-law writ system provided the basis for the development of this methodology.

---

which would be very modern indeed. However, such contracts were limited to partnership, mandate, sale and hire transactions. "Innominate" contracts were not limited to particular types of transactions and they depended upon an exchange, a *quid pro quo*. However, they were enforceable only when they were half completed, i.e., when one of the parties had fully performed one side of the contract. *See* F. LAWSON, A COMMON LAWYER LOOKS AT THE CIVIL LAW 113-37 (1955).

[15] "The dependence of right upon remedy has a vivid illustration in the system of 'forms of action,' which embraces the occasions of remedy in the English common law. The question whether a man can bring this or that action, trespass, trover, assumpsit, etc., is the way the question of liability and substantive right presents itself. There ought indeed to be a remedy for every wrong (ubi jus, ibi remedium), yet the right of action at common law depends upon whether the case fits anywhere in a limited and arbitrary list of writs, within the scope and theory of which the facts may be brought. There are only so many rights of action, as there are forms of action. This system of forms of action persisted in actual use in English procedure for six centuries, from the time of Henry II and Edward I until the Judicature Acts (in force in 1875). Most states have abolished the necessity of choosing one of these specified theories in commencing suit. The forms of action we have buried. Yet, though we have buried them, says Professor Maitland [Maitland, Equity 296], 'they still rule us from their graves.'" B. SHIPMAN, HANDBOOK OF COMMON-LAW PLEADING 54 (3d ed. 1923).

[16] The name is derived from *pie poudre,* meaning "dusty foot," since the shoes of the merchant litigants were often dusty.

[17] The classic work in this area is Malnyes' LEX MERCATORIA, published initially in England in 1622. The author explains a system of law created by merchant custom quite separate from the common law.

[18] "[I]t is even possible that the decisive argument in favor of extending the action on the case to cover nonfeasance was that the Chancellor was going to annex the whole field of commercial law if the extension were not made." Barton, *The Early History of Consideration,* 85 LAW Q. REV. 372, 378 (1969).

Modern substantive classifications of the law, such as contract and tort, were unknown to the early common lawyer, who focused exclusively upon the availability of the proper writ that would fit each case. Absent such a writ, there was no cause of action at common law. There were, essentially, three forms of action or writs available to the early common lawyer: covenant, detinue, and debt.

Covenant was limited to enforcement of promises that adhered to a particular form — the promise under seal (a "specialty").[19] The seal was wax containing the insignia of the promisor. A written promise under seal provided evidence of the existence of the promise and precluded unconsidered action, since it would take time to heat the wax and deliberate action to place one's insignia on the wax. Modern scholars also recognize another function of the seal — it furnished a simple test of the enforceability of the promise.[20] Like the Roman *stipulatio,* the promise under seal was enforced exclusively because of the form of the promise. Though an attempt was made to make the writ available beyond formalistic promises under seal, by the fourteenth century it became clear that the only acceptable evidence for the use of the writ of covenant was the seal.[21]

Detinue was a form of action or writ used essentially in bailment contracts. If the defendant possessed goods owned by the plaintiff who had voluntarily surrendered possession ("bailed") the goods to the defendant, a refusal by the defendant to surrender the goods to the plaintiff-owner permitted the action for detinue, which charged the defendant with unlawful detainer. Thus, the action of detinue would lie only for the recovery of specific chattels. Great certainty was required in identifying the chattels to be recovered.[22] One of the defects in this action was the conditional judgment against such a defendant, i.e., the defendant could choose either to surrender the goods or to retain the goods and pay for them. A much more serious defect attended detinue as well as other forms of action that antedated trial by jury. "Wager of law" permitted the defendant to make his oath that he did not detain the goods. If he could produce twelve oath helpers or compurgators to swear that they believed the defendant, the defendant prevailed.[23] This has been called a form of "licensed perjury"[24] since the oath of the defendant and the oaths of his twelve friends were conclusive. The limitation of detinue to the bailment situation and "wager of law" made detinue useless for those who attempted to enforce the typical executory contract promise as we know it today.

Debt was the most common action for breach of contract at early common law. It was an action for a "sum certain" (liquidated amount) of money due for

---

[19] "It appears for a time as if the covenant might be of general use wherever there is an agreement (*conventio*), might become, in fact, a general action for breach of contract; but the practice of the thirteenth century decides that there must be a sealed writing." F. MAITLAND, THE FORMS OF ACTION AT COMMON LAW 52 (1909).

[20] *See* Fuller, *Consideration and Form,* 41 COLUM. L. REV. 799, 800-01 (1941).

[21] *See* B. SHIPMAN, HANDBOOK OF COMMON LAW PLEADING 141-43 (3d ed. 1923).

[22] *Id.* at 114-19, 231-32.

[23] "Attempts have been made to rationalize and explain this fact. It has been said that debt and detinue were matters more particularly within the knowledge of the parties, and so on, but the simple explanation is that detinue and debt were older than trial by jury." F. MAITLAND, THE FORMS OF ACTION AT COMMON LAW 51 (1909).

[24] *Id.* at 34.

any reason. The plaintiff was held to a strict standard of proof of the exact amount alleged to be due. The essence of the debt action was the fact that the exchange between the parties was "half-completed," i.e., the contract had been performed on one side and a "sum certain" was owing to the promisee.[25] Thus, the defendant's liability depended upon his having received what he had sought in exchange for his promise, the quid pro quo. Like detinue, debt was viewed as the unjust detention of a sum of money. In fact, the action of debt was originally available to plaintiffs who sought to recover either a specific chattel or money. Later, detinue was used for chattels and debt was relegated to the recovery of money in the possession of the defendant. Debt was viewed in what modern lawyers would characterize as a tortious sense, and the recovery of the sum certain from the defendant may have been considered a form of restitution, except that the recovery was not limited to the value of the benefit conferred. Rather, it was the amount the defendant had promised to pay. Thus the action of debt produced a specific performance recovery, i.e., "the recovery of a debt *eo nomine et in numero,* and not merely the recovery of damages."[26]

In covenant, detinue, and debt, the common-law courts afforded no mechanism for the enforcement of executory promises. Further imaginative extensions of the forms of action would be required to demonstrate an effective mechanism to make such promises enforceable.

§ 3. The Enforcement of Promises — Assumpsit, Common Counts, Slade's Case.

The most significant extension of the common-law writs occurred in the extension to the action of assumpsit. At early common law, all civil injuries were divided into those with force or violence and those without force or violence. Thus battery was an injury to the person involving force or violence, whereas slander was an injury not involving physical force or violence. There were two essential remedies for civil wrongs based upon the distinction. Violent wrongs were remedied through the action of trespass while non-violent wrongs found remedies in actions of trespass on the case. Trespass on the case was developed through the statute of Westminster II, which provided clerks of the chancery with power to develop new writs or forms of action that were analogous (consimili casu) to existing writs. To permit what would be today called a tort recovery in a non-violent tort, i.e., one without force, the writ of trespass on the case (brevia de transgressione super casum) was created. Among the species of trespass on the case, the most important was *assumpsit.* As in other stages of the extension of common-law writs, the Court of King's Bench had begun to use this flexible generic writ of trespass on the case to generate more business for the Court. If someone undertook the performance of a service (e.g., to shoe a horse) and performed the undertaking badly, this *misfeasance* was the basis for an action of trespass on the case against the blacksmith.[27] The action was in that form of trespass on the case known as

---

[25] "As a rule the *quid pro quo* needed to support an action of Debt must be something actually given or done." Holdsworth, *Debt, Assumpsit, and Consideration,* 11 Mich. L. Rev. 347, 348 (1913).

[26] *Id.* at 133. *See also* Ames, *Parol Contract Prior to Assumpsit,* 8 Harv. L. Rev. 252, 260 (1894).

[27] "If on the other hand, one saw fit to authorize another to come into contact with his person or property, and damage ensued, there was, without more, no tort. The person injured took the risk

special assumpsit (he undertook or he promised). When the blacksmith performed badly or misfeased, there was a *detriment* to the promisee, the owner of the horse. As long as the emphasis was upon the *misfeasance* of the promisor, the action in special assumpsit sounded more in tort (*ex delicto*) than contract (*ex contractu*). To move to the goal of the enforcement of the purely executory exchange of promises, further development was essential.

If the promisor did not perform badly but failed to perform at all, would a remedy lie in special assumpsit not only for misfeasance but also for *nonfeasance*? If the defendant had performed no act at all, there was a problem in relating it to the concept of trespass on the case and, therefore, special assumpsit. The connection was found by suggesting that failure to perform (nonfeasance) was a form of deceit. Thus where a defendant promised to sell a horse to plaintiff and, instead, sold it to a third party, the allegation included deceit. Gradually, the emphasis was shifted from the "deceit" of the defendant to the failure to perform the promise. The emphasis in assumpsit was correspondingly shifted from the performance stage of the undertaking to the initial stage of the undertaking, i.e., to the formation stage. It is at this point that special assumpsit becomes an action *ex contractu*.[28] At the end of the sixteenth century, it was recognized that a party who had made a promise in exchange for the promise of the other party had suffered a detriment since he was bound by his own promise. Notwithstanding the circularity of reasoning, this rationale permitted courts to enforce purely executory promises which had been exchanged for each other[29] rather than merely half-completed exchanges (debt), promises under seal (covenant) or situations where goods were in the hands of a bailee (detinue).

Unfortunately, one problem still plagued parties who sought to bring actions in special assumpsit. If the old action of debt were available, one could not bring the action in assumpsit. This was devastating to some creditors since the action of debt was subject to the "licensed perjury" of "wager of

---

of all injurious consequences, unless the other expressly assumed the risk himself, or unless the peculiar nature of one's calling, as in the case of the smith, imposed a customary duty to act with reasonable skill." Ames, *The History of Assumpsit,* 2 HARV. L. REV. 1, 3 (1888).

[28] "[I]f money was in fact paid for a promise to convey land, the breach of the promise by a conveyance to a stranger was certainly, as already seen, an actionable deceit by the time of Henry VII. This being so, it must, in the nature of things, be only a question of time when the breach of such a promise, by making no conveyance at all, would also be a cause of action. The mischief to the plaintiff was identical in both cases. The distinction between misfeasance and nonfeasance, in the case of promises given for money, was altogether too shadowy to be maintained. It was formally abandoned in 1504, as appears from the following extract from the opinion of Frowyk, C.J.: 'And so, if I sell you ten acres of land, parcel of my manor, and then make a feoffment of my manor, you shall have an action on the case against me, because I received your money, and in that case you have no other remedy against me. And so, if I sell you my land and covenant to enfeoff you and do not, you shall have a good action on the case, and this is adjudged.... And if I covenant with a carpenter to build a house and pay him £20 for the house to be built by a certain day, now I shall have a good action on my case because of payment of money, and still it sounds only in covenant and without payment of money in this case no remedy, and still if he builds it and misbuilds, action [on] the case lies. And also for nonfeasance, if money paid case lies.'" *Quoted in* Ames, *The History of Assumpsit,* 2 HARV. L. REV. 1, 13 (1888) (*citing* Keilw. 77, pl. 25, which seems to be the same case as Y.B. 20 H. VII. 8, pl. 18. 21 H. VII. 41, pl. 66, per Fineux, C.J., *accord. See also* Brooke's allusion to an "action on the case upon an *assumpsit pro tali summa.*" Br. Ab. Disceit, pl. 29).

[29] *See* Strangborough v. Warner, 4 Leo. 3, 74 Eng. Rep. 686 (K.B. 1588).

law"[30] whereas the more modern writ of assumpsit, developed after the trial by jury, was not subject to "wager of law." The common-law courts permitted assumpsit instead of debt where a party already indebted (indebitatus) undertook (assumpsit) to pay the "sum certain." This was known as *indebitatus assumpsit* or *general assumpsit* to distinguish it from *special assumpsit,* which lies only for breach of an actual promise in an express contract. General assumpsit does not depend upon an actual promise or a real contract. It is based upon a promise implied in law where one party has already performed part of the contract (like debt, it depends upon some portion of the exchange being completed) or from some other debt resting upon the defendant. Since it was developed to provide an alternate to the cumbersome action of debt, it attempts to secure repayment of amounts owed though, unlike debt, it does not require a "sum certain." Quasi contract actions are actions to recover sums due from defendants who are unjustly enriched at the expense of the plaintiff. "Quasi" ("something like") modifies the term "contract" since they are not real contracts. There is neither express nor implied mutual assent or exchange of promises. Rather, there is a recognition that the defendant has money that belongs to the plaintiff for work and labor done (quantum meruit) with the expectation of payment, or for goods sold and delivered (quantum valebat) or for another reason, defendant has received money that belongs to the plaintiff (money had and received or money paid). While general assumpsit would lie for a partially executed express contract, it also provided a desirable alternative remedy where such an express promise could not be shown though the indebtedness from the defendant to the plaintiff was clear. The action would be brought in general assumpsit using one of the "common counts" (quantum meruit, quantum valebat, money had and received, or money paid) to plead the cause of action.

A debate between the courts of Common Pleas and King's Bench raged for many years concerning the use of the new form of assumpsit, general or indebitatus assumpsit, in place of debt. Common pleas urged a continuation of the conservative view that assumpsit would not lie where debt would lie since assumpsit was permitted only to provide a remedy where none was available. King's Bench, however, was not concerned with a fastidious preservation of distinctions between forms of action. It simply permitted assumpsit to recover debts. A suggestion that this was simply another King's Bench effort to procure additional revenue through fees has been rejected.[31] "The debate seems rather to have been symptomatic of a more intellectual conflict, a final confrontation between the old learning and the new. It may perhaps be regarded as the last stand of Tudor legal conservatives against the legal renaissance of the sixteenth century, and the reformation of the old Year Book learning which this entailed."[32]

The resolution occurred in the most famous case of its era, *Slade's Case,* decided by all of the judges of the central courts of England in an argument

---

[30] See the preceding section, which, inter alia, deals with the action of debt and "wager of law." *But see* Baker, *New Light on Slade's Case, Part II,* 29 CAMBRIDGE L.J. 213, 228-30 (1971), where the author concludes: "There is no clear evidence that wager of law did not work well."

[31] *See id.* at 215.

[32] *Id.* at 216.

won by Sir Edward Coke, then Attorney General, and lost by Sir Francis Bacon, his rival.[33] Much has been made of the statement of the words of Popham, C.J., "Every contract executory imports in itself an assumpsit."[34] One interpretation is that this statement is evidence of final recognition of the enforcement of mutual promises, but this interpretation can no longer stand.[35] The more pervasive view of *Slade's Case* was that it disposed of the necessity of implying a fictional subsequent promise to pay the debt. Why was a subsequent promise necessary? One explanation suggests the importance of the deceit concept.[36] The main question in the case was whether the parties could be said to have undertaken a legally enforceable obligation though they failed to use express promissory language. Again, the more penetrating conflict raged between Common Pleas and King's Bench concerning the availability of assumpsit to recover debts. Notwithstanding misinterpretations, it cannot be gainsaid that *Slade's Case* marked a critical passage in the common law of contract.[37] Indebitatus assumpsit (general assumpsit) became available in actions to recover debts, and the ineluctable movement toward the recognition and enforcement of executory promises continued. The term "consideration" was found in many of the lawyer's arguments of this time. In *Slade's Case* itself, Sir Francis Bacon used the term in arguing for the defendant.[38] "Consideration" was used to express vaguely the concept that there had to be some reason for enforcing a promise. Good and sufficient reasons for common lawyers were to be found in their old friends, the forms of action.

---

[33] Slade's Case, 4 Co. Rep. 92b, 76 Eng. Rep. 1074 (1602).

[34] *Id.* at 94a and 1077.

[35] *See* Baker, *supra* note 30, at 226.

[36] "Why was the subsequent promise sufficient for that purpose? In the litigation between Tom and Dick, how was Tom's case notionally put? To say that by the middle of the sixteenth century *assumpsit* had become a purely contractual action, and that a debt precedent was accepted as a sufficient consideration, is an unsatisfying restatement; it also supposes that *assumpsit* had forgotten its parentage with unfilial alacrity. The likely answer is that here was another and more recondite application of the deceit ploy, and that Tom put his case like this: 'I had sold Dick goods and could have got my money from him by an action of debt; but because of his promise I did not do so, and have been kept out of my money for a time by his deceit.' Put in modern terms, the suggestion is that the subsequent promise really worked because made in consideration of forbearance of the debt. Expressed in terms of tortious deceit, it will be noticed that Tom was formally complaining of damage in being kept out of his money for a time rather than of the loss of the amount of the debt; and this explains the opening words of the fourth resolution in *Slade's Case*: 'that the Plaintiff in this Action on the Case in *Assumpsit* should not recover only Damages for the special Loss (if any be) which he had, but also for the whole Debt....' If this is right, the allegations of deceit found in every *indebitatus* count were not mere abuse of the defendant for breaking his promise, but, in principle, the assertion of a definite wrong causing definite harm; and their original purpose was to express the matter as something other than mere non-payment of the debt for which the action of debt properly lay." *Quoted in* Milsom, *Not Doing Is No Trespass?: A View of the Boundries of Case,* 1954 Cambridge L. Rev. 105 (this applies to the question of why a second promise (on top of the original debt) was needed in the first place) (*citing:* Rastell's Entrees, 1574 ed., f. 4 *sub. tit. Action sur le case in lieu de action de dett;* Coke's Entries, f. 1, *Action sur le case 1 (Pinchon's Case)* 4 Co. Rep. 91 at 94b).

[37] *See* Simpson, *The Place of Slade's Case in the History of Contracts,* 74 Law Q. Rev. 381 (1958).

[38] "And we put that a man, in consideration of certain corn delivered to him by the plaintiff will acknowledge himself to be indebted in 120...." *See* Baker, *supra* note 30, at 61.

§ 4. Contract Law and Economics — Economic Organization.

In recent years, considerable interest has been shown in scholarship concerning law and economics.[39] While students of antitrust law have often considered economic theory, other traditional law school subjects did not include an inquiry into their underlying economic philosophies until legal scholars began to suggest this dimension. Even now, the dimension of economic theory in a given course in contracts, torts, property, or other traditional courses will depend heavily upon the significance of economic theory to the teacher. A text that attempts to deal with a subject as broad as the law of contracts cannot pursue this dimension comprehensively. However, it is important to introduce the economic dimension at this stage and to suggest additional aspects of economic theory at relevant places throughout this volume.

Any form of economic organization must be concerned with three basic problems: (1) *what* products shall be produced and how much of each product shall be produced; (2) *how* society shall produce such products and how the scarce resources of society shall be allocated to such production; (3) *for whom* the products shall be produced, i.e., how shall societal production be distributed among the members of society.[40] These problems can be approached through three fundamentally different forms of economic organization. An early form was based on *status*, which answered the *what, how* and *for whom* questions through tradition. The manorial economic organization of feudal times or the more modern caste system of occupational choice in India are examples. Another approach is *centralized planning,* as evidenced by the decision of what to produce, how to produce, and how to distribute the production as found in the Soviet Union. Except in isolated contexts, Americans are not familiar with these systems, as the economic organization of the United States is the *market* system.[41]

The market system depends upon atomistic decisionmaking by innumerable consumers and producers instead of central planning. Economists have supplied economic models that indicate that no single consumer or producer makes the decision as to what shall be produced, how it shall be produced, or how the production shall be distributed. These questions are answered by the market process, which involves utility maximization by millions of consumers and profit maximization by innumerable producers. The interface of supply and demand forces will not only determine which products will be made; it

---

[39] For a discussion of the development of the discipline of law and economics, *see* Kitch, *The Fire of Truth: A Remembrance of Law and Economics at Chicago 1932-1970,* 26 J.L. & ECON. 273 (1983). For a discussion of law and economics generally, *see* A. KRONMAN & R. POSNER, THE ECONOMICS OF CONTRACT LAW (1979); SCHWARTZ & SCOTT, COMMERCIAL TRANSACTIONS (1982); Note, *Efficiency and a Rule of "Free Contract": A Critique of Two Models of Law and Economics,* 97 HARV. L. REV. 978 (1984); J. Dawson, *Economic Duress — An Essay in Perspective,* 45 MICH. L. REV. 253 (1947). Various aspects of this topic are discussed in Horowitz, *Reviving the Law of Substantive Unconscionability: Applying the Implied Covenant of Good Faith and Fair Dealing to Excessively Priced Consumer Credit Contracts,* 33 UCLA L. REV. 940 (1986) (unconscionability); Shadowen & Voytek, *Economic and Critical Analyses of the Law of Covenants Not to Compete,* 72 GEO. L. REV. 1425 (1984) (antitrust); Caselton, *Lost Profits Damage Awards Under U.C.C. 2-708(2),* 37 STAN. L. REV. 1109 (1985) and Yorio, *In Defense of Money Damages for Breach of Contract,* 82 COLUM. L. REV. 1365 (1982) (remedies).

[40] *See* F. SCHERER, INDUSTRIAL MARKET STRUCTURE AND ECONOMIC PERFORMANCE 11-12 (1970).

[41] *Ibid.*

will also determine the *price* at which such products will be sold and the *quantity* that will be bought and sold. In their quest to maximize utility and profits, consumers and producers engage in *competition,* which has been described as a form of economic organization, a process of selection, and an agency of social development.[42] The form of economic organization that allocates resources through the invisible hand of the market place — the competitive model — evolved from the development of petty trade after the passage of the medieval regime of prelate and baron. Essentially, it consists of two pairs of institutions: property and contract; profit-making and freedom of trade. Private property determines who is to possess and control the resources of society. Contract determines how persons and resources are brought together in the productive and allocation processes. Property and contract together constitute the mechanism of competition. Profit and utility maximization compel firms and consumers to produce and to buy. Freedom of trade ensures that industry and markets will be open to those who seek to maximize their profits and utilities.

Economists construct models that range from the *perfectly competitive* to the *monopoly* model. In the perfectly competitive model, the market is characterized by a large number of buyers and sellers, all of whom have perfect knowledge of prices and quantities of standardized products, and there is perfect mobility of resources into and out of an industry. Though the perfectly competitive model has never existed, since one or more of the conditions of such a model will invariably be absent, economists project this model as an aspiration that might be approached but never actualized. In such a perfectly competitive market, no single buyer or seller could affect the price, buyers would be indifferent in their choice of sellers since the goods would always be standardized, it would be irrational for any seller to charge higher prices since buyers would have perfect knowledge of prices and quantities, perfect mobility of resources would ensure the immediate shift of resources to any production that suggested a potential shortage, and buyers would always buy at the lowest price. In the monopoly model, a single firm produces a product for which there are no substitutes. The industry and the firm are coextensive and the firm exercises complete control over price since the buyer has no alternative source of supply. The monopolist does not "take" a price as determined by the market; the monopolist is a price "maker." A comparison of the monopoly model with the perfectly competitive model clearly suggests that monopolists produce less at higher prices. The rational monopolist will restrict output when necessary to preserve monopolistic profits and thereby misallocate the resources of society. The income to purchasers found in the perfectly competitive model becomes profit to the monopolist. Since this comparison obviously suggests a preference for competition over monopoly, the United States has enacted antitrust laws, which are original legal products of the United States.[43] The antitrust laws seek to maintain competition and thereby pre-

---

[42] Hamilton, *Essay on Competition,* 4 ENCYCLOPEDIA OF THE SOCIAL SCIENCES 141 (1931).

[43] The Federal Antitrust Laws include the Sherman Act, 15 U.S.C. §§ 1-11, first enacted in 1890. The basic provisions of the Sherman Act prohibit contracts, combinations or trusts (agreements) in restraint of trade (Section 1) and monopolizing in restraint of trade (Section 2). Two or more parties are required to violate Section 1 while one party or more than one party can violate

serve impersonal market control.[44] The objective is not perfect competition but some realistic form of imperfect competition, which is often called effective or workable competition.

§ 5. Contract Law and Economics — "Exchange" — "Promises" and the Purpose of Contracts.

The social institution of contract is found in every society.[45] The law of contracts, like any other segment of law, can be pursued successfully only if its purpose is understood. Why is the institution of contract essential in society? There are phenomena in every society more fundamental than contract. One is economic exchange — one person giving something of economic value to another in return for something of economic value. Before economic exchange can exist, the parties must have control over the subject matter of the exchange. Without a legal system, such control may be accomplished by force. With a legal system, the control occurs through recognition of rights in each person to control the subject matter of the exchange. Once it is recognized that the wheat possessed by one farmer belongs to him and the cow possessed by another farmer belongs to him, there is societal recognition of one of the basic requirements for a legally recognized system of exchange. This requirement is characterized as rights in property. The next step is the recognition that the holders of these rights (the owners of the property) may *exchange* their property. Both the recognition of property rights and the recognition of the right to exchange property can occur without the social institution of contract.

The mere economic exchange of property rights, however, is an exchange of *existing* property, a system of *barter*. In a barter system, myriad advantageous economic exchanges will simply not occur. The owner of the cow may be reluctant to surrender it in exchange for a mere *assurance* that he will receive wheat harvested months later by his neighboring farmer. The owner's family may be in need of clothing, utensils, or other commodities or services, but, again, he will be reluctant to surrender the cow for assurances that the eco-

---

Section 2. The Sherman Act contains criminal provisions. In 1974, fines were increased to $1,000,000 for corporations and $100,000 for other persons, and prison terms were increased from a maximum of one year to a maximum of three years in 1974. The Clayton Act of 1914, 15 U.S.C. §§ 12-27, was designed as a supplement to the Sherman Act. The Clayton Act proscribes exclusive dealing agreements (Section 3), price discrimination (Section 2, which was amended in 1936 by the Robinson-Patman Act) and mergers (Section 7, amended in 1950 by the Celler-Kefauver Amendment) which may substantially lessen competition. The Clayton Act contains no criminal provisions. Section 4 of the Clayton Act allows for the recovery of treble damages plus reasonable attorney's fees for any person injured by the violation of any antitrust law. The Federal Trade Commission Act (15 U.S.C. §§ 41-58), establishing the FTC, was also enacted in 1914 to further supplement the Sherman Act. Section 5 of the FTC Act proscribes unfair methods of competition. The Act does not contain criminal sanctions. The federal antitrust laws are enforced by the Antitrust Division of the Department of Justice and by the Federal Trade Commission though violations of Sections 1 and 2 of the Sherman Act are enforced exclusively by the Department of Justice because they contain criminal sanctions. Beyond the federal antitrust laws, states have enacted antitrust laws to supplement the federal statutes.

[44] For an excellent analysis of federal antitrust law, *see* P. AREEDA & D. TURNER, ANTITRUST LAW (1978).

[45] Farnsworth, *The Past of Promise: An Historical Introduction to Contract,* 60 COLUM. L. REV. 576, 578-82 (1969). "The attempt by the Soviet Union to administer the economy without the institution of contract failed." *See* Loeber, *Plan and Contract Performance in Soviet Law* in LAW IN THE SOVIET SOCIETY 128-29 (La Fave ed. 1965).

nomic goods he needs or desires will be delivered at some future time. To overcome this reluctance, the assurances offered to the owner of the cow must become binding assurances. If the legal system places its force behind the assurances to ascertain their fulfillment, the owner no longer must rely upon mere hope. He will have a legally recognized right creating a correlative duty in those who have provided the assurances. He will have the right to expect that assurances made to him in exchange for his present delivery of goods will be fulfilled.

Once a society moves from a primitive form of present economic exchange, a barter system, to a system of assured future exchange, a new dimension of economic exchange creating geometric economic benefits exists. Innumerable advantageous economic exchanges become available to all members of society. They may engage in future exchanges as to property that does not yet exist. Parties may give assurances of property exchanges that they expect to acquire in exchange for property that does not yet exist. Parties will commit themselves to future exchange by their exchange of promises and the assurance that their promises will be performed permits the parties to the exchange to design their economic futures. It also lets the other members of society recognize that the promises are valuable *in themselves*.[46] The wealth of any modern society is composed of such promises. The assurance that something will or will not happen in the future is nothing more than a promise. A promise is a voluntary commitment or undertaking by the party making it (the promisor) addressed to the other party (the promisee) that the promisor will perform some action or refrain from some action in the future.[47] A reliable system of assured future exchanges provides a basis for understanding the purpose of contract law: to ascertain the fulfillment of those expectations that have been induced in the promisee by the voluntary conduct of the promisor in making the promise.[48]

A complex industrial society cannot operate on the basis of barter. Sophisticated economic planning requires a comprehensive system of future exchange. The institution of contract brings persons and resources together as a necessary condition to the operation of the market system because the institution of contract facilitates future exchanges. The enhancement of the resources of society and the maximizing of these resources to all members of society is illustrated by a simple example.

Suppose X owns property which he values at $1,000 while the same property is worth $2,000 to Y. X has goods worth $1,000 and Y has cash valued at $2,000. Absent any present or future exchange, the total wealth of X and Y is $3,000. If the legal system facilitates an exchange between these parties at a price of $1,500 for X's goods, X now has $1,500 and Y has goods worth $2,000 to Y for a total of $3,500. Assuming no detrimental effects to non-parties and

---

[46] R. POUND, AN INTRODUCTION TO THE PHILOSOPHY OF LAW 133 (rev. ed. 1954).

[47] RESTATEMENT OF CONTRACTS § 2(1) (hereinafter cited as FIRST RESTATEMENT); RESTATEMENT (SECOND) OF CONTRACTS § 2(1) (hereinafter cited as RESTATEMENT 2d). For an explanation of the original RESTATEMENT OF CONTRACTS and the RESTATEMENT 2d, *see infra* § 9.

[48] 1 CORBIN, CONTRACTS § 1 (1963) (hereinafter cited as CORBIN). "[C]ontract law provided a framework of reasonably assured expectations within which men might plan and venture." J. HURST, LAW AND ECONOMIC GROWTH: THE LEGAL HISTORY OF THE LUMBER INDUSTRY IN WISCONSIN 1836-1915, at 297 (1964).

recognizing that the values to X and Y are values that they assume, the facilitation of this exchange has increased individual values *and* the value of the resources of society of which X and Y are members. After the exchange, if X and Y each consider themselves at least no worse off than they were prior to the exchange, and if either party assumes that he is better off as a result of the exchange, economists would refer to this situation as a "Pareto-superior" outcome.[49] The psychology of exchange was long ago recognized by Adam Smith, who suggested that one cannot depend upon the benevolence of others. Rather, the appeal must be to the self-love of others rather than one's own necessities.[50]

§ 6. Contract Law and Economics — "Efficient Breach."

One of the fundamental rubrics of the social institution of contract is that promises ought to be kept — *pacta sunt servanda.* Yet not all promises will be legally enforced, for a variety of reasons that will be discussed in great detail later in this volume. One of the principal questions of contract law is, what promises shall be enforced? Assuming that a particular promise is within the scope of those the legal system deems enforceable, society obviously supports the performance of such a promise. Yet, from an economic perspective, a refusal to perform a particular promise may not only be defensible but desirable. If X and Y exchange promises and X later discovers that the future exchange to which he has agreed will be detrimental rather than beneficial to him, X may breach the contract so made by the exchange of promises. If X's refusal to perform his promise is accompanied by sufficient compensation to Y, the result may be economically efficient, whereas a legal insistence that X's promise be performed would be inefficient. "Efficiency" may be viewed as the utilization of economic resources in such a fashion that "value " — human satisfaction as measured by aggregate consumer willingness to pay for resources — is maximized.[51] Normally, a refusal to perform a future exchange will result in loss to the non-breaching party that must be compensated to fulfill the expectations of that party. Thus if X agrees to supply 1,000 tape recorders to Y, a refusal by X to perform will require Y to seek an alternative supplier of the recorders. If Y must pay a higher price, the difference between the contract price and the higher (substitute purchase) price will make Y whole in terms of fulfilling Y's reasonable expectations. However, assume that X has agreed to deliver the 1,000 recorders of a particular brand with a peculiar feature to Y at $200 per unit. Before the future exchange is to be performed, Z requires 1,000 recorders with the peculiar feature of the models X has promised to sell to Y. X has no more of these or any other recorders. Since Y has no interest in the peculiar feature, Y can purchase substitute recorders that will serve him at least as well as X's recorders at $210 per unit. However, no substitutes would satisfy the needs of Z. Z is willing to pay X

---

[49] Pareto's view was that resources are not *optimally* employed if it is possible to make someone better off without making anyone worse off. V. Pareto, Courts D'Economic Politique (1896-1897); Manuel D'Economie Politique (2d ed. 1927).

[50] A. Smith, An Inquiry into the Nature and Causes of the Wealth of Nations 19 (1811 ed.).

[51] R. Posner, Economic Analysis of Law 10 (2d ed. 1977).

$220 per unit. If X refuses to perform his promise to Y, Y may be compensated by a $10,000 payment from X. Having received $220 per unit from Z, X receives a net of $10,000 more than he would have received from Y though Y, again, has been compensated. Thus Y is made whole, X receives expected value, and Z is satisfied. Not only are the parties better off; the society in which the parties live is also better off in terms of efficiency or value maximization. This situation is often described as one of "efficient breach" of contract.[52] This economic analysis is consistent with the fundamental concept of contract remedies, i.e., to compensate the injured party by placing him in the position he would have occupied had the contract been performed. The protection of the injured party's expectation interest provides an incentive for the other party to breach *only* if the gain from the breach (notwithstanding compensation to the injured party) is greater than the gain from contract performance.

§ 7. Contract Law and Economics — Conclusions.

The institution of contract permits the market system to operate effectively with innumerable decisions made by the members of this exchange society. Each member seeks to maximize his individual welfare. The resources of society are allocated by its members in a relatively unfettered fashion, with the market mechanism incorporating the subjective value judgments of each decisionmaker and creating an objective determinant — the "price" — for all of the resources of that society. The judgment of any member of this exchange society may be less than voluntary if there is state regulation of particular resources. The individual judgment may also be hampered, if not destroyed, by elements of misrepresentation, duress, unconscionability, or similar factors. The market system itself may be undermined by activities that would hamper or destroy the automatic, self-regulating process of the market — behavior that is proscribed by the antitrust laws. The social institution of contract is obviously affected by such activity. Thus, absent an effective — albeit imperfect — market structure, the social institution of contract and the consequent freedom of the members of society is at least impaired, if not destroyed. A relatively free market depends upon the mechanism known as the institution of contract. Absent such a market, there is no raison d'être for the institution of contract as it is currently known in the United States. This is not to say, however, that it would be possible for a modern society to proscribe all forms of present, future, direct, or indirect exchange. The most significant evidence in support of this view is found in the attempt by the Soviet Union to eliminate the institution of contract by relying entirely upon the central distribution of the resources of that society. In 1921, Lenin admitted that the experiment had failed since "the private market proved to be stronger than we and ... we ended up with ordinary purchase and sale,

---

[52] *See* Birmingham, *Breach of Contract, Damage Measures, and Economic Efficiency*, 24 RUTGERS L. REV. 273 (1970). *But see* Macneil, *Efficient Breach of Contract: Circles in the Sky*, 68 VA. L. REV. 947 (1982), in which the author criticizes the "simple-efficient-breach" analysis on the footing that it assumes a world in which all relations between the parties can be conducted without transaction costs.

trade."[53] Recent events in the Soviet Union and other parts of the world are clear evidence of the indispensability of the "private market" as a necessary condition to freedom, itself.

§ 8. Meaning of the Word "Contract."

We distinguish those promises that the law enforces from those that it does not by calling the former "contracts." For practical purposes, a contract is a promise, or group of promises, that the law will enforce, or the performance of which it in some way recognizes as a duty.[54] This could hardly be called a definition, since it does not purport to set forth and delimit the constituent elements of the thing described. In fact it is not practicable to state all the pertinent operative facts that are essential to create a contract, or all of the legal relationships that result from it, within the necessary limits of a definition. This will have to be left for detailed development in the sections that follow. In recent years, there has been a tendency to think of contract in different terms. The Uniform Commerical Code (UCC), which has been enacted into law by every state (Louisiana has enacted only parts of the Code) does not speak in terms of promises. The basic term used in the UCC is "agreement," which is further defined in the Code as "the bargain of the parties in fact as found in their language or by implication from other circumstances including course of dealing or usage of trade or course of performance."[55] The insistence on thinking of contract as emanating from agreements-in-fact is an effort to view the law of commercial contracts in a transactional and more realistic context. It is premised on the observation that business deals are initiated by various expressions of agreements involving not only words but acts and prior understandings between the contracting parties as well as the custom and usage surrounding the transaction. This functional view of contract excludes the use of "promise" on the footing that "promise" suggests a fictitious concept of agreements-in-fact that creates the need to find a definite promise even though a real promise does not exist in the particular transaction.[56] The new description of contract in the Code is the first and perhaps most basic change among the radical changes in commercial contracts (contracts for the sale of goods) manifested by the Code.[57] The influence of the Code on the law of contracts will be emphasized throughout this volume since the influence is substantial. There are philosophical changes in the law

---

[53] Loeber, *Plan and Contract Performance in Soviet Law*, in LAW IN THE SOVIET SOCIETY 128-29 (La Fave ed. 1965).

[54] *See* FIRST RESTATEMENT § 1 and RESTATEMENT 2d § 1. "'Contract' means the total legal obligation which results from the parties' agreement as affected by this Act and any other applicable rules of law." UNIFORM COMMERCIAL CODE § 1-201(11). For an explanation of the UCC, *see infra* §§ 9 and 10. For various definitions of "contract" discussed, see Snyder, *Contract — Fact or "Legal Hypothesis?"* 21 MISS. L.J. 304 (1949).

[55] UCC § 1-201(3). *See infra* §§ 10-13.

[56] *See* Mooney, *Old Kontract Principles and Karl's New Kode: An Essay on the Jurisprudence of Our New Commercial Law*, 11 VILL. L. REV. 213 (1966). *See also* Carroll, *Harpooning Whales; or Searching for More Expansion Joints in Karl's Crumbling Cathedral*, 12 B.C. INDUS. & COM. L. REV. 139 (1970).

[57] *See* Murray, *The Realism of Behaviorism Under the Uniform Commercial Code*, 51 OR. L. REV. 269 (1972); Murray, *The Article Two Prism: The Underlying Philosophy of Article 2 of the Uniform Commercial Code*, 21 WASHBURN L.J. 1 (1981).

of contracts initiated by the Code the impact of which has barely been felt at the time of this writing.[58] These changes are largely the product of the scholarship of the late Professor Karl N. Llewellyn, who attacked the basic structure of traditional contract law as early as the 1930s. Whether the Llewellyn change in the description of contract (and particularly the elimination of the term "promise" from that description) will ultimately succeed is questionable. The most recent description of contract by a number of the contract scholars in the United States suggests that "promise" is still an indispensable term in any attempted definition of contract.[59] At this point, it is important to keep in mind two elements of a contract that are critical: (1) It involves an undertaking or commitment that something shall or shall not be done in the future; and (2) the law sanctions such undertaking or commitment and puts its coercive machinery behind it.

Unfortunately, the use of the term "contract" as just described is not consistently adhered to. Lawyers as well as laymen frequently use it to express other and quite different thoughts. This may not be terribly harmful if the connotation of the word in the particular situation is observed. However, the neophyte must be aware of the careful distinctions in the use of the word that may be properly raised. To prevent needless confusion in the sections that follow, attention will now be directed to some of the other senses in which the word is commonly, though imprecisely, employed.

Frequently the word "contract" is used to refer to the written memorial[60] (the signed writing) or other utterance that evidences a legally enforceable promise or group of promises. The writing is not the contract; the words the parties use if they contract orally is not the contract; the conduct or customs of the parties that manifest their legally enforceable agreement are not the contract. All of these manifestations are mere *evidence* of the contract. Where is the contract? One cannot touch, hear, smell, or feel the contract. The evidence of the contract is subject to sensory perception, but the contract is an abstract legal relationship between the parties. The legal relationship is composed of enforceable rights and correlative enforceable duties. If *A* and *B* enter into a contract for the purchase and sale of *A*'s auto, they may reduce their understanding to writing. They may agree orally. It is even possible for them to agree without any words oral or written. *A* may be showing the car to a number of prospective purchasers. *B*, a close friend of *A*, observes the display to potential buyers. *A* notices *B* standing nearby and *B* points to himself, then

---

[58] Llewellyn, *On Our Case-Law of Contract: Offer and Acceptance* (pts. 1, 2), 48 YALE L.J. 1, 779 (1939).

[59] "A contract is a promise or a set of promises for the breach of which the law gives a remedy, or the performance of which the law in some way recognizes as a duty." RESTATEMENT 2d § 1. Professor Ian Macneil believes that the RESTATEMENT 2d § 2(1) definition of "promise" ("manifestation of intention to act or refrain from acting in a specified way, so made as to justify a promisee in understanding that a commitment has been made") is "merely a Gertrude Steinian 'a promise is a promise is a promise.'" Macneil's preferred definition is "present communication of a commitment to engage in a reciprocal measured exchange." He also argues that contract cannot be understood as the relations among parties to the processes of future exchange unless a number of nonpromissory exchange-projectors are also considered. These include custom, status, habit, the internal hierarchies of corporations and bureaucracies, and ongoing contractual relations. *See* I. MACNEIL, THE NEW SOCIAL CONTRACT 5-8 (1980).

[60] *See* Simpson v. Dyer, 268 Mich. 328, 256 N.W. 341 (1934); Southern R.R. v. Huntsville Lumber Co., 191 Ala. 333, 67 So. 695 (1914).

extends three fingers in the air. *A* understands that *B* wants to buy the car for $300. *A* extends his fingers in the familiar "O.K." sign. This may be called sign language, but it is not reduced to words, written or spoken. This manifestation of agreement, like the written or spoken words of agreement, is not the contract. It is merely evidence of the contract.

Sometimes the word "contract" is used to designate a transaction involving the exchange of goods or land for money. When money is exchanged for goods, this constitutes a sale. When money is exchanged for land, this constitutes a conveyance. Sales and conveyances may be the result of a previous contract, but they are not contracts in themselves. There is no undertaking or commitment to do or refrain from doing anything in the future. This indispensable element of contract is missing. If *A* sells and delivers an automobile to *B* and is paid a price in exchange for the car, it is incorrect to suggest that a "contract" results from this sale.[61] There is a present transfer of property rights leaving nothing to be done in the future. The legal rights that are created by a sale of goods or conveyance of land are rights *in rem*[62] or rights in the property itself. There are no special rights *in personam* between the parties to the transaction. If *A* should deprive *B* of the automobile after selling and delivering it to him, *B* could not maintain an action for breach of contract but would be relegated to an action in tort for wrongful conversion of the auto. If a total stranger to the transaction, *C*, should deprive *B* of the auto, *B* would have the same right against *C* in tort. The legal relations created by the sale are relations *in rem* affecting not only the two parties involved in the transaction but all other members of society. If *A* had only *promised* to sell and deliver the auto to *B* in return for *B's* promise[63] to pay the agreed price, the legal relations created would be special *in personam* rights and correlative duties between *A* and *B*. If either party refused to perform his promise, the other would have the exclusive *in personam* right to bring an action in contract for breach.

It is possible to couple an undertaking for the future with a sale, as when the future delivery of the goods, or the future payment of the price or a warranty is provided for. In such a case, a contract in the sense indicated results, as well as a sale.

§ 9. Sources of the Law of Contracts.

The fundamental principles of contract law developed at common law.[64] The principles evolved from innumerable decisions resolving countless disputes. It was, therefore, appropriate to think of contract law as a common-law subject with a few statutory modifications of the fundamental principles. Since the

---

[61] *But see* W.F. Boardman Co. v. Petch, 186 Cal. 476, 482, 199 P. 1047, 1050 (1921); White v. Treat, 100 F. 290, 291 (2d Cir. 1900). Sometimes such a transaction is referred to as an executed contract. *See* 2 BLACKSTONE'S COMMENTARIES 443 (1941); Mettel v. Gales, 12 S.D. 632, 639, 82 N.W. 181 (1900).

[62] 1 CORBIN § 4 (1963).

[63] *See* Douglass v. W.L. Williams Art Co., 143 Ga. 846, 85 S.E. 993 (1915); Lords Buller & Kenyon in Cooke v. Oxley, 3 Term. Rep. 653, 1 R.R. 783 (1790).

[64] "Roman concepts of contract were known in England in the twelfth and thirteenth centuries. But although they inspired the comparable evolution of a general theory of contract in the civil law systems of the Continent, they exercised no significant influence on the common law. The common law was thus able to chart its own peculiar course in the direction of a general basis of the enforcement of promises." *See* Farnsworth, *supra* note 45, at 591.

enactment of the UCC in fifty-one jurisdictions,[65] it is no longer possible to think of contract law exclusively as a common-law subject. Though the Code is technically applicable only to contracts for the sale of goods, there is little doubt that courts will be inclined to apply it analogously to other types of contracts.[66] This probability is reinforced by the current development of the RESTATEMENT 2d,[67] which is a systematic and modern statement of the principles of contract law including comments and illustrations. The RESTATEMENT 2d incorporates the major changes of the Code for all contracts not otherwise covered by the Code.

The original RESTATEMENT was published in 1932 by the American Law Institute for the guidance of the bench and bar. Since the Institute is a private organization, the FIRST RESTATEMENT did not have the force of law. However, the Chief Reporter for the original RESTATEMENT was Professor Samuel Williston, who was generally regarded as the leading contracts expert in America at that time. With the assistance of other luminaries, particularly Professor Arthur Linton Corbin, Professor Williston directed the effort to analyze the existing judicial decisions and to distill therefrom sound principles of contract law. The effect was more than substantial. Courts and lawyers have relied heavily on the RESTATEMENT to furnish guidance in the analysis of contracts questions, and the citations to the RESTATEMENT as sound authority in contracts cases are legion. With the enactment of the UCC throughout the country and with new conflicts among jurisdictions developing in various contracts cases, the American Law Institute undertook the compilation of a new RESTATEMENT OF CONTRACTS. The RESTATEMENT 2d was completed in 1980, and incorporated the major changes in contract law effected by the Code. Beyond this effort, the RESTATEMENT 2d performs the more traditional task of promoting sound resolutions of conflicting judicial decisions in contracts cases that have emerged since the publication of the FIRST RESTATEMENT. It promises to have a highly significant influence on courts in their adjudications of contracts questions.

In addition to the RESTATEMENT 2d, the development of a scholarly contracts analysis has been immensely aided by the production of two monumental, multi-volume treatises. The treatise by Professor Williston (first published in 1920)[68] was almost exclusively relied upon by courts and lawyers seeking a discourse on any topic in the field. More recently, the treatise of Professor Corbin (first published in 1950)[69] tends to be regarded as the principal comprehensive work on the subject. It is difficult to overestimate the contribution of these two giants of contract law. There is, however, a substantial difference

---

[65] 1 UNIFORM LAWS ANNOTATED 5 (Supp. 1972).

[66] In Discount Fabric House v. Wisconsin Tel. Co., 113 Wis. 2d 258, 334 N.W.2d 922 (1983), the telephone company sought to exculpate itself for liability under a Yellow Pages contract by inserting a fine print clause. The court included § 2-302 of the UCC in its analysis of unconscionability. In Olean v. Treglic, 190 Conn. 756, 463 A.2d 242 (1983), the court, in an opinion by Judge Peters, who formerly taught commercial law at the Yale Law School, used UCC § 9-311 to support the view that secured creditors have a right to accelerate the due date of unpaid debts upon alienation of property.

[67] See Braucher, *Freedom of Contract and the Second Restatement,* 78 YALE L.J. 598 (1969).

[68] WILLISTON, CONTRACTS (1920) [hereinafter cited as WILLISTON]. Subsequently revised in 1936. The third edition, begun in 1957, was completed in 1979.

[69] Most volumes of the treatise were revised in 1963.

in perspective between them. The Williston view tends to be more rigid and rule-oriented than the Corbin view. Often characterized as a positivist view, the Williston analysis suggests a system of rules or compartments into which any fact situation can be fit (or to use the terminology of certain critics, "squeezed"). The Williston position has undergone considerable criticism to the effect that it is mechanical and monistic.[70] On the other hand, Professor Corbin enjoys wide approval at the present time. In the American "Legal Realist" tradition, the Corbin approach is much more flexible in that it incorporates economic, social, moral, and ethical considerations. It recognizes the frailty of human institutions in judicial decisionmaking. It suggests that rules of law should be pliable and workable. It is willing to sacrifice some of the values of certainty and predictability in exchange for what Professor Corbin would hope are more relevant rationales and just results. The traditional criticism of the Corbin approach is its lack of certainty and predictability and its incorporation of extra-legal concepts into the "science" of law. For those who believe that certainty in the law is largely an illusion,[71] the Corbin approach is the clear choice. Since the RESTATEMENT 2d follows the Corbin tradition, that influence is destined to prevail for a considerable time. Notwithstanding the current dominance of the Corbin approach, there are other perspectives that suggest alternative, significant analyses of contract law.[72] Their ultimate course of development is a matter of speculation.

§ 10. The Uniform Commercial Code — History.

The UCC is the product of two distinguished organizations.[73] The National Conference of Commissioners on Uniform State Laws is composed of Commissioners from each of the states as well as the District of Columbia and Puerto Rico. Its principal purpose is the promotion of uniformity in state laws. The American Law Institute is a voluntary organization composed of some 1500 judges, law professors, and leading practitioners. The Institute is concerned with the improvement and clarification of American law. It is widely known and respected for its production of Restatements of the law in various subjects including contracts.[74] There is clear and convincing evidence of the significance of the Restatements in the many thousands of judicial opinions that rely upon them.

In 1938, the Merchants Association of New York City sponsored a proposal for a federal law to govern all interstate sales of goods. This proposal gave rise to an effort by the National Conference of Commissioners on Uniform State

---

[70]See F. KESSLER & G. GILMORE, Contract as a Principle of Order, CONTRACTS, CASES AND MATERIALS (2d ed. 1970).

[71]1 CORBIN § 1 (1936). "But certainty generally is illusion, and repose is not the destiny of man." Holmes, The Path of the Law, 10 HARV. L. REV. 457, 466 (1897).

[72]See I. MACNEIL, THE NEW SOCIAL CONTRACT (1980); Friedman & Macaulay, Contract Law and Contract Teaching: Past, Present and Future, 1967 WIS. L. REV. 804; Macaulay, The Use and Non-Use of Contracts in the Manufacturing Industry, 9 PRAC. LAW. 13 (No. 7, 1963); Friedman & Macaulay, Contract Law and Contract Research, 20 J. LEGAL EDUC. 452 (1968); Mueller, Contract Remedies; Business Fact and Legal Fantasy, 20 J. LEGAL EDUC. 469 (1968).

[73]See generally Malcolm, The Uniform Commercial Code in the United States, 12 INT'L & COMP. L.Q. 226 (1963); Schnader, A Short History of the Preparation and Enactment of the Uniform Commercial Code, 22 U. MIAMI L. REV. 1 (1967).

[74] See supra § 9.

Laws to revise the Uniform Sales Act that had been promulgated by the National Conference in 1906 and was subsequently enacted in thirty-seven states. In 1940, the National Conference adopted a proposal to undertake the preparation of a uniform commercial code that would not only encompass the law of sales but other commercial problems such as negotiable instruments, bills of lading, warehouse receipts, and related problems. The following year, the American Law Institute joined the National Conference in this effort, and work on the enlarged product started in 1945. The project was financed by grants from private foundations as well as business concerns and law firms. Many drafts of parts of the proposed uniform commercial code were prepared by committees of both organizations. Various advisory groups composed of judges, law professors, lawyers, and businessmen considered these drafts. The drafts were submitted to the general memberships of the National Conference and the Institute. Consultation with various individuals and organizations in the commercial world accompanied this effort. Finally, the first complete draft of the new Code was promulgated in 1949. A final draft was completed in 1951 that was approved not only by the National Conference and the Institute but also by the House of Delegates of the American Bar Association. A few amendments to the 1951 draft were made leading to an "official" edition of the new Code in 1952. The 1952 draft was then submitted to various state legislatures for enactment.

The first state to enact the Code was Pennsylvania in 1953 (effective July 1, 1954). In New York the governor referred the official text to the New York Law Revision Commission, which employed a large staff of consultants to study the Code. In 1956, the report of the Commission applauded the concept of a uniform commercial code but stated that the current (1952) official text required substantial revision.[75] During the time the Law Revision Commission study was proceeding, Pennsylvania was operating under the 1952 edition, and it was therefore important to consider the actual experience under the new Code in Pennsylvania. The experience in Pennsylvania was quite favorable. The National Conference and the Institute carefully considered both the New York study and the Pennsylvania experience in preparing and promulgating a revised edition of the Code to be known as the 1958 Official Text of the Code.

Though fourteen states had enacted the Code prior to 1962, the enactment in New York in that year prompted enactment throughout the country. In 1963, eleven states adopted the Code, and by 1968, forty-nine states had done so. Finally, in 1974, Louisiana adopted parts of the Code (Articles 1, 3, 4, 5, 7, and 8).[76]

In 1961, the Code sponsors established a Permanent Editorial Board to promote uniformity in state enactments and interpretation of the Code.[77] The Board was also concerned with the evaluation of the operation of the Code in

---

[75] N.Y. State Law Revision Comm'n, 1956 Report 56 (1956). These reports can provide insight in an analysis of the "purpose" of various Code sections.

[76] The jurisdictions enacting the UCC and the dates of such enactments are listed in 1 U.L.A. 1 (master ed. 1976).

[77] Schnader, *The Permanent Editorial Board for the Uniform Commercial Code: Can It Accomplish Its Object?*, 3 Am. Bus. L.J. 137 (1965).

the various states to fulfill its continuing duty to prepare proposals for revision of the official text. In 1971, the Board submitted a revision of Article 9 of the Code (dealing with security interests in personal property) that the sponsoring organizations approved in 1972. The 1972 Official Text of the Code included this revised version of Article 9. A revised version of Article 8 (Investment Securities) was recommended by a committee of the Permanent Editorial Board, and the Code sponsors adopted this new version in 1978. A new Article on personal property leasing, Article 2A, was adopted in 1987.

§ 11. The Uniform Commercial Code — Overview.

The UCC[78] is divided into twelve articles. Article 10 is designed to set forth the effective date of the Code in the particular jurisdiction and to allow for transition from pre-Code law. Article 11 is also concerned with transition — the transition to the 1972 version from earlier versions to allow for the revised Article 9. The other nine articles are substantive, and a summary of the coverage of each of these articles will provide an overview of the entire Code.

Article 1. General Provisions. Article 1 sets forth statements of the underlying purposes and policies of the Code. It also contains many useful definitions of terms used throughout the entire Code. It provides for conflict-of-laws problems,[79] interpretation guidelines,[80] and a statement of the underlying purpose of Code remedies.[81] A particularly important section, § 1-103, allows for the application of pre-Code law (general supplementary principles of law) that has not been displaced by the Code. The other critical section of Article 1 is § 1-201, which contains forty-six definitions of terms used throughout the Code.

Article 2. Sale of Goods. The student of contract law will be particularly interested in Article 2, since it governs the sale of, and contracts for the sale of, tangible personal (moveable) property. Not only is it simplistic to suggest that Article 2 of the Code merely replaces the Uniform Sales Act (1907), it is incorrect to characterize the change in this fashion. The law of sales of goods under the old Sales Act was based upon a property orientation in which questions as to which party had "title" to the goods were critical. Article 2 radically changes this property orientation to a contracts orientation, where questions of "title" are largely irrelevant. Numerous changes in classical contract

---

[78] The Code itself is not a traditional, authentic code. A genuine code totally displaces any preexisting law. The UCC depends upon supplementary principles of law and equity not displaced by its provisions (§ 1-103). A genuine code directs courts to look at the statute afresh in each case, regardless of prior interpretations. The UCC must be read in the light of the precedents that have provided interpretations of the statutory language. It is clear that our courts, proceeding from the common-law tradition, continue the concept of *stare decisis* in their interpretations. One of the principal draftsmen and commentators on the UCC, Professor Grant Gilmore, suggests, "We shall do better to think of it as a big statute — or as a collection of statutes bound together in the same book — which goes as far as it goes and no further." Gilmore, *Article 9: What It Does for the Past,* 26 LA. L. REV. 285, 285-86 (1966). *But see* Hawkland, *Uniform Commercial "Code" Methodology,* 1962 U. ILL. L.F. 291 (1962), where the author argues that the UCC is a true code in the classical sense.

[79] UCC § 1-105. Unless otherwise indicated, all references to the UCC in this book are to the 1972 Official Text.

[80] UCC § 1-102(3), (4), (5).

[81] UCC § 1-106.

law are wrought by Article 2. These changes may be viewed as more or less radical depending upon the particular aspect of classical contract law involved. Where the parties failed to include all of the terms of the contract, pre-Code courts would permit some terms to be implied, i.e., supplied by the court on a reasonable basis.[82] Article 2 liberalizes that view and permits virtually any term (with the exception of the quantity term) to be implied. Thus if the parties intend to make a contract and there is a reasonable basis for a court to provide a remedy for the breach of that contract,[83] the failure to include terms such as price, time of delivery, place of delivery, or other details of the bargain will not constitute fatal indefiniteness. The precise time of contract formation need not be provable.[84] A party may accept an offer in any reasonable manner or medium.[85] The parties may have an enforceable contract even though there are some additional or different terms in the acceptance of the offer.[86] This repudiation of the so-called "matching acceptance" rule of classical contract law is one of the more radical changes in Article 2. Similarly, a court may refuse to enforce all or part of a contract if the court deems the whole or part to be "unconscionable."[87] The pre-Code Statute of Frauds is substantially modified in the Article 2 version.[88] These are just some of the changes which Article 2 effectuates. Each of them will be considered in detail in the appropriate sections of this work. Finally, it is important to understand the basic concern of Article 2, which can be illuminated through an understanding of the pre-Code work of Karl Llewellyn, the principal draftsman of Article 2 and the father of the UCC. Llewellyn was concerned with the "bargain-in-fact" of the parties and believed that the identification of the factual bargain (the agreement) of the parties should not be fettered with technical rules of pre-Code contract law, because the application of these technical rules might well lead to a failure to recognize the true agreement or understanding of the parties.[89] Much of Article 2 can be appreciated only with an understanding of this basic philosophy of the law of contract in society. Finally, while Article 2 technically applies only to contracts for the sale of goods (and the sale of goods), the incorporation of many Article 2 concepts in the RESTATEMENT 2d will assure their application to all contracts.

Article 2A. Leases. In 1987, the American Law Institute and National Conference of Commissioners on Uniform State Laws approved this new Article dealing with the leasing of personal property. Leasing accounts for approximately $100 billion per year spent by business on equipment. Equipment leasing was particularly advantageous prior to the Tax Reform Act of 1986 due to the investment tax credit. Though the investment tax credit has been absolished, the popularity of leasing will continue. Another factor for the use of equipment leases is the avoidance of certain requirements of Article 9 of the

---

[82] *See infra* § 90.
[83] UCC § 2-204(3).
[84] UCC § 2-204(2).
[85] UCC § 2-206(1)(a).
[86] UCC § 2-207.
[87] UCC § 2-302.
[88] UCC § 2-201.
[89] *See generally* Llewellyn, *Why a Commercial Code?*, 22 TENN. L. REV. 779 (1953); K. LLEWELLYN, THE COMMON LAW TRADITION: DECIDING APPEALS 370 (1960).

UCC. This type of leasing was governed partly by the common law and partly by Articles 2 and 9 of the Code. The governance, however, was spotty and confusing. Article 2A is the first comprehensive effort to deal with personal property leasing. At the time of this writing, fourteen states have adopted Article 2A.[90]

Article 3. Commercial Paper. This article deals with all forms of negotiable instruments, including checks, promissory notes, drafts, and certificates of deposit. It replaces the 1897 Uniform Negotiable Instruments Law, though it does not govern bank deposits and collections, letters of credit, or corporate securities. Other articles of the Code (4, 5, and 8) deal with these questions. Commercial paper (negotiable instruments) problems are dealt with either in separate or combined courses taken in the second or third year of law school.

Articles 4 and 4A. Bank Deposits and Collections. Article 4 deals with all of the problems that can occur between the bank and its customer (e.g., checking account problems such as stop-payment orders) as well as the numerous problems that may occur when a check is deposited for collection. From the time a check is deposited in the customer's bank until it is finally paid by the bank upon which the check was drawn (perhaps necessitating a journey through one or more intermediate banks), problems may arise. Article 4 deals with those problems. New Article 4A was recently promulgated by the National Conference of Commissioners on Uniform State Laws to provide a comprehensive body of law defining the rights and duties of parties arising from *wire transfers* which currently account for trillions of dollars of payments each day.

Article 5. Letters of Credit. A letter of credit is simply a promise by a bank to pay a seller if and when certain specified conditions are met, i.e., the delivery of the goods ordered by the buyer and all necessary accompanying documentation. It assures the seller of payment through the credit of a party with impeccable credit standing (a bank) when the goods and documents are properly delivered. In overseas or long-distance contracts for the sale of goods, many sellers insist upon the supporting credit of a bank through the letter of credit device that the buyer will have its bank issue before the goods are shipped. There is a rough similarity between letters of credit issued by a bank and credit cards (*e.g.,* Visa or MasterCard) issued by a bank that permit the seller to rely upon a presumably solvent party, the bank. This article of the Code is normally considered in courses that combine coverage of several Code articles.

Article 6. Bulk Transfers. The original Article 6 of the Code was designed to complement other statutes (fraudulent conveyance and bankruptcy laws) in protecting unsecured creditors against sales of major parts of their debtors' inventories outside the ordinary course of business by placing notification

---

[90] *See* Cooper, *Identifying a Personal Property Lease Under the UCC,* 49 Оню St. L.J. 195 (1988); Comment, *A Unified Treatment of Finance Lessees' Revocation of Acceptance Under the Uniform Commercial Code,* 137 U. Pa. L. Rev. 967 (1989); Note, *Article 2A of the Uniform Commercial Code: An Unnecessary Perpetuation of the Lease-Sale Distinction.* There are few cases dealing with or mentioning Article 2A to this time. Among the more helpful, *see* Crumley v. Berry, 298 Ark. 112, 766 S.W.2d 7 (1989); Midwest Precision Servs. v. PTM Indus. Corp., 887 F.2d 1128 (1st Cir. 1989); *In re* Charles Cole v. Ford Motor Credit Co., 100 Bankr. 561 (N.D. Okl. 1989).

requirements and other restrictions on such sales. Because today's creditor is in a much better position to make informed judgments about whether to extend credit (through technology, reporting services and the like), the National Conference of Commissioners on Uniform State Laws has recently taken the position that regulation of bulk sales is unnecessary and Article 6 should be repealed. Recognizing, however, that bulk sales may present particular problems in certain states and others may be disinclined to repeal the original Article 6, the Conference has recently promulgated a revised version of Article 6 "designed to afford better protection to creditors while minimizing the impediments to good-faith transactions."

Article 7. Documents of Title. Documents of title are receipts for goods, typically issued by public warehouses where the owner of the goods decides to store them (warehouse receipts) or by public carriers who issue documents of title called bills of lading when goods are placed with the carrier (railroad, trucking company, airline) for transportation. These documents of title take on great importance, particularly if they are negotiable, as they will control the disposition of the goods. Article 7 deals with the purchase and sale of these documents: the rights and duties of the issuer of the document and the holder of the document as well as the owner of the stored or transported goods. Article 7 replaces the Uniform Warehouse Receipts Act and the Uniform Bills of Lading Act, both of which were produced by the National Conference of Commissioners on Uniform State Laws, and is considered in courses dealing with several articles of the Code.

Article 8. Investment Securities. Article 8 is designed to govern transactions in securities (stocks, bonds, and other securities that serve as investment devices). It is not a regulatory statute; with some justification it has been called a negotiable instruments law for investment securities. It replaces the Uniform Stock Transfer Act. Article 8 was revised in 1978 so as to permit it to deal with "uncertificated" or paperless securities and is typically covered in courses dealing with commercial paper.

Article 9. Secured Transactions. Many lawyers think that Article 9 is the most significant contribution of the Code. It deals with security interests in personal property that, prior to the Code, were a curious assortment of conditional sales, factor's liens, chattel mortgages, and trust receipts. Each of these security devices was designed to accomplish the same purpose: to assure the repayment of outstanding indebtedness to the seller who sold the goods on *secured* credit, or to the bank or other lending institution that lent the money with which the goods were purchased. Secured transactions reflect the way business is done in America. The inventory on the floor of an auto dealer or appliance or other retail store is typically purchased with funds borrowed from a commercial lender or on credit extended by the seller of those goods. The seller or lender takes a security interest in the goods and is repaid as those goods are resold. Security interests may be taken in the raw materials of manufacturing concerns to assure repayment when the goods are manufactured and sold. Security interests may be taken in intangible property such as accounts and general intangibles. If the outstanding loan is not repaid, the secured party may look to the collateral (the specific, identified tangible, or intangible property) in which the secured party has its security interest. The property will be repossessed (perhaps without any judicial proceeding), and the collateral will be sold to assure the repayment of the outstanding indebtedness. Article 9 of the Code deals with all aspects of secured transactions and is normally the subject of a separate law school course or a course covering several Code articles.

§ 12. Uniform Commercial Code — Scope of Article 2.

Since Article 2 of the Code plays such a prominent part in the law of contracts, it is important to consider its scope. Section 2-102 of the Code states that it applies to *transactions* in goods, but such transactions do not include security interests in goods that are governed by Article 9. There can be no doubt that "transactions" includes contracts for the sale of goods. But the question arises, does Article 2 apply to bailments and leases of goods? Since Article 7 deals with bailments to warehousemen or carriers, such bailments are necessarily excluded from the scope of Article 2. Article 2 refers to "buyer" and "seller," thereby negating the possibility of including leases of goods within its scope.[91] There is another problem in determining the scope of Article 2. Section 2-102 refers to transactions in "goods" and the term "goods" is defined in § 2-105: "[A]ll things (including specially manufactured goods) which are moveable at the time of identification to the contract for sale other than money in which the price is to be paid, investment securities (Article 8) and other things in action. 'Goods' also includes the unborn young of animals and growing crops and other identified things attached to realty as described in the section on goods to be severed from realty (Section 2-107)." While § 2-105 is helpful, it does not provide self-evident boundaries for Article 2. It emphasizes the inclusion of "moveable" goods, but some "moveables" such as investment securities are excluded because they are dealt with in Article 8. This structure may appear watertight but it is not. Thus in an action for breach of contract to purchase securities, the court first recognized that Article 2 does not apply to investment securities. However, it further recognized that Article 8 contains no provisions for buyer's remedies when the seller breaches such a contract.[92] The court applied the remedy provisions of Article 2, finding support in a comment to § 2-105 which expressly recognizes the possibility that a court may wish to apply an Article 2 section to an Article 8 situation by analogy.[93]

If there is authority, albeit in the unenacted comment, for the application of Article 2 by analogy, it is important to consider the extent of that analogous application. Courts have had little difficulty applying the significantly modified concepts of contract law in Article 2 to contracts that are not concerned with the sale of goods.[94] Again, the incorporation of Article 2 guidelines in the RESTATEMENT 2d assures a continuation of this application of Article 2 con-

---

[91] Leases of goods are now dealt with in new Article 2A.

[92] G.A. Thompson & Co. v. Wendell J. Miller Mtg. Co., 457 F. Supp. 996, 998 (S.D.N.Y. 1978).

[93] *Id.* at 999.

[94] *See, e.g.,* Zamore v. Whitten, 395 A.2d 435 (Me. 1978) (sale of stock certificates); Kroeze v. Chloride Group, Ltd., 572 F.2d 1099 (5th Cir. 1978) (tender offer for shares of stock); Fairfield Lease Corp. v. U-Vend, Inc., 14 UCC REP. SERV. (CALLAGHAN) 1244 (N.Y. 1974) (lease of a soda machine).

cepts outside its technical scope. The warranty provisions of Article 2 have been applied to real property transactions though the name of the warranty may have been altered to reflect the nature of the transaction.[95] An express invitation to apply a provision beyond its technical application is found in the comments to § 2-313 dealing with express warranties. While the section refers to "buyers" and "sellers," thereby limiting its technical operation to the sale of goods, the comment expressly recognizes "those lines of case law growth which have recognized that warranties need not be confined either to sales contracts or to the direct parties to such a contract. They may arise in other appropriate circumstances such as in the case of bailments for hire."[96] With some exceptions, courts appear willing to apply Article 2 provisions analogously to leases of goods.[97] Even with respect to mixed or hybrid transactions involving goods and services or goods and real estate, courts generally take an expansive view of the analogous application of Article 2. When a wine glass broke in the hand of a diner, the restaurant was held liable under the warranty provisions of Article 2.[98] Where a customer of a beauty shop suffered injury from the application of a certain product as part of a permanent wave treatment, the court held the Code applicable though it recognized the hybrid nature of the transaction.[99] Where the contract involves goods and services, some courts consider the dominant purpose of the contract to determine whether it is a contract for goods to which the Code applies or to services to which the Code does not apply.[1] Other courts apply Code provisions though the majority of the price is allocable to the services portion of the contract. The spraying of crops has been held to be a sale of goods[2] as has the delivery of electricity[3] and natural gas.[4] The complex policy issues in determining whether blood transfusions should be regarded as sales of goods perplexed several courts.[5] However, those questions have largely been resolved by statute.[6] In summary, courts have demonstrated a definite proclivity to apply Article 2 provisions well beyond technical sale-of-goods contracts.[7]

---

[95] *See infra* § 100.

[96] UCC § 2-313 comment 2.

[97] Baker v. City of Seattle, 79 Wash. 2d 198, 484 P.2d 405 (1971) (lease of a golf cart); Hertz Commercial Leasing Corp. v. Transportation Credit Clearing House, 59 Misc. 2d 226, 298 N.Y.S.2d 392 (1969), *rev'd on other grounds*, 64 Misc. 2d 910, 316 N.Y.S.2d 585 (1970) (lease of equipment); Redfern Meats, Inc. v. Hertz Corp., 134 Ga. App. 381, 215 S.E.2d 10 (1975) (lease of truck). *See also* Murray, *Under the Spreading Analogy of Article 2 of the Uniform Commercial Code*, 39 FORDHAM L. REV. 447 (1971). *Contra* Bona v. Graefe, 264 Md. 69, 285 A.2d 607 (1972) (lease of golf cart not covered by UCC).

[98] Shaffer v. Victoria Station, Inc., 91 Wash. 2d 295, 588 P.2d 233 (1978).

[99] Newmark v. Gimbel's, Inc., 102 N.J. Super. 279, 246 A.2d 11 (1968), *aff'd*, 54 N.J. 585, 258 A.2d 697 (1969).

[1] Glover School & Office Equip. Co. v. Dave Hall, Inc., 372 A.2d 221 (Del. Super. 1977); Bonebrake v. Cox, 499 F.2d 951 (8th Cir. 1974).

[2] Eichenberger v. Wilhelm, 244 N.W.2d 691 (N.D. 1976).

[3] Rochester Gas & Elec. Corp. v. Public Serv. Comm'n, 404 N.Y.S.2d 801 (Sup. Ct. 1978).

[4] University of Pittsburgh v. Equitable Gas Co., 5 Pa. D. & C. 3d 303 (1978).

[5] Perlmutter v. Beth David Hosp., 308 N.Y. 100, 123 N.E.2d 792 (1954) (blood transfusion is a service contract). *Accord* White v. Sarasota County Pub. Hosp. Bd., 206 So. 2d 19 (Fla. App. 1968). *Contra* Jackson v. Muhlenberg Hosp., 96 N.J. Super. 314, 232 A.2d 879 (1967) (sale of goods).

[6] Note, *Pricing Bad Blood: Re-Assessing Liability for Post-Transfusion Hepatitis*, 15 HARV. J. LEGIS. 557 (1978).

[7] *See* Note, *Contracts for Goods and Services and Article 2 of the U.C.C.*, 9 RUT.-CAM. L. REV. 303 (1978).

Other questions regarding the scope of Article 2 are dealt with more directly by specific sections within that Article. Thus a contract requiring a farmer to sell all of the crops from a certain tract of land is within Article 2 even though the crops have not yet been planted at the time the contract is made.[8] Since the goods did not exist at the time of contract formation, the Code would characterize them as "future" goods that make the agreement a "contract to sell." Since growing crops are considered goods under Article 2, the contract would be viewed as a contract to sell future crops and would clearly come within Article 2. However, a contract for the sale of minerals (including oil and gas) would be characterized as a contract for the sale of realty if the buyer was to sever such goods from the land.[9] If the contract provides for the seller to sever, the Code would characterize the contract as one for the sale of goods.[10] Under the 1962 version of the Code, timber was treated like minerals, i.e., whether it was a goods or land contract depended upon who was to sever the timber. However, under the revised (1972) version, timber is treated as goods (analogous to growing crops) regardless of which party severs.[11] It must be remembered that, at the time of this writing, only about half the jurisdictions have enacted the revised (1972) version of the Code, which deals extensively with the revision of Article 9 and only incidentally with other sections including the Article 2 section relating to the treatment of timber.

§ 13. The Uniform Commercial Code — Comments.

Each section of the UCC is followed by "official comments" that elaborate on the purpose and application of the section. They vary in length, clarity, and sophistication. It is important to recognize that these "official" comments are not part of the enacted law, i.e., the various legislatures enacted only the sections of the Code — not the comments. Moreover, the Permanent Editorial Board added comments after the Code had been enacted in many states. The comments, therefore, do not have the weight of "legislative history" in the interpretation of Code sections. An early version of the Code contained a section that stated that the comments "may be consulted in the construction and application of this Act."[12] However, that section was deleted in 1956, and no similar section was inserted in subsequent drafts. In theory, the comments may be ignored. However, many courts have relied heavily upon the comments in their construction and application of particular sections of the Code. Judicial adoption of the comments provides them with precedential force. The comments contain a wealth of material, but it must always be remembered that the comments are not legislation. Moreover, they are not exhaustive. One of the more useful aspects of the comments is their cross-reference to statutory definitions found in other Code sections. Again, the warning is that these cross-references are not always exhaustive. Since the comments are not part

---

[8] UCC § 2-107(1).

[9] *Id.*

[10] *Id.* Coos Lumber Co. v. Builders Lumber & Supply Corp., 104 N.H. 404, 188 A.2d 330 (1963) (sale of logs).

[11] UCC § 2-107(2).

[12] UCC § 1-102(3)(f) in the 1952 version.

of the enacted law, should there be any conflict between the enacted section language and comment language, there is no question that the section language controls and the comment language must be rejected.

§ 14. Contracts Classified.

For the sake of analysis, contracts are classified in various ways. With relation to the mode of their formation, they are classified as formal or informal. From the point of view of the time of formation, classical contract law characterized them as unilateral or bilateral. In terms of the legal sanctions involved, contracts are enforceable, voidable, or unenforceable. An understanding of the meaning of these terms will facilitate our discussion of more specific problems.

§ 15. Formal and Informal Contracts.

In general, it can be said that our law recognizes two ways in which a promise may become legally obligatory. On the one hand, we have the formal method, the essence of which is the observance of certain prescribed formalities in connection with the making of the promise. On the other hand, there is the informal method, which depends for its efficacy upon the presence in the transaction of certain elements that may be said to be the normal concomitants of a promise that is made with binding intent.

The formal method of making a contract is historically the older. In the early stages of our law, a promise had no binding force unless its making was accompanied by the observance of certain set formalities.[13] Whether this was due to the fact that it was realized that untutored men would be more likely to carry out an undertaking that was entered into with the accompaniment of certain more or less solemn acts, we do not know. Of the formal contracts known to the early law, four are of importance to the present day lawyer. These are: (1) the contract under seal; (2) the recognizance; (3) the negotiable instrument and document; and (4) the letter of credit.[14]

The antithesis of the formal contract is the informal contract, which is sometimes also called a simple contract or bargain.[15] The informal contract, as has already been indicated, derives its force not because certain formalities have been observed, but because of the presence in the transaction of certain elements that are usually present when people make promises with binding intent. These elements have been generalized by our law and made essential in practically all cases. They are mutual assent and consideration (or a device other than consideration), which will be examined in detail when we come to consider the question as to how an informal contract is consummated.[16] The

---

[13] See Hazeltine, *The Formal Contract of Early English Law*, 10 COLUM. L. REV. 806 (1910), SELECTED READINGS ON CONTRACTS 1 (1931); Pollock, *Contracts in Early English Law*, 6 HARV. L. REV. 389 (1892), SELECTED READINGS ON CONTRACTS 10 (1931).

[14] RESTATEMENT 2d § 6 comments c, d, e, and f.

[15] See RESTATEMENT 2d § 6 comment a (1973) indicating that the "formal" and "informal" usage is avoided. For historical background, see Ames, *Parol Contracts Prior to Assumpsit*, 8 HARV. L. REV. 252 (1894), SELECTED READINGS ON CONTRACTS 23 (1931); Ames, *The History of Assumpsit*, 2 HARV. L. REV. 1, 53 (1888), SELECTED READINGS ON CONTRACTS 33 (1931).

[16] See infra Chapter 2.

informal contract may exist either with or without a writing or any other formality, except insofar as statutes have been passed changing the common-law rules. It is true that in most jurisdictions statutes have been passed, known as Statutes of Frauds, which require that certain kinds of informal contracts be evidenced by a writing in order that they may be legally enforceable.[17] While it might be thought that these statutes make formal contracts out of those undertakings that are comprehended within their terms, it is incorrect to classify them as formal contracts.

§ 16. Unilateral and Bilateral Contracts.

Traditional contract law emphasized the distinction between contracts involving two promises, which were said to be bilateral, and contracts involving only one promise, which were called unilateral.[18] While the student should be aware of this distinction, neither the UCC nor the RESTATEMENT 2d classifies contracts in this fashion. The reporter's note in the RESTATEMENT 2d suggests that the reasons for the deletion of this classification included serious doubt as to its utility as well as the confusion it was capable of producing.[19] As subsequent sections suggest, the result is that the true unilateral contract is rare under either the UCC or the RESTATEMENT 2d. Yet, the traditional classification may appear in the case law or elsewhere in the future. Moreover, the student must be able to recognize the true unilateral contract even though it will be a rarity under the UCC or RESTATEMENT 2d. Therefore, the student should be aware of the traditional analysis that follows. The new analysis is found in the sections dealing with the acceptance of the offer.[20]

If the parties to a contract exchange promises, the contract is formed as soon as the promises are exchanged. At that point there are two outstanding obligations since both promises remain to be performed or, as it is sometimes put, the contract is executory on both sides. When there are two outstanding obligations resulting from an exchange of promises, the contract is said to be bilateral or two-sided. There are two rights and two duties in such a contract since each of the parties has a right against the other and each has a duty of performance to the other. Another characteristic of a bilateral contract is that there are two promisors and two promisees. Since each party has made a promise to the other, each has given a promise and a promise has been addressed to each of the parties.

A simple example of the bilateral contract is a promise by *A* to sell his auto to *B* for $2000 in exchange for *B*'s promise to buy *A*'s car for $2000. As soon as the promises are exchanged, a bilateral contract exists. *A* is a promisor whose duty is to deliver the car to *B*. *A* is also a promisee since he has received *B*'s promise to pay the price. As a promisee, *A* has the right to collect $2000 from *B*. *B* is a promisor whose duty is to pay the price to *A*. *B* is also a promisee since he has received *A*'s promise to deliver the car. As a promisee, *B* has the right to the auto. Thus, both *A* and *B* are promisors and promisees; moreover,

---

[17] See *infra* Chapter 12.

[18] FIRST RESTATEMENT § 12.

[19] See RESTATEMENT 2d, reporter's note at 17.

[20] See RESTATEMENT 2d, reporter's note at 17; Murray, *Contracts: A New Design for the Agreement Process,* 53 CORNELL L. REV. 785 (1968).

A and *B* both have rights and duties so that there are two rights and two duties.

In unilateral or one-sided contracts, there is only one promise. Therefore, there is only one promisor and one promisee.[21] The promisor manifests his intention that he does not wish a promise in exchange for his promise. Rather, he wants an act or performance. The classic illustration of the unilateral contract finds *A* saying to *B*, "If you will walk across the Brooklyn Bridge I will pay you $100." *A* does not wish *B* to promise to walk across the bridge. He requires the act or performance of walking across the bridge. The contract will be *formed* when *B* successfully traverses the bridge. *A* will have already received that which he wanted in exchange for his promise. *B* will have already performed the act requested by *A* at the moment the contract is formed. Therefore, at the time the unilateral contract is formed, there is only one right and one correlative duty. *B,* who has already performed, has a right against *A* to collect the $100, and *A,* who has already received the performance requested, has a correlative duty to pay the $100.

§ 17. Void and Voidable Contracts.

In certain types of contracts, one or more of the parties may have the power to put an end to the contract simply by manifesting an election to do so. This is known as a "voidable" contract since it can be avoided by one or more of the parties. Until the party who has the power of avoidance elects to exercise it, the contract remains intact. Moreover, even though one of the parties has the power of avoidance, he may extinguish that power by ratification of the contract.[22]

Illustrations of voidable contracts include those where one party is an infant[23] (i.e., one who has not attained the age providing full capacity to enter

---

[21] *See* FIRST RESTATEMENT § 12; 1 CORBIN § 21 (1963). The distinction between a unilateral and a bilateral contract is frequently, although somewhat inaccurately, expressed by saying that a unilateral contract is one in which the requested consideration for the promise is some act or forbearance other than the making of a promise, whereas a bilateral contract is one in which the consideration consists of a return promise. Thus in Brackenbury v. Hodgkin, 116 Me. 399, 102 A. 106, 107 (1917), it is said, "The offer was the basis, not of a bilateral contract, requiring a reciprocal promise, a promise for a promise, but of a unilateral contract requiring an act for a promise." *See also* Port Huron Mach. Co. v. Wohlers, 207 Iowa 826, 221 N.W. 843 (1928); Petterson v. Pattberg, 248 N.Y. 86, 161 N.E. 428 (1928). This usage of these terms, while of comparatively recent origin, is very common at the present time. In the older cases, the term "unilateral contract" was frequently used to refer to a promise that had no consideration to support it and therefore was not legally enforceable, unless it had been put in the form of a formal contract. *See* Great N. Ry. v. Witham, L.R. 9 C.P. 16 (1873). Unfortunately, it is still sometimes used with this connotation. *See* SALMOND & WINFIELD, LAW OF CONTRACTS 14 (1927); Perfection Mattress & Spring Co. v. Dupree, 216 Ala. 303, 113 So. 74 (1927); Edwards v. Roberts, 209 S.W. 247, 250 (Tex. 1919); Cal Hirsch & Sons Iron & Rail Co. v. Paragould & M.R.R., 148 Mo. App. 173, 127 S.W. 623 (1910). Where there is no legal obligation the transaction may perhaps be properly called a "unilateral promise" or an "offer looking to the formation of a unilateral contract" but it can hardly be correctly called a "unilateral contract." *See* High Wheel Auto Parts Co. v. Journal Co., 50 Ind. App. 396, 98 N.E. 442 (1912), where the court said of the term "unilateral contract" when so used that it is a "legal solecism."

[22] *See* FIRST RESTATEMENT § 13; RESTATEMENT 2d § 7; 1 CORBIN § 6 (1963). *See also* Stabbert v. Atlas Imperial Diesel Engine Co., 39 Wash. 2d 789, 238 P.2d 1212 (1951). Sometimes the phrase "void contract" is used incorrectly to mean "voidable contract." *See generally* Levin, *The Varying Meaning and Legal Effect of the Word "Void,"* 32 MICH. L. REV. 1088 (1933).

[23] *See infra* § 23.

into contracts) or contracts induced by fraud, mistake, or duress. If a sixteen-year-old infant enters into a contract with an adult, the adult is bound to the contract but the infant has the power of avoidance. This power continues until the infant reaches the age of full capacity, at which time he will either affirm (ratify) the contract or disaffirm it, thereby avoiding any obligations thereunder. If the infant does not disaffirm within a reasonable time after reaching maturity, his silence will operate as an affirmance of the contract.

If a party is induced to enter into a contract by fraud, there is a contract, but the fraudulent representations of the other party give the defrauded party a power of avoidance or disaffirmance. On the other hand, the defrauded party may wish the contract to be performed because, notwithstanding the fraud, he believes the contract to be beneficial to him. In that situation, he simply does not exercise the power of avoidance; instead, he affirms or ratifies the contract. The identical analysis would apply to a contract induced by mistake or duress. The policy reasons underlying various types of voidable contracts will be discussed in subsequent sections.

"Void" contracts are not contracts at all.[24] The phrase is a contradiction since any promise under a void contract that is breached will not give rise to any remedy nor will the law recognize any duty of performance by the promisor. Sometimes "void contracts" are referred to as "illegal contracts." While public policy may dictate that a particular bargain that has all the earmarks of a contract receive no legal sanction whatsoever because the bargain, if performed, would result in an illegal act, the phrase "illegal contract" used synonymously with "void contract" may be inaccurate.[25] While certain illegal bargains are clearly "void" in the sense that there is no legal sanction attached to them, there are certain kinds of "illegal contracts" that are merely voidable bargains. As to these contracts, the phrase "illegal contract" does not properly designate the transaction.

§ 18. Enforceable and Unenforceable Contracts.

The law treats contracts differently with respect to their performance. If a promisor breaches his promise, various consequences may result, depending upon the particular contract. The normal situation involves an award of money (damages) to the injured promisee for the breach by the promisor. This is often the only remedy open to the promisee. In other situations, the injured promisee may be entitled to another remedy, i.e., other than damages. One additional remedy is specific performance of a promise that is available only in certain situations. An example of this remedy occurs in relation to a breach of a promise to sell land. The injured buyer may successfully ask a court of equity to decree (order) the defaulting promisor to convey the land itself rather than pay damages to the injured promisee. Of course, the buyer must pay the purchase price of the land as set forth in the contract. However, if he receives the very land for which he contracted, he is being placed in exactly the same position he would have been in had the promise to sell the land been

---

[24] This phraseology is frequently used in statutes that prohibit the making of certain kinds of contracts, or make certain kinds of agreements unenforceable. Sometimes it is used as synonymous with "voidable contract." See supra note 22.

[25] See infra § 18.

performed. One of the reasons for permitting this unusual remedy in land contracts is that land is unique and money (damages) would not place the promisee in the position he would have been in had the promise been performed since this particular tract could not be purchased elsewhere at any price. Therefore, the usual remedy at law (damages) is inadequate. Again, the normal remedy for breach of contract is money (damages), which constitutes substitutional relief to protect the reasonable expectations of the injured promisee. When either remedy (damages or specific performance) is available, the contract is said to be "enforceable."

In other situations, the law will recognize the existence of the contract but refuse to enforce it when it is breached. Here, the contract is said to be "unenforceable."[26] Since the court will not enforce the contract, neither the remedy of damages nor the remedy of specific performance is available. However, the court still recognizes, in some fashion, that a duty of performance has been created.[27] An illustration of this situation occurs in relation to certain types of contracts that are not enforceable unless there is a signed writing to evidence the contract. Contracts for the sale of land or contracts for the sale of goods priced at $500 or more fall into this category. Therefore, an oral contract for the sale of land or an oral contract for the sale of goods at $500 or more that fulfills all of the requirements of a contract will still not be enforceable unless there is some writing to evidence it. If either the seller or the buyer breaches and the other party seeks damages or (in the land contract) specific performance, the breaching party may simply raise what is known as the Statute of Frauds as a defense. The Statute of Frauds requires certain types of contracts to be evidenced by writing. The policy reasons underlying the Statute of Frauds will be discussed in the chapter dealing with that subject. At this point, the student should regard this discussion as simply an illustration of an unenforceable contract. Again, it is important to emphasize the fact that courts refusing to enforce such oral contracts are not deciding that the contracts do not exist. They simply hold that even if the contracts do exist, they are unenforceable.

It is important to distinguish "unenforceable" contracts from "voidable" contracts. As suggested in the preceding section,[28] a voidable contract is one that allows one of the parties to the contract to avoid it. The party with the power of avoidance may elect to either avoid the contract or affirm it. An unenforceable contract is one in which the duty of performance does not depend solely on the election of one party. If *A*, an infant, enters into an oral contract with *B*, an adult, whereby *B* agrees to sell and *A* agrees to buy a tract of land, *A*'s promise is voidable because of his infancy and it is unenforceable under the Statute of Frauds. *B*'s promise to sell the land is also unenforceable because of the Statute of Frauds but it is not voidable since *B* is an adult. Assume that *A* delivers to *B* a signed writing stating the terms of the contract.

---

[26] *See, e.g., infra* Chapter 12. Such agreements are sometimes called "agreements of imperfect obligation." *See* POLLOCK, CONTRACTS 682 (8th ed. 1921). *See also* FIRST RESTATEMENT § 14; RESTATEMENT 2d § 8.

[27] "An unenforceable contract is one for the breach of which neither the remedy of damages nor the remedy of specific performance is available, but which is recognized in some other way as creating a duty of performance, though there has been no ratification." RESTATEMENT 2d § 8.

[28] *See infra* § 17.

At this point, the contract is enforceable since the Statute of Frauds writing requirement has been satisfied; but the contract is still voidable by *A*. *A* may choose to avoid the contract or to ratify it. If he chooses the former, the contract is enforceable but avoided since *A* has elected to exercise his power of avoidance. On the other hand, if *A* chooses to affirm or ratify the contract, the enforceable contract is no longer subject to the power of avoidance since that power has been extinguished by *A's* affirmance or ratification.

Oral contracts subject to the Statute of Frauds constitute only one illustration of unenforceable contracts. At this point, it is important for the student to understand the concept of "unenforceable" contracts and to be able to distinguish that classification from "void" and "voidable" contracts.

§ 19. Express and Implied Contracts.

Contracts are sometimes classified as being either express or implied. Implied contracts are in turn classified as implied in fact or implied in law.

A contract is said to be "express" when it has been stated in oral or written words, as distinguished from an "implied-in-fact" contract in which the undertaking is inferred from conduct other than the speaking or writing of words.[29] It is submitted that this classification, at its best, is of no practical value and may even mislead. All true contracts are necessarily express contracts, in that they must arise out of an expressed intention. It is true that the undertaking that the law sanctions and calls a contract does not have to be manifested in language but may be evidenced by conduct. However, this does not militate against the conclusion that the undertaking is in all cases one that has been expressed. To speak of it as "implied in fact," when it has been expressed in ways other than through the use of language, is simply to confuse the real issue, which is in all cases one of determining whether an intention to assume the alleged undertaking has been manifested in some way.[30] So-called "implied-in-fact" contracts occur in many contexts. A wife requests a husband to stop at the local grocery on his way from work to purchase one or more small items. When the husband stops at the store, he finds a large crowd. He knows the owner of the store. He picks up the small items and holds them high to attract the owner's attention. The owner nods or in some other fashion indicates that he agrees to the transaction. The husband leaves with the items. A contract is formed, the clear implication of which is that the husband has promised to pay for the items at some more convenient time and the owner has accepted the promise. No words were spoken or written and, therefore, the traditional characterization would be a contract "implied in fact." However, the outward manifestations of the parties clearly expressed the consensual elements necessary for a genuine contract. The parties expressed themselves

---

[29] *See* Bush v. Lane, 161 Cal. App. 2d 278, 326 P.2d 640 (1958); Miller v. Stevens, 224 Mich. 626, 195 N.W. 481 (1923); and the cases cited in the following notes to this section.

[30] Desny v. Wilder, 46 Cal. 2d 715, 299 P.2d 257 (1956); Lombard v. Rahilly, 127 Minn. 449, 149 N.W. 950 (1914). In Francis v. St. Louis Cty. Water Co., 322 S.W.2d 724, 726 (Mo. 1959), the court said, "And as a matter of fact there is no difference in the legal effect between an express contract and an implied contract; if there was a contract it was of course an express contract whether the agreement was in writing, verbal, or an inference from the acts and conduct of the parties. The distinction lies in the manner of manifesting mutual assent."

through their conduct just as effectively, if not more effectively, than they would have expressed themselves through language.

The phrase "implied-in-law" contract is even more unfortunate. The phrase is intended to designate certain legal obligations that are enforceable on the basis of unjust enrichment. If one party, reasonably expecting to be compensated, confers a benefit upon another, the party receiving the benefit will be unjustly enriched at the expense of the other. To avoid unjust enrichment, the law permits the party who has conferred the benefit to recover the reasonable value of the benefit. Through this action, he is restored to status quo, i.e., he is placed in the position he would have been in if there had been no unjust enrichment. At common law, this restitutionary action was brought in the form of a contract action (assumpsit) with a fictitious promise implied in law to permit the recovery. There is no real promise and none of the other elements of a real contract is present.[31] The exclusive connection between this kind of action and a real contract is the historic accident of the form of action that was used to accomplish restitution. Since there is no true contract involved, the enforceable obligation came to be known as a "contract implied in law" or "quasi-contract."[32] Though the common-law forms of action have been abolished, this anomaly continues at the present time and is traditionally dealt with in courses and books dealing with contract law. The purpose of quasi-contracts is to accomplish restitution, i.e., to place the parties in status quo as if no unjust enrichment had occurred. The purpose of true contracts is to fulfill those reasonable expectations that have been induced by the making of a promise. It would be preferable if a wholly different name were adopted for the restitutionary device so that it would be clear that this type of obligation (which is controlled by entirely different principles) has no relationship to contract.

Quasi-contract can arise in innumerable situations. For the sake of clarity, one example of its use follows. The student is cautioned against viewing this example as the only kind of situation in which this restitutionary device can be used.[33] A statute in Ohio provided that a county board of education had a duty to provide transportation to schoolchildren within the county who resided more than four miles from the appropriate school. A and his family resided more than four miles from the appropriate school. The county board refused to perform its statutory duty of providing transportation for A's children. A transported the children to school during the academic year and then presented his bill to the board. The board refused to pay. In an action by A, the court held that A conferred a benefit upon the board by performing the board's statutory duty to transport the children. The board was, therefore, unjustly enriched at the expense of A. A was a proper person to perform the duty since he was the father and a taxpayer in the county. Therefore, A did not confer

---

[31] Hill v. Waxberg, 16 Alaska 477, 237 F.2d 936 (9th Cir. 1956); People v. Dummer, 274 Ill. 637, 113 N.E. 934 (1916); Continental Forest Prods., Inc. v. Chandler Supply Co., 95 Idaho 739, 518 P.2d 1201, 1205 (1974): "However, a contract implied in law is not a contract at all, but an obligation imposed by law for the purpose of bringing about justice and equity without reference to the intent or the agreement of the parties and, in some cases, in spite of an agreement between the parties."

[32] See F. Woodward, The Law of Quasi-Contracts § 4 (1913).

[33] See infra § 126(D)(1).

the benefit upon the board gratuitously; he reasonably expected to be compensated. In the quasi contract action, *A* recovered the reasonable value of the benefit conferred.[34]

§ 20. Parties to Contracts.

At least two persons, either natural or artificial (one a promisor and the other a promisee), are necessary to the making of a contract, although any number greater than two may participate.[35] When there is more than one promisor or more than one promisee, the promisors or the promisees may act together as a unit, they may act separately as individuals, or they may act together and separately. Traditionally the obligation is said to be either "joint," "several," or "joint and several," depending upon the circumstances.[36] The RESTATEMENT 2d avoids the terminology "joint," "several," and "joint and several" because of their obsolete connotations.[37] The RESTATEMENT 2d substitutes "multiple promisors and promisees."[38]

§ 21. Requirement of Capacity to Contract.

Persons who make contracts differ markedly as to their intelligence, background, experience, judgment, and maturity. In general, the law does not take these differences into account because it would be impossible to do so. If there is a clear impairment of the ability to participate in the contracting process, however, the law will consider such impairment and find a lack of capacity to make a contract.[39] The basic requirement of any contract is an objective manifestation of intention to be bound to a bargain. An objective manifestation of assent may be impossible if physical or mental impairment is so extreme that the person cannot form the necessary intent. In such cases, there is a *total* lack of capacity and no contract is formed. Sometimes the effect of finding a total lack of capacity is characterized as a "void contract." This usage should

---

[34]Sommers v. Putnam Cty. Bd. of Educ., 113 Ohio St. 177, 148 N.E. 682 (1925).

[35]RESTATEMENT 2d § 9. "It is a first principle, that in whatever different capacities a person may act, he never can contract with himself nor maintain an action against himself. He can in no form be both obligor and obligee." Eastman v. Wright, 23 Mass. (6 Pick.) 316, 320 (1828). *Accord* Peoples Bank v. Allen, 344 Mo. 207, 125 S.W.2d 829 (1939); Dotson v. Skaggs, 77 W. Va. 372, 87 S.E. 460 (1915); Gorham's Adm'r v. Meacham's Adm'r, 63 Vt. 231, 22 A. 572 (1891). *But see* Breedlove v. Freudenstein, 89 F.2d 324 (5th Cir. 1937), *commented on,* 51 HARV. L. REV. 351 (1937), in which it was held that a national bank that was authorized by statute to act as executor of an estate could make a binding contract for the borrowing of money in its capacity as executor with itself as a bank. So, also, it apparently was not possible, in the earlier law, for one member of an unincorporated group to contract with the group as a whole. There was no such thing as group entity at the common law. *See* Faulkner v. Lowe, 2 Exch. 593, 154 Reprint 628 (1848); Napier v. Williams, 1 Ch. 361 (1911); Ellis v. Kerr, 1 Ch. 529 (1910). However, there is a tendency at the present time to recognize such bargains as contracts, although there may still be some procedural difficulties in the way of their enforcement where the common-law rules as to parties and joint obligations still prevail. *See In re* Estate of Talbott, 200 Iowa 585, 203 N.W. 303 (1925); Anderson v. Amidon, 114 Minn. 202, 130 N.W. 1002, 34 L.R.A. (n.s.) 647 (1911); FIRST RESTATEMENT § 17.

[36]*See infra* Chapter 13.

[37]RESTATEMENT 2d § 10, reporter's note at 26.

[38]RESTATEMENT 2d § 10.

[39]RESTATEMENT 2d § 12.

be avoided because the phrase, "void contract," is a contradiction.[40] A total lack of capacity will preclude the formation of any contract.

If the lack of capacity is merely *partial,* a contract will be formed but it is properly characterized as "voidable" since the party who suffers from some impairment of capacity will have a legal power of avoidance or, as it is often called, a power of disaffirmance. Where the capacity impairment is partial, the power of disaffirmance will be available to the impaired party in certain transactions, but not in others. Under certain circumstances, the power of disaffirmance will be limited or unavailable. It is essential that the student of contract law become aware of how the law has dealt with impairment of the capacity to contract. To facilitate that understanding, we will consider the types of persons whose capacity to contract has been questioned by the courts. The traditional classification of such persons includes (1) married women; (2) artificial persons (*e.g.,* corporations); (3) infants (minors); (4) mentally ill persons; (5) persons whose capacity is affected by alcohol or drugs; (6) persons under legal guardianship.

§ 22. Married Women and Artificial Persons.

There are no longer significant problems involving married women and artificial persons. At common law, a *married woman* had no capacity to bind herself by contract during the life of her husband.[41] Her promises were regarded as totally ineffectual. Courts of equity did recognize a limited capacity in a married woman to contract with reference to property conveyed to her separate use (her equitable separate estate). The enactment of Married Women's Acts throughout the country provided women with full power to contract though some restrictions such as interspousal immunity for contract or tort actions predicated upon the "unity" of married persons remained. These common law throwbacks have been eroded through new interpretations of the original legislation, judicial recognition of the modern status of women, equal rights amendments, and equal protection arguments.[42] *Any* restriction on the capacity of a married woman to contract, however, is of highly questionable constitutional validity.[43]

Artificial persons such as corporations and government agencies were traditionally limited to such powers as were conferred upon them by the sovereign that created them. Their power to make contracts, therefore, had to be within the limits of those conferred powers. If they attempted to contract, they were

---

[40] *See supra* § 17.

[41] "At common law, when a woman married, she lost her separate legal identity. It became merged in the husband during coverture. Husband and wife were but one person in the law." 2 COKE ON LITTLETON § 187a; 2 BLACKSTONE COMMENTARIES 182. *See also,* Currie, *Married Women's Contracts,* 25 U. CHI. L. REV. 227 (1958).

[42] For some recent cases discussing this erosion of any remaining limitations upon the rights of married women, *see* Burns v. Burns, 518 So. 2d 1205 (Miss. 1988); Garrity v. Garrity, 399 Mass. 367, 504 N.E.2d 617 (1987) (Note 12 of this opinion lists states with statutes similar to Massachusetts which have interpreted such statutes as granting married women the broad, unimpeded right to contract); Boblitz v. Boblitz, 296 Md. 242, 462 A.2d 506 (1982); Memorial Hospital v. Hahaj, 430 N.E.2d 412 (Ind. App. 1982).

[43] *See, e.g.,* Cleveland Bd. of Educ. v. La Fleur, 414 U.S. 632 (irrebuttable presumption); Reed v. Reed, 404 U.S. 71 (1971) (irrational classification). *See also* Craig v. Boren, 429 U.S. 190 (1976) and Frontiero v. Richardson, 411 U.S. 677 (1973).

said to be operating *ultra vires,* i.e., beyond their conferred powers, and any such attempt would be unlawful. Modern legislation, however, has significantly restricted the *ultra vires* limitation to provide, in effect, full capacity to such persons.[44] Other forms of business organization such as partnerships or unincorporated associations may have no power to make contracts in certain situations. Where this is so, their attempted contracts may bind their individual members.[45]

§ 23. Infants (Minors).

At common law, a person was an infant (minor) until he reached the age of twenty-one.[46] The rule continues at the present time, though by statute in virtually all states the age has been lowered to eighteen.[47] At common law, the capacity of an infant or minor to make a contract was considered impaired. The older common law view was that infants' contracts were void, voidable, or invalid.[48] The modern view, however, clearly makes such contracts voidable, i.e., the infant has a power of disaffirmance.[49] To suggest that a person who has yet to reach the statutory age of majority is necessarily impaired in his judgment or maturity and, therefore, must be protected against his own improvidence, is quite arbitrary. A seventeen-year-old may possess greater maturity, judgment, and even business acumen than most adults. The costs and uncertainties of distinguishing the capacities of minors, however, preclude any rule except an arbitrary one. The law, therefore, indulges what amounts to a conclusive presumption concerning the capacity of minors. A minor may disaffirm a contract he has made even though he is experienced and knowledgable, successful in business, emancipated by his parents, or married.[50] There is an argument that the infant's power of disaffirmance is not a limitation of his capacity, i.e., a disability. Rather, it is a power possessed by the infant in addition to his normal capacity and the suggestion that the infant has less than full capacity is erroneous. This perspective fails

---

[44] MODEL BUSINESS CORPORATION ACT § 3.02 (1984). Even in the absence of legislation, the defense of *ultra vires* is not favored by the courts. *See, e.g.,* Stadium Realty Corp. v. Dill, 233 Ind. 378, 119 N.E.2d 893 (1954); Valley Stream Teachers Fed. Credit Union v. Commissioner of Banks, 384 N.E.2d 200 (Mass. 1978).

[45] *See* RESTATEMENT 2d AGENCY § 20, and RESTATEMENT 2d TRUSTS §§ 97 and 98.

[46] RESTATEMENT 2d § 14.

[47] The twenty-sixth amendment to the U.S. Constitution lowered the voting age to 18. This prompted almost all of the states to enact statutes reducing the age of majority for contracting to 18. *See, e.g.,* PA. STAT. ANN. tit. 73 § 2021. A representative list of other statutes may be found in RESTATEMENT 2d § 14 in the Reporter's Note. Such statutes do not affect preexisting rights, Prinze v. Jonas, 38 N.Y.2d 570, 381 N.Y.S.2d 824, 345 N.E.2d 295 (1976).

[48] As early as the fifteenth century, there were decisions holding an infant's contract to be voidable. 2 WILLISTON § 223 (3d ed. 1959).

[49] RESTATEMENT 2d § 14 comment b. Moreover, many states have enacted statutes recognizing the power of disaffirmance in infants.

[50] Statutes, however, may provide that majority is reached upon marriage, *e.g.,* ALASKA STAT. § 25.20.020 (1977), or that the infant is bound by his contract if the other party had good reason to believe that the infant had reached majority because the infant was engaged in business as an adult, *e.g.,* KAN. STAT. ANN. § 38-103 (1981). If a minor engaged in business fails to post a sign conspicuously at the place of business and publish a notice of his status as an infant, he will lose his power of disaffirmance under VA. CODE § 8.01-278 (1984). A Georgia statute holds infants to their contracts if the minor is operating in a profession, trade or business as an adult through the permission of his parents, GA. CODE ANN. § 13-3-21 (1982).

to consider the fact that numerous parties will not deal with infants simply because the law has conferred this one-sided power of disaffirmance on them. Infants cannot surrender the power of disaffirmance during their minority since the surrender, itself, would be subject to the power of disaffirmance.[51] In the eyes of the law, the infant must be protected against his own improvidence. Any adult who deals with an infant, therefore, must assume the risk that the infant may decide to disaffirm the contract. Consequently, the very power of disaffirmance conferred by the law creates a limitation on the capacity of the infant since the infant, again, is incapable of forming a contract absent the power of disaffirmance.[52]

It is important to consider how the infant may exercise his power of disaffirmance. The infant may disaffirm before or after he attains majority except in real estate conveyances.[53] Any such disaffirmance is irrevocable.[54] There are no formal requirements for disaffirmance; any manifestation of intention not to be bound to the contract is sufficient. Disaffirmance may be oral or in writing[55] and it may be manifested by conduct.[56] A minor may not disaffirm burdensome portions of a contract and affirm beneficial portions.[57] If the infant chooses to surrender the power of disaffirmance, he may *ratify* the contract. Unlike the power of disaffirmance, any attempt to ratify, i.e., to surrender the power of disaffirmance prior to majority, will be ineffective since such an act of ratification would, itself, be voidable. There are no formal requirements for ratification. Any manifestation of intention to be bound to the voidable contract will be sufficient. Absent a statutory requirement that such ratification be evidenced by a writing,[58] the ratification may be oral. Generally, however, a promise to perform rather than a mere acknowledgment of the contractual obligation is required.[59] Since a ratification is, essentially, a

---

[51] One writer suggests, "[T]he law confers a privilege rather than imposes a duty." L. SIMPSON, CONTRACTS 216 (2d ed. 1965). This is criticized in J. CALAMARI & J. PERILLO, CONTRACTS 200 (1970). However, the criticism suggests only the pragmatic disability. There is, however, a legal disability.

[52] Bancredit, Inc. v. Bethea, 65 N.J. Super. 538, 168 A.2d 250 (1961).

[53] "Any disaffirmance (which necessarily would have to be by the execution of another deed) made by the infant alone before reaching his majority, would be of the same voidable nature, and for that reason the courts generally hold that such attempted disaffirmances are not effectual for that purpose." New Domain Oil & Gas Co. v. McKinney, 188 Ky. 183, 221 S.W. 245 (1920).

[54] Smith v. Wade, 169 Neb. 710, 100 N.W.2d 770 (1960). Michigan takes the unusual position that no disaffirmance can occur until majority. Poli v. National Bank, 355 Mich. 17, 93 N.W.2d 929 (1959).

[55] For an illustration of an effective oral disaffirmance, *see* Tracy v. Brown, 265 Mass. 163, 163 N.E. 885 (1928).

[56] A minor injured by defendant's truck signed a discharge of all claims and received payment for medical expenses and a small payment. Nonetheless, the minor brought a negligence action against defendant and the court treated his conduct in bringing the action as a disaffirmance of the contract discharging all claims. Tharpe v. Cudahy Packing Co., 4 S.E.2d 49 (Ga. App. 1939).

[57] "This is not a case in which a minor seeks to disaffirm a contract. He may, of course, do so.... Such a course, however, would leave plaintiff with *no* insurance. What he seeks here, by whatever name it is called, is to retain the benefits of the policy but to avoid the one provision which has become burdensome. Disaffirmance, if asserted, goes to the whole contract." Langstraat v. Midwest Mut. Ins. Co., 217 N.W.2d 570, 571 (Iowa Sup. 1974).

[58] *See, e.g.,* S.C. CODE § 32-5-10 (1977); MISS. CODE ANN. § 15-3-11 (1972). *See also* RESTATEMENT 2d § 89 comment b.

[59] "In general, a mere partial payment by a person, after coming of age, on a contract made by him during infancy, without an express promise or intention to ratify, does not constitute a

promise to perform a voidable duty, like other such promises,[60] it needs no consideration or other validation device to support it. Beyond an express ratification whereby the infant, after attaining majority, expressly promises to perform, ratification may be implied from the infant's conduct. For example, if the infant reaches majority and then retains and enjoys the use of property received under the contract, ratification will have occurred absent his express promise to perform.[61] If the infant has not received and enjoyed the property but partly performs (*e.g.*, part payment), this alone will not constitute ratification.[62] The question arises, if ratification can occur through the conduct of the infant, does such "conduct" include inaction, i.e., will the infant be said to have ratified the contract by failing to disaffirm the contract within a reasonable time after reaching majority? It is not difficult to find statements in the case law to the effect that the infant has only a "reasonable time" to disaffirm upon attaining majority. Otherwise, he will be said to have ratified. Such statements must be carefully applied to particular fact situations since an absence of benefit to the infant and lack of prejudice to the adult may lead a court to permit disaffirmance a number of years after the infant has attained majority.[63] If the contract has been completely performed (executed) and the infant has received a benefit that he has retained after reaching majority, he will have to be prompt in disaffirming. However, if the contract is wholly executory or has been performed only by the infant, there is no reason to insist upon prompt disaffirmance when the infant reaches majority. The preferable view considers the effect on the adult caused by the inaction of the infant under all of the circumstances rather than a mechanical test of whether the contract has been executed.[64] Reliance by the adult for some period after the infant has attained majority may very well result in the infant's loss of the power of disaffirmance.[65]

---

ratification of the contract." Bronx Sav. Bank v. Condruff, 78 N.M. 216, 430 P.2d 374, 375 (1967). *See also* Derouen's Estate v. General Motors Acceptance Corp., 245 La. 615, 159 So. 2d 695 (1964).

[60] RESTATEMENT 2d § 85.

[61] "Affirmance is not merely a matter of intent. It may be determined by the actions of a minor who accepts the benefits of a contract after reaching the age of majority, or who is silent or acquiesces in the contract for a considerable length of time. What act constitutes ratification or disaffirmance is ordinarily a question of law to be determined by the trial court.... We agree that what constitutes a reasonable time for affirmance or disaffirmance is ordinarily a question of fact to be determined by the facts in a particular case." Jones v. Dressel, 623 P.2d 370, 374 (Colo. Sup. 1981). *See also* Bobby Floars Toyota, Inc. v. Smith, 48 N.C. 580, 269 S.E.2d 320 (1980) and Cassella v. Tiberio, 150 Ohio St. 27, 80 N.E.2d 426, 5 A.L.R.2d 1 (1948).

[62] *Supra* note 59. *See also* Lee v. Thompson, 124 Fla. 494, 168 So. 848 (1936).

[63] In Harrod v. Kelly Amusement Co., 179 A.2d 431, 432-33 (D.C. Cir. 1962), defendant-minor purchased a watch in 1951. A few months later he lost it. An action was brought in 1961 pursuant to a twelve-year statute of limitations for sealed instruments. The court applied what it termed the "general rule" that ratification will not be implied from a party's inaction or silence no matter how prolonged after majority. The court, however, added, "It would be altogether different had appellant accepted, retained, or used the benefits of the contract during all this time...." *See also* Warwick Mun. Emps. Credit Union v. McCallister, 110 R.I. 399, 293 A.2d 516 (1972).

[64] *See* Walker v. Stokes Bros. & Co., 262 S.W. 158 (Tex. Civ. App. 1924).

[65] *See* Jones v. Godwin, 187 S.C. 510, 198 S.E. 36 (1938) in which a mortgagee made loans for many years after a mortgagor attained majority and the mortgagor remained silent. *See also* Martin v. Elkhorn Coal Corp., 227 Ky. 623, 13 S.W.2d 780 (1929) where an adult incurred considerable expense installing a mine operation for eight years after the minor attained majority.

§ 24. Infants' Liability for Necessaries and Restitution.

An infant is liable for necessaries furnished him, but he is not liable on the contract. Instead, the infant is liable for the reasonable value of the necessaries in a quasi contract action rather than for the contract price.[66] The word "necessaries" creates problems because it is a relative term that depends upon the particular situation of the infant, including his social position. The question is often going to be one of fact, though it is usually clear that food, clothing, and shelter are necessaries.[67] It is the quality of these items that can create problems because the infant's particular status must be considered.[68]

There has been considerable controversy and consequent conflicting decisions as to what occurs after the infant has effectively disaffirmed. If an infant purchases goods on credit and refuses to pay for them, an action by the adult seller is subject to the infant's power of avoidance. However, if the infant still possesses the goods, he must return them.[69] If the infant no longer has the goods, he is under no liability, according to the prevailing view, even though he has negligently destroyed or wasted them.[70] The infant may have paid for

---

[66]*See* Fellows v. Cantrell, 143 Colo. 126, 352 P.2d 289 (1960); Doenges-Long Motors, Inc. v. Gillen, 138 Colo. 31, 328 P.2d 1077 (1958) (damages); Dixon Nat'l Bank v. Neal, 5 Ill. 2d 328, 125 N.E.2d 463 (1955). *See also* Comment, *Infants' Contracts: Rights and Remedies,* 28 TENN. L. REV. 395 (1961); Gastonia Personnel Corp. v. Rogers, 276 N.C. 279, 172 S.E.2d 19 (1970) (contract for services of employment agency. Infant was 19, married, high school graduate earning $5000 per year. The court held that, despite minority, as a matter of law he cannot disaffirm. The court characterized this contract as a type of necessary — "such articles of property and such services as are reasonably necessary to enable the infant to earn the money required to provide the necessities of life for himself and those who are legally dependent on him." This was to protect "older minors" so they may contract.).

[67]*See, however,* Webster Street Partnership Ltd. v. Sheridan, 220 Neb. 9, 368 N.W.2d 439 (1983), in which the court held that an apartment was not a necessary for two infants who had voluntarily chosen to leave home and could return whenever they wished. On the other hand, in Rose v. Sheehan Buick, Inc., 204 So. 2d 903 (Fla. App. 1967), where a minor used an automobile for school, social, and business activities, the court found the car to be a necessary. However, in Valencia v. White, 134 Ariz. 139, 654 P.2d 287 (1982), the repair of a truck was not a necessary for the minor's trucking business since board, room, clothing, medical needs, and education were provided for him and it was not necessary that he engage in business.

[68]"While the work, labor, and professional services alleged in the complaint do not fall within the generally accepted notion of what constitutes necessaries, and might not be for a minor of *average* talents, the infant defendant, according to the complaint, is no ordinary child. The educational opportunities which should be afforded to a child whose gift holds promise of success in the entertainment world might, in part, well be of a type radically different from those educational opportunities and the kind of training which should be afforded to a child whose talents are directed along more traditional lines." Siegel & Hodges v. Hodges, 20 Misc. 2d 243, 191 N.Y.S.2d 984, 987-88 (1959). "What constitutes necessaries is a relative, somewhat flexible term, depending upon social position, the infant's fortune and situation in life." Daubert v. Mosley, 487 P.2d 353, 356 (Okl. 1971). *See also* Robertson v. King, 225 Ark. 276, 280 S.W.2d 402, 52 A.L.R.2d 1108 (1955); Fisher v. Cattani, 53 Misc. 2d 221, 278 N.Y.S.2d 420 (1966): "An infant may not, however, disaffirm contracts for necessaries. Even here, the phrase necessaries, does not possess a fixed interpretation, but must be measured against both the infant's standard of living, and the ability and willingness of his guardian, if he has one, to supply the needed services or articles."

[69]Though the infant should restore any value that he has received if he still possesses it, that may not be a condition precedent to the exercise of his power of avoidance. Weathers v. Owen, 78 Ga. App. 505, 51 S.E.2d 584 (1949).

[70]Taylor v. Grant, 220 Or. 114, 349 P.2d 282 (1960); Russell v. Buck, 116 Vt. 40, 68 A.2d 691 (1949); Kiefer v. Fred Howe Motors, Inc., 39 Wis. 2d 20, 158 N.W.2d 288 (1968) (good discussion of issues and policy questions involved in infancy cases. Kiefer (20 years old) bought a car that had a cracked block. Subsequently, he disaffirmed the contract and sued for the purchase price. Held, he could disaffirm despite the fact that he was married and had a child.).

the goods in advance and, upon disaffirmance, he may seek to recover that payment in a restitutionary action. Here, the infant is a plaintiff and to many courts the traditional view should prevail, i.e., the infant need only account for any goods or other value he retains after disaffirmance and therefore is entitled to the return of the prior payment.[71] This view has been seriously questioned and a sizeable number of courts are willing to take a different position when the infant is a plaintiff, i.e., suing to recover prior payments.[72] If an infant purchases an automobile for $3000 and pays the purchase price at the time of delivery, many courts hold that, upon his disaffirmance, his recovery of the purchase price will be offset by either the depreciation in the value of the car, the value of the use of the auto to the infant, or both.[73] It may seem anomalous to suggest a different result when the infant is a defendant (i.e., being sued by a seller to enforce the contract) from the result that an increasing number of courts are willing to take when the infant is a plaintiff (attempting to recover prior payments). Yet, there are decisions that clearly recognize this distinction and, from the standpoint of risk allocation, it may suggest considerable merit.[74] Some sellers would not extend credit to infants because of the infancy but would sell to an infant for cash. Those courts that recognize a distinction between the infant as plaintiff and the infant as defendant are protecting the infant from improvident commitments but not from equally improvident expenditures. An extrapolation of this position, often called the New Hampshire view (where it was pioneered), would allow a recovery in restitution for the value of any benefits conferred upon the infant, whether or not the benefit conferred constitutes necessaries.[75]

In Halbman v. Lemke, 99 Wis. 2d 241, 298 N.W.2d 562 (1980), the plaintiff (infant) bought a car from the defendant for $1200. After paying substantially the full amount, plaintiff had car trouble, which cost $700 to repair. Plaintiff did not pay repairs but disaffirmed the contract and demanded his money back. The court followed RESTATEMENT 2d § 15 — minor may disaffirm but he must return property to vendor. However, plaintiff was entitled to the return of his money, and did not have to make "restitution" for value of depreciation of the vehicle. "[W]e believe that to require a disaffirming minor to make restitution is, in effect, to bind the minor to a part of the obligation which by law he is privileged to avoid." *Id.* at 567. *Accord,* Weisbrook v. Clyde C. Netzley, Inc., 58 Ill. App. 3d 862, 374 N.E.2d 1102 (1978); Boudreaux v. State Farm Mut. Auto. Ins. Co., 385 So. 2d 480 (La. App. 1980).

[71] Loomis v. Imperial Motors, Inc., 88 Idaho 74, 396 P.2d 467, 12 A.L.R.3d 1166 (1964). *See* Annot., 12 A.L.R.3d 1174 (1967). An Arkansas statute (§ 68-1601) requires infants to make "full restitution" upon disaffirmance. "Full restitution of property means that the property must be returned in substantially the same condition as received; or if this cannot be done, there must be returned the property plus a sum of money which equals the difference between the fair market value of the property at the time the ... contract was made and its fair market value at the time of the rescission." *See* Wheeless v. Eudora Bank, 256 Ark. 644, 509 S.W.2d 532 (1974). In New York, a married infant may not avoid contracts for real property or hospital care. There are also restrictions on infants who are veterans, professional athletes, or performing artists as to the exercise of their powers of avoidance. N.Y. GEN. OBLIG. LAW § 3-105.

[72] Boyce v. Doyle, 113 N.J. Super. 240, 273 A.2d 408 (1971); Keser v. Chagnon, 159 Colo. 209, 410 P.2d 637 (1966); Porter v. Wilson, 106 N.H. 270, 209 A.2d 730, 13 A.L.R.3d 1247 (1965).

[73] The cases are unclear as to whether both depreciation and the use value may be recovered or, if only one of the measures is recoverable, which one is preferable. One problem is that courts often equate the two measures. Another problem is that the allowance of either measure normally exhausts the amount paid by the infant. For further discussion *see* Annotation, 12 A.L.R.3d 1174, 1187 *et seq.* (1967).

[74] Rodriguez v. Northern Auto Auction, Inc., 35 Misc. 2d 395, 225 N.Y.S.2d 107 (1962); Pettit v. Liston, 97 Or. 464, 191 P. 660 (1920); Rice v. Butler, 160 N.Y. 568, 55 N.E. 275 (1899).

[75] Porter v. Wilson, 106 N.H. 270, 209 A.2d 730, 13 A.L.R.2d 1247 (1965). *See also* Pankas v. Bell, 413 Pa. 494, 198 A.2d 312 (1964).

The courts have been troubled by the situation in which the infant intentionally misrepresents his age and the other party reasonably and in good faith relies upon that misrepresentation, thereby suffering a substantial loss. Notwithstanding the fraud of the infant, some courts have continued to permit the infant to disaffirm the contract whether the plaintiff has brought an action at law or suit in equity.[76] Other courts have expressly or impliedly followed the view of Lord Mansfield that the power of disaffirmance is a shield and not a sword and should never be permitted to be used as an offensive weapon of fraud or injustice.[77] Thus, where an infant misrepresented his age in purchasing an automobile and was no longer in possession of it, the infant was estopped from pleading the defense of infancy since the seller acted in good faith and would have suffered a substantial loss because the infant could not return the auto. To permit the defense of infancy in such a case would place the court in the position of providing a "weapon of injustice."[78] The case law suggests that modern courts are more receptive to the Mansfield view of disallowing the power of avoidance where the elements of conscious misrepresentation by the infant and reasonable and good faith reliance causing substantial detriment to the other party are present.[79]

§ 25. Mentally Ill and Mentally Defective Persons.

The older cases suggest that contracts as well as executed transactions of mentally incompetent parties are void rather than voidable.[80] However, as in the case of infants, the prevailing view today is that such contracts are merely voidable.[81] There are other similarities between infants' contracts and contracts involving the mentally incompetent. The incompetent is liable in a quasi-contract action for necessaries furnished him or his family.[82] Like an infant, the mental incompetent has a power of avoidance, but the other party to the contract (the competent party) does not. If the incompetent recovers from his illness or defect, he may ratify the contract. Only the recovered incompetent, his heirs, or his personal representative after death may exercise the power of avoidance or ratification.[83] The test of contractual mental competency has been the subject of some judicial dispute. The traditional test is known as the *cognitive* test, i.e., did the party understand the nature and consequences of the transaction? One court was asked to reject the cognitive test in favor of what the court characterized as a motivational test, i.e., but for the mental illness, the contract would not have been entered into, so the contract is voidable. The court refused to adopt the new test and confirmed the cognitive (understanding) test.[84] Another court characterized the cognitive

---

[76]*See* Gillis v. Whitley's Discount Auto Sales, 319 S.E.2d 661 (N.C. App. 1984).
[77]Zouch *ex dem.* Abbot & Hallet v. Parsons, 3 Burr 1794, 97 Eng. Rep. 1103 (1765).
[78]Haydocy Pontiac, Inc. v. Lee, 19 Ohio App. 2d 217, 250 N.E.2d 898, 901 (1969). *See also* Johnson v. McAdory, 88 So. 2d 106 (Miss. 1956).
[79]*See* Annotation, *Infant's Misrepresentation as to His Age as Estopping Him from Disaffirming His Voidable Transaction,* 29 A.L.R.3d 1270 (1970).
[80]*See Mental Illness and the Law of Contracts,* 57 Mich. L. Rev. 1020 (1959).
[81]Restatement 2d § 15.
[82]*See* Restatement 2d § 12 comment f.
[83]Restatement 2d § 15 comment d.
[84]Smalley v. Baker, 262 Cal. App. 824, 69 Cal. Rptr. 521 (1968); *see also* Matter of Guardianship of Collins, 327 N.W.2d 230 (Iowa 1982) and Ludwig v. Hart, 40 N.C. App. 188, 252 S.E.2d 270

test as "nineteenth century psychology" and, persuaded by the RESTATEMENT 2d, applied another test: Even though a party may have a complete understanding of the transaction, if he lacks the ability to control his acts in a reasonable manner because of mental illness, the contract is voidable if the other party has reason to know of this condition.[85] The RESTATEMENT 2d adopts the traditional cognitive test and also recognizes the uncontrolled manner of acting test.[86] The RESTATEMENT 2d position is well conceived as an effective reaction to a modern understanding of mental illness.

The contract standard of mental incompetency applied today recognizes a wide range of mental illnesses or defects including congenital deficiencies in intelligence, brain damage caused by organic disease or accident, deterioration caused by old age, and various mental illnesses giving rise to symptoms such as hallucinations, delusions, confusion, or depression. It is important to emphasize that there is complete capacity to contract unless the mental illness or deficiency has affected the particular contract.[87] Certain persons may be able to contract normally in relation to simple or even complicated transactions. Their mental incompetency may be activated only in relation to certain types of transactions, and it is only these contracts that are voidable.[88] Unless there has been a prior adjudication of incompetency, the party asserting the incompetency has the burden of proving it.[89]

When a mentally incompetent person enters into a contract, the other party to the contract may be unaware that the first party suffers from such illness or deficiency. Under an objective standard that is generally applied in contract law, it is the manifestation of assent rather than actual, subjective assent that is operative. Therefore, if the competent party is unaware of the deficiency of the other and makes a fair contract with the incompetent, there is a strong argument that the policy of protecting reasonable expectations and the security of transactions should prevail and the contract should, therefore, be enforced. On the other hand, a mentally ill or defective person may have to be protected against his own improvidence (similar to an infant) because of deficiencies in his judgment in relation to the particular transaction. The evolving case law has attempted to reconcile these policies.[90]

When the incompetent regains full capacity, he may either affirm (ratify) or disaffirm (exercise the power of avoidance) the contract. The reconciliation of

---

(1979). The cognitive test has been equated with the highly criticized *M'Naghten* test in criminal law. *See* M'Naghten's Case, 10 Clark & Fin. 200, 8 Eng. Rep. 718 (1843).

[85] Ortelere v. Teachers' Retirement Bd., 25 N.Y.2d 196, 303 N.Y.S.2d 362, 250 N.E.2d 460 (1969). *See also* Krasner v. Berk, 366 Mass. 464, 319 N.E.2d 897 (1974), which also recognizes the uncontrolled manner of acting test expressly following RESTATEMENT 2d § 15(c)(1)(b).

[86] RESTATEMENT 2d § 15C(1)(a) and (b).

[87] "The test of contractual capacity is whether a person is able to understand the nature of his action and apprehend its consequences.... This capacity is measured at the time of the execution of the contract.... Even where there are substantial indications of mental incompetence, it is possible that a person may have 'lucid intervals' during which he possesses requisite capacity." Urbie v. Olson, 42 Or. App. 647, 601 P.2d 818 (1979). In Van Wagoner v. Van Wagoner, 131 Mich. App. 204, 346 N.W.2d 77, the court applied the "cognitive" or "understanding" test and held that emotional disorders, alone, will not invalidate a contract.

[88] RESTATEMENT 2d § 15 comment b.

[89] RESTATEMENT 2d § 15.

[90] *See* Virtue, *Restitution From the Mentally Infirm* (pts. 1-2), 26 N.Y.U. L. REV. 132, 291 (1951).

the policies just set forth has resulted in a compromise in the case law. Where the contract is executory (not performed), the result is exactly the same as the infant contract, i.e., it is voidable. However, if the contract has been executed in whole or in part, the power of avoidance may be exercised only on equitable terms. If the competent party was unaware of the mental illness or deficiency and did not take unfair advantage of the incompetent, the contract is voidable only if the incompetent can restore the other party to status quo. For example, in a contract for the sale of land where the buyer was incompetent, the seller did not know of the incompetency and the price was fair. The incompetent died shortly after title to the land was transferred. The personal representative of the incompetent could recover the part payment made by the incompetent only upon reconveyance of the land to the seller. Since the reconveyance was possible in this case, the contract was voidable.[91] However, there are situations in which the exercise of the power of avoidance would be inequitable. For example, an incompetent and her husband mortgaged land on fair terms to a bank, and with the acquiescence of the incompetent, the money was paid to her and her husband. When the money was substantially squandered by the husband, the court held the contract was not voidable.[92] This is to be contrasted with situations wherein the competent party knows or reasonably should know of the other's incompetency at the time of contracting or takes unfair advantage of the incompetent. In such cases, any value received by the incompetent that he has dissipated need not be restored.[93]

§ 26. Persons Under the Influence of Alcohol or Drugs.

There have been numerous contracts cases dealing with the effects of alcoholism on one of the parties to the contract. There will undoubtedly be cases involving the use of drugs where arguments will be made relating to the capacity of the drug user. Since courts reason by analogy, the probabilities are great that the concepts developed in relation to mental illness, mental deficiency, and intoxication will be applied to the arguments dealing with the capacity of the drug user. Therefore, the following discussion dealing with intoxication may be viewed as a reliable guide to the reaction of courts in the area of contracts by drug users.

If compulsive alcoholism or drug addiction qualifies as a type of mental illness, the same concepts apply as those set forth in the previous section. It would be possible to consider any voluntary intoxication or drug use as a form of mental illness, but the courts have not yet done so, apparently on the ground that the one who voluntarily becomes drunk (or uses drugs) has less reason to be excused than the party who is mentally ill or mentally defective.[94] Therefore, most courts take the position that the contract will be en-

---

[91] Verstandig v. Schlaffer, 296 N.Y. 62, 70 N.E.2d 15 (1946).

[92] Sparrowhawk v. Erwin, 30 Ariz. 238, 246 P. 541, 46 A.L.R. 413 (1926). *Contra* Jordan v. Kirkpatrick, 251 Ill. 116, 95 N.E. 1079 (1911).

[93] Brandt v. Phipps, 398 Ill. 296, 75 N.E.2d 757 (1947); Spence v. Spence, 239 Ala. 480, 195 So. 717 (1940); Fecht v. Freeman, 251 Ill. 84, 95 N.E. 1043 (1911).

[94] "Drunkenness may be insanity, but it is voluntary. If it is no excuse from the consequences of a crime, why should it be against those acts affecting property? Sound policy requires that it should not, unless brought about by the other party, or unless it was so total as to be palpable evidence of fraud in the person entering into a contract with one so intoxicated." Burroughs v.

forceable (including even executory contracts) if the other party to the contract had no reason to know of the intoxication.[95] This situation tends to be rare because of the standard established as to the degree of intoxication that must occur in any event to avoid a contract. The intoxicated party must not be able to understand the nature and consequences of the transaction.[96] Normally, the other party to the contract will be aware of such a degree of intoxication. However, if the competent party is not reasonably aware of the intoxication, the contract is enforceable. An intoxicated party has a power of avoidance only if he is sufficiently intoxicated and the competent party has reason to know of the intoxication. Situations do arise in which the competent party induces the intoxication before the drunken party signs the contract or, in some fashion, exploits the afflicted party's need for alcohol or drugs. These cases are really not decided on grounds of lack of capacity; they may speak of mistake or a species of fraud on the part of the competent party.[97] In any such case, the intoxicated party may avoid the contract since his intoxicated condition has been consciously induced by the other party to the contract. When the intoxicated person does have the power of avoidance, the normal rules as to ratification or avoidance of the contract are applied. Upon regaining a sober condition, the afflicted party must act promptly to disaffirm, and he must offer to restore any value received. However, if the value has been squandered or otherwise dissipated during the period of drunkenness, the afflicted party may not have to offer the return of any value received.[98]

The cases involving the exploitation of alcoholics or drug users are quite similar to cases involving parties suffering from other kinds of infirmity, such as the aged and bedridden, as well as those suffering other infirmities that may indicate that they are in a state of shock or great pain. The trend is clear that some infirmity coupled with overreaching on the part of the competent party will provide the court with a sufficient base to avoid the enforcement of the contract. The fact situations are myriad and the case may ultimately be captioned under a heading such as "fraud," "unconscionability," "intoxication," or some form of mental infirmity.[99] Regardless of the caption, the courts have little difficulty in avoiding the contract if the two elements of infirmity and overreaching are present.

Richman, 13 N.J. (1 Green) 233, 23 Am. Dec. 717 (1832). *See also,* Cook v. Bagnell Timber Co., 78 Ark. 47, 94 S.W. 695 (1906).

[95] RESTATEMENT 2d § 16; Scherer v. Scherer, 76 Ind. Dec. 260, 405 N.E.2d 40, 47 (1980) (dicta). Husband who signs divorce papers while drunk and under influence of valium is estopped from raising this defense of incapacity if he later acts (prior to bringing suit) inconsistent with his objections. "Tacit encouragement test."

[96] Williamson v. Matthews, 379 So. 2d 1245 (Ala. 1980); Olsen v. Hawkins, 90 Idaho 28, 408 P.2d 462 (1965).

[97] *See, e.g.,* Stacey v. Mikoloski, 367 Mich. 550, 116 N.W.2d 757 (1962).

[98] RESTATEMENT 2d § 16 comment c.

[99] *See* Virtue, *supra* note 90.

§ 27. Persons Under Guardianship.

If a party suffering from mental illness or defect or a party who is an habitual drunkard, a drug addict, a spendthrift, or an aged person is adjudicated incompetent and a guardian is appointed, any contracts made by such a person are void since he has absolutely no capacity to incur contractual duties.[1] The purpose of guardianship is to protect the property from being squandered or in some other fashion improvidently used. The adjudication of guardianship is public notice of the incapacity of the ward. Therefore, even though the other party to the contract may be unaware of the guardianship, there is no contract with the ward. The ward's property is under the control of the guardian subject to the supervision of the court. Until the guardianship is either judicially terminated or otherwise abandoned,[2] the ward is totally incapable of contracting. His contracts are not merely voidable; they are void, which suggests that there never was a contract to either avoid or to ratify. Under certain circumstances, property under guardianship may be available to satisfy quasi-contractual obligations of the ward.[3] However, if the ward has received any value, an innocent party who has contracted with the ward may reclaim any value received by the ward if it is still available.[4] In the case of necessaries, the competent party may recover the fair value of the consideration received to avoid the unjust enrichment of the ward. It must be emphasized that simply committing a person to an asylum or hospital where no guardian has been appointed does not make the contracts of the afflicted person void. In such cases, the contracts are voidable.[5] Another classification is the appointment of a guardian of the person as contrasted with the guardian of the property. Unless there has been an adjudication that a party has been named as guardian of the afflicted person's property, the principles set forth in this section are not applicable.[6]

---

[1] Cottrell v. Conn. Bank & Trust Co., 175 Conn. 257, 398 A.2d 307 (1978). *See also* RESTATEMENT 2d § 13. As to contractual capacity of convicts, *see* 2 WILLISTON § 272 (3d ed. 1959); Freshour v. Aumack, 567 S.W.2d 176 (Tenn. App. 1977).

[2] When the ward recovers from his infirmity, the guardianship should be terminated by decree of a court. However, the guardianship may be abandoned informally, i.e., absent any adjudication. If the ward resumes control over the property without interference, or if the guardian dies and a successor is not appointed, the incapacity may terminate.

[3] *See* RESTATEMENT 2d § 13, comment b, and § 18 comment f.

[4] Reeves v. Hunter, 185 Iowa 958, 171 N.W. 567 (1919).

[5] G.A.S. v. S.I.S., 407 A.2d 253 (Del. Ch. 1978).

[6] Finch v. Goldstein, 245 N.Y. 300, 157 N.E. 146 (1927).

Chapter 2

THE AGREEMENT PROCESS

§ 28. The Essential Elements of Contract Formation.

There are six essential elements to the formation of the typical[1] contract. They are (1) mutual assent;[2] (2) consideration or some other validation device;[3] (3) two or more contracting parties;[4] (4) an agreement that is sufficiently definite;[5] (5) parties that have legal capacity to make a contract;[6] (6) no legal prohibition precluding the formation of a contract.[7] In this Chapter, the concept of mutual assent and the requirement that the agreement be sufficiently definite will be explored. The other elements have either been explored in Chapter 1 or will be analyzed in subsequent chapters.

§ 29. Mutual Assent — Agreement — Promise — Offer — Acceptance.

The concept of future economic exchange which is essential in our society has already been explored.[8] Parties must be willing to commit to future exchanges and the legal system must assure the performance of these exchanges. In a society of free economic exchange, each party decides whether to commit to do or not to do some act at some future time. Such a commitment will usually be induced by a counter commitment from another party. If Ames commits herself to sell her used automobile to Barnes because Barnes commits himself to pay $5000 to Ames, the parties have committed themselves to a future economic exchange. When parties make commitments to each other to act or refrain from acting in a certain way in the future, they have expressed their *mutual assent* concerning such actions or inactions. Mutual assent is simply an expression of *agreement* between or among parties.[9]

Whether an agreement is a contract depends upon whether the parties intend that legal consequences attach to that agreement. A social or domestic agreement is a manifestation of future exchange but it is not a contract because the parties do not intend legal consequences to attach to their agreement.[10] On the other hand, agreements to buy or sell goods or services, to construct a building, to become an employee for a particular firm, and similar agreements are typically based on the conscious or unconscious assumption that legal consequences will attach to such agreements.

A basic question of contract law is whether two or more parties arrived at an agreement, i.e., whether the parties have expressed their mutual assent concerning their future conduct. The anatomy of the agreement process has been developed by innumerable courts over many centuries. Central to the agreement process is the concept of *promise,* which is "a manifestation of intention to act or refrain from acting in a specified way, so made as to justify

---

[1] The typical contract is the "informal" contract as contrasted with the "formal" contract. The "formal" contract is validated by the seal or a modern substitute for the seal. *See* Chapter 1, § 15.

[2] *See infra* § 29.

[3] Consideration and other validation devices are explored in Chapter 3.

[4] A party may not contract with himself. *See* Chapter 1, § 21. *See also* United States v. Alaska S.S. Co., 491 F.2d 1147 (10th Cir. 1975) and RESTATEMENT 2d § 9.

[5] *See infra* § 38.

[6] *See* Chapter 1, §§ 21-27.

[7] *See* Chapter 1, §§ 17-18.

[8] *See* Chapter 1, § 5.

[9] *See* Dixie Ag Supply, Inc. v. Nelson, 500 So. 2d 1036 (Ala. 1986).

[10] *See infra* § 31.

a promisee [the party to whom the promise was made by the promisor] in understanding that a commitment has been made."[11] When parties desire future economic exchange, they typically negotiate until one party *promises* to act or refrain from acting in a certain way in exchange for an act, inaction or promise from the other party. Expressions of agreement or mutual assent typically are evidenced in the spoken or written language of the parties but may also be found in other conduct.[12] When Ames promised to sell her car to Barnes, she was induced by his promise to pay her $5000. The parties exchanged promises and committed themselves to future action. If Ames wanted her lawn to be cut, she could have promised to pay Barnes $25 to cut the lawn. Even if Barnes then simply cut the lawn without promising to do so, the parties manifested their intention to have an agreement. In this situation, however, Barnes eliminated the typical manifestation of promise prior to performance, but he manifested his agreement by his action, i.e., performance. Ames received the desired performance from Barnes and her promise should be enforced by the legal system. If Barnes owned property adjacent to the residence of Ames and Ames discovered that Barnes intended to cut certain trees on his property that Ames found useful for her privacy, the parties could agree that Ames would pay Barnes a certain sum in exchange for his promise to forebear cutting his trees, i.e., Barnes would perform his promise by inaction. Here, his inaction would be the performance of his promise not to do something which he had a legal right to do.

Courts have further structured the agreement process by developing a step-by-step analysis of the promissory process. The agreement process is initiated by the discovery of an *offer*. Almost invariably, an offer is created by a promise,[13] i.e., the initial promise is the offer and the party making that promise is both a promisor and an offeror. The party to whom the promise/offer is made is both a promisee and an offeree. When the offeree performs an act, forebears from acting, or makes a counter promise in accordance with the offer, the offeree has *accepted* the offer.[14] The parties have expressed their mutual assent by making an agreement — a bargain or deal. If the other elements necessary for the formation of a contract are present,[15] the parties have made a legally enforceable agreement — a contract. Consequently, the mutual as-

---

[11] RESTATEMENT 2d § 2.

[12] The UCC defines "Agreement" as "the bargain of the parties in fact as found in their language or by implication from other circumstances including course of dealing or usage of trade or course of performance." UCC § 1-201(3).

[13] A rare situation suggests the possibility that the offer is not a promise. For example, if Ames had lent a book to Barnes and, while the book was still in Barnes' possession, Ames said, "Promise to pay me $50 and the book is yours," the promise by Barnes would form a contract. It is suggested that the offer is one of performance in exchange for a promise and ownership of the book is transferred immediately upon the promise by Barnes. This type of agreement is also called a "reverse unilateral contract" since the normal unilateral contract involves a promise by the offeror requiring an acceptance by performance whereas this agreement involves performance by the offeror and a promissory acceptance by the offeree. RESTATEMENT 2d, § 55; *see also* § 24 comment a. Yet the transaction may be viewed as a promise by Ames to transfer ownership of the book (which happens to be in the possession of Barnes) to Barnes in exchange for Barnes' promise to pay $50 to Ames. Williston refers to such an offer as a promise though it is "self-operating." 1 S. WILLISTON, CONTRACTS § 29A (3d ed. 1957).

[14] In the sections that follow, the concepts of offer and acceptance will be fully analyzed.

[15] *See supra* § 28.

sent which the law requires for the formation of an informal contract is an agreement which is found in the usual bargain of the parties and is normally expressed through an offer by one and an acceptance by the other.[16]

It is possible to discover a manifestation of mutual assent though neither the offer nor the acceptance can be identified as such, and/or the precise moment of contract formation cannot be determined.[17] In the typical case, however, the offer and acceptance as well as the moment of contract formation can be identified and the acceptance invariably follows the offer.[18] Since virtually all negotiations leading to contract formation can be analyzed in terms of offer and acceptance, they have become the traditional analytical tools used by courts in formation questions. It is essential to have a clear understanding of their characteristics and operation. Before proceeding to an exploration of offer and acceptance, however, certain preliminary matters must be understood to avoid unnecessary confusion in subsequent sections.

§ 30. Objective Versus Subjective Assent — "Meeting of the Minds."

The requirement of mutual assent explored in the previous section is complicated by the question of *when* that mutual assent must occur. Older common law cases contained statements suggesting not only the requirement of mutual assent, but simultaneous mutual assent.[19] This "requirement" was typically expressed as requiring a "meeting of the minds." The phrase, "meeting of the minds" is capable of creating a great deal of mischief.[20] If understood literally, it suggests that the mutual assent of the parties must be *actual*

---

[16] Section 3 of the RESTATEMENT 2d defines "agreement" as a manifestation of mutual assent on the part of two or more persons. It defines "bargain" as an agreement to exchange promises or to exchange a promise for a performance or to exchange performances. The "mode of assent" ordinarily takes the form of an offer or proposal by one party followed by an acceptance by the other party or parties. RESTATEMENT 2d § 22. *See* I.M.A., Inc. v. Rocky Mt. Airways, 713 P.2d 882 (Colo. 1986); Dixie Ag Supply, Inc. v. Nelson, 500 So. 2d 1036 (Ala. 1986); Kristerin Dev. Co. v. Granson Inv., 394 N.W.2d 325 (Iowa 1986).

[17] For example, two parties may sign a writing manifesting agreement without identifying themselves as offeror or offeree. Parties may agree that a contract will be formed when a particular official of one of the contracting companies signs the writing evidencing the agreement. Subsequently, it may not be possible to prove the exact moment of that signing though it did occur. A contract has been formed notwithstanding the inability to prove the precise moment in time the signing occurred. Section 2-204(2) of the UCC supports this analysis: "An agreement sufficient to constitute a contract for sale may be found even though the moment of its making is undetermined." A comment to this section indicates that exchanged correspondence may not disclose the exact point at which the deal was closed, but the actions of the parties may be sufficient evidence that a binding obligation was undertaken.

[18] Professor Corbin suggests the hypothetical of a document expressing agreement between *A* and *B,* prepared in advance by a third party, *C.* After reading the document, *A* and *B* stand in each other's presence and, in unison, say, "We mutually agree in accordance with the terms prepared for us by *C.*" Corbin can find no recorded instance of such a case, but concludes that a contract would be formed. He then suggests that, "Offer followed by acceptance is the substantially universal method." 1 CORBIN ON CONTRACTS § 12 (1963).

[19] *See, e.g.,* Thesiger, L. J., in Household Fire Ins. Co. v. Grant, 4 Ex. D. 216, 220 (1879): "Now, whatever in abstract discussion may be said as to the legal notion of its being necessary, in order to the effecting of a valid and binding contract, that the minds of the parties should be brought together at one and the same moment, that notion is practically the foundation of English law upon the subject of the formation of contracts."

[20] Professor Farnsworth suggests that the origins of "meeting of the minds" are traceable to the unwarranted assumption that the term, "agreement" was derived from *aggregatio mentium,* a meeting of the minds. Farnsworth, *"Meaning" in the Law of Contracts,* 76 YALE L.J. 939, 943-44 (1967).

(subjective) mutual assent, i.e., the thought processes of the parties must be identical with respect to their bargain at the same moment in time. A moment's reflection suggests the folly of this notion. If an offer is sent on Monday and arrives on Wednesday, the offeree may decide to accept the offer on Thursday by making on that day the necessary promise to perform. If, upon receipt of the acceptance, the offeror would notify the offeree that he, the offeror, had changed his mind before the offeree had accepted, the literal "meeting of the minds" requirement would preclude the formation of a contract. Yet, the only evidence of the mind change by the offeror would be the offeror's subsequent statement that he had changed his mind prior to the acceptance. Under that analysis, no system of contract law could ever prove workable since it would be impossible to prove the subjective intention of either party at any time. Notwithstanding this obvious fundamental flaw, a great deal of controversy was spawned over the question of whether the actual mental assent (subjective) of the parties was required, or whether the *expression* or *manifestation* of that assent (objective) would control regardless of any alleged subjective intention.[21] Long before this debate, courts had always taken the pragmatic view that unmanifested intention could not be the basis for making or accepting an offer. If a party had the thought of making an offer and did not communicate that thought to the offeree, no offer would result. Similarly, if a party received an offer, his thought of acceptance absent a manifestation of that acceptance would create no contract. Any other rule would be wholly impracticable. The difficult question, however, was whether manifested mutual assent had to correspond to the subjective intention of the parties. If, for example, a party appeared to manifest assent to a bargain and later claimed, quite honestly, that he intended only a joke or did not intend to be bound for other reasons, should he escape contractual consequences even though the other party reasonably understood and honestly believed that a contract had been formed? Thus, the question became, does a party have a right to rely upon the *apparent* manifestation of intention by the other party, regardless of that party's subjective state of mind? If one has this right, it is the *expression* or *manifestation* of assent, rather than assent itself, that is the essential element of contractual obligation.

Until the middle of the nineteenth century, courts generally accepted the view that a subjective "meeting of the minds" as well as an expression of mutual assent was essential to the consummation of a contract.[22] It became painfully clear, however, that such a view could lead to serious injustice for the reasons suggested earlier. Again, if A makes an offer to which B manifests assent, may A later say, "I'm sorry, but we have no contract since I changed

---

[21] *See* the famous concurring opinion of Judge Jerome Frank in Ricketts v. Pennsylvania R.R., 153 F.2d 757, 760-62 (2d Cir. 1946). Judge Frank agreed that the actual intent theory of the "subjectivists" had been carried too far. However, he felt that those who supported only the manifested (expressed) intent of the parties (the "objectivists") also went too far by excluding any evidence of the actual intention of the parties. He accused the objectivists of importing "that stubborn anti-subjectivist, the 'reasonable man'" from the law of torts apparently because they desired "legal symmetry." A complete recent judicial analysis of the objective/subjective controversy is found in Newman v. Schiff, 778 F.2d 460 (8th Cir. 1985).

[22] *See* Williston, *Mutual Assent in the Formation of Informal Contracts,* 14 ILL. L. REV. 85 (1919), SELECTED READINGS ON CONTRACTS 119 (1931).

my mind a moment before you announced your acceptance?" The possible hardship to one who had relied upon what had been expressed, only to discover that he had built his house of expectations upon the shifting sands of subjective intention, was unacceptable. The controversy has been resolved. Modern contract law has abandoned the theory of subjective intention as unworkable. Innumerable cases support the view that it is the outward manifestations of the parties — their expressions — that will be viewed as the exclusive evidence of the parties' intentions rather than assertions of their subjective intention.[23] Unfortunately, the mischievous phrase, "meeting of the minds," continues to appear in modern contracts cases.[24] There can be no

---

[23] One of the classic expressions of this view is from the pen of Judge Learned Hand: "A contract has, strictly speaking, nothing to do with the personal, or individual, intent of the parties. A contract is an obligation attached by the mere force of law to certain acts of the parties, usually words, which ordinarily accompany and represent a known intent. If, however, it were proved by twenty bishops that either party, when he used the words, intended something else than the usual meaning which the law imposes upon them, he would still be held, unless there were some mutual mistake, or something else of the sort. Of course, if it appears by other words, or acts, of the parties, that they attribute a peculiar meaning to such words as they use in their contract, that meaning will prevail, but only by virtue of the words, and not because of their unexpressed intent." Hotchkiss v. National City Bank, 200 F. 287, 293 (S.D.N.Y. 1911). Almost two decades later, Judge Hand wrote "It is quite true that contracts depend upon the meaning which the law imputes to the utterances, not what the parties actually intended; but, in ascertaining what meaning to impute, the circumstances in which the words are used is always relevant and usually indispensable. The standard is what a normally constituted person would have understood them to mean, when used in their actual setting." New York Trust Co. v. Island Oil & Transp. Corp., 34 F.2d 655, 656 (2d Cir. 1929). Innumerable opinions contain similar statements. "The law of contracts is not concerned with the parties' undisclosed intents and ideas. It gives heed only to their communications and overt acts." Kitzke v. Turnidge, 209 Or. 563, 307 P.2d 522 (1957). "[M]utual assent is, however, unimportant except as it is manifested by one party to the other, generally by a communicated offer and acceptance.... So, the obligations depend not on the so-called real intent of a party, but on that expressed.... The phrase 'meeting of the minds,' can properly mean only the agreement reached by the parties as expressed, i.e., their manifested intention.... Frequently ['meeting of the minds'] is misapplied seemingly to impose the requisite that there is no contract unless both parties understood the terms alike, regardless of the expressions they manifested.... The mere fact that each had a different subjective idea of what the term included did not prevent a binding agreement on this objective basis." Leitner v. Braen, 51 N.J. Super. 31, 143 A.2d 256, 260 (1958). "If a party's words or acts, judged by a reasonable standard, manifest an intention to agree to the matter in question, that agreement is established, and it is immaterial what may be the real but unexpressed state of the party's mind on the subject." Wesco Realty, Inc. v. Drewry, 9 Wash. App. 734, 735, 515 P.2d 513, 515 (1973). The most comprehensive judicial analysis is found in Newman v. Schiff, 778 F.2d 460 (8th Cir. 1985). See also Chemical Realty Corp. v. Home Fed. Sav. & Loan Ass'n of Hollywood, 84 N.C. App. 27, 351 S.E.2d 786 (1987); Zeman v. Lufthansa German Airlines, 699 P.2d 1274 (Alaska 1986); Dumas v. Kessler & Maguire Funeral Home, 380 N.W.2d 544 (Minn. 1986).

[24] See, e.g., Jack V. Heard Contrs. v. A.L. Adams Constr. Co., 155 Ga. App. 409, 271 S.E.2d 222, 225 (1980), in which the court may appear to be retrogressing: "It is essential to the validity of a contract that the minds of the contracting parties meet on the same subject matter, at the same time, and in the same sense." A more than occasional use of "meeting of the minds" as meaning "mutual assent" will appear. See, e.g., Bejmuk v. Russell, 734 P.2d 122 (Colo. App. 1986); Mendes Bros. Dairy v. Farmers Nat'l Bank, 111 Idaho 511, 725 P.2d 535 (1986); Herman R. Rasch v. City of E. Jordan, 141 Mich. App. 336, 367 N.W.2d 856 (1985); Normile v. Miller, 313 N.C. 98, 326 S.E.2d 11 (1985). While little harm may be perceived from the use of the phrase on the assumption that those using it understand the dominance of the objective theory of contract law and use it without the intention of asserting the necessity of subjective intention, it is unnecessary and could be misleading absent explanation. See Johnson v. Mineral Estate, Inc., 371 N.W.2d 136 (N.D. Or. 1985). Thus, the continued use of the phrase in terms of any useful purpose is, indeed, puzzling.

doubt, however, that the objective theory is clearly established throughout the country.[25]

§ 31. Intention of Legal Consequences.

It has generally been asserted that, even though all of the elements of a contract are present, there is no contract unless the parties also intend their agreement to be legally binding.[26] Like other general statements, this statement fails to consider numerous complexities which appear to contradict the statement in specific situations. The first major difficulty is clearly seen in the overwhelming majority of contracts in which the parties do not consider, much less express, any intention concerning legal consequences at the time of contract formation. As the contract is formed, the typical party is contemplating the performance he expects in return for his performance and does not consciously advert to the legal consequences of the agreement. In analyzing the so-called requirement that legal consequences must be intended by the parties as a prerequisite to any contract, four general situations are readily conceivable: (A) the parties express their intention to be legally bound; (B) the parties express their intention not to be legally bound; (C) the expressions of the parties are properly interpreted as either intending or not intending legal consequences; (D) the parties manifest no intention whatsoever in relation to legal consequences. Each of these situations will now be considered in light of recurring problems.

A. *The Parties Express Their Intention to Be Legally Bound.*

Since parties to a typical contract do not consciously consider the legal consequences of their agreement, it will be rare for such parties to include a statement to the effect that they intend their agreement to be legally binding. Should they include such a statement, however, the parties have eliminated any question as to their intention of legal consequences if all of the other elements of an enforceable contract are in place. A court should enforce the manifested intention of the parties in such a case, but the qualification of the foregoing statement must be kept in mind. Parties to an agreement that is unenforceable because of public policy reasons may not make such an agreement enforceable simply by including a statement that they intend legal consequences to attach to that agreement. An agreement to perform an illegal bargain would not admit of legal sanction even if that agreement contained a provision that the parties intended legal consequences to attach. The agreement would still be unenforceable.[27]

---

[25] In addition to the cases cited *supra* note 23, *see* Zeman v. Lufthansa German Airlines, 699 P.2d 1274 (Alaska 1986); Dumas v. Kessler & Maguire Funeral Home, 380 N.W.2d 544 (Minn. App. 1986); Hoffman v. Ralston Purina Co., 86 Wis. 2d 445, 273 N.W.2d 214 (1979); Alteri v. Layton, 35 Conn. Supp. 258, 408 A.2d 17 (1979); Kabil Dev. Corp. v. Mignot, 279 Or. 151, 566 P.2d 505 (1977).

[26] CLARK ON CONTRACTS § 27 at 53 (4th ed. 1931); *see also* ANSON ON CONTRACTS 4 (Corbin's 5th Am. ed. 1930). *But see* criticism of this statement in 1 CORBIN ON CONTRACTS § 34 (1963).

[27] An obvious example would be an agreement between parties whereby one promised to murder the spouse of the other. Such an agreement would be void and no statement concerning the intention of legal consequences would be sufficient to convert that void understanding into an enforceable contract. A less obvious example would be an agreement between married persons

B. *The Parties Express Their Intention Not to Be Legally Bound — Employee Benefits.*

On the surface, the second situation appears as free from doubt as the first, i.e., if the parties clearly state their intention not to be legally bound, again, the courts have no need to discover their intention. The intention of the parties should be effectuated since courts ought to respect the manifested intention of the parties even though the bargain they have made appears to be the kind that is normally enforced at law. In general, the courts have adopted this position in finding a "gentleman's agreement" not binding at law.[28] Considerations of fairness, however, may limit the application of a clause negating legal obligation. Thus, if an agreement containing a "not legally binding" clause has been performed by one of the parties and a refusal to enforce it against the other party would result in manifest unfairness, as in some employee death benefit or bonus cases, some courts will enforce the agreement notwithstanding the clause.[29] In such cases, courts do not always articulate the rationale effectively. It is clear, however, that the rationale emphasizes reliance by one party who may not have read or understood the "not legally binding" clause. When the other party later raises the clause in defense, the reliance factor overcomes the technical defense and the enforcement of the "not legally binding" clause may also be unconscionable.

---

that would be considered unenforceable because it would change an essential element of the marriage relationship. *See* RESTATEMENT 2d § 190.

[28] The classic exposition of this principle is found in Rose & Frank Co. v. J.B. Crompton Bros., [1923] 2 K.B. 261 (C.A.). A common example is found in "letters of intent" which expressly state that the parties intend no liability or legal obligation. *See, e.g.,* Dunhill Secs. Corp. v. Microthermal Applications, Inc., 308 F. Supp. 195 (S.D.N.Y. 1969). "Letters of intent" or similar documents containing express negations of legal obligation must, however, be carefully interpreted. The conduct of the parties or their language may suggest some legal obligation. Thus, in Itex Corp. v. Chicago Aerial Indus., 248 A.2d 625 (Del. 1963), the court found a duty to bargain in good faith despite language in the letter of intent negating any legal obligation. *See also* Garner v. Boyd, 330 F. Supp. 22 (N.D. Tex. 1970), *aff'd per curiam,* 447 F.2d 1373 (5th Cir. 1971), which held that a document was evidence of a contract notwithstanding its caption of "letter of intent."

[29] The classic illustration is Tilbert v. Eagle Lock Co., 116 Conn. 357, 165 A. 205 (1933), where an employee received a "certificate of benefit" stating that his beneficiary would receive a certain sum upon his death if he should die while an employee of the company. The certificate stated that it was not a contract and conferred no legal rights on the employee. When the company decided to withdraw the benefit some eight years later, it posted notices of withdrawal. However, the employee died at 2 A.M. on the day such notices were posted and the court held the notices of withdrawal ineffective until the end of the day on which they were posted. The court in Spooner v. Reserve Life Ins. Co., 47 Wash. 2d 454, 287 P.2d 735 (1955), distinguished the death benefit case where a living employee claimed a bonus. *See also* Finnell v. Cramet, Inc., 289 F.2d 409 (6th Cir. 1961), in which a "not legally binding" clause was upheld under an employee plan where the plaintiffs were living. RESTATEMENT 2d § 21 comment b, suggests that parties are free to include "not legally binding" clauses which are normally enforced. However, they may raise difficult questions of interpretation, misrepresentation, mistake, or overreaching, i.e., unconscionability. For a modern judicial analysis indicating a greater willingness on the part of courts to enforce such agreements, *see* Hoefel v. Atlas Tack Corp., 581 F.2d (1st Cir. 1978). The Employee Retirement Income Security Act of 1974, § 2(c), 29 U.S.C.A. § 1101 et seq., was designed, in part, to overcome the abuse of a "not legally binding" clause in employee pension plans. *See* Annotation, 28 A.L.R.3d (1969).

C. *The Expressions of the Parties Are Interpreted as Intending or Not Intending Legal Consequences — Jest, Physicians' Statements.*

Where the parties have not clearly indicated their intention whether or not to be legally bound, courts are faced with the usual task of interpreting all of their manifestations of intention under all of the circumstances to determine the underlying question of whether they intended to be legally bound. There are two kinds of cases, in particular, that raise this question. In the first type, one of the parties to an agreement insists that he was only joking or bragging and should not have been taken seriously, i.e., he intended no legal consequences. When confronted with these cases, courts have considered all of the relevant circumstances and applied the following test: should the party alleging that he was only jesting or bragging have been reasonably understood as expressing himself in that fashion so that the other party would be unreasonable in assuming that a binding agreement had been formed?[30] If a party is reasonable in assuming that the other party was serious, i.e., not joking or bragging, then a contract will have been formed regardless of the secret, undisclosed intention of the other party. The objective test, again, prevails, and legal consequences will attach to an apparently serious statement that would normally be understood as sufficient to form a contract.

The second type of case that has proven difficult under this third classification involves statements by physicians concerning the cure of a particular malady or related matters such as the duration of a hospital stay. It is unusual for a court to find that a physician has made a clear and unambiguous promise to cure a patient even though the physician may have made statements of assurance that the patient may have understood as promissory. The physician may suggest a surgical procedure to cure the condition and may respond to questions concerning the period of recovery with some manifestation of assurance that the period will not exceed a certain time. Whether the physician has made a promise to the patient as contrasted with a professional opinion or judgment is a question of fact. Courts require clear proof that a promise was made in such cases.[31] Even if the physician has used promissory language, courts typically hold that the patient should not have understood the physician as undertaking a legal obligation in the same sense that a merchant makes a legally binding promise in a commercial transaction.

---

[30]Cases involving alleged jesting include Lucy v. Zehmer, 196 Va. 493, 84 S.E.2d 516 (1954); Davis v. Davis, 119 Conn. 194, 175 A. 574 (1934); Chiles v. Good, 41 S.W.2d 738 (Tex. Civ. App. 1931); Deitrick v. Sinnott, 189 Iowa 1002, 179 N.W. 424 (1920); McClurg v. Terry, 21 N.J. Eq. 225 (1870); and Keller v. Holderman, 11 Mich. 248, 83 Am. Dec. 737 (1863). Cases involving "bragging" include Lucy v. Zehmer, *supra,* and Newman v. Schiff, 778 F.2d 460 (8th Cir. 1985), in which Schiff, a "tax rebel," appeared on a television news program and offered to pay $100,000 to anyone who could disprove his theory that the Internal Revenue Code contained no provision making the payment of taxes mandatory. The court held that the statement, albeit a bragging one, was an offer. The segment of that program containing the offer was rebroadcast on a news program by the same network (CBS) where Newman saw it. Newman attempted to accept the offer because he had become aware of it on the rebroadcast. The court held the rebroadcast was not a renewal of the offer but only a news report of the original offer that terminated at the end of the "call-in" program. In Barnes v. Treece, 15 Wash. App. 437, 549 P.2d 1152 (1976), the court found a statement made by a promoter of punch boards that he would pay a certain sum if anyone could prove that such devices were "crooked" to be an effective offer which was accepted. *See also* Higgins v. Lessig, 49 Ill. App. 459 (1893), Weeks v. Tybald, Noy 11 (1605).

[31]*See* Sullivan v. O'Connor, 363 Mass. 579, 296 N.E.2d 183 (1973).

Rather, the patient should have understood the physician's statements only as statements of what is likely to occur notwithstanding language that, in other contexts, would be interpreted as promissory. A therapeutic reassurance should not be understood as a contractual promise.[32] Courts are reluctant to cast contractual liability upon physicians because they recognize that physicians necessarily make judgmental and predictive statements to their patients. Courts also recognize the special relationship of doctor and patient that may permit a physician to refrain from discussing all of the dangers that may be present even in a relatively simple surgical procedure. Excessive candor may create a psychic reaction which would seriously impair the success of the treatment.[33] Nor is a physician liable in contract for failure to possess skill commensurate with the skill of his colleagues in similar localities. An effort to find an implied promise by a physician with respect to such skill will not succeed. The customary remedy for failure to meet such a standard is a malpractice action in Tort.[34] Notwithstanding the reluctance of courts to find a breach of promise by a physician, if the promise is abundantly clear, a physician is capable of making an enforceable promise to which legal consequences will attach to effectuate a cure or result.[35]

D. The Parties Manifest No Intention About Legal Consequences — Social Agreements, Agreements Between Married Persons and Cohabitants.

If the parties have not manifested any intention concerning legal consequences so that courts may not legitimately find such an intention through interpretation of the parties' expressions, courts have generally concluded that legal consequences should attach. Since the typical agreement involves no thought about legal consequences, courts are faced with the necessity of deciding what reasonable parties would have intended had they considered the matter at all. The judicial assumption that the parties would have in-

---

[32] *Ibid.*

[33] Gault v. Sideman, 42 Ill. App. 2d 96, 191 N.E.2d 436 (1963). *See* Annotation, *Recovery Against Physician on Basis of Breach of Contract to Achieve Particular Result or Cure*, 43 A.L.R.3d 1221 (1972).

[34] *See* Note, *Contractual Liability in Medical Malpractice — Sullivan v. O'Connor*, 24 DE PAUL L. REV. 212, 214 (1974); Note, *Physicians and Surgeons — Sullivan v. O'Connor: A Liberal View of the Contractual Liability of Physicians and Surgeons*, 54 N.C.L. REV. 885, 887 (1976).

[35] The celebrated case is Hawkins v. McGee, 84 N.H. 114, 146 A. 641 (1929), where a boy suffered a severe scar on his hand resulting from a burn. The physician attempted to persuade the parents for several years to permit an operation to remove the scar although skin specialists had advised against surgery. The parents resisted these efforts. The physician had claimed expertise and, when the boy turned eighteen, he agreed to the surgery. The physician stated that the operation would be simple, quick, and effective and said, "I will guarantee to make the hand a hundred percent perfect hand." He also told the father that the boy would be hospitalized no more than four days. After the operation, the patient bled badly for several days, the hand was partially closed and the scar worsened. Moreover, the hand was densely covered with hair. Other specialists stated that nothing could be done to remedy the problem. The physician claimed that his statements were mere opinions or predictions rather than promises. With respect to the statement that the hand would be "a hundred percent perfect hand," the court disagreed since the physician was so persistent and had clearly gone beyond statements of opinion or prediction. However, with respect to the duration of the hospital stay, the court held that statement to be prediction rather than promise. *See also* Sullivan v. O'Connor, 363 Mass. 579, 296 N.E.2d 183 (1973) (promise to make patient more beautiful), and Stewart v. Rudner, 349 Mich. 459, 84 N.W.2d 816 (1957) (promise to perform Caesarian section).

tended legal consequences had they thought about it may be said to lead to the conclusion that no genuine intent concerning legal consequences is essential. This apparent conundrum is overcome through the practical necessity of attaching legal consequences to the overwhelming majority of agreements in which the parties do not manifest any such intention. Absent the presumption, the majority of agreements would not be contracts. Thus, the simple statement that the parties must intend legal consequences to attach before any contract can be recognized has been replaced with the modern view: "Neither real nor apparent intention that a promise be legally binding is essential to the formation of a contract, but a manifestation of intention that a promise shall not affect legal relations may prevent the formation of a contract."[36] Thus, the general rule is that legal sanctions attach unless the parties manifest their intention that they shall not attach. This general rule, however, is subject to exceptions.

If parties agree to a social engagement, no legal obligation attaches. If A invites B to dinner or another social engagement and B accepts the invitation, there is no manifestation of intention regarding legal consequences. Under the general rule that legal obligation attaches absent express negation by the parties, legal obligation would attach. But that result is contrary to the reasonable expectation of parties to the typical social engagement. The law recognizes the normal understanding of parties in such circumstances, that, had they thought about the matter at all, they would have regarded such an engagement as binding only in honor.[37] In effect, the law substitutes the normal understanding of parties in social engagements for an expression manifesting their intention that legal consequences should not attach.

A similar conclusion is found in domestic arrangements. Where a husband and wife are living in harmony, the normal understanding is that agreements between spouses are ordinarily not intended to be legally binding.[38] Even where the family relationship is not as close as the husband and wife relationship, the normal understanding is that such agreements are binding only in honor. If, however, members of the same family were to enter into a business arrangement, the result could change if the inference were unwarranted.[39]

A relatively recent spate of cases involve unmarried cohabitants. The best-known case involves the well-known actor Lee Marvin, who lived with Michelle Marvin for seven years. Title to all property was held by Lee Marvin. Michelle alleged an oral contract that they would share equally any property accumulated while cohabiting. She further alleged the parties had agreed to represent themselves as a married couple, and that her contribution was that

---

[36] RESTATEMENT 2d § 21.

[37] "There are agreements between parties which do not result in contract within the meaning of that term in our law. The ordinary example is where two parties agree to take a walk together, or where there is an offer and an acceptance of hospitality. Nobody would suggest in ordinary circumstances that those agreements result in what we know as a contract." Balfour v. Balfour, 2 K.B. 571 (1919). See also Mitzel v. Hauck, 78 S.D. 543, 105 N.W.2d 378 (1960) (promise to go duck hunting was not a contractual promise — it was a social engagement). Nor is a politician liable for campaign promises: O'Reilly v. Mitchel, 85 Misc. 176, 148 N.Y.S. 88 (1914).

[38] Balfour v. Balfour, 2 K.B. 571 (1919). See also In re Weide's Estate, 73 S.D. 448, 44 N.W.2d 208 (1950) (wife, a registered nurse, presented a bill to the estate for caring for husband-decedent. Held: the services were presumed to be gratuitous).

[39] See Boston v. Boston, 1 K.B. 124 (1904).

of companion, homemaker, housekeeper and cook. This and similar cases focus on the question of whether such agreements violate public policy or even criminal statutes proscribing fornication or adultery. In *Marvin,* the court held that a relationship that appears conventional and does not flout public standards should not be characterized as contrary to public policy on the ground that it is meretricious unless the contract is explicitly founded on payment for sexual services.[40] Another court held that the contract may contemplate sexual intercourse as part of cohabitation and is still enforceable if the sole or dominant consideration is not sexual intercourse.[41] The overwhelming majority of courts favor the *Marvin* rationale at this time.[42] The contrary view representing an extreme minority is expressed in *Hewitt v. Hewitt,*[43] where the court discovered an implicit public policy in its statutes involving marriage:

> We cannot confidently say that judicial recognition of property rights between unmarried cohabitants will not make that alternative to marriage more attractive by allowing parties to engage in such relationships with greater security [than the marriage relationship]. . . . In thus potentially enhancing the attractiveness of a private arrangement over marriage, we believe that the appellate court decision in this case contravenes the [legislative] policy of strengthening and preserving the integrity of marriage.[44]

Since the great majority of courts hold that legal consequences should attach to agreements between unmarried cohabitants, in this situation they may be said to have returned to the general rule that legal consequences attach in the absence of a contrary manifestation. This shift, however, is predicated upon the assumption that, had the parties thought about the matter at all, they would have intended legal consequences. In contrast, the agreement between married persons living in harmony suggests the contrary assumption, i.e., that the agreement is binding only in honor. The indefinite duration of relationships between unmarried cohabitants and the lack of non-contractual legal sanctions attending such relationships suggests that agreements between such persons would have been thought legally binding had the parties consciously considered the matter. Lawyers have begun to counsel those contemplating such relationships to put their agreements in writing to avoid misunderstandings and evidentiary problems. Written evidence of the agreement, if enforceable, will more clearly provide a remedy in a situation that might otherwise be remediless.[45] Thus, agreements between unmarried cohabitants concerning the ownership of property or other economic concerns should

---

[40] Marvin v. Marvin, 134 Cal. Rptr. 815, 557 P.2d 1106 (1976).

[41] Latham v. Latham, 274 Or. 421, 547 P.2d 144 (1976).

[42] *See* Boland v. Catalano, 202 Conn. 333, 521 A.2d 142 (1987), in which the court provides a full discussion of the *Marvin* rationale which it adopts and then lists numerous cases in conformity with the *Marvin* rationale throughout the country.

[43] 77 Ill. 2d 49, 394 N.E.2d 1204 (1979).

[44] *Id.* at 1209.

[45] The *Marvin* opinion recognizes a restitutionary (quantum meruit) possibility in terms of the reasonable value of the services if plaintiff can show the normal requirement that such services were rendered with the expectation of payment. Marvin v. Marvin, *supra* note 40. However, *Morone v. Morone,* 50 N.Y.2d 481, 429 N.Y.S.2d 592, 413 N.E.2d 1154 (1980), suggests difficulty with that approach.

come within the general assumption that legal consequences are intended where the express agreement is silent as to legal consequences. Married persons living in harmony typically make no such agreements since there is a body of non-contractual law that will deal with these problems should the marriage be dissolved. On the other hand, if marital discord prompts a separation agreement or should parties contemplating marriage enter into an antenuptial agreement, the assumption of intended legal consequences is appropriate. These arrangements are intended to substitute the private agreement between the married parties for the legal apportionment of property that would otherwise occur. In the case of unmarried cohabitants, an agreement apportioning property is not intended as a substitute since no other sanction would be invoked upon the dissolution of such a relationship.[46]

§ 32. Final Writing Contemplated by the Parties — "Agreement to Agree."

Parties to an agreement often contemplate that their agreement will be put into the form of a final written statement. This raises the question of whether the contract was formed as soon as the agreement was reached or not until the contemplated writing had been executed (signed) by the parties. If the parties have manifested their intention as to when their undertaking shall be legally obligatory, the question is easily answered as in other cases in which the parties articulate their intention. If their expressions of agreement indicate that they understood themselves to be bound as soon as the agreement occurred and before the final writing, a contract existed as soon as they reached agreement whether or not any writing is ever created.[47] On the other hand, if their expressions indicate that they mutually understood no binding obligation to exist until the writing was executed, the law will give effect to that intention. In that situation, what occurred prior to the writing would be viewed as mere preliminary negotiations.[48] The problem arises where the parties express neither intention, leaving the courts with the same fundamen-

---

[46] To this point, courts have been unwilling to apportion property between unmarried cohabitants as if they were married. Thus, upon dissolution of such a relationship, one of the parties will seek a contractual or quasi-contractual remedy.

[47] In Kazanjian v. New England Petr. Corp., 480 A.2d 1153, 1157 (Pa. Super. 1984) the court stated: "If the parties orally agree to all of the terms of a contract between them and mutually expect the imminent drafting of a written contract reflecting their previous understanding, the oral contract may be enforceable." See also Courtin v. Sharp, 280 F.2d 345 (5th Cir. 1960); Smith v. Onyx Oil & Chem. Co., 218 F.2d 104 (3d Cir. 1955). See RESTATEMENT 2d § 27.

[48] Barry v. James, 31 Ill. Dec. 139, 394 N.E.2d 55 (1979) (a written memorial was a condition precedent to contract formation). See also Southwestern States Oil & Gas Co. v. Sovereign Resources, Inc., 365 S.W.2d 417 (Tex. Civ. App. 1963). The classic statement is found in Miss. & Dominion S.S. Co. v. Swift, 86 Me. 248, 258-59, 29 A. 1063, 1066-67 (1894): "If the party sought to be charged intended to close a contract prior to the formal signing of a written draft, or if he signified such an intention to the other party, he will be bound by the contract actually made, though the signing of the written draft be omitted. If, on the other hand, such party neither had nor signified such an intent to close the contract until it was fully expressed in a written instrument and attested by signatures, then he will not be bound until the signatures are affixed.... [I]f the written draft is viewed by the parties merely as a convenient memorial or record of their previous contract, its absence does not affect the binding force of the contract; if, however, it is viewed as the consummation of the negotiation, there is no contract until the written draft is finally signed." See also Massee v. Gibbs, 169 Minn. 100, 210 N.W. 872 (1926).

tal problem encountered in much of the agreement process, i.e., effectuating the intention of the parties which is a question of fact.[49]

The most important of the factors that courts view as significant in this determination is whether the parties have reached agreement on all essential terms prior to the consummation of the formal document evidencing their agreement.[50] Courts will also consider the nature of the transaction and the circumstances surrounding it since they may be sufficient to convince the fact finder of the parties' intention. In *Lambert Corp. v. Evans*,[51] the defendant had exchanged correspondence with the plaintiff concerning the acquisition of a particular line of products owned by the plaintiff. The defendant's vice-president visited the plaintiff for an entire day and discussed the proposed acquisition. This was followed by further correspondence and later by a telephone exchange during which the parties agreed to execute a formal document but also congratulated each other on having reached agreement. Defendant argued that the parties were not bound at that point since a more extensive review of the product line and related matters by engineers, accountants, and lawyers would be appropriate in such an acquisition. The court rejected this argument on the ground that a sensible businessman would not engage in such a costly review for an acquisition valued at only $20,000. Moreover, this was not the procedure defendant itself had followed in small acquisitions.[52]

Beyond the guides suggested previously (whether all essential terms have been agreed upon prior to the writing and the size of the transaction), courts will consider the complexity of the transaction and apply a common sense guideline: the more detailed the transaction, the less likely is the parties' intention to be bound prior to the execution of the formal document they contemplated.[53] Another guide is found in the partial performance of the par-

---

[49] *See* Burkett v. Morales, 128 Ariz. 417, 626 P.2d 147 (1981) (parties executed a memorandum which was to be followed by a formal document to be drafted by the lawyer of one of the parties. The court held that whether the parties intended to be bound only after the execution of the formal document was a question of fact). *See also* Arnold Palmer Golf Co. v. Fuqua Indus., 541 F.2d 584 (6th Cir. 1976).

[50] If the writing is to contain a material term upon which agreement has not been reached previously, courts typically regard the parties as intending no legal consequences until the writing is executed. *See* Scholnick's Importers v. Lent, 130 Mich. App. 104, 343 N.W.2d 249 (1983). It should be noted, however, that the parties may have manifested their intention to be bound prior to a formal writing even though they have left a material term for future agreement. *See* UCC § 2-305 which permits parties to conclude a contract for sale even though the price is not settled. The critical language is in subsection (1): "if they [the parties] so intend...."

[51] 575 F.2d 132 (7th Cir. 1978).

[52] *See* Jolly Elev. Co. v. Schweggmann Bros. Giant Super Mkts., 230 So. 2d 640 (La. App. 1970) (size of transaction was $12,376 and court found a contract when parties shook hands and said they had a deal). In Michigan Broadcasting Co. v. Shawd, 352 Mich. 453, 90 N.W.2d 451 (1958), the court found that the parties did not intend to be bound until the formal document was executed in a transaction valued at $230,000. *See also* Ryan v. Shott, 109 Ohio App. 317, 159 N.E.2d 907 (1950) (in a contract for the purchase of stock which would provide the buyer with a large office building, court held no contract upon a hand shake and statement that a deal had been made).

[53] *See* Michigan Broadcasting Co. v. Shawd, 352 Mich. 453, 90 N.W.2d 451 (1958); Blair v. Dickinson, 54 S.E.2d 828 (W. Va.), *cert. denied*, 338 U.S. 904 (1949), and RESTATEMENT 2d § 27, in particular comment c, which contains a sound statement of the various circumstances a court should consider in determining whether a contract has been concluded prior to the execution of the final writing. The writing itself may be so cursory, omitting essential elements, that a court may not be convinced that the parties intended such a writing as evidence of an enforceable agreement. *See* Hill v. McGregor Mfg. Corp., 23 Mich. App. 342, 178 N.W.2d 553 (1970). A court

ties. If the parties contemplate a writing but, prior to its execution, they begin to perform, their course of performance may indicate that they either intended the contract to be formed prior to the final writing, or they have modified their agreement to dispense with the final writing as a necessary condition to contract formation.[54]

Where neither the expression of the parties nor the surrounding circumstances provide any convincing evidence of the parties' intention to be bound or not to be bound until a final document has been executed, some courts have taken the position that the mere contemplation of a writing by the parties is sufficient evidence of their intention not to be bound until the writing is executed.[55] Thus, no contract would exist prior to the writing unless the inference drawn could be overcome by some other affirmative evidence. Such an inference or presumption is unwarranted. The isolated fact that the parties contemplated a writing sheds little or no light on the question of their intention as to when legal obgliation shall attach. It is just as likely that the parties desired the writing as a mere memorial of their agreement, i.e., as satisfactory evidence of a contract already consummated. In the preceding section, we discovered that parties need not consciously intend legal consequences to attach to an agreement in order that a contract be said to exist. It follows that, in cases where the parties merely indicate that a writing is contemplated and the circumstances do not allow for the application of the guides suggested earlier in this section, a contract is formed as soon as agreement on all essential terms has been reached even though the contemplated final document has not yet been executed. While the problem has not always been analyzed in this fashion, this view accords with the results reached in most of the decided cases.[56]

Again, it must be remembered that this analysis proceeds on the assumption that the parties have reached agreement upon all essential matters in-

---

may, however, find that the parties have concluded a contract notwithstanding a statement in a "confirmation" or "letter agreement" that they intended an even more formal and final writing. *See* Lambert Corp. v. Evans, *supra* note 51, in which a confirming letter was "subject to completion of such documents, papers and formal written agreement satisfactory to our counsel." *See also* Field v. Golden Triangle Broadcasting, 451 Pa. 410, 305 A.2d 689 (1973), *cert. denied,* 414 U.S. 1158 (1974) in which a letter agreement was subject to a final agreement, but the letter agreement was so complete in its terms and executed with such extraordinary care and finality that the court held the parties intended to be bound at the time they executed it, i.e., prior to the "final" agreement.

[54] *See* Dunkel Oil Corp. v. Independent Oil & Gas Co., 70 F.2d 967 (7th Cir. 1934); Jolly Elevator Co., *supra* note 52.

[55] Some cases suggest that the contemplation of a writing, by itself, is "some evidence" of the intention not to be bound until the writing is executed. Berman v. Rosenberg, 115 Me. 19, 97 A. 6 (1916). Other courts suggest that "strong evidence" is necessary to overcome the "presumption" that no final contract has been formed until the writing is executed. Atlantic Coast Realty Co. v. Robertson's Ex'r, 135 Va. 247, 116 S.E. 476 (1923). *See also* Blair v. Dickinson, *supra* note 53.

[56] Recognizing the scholarship of Professor Williston and Professor Corbin in this area, the United States Court of Appeals for the Third Circuit suggests: "The emphasis of these two eminent writers is, it seems to us, inclined toward finding the formation of a contract prior to the signing of the document unless the parties pretty clearly show that such signing is a condition precedent to legal obligation. And since contract law has passed the formalism of elaborate doctrines pertaining to sealed instruments, it seems to us such emphasis is quite natural and quite correct." Smith v. Onyx Oil & Chem. Corp., 218 F.2d 104, 108 (3d Cir. 1955). *See also* Barton Chem. Co. v. Penwalt Corp., 79 Ill. App. 3d 829, 399 N.E.2d 288 (1979); W. Bank v. Morrill, 245 Or. 27, 420 P.2d 119 (1966); Dorhman v. Sullivan, 310 Ky. 463, 220 S.W.2d 973 (1949).

tended to be agreed upon prior to the execution of the formal document. The only question is the moment legal obligation is intended to attach. If the parties have not reached agreement on all essential terms prior to the execution of the final writing, other complex issues may arise. The parties may not have reached the stage of mutual assent, i.e., they may still be in the preliminary negotiation stage, or the parties may have come to an agreement on most of the terms but have left the remaining terms to be agreed upon at a later time. The traditional judicial reaction to such an "agreement to agree" was to find no contract on the grounds that an "agreement to agree" is a contradiction in terms, since parties cannot be contractually bound until they arrive at a final agreement.[57] It is clear, however, that this strict position is not in accordance with modern contract law, in which many contracts may be found to exist even though some terms, including material terms, are left for future agreement between the parties.[58] These matters have not been addressed in this section, but will be explored in later sections.

§ 33. The Effect of Offers — Power of Acceptance.

To this point, we have explored the requirement of mutual assent and concluded that the parties must manifest such mutual assent by arriving at an agreement to form a contract. We explored the fundamental requirements of an agreement and the traditional fashion in which courts discover an agreement — the existence of offer and acceptance. The determination of whether an offer exists can be difficult and complex, and the two sections which follow will explore this question in detail. Before considering the ways in which courts determine whether an offer exists, however, it is of vital importance that the *legal effect* of an offer be understood.

An offer may be defined as a manifestation of assent to a bargain proposed by one party in exchange for a manifestation of assent to the same bargain by the other party. The expression of assent may be oral or written; no particular form is required. By far, the typical manifestation of assent is by promise. As suggested earlier, a promise is a commitment or undertaking to act or refrain from acting in a particular fashion.[59] If Ames makes a promise to Barnes to

---

[57] "[A]n agreement that [the parties] will in the future make such a contract as they may then agree upon amounts to nothing. An agreement to enter into negotiations, and agree upon the terms of a contract, if they can, cannot be made the basis of a cause of action. There would be no way by which the court could determine what sort of a contract the negotiations would result in; no rule by which the court could ascertain whether any, or, if so, what damages might follow a refusal to enter into such future contract. So, to be enforceable, a contract to enter into a future contract must specify all its material and essential terms, and leave none to be agreed upon as the result of future negotiations." Shephard v. Carpenter, 54 Minn. 153, 55 N.W. 906 (1893), *quoted with approval in* St. Louis & S.F.R.R. v. Gorman, 79 Kan. 643, 100 P. 647 (1909). The concept can be found at least as early as Ridgway v. Wharton, 6 Clark's H.L. Cases 238, 306 (1857), in which the court states the strict view that "[a]n agreement to enter into an agreement upon terms to be afterward settled between the parties is a contradiction in terms."

[58] *See, e.g.,* § 2-204(3) of the UCC: "Even though one or more terms is left open a contract for sale does not fail for indefiniteness if the parties have intended to make a contract and there is a reasonably certain basis for giving an appropriate remedy." One of the "gap-filling" terms, in particular, of part 3 of Article 2 of the Code suggests that the parties may "agree to agree": § 2-305 permits parties to conclude a contract and later agree upon a price. These matters will be discussed later. *See also* RESTATEMENT 2d §§ 33 and 54.

[59] *See* RESTATEMENT 2d § 2.

sell Ames' automobile to Barnes for $5000, Ames is an *offeror* and Barnes is an *offeree*. Before making the promise to sell her car to Barnes, Ames may have discussed the possibility of the sale; she may have negotiated with Barnes, who may have originally suggested an unwillingness to pay more than $4500 for the automobile. At a particular point in these negotiations, if Ames said, "I will sell my car to you for $5000," or a similar expression with the same meaning, Ames has made the first *legally operative* statement in the negotiations. She has made an offer which *creates a power of acceptance* in the offeree, Barnes. A statement is operative when it creates a legal effect. All of the preliminary discussion prior to the offer created no legal effect. Once an offer is made, however, the offeree, Barnes, now has something which he did not have prior to the offer. He has a legal *power,* a power of acceptance. Barnes now has a choice: he may or may not choose to *exercise* his power of acceptance. If he decides to exercise the power conferred on him by Ames by stating, "I will buy your car for $5000," or a similar expression with the same meaning, a contract is formed. It is important to emphasize that a contract is formed at that point in time even though Ames has decided that she does not want to sell her car for $5000. She may have decided to withdraw (revoke) her offer to sell at that price. Before she had time to express her revocation, however, Barnes exercised his power of acceptance and formed a contract. Once a contract is formed, there is no offer or acceptance; they have been merged into the contract and Ames is now bound to sell the car to Barnes for $5000. By creating a power of acceptance in Barnes, Ames has made herself *susceptible* to Barnes with respect to her car. By exercising his power of acceptance, Barnes has made the second *operative* statement in the transaction. His acceptance has the legal effect of forming a contract. By the exchange of their expressions of offer and acceptance, the parties have created a legal relationship between them. Prior to Barnes' exercise of the power of acceptance, there was a power-susceptibility relationship between Ames and Barnes, but there were no legal rights and duties. As soon as the contract was formed through the exercise of Barnes' power, however, both parties acquired legal rights and duties. Barnes has the right to become the owner of Ames' auto and he has the duty to pay Ames $5000. Ames has the right to Barnes' $5000 and she has the duty to transfer ownership of her automobile to Barnes. The creation of the power of acceptance in Barnes created a pre-contractual relationship, i.e., a power in Barnes and susceptibility in Ames. Once the power was exercised by Barnes, the relationship between the parties became a right/duty relationship, i.e., a relationship of correlative rights and duties.[60]

---

[60]These relationships were described by Professor Wesley Hohfeld in FUNDAMENTAL LEGAL CONCEPTS AS APPLIED IN JUDICIAL REASONING (1919). Hohfeld suggested that fundamental legal relations are *sui generis,* i.e., unique of their own kind and class. Therefore, he felt that attempts at formal definition are unsatisfactory and probably useless. Rather than definitions, Hohfeld provided an analysis of all of the various legal relations in terms of "jural opposites" and "jural correlatives":

Jural opposites: right/no-right; privilege/duty; power/disability; immunity/liability.

Jural correlatives: right/duty; privilege/no-right; power/liability; immunity/disability.

The Hohfeld analysis provides an explanation of each "opposite" and "correlative." As to "power," he suggests that the party whose volitional control is paramount may be said to have the (legal) power to effect the particular change of legal relations involved in the problem. When an offer is made, the offeror has created a power of acceptance in the offeree and the correlative of

The cases are now legion in which the legal effect of an offer is characterized as the creation of a "power of acceptance."[61]

A. *Criticism of Traditional Analysis — Relational Contracts.*

While the agreement process continues to be analyzed in terms of offer and acceptance, this approach has generated criticism among some contemporary writers. One criticism points to the practice in large-scale transactions of producing a series of preliminary drafts of potential contracts prepared by lawyers on either side, and simultaneously executing those drafts, so that it may be difficult to determine which party made the offer and which exercised the power of acceptance. Attempts to analyze this kind of transaction in traditional offer/acceptance fashion are unrealistic.[62] The criticism may be countered by recognizing simultaneous signing of such documents as quite rare. No recorded case is suggested. It would, therefore, be possible to characterize the first signer as the offeror and the last signer as the offeree, assuming, of course, that the parties had not agreed to be bound prior to the signing, in which case the execution of the document would constitute a mere memorial to their agreement.[63] There is, however, little or no point in dissecting this type of transaction to discover the offeror and offeree. Mutual assent is clear and it is neither necessary nor desirable to discover which party was the offeror, since the discovery of one party as offeror and the other as offeree has never been a requisite to finding a contract where mutual assent is otherwise clear. Whatever the issues in such a transaction, the question of which party was the offeror simply will not arise.

Another contemporary writer is highly critical of neoclassical contract concepts as found in the RESTATEMENT 2d and other works because they are predicated upon a discrete transaction concept, i.e., the isolated agreement to purchase and sell the automobile or similar discrete transactions, as contrasted with *relational* contracts. A relational contract is one of relatively long duration. Thus, if an engineer is employed by a large corporation with the expectation of remaining in that employment indefinitely, such a contract should be viewed as only the beginning of a possible long-term relationship between the engineer and the corporation. Many changes in that relationship may occur over a period of time, and these changes cannot be presentiated and brought into the present at the time the contract is formed.[64] Thus, contracts must be viewed on a spectrum of transactional and relational behavior. At one

---

"power" is "liability" in the offeror. It may be more precise to refer to the status of the offeror as one of "susceptibility" as suggested in the text, since the offeree may exercise the power and form a contract even though, at the moment of contract formation, the offeror is contemplating the revocation of the offer. (Revocations of offers will be explored in a subsequent section.) Once a contract is formed, the parties then have a right-duty correlative relationship.

[61] *See, e.g.,* Contempo Constr. Co. v. Mountain States Tel. & Tel. Co., 736 P.2d 13 (Ariz. App. 1987); Eakins v. New England Mutual Life Ins. Co., 130 Ill. App. 3d 65, 473 N.E.2d 439 (1984); Foremost Pro Color, Inc. v. Eastman Kodak Co., 703 F.2d 534 (9th Cir. 1983) (no power of acceptance created). The classic analysis is found in Corbin, Offer and Acceptance and Some of the Resulting Legal Relations, 26 YALE L.J. 169, particularly at 199-200 (1917).

[62] *See* 2 FORMATION OF CONTRACTS: A STUDY OF THE COMMON CORE OF LEGAL SYSTEMS 1585 (R. Schlesinger ed. 1968).

[63] *See supra* § 31.

[64] *See* Macneil, *Restatement (Second) of Contracts and Presentation,* 60 VA. L. REV. 589 (1974).

end we find discrete transactions of short duration, limited interpersonal relationships, and easily measured objectifications of exchange, e.g., the purchase and sale of a television set for $300. At the opposite end of the spectrum we find long-term relationships such as the employment contract involving the engineer and the large corporation. This agreement presents difficult problems in measuring performance and numerous entangling possibilities that cannot be projected with definiteness and accuracy at the time of contract formation.[65] This critic sees neoclassical contract law, with its emphasis upon the "promise" concept and the attendant offer/acceptance analysis, as inadequate to deal with modern contracts of a relational character. Certainly, questions of measurement and sufficient definiteness can be very difficult within the neoclassical tradition. Notwithstanding these difficulties, it remains necessary to determine whether the parties formed a contract initially, regardless of the inability to "presentiate" a long-term, relational contract several years into the future. Whether neoclassical doctrines will ultimately fail when applied to complex relational contracts, neoclassical concepts have proven remarkably flexible. With the continued assistance of critics, the prognosis is highly favorable that they will continue to accommodate the demands of an increasingly complex society.[66]

§ 34. Tests to Determine Whether an Offer Has Been Made.

The scores of cases that have sought to determine whether, in a given set of facts, an offer has been made, are notoriously deficient in suggesting clear guidelines to determine whether an offer exists. A glance at modern cases often reveals an admission that "[i]t is impossible to formulate a general principle or criterion for its determination."[67] The rationale for this less than helpful conclusion is based on the nature of the question to be determined, which is a question of intention — a question of fact[68] — that can only be determined by considering the objective manifestations of the parties and

---

[65] *See* Macneil, *Ibid.,* and also Macneil, *The Many Futures of Contract,* 47 S. CAL. L. REV. 691 (1974); I. MACNEIL, THE NEW SOCIAL CONTRACT (1980); Macneil, *Economic Analysis of Contractual Relations: Its Shortfalls and the Need for a Rich Classificatory Apparatus,* 75 NW. U.L. REV. 1018 (1981).

[66] Professor Macneil suggests no substitute for current neoclassical contract law to meet the needs of a society filled with relational contracts. His writings, however, have provided neoclassical scholars with considerable insight that has proven particularly useful in extending the neoclassical doctrines more effectively to relational concepts.

[67] R.E. Crummer & Co. v. Nuveen, 147 F.2d 3, 5 (7th Cir. 1945) *quoted in* Maryland Supreme Corp. v. Blake Co., 279 Md. 531, 369 A.2d 1017 (1977) *and* Interstate Indus. v. Barclay Indus., 540 F.2d 868 (7th Cir. 1976).

[68] The determination of whether a question is one of fact or law is a topic dealt with in civil procedure texts. The law/fact dichotomy may be seen as false when questions are characterized as questions of law rather than questions of fact on the basis of who is to decide the questions. The shibboleth is that questions of fact are decided at the trial level by juries or judges sitting without juries. Questions of law, on the other hand, are decided by judges, and appellate courts deal only with "law" questions — questions of fact are not reviewable absent an abuse of discretion by the fact finder. Yet, in many situations factual questions will be resolved by judges, although such questions will be called questions of law because the judge decides them and they are reviewable by appellate courts. The interpretation of a writing susceptible to different interpretations raises questions normally reserved to judges. The question "What happened?" is one of fact that should be decided exclusively by the trier of fact and should not be susceptible to judicial review, again, absent a manifest abuse of discretion.

circumstances under which those manifestations occurred. The only guide suggested by the RESTATEMENT 2d is of limited assistance, i.e., whether a purported offeree was justified in understanding a manifestation of intention as creating a power of acceptance.[69] Notwithstanding the legitimate insistence that the question is one of manifested intention, i.e., one of fact, and the assertion that no general principle can be stated, there are discernible guidelines in the case law that will now be examined.

A. *Present Intention Versus Promises — Advertisements — Definiteness — Identifiable Offerees.*

A basic distinction is made between *statements of present intention* on the one hand and *commitments or promises* on the other. As suggested in the preceding section, if A says to B, "I intend to sell my car for $5000," and B replies, "I will buy it for $5000," there is no contract if these statements are taken at face value. A's statement involves no promise, commitment or undertaking; it is merely a statement of present intention. B is not justified in understanding that he has the power to conclude a contract with A. A's statement is not an offer because, on its face, it cannot reasonably be interpreted to mean, "I will sell this car to you, B, for a price of $5000." Rather, A's statement may indicate A's intention either to make an offer at some future time, or to receive an offer at $5000 to sell his car. Neither manifestation of intention is, itself, an offer. This analysis is found in myriad cases involving advertising appearing in newspapers, catalogs, trade circulars and the like, or with respect to goods displayed in stores. Such advertising or display of goods is generally construed to constitute mere solicitation of offers rather than offers.[70] In a narrow range of other advertisement cases, courts have found offers by suggesting that the advertisement was sufficiently clear, definite and explicit.[71] Yet, much advertising contains considerable detail concerning the advertised goods and states a definite price. It is sufficiently clear, definite and explicit, though no offer is found. Where a court finds that an advertisement constitutes an offer, the critical manifestation of intention in such an advertisement is a statement of promise, i.e., that the party issuing the statement will perform or refrain from performing an act in the future. Where a store advertised three sufficiently described items at a definite price with the commitment "First Come First Served,"[72] the court found that offers had been made. While the court's conclusion was correct, it failed to provide the appropriate analysis. It is at least doubtful that a finding of an offer would have been justified absent a limitation on the number of advertised items and the "First Come First Served" language in the advertisement. A reasonable interpretation of that language indicates a commitment by the advertiser to sell

---

[69] "An offer is the manifestation of willingness to enter a bargain, so made as to justify another person in understanding that his assent to that bargain is invited and will conclude it." RESTATE-MENT 2d § 24.

[70] *See* Foremost Pro Color, Inc. v. Eastman Kodak Co., 703 F.2d 534 (9th Cir. 1983) (information circular, like other trade circulars, catalogs, and advertisements which are uniformly regarded as mere preliminary negotiations creating no power of acceptance in the recipient, was not an offer).

[71] *See* Lefkowitz v. Great Minneapolis Surplus Store, 251 Minn. 188, 86 N.W.2d 689 (1957).

[72] *Ibid.*

the described goods to the first three buyers who present the advertised price for the goods. The advertisement is seen as a promotional device whereby the store is promising to sell valuable goods at a price far below market value. A prospective buyer who may expend considerable energy and time to ascertain that he or she is one of the first three customers to enter the store when it opens on the day of the sale would be legitimately disappointed if the tender of the advertised price would be viewed as a mere offer. Such customers reasonably understand that they have powers of acceptance.

Since store advertising of specific goods at specific prices is addressed to the public at large rather than specific parties, it is sometimes suggested that the risk to the store would be unreasonably large if advertisements were construed as offers. This view is based upon two concerns: (1) the offerees are not identified, which suggests that the advertisement was not designed as an offer, and (2) the number of offerees is left uncertain, which creates an unreasonable risk for the purported offeror-shopkeeper.[73] With respect to the first concern, there is no indefiniteness if the offeree is *identifiable.* In the "First Come First Served" advertisement, the offerees will be the three customers who first present themselves as prospective buyers of the goods, conditioned only upon their tendering the advertised prices. Similarly, where rewards are made to the public, the lack of identity of the offeree at the time the offer is made is no bar to finding a contract. One of the most famous cases in the law of contracts is illustrative.

In *Carlill v. Carbolic Smoke Ball Co.,*[74] the advertisement read:

> £100 reward will be paid by the Carbolic Smoke Ball Company to any person who contracts the increasing epidemic influenza, colds or any disease caused by taking cold after having used the ball three times daily for two weeks according to the printed directions supplied with each ball. £100 is deposited with the Alliance Bank, Regent Street, shewing our sincerity in the matter.

The court did not question whether the language of the advertisement was promissory since the language clearly evidenced a commitment by the advertiser. The opinion carefully considered the deposit with the Alliance Bank as a manifestation of sincerity — the advertisement was not mere "puff." Moreover, there was no question concerning the proper interpretation of this advertisement as an offer notwithstanding the lack of identified offerees at the time the offer was made.[75] The case is also instructive with respect to the second concern: the risk assumed by the manufacturer of the product arising from the

---

[73] The classic statement is found in Crawley v. Rex (1909) Transvaal 1105 (S. Africa): "It would lead to most extraordinary results if that were the correct view of the case. Because then supposing a shopkeeper were sold out of a particular class of goods, thousands of members of the public might crowd into the shop and demand to be served, and each one would have a right of action against the proprietor for not performing his contract."

[74] 1 Q.B. 256 (1893).

[75] Since the act required by the offer was the use of the product (the smoke ball) in accordance with directions for the period stipulated, all members of the public were potential offerees and those who used the product accordingly were offerees who accepted the offer. The proper use of the product formed a contract between the company and all such users. The company thereby had a duty to pay the reward to any such user, but the company's duty was conditioned on the involuntary act of contracting influenza.

potentially large number of offerees. The risk of a large number of offerees who met the condition of contracting influenza was clearly assumed by the offeror. While the typical shopkeeper may not be said to have assumed the risk of an unlimited number of offerees, such an offeror could place a reasonable limitation on the number of advertised items. In the absence of an express limitation, the shopkeeper should not be confronted with the risk of having an unlimited number of such items available for an unexpected number of customers, because the number of available items would be subject to a reasonable limitation under the circumstances.[76]

The advertisment cases dealing with statements to an indefinite number of prospective parties may be seen as containing a negative implication that a statement addressed to a definite party should necessarily be construed as an offer. This is an unreliable suggestion. Even where parties are dealing exclusively with each other, what may appear to be an offer may, upon careful examination, be a mere invitation for an offer.[77]

The unpersuasive rationales found in numerous cases involving the question of whether an offer exists and the insistence that no general principle can be stated because the question is one of fact, do not deter the judicial search for a promise or commitment to future action. Thus, in a case suggesting the futility of discovering a general principle, the court quotes from an earlier opinion:

> In order to hold that the parties entered into a contract to buy and sell at the [quoted] prices, there must be evidence of an offer. . . . Such an offer must have manifested a present intention of a *promise* to sell. . . .[78]

The requirement of a promise is the pervasive element in the entire body of case law distinguishing offers from preliminary negotiations. If a general

---

[76] Where a party has only one item for sale, *e.g.*, a tract of land, it is possible for that party to make offers to innumerable offerees. If more than one offeree accepts, the offeror has contracts with all of the offerees. He can perform only one of the contracts and must breach the others. The question remains, did the owner of the land make an offer to anyone? In Lonergan v. Scolnick, 129 Cal. App. 2d 179, 276 P.2d 8 (1954), the owner placed an ad in a newspaper describing the land. The ad prompted an inquiry from the plaintiff to which the owner responded with directions to the land, a "rock-bottom price," and the following statement: "This is a form letter." Plaintiff responded with further questions concerning the topography and a particular bank as escrow agent. The owner replied with further information concerning the land and indicated that the named bank would be a satisfactory escrow agent. This letter ended with "If you are really interested, you will have to decide fast, as I expect to have a buyer in the next week or so." The court held that the owner had made no offer to the plaintiff. The owner's first letter ending with "This is a form letter" clearly indicated that the owner made no commitment to the plaintiff. The second letter from the owner made it clear that the owner reserved the right to sell the land to another buyer, i.e., the buyer who first tendered the "rock-bottom" price, who was, necessarily, unidentified but identifiable. The owner's statements were, in effect, treated by the court as a "first come, first served" expression which would constitute an offer to any such offeree. Since the land was sold to another prior to the receipt of any tender from the plaintiff, the owner was free to sell to the party who first tendered the price.

[77] *See* Rhen Marshall, Inc. v. Purolator Filter Div., 211 Neb. 306, 318 N.W.2d 284 (1982), relying upon the classic case of Nebraska Seed Co. v. Harsh, 98 Neb. 89, 152 N.W. 310 (1915), in which the defendant sent a letter to the plaintiff which stated, in pertinent part, "I want $2.25 per cwt. for this seed f. o. b. Lowell." The attempted acceptance by the plaintiff was ineffective since the plaintiff had no power of acceptance. The defendant's letter was a mere invitation to plaintiff to make an offer at the stated price. *See also* Lonergan v. Scolnick, *supra* note 76.

[78] Thos. J. Sheehan Co. v. Crane Co., 418 F.2d 642, 644 (8th Cir. 1969), *as quoted in* Interstate Indus. v. Barclay Indus., 540 F.2d 868 (7th Cir. 1976) (emphasis added).

contractor desires to place a bid for a particular construction project, his invitation to various subcontractors to bid on various parts of the project is seen as his invitation for offers, i.e., he is asking subcontractors to promise that they will supply certain goods or services at definite prices to enable him to bid on the project. He is not committing himself to the lowest bidder.[79]

B. *Opinions and Predictions — Express Warranties Distinguished.*

If a party makes a statement of *prediction* or *opinion,* it is not a promise and the party making the statement is not an offeror. In a well-known case, a tenant farmer worried about the water supply before making a decision concerning the purchase of cattle. His landlord said, "Never mind the water, John, I will see that there will be plenty of water because it never failed in Minnesota yet." The farmer purchased more than 100 cattle and later suffered a loss when the water supply failed. In an action against the landlord, the court found the landlord's statement to be mere prediction and the farmer was not justified in relying upon it.[80] If the landlord had said, "Don't worry, John. If you suffer any loss as a result of a water shortage, I will reimburse you" (or words to that effect), this would have been a promise upon which the farmer could justifiably rely. Earlier in this chapter, cases involving alleged promises by physicians concerning the recovery time or chance of recovery by patients were explored.[81] Those cases typically involve the question of whether a physician is merely stating an opinion or prediction concerning a cure or period of recovery rather than a promise. As the prior discussion indicates, such statements by a physician will be viewed as statements of opinion or prediction absent clear and convincing evidence that the physician's statement constituted a promise. In a related situation, the UCC requires statements of *fact* as contrasted with statements of opinion or commendation by the seller.[82] If a seller of goods informed a prospective buyer of how "wonderful" or "great" the goods are, or how extremely valuable they are, such statements would be statements of the seller's opinion or commendation. Earlier courts would refer to such statements as mere "puff," i.e., statements with no legal effect. If, however, the seller provides statements of fact, descriptions,[83] specifications, blueprints, samples or models[84] which become part of the basis of the bargain, they are factual assertions by the seller and, as such, constitute express warranties under the UCC.

C. *Summary of Guidelines — Application — Harvey v. Facey.*

The effort to discover criteria or guides to be applied to myriad fact situations that are effective in distinguishing offers from preliminary negotiations

---

[79] Milone & Tucci, Inc. v. Bona Fide Bldrs., Inc., 49 Wash. 2d 363, 301 P.2d 759 (1956); Anderson v. Board of Pub. Schs., 122 Mo. 61, 27 S.W. 610 (1894).

[80] Anderson v. Backlund, 159 Minn. 423, 199 N.W. 90 (1924).

[81] *See supra* § 31.

[82] *See* UCC § 2-313(2). It should be noted that express warranties may be created not only by promises relating to the quality of the goods that become part of the basis of the bargain, but also by affirmations of fact relating to the goods that become part of the basis of the bargain, § 2-313(1)(a). For a discussion of the elusive concept of "basis of the bargain," *see* Murray, *Basis of the Bargain: Transcending Classical Concepts,* 66 U. MINN. L. REV. 283 (1982).

[83] § 2-313(1)(b).

[84] § 2-313(1)(c).

is not in vain. A summary of the guides developed to this point is in order. It is fashionable to begin with the basic test found in the RESTATEMENT 2d: Is there a manifestation of willingness to enter into a bargain that would justify the party to whom it is made in understanding that his assent to that bargain is invited and will conclude it?[85] We have seen that this definition of an offer is almost a tautology, i.e., the manifestation will be an offer if a reasonable party would have understood it as an offer. But, what is the basis for such a reasonable understanding? Since modern contract law tolerates considerable indefiniteness in contract formation,[86] one of the guides found in numerous cases is not particularly helpful, i.e., the more definite the statement, the more likely that the statement is an offer.[87] In light of innumerable advertisements and other preliminary statements that provide more detail than any reasonable potential buyer desires to know, it is misleading to suggest that the likelihood of an offer depends upon the definiteness of the statement. Offers must be sufficiently definite. An advertisement or other solicitation of an offer, however, will not be construed as an offer regardless of extreme definiteness. Another guide suggests that the more definite the party or parties to whom the statement is addressed, the more likely it is that an offer will be found. Yet, the reward cases and other cases involving advertisement offers to the public make that guide usable only if the offeree is not *identifiable*, i.e., the fact that the party to whom the expression is addressed is not identified at the moment the expression occurs does not suggest that the manifestation cannot be an offer. There is only one, constant, unexcepted criterion that can be stated: the expression must be a promise. From this base, the following guide can be constructed: If a statement is sufficiently definite and there is a manifestation of commitment, a promise designed to induce action or forebearance which the promisor desires,[88] an offer exists, because the party to whom such a statement is addressed reasonably assumes that his assent will form a contract. Even this reliable guide, however, must not be viewed algebraically — it is not a litmus test, since the discipline is law and not science. It must be remembered that the question is still one of manifested intention, a question of fact,[89] and that courts will decide this question of fact. Two or more courts could apply the suggested guide to virtually identical fact

---

[85] RESTATEMENT 2d § 24. In Barnum v. Review Bd. of Ind. Emp. Sec. Div., 478 N.E.2d 1243 (Ind. App. 1985), the RESTATEMENT 2d definition was applied and the court found no offer because the party to whom the statement was addressed would not have been reasonable in understanding that his assent would conclude a contract. *See also* Contempo Constr. Co. v. Mountain States Tel. & Tel. Co., 736 P.2d 13 (Ariz. App. 1987).

[86] UCC § 2-204(3) expressly permits such indefiniteness. When one or more terms are left open, a contract will be formed if (1) the parties intended to make a contract, and (2) there is a reasonably certain basis for giving an appropriate remedy. The same concept is found in RESTATEMENT 2d § 33(2). The concept of indefiniteness will be explored in detail in later sections.

[87] In Chasan v. Village Dist. of Eastman, 523 A.2d 16 (N.H. 1986), the court's finding of no offer relies almost entirely upon the lack of definiteness of the language. Numerous cases, however, do not find a missing term fatal in their quest to discover an offer. *See, e.g.,* Wilcom v. Wilcom, 66 Md. App. 84, 502 A.2d 1076 (1986), where the failure to identify the price or the number of shares of stock to be sold did not deter the court from discovering an offer where the necessary information was ascertainable from facts beyond the writing.

[88] A promise that induces action or forebearance desired by the promisor is a partial statement of the requirement of consideration, to be discussed in the next chapter dealing with the validation process.

[89] *See supra* note 68.

situations and arrive at opposite conclusions. There is no mathematical formula that promises a certain and just result in all cases.[90] One of the classic cases in contract law, *Harvey v. Facey,* demonstrates this difficulty.[91]

Facey owned certain property known as Bumper Hall Pen. He had been negotiating with the town council for the sale of the property. Harvey and another were interested in the property and telegraphed Facey as follows: "Will you sell us Bumper Hall Pen? Telegraph lowest cash price — answer paid." Facey replied by telegram: "Lowest cash price for Bumper Hall Pen £900." Harvey assumed this was an offer by Facey — a commitment to sell the property to Harvey justifying him in assuming that his assent would form a contract for the property. He replied, "We agree to buy Bumper Hall Pen for the sum of nine hundred pounds asked by you." Facey refused to convey the property and Harvey sued. The issue was whether Facey's telegram to Harvey constituted an offer. The court analyzed the first telegram from Harvey as containing two questions: (1) would Facey sell the property to Harvey, and (2) what was the lowest price Facey would accept? Since Facey answered only the second question ("Lowest cash price for Bumper Hall Pen £900"), the court found that Facey had made no offer; he had merely quoted the price. Facey had not, for example, started his telegraphic answer with, "Yes, I will sell Bumper Hall Pen to you." Absent that kind of statement or, at least, the word "Yes" before announcing the price, the court found no offer. The court's analysis may be criticized as too rigid because it failed to consider the medium used — telegrams — which promote relatively cryptic messages since every additional word adds to the cost, regardless of which party is paying the fee. Even parties who are not concerned about cost may feel compelled to sound cryptic in telegraph or mailgram messages, as that is the accepted style of communicating in that medium. The court in *Harvey* also seemed to be asking the parties to express themselves comprehensively. Such rigidity and insistence upon completeness would necessarily result in finding many expressions ineffective as offers. The court also failed to consider the possible motivation of Facey in bothering to respond at all to the Harvey telegram.[92] This raises the test question: would a reasonable party in Harvey's position understand that he had a power of acceptance? Other courts, particularly modern courts, might find an offer in Facey's response in light of the questions to which that response was addressed and the medium of communication. The factual patterns illustrating this kind of borderline or "gray area" case are myriad, and the judicial task is essentially the same in each: to approximate, as closely as possible, the manifested intentions of the parties, which are more often than

---

[90] "Since two cases are never identical in the exact words used, in the existing relations and history of the parties, in the circumstances surrounding the communication, the decision made in one of them can never be regarded as a conclusive precedent for the other. Nevertheless, it may be suggestive and enlightening precedent." 1 CORBIN § 23 at 68-69.

[91] 62 L.J., P.C. 127, A.C. 552 [1893].

[92] Other facts in *Harvey v. Facey* could justify the conclusion reached by the court. There was public knowledge that the defendant had offered the property to the City the day before plaintiffs sent their telegram. Plaintiffs' knowledge of this fact could lead to the conclusion that plaintiffs should not have viewed defendant's telegram response as an offer if they knew that defendant had already made an offer to the City. The court does not indicate whether plaintiffs had knowledge of the offer to the City. Moreover, the court does not present its analysis on the basis of these additional facts.

not imperfectly expressed. The use of the guide suggested in this section should prove helpful to courts in their performance of this task. Again, it is no more than a guide, since, as Aristotle and others remind us, we should not expect as much certainty in our law as we expect in our physics.

§ 35. The Effect of Captions and Headings — "Quotation," Purchase Order, Etc.

A prospective buyer of goods or services may solicit a price quotation or "quote" from one or more vendors. The solicitation is not an offer. It is an invitation to negotiate or, in antiquated usage, "an invitation to treat." In response to the solicitation, the vendor may send a document captioned "quotation". There are many cases suggesting that a mere "price quotation" is not an offer,[93] that a "purchase order" is an offer[94] and that documents with other captions may or may not be offers.[95] There are other cases construing documents captioned "quotation" to be offers[96] and construing purchase orders to be acceptances rather than offers.[97] It is particularly important to emphasize a pervasive truth emanating from all of the cases that require courts to construe various documents: *the caption or other characterizing language of the document will not be conclusive of the legal effect of that document.* The entire

---

[93]*See, e.g.,* Interstate Indus. v. Barclay Indus., 540 F.2d 868 (7th Cir. 1976). When a court has concluded that a price quotation is not an offer in a given case, it almost invariably refers to such a price quotation as a "mere" price quotation. On its face, a "quote" or quotation may appear to solicit an offer. *See* RESTATEMENT 2d § 26 comment c. It is not intended to be binding when the purchaser reacts by sending its order in response to the quotation. However, if a document referred to a price quotation as a manifested binding intention upon submission of the buyer's order through the typical purchase order, such a quotation would be an offer. *See* McCarty v. Verson Allsteel Press Co., 89 Ill. App. 3d 498, 411 N.E.2d 936 (1980).

[94]*See, e.g.,* J. B. Moore Elec. Contr. v. Westinghouse Elec. Supply Co., 221 Va. 745, 273 S.E.2d 553 (1981).

[95]*See, e.g.,* Paloukos v. Intermountain Chevrolet Co., 99 Idaho 740, 588 P.2d 939 (1978) ("worksheet" construed as evidence of contract rather than mere preliminary negotiations); J. B. Moore Elec. Contr. v. Westinghouse Elec. Supply Co., 221 Va. 745, 273 S.E.2d 553 (1981) (purchase order form supplied by seller construed to be an offer rather than an invitation to the buyer to make an offer because it did not contain a purchaser's signature line). In Three-Seventy Leasing Corp. v. Ampex Corp., 528 F.2d 993 (5th Cir. 1976), a purchase order submitted by a seller was held to be an offer by the purchaser because it had a signature line where buyer signed. *Accord* Antonucci v. Stevens Dodge, Inc., 73 Misc. 2d 173, 340 N.Y.S.2d 979 (Civ. Ct. N.Y.C. 1973).

[96]Perhaps the most famous case among the older decisions is Fairmount Glassworks v. Crunden-Martin Wooden Ware Co., 106 Ky. 695, 51 S.W. 196 (1899) where a response to a price solicitation provided a series of prices on various sizes of jars, but ended with, "for immediate acceptance" which was sufficient for the court to conclude that the seller had made an offer. Presumably, the court felt that this phrase indicated the seller's promise or commitment to sell. RESTATEMENT 2d § 26 ill. 3, suggests that a letter from A to B stating, "I can quote you flour at $5 per barrel in carload lots" would not, itself, be an offer in view of the word "quote" and incompleteness of the terms. However, the same letter in response to an inquiry specifying detailed terms "would probably" convert the letter into an offer. Moreover, if A had added, "for immediate acceptance," the RESTATEMENT 2d suggests that an intention to make an offer would then be "unmistakable." *See also* Maryland Supreme Corp. v. Blake Co., 279 Md. 531, 369 A.2d 1017 (1977) where the "quotation" was construed to be an offer.

[97]*See, e.g.,* Island Creek Coal Co. v. Lake Shore, Inc., 636 F. Supp. 285 (W.D. Va. 1986); Daitom, Inc. v. Pennwalt Corp., 741 F.2d 1569 (10th Cir. 1984); Mead Corp. v. McNally-Pittsburgh Mfg. Corp., 654 F.2d 1197 (6th Cir. 1981); Idaho Power Co. v. Westinghouse Elec. Corp., 596 F.2d 924 (9th Cir. 1979); Earl M. Jorgensen Co. v. Mark Constr. Inc., 56 Hawaii 466, 540 P.2d 978 (1975). In particular, *see* Phillips Petr. Co. Norway v. Bucyrus-Erie Co., 125 Wis. 2d 418, 373 N.W.2d 65 (1985), *rev'd on other grounds,* 1 U.C.C. Rep. Serv. 2d (Callaghan) 667 (Wis. Sup. 1986).

document must be considered in light of the surrounding circumstances, i.e., interpretation or construction must occur in *context*. In a classic case, the phrase, "for immediate acceptance" at the end of what otherwise appeared to be a price quotation converted the preliminary negotiation into an offer.[98] In another case, a document captioned "quotation" was construed to be an offer because the parties manifested their intention that it operate as an offer.[99] Even the term "offer" may not be sufficient to create a power of acceptance if the statement otherwise suggests that it sought to induce offers and was not, therefore, itself an offer.[1] While captions and characterizing terms within a statement are not conclusive of the legal effect to be accorded a statement, it would be foolhardy to characterize a statement as a "quotation" if an offer were intended, or to characterize it as an "offer" if a preliminary negotiation were intended. In an otherwise close case, the use of a term normally associated with offers or non-offers can be persuasive.[2] Yet, the general principle remains: whether a particular manifestation of intention is an offer as contrasted with a preliminary negotiation will depend upon the proper interpretation of the entire statement within the surrounding circumstances as one which is sufficiently definite to permit a remedy to be fashioned and, in particular, whether the statement is promissory in character, i.e., whether it manifests a definite commitment of future action or inaction on the part of the promisor in exchange for a promise or performance by the party to whom it is addressed.[3] Only then will the promisee be reasonable in assuming that his promise or performance in reply will form a contract.

§ 36. Auction Sales and Self-Service Transactions.

A. *Auction Sales.*

The determination of who makes the offer at the typical auction sale was the subject of considerable controversy at one time. When the auctioneer places goods up for sale, is he making an offer to sell to the highest bidder, or is he merely inviting bidders to make offers? An early case took the view that the typical auction sale is one in which the auctioneer merely invites offers, i.e., the auctioneer is saying, "What am I bid?"[4] Under this view, if the auctioneer is dissatisfied with the level of bidding, he need not accept any bid and can withdraw the item. To avoid negative public relations, the auctioneer may even resort to employing an agent or "shill" to increase the bidding. If the agent does not succeed in elevating the bidding to a level satisfactory to the auctioneer, the auctioneer may then pretend to sell the item to his agent.

---

[98] *See* Fairmount Glassworks v. Crunden-Martin Wooden Ware Co., 106 Ky. 659, 51 S.W. 196 (1899), discussed in *supra* note 96.

[99] *See* Earl M. Jorgensen Co. v. Mark Constr., Inc., 56 Haw. 466, 540 P.2d 978 (1975) and cases cited *supra* note 16.

[1] *See supra* § 34.

[2] For example, in Interstate Indus. v. Barclay Indus., 540 F.2d 868 (7th Cir. 1976), the reference to the contents of a letter as a "price quotation" was one of four factors leading a court to conclude that the statement was not an offer. In Chasan v. Village Dist. of Eastman, 523 A.2d 16 (N.H. 1986), the court points to the fact that the document did not purport to be an offer and, while not dispositive, the court was somewhat persuaded by that fact.

[3] *See supra* § 34.

[4] Payne v. Cave, 3 Term. Rep. 148 (1789).

While this is not a straightforward method of withdrawing the item from sale, it has the same effect.[5] The early interpretation of the typical auction sale as one where the bidder is the offeror and the acceptance of the offer does not occur until the auctioneer brings down the hammer or in some other customary manner manifests acceptance[6] has been uniformly accepted. Since the bidder is the offeror, he may revoke his offer prior to its acceptance, i.e., he may withdraw (revoke) his offer at any time prior to the fall of the hammer or the completion of the sale in some other customary manner. It is important to emphasize that the typical auction sale is one "with reserve," i.e., the auctioneer is not compelled to sell anything to anyone. *Auction sales are presumed to be "with reserve" unless they are expressly announced to be "without reserve."*[7] Bids are merely offers at a "with reserve" sale and any offer may be rejected by the auctioneer. This view was adopted by the old Uniform Sales Act[8] and has been recodified in its successor, the UCC.[9]

In auctions expressly announced to be "without reserve" or sufficiently similar language,[10] the offer-acceptance analysis changes dramatically. In "with reserve" sales, the auctioneer is saying, "What am I bid," but in "without reserve" sales, the auctioneer is saying, "I will sell to the highest bidder." The offeree is not identified until he makes a bid, but he is *identifiable* as the highest bidder.[11] Thus, in "without reserve" sales, the auctioneer is making an offer, i.e., creating a power of acceptance, in any prospective bidder. Moreover, when the auctioneer calls for bids in a "without reserve" sale, the offer is open for a reasonable time and the item may not be withdrawn from sale unless no bid is made within a reasonable time.[12] The first bidder at such a sale is, necessarily, the highest bidder since it is possible that no other bids may be made. There is, therefore, a contract with that first bidder who has exercised his power of acceptance. If no other bid is made, that contract is completed. If

---

[5]*See* Freeman v. Poole, 37 R.I. 489, 93 A. 786 (1915).

[6]Section 2-328(2) of the UCC indicates that the typical auction sale "is complete when the auctioneer so announces by the fall of the hammer or in some other customary manner." In Bradshaw v. Thompson, 454 F.2d 75 (6th Cir. 1972), the court applied this section of the Code pursuant to the sale catalogue in a horse auction which, in boldface, indicated that the horse could be withdrawn even after the fall of the hammer so long as the horse had not been taken from the sale ring.

[7]UCC § 2-328(3). *See* Sly v. First Nat'l Bank of Scottsboro, 387 So. 2d 198 (Ala. 1980).

[8]Uniform Sales Act § 21.

[9]UCC § 2-328(2). *See also* RESTATEMENT 2d § 28(1)(a).

[10]*See* Sly v. First Nat'l Bank of Scottsboro, 387 So. 2d 198 (Ala. 1980) where the public notice stated that the sale was to be "at public outcry to the highest, best and last bidder." The court held this notice to be insufficient notice of a "without reserve" sale; therefore, the sale was automatically "with reserve". The court appeared to insist upon the literal phrase, "without reserve", in the notice to constitute such a sale, i.e., no substitute phrase would accomplish this result. However, in Dublin Livestock & Comm'n Co. v. Day, 178 Ga. App. 50, 341 S.E.2d 913 (1986), an announcement that the auction would be "absolute" and that everything would be sold for the highest dollar bid was construed to be an announcement of an auction sale "without reserve." Courts will generally accept clear language in substitution for the literal phrase, "without reserve." *See* Chevalier v. Town of Sanford, 475 A.2d 1148, 1149 (Me. 1984): "The advertisement in the present case did not expressly state that the forthcoming sale was without reserve nor did it contain any language subject to the interpretation that the right to reject any and all bids was not reserved."

[11]*See* discussion of *identifiable* offerees *supra* § 34.

[12]UCC § 2-328(3). *See* Dublin Livestock & Comm'n Co. v. Day, 178 Ga. App. 50, 341 S.E.2d 913 (1986).

one or more higher bids are made thereafter, there is a contract with each subsequent higher bidder. The contract formed by the previous bid is discharged as soon as the higher bid is made. Thus, a contract formed by the making of the current highest bid at a "without reserve" sale is conditioned upon no higher bid being made.

The application of the traditional offer-acceptance analysis to "with reserve" auction sales needs no accommodation since the bidder is the offeror who may withdraw (revoke) his bid/offer at any time before the manifestation of acceptance by the auctioneer. The making of a bid creates a power of acceptance in the auctioneer/offeree which he need not exercise if he is dissatisfied with the level of bids. In "without reserve" sales, however, the accommodation to traditional offer-acceptance analysis becomes difficult, if not impossible. A minor problem occurs in the insistence that the auctioneer who is making the offer must keep the offer open for a reasonable time.[13] Normally, the offeror can revoke his offer at any time after it is made, even a moment after it is made, if that is his preference.[14] By precluding the auctioneer from revoking the offer for a reasonable time, any potential offeree has an irrevocable power of acceptance at such an auction — i.e., the bidder has what amounts to an option contract.[15] A genuine option contract requires that value be given (consideration). One could construe the "without reserve" announcement as saying, "If you come to this auction, we will sell to the highest bidder, i.e., we place no reserve on any item to be sold, *and* we will give any bidder a reasonable opportunity to bid before withdrawing the item from sale." This construction would find the prospective bidders "giving value" for their right to have a reasonable time to bid by taking the time and trouble to come to the auction. The next analytical problem, however, is much more serious.

If a contract is formed upon the making of the first and any subsequent higher bid, it should be impossible for either party, highest bidder or auctioneer, to withdraw from that contract. The older law represented in the Uniform Sales Act precluded the auctioneer from withdrawing the goods from sale once a bid was made in a "without reserve" sale. This was conceptually essential, in terms of traditional contract law, since a contract is formed once the bid is made. After a contract is formed, there is no possibility of either party unilaterally withdrawing from the contract. Yet, the Sales Act permitted the bidder to withdraw his bid so long as the auctioneer had not announced the sale to have been completed.[16] Under this theory, the auctioneer (offeror) is bound as soon as the bid is made, but the bidder (who is supposed to be the offeree and who accepted the offer by making the bid) is free to retract the bid until completion of the sale. The result is that one party is bound to a contract but the other may withdraw unilaterally from the contract. Recognizing the irrec-

---

[13] *Ibid.*

[14] Revocations of offers will be explored in subsequent sections.

[15] The purpose of an option contract is to keep an offer open. For example, *A* offers to sell property to *B* who is interested and would like a week to think about it. *B* also worries that *A* might sell the property to another during the week. Therefore, *B* offers to pay *A* a sum of money to keep the offer to sell the property open. *A* accepts *B*'s offer and an option contract is formed. The offer to sell the property is now irrevocable for the duration stated in the option contract, i.e., one week. Option contracts will be discussed fully later in this volume.

[16] Uniform Sales Act § 21.

oncilability of this proposition with fundamental contract concepts of offer and acceptance, an early version of the UCC prohibited *both* the auctioneer and the bidder from withdrawing.[17] The purification of "without reserve" rules to coincide with traditional contract theory was, however, of short duration. The Code was subsequently revised to conform to the theoretical anomaly of the old Sales Act and the current version retains that anomaly.[18] One speculative explanation is that, "without reserve" sales are designed to attract potential bidders who would not attend ordinary "with reserve" sales. Since "without reserve" sales promise to sell to the highest bidder even though the highest bid may be low, one may be induced to attend such a sale in the hope of a considerable bargain. This inducement would be mitigated, however, under a rule that binds a bidder as soon as the bid is made. The excitement and hurried atmosphere of auction sales could induce intemperate bids. If such bids could not be withdrawn by the bidders, they may feel insecure about attending such sales. Whether this speculative rationale has any bearing on the return of the Code to the old Sales Act anomaly,[19] the current posture is, again, inconsistent with traditional contract law. There is, however, a consistent analysis which may also be useful in at least one other context. It is desirable to develop the analysis in the other context, *self-service transactions,* before applying it to the auction "without reserve" situation.

B. *Self-Service Transactions.*

Several cases have confronted the question of who makes the offer in a self-service transaction such as a supermarket transaction. Typically, these cases are concerned with the application of warranty protection for buyers under the U.C.C. If a shopper in a supermarket takes a carton of cola from the shelves and one or more of the bottles explode, injuring the shopper before he has presented the cola and other items in the shopping cart to the checker for payment, questions of contract formation become highly relevant. The UCC provides an implied warranty of merchantability for purchasers of such goods if a contract for the sale of the goods has been made.[20] Though such buyers may also be able to resort to tort remedies,[21] an action under the UCC may be a desirable alternative in certain situations.[22]

When courts have been confronted with the necessity of applying the offer-acceptance analysis to the self-service situation, they have suggested two views, both analytically flawed. The first view is illustrated by a decision of

---

[17]UCC § 2-328(3) (Final Draft No. 1, 1944).

[18]UCC § 2-328(2).

[19]The RESTATEMENT 2d, a creation of the American Law Institute that was half responsible for the UCC, was destined to comply. RESTATEMENT 2d § 28(1)(c).

[20]UCC § 2-314(1).

[21]In addition to a tort theory based upon negligence (which may be difficult to prove), the injured party in such a situation may be able to resort to the strict liability theory, of the RESTATEMENT 2d OF TORTS § 402A (1977), which has been adopted throughout the country as part of the products liability revolution.

[22]For example, in some jurisdictions, a plaintiff in such an action who waits beyond the torts statute of limitations (often two years for personal injury) may still be able to take advantage of the UCC where § 2-725 provides a statute of limitations of four years from the time the goods are delivered. *See* Williams v. West Penn Power Co., 460 A.2d 278 (Pa. 1983).

Queen's Bench[23] where the defendant operated a self-service chemists' shop. Certain shelves contained drugs found on the Poisons List of the British Pharmacy and Poisons Act which required the sale of any listed drugs to be made under the supervision of a registered pharmacist. The pharmacist was at the check-out counter. The customer took the listed drug from the shelf and placed it in her basket. The question was whether the contract of sale was made under the supervision of a registered pharmacist as required by the statute. If the shop was making an offer by placing the goods on the shelves, and the customer was accepting the offer by taking the goods off the shelves, the contract for sale was not made under the supervision of a registered pharmacist. If, however, the customer made no contract until she offered to pay for the goods at the check-out counter and the shop accepted that offer, the contract was made under appropriate supervision and no violation of the statute occurred. The court held that the contract was made at the check-out counter in this case. This view of the agreement process in self-service stores comports with the trade usage of customers replacing goods on shelves after changing their minds about purchasing such goods. Theoretically, however, the customer would have no right to purchase the goods from the store, i.e., the customer could only offer to purchase and the store could reject the offer. Moreover, the customer would have no right to the goods in her basket while shopping, i.e., store officials or, perhaps, other customers, could take a scarce good from a customer's basket. This could generate unwelcome disputes in supermarkets and other self-service stores. American courts have analyzed the situation differently.

In a products liability context, American courts have found a contract to have been made when the buyer takes the goods from the shelves. The display of the goods on the shelves constitutes an offer and the customer's act of taking the goods from the shelves constitutes an acceptance of the offer by the implication of a promise to pay for the goods at the check-out counter.[24] This theory supports recovery by plaintiffs in products liability situations, pursuant to the implied warranty of merchantability under the UCC, by finding a contract for sale when the customer reduces the goods to possession and is injured by them before presenting them at the check-out counter. Whatever may be said for the desirability of protecting such customers, the analysis is flawed. If a contract is formed as soon as a customer takes goods from the shelves of a self-service store, the customer should be said to have breached that contract by changing his mind and returning the goods to the shelves. Yet, the trade usage is clear that innumerable customers do return goods to shelves and make the reasonable assumption that they may do so without liability. While efforts have been made to overcome the analytical flaw in this analysis, they have been less than persuasive.[25] There is another analysis that

---

[23] Pharmaceutical Soc'y of Great Britain v. Boots Cash Chemists (Southern) Ltd., [1953] 1 Q.B. 401.

[24] See, e.g., Barker v. Allied Supermarket, 596 P.2d 870 (Okla. 1979). See also Sheeskin v. Giant Food, Inc., 20 Md. App. 611, 318 A.2d 874 (1974).

[25] In Barker, ibid., the court recognized this usage and attempted to overcome it by finding a power of termination in the customer as defined in UCC § 2-106(3): "Termination occurs when either party pursuant to a power created by agreement or law puts an end to the contract otherwise than for its breach...."

may achieve the ends sought by American courts prone to extensions of product liability protection. This analysis may, serendipitously, provide a more cohesive view of the auction "without reserve" situation with respect to the bidder's right to withdraw after the contract has been formed.

C. *A Suggested Analysis.*

In the self-service situation, the customer could be said to have an irrevocable power of acceptance for a reasonable time upon taking possession of goods from a shelf. The store would be seen as making an irrevocable offer for a reasonable (shopper's) time. In effect, an option contract would be formed and the value the customer would be said to have provided in exchange for the implied promise of the store to forebear revocation of the offer would be the customer's choice of *that* store rather than other stores the customer could have chosen. Advertising by the chosen store could be said to have induced the choice. The customer could then replace goods on the shelf (not exercising the power of acceptance) with impunity, or exercise the power of acceptance by tendering payment for the goods at the check-out counter. The store could not refuse the tender since the power of acceptance is irrevocable. Moreover, the bizarre possibility of others taking the goods from the customer's basket would be eliminated. For products liability purposes, courts would simply have to read the requirement of a contract of sale in the UCC as being satisfied through an *option* contract for sale. This theory comports with the reasonable understanding of self-service customers and stores. Since such stores long antedated any legal theory, the law should react to this situation in accordance with the reasonable understanding of the actors in such a setting. As is often the case, the law, here, is the creature rather than the creator of events.

With respect to the right of bidders to withdraw bids in "without reserve" auction sales, the same theory may prove useful. By characterizing the bid at a "without reserve" sale as providing the bidder with an irrevocable power of acceptance to purchase the item for a reasonable time (subject to no higher bid being made), the bidder could, consistent with contract theory, withdraw the bid prior to the completion of the sale but the auctioneer could not withdraw. The same option contract analysis would apply to create an irrevocable power of acceptance in the bidder.[26] If the bidder failed to withdraw prior to the completion of the sale, he would have impliedly exercised his power of acceptance and would be bound to purchase the item at the bid price. While the results reached in "without reserve" bidder withdrawal cases and self-service cases are justifiable, the underlying theories do not promote law settlement. The suggested analysis relies upon implication since it is sometimes necessary to create appropriate theories to avoid manifest injustice and to promote a cohesive analysis with precedential value. The suggested analysis overcomes

---

[26] By attending the sale "without reserve," the bidder has provided the "value" sought by the seller who sought to induce the bidder to attend. The seller would not only be promising to sell without reserve to the highest bidder; he would also be promising not to revoke his offer for a reasonable time after the item is placed up for sale as well as permitting the then highest bidder to announce that he would not exercise his irrevocable power of acceptance and, thereby, withdraw from the transaction.

blatant disregard for contract theory while achieving the necessary results in conformity with accepted trade usage.

§ 37. Assent Through Conduct.

The normal exchange of offer and acceptance is by language, oral or written. The offeror promises to purchase goods or services at a certain price and the offeree promises to supply the offeror with such goods or services at the price offered. Such verbal exchanges, however, do not constitute the exclusive mode of expressing mutual assent.[27] Acts or conduct may evidence mutual assent. Assume neighbors have discussed the possibility of the erection of a party wall between their properties that will provide mutual benefit, and both neighbors have reason to know[28] that the cost of the wall will be shared. They have reached no contract through their discussions, i.e., there is no commitment by either party concerning this project; it is a mere possibility. Later, one of the parties begins to construct the wall with the full knowledge of the other party who does not object. Under these circumstances, an agreement between these parties concerning the sharing of costs for the party wall can be found through their conduct.[29] The neighbor commencing work on the wall could be viewed as offering to build it in exchange for one-half of its cost. The knowing silence of the other neighbor could be viewed as an acceptance of the offer,[30] just as the display of goods on shelves in a supermarket or other self-service store could be viewed as an offer.[31] Millions of shoppers make contracts to purchase goods from innumerable self-service stores with no language manifestation of their agreement. Yet, mutual assent, agreement, and bargain are present in each of those transactions. Whether particular conduct expresses an offer and acceptance must be determined on the basis of what a reasonable person in the position of the parties would be led to understand by such conduct under all of the surrounding circumstances.[32] In keeping with this standard, a party will be responsible for creating the appearance of an offer

---

[27] RESTATEMENT 2d § 19.

[28] RESTATEMENT 2d § 19, comment b, suggests that a person has "reason to know" a fact, present or future, if he has information from which a person of ordinary intelligence would infer that the fact in question does or will exist. Moreover, if the inference would be that there is such a substantial chance of the existence of the fact that, if exercising reasonable care with reference to the matter in question, the person would predicate his action upon the assumption of its possible existence.

[29] See Day v. Caton, 119 Mass. 513, 20 Am. Rep. 347 (1876). See also Earhart v. Williams Low Co., 23 Cal. 3d 503, 600 P.2d 1344 (1979). The contract between the parties will often be characterized as an "implied-in-fact" contract which simply means that the manifestation of mutual assent was not in language, oral or written. There is no difference in legal effect between an "express" contract and an "implied-in-fact contract." See Francis v. St. Louis Cty. Water Co., 322 S.W.2d 724, 726 (Mo. 1959). One must also be careful to distinguish so-called implied-in-fact contracts from "implied-in-law" contracts which are not contracts in any sense but are judicial constructions to avoid unjust enrichment.

[30] The question of silence as acceptance requires separate exploration. A conduct acceptance may be found where goods are shipped to a party who exercises dominion and control over them. See Preston Farm & Ranch Supply, Inc. v. Bio-Zyme Enters., 625 S.W.2d 295 (Tex. 1981). This situation is explored infra.

[31] See Barker v. Allied Supermarket, 596 P.2d 870 (Okla. 1979). However, see the criticism of the analysis in the Barker case and the suggested analysis of self-service transactions in the preceding section.

[32] See Rainier Fund, Inc. v. Bloomfield Real Estate Co., 717 P.2d 850 (Alaska 1986).

whether done so intentionally or negligently. Assume that Ames writes a letter to Barnes containing an offer. She encloses the letter in a properly addressed and stamped envelope. Later, she decides not to mail it. By mistake, she includes the letter in a group of other letters she does intend to mail. Barnes receives the mistakenly mailed letter and accepts the offer by return mail. Unless Barnes knows or has reason to know of Ames' mistake, a contract results because Ames is responsible for negligently creating the appearance of an offer.[33] This analysis is in keeping with the objective theory of contract law[34] since the undisclosed intention of Ames is irrelevant; her manifested intention to make an offer created a reasonable understanding in Barnes that his assent would conclude a contract.

§ 38. Reasonable Certainty — Indefiniteness.

A. *General Requirement of Definiteness.*

The general principle may be stated as follows: Even though parties intend to form a contract, if the terms of their agreement are not sufficiently definite or reasonably certain, no contract will be said to exist.[35] This general statement, like others, is of little assistance absent an elaboration of the somewhat elusive modifying terms, "sufficiently" and "reasonably." If the terms of the contract need not be absolutely certain or definite but only "reasonably" certain or "sufficiently" definite, courts will enforce contracts containing terms that lack clarity and courts will also enforce contracts that do not contain all of the terms of the agreement. At some point, however, the terms of the agreement may be so unclear, or the agreement may be silent on such important terms or so many terms, that courts will not be able to determine whether any breach occurred because they cannot be certain of what may have been breached. Therefore, it will be impossible for a court to fashion an appropriate remedy.[36] Many older cases found indefiniteness to be fatal.[37] Yet, the applied standards were so vague that it is possible to discover cases that appear to be contradictory. One court construed an agreement to erect a structure in accordance "with plans to be approved by your company" and to con-

---

[33] *See* RESTATEMENT 2d § 19 ill. 3.

[34] *See supra* § 30.

[35] *See, e.g.,* Ault v. Pakulski, 520 A.2d 703 (Me. 1987); Bishop v. Hendrickson, 695 P.2d 1313 (Mont. 1985); North Coast Cookies, Inc. v. Sweet Temptations, Inc., 16 Ohio App. 3d 342, 476 N.E.2d 388 (1984); Arrowhead Constr. Co. v. Essex Corp., 233 Kan. 241, 662 P.2d 1195 (1983); Almeida v. Almeida, 4 Haw. App. 513, 669 P.2d 174 (1983); Porter v. Porter, 637 S.W.2d 396 (Mo. App. 1982).

[36] RESTATEMENT 2d § 33(2) suggests, "The terms of a contract are reasonably certain if they provide a basis for determining the existence of a breach and for giving an appropriate remedy." Section 2-204(3) of the UCC provides: "Even though one or more terms is left open, a contract for sale does not fail for indefiniteness if the parties have intended to make a contract and there is a reasonably certain basis for giving an appropriate remedy."

[37] *See, e.g.,* Klimek v. Perisich, 231 Or. 71, 371 P.2d 956 (1962) (vague agreement to remodel house at cost not exceeding $10,000 with prices of certain items to be agreed upon at most reasonable price available); Smith v. Chickamauga Cedar Co., 263 Ala. 245, 82 So. 2d 200 (1955) (agreement to furnish logs in quantities deemed "feasible and economical" by lumberman); Hardman v. Polino, 113 W. Va. 404, 168 S.E. 384 (1933), (agreement to loan money to develop farms to their highest efficiency); Varney v. Ditmars, 217 N.Y. 223, 111 N.E. 822 (1916) (promise to pay "a fair share of my profits").

form "to the most recent stores" as fatally indefinite.[38] Similarly, another
court held an agreement to erect "a permanent and first-class hotel" as fatally
indefinite.[39] Yet, another case involved a promise to erect "a first-class theatre" and the court held the agreement to be sufficiently definite to be enforced because "first-class theatre" could refer to a similar theatre owned by
the promisor and local building codes could be used to establish construction
standards.[40] Whether the facts of these and similar cases are sufficiently dis-
parate to make them irreconcilable, the general observation that modern
courts are much less willing than their predecessors to regard indefiniteness
as fatal cannot be gainsaid.[41] Much of the willingness of modern courts to find
enforceable agreements where prior courts would not have found them is due
to the general and specific directives against fatal indefiniteness in the
UCC.[42] The general requirement that a court should find an enforceable
agreement if it discovers (a) a manifested intention to be bound, and (b) a
reasonable basis to afford a remedy[43] served as a catalyst to chart a new, anti-
technical[44] course away from fatal indefiniteness so as to promote the effectuation of the factual bargain of the parties in accordance with the underlying
philosophy of Article 2 of the Code.[45] The influence of this initiative is clearly
seen in the RESTATEMENT 2d as applied to non-sale of goods contracts.[46] The
initiative recognizes that parties often and, perhaps, typically, do not express
themselves precisely or comprehensively when they make an agreement.

---

[38] Peoples Drug Stores v. Fenton Realty Corp., 191 Md. 489, 62 A.2d 273 (1948).

[39] Hart v. Georgia R.R., 101 Ga. 188, 28 S.E. 637 (1897).

[40] Bettancourt v. Gilroy Theatre Co., 120 Cal. App. 2d 364, 261 P.2d 351 (1953).

[41] A modern court is apt to suggest the following policy: "[T]he law leans against the destruction
of contracts for uncertainty" and "[c]ourts favor the determination that an agreement is sufficiently definite." *In re* Sing Chong Co., 1 Haw. App. 236, 239, 617 P.2d 578, 581 (1980). This is not
to suggest that modern courts will always err on the side of discovering sufficient certainty. For
example, while indicating its policy to enforce contracts in spite of indefiniteness, the court in
Almeida v. Almeida, 4 Haw. App. 513, 669 P.2d 174 (1983), could not find sufficient definiteness
to enforce an agreement to care for a person. In Bishop v. Hendrickson, 695 P.2d 1313 (Mont.
1985), though it applied § 33 of the RESTATEMENT 2d provision concerning reasonable certainty,
the court could not discover sufficient certainty to enforce an agreement between partners in a
law firm that, "in the event any of their children ever became lawyers and wanted to practice law
with the firm that there would be a place for such child or children in the law firm."

[42] In addition to the general prescription of the UCC found in § 2-204(3), *supra* note 36, Part 3 of
Article 2 of the Code contains numerous gap-filling terms. The fact that terms such as price
(§ 2-305), place of delivery (§ 2-308), and time of delivery (§ 2-309) are missing will not cause the
agreement to fail for indefiniteness if the two critical conditions of § 2-204(3) are present: (a) a
manifested intention to be bound, and (b) a reasonably certain basis for giving a remedy. Output
and requirements contracts (§ 2-306) that preclude even a certain quantity term at the time of
formation though the quantity will be ascertained at the conclusion of the contract are "not too
indefinite" (comment 2 to § 2-306). If the parties leave particulars of performance to be specified
by one of the parties, the contract does not fail for indefiniteness under § 2-311. For an examination of these and other Article 2 changes, *see* Murray, *The Article 2 Prism: The Underlying
Philosophy of Article 2 of the Uniform Commercial Code,* 21 WASHBURN L.J. 1 (1982).

[43] UCC § 2-204(3).

[44] Section 2-204(3) is one of several sections illustrating the purposeful, anti-technical nature of
Article 2 of the UCC. Subsequent sections of this book will explore other anti-technical sections
including § 2-206 which expressly warns against formal technical rules as to offer and acceptance
(comment 1 to § 2-206) and § 2-209(1) which expressly eschews "the technicalities which presently
hamper" modifications of contracts without consideration (comment 1 to § 2-209).

[45] *See* the definition of "agreement" in § 1-201(3) defined as "the bargain of the parties in fact as
found in their language or by implication from other circumstances including course of dealing,
usage of trade or course of performance...". *See also* Murray, *supra* note 42.

[46] RESTATEMENT 2d § 33.

Rather than focusing upon what parties failed to say, the Code and RESTATE-MENT 2d focus upon the overriding question of whether the parties manifestly intended to make a binding arrangement. If that manifestation is present, the only remaining concern is whether the terms are definite enough to permit courts to afford an appropriate remedy. The second requirement assists courts to determine the degree of permissible indefiniteness. If an appropriate remedy cannot be fashioned, that, alone, may be sufficient to indicate that the parties have not manifested their intentions adequately and, therefore, it is impossible for a court to discover the agreement or "deal" which the parties may have intended as binding. As usual, Professor Corbin provides the cryptic but penetrating analysis: "A court cannot enforce a contract unless it can determine what it is."[47]

Since determinations of sufficient definiteness necessarily require interpretations of language and the surrounding circumstances, it is important to consider certain clusters of cases that have focused on these questions.

B. *Agreements to Agree.*

The cases are legion in which courts have held that an "agreement to agree" upon a *material* term is not a contract.[48] Courts have never experienced much difficulty enforcing agreements where all of the essential (material) terms such as subject matter, quantity, and price have been agreed upon, though the parties have, either inadvertently or purposely, left relatively insignificant matters for future determination.[49] Even with respect to material terms, the indefiniteness of an agreement may be cured by the parties' performance which permits courts to interpret the indefinite term in accordance with that performance.[50] Similarly, if one party is willing to eliminate the risk of indefi-

---

[47] 1 A. CORBIN CONTRACTS § 95 at 363 (1963).

[48] *See, e.g.,* Belitz v. Riebe, 495 So. 2d 775 (Fla. App. 1986); Gregory v. Perdue, Inc., 47 N.C. App. 655, 267 S.E.2d 584 (1980); Burgess v. Rodom, 121 Cal. App. 2d 71, 262 P.2d 335 (1953); Machesky v. City of Milwaukee, 214 Wis. 411, 253 N.W. 169 (1934); Sun Printing & Pub'g Ass'n v. Remington Paper & Power Co., 235 N.Y. 338, 139 N.E. 470 (1923). This situation should be distinguished from the problem explored earlier concerning the intention of the parties to be bound either before or only upon the execution of a written memorial of their agreement, *see supra* § 31. If the parties have come to an agreement on all essential terms and leave only the written memorial of that agreement for the future, absent an expression of their intention not to be bound until the writing is executed, they will be bound at the time of their agreement. As will be seen later in this section, it is possible to effectuate the intention of parties to be bound though they leave a material term for future agreement. Typically, if parties contemplate a future writing to evidence their agreement *and* have yet to agree on a material term, courts will hold that they do not intend to be bound until the writing is executed, i.e., the situation combines the contemplation of a writing and the "agreement to agree" which is sufficient to negate the assumption that parties intend to be bound prior to a written memorial. It is conceivable that parties could intend to be bound immediately though they have left a material term for future agreement *and* they contemplate a written memorial of that agreement. In this situation, however, it would seem necessary to produce clear and convincing evidence of that intention.

[49] "Even if the contract were indefinite as to some items, it must appear that such terms were so essential to the contract that it would be unfair to enforce the remainder." Palmer v. Aeolian Co., 46 F.2d 746, 753 (8th Cir. 1931).

[50] "The courts should be extremely hesitant to hold a contract void for indefiniteness, particularly when one party has performed under the contract and allowed the other party to obtain the benefit of his performance." Blackhawk Heating & Plumbing Co. v. Data Lease Fin. Corp., 302 So. 2d 404, 408 (Fla. 1974). *See also* Florida Fruit, Etc. v. Rolling Meadow Ranch, 424 So. 2d 195 (Fla. App. 1983) in which the indefinite term in an agreement concerning workmen's compensa-

niteness by undertaking to expand his obligation, indefiniteness would be cured. Thus, where one party held an option to purchase land and the parties had left the terms of payment for future agreement, the indefiniteness was cured when the option holder agreed to pay cash or to make payments on terms imposed by the seller.[51] If, however, the parties have left a material term for future agreement and the indefiniteness of that term has not been cured, we are left with the traditional view that an agreement to agree is not a contract even if the parties intended to be bound immediately.

It is important to emphasize the underlying assumption of the traditional view, i.e., since the parties may subsequently fail to agree on the postponed material term, the court would have no basis for supplying the missing term and enforcing the contract.[52] If the parties had clearly manifested their intention to be bound but had simply *forgotten* to include the term, a modern court could supply the missing term, e.g., by implying a reasonable term, without violating the intentions of the parties. The reasonable term could be supplied by the court on the footing that it is probably the term the parties would have inserted had they thought about the matter at all. But when the parties manifest *their* intention to agree later on a material term, they *have* thought about the matter. For example, if they intended to agree upon the same price that would otherwise be supplied by a court, i.e., a reasonable market price, they could have easily indicated that intention and dismissed any necessity of further agreement. Rather, they chose to agree upon a specific process for determining the price, i.e., *their* future agreement as to the price. Moreover, they have not expressed their intention as to the status of their otherwise binding agreement if that process fails, i.e., if they fail to agree on a price, should a court then imply a "reasonable price"? For some courts, such an implication is beyond the pale since the parties have insisted upon a particular process for determining a material term. For these courts, the judicial implication of a price would be a blatant illustration of a court making a contract for the parties, i.e., contradicting the express intention of the parties.[53] It is instructive to consider this view and contrasting judicial approaches.

1. Future Agreements as to Rental Payments.

The traditional view that courts may not imply a reasonable term if the parties fail to agree and, therefore, the agreement is fatally indefinite from the inception, has been adopted by a number of courts with respect to re-

---

tion was the term "premium." However, premium payments were made and submitted claims were paid. Thus, the court was willing to interpret the indefinite term in accordance with the parties' course of performance. If trade usage or prior course of dealing evidence were sufficient to make a superficially indefinite term sufficiently definite, there would be no indefiniteness problem from the inception since parties are assumed to have used any contract term in accordance with such trade usage or prior course of dealing unless the contract expressly negates such evidence. *See* Columbia Nitrogen Corp. v. Royster Co., 451 F.2d 3 (4th Cir. 1971).

[51] Morris v. Ballard, 16 F.2d 175 (D.C. Cir. 1926). *See also* Shull v. Sexton, 154 Colo. 311, 390 P.2d 313 (1964).

[52] "Since either party by the terms of the promise may refuse to agree to anything to which the other party will agree, it is impossible for the law to fix any obligation to such a promise." Ablett v. Clauson, 43 Cal. 2d 280, 272 P.2d 753 (1954).

[53] *See* Walker v. Keith, 382 S.W.2d 198 (Ky. 1964).

newals or extensions of leases where the parties have left the rental to future agreement.[54] A second group of courts in this situation has adhered to the traditional view with what some may view as a slight modification. If the lease contains a methodology[55] for determining the new rental, these courts have no difficulty in discovering the rental term based on the methodology the parties have expressed in their lease agreement.[56] To suggest that this view is even a slight modification of the traditional view may be too generous. If the lease contains objective standards or even sufficiently definite guidelines for determining the new rental under the extension of the lease period, one should question whether any problem of indefiniteness exists. A third group of courts has taken a position in lease renewal cases that coincides with the view found in the UCC. If the parties have simply left the new rental for future agreement, these courts will enforce the lease contract even though it contains no method or guideline for determining the new rental when the parties fail to agree. These courts will imply a reasonable rental payment without regret that they are making a contract for the parties, i.e., allegedly going beyond their judicial function in implying a term.[57] Before considering the application of this view in contracts for the sale of goods under the UCC, it is important to consider why it is preferable.

If a lessee has an option to extend a lease contract for a definite period of time, a provision in the lease leaving the rental amount for the extension to future agreement can be justified on numerous bases. It is typically difficult to foresee economic conditions at the time the extension would take effect. Fairness to both the lessee and lessor should permit the parties to postpone the determination of the future rental so that they may, in good faith, agree upon a rental that is reasonable under changed market conditions.[58] If the lessee has an option to renew the lease, the lessee may very well have relied upon that option for which value has been already given.[59] To permit the lessor to

---

[54] In addition to Walker v. Keith, *ibid., see* Rosenberg v. Gas Serv. Co., 363 S.W.2d 20 (Mo. App. 1962).

[55] For example, the lease may state that the new rental can be determined by arbitration, by reference to fair rental values for similar properties, or by the appraisal of experts.

[56] *See* Etco Corp. v. Hauer, 161 Cal. App. 3d 1154, 208 Cal. Rptr. 118 (1984); Joseph Martin, Jr. Delicatessen, Inc. v. Schumacher, 52 N.Y.2d 105, 417 N.E.2d 541 (1981).

[57] *See* City of Kenai v. Ferguson, 732 P.2d 184 (Alaska 1987); Cassinari v. Mapes, 91 Nev. 778, 542 P.2d 1069 (1975); Moolenaar v. Co-Build Cos., 354 F. Supp. 980 (1973) (analogizing to § 2-305 of the UCC); Playmate Club Inc. v. Country Clubs, Inc., 62 Tenn. App. 383, 462 S.W.2d 890, 58 A.L.R.3d 494 (1970); Chaney v. Schneider, 92 Cal. App. 2d 88, 206 P.2d 669 (1949); Moss v. Olson, 148 Ohio St. 625, 76 N.E.2d 875 (1947).

[58] "Good faith is a term implied in every contract. In this context, good faith requires the parties to attempt to reach agreement as to rent for the property for the five-year period in question. Forcing Ferguson to quit the property after his substantial reliance on the fifty-five year length of the lease would be inequitable, as would be allowing Ferguson to continue using the property without reasonably compensating the City," City of Kenai v. Ferguson, 732 P.2d 184 (Alaska 1987). Another situation involving the requirement of good faith must be distinguished. If parties have agreed to negotiate in good faith, i.e., they have not agreed to agree with respect to a lease nor have they entered into any lease agreement, but simply agreed to negotiate in good faith, if one of the parties unilaterally terminates negotiations and enters a lease agreement with another, that party has breached the obligation to negotiate in good faith as that obligation was found in a document called a "letter of intent." *See* Channel Home Centers v. Grossman, 795 F.2d 291 (3d Cir. 1986).

[59] The payment of the rental under the original lease has been exchanged not only for the present occupancy of the premises, but, in an indivisible fashion, for the right of the lessee to exercise the option for renewal.

escape the bargain on the technical ground that the payment term is indefinite — because it is possible that the parties will fail to agree upon that term — would frustrate the reasonable expectation and reliance of the lessee.[60] Either party to the contract could have relied upon an extension agreement only to have expectations frustrated by the traditional view. Since the indefiniteness argument typically will be raised as a technical defense to the claim of the other party with reasonable expectations and reliance, it should be rejected. The cost of rejection is not excessive but it should be understood. By imposing a "reasonable rental" term upon the parties due to their failure to agree, the court is not necessarily supplying a term the parties expected at the time of contract formation. The court *is* making a contract for the parties to the extent that it is supplying a term that the parties may not have supplied themselves. This, however, is highly preferable to the destruction of expectation or reliance interests that might otherwise result. To achieve this preferable result, courts must assume that, had the parties considered the possibility that they would not reach agreement concerning the new rental, they would have agreed to permit a reasonable rental to be fixed by the court. This assumption is sound wherever intention to renew was the essence of the contract.[61]

2. Uniform Commercial Code — Implying Reasonable Price.

Article 2 of the UCC, which encompasses contracts for the sale of goods, is predicated upon a more precise and fair identification of the actual or presumed mutual assent of the parties.[62] The "agreement" of the parties is their factual bargain unfettered by technical constraints.[63] With respect to missing terms, a comment to § 2-204(3) expresses the Code philosophy:

> If the parties intend to enter into a binding agreement, this subsection recognizes that agreement as valid in law, despite missing terms, if there is any reasonably certain basis for granting a remedy. The test is not certainty as to what the parties were to do nor as to the exact amount of damages due the plaintiff. Nor is the fact that one or more terms are left to be agreed upon enough itself to defeat an otherwise adequate agreement. Rather, commercial standards on the point of "indefiniteness" are intended

---

[60] "There is even greater reason to declare a rental term when, as here, parties under a long-term lease are unable to reach agreement, since there are correspondingly greater reliance expectations created in the continuing use of the property." City of Kenai v. Ferguson, *supra* note 58 at 187. *See also* 1 A. CORBIN, CORBIN ON CONTRACTS, § 97 at 432-33 (1960).

[61] [I]ntent is to be determined from a view of the instrument as a whole, and a consideration of all of the facts in the case. If the agreement to renew was the essence of the contract, and the terms of the lease or the rental to be paid thereunder were to be fixed by agreement ... then failure of the parties to so agree, or to fix particular terms, does not avoid the lease. In such a case, the courts will declare the terms upon which the parties fail to agree." Chaney v. Schneider, 92 Cal. App. 2d 88, 206 P.2d 669, 671 (1949).

[62] *See* R. SPEIDEL, R. SUMMERS & J. WHITE, COMMERCIAL AND CONSUMER LAW, 677 (3d ed. 1981) quoting Murray, *The Realism of Behaviorism Under the Uniform Commercial Code,* 51 OR. L. REV. 269, 297 (1972). *See also* Murray, *The Underlying Philosophy of the Uniform Commercial Code,* 21 WASHBURN L.J. 1 (1981) and Murray, *The Chaos of the Battle of the Forms,* 39 VAND. L. REV. 1307, 1311-15 (1986).

[63] *See* UCC § 1-201(3).

to be applied, this Act making provision elsewhere for missing terms needed for performance, open price, remedies and the like.[64]

Again, the general directive of § 2-204(3) is that missing terms will not cause a contract to fail for indefiniteness if (a) the parties intend to make a contract, and (b) there is a reasonably certain basis for affording a remedy. The Code provision found "elsewhere" for a missing price term is § 2-305. A comment to that section is particularly revealing:

> This section applies when the price term is left open on the making of an agreement which is nevertheless intended by the parties to be a binding agreement. *This Article [2] rejects in these instances the formula that "an agreement to agree is unenforceable"* if the case falls within subsection (1) [the parties intend to conclude a contract].[65]

Section 2-305 of the Code was designed to deal not only with the relatively simple situation of a missing price term;[66] it also sought to deal with agreements to agree upon a future price[67] and agreements to have the price established by an objective standard when that objective standard fails.[68] The Code solutions are conditioned upon a finding that the parties intended to conclude a contract though the price was not settled.[69] This requirement is also found, somewhat redundantly and emphatically, in the last subsection of § 2-305.[70] Section 2-305 is not radical in permitting courts to imply a reasonable price when the parties have simply omitted the price term though otherwise manifesting an intention to be bound. Prior to the Code, price and other terms could be supplied in accordance with standards of fairness.[71] Section 2-305 is

---

[64] UCC § 2-204(3), second paragraph of comment thereto.

[65] § 2-305, comment 1.

[66] § 2-305(1)(a).

[67] § 2-305(1)(b).

[68] § 2-305(1)(c).

[69] § 2-305(1).

[70] § 2-305(4). If the buyer has already received goods, the buyer must return them or, if unable to do so, must pay the reasonable value of the goods received.

[71] In his analysis of certain sections of UCC Article 2 for the New York Law Revision Commission that was charged with the responsibility of studying the Code when it was considered for enactment in New York, Professor Edwin Patterson of Columbia Law School concluded that the implication of a price term under § 2-305(1)(a) — nothing is said as to price — "is supported by respectable authority [in New York]...." 1 STUDY OF THE UNIFORM COMMERCIAL CODE, STATE OF NEW YORK, LAW REVISION COMMISSION 329 (1955). For a modern treatment of the implication of missing terms, *see* RESTATEMENT 2d § 204 comment d, dealing with supplying an omitted term and referring to UCC sections which supply missing terms such as § 2-309, a "reasonable" time implication and § 2-305, "reasonable" price implication. *See also* UCC § 2-306, setting forth criteria in output and requirements contracts where there is no stated estimate, § 2-307, dealing with the number of deliveries and payment for such deliveries where the agreement is silent, § 2-308, providing for the place of delivery where the agreement is silent, § 2-310(a), providing for the time when and place where payment is due where the agreement is silent, and § 2-311, providing for particulars of performance to be specified by one of the parties. One could also include the warranty of title (§ 2-312) which is not captioned, "implied" because it contains its own requirements for disclaimer in § 2-312(2) but is, nonetheless, an implied warranty, as well as the implied warranty of merchantability (§ 2-314) and the implied warranty of fitness for a particular purpose (§ 2-315). Much of Part 3 of Article 2 can, therefore, be characterized as containing Code "gap-fillers" where the parties have failed to manifest their agreement. Other gap-fillers are derivable from other sections or comments to the Code. For example, where the parties have not expressed an FOB term which, under the Code will determine risk of loss, comment 5 to § 2-503 indicates that "the 'shipment' contract is regarded as the normal one and the 'destination' contract as the variant type." Thus, absent the parties' expression to the contrary, the FOB term will be the

not particularly progressive in permitting the parties to agree that the price will be established by some objective standard and then permitting a court to establish the price when that standard fails though pre-Code law would excuse the parties from performance if the external standard failed.[72] In that situation, the parties had not intended to fix the price by their own subsequent agreement. They had agreed upon an objective standard that failed and the court simply created a substitute for that objective standard. In the third situation, however, by allowing courts to imply a reasonable price when the parties fail to agree, the Code cuts deeply against the tradition precluding so-called agreements to agree.[73] Again, however, if the parties manifest their intention to be bound to a contract though they postpone the time for agreement upon the price, the protection of reliance interests and fairness to both parties suggests that such an agreement should not fail for indefiniteness simply because the parties may later fail to agree upon the price. Such a failure may be caused by the refusal of the other party to bargain in good faith concerning the price term[74] or simply because one party seeks to avoid his contractual obligation though the other party is suggesting reasonable terms in good faith.[75] Whatever the reason, the courts have demonstrated little difficulty in the application of § 2-305 where the parties have failed to agree upon a price term for their previously formed contract, or where they have simply omitted the price term,[76] or left it to be determined by an external

---

"FOB shipment" contract which, pursuant to § 2-509(1)(a) places the risk of loss on the buyer when the goods are duly delivered to the independent carrier. See Ninth Street East, Ltd. v. Harrison, 5 Conn. 597, 259 A.2d 772 (1968). The implication of various terms where the parties have omitted such terms but otherwise intend to form a contract will be dealt with later in this volume.

[72] See the New York Law Revision analysis by Professor Patterson, ibid., at 331 where he suggests that the recognition of an external (objective) standard to determine price does not conflict with pre-Code New York law. However, New York courts had not gone so far as to permit substitution of a "reasonable" price where the external standard failed. Patterson then adds his view that, if a contract were discovered in this situation, failure of the objective standard "would let in the current or market price." However, in Interstate Plywood Sales Co. v. Interstate Container Corp., 331 F.2d 449 (9th Cir. 1964), the court held that a pricing formula was intended as the only binding method of determining price and, when it failed, the contract was unenforceable. Thus, there was a contract when the parties fixed the pricing formula, which contract became unenforceable upon failure of the external standard. See also Turman Oil Co. v. Sapulpa Ref. Co., 124 Okla. 150, 254 P. 84 (1926). The UCC continues to permit the parties to be bound only by a price set by a particular third person's judgment. If the parties so intend, no reasonable substitute is available when that party is not available. The distinction is one between choosing a barometer or index of a fair price as contrasted with the particular, subjective judgment of a named third party. An example of the latter is rather rare, under the Code, as in the case of the determination of the value of a painting by a known and trusted expert. UCC § 2-305 comment 4.

[73] In the analysis by Professor Patterson (see supra note 71), at 329-31, Professor Patterson found "some" New York authority contrary to § 2-305(1)(b) as an "agreement to agree." In particular, he mentioned the dissenting opinion of Judge Cardozo in Varney v. Ditmars, 217 N.Y. 223, 111 N.E. 822 (1916) and Cardozo's opinion for the court in Sun Printing & Pub'g Ass'n v. Remington Paper & Power Co., 235 N.Y. 338, 139 N.E. 470 (1923).

[74] See Schmeider v. Standard Oil, 69 Wis. 2d 419, 230 N.W.2d 732 (1975) which provided Standard with an option to purchase certain equipment of Schmeider on a price to be mutually agreed upon. Schmeider submitted a price that was, according to the evidence, filled with discrepancies and Standard sought to withdraw from the arrangement because the parties could not agree upon a price. The court held that § 2-305(1)(b) supplies a reasonable price in such circumstances.

[75] See D.R. Cursi Co. v. Mathews, 653 P.2d 1188 (Idaho App. 1982).

[76] See, e.g., Robinson v. Stevens Indus., 162 Ga. App. 132, 290 S.E.2d 336 (1982).

standard that subsequently failed.[77] At the same time, courts have adhered to the Code directive that the parties must intend to be bound, notwithstanding a missing price term, if § 2-305 is to apply.[78]

3. Uniform Commercial Code: Missing Performance Terms.

The UCC makes provision for numerous "gap-filling" terms beyond the price term where the parties have omitted such terms and still intend to be bound to their agreement.[79] For example, where the contract is silent concerning delivery in single lots or installments,[80] the place for delivery,[81] or the time for delivery,[82] the contract does not fail for indefiniteness. These Code provisions manifest little or no change from pre-Code law, whether or not the contract was one for the sale of goods.[83] There is, however, one situation where the pre-Code case law was split. It is illustrated by a well-known case involving a contract for the sale of definite quantities of motor oil. Though the prices were definitely established, they depended upon the weight or viscosity of the oil to be chosen by the purchaser, i.e., the higher the weight, the higher the price. When the seller telephoned the buyer to determine the buyer's selection, the buyer refused to select and "cancelled" the contract. The court held the contract to be fatally indefinite with regard to buyer's choice of weights.[84] This result is obviously unfair to the seller who reasonably assumed that he and the buyer were bound to a contract. The buyer was permitted to withdraw from the bargain simply by refusing to cooperate in choosing the weights of the motor oil. Other courts saw no difficulty with indefiniteness in holding sellers to such arrangements where the buyer notified the seller of the selection.[85] The difficulty in affording a remedy where the buyer refuses to exercise the right to select should not be seen as insuperable. A solution that cannot be unfair to the breaching buyer is to afford the seller the least profit the seller would have received.[86] The UCC, however, permits the aggrieved party to

---

[77] See North Cent. Airlines, Inc. v. Continental Oil Co., 574 F.2d 582 (D.C. Cir. 1978).

[78] See In re Glover Constr. Co., 49 Bankr. 581 (Bankr. W.D. Ky. 1985) and Billings Cottonseed, Inc. v. Albany Oil Mill, Inc., 173 Ga. App. 825, 328 S.E.2d 426 (1985).

[79] See supra note 71.

[80] See Luedtke Eng'g Co. v. Indiana Limestone Co., 740 F.2d 598 (7th Cir. 1984).

[81] See Dura-Wood Treating Co. v. Century Forest Indus., 675 F.2d 745 (5th Cir. 1982).

[82] See Southern Utils. Inc. v. Jerry Mandel Mach. Corp., 71 N.C. App. 188, 321 S.E.2d 508 (1984).

[83] See, e.g., Orlowski v. Moore, 198 Pa. Super. 360, 181 A.2d 692 (1962) (lease providing lessee with first refusal had to be exercised within a reasonable time under all of the circumstances); Marsh v. Brown-Crummer Inv. Co., 138 Kan. 123, 23 P.2d 465 (agreement to repurchase bonds on demand, no time being fixed within which demand was to be made); Cameron Coal & Mercantile Co. v. Universal Metal Co., 26 Okla. 615, 110 P. 720 (1910) (contract for sale of goods). The presumption of a "reasonable time" where the parties had not otherwise specified was a continuation of the presumptions throughout the Uniform Sales Act: §§ 19, 43(2), 47(1), 48, 49 and 69(3). The presumption concerning the place of delivery under § 2-308 of the Code was a continuation of § 43(1) of the Uniform Sales Act and pre-Code case law. The presumption concerning delivery in single lots in § 2-307 was, essentially, a continuation of § 45(1) of the Uniform Sales Act and interpretations thereof.

[84] See Wilhelm Lubrication Co. v. Brattrud, 197 Minn. 626, 268 N.W. 634 (1936).

[85] See Fairmount Glass Works v. Crunden-Martin Woodenware Co., 106 Ky. 659, 51 S.W. 196 (1899) where the buyer brought an action for the buyer's selection of glass containers in a case that focused upon whether the seller's quotation was an offer.

[86] See, e.g., Dolly Parker Motors v. Stinson, 220 Ark. 28, 245 S.W.2d 820 (1952).

perform in any reasonable manner which would, presumably, permit the selection to be made by the aggrieved seller in substitution for the buyer's selection. If the buyer refuses to accept the goods as selected by the seller, all of the seller's UCC remedies are available.[87] The seller would proceed to recover based upon a commercially reasonable selection which necessarily includes good faith[88] rather than the selection that would have netted the "lowest profit." This analysis is more in keeping with the protection of the seller's reasonable expectations.[89]

4. Terminable-at-Will Contracts.

Earlier in this section we suggested the general willingness of courts to imply a reasonable time in contracts where the parties have not manifested their intention. One of the stark exceptions to this generally accepted practice occurs in employment contracts with no specified duration. By the end of the nineteenth century, most American courts adopted the following principle: If an employee is hired, absent language or circumstances identifying the duration of that employment, the employment is terminable at the will of either party.[90] This view is traceable to the unwarranted utterances of a text book writer[91] and the laissez-faire philosophy of the period which reserved absolute power to the employer to dismiss the employee because it was essential to preserve the autonomy of managerial discretion as well as the freedom of the parties to make their own contract.[92] As early as 1562, an English statute prohibited the discharge of an employee except for reasonable and sufficient cause[93] and even after that statute was repealed, English courts presumed that an employment contract of indefinite duration continued for one year.[94] Notwithstanding this precedent, American courts adhered to the flat rule that such contracts are terminable at will "for good cause, for no cause, or even for cause morally wrong."[95] Even if the contract was one for "permanent"[96] or

---

[87] The remedies of the seller are listed in UCC § 2-703. Sections 2-704 through 2-710 adumbrate the generic list in § 2-703.

[88] See UCC § 2-103(1)(b): "'Good faith' in the case of a merchant means honesty in fact and the observance of reasonable commercial standards of fair dealing in the trade." Contrast this definition of "merchant" good faith with the general requirement of good faith that applies to non-merchants in § 1-201(19): "'Good faith' means honesty in fact in the conduct or transaction concerned." The latter definition is sometimes referred to rather whimsically but pointedly as the "Pure heart, empty head" standard.

[89] The general policy of the Code concerning remedies for breach of contract is found in § 1-106, "Remedies to be Liberally Administered." "(1) The remedies provided by this Act shall be liberally administered to the end that the aggrieved party may be put in as good a position as if the other party had fully performed...."

[90] See Magnan v. Anaconda Indus., 193 Conn. 558, 479 A.2d 781 (1984) and Toussaint v. Blue Cross & Blue Shield of Mich., 408 Mich. 579, 292 N.W.2d 880 (1980) which trace the history of the "terminable at will" concept.

[91] H.G. WOOD, MASTER AND SERVANT § 134 (1877): "With us the rule is inflexible, that a general or indefinite hiring is prima facie a hiring at will, and if the servant seeks to make it out a yearly hiring, the burden of proof is upon him to establish it by proof."

[92] Coppage v. Kansas, 236 U.S. 1, 10 (1915).

[93] Statute of Labourers, 5 Eliz. C. 4 (1562) found in Pickering's Statutes 159-60 (1763).

[94] The rule was premised "upon a principle of natural equity, that the servant shall serve, and master maintain him, throughout all the natural revolutions of the respective seasons, as well when there is work to be done, as when there is not...." 1 BLACKSTONE'S COMMENTARIES 335 (1832). See The King v. Inhabitants of Hampreston, 5 TR 205, 101 Eng. Rep. 116 (1793).

[95] Payne v. Western & Atlantic R.R., 81 Tenn. 507, 519-20 (1884), overruled on other grounds, Hutton v. Watters, 132 Tenn. 527, 179 S.W. 134 (1915).

[96] See Newfield v. Insurance Co. of the West, 156 Cal. App. 3d 440, 203 Cal. Rptr. 9 (1984);

"lifetime"[97] employment, absent other circumstances,[98] the contract would be terminable at will. The rationale usually suggested that "permanent" or "lifetime" referred to the position as steady employment rather than the tenure of the employee in that position. If the parties agreed that the employee would be paid for his services on a daily, weekly, monthly or yearly basis, many courts refused to imply an understanding that the duration of the contract was intended to be for the payment period — again, it was terminable at will.[99] It is difficult to determine whether the specification as to salary is simply to fix the rate of pay or is intended to indicate that the employment is to continue for at least one pay period. The question is one of interpretation of the parties' manifestations. Yet, the employee confronted the strong presumption in favor of the terminable-at-will construction for the policy reasons already set forth.

The terminable-at-will presumption has eroded over the years and the erosion is particularly strong at the time of this writing. There are numerous statutory and judicial restrictions protecting employees from arbitrary discharge[1] or from discharge for reasons against public policy.[2] A flood of litiga-

---

Fisher v. Jackson, 142 Conn. 734, 118 A.2d 316 (1955); Arentz v. Morse Dry Dock & Repair Co., 249 N.Y. 438, 164 N.E. 342 (1928); Rape v. Mobil & Ohio R.R., 136 Miss. 38, 100 So. 585, 35 A.L.R. 1422 (1924).

[97] See Page v. Carolina Coach Co., 667 F.2d 1156 (4th Cir. 1982) (statements of employer could not reasonably be interepreted as promise of lifetime appointment; rather, they were words of encouragement); Brown v. Safeway Stores, Inc., 190 F. Supp. 295 (E.D.N.Y. 1960) (employer said he needed district managers to stay with them and there would always be a job for them, and said to plaintiff, "You will always be one of us", held not a promise for lifetime employment since the language was not sufficiently clear and unequivocal to create a lifetime contract which is unusual and extraordinary.)

[98] For example, if consideration beyond the employment services was provided by the employee, a "lifetime" contract would be enforced. See C & P Tel. Co. v. Murray, 198 Md. 526, 84 A.2d 870 (1951). An employee will sometimes argue that he left his former position to take the new job and that detriment should be viewed as consideration. As will be seen in the sections dealing with consideration in the next chapter, the detriment suffered in such cases by the employee is simply a necessary condition to accepting the new position since the employee is typically incapable of maintaining two employments simultaneously. Such a detriment is not "bargained-for" and does not constitute consideration. If, however, an employee has a position that appears secure or is, in fact, a lifetime or permanent position, if he is induced to leave that position by the new employer, consideration may be found.

[99] See Boatright-Steinite Radio Corp., 46 F.2d 385 (10th Cir. 1931). Contra Southwell v. Parker Plow Co., 234 Mich. 292, 207 N.W. 872 (1926) and RESTATEMENT 2d § 33 ill. 6.

[1] See, e.g., 5 U.S.C. § 7513 which requires a showing of "such cause as will promote the efficiency of the service" to dismiss a civil servant.

[2] It is impossible to list all of the various possibilities of public policy violations, whether in statutory or case law form. The following are merely illustrative. Discharge for reasons of race, color, religion, sex, or national origin is prohibited by 42 U.S.C. 2000(e) — (2)(a)(1). See Rosemond v. Cooper Indus. Prods., 612 F. Supp. 1105 (D.C. Ind. 1985). Discharge for reasons of age is prohibited by 29 U.S.C.A. § 623(a)(1). See McNeil v. Economics Lab., Inc., 800 F.2d 111 (7th Cir. 1986). A discharge of an employee who is responding to a notice of jury service is against public policy, Reuther v. Fowler & Williams, Inc., 255 Pa. Super. 28, 386 A.2d 119 (1978). A cause of action existed for tortious discharge where the employee was discharged for refusing to take a polygraph examination in violation of a state statute. Perks v. Firestone Tire & Rubber Co., 611 F.2d 1363 (3rd Cir. 1979). A discharge because of union activities will be prohibited. See 29 U.S.C.A. § 158(a)(3). See also Cleary v. Am. Airlines, Inc., 11 Cal. App. 3d 443, 168 Cal. Rptr. 722 (1980). Discharge of an employee who refuses to cooperate in an alleged antitrust violation may state a cause of action in tort for wrongful discharge, McNulty v. Borden, Inc., 474 F. Supp. 1111 (E.D. Pa. 1979). See Note, Protecting Employees at Will Against Wrongful Discharge: The Public Policy Exception, 96 HARV. L. REV. 1931.

tion has addressed the question of the effect of statements in employee hand-books, manuals or policy statements from the employer which may preclude discharge except for good cause. The overwhelming majority of the courts addressing this question have concluded that such statements may give rise to contractual obligations of the employer, thereby substantially modifying the otherwise intact terminable-at-will rule.[3] To this point, however, most courts have stopped short of implying a requirement that discharge can only be for good cause in the absence of public policy reasons against a particular discharge, or employer's statements in handbooks or otherwise that could give rise to greater contractual obligations.[4] While the terminable-at-will presumption has been severely tested and modified, it continues to be the general rule because of the great reluctance of courts to thrust an unwanted employee upon an employer.[5] As in many other contexts, this situation requires courts to balance legitimate needs and desires against legitimate expectation and reliance interests.[6] There is a recognition that "freedom of contract" may be illusory where the employee is not protected by a collective bargaining agreement.[7] If the employer induces the employee to believe that he has job security, a court may find a contract to that effect. The judicial willingness to do so, however, is often couched in terms requiring sufficient definiteness[8] as courts begin to move away from the rigidity of the terminable-at-will rule as originally conceived in this country. Absent decisive state or federal legisla-

---

[3] The analysis is in terms of a unilateral contract which was described *supra* § 16, and will be further explored *infra*, or in terms of the employee's reliance (to be explored in the next chapter). *See, e.g.,* Toussaint v. Blue Cross & Blue Shield of Mich., 408 Mich. 579, 292 N.W.2d 880 (1980); Pine River State Bank v. Mettille, 333 N.W.2d 622 (Minn. 1983); Finley v. Aetna Life & Cas. Co., 5 Conn. App. 394, 499 A.2d 64 (1985); Woolley v. Hoffman-La Roche, Inc., 99 N.J. 284, 491 A.2d 1257 (1985); Duldulao v. Saint Mary of Nazareth Hosp., 115 Ill. 2d 482, 505 N.E.2d 314 (1987). Cases taking a contrary position include White v. Chelsea Indus., 425 So. 2d 1090 (Ala. 1983); Heidek v. Kent Gen. Hosp., 446 A.2d 1095 (Del. 1982); Johnson v. National Beef Packing Co., 220 Kan. 52, 551 P.2d 779 (1976). *See* Annotation, *Right To Discharge Allegedly "At-Will" Employee as Affected by Employer's Promulgation of Employment Policies as to Discharge,* 33 A.L.R.4th 120 (1984). With the trend suggesting contractual obligations conferred by employee handbooks, manuals, or policy statements by the employer, it was probably inevitable that such books or statements would include conspicuous disclaimers of any contractual intent. Such disclaimers have been upheld. *See* Castiglione v. Johns Hopkins Hosp., 69 Md. App. 325, 517 A.2d 786 (1986).

[4] *See* Brockmeyer v. Dun & Bradstreet, 113 Wis. 2d 561, 335 N.W.2d 834 (1983); Parnar v. American Hotels, Inc., 65 Haw. 370, 652 P.2d 625 (1982); Magnan v. Anaconda Indus., Inc., 193 Conn. 558, 479 A.2d 781 (1984). See, however, Monge v. Beebe Rubber Co., 114 N.H. 130, 316 A.2d 549 (1974).

[5] For a recent judicial defense of the terminable-at-will rule, see the opinion of President Judge Cirillo in Greene v. Oliver Realty, Inc., 363 Pa. Super. 534, 526 A.2d 1192 (1987) citing sections of the second revised edition of this book with respect to unilateral contracts and the terminable-at-will rule.

[6] The purpose of the "exception" to the terminable-at-will rule based upon employers' statements of personnel policy "is to protect the legitimate expectations of employees who have justifiably relied on manual provisions precluding job termination except for cause." *Castiglione, supra* note 3, at 793.

[7] The overwhelming majority of collective bargaining agreements require dismissal to be for cause or just cause. Peck, *Unjust Discharges From Employment: A Necessary Change in the Law,* 40 Ohio St. L.J. 1, 8 (1979). However, in 1981, only twenty-five percent of the nonagricultural work force was covered by a collective bargaining agreement. *See* Note, *Protecting Employees at Will Against Wrong Discharge: The Public Policy Exception,* 96 Harv. L. Rev. 1931, 1934 (1983).

[8] *See, e.g.,* Finley v. Aetna Life & Cas. Co., 5 Conn. App. 394, 499 A.2d 64 (1985) in which the court made a point of requiring an offer in definite form that was communicated to the employee.

tion, the judicial ferment will continue as the common law tradition strives to develop more effective reactions to the myriad complexities of the employment-at-will relationship.[9]

§ 39. To Whom an Offer Is Addressed — Who Is the Offeree?

As the master of the offer, the offeror creates a power of acceptance exclusively in the party or parties to whom the offer is addressed and the offer is addressed to the party who will provide the exchange sought by the offeror.[10] While the general principle may appear self-evident, there are problems in the identification of the offeree.

In our prior discussion of guides to distinguish preliminary negotiations from offers,[11] we suggested that courts have often considered whether the proposal was addressed to a specified person or persons on the assumption that, the more definite the addressee of the proposal, the more likely the proposal would constitute an offer. We regarded that guide as anything but conclusive since we found that a proposal to an indefinite party or parties could be an offer to one or all such parties. In cases of reward offers or the unusual situation involving an advertisement offer, where the power of acceptance is restricted to one or several *identifiable* parties, such proposals to the public may constitute offers.[12] It is possible to create powers of acceptance in an unlimited number of persons and the exercise of that power by one person may or may not have an effect on the continuation of the power in the others. Thus, where a reward offer is made, any party who knows of the offer[13] and is not disabled from accepting[14] may accept the offer. The language or circumstances of such an offer may, however, indicate that the offeror will pay only once. If Ames offers $10,000 for information leading to the arrest and conviction of the murderer of Ames' brother, the first person providing that information would be viewed as an offeree and the exercise of that power would terminate the powers in other offerees, i.e., members of the public who had become aware of the offer.[15] On the other hand, if a manufacturer of a cold remedy promised to pay $100 to any party contracting a cold after using the remedy in accordance with directions, the offer is made to an unlimited number of parties. If one or one thousand or more use the preparation in accor-

---

[9]Problems of indefinite duration are also troublesome in franchise agreements. These problems will be explored *infra* § 57(D)(2).

[10]*See* RESTATEMENT 2d § 52. Ill. 3 to this section is based upon the well known case, Boston Ice Co. v. Potter, 123 Mass. 28 (1877). The illustration reads as follows: "*A* promises *B* that *A* will sell and deliver a set of books to *B* if *B*'s father *C* will promise to pay $150 for the set. *B* is the promisee of *A*'s promise; *C* is the offeree of *A*'s offer. Only *C* can accept the offer by making the return promise invited by *A*."

[11]*See supra* § 34.

[12]Thus, in a "First Come, First Served" advertisement, the identifiable parties would be offerees. *See* Lefkowitz v. Great Minneapolis Surplus Store, 251 Minn. 188, 86 N.W.2d 689 (1957). We discovered an offer via advertisement in the famous case of Carlill v. Carbolic Smoke Ball Co., 1 Q.B. 256 (1893).

[13]*See* RESTATEMENT 2d § 23. One cannot accept an offer unless one is aware of it, since no mutual assent would be possible, otherwise. This concept will be discussed further in this chapter.

[14]For example, a police officer who has the duty to discover an alleged murderer would not be able to accept an offer for the capture of that party because he has a pre-existing duty to perform the act in any event. *See* RESTATEMENT 2d § 73 ill. 1.

[15]*See* RESTATEMENT 2d § 29 ill. 1.

dance with directions, they are offerees who have exercised their powers of acceptance.[16]

A problem may arise where the offeror contemplates the payment of one sum to one identifiable party, e.g., the first person to provide information leading to the arrest and conviction of the murderer from innumerable offerees. If more than one of the offerees provide the information sought by the offeror, how is the duty of the offeror to be performed? The problem has rarely come before the courts so that there is no dispositive case law. Professor Corbin recommends a pro rata distribution among the claimants to the extent of the information provided[17] and Corbin's recommendation, not remarkably, appears sound.

Perhaps the most difficult problem concerning the person or persons entitled to exercise a power of acceptance occurs when the offer is made to an impersonal entity, e.g., a business whether or not it is incorporated. In a famous case,[18] the plaintiff had been the foreman and manager for a manufacturer with whom defendants had dealt. The plaintiff bought the business and, thereafter, defendants ordered goods from the manufacturer without knowledge that the business had been sold. The plaintiff struck the name of his former employer and inserted his own on the order as he supplied the goods. The court held that the plaintiff was not entitled to accept the offer, though the judges were split on the preferable rationale for the result and none suggested a desirable rationale.[19] The determination of who has a power of acceptance must be found in the manifested intention of the offeror since the offeror is the master of the offer and may create a power of acceptance in any person or persons he chooses.[20] In accordance with the overriding objective test,[21] the offeror is also responsible for creating the appearance of an offer, i.e., if he knows or has reason to know that he is creating the appearance of having made an offer to a particular person or persons, he is bound by that outward manifestation of appearance.[22] These fundamental principles provide a basis for deciding the question at issue. In a more contemporary illustration, if a customer makes a catalogue offer to purchase goods from Sears & Roebuck

---

[16]*See* RESTATEMENT 2d § 29 ill. 3. While each user of the remedy has exercised his or her power of acceptance and has, therefore, formed a contract with the manufacturer, a condition to the manufacturers' contractual duty must occur before that duty is activated, i.e., the user must catch a cold. The illustration is based on the famous *Carbolic Smoke Ball* case, *supra* § 34. For another offer to the public with unlimited offerees, consider Rosenthal v. Al Packer Ford, Inc., 36 Md. App. 349, 374 A.2d 377 (1977) (offer of $20,000 to anyone who could prove it was not "absolutely true" that cars were being sold for $89 over the invoice price.) *See also* Newman v. Schiff, 778 F.2d 460 (8th Cir. 1985) (offer to pay anyone $100,000 if they could disprove offeror's theory that the Internal Revenue Code contained no provision making the payment of taxes mandatory.).

[17]1 CORBIN ON CONTRACTS, § 64 at 268 (1963).

[18]Boulton v. Jones, 2 H. & N. 564 (Ex. 1857).

[19]One judge took the straightforward view that the defendants had intended to deal with the plaintiff's predecessor; thus precluding a power of acceptance in the plaintiff. Another judge discussed setoffs and concluded that the identity of the offeree was material to the defendants. A third judge thought that the plaintiff should have notified the defendants of the change in ownership prior to shipment of the goods.

[20]*See* RESTATEMENT 2d § 29(1) and comment a.

[21]*See supra* § 30.

[22]RESTATEMENT 2d § 29 comment a. *See also* RESTATEMENT 2d §§ 52 and 53 comment g. The issue may be seen as, "Who may accept an offer," and that issue may involve a unilateral mistake of identity to be considered later in this volume.

Co., and if she did so because her relative worked at the company but, prior to the acceptance of the offer by Sears, the relative had been discharged from employment, would a contract be formed? Unless the customer had informed Sears that the offer was based upon the continuation of the relative's employment, Sears would be justified in assuming the continuation of its power of acceptance even though it had discharged the relative. On the other hand, if customers of a local druggist are willing to place orders for over-the-counter drugs at somewhat higher prices than would be available in impersonal self-service stores because of their personal affection for the local druggist who has served the community for many years, the party who purchases that business may have reason to know that the offers were being made only to the former owner. The question is one of fact, i.e., did the purported offer intend to create a power of acceptance in a particular party, and the attendant test: did such party reasonably understand that (s)he had a power of acceptance? The language of the offer and all of the surrounding circumstances must be considered to determine that question of fact.

§ 40. Offers Proposing One Contract Versus a Series of Contracts.

The typical offer contemplates a single acceptance forming one contract. It is, however, possible that the offer is divisible, i.e., it contemplates a series of acceptances forming a series of contracts. Thus, where the seller of goods undertook to supply the offeree "with such quantities of each or any of several articles named in the attached specification as the company's storekeeper may order from time to time, at the price set opposite each article respectively" for a period of one year, it was held that a separate and distinct bilateral[23] contract was made every time the offeree sent an order for goods.[24] On the other hand, where an offeror wrote, "We hereby agree to receive ... and transport ... not exceeding six thousand tons gross (2,240 lbs.) in and during the months of April, May, June, July and August ... upon the terms and for the price hereinafter specified," the proposal was held to embody a single offer.[25] Whether the proposal embodies but one offer or a series of offers is a problem of interpretation that is not always easily solved. It must be solved as analogous problems are solved on the basis of what a reasonable person in the position of the offeree would understand.[26] The offer may contemplate a series of acceptances that will not occur at the same time. The common example is an offer of guaranty, i.e., a promise to guarantee payment for goods to be sold or money to be advanced at intervals to a third party. Assume that Ames says to

---

[23] See supra § 16, for the basic distinction between bilateral and unilateral contracts.

[24] Strang v. Witkowski, 138 Conn. 94, 82 A.2d 624 (1951). See also Merit Specialties Co. v. Gilbert Brass Foundry Co., 362 Mo. 325, 241 S.W.2d 718 (1951); Oscar Schlegel Mfg. Co. v. Peter Cooper's Glue Factory, 231 N.Y. 459, 132 N.E. 148 (1921). See RESTATEMENT 2d § 31.

[25] American Pub'g & Engraving Co. v. Walker, 87 Mo. App. 503 (1901).

[26] McCullough v. Cashmere Sch. Dist. 222 of Chelan Cty., 115 Wash. App. 730, 551 P.2d 1046, 1049 ((1976): "Whether an offer contemplates more than one acceptance depends upon the intent of the parties to be discovered by reading the document as a whole, together with surrounding facts and circumstances, if necessary." (Two teachers were offered reemployment contracts including their traditional curricular positions but adding extracurricular duties. The teachers deleted the extracurricular duties and signed the contracts. Held: though the assignments offered could have been handled as separate contracts, i.e., offers contemplating two acceptances, that was not the intention of the parties.)

Barnes, "I will be out of the country for a year. If, during that time, my brother needs money, let him have it and I will see to it that you suffer no loss." During the year, Barnes lends Ames' brother $1000 on each of five separate occasions.[27] Ames' offer in this case would be seen as, "A continuing guaranty of debts [which] is, in effect, an offer accepted serially by each extension of credit."[28] A continuing guaranty contemplates a series of transactions or succession of credits, whereas a restricted guaranty is limited to either a single transaction or to a number of specific transactions.[29] By lending Ames' brother the first $1000, Barnes was accepting Ames' offer of guaranty, and each successive loan was a separate acceptance. Since Barnes' acceptance was not promissory, each loan created a unilateral contract, i.e., the acceptance was by performance.[30] As will be seen in subsequent sections, questions of notice of acceptance arise when the acceptance is by performance.[31] Even if notification of the act of acceptance is essential, however, a single notice of intention to act, e.g., one notice from Barnes to Ames of his intention to lend the money, will be viewed as sufficient with respect to the series of loans.[32] Since guaranty proposals constitute offers, they are, like other offers, revocable.[33]

----

[27] See Offord v. Davies, 12 C.B. (n.s.) 748 [1862].

[28] Georgia-Pacific Corp. v. Levitz, 149 Ariz. 120, 716 P.2d 1057, 1059 (1986).

[29] Iola State Bank v. Biggs, 233 Kan. 450, 662 P.2d 563, 568 (1983). In Birdsall v. Heacock, 32 Ohio St. 177, 30 Am. Rep. 572 (1877), an offer reading, "Please send my son the lumber he asks for, and it will be all right," was held to be an offer to guarantee payment for only one delivery. On the other hand, in Newcomb v. Kloeblen, 77 N.J.L. 791, 74 A. 511 (1909), the offer read, "I will be responsible for any bill that my son James will make." Held: the proposal was a continuing guaranty subject to an indefinite number of acceptances. See also Roberson v. Liberty Nat'l Bank & Trust Co., 88 Ga. App. 271, 76 S.E.2d 522 (1953). Modern guaranty agreements intending a series of acceptances are clearly captioned, "continuing guaranty" and other language of such agreements leave no doubt as to the manifested intention of the parties.

[30] See supra § 16 for the fundamental distinction between unilateral and bilateral contracts. Note, however, that a performance acceptance may create a bilateral contract where the offeree may accept in any reasonable manner, i.e., by promising or by performing. Typically, offers permit that choice. This concept will be explored in detail in subsequent sections.

[31] The classic case involving an offer of guaranty is Bishop v. Eaton, 161 Mass. 496, 37 N.E. 665 (1894), in which the court dealt with the notice question as follows: "It was an offer to be bound in consideration of an act to be done, and in such a case the doing of the act constitutes the acceptance of the offer.... Ordinarily there is no occasion to notify the offeror of the acceptance of such an offer, for the doing of the act is a sufficient acceptance, and the promisor knows that he is bound when he sees the action has been taken on the faith of his offer. But if the act is of such a kind that knowledge of it will not quickly come to the promisor, the promisee is bound to give him notice of his acceptance within a reasonable time after doing that which constitutes the acceptance." This principle is effective at present as will be seen in the exploration of performance acceptances in subsequent sections.

[32] See RESTATEMENT 2d § 30 comment b.

[33] Iola State Bank, supra note 29, at 568. An exploration of revocation will be found in subsequent sections.

§ 41. Duration of Power of Acceptance.

A. *The Early Law.*

Assuming that an offer has been made, how long does the power of acceptance created by the offer continue? The early law proceeded on the theory of subjective assent, i.e., an actual "meeting of the minds." As such, it was unwilling to admit the possibility that an offer could create a continuing power of acceptance in the offeree. Even if the offeror had stated that the offer would continue and could be accepted during a specified period and manifested no change of intention in the meantime, early courts felt conceptually barred from treating the offer as remaining open during that period if the offeror subjectively changed his mind.[34] The result was that an offer had to be accepted practically on the spot if any contract was to result from it. A subjective theory of mutual assent supports that view since an offer may be said to indicate the offeror's true state of mind only at the moment it is made. This mode of dealing with the problem is, of course, unsatisfactory because the subjective theory of contract is impracticable.[35] The impracticability was recognized early with respect to contracts by correspondence. A considerable period of time must elapse between the sending of an offer by mail and its receipt by the offeree. Subjectively, the offeror could change his mind a moment after posting the offer. Certainly he could change his mind prior to any acceptance by the offeree. There was a grudging recognition that the acceptance may occur though the offeror had changed his mind prior to the acceptance. To reconcile this practicable and necessary result with the subjective theory, one court indulged the fiction that the offeror, in such a situation, "must be considered in law as making, during every instant of the time [his] letter is traveling, the same identical offer."[36] On its face, the statement is ridiculous since the addressee of an offer must receive it before (s)he can possibly have any power of acceptance. Apparently, the court meant to suggest that it must be conclusively presumed that the offeror is still willing to contract at the time his proposal reaches the offeree, regardless of the actual state of mind of the offeror at that moment. While the court's attempt to accommodate practicability and the subjective theory is awkward, it was inevitable that courts would recognize a continuing power of acceptance. This is universally recognized today.[37]

B. *Offers With a Specified Time Limit.*

One of the traditional statements about the agreement process is as true today as it ever was: *The offeror is the master of the offer.*[38] The offeror may, therefore, make any offer she pleases and may place whatever time limitation upon it that seems desirable to her.[39] Thus, if Ames offers to sell Blackacre to

---

[34] Head v. Diggon, 3 M. & R. 97 (1828); Cooke v. Oxley, 3 Term. Rep. 653 (1790).
[35] *See supra* § 30.
[36] Adams v. Lindsell, 1 Barn. & Ald. 681 (1818).
[37] RESTATEMENT 2d § 35(1).
[38] *See* RESTATEMENT 2d § 29 comment a. The statement may be even more true today than heretofore. *See* the discussion of the manner of acceptance *infra* § 45.
[39] *See* Cain v. Noel, 268 S.C. 583, 235 S.E.2d 292 (1977). *See also* RESTATEMENT 2d § 41 comment a.

Barnes for a certain price, the offer to be open for one hour, Barnes' power of acceptance lasts for only one hour. The late acceptance is totally ineffective as an acceptance though it may operate as a new offer.[40] Since Ames creates the power of acceptance, she is entitled to decide its duration even though that duration may seem unreasonable under the circumstances. Moreover, even though the power of acceptance will terminate after the time stated in the offer, absent other circumstances,[41] the offeror may revoke the offer prior to the end of the time stated, as will be shown subsequently.[42]

The problem that has occurred most often in the application of this rule is a problem of interpretation. The offer may specify a time limit in ambiguous or indefinite fashion. If, for example, the offer states that it must be accepted "by return mail," should that phrase be taken to mean that the offeree must immediately write a letter of acceptance and hurry to the mailbox? Or, could "by return mail" permit the offeree to consider the offer in the morning and send a letter of acceptance by afternoon mail? Since the offeree is mailing the letter on the same day he received the offer, though he misses the first possible return mail, there is a basis for concluding that the offeree has met the basic requirement of "by return mail," in the absence of other circumstances.[43] Again, the test can only be the understanding of a reasonable person in the position of the offeree under all of the surrounding circumstances, including any trade usage, prior course of dealing, and the like. What the offeror in fact actually intended is, as usual, irrelevant since it is his manifestation of intention as reasonably understood by the offeree that must control.[44] Even where

---

[40] If the offeree attempts to accept after the time prescribed in the offer, there is no acceptance since the offeree lacks the power to accept. Such an ineffective attempt at acceptance, however, may constitute a new offer, which would be accepted through a manifestation of assent by the original offeror. See RESTATEMENT 2d § 70 comment b. See also Houston Dairy v. John Hancock Mut. Life Ins. Co., 643 F.2d 1185 (5th Cir. 1981); Cain v. Noel, 268 S.C. 583, 235 S.E.2d 292 (1977) (characterizing the late acceptance as a counter offer). The RESTATEMENT 2d rejects the view that the offeror can regard the late acceptance as an acceptance by "waiving" the requirement that the acceptance occur within the time prescribed by the offer and, by remaining silent, treat the acceptance as effective. Generally, acceptances must be communicated. Another problem addressed in § 70 of the RESTATEMENT 2d involves an offeree who "erroneously but plausibly" believes he has accepted within the time prescribed by the offer, § 70 comment a. Here, the RESTATEMENT 2d places a duty upon the offeror to speak. The reference to § 20 dealing with the effect of misunderstanding suggests that the duty is predicated upon the offeror knowing or having reason to know that the offeree has made a mistake and should be informed of that mistake. Thus, the offeror could not remain silent in the face of an understanding by the offeree that a contract had been formed.

[41] For example, an option contract or a statutory firm offer to be explored later in this chapter, will make the offer irrevocable.

[42] See RESTATEMENT 2d § 42 and the discussion of termination of offers infra § 42.

[43] RESTATEMENT 2d § 41 comment e suggests the "normal understanding that mail is promptly answered if a reply is mailed at any time on the date of receipt."

[44] See Wertheimer, Inc. v. Wehle-Hartford Co., 126 Conn. 30, 9 A.2d 279 (offer requiring "immediate confirmation"); Cheesbrough v. Western Union Tel. Co., 76 Misc. 516, 135 N.Y.S. 583 (1912), aff'd, 157 App. Div. 914, 142 N.Y.S. 1112 (1913) (offer calling for "immediate reply by wire" delayed in transmission without offeree's knowledge. Acceptance on receipt held to be on time.) Maclay v. Harvey, 90 Ill. 525, 32 Am. Rep. 35 (1878) ("return mail"); Palmer v. Phoenix Mut. Life Ins. Co., 84 N.Y. 63 (1881) ("return mail"). See RESTATEMENT 2d § 41 comment e, ibid. and RESTATEMENT 2d § 60 comment a ill. 1 which suggests that a reasonable interpretation of, "I must receive your acceptance by return mail" would include other means of communication which reaches the offeror as soon as a letter sent by return mail would normally arrive because a fair interpretation of the offer requires only acceptance within the time required rather than the method suggested.

the offeror attempts to be more definite, ambiguity may intrude. In the well-known case of *Caldwell v. Cline*,[45] the offeror gave the offeree "eight days in which to accept the offer." Did the offeror mean (a) eight days from the date of the letter, (b) eight days from the time the letter was received, (c) eight days in which to decide whether to accept and then to notify the offeror on the ninth day, (d) that the letter of acceptance had to be posted on the eighth day from either (i) the date of the offer, or (ii) the date the offer was received, (e) that the letter of acceptance had to be received by the offeror on the eighth day from either (i) the date of the offer, or (ii) the date the offer was received or, finally, (f) none of the above? Thus, even in an expression as superficially innocent as, "eight days in which to accept the offer," the ambiguities may become exponential. In *Caldwell v. Cline*, the court interpreted the phrase as permitting the offeree eight days from the time the offer was received on the footing that the power of acceptance did not exist in the offeree until the offeree received the offer. This is a somewhat mechanical view though the result may have been correct. It is conceivable that a given offeree could reasonably interpret the phrase in the offer differently. Again, the test should be the reasonable understanding of the offeree under all of the circumstances. If the offeror writes, "You will do me a favor by sending your reply by the 10th," should this be interpreted as an absolute restriction on the power of acceptance after the 10th, even though phrased in polite and friendly language,[46] or should it be interpreted as urging a response by the 10th but permitting the power of acceptance to continue thereafter, at least for a short period? There is, obviously, no conclusive answer one way or the other. Focusing upon the reasonable understanding of the offeree in such circumstances is the most reliable test though it does not promise algebraic solutions.

Other ambiguities arise in relation to the computation of the period of acceptance. Where the offer states that it "expires July 1," does the offeree have until midnight of July 1 to accept, i.e., is the day of acceptance counted in its entirety? Courts generally hold that the first day of the period is excluded and the last day is included in its entirety.[47] Again, the rule is somewhat arbitrary and should give way to other manifestations of intention.

Still another problem arises in relation to an offer with a specified time that is delayed in transmission. If an offer is delayed and the offeree knows or has reason to know it has been delayed, the power of acceptance is not extended, i.e., the offeree has only the same time to accept as if the offer had not been delayed.[48] Thus, if an offer dated January 3 states that the power of acceptance must be exercised within 10 days from the date of the letter and the letter is not received until January 20, the offeree has no power of acceptance upon learning of the offer. Moreover, the same analysis applies even though

---

[45] 109 W. Va. 553, 156 S.E. 55 (1930).

[46] *See* Howells v. Stroock, 50 App. Div. 344, 63 N.Y.S. 1074 (1900).

[47] Thus, in an offer that became effective on January 5, if the offeree had to accept on the tenth day, the count would begin with January 6 and the power of acceptance could be exercised until midnight on January 15. *See* Dobson & Johnson, Inc. v. Waldron, 47 Tenn. App. 121, 336 S.W.2d 313 (1960); Housing Auth. v. T. Miller & Sons, 239 La. 966, 120 So. 2d 494 (1960). *See also* Clements v. Pasadena Fin. Co., 376 F.2d 1005 (9th Cir. 1967) applying Section 10 of the Cal. Civ. Code to the same effect.

[48] Restatement 2d § 49.

the delay in transmission is exclusively the fault of the offeror. If, however, the offeree neither knows nor has reason to know of the delay in transmission, his power of acceptance lasts for as long as it would normally last except that the period is measured from the time it *appears* to have been sent rather than from the time it was actually sent.[49] This analysis is in strict conformity with the preferable test, i.e., the reasonable understanding of the offeree.

C. *Offers Without a Specified Time Limit.*

If an offer contains no specified duration of the power of acceptance, it might be supposed that the offer continues indefinitely unless revoked by the offeror. Such a rule would lead to manifestly unjust results. After a period of time has elapsed, if the offeror has heard nothing from the offeree, the offeror naturally assumes that the offeree is not interested in the proposed deal, and is, therefore, reasonable in assuming that it is unnecessary to notify the offeree that the offer is no longer open. Under these circumstances, it would be eminently unfair to permit the offeree to bind the offeror by a purported acceptance of the offer. To avoid such an unfair result, the cases are legion which hold that a power of acceptance created by an offer without a specified time limit continues only for a reasonable time.[50] This rule provides a result in keeping with the presumable intention of the parties had they consciously adverted to the question.

The principal difficulty in the application of the rule comes in determining what constitutes a reasonable time in a given case. A court must consider a wide range of circumstances in making this determination, including the nature of the proposed contract and the purposes of the parties, as well as any trade usage or prior course of dealing between the parties. Again, the general test is, how much time for acceptance would a reasonable person in the position of the offeree assume he had under all of the circumstances?[51] A reasonable time in one case may be only a few moments, whereas in another case it may be several days or even years.[52] In offers to the public such as reward

---

[49] *Ibid.*

[50] *See, e.g.,* Stern v. Wesner, 395 N.W.2d 585 (S.D. 1986); Miller v. Campello Co-operative Bank, 344 Mass. 76, 181 N.E.2d 345 (1962); Fortin v. Wilensky, 142 Me. 372, 53 A.2d 266 (1947); RESTATEMENT 2d § 41(1).

[51] *See* RESTATEMENT 2d § 41 comment b.

[52] *See* Textron, Inc. v. Froelich, 223 Pa. Super. 506, 302 A.2d 426 (1973) (seller offered steel at certain prices in a telephone conversation. Buyer replied that he wanted time to check with his customers. Five weeks later, buyer attempted to accept and seller responded, "Fine, thank you." Court held that while telephone offers may generally end with the completion of the conversation, the facts suggest that a jury could have found the offer still open at the time of buyer's acceptance. In any event, since buyer and seller manifested mutual assent five weeks later, there was a contract. In Orlowski v. Moore, 198 Pa. Super. 360, 181 A.2d 692 (1962), the lessee of property had an option to purchase in the form of a right of first refusal, i.e., the lessee had to be informed of the availability of another purchaser willing to buy at a certain price and then given a reasonable time (in the absence of a stated time) to exercise his power of acceptance to purchase the property. In mid-January, the owners notified the lessee that they had a willing purchaser at a certain price and the lessee should decide whether to exercise his right to purchase. The lessee had been unable to pay the modest monthly rental for the months of December and January on time. He finally paid the overdue rent in early February, at which time the owners, again, informed him of the willing purchaser. At that time, he told the owners that his attempt to secure a loan from the bank was unsuccessful but that he would continue his effort to obtain a loan. On February 10, the owners, believing that the lessee could not obtain a loan, agreed to sell the house

offers, an offer of reward for information leading to the arrest and conviction of the party guilty of a crime may last only as long as the statute of limitations for that crime, but it could be considerably shorter. If a municipality has been experiencing a series of arson crimes and the city officials post a reward for information leading to the arrest and conviction of the arsonist, if no arson occurs for several years, the offer may have lapsed before an attempted exercise of the power of acceptance based upon a current commission of arson because the apparent purpose of the offeror was to deal with a particular problem at a particular time.[53] The purpose of the offeror and the communication of that purpose to the offeree is often critical in determining the duration of the power of acceptance.[54] Where the parties are bargaining face-to-face or by the telephone, the general rule is that the time for acceptance does not extend beyond the end of the conversation[55] unless there is a manifestation of intention to the contrary.[56] If the subject matter of the transaction involves great fluctuations in price such as securities or goods on a commodities exchange, the reasonable time for acceptance will be very short, perhaps instantaneous through an appropriate means of telecommunication. The duration of the power of acceptance will be much greater with respect to subject matter that does not fluctuate rapidly in value.[57] These common sense guides are in keeping with the overriding test of what a reasonable offeree should assume with respect to a reasonable time for acceptance. The offeree should not, for example, expect to enjoy a period of time to speculate at the expense of the offeror.[58]

We have provided only a few examples of circumstances that must be considered in determining the duration of the power of acceptance when the offer has not specified it. They should, however, provide a sufficient analytical framework in which to determine a reasonable time for acceptance in myriad fact situations.

---

to the other purchaser. Before title was conveyed, the lessee informed the owners that he had secured a loan. In determining whether the lessee had been given a reasonable time to exercise his right of first refusal, the court considered all of these facts and concluded that the lessee had been given a reasonable time though the total time involved was less than one month. If the lessee had been able to pay the prior rental on time and had not been unsuccessful in his first attempt to secure a loan, a court could have decided that the time provided was not reasonable.

[53] See Loring v. City of Boston, 48 Mass. (7 Met.) 409 (1844). RESTATEMENT 2d § 41 ill. 2. If, however, the apparent purpose of the offeror is to deal with a continuing problem over a long period of time such as an offer by a group of banks concerning bank robbery, the reasonable duration of the power of acceptance could be much longer. See Carr v. Mahaska Cty. Bankers Ass'n, 222 Iowa 411, 269 N.W. 494 (1936) and RESTATEMENT 2d § 41 ill. 3.

[54] See, e.g., Beiriger & Sons Irrigation, Inc. v. Southwest Land Co., 705 P.2d 532 (Colo. App. 1985) (where the seller of a sprinkler system had not been informed that it was to be used on an oat crop which had to be planted by June 1, the delivery of the system was not late).

[55] RESTATEMENT 2d § 41 comment d and ill. 4.

[56] See Textron, Inc. v. Froelich, supra note 52.

[57] RESTATEMENT 2d § 41 comment f.

[58] Thus, in an offer to sell securities not listed on an exchange, if the offeree waits for two days and then, learning of a sharp rise in the price of the stock, attempts to accept, the acceptance may be too late because the period exposed the offeror to an unwarranted risk. See RESTATEMENT 2d § 41 comment f and ill. 8.

1. Acceptance Beyond a Reasonable Time That Is Effective — Cross-Offers Distinguished.

Having seen that an offer without a specified duration is open for a reasonable time, it is clear that the offeror may either extend or decrease that duration. As the master of the offer, the offeror may extend the duration of the offer, whether the offer contained a specified time for acceptance or was subject to the substituted reasonable time where no time was specified.[59] Similarly, since an offeror may revoke the typical offer at any time after it is made, even if it contained a specified time limit or the revocation occurred long before what would have been a reasonable time for acceptance,[60] the offeror may shorten the time for acceptance by communicating that intention to the offeree. The more difficult question is whether the life of the offer may be extended or shortened through the manifested but uncommunicated intention of the offeror. In the well-known case of *Mactier's Administrators v. Frith*,[61] an offer had been before the offeree for a period of two and one-half months before he purported to accept it. In the light of the surrounding circumstances and the nature of the offer involved, it seemed clear that more than a reasonable time for acceptance had passed. In the meantime, however, the offeror had written indicating his intention that the offer was still open. Had this communication reached the offeree, there would have been no question that the duration of the power of acceptance had been extended. The communication, however, had not reached the offeree. Thus, there was a manifestation of intention on the part of the offeror of which the offeree was unaware. The court, nevertheless, held that the acceptance was timely.[62] At first blush, the result reached in this case may appear to support the outmoded subjective theory of mutual assent. A more careful analysis, however, belies that appearance. There was an objective manifestation from the offeror to extend the duration of the power of acceptance. The problem was that this objective manifestation was not communicated to the offeree prior to his otherwise untimely exercise of the power of acceptance. As will be seen subsequently, normally an offer cannot be accepted unless the offeree is aware of the offer since mutual assent requires each party to manifest assent with reference to the manifestation of the other.[63] The classic illustration involves a party who provides information leading to the arrest and conviction of a murderer without knowledge of the reward.[64] It is quite another matter, however, to know of

---

[59] Even if an offer lapses, the offeror may recreate the offer though it would be preferable, in such a case, to regard the recreation as a new offer creating a new power of acceptance. *See* Averill v. Hedge, 12 Conn. 424 (1828); Tinn v. Hoffman, 29 L. T. 271 [1873].

[60] *See* RESTATEMENT 2d § 42 ill. 1.

[61] 6 Wend. 103, 21 Am. Dec. 262 (N.Y. 1830).

[62] The opinion stated, "Then we are to determine, as a matter of fact, whether Frith's offer was held out for Mactier's acceptance until the thirty-first of March, if Frith intended it should stand so, and he viewed himself as tendering it to Mactier down to that time, we are bound to regard it as standing, unless his intention was the result of the fraudulent conduct of Mactier. The acts of Frith after the death of Mactier, could do nothing towards completing an unfinished contract; but I think they may be fairly adverted to for the purpose of ascertaining his intentions in relation to the continuance of his offer." Marcy, J., *id.* at 274. *Accord,* RESTATEMENT 2d § 13 comment d and ill. 6.

[63] RESTATEMENT 2d § 23.

[64] *See* Glover v. Jewish War Veterans of United States, Post No. 58, 68 A.2d 233 (D.C. Mun. 1949). This situation will be analyzed later in this chapter.

an offer and to attempt to accept it beyond what may be a reasonable time where there has been a manifestation of extension of that period though the manifestation was not communicated to the offeree. As suggested earlier, in the absence of a specified duration of the offer, the obvious purpose of the reasonable time limitation is to protect the offeror since a reasonable offeror would assume that the offeree chose not to accept the offer after a reasonable time. If, however, the offeror has manifested his intention to extend the normal reasonable time duration of the offer, the purpose of protecting the offeror by the original reasonable time limitation is unnecessary, even though the offeree has not become aware of the extension. Where the purpose of the rule stops, so should the rule. There is, therefore, no unfairness in permitting the acceptance to be effective under such circumstances. If, however, the offeror had manifested his intention to shorten the reasonable time for acceptance and the offeree had not received that communication, that manifestation should not be effective because there is another purpose behind the rule permitting a reasonable time for acceptance. The rule protects not only the offeror; it protects the offeree who is entitled to assume a reasonable time for acceptance. If the offeree manifests acceptance within a reasonable time, the expectation and possible reliance of the offeree should not be frustrated when a manifestation of a shortening of the duration of the offer that had not been received prior to acceptance is later discovered.

This situation should not be confused with the rare problem of cross-offers, i.e., identical offers crossing in the mails. If Ames sends a letter to Barnes offering to sell Ames' auto for $5000 and Barnes, without knowledge of the Ames offer, sends a letter to Ames offering to purchase Ames' auto for $5000, two powers of acceptance have been created but there is no contract because the mutual assent of each party was not manifested with reference to the mutual assent of the other.[65] The parties have not made a bargain[66] and, normally, promises must be bargained for.[67] In the situation involving an otherwise late acceptance after an uncommunicated manifestation of extension of the duration of the offer, however, there clearly is a bargained-for exchange.

§ 42. Termination of the Power of Acceptance.

A. *Introduction — Methods of Termination.*

We have seen that the typical power of acceptance created by an offer comes to an end at the time set forth in the offer or, in the absence of a specified time, at the completion of a reasonable time.[68] As the master of the offer,[69] the offeror may revoke the offer at any time, even if a time for acceptance has

---

[65] *See* RESTATEMENT 2d § 23 comment d and ill. 4. *See also* Tinn v. Hoffman, 29 L. T. 271 [1873].

[66] "Bargain" is defined as an agreement to exchange promises or to exchange a promise for a performance or to exchange performances. RESTATEMENT 2d § 3.

[67] As will be seen in the next chapter dealing with the Validation Process, one of the requirements for an enforceable agreement, i.e., a contract, is the requirement of consideration though there are additional validation devices under certain circumstances. *See* RESTATEMENT 2d § 71.

[68] *See supra* § 41.

[69] *See* RESTATEMENT 2d § 29 comment a.

been previously specified.[70] The power of acceptance will come to an end if it is rejected by the offeree[71] either by a manifestation not to accept or by the submission of a substitute bargain, i.e., a counter-offer.[72] Death or incapacity of either the offeror or offeree will terminate the power of acceptance.[73] The power of acceptance in a given situation may be subject to a supervening event that operates to terminate the power.[74] Each of these methods of terminating the power of acceptance will be explored. As this exploration proceeds, it must be remembered that an offer can be made irrevocable in various ways, which will be analyzed in the next section.

B. *The Power of Revocation — Direct and Indirect.*

A manifestation by the offeror to withdraw the offer prior to the moment of acceptance terminates the offeree's power of acceptance.[75] The common law principle that offers are revocable is not universally shared as evidenced by the civil law principle that offers are irrevocable.[76] The preferable rationale is one of fairness to the offeror, i.e., if offers were irrevocable, the offeror would be bound but the offeree would not be bound, thus violating the common law principle of "mutuality of obligation": either both parties are bound or neither is bound.[77] To be effective, a revocation must be received by the offeree.[78] Without knowledge of a revocation, an offeree may accept the offer and reasonably assume there is a binding agreement. To protect reasonable expectations and possible reliance, the revocation of the offer must be received by the offeree to be effective. An oral notice of revocation is received when the offeree or his agent learns of it or has reason to know it exists.[79] A written revocation

---

[70] RESTATEMENT 2d § 42 comment a. Exceptions to this general rule whereby the offer will be irrevocable will be explored in Section 43.

[71] RESTATEMENT 2d § 38.

[72] RESTATEMENT 2d § 39.

[73] RESTATEMENT 2d § 48.

[74] We have already seen examples in auctions without reserve where the power of acceptance is subject to no higher bid being made, *supra* § 36, and reward offers which contemplate the exercise of the power of acceptance only by the first party to exercise it, *supra* § 39.

[75] *See* R.J. Taggart, Inc. v. Douglas County, 31 Or. App. 1137, 572 P.2d 1050 (1977). *See also* Pribil v. Ruther, 200 Neb. 161, 262 N.W.2d 460 (1978) (indicating that a revocation communicated prior to the deposit of the acceptance in the mail would be effective); RESTATEMENT 2d, § 42 and Wagner, *Some Problems of Revocation and Termination of Offers,* 38 N.D.L. REV. 138 (1963).

[76] *See* 1 FORMATION OF CONTRACTS: A STUDY OF THE COMMON CORE OF LEGAL SYSTEMS 780-83 (R. Schlesinger ed. 1968).

[77] The principle of "mutuality of obligation" will be considered in the next chapter.

[78] The classic case is Byrne & Co. v. Leon Van Tienhoven & Co., L.R. 5 C.P.D. 344 (1880) (letter of acceptance mailed before letter of revocation was received). *See also* L. & E. Wertheimer v. Wehle-Hartford Co., 126 Conn. 30, 9 A.2d 279 (1939), Annotation 125 A.L.R. 985 (1940); Jennette Bros. Co. v. Hovey & Co., 184 N.C. 140, 113 S.E. 665 (1922); RESTATEMENT 2d § 42 comment b. Under the influence of the "Field Code" which was drafted pursuant to the subjective theory, some Western states have adopted legislation making revocations effective when they are put in the course of transmission to the offeree. *See, e.g.,* CAL. CIV. CODE §§ 1583, 1587; MONT. CODE ANN. §§ 13-319, 13-323, N.D. CENT. CODE §§ 9-03-19, 9-03-23, S.D. CODIFIED LAWS §§ 53-7-2, 53-7-6.

[79] *See* UCC § 1-201(25): "A person has 'notice' of a fact when (a) he has actual knowledge of it; ... or (c) from all the facts and circumstances known to him at the time in question he has reason to know that it exists," and § 1-201 (26)(a) to the effect that a person "receives" a notice when "it comes to his attention...."

is received when it comes into the possession of the offeree or his agent, or when it is deposited in an authorized place.[80]

One of the classic problems concerning notification to the offeree was confronted in the well-known case of *Dickinson v. Dodds*.[81] The owner of land created a power of acceptance with a specified time limit. Before the offer had expired according to its terms, the offeree's agent told the offeree that the offeror "had been offering or agreeing to sell the property" to another. The court interpreted the communication as making the offeree aware that the offeror no longer intended to sell the property to the offeree and this knowledge constituted an *indirect* revocation of the offer. It is clear that knowledge by the offeree that the offeror has taken action inconsistent with the continuation of the power of acceptance in the offeree constitutes a revocation of the offer as effectively as direct communication from the offeror to the offeree that the offer is revoked.[82] The first question, however, is, what constitutes *knowledge* on the part of the offeree? Must the offeree investigate every rumor about actions on the part of the offeror? The question scarcely survives its statement. We turn to our old friend, the reasonable person, and place the offeree in that position. A reasonable offeree need not be concerned about statements by third parties who would not be viewed as *reliable* sources. The town gossip who is known for making statements that turn out to be false need not be relied upon, even if the information he conveys turns out to be true on this occasion. Even if the source is reliable, i.e., someone who normally would be viewed as a trusted and reliable source of information, there is no effective revocation if the information, though submitted in good faith, is erroneous. The power of acceptance cannot be terminated by incorrect information even from a reliable source. Moreover, even if the information is correct and the source reliable, the information must amount to a definite manifestation of intention by the offeror that he no longer intends to form a contract with the offeree. Thus, if the information conveyed in *Dickinson v. Dodds* were interpreted as the offeror merely having made an additional *offer* to sell the property to another, such an act by the offeror is not inconsistent with the continuation of the offer in the original offeree since an offeror may create more than one power of acceptance as to the same subject matter though he runs the risk of having both powers exercised, thereby forming two contracts for the same subject matter.[83] The same principle would apply with respect to *direct* revocations, i.e., the offeror's manifestation of intention not to enter into the proposed contract must be sufficient to indicate to a reasonable of-

---

[80] *See* RESTATEMENT 2d § 68 and Night Commander Lighting Co. v. Brown, 213 Mich. 214, 181 N.W. 979 (1921) (revocation effective when received by agent who took order for his company). *See also* UCC § 1-201 (25)(b) to the effect that a person has notice when "he has received a notice or notification," and § 1-201 (26)(b): "A person 'receives' a notice or notification when ... (b) it is duly delivered at the place of business through which the contract was made, or at any other place held out by him as the place for receipt of such communications."

[81] 2 Ch. D. 463 (1876).

[82] *See* RESTATEMENT 2d § 43. *See* Berryman v. Kmoch, 221 Kan. 304, 559 P.2d 790 (1977) (offeree informed by a reliable source that land had been sold before offeree attempted to accept).

[83] *See* RESTATEMENT 2d § 43 comment d and CALAMARI & PERILLO, CONTRACTS 98 (3d ed. 1987) citing the prior edition of this book. *A fortiori*, mere negotiations with another potential purchaser of the property would not constitute sufficient information of an intention to revoke the offer.

feree that the offeror no longer intends to form the contract though the statement may be somewhat indefinite and need not take a definite form such as use of the term "revocation."[84] If a reliable third party informs the offeree that the offeror has made a binding contract with another, and the information is correct, such information normally would be effective to constitute a revocation of the offer.[85] Yet, the contract made with another may be expressly conditioned upon the offeree's failure to exercise the power of acceptance within the time stated in the original offer. Thus, the "correct" information would then be incomplete and a timely exercise of the power of acceptance would still be effective.[86] With these qualifications in mind, the *indirect revocation* principle is firmly ensconced and applies beyond the narrow range of contracts for the sale of land to which the original RESTATEMENT had limited it.[87]

A final problem is encountered with offers to the public, such as reward offers. If an offer is made to the world at large, an obvious difficulty is encountered if the manifested intent to revoke the power of acceptance is not learned by a particular offeree who exercises a power of acceptance. To require communication to each member of the public would be ridiculous. The pragmatic reaction to this problem is to require the offeror to promulgate the intention to revoke to the same extent and through the same media through which the original offer was published since no better means of notification is available.[88] If, however, it is practicable to notify a number of offerees individually, i.e., the number is not so great as to make individual notification prohibitively difficult, a general publication of revocation would be ineffective.[89] Finally, if a general notice of revocation would otherwise be acceptable but the medium used to announce the offer is not available, the same pragmatism would suggest an alternate medium of similar scope as an effective device to communicate the revocation.[90]

---

[84] If the offeror equivocates, a difficult question of interpretation may arise. In Hoover Motor Express Co. v. Clements Paper Co., 193 Tenn. 6, 241 S.W.2d 851 (1951), the court found that a statement by the offeror to the effect that it "didn't think they would go through with the proposal" was sufficient to indicate to the offeree that the offer was revoked. Lesser statements, however, may not be sufficient to constitute a revocation.

[85] In addition to *Dickinson v. Dodds, see* Watters v. Lincoln, 29 S.D. 98, 135 N.W. 712 (1912); Frank v. Stratford-Handcock, 13 Wyo. 37, 77 P. 134 (1904); Coleman v. Applegarth, 68 Md. 21, 11 A. 284 (1887); RESTATEMENT 2d § 43.

[86] *See* RESTATEMENT 2d § 43 comment d.

[87] *See* FIRST RESTATEMENT § 43 and RESTATEMENT 2d § 43 comment c. An interesting question arises concerning the possibility of an indirect communication of an offer. If *A* tells *B* of *A*'s intention to offer *A*'s auto to *C* for a certain price but does not empower *B* to communicate such an offer to *C, if B* informs *C* of *A*'s intention, does *C* have a power of acceptance? This problem is suggested in J. MURRAY, CASES AND MATERIALS ON CONTRACTS 94 (3d ed. 1983). Under these circumstances, *C* should not have a power of acceptance since *A* has not made an offer to *C* or any other party.

[88] *See* Shuey v. United States, 92 U.S. (2 Otto) 73 (1876) (ineffective attempt to accept reward offered for apprehension of accomplice of John Wilkes Booth) and FIRST RESTATEMENT § 43. *See also* Carr v. Mahaska Cty. Bankers Ass'n, 222 Iowa 411, 269 N.W. 494 (1936).

[89] *See* Long v. Chronicle Pub'g Co., 68 Cal. App. 171, 228 P. 873 (1924).

[90] An offer made through a national publication might be effectively revoked through a similar, national publication when the first publication either ceased to exist or was unavailable for a period of time.

C. *Rejection Terminating the Power of Acceptance.*

An offeree has a power of acceptance, but the power does not have to be exercised. If an intention not to exercise the power of acceptance is manifested by the offeree, the offeree has rejected it and the power of acceptance is terminated.[91] Any other rule would subject the offeror to undue risk. When the offeree informs the offeror by words or conduct[92] that the offeree is not interested in the proposal, the offeror may change plans in reliance on the rejection without bothering to revoke the rejected offer. Revocation in such a case would appear to be a useless gesture. The reliance of the offeror on the rejection may be difficult to prove. If the offeree were then permitted to change his mind and exercise a power of acceptance after putting the offeror off guard, obvious injustice could result. Thus, the firm principle has been established that rejection of an offer terminates it, and the principle is not affected by the inclusion of a definite time for acceptance in the offer if the rejection occurs before that time has expired.

There are, however, two situations that must be distinguished. The first involves a manifestation in the offer that the offer will not be terminated for a definite time notwithstanding earlier rejections by the offeree. Thus, if *A* offers to sell *A*'s auto to *B* for $5000 and also states, "This offer will expire 90 days from its date regardless of any statement of rejection on the part of *B*," would a rejection by *B* on the 45th day terminate *B*'s power of acceptance? The answer must be, no. We return to the general principle that the offeror, *A*, is master of the offer and may create a power of acceptance which includes abnormal risks for the offeror. As suggested earlier, the rule that rejection terminates an offer is designed to protect the offeror. The offeror is free to create a power of acceptance that eliminates that protection.[93] A similar effect occurs where an offeree responds to an ordinary offer by stating "I reject it for the time being, but will reconsider it later." Assuming the power of acceptance would not have lapsed at the time of reconsideration by the offeree, the power of acceptance is not terminated by such a statement.[94] In this situation, it is unfortunate to characterize the offeree's response as a rejection even though the term, "rejection" is used. A proper interpretation of the response would be, "I am not rejecting your offer but I cannot accept at this time. I would like to consider accepting at a later time." In either of these distinguishable situations, i.e., the offeror eliminating the protection normally enjoyed through a rejection, or the offeree indicating the possibility of acceptance at a subsequent time, the offeror may not justifiably rely upon the offeree's response as a termination of the power of acceptance. Since the reason for the rule is absent, the rule should not apply. It should be noted, however, that the offeror

---

[91] *See* Chaplin v. Consolidated Edison Co. of N.Y., 537 F. Supp. 1224 (S.D.N.Y. 1982) (offer of settlement stated that, if not satisfactory, all offers would be withdrawn; reply that attorney could not get clients to agree constituted rejection); Nabob Oil Co. v. Bay State Oil & Gas, 208 Okla. 296, 255 P.2d 513, 515 (1953) ("It is elementary that plaintiff could not revive the offer by orally accepting it ... after its rejection....") *See also* RESTATEMENT 2d § 38. Normal rejection rules are overcome by the policies of the National Labor Relations Act governing collective bargaining. *See* Pepsi-Cola Bottling Co. v. N.L.R.B., 659 F.2d 87 (8th Cir. 1981).

[92] *See* Smaligo v. Fireman's Fund Ins. Co., 432 Pa. 133, 247 A.2d 577 (1968).

[93] RESTATEMENT 2d § 38 comment b.

[94] RESTATEMENT 2d § 38(2) and comment b thereto.

has not surrendered the power to *revoke* the offer in either situation.[95] Only the effect of rejection on the power of acceptance has been abrogated.

D. *Counter Offer Terminating Power of Acceptance — "Grumbling Acceptance."*

Upon receiving an offer, an offeree may choose to propose a different bargain to the offeror relating to the same subject matter. If *A* offers to sell her auto to *B* for $5000, *B* may choose to reply, "Your price is much too high. I will give you $4000 for the car." *B*'s reply is a counter offer which normally has the same effect as an outright rejection, i.e., it terminates *B*'s power of acceptance because it manifests *B*'s intention not to accept *A*'s offer.[96] Yet, *B*'s response is different from an outright rejection in that the counter offer is, itself, an offer that creates a power of acceptance in the original offeror.[97] The intention is to continue negotiations rather than to break them off.[98] The counter offer may indicate that it is an acceptance with qualifications, i.e., that the offeree manifests its assent to most but not to all of the terms and insists upon some modification of the offer. Such a "qualified acceptance" is a counter offer that operates as a rejection of the original offer notwithstanding language of "acceptance."[99] If, on the other hand, the acceptance merely requests or suggests a change or addition to the terms of the offer but does not indicate that the acceptance is conditional on such change, the acceptance is effective to form a contract on the terms of the offer.[1] Thus, if *A* offers to sell *A*'s auto to *B* for $5000 and *B* replies, "I will pay your very high price and we have a deal. I think it would be nice if you would let me have it for $4500, however," there is an acceptance which may be viewed as a "grumbling acceptance" with a suggestion or request for a discount.[2] It is, nonetheless, an acceptance of the offer on the terms of the offer. If an offeree accepts the offer on the terms specified

---

[95] This statement assumes that the offer stating the duration of the power of acceptance at 90 days is not a "firm offer" that is statutorily irrevocable. The "firm offer" concept will be explored in the next section.

[96] *See* Dataserv Equip., Inc. v. Technology Fin. Leasing Corp., 364 N.W.2d 838 (Minn. App. 1985); Normile v. Miller, 313 N.C. 98, 326 S.E.2d 11 (1985); Glende Motor Co. v. Superior Court of Sutter Cty., 159 Cal. App. 3d 389, 205 Cal. Rptr. 682 (1984); Duval & Co. v. H. A. Malcom, 233 Ga. 784, 214 S.E.2d 356 (1975) and Ebline v. Campbell, 209 Md. 584, 121 A.2d 828 (1956), all of which involve purported acceptances adding qualifications or otherwise changing the terms of the offer. In these and similar cases, courts hold the response to be a counter offer which has the effect of terminating the power of acceptance. *See* RESTATEMENT 2d § 39.

[97] *See* Hall v. Add-Ventures, Ltd., 695 P.2d 1081 (Alaska 1985); Steele v. Harrison, 220 Kan. 422, 552 P.2d 957 (1976).

[98] RESTATEMENT 2d § 39 comment a.

[99] *See* the cases *supra* note 96, and, in particular, the *Glende Motor Co.* case therein. *See also* RESTATEMENT 2d § 39 comment b. *See also* Ardente v. Horan, 117 R.I. 254, 366 A.2d 162 (1976) (acceptance accompanied by cover letter asking vendors to confirm that furniture was included in the sale of real property. The reply was interpreted as a counter offer).

[1] A typical illustration of this situation occurs where the offeree unequivocally accepts the offer and then suggests a means of payment. *See, e.g.,* Kodiak Island Borough v. Large, 662 P.2d 440, 448 (Alaska 1981) ("Here, Large unequivocally accepted the Borough's offer. The fact that the assent was accompanied by a suggestion as to terms of payment, a detail not inconsistent with the Borough's offer, did not convert it into a counter offer."); Martindell v. Fiduciary Counsels, Inc., 131 N.J. Eq. 523, 26 A.2d 171, *aff'd,* 30 A.2d 281 (1943), and Rucker v. Sanders, 182 N.C. 607, 109 S.E. 857 (1921), both of which involve a sale of stock where buyer suggested method of payment. *See also* RESTATEMENT 2d § 61.

[2] *See* Brangier v. Rosenthal, 337 F.2d 952 (9th Cir. 1964).

in the offer but then proposes an additional arrangement consistent with the offer, there is an acceptance and a new offer for the additional item.[3] If the offer or acceptance expresses a term that is implied in the other manifestation of assent, there is no difference in terms so that no question of a counter offer or other failure of mutual assent occurs.[4] It must be emphasized, however, that a counter offer that changes some terms in the original offer will not be said to incorporate terms of the original offer that were not expressly changed in the counter offer. Thus, where a vendor of property responded to a purchaser's offer with several material changes but the response was silent with respect to the duration of the power of acceptance, the counter offer did not incorporate the time-for-acceptance provision in the original offer.[5]

While a counter offer normally rejects the original offer, it need not do so. Just as an offer can state that it will remain open for a period of time notwithstanding earlier rejections,[6] an offeror can manifest an intention to continue the power of acceptance in the offeree notwithstanding counter offers.[7] Thus, an offeree may state a desire to consider the offer but may also propose a counter offer. Thus, if *A* offers to sell her auto to *B* for $5000, *B* might respond, "I am interested in your offer and will take it under advisement. In the meantime, I am willing to pay $4500 for your car right now." Here, the offeree is not accepting the original offer and is making a counter offer that does not reject the original offer.[8] Each party now has a power of acceptance, i.e., *A* to accept *B*'s counter offer at $4500, and *B* to accept *A*'s original offer at $5000. In both of these situations, i.e., a contrary intention expressed by either the offeror or offeree concerning the normal operation of counter offers as rejections of the original offers, the parties have clearly manifested their intention that the counter offer should not be understood as a rejection of the original offer. They have, therefore, overcome the normal understanding that, by making a counter offer, the offeree intends to reject the original offer and the offeror will reasonably understand the counter offer as having that effect.

E. *Termination of Power of Acceptance by Death or Incapacity.*

It has generally been held that death[9] or incapacity[10] terminates the power of acceptance. As an original question, there is grave doubt whether this rule

---

[3]*See* McAfee v. Brewer, 214 Va. 579, 203 S.E.2d 129 (1974) (acceptance of terms specified in offer plus a request that "the red secretary" be included). *See* RESTATEMENT 2d § 61, ill. 2.

[4]*See* United States v. National Optical Stores Co., 407 F.2d 759 (7th Cir. 1969); Burkhead v. Farlow, 266 N.C. 595, 146 S.E.2d 802 (1966); RESTATEMENT 2d § 59 and, particularly, ill. 3.

[5]Normile v. Miller, 313 N.C. 98, 326 S.E.2d 11 (1985). The court took the strict position that the "qualified acceptance" as a counter offer rejected all of the terms of the original offer and the only terms that were operative thereafter were the terms of the counter offer. It is, of course, possible to discover a manifestation of intention on the part of the offeree to maintain certain terms in the original offer so that his counter offer would continue any unchanged term.

[6]*See supra* text at note 93.

[7]*See* RESTATEMENT 2d § 39(2) and comment c.

[8]*Id.*

[9]Estate of Beverly Watts, 162 Cal. App. 3d 1160, 208 Cal. Rptr. 846 (1984); Beall v. Beall, 434 A.2d 1015 (Md. App. 1981); New Headley Tobacco Whse. Co. v. Gentry's Ex'r, 307 Ky. 857, 212 S.W.2d 325 (1948); Jordan v. Dobbins, 122 Mass. 168 (1877). RESTATEMENT 2d § 48.

[10]Capacity to contract is explored *supra* §§ 21-27, Chapter 1. *See* Union Trust & Sav. Bank v. State Bank, 188 N.W.2d 300 (Iowa 1971) (before acceptance of guaranty offer, a conservator of the guarantor was appointed. Held: appointment of conservator for guarantor with plaintiff's knowl-

is desirable. It is a product of the outmoded subjective theory of mutual assent[11] and a logical application of that theory. Long ago, Professor Corbin provided the telling criticism: while one cannot contract with a dead man, there is no obstacle in creating legal relations with the personal representative who will be responsible for paying the debts of the estate.[12] Professor Williston would have preferred a different rule in the FIRST RESTATEMENT[13] but, remarkably, failed to convince the Council of the American Law Institute.[14] The RESTATEMENT 2d retains the rule but suggests no support for this "relic of the obsolete view that a contract requires a 'meeting of the minds.'"[15] The application of the rule is particularly egregious in the following situation: A offers to guaranty the payment to B of loans or other credit extended to C. A will not become aware of any extensions of credit or loans to C. B provides C with credit or loans unaware of the fact that, prior to the first extension of credit or loan, A had died in a distant land. Since death revokes an offer, regardless of the offeree's awareness of the offeror's death, there was no power of acceptance in B.[16] Under an objective theory, the contrary holding can readily be justified since there is no difficulty in establishing manifested mutual assent even though the offeror has died or become incapacitated, assuming only that the offeree is not aware of the fact. If the offeree is aware of it, clearly there should no longer be a power of acceptance. Under the existing rule, however, an offeree who performs, unaware of the death of the offeror, may in good faith proceed to perform in reliance on the offer only to find, after doing the requested act, that no contractual rights exist under which he can claim compensation for performance. Notwithstanding universal criticism, the rule remains intact except for isolated statutory changes.[17]

§ 43. Irrevocable Power of Acceptance.

A. *Need and Methods.*

Under the common law system, offers are revocable even if they contain a specified period for acceptance and the offeror promises not to revoke during that period.[18] Since offers are considered to be promises, a promise unsupported by consideration, i.e., something of value given in exchange for the

---

edge served to revoke the then unaccepted guaranty offer). In Swift v. Smigel, 115 N.J. Super. 391, 279 A.2d 895 (1971), aff'd, 60 N.J. 348, 289 A.2d 793 (1972), however, the court held that while guarantor was incompetent at the time the guaranty offer was accepted, there was an acceptance unless plaintiff should have been aware of guarantor's incompetency. *See* RESTATEMENT 2d § 48.

[11] *See supra* § 30.

[12] Corbin, *Offer and Acceptance and Some of the Resulting Legal Relations*, 26 YALE L.J. 169, 198 (1917).

[13] AM. L. INST. PROC. 198 (1925).

[14] The authority of Professor Williston was rarely questioned with respect to the FIRST RESTATEMENT.

[15] RESTATEMENT 2d § 48 comment a.

[16] See, in particular, Jordan v. Dobbins, *supra* note 9.

[17] *See, e.g.,* UCC § 4-405(1): "Neither death nor incompetence of a customer revokes such authority to accept, pay, collect or account until the bank knows of the fact of death or of an adjudication of incompetence and has reasonable opportunity to act on it." *See also* with respect to incompetency, Swift & Co. v. Smigel, discussed *supra* note 10.

[18] *See* RESTATEMENT 2d § 42 comment a: "... [T]he ordinary offer is revocable even though it expressly states the contrary...."

promise,[19] is unenforceable. Consequently, the offeror's promise not to revoke the offer for a stated time is necessarily unenforceable if it is not supported by consideration.[20] There was no need to treat offers as revocable[21] as evidenced by the irrevocability of offers (absent a manifestation of the offeror's contrary intention) in civil law systems.[22] Notwithstanding the common law insistence upon revocable offers, the need for an irrevocable power of acceptance in myriad situations was clear. The offeree may be very interested in a proposal but require time to make a final decision as to whether to accept it. The offeree may require time to determine whether necessary funds can be raised, or may have to await the occurrence or nonoccurrence of other events before deciding to accept. While in the process of deciding, the offeree does not want to assume the risk that the offer may be revoked. To provide the offeree with a dependable basis for decision, it was inevitable that devices would be developed to ascertain that the power of acceptance would be irrevocable. The original common law device which allowed for the desired result while adhering to the common law requirement that a promise must be supported by consideration to be enforceable was the *option contract.* We will explore the problems connected with the option contract in this section, and will then explore other, more modern devices to achieve an irrevocable power of acceptance: the *firm offer, irrevocability through part performance,* and *irrevocability through reliance.* As will be seen, these devices are predicated essentially on protection of the offeree in situations where revocation of the power of acceptance would lead to manifestly unjust results.

B. *Option Contracts.*

If *A* offers to sell Blackacre to *B* for $100,000, *B* may be quite interested in the offer but may require time to make a final acceptance decision. If *B* does not want to lose this opportunity, *B* may offer to pay *A* a relatively small amount, *e.g.,* ten dollars, in exchange for *A's* promise not to revoke the offer for a stated period, *e.g.,* 30 days. If *A* accepts *B's* offer, the parties have formed an *option contract*[23] which has only one purpose: to create an irrevocable power of acceptance in *B* with respect to the main offer,[24] i.e., *A's* offer to sell Blackacre to *B* for $100,000, for thirty days.[25] Not only is the power of accep-

---

[19] Consideration and other validation devices will be explored in Chapter 3.

[20] *See, e.g.,* Crowley v. S.E. Bass, 445 So. 2d 902 (Ala. 1984); Beall v. Beall, 45 Md. App. 489, 413 A.2d 1365 (1980), *rev'd,* 291 Md. 224, 434 A.2d 1015 (1981).

[21] *See* J. DAWSON, GIFTS AND PROMISES 213 (1980) suggesting that the difficulties were manufactured by viewing offers as subsidary forms of promises.

[22] 1 FORMATION OF CONTRACTS: A STUDY OF THE COMMON CORE OF LEGAL SYSTEMS, 780-83 (R. Schlesinger, ed. 1968).

[23] "One method by which an offer is rendered irrevocable is by the acceptance of consideration by the offeror in exchange for his promise to keep the offer open." Northwestern Bell Tel. v. Cowger, 303 N.W.2d 791, 794 (N.D. 1981).

[24] "An option contract has two elements: 1) the underlying contract which is not binding until accepted; and 2) the agreement to hold open to the optionee the opportunity to accept." Plantation Ket Devs. v. Colonial Mtg., Etc., 589 F.2d 164, 168 (5th Cir. 1979).

[25] *See* West Caldwell v. Caldwell, 26 N.J. 9, 138 A.2d 402 (1958). The RESTATEMENT 2d § 25, states the purpose of an option contract as follows: "An option contract ... limits the promisor's power to revoke an offer." Presumably, this language is designed to ascertain that while the power of acceptance cannot be terminated through the offeror's revocation, it can be terminated in any way in which any contractual duty can be terminated. However, comment d to this section

tance not terminated by the offeror's attempted revocation; neither is it terminated by rejection, counter offer or the death or incapacity of the offeror.[26] An early theoretical argument threatened the effectiveness of this device: If the offeror attempts to revoke the irrevocable power of acceptance, he is merely breaching the *duty* not to revoke, i.e., the *power* to revoke remains, though he is liable for whatever damages the offeree may prove for the breach of the option contract. This view was based on the notion that an "irrevocable offer" is contrary to the legal conception of an offer — it is a legal impossibility because of the subjective theory that an acceptance is impossible where one of the parties is expressing unwillingness to contract.[27] The argument has long been put to rest.[28] It is clear that, by entering into an option contract, the offeror has made a promise not to revoke which creates a duty not to revoke, *and* has surrendered the power to revoke, thereby creating an irrevocable power of acceptance in the offeree.

The example used to illustrate this point is the classical option contract with a separate consideration, i.e., ten dollars paid to the offeror to keep the main offer open for thirty days. It makes no difference whether the ten dollars was simply paid in response to the offeror's statement, "If you will pay me $10, I will keep the offer to sell Blackacre to you for $100,000 open for thirty days," or if the offeree *promised* to pay the ten dollars in exchange for the promise of irrevocability by the offeror. In the first instance, traditional contract law would characterize the contract as unilateral since there is a promise exacting a performance and creating a contract upon the payment of the ten dollars with one right in the offeree/optionee and one duty in the offeror/optionor. In the second situation, the parties have exchanged promises creating a bilateral contract with correlative rights and duties in both parties.[29] In both situa-

---

suggests that, "A revocation by the offeror is not of itself effective, and the offer is properly referred to as an irrevocable offer."

[26] RESTATEMENT 2d § 37. However, the offeror's duty under the option contract may be discharged. If, for example, the offeree were to inform the offeror that he does not intend to exercise his irrevocable power of acceptance to permit the offeror to convey the land to another, the offeror may justifiably rely upon the offeree's rejection of the offer in selling the land to another and the offeree's power of acceptance is terminated. *See* RESTATEMENT 2d § 37 ill. 2. If, however, the main offer included terms for payment at a 7½ percent interest rate and, during the option period, the offeree made a counter offer to purchase at a four percent interest rate, this counter offer would not terminate the irrevocable power of acceptance to purchase at the higher interest rate. *See* Kidd v. Early, 289 N.C. 343, 222 S.E.2d 392 (1976). *See also* Title Ins. & Guar. Co. v. Hart, 160 F.2d 961 (9th Cir.), *cert. denied*, 332 U.S. 761 (1947). Though death revokes the typical offer, Bruce v. Dyer, 309 Md. 421, 524 A.2d 777 (1987) and see *supra* § 42(E), death does not revoke an irrevocable power of acceptance. *See, e.g.,* Crowley v. S.E. Bass, 445 So. 2d 902 (Ala. 1984).

[27] This suggestion is primarily attributable to C. LANGDELL, SUMMARY OF THE LAW OF CONTRACTS § 178 (1880).

[28] *See* McGoveny, *Irrevocable Offers*, 27 HARV. L. REV. 644 (1914). *See also* the concurring opinion in Solomon Mier Co. v. Hadden, 148 Mich. 488, 111 N.W. 1040, 1043 (1907): "While it may seem at first blush a legal paradox that a contract for the sale of land, mutual and enforceable, can be made when at the time it is claimed to have been made one party to it is openly protesting that he will make no such contract, and while reasons may be advanced to support the proposition that the option holder should be in such a case remitted to an action for damages for refusal to hold the offer open for the stipulated time, there is reason and precedent for holding that the offer to sell, if paid for, may not be withdrawn during the stipulated time, being, in law, a continuing offer to sell."

[29] A bilateral contract also manifests two promisors and two promisees, whereas a unilateral contract has only one promisor and one promisee. This distinction is set forth *supra* § 16, and

tions, an option contract has been created. There need be no separate consideration, however, since option arrangements often arise in other contexts, e.g., lease contracts where, as an indivisible part of the rental payments, the lessee is paying for the right to purchase the property whenever the owner notifies the lessee that the owner has found a prospective buyer to whom the owner is willing to sell at a certain price. The lessee then has what is often called a right of first refusal to purchase the property.[30] Returning to the typical situation, the consideration for an option contract is often found in what are called "recital clauses," e.g., "In consideration of ten dollars in hand paid." If the ten dollars was not really bargained for but was intended only as "sham" consideration, or if the recited amount was not, in fact, paid, serious questions arise as to the enforceability of the option contract.[31] These questions will be explored in the analysis of consideration later in this volume.[32]

Courts are generally quite insistent that the exercise of an irrevocable power of acceptance conform precisely to the terms of the main offer,[33] that it be exercised in timely fashion,[34] and that the normal rule permitting an acceptance to be effective upon dispatch[35] does not apply to an irrevocable power of acceptance that must be received to be effective.[36]

C. *Firm Offers.*

As we have just seen, at common law, if an offer stated that it would be irrevocable for a certain time it still could be revoked unless the promise not to revoke was supported by consideration forming an option contract. Though

---

further elaboration of acceptance by promise vs. acceptance by performance appears later in this chapter.

[30] In Park-Lake Car Wash, Inc. v. Springer, 352 N.W.2d 409 (Minn. 1984), the court distinguished the right of first refusal provision in a lease by suggesting that such a right requires a condition precedent before it may be exercised, i.e., the owner must have received a bona fide offer from a third party which he or she is willing to accept. Except for this distinction, the court indicates that such a right of first refusal is like any other option. See, however, 1A CORBIN at § 261, where Professor Corbin distinguishes a number of situations under the generic caption, right of first refusal, which are not option contracts.

[31] *See, e.g.,* Hamilton Bancshare, Inc. v. Leroy, 131 Ill. App. 3d 907, 476 N.E.2d 788 (1985).

[32] *See infra* § 61(C).

[33] *See, e.g.,* Westinghouse Broadcasting Co. v. New England Patriots Football Club, Inc., 10 Mass. App. 70, 406 N.E.2d 399, 491 (1980) in which the court stated, "Generally, conditions for the exercise of an option require a more strict degree of adherence than may be the case in provisions of a bilateral contract.... The rationale for the lesser inclination of courts to inquire into the materiality of a breach of an option condition is that an optionee has a unilateral right.... He may choose to compel or not to compel the optionor to a course of performance which intervening facts (*e.g.,* an increase in the value of the optioned rights) may have been made unpalatable to the latter. In the circumstances it may not be too much to ask that a person seeking to keep alive and to exercise option rights turn his corners squarely."

[34] *See* Trueman-Aspen Co. v. North Mill Inv. Corp., 728 P.2d 343 (Colo. App. 1986). *See also* Westinghouse Broadcasting, *supra* note 33.

[35] As will be seen later in this chapter, the so-called "dispatch" or "mailbox" rule makes acceptance effective upon dispatch or mailing in contracts by correspondence unless the offeror otherwise indicates. *See infra* § 47.

[36] *See* Smith v. Hevro Realty Corp., 199 Conn. 330, 507 A.2d 980 (1986). *Contra see* Palo Alto Town & Country Village, Inc. v. BBTC Co., 11 Cal. 3d 494, 113 Cal. Rptr. 705, 521 P.2d 1097 (1974). *See* RESTATEMENT 2d § 63, comment f, which suggests that acceptances under option contracts must be received because the offeree may not speculate at the expense of the offeror since the offeror has already assumed the risk of such speculation by providing an irrevocable power of acceptance for the time stated in the offer.

no payment had been made to keep the offer open, the offeree may have in good faith relied upon the promise of irrevocability. Nonetheless, the offer was still revocable. The manifest injustice of this result has led, *inter alia,* to statutory reforms. The best-known statutory response is found in the UCC. Under the UCC, if a merchant[37] makes an offer in a signed[38] writing[39] which, by its terms, gives assurance that it will be held open, the offer will then be irrevocable for the time stated in the writing or for a reasonable time, but in no event to exceed three months.[40] Since merchants sometimes make offers by signing printed forms supplied by the other party, such a form may contain a "firm offer" provision to which the merchant/offeror may not consciously advert. To avoid the making of inadvertent firm offers, another provision in § 2-205 requires "any such term of assurance on a form supplied by the offeree [to be] separately signed by the offeror."[41]

The purpose of the firm offer provision is to effectuate the deliberate intention of a merchant to make an offer binding for a specified time or a reasonable time since the common law rule that offers assuring irrevocability are still revocable is contrary to modern business practice, i.e., the reasonable understanding of merchants.[42] The basic requirement of the "firm offer" is a deliberate intention to keep an offer open. Absent a manifestation to that effect, the offer will be revocable.[43] If an offer from a merchant in a signed writing merely states the time when the offer will lapse, the offer does not contain the necessary assurance that it will be held open and is, therefore,

---

[37]"Merchant" is defined in § 2-104 of the Code. For most of the sections of Article 2, including the "firm offer" section (2-205), the definition of merchant is so broad that it includes virtually anyone in business. With respect to the implied warranty of merchantability in § 2-314, however, the merchant must be one who regularly deals in goods of that kind. *See* comment 2 to § 2-104.

[38]*See* UCC § 1-201(39) which includes a very broad definition of "signed," i.e., "any symbol executed or adopted by a party with present intention to authenticate a writing." Comment 39 indicates that this would include a printed, stamped or written signature, initials or thumbprint, and in appropriate cases may be satisfied by the printed billhead or letterhead of the purported signer.

[39]*See* UCC § 1-201(46) defining "written" or "writing" as including printing, typewriting or any other intentional reduction to tangible form.

[40]UCC § 2-205. Under the N.Y. GEN. OBL. LAW § 5-1109, a written and signed offer stating that it will be irrevocable for a stated period will be irrevocable for the period stated or, if no time is stated, for a reasonable time, without any limitation to three months or otherwise. The statute, however, expressly excepts offers by merchants in contracts for the sale of goods under the UCC since New York, like all other states in the United States except Louisiana, has adopted Article 2 of the Code and § 2-205, therefore, applies exclusively to such offers.

[41]*See* UCC § 2-205 and particularly comment 4 to that section. The broad definition of "signed" suggested *supra* note 38, suggests that the offeror may meet this requirement by the normal device of inserting his or her initials in the space adjacent to the firm offer provision in the printed form supplied by the offeree. This is the normal practice though other forms of separate signing would be acceptable. The separate signing requirement is one of several safeguards found in Article 2 of the Code. A similar requirement is found in § 2-209(2) where a "no oral modification" clause on a form supplied by a merchant must be separately signed by a non-merchant. Still another safeguard is found in § 2-316(2), requiring a written disclaimer of the implied warranty of merchantability to be "conspicuous" as defined in § 1-201(10). These and other safeguards are in keeping with the underlying philosophy of Article 2 to identify, more precisely and fairly, the factual bargain of the parties, i.e., their actual or fairly presumed manifestation of mutual assent. *See* Murray, *The Article 2 Prism: The Underlying Philosophy of Article 2 of the Uniform Commercial Code,* 21 WASHBURN L.J. 1 (1982).

[42]*See* comment 2 to UCC § 2-205 and E. A. Coronis Assocs. v. M. Gordon Constr. Co., 90 N.J. Super. 69, 216 A.2d 246 (1966).

[43]*See* Janke Constr. Co. v. Vulcan Materials Co., 386 F. Supp. 687 (W.D. Wis. 1974).

revocable.[44] Otherwise, offerors who intend to make revocable offers lasting for a certain period would be surprised to discover they had made irrevocable offers simply by stating the period after which the offer will lapse. This was not the intention of the drafters of § 2-205, but interpretation problems remain[45] and the case law has yet to focus upon these problems. It is clear that the assurance of irrevocability must be expressly stated; it will not be implied.[46] Often, however, the question will be left to the trier of fact.[47]

A UCC firm offer will become revocable at the end of three months regardless of whether it stated a term of irrevocability longer than three months, or whether, in the absence of a stated period, a reasonable time under the circumstances would exceed three months.[48] The section was not designed for long term options[49] and the three month period is considered an absolute limitation. If the offer is "firm" until the occurrence of a contingency that will

---

[44]This is an important distinction that should not be overlooked. If the offer merely states that it is open for a specified time, it should be construed to lapse at the end of that period and it should be revocable during that period. Whether the time is fixed for lapse or for irrevocability is a question of interpretation. This question was addressed in the creation of Article 16 of the United Nations Convention on Contracts for the International Sale of Goods (effective in the United States as of January 1, 1988) which reads as follows:

(1) Until a contract is concluded an offer may be revoked if the revocation reaches the offeree before he has dispatched an acceptance.
(2) However, an offer cannot be revoked:
(a) if it indicates, *whether by stating a fixed time limit or otherwise, that it is irrevocable;* or
(b) if it was reasonable for the offeree to rely on the offer as being irrevocable and the offeree has acted in reliance on the offer. (emphasis added)

Professor Farnsworth suggests that this language is not entirely clear and further suggests that an offeror wishing to fix a time for lapse and not for irrevocability should make his intention plain under the Convention. *See* Farnsworth, *Formation of Contract,* § 3.04, 3-11-3-12 in INTERNATIONAL SALES: THE UNITED NATIONS CONVENTION ON CONTRACTS FOR THE INTERNATIONAL SALE OF GOODS (Galston & Smit eds. 1984).

[45]In comparing § 2-205 with the similar N.Y. GEN. OBL. LAW § 5-1109 when the UCC was under study for enactment in New York, Professor Patterson of the Columbia Law School suggested the following: "Since both statutes recognize that offers are 'ordinarily' revocable, by what criterion shall a court or a counselor determine when an offer is 'firm'? The New York statute may be construed to require an explicit statement in the writing, such as: 'This offer shall be irrevocable for ten days,' or 'This offer shall be irrevocable,' or 'We offer you irrevocably,' or 'The foregoing offer is not to be withdrawn before November 1st.' All of these would, it seems, satisfy the requirement of Section 2-205. Now consider this statement: 'This offer will not be kept open after November 1st.' This seems insufficient under [the New York statute]; does it 'give assurance that it will be held open' until November 1st? Probably not; but a decision of the highest court might be necessary to settle such cases. Suppose the offer is 'We offer you for acceptance within ten days.' Does this 'give assurance' that it will be kept open? It might be so held under Section 2-205; but surely not under [the New York statute]. A time limitation is often inserted to protect the *offeror,* so that the offer will lapse unless accepted within that time." Statement of Professor Edwin Patterson, 1 STATE OF NEW YORK LAW REVISION COMMISSION REPORT, STUDY OF THE UNIFORM COMMERCIAL CODE 614 (1955).

[46]Ivey's Plumbing & Elec. Co. v. Petrochem Main., Inc., 463 F. Supp. 543 (N.D. Miss. 1978). If the offer states that the offeree has "the non-exclusive right to purchase ... for a period of thirty (30) days," it is not a firm offer since it expressly provided that it was non-exclusive. Friedman v. Sommer, 63 N.Y.2d 788, 471 N.E.2d 139 (1984). It is noteworthy that the court in this case applied § 2-205 to a sale of a cooperative apartment which was, according to the court, in reality a sale of securities in a cooperative corporation. The court relied upon Weiss v. Karch, 62 N.Y.2d 849, 477 N.Y.S.2d 615, 466 N.E.2d 155 (1984).

[47]*See* City Univ. of New York v. Finalco, Inc., 93 App. Div. 2d 792, 461 N.Y.S.2d 830 (1983).
[48]*See* Mid-South Packers, Inc. v. Shoney's, Inc., 761 F.2d 1117 (5th Cir. 1985).
[49]*See* comment 3 to UCC § 2-205.

occur within three months, the offer will remain irrevocable until that time.[50] Thereafter, if the offer has not lapsed, it is revocable.[51]

It is appropriate to characterize the UCC firm offer as an option contract, since it has the effect of such a contract, with the limitations noted above. Similarly, other "statutory firm offers"[52] may also be viewed as option contracts in terms of their effect.[53] These statutes simply remove the consideration requirement of classical option contracts. Again, it must be emphasized that the particular firm offer statute may be limited in ways similar to the UCC with respect to the type of contract involved, qualifications of the offeror, formal requirements of a writing that must be signed, and even an outside time limitation. Different statutes will have different limitations.[54] Whether the device is the classical option contract, a statutory firm offer, or one of the devices yet to be discussed in this section, the purpose is the same: to protect the justifiable reliance and expectations of the offeree.

D. *Irrevocability Through Part Performance — Section 45 of the* RESTATE-MENT *2d.*

The typical offer is indifferent as to how it may be accepted, i.e., by promise or by performance.[55] With respect to such offers, the power of acceptance may be exercised in any reasonable manner.[56] As master of the offer, however, the offeror may prescribe a particular manner of acceptance and the offeree must comply with that prescription in order to accept the offer.[57] The case law suggests that it is rare for an offeror to insist upon a performance acceptance, but if the offeror prescribes that exclusive manner of acceptance, acceptance can occur only in that fashion.[58] The nature of the offer may dictate the manner of acceptance though there is no express limitation found in the offer. The obvious example is an offer to the public such as a reward offer which does not contemplate a promissory acceptance.[59] Where the offer can be ac-

---

[50] *Ibid.*

[51] *See* Mid-South Packers, Inc. v. Shoney's, Inc., *supra* note 48.

[52] *See supra* note 40, which contains an analysis of the statutory firm offer in New York.

[53] RESTATEMENT 2d § 87(2) so views statutory firm offers.

[54] *See supra* note 40. In an auction without reserve, the offer is irrevocable for the reasonable time of the bidding. UCC § 2-328(3). For an analysis of auctions without reserve, *see supra* § 36 A. Under statutes authorizing or requiring government units to award contracts on the basis of competitive bidding, the public officials may refuse to permit the withdrawal of a bid after it is opened. *See* RESTATEMENT 2d § 87 comment d.

[55] *See* Murray, *Contracts: A New Design for the Agreement Process,* 53 CORNELL L. REV. 785 (1968).

[56] *See* UCC § 2-206(1) and RESTATEMENT 2d § 30(2). *See also* Deukmejian v. Cory, 155 Cal. App. 3d 494, 202 Cal. Rptr. 611 (1984).

[57] RESTATEMENT 2d § 60 indicating that the offer may prescribe the place, time or manner of acceptance, all of which must be complied with if the power of acceptance is to be exercised. If the offeror merely *suggests* a permitted place, time or manner of acceptance, however, other methods of acceptance are not precluded. *See also* § 30 and comment a. *See* Overman v. B.G. Brown, 220 Neb. 788, 372 N.W.2d 102 (1985). *See also* Panhandle Eastern Pipe Line Co. v. Nowlin Smith, Jr., 637 P.2d 1020 (Wyo. 1981) (where there is a dispute concerning the mode of acceptance, the offer itself must clearly and definitely express an exclusive mode of acceptance).

[58] *See, e.g.,* BC Tire Corp. v. GTE Directories Corp., 46 Wash. App. 351, 730 P.2d 726 (1987).

[59] Another example is the promise of guaranty which is accepted by the promisee or extending credit to a third party pursuant to the assurance of the guarantor to pay the promisee if the third party fails to pay.

cepted exclusively by performance, the contract will be formed when performance is completed. At that time, a unilateral contract will be formed with one right in the former offeree, and one duty in the former offeror. An attempt by the offeree to accept such an offer by promising would be ineffective. Therefore, if the offeree wishes to accept, he or she must perform the act required by the offeror in exchange for the offeror's promise. There is only one promisor and one promisee in such a contract. On the basis of this analysis, and remembering the common law obsession that offers are revocable absent an option contract, a classic problem arises. The best-known exposition of this problem is found in Professor Wormser's analysis utilizing the following hypothetical:

A offers to pay B $100 if B will walk across the Brooklyn bridge and B can accept only by performing, i.e., walking across the bridge. B wants to accept the offer and begins walking across the bridge. When B is halfway across, A shouts, "I revoke the offer." At this point, there is no contract since A did not offer to pay B in exchange for B's walking partway across the bridge. B must complete the act to accept the offer and form the contract. A's duty and B's correlative right to payment, therefore, do not arise until B completes the walk across the bridge.

Classical contract theory requires the revocation to be effective since the offer was revocable. Yet, the result appears harsh to B who has begun to perform in the only manner possible to accept the offer and, while in the process of performing, B's power to accept has been withdrawn by A's revocation. Notwithstanding the harshness of the result, Professor Wormser insisted that the revocation was effective since the offeree, B, was under no contractual duty to complete the walk across the bridge and had not promised to complete the walk. Of course, B's promise would be ineffective to exercise the power of acceptance. Wormser believed that since B was not bound to complete the walk, A should not be bound by any contractual duty prior to the completion of the walk by B. Otherwise, one party would be bound and the other party would not be bound.[60]

The classic exposition of the problem did not consider a number of factors. While it is possible for an offeree who is in the process of performing the requested act to have a change of heart and fail to complete the act, that result is unlikely. The probabilities are strong that the offeree intends to complete the act once beginning to perform. By starting to perform, B evidences a present intention to complete performance in reliance on the offer, and has a reasonable expectation that there will be the opportunity to complete performance, thereby forming the contract and obtaining the right to the performance promised by the offeror. In the bridge hypothetical, if the offeree is prevented from completing performance through the offeror's revocation, there is no remedy available. If the offer was to paint the offeror's house with a promise to pay $1000 upon the completion of the painting and acceptance could occur only through performance, and if the offer was revoked after the house was half-painted, it is possible that the offeree could recover the reasonable value of the benefit conferred on the offeror through an action protecting

---

[60]Wormser, *The True Conception of Unilateral Contracts*, 26 YALE L.J. 136 (1916).

the offeree's restitution interest.[61] In the bridge example, however, no measurable benefit is conferred on the offeror. A restitutionary remedy is, therefore, precluded. Yet, the offeree has suffered a detriment, i.e., the offeree has expended time and effort in performing up to the point of revocation and the act the offeree was in the process of performing was an act requested by the offeror. It was inevitable that the manifest injustice resulting from permitting the offeror to revoke as the offeree is attempting to complete performance would be overcome. The only question was, what theory would be devised to support the inevitable result?

One of the earliest theories solved the problem very simply: When the offeree begins performance, the contract takes on a bilateral character, i.e., we will treat the beginning of performance as the offeree's promise to complete performance.[62] There is considerable difficulty in discovering how an offer for a unilateral contract takes on a bilateral character through the offeree's part performance.[63] Moreover, if the offeree who has not promised to complete performance decides, after part performance, to stop performing, the offeree would have breached the contract formed by the part performance. It was important to develop another theory that did not contain these analytical and practical impediments.

The FIRST RESTATEMENT announced its theory in what may have become the most familiar section of that work, Section 45.[64] Under this theory, a contract is formed upon part performance, but the offeror's duty under that contract is conditioned upon his receiving the completed performance requested in the offer within the time stated in the offer or, in the absence of a stated time, within a reasonable time. A case which antedated the original § 45 disclosed an offer to the offeror's son-in-law which stated that if he would move from Missouri to Maine and care for the offeror for the remainder of her life, he would have the offeror's farm upon her death. The court held that the contract was complete when the offeree moved from Missouri to Maine but the offeree would not be entitled to the farm unless he performed the condition to the offeror's duty, i.e., caring for her until her death.[65] While this theory is somewhat superior to the "bilateral" theory, it is still not in keeping with the manifested intention of the offeror who did not want part performance as an acceptance, but full performance. In the offer to the son-in-law, full perfor-

---

[61] In such a case, no genuine contract would exist since the act was not completed. However, when one party confers a benefit on another at the request of the other, and there is a contemplation that the performing party expects to be compensated, an action in quasi contract may lie to prevent the unjust enrichment of the offeror at the expense of the offeree. The restitution interest of the offeree is thereby protected. An analysis of the restitution interest and devices to accomplish it, such as quasi contract, will be found later in this volume.

[62] See Los Angeles Traction Co. v. Wilshire, 135 Cal. 654, 67 P. 1086 (1902).

[63] "This is a remarkable instance of confusion of thought. By what magic the offer had been turned into a 'contract' does not appear." Ashley, *Offers Calling for a Consideration Other Than a Counter Promise,* 23 HARV. L. REV. 159, 164 (1910).

[64] Section 45 of the FIRST RESTATEMENT reads as follows: "If an offer for a unilateral contract is made, and part of the consideration requested in the offer is given or tendered by the offeree in response thereto, the offeror is bound by a contract, the duty of immediate performance of which is conditioned on full consideration being given or tendered within the time stated in the offer, or, if no time is stated, within a reasonable time."

[65] Brackenbury v. Hodgkin, 116 Me. 399, 102 A. 106 (1917). *See also* Winslow v. White, 163 N.C. 29, 79 S.E. 258 (1913).

mance could not possibly occur until the death of the offeror. By placing a duty on the offeror when the offeree performed in part, however, the theory manages to avoid revocation of the offer, thereby protecting the offeree against harsh results. At the same time, by implying a condition to the constructed duty of the offeror upon part performance that the remainder of performance must occur before the duty is activated, the original § 45 achieves the necessary result and still permits the offeree to refuse to complete performance with impunity. Though the result is just, there was no need to resort to several fictions antagonistic to otherwise desirable contract theory. This was particularly true in light of a more desirable theory set forth in the comment to the original § 45:

> The main offer includes as a subsidiary promise, necessarily implied, that if part of the requested performance is given, the offeror will not revoke his offer, and that if tender is made it will be accepted.[66]

While this theory implies a promise, it is a more than plausible implication and arrives at the desired result without the necessity of any further implication or fiction. Moreover, it preserves the intention of the offeror and the reasonable understanding of the offeree that no contract is formed until performance is completed. This analysis is indistinguishable from that set forth in the RESTATEMENT 2d § 45 which implies a subsidiary promise not to revoke the offer. The implied subsidiary promise is accepted by part performance forming an option contract.[67]

Section 45, in its original FIRST RESTATEMENT form or in the option contract mode of the RESTATEMENT 2d, can be applied to any offer requiring a performance acceptance where the question of revocability of the offer occurs. It has been applied in a cluster of cases involving performance by real estate brokers under exclusive agency or exclusive right to sell arrangements.[68] It also appears in cases involving services by employees pursuant to retirement plans or other employee benefits[69] and sundry other applications. There is no question that the concept is universally accepted.[70] Any problems connected with a § 45 theory are now interpretation problems.

---

[66] FIRST RESTATEMENT § 45 comment b.

[67] RESTATEMENT 2d § 45 states:

(1) Where an offeror invites an offeree to accept by rendering a performance and does not invite a promissory acceptance, an option contract is created when the offeree begins the invited performance or tenders part of it.

(2) The offeror's duty of performance under any option contract so created is conditional on completion or tender of the invited performance in accordance with the terms of the offer.

[68] Under an "exclusive agency," the owner may still sell the property himself. Under an "exclusive right to sell," he may not do so. Cases applying § 45 in situations involving performance by real estate brokers include Rainier Fund, Inc. v. Bloomfield Real Estate Co., 717 P.2d 850 (Alaska 1986); Ladd v. Teichman, 359 Mich. 587, 103 N.W.2d 338 (1960); Hutchinson v. Dobson-Brainbridge Realty Co., 31 Tenn. App. 490, 217 S.W.2d 6 (1946). It has also been applied to a real estate broker's situation involving a non-exclusive agency: Marchiondo v. Scheck, 78 N.M. 440, 432 P.2d 405 (1967).

[69] See, e.g., Marvel v. Dannemann, 490 F. Supp. 170 (D. Del. 1980); Cangott v. ASG Indus., 558 P.2d 379 (1976); Taylor v. Multnomah Cty. Deputy Sheriff's Ret. Bd., 265 Or. 445, 510 P.2d 339 (1973); Sylvestre v. State, 298 Minn. 142, 214 N.W.2d 658 (1973).

[70] Even Professor Wormser, who created the famous Brooklyn bridge hypothetical, recanted more than three decades later: "[N]ow, clad in sackcloth, I state frankly, that my point of view has

1. Starting Performance Versus Preparation.

For an offer to become irrevocable under § 45, performance, as contrasted with mere preparation for performance, must have begun. The line between performance and mere preparation, in a given case, may not be very bright. It can be particularly difficult when the act requested by the offer is one that can be performed almost instantaneously. The classic example is found in the well-known case of *Petterson v. Pattberg*[71] in which the holder of a mortgage (the mortgagee) offered to accept a lesser amount than the full amount due on the mortgage debt if the debt was paid in advance of the original maturity date. The offeree (mortgagor) proceeded to raise the money which he brought to the residence of the offeror and, after identifying himself said, "I have come to pay off the mortgage." The offeror answered, "I have sold the mortgage," which was equivalent to revoking the offer. If performance had begun, the offer could not be revoked. What was the performance required by the offer? The court held that the required performance was the act of "payment" which required the cooperation of the offeror, i.e., the act of payment requires a tender of the payment (by the offeree) *and* the acceptance of that payment by the offeror. By presenting himself at the door of the offeror and announcing that he had come to pay off the mortgage, the court held that the offeree had not even tendered payment but had merely taken the necessary preparatory step to make a tender. From this perspective, the case was easily decided. The member of the court who wrote the majority opinion, however, stated his individual view that the result would not have changed even if the offeree had made a tender of payment.[72] It cannot be gainsaid that this analysis is unsound. The court had no difficulty in deciding that an offer had been made. Yet, the acceptance of that offer required the cooperation of the offeror, i.e., he must assent to the payment tendered by the offeree. The fundamental flaw in this analysis is its failure to consider the legal effect of any offer: the creation of a power of acceptance in the offeree which makes the offeror susceptible to the exercise of that power. A contract may be formed regardless of the desire of the offeror at the moment of acceptance. If the offeree in *Petterson* had a power of acceptance, the only act he could perform to exercise that power was the tender of payment. He could not thrust the money on the offeror. If the offeror refused to cooperate in accepting the money, the offeree was powerless to insist that it be taken. Thus, if a tender of payment had occurred in this case, the offeree would have done more than begin performance by such a tender; he would have *completed* performance by that tender since he could perform no other or additional act to accept the offer. The RESTATEMENT 2d deals effectively with this situation by finding an acceptance upon tender.[73]

---

changed. I agree, at this time, with the rule set forth in the Restatement...." Book Review, 3 J. LEGAL EDUC. 145, 146 (1950).

[71] 248 N.Y. 86, 161 N.E. 428 (1928).

[72] Justice Kellogg stated this view.

[73] *See* RESTATEMENT 2d § 45(1), "... an option contract is created when the offeree *tenders* or begins performance" (emphasis added) and comment c. Nine years after the *Petterson* case, New York enacted a statute precluding revocation of a signed offer after tender, N.Y. GEN. OBL. LAW § 15-503.

Since the entire act of tender is completed in a moment, it is difficult to apply a § 45 analysis to this type of act though it is theoretically possible to do so.[74] Again, however, mere preparation for performance, though it may be essential to performing the act required by the offer, is not performance and such preparation will not cause the offer to become irrevocable.[75] Some assistance in drawing the line between preparation and performance may be found in a well-known case dealing with that question. In *White v. Corlies*,[76] the offeror desired the remodeling of his office and received specifications from the offeree. Satisfied with the specifications, the offeror stated, "You may begin at once." The offeree purchased lumber and began to work on the lumber prior to the revocation. The work he performed, however, was suitable for many other applications, i.e., it was not specifically referable to the performance required by the offer. The court, therefore, held that performance had not begun. The RESTATEMENT 2d adopts this illustration[77] and suggests that the distinction between preparing for performance and beginning performance may turn on, *inter alia*, "the extent to which the offeree's conduct is clearly referable to the offer."[78]

2. Reconciling the Mitigation Principle.

A final problem is raised in reconciling the § 45 theory with the general principle of contract law concerning the mitigation of damages. Where *A* and *B* have formed a contract and before the performance by *B* is complete *A* informs *B* that *A* will not perform, i.e., *A* repudiates the contract, the innocent party, *B*, may not recover any damages he could have avoided had he stopped performing at the time of repudiation.[79] Under § 45, the main contract is not formed until *B* completes his performance. If *A* attempts to revoke after performance has begun but before it is completed, surely *A* does not wish the contract to continue. *A*'s attempted revocation may not be arbitrary; he could have a sound reason for his announced desire that *B* cease performing.[80] If the condition to *A*'s duty is the completion of performance by *B*, on the face of § 45, *B* would face the dilemma of either completing performance and violating the

---

[74] Tender of payment would be accomplished by the act of attempting to hand the money to the offeror. Though the act is accomplished almost instantaneously, it is conceivable that sufficient evidence could be adduced that tender had begun before the attempted revocation, thereby precluding an effective revocation. Thus, if the offeror had come to the door after the offeree identified himself and announced that he had come to pay off the mortgage, and if the offeree, with the cash in hand had started his arm in motion to hand it to the offeror at which moment the offeror had said, "Offer revoked" or "I have sold the mortgage," the offer could be said to have been irrevocable before the attempted revocation.

[75] *See* RESTATEMENT 2d § 45 comment f.

[76] 46 N.Y. 467 (1871).

[77] *See* RESTATEMENT 2d § 62 ill. 1.

[78] RESTATEMENT 2d § 45 comment f.

[79] There is no "duty" on the part of the innocent party, *B*, to mitigate (lessen) damages by acting reasonably after the breach. However, *B* may not recover damages he could have avoided after that time. The mitigation principle will be fully explored in the later chapter on contract remedies.

[80] Though it was not a unilateral contract situation, in the well-known case of Rockingham Cty. v. Luten Bridge Co., 35 F.2d 301 (4th Cir. 1929), the county commissioners informed a bridge builder before completion of the bridge to stop building because no road would connect to the bridge, i.e., it would be a bridge to nowhere.

mitigation principle, or ceasing performance and not fulfilling the condition to
A's duty. The problem is solved by *excusing* the condition to the activation of
A's duty if the offeror prevents performance or repudiates the contract.[81] B
would, in such a case, recover the contract price promised by A, less any
amount saved by not having to perform the remainder of the contract.

E. *Irrevocability Through Reliance.*

One of the major validation devices that will be explored in the chapter
dealing with the validation process is detrimental reliance, popularly known
as "promissory estoppel." In essence, that device will make a promise enforceable if the promisee justifiably suffers a detriment by changing his position in
reliance on the promise where the promisor should reasonably expect his
promise to induce such reliance.[82] The question arises, may an offer become
irrevocable if the offeree has relied on that offer? It would be a simple matter
for any offeree to rely upon any offer and thereby attempt to make an otherwise revocable offer irrevocable. Absent one or more of the devices explored in
this section, the common law principle that offers are revocable remains
steadfast. If the X Corporation offers to sell steel to the Y Corporation, Y may
pursue activity with the expectation of accepting the X offer. It may prepare
to receive steel from X; it may reject an offer from another potential supplier
because it intends to accept X's offer; Y may even change its production plans
in anticipation of receiving the steel from X. Absent other circumstances, this
type of reliance on a typical offer in a commercial transaction is not justifiable. Y may engage in any number of preparatory steps which, we have seen,
will not make the offer irrevocable since performance has not begun. Whatever activity Y may pursue in anticipation of a contract with X, it is commercially unreasonable to pursue such action before exercising its power of acceptance in response to X's offer. X has no reason to assume that its offer has
induced Y to change its position in reliance on the offer. Thus, regardless of
Y's activity, X may revoke the offer. There are, however, situations where
reliance on an offer may be justifiable.

The paradigm involves an offer by a subcontractor to a general contractor
who intends to submit a bid (offer) on a particular building project. General
contractors must assemble their bids from a series of subcontractors' bids —
the plumbing, electrical, carpentry, masonry and other necessary parts of a
building project. Having assembled all of the sub bids, the general contractor
then submits his or her bid/offer for the complete project. Typically, the general's bid/offer will be irrevocable.[83] Each subcontractor submitting a bid
knows or has reason to know that the general's bid is irrevocable. The general
contractor is in no position to accept the bids of the subcontractors used in

---

[81] *See* RESTATEMENT 2d § 45 comment e.

[82] *See* RESTATEMENT 2d § 90.

[83] "[W]hen statutes authorize or require that government work be awarded to contractors on the
basis of competitive bidding, it may be fairly implied that the public officials in charge may
protect the integrity of the competition by refusing to allow a bid to be withdrawn after bids are
opened." RESTATEMENT 2d § 87 comment d. General contractors may have to submit a bid bond
issued by a bonding company in the business of assuring the performance of the building contract
according to the bid price if the general is awarded the contract and fails to perform.

making the general bid because he or she may not be awarded the contract and would have no use for the labor and materials to be supplied by the subcontractors. If, however, the general is the winner of the competitive bidding contest, he or she is then committed to performing the entire job at the total bid price, and that price is predicated upon the various bids of subcontractors the general has used in computing the final, total bid. The question arises, if the general is awarded the contract, should one or more subcontractors be able to revoke their offers before the general has an opportunity to accept the very offers used in computing his bid?

This was the issue in two cases which came before courts numbering among their judges two of the judicial giants of the twentieth century, Judge Learned Hand of the United States Court of Appeals for the Second Circuit, and Justice Roger Traynor of the Supreme Court of California. These brilliant judges wrote the opinions for their courts in these cases where the issue was whether the relatively new validation device of detrimental reliance (promissory estoppel)[84] which had been applied to unbargained-for promises, i.e., otherwise gratuitous promises which had been justifiably relied upon,[85] should now be applied to a commercial transaction in a bargained-for exchange context. In *James Baird Company v. Gimbel Brothers, Inc.*, Judge Hand wrote:

> Offers are ordinarily made in exchange for consideration, either a counter-promise or some other act which the promisor wishes to secure. In such cases they propose bargains; they presuppose that each promise or performance is an inducement to the other.... But a man may make a promise without expecting an equivalent; a donative promise, conditional or absolute. The common law provided for such by sealed instruments, and it is unfortunate that these are no longer generally available. The doctrine of "promissory estoppel" is to avoid the harsh results of allowing the promisor in such a case to repudiate when the promisee has acted in reliance upon the promise. . . . But an offer for an exchange is not meant to become a promise until a consideration has been received, either a counter-promise or whatever else is stipulated. To extend it would be to hold the offeror regardless of the stipulated condition of his offer. . . . There is no room in such a situation for the doctrine of "promissory estoppel."[86]

Justice Traynor did not agree:

> When plaintiff [general contractor] used defendant's [subcontractor's] offer in computing his own bid, he bound himself to perform in reliance on defendant's terms. Though defendant did not bargain for this use of its bid neither did defendant make it idly, indifferent to whether it would be used or not. On the contrary, it is reasonable to suppose that defendant submitted its bid to obtain the subcontract. It was bound to realize the substantial possibility that its bid would be the lowest, and that it would be included by plaintiff in his bid. It was to its own interest that the contractor

---

[84] As will be seen, the antecedents of promissory estoppel are very old, even older than the traditional validation device, consideration.

[85] The typical case was a gift promise with reliance, such as a charitable subscription promise. See the most famous exposition of this doctrine in such a context in the opinion by Benjamin Cardozo in Allegheny College v. National Chautauqua Cty. Bank, 246 N.Y. 369, 159 N.E. 173 (1927).

[86] 64 F.2d 344, 346 (2d Cir. 1933).

be awarded the general contract; the lower the subcontract bid, the lower the general contractor's bid was likely to be and the greater its chance of acceptance and hence the greater the defendant's chance of getting the . . . subcontract. Defendant had reason not only to expect plaintiff to rely on its bid but to want him to. Clearly defendant had a stake in plaintiff's reliance on its bid. Given this interest and the fact that plaintiff is bound by his own bid, it is only fair that plaintiff should have at least an opportunity to accept defendant's bid after the general contract has been awarded to him.[87]

Justice Traynor analogized the situation to a § 45 situation making the offer irrevocable upon part performance, and specifically relied upon a Comment to § 45 in the original RESTATEMENT: "[M]erely acting in justifiable reliance on an offer may in some cases serve as sufficient reason for making a promise binding (see § 90)."[88] That concept is now reflected in a subsection of the RESTATEMENT 2d.[89] Traynor discovered an implied subsidiary promise on the part of the subcontractor not to revoke the offer since the subcontractor must have foreseen the reasonable change of position in reliance upon the offer by the general contractor whose foreseeable course of performance was to include the subcontractor's bid in the general bid. Having implied the subsidiary promise, the detrimental reliance of the general contractor was sufficient to make the subcontractor's offer irrevocable for a reasonable time. In effect, an option contract was created through detrimental reliance rather than part performance, providing the offeree/general contractor with an irrevocable power of acceptance for a reasonable time after being awarded the general contract.

Both solutions to the subcontractor/general contractor problem suggest negative ramifications. If the Hand approach is followed, the general contractor will have no legal remedy if the subcontractor revokes before the general accepts the sub's offer but after the general's bid has been accepted. A subcontractor who becomes known for pursuing such practice may face extra-legal sanctions affecting his business, but the general contractor remains affected. If the Traynor approach is followed, the general need not accept the bid of the subcontractor after being awarded the contract since the general made no promise to the subcontractor.[90] This creates the unfortunate situation of one party being bound while the other (general) is not bound. Some general contractors may use the lowest subcontractors' bids in order to get the job and then make contracts with other subcontractors with whom they intended to contract from the inception. This practice and others favoring the general contractor, who often has superior bargaining power in any event, wars against the application of the Traynor position.[91] Justice Traynor sought to overcome some of the potential inequities in his analysis by insisting that a general contractor is not free to delay acceptance after being awarded the

---

[87] Drennan v. Star Paving Co., 51 Cal. 2d 409, 333 P.2d 757, 760 (1958).

[88] FIRST RESTATEMENT § 45 comment b.

[89] RESTATEMENT 2d § 87(2).

[90] Milone & Tucci, Inc. v. Bona Fide Bldrs., 49 Wash. 2d 363, 301 P.2d 759 (1956); Williams v. Favret, 161 F.2d 822 (5th Cir. 1947).

[91] See Schultz, The Firm Offer Puzzle: A Study of Business Practice in the Construction Industry, 19 U. Chi. L. Rev. 237 (1952). See also Note, Another Look at Construction Bidding and Contracts at Formation, 53 VA. L. REV. 1720 (1967).

general contract, nor can the general reopen bargaining with the subcontractor and still claim an irrevocable power of acceptance with respect to the original offer, i.e., delays in acceptance or attempts to "chisel" the price with the subcontractor will result in the loss of the irrevocable power of acceptance.[92] Statutory protection of subcontractors is also afforded in some jurisdictions by requiring that the general list the names of the subcontractors in his bids[93] and that such named subcontractors may not be changed by the general contractor without the consent of the owner.[94]

The overwhelming majority of courts considering this question have adopted the Traynor position.[95] That position is also supported by the RESTATEMENT 2d which characterizes an offer by a subcontract or made irrevocable by detrimental reliance as another form of option contract.[96] In keeping with its general concept of detrimental reliance to be explored later in this volume, the RESTATEMENT 2d limits the option contract protection "to the extent necessary to avoid injustice."[97] Presumably, any nefarious activity on the part of the general contractor after being awarded the general contract by, for example, unnecessarily delaying the acceptance of the subcontractor's offer or attempting to renegotiate with the subcontractor for a lower price, would immediately eliminate the protection of an irrevocable offer enjoyed by the general contractor under this RESTATEMENT provision.

There can be no question that the concept of detrimental reliance is now available to protect reliance interests in pre-formation situations other than the subcontractor-general contractor model, even where there may be no offer.[98] That doctrine will be fully explored in the next chapter dealing with the Validation Process.[99]

---

[92] 333 P.2d 757, 760.

[93] See MASS. ANN. LAWS ch. 149, §§ 44A-44I and particularly § 44F (1980).

[94] See Subletting and Subcontracting Fair Practices Act, CAL. GOV'T CODE § 4100 et seq., particularly § 4107 proscribing the substitution by the prime contractor of a subcontractor listed in the original bid. See Coast Pump Assocs. v. Stephen Tyler Corp., 62 Cal. App. 3d 421, 133 Cal. Rptr. 88 (1976).

[95] Arango Constr. Co. v. Success Roofing, Inc., 46 Wash. App. 314, 730 P.2d 720 (1986); Powers Constr. Co. v. Salem Carpets, Inc., 283 S.C. 302, 322 S.E.2d 30 (1984); Illinois Valley Asphalt, Inc. v. I. F. Edwards Constr. Co., 90 Ill. App. 3d 768, 413 N.E.2d 209 (1980); Montgomery Indus. Int'l, Inc. v. Thomas Constr. Co., 620 F.2d 90 (5th Cir. 1980) (Texas law); Janke Constr. Co. v. Vulcan Materials Co., 386 F. Supp. 687 (W.D. Wis. 1974); James King & Son, Inc. v. DeSantis Constr. No. 2 Corp., 97 Misc. 2d 1063, 413 N.Y.S.2d 78 (Sup. Ct. 1977); Constructors Supply Co. v. Bostrom Sheet Metal Works, Inc., 291 Minn. 113, 190 N.W.2d 71 (1971); N. Litterio & Co. v. Glassman Constr. Co., 319 F.2d 736 (D.C. Cir. 1963).

[96] RESTATEMENT 2d § 87(2) and comment e.

[97] Id.

[98] See Hoffman v. Red Owl Stores, Inc., 26 Wis. 2d 683, 133 N.W.2d 267 (1965); Wheeler v. White, 398 S.W.2d. 93 (Tex. 1965); Goodman v. Dicker, 269 F.2d 684 (1948). For an analysis of such cases, see Henderson, Promissory Estoppel and Traditional Contract Doctrine, 78 YALE L.J. 343, 360 (1969).

[99] Infra Chapter 3.

§ 44. Nature of an Acceptance.

A. *The Essence of Acceptance.*

We have already seen that an offer confers upon the offeree a power — the power to cause a contract to come into being by giving the act, forebearance or promise required or invited by the offer *and* by manifesting assent to the offer.[1] It is important to emphasize the dual nature of the act of acceptance. Normally, when the offeree makes the promise or performs the act required or invited by the offer, the promise or act, itself, manifests assent to the offer. There are, however, some cases in which this is not so as will appear from the exploration that follows.

B. *Can an Offer Be Accepted Without Knowledge of Its Existence?*

It is possible for a person to perform an act required to accept an offer without knowledge that the offer exists. A person may, for example, bring about the arrest and conviction of a criminal not knowing that a reward has been offered for the act which has been performed. Does a contract come into being under these circumstances? If the reward offer was private, it contemplated a bargain, i.e., it sought to induce action on the part of any member of the public capable of such action. If a person acted without knowledge of the reward, he was not induced to act by the reward offer and had no expectation of receiving payment under the reward offer when he completed the act. He had, therefore, no power of acceptance; he was not an offeree. The case law is clear that no contract can come into existence unless the offeree knew of the offer when he or she performed the act required by the offer.[2] Governmental bodies may provide standing reward offers to create an atmosphere in which people do certain acts with the hope of earning unknown rewards and the performance of the required act without knowledge of the reward may, in such "public" reward cases, give rise to recovery of the offered amount.[3] If a person performs such an act with the hope that he will subsequently discover a standing public reward offer, it is theoretically possible to view the act as an exchange for the reward offer and, therefore, a bargain between the offeror and the party performing the act. If the same act were performed with respect to a specific, private reward offer, however, there is no basis for suggesting a bargain and there is no acceptance of the offer. Even in the standing government reward offer situation, the preferable analysis is that the reward is paid for policy reasons, e.g., creating an atmosphere of assistance in the minds of

---

[1] *See* Contempo Constr. Co. v. Mountain States Tel. & Tel. Co., 736 P.2d 13 (Ariz. 1987), RESTATEMENT 2d § 50 and *supra* § 33.

[2] *See* Alexander v. Russo, 1 Kan. App. 546, 571 P.2d 350 (1979); Summerel v. Pinder, 83 So. 2d 692 (Fla. 1955); Glover v. Jewish War Veterans of United States, Post No. 58, 68 A.2d 233 (D.C. App. 1949); Broadnax v. Ledbetter, 100 Tex. 375, 99 S.W. 1111 (1907). *Accord* RESTATEMENT 2d § 23 comment c and RESTATEMENT 2d § 51 comment a. Some older cases take a contrary position. *See, e.g.,* Sullivan v. Phillips, 178 Ind. 164, 98 N.E. 868 (1912); Russell v. Stewardt, 44 Vt. 170 (1872); Gibbons v. Proctor, 64 L.T. 594 [1891].

[3] For an analysis of different views of such government reward offers, *see* State v. Malm, 143 Conn. 462, 123 A.2d 276 (1956).

the citizenry in assisting governmental authorities to bring criminals to justice, beyond a contractual analysis.[4]

The theoretically correct contractual analysis may lead to an anolmalous result. If a party knows of an offer and, with mercenary motivation, performs the requested act, he will have accepted the reward offer. Another party who performs the identical act out of a sense of civic duty alone will not be considered as having accepted the offer. It may be desirable to treat reward offers, private or governmental, as payable to parties who perform the desired act regardless of knowledge, i.e., to treat all reward cases beyond the traditional categories of offer and acceptance. A party who performs the requested act, albeit without knowledge of the reward, may reasonably expect to receive the reward for his services when he subsequently learns of it. The case law denying such recoveries at present is based on the offer/acceptance analysis which appears sound because it is the only analysis that appears to fit. The case law development, however, suggests a procrustean quality, i.e., it has made reward offers fit the bed of contracts analysis without regard for the disappointment it may engender. Perhaps it is time to recognize that such an analysis need not be mandated in the reward offer situation.[5]

Since an offer cannot be accepted without knowledge of its existence, offers which cross each other in the mail do not create a contract though they happen to contain identical terms.[6] If, however, one party creates a reasonable understanding in the other that an offer or acceptance exists, that reasonable understanding will be protected. If A sends what appears to be an offer to B even though the writing sent by A was drafted by a third party and A was unaware of its contents, B has a power of acceptance. Similarly, if A intentionally sends an offer in a letter to B who decides to manifest acceptance without reading the letter, there is a contract though B literally did not know of the offer.[7] This is in keeping with the necessary objectivity of regarding the manifestations of the parties as controlling[8] and permitting manifestations of assent to be operative in accordance with the intention of the party who neither knew nor had reason to know of the other party's lack of intention to assent.[9]

A final problem in this area is whether an act that is begun without knowledge of the offer but completed with knowledge of the offer constitutes accep-

---

[4] *See* RESTATEMENT 2d § 23 comment c.

[5] Analogously, in dealing with express warranties, comment 7 to UCC § 2-313 allows for the creation of post-formation express warranties on the footing that, "The precise time when words of description or affirmation are made or samples are shown is not material. The sole question is whether the language or samples or models are fairly to be regarded as part of the contract." For an elaboration of this concept, *see* Murray, *Basis of the Bargain: Transcending Classical Concepts,* 66 MINN. L. REV. 283 (1982).

[6] *See* RESTATEMENT 2d § 23 comment d and *supra* § 30.

[7] RESTATEMENT 2d § 23 comment b.

[8] *See supra* § 30.

[9] *See* RESTATEMENT 2d § 20(2):

The manifestations of the parties are operative in accordance with the meaning attached to them by one of the parties if:

(a) that party does not know of any different meaning attached by the other, and the other party knows the meaning attached by the first party; or

(b) that party has no reason to know of any different meaning attached by the other, and the other has reason to know the meaning attached by the first party.

tance. Assume that *A* offers a reward for the apprehension of the murderer of *A*'s brother. *B,* without knowledge of the reward offer, is in the process of apprehending the criminal when a radio announcement informs him of the reward offer. *B,* therefore, completes the act required by the offer, i.e., apprehension, after learning of the reward offer. Has *B* accepted the offer? The FIRST RESTATEMENT answered "no," since assent to the entire proposal was lacking.[10] Professor Corbin criticized this view severely on the footing that the normal person who learns of the reward after beginning performance will proceed with that performance relying upon the offer with expectation of receiving the reward.[11] The RESTATEMENT 2d adopts the Corbin view with the suggestion that knowledge of the offer after part performance can induce the offeree to complete performance and, since part performance is valueless to the offeror, there is a reasonable inference that the offeror intends to create a power of acceptance in a party who has yet to complete the performance required by the offer.[12]

C. *Intention to Exercise Power of Acceptance — Motivation.*

It is often suggested that an offeree must demonstrate an intention to accept the offer.[13] In promissory acceptances, the promise, itself, is an objective manifestation of this intention. The problem arises in performance acceptances. With knowledge of an offer, the offeree may perform the required act but may do so for reasons apart from the offer. At the moment the offeree performs the act, notwithstanding his knowledge of the offer, he may not be consciously adverting to the offer but may be performing the act for other reasons. An employee who knew of his employer's reward offer of $5000 in exchange for information leading to the arrest and conviction of persons stealing from the employer did not rely upon the offer at the time he gathered the information. As a supervisor, he may have gathered the information in any event. The court, nonetheless, followed the generally accepted view that, in rendering the performance requested in the offer, "... it is not necessary that the *sole* motive of the offeree shall be his desire for the offered reward."[14] Similarly, where a prize was offered to anyone who caught a particular, tagged fish, a fisherman who caught the fish need not have been consciously adverting to the offer at that moment if he had been aware of the offer but had gone fishing for pleasure.[15] The offeror or the offeree may have many different reasons or motives for creating or exercising a power of acceptance and the motivation to enter into a contract may be quite subsidiary to other motivations.[16] Prizes in golf or

---

[10]*See* FIRST RESTATEMENT § 53.

[11]1 CORBIN § 60.

[12]RESTATEMENT 2d § 51 comment b. *See* Hoggard v. Dickinson, 180 Mo. App. 70, 165 S.W. 1135, 1138 (1914). *Cf.* Henderson Land & Lumber Co. v. Barber, 17 Ala. App. 337, 85 So. 35 (1920) (employee entitled to bonus which he learned of after the contract was formed but which he intended to accept after knowledge of offer). Similarly, *see* Miller v. Dictaphone Corp., 334 F. Supp. 840 (D. Or. 1971).

[13]*See* FIRST RESTATEMENT § 55. *See also* Braun v. Northeast Stations & Servs., 93 A.D.2d 994, 461 N.Y.S.2d 623, 624 (1983).

[14]Consolidated Freightways Corp. of Del. v. Williams, 139 Ga. App. 302, 228 S.E.2d 230, 233 (1976).

[15]*See* Simmons v. United States, 308 F.2d 160 (4th Cir. 1962).

[16]*See* Consolidated Freightways Corp., *supra* note 14.

tennis tournaments may be offered and accepted though the offerors and offerees may be much more concerned about support for a given charity that will benefit from a given tournament, or the prestige connected with sponsoring or winning the tournament. The fact that an act is performed with numerous motivations, some or all of which are superior to a motivation to accept the offer, should not preclude an effective exercise of the power of acceptance. On this basis, it is often suggested that the motivation of a party who performs the requested act with knowledge of the offer is irrelevant.[17] There are, however, cases to the contrary.

In *Vitty v. Eley*,[18] the plaintiff was aware of a reward offer but was afraid to provide the information to the police for fear of retaliation. When threatened with arrest, the plaintiff provided the information. The court denied a recovery of the offered reward on the footing that the plaintiff had not provided the information voluntarily, i.e., it had been "corkscrewed out of him." The court also stated its disagreement with a well-known English case where motiviation had been deemed irrelevant.[19] The RESTATEMENT 2d utilizes the facts of both cases as the bases for illustrations.[20] It is possible to read the illustration based on the *Vitty* case as a modification of the actual facts in *Vitty*. A comparison of the actual facts of the two cases, however, reveals an irreconcilability that the RESTATEMENT illustrations cannot overcome. It would have been highly preferable for the RESTATEMENT 2d to emphasize the language in § 53(3):

> Where an offer of a promise invites acceptance by performance ..., the rendering of the invited performance does not constitute acceptance if before the offeror performs his promise, the offeree manifests *an intention not to accept*.[21]

This language manifests a major shift from the FIRST RESTATEMENT requirement that the offeree manifest an intention to accept to a rebuttable presumption of acceptance arising from performance by the offeree.[22] Notwithstanding its somewhat confusing illustrations, the RESTATEMENT 2d focuses upon the

---

[17] *See* RESTATEMENT 2d § 53 comment c: "[I]nquiry into his motives is unnecessary." *See also* Hamilton v. Oakland Sch. Dist. of Alameda Cty., 219 Cal. 322, 26 P.2d 296 (1933) and Braun v. Northeast Stations & Servs., *supra* note 13, at 461 N.Y.S.2d 624: "It is well settled, however, that 'motivation of a person performing the acts required by an offer of a reward is immaterial, but consent to the offer is vital'" citing Reynolds v. Eagle Pencil Co., 285 N.Y. 448, 35 N.E.2d 35 (1941).

[18] 51 A.D. 44, 64 N.Y.S. 397 (1900).

[19] Williams v. Cawardine, 4 B. & Ad. 621 [1833]. *See*, however, Braun v. Northeast Stations & Servs., *supra* note 13, a recent New York case in which the court states that motivation *is* irrelevant and citing for that proposition, Reynolds v. Eagle Pencil Co., 285 N.Y. 448, 35 N.E.2d 35 (1941). In their recent book, however, Professor Calamiri and Professor Perillo cite the Reynolds case and Vitty v. Eley as support for the relevance of motivation, CALAMIRI & PERILLO, CONTRACTS at 76 n.15 (3d ed. 1987).

[20] Illustration 1 is said to be based on the facts of Williams v. Cawardine, and ill. 2 is said to be based on the facts of Vitty v. Eley.

[21] Emphasis added.

[22] "[T]he favored rule shifts the emphasis away from a manifestation of intent to accept to a manifestation of intent not to accept, thereby establishing, it would appear, a rebuttable presumption of acceptance arising from performance when the offer invites acceptance by performance." "Industrial America," Inc. v. Fulton Indus., 285 A.2d 412, 416 (Del. 1971), quoted with apparent approval in Reporter's Note to RESTATEMENT 2d § 53. *See* FIRST RESTATEMENT § 55.

virtual impossibility of finding no intention to accept absent an explicit disclaimer by the purported offeree to the effect that he has no intention of accepting the offer by rendering the performance requested in the offer.[23] If, therefore, the act requested in the offer is performed by a party who has knowledge of the offer, the presumption is very strong that he or she acted with some reference to the offer though perhaps having had one or more superior motivations for performance of the requested act. Absent a clear manifestation of no intention to accept the offer, the performance evidences to acceptance of the offer.

D. *Who May Accept the Offer?*

Earlier we considered to whom an offer is addressed and that analysis explored certain problems in identifying the party or parties with a power of acceptance.[24] There, we suggested that since the offeror is master of the offer, it is the offeror's manifestation of intention that determines the person or persons in whom a power of acceptance is created.[25] It is, therefore, clear that only such a person or persons may exercise the power of acceptance and that power is not assignable by the offeree to another.[26] The earlier analysis should be reconsidered at this point since it necessarily deals with the problems relating to the identification of the person or persons holding a power of acceptance. One of the points emphasized in that analysis bears repetition: whether a particular party has the power of acceptance will often be a question of interpretation of the language of the offer under all of the surrounding circumstances. Thus, where a reward offer was made by an employer to pay $5000 to the person providing information leading to the arrest and conviction of the party or parties stealing from the employer, and the reward notice ended with the statement, "Contact your supervisor," the question before the court was, did the plaintiff who was a supervisor have a power of acceptance? In holding that the plaintiff had a power of acceptance, the court applied generally accepted guides to interpretation.[27]

Other questions concerning the power of acceptance where the offeror has made a mistake of identity will be considered in the sections dealing with mistake in the agreement process.[28]

---

[23]*See* comment c. and ill. 3 to RESTATEMENT 2d § 53.

[24] *See supra* § 39.

[25]*See* RESTATEMENT 2d § 29.

[26]RESTATEMENT 2d § 52. With respect to the non-assignability of the power of acceptance, *see* Ott v. Home Sav. & Loan Ass'n, 265 F.2d 643 (9th Cir. 1958). Agents may accept offers for their principals, *see* RESTATEMENT 2d AGENCY § 292. If an agent does not have agency authority in a given case, the principal/offeree may ratify the acceptance. RESTATEMENT 2d AGENCY §§ 82-104.

[27]Consolidated Freightways Corp. of Del. v. Williams, 139 Ga. App. 302, 228 S.E.2d 230 (1976) wherein the court applied the following generally accepted interpretation guides: the writing (the reward notice) must be construed against the party drafting it; a construction should be given that will enhance the beneficial purpose of the contract; the promise must be construed in light of the substantial purpose which influenced the parties to enter the contract.

[28]*See infra* § 91(F).

§ 45. The Manner and Medium of Acceptance.

A. *Introduction: Manner Versus Medium.*

The *manner* of acceptance refers to the way in which an offer may be accepted, i.e., by *promising* to perform or actually *performing* the act requested in the offer. The *medium* of acceptance refers to the means used to communicate acceptance. As master of the offer, the offeror may specify the manner and/or medium of acceptance. Absent such a requirement in the offer, however, questions arise concerning both. Currently, there is little difficulty concerning the medium of acceptance. Starting with the general proposition that any reasonable medium of acceptance will be effective,[29] the case law supports common sense guidelines in the determination of what is reasonable. If, for example, the offeror uses the mail to make an offer, it would be reasonable for the offeree to adopt the mail as a reasonable medium of acceptance. A telegram, mailgram or other reliable medium would also be a reasonable medium of acceptance since they are typically faster than the post. A private but reliable service that is customarily used in commercial dealings would also be a reasonable medium.[30] The subject matter of the contract may require a faster medium than the post. An offer to sell securities listed on an exchange may suggest the use of the telegraph rather than the mail. The problem, however, may deal with another question, i.e., what is a reasonable time for acceptance in the absence of a specified time in the offer? If an offeree waits beyond the reasonable time, the use of the telegram will not remedy a lapsed power of acceptance.[31] Further problems of the appropriate medium of acceptance will be explored as part of the analysis of the "dispatch" or "mailbox" rule in contracts by correspondence later in this chapter.[32]

While the question of a reasonable medium of acceptance is not terribly difficult under modern case law, there are a number of questions surrounding the proper *manner* of acceptance. The UCC, which governs contracts for the sale of goods, and the RESTATEMENT 2d, which is highly influential with respect to all other contracts, have wrought significant changes in the traditional structure of the agreement process with respect to the *manner* of acceptance.[33] These major modifications of common law contract doctrine cannot be understood unless the common law principles relating to the manner of acceptance as found in the FIRST RESTATEMENT are first understood.

B. *Manner of Acceptance — Common Law — FIRST RESTATEMENT — "Bilateral"/"Unilateral."*

If the offer does not specify a particular manner of acceptance, i.e., it requires neither a promise nor performance but is silent as to the manner of

---

[29] RESTATEMENT 2d § 30(2); UCC § 2-206(1)(a).

[30] RESTATEMENT 2d § 65 comment b suggests a less than exhaustive list of circumstances relating to the reasonableness of a particular medium: speed, reliability of the medium, prior course of dealing between the parties, and usage of trade. The RESTATEMENT recognizes the likelihood that new media will develop, or that existing media will become more reliable or faster.

[31] *See* RESTATEMENT 2d § 41 ill. 7.

[32] *See infra* § 47.

[33] For an exploration of these changes and their effects, *see* Murray, *Contracts: A New Design for the Agreement Process,* 53 CORNELL L. REV. 785 (1968).

acceptance, it would seem a relatively simple matter to generate a workable rule to be used in such cases. The traditional common law view set forth in the FIRST RESTATEMENT, however, assumed that the great majority of offers could be separated into (a) those which requested a promise to exercise the power of acceptance to form a *bilateral* contract, and (b) those which requested the ultimate performance sought by the offeror as the acceptance, thereby forming a *unilateral* contract.[34] The bilateral/unilateral dichotomy was clear. In a bilateral contract, the contract was formed by a promissory acceptance and the resulting contract manifested two rights and two correlative duties as well as two promisors and two promisees. In a unilateral contract, as we have seen in earlier analyses, the acceptance occurred upon complete performance of the requested act (though the offer became irrevocable upon part performance),[35] and a contract was formed with one right in the former offeree and one correlative duty in the former offeror. In such contracts, there was only one promisor (the offeror) and one promisee (the offeree).[36] Certainly, if the offeror as master of the offer specified the particular manner of acceptance, there was usually no problem since no contract would exist until the acceptance was exercised in the specified manner. If, however, the offer did not specify the manner of acceptance, a workable rule as to the proper manner of acceptance was essential. Such an offer was characterized as ambiguous or "doubtful" with respect to the manner of acceptance. The doubt was resolved by presuming that the offer invited a promissory acceptance because of the assumption that a promissory acceptance immediately and fully protects both parties to the contract.[37] At this point, another assumption should be emphasized, i.e., that doubtful offers, i.e., those not specifying a particular manner of acceptance, were relatively rare. Another problem with respect to the doubtful offer arose when the offeree did not make a promise to accept, but simply performed the act requested in the offer. Since the presumption was that a doubtful offer requires a promissory acceptance, the application of that presumption would result in no acceptance where the offeree performed rather than promised. This problem was overcome through the creation of an exception to the presumption. By receiving the performance without a prior promise, the offeror was said to have received something better than the promise he presumably requested, i.e., the actual performance underlying the promise which was, after all, the ultimate desideratum of the offeror.[38] The exception applied even where the offeror had specified a promissory acceptance, i.e., it applied beyond

---

[34] FIRST RESTATEMENT § 52.

[35] *See supra* § 43.

[36] If there is a "non-promissory" offer, a unilateral contract may be formed where the promisor is the offeree and the promisee of the offeror. Thus, if *A* owns a book that is in *B*'s possession and *A* offers to sell the book to *B* by saying, "If you promise to pay me $10 for that book which you now possess, the book is yours," upon *B*'s promise to pay the $10, a contract is formed. There is one right in the offeror/promisee to receive the $10, and one duty in the offeree/promisor to pay the $10. Since there is one right and one correlative duty as well as one promisor and one promisee, the contract is "unilateral." However, since the normal unilateral situation has the right in the offeree/promisee and duty in the offeror/promisor, the reversing of the parties has led to the characterization of this type of contract as a "reverse unilateral." *See* RESTATEMENT 2d § 55 comment a.

[37] FIRST RESTATEMENT § 31. *See also* Davis v. Jacoby, 1 Cal. 2d 370, 34 P.2d 1026 (1934).

[38] FIRST RESTATEMENT § 63.

doubtful offers. This, in turn, raised a theoretical difficulty: if the offeror is the master of the offer, and the master requires a promise as the exclusive manner of acceptance, how can a non-promissory acceptance be effective? This objection was viewed as a peccadillo and was ignored in light of the rationale that the offeror should be pleased to receive the actual performance desired, and the fact that no promise was made should be irrelevant. Other difficulties such as the offeror not hearing from the offeree (who was in the process of performing) and proceeding to contract with another[39] were also dismissed. The theoretical and practical problems, however, remained.[40]

C. Manner of Acceptance — Uniform Commercial Code — RESTATEMENT 2d — Indifferent Offers.

The fundamental change effected by the UCC, which was subsequently incorporated into the RESTATEMENT 2d, is a major change in assumption concerning the doubtful offer. Unlike their predecessors, the Code and RESTATEMENT 2d proceed on the assumption that the doubtful offer, i.e., the offer not requiring a particular manner of acceptance, is the normal or typical offer rather than the relatively rare offer assumed by the FIRST RESTATEMENT. The assumption is that, in the overwhelming majority of cases, offerors are indifferent as to the manner of acceptance. Based on this assumption, the fundamental policy change is set forth: "Unless otherwise indicated by the language or the circumstances, an offer invites acceptance in any manner and by any medium reasonable in the circumstances."[41] Having restructured the basic concept of the manner of acceptance, other specific changes were essential. Thus, a "doubtful" offer, i.e., the typical offer where the offeror is indifferent as to the manner of acceptance, could now be accepted by the offeree choosing either to promise to perform or to perform.[42] If the offeror is not indifferent as to the particular manner of acceptance required, the offeror is now the absolute master of the offer, i.e., there is no exception to the requirement that the exclusive manner of acceptance is that required by the offeror.[43]

---

[39] See Goble, Is an Offer a Promise? 22 ILL. L. REV. 567 (1928) and the reply by Professor Williston in 22 ILL. L. REV. 788 (1928).

[40] Courts managed to achieve just results in most cases without a consistent theoretical base. There was a lack of law settlement with courts only sometimes using various sections of the FIRST RESTATEMENT in accordance with their stated purposes. See Murray, supra note 33, at 792.

[41] RESTATEMENT 2d § 30(2). The UCC formulation is almost identical: "Unless otherwise unambiguously indicated by the language or circumstances an offer to make a contract shall be construed as inviting acceptance in any manner and by any medium reasonable in the circumstances." UCC, § 2-206(1)(a). RESTATEMENT 2d § 32 elaborates the basic principle in terms of the new assumption concerning doubtful (indifferent) offers: "In case of doubt an offer is interpreted as inviting the offeree to accept either by promising or by rendering the performance as the offeree chooses." In the Reporter's Note to § 32, the following appears: "This Section is derived from former § 31 [First Restatement], but replaces that Section's presumption that an offer invited a bilateral contract with the present formulation."

[42] RESTATEMENT 2d § 32; UCC § 2-206(1)(b). For a UCC application, see Maryland Supreme Corp. v. Blake Co., 279 Md. 531, 369 A.2d 1017 (1977).

[43] The following statement appears in the Reporter's Note to RESTATEMENT 2d § 62: "This Section [62] is modified from former [First Restatement] § 63. That Section stated that performance is an effective acceptance even if the offer requires acceptance by promise. Thus the rule was made an exception to former [First Restatement] §§ 52 and 59. Those exceptions mitigated the effect of former [First Restatement] § 31, which stated a presumption that an offer invites acceptance by promise. Section 32 of the present [Second] Restatement states that in case of doubt an

Under the new structure of the agreement process, if the offer is indifferent as to the manner of acceptance and the offeree chooses to promise to perform, the contract is formed by a promissory manner of acceptance. Under traditional labels which neither the Code nor the RESTATEMENT 2d apply, the contract would be a bilateral contract with two rights, two correlative duties, two promisors and two promisees. If, however, the offeree chooses to accept such an indifferent offer by performance, the question arises, when is the contract formed? The RESTATEMENT 2d clearly indicates that such a contract is formed upon the beginning of the requested performance or a tender of performance[44] and such an acceptance (the beginning of performance or tender of performance) operates as a promise to render complete performance,[45] thereby creating, in traditional terms, a *bilateral* contract. It is important to emphasize a basic distinction between this situation, i.e., beginning performance in response to an indifferent offer, and the situation discussed earlier, beginning performance in response to an offer requiring performance as the exclusive manner of acceptance. In the first situation, the offeree could either promise to perform or start to perform. Since the offeree has this choice, an implication that such beginning performance constitutes a promise to complete performance is warranted. In the second situation where the offeree must complete performance to form a *unilateral* contract, there is no choice as to the manner of acceptance. The offeror has relegated acceptance to one, exclusive manner, i.e., complete performance. The beginning of performance cannot be acceptance of such an offer, even if the offeree desired it to be so. To imply a promise by the offeree under such circumstances, therefore, thrusts an unwarranted risk on the offeree and has no effect in the formation of a contract. The offer becomes irrevocable upon part performance to protect the offeree from an unwarranted revocation by the offeror before the offeree has an opportunity to accept by completing performance. Again, however, the beginning of performance in response to an offer demanding performance as the exclusive manner of acceptance cannot form a contract and the implication of a promise from such part performance is unwarranted.[46]

The UCC was primarily responsible for this change since it preceded the RESTATEMENT 2d which has adopted most of the substantial changes in classical contract law effected by Article 2 of the Code. Under the Code, where the offer is indifferent as to the manner of acceptance, the offeree may choose to promise or to perform, and the beginning of performance will form the con-

---

offer invites either acceptance by promise or acceptance by performance as the offeree chooses. This change makes unnecessary these departures from the basic principle that the offeror is master of his offer." Cases holding that § 2-206(1)(a) of the Code permits the offeror to insist upon a particular manner of acceptance include Southwestern Stationery & Bank Supply, Inc. v. Harris, 624 F.2d 168 (10th Cir. 1980); Nations Enters. v. Process Equip. Co., 579 P.2d 655 (Colo. 1978); Empire Mach. Co. v. Litton Bus. Tel. Sys., 115 Ariz. 568, 566 P.2d 1044 (1977). For a discussion of the absolute requirement that the offeror is the master of the offer principle under the UCC and RESTATEMENT 2d and some inferences therein, *see* Murray, *supra* note 33, at 800-01.

[44] RESTATEMENT 2d § 62(1).

[45] RESTATEMENT 2d § 62(2).

[46] It should be recalled that an early theory converting part performance into an implied promise creating a bilateral contract where the offer could be accepted by performance alone was severely criticized. *See supra* § 43(D).

tract.[47] A comment to this section, however, suggests, "Such a beginning of performance must unambiguously express the offeree's intention to engage himself."[48] Presumably, such a beginning of performance would be tested according to the reasonable understanding of the merchant-offeror, i.e., if such an offeror would regard the start of performance as an expression of the offeree's intention to complete the performance, the beginning of performance would constitute an implied promise to complete and, in the traditional usage, a bilateral contract would be formed at that time.[49] If, however, the offeror knew or had reason to know that the offeree was not engaging upon the start of performance, no contract would be formed until performance was complete. Thus, if the offeree indicated some doubt as to whether he could complete performance, his beginning of performance would not be an engagement or implied promise to complete performance. If the offeree expressly indicated that performance was not to be construed as an acceptance, his manifested intention would be respected. The Code drafters were very much aware of this situation in the shipment of goods as an acceptance of an offer.

The Code emphasizes that an order or other offer to purchase goods for prompt or current shipment may be accepted either by a prompt promise to ship or by prompt or current shipment.[50] This provision may be seen as nothing more than a specific example of the general rule that indifferent offers may be accepted by promising or by performing. But the Code provision adds an important element: if the offeree chooses to accept by the prompt shipment of goods rather than by promising to ship, he accepts the offer by the prompt shipment of conforming *or nonconforming* goods.[51] Under pre-Code law, if a seller shipped nonconforming goods, i.e., goods that were different from the goods required by the offer, the seller was not accepting the offer; he was making a counter offer, and if the buyer accepted the nonconforming goods, the buyer was accepting the seller's counter offer. Under the Code, however, when the seller ships even nonconforming goods in response to the buyer's offer, such a shipment is normally understood "to close the bargain."[52] The ramifications of this change over pre-Code law are radical. Assume, for example, that the buyer offers to purchase model X-35 widgits and, in response to this order, the seller ships X-36 widgits, i.e., nonconforming goods. A court applying the Code provision would find that a contract has been formed for the X-35 widgits and that contract has been, simultaneously, breached by the shipment of the nonconforming goods.[53] The buyer may reject the nonconforming goods,[54] but the seller typically has the right to "cure" the defect[55] if that

---

[47] UCC § 2-206(2).

[48] *See* comment 3 to UCC § 2-206.

[49] *See* Nasco, Inc. v. Dahltron Corp., 74 Ill. App. 3d 302, 392 N.E.2d 1110 (1979) (on the assumption that there was merely an offer to purchase goods, the contract came into being when the seller began to execute the buyer's order).

[50] UCC § 2-206(1)(b).

[51] *Id.*

[52] UCC § 2-206 comment 4.

[53] Comment 4 to UCC § 2-206 suggests: "Such a non-conforming shipment is normally to be understood as intended to close the bargain, even though it proves to have been at the same time a breach."

[54] UCC § 2-601.

[55] UCC § 2-508.

can be accomplished prior to the time conforming goods should have been shipped. The seller can also avoid the effect of forming a contract in shipping nonconforming goods by notifying the buyer that the shipment of nonconforming goods is sent as an accommodation to the buyer.[56] A seasonable[57] notification to the buyer that the shipment of nonconforming goods was intended to accommodate the buyer constitutes a counter offer by the seller. The buyer need not accept such nonconforming goods, but if he does so, he has accepted the seller's counter offer.

Other ramifications of the structural change in the Code and RESTATEMENT 2d should not be overlooked. If a seller chooses to accept an indifferent offer by performance and later sends written terms, such terms will be inoperative. Consider, for example, an order (offer) sent by the purchaser to which the seller responds by shipping all or a portion of the goods. After shipment, the seller sends an invoice or similar document that contains certain terms favorable to the seller, e.g., a clause excluding liability for consequential damages. Under the Code, the contract was formed upon shipment by the seller and the attempt by the seller to insert new or different terms in the contract thereafter is too late. The terms of the contract are those found in the buyer's offer (e.g., a purchase order) and any supplemental terms implied by the Code which are typically favorable to the buyer. Such implied terms would provide the buyer with a right to consequential damages.[58] Therefore, the importance of treating the performance — shipment — as acceptance has been emphasized in several cases.[59]

It is, of course, still possible for an offeror to require performance as the exclusive manner of acceptance. We have already dealt with the analysis of part performance in response to such offers under § 45 of the RESTATEMENT 2d.[60] Should such an offer be made in a contract for the sale of goods, it is clear that the same analysis would apply under the Code.[61] It is particularly unusual for an offeror to state that performance is the exclusive manner of acceptance.[62] More often, the nature of the offer will suggest that a promissory acceptance would be worthless to the offeror as in the case of reward

---

[56] UCC § 2-206(1)(b) and comment 4.

[57] Under the Code, an action is taken "seasonably" when it is taken at or within the time agreed, or if no time is agreed, within a reasonable time. § 1-204.

[58] Consequential damages are defined in § 2-715 of the UCC and will be explored in the Chapter dealing with contract remedies.

[59] See, e.g., Wheaton Glass Co. v. Pharmex, Inc., 548 F. Supp. 1242 (D.N.J. 1982) (consequential damages limitation in seller's "order-billing" was inoperative because the shipment of some 50,000 bottles in response to a purchase order (offer) to buy 216,000 bottles was an acceptance of the offer); In re Isis Foods, Inc., 38 Bankr. 48 (B.C. W.D. Mo. 1983) (offer stated an "FOB St. Louis" term, i.e., buyer's location, which was an offer to sell on the basis of a "destination" contract. The risk of loss would not, therefore, pass to the buyer until the goods were tendered to the buyer in St. Louis as contrasted with the usual FOB "shipment" contract where the risk of loss passes to the buyer at the seller's location upon delivery to the independent carrier. By shipping the goods, the seller accepted the buyer's offer including the FOB destination term. See UCC § 2-509(1)(a) and (b).).

[60] See supra § 43(D).

[61] The UCC does not change any law that it does not expressly replace. UCC § 1-103. Moreover, § 2-206 comment 3 indicates: "Nothing in this section however bars the possibility that under the common law performance begun may have an intermediate effect of temporarily barring revocation of the offer...."

[62] See, e.g., BC Tire Corp. v. GTE Directories Corp., 46 Wash. App. 351, 730 P.2d 726 (1987).

offers or other offers to the public such as prizes in a contest requiring the performance of certain acts[63] or offers of guaranty.[64] Though the term "unilateral" contract is not mentioned in the UCC and has been intentionally omitted from the RESTATEMENT 2d,[65] a plethora of cases has recently appeared and more are in the process of litigation which utilize a theory of unilateral contract. The cases involve the problem of terminable-at-will employment contracts explored earlier.[66] If an employer provides an employee handbook or manual or otherwise issues a statement of policy concerning procedures for termination, severance pay, probation or other matters, a number of courts have indicated a willingness to discover a unilateral contract by characterizing the handbook, manual or statement as an offer and the employee's starting or continuing employment with knowledge of the offer an acceptance by performance.[67] The unilateral contract, so formed, modifies the former contract that was terminable-at-will by the employer. Since the employer decided to issue the handbook, manual or policy statement, it is now bound to follow whatever procedures for termination, for example, are found therein. The consideration supporting the promise of the employer is found in the continuing performance of the employee with knowledge of the offer. A minority of courts have found the unilateral construct to be unpersuasive. At least with respect to a manual published after the plaintiff had been employed for some time, one court suggested that the manual was "only a unilateral expression of company policy and procedures. Its terms were not bargained for by the parties and any benefits conferred by it were gratuities. Certainly, no meeting of the minds was evidenced by the defendant's unilateral act of publishing company policy."[68] While the judicial debate is bound to continue, the use of a unilateral contract concept may be a mechanistic expression of a judicial desire to protect any reasonable reliance on the part of the employee. There is some difficulty in discovering an offer from a manual as evidenced by those courts that have insisted that the communication be sufficiently definite to the employee to constitute an offer.[69] Moreover, employment manuals may

---

[63]*See* RESTATEMENT 2d § 32 comment b. *See also* Rosenthal v. Al Packer Ford, Inc., 36 Md. App. 349, 374 A.2d 377 (1977); Grove v. Charbonneau Buick-Pontiac Inc., 240 N.W.2d 853 (N.D. 1976).

[64]*See, e.g.,* King v. Industrial Bank of Wash., 474 A.2d 151 (1984).

[65]*See* Reporter's Note to comment f of RESTATEMENT 2d § 1 which indicates that the "unilateral"/"bilateral" definitions of the FIRST RESTATEMENT have not been "carried forward because of doubt as to the utility of the distinction, often treated as fundamental, between the two types." While not using these captions, the RESTATEMENT 2d clearly recognizes that an offer may require an exclusive manner of acceptance by promise, or an exclusive manner of acceptance by performance as well as being indifferent to the manner of acceptance as suggested in the analysis of the UCC and RESTATEMENT 2d modifications of traditional contract theory found in the current section of this volume.

[66]*See supra* § 38(B)(4).

[67]*See* Continental Air Lines, Inc. v. Keenan, 731 P.2d 708 (Colo. 1987); Bachelder v. Communications Satellite Corp., 657 F. Supp. 423 (D. Me. 1987); Duldulao v. Saint Mary of Nazareth Hosp., 115 Ill. 2d 482, 505 N.E.2d 314 (1987); Wagner v. City of Globe, 150 Ariz. 82, 722 P.2d 250 (1986); Woolley v. Hoffman-La Roche, Inc., 99 N.J. 284, 491 A.2d 1257 (1985); Finely v. Aetna Life & Cas. Co., 5 Conn. App. 394, 499 A.2d 64 (1985); Pine River State Bank v. Mettille, 333 N.W.2d 622 (Minn. 1983); Toussaint v. Blue Cross & Blue Shield of Mich., 408 Mich. 579, 292 N.W.2d 880 (1980).

[68] Johnson v. National Beef Packing Co., 220 Kan. 52, 551 P.2d 779 (1976). *See also* White v. Chelsea Indus., 425 So. 2d 1090 (Ala. 1983); Heidek v. Kent Gen. Hosp., 446 A.2d 1095 (Del. 1982).

[69]*See* Finley v. Aetna Life & Cas. Co., 5 Conn. App. 394, 499 A.2d 64 (1985).

avoid contractual obligation by clear expressions negating any contractual intent.[70] Attacks on the terminable-at-will rule might, therefore, proceed more effectively and with more precision if based upon possible justifiable reliance by the employee.

§ 46. Notice of Acceptance.

A. *General Principles in Bilateral Versus Unilateral Contracts.*

As the master of the offer, the offeror may insist that the offeree's assent be communicated before a contract can exist. To exercise the power of acceptance, the offeree must comply with this requirement and any other requirements concerning the notice of acceptance stated in the offer.[71] This is simply an expression of the general principle that the offeree must comply with the place, time, manner or medium of acceptance mandated by the offeror.[72] Often, however, the offer does not expressly indicate that notice of acceptance is necessary. In that situation, must the offeree notify the offeror of the acceptance? There is some confusion in this area resulting from an antiquated view that notice of acceptance is always required.[73] This "rule," however, is emasculated where the offer requires a performance acceptance. In such a contract, the performance, itself, is the consideration for the offeror's promise and it is also the offeree's manifestation of assent.[74] Notice of assent in such cases should, therefore, be required only where the offeror would not be aware of the performance.[75] Where the offer requires or allows for a promissory acceptance, however, notice of acceptance is usually required.[76] A promise may be inferred by conduct. The typical promise, however, involves communication in language and it is, therefore, generally understood that acceptance requires communication of the offeree's manifestation of assent to the offeror. Yet, we will later explore situations where the offeree has pursued reasonably diligent efforts to communicate acceptance to the offeror but, through no fault of the offeree, such efforts have failed.[77] The acceptance will be said to be effective in those situations. The RESTATEMENT 2d formulation of the guiding principle, therefore, seems preferable, i.e., acceptance by promise requires either a reasonably diligent effort to notify the offeror, or the offeror's receipt of the notice of acceptance within the time stated in the offer (or a reasonable time).[78] The difference between acceptance by promise and acceptance by performance caused some courts to state different notice requirements depending upon whether the contract was "bilateral" or "unilateral." Since it is now clear that

---

[70] *See* Castiglione v. Johns Hopkins Hosp., 669 Md. App. 325, 517 A.2d 786 (1986).

[71] *See* Dempsey v. King, 662 S.W.2d 725 (Tex. App. 1983); Crockett v. Lowther, 549 P.2d 303 (Wyo. 1976).

[72] *See* RESTATEMENT 2d §§ 58 and 60.

[73] *See* the opinion by Bramwell, J., in Household Fire Ins. Co. v. Grant, 4 Ex. D. 216, 233 [1879].

[74] Hauk v. First Nat'l Bank of St. Charles, 680 S.W.2d 771 (Mo. Ct. App. 1984).

[75] *See* subsection C of this section for an exploration of this concept.

[76] *See* Normile v. Miller, 313 N.C. 98, 326 S.E.2d 11 (1985); Hauk v. First Nat'l Bank of St. Charles, 680 S.W.2d 771 (Mo. Ct. App. 1984); Mintzberg v. Golestaneh, 390 So. 2d 759 (D. Fla. 1980).

[77] For example, where the offer is by post and the offeree deposits his letter of acceptance in the mailbox but the letter is lost in the mails.

[78] RESTATEMENT 2d § 56.

a "bilateral" contract can be formed by the *performance* of the offeree where the offeror is indifferent as to how it is accepted,[79] that distinction is no longer viable. A modern restatement of the rule should eschew "bilateral" or "unilateral" characterizations. It might be stated as follows: Where acceptance occurs through performance, notice of acceptance is usually not required; where acceptance occurs through promising, notice to the offeror or a reasonably diligent effort to notify the offeror is required.

B. *May the Offeror Dispense With the Necessity of Notice of Acceptance?*

As master of the offer, the offeror may dispense with any notice of acceptance. If the offeror manifests a willingness to be bound without any communication or manifestation of acceptance by the offeree, the law takes him at his word.[80] Unfortunately, this situation often occurs where a seller of goods or services presents the seller's printed form to the prospective buyer. The form contains a critical clause which the buyer has ignored. The buyer signs this form and typically assumes she has formed a contract with the seller. Had she read all of the provisions of the form carefully, however, the buyer would have discovered a clause stating that the agreement evidenced by this document does not become a contract until it is approved or signed by an officer of the seller at its home office. The buyer, perhaps unwittingly, has made an offer and the power of acceptance is in the seller. That power is exercised when the seller, through one of its officers, signs the document at the home office even though at the moment of formation, the buyer (offeror) is unaware of that signing and consequent exercise of the power of acceptance. Notification to the buyer is unnecessary simply because the offer made by the buyer dispenses with such notification.[81] The only problem that may arise is whether the offeror has manifested an intention to dispense with the requirement of notification and that is a question of the proper interpretation of the offer.

C. *Notice in Offers Requiring Acceptance by Performance — RESTATEMENT 2d and Uniform Commercial Code.*

As suggested earlier, the general rule is that notice is not required in a performance acceptance.[82] Where an offer requires or permits acceptance by performance, it is the performance, itself, that manifests the offeree's assent

---

[79] *See supra* § 45(C).

[80] *See* RESTATEMENT 2d § 54(2)(c) and § 56 comment a.

[81] The classic case is International Filter Co. v. Conroe, Gin, Ice & Light Co., 277 S.W. 631 (Tex. Civ. App. 1925). There are, however, many illustrations of this arrangement in the case law. *See, e.g.,* Pacific Photocopy, Inc. v. Cannon U.S.A., Inc., 57 Or. App. 752, 646 P.2d 647 (1982), *rev. denied,* 293 Or. 635, 652 P.2d 810 (1982); Empire Mach. Co. v. Litton Bus. Tel. Sys., 115 Ariz. 568, 566 P.2d 1044 (1977) (where court held that buyer/offerer waived this particular manner of acceptance); Three-Seventy Leasing Corp. v. Ampex Corp., 528 F.2d 993 (5th Cir. 1977); Antonucci v. Stevens Dodge, Inc., 73 Misc. 2d 173, 340 N.Y.S.2d 979 (1973). *See also* J.B. Moore Elec. Contr. v. Westinghouse Elec. Supply Co., 221 Va. 745, 273 S.E.2d 553 (1981) where, in a curious analysis of a printed form supplied by the seller containing the provision, "This Order is subject to the Company's acceptance at its office . . . ," the court distinguished similar cases on the footing that this form contained no signature line for the seller whereas other cases holding such forms to be offers when signed by the buyer contained such lines for the seller's signature.

[82] *See supra* subsection A.

and the contract should be said to be formed without notice of acceptance.[83] There are, however, situations in which the offeree knew or reasonably should have known that the offeror would not learn of the offeree's performance with reasonable promptness or certainty. For example, if the offeree knows that the offeror will be located at a considerable distance when the performance occurs and will not, therefore, be aware of the offeree's performance/acceptance, should notice be required in such a case? Some cases took the position that, even in that situation, notice was not essential since the offeror could have insisted upon notice and chose not to do so.[84] Other cases went so far as to hold that no contract was formed until notice was communicated.[85] Under this view, if the offeree performed the act required by the offeror, there would be no contract until notice of performance had been communicated to the offeror. A third view, though announced even earlier, presented a sound analysis. In the well-known case of *Bishop v. Eaton*,[86] the court rejected an all-or-nothing approach in suggesting that, ordinarily, there is no necessity to notify an offeror that the act requested in the offer has been performed because the offeror is bound when he or she sees the act performed. If, however, the act is of such a kind that knowledge of its performance will not reach the offeror promptly, the offeree must provide notice. The court further insisted that the doing of the act, the performance, was the acceptance of the offer, i.e., a contract is formed at that point, even though the situation is one requiring notice within a reasonable time. This analysis withstood the test of time and has become the prevailing view.[87] It is important to recognize the significance of treating the performance as the acceptance forming the contract even though the situation calls for notice to the offeror. If *A* tells *B*, "I am going away for a few months during which time my brother, Harry, may need money. If he needs it, let him have it and, if he does not repay you with interest, I will." Assume that *B* lends money to Harry while *A* is away. *B* is about to send notice to *A* that he has lent the money when he receives a note from *A* revoking the offer. If the acceptance was not effective until notice was either sent or received by *A*, the revocation could be said to be effective unless the act of lending was seen as partial performance making *A*'s offer irrevocable so that *B* would have a reasonable time to complete performance by sending the notice. Even if § 45 of the RESTATEMENT 2d or other irrevocable offer theory[88] applied to a situation where the offer could be accepted only by performance, however, such theories do not apply to a performance acceptance of an indifferent offer, i.e., one that could be accepted either by promising or performing.

---

[83] *See* Compton v. Shopko Stores, Inc., 93 Wis. 2d 613, 287 N.W.2d 720 (1980). *See also* RESTATEMENT 2d § 54(1).

[84] *See* Midland Nat'l Bank v. Security Elev. Co., 161 Minn. 30, 200 N.W. 851 (1924); City Nat'l Bank v. Phelps, 86 N.Y. 484 (1881).

[85] *See* Kresge Dept. Stores v. Young, 37 A.2d 448 (App. 1944); German Sav. Bank v. Drake Roofing Co., 112 Iowa 184, 83 N.W. 960 (1900).

[86] 161 Mass. 496, 37 N.E. 665 (1894).

[87] *See* RESTATEMENT 2d § 54, particularly, ills. 5 and 6.

[88] *See supra* § 43(D).

Under the UCC and RESTATEMENT 2d the typical, indifferent offer may be accepted by a promise or by performance.[89] If an offeree chooses to accept such an offer by performance, the question of notice should be analyzed in precisely the same fashion as if the offer could be accepted exclusively by performance, i.e., the *Bishop v. Eaton* analysis applies to *any* performance acceptance whether it is an acceptance of an indifferent offer, or an acceptance of an offer that can be accepted exclusively by performance.[90] Moreover, notice is not part of the acceptance since the acceptance was completed upon performance. If notice is not part of the acceptance, what is it?

The UCC is particularly troubling with respect to the notice requirement where the offeree chooses to accept by performance. Section 2-206(2) of the Code states: "Where the beginning of a requested performance is a reasonable mode of acceptance, an offeror who is not notifed of acceptance within a reasonable time may treat the offer as having lapsed before acceptance." If beginning performance constitutes acceptance, there is no longer any offer to lapse. Both the offer and acceptance have merged into a contract. To suggest, therefore, that an offer is accepted by performance but, because the former offeree failed to provide the notice that should have been provided, the "offer lapses," is theoretically impossible. The situation is worsened by a comment to this section of the Code.[91] Again, the offeror does not seek notice; he or she does not bargain for notice where the acceptance is by performance. If the offer is indifferent as to the manner of acceptance and the offeree chooses to accept by performance, notification will not be essential unless the offeror would not learn of the performance/acceptance with reasonable promptness. The contract is formed upon the start of performance in that situation as both the UCC and the RESTATEMENT 2d indicate.[92] If notice is necessary in such a situation, notice is not part of the acceptance; it is a *condition precedent* to the

---

[89] *See supra* § 45(C).

[90] RESTATEMENT 2d § 54 comment b appears to support this view. However, it suggests that a performance acceptance dispensing with notification would be rare because a performance acceptance of an indifferent offer "often carries with it a return commitment" pursuant to § 62. Subsection (2) of § 62 indicates that a performance acceptance of an indifferent offer "operates as a promise to render complete performance." To provide such performance with the operative effect of a promise merely binds the offeree to complete performance. It is submitted that an offeree, by starting to perform in response to an offer that can be accepted exclusively by performance, may manifest the same intention of completing performance as does an offeree who begins to perform in response to an indifferent offer. Yet, no contract will be formed by such part performance in the first situation while a contract will be formed in the second situation. The real difference is that the offeree who decides to accept by performance in response to an indifferent offer could have chosen to promise performance. An implication of promise from part performance in response to such an offer is, therefore, warranted. Where the offer requires performance as the exclusive manner of acceptance and the offeree, therefore, cannot possibly accept prior to completing performance, an implication of promise from the start of performance is not warranted. Notwithstanding the inexplicable language in comment b to § 54 of the RESTATEMENT 2d, there is no question that it supports the view that the notice requirement analysis is the same whether the performance acceptance refers to an indifferent offer or an offer requiring only a performance acceptance.

[91] Comment 3 to UCC § 2-206 states: "The beginning of performance by an offeree can be effective as acceptance so as to bind the offeror only if followed within a reasonable time by notice to the offeror. Such a beginning of performance must unambiguously express the offeree's intention to engage himself. For the protection of both parties it is essential that notice follow in due course to *constitute acceptance*." (emphasis added).

[92] UCC § 2-206(2) and RESTATEMENT 2d § 62.

duty of the former offeror. That duty of the former offeror was created when the contract was formed, and the contract was formed upon part performance by the former offeree. A contract existed at that moment in time, else there would be no contractual duty. The analysis indicating that notice is a condition precedent to the former offeror's duty is the primary analysis in the RESTATEMENT 2d[93] though it nods in an illustration by resorting to the intellectually untidy, "lapsed offer" notion of its half-brother, the UCC.[94]

Perhaps a more important problem in the Code formulation is Comment language that may be read to suggest that notice of performance by an offeree who chooses to accept in that manner is always essential.[95] The RESTATEMENT 2d does not even attempt to deal with this Code defect. It insists that notice is essential as a condition after a performance acceptance *only* where the former offeror will not learn of the performance/acceptance promptly and with reasonable certainty.[96] Fortunately, the Code language that may be read to require notice in all performance acceptance situations is in a comment which is not part of the enacted law. Preferably, the comment should be ignored since it is analytically unsound. If courts choose to consider it, it could be interpreted as not requiring notice in all performance acceptance situations. At least courts should be persuaded by the sound analysis of the RESTATEMENT 2d even if they read the Code comment to insist upon notice as part of the acceptance in all performance acceptance situations.[97] It is reasonably certain that Karl Llewellyn, the father of the Code and the principal draftsman of Article 2, did not intend notice to be part of the acceptance so as to permit revocation by the offeror after part performance.[98] It is important to consider the case law under the Code to this time.

---

[93] "If an offeree who accepts by rendering a performance has reason to know that the offeror has no adequate means of learning of the performance with reasonable promptness and certainty, the *contractual duty* of the offeror is discharged...." RESTATEMENT 2d § 54(2).

[94] *See* ill. 1 to § 54 which indicates that the absence of notice discharges the contractual duty, but then, sadly, it adds, "... and he [the former offeror] may treat the offer as having lapsed before acceptance unless within a reasonable time [the former offeree] sends notification of acceptance...." It is clear that the drafters of the RESTATEMENT 2d felt considerable pressure to create a new Restatement reconcilable with the UCC wherever possible. Since the Code is the controlling statute in contracts for the sale of goods, it was obviously desirable to present as much uniformity for all contracts as possible. Moreover, Article 2 of the Code generally presents a highly desirable movement toward a more effective system of modern contract law. *See* RESTATEMENT 2d, *Legislation,* in Introduction, at page 2. On occasion, however, another motivation may have moved the RESTATEMENT 2d drafters to the Code view, to wit, the fact that the American Law Institute is fully responsible for the RESTATEMENTS and it was also partly responsible for the UCC.

[95] *See* comment 3 to § 2-206 of the Code quoted *supra* note 91.

[96] RESTATEMENT 2d § 54(2).

[97] *See* Murray, *Contracts: A New Design for the Agreement Process,* 53 CORNELL L. REV. 785, 796-800 (1968).

[98] In the earliest draft of Article 2 which is regarded as the work of Llewellyn exclusively, a comment to then § 3-F suggests his thinking: "The giving of such notice, however, is a matter which has no need at all to coincide with the moment at which revocation is barred. And it repeatedly happens that the seller's reasonably invited action, even before time for reply or for sending notice has expired, is both a material disarrangement of *his* affairs and an unambiguous expression of intention to perform. In such case, the seller needs protection, *even though* a communication of notice may still be due the buyer, and may be due promptly.... The matter of notification is here treated as one of completing acceptance, rather than as one of breach, because it deals with the effective creation of the offeror's expectations, and because it commonly comes within the time for promissory acceptance." NATIONAL CONFERENCE OF COMMISSIONERS ON UNIFORM STATE LAWS, REPORT ON AND SECOND DRAFT OF A REVISED UNIFORM SALES ACT 77-78 (1941).

If a buyer offers to purchase goods to be manufactured and indicates that manufacturing should begin, the start of manufacturing will be viewed as an acceptance because beginning performance in response to such an offer will be considered a "reasonable mode" of acceptance under the Code.[99] Since the typical, indifferent offer can be accepted in any reasonable manner under the Code and the "prompt shipment" of goods is expressly regarded as a reasonable manner of acceptance, where the seller promptly ships in response to a purchase order (offer), shipment constitutes acceptance.[1] The case law is scant with respect to potentially troublesome problems concerning a notice requirement where the seller accepts an offer by "shipment." If a seller chooses to accept an indifferent offer by shipping the goods, it is important to recognize "shipment" as complete performance if the goods are delivered by the seller to an independent carrier under an FOB "shipment" contract. The act of shipment under these circumstances is not simply the beginning of performance as it would be if the seller began loading the goods on his own truck for delivery to the buyer.[2] Section 2-206(2) which contains an express notice requirement would apply only to acceptances by "beginning of a requested performance" and not to performance which is complete. If, therefore, the seller completes his performance by "shipment," must he then notify the buyer of such shipment? There is no answer in the section language of § 2-206. A comment, however, suggests that "shipment" is used in § 2-206(1)(b) in the same fashion as it is used in another section of Article 2 dealing with the duties of the seller in an FOB "shipment" contract. That section requires the seller to (a) make an appropriate contract with a reasonable independent carrier,[3] (b) obtain any necessary documents, e.g., a bill of lading, and promptly deliver such documents to enable the buyer to receive the goods,[4] and (c) *promptly notify the buyer of the shipment.* If, however, the seller fails to carry out the third requirement of notification, the last paragraph of this section indicates that the buyer may reject the goods "only if material delay or loss ensues."[5] The RESTATEMENT 2d suggests that, in the normal situation of

---

§ 3-F, itself, envisioned making the offer irrevocable upon part performance by the offeree, and the "perfection" of that part performance "acceptance" by notifying the offeror of such acceptance. It is therefore clear that, once performance had begun, Llewellyn would not permit a revocation of the offer.

[99] *See* American Bronze Corp. v. Streamway Prod., 8 Ohio App. 3d 223, 456 N.E.2d 1295 (1982).

[1] *See* Home Lumber Co. v. Appalachian Reg'l Hosps., 722 S.W.2d 912 (Ky. App. 1987); Rangen, Inc. v. Valley Trout Farms, Inc., 104 Idaho 284, 658 P.2d 955 (1983) (separate contracts formed through sending of purchase order by buyer and shipment seller).

[2] Under an FOB "shipment" contract (the normal contract when goods are to be shipped through an independent carrier to the buyer), the seller's performance is complete when he delivers the goods to the carrier at which time the risk of loss passes to the buyer. *See* UCC §§ 2-504 and 2-509(1)(a). If, however, the seller is to deliver by his own truck, the risk of loss will not pass to the buyer until the buyer receives the goods and the seller will be obligated to make a reasonable tender of the goods to the buyer. *See* §§ 2-503 and 2-509(3). *See also* comment 2 to § 2-206.

[3] *See, e.g.,* Larsen v. A.C. Carpenter, Inc., 620 F. Supp. 1084 (E.D.N.Y. 1985) (seller of seed potatoes had responsibility to secure refrigerated transportation as the reasonable if not quite customary mode of transportation to ascertain the safe carriage of such perishable goods even though refrigeration was not expressly required under the contract).

[4] In a documentary transaction, the party in possession of a document of title such as a bill of lading or warehouse receipt is normally entitled to receive, hold, and dispose of the document and the goods represented by the document. UCC § 1-201(15). Thus, to receive the goods in such a transaction, the buyer should have possession of the document of title, i.e., the bill of lading.

[5] UCC § 2-504. The last paragraph of this section also applies to (a), i.e., if the seller fails to make an appropriate contract with a reasonable carrier. It does not, however, apply to (b), i.e., a

"shipment" of goods as an acceptance of the offer, notice is not necessary because the acceptance (shipment) "... will come to the offeror's attention in normal course."[6] Since the UCC is a statute and will govern in cases of contracts for the sale of goods, the notice requirement cannot be ignored and a court may find that a failure of prompt notice of shipment permits the buyer to reject the goods, thereby shifting the risk of loss to the seller when the goods suffer casualty in transit.[7] While the failure to notify is a ground for rejection only if material loss or delay ensues, and such a failure of one of the seller's obligations under an FOB "shipment" contract must *cause* the material loss or delay,[8] there is no escape from the notice requirement under the Code, notwithstanding the contrary view expressed in the RESTATEMENT 2d.

The discrepancies between the Code and RESTATEMENT 2d concerning notice and the awkward language of § 2-206 of the UCC concerning the requirement of notice should not undermine the significance of the basic change in traditional contract law effected by the UCC and supported by the RESTATEMENT 2d. Treating the indifferent (doubtful) offer as the typical offer that may be accepted in any reasonable manner while preserving the absolute mastery of the offer in the offeror constitutes a highly desirable modification of classical contract law. The new concept is a more realistic reaction to the felt needs of a contracts society, and the theory supporting this change is analytically sound.

§ 47. Acceptance in Contracts by Mail and Other Media — The "Mailbox" or "Dispatch" Rule.

A. *The Problem and Original Solutions.*

We have seen that the offeror, as master of the offer, may insist that acceptance be communicated through a particular medium such as the post or telegraph.[9] We have also considered the situation where the offeror does not specify such a medium. There, we concluded that the power of acceptance may be exercised through any medium reasonable under the circumstances.[10] We then noted the requirement that, normally, notice of acceptance be communi-

---

failure by the seller to deliver any necessary documents to enable the buyer to obtain possession of the goods.

[6] RESTATEMENT 2d § 62 comment b.

[7] *See* Rheinberg-Kellerei GMBH v. Vineyard Wine Co., 53 N.C. App. 560, 281 S.E.2d 425 (1981). If the buyer has the right to reject because the seller has failed to comply with § 2-504 of the Code, even under an FOB shipment contract, the buyer may treat the risk of loss as remaining on the seller until cure or acceptance under § 2-510(1).

[8] *See* Monte Carlo Shirt, Inc. v. Daewoo Int'l (Am.) Corp., 707 F.2d 1054 (9th Cir. 1983).

[9] *See* RESTATEMENT 2d § 2-206 and the earlier discussion *supra* § 45(A). If, however, the offer may be fairly interpreted as merely suggesting a particular medium of acceptance, another medium of equal reliability and speed will suffice. Thus, if an offer states that the offeror must receive acceptance by return mail, the offer may be interpreted as referring to the speed of acceptance rather than the particular medium. In such a case, a telegraph or mailgram or Federal Express response would be sufficient if sent within the time the return mail would arrive. If, however, an offer by mail to sell a commodity which fluctuates in price such as securities is received and the offeree waits two days and then, after learning of a sharp rise in the price of the securities, sends a telegraph acceptance, the acceptance will be too late though it arrives in the same time as a prompt acceptance by mail would have arrived. The offeree should not be permitted to speculate at the offeror's expense. *See* RESTATEMENT 2d § 41 ill. 8.

[10] *See* RESTATEMENT 2d §§ 30 and 65, and UCC § 2-206(1)(a) and discussion of this topic *supra* § 45(A).

cated in contracts requiring or permitting a promissory acceptance.[11] If, therefore, the offeror does not require a particular medium of promissory acceptance, the offer is made by mail, and notice of acceptance is required because the acceptance is promissory, how shall that acceptance requirement be fulfilled? It is almost painfully clear that, absent contrary requirements stated in the offer, an acceptance by mail should be effective where the offer came by mail since the mail would certainly be a reasonable medium of acceptance. That conclusion may be supported by the assumption that the offeror has impliedly authorized the mail as a reasonable medium of acceptance by using the mail to make the offer.[12] Yet, a problem remains.

If the mail or other medium is a reasonable medium of acceptance, suppose the offeree uses such a medium but the letter or other communication does not reach the offeror, *e.g.,* it is lost in the mail. In contracts by correspondence, there is a risk of transmission and the question arises, who bears that risk? To put the question another way, is an acceptance dispatched through a reasonable medium effective when dispatched, *e.g.,* when a letter of acceptance is placed in the mailbox, or is it not effective until received by the offeror?

If the acceptance is effective when posted or dispatched, certain ramifications are clear. When a letter of acceptance is lost in the mail, the offeror is unaware that the offer has been accepted, and on the assumption that the offeree is not interested in the proposal, may make a contract with another. The offeree, however, may reasonably assume that a contract has been formed and may proceed to rely on that assumption. There is also the problem of revocation of offers. If the offeror has not yet received the acceptance by mail, he or she may send a letter to the offeree revoking the offer. Revocations, however, must be received to be effective.[13] If the offeree has already accepted by posting the letter of acceptance, the revocation comes too late, i.e., the offer has already been accepted and there is, therefore, no offer to revoke.[14]

If the opposite rule is chosen, i.e., if the dispatched acceptance is not effective until it is received by the offeror, equally difficult problems may occur. Such a rule places the risk of transmission on the offeree. If an offeree mailed a letter of acceptance, he or she could not rely upon having any contractual right until the letter was received by the offeror, and that letter would have to be received before the offeree received any letter of revocation from the offeror. How would the offeree learn that the offeror had received the letter of acceptance? We might require the offeror to notify the offeree. If this notice of receipt of acceptance were lost in the mail, the offeree would not learn that the letter of acceptance was received. Assuming the notice from the offeror (that the offeror had received the letter of acceptance) was received by the offeree, how would the offeror learn that the offeree had received such notice? Another notice would be in order. Again, any of these notices could be lost in transmission. The *ad nauseam* replication of notice upon notice was recognized very

---

[11] *See supra* § 46(A) and text accompanying note 78.

[12] *See, e.g.,* Farley v. Champs Fine Foods, 404 N.W.2d 493 (N.D. 1987).

[13] *See supra* § 42(B) and text accompanying note 78.

[14] *See* Farley v. Champs Fine Foods, *supra* note 12, where the revocation was effective before the acceptance was mailed.

early in the landmark case of *Adams v. Lindsell*.[15] That case was decided when the subjective theory of mutual assent was still prevalent and when it was still doubtful whether an offer could ever be said to create a continuing power of acceptance in the offeree. As suggested earlier,[16] that view would have made it practically impossible to consummate a contract by correspondence. A compromise was inevitable. While the *Adams* court was prepared to go as far as was absolutely necessary in the direction of admitting the possibility of a continuing offer in contracts by mail, it was unwilling to go any farther. The court held that the offer would be operative until the offeree had an opportunity to manifest acceptance by an unequivocal overt act, but the power of acceptance would not last beyond that moment. Thus, once the offeree had performed that overt act by placing the acceptance letter in the post, the contract was formed. Three decades later, the House of Lords reaffirmed the rule[17] and it has never been doubted in England since that time. A few attempts to overcome the rule[18] were unsuccessful in this country where the rule has achieved overwhelming acceptance.[19] It is important to consider the appropriate rationale for its continued application.

There is difficulty in suggesting that the offeree has manifested assent to an offeror by the posting of a letter which may never be received by the offeror. In an ineffective attempt to harmonize the dispatch rule with the requirements of mutual assent, arguments were advanced that the postal service is the "agent" of the offeree or the mutual agent of both parties, or that mutual assent is manifested upon the "loss of control" of the letter of acceptance once it is mailed.[20] The RESTATEMENT 2d does not attempt a significant rationale. It merely suggests that, "the offeree needs a dependable basis for his decision whether to accept."[21] There is, however, a rationale for the rule beyond certainty and stability that is found in the phrase used earlier, "risk of transmission."

B. *A Modern Rationale for the "Dispatch" Rule.*

A contract by correspondence involves two innocent parties. The risk that the communication of acceptance through a reasonable medium will be lost or

---

[15] 1 B. & Ald. 681 [1818].

[16] *See supra* § 30.

[17] *See* Dunlop v. Higgins, 1 H.L. Cas. 381 [1848].

[18] Rhode Island Tool Co. v. United States, 130 Ct. Cl. 698, 128 F. Supp. 417 (1955); Guardian Nat'l Bank v. Huntington Cty. State Bank, 206 Ind. 185, 187 N.E. 388 (1933). Both cases were based on the ability to recall a letter after it was mailed by following postal regulations for such recall. This rationale has been rejected by other courts and commentators as well as the RESTATEMENT 2d. *See* RESTATEMENT 2d § 63 comment a. For a suggestion that the postal acceptance exception to the normal rule requiring communication of promissory acceptances is unwarranted, *see* Samek, *A Reassessment of the Present Rule Relating to Postal Acceptance*, 35 AUSTL. L.J. 38 (1961). For a more flexible approach, *see* Macneil, *Time of Acceptance: Too Many Problems for a Single Rule*, 112 U. PA. L. REV. 947 (1964).

[19] For an extensive analysis of the "deposited acceptance" ("mailbox") rule, *see* Morrison v. Thoelke, 155 So. 2d 889 (Fla. App. 1963). More recent analyses include Nature's Farm Prods., Inc. v. United States, U.S. Ct. Int'l Trade, 648 F. Supp. 6 (1986) and Farley v. Champs Fine Foods, *supra* note 12. *See also,* RESTATEMENT 2d § 63. The mailbox rule has been codifed, *e.g.,* in North Dakota. *See* N.D. CENT. CODE §§ 9-03-18 and 9-03-19.

[20] *See* Morrison v. Thoelke, 155 So. 2d 889 (Fla. App. 1963) for an analysis of these and other earlier theories. The "loss of control" theory was overcome by postal regulations permitting the offeree to withdraw the letter of acceptance from the mail.

[21] *See* RESTATEMENT 2d § 63 comment a.

delayed on its journey to the offeror must be allocated to one of the parties. Since we are forced to choose one of two innocent parties as the recipient of this risk of transmission, we can find some justification for allocating the risk to the offeror. As master of the offer, the offeror can insist that no acceptance will be effective until it is received. If he chooses not to require receipt of acceptance, he should bear the risk of transmission since, as between the offeror and offeree, only the offeror had the power to control that risk.[22]

It is important to recognize that, for almost all other purposes other than acceptance of an offer, mailing a letter is insufficient to make an action legally operative.[23] In particular, there is a superficial inconsistency between the acceptance-upon-dispatch rule and the rules that a revocation of an offer must be received. This alleged inconsistency disappears, however, when we remember that an offeror invites acceptance by post if he or she makes the offer in that fashion, but an offeree does not invite and perhaps, does not expect, a revocation. Similarly, a rejection of an offer must be received.[24] The offeror does not invite a rejection any more than the offeree invites a revocation.

C. *Non-Application in Option Contracts.*

As suggested earlier, the singular exception to the dispatch rule is found in an irrevocable power of acceptance created by an option contract.[25] This is predicated upon the normal understanding that notification of acceptance must be communicated to the offeror within the time limit prescribed in the option or, if no time is stated, within a reasonable time.[26] The parties may, of course, manifest a different intention and that manifestation will control.[27]

D. *"Implied Authorization" to "Reasonable Medium."*

The preferable caption for the rule is the "dispatch" rather than the "mailbox" rule since the rule applies to media other than the post. A telegram of

---

[22]This analysis proceeds from the analysis by Professor Corbin who indicates that we can place the risk on either the offeror or offeree, but we must choose one in the interest of certainty and stability. Corbin supports the choice of the mailbox rule because it closes the deal more quickly and enables performance to proceed more promptly. Moreover, he suggests that communications of acceptance through reasonable media are rarely lost or delayed. 1 CORBIN § 78.

[23]*See* Farley v. Champs Fine Foods, 404 N.W.2d 493 (N.D. 1987) quoting Professor Corbin at § 80 of his treatise in suggesting that the mailing of a letter is insufficient notice to quit a tenancy, not the actual payment of money enclosed in the letter, not sufficient to transfer title to a negotiable instrument, and not sufficient notice required as a condition precedent to a contractual duty.

[24]RESTATEMENT 2d § 68.

[25]*See supra* § 43(B), and text accompanying note 36. *See also* Romain v. A. Howard Whsle. Co., 506 N.E.2d 1124 (Ind. App. 1987) citing the previous edition of this book.

[26]RESTATEMENT 2d § 63 comment f suggests that the offeror who has assumed the risk of the power of acceptance being exercised during a specified period regardless of the offeror's intention during that period should not assume the further risk that the power of acceptance could be exercised without his knowledge.

[27]*See* McTernan v. LeTendre, 4 Mass. App. 502, 351 N.E.2d 566 (1976) where an irrevocable offer under an option contract had to be "accepted" within 60 days. The offeree mailed the acceptance on the 60th day and the court interpreted the term "acceptance" as intending the application of the usual "mailbox" rule.

acceptance is effective upon dispatch,[28] and cases that conditioned the rule upon the use of the precise medium of acceptance,[29] i.e., holding that a telegram acceptance would not be effective upon dispatch when the offer was by mail, have been overcome by contrary decisions[30] and particularly by liberalization of the rule found in the UCC and the RESTATEMENT 2d. Older cases proceeded on the footing that an offeror who did not specify a particular medium of acceptance "impliedly authorized" the same medium.[31] The UCC and RESTATEMENT 2d change is part of the major restructuring of offer and acceptance law. Unless otherwise indicated, an offer is accepted in any reasonable manner and by any *reasonable medium*.[32] In the normal case, it would certainly be reasonable to respond to a mailed offer by telegram, mailgram or another generally accepted medium.[33] It is, however, important to note that, while the dispatch rule would be applied even when a private messenger is used by the offeree, such a messenger would have to be independent and maintain accurate records of its activities.[34]

E. *Reasonable Medium — Proper Address and Payment of Charges.*

The reasonableness of the particular medium of acceptance chosen by the offeree would depend in large part on its reliability and speed as well as any prior dealings with the offeror or usage of trade.[35] Assuming the choice of a reasonable medium, it is essential that the offeree properly address the communication and pay any charges so that it will be delivered in due course. If, for example, a letter of acceptance is delayed, because of insufficient postage or because it is misaddressed, the offeror does not assume the risk of such defects in the communication and the dispatch rule would not apply. Acceptance would become effective in such a case only upon receipt by the offeror, assuming that offer had not lapsed by that time.[36] It should be noted, however, that the failure to use a reasonable medium of acceptance or the defective use

---

[28] *See* L. & E. Wertheimer v. Wehle-Hartford Co., 126 Conn. 30, 9 A.2d 279 (1939); Williams v. A.C. Burdick & Co., 63 Or. 41, 125 P. 844, 126 P. 603 (1912); Haas v. Myers, 111 Ill. 421, 53 Am. Rep. 634 (1884); Trevor v. Wood, 36 N.Y. 307, 93 Am. Dec. 511 (1867).

[29] *See, e.g.,* Dickey v. Hurd, 33 F.2d 415 (1st Cir. 1929), noted in 39 YALE L.J. 424 (1929) and Lucas v. Western Union Tel. Co., 131 Iowa 669, 109 N.W. 191 (1906).

[30] *See, e.g.,* Stephen M. Weld & Co. v. Victory Mfg. Co., 205 F. 770 (E.D.N.C. 1913).

[31] A more liberal rationale, however, is found in Henthorn v. Fraser, 2 Ch. 27 [1892]: "I should prefer to state the rule thus: Where the circumstances are such that it must have been within the contemplation of the parties that, according to the ordinary usages of mankind, the post might be used as a means of communicating the acceptance of an offer, the acceptance is complete as soon as it is posted."

[32] *See* UCC § 2-206 and RESTATEMENT 2d § 30(2). There is no specific language adopting the dispatch rule under Article 2 of the Code. Under § 1-103, however, since the dispatch rule is not displaced, it remains intact under the Code. See the definition of "notifies" in § 1-201(26): a person notifies or gives notice "by taking such steps as may be reasonably required to inform the other in ordinary course whether or not such other actually comes to know of it." *See also* Barclays Am./Bus. Credit, Inc. v. E & E Enters., 697 S.W.2d 694 (Tex. App. 1985), applying UCC § 2-206 and holding acceptance was effective when acknowledgment was mailed.

[33] *See* RESTATEMENT 2d § 65 comment d.

[34] *See* RESTATEMENT 2d § 63 comment e and ill. 11 thereto which suggests that an acceptance sent through the offeree's own employee would not permit the application of the dispatch rule. In such a situation, the acceptance would not be effective until received.

[35] RESTATEMENT 2d § 65 comment b.

[36] RESTATEMENT 2d § 66. *See supra* note 57.

of a reasonable medium by, *e.g.,* misdirecting the letter or telegram or failure to pay necessary charges, will still be operative upon dispatch if it is received when a properly dispatched acceptance would have been received.[37]

F. *Proving the Acceptance Was Dispatched.*

There is a rebuttable presumption that a mailed or otherwise dispatched item has been received.[38] That presumption is not rebutted by the offeror's testimony denying receipt of the item.[39] There must, however, be evidence that the item was mailed. In a business setting, evidence that a letter was written and signed in the ordinary course of business and placed in the usual place for mailing is receivable as evidence that the item was duly mailed.[40] Such evidence is sufficient to create the rebuttable presumption that the item was received.

G. *Application of Dispatch Rule to Telephone, Teletype, or Other Instantaneous Media — "Presence" Versus "Distance."*

If the offeror and offeree are in each others' presence rather than at some distance, there is virtually no risk in the transmission of the acceptance. Consequently, there is no need to apply the dispatch rule. In a face-to-face situation, the acceptance will be effective when *heard* by the offeror rather than when it was *spoken* by the offeree.[41] The question then arises, if the offeror will receive the communication of acceptance instantaneously through the use of a telephone, teletype, telex, radio, or other telecommunication device, is the acceptance effective when spoken or sent (the "distance" rule), or is it effective only when heard or received (the "presence" rule)? If the situation is treated as if the parties were in the presence of each other, the acceptance would be effective when heard or received. If, however, the distance rule were applied as it is in the application of the dispatch rule, the acceptance would be effective when it was spoken or sent. While the RESTATEMENT 2d adopts the rule of the FIRST RESTATEMENT[42] in conformity with the views of the giants of Contract law[43] who were persuaded that the "presence" rule should apply to such instantaneous communications, the case law adopts the "distance" rule, though there is some recognition that the "presence" rule is theoretically preferable.[44] The distance rule is adopted because of the pervasiveness of the

---

[37] RESTATEMENT 2d § 67. *See supra* note 57.

[38] Commonwealth v. Brayman Constr. Corp.—Bracken Constr. Co., 513 A.2d 562 (Pa. Commw. 1986).

[39] *See* Berkowitz v. Mayflower Secs., Inc., 455 Pa. 531, 317 A.2d 584 (1974).

[40] *See* Christie v. Open Pantry Marts, 237 Pa. Super. 243, 246, 352 A.2d 165, 1166-67 (1975) relying upon McCORMICK, EVIDENCE, § 195 at 464 (2d ed. 1972).

[41] 1 CORBIN § 79. RESTATEMENT 2d § 64 comment a. If, however, the offeree knows or has reason to know that his spoken words have not been heard or understood by the offeror, there is no acceptance.

[42] RESTATEMENT 2d § 64; FIRST RESTATEMENT § 65.

[43] 1 CORBIN § 79 and 1 WILLISTON § 82A.

[44] Lipshutz v. Gordon Jewelry Corp., 373 F. Supp. 375 (S.D. Tex. 1974); Pierce v. Foley Bros., 283 Minn. 360, 168 N.W.2d 346 (1969); Linn v. Employers Reins. Co., 392 Pa. 58, 139 A.2d 638 (1958); Ward Mfg. Co. v. Miley, 131 Cal. App. 2d 603, 281 P.2d 343 (1955); United States v. Bushwick Mills, 165 F.2d 198 (2d Cir. 1947). *But see* Entores Ltd. v. Miles Far East Corp., 2 Q.B. 327 (1955).

dispatch rule and the desire for uniformity. In practical terms, the distinction will be important to determine *where* the contract was made if there is a conflict between the laws of the jurisdiction where the acceptance was spoken or dispatched through an instantaneous device, and the jurisdiction where the acceptance was heard or received.[45] In cases where the dispatch rule clearly applies, *e.g.*, an offer and acceptance by mail, the contract will be said to have been formed in the jurisdiction where the letter of acceptance was mailed.[46] By applying the same rule to instantaneous media including the telephone, the result will be the same, i.e., the acceptance will have occurred where and when the acceptance was spoken or sent.

1. Breaks in Communication — Telephone, Telecommunications or Similar Devices.

Other problems that may arise in the use of the telephone or other instantaneous devices include breaks in connection. The increasing use of computers for telecommunication purposes may present even more obvious illustrations of a break in the connection since telephone lines are used for such communications and the break in connection may be visible on the computer screen. If an offer is made through the use of such a device and the offeree speaks or sends an acceptance but knows or has reason to know that the acceptance has not been heard or received, the acceptance is not effective when spoken or dispatched. Absent such actual knowledge or reason to know on the part of the offeree, however, the acceptance is effective when and where spoken or sent, i.e., the allocation of the risk of transmission is identical to the traditional operation of the dispatch rule — the offeror bears that risk.[47] Finally, if the offeror and offeree are equally at fault in not pursuing further communication after a break in transmission, the RESTATEMENT 2d suggests that no contract results.[48] This is in keeping with the usual rule that misunderstanding between parties where both are equally at fault precludes the formation of a contract between such parties.[49]

H. *Interference With Normal Operation of the Dispatch Rule — Overtaking Rejections, Etc.*

We have just seen that a break in a telephone or similar connection that is known to one party but not the other will prevent the knowing party from insisting that a contract was formed. There is a pervasive concept of fault at

---

[45]Thus, in the *Linn* case, *supra* note 44, the plaintiff, in Pennsylvania, made an offer with respect to insurance contracts and defendant, in New York, telephoned his acceptance. There was no written evidence of this contract and New York law required such contracts to be evidenced by a writing to be enforceable. No such requirement existed in Pennsylvania. Defendant failed to perform the oral contract and plaintiff brought an action. The defense was that there was no written evidence of the contract and New York law applied making the alleged oral contract unenforceable. The success of that defense depended upon the choice of law and the court chose New York law because New York was the place where the acceptance was *spoken* and the contract was formed at that point in time where the defendant was located, i.e., New York.

[46]*See* Erie Press Sys. v. Schultz Steel Co., 548 F. Supp. 1215 (W.D. Pa. 1982).

[47]*See* RESTATEMENT 2d § 64 ills. 1 and 2.

[48]RESTATEMENT 2d § 64 comment b.

[49]RESTATEMENT 2d § 20. This concept will be explored later in this volume.

work in contract law. If *A* knows or has reason to know that *B* is laboring under a mistake but chooses not to inform *B* of any misunderstanding, *A* will not be permitted to enforce a contract on *A*'s terms. In fact, *A* may be subject to a contractual duty on *B*'s terms.[50] Similarly, if an offeree chooses to interfere with the normal and reasonable operation of the "mailbox" rule, her acceptance may not be effective on dispatch. Suppose an offeree decides to reject an offer and sends a notice of rejection to the offeror. The offeree then changes her mind and decides to accept. Rejections must be received to be effective while acceptances are effective upon dispatch. If these rules are applied algebraically, an acceptance would be effective if it were dispatched before the rejection were received. The obvious problem arises if the offeror receives the rejection not knowing the acceptance has been mailed. He may very well rely upon the rejection and make an agreement with another. If the acceptance had been received before the rejection, the offeror would assume a contract has been formed with the offeree. To avoid harm to the innocent offeror, the operation of the dispatch rule is modified. An acceptance started *after* the sending of an outright rejection or a counter offer rejection is, itself, a counter offer unless the acceptance is received by the offeror before receipt of the rejection or counter offer.[51] Since the offeree first sent a rejection before sending an acceptance, the dispatch rule does not apply to her acceptance. The acceptance will have to be received to be effective and it will not be effective unless it is received first, i.e., before the rejection is received.[52] If an offeree decides to post a letter manifesting her acceptance of an offer and then changes her mind, the acceptance is effective even though the offeree meets the requirements of the U. S. Postal Service or other medium of acceptance in reclaiming her letter of acceptance from the mail. The offeree may not speculate at the expense of the offeror. Therefore, if the offeror can prove that an acceptance was mailed, a contract was formed regardless of legal reclamation of the letter by the offeree.[53] If the offeree decides to mail her letter of acceptance and then, having changed her mind, to overtake that letter of acceptance with a faster medium such as a mailgram which states that the offer is rejected, it is important to hold that a contract has been formed at the moment the offeree mailed an acceptance even in this situation. Again, however, it is necessary to protect an offeror who has justifiably relied upon a communication of rejection. In that situation, it is not said that a contract has not been formed, but that the offeree is estopped from enforcing the contract against the innocent offeror who has relied on the offeree's overtaking mailgram of rejection.[54] On the other hand, we prevent the offeree from taking the position that a contract was not formed when she mailed the acceptance because she later overtook the acceptance with a mailgram of rejection. If that position were countenanced, the offeree could speculate at the expense of the offeror. Absent reliance by the offeror, the contract that was formed when the accep-

---

[50] *See* § 20 of the RESTATEMENT 2d. This concept will be explored thoroughly in subsequent sections dealing with mistake.

[51] RESTATEMENT 2d § 40.

[52] *Ibid.,* comment b.

[53] RESTATEMENT 2d § 63 comment c.

[54] *See* RESTATEMENT 2d § 63 comment c.

tance was mailed is effective. The offeree's attempt to revoke the acceptance of the offer could be interpreted as a repudiation of her duties under the contract, i.e., the duties created upon posting the letter of acceptance. The arrival of a mailgram containing the proposal of the offeree that the parties surrender their mutual rights and duties that were created when the offeree mailed her acceptance (which has not yet been received by the offeror) should be viewed as an offer to rescind the recently formed contract. If the offer of rescission is accepted, the recently formed contract is discharged.[55]

In any permutation of the "mailbox" rule, the purpose of the rule must be kept in mind, i.e., the risk of transmission is normally allocated to the offeror, not because the offeror is at fault in any real sense, but only because the offeror could have controlled the risk of transmission and chose not to do so. The risk of transmission should not go beyond loss or delay in a properly addressed and stamped letter or other medium where the dispatch by the offeree was proper.[56] If the offeree, however, interferes with the operation of the rule, modifications of the rule to protect the offeror against unwarranted risk will appear.[57] Like any other workable rule of contract law, the "mailbox" rule is not sacred. When it ceases to function as it should because it is not properly utilized, the rule will terminate or, at the very least, will be modified to avoid injustice to innocent parties. The rationale is obvious in light of a hypothetical which has no basis in the extant case law to the present time. An offeree places her letter of acceptance with correct address and proper postage in the usual mailbox. As she is walking away from the mailbox, she notices some children playing with matches, one of which is lighted and tossed into the mailbox. Billows of smoke are forthcoming. The offeree knows that her letter of acceptance will never be received by the offeror. She later argues, "I knew the offeror would never get my offer, but that's not my problem." Should that argument be effective as a matter of law? The question scarcely survives its statement.

---

[55] See RESTATEMENT 2d § 63 comment c which, without elaboration, suggests the possibility of an overtaking communication of revocation operating either as a repudiation of the contract or an offer to rescind it.

[56] RESTATEMENT 2d § 66.

[57] If the offeree misdirects the letter of acceptance or fails to place proper postage thereon, RESTATEMENT 2d § 66 indicates that the dispatch ("mailbox") rule is inoperative. In § 67, however, the RESTATEMENT 2d indicates that, if the misaddressed letter of acceptance manages to arrive when it would have arrived if properly addressed, the dispatch rule would be applicable. This rule is designed to avoid the possibility of the offeree's "disavowal" of acceptance upon mailing. (Comment a to § 67). Thus, if a letter with insufficient postage or the incorrect address were mailed on Monday and arrived when it would have arrived with proper address and postage, e.g., on Wednesday, the FIRST RESTATEMENT, § 67, would make the acceptance effective only upon receipt because the offeree failed to accept properly and, therefore, should lose the advantage of the "mailbox" rule. Suppose, however, that on Tuesday the offeree changed her mind and sent a telegram rejecting the offer. Such a result permits the offeree to speculate at the offeror's expense only because the offeree has misaddressed the letter of acceptance or failed to provide proper postage. The RESTATEMENT 2d avoids that possibility in new § 67. The identical analysis applies if the offeree used an uninvited medium of acceptance.

§ 48. "Matching Acceptance" — Qualified or Conditional Acceptance — Equivocal Acceptance — Acceptance Requesting Additional Terms — "Grumbling Acceptance."

A. *The Matching Acceptance or "Mirror Image" Rule.*

If the offeror is the master of the offer,[58] the offeree may exercise the power of acceptance created by the offer only by complying with the requirements of the offer. Any attempt by the offeree to change the terms of the offer and, simultaneously, exercise the power of acceptance would appear to be impossible. The offeror has assumed a risk of a certain scope by making the offer. Again, it would seem impossible for the offeree to enlarge the scope of that risk by varying the terms of the offer in attempting to accept it because the only power conferred upon the offeree by the offeror is the power to accept the offer. This is the inexorable logic underlying the so-called "matching acceptance" or "mirror image" rule: the acceptance must exactly match the terms of the offer.[59] The rule, however, is often easier to state than to apply. The express terms of any offer may be subject to interpretation. The offer may have been silent with respect to certain terms and the offeree may indicate his intention to proceed according to reasonable terms not mentioned in the offer. The offeree may manifest an intention to accept the offer while indicating his displeasure with the offer or suggesting additional arrangements between the parties. Finally, the manifestation of acceptance may be anything but clear. It is important to distinguish among qualified or conditional acceptances, equivocal acceptances, acceptances which suggest additional or different terms and "grumbling acceptances." Some of these responses to offers are operative acceptances and others are not.

B. *Qualified or Conditional Acceptance.*

We have already explored the situation involving a purported acceptance that adds terms or changes terms in the offer and manifests the offeree's intention to be bound, conditioned upon the new or different terms.[60] We concluded that such a purported acceptance is not an acceptance. Since it is not an acceptance, the common law requires it to be placed in another category. Thus, it is a counter offer.[61] To constitute a qualified or conditional

---

[58] RESTATEMENT 2d § 29.

[59] What has become the classic case illustrating this rule is Poel v. Brunswick-Balke-Collender Co., 216 N.Y. 310, 110 N.E. 619 (1915) in which the purported acceptance contained a printed clause requiring acknowledgment by the other party. Since a literal application of this requirement would place the power of acceptance in that party, the purported acceptance was a conditional acceptance and, therefore, a counter offer. In § 58 of the RESTATEMENT 2d, the requirement is stated as follows: "An acceptance must comply with the requirements of the offer as to the promise to be made or the performance to be rendered." Then, in § 59, "A reply to an offer which purports to accept it but is conditional on the offeror's assent to terms additional to or different from those offered is not an acceptance but is a counter offer." For a modern narrative of the "ribbon matching" or "mirror" rule of common law, *see* Dorton v. Collins & Aikman Corp., 453 F.2d 1161 (6th Cir. 1972).

[60] *See* § 42(D) and text accompanying note 96.

[61] *See* RESTATEMENT 2d § 39 comment b and § 59 comment a. *See also* Davis v. Satrom, 383 N.W.2d 831 (N.D. 1986); Dataserv Equip. Inc. v. Technology Fin. Leasing Corp., 364 N.W.2d 838 (Minn. App. 1985); Normile v. Miller, 313 N.C. 98, 326 S.E.2d 11 (1985); Glende Motor Co. v.

"acceptance" which is not an acceptance but a counter offer, the response to the offer must expressly condition the offeree's assent to the variant terms in the offeree's response. Such a response must be carefully distinguished from other types of responses.

C. *Equivocal Acceptance.*

Where the offer requires or permits an acceptance by promise, thereby necessitating notice of acceptance,[62] it is often suggested that the acceptance must be unequivocal, i.e., that the offeror is entitled to a clear manifestation of acceptance by the offeree before the offeror will be said to be bound to a contract.[63] The offeror is not required to guess or draw inferences of assent from the offeree's response to the offer. If the offeror receives a response in the form of an acknowledgment merely stating that the offer has been received, such a response is equivocal and does not bind the offeror.[64] If, however, the offeror reasonably relies on certain manifestations of the offeree that indicate acceptance of the offer, the offeror will be protected. A court will find a contract formed though the manifestation of acceptance is ambiguous.[65] The concept is based upon fairness to an offeror who neither knows nor should know the meaning attached by the offeree to the offeree's equivocal response to the offer.[66] If, therefore, the offeror may justif(i)ably infer assent to his offer from the offeree's response and he acts on that justifiable inference, a contract will be formed to protect the offeror. He need not, however, infer assent from an equivocal response, but may reasonably assume his offer has not been accepted. The test to be applied is the reasonable understanding of the offeror.[67]

D. *Acceptance Merely Suggesting Variant Terms.*

If an acceptance is stated in clear, unequivocal terms but suggests or requests terms different from the offer as contrasted with conditioning or qualifying the response on the offeror's assent to the different terms, the acceptance is effective and the suggested or requested terms are mere proposals for addition to the contract.[68] A clear illustration is an offer that does not contain any terms relating to a method of payment and a response that unequivocally accepts the offer but adds a suggested method of payment.[69] Conversely, if a buyer unequivocally accepts a seller's offer to sell goods but adds a desire to purchase other goods not mentioned in the original offer, there is an accep-

---

Superior Court of Sutter Cty., 159 Cal. App. 3d 389, 205 Cal. Rptr. 682 (1984); Duval & Co. v. H. A. Malcom, 233 Ga. 784, 214 S.E.2d 356 (1975); Ebline v. Campbell, 209 Md. 584, 121 A.2d 828 (1956).

[62] *See supra* § 46.

[63] *See* Kurio v. United States, 429 F. Supp. 42, 66 (S.D. Tex. 1970). *See also* RESTATEMENT 2d § 57.

[64] *See* RESTATEMENT 2d § 57 ill. 1.

[65] *See* Empire Mach. Co. v. Litton Bus. Tel. Sys., 115 Ariz. App. 568, 566 P.2d 1044 (1977) and RESTATEMENT 2d § 57 comment b.

[66] *See* RESTATEMENT 2d § 20.

[67] *See* Murray, *The Standardized Agreement Phenomena in the Restatement (Second) of Contracts,* 67 CORNELL L. REV. 735, 756-58 (1982).

[68] RESTATEMENT 2d § 61.

[69] *See* Kodiak Island Borough v. Large, 662 P.2d 440 (Alaska 1981); Martindell v. Fiduciary Counsels, Inc., 131 N.J. Eq. 523, 26 A.2d 171, *aff'd,* 30 A.2d 281 (1943); Rucker v. Sanders, 182 N.C. 607, 109 S.E. 857 (1921).

tance of the original offer and a new offer to purchase the other goods.[70] Whether the offeree's response unequivocally accepts the offer and merely suggests or requests additional or different terms as contrasted with conditioning the "acceptance" on the offeror's assent to the variant terms is a question of the fair interpretation of the response according to the reasonable understanding of the offeror.[71] Finally, a response to an offer that suggests terms consistent with trade usage [72] or prior course of dealing[73] is an operative acceptance since such terms become part of the contract absent any contrary expression in the offer.[74]

E. *"Grumbling Acceptance."*

If the response to an offer indicates dissatifaction or displeasure with the offer but still manifests an unequivocal and unconditional acceptance, it operates as an acceptance nowithstanding the "grumbling" statements of the offeree. An offeree need not be pleased with an offer; he need not like the offer and may harbor ill feelings toward the offeror. Nonetheless, he has a power of acceptance and may exercise it though adding an expression of discontent in an otherwise clear manifestation of acceptance. Thus, where an employee responded to a renewal of his contract for another term by suggesting, in effect, "I don't like your offer, I don't think it's right or fair, but I accept it," the court rejected the employer's claim that this response was a qualified or conditional acceptance amounting to a counter offer. Rather, these expressions of dissatisfaction constituted a "grumbling acceptance" but acceptance nonetheless.[75]

§ 49. The "Battle of the Forms" Problem — Bound by What Is Signed.

In the last section, we saw that a conditional or qualified "acceptance" was not an acceptance because it did not match the terms of the offer. Such an "acceptance" is a counter offer. It is abundantly clear that, if *A* offers to sell 1000 units of plastic to *B* at $10 per unit for a total price of $10,000, a purported acceptance by *B* which states that he "accepts" the offer but will take only 500 units at $10 per unit, or that he will take 1000 units at $9 per unit, would not be an acceptance of the offer. Neither response could possibly be an acceptance of *A*'s offer because the response to the offer changed terms that are obviously important to the offeror. Terms such as price or quantity are consciously intended as terms that circumscribe the power of acceptance. *B*

---

[70] *See* McAfee v. Brewer, 214 Va. 579, 203 S.E.2d 129 (1974). Even though this case involved an analysis of UCC § 2-207, to be explored in the next section of this volume, the analysis presented in this section would be effective dehors the Code section.

[71] *See* Murray, *supra* note 67, at 758 and RESTATEMENT 2d § 61 comment a.

[72] *See* UCC § 1-205(2) which defines "usage of trade" as "any practice or method of dealing having such regularity of observance in a place, vocation or trade as to justify an expectation that it will be observed with respect to the transaction in question."

[73] UCC § 1-205(1) defines "course of dealing" as "a sequence of previous conduct between the parties to a particular transaction which is fairly to be regarded as establishing a common basis of understanding for interpreting their expressions and other conduct."

[74] *See* Columbia Nitrogen Corp. v. Royster Co., 451 F.2d 3 (4th Cir. 1971) suggesting that such terms automatically become part of the contract unless they are expressly negated.

[75] Price v. Oklahoma College of Osteopathic Med. & Surgery, 733 P.2d 1357 (Okla. App. 1987).

had no power of acceptance in either of the ways he attempted to exercise it. To suggest that B could "accept" in either of these ways would create a new risk to the offeror, which A never created by his offer. These cases raise few, if any, problems.[76] There is, however, a common problem in which the response to the offer reasonably *appears* to manifest the offeree's acceptance of the offer though subsequent investigation reveals that there were, indeed, terms in that response which varied the terms of the offer. This situation occurs innumerable times each business day where buyers and sellers of goods and services exchange printed forms.

The written evidence of the overwhelming majority of the contracts in our society is found in standardized, printed forms.[77] The print on such forms is often faint and small. Moreover, it contains language attempting to create legal effects which reasonable parties, whether consumers or merchants, would not understand even if they took the time to read the clauses.[78] It is clear beyond peradventure that reasonable parties, including merchants in commercial transactions, do not read the fine print "boilerplate" on the forms received in response to their proposals.[79] The paradigm is an offer in the form of a purchase order sent to a seller who responds with an acknowledgment form manifesting acceptance[80] of the negotiated terms of the offer, i.e., the subject matter, the quantity, the price and, perhaps, certain delivery terms. These are the terms of either form which have been consciously considered by the offeror-buyer and the offeree-seller—the negotiated or "dickered" terms.[81] The seller's acknowledgment form, in effect, states that the seller will ship the goods which the buyer offered to buy in his purchase order at the price and on

---

[76] *See* Koehring Co. v. Glowacki, 77 Wis. 2d 497, 253 N.W.2d 64 (1977) (purported acceptance in a telegram adds a condition to the terms of the offer changing the terms of the offer); Duval & Co. v. H. A. Malcom, 233 Ga. 784, 214 S.E.2d 356 (1975) (purported acceptance contained a material alteration in the quantity term).

[77] Professor W. David Slawson suggests that standard forms are probably the written evidence of the contract in up to 99% of all contracts. Slawson, *Standard Form Contracts and Democratic Control of Lawmaking Power,* 84 HARV. L. REV. 529 (1971).

[78] Among the typical clauses on sellers' forms are attempts to disclaim or exclude implied warranties that would otherwise automatically attach under the UCC (e.g., the implied warranty of merchantability under UCC § 2-314 and the implied warranty of fitness for a particular purpose under § 2-315), the recovery of consequential damages as defined in § 2-715 of the Code, the 'lowance of a four-year statute of limitations which the Code provides in § 2-725, and the insertion of a clause requiring arbitration in the event of any dispute rather than permitting the judicial remedies of the buyer which are listed in § 2-711 of the Code.

[79] *See* Macaulay, *Non-Contractual Relations in Business: A Preliminary Study,* 28 AM. SOC. REV. 55, 59-62 (1963). *See also* Murray, *Standardized Agreement, supra* note 67, at 778-79, n.207.

[80] A response that merely acknowledges receipt of the order (offer) is not an acceptance. *See* § 48(C), text accompanying note 64.

[81] The father of the UCC and principal draftsman of Article 2 of the Code, Professor Karl Llewellyn, suggested that "dickered" terms were the terms to which the parties consciously adverted.

"The answer, I suggest, is this: Instead of thinking about 'assent' to boiler plate clauses, we can recognize that so far as concerns the specific, there is no assent at all. What has in fact been assented to, specifically, are the few dickered terms, and the broad type of the transaction, and but one thing more. That one thing more is a blanket assent (not a specific assent) to any not unreasonable or indecent terms the seller may have on his form, which do not alter or eviscerate the reasonable meaning of the dickered terms. The fine print which has not been read has no business to cut under the reasonable meaning of those dickered terms which constitute the dominant and only real expression of agreement, but much of it commonly belongs in." K. LLEWELLYN, THE COMMON LAW TRADITION: DECIDING APPEALS 370 (1960).

the delivery terms found in that purchase order. A comparison of the "dickered" terms of both forms, i.e., the terms that were typewritten or word processed on the blank spaces of the forms, clearly manifests a "matching acceptance" of an offer. The acknowledgment form, however, contains other terms, terms that were not placed in the blank spaces of the acknowledgment through the use of a typewriter or word processor. These other terms were prefabricated — the pre-printed terms on the form the seller sent to the buyer. These are the terms the buyer did not read, and it is just as likely that the seller neither read nor understood such printed terms albeit they appear on his own form. These are the printed terms drafted by lawyers in their attempts to protect their clients against any contingency.[82] Should the buyer be bound by material, risk-shifting provisions on the seller's form that a reasonable buyer would not have read or understood? It is important to understand the common law reaction to a simpler situation before continuing with our discussion of the "battle of the forms" problem.

If only *one* document containing printed clauses was signed by both parties and represented the exclusive written evidence of the contract, the common law treated the document as binding the parties to its "dickered" *and* printed clauses though there may have been good reason to believe that one of the parties, *e.g.,* a consumer, would not have read or understood one or more clauses, shifting a material risk to that party. This result was predicated upon the seemingly compelling logic of the old common law rule that one is bound by what he signs:

> It will not do for a man to enter into a contract and, when called upon to respond to its obligations, to say that he did not read it when he signed it, or did not know what it contained. If this were permitted, contracts would not be worth the paper on which they were written. But such is not the law. A contractor must stand by the words of his contract; and if he will not read what he signs, he alone is responsible for his omission.[83]

A modern restatement of the same rule would invariably emphasize exceptions for fraud,[84] duress[85] or even unconscionability.[86] Beyond these excep-

---

[82] "[T]he form document is not the direct product of the businessman's knowledge. Rather, it is the product of the draftsman's art. Between the drafting party and the actual draftsman, much knowledge, and much of the sense of fairness, may be lost. More importantly, the professional draftsman's goal is to protect his client as fully as possible from legally enforceable obligations, including some relating to risks that the businessman might be willing to accept. In this process, the temptation, and indeed the art, is to draft up to the limit allowed by law, rather than to change only those features of the background law that must be altered for the trade reasonably to proceed." Rakoff, *Contract of Adhesion: An Essay in Reconstruction,* 96 HARV. L. REV. 1173, 1205 (1983). This is an elaboration of the insight of Karl Llewellyn, "Business lawyers tend to draft to the edge of the possible." Statement of K. Llewellyn in 1 STATE OF NEW YORK LAW REVISION COMMISSION HEARINGS ON THE UNIFORM COMMERCIAL CODE 113 (1954). Further support is found in Murray, *The Chaos of the Battle of the Forms: Solutions,* 39 VAND. L. REV. 1307, 1350-51 (1986) (hereinafter cited as Murray, *Chaos*).

[83] Upton v. Tribilcock, 91 U.S. 45, 50 (1875).

[84] *See* Pioneer Credit Co. v. Medalen, 326 N.W.2d 717, 719 (N.D. 1982): "Failure to read a document before signing it does not excuse ignorance of its contents unless the party shows that 'he was prevented from reading it by fraud, artifice or design by the other party or his authorized representative,'" citing Oliver-Mercer Elec. Coop. v. Fisher, 146 N.W.2d 346, 357 (N.D. 1966).

[85] Colburn v. Mid-State Homes, Inc., 266 So. 2d 865, 868 (Ala. 1972): "If no duress or fraud has been exercised, ... he is ... presumed to know what it was that he signed."

[86] *See* Richardson Greenshields Secs., Inc. v. Metz, 566 F. Supp. 131, 133 (S.D.N.Y. 1983): The failure to discuss or negotiate the terms of an agreement and the fact that no one explained the

tions, a modern court may decide that a particular printed clause should not be binding on the party against whom it was designed to operate simply because such a party cannot be fairly said to have manifested assent to a particular clause.[87] Thus, the general rule remains that one is bound by what he or she signs, but courts have recognized an increasing number of exceptions to that rule over the years.

In the "battle of the forms" problem, there are *two* forms, typically, the buyer's purchase order and the seller's acknowledgment which manifests an acceptance of the offer with respect to the "dickered" terms. Typically, neither party signs the form of the other, i.e., the forms are simply exchanged. If the "dickered" terms on both forms match, should a contract be said to exist, notwithstanding non-matching printed clauses? Such a result was anathema to the common law mind. Again, the insuperable obstacle was the "matching acceptance" or "mirror image" rule — the acceptance had to match the terms of the offer. If the printed clauses in the seller's acknowledgment were different from the terms of the offer, the "matching acceptance" rule was violated and the seller's response could not possibly be an acceptance. The compartmentalized thinking of common law judges compelled another conclusion.

If the response to an offer did not match and, therefore, did not constitute an acceptance, the response had to be something other than an acceptance. The only other available common law compartment in this situation was the counter offer. A non-matching acceptance had to be a counter offer because it appeared to be a qualified or conditional acceptance which is, necessarily, a counter offer.[88] The typical counter offer rejects the original offer and creates a new power of acceptance.[89]

To continue the paradigm, it must be recalled that the buyer and seller were totally unaware of these manufactured legal effects of their effort to manifest a closed deal. Both parties assumed they had made a contract by their exchange of the purchase order and acknowledgment forms because the "dickered" terms of both forms — the terms they noticed — were identical. Thus, after the seller sent its acknowledgment, it shipped the goods and the buyer received and accepted the goods. Later, the buyer discovered a defect in the goods, *e.g.*, a breach of the implied warranty of merchantability.[90] The buyer complained to the seller who, for the first time, read the printed provisions in his own acknowledgment form in a belated attempt to discover an

---

agreement to the signer does not make the agreement unenforceable unless it rises "to the level of fraud, overreaching or unconscionability." The concept of unconscionability permits a court to declare a part or all of a contract inoperative if it would result in "unfair surprise" or if it would be "oppressive" to the signer. It is an elusive concept that will be explored in detail later in this volume. *See* UCC § 2-302 and the comments thereto.

[87] *See* Parton v. Pirtle Oldsmobile-Cadillac-Isuzu, 730 S.W.2d 634, 637-38 (Tenn. App. 1987) holding that a clause exculpating a dealer from any loss or damage to a vehicle was not enforceable. Though recognizing that its fomulation may appear to be based on the doctrine of unconscionability, the court emphasized that it did not intend to predicate its holding on that doctrine in this case. Rather, "[I]t is simply a matter of ascertaining the agreement of the parties in light of modern notions of fair play: a matter of finding the elusive 'circle of assent' which contains the agreement of the parties." The "circle of assent" analysis quoted in part by the court at 637 of its opinion is taken from the second edition of this book at §§ 352-353.

[88] *See supra* § 48(B).

[89] *See supra* § 42(D).

[90] The implied warranty of merchantability is currently set forth in UCC § 2-314.

escape clause which would relieve him from any liability under the normal implied warranty of merchantability. The seller breathed a sigh of relief when he discovered a clause disclaiming the implied warranty of merchantability. The buyer's purchase order either expressly reserved this warranty or it was necessarily implied as it would be in any typical offer to purchase goods. The warranty term in the buyer's form and the disclaimer of warranty in the seller's form clashed — the paradigmatic "battle of the forms" problem. With appropriate counselling from his attorney, the seller would not argue that his form was superior to the buyer's purchase order. Rather, the seller would pursue the inexorable logic of the common law, i.e., the seller's acknowledgment did not match the terms of the offer. It was, therefore, a counter offer which had the effect of rejecting the buyer's offer. The only extant offer was the seller's new (counter) offer creating a power of acceptance in the former offeror. The buyer was now an offeree and could exercise that power of acceptance in any reasonable manner, i.e., by promising to purchase the goods on the terms of the seller's acknowledgment, or simply by accepting the goods since an acceptance by conduct is an effective acceptance.[91] By accepting the goods shipped by the seller, the buyer had accepted the seller's counter offer to ship on the terms of the seller's acknowledgment. Since the terms of that counter offer acknowledgment disclaimed the implied warranty of merchantability, the contract contained no such warranty and the buyer's effort to recover for breach of that warranty was in vain. The traditional common law analysis was based on unassailable logic,[92] but it ignored the agreement that the parties thought they had made when they exchanged their forms, i.e., it ignored the factual bargain,[93] or "true understanding"[94] or "genuine assent"[95] of the parties. The analysis compelled a result based upon technical constraints of the common law.[96] These technical constraints created a contract for the parties — a contract the parties never made. By regarding the unread, printed clauses of the acknowledgment form as operative, the common law discovered a "conditional" or "qualified" acceptance, i.e., a counter offer. The offeror did not understand the acknowledgment as a counter offer. He assumed it was an acceptance and that both parties understood the deal was closed. Moreover, the seller was operating under the same assumption at the moment the forms were exchanged. No reasonable businessman would have discovered a condition to the seller's acceptance of the buyer's purchase order in such printed clauses that were ignored by both parties when the forms were

---

[91] See RESTATEMENT 2d § 19. See also supra § 45.

[92] For an application of these concepts to a real estate lease, see Griggs v. Oak, 164 Neb. 296, 82 N.W.2d 410 (1957).

[93] See the definition of "agreement" in § 1-201(3) of the UCC, i.e., "the bargain of the parties in fact." See also Murray, The Article 2 Prism: The Underlying Philosophy of Article 2 of the Uniform Commercial Code, 21 WASHBURN L.J. 1 (1981) and Murray, The Standardized Agreement Phenomenon in the Restatement (Second) of Contracts, 67 CORNELL L. REV. 735 (1982).

[94] See comment 2 to UCC § 2-202 which states the objective as arriving at the "true understanding" of the parties' agreement.

[95] See Parton v. Pirtle Oldsmobile-Cadillac-Isuzu, 730 S.W.2d 634, 637 (Tenn. App. 1987) relying upon §§ 352-353 of the second edition of this book in which the concept of "genuine" assent is distinguished from "apparent assent."

[96] For several illustrations of the attempt to overcome the technical constraints of the common law of contracts which interfere with the effectuation of the factual bargain or "true understanding" or "genuine assent" of the parties, see Murray, Chaos, supra note 82, at 1312, n.18.

exchanged.[97] The manifest injustice to buyers in the paridigmatic case was equally applicable to sellers in other fact situations.[98] If the seller was the original offeror and the buyer sent what reasonably appeared to be an acceptance, the response was converted into a counter offer because it contained variant terms. No contract was formed and the buyer could escape the genuine bargain to which the buyer and the seller had cleary assented. Returning to the paradigm, if the seller's response appeared to be an acceptance but contained variant terms in the seller's printed clauses to which neither party paid any attention, no contract was formed by the exchange of the offer and technical counter offer. Both parties assumed a contract had been made. This conclusion is evidenced by the fact that the seller would invariably ship the goods and the buyer would invariably accept them. Shipping and accepting the goods formed a contract, but, though surprising to the buyer and only belatedly discovered by the seller, the terms of that contract were the terms of the seller's counter offer. Since the seller's counter offer was the "last shot" fired in the battle of the forms and the parties then proceeded to perform what they had reasonably but mistakenly understood to be their contractual duties resulting from their exchange of forms, the seller prevailed because the buyer accepted the counter offer. The "last shot" principle was firmly embedded in the very common situation of exchanged forms where the "dickered" terms were identical but the printed clauses did not match. It was abundantly clear to Professor Karl Llewellyn, who was to become the father of the UCC and the principal draftsman of Article 2 of the Code where this problem had to be addressed, that a party should not win the "battle of the forms" simply because he fired the last shot in that battle.[99] Moreover, Llewellyn recognized the total lack of assent to any bargain other than the bargain which the parties thought they had made. He was eager to change the procrustean rules of common law to have it recognize the bargain the parties reasonably thought they had made — the factual bargain. He knew that this effort would require a radical transformation of classical contract law with respect to the "matching acceptance" rule.[1]

---

[97] In dealing with this problem with respect to the then new UCC, Professor Karl Llewellyn stated, "Those unhappy cases which find a condition where no businessman would find one are carefully disapproved." 1 STATE OF NEW YORK LAW REVISION COMMISSION HEARINGS ON THE UNIFORM COMMERCIAL CODE 55 (1954).

[98] Thus, in a classic illustration of the injustice of the common law analysis of the battle of the forms, a buyer escaped a contract that the buyer and seller thought they had made. As an afterthought, the buyer discovered a printed clause on the purchase order form it had intended as an acceptance of the seller's offer. The clause required an acknowledgment of the buyer's order since, when the form was used as an offer, such an acknowledgment was necessary. Notwithstanding compelling evidence that neither party regarded the printed clause in the purchase order as operative, the court held that it was, necessarily, a counter offer. No contract was formed and the buyer escaped the closed deal that both parties had assumed. Peol v. Brunswick-Balke-Collender Co., 216 N.Y. 310, 110 N.E. 619 (1915). The case is analyzed in Murray, Chaos, supra note 82, at 1315-18.

[99] Professor Grant Gilmore, who is best known for his remarkable scholarship with respect to security interests in personal property, was one of Professor Llewellyn's co-workers in creating the UCC. With respect to the "battle of the forms" problem he commented that it was a problem that Professor Llewellyn "dearly loved." See Coogan, Dunn, Farnsworth, Gilmore, Hogan, Kripke, Leary & Sachse, Advanced ALI-ABA Course of Study on Banking and Secured Transactions Under the Uniform Commercial Code, Transcript at 108 (1968).

[1] Professor Llewellyn was disturbed by suggestions that the changes he contemplated in Article 2 and Sales law in general were misunderstood as merely changing the law in "a few particulars."

§ 50. "Battle of the Forms": Solutions — Section 2-207 of the Uniform Commercial Code.

A. *The Essential Section 2-207.*

In the previous section, we traced the problems created by the application of traditional contract doctrine to the situation in which parties apparently intend to make a contract through the exchange of forms which contain identical negotiated or "dickered" terms, but also contain non-matching printed clauses to which the parties pay little, if any, attention. To overcome these problems, it was essential to deprive such clauses of any operative effect unless the parties agreed to them. It was particularly important to deprive such clauses of the traditional common law effect of converting the response to a counter offer and, after the parties had performed, finding a contract on the terms of the last form sent by the offeree simply because it was the last form or "last shot" in the "battle of the forms." To understand the attempt to solve the problem, there is no escape from a detailed exploration of the statutory language in what is generally regarded as the most difficult and controversial section of the UCC, § 2-207.

1. Section 2-207 — Additional Terms in Acceptance or Confirmation.

A definite and seasonable expression of acceptance or a written confirmation which is sent within a reasonable time operates as an acceptance even though it states terms additional to or different from those offered or agreed upon, unless acceptance is expressly made conditional on assent to any different or additional terms.

The additional terms are to be construed as proposals for additions to the contract. Between merchants, such terms become part of the contract unless:

(a) the offer expressly limits acceptance to the terms of the offer;

(b) they materially alter it; or

(c) notification of objection to them has already been given or is given within a reasonable time after notice of them is received.

Conduct by both parties which recognizes the existence of a contract is sufficient to establish a contract for sale although the writings of the parties do not otherwise establish a contract. In such case the terms of the particular contract consist of those terms on which the writings of the parties agree, together with any supplementary terms incorporated under any other provision of this Act.[2]

He made it clear that the Code would "remake" sales law *"vigorously and over the whole field* in order that the law may be made to conform to commercial practice, and may be read and make sense.... The changes are, in fact, deep, wide, vital. And they are utterly needed in order to produce intelligent and workable commercial law. Professor Mentshikoff's [Professor Menshikoff is well-known for her major contributions to the UCC while working with her husband, Karl Llewellyn] comments in your final session are peculiarly on point: The present law 'works' by being *ignored* by the *decent* business man." 1 STATE OF NEW YORK LAW REVISION COMMISSION HEARINGS ON THE UNIFORM COMMERCIAL CODE 49 (1954) (emphasis in original).

[2] This is the current version of § 2-207 of the UCC. For an analysis of earlier drafts of § 2-207, see Murray, *Chaos, supra* note 82, at 1319-30.

   This statutory language has been the subject of considerable criticism, at least some of which is warranted.[3] There can be little question that the concepts and the statutory language of § 2-207 have created the most difficult set of problems in Article 2 of the Code. Subsection (1) manifests the radical transformation of the "matching acceptance" rule. To suggest that a response to an offer ("a definite and seasonable expression of acceptance") can have the effect of an acceptance ("operates as an acceptance") even though that response contains terms that are different from or additional to the terms of the offer, appears to strike at the very heart of the matching acceptance rule. Indeed, the conventional wisdom found in current case law interpreting this language of § 2-207(1) insists that the fundamental change of the Section is the emasculation of the "matching acceptance" or "mirror image" rule of classical contract law.[4] Even Karl Llewellyn would not claim that such an expression of acceptance *is* an acceptance. He softened the effect of the change by having the response *operate* as an acceptance. He may have recognized the traumatic effect that a more direct approach would engender. The effect on the vested notions of classical contract law was particularly evident in the first major judicial interpretation of § 2-207.

   In *Roto-Lith, Ltd. v. F. P. Bartlett & Co.,*[5] the response to the offer appeared to manifest acceptance but contained the usual disclaimer of warranty provision found in the typical seller's acknowledgment form. The offeror argued that the response was a definite expression of acceptance notwithstanding the different warranty term, and that the warranty term should not become a part of the contract since it constituted a material alteration of the terms of the offer.[6] While the court recognized the disclaimer of warranty as a material alteration, it could not bring itself to find that a response containing such a term constituted an acceptance resulting in a contract without that term. The court appeared to be so imbued with traditional notions of offer and acceptance law that it simply could not assimilate the seemingly radical changes effected by § 2-207. It insisted that § 2-207 would not permit a response with a *materially* altering term to operate as an acceptance. Such a response had to be a counter offer in the eyes of this court. The effect of the holding is to

----

   [3]The statute is a "murky bit of prose," Southwest Eng'g Co. v. Martin Tractor Co., 205 Kan. 684, 694, 473 P.2d 18, 25 (1970); "The statute is not too happily drafted," Roto-Lith, Ltd. v. F. P. Bartlett & Co., 297 F.2d 497, 500 (1st Cir. 1962); § 2-207 is "[a]n enigmatic section of the Code," Ebasco Servs., Inc. v. Pennsylvania Power & Light Co., 460 F. Supp. 163, 205 (E.D. Pa. 1978); Section 2-207 is "one of the most important, subtle and difficult in the entire Code, and well it may be said that the product as it finally reads is not altogether satisfactory." R. Deusenberg & L. King, *Sales and Bulk Transfers,* 3 Bender's U.C.C. Serv. § 3.02 (1986); "The 1952 version of 2-207 was bad enough ... but the addition of subsection (3) without the slightest explanation of how it was supposed to mesh with (1) and (2) turned the section into a complete disaster," Professor Grant Gilmore (who worked with Karl Llewellyn) in a letter to Professor Robert Summers of the Cornell Law School, quoted in R. Speidel, R. Summers & J. White, Commercial and Consumer Law 54-55 (3d ed. 1981).

   [4]*See, e.g.,* Diamond Fruit Growers, Inc. v. Krack Corp., 794 F.2d 1440 (9th Cir. 1986); C. Itoh & Co. (American) Inc. v. Jordan Int'l Co., 552 F.2d 1228 (7th Cir. 1977); Hohenberg Bros. v. Killebrew, 505 F.2d 643 (5th Cir. 1974); Uniroyal, Inc. v. Chambers Gasket & Mfg. Co., 380 N.E.2d 571 (Ind. App. 1978); Steiner v. Mobil Oil Corp., 20 Cal. 3d 90, 141 Cal. Rptr. 157, 569 P.2d 751 (1977); Dorton v. Collins & Aikman Corp., 453 F.2d 1151 (10th Cir. 1972).

   [5]297 F.2d 497 (1st Cir. 1962).

   [6]As will be seen later in this section, § 2-207(2)(b) would eliminate any such materially altering term from the contract terms which a court should recognize.

frustrate the essential purpose of § 2-207 whenever a response to an offer which reasonably appears to be an acceptance happens to contain a materially variant term in a printed clause ignored by both parties. Fortunately, the *Roto-Lith* case has virtually no precedential value.[7]

An examination of the *purpose* of § 2-207 may suggest that it is not radical if it is seen in the context of the underlying purpose of Article 2 of the Code to effectuate the factual bargain of the parties, i.e., their manifestly intended bargain as contrasted with the technical contract found through classical contract rules.[8] The common law contracts lawyer finds a contradiction in an "acceptance" when applied to an expression containing terms that are different from the terms of the offer. In his mind, such terms mandate the characterization of "counter offer" rather than "acceptance." This is precisely where orthodox contract theory and the policy of effectuating the factual bargain collide. The old "matching acceptance" rule is sensible in precluding the imposition of additional or different terms on the offeror. It departs from reality and becomes a technical construct, however, where it precludes the recognition of a contract that both parties reasonably assume they have made simply because there are some ignored terms in the fine print of a form, typically the seller's acknowledgment, that do not match the terms of the offer.[9] Comments to § 2-207 clearly support this analysis.

One comment recognizes the commercial reality that, "Because the [printed] forms are oriented to the thinking of the respective drafting parties, the terms contained in them often do not correspond. Often the seller's form contains terms different from or additional to those set forth in the buyer's form. Nevertheless, the parties proceed with the transaction." [10] Another comment supports the underlying philosophy of Article 2 of the Code in suggesting, "Under this Article a proposed deal which in commercial understanding has in fact been closed is recognized as a contract." [11] Thus, if the exchanged forms manifest identity in the terms the parties have consciously considered, leading them to the reasonable belief that they have an operative agreement, there is a *substantive* matching acceptance of the offer that should not be denied operative effect on the artificial basis that the acceptance also contains additional or different terms in unread and otherwise ignored clauses. Thus, such an expression of acceptance will operate as an acceptance; it will not be a counter offer. In summary, it is suggested that the basic purpose of § 2-207 was to change the assumption that variant terms in the response to an offer

---

[7]Criticisms of *Roto-Lith* will be found in C. Itoh & Co. (America) v. Jordan Int'l Co., 552 F.2d 1228, (7th Cir. 1977); Dorton v. Collins & Aikman Corp., 453 F.2d 1161, 1168 & n.5 (6th Cir. 1972); Ebasco Servs. v. Pennsylvania Power & Light Co., 402 F. Supp. 412, 437-38 (E.D. Pa. 1975); Steiner v. Mobil Oil Corp., 70 Cal. 3d 70, 107, 569 P.2d 751, 763, 141 Cal. Rptr. 157, 169 (1977); Uniroyal, Inc. v. Chambers Gasket & Mfg. Co., 177 Ind. App. 508, 517-18, 380 N.E.2d 571, 578 (1978).

[8]*See* the discussion of the factual bargain analysis in the preceding section.

[9]For an elaboration of this concept, *see* Murray, *Section 2-207 of the Uniform Commercial Code: Another Word About Incipient Unconscionability*, 39 U. PITT. L. REV. 597, 601 *et seq.* (1978).

[10]UCC § 2-207 comment 1. The implication is clear: § 2-207 recognizes the commercial reality that parties, including merchants, do not read or understand such non-matching, printed, clauses and that this conduct is not unreasonable.

[11]UCC § 2-207 comment 2. *See also* Murray, *The Article 2 Prism: The Underlying Philosophy of Article 2 of the Uniform Commercial Code*, 21 WASHBURN L.J. 1 (1981).

necessarily create a counter offer to the assumption that a response to an offer is an acceptance unless a reasonable offeror would understand it to be a counter offer.[12]

2. Variant Terms in the Response — "Material" Versus "Immaterial."

If a response to an offer containing different or additional terms operates as an acceptance, what shall be done with the different or additional terms in that response?[13] Subsection (2) of § 2-207 is designed to deal with variant terms in an otherwise definite expression of acceptance. It begins with the directive that the additional terms[14] are to be viewed as mere proposals of addition(s) to the contract. The application of this directive, however, is immediately narrowed by the next sentence in subsection (2) indicating that additional terms "become part of the contract" if the contract is "between merchants." Reading the two sentences together, it becomes clear that the first directive that additional terms are mere proposals (that would have to be accepted by the party to whom they are proposed if they are to become part of the contract) would be applied only if one or both parties were not merchants.[15] While the second sentence begins with the directive that additional terms become part of the contract between merchants, if it said no more, we would have the party firing the "last shot" winning the battle of the forms since those additional terms would become operative terms of the contract. The second sentence of subsection (2), however, is heavily qualified. The additional terms will become part of a contract between merchants *unless* any one of three conditions is met. One of the three conditions is so likely to be present that the conditions tend to swallow the first part of this prescription that additional terms become part of the contract between merchants.

The first condition is that the offer does not contain a provision expressly limiting acceptance to its terms.[16] This condition can be seen as a restatement of the usual rule that the offeror is master of the offer and may, therefore, insist that the acceptance be in precise conformity with the offer. Under even modern analyses of the agreement process, however, such an offer could be

---

[12] *See Murray, Chaos, supra* note 82, at 1372.

[13] It would have been preferable for subsection (1) of § 2-207 to use the term "response" instead of the term "acceptance." "Response" is a neutral term. A response to an offer containing different or additional terms may or may not operate as an acceptance, depending upon the different or additional term in that response. Thus, in an offer to purchase 1000 widgits at $10 per widgit, a response that changes the price or quantity terms, or a response that changes the very subject matter of the contract, would not be a definite expression of acceptance. *See supra* § 49 and text accompanying note 76. However, a response in which the seller agrees to ship 1000 widgits at $10 per widgit and which is otherwise in conformity with any consciously considered term may be a definite expression of acceptance and operate as an acceptance although the response also contains a clause limiting warranty liability, or a clause indicating that, in the event of a dispute over the contract, the parties agree to submit their dispute to arbitration, or another term typically found in the "boilerplate" of sellers' acknowledgment forms.

[14] Subsection (2) mentions only "additional" terms while subsection (1) of § 2-207 deals with "different" *or* "additional" terms. The omission of "different" in subsection (2) has caused a great deal of controversy which will be addressed later in this discussion of the "battle of the forms."

[15] The broad definition of "merchant" under § 1-204 would apply to the use of the term in § 2-207, i.e., virtually anyone in business would be a "merchant" for the purposes of this Article 2 section.

[16] Section 2-207(2)(a).

said to insist upon such precise conformity with its terms that *any* purported acceptance containing *any* different or additional term could not possibly operate as an acceptance, i.e., such a clause in an offer would prevent a response from operating as an acceptance under § 2-207(1) if it contained *any* change in the offer. At this point in our analysis, it is critically important to emphasize the fact that subsection (2) of § 2-207 *does not apply at all unless there has been a definite expression of acceptance containing different or additional terms in response to the offer.* We will, therefore, never reach any part of subsection (2) unless we first discover such an acceptance under subsection (1). Consequently, it would be ludicrous to interpret § 2-207(2)(a) as precluding an acceptance absent precise conformity to the offer.[17] Subsection (2)(a) is designed to permit the offeror to notify the offeree that any additional terms in the response to the offer will not become part of the contract even though the response otherwise operates as an acceptance. It is, therefore, somewhat redundant to have included § 2-207(2)(c), which permits the offeror to notify the offeree of objection to any variant terms either before the offeror receives the response or within a reasonable time thereafter.[18] At first glance, it may also appear that neither subsections (2)(a) or (c) are necessary since subsection (2)(b) automatically excises any additional term in the response to the offer if that term "materially alters" the terms of the offer. If, for example, the response to the offer disclaims the usual implied warranties of merchantability or fitness for a particular purpose that attend the buyer's offer, such disclaimers would be regarded as material alterations.[19] Professor Llewellyn was particularly concerned that the offeror not be burdened with any substantial or material additions to the risks he or she assumed as offeror.[20] The primary

---

[17] It should be emphasized, however, that if an offer is almost painfully clear in its insistence that, literally, *any* deviation from the terms of the offer will cause the response to be ineffective as an acceptance, the response will not be an acceptance. Traditional contract law would then require the response to be characterized as a counter offer. In Salt River Project Agrl. Dist. v. Westinghouse Elec. Corp., 143 Ariz. 437, 695 P.2d 267 (1983) *modified en banc,* 143 Ariz. 368, 694 P.2d 198 (1984), the buyer sent its offer through the use of its printed purchase order which contained the following language: "Acceptance of this Purchase Order must be made on its exact terms and if additional or different terms are proposed by Seller, such response will constitute a counter-offer." The response by the seller was through its printed acknowledgment form which may not have been construed as a counter offer. It did, however, contain the usual different or additional terms. The court construed the seller's response as a counter offer because the buyer's purchase order (offer) required that characterization of any response containing any different or additional terms. For a more complete analysis of this opinion, *see* Murray, *Chaos, supra* note 82, at 1352-54.

[18] Section 2-207(2)(c) is only *somewhat* redundant since, in the absence of any notification of objection clause in the offer, the offeror may subsequently notify the offeree of objection to variant terms in the response within a reasonable time after the offeror learns of such variant terms.

[19] *See, e.g.,* Twin Disc, Inc. v. Big Bud Tractor, 772 F.2d 1329, 1334 (7th Cir. 1985).

[20] "In a word, the existing law is confused and uncertain. Some improvement is to be hoped from the provision of § 2-207(2) which allows minor additional terms to enter the contract without the express consent which (more frequently than not) never occurs. What terms will be construed as 'materially' altering the contract is indeed a question for the courts' determination; but at least the Code focuses the question." Statement of Karl Llewellyn, 1 NEW YORK LAW REVISION COMMISSION HEARINGS ON THE UNIFORM COMMERCIAL CODE 56 (1954). The comments to § 2-207 contain illustrations of material versus immaterial alterations. A prime example of a material alteration is a disclaimer of warranty clause and another is a cancellation clause (comment 4). If an additional term merely specified a reasonable time for part of the performance within customary time limits, it would be an immaterial addition and would not be subject to excision under § 2-207(2)(b) comment 5.

purpose of § 2-207 is the avoidance of oppression and unfair surprise.[21] That purpose is effectuated if material alterations of the offer are excised. If, therefore, any material alterations in the response to the offer will be excised under § 2-207(2)(b) without any mention of that safeguard in the offer, why should an offeror bother to include a § 2-207(2)(a) clause expressly limiting acceptance to the terms of the offer, or a § 2-207(2)(c) clause providing advance notification of objection to any different or additional terms? The explanation lies in the recognition that the proper interpretation of the context of § 2-207(2) requires *immaterial* additional terms in the merchant-offeree's response to the offer to become part of the contract absent a clause in the offer limiting acceptance to the terms of the offer or a notification of objection to variant terms in the response. It may be assumed that there is no harm to the offeror in permitting such immaterial terms to be added to the contract since the risk of the offeror is not substantially enlarged by the inclusion of such terms. That seemingly plausible assumption is undermined, however, when we recall that courts will decide whether a particular additional term is material or immaterial. There can be some highly questionable characterizations of immateriality of particular additional terms. Thus, one court held that a clause in a response excluding the buyer's normal recovery of consequential damages is an immaterial term,[22] while other courts have recognized the substantial nature of such clauses and characterized them as material terms.[23] A response to an offer may contain an arbitration clause. If it were an operative term of the contract, such a clause would require the parties to submit any dispute under their contract to the arbitration process rather than the normal judicial process. Some courts have held that the determination of whether such clauses constitute material vs. immaterial alterations is a question of fact [24] while other courts have determined such clauses to be material alterations.[25] An offeror may, therefore, avoid a judicial determination of ma-

---

[21] Comment 4 to § 2-207 indicates that the test for a material alteration is "whether the variant term in the acceptance would result in surprise or hardship if incorporated without express awareness by the other party...." Comment 5, dealing with immaterial alterations, suggests the converse, i.e., "clauses which involve no element of unreasonable surprise and which therefore are to be incorporated in the contract unless notice of objection is seasonably given...." Cases testing the materiality of the alteration in terms of unreasonable surprise or hardship include Luedtke Eng'g Co. v. Indiana Limestone Co., 740 F.2d 598, 600 (7th Cir. 1984), and Ebasco Servs. v. v. Pennsylvania Power & Light Co., 402 F. Supp. 421, 442 (E.D. Pa. 1975). The principle of avoiding oppression and unfair surprise also underlies the UCC concept of unconscionability in UCC § 2-302. There is considerable overlap between §§ 2-207 and 2-302. The essential difference may be seen as avoiding unfair surprise and hardship as a threshold matter by precluding certain terms from becoming operative terms of the contract *ab initio* under § 2-207, and then, under § 2-302, permitting courts to excise terms from an existing contract if their operation would cause unfair surprise or hardship to the party against whom they are designed to operate. *See* comment 1 to § 2-302 suggesting that the principle of unconscionability "is one of the prevention of oppression and unfair surprise...." For an analysis of the sections in terms of the identity of underlying principle, *see* Murray, *Section 2-207 of the Uniform Commercial Code: Another Word About Incipient Unconscionability,* 39 U. Pitt. L. Rev. 597, 606-608 (1978).

[22] *See* Hydraform Prods. Corp. v. American Steel & Alum. Corp., 498 A.2d 339 (N.H. 1985) and Kathenes v. Quick Check Food Stores, 596 F. Supp. 713, 718 (D.N.J. 1984).

[23] *See* Western Indus. v. Newcor Canada, Ltd., 739 F.2d 1198, 1205 (7th Cir. 1984); Transamerica Oil Corp. v. Lynes, Inc., 723 F.2d 758 (10th Cir. 1983); Album Graphics, Inc. v. Beatrice Foods Co., 87 Ill. App. 3d 338, 408 N.E.2d 1041 (1980).

[24] *See* Dorton v. Collins & Aikman Corp., 453 F.2d 1161 (6th Cir. 1972).

[25] *See, e.g.,* Marlene Indus. v. Carnac Textiles, 45 N.Y.2d 327, 380 N.E.2d 239 (1978); N. & D. Fashions, Inc. v. D. H. J. Indus., 548 F.2d 722 (8th Cir. 1976); Frances Hosiery Mills, Inc. v.

teriality concerning one or more additional terms in the response to the offer by inserting a § 2-207(2)(a) clause limiting acceptance to the terms of the offer or taking advantage of § 2-207(2)(c) by advance or subsequent notification of objection to any variant terms in the response. A limitation to the terms of the offer or notification of objection to variant terms will preclude such terms from becoming operative regardless of their materiality.

3. Confirmation Operating as an Acceptance — Statute of Frauds Distinguished.

Having seen the basic operation of § 2-207(1) and (2) where the response to the offer is characterized as an acceptance though it contains different or additional terms, it is important to consider another matter which was very troublesome to Professor Llewellyn as he set about to construct what has become § 2-207 of the Code. Contracts are often formed orally, i.e., in person or by telephone. As will be seen later in this volume, certain kinds of contracts must be evidenced by a writing to be enforceable pursuant to the Statute of Frauds which began in Seventeenth Century England and was adopted in this country as part of our English legal heritage.[26] Contracts for the sale of goods with a price of $500 or more must be evidenced by a writing. The written evidence of the contract, however, need not exist at the moment of contract formation. A memorandum of a prior oral contract will be sufficient to satisfy the Statute of Frauds. When parties form their contract orally, therefore, it is common practice for one or both parties to send a confirmation of the oral contract to provide reliable written evidence of that contract. It must be remembered that the confirmation is subsequent to the formation of the oral contract. The "battle of the forms" problem enters in the following situation: *A* and *B* have a luncheon meeting (or a telephone discussion) during which *A* agrees to sell 1000 units of X-35 plastic to *B* at a price of ten dollars per unit for a total price of $10,000. The parties have evidenced their mutual assent to this arrangement by discussing the subject matter, the quantity and the price. They may have also discussed certain delivery terms such as the time and place of delivery and, perhaps, even the method of delivery. It would be unusual, however, for the parties to have discussed warranty terms, terms dealing with judicial remedies such as the allowance or exclusion of consequential damages, or an arbitration term. Having formed their oral contract, the parties return to their respective offices and immediately send documents to each other confirming the oral contract they made during their luncheon meeting. Each of these parties is an agent for their respective firms and they follow the standard procedure of sending the printed purchase order and acknowledgment forms their firms have provided to evidence contracts they make for their companies. Had there been no prior oral agreement and the buyer *(B)* wanted to purchase 1000 units of X-35 plastic at $10 per unit from *A*, *B* would have sent its purchase order as an offer to purchase the plastic. If *A* desired to enter into such a contract with *B*, *A* would have responded through his ac-

---

Burlington Indus., 285 N.C. 344, 204 S.E.2d 834 (1974). *See* Furnish, *Commercial Arbitration Agreements and the Uniform Commercial Code,* 67 CALIF. L. REV. 317 (1979).

[26] The Statute of Frauds is explored in Chapter 4.

knowledgment form. In that situation, the offer would have been evidenced by the purchase order and, assuming the acknowledgment constituted a definite expression of acceptance, the acknowledgment would have served as an acceptance even though it contained different or additional terms. Such terms would have been dealt with under § 2-207(2) as we saw earlier in this Section. Where there has been a prior oral agreement to purchase and sell the plastic, however, the exchange of purchase order and acknowledgment forms constitute an exchange of confirmations of a prior oral contract. The confirmations contain the terms that were discussed — the "dickered" terms — and they are identical on the printed forms. Typically, however, the seller's acknowledgment will contain what have become the usual printed clauses disclaiming warranties, excluding certain damages such as consequential damages and, perhaps, requiring arbitration of any disputes between the parties to the contract. Section 2-207(1) deals not only with written offers and acceptances; it also deals with written confirmations and the statutory language is curious. "A definite and seasonable expression of acceptance *or a written confirmation* ... operates as an acceptance even though it states terms additional to or different from those offered *or agreed upon. . . .*" [27]

The problem is, how can a written confirmation of a contract *operate as an acceptance*? The contract has already been formed and the written confirmation, therefore, must be confirming a contract. Professor Llewellyn was particularly eager to deal with this problem which he felt was "hopelessly confused" under pre-Code law.[28] The factual bargain was the bargain the parties made during their luncheon conversation. Thus, any different or additional terms in one or more confirmations of that oral contract should not be made operative. To effectuate that result, § 2-207(1) treats a confirmation as if it were an acceptance and deals with any different or additional terms under § 2-207(2). Any materially altering terms in a seller's confirmation would be excised under § 2-207(2)(b). Moreover, the conflicting terms in the confirmation may be seen as an implied notice of objection to such additional or different terms, i.e., having the same effect as a notice of objection clause pursuant to § 2-207(2)(c).[29] The result is to effectuate the purpose of § 2-207 in finding a

---

[27] UCC § 2-207(1) (emphasis added).

[28] *See* statement of Professor Llewellyn at 1 STATE OF NEW YORK LAW REVISION COMMISSION HEARINGS ON THE UNIFORM COMMERCIAL CODE 55-56 (1954).

[29] Comment 6 to § 2-207 begins with the enigmatic statement, "If no answer is received within a reasonable time after additional terms are proposed, it is both fair and commercially sound to assume that their inclusion has been assented to." This initial statement is not designed to deal with written confirmations of an existing oral contract. Rather, it seems to suggest that silence by the offeror will manifest assent to additional terms in the offeree's expression of acceptance. As one commentator observed, this is not true except as to immaterial additional terms and even those terms may be made inoperative by the offeror's limitation of acceptance to the terms of the offer or notice of objection to such additional terms. Comment 6 then attempts to deal with the situation involving written confirmations of oral contracts which confirmations contain additional or different terms: "Where clauses on confirming forms sent by both parties conflict each party must be assumed to object to a clause of the other conflicting with one on the confirmation sent by himself. As a result the requirement that there be notice of objection which is found in subsection (2) is satisfied and the conflicting terms do not become part of the contract. The contract then consists of the terms originally expressly agreed to, terms on which the confirmations agree, and terms supplied by this Act, including subsection (2)." As to this statement, the same commentator suggests that the Code will fill gaps left by the excision of conflicting terms under § 2-207(3) rather than § 2-207(2) whereas this comment indicates that it is dealing with

contract according to the factual bargain of the parties rather than one including additional terms to which the parties had not consciously adverted when they made their oral contract.

Some courts fail to distinguish between the "battle of the forms" under § 2-207 and the quite distinct requirement under UCC § 2-201 that an oral contract for the sale of goods priced at $500 or more must be evidenced by a writing sufficient to show that the parties intended to be bound by such an agreement. The Statute of Frauds requires a sufficient memorandum evidencing a contract for the sale of goods which identifies the parties, the subject matter, states the quantity and is properly signed.[30] If such a memorandum is present, the party attempting to persuade the court that an oral contract was made has overcome the initial hurdle of complying with this requirement of a sufficient writing. This, however, is not a § 2-207 problem. An acknowledgment form, for example, may be sufficient to satisfy the Statute of Frauds but it may also contain terms additional to or different from the terms the parties discussed while forming their oral contract. The problem is now a "battle of the forms" problem to be dealt with under § 2-207. There is no longer any Statute of Frauds problem though some courts became hopelessly confused in this area.[31]

If only one written confirmation of the oral contract is evident, it is important to remember the initial Statute of Frauds problem. Thus, if the only confirmation is the buyer's purchase order, such a document may only evidence an *offer* while the Statute of Frauds requires a writing to evidence a *contract*.[32] An acknowledgment from the seller, however, typically evidences a contract between the parties which satisfies the Statute of Frauds. If that form contains terms not discussed when the oral contract was formed, the terms of the oral agreement evidenced by the confirmation should be enforced as the contract, but the additional or different terms should be deemed inoperative.[33]

B. *The Counter Offer Riddle — Contract by Conduct.*

We have seen that a seller accepts the buyer's offer on the buyer's terms where the seller sends an acknowledgment containing identical "dickered"

---

subsection (2). He concludes, "As a comment on the section, this is a poor one." Duesenberg, *Contract Creation: The Continuing Struggle with Additional and Different Terms Under Uniform Commercial Code Section 2-207*, 34 Bus. Law. 1477, 1485 (1979). While the commentator is undoubtedly correct in his criticism of the opening sentence of comment 6 and equally sound in his suggestion that inclusion of supplementary terms under the Code is an application of subsection (3) of § 2-207 (to be discussed later in this section), this otherwise flawed comment appears helpful in dealing with written confirmations containing conflicting terms.

[30] UCC § 2-201, comment 1. The Statute of Frauds will be explored in detail in Chapter 4.

[31] *See, e.g.,* Marlene Indus. v. Carnac Textiles, 399 N.Y.S.2d 229 (1977) which was, fortunately, reversed by a court that understood the distinction: 45 N.Y.2d 327, 380 N.E.2d 239 (1978). Another illustration of confusion is found in Campanelli v. Conservas Altamira, S.A., 477 P.2d 870 (Nev. 1970).

[32] This distinction is mentioned in Harry Rubin & Sons v. Consolidated Pipe Co., 396 Pa. 506, 153 A.2d 472 (1959).

[33] *See* American Parts Co. v. American Arb. Ass'n, 8 Mich. App. 156, 154 N.W.2d 5, 12 (1967): "[P]arties should be able to enforce their agreement whatever it is, despite discrepancies between the oral agreement and the confirmation (or between an offer and acceptance) if enforcement can be granted without requiring either party to be bound to a material term to which he has not agreed. Applying this policy to this case, if as the seller contends, there was a firm oral agreement ... which was later confirmed, *it is that agreement which should be enforced.*" (emphasis added).

terms even though his printed form contains different or additional terms such as a warranty disclaimer, exclusion of consequential damage or other terms that will be deemed inoperative under subsection (2) of § 2-207. In one sense, the seller is wasting its time by including such clauses in an otherwise definite expression of acceptance since the fundamental change effected by § 2-207(1) is that such additional or different terms do not convert the seller's response to a counter offer because the buyer will pay no attention to these printed terms. He will reasonably assume a contract was formed on the terms to which both parties consciously adverted, i.e., the "dickered" terms. Though undickered additional or different terms, alone, will no longer create a counter offer, § 2-207 *does* permit a party to make a counter offer. In that portion of § 2-207(1) which may be called the "proviso" or, less artfully, the "language after the comma," the section permits an offeree to make the acceptance "expressly conditional on assent to the additional or different terms." [34] It is clear that Professor Llewellyn and his associates intended this language to permit an offeree to make a counter offer.[35] If an offeree will not prevail in the "battle of the forms" because his response appears to be a definite expression of acceptance resulting in the exclusion of certain terms highly favorable to him, it was inevitable that offerees would attempt to "win the battle" in other ways. In the typical situation, the buyer makes an offer through his purchase order and the seller responds with his acknowledgment form. By converting the acknowledgment to a counter offer, the seller hopes to achieve the goal of rejecting the buyer's offer, thereby creating a new power of acceptance in the buyer which will be exercised when the buyer accepts the goods shipped by the seller pursuant to the seller's counter offer. The resulting contract would contain the seller's terms. The logic of this approach appears unassailable. Sellers quickly discovered serious obstacles, however.

Sellers who seek to win the battle of the forms by making counter offers invariably avoid placing a conspicuous statement on their responses such as, "This is a counter offer." There is more than a suspicion that acknowledgment forms are drafted to avoid the possibility that the offeror will clearly understand the response as a counter offer since an understandable counter offer may induce the offeror to shop elsewhere for the goods he wishes to purchase. The typical effort to make a counter offer contains language that could manifest acceptance but contains certain terms designed to have the technical effect of creating a counter offer. Thus, an acknowledgment might suggest that the "acceptance is subject to the terms and conditions contained on the front or reverse side" of the acknowledgment form.[36] The obvious purpose is to have a court characterize the response as a "conditional" or "qualified" acceptance which constitutes a counter offer thereby elevating the terms of the

---

[34] UCC § 2-207(1).

[35] "We are attempting to say, whether we got it said or not, that a document which said, 'This is an acceptance only if the additional terms we state are taken by you' is not a definite and seasonable expression of acceptance but is an expression of a counter-offer." Statement of Karl Llewellyn, 1 New York Law Revision Commission Hearings on the Uniform Commercial Code 117 (1954). For an exploration of the history of this proviso, *see* Murray, *Chaos, supra* note 82, at 1322-30.

[36] *See, e.g.,* the acknowledgment as quoted in Dorton v. Collins & Aikman Corp., 453 F.2d 1161 (6th Cir. 1972).

acknowledgment to the dominant position in the battle of the forms. Various drafting efforts of this sort have resulted in numerous cases where courts are forced to interpret the language of acknowledgment forms to determine whether certain conditional language *is the equivalent* of the statutory language in the proviso of § 2-207(1). If the language used in a response to an offer is the equivalent of, "This acceptance is expressly conditioned on buyer's assent to any different or additional terms contained on the front or reverse side(s) of this acknowledgment," the response will be a counter offer. The extant case law suggests that courts will typically insist upon language that closely tracks the language of the statutory proviso though there are interpretations that are more than difficult to reconcile.[37] Faced with this uncertainty and still desirous of making a counter offer, sellers will take the safe route of tracking the language of the Code. Thus, if the acknowledgment states, "Seller's acceptance is ... expressly conditioned on Buyer's assent to the additional or different terms and conditions set forth below and printed on the reverse side," the comparison of this language with the statutory language compels a court to conclude that the acknowledgment constitutes a counter offer.[38] The statutory proviso language is anything but clear since it suggests that an "acceptance" that is expressly conditioned on the offeror's assent to any different or additional terms is *not* an acceptance. If it is not an acceptance, it is a counter offer, but sellers' forms studiously avoid the clear term, "counter offer." It is, therefore, unlikely that the response will be clearly understood as a counter offer by the typical merchant-offeror. At this point, it should be recalled that whether a response to an offer is an acceptance, a rejection, a qualified acceptance which constitutes a counter offer or an equivocal acceptance, depends upon the fair interpretation of that response as the response would be understood by a reasonable offeror.[39] If, therefore, a reasonable offeror would not understand the response to the offer as a counter offer, *even though the response stated that it was expressly conditioned on the offeror's assent to any additional or different terms found in the response,* such a response should not be effective as a counter offer. An offeror, for example, may be justified in treating the response containing such language

---

[37] In Boese-Hilburn Co. v. Dean Mach. Co., 616 S.W.2d 520, 525 (Mo. App. 1981), the court recognized that "[j]udicial interpretation of the language 'expressly made conditional' contained in UCC § 2-207(1) ranges across a broad spectrum." The language in *Dorton, id.,* "subject to all of the terms and conditions on the face and reverse side hereof" was held insufficient to create a counter offer because it did not emphasize that it was conditional on buyer's *assent* to such different or additional terms. "Our acceptance of the order is conditional on the buyer's acceptance of the conditions of sale printed on the reverse side hereof" was sufficient to create a § 2-207(1) counter offer in Uniroyal, Inc. v. Chambers Gasket & Mfg. Co., 380 N.E.2d 571 (Ind. App. 1978). Acceptance "predicated on the following clarifications, additions or modifications to the order" held sufficient in Construction Aggregates Corp. v. Hewitt-Robins, Inc., 404 F.2d 505 (7th Cir. 1968); "[A]cceptance of this order shall be deemed to constitute an agreement ... to the conditions named hereon and supersedes all previous agreements" held not expressly conditional in Idaho Power Co. v. Westinghouse Elec. Corp., 596 F.2d 924 (9th Cir. 1979); "Acceptance of this order is expressly limited to the conditions of purchase printed on the reverse side" was held sufficiently similar to the "expressly conditional" language of § 2-207(1) in Reaction Molding Techs., Inc. v. General Elec. Co., 585 F. Supp. 1097 (E.D. Pa. 1984), but, upon reconsideration, it was held insufficiently similar to the statutory language, 588 F. Supp. 1280 (E.D. Pa. 1984).

[38] This is the holding in C. Itoh & Co. (Am.) v. Jordan Int'l Co., 552 F.2d 1228 (7th Cir. 1977) based upon the quoted language.

[39] All of these matters are explored *supra* § 48.

as an equivocal acceptance from which the offeror may infer assent.[40] Curiously, in their interpretations of the proviso language of § 2-207(1), courts have not addressed that question. Instead, they have focused exclusively upon the language in the response to the offer and applied a mechanical test, again, whether the language is sufficiently similar to the language of the statutory proviso. If there is sufficient similarity, the response is a counter offer, regardless of the reasonable understanding of the offeror.[41]

If a court insists that a response is a counter offer because it tracks the language of § 2-207(1) notwithstanding the probability that the offeror will not understand the response as a counter offer, the counter offer should have the usual effect of counter offers, i.e., it should reject the original offer including all of the express and implied terms of that offer such as the implied warranty of merchantability. There is no indication that normal counter offer law is changed in the UCC. Thus, if the seller makes a statutory counter offer, the only power of acceptance should be in the former offeror. If the seller then ships the goods and the buyer accepts them, the acceptance of the goods should be construed as an acceptance of the seller's counter offer through the conduct of the buyer.[42] The acceptance of the seller's counter offer would include all of the seller's printed terms, such as the warranty disclaimer, exclusion of damages, perhaps an arbitration clause and other terms that materially altered the terms of the offer. In effect, the seller should win the battle of the forms. While this analysis may appear unassailable, it would have the effect of returning the law to the "last shot" principle. For this and other reasons about to be explored, it is not the analysis found in the case law at this time.

Having curiously ignored the reasonable understanding of the offeror as to whether a response containing the statutory proviso constituted a counter offer, the courts have augmented the disconcertion in this area. Once they conclude that the language of a response is sufficient to constitute a counter offer (without any authority under the Code), they reject the normal view that the buyer's acceptance of the goods constitutes an acceptance of the counter offer.[43] They insist that the buyer should not be said to have accepted the counter offer unless the buyer expressly assents to the terms of the counter offer, i.e., the buyer must manifest assent in some form of language rather than conduct. The most obvious method of express acceptance would have the buyer sign the seller's counter offer and return it. The buyer, of course, is more than unlikely to express assent to the seller's counter offer because the buyer does not recognize the response as a counter offer. The probabilities are

---

[40] See RESTATEMENT 2d § 57 comment b. It is more than interesting to note that one of the major cases supporting the view that an expressly conditional clause tracking the language of the § 2-207(1) proviso expressly characterizes such a response to an offer as "ambiguous": '... [T]he seller injected ambiguity into the transaction by inserting the 'expressly conditional' clause in his form...." C. Itoh & Co. (Am.) v. Jordan Int'l Co., 552 F.2d 1228, 1238 (7th Cir. 1977).

[41] A trilogy of cases which manifest high precedential value supports this assertion. See Dorton v. Collins & Aikman Corp., 453 F.2d 1161 (6th Cir. 1972); C. Itoh & Co. (Am.) v. Jordan Int'l Co., 552 F.2d 1228 (7th Cir. 1977); Uniroyal, Inc. v. Chambers Gasket & Mfg. Co., 380 N.E.2d 571 (Ind. App. 1978). For a comprehensive analysis see Murray, Chaos supra note 84, at 1330-43.

[42] The UCC does not change the normal rules concerning a manifestation of assent through conduct. See RESTATEMENT 2d § 19.

[43] See supra note 41.

great that the buyer and the seller assumed they formed a contract through their exchange of forms, notwithstanding the inclusion of the statutory proviso which was inserted by the seller's lawyer. It is clear, however, that current judicial interpretations would find no contract through the exchange of forms. Having made a counter offer, the seller is under no obligation to the buyer unless the buyer has expressly assented to the terms of the counter offer.[44] Again, the buyer is unlikely to assent since she is typically unaware that a counter offer has been made.[45] After making the counter offer, if the seller ships the goods and the buyer accepts the goods, the buyer has not accepted the seller's counter offer. A contract, however, is formed at this point since the parties have shipped and accepted goods. It is a contract by conduct under subsection (3) of § 2-207 which indicates that the terms of such a contract will be the matching terms of the previously exchanged forms which did not manifest a contract because the seller's form was a counter offer. The non-matching terms of the exchanged forms are excised. If the offer expressly or impliedly contained warranty provisions, remedial provisions and the like, the seller's form disclaimed warranties and excluded remedies. Since these non-matching terms are excised under § 2-207(3), "gaps" remain and the gaps are filled with the supplementary terms of Article 2 of the Code. Article 2 terms typically favor the buyer, e.g., they include implied warranties [46] and a comprehensive list of buyer's remedies.[47] Since the contract by conduct under § 2-207(3) requires the "gap-filling" terms of Article 2, the terms supplied by the Code will be terms favorable to the buyer. The net effect is that once § 2-207(3) is activated in a contract by conduct, the buyer will prevail in the battle of the forms.

This tortured judicial analysis is the product of the fatal analytical flaw of disregarding the reasonable understanding of the offeror [48] and finding a counter offer simply because the response to the offer used formula language from the statute. Having made that fatal error, but recognizing that the offeror would not understand the counter offer effect of the fomula language in the response, these courts suggest that it would be patently unfair to the offeror to saddle him with the offeree's terms. The only way to avoid such an unfair result is to change, again without any UCC authority, the normal contract

---

[44] In C. Itoh & Co. (Am.) v. Jordan Int'l Co., 552 F.2d 1228, 1237-38 (7th Cir. 1977), the court stresses the freedom of the seller "to walk away from the transaction without incurring any liability so long as the buyer has not in the interim expressly assented to the additional terms."

[45] A recent illustration of the buyer's lack of awareness of the meaning of the statutory proviso in § 2-207(1) occurred in Diamond Fruit Growers, Inc. v. Krack Corp., 794 F.2d 1440 (9th Cir. 1986) where an acknowledgment form contained the "expressly conditional" language of § 2-207(1) as well as an exclusion of consequential damages. The parties were in a continuous relationship and the buyer negotiated with the seller to have the seller remove the exclusion of consequential damages clause from the seller's form. The seller refused. The parties then continued to deal with each other using the same forms. When consequential damages occurred, the buyer brought an action against the seller who insisted that his clause should be enforced as a term of the contract since the parties had consciously negotiated with respect to this clause and the buyer clearly understood that the clause was a term of the contract and continued to deal with the seller with such actual knowledge. However, the acknowledgment contained counter offer language and the buyer had never expressly assented to the terms of the seller's counter offer.

[46] See UCC § 2-312 (warranty of title) § 2-313 (express warranties) § 2-314 (implied warranty of merchantability) and § 2-315 (implied warranty of fitness for a particular purpose).

[47] The remedies of the buyer under Article 2 are listed in § 2-711.

[48] See discussion of C. Itoh, supra 44.

rules concerning acceptance of offers or counter offers by conduct. By insisting that the only manner of accepting the seller's formula counter offer is by express assent, the offeror will be treated fairly since, by expressly assenting to a counter offer, the offeror manifests his understanding that the offeree has made a counter offer. This intellectually untidy analysis is at least unnecessary and could result in manifest injustice to an offeror.

The analysis is unnecessary because the offeror could treat the response to his offer as a definite and seasonable expression of acceptance, i.e., the inclusion of formula statutory language using the term, "acceptance," should not convert an otherwise definite expression of acceptance to a counter offer. Thus, in the typical situation, a buyer-offeror would prevail in the battle of the forms under § 2-207(1) with the seller's additional terms treated as inoperative under subsection (2). The only type of counter offer that should be recognized is the true counter offer, i.e., one that would be reasonably understood as such by the offeror. If a genuine counter offer were made by the seller, there would be no contract via the exchange of forms and both parties would understand that no contract existed. The current judicial analysis allows for a result that is oppressive to the offeror if he or she reasonably believes that the exchange of forms has produced what the UCC would term a "closed deal." Instead of a binding agreement, there is no contract because the seller will be said to have made a counter offer. The buyer's reasonable expectation and reliance are emasculated if the seller chooses not to perform even though there is a judicial recognition that it is the seller who has injected ambiguity into the transaction by using the "expressly conditional" clause of § 2-207(1).[49] Thus, a seller who subsequently decides he has made a bad deal may extricate himself from what reasonably appeared to be a closed deal because he inserted ambiguous formula language in the response to a buyer's offer. Neither the result nor the analysis has any redeeming virtue.

C. The Offeror Prevails in the "Battle of the Forms."

A recent development in the § 2-207 case law exacerbates the already difficult interpretation and construction of that section. It is best understood through a comparison of hypothetical situations.

(1) A purchase order offer to purchase certain goods is silent concerning warranties, remedies and arbitration. The response is an acknowledgment that appears to be a definite expression of acceptance because it contains the identical "dickered" terms found in the offer though it also contains the usual clauses disclaiming warranties, excluding remedies and an arbitration clause. The acknowledgment does not contain any counter offer language. In this situation, there will be a contract on the express and implied terms of the offer; the additional or different terms in the acknowledgment will not become part of the contract under § 2-207.

(2) We now assume that the same buyer sends the same purchase order. In this case, however, the seller had previously sent a document captioned, "quo-

---

[49] C. Itoh & Co. (Am.) v. Jordan Int'l Co., 552 F.2d 1228, 1238 (7th Cir. 1977): "Since the seller injected ambiguity into the transaction by inserting the 'expressly conditional' clause in his form, he, and not the buyer, should bear the consequence of that ambiguity under subsection (3)."

tation." The seller's quotation contained all of the clauses disclaiming warranties, excluding remedies and the arbitration clause found in the seller's acknowledgment in situation (1). The quotation is construed by the court to be an offer and the purchase order in this situation is construed to be an acceptance of the offer.[50] If the purchase order (now an acceptance) is construed as containing the usual implied warranties as well as an implication of normal Code remedies and the negation of arbitration, it would be said to contain terms that varied the terms of the offer. Such variant terms will be excised pursuant to subsection (2)(b) since they are material alterations of the quotation/offer. The purchase order/acceptance may, on the other hand, be construed to be silent as to any implied terms. Thus, one court has implied the usual UCC terms in a purchase order when it was an offer, but refused to imply such terms in the same purchase order when it was construed to be an acceptance.[51]

It is absurd to include implied UCC terms in a purchase order functioning as an offer and to exclude the same terms in the same purchase order when it is construed as an acceptance. The foregoing hypotheticals should indicate the extreme confusion surrounding battle of the forms problems. Characterizing a purchase order as an offer or acceptance has little if anything to do with a merchant-buyer's conscious use of that form. Rather, the characterization is a judicial afterthought. Moreover, the net effect is to permit the offeror, whether the offeror is the buyer or seller, to prevail simply because he or she is the offeror in a situation where the parties have paid no attention to which of them happened to be the offeror.[52] This analysis is the consummate elevation of form over substance and, in terms of the purpose of § 2-207 as a species of the underlying philosophy of Article 2 of the Code to effectuate the factual bargain of the parties, it stands that section on its head. If § 2-207 is to be applied in accordance with its purpose, a major change in its current interpretation and construction is required.

---

[50] Though a purchase order may appear to be an offer on its face, it will be construed as an acceptance if the parties "intended" that effect. *See, e.g.,* Daitom, Inc. v. Pennwalt Corp., 741 F.2d 1569 (10th Cir. 1984); Mead Corp. v. McNally-Pittsburgh Mfg. Corp., 654 F.2d 1196 (6th Cir. 1981); Idaho Power Co. v. Westinghouse Elec. Corp., 596 F.2d 924 (9th Cir. 1979); Earl M. Jorgensen Co. v. Mark Constr., Inc., 56 Haw. 466, 540 P.2d 978 (1975). In particular, *see* Phillips Petr. Co., Norway v. Bucyrus-Erie Co., 125 Wis. 2d 418, 373 N.W.2d 65 (App. 1985), *rev'd on other grounds,* 388 N.W.2d 584 (Wis. 1986).

[51] *See* Phillips Petr. Co., Norway v. Bucyrus-Erie Co., *supra* note 50, at 590. When the Wisconsin Supreme Court reversed the intermediate appellate court in that case, the supreme court expressly avoided § 2-207 problems, stating, "[W]hatever Byzantine complexities the original exchange of contract documents might pose, ... a rather simple straight-forward modified contract arose during the course of negotiations...".

[52] *See* Southern Idaho Pipe & Steel Co. v. Cal-Cut Pipe & Supply, Inc., 98 Idaho 495, 567 P.2d 1246, 1253-1254 (1977) where the court comments: "Cal-Cut makes the argument that since its document was the offer, Southern Idaho's expression of acceptance was an acceptance of all the terms on this form.... Under this argument, the first party to a sales transaction will always get his own terms. In most commercial transactions, which party processes its form first is purely fortuitous. To allow the contents of a contract to be determined on this basis runs contrary to the underlying purposes of the Uniform Commercial Code of modernizing the law governing commercial transactions.... We cannot accept such an arbitrary solution." *See also* McCarty v. Verson Allsteel Press Co., 89 Ill. App. 3d 498, 411 N.E.2d 936 (1980). For a criticism of this view *see* Deusenberg, *supra* note 29, at 1485. For an analysis supporting the view that the printed form of one party should not control simply because that party is the offeror, *see* Murray, *Chaos, supra* note 82, at 1366-72.

D. *"Different" Versus "Additional" Terms.*

Section 2-207(1) permits an operative acceptance that contains *different* or *additional* terms.[53] If a definite and seasonable expression of acceptance is found, it is necessary to deal with different or additional terms in the expression of acceptance. Subsection (2) of § 2-207 deals with *additional* terms, but it fails to mention *different* terms. Moreover, there is no other statutory language dealing with "different" terms. A comment to § 2-207 is particularly helpful: "Whether or not additional or different terms will become part of the agreement depends upon the provisions of subsection (2)." [54] If the comment language were accepted, the problem of dealing with "different" terms is solved since subsection (2) would be treated as dealing with both "additional" and "different" terms.[55] Because this UCC comment, like other Code comments, is not part of the enacted law, it has been disregarded by some courts.[56] An influential Commercial Law text has persuaded a number of courts that subsection (2) does not apply to "different" terms.[57] The authors, however, disagree on the proper treatment of "different" terms in an otherwise definite and seasonable expression of acceptance.[58] Courts and scholars have recognized the difficulty in distinguishing additional from different terms.[59] Per-

---

[53] See the statutory language of § 2-207(1) set forth at the beginning of this section.

[54] Comment 3 to § 2-207.

[55] There is a suggestion that the omission of "different" in § 2-207(2) was an inadvertent printer's error. *See* Utz, *More on the Battle of the Forms: The Treatment of "Different" Terms Under the Uniform Commercial Code,* 16 U.C.C. L.J. 103, 111-12 (1983). Further support for the view that "different" should be treated as coming within § 2-207(2) is found in Murray, *Chaos, supra* note 842, at 1355. *See also* Steiner v. Mobil Oil Corp., 141 Cal. Rptr. 157, 569 P.2d 751 (1977).

[56] *See, e.g.,* Daitom, Inc. v. Pennwalt Corp., 741 F.2d 1569 (10th Cir. 1984).

[57] *See* J. WHITE & R. SUMMERS, UNIFORM COMMERCIAL CODE 27-31 (2d ed. 1980).

[58] The view of Professor White has been christened the "knockout" view. If an offer contains a term (*e.g.,* an arbitration clause) and the otherwise definite expression of acceptance contains a contradictory term (an anti-arbitration clause), the "knockout" view would have these contradictory clauses cancel each other. There is judicial support for this view: *Daitom, supra* note 56; Idaho Power Co. v. Westinghouse Elec. Corp., 596 F.2d 924 (9th Cir. 1979); Lea Tal Textile Co. v. Manning Fabrics, Inc., 411 F. Supp. 1404 (S.D.N.Y. 1975); Southern Idaho Pipe & Steel Co. v. Cal-Cut Pipe & Supply, Inc., 98 Idaho 495, 567 P.2d 1246 (1977), *cert. denied,* 434 U.S. 1056 (1978); Challenge Mach. Co. v. Mattison Mach. Works, 138 Mich. App. 15, 359 N.W.2d 232 (Mich. App. 1984). Under his co-author's "fall out" view, the contract would contain an arbitration clause because the different term in the acceptance would simply "fall out." Professor White relies upon comment 6 to § 2-207 to support his "knockout" view, but Professor Summers reminds him that comment 6 deals with "confirming forms." White complains that Summers' "fall out" view provides the offeror with an "unearned advantage" and Summers responds that the advantage is not entirely unearned since the offeree could have perused the offeror's terms and refused to contract on that basis. (White & Summers, *ibid.* at 29). Summers is discontent with his own "fall out" view, however, since he suspects that the offer contains implied terms such as warranty and remedial protection of the buyer. Thus, any expressly different term in a seller's acceptance would simply "fall out" and the buyer would always win the battle of the forms. In some frustration, Summers would suggest that the statute be redrafted (White & Summers, *ibid.* at 30). Under White's "knockout" view, the problem is solved since implied terms that are contradicted by express terms of the acceptance simply cancel each other. Where the offer contains an arbitration clause and the acceptance is silent on arbitration, White happily finds an arbitration clause in the contract. White is uncomfortable with his "knockout" view when applied to this situation since an extrapolation of his view would result in an acceptance of only those terms on which both documents agree (White & Summers, *Ibid.* at 31), yet he would agree with Summers' result that the contract should contain the arbitration term. Like Summers, White "would write the law differently if he could do so." *Id.*

[59] *See Daitom, supra* note 56, at 1578-79; *Steiner, supra* note 55, at 759-60; Boise-Hilburn Co. v. Dean Mach. Co., 616 S.W.2d 520, 527 (Mo. App. 1981). *See also* R. ALDERMAN, 1 A TRANSACTIONAL GUIDE TO THE UNIFORM COMMERCIAL CODE 21, n.54 (1983) (formerly Hawkland).

haps it is more important to focus on the distinction between material and immaterial terms. An additional term does not change the offer in the sense of altering it. A nonmatching term in an acceptance is necessarily different if it is a material term.[60] Moreover, subsection (2)(b) of § 2-207 eliminates terms in the acceptance that "materially alter" the terms of the offer. The common definition of "alter" is "to change, to make different." [61] There is no need, therefore, to resort to comment language to discover a basis for including "different" terms in § 2-207(2). The elimination of "different" terms from the operation of subsection (2) virtually emasculates the subsection because so many variant terms in responses to offers are necessarily "different". We are then left with views such as those suggested by text writers who are, themselves, uncomfortable with their individual views and suggest statutory change.[62] Since the legislative history does not support the exclusion of "different" any more than its inclusion, comments to § 2-207 clearly assume that "different" as well as "additional" terms will be treated under subsection (2), there is support for an emphasis upon material versus immaterial terms rather than different versus additional terms,[63] and, finally, the exclusion of "different" terms has violated and will continue to violate one of the underlying purposes of the UCC,[64] future interpretations of § 2-207(2) would do well to include "different" as well as "additional" terms.

§ 51. Silence, Inaction, Retention of Benefits and Exercise of Dominion as Acceptance — Unsolicited Goods.

A. Silence.

It has often been asserted that, as a general rule, silence may not constitute acceptance of an offer.[65] Numerous exceptions to this general rule, however, quickly appear. A more cautious statement found in numerous cases is that silence will not constitute acceptance of an offer unless there is a duty to speak.[66] This immediately raises the question, when does an offeree have a duty to inform the offeror that the offeree does not intend to accept the offer? If *A* offers to sell an automobile to *B* at a certain price and concludes the offer with the following statement, "If I do not hear from you within 10 days from

---

[60] For analysis of this view, *see* Murray, *Chaos, supra* note 82, at 1364-65.

[61] WEBSTER'S THIRD NEW INTERNATIONAL DICTIONARY 63 (1965).

[62] *See* discussion of "knockout" and "fall out" views of Professor White and Professor Summers, *supra* note 58.

[63] Support for the view that "additional" terms were viewed as immaterial is found in the statement of Karl Llewellyn: "Some improvement is to be hoped for from the provision of § 2-207(2) which allows minor additional terms to enter into the contract without that express consent which (more frequently than not) never occurs. What terms will be construed as 'materially' altering the contract is ... a question for the courts' determination." 1 STATE OF NEW YORK LAW REVISION COMMISSION HEARINGS ON THE UNIFORM COMMERCIAL CODE 56 (1954). Since § 2-207(2)(b) deals with "material alterations" in an otherwise definite and seasonable expression of acceptance and, in conformity with the statement of Professor Llewellyn, such terms do not become part of the contract absent express consent, it is clear that materially altering terms, which are necessarily "different" terms, are included within subsection (2).

[64] *See* § 1-102(2)(a) which states one of the underlying purposes of the Code as follows: "to simplify, clarify and modernize the law governing commercial transactions...."

[65] *See, e.g.,* Bestor v. American Nat'l Stores, Inc., 691 S.W.2d 384 (Mo. App. 1985); Rosin v. First Bank of Oak Park, 126 Ill. App. 3d 230, 466 N.E.2d 1245 (1984).

[66] *See, e.g.,* Chorba v. Davlisa Enters., 303 Pa. Super. 497, 450 A.2d 36 (1982).

the date you receive this letter, I will assume you have accepted my offer," should B's silence indicate assent so that he will be said to have accepted the offer? On the face of this offer, B's silence cannot be construed as a manifestation of acceptance. But, neither can B's silence be viewed as a rejection of the offer. Assuming an offer has been communicated to the offeree, the offeree's silence, by itself, is ambiguous because it does not indicate the offeree's state of mind. His silence may indicate that he is ignoring the offer or that he desires to reject it. It may, however, indicate that he intends to accept the offer and is silent because he is following the command of the offeror in exercising the power of acceptance. The offeror has no right to compel the offeree to speak. The offeror may not, therefore, infer assent to the offer from the offeree's silence. If, however, the offeree intends to accept through silence, he exercises the power of acceptance through silence though he does not manifest his intention in any other objective fashion.[67] In such a case, there is no evidence of B's exercise of his power of acceptance other than the ambiguous act of silence and subsequent claim that he intended to accept through such silence. The offeror, however, will not be heard to complain that an unambiguous manifestation of acceptance is lacking since the offeror, as master of the offer, created the predicament in which he now finds himself. If an offeror decides to create a power of acceptance that can be exercised by silence or any other ambiguous action or inaction, the power can be exercised by the offeree in that fashion, but he will not be bound unless he intends to be bound, and such intention can be adduced in this situation only by the subsequent statement of the offeree.[68]

The ambiguity surrounding silence or inaction on the part of the offeree may be removed in certain situations. The classic case involves a prior course of dealing between the parties. Where a seller of goods solicited offers from a merchant and, on repeated occasions, the seller had shipped the ordered goods within a certain period absent any notification other than the bill accompanying shipment, the merchant was justified in relying upon the silence of the seller as acceptance of the latest order. Such silence will constitute acceptance because the parties' prior relationship creates a reasonable obligation on the offeree to speak, i.e., to notify the offeror, if he does not intend to accept.[69] A

---

[67] See RESTATEMENT 2d § 69(1)(b) and comment c. See Cavanaugh v. D. W. Ranlet Co., 229 Mass. 366, 118 N.E. 650, 651 (1918), (Where the offer stated, "This is a contract and will be considered mutually binding unless we are advised of its nonacceptance by wire," the court held it was a jury question as to whether plaintiffs' silence constituted assent). Contra Prescott v. Jones, 69 N.H. 305, 41 A. 352 (1898) in which the court insisted upon written or spoken words or some other overt act to constitute acceptance.

[68] If an offeror insists that the only way in which his offer can be accepted is by the offeree's eating or not eating breakfast on a given day, the action or inaction required by the offer is an ambiguous act. If performed, a contract will be formed if the offeree intended to accept by such action or inaction, but it will not be formed absent such intention.

[69] See Ammons v. Wilson, 176 Miss. 645, 170 So. 227 (1936). See also RESTATEMENT 2d § 69(1)(c) and comment d and R.A. Berjian, D. O., Inc. v. Ohio Bell Tel., 54 Ohio St. 2d 147, 375 N.E.2d 410 (1975). See also Laredo Nat'l Bank v. Gordon, 61 F.2d 906 (5th Cir. 1932): "It is true that, generally speaking, an offeree has a right to make no reply to offers and intends that his silence is not to be construed as an acceptance. But where the relation between the parties is such that the offeror is justified in expecting a reply, or the offeree is under a duty to reply, the latter's silence will be regarded as an acceptance." Trade usage could also serve as a basis for a justifiable assumption that silence constitutes acceptance. Section 1-205(2) of the UCC defines trade usage as "any practice or method of dealing having such regularity of observance in a place, vocation or

similar analysis is found in cases where an insurance company fails to respond to an application for an unreasonable length of time. The applicant may be justified in understanding that he is insured, particularly where a premium has been paid and retained by the insurance company.[70]

Another situation in which the ambiguity of silence is removed occurs where the parties enter into a contract and, as part of that contract, agree that a subsequent offer to modify their contract will be accepted by silence.[71] As in the previous situation, silence can operate as acceptance here because the parties already have a contractual relationship which manifests their intention that silence will constitute acceptance. Similarly, if an offeree tells an offeror that the offeree's silence will constitute acceptance, the ambiguity of silence disappears. Thus, where the owner of a yacht requested that his insurer extend the insurance coverage on the yacht for a certain journey and the response indicated that existence of the extended coverage depended upon a survey of the yacht which was performed and was favorable, the court held that the offeree had authorized the offeror to believe that the silence of the insurer thereafter amounted to an acceptance.[72]

B. Retention of Benefits — "Implied-in-Fact" Versus "Implied-in-Law."

Even where the parties have no prior relationship, silence or inaction in conjunction with acceptance of valuable goods or services will evidence an agreement between the parties.[73] In a well-known case,[74] a court inferred a promise to pay on the part of the recipient of valuable services who had an opportunity to reject them, but accepted them knowing or having reason to know that the other party expected to receive compensation. The silence or inaction of the recipient of such benefits is not ambiguous since he knows or has reason to know he is receiving benefits and could, without difficulty or expense, inform the other party that he rejects them. Failing to speak and the retention of benefits in such circumstances manifests an acceptance of the offer.[75]

---

trade as to justify an expectation that it will be observed with respect to the transaction in question."

[70] See American Life Ins. Co. v. Hutcheson, 109 F.2d 424 (6th Cir. 1940). See also RESTATEMENT 2d § 69 comment d: "In many states by statute or decision an insurance company is under a duty to act without unreasonable delay on insurance applications solicited by its agents...." See Annotation, 32 A.L.R.2d 487 (1953).

[71] See Fineman v. Citicorp USA, Inc., 137 Ill. App. 3d 1035, 485 N.E.2d 591 (1985) (credit card contract contained amendment provision concerning finance charges and annual percentage rate that required cardholder to notify issuer of card of objection to any changes. Absent notification, the provision indicated that the issuer "will understand that you agreed to the changes in the notice." Held: silence was effective as a matter of contract law and there was no violation of the Illinois consumer protection law, ILL. REV. STAT. 1981, ch. 12, pars. 261 et seq. and 311 et seq.).

[72] See Freimuth v. Glens Falls Ins. Co., 50 Wash. 2d 621, 314 P.2d 468 (1957) citing 1 WILLISTON ON CONTRACTS § 91C.

[73] See Bump v. Robbins, 24 Mass. App. 296, 509 N.E.2d 12 (1987) (finding that, notwithstanding the possibility of discovering an agreement through silent retention of services, such a finding was not justified in a situation involving a brokerage commission since brokerage agreements involve a high risk of noncompensation).

[74] Day v. Caton, 119 Mass. 513, 20 Am. Rep. 347 (1876).

[75] See RESTATEMENT 2d § 69(1)(a) and comment b. See also Laurel Race Course, Inc. v. Regal Constr. Co., 274 Md. 1412, 333 A.2d 319 (1975).

It is important to distinguish the type of contract in this situation from one where there will be restitutionary relief for unjust enrichment. If a court implies a promise to pay for services rendered because the recipient had an opportunity to reject the services but chose not to do so and had knowledge or reason to know that the other party expected to be paid, the court is discovering a genuine contract — a contract by conduct. It is often called an "implied-in-fact" contract because the acceptance is not expressed in language; it is expressed by the action or, in this case, the inaction of the offeree where he should manifest an objection if he does not intend to accept. Where facts do not permit such an inference but benefits are knowingly received at the expense of the party conferring such benefits and such party is neither officious nor should have been understood to be conferring such benefits gratuitously, an action in restitution will normally lie. Such an action is not an action on a real contract. Rather, it is an action to prevent the unjust enrichment of the party who has received the benefits. The action is often referred to as one in *quasi contract*, a so-called implied-in-law contract constructed by the court, again, to prevent unjust enrichment.[76] The recovery under quasi contract will be measured by the reasonable value of the benefits conferred rather than any contract price since there is no contract. If, however, a court finds an acceptance of an offer, though it discovers that acceptance inferentially from the conduct of the parties and the surrounding circumstances rather than the oral or written expressions of the offeree, a real acceptance has occurred forming a genuine contract albeit one implied from conduct. The duty of the offeree under such a contract is not merely to pay the reasonable or fair value of the benefits conferred; it is a duty to pay whatever price is found in the terms of the offer since that offer has been accepted.[77] Quasi-contractual recovery for benefits conferred will be considered later in this volume in the exploration of the restitution interest.[78]

If a seller ships goods to a buyer who has not ordered them, the mere receipt of the goods is not a manifestation of acceptance of the seller's offer since the buyer must have an opportunity to discover that he has received unordered goods.[79] Once the buyer knows or should know that he has received unordered

---

[76] For an exploration of the distinction between "implied-in-fact" and "implied-in-law" ("quasi") contracts, *see supra* § 19.

[77] *See* RESTATEMENT 2d § 69 comment b.

[78] *See* the exploration of the distinction between implied-in-fact contracts and implied-in-law (quasi) contracts in § 19, Chapter 1. *See also* Chapter 9 dealing with all contract remedies, including the protection of the restitution interest. In a given fact situation, the line between a genuine contract, albeit one implied-in-fact, and a quasi contract (which is not a contract but goes under the name of contract only because relief for unjust enrichment was brought under a common law form of action which was used for true contracts, i.e., assumpsit) is extremely difficult to draw. The RESTATEMENT 2d suggests that in certain cases, the line is "often indistinct." *See* RESTATEMENT 2d § 4 comment b and § 19 comment a.

[79] Even where the parties had a prior contract to buy and sell goods, the buyer's receipt of the goods does not amount to acceptance *of the goods.* The buyer is normally entitled to inspect the goods before he will be said to have accepted them. *See* UCC §§ 2-513(1) and 2-606(1)(a) and (1)(b). Acceptance of the goods pursuant to a prior contract of sale must be distinguished from acceptance of unordered goods. Where the buyer accepts unordered goods, he is accepting the seller's offer made through the seller's conduct of tendering unordered goods to the buyer and, simultaneously, he is accepting the goods, themselves, which precludes a right of rejection that must occur within a reasonable time after delivery or tender of the goods. UCC § 2-602(1). If the

goods, he may, of course, reject them though, while they are in his possession, he will have certain duties with respect to such goods.[80] If the buyer does not reject unordered goods but chooses to use them or otherwise exercise dominion or control over them by doing something to or with the goods that is inconsistent with the seller's ownership, the buyer may be said to have accepted the seller's offer to sell the unordered goods.[81] If the offer to sell the unordered goods states a price, the use of the goods will constitute an acceptance of the offer at the price stated in the offer, i.e., the offeree may not use the goods and simultaneously pay a price he deems fair if that price is less than the price at which the goods were offered.[82] In such a situation, the offeror has the choice of treating the offeree as a tort-feasor who has converted the goods, or an offeree who has exercised his power of acceptance by accepting the goods. If the offeror chooses to treat the offeree as having contracted to purchase the goods, the offeree is bound to pay the price stated in the offer.[83]

One of the problems faced by parties who receive unordered goods is that the application of contracts principles will result in their being held to a contract if they use the goods.[84] Merely inspecting the goods does not amount to acceptance nor does storing the goods for the offeror. Sellers of unsolicited goods, however, may attempt to thrust their products on an unsuspecting party who is unaware of these distinctions. There have, therefore, been a number of statutory modifications of the basic contracts rule to protect the public against contract liability for unsolicited goods. The most pervasive statutory change is found in U.S. Postal Regulations which now permit a party receiving unordered merchandise *through the mail* to retain, use or dispose of it without obligation.[85] There are also state statutes which relieve the recipient of the obligation to pay for unsolicited goods when the goods have been received through the mail or otherwise.[86]

---

buyer has accepted the goods, he may not reject them but may, under appropriate circumstances, revoke his acceptance of the goods under UCC § 2-608.

[80] *See* §§ 2-603 and 2-604 of the UCC which place certain duties on a buyer who rejects concerning perishable goods or goods that are not perishable but threaten to decline in value speedily. Where the seller has no place or business or agent at the buyer's location, the rejecting buyer must follow any reasonable instructions from the seller and, in the absence of such instructions, may have to dispose of the goods for the seller's account. Typically, the buyer may either store the goods, reship them, or resell them as commercial reasonableness requires.

[81] *See* Pace v. Sagebrush Sales Co., 114 Ariz. 271, 560 P.2d 789 (1977); European Import Co. v. Lone Star Co., 596 S.W.2d 287 (Tex. App. 1980).

[82] *See* RESTATEMENT 2d § 69 ill. 9.

[83] *Id.*

[84] *See* Austin v. Burge, 156 Mo. App. 286, 137 S.W. 618 (1911) in which the recipient of a newspaper continuously complained that he had not ordered it. Since, however, he read the newspaper, he was said to have accepted it.

[85] 39 U.S.C. § 3009.

[86] *See, e.g.,* NEB. REV. STAT. § 63-101; 73 PA. CONS. STAT. 2001; N.Y. GEN. BUS. LAW § 396.

Chapter 3

THE VALIDATION PROCESS

§ 52. The Enforceability of Promises — "Pacta Sunt Servanda."

A. *Problems in the Enforcement of All Promises — The Validation Process.*

In a society requiring literal adherence to the concept, "pacta sunt servanda" (all promises must be kept), that portion of the legal system dealing with the enforcement of promises may, at first glance, appear to be uncomplicated. The only question in such a society would be whether a member of that society made a promise. With sufficient evidence of a promise, the promise would be enforced. A moment's reflection, however, suggests myriad complications. If the promise was made under duress or induced by fraud, should the promise be enforced at law?[1] If the promisor did not intend to be bound until a more formal agreement was executed, should his promise be enforced prior to that formal agreement?[2] If the promise was made in jest and would have been reasonably understood as a joke, should that promise be enforced?[3] If the promise was made to a member of the promisor's family or to his friend and dealt with ordinary domestic or social matters, should the legal system enforce that kind of promise?[4] And, what of promises to make gifts? A promisor may have every intention of performing a donative promise before encountering unforeseen difficulties which prohibit performance of that promise. Should the promisor now be subject to a legal proceeding for nonperformance even though the promisee has lost nothing as a result of the donative promise?[5]

---

[1] *See infra* Chapter 6.

[2] On the question of intention to be legally bound before a final writing is executed, *see supra* § 32. This question arose in the much publicized dispute between the Texaco Corp. and the Pennzoil Co. Pennzoil made several attempts to take control of the Getty Oil Corp. and its final attempt resulted in what was characterized as "an agreement in principle" for the merger of Getty Oil and a newly formed entity to be owned jointly by Pennzoil and Gordon P. Getty as trustee of a family trust and a charitable trust. While lawyers worked on the implementation of that plan, Getty's representatives were considering the possibility of a better arrangement and began discussions with Texaco. Shortly thereafter, it was announced that Getty would be acquired by Texaco. After unsuccessful attempts to enjoin this merger, Pennzoil brought an action in a district court in Texas on a theory of tortious interference with Pennzoil's rights under its contract with Getty. The critical question in the case was whether the "agreement in principle" was a binding agreement before all of the details to implement the arrangement were effectuated. The jury awarded Pennzoil $7.53 billion in actual damages and $3 billion in punitive damages which, according to the Wall Street Journal (Nov. 20, 1985), was the largest civil judgment in history. To appeal this judgment in Texas, Texaco would have been forced to post an appeal bond equal to the amount of the judgment plus interest and costs, totaling over $12 billion. Texaco, therefore, sought relief in the federal courts (Texaco Corp. v. Pennzoil Co., 784 F.2d 1133 (2d Cir. 1986). At the time of this writing, however, Texaco found it necessary to seek protection under the Federal Bankruptcy Reform Act of 1978 (Title 11 of the U.S.C.).

[3] *See supra* § 31(C).

[4] *See supra* § 31(D).

[5] For an analysis of why donative promises should not be enforceable, *see* Eisenberg, *Donative Promises*, 47 U. CHI. L. REV. 1 (1979). Professor Eisenberg suggests that the legal system may fairly take the position that its compulsory processes will be invoked only to remedy injuries of a certain intensity, *e.g.*, the prevention of unjust enrichment or the promotion of a social policy such as the promotion of the economy and the injury to the donative promisee is typically slight, involving defeated expectations in the form of disappointment. Typically there will be no unjust enrichment of the promisor and, while the author would not go so far as to suggest that a gift is a sterile transmission from an economic perspective because they do have a wealth redistribution effect, the enforcement of gratuitous promises would have a relatively insignificant effect in achieving wealth redistribution as a goal of contract law. While his thesis suggests that our legal system is correct in withholding legal enforcement from gratuitous promises, Professor Eisenberg emphasizes the distinction between the questions, what promises should the *law* enforce, and what promises should people keep? There are myriad extra-legal sanctions for breaking a promise

These and other questions support the view that, "No legal system does or can attempt to enforce all promises."[6]

If a basic principle of any legal system is that it cannot enforce all promises, a question that can be viewed as the most important question in contract law immediately arises: Of all the promises made in a given society, which promises should be enforced at law? That fundamental question immediately suggests the necessity of determining the criteria to be used to separate those promises which the law will enforce from those that it will not recognize in terms of legal sanctions. Our legal system has never confronted the underlying question of whether all promises should be enforced. Rather, it has operated on the assumption that legal sanctions should not attach to every promise. In common law fashion, it has evolved the criteria for deciding which promises should have the force of law attached to them. The decisions in which this evolution has occurred evidence a curious mixture of rationality, pragmatism and historic accident. Something more than mutual assent, as manifested, typically, in offer and acceptance, has always been necessary to create an informal contract, i.e., the typical contract involving a bargain.[7] Long before the simple or informal contract was known to the common law, however, the process for making a promise enforceable was formal or ritualistic. It did not focus upon any bargained-for-exchange between the parties. Rather, it relied upon certain prescribed formalities.[8] At any given time in the history of our legal system, it has been possible to identify the recognized criteria used in that system to answer the fundamental question: which promises ought to be enforced? At this time, therefore, we find certain devices which are currently used in our system to validate promises, i.e., to make them legally enforceable. In this book, these validation devices are grouped under the caption, "The Validation Process," because that process explores all of the current devices used to make promises enforceable.[9] The validation process is not static. Certain promises that were not enforceable in the past are enforceable at this time, and it is more than probable that some promises which are not recognized as enforceable at this time will be validated in the future. In this chapter, we will explore all of the current validation devices and we will suggest the possibility of future validation devices.

B. *Current Validation Devices.*

1. The Seal and Other Formalistic Devices.

If a promise is to be enforced simply because it adheres to certain formalities, *e.g.*, it is evidenced by a writing that contains certain formal language or

---

that is not legally enforceable, *e.g.*, loss of business, loss of friends, loss of self-respect, and other, difficult-to-measure, losses. In a given situation, one of these sanctions may be a more effective deterrent to promise-breaking than the mere payment of money damages which is the typical legal sanction for failure to perform one's legally enforceable promise.

[6] *See* Cohen, *The Basis of Contract*, 46 HARV. L. REV. 553 (1933).

[7] The basic distinction between "formal" and "informal" contracts is found *supra* § 15.

[8] *See* Hazeltine, *The Formal Contract of Early English Law*, 10 COLUM. L. REV. 806 (1910); Pollock, *Contracts in Early English Law*, 6 HARV. L. REV. 389 (1892).

[9] It is, therefore, historically and analytically unsound to suggest that consideration is necessary to make a promise enforceable. As will be seen, consideration is one of several validation devices.

symbols or deals with a certain type of promise, the exclusive reason for enforcing that promise is that it meets the prescribed formalities. Thus, a formalistic validation device supports such promises. The oldest formalistic validation device is the seal which will be examined in the next section. We will also examine modern formalistic validation devices that became necessary after the seal was either abolished or severly restricted in scope.

2. Consideration.

Without question, consideration is the best-known validation device. It does not rest on any prescribed formalities. Rather, it requires an agreement between two or more parties evidencing a bargained-for-exchange of value between or among the parties. The consideration device is so well-known that it is often mistakenly viewed as the only validation device. Yet, long prior to the development of the consideration concept, promises were enforced on other bases. Because consideration has produced innumerable cases and its application can be difficult in given fact situations, this particular validation device will occupy more space in this chapter. That necessity, however, should not mislead the student of contract law into believing that consideration is a stronger or more important validation device than the others.

3. Detrimental Reliance (Promissory Estoppel).

Like consideration, the validation device preferably called "deterimental reliance," popularly known as "promissory estoppel," does not depend upon adherence to any prescribed formalities. It requires a promise (in no particular form) inducing the promisee to rely to his or her detriment where the promisor should have foreseen such reliance. While detrimental reliance is sometimes viewed as a relatively recent addition to recognized validation devices, our exploration of this device later in this chapter will reveal antecedents of detrimental reliance which antedate consideration.

4. Moral Obligation.

While it is often suggested that circumstances giving rise to a moral as contrasted with a legal obligation will not make a promise enforceable, later in this chapter we will identify clusters of cases which evidence promises enforceable exclusively on the basis of moral obligation. Thus, moral obligation is entitled to be listed among currently recognized validation devices.

§53. Contracts Under Seal — Formalistic Validation Devices.

A. *The Functions of Formalistic Validation Devices.*

We have already suggested that the oldest formalistic validation device, the seal, has been abolished or significantly diminished in importance in most jurisdictions. We will explore the reasons for that development in this Section. It is, however, important to begin our exploration of formalistic validation devices with an examination of the functions they serve. The fact that the abolishment or severe weakening of the seal led to the development of substitute formalistic devices, itself, suggests the need for such devices. The reasons for that felt need are found in the functions they serve. The classic exposition of the functions of formalities was supplied by Professor Lon L. Fuller.[10] He suggested three functions that are performed by formalistic devices: (1) the evidentiary function, (2) the cautionary function, and (3) the channeling function.

The *evidentiary* function is the obvious function of a legal formality. In the event of controversy, a writing, attestation or some official certification provides reliable evidence of a contract and its terms, not subject to the favorable or unfavorable recollection of witnesses. The evidentiary function could, however, be served in other ways. For example, Professor Fuller mentions the Roman *stipulatio* which required the oral statement of the promise in significant ceremony.[11] The second function of formalities, the *cautionary* function, is described by Fuller in terms of deterrence against inconsiderate or impulsive action. The affixing of the seal, for example, required the heating of wax, placing the wax on the writing and impressing it with one's seal which may have been a ring worn by the promisor containing his unique inscription.[12] This or a similar act required time and allowed the promisor to carefully consider the action.[13] Fuller believed that the affixing and impressing of a wax wafer was a splendid device for creating that circumspective frame of mind to guard against pledging the promisor's future performance without some contemplation of the potentially serious consequences. One of the reasons for the demise of the seal was the elimination of the wax and the impression thereon and the substitution of pre-printed forms with the word "seal" or simply the initials "l.s." (locus sigilli — the place of the seal). Signing such a printed form carried with it none of the cautionary function of the original ceremony of the seal. The third function, the *channeling* function, is one that Professor Fuller accurately described as essentially overlooked in discussions of legal formalities. The channeling function permits one to simply look at the document and, observing compliance with prescribed formalities, to recognize the document as containing an enforceable promise.[14] In summary, Fuller suggests that a

---

[10] Fuller, *Consideration and Form*, 41 COLUM. L. REV. 799 (1941).

[11] A conveyance of land with the handing of soil from the land to the grantee with a young witness who is likely to be alive in the event of controversy is another manifestation of ceremonial conduct serving an evidentiary function. Religious ceremonies such as the conferring of the Sacrament of Confirmation in the Roman Catholic religion manifest functions similar to those suggested by Professor Fuller.

[12] The term "signet" ring is a modern manifestation of the instrument used by many illiterate promisors to impress the wax with their "seals."

[13] Wedding ceremonies involve the most serious exchange of promises. The length of the ceremony may be said to allow for the cautionary function.

[14] The channeling function is found in the formal requisites of a negotiable instrument such as the ordinary check. The formal requisites are set forth in § 3-104 of the UCC: (a) signed by the maker or drawer; (b) contain an unconditional promise or order to pay a sum certain in money and no other promise, order, obligation or power given by the maker or drawer except as authorized by this Article; and (c) be payable on demand or at a definite time; and (d) be payable to order or bearer. Students unfamiliar with negotiable instruments law will still recall that their checks contain the "words of negotiability," "Pay to the order of...." This and the other formal requisites present the necessary test to determine whether a particular writing is negotiable so that a party who is asked to purchase such an instrument can know that if he or she purchases it for value, in good faith, and without notice of any claims or defenses, he or she can become a holder in due course (§ 3-302) and take the instrument free of most of the typical claims and defenses of prior parties to such instruments (§ 3-305). If the instrument is not a negotiable instrument, the purchaser would be subject to such claims as a mere transferee or assignee of the

formalistic validation device such as the seal "not only insures a satisfactory memorial of the promise [evidentiary] and induces deliberation in making the promise [cautionary]. It also serves to mark or signalize the enforceable promise; it furnishes a simple and external test of enforceability [channeling]."[15]

B. *The Essential Formalities of the Contract Under Seal.*

The essence of a contract under seal was a promise, in writing, evidencing certain prescribed formalities. The contract under seal was frequently called a deed, specialty or covenant. At early common law, if all of the formalities were met, the promise was enforceable even in light of evidence that the seal was lost or stolen and affixed by another, or induced by fraud.[16] If one or more of the required formalities was not observed, however, the early law refused legal enforcement of the sealed promise. It is essential to examine the essential formalities of a contract under seal: (1) the writing, (2) sealing, and (3) delivery.

1. What Is a Sufficient Writing?

Though *Blackstone's Commentaries* requires a contract under seal to be written on paper or parchment,[17] it is doubtful that another relatively permanent surface would be insufficient. Whatever the surface upon which it is written, it is clear that the writing must be complete in itself, i.e., it must contain a sufficiently definite promise and must identify the promisor and promisee.[18] A signature, however, is not required because one of the original functions of the seal was to authenticate a document without the signature of an illiterate promisor who found the seal to be an effective substitute for his inability to sign his name. Thus, while modern contracts under seal are invariably signed, a signature is not required.[19] Rather than a signature, authentication of the writing was supplied by other formalities which we will explore, i.e., sealing and delivery.

---

instrument. Therefore, whether he or she will purchase it may very well depend upon its negotiability, and whether it is negotiable will depend upon its external manifestation of compliance with the formal requisites set forth above.

[15] Fuller, *supra* note 10, at 801.

[16] *See, e.g.,* Mason v. Ditchbourne, 1 Mo. & R. 460, 174 Eng. Rep. 158 (1835) and Wright v. Campbell, 1 F. & F. 393, 175 Eng. Rep. 1111 (1861) holding that fraud is not a defense to a sealed instrument. *See generally* J. AMES, LECTURES ON LEGAL HISTORY 98 (1913).

[17] 2 BLACKSTONE'S COMMENTARIES, 297 (1765) suggest that a "deed must be written, or I presume printed, for it may be in any character or any language; but it must be upon paper or parchment. For if it be written on stone, board, linen, leather, or the like, it is no deed."

[18] *See* RESTATEMENT 2d §§ 95(1)(c) and 108 which indicate that the promisor and promisee must be named in the document or so described as to be capable of identification when the document is delivered. *See also* Green v. Horne, 1 Salk 197 [1965] where the deed contained a promise but did not name or describe the promisee. Held: the obligation was not enforceable as a deed. Comment a to § 108 of the RESTATEMENT 2d refers to the RESTATEMENT 2d AGENCY §§ 151, 191 and 296, which indicate that a principal is not a party to a sealed instrument unless he appears in the instrument as a party.

[19] *See* RESTATEMENT 2d § 95 comment c.

2. Sealing — Nature of the Seal.

Lord Coke informs us that a seal is composed of two elements: wax attached to the writing and an impression upon the wax.[20] That ancient form, however, was relaxed no later than the nineteenth century: "Anciently a seal was defined to be an impression on wax; but it has long been held, that a seal by a wafer, or other tenacious substance, upon which an impression is or may be made is a valid seal."[21] The evolution continued to permit an impression on the writing, itself, rather than something attached to the writing.[22] The final extension of the early common law rule is manifested by writings containing a scrawl or scroll or other mark or symbol, made with pen or pencil, or printed on the document with the apparent intention that such mark or symbol constitute a seal. Earlier cases tended to view such marks as insufficient,[23] but later cases generally held them adequate to constitute seals when used or adopted for that purpose.[24] The word "seal" has been held sufficient[25] and by judicial decision or statute, the term "seal", "locus sigilli" (the place of the seal), its abbreviation, "L.S.," "scroll" or "scrawl" may be sufficient.[26] Even if the word "seal" or a substitute such as "L.S." is printed on a standardized form, it will often be sufficient.[27] The modern relaxation of the form of the seal has substantially affected its significance. It is commonplace for pre-printed forms containing "seal" to be signed without the reflection required under the ancient form of the wax impression. The functions of formalistic validation devices explored in the previous section are compromised by permitting the seal to be affixed in this fashion. The cautionary function is destroyed when documents containing the preprinted word, "seal," are signed without reflection on the significance of that term. It is difficult to treat such a form of sealed instrument as manifesting anything like conclusive evidence that the writing was intended by the signer to have any special significance. Thus, the channeling function is severely mitigated, if not destroyed. Even the evidentiary function is made ineffective through such unconscious adoption of the writing as a sealed instrument, i.e., just because it contains a printed term such as "seal" or "L.S." that the typical signer does not understand. Such "sealing," unlike the affixing of the wax impression, can no longer be considered conclusive evidence that the signer intended the sealed instrument to contain an enforceable promise just because it is sealed. For the most part, signers appear

---

[20] 3 COKE'S INSTITUTES 169.

[21] Tasker v. Bartlett, 59 Mass. (5 Cush.) 359 (1850). *Accord* Maddocks v. Keene, 114 Me. 469, 96 A. 785 (1916).

[22] Hendee v. Pinerton, 96 Mass. (14 Allen) 381 (1867); Hastings v. Vaughn, 5 Cal. 315 (1855); Allen v. Sullivan R.R., 32 N.H. 446 (1855). *See also Seals*, 1 AM. L. REV. 638 (1866) in which it is sought to be established that the essential characteristic of the early seal was the impression rather than the substance on which the impression was made.

[23] *See, e.g.,* McLaughlin v. Randall, 66 Me. 226 (1877); Bates v. Boston & N.Y.C.R.R., 92 Mass. (10 Allen) 251 (1865); Warren v. Lynch, 5 Johns. 239 (N.Y. 1810).

[24] *See, e.g.,* Appeal of Hacker, 121 Pa. St. 192, 15 A. 500 (1888) (dash one-eighth of an inch long following signature); Pitts v. Pitchford, 201 So. 2d 563 (Fla. App. 1967) (L.S. — abbreviation for *locus sigilli* — the place of the seal, scrawl or scroll would be sufficient).

[25] *See, e.g.,* Avery v. Kane Gas Light & Heating Co., 403 F. Supp. 14 (W.D. Pa. 1975).

[26] A list of statutory modifications of the *form* of the seal is found in RESTATEMENT 2d, § 94 as part of the "statutory note" to that section.

[27] *See* Warfield v. Baltimore Gas & Elec. Co., 307 Md. 142, 512 A.2d 1044 (1986); Felix v. Evangelist, 71 N.C. App. 35, 321 S.E.2d 524 (1984).

to pay no attention to such printed terms on the documents they are signing. It was inevitable that courts and legislatures would begin to recognize this reality. The focus shifted from the mere form of the document, which could no longer be relied upon as evidence of the signer's intention to adopt the writing as a sealed instrument, to other evidence of the promisor's intention. Intention became the crucial factor since it could no longer be presumed conclusively from the form of the writing.

3. Reciting the Fact that the Writing Is Sealed.

When the wax impression was the exclusive manner of sealing, it would have been superfluous for the writing to contain a statement that the promisor intended the writing to be sealed. Whether a writing was sealed had to be determined from an inspection of the document itself; extrinsic evidence was not admissible to prove the fact of sealing.[28] The strict rule was totally compatible with the channeling function of such a formalistic validation device, i.e., if a writing had the wax impression containing the insignia of the promisor, it was conclusively presumed to evidence an enforceable obligation. With the relaxation of the form of the seal and the consequent shift to focusing upon the intention of the promisor, courts sought other evidence of that intention. Once it became permissible to make use of virtually any mark or device as a seal, the question of intention became much more difficult to determine. The mere presence of a scrawl or scroll or, in particular, the printed term "seal" or a substituted printed term was very little evidence that the mark was intended as a seal. In search of other evidence that the writing was intended to be a sealed instrument, courts began considering the effect of a statement in the writing manifesting the intention of the promisor that the writing should be considered sealed. Some courts were so taken with this substitute evidence that they took an extreme position, i.e., a recital was *always* necessary.[29] However, other courts did not view the recital as either necessary or conclusive, i.e., they did not require recitals to hold promises binding under seal,[30] and where the writing recited that it was sealed, they did not view the recital as conclusive evidence that the promise was under seal since recitals can be false.[31] A recital of sealing, however, may be the equivalent of a seal according to some statutes or case law.[32]

The movement away from a mere inspection of the document to determine its validity to the admissibility of extrinsic evidence to determine the inten-

---

[28] *See* Jacksonville Mayport, Pablo Ry. & Nav. Co. v. Hooper, 160 U.S. 514 (1895); Corlies v. Vannote, 16 N.J.L. 324 (1838). The strict position was that extrinsic evidence was not admissible even to show that the instrument was voidable for fraud. RESTATEMENT 2d § 108 comment a.

[29] *See, e.g.*, Baxley Hardware Co. v. Morris, 165 Ga. 359, 140 S.E. 869 (1927) (statutory requirement); Dawsey v. Kirven, 203 Ala. 446, 83 So. 338, 7 A.L.R. 1658 (1919); Bradley Salt Co. v. Norfolk Importing & Exporting Co., 95 Va. 461, 28 S.E. 567 (1897).

[30] *See* Warfield v. Baltimore Gas & Elec. Co., 307 Md. 142, 512 A.2d 1044 (1986) and cases cited therein.

[31] RESTATEMENT 2d § 100. *But see* Mobil Oil Corp. v. Wolfe, 297 N.C. 36, 252 S.E.2d 809 (1979) holding that a recital is conclusive evidence that the promise is under seal.

[32] *See* RESTATEMENT 2d § 100 comment b. *See* ALA. CODE § 35-4-22; MASS. GEN. LAWS ANN. ch. 4, § 9A; *see also* Morad v. Silva, 331 Mass. 94, 117 N.E.2d 290 (1954).

tion of the promisor is clear from numerous cases permitting such evidence under myriad circumstances.[33]

4. What Constitutes Sealing? — Adoption of a Seal — Corporate Seals Distinguished.

It has long been held that an obligor need not place the seal on the document — he may adopt as his own a seal already on the writing.[34] Moreover, the fact of adoption may be shown by extrinsic evidence.[35] Where several persons execute the instrument, a separate seal for each obligor is not necessary; one seal will serve for any number of persons.[36] If the previously attached or printed seal appears to refer to the signature of the obligor, there is an inference that the signer has adopted it.[37] In the case of multiple obligors with only one seal or, at least, fewer seals than the number of obligors, the inference of adoption may be found if a seal follows the signature of the first signer so that all those signing after him or her would be presumed to have adopted it.[38] Since the question of adoption is one of intention, a recital of sealing by all signers would remove any doubt that each signer intended to adopt the seal.[39]

Finally, it should be noted that a number of cases distinguish the situation involving writings containing corporate seals. The seal of a corporation is typically not intended to perform the function of a seal as a validation device. A corporate seal will identify a document as an official document of the corporation whose seal is printed thereon. Neither the corporation nor a party signing a document containing the corporate seal normally intends to adopt such a seal as validating any obligation evidenced by that writing.[40]

5. Delivery.

We have considered the first and second elements necessary to make a promise binding under the formalistic validation device traditionally called

---

[33] For example, see Garrison v. Blakeney, 37 N.C. App. 73, 246 S.E.2d 144, cert. denied, 295 N.C. 646, 248 S.E.2d 151 (1978), denying summary judgment with respect to the issue of the promisor's intent to adopt the term "sign" as his seal. See also Transbel Inv. Co. v. Venetos, 279 N.Y. 207, 18 N.E.2d 129 (1938) admitting extrinsic evidence; Graybill v. Juniata Cty. Sch. Dist., 21 Pa. Commw. Ct. 630, 347 A.2d 524 (1976) (dicta).

[34] For example, in Loraw v. Nissley, 156 Pa. 329, 27 A. 242 (1893), the printed word "seal" after the signature was held valid by adoption. See also Warfield v. Baltimore Gas & Elec. Co., 207 Md. 142, 512 A.2d 1044 (1986); Van Domelen v. Westinghouse Elec. Corp., 382 F.2d 385 (9th Cir. 1967).

[35] See Transbel Inv. Co. v. Venetos, 279 N.Y. 207, 18 N.E.2d 129 (1938) and Pickens v. Rymer, 90 N.C. 282, 47 Am. Rep. 521 (1884). See also RESTATEMENT 2d § 98.

[36] Gilderhorn v. Columbia Real Estate Title Co., 271 Md. 387, 317 A.2d 836 (1974); McNulty v. Medical Serv. of D.C., 176 A.2d 783 (D.C. App. 1962). See also RESTATEMENT 2d § 99.

[37] RESTATEMENT 2d § 98.

[38] See RESTATEMENT 2d § 98 ill. 2. See, however, Eames v. Preston, 20 Ill. 389 (1858) (semble), suggesting that, if the seal appears after the name of one of the signers, it will be presumed that all whose signatures follow his have adopted the seal, whereas those whose names come before his are not presumed to have adopted it.

[39] See RESTATEMENT 2d § 99 ill. 1.

[40] See, e.g., Square D Co. v. Kern Contrs., 314 N.C. 423, 334 S.E.2d 63 (1985); Georgetown College v. Madden, 505 F. Supp. 557 (D. Md. 1980) (corporate seal alone is insufficient — the body of the contract must indicate that the parties intended to establish an agreement under seal); Mayor & Council of Federalsburg v. Allied Contrs., 275 Md. 151, 338 A.2d 285, cert. denied, 423 U.S. 1017 (1975).

the sealed contract: (1) a sufficient writing, and (2) the fact of sealing. The third and final element is the requirement of delivery. The delivery of the sealed writing is the final act required to consummate a contract under seal.[41] The early law merely required the obligor voluntarily to hand over the writing, i.e., to part with physical possession of it. It quickly became apparent, however, that the document may have been handed over merely for inspection. Consequently, it soon became the rule that delivery involved two elements: (a) surrendering physical possession of the writing accompanied by (b) the apparent intention that the writing should evidence an immediately binding obligation.[42] The second of these two elements has become, by far, the more important. For some time, English courts have taken the position that the second element is the only essential element, i.e., evidence of the obligor's intention that the instrument shall be presently binding consummates the contract under seal even though the instrument is not physically transferred. Thus, where the officers of an insurance company executed a burglary policy and left it with the secretary for delivery, it was held to be a binding contract although the policy at all times remained in the hands of the secretary.[43] There is substantial support for this view in American case law.[44] The Restatement 2d, however, clings to the requirement that the promisor put the writing out of his possession.[45] Professor Corbin insists upon the view supported by English and some American case law, i.e., an overt manifestation of the obligor's intention to make the sealed document immediately operative should be effective even without a manual transfer of the document.[46] Thus, "delivery" may be evidenced by a manifestation of intention other than physical transfer of the writing. As is almost always the case, the Corbin view appears preferable.

6. Conditional Delivery — Escrow Delivery.

If a promisor signs a sealed writing and delivers it to the obligee with the understanding that the obligation is irrevocable but that it will not be activated until a certain event occurs, delivery of the sealed writing is effective even though it is conditional upon the occurrence of the particular event.[47]

---

[41] See RESTATEMENT 2d § 95(1)(b).

[42] RESTATEMENT 2d § 102.

[43] Roberts v. Security Co., 1 Q.B. 111 [1897]. See also Xenos v. Wickham, L.R. 2 H.L. 2296 [1866].

[44] See, e.g., Twining v. National Mtg. Corp., 268 Md. 549, 302 A.2d 604 (1973) where the sealed writing was not handed over manually but the court relied heavily upon the scholarship of Professor Corbin at 1A, § 244 of his treatise. Professor Corbin suggests that, while "delivery" is usually a manual delivery of the writing, "the operative fact is overt action by the obligor expressing an intention to make the sealed document at once operative and justifying the obligee in relying upon it." Thus, courts "do not abandon the word ['delivery'] when they hold that another mode of expression is effective; instead, they merely stretch the word 'delivery' so as to include facts other than a manual transfer of possession." In La Fleur v. All Am. Ins. Co., 157 So. 2d 254 (La. App. 1963) an insurance policy in the hands of insurance company's general agent was in force though insured died before physical delivery could be accomplished. See also McMahon v. Dorsey, 353 Mich. 623, 91 N.W.2d 893 (1958); Gurley v. Life & Cas. Ins. Co., 132 F. Supp. 289 (M.D.N.C. 1955), aff'd, 229 F.2d 326 (4th Cir. 1956) (constructive delivery).

[45] RESTATEMENT 2d § 102 comment b.

[46] See discussion of the Corbin position in supra note 44.

[47] See RESTATEMENT 2d § 103(2).

Such a *conditional delivery* is effective since the obligor is irrevocably bound unless the condition does not occur.[48] If the condition does not occur, the duty of the obligor is discharged by the failure of a condition over which he or she had no control, i.e., it is not discharged by any act of the obligor.[49] A typical situation would be the handing over of a sealed promise to sell or buy land if the other party pays a certain sum or transfers a deed to the land within a certain time.[50] Such a promise under seal (where the seal is still effective) would create an option contract, i.e., it would provide the other party with an irrevocable power of acceptance during the time stated in the writing. Thus, the obligor manifests a willingness to provide a binding assurance but insists that he will not be liable until he receives a particular value from the obligee in exchange for his commitment. The obligee is assured that if she relies upon the promise and provides the necessary exchange, she will receive what is promised in the writing with no concern that the obligor will revoke the power of acceptance during the time stated. When the conditions attached to the sealed promise have been fulfilled, the sealed writing becomes effective without any further act or delivery by anyone.[51]

A virtually identical analysis applies to a *delivery in escrow.* "Escrow" is derived from the Norman-French term for a writing,[52] but the term has come to be understood as describing the delivery of property or a writing intended to benefit the obligee to a third party who holds the property or writing until a conditioning event has occurred or failed to occur. If the condition occurs, the title to the property held by the third party passes to the grantee. If the third party is holding a sealed writing, the document takes effect according to its terms when the condition occurs. Lawyers often refer to the property held by the third party as "the escrow" while the delivery of the writing or property is characterized as a delivery "in escrow." Thus, a sealed promise delivered "in escrow" is delivered to a third party, i.e., a party other than the promisee. As in the conditional delivery to the promisee, the sealed promise is not revocable by the promisor[53] and there is an intention manifested that it is to become effective upon the occurence of a certain condition. Such a delivery "in escrow" is an effective delivery.[54] Since the same operative effects flow from either a conditional delivery to the promisee or a delivery "in escrow," it is possible to discover a court mischaracterizing a conditional delivery as an escrow delivery.[55] The RESTATEMENT 2d, however, properly insists upon the foregoing distinction between the two forms of delivery.[56]

---

[48] *See* Hudson v. Hudson, 287 Ill. 286, 122 N.E. 497 (1919).

[49] If the "condition" required the obligor to manifest assent to the obligation at some later time, the obligation would simply be a revocable promise by the obligor and delivery would not have occurred. *See* RESTATEMENT 2d § 103 comment c.

[50] Conditional delivery of a sealed promise is irrevocable for the time stated by the promisor or, if no time is specified, for a reasonable time. RESTATEMENT 2d § 103(4). The performance of the condition on time may be waived by the promisor, thus extending the time for its occurrence. *See* Sunset Beach Amusement Corp. v. Belk, 31 N.J. 445, 158 A.2d 35 (1960).

[51] *See* Gardiner v. Gardiner, 36 Idaho 664, 214 P. 219 (1923); Craddock v. Barnes, 142 N.C. 89, 54 S.E. 1003 (1906).

[52] The terms "scroll" or "scrawl" are similarly derived. RESTATEMENT 2d § 103 comment a.

[53] If the promisor had reserved a power of revocation, the third party would operate as the *agent* of the promisor. *See* RESTATEMENT 2d AGENCY § 14D.

[54] RESTATEMENT 2d § 103(1).

[55] *See, e.g.,* Whitaker & Fowle v. Lane, 128 Va. 317, 104 S.E. 252, 11 A.L.R. 1157 (1920).

[56] RESTATEMENT 2d § 103 comment d.

The only difficulty that arises in relation to the foregoing analysis is the possible inconsistency with a rule concerning the admissibility of evidence that would change or vary the terms of the writing. The "parol evidence rule" might be said to preclude the admission of evidence of an oral condition since the writing is absolute on its face.[57] The complexities of the parol evidence rule will be explored later in this volume.[58] At this time, it is sufficient to report that, with respect to conditional delivery or escrow delivery of a sealed promise, the views of Professor Corbin have prevailed, i.e., evidence of such a condition will be admissible because to deny it would be to frustrate the intentions of the parties in too many cases.[59]

7. Acceptance by the Promisee.

The earliest recorded cases involving sealed promises made it clear that acceptance of the promise or assent by the promisee has never been essential to the consummation of a contract under seal.[60] Some American courts, apparently pursuing the requirement of mutual assent in informal (unsealed) contracts, required assent by the promisee but quickly nullified the effect of that requirement by holding that, in the absence of a disclaimer by the promisee, acceptance would be presumed.[61] It is, however, more accurate to state that acceptance is simply unnecessary.[62] Just as an offer can be rejected by an offeree, a promisee may disclaim the benefit of the obligation created by the sealed promise. Unless the promisee disclaims within a reasonable time after learning of the existence and terms of the promise, however, the promise is enforceable without any manifestation of assent by the promisee.[63] The only situation requiring a communication of acceptance by the promisee is one which contemplates a return promise. Thus, if the sealed promise is one providing the promisee with thirty days to accept an offer to purchase the promisee's land for $50,000, the sealed promise creates an option contract making the promise irrevocable for thirty days *and* the sealed promise manifests the contemplation of an acceptance of the irrevocable offer if the promisee chooses to accept. In such a situation, acceptance by the promisee would be essential.[64] Where the sealed promise does not require acceptance, the promisee may still manifest acceptance. Whether or not acceptance is required, once it is manifested, a disclaimer would, thereafter, be ineffective. Similarly, if the prom-

---

[57] *See, e.g.,* Hume v. Kirkwood, 216 Ala. 534, 113 So. 613 (1927).

[58] *See infra* §§ 82-84.

[59] *See* CORBIN, *Conditional Delivery of Written Contracts,* 36 YALE L.J. 443 (1926). *See also* RESTATEMENT 2d § 217 comments a and b.

[60] *See* Butler v. Baker's Case, 3 Coke 25a, 26b [1591] in which delivery of the instrument to a third person, without the knowledge of the obligee, was held effective to bind the obligor unless and until the obligee disclaimed. *See also* Malott v. Wilson, 2 Ch. 494 [1903].

[61] The American cases so holding involve conveyances. There is, however, no reason to suppose that a different rule would have been said to apply in the case of a contract. The cases are collected in 4 TIFFANY, REAL PROPERTY § 1057 (3d ed. 1939).

[62] *See* RESTATEMENT 2d § 104 comment a.

[63] RESTATEMENT 2d § 104.

[64] RESTATEMENT 2d § 105.

isee disclaims the benefit contained in a sealed promise, the disclaimer is irrevocable.[65]

8. Necessity for Consideration in Sealed Contracts.

Since contracts under seal long antedated the doctrine of consideration, it is absurd to suggest that the seal "imports consideration" or that the seal is the "real consideration" for a particular contract.[66] Since a sealed contract is binding absent consideration,[67] there is no need to mention consideration in holding that the sealed promise is binding. Apparently, some courts have "imported" or "presumed" consideration in sealed promises either because they have momentarily forgotten the independence of the seal as a validation device, or because they wish to harmonize that validation device with the mutually exclusive validation device called consideration. These unfortunate utterances should be eschewed because they are historically and analytically unsound.

There is, however, a situation that may appear as an exception to the rule that sealed promises (again, where the seal is still effective) are enforceable without consideration. If an aggrieved party is not seeking ordinary relief in the form of money (damages), but is seeking equitable relief in the form of specific performance or an injunction, the remedy may not be granted unless there is consideration for the sealed promise, some prior benefit to the promisor or detriment to the promisee, or evidence of a substantial change of position by the promisee in reliance on the sealed promise.[68]

9. Parties with Rights and Duties Under a Sealed Contract — Agent's Authority.

Before one can be held on a contract under seal, he must make a promise in writing in his own name and seal and deliver the instrument.[69] Therefore, if the contract is "bilateral" in operation, i.e., it is intended to contain reciprocal

---

[65] RESTATEMENT 2d § 104(3).

[66] See In re Conrad's Estate, 333 Pa. 561, 3 A.2d 697 (1933) ("seal imports consideration"); Hartford-Connecticut Trust Co. v. Divine, 97 Conn. 193, 116 A. 239, 21 A.L.R. 134 (1922) ("real consideration").

[67] RESTATEMENT 2d § 95(1).

[68] See Russ v. Barnes, 23 Md. App. 691, 329 A.2d 767 (1974); Community Sports, Inc. v. Denver Ringsby Rockets, 429 Pa. 565, 240 A.2d 832 (1968) (holding that even a "past" consideration would not be effective for a sealed promise when the relief sought is specific performance). RESTATEMENT 2d § 364 comment b suggests, "A contract, other than an option contract on fair terms ... that is binding solely because of a nominal payment or by reason of some formality such as a seal ... will not ordinarily be enforced by specific performance or an injunction." See, however, Marine Contrs. Co. v. Hurley, 365 Mass. 280, 310 N.E.2d 915, 919 (1974) where the defendant urged that a contract under seal should not be specifically enforced, relying upon § 366 of the FIRST RESTATEMENT and citing Professor Corbin's treatise, 1A at § 252. The court replied, "The short answer to this argument ... is that the rule of the Restatement is not the law of Massachusetts."

[69] Therefore, a principal cannot be held on a contract under seal executed by his agent in the agent's own name. See RESTATEMENT 2d AGENCY §§ 151, 191 and 296 where a principal is not a party to a sealed instrument unless he appears in the instrument as a party. See, however, Nalbandian v. Hanson Restaurant & Lounge, Inc., 369 Mass. 150, 338 N.E.2d 335 (1975) in which the Supreme Judicial Court of Massachusetts overruled prior law and held that, upon proof of its identity, an undisclosed principal could be held liable on a sealed contract to the same extent that it could be held on an unsealed contract.

promises, then both parties must seal and deliver the writing.[70] If both parties have sealed and delivered their written promises, they are both bound by the formalities of the sealed instrument.[71] If, however, the promise is unilateral in its operation, only the promisor need seal and deliver it because the promisee/obligee need not execute the instrument to have rights under it.[72] Since the early common law viewed the sealed instrument as *the* contract, a party not named in the instrument could not have rights under it.[73] Some of the earlier authorities extended this rule. If a deed, bilateral in form, stated on its face that it was made between certain persons, these authorities held that only those persons (between whom the deed was stated to have been made) could have any rights under it. Thus, even a promisee named in the deed would have no rights under it if he was not one of the persons between whom the contract was stated to have been made.[74] Modern courts may permit even an unnamed party to bring an action on a sealed contract[75] and, in light of the widespread changes in the effects of the seal, an application of the strict rules would be difficult to discover in modern case law.

While the common law required no formality for the appointment of an agent to make an informal contract on behalf of the principal, authority to execute a sealed contract for a principal could be conferred only by an instrument under seal.[76] Where the seal retains its common law effect, this rule obtains, except in the case of an agent executing a sealed contract on behalf of a corporation.[77]

10. Effect of the Seal — Statutes of Limitations.

As we have seen, the principal effect of the seal, where still effective, is to make a promise enforceable simply because it conforms to the form of the seal. As will be seen in the next subsection, statutory changes have either abolished this effect or reduced it to a presumption of consideration. Modern cases

---

[70] Such an instrument is often referred to as an *indenture* to distinguish it from an instrument executed only by one party which is called a *deed poll*. The term, "indenture" comes from the early practice followed when two parties executed a deed. Two copies of the deed were usually written on the same piece of parchment and then cut apart in a waving or serrated line. The "deed poll" which involved a sealed promise by only one party was cut evenly.

[71] If an obligee is supposed to make a reciprocal promise and does so without sealing and delivery, he may still be liable on his *informal* promise, i.e., if it is supported by a validation device other than the seal. However, he is not liable on the sealed contract, alone, i.e., he would not be liable in the common law action called "covenant."

[72] RESTATEMENT 2d § 109.

[73] Exchange Realty Co. v. Bines, 302 Mass. 93, 18 N.E.2d 425 (1939); Case v. Case, 203 N.Y. 263, 96 N.E. 440 (1911); Harvey v. Maine Condensed-Milk Co., 92 Me. 115, 42 A. 342 (1898); Newberry Land Co. v. Newberry, 95 Va. 119, 27 S.E. 899 (1897). *Accord* RESTATEMENT 2d § 108.

[74] Scudamore v. Vandenstone, 2 COKE'S INSTITUTES 673 [1587]; Chesterfield & Midland Silkstone Colliery Co. v. Hawkins, 3 H. & C. 677 [1865].

[75] *See, e.g.,* Philipsborn v. 17th & Chestnut Streets Holding Corp., 111 Pa. Super. 9, 169 A. 473 (1933). *See also* Annotation in 170 A.L.R. 1299 (1947). While the RESTATEMENT 2d clings to the strict rule requiring all parties to be named, it admits that the rule is a remnant of medieval strictures. RESTATEMENT 2d § 108 comment a.

[76] RESTATEMENT 2d AGENCY § 28(1).

[77] RESTATEMENT 2d AGENCY § 28(2)(b). It should also be noted that where the agent acts in the presence of his principal, he can bind the principal on a sealed contract even without sealed authority. Here, the theory is that the agent is the mere mechanical instrument through which the principal himself executes the sealed instrument. RESTATEMENT 2d AGENCY § 28(2)(a).

dealing with the seal in jurisdictions in which it retains its effectiveness are often concerned with the applicable statute of limitations. Since a writing under seal provides a permanent and, presumably, careful manifestation of a promise that the promisor intends to be enforceable, it has often been asserted that an action on a written contract under seal should enjoy a long statute of limitations.[78] The RESTATEMENT 2d indicates that contracts under seal are clearly recognized in the statutes of limitations of twenty jurisdictions and in five other states where there is no special limitations period governing contracts under seal.[79] In these jurisdictions, a case may turn on whether the promise is under seal, thereby activating a much longer limitations period.[80]

11. Statutory Modification and Substitutes for the Seal.

At the beginning of our discussion of formalistic validation devices, we explored the functions of these formalities, the evidentiary, cautionary and channeling functions. The original wax impression attached to a writing fulfilled all of these functions. When, however, the ritual attending the affixation of the seal evolved from the reflective effort of heating wax and imprinting it to the modern, pre-printed form containing the word "seal" or a substitute, we saw the erosion of these functions since printed forms were typically signed with little or no thought given to the nature of the seal or its possible effect on the promise evidenced by the signature of the promisor. This evolution caused numerous modifications, typically statutory, of the effect of the seal. Some statutes modified the form of the seal, i.e., permitting various kinds of marks such as the word "seal," the abbreviation for *locus sigilli* or statements in the writing that it was intended to be under seal to be effective.[81] The RESTATEMENT 2d reports that, at least twenty-four states purport to abolish the seal or, as it is often put, they have abolished any distinction between sealed and unsealed instruments.[82] The most significant statutory abolition of the seal is found in the UCC which makes "seals inoperative", i.e., affixing a seal to a writing evidencing a contract for the sale of goods or to an offer to buy or sell goods does not make the writing a sealed instrument and the law of sealed instruments does not apply to such a contract or offer.[83] Since all American jurisdictions except Louisiana have enacted Article 2 of the

---

[78] *See* Solomon v. Birger, 19 Mass. App. 634, 477 N.E.2d 137 (1985) quoting 118 WILLISTON, CONTRACTS § 2020, at 678.

[79] RESTATEMENT 2d § 94, *Statutory Note.* This Note contains a list of jurisdictions setting forth periods of limitation ranging from 5 to 20 years. The RESTATEMENT 2d indicates that there is no specified statute of limitations on sealed contracts in Delaware, but there is a common law presumption of payment after 20 years. *See* Di Biase v. A & D, Inc., 351 A.2d 865 (Del. Super. 1976).

[80] *See, e.g.,* Warfield v. Baltimore Gas & Elec. Co., 307 Md. 142, 512 A.2d 1044 (1986) (12 years); Biggers v. Evangelist, 71 N.C. App. 35, 321 S.E.2d 524 (1984) (10 years); Telefair Fin. Co. v. Williams, 172 Ga. App. 489, 323 S.E.2d 689 (1984) (20 years).

[81] See the list of modified forms in RESTATEMENT 2d § 94, *Statutory Note.*

[82] *Id.*

[83] UCC § 2-203. *See* Osguthorpe v. Anschutz Land & Livestock Co., 456 F.2d 996 (10th Cir. 1972); Associates Disct. Corp. v. Palmer, 47 N.J. 183, 219 A.2d 858 (1966). See, however, North Carolina Nat'l Bank v. Holshouer, 38 N.C. App. 165, 247 S.E.2d 645 (1978) refusing to apply the four-year statute of limitation under § 2-725 of the UCC to an Article 9 security agreement under seal to which the court applied the North Carolina 10-year statute of limitation, expressly rejecting the holding and rationale in *Associates Disct. Corp.*

Code, and Louisiana never adopted the seal, the seal is abolished with respect to contracts for the sale of goods (or offers to buy or sell goods) throughout the United States. Some statutes have reduced the seal to "presumptive evidence of consideration"[84] while others have abolished the seal but presume consideration with respect to written promises.[85] The statutes are not always drafted in clear and precise terms, so their effects are not always certain.

Notwithstanding the abolition or diminishing effects of the seal in many jurisdictions, the need for formalistic validation devices is clear. Thus, even though the UCC made seals inoperative, we have already explored the inclusion of a formalistic validation device to permit offers to become irrevocable (the "firm offer")[86] and we will explore another UCC device to permit subsequent modifications of a contract to be enforceable without consideration.[87] Other state statutes permitting "firm offers" without consideration[88] or, a *fortiori*, statutes directing that any contract in writing "shall import consideration in the same manner and as fully as sealed instruments have heretofore done"[89] are clear illustrations of a statutory reaction to the felt need for other formalistic validation devices. The most significant device which was presented prior to the general abolition or weakening of the seal was a legislative innovation originally captioned, the Uniform Written Obligations Act, a product of the National Conference of Commissioners on Uniform State Laws. Since Pennsylvania is the only state that currently features this Act, its title has been changed to the Model Written Obligations Act.[90] It permits a written release or promise, signed by the releasing or promising party, to be enforceable without consideration if it contains an express statement, in any form of language, that the signer intends to be legally bound.[91] The Model Act appears to be an effective and modern substitution for the seal. The failure of many jurisdictions to enact it appears to be due, in large measure, to legislative inertia. There is a need for formalistic validation devices, but that need seems to be addressed to specific kinds of promises such as firm offers rather than a general requirement for an effective and modern formalistic device.

§ 54. Consideration — Origins.

Although consideration is only one of the validation devices recognized to make a promise enforceable, it is often remembered as the dominant validation device because it is more complex in its application than other validation devices. Its complexity leads to difficulty in understanding. That difficulty is due, in some measure, to a failure to understand the origins of consideration.

---

[84] RESTATEMENT 2d § 94 *Statutory Note.*

[85] *Id.*

[86] UCC § 2-205. *See supra* § 43(C).

[87] UCC § 2-209.

[88] *See, e.g.,* N.Y. GEN. OBLIG. LAW § 5-1109.

[89] N.M. STAT. ANN. § 38-7-2. It is unfortunate that this New Mexico statute suggests that the seal "imported consideration" since, as suggested at the commencement of our exploration of the seal, the seal antedates consideration. While the enactment is historically untidy, the point is clear.

[90] Utah had enacted the "Uniform" Act but later repealed it.

[91] PA. STAT. ANN. tit. 33 § 6.

Consideration may be viewed as an historic accident. In Chapter One, we saw the development of the common law writ system which permitted the enforcement of formal promises under seal through the writ called *covenant*, the use of the writ *detinue* essentially in bailment contracts where the defendant was charged with unjust detention of the plaintiff's property, and the action in *debt* which could be used only where the exchange between the parties was half-completed. In addition to the intrinsic limitations on the actions in detinue and debt, both were subject to "wager of law" allowing the defendant to defeat recovery by securing twelve persons who would swear that the defendant told the truth. The need for a flexible writ or form of action to permit the enforcement of informal promises was clear. That development occurred through the writ of *trespass on the case* which was being developed in the Court of King's Bench. Trespass on the case was expanded to permit the development of the action in *special assumpsit* which involved an *undertaking* (assumpsit — he undertook) by a party who performed the undertaking badly, i.e., he committed *misfeasance.* The blacksmith, for example, undertook to shoe a horse and he performed badly, injuring the horse. The undertaking coupled with the blacksmith's misfeasance permitted the action in special assumpsit. Because he had performed badly, there was a *detriment* to the promisee, the owner of the horse. Thus, the origins of special assumpsit were what modern lawyers would call tort (*ex delicto*) since the emphasis was upon the *misfeasance* of the promisor.

If the party who undertook to perform (the promisor) did not misfease, i.e., did not perform badly, but simply failed to perform at all, there would be no connection to the basic concept of trespass — even an expansion of trespass on the case in the form of special assumpsit — because there would be no deviant conduct. Some connection had to be found. The connection was discovered by finding the defendant who failed to perform at all guilty of *deceit.* In a simple case involving a promise to sell a house, if the defendant breached the promise by selling the house to a third party, there was an allegation that this constituted deceit to the plaintiff. Gradually, the emphasis shifted from the performance stage where the defendant was guilty of deceit to the initial stage of the undertaking itself. At this point, assumpsit became an action *ex contractu* rather than *ex delicto.*

There was competition in the English courts concerning the actions in *debt* and *assumpsit.* King's Bench was particularly eager to continue the development of assumpsit because it derived remuneration from the fees paid by the parties in litigation. In 1602, *Slade's Case*[92] provided a quantum leap in this development. If a chattel were purchased from the plaintiff and defendant breached the agreement to pay for it, unless the promise of the defendant were under seal, the only action that would lie was the action in debt. *Covenant* would not lie for an unsealed promise, and *detinue* was unavailable absent an unjust detainer. If, however, the defendant subsequently *promised* to pay a second time, the second promise would permit an action in *indebitatus assumption* (being indebted, he undertook). In *Slade's Case,* the court held that the second promise need only be alleged and not proved, thus permitting the

[92] 4 Coke 92b [1602].

writ of assumpsit in actions where debt alone had previously been available. Assumpsit became the popular remedy for breach of contract since it could be brought without the limitations of earlier writs.

The new action created significant problems. Would assumpsit lie for breach of *any* promise, or would there be limitations? The term "consideration" was first used in pleadings suggesting different contents. For example, the pleadings might state, "In consideration that the buyer had paid £100, the seller promised to deliver his horse and car to the buyer." The term was used to express vaguely the concept that there had to be some reason for enforcing the promise. What were good and sufficient reasons for enforcing a promise? Once again, the common lawyers resorted to their familiar forms of action. They recognized that assumpsit had been applied to situations where the action of debt had been applied, i.e., situations involving an exchange, a *quid pro quo,* where the defendant had already received a *benefit* — the half-completed exchange. They also recognized that assumpsit had been applied to the misfeasance situations where the promise or undertaking by the defendant had been performed badly resulting in a *detriment* to the promisee. Thus, if there were an *exchange* resulting in *either* a *benefit* to the promisor or a *detriment* to the promisee, there was reason for enforcing the promise. The characterization that developed from this formula was *consideration*. What has become the traditional formula for consideration — bargained for exchange plus either a benefit to the promisor or a detriment to the promisee — was not easily developed. It can, however, be traced to the historical development we have just sketched.

A related theory of the origins of consideration emanates from the reflection of Holmes who argued that the "quid pro quo" requirement fulfilled an evidentiary function.[93] Since witnesses could testify only to facts within their personal knowledge, they could testify that the performance on one side was in exchange for performance on the other in an action for *debt.* The evidentiary function in actions on a sealed instrument under the writ called *covenant* was fulfilled by the prescribed form of the promise. Still another theory emanates from the Roman law concept of "causa." Though quite distinct from consideration, "causa" is another suggested basis for the eventual development of consideration on the footing that "causa" found its way into canon law and, from there, to the consciousness of English chancellors who influenced English common law.[94] There are, however, important assertions that consideration is not traceable to either debt or causa.[95] There is an amusing view that the bargain theory of consideration can be traced only as far back as 1881, i.e., to the alleged creator of this revolutionary concept, O. W. Holmes, Jr.[96] The evidence, however, is compelling that at least as early as the sixteenth century, English courts had discovered the central device for determining which

---

[93] O. HOLMES, THE COMMON LAW 254-59 (1923).

[94] J. SALMOND, JURISPRUDENCE AND LEGAL HISTORY ch. iv, 27 (London: Stevens & Haynes 1891).

[95] INTRODUCTION TO THE REPORTS OF SIR JOHN SPELMAN 292-97 (Selden Society, J. H. Baker, ed. 1978).

[96] GILMORE, THE DEATH OF CONTRACT 19-21 (1974) in which the author relies essentially upon two sentences from HOLMES' COMMON LAW at 230 (Howe ed. 1963).

promises were enforceable: "[E]ach party had in fact desired some act or abstention of the other in return for which he had agreed to perform his own."[97]

In the eighteenth century, Lord Mansfield, Chief Justice of King's Bench from 1756 to 1788, was almost solely responsible for the erosion of the doctrine of consideration for a period of approximately thirteen years. In 1765, Mansfield suggested that a promise should be enforced simply because it was in writing. Consideration only afforded evidence of the contract. Since a writing provided sufficient evidence, consideration was unnecessary.[98] This view, however, was rejected in 1778 when the House of Lords emphatically reinstated the requirement of consideration.[99] In its 1937 Report, the British Law Revision Committee was highly critical of consideration and recommended significant limitations though many members of the Committee would have preferred the abolition of the doctrine.[1] The recommendations included making agreements in writing enforceable without consideration as well as other substantial incursions. The recommendations were not adopted.

There have been vigorous debates over the origins of consideration for many years.[2] The foregoing summary of a number of views should convince the student that consideration was not a well-planned, rationally conceived device for deciding which promises are enforceable. Notwithstanding its origins, the pervasive notion of bargained-for exchange seems to reflect a felt need to retain consideration at least as one of the devices to determine the enforceability of promises. The student of contract law will be in a position to decide whether consideration is a desirable validation device only through an examination of the doctrine in operation.

§ 55. The Elements of Consideration.

The classic formula of consideration, which we have just traced to its historic origins, is composed of two elements: (1) something which the law regards as valuable — a benefit to the promisor or a detriment to the promisee; and (2) must be exchanged, i.e., dealt with by the parties to the agreement as the agreed price or exchange for the promise. Thus, there must be a "bargained-for-exchange" of something which, in the eyes of the law, is of some value. Neither the FIRST RESTATEMENT nor RESTATEMENT 2d defined consideration in terms of benefit to the promisor or detriment to the promisee. The RESTATEMENT 2d defines consideration simply: "[A] performance or a return

---

[97] J. DAWSON, GIFTS AND PROMISES 203 (1980). Another scholar suggests that the concept of "bargain" is found in fourteenth and fifteenth century English cases, K. SUTTON, CONSIDERATION RECONSIDERED 6, 13-18 (1974). For another view contrary to the assertion of Gilmore, see Speidel, *An Essay on the Reported Death and Continued Vitality of Contract,* 27 STAN. L. REV. 1161 (1975). Note also that there are American cases prior to 1881 suggesting the necessity of a bargain theory of consideration: Hardesty v. Smith, 3 Ind. 39 (1851).

[98] Pillans & Rose v. Van Mierop & Hopkins, 3 Burr. 1663, 97 Eng. Rep. 1035 (K.B. 1765).

[99] Rann v. Huges, 7 T.R. 350, 101 Eng. Rep. 1014 (1778).

[1] LAW REVISION COMMITTEE (GREAT BRITAIN) SIXTH INTERIM REPORT (1937).

[2] *See* Dawson, *supra* note 97, particularly at 199-221. *See also* Patterson, *An Apology for Consideration,* 58 COLUM. L. REV. 929 (1958); Sharp, *Pacta Sunt Servanda,* 41 COLUM. L. REV. 783 (1941); Llewellyn, *Common Law Reform of Consideration: Are There Measures?* 41 COLUM. L. REV. 863 (1941); Wright, *Ought the Doctrine of Consideration To Be Abolished,* 49 HARV. L. REV. 1225 (1936), and the sources cited earlier in the notes to this section.

promise must be bargained for."[3] Yet, the cases are legion in which courts describe consideration in terms of a benefit to the promisor or detriment to the promisee.[4] Fewer courts appear to remember the necessity of stating the other element, bargained-for-exchange, as part of the formula,[5] though there is little doubt that they would consider the bargained-for-exchange element essential.

There is significant difficulty in discovering definitional terminology sufficient to encompass all that is meant by "consideration." As usual, definitions in the study of law are of little assistance. The consensus is clear that the two elements are essential. To understand those elements beyond any attempted definition, it is important to examine them in operation, i.e., as applied by courts in myriad circumstances.

§ 56. The First Element: Legal Value — "Benefit" or "Detriment."

A. *Generally.*

The classic description of the legal value element of consideration is found in *Currie v. Misa*,[6] where the Court of Exchequer stated, "A valuable consideration, in the sense of the law, may consist either in some right, interest, profit or benefit accruing to the one party, or some forbearance, detriment, loss or responsibility, given, suffered, or undertaken by the other."[7] While the formula for this element is stated in the alternative, benefit to the promisor *or* detriment to the promisee, the typical contract will manifest *both* benefits and detriments. If, for example, Ames agrees to purchase Barnes' car at a price of $10,000, there are benefits and detriments to both parties. The benefit to

---

[3] RESTATEMENT 2d § 71(1). In subsection (2), the RESTATEMENT 2d defines "bargained for" and in subsection (3), it states that the performance bargained for may consist of an act other than a promise, or a forbearance, or the creation, modification, or destruction of a legal relation. Subsection (4) states that the performance or return promise may be given to the promisor or to some other person, and it may be given by the promisee or by some other person. Each of these elements will be explored in the discussion to follow.

[4] Examples of recent cases suggesting this traditional formula include USLIFE Title Co. of Ariz. v. Gutkin, 152 Ariz. 349, 732 P.2d 579 (1986); Vogelhut v. Kandel, 308 Md. 183, 517 A.2d 1092 (1986); Chasan v. Village Dist. of Eastman, 128 N.H. 807, 523 A.2d 16 (1986); Cook v. Heck's, Inc., 342 S.E.2d 453 (W. Va. App. 1986); Nordwick v. Berg, 725 P.2d 1195 (Mont. 1986); Artoe v. Cap, 140 Ill. App. 3d 980, 489 N.E.2d 420 (1986); Hyde v. Shapiro, 216 Neb. 785, 346 N.W.2d 241 (1984); Koehler Constr. Co. v. Medical Center of Blue Springs, 670 S.W.2d 558 (Mo. App. 1984); R & L Farms, Inc. v. Windle, 653 F.2d 328 (8th Cir. 1981).

[5] *See, e.g.,* Saikowski v. Manning, 720 S.W.2d 275 (Tex. App. 1986); Twin City Fire Ins. Co. v. Philadelphia Life Ins. Co., 795 F.2d 1417 (9th Cir. 1986). A case that suggests confusion between the bargained-for-exchange element and the benefit to the promisor or detriment to the promisee element is United States v. Meadors, 753 F.2d 590 (7th Cir. 1985).

[6] L.R. 10 Ex. 153, 162 [1875].

[7] Identical statements can be found in modern cases. *See, e.g.,* Cook v. Heck's, Inc., 342 S.E.2d 453 (W. Va. App. 1986) ("some right, interest, profit, or benefit accruing to one party, or some forbearance, detriment, loss or responsibility given, suffered or undertaken by another"); Artoe v. Cap, 140 Ill. App. 3d 980, 489 N.E.2d 420 (1986) ("some right, interest, profit or benefit accruing to one party or some forbearance, disadvantage, detriment, loss or responsibility given, suffered or undertaken by the other"). Other statements of the "legal value" element are often truncated. *See, e.g.,* United States v. Meadors, 753 F.2d 590 (7th Cir. 1985) ("the one who made the promise receives consideration if he gets something, or if the one to whom he makes the promise gives something up. Either alternative will do."); Hyde v. Shapiro, 216 Neb. 785, 346 N.W.2d 241 (1984) ("there is a consideration if the promisee does anything legal which he is not bound to do or refrains from doing anything which he has a right to do....").

Ames is the receipt of Barnes' car. The benefit to Barnes is the receipt of Ames' $10,000. The detriment to Ames is the surrender of $10,000, and the detriment to Barnes is the surrender of his car.

B. *Either Benefit or Detriment — "Legal" Detriment.*

1. The Absence of Benefit.

We have just illustrated the typical contract that provides benefits and exacts detriments from both parties. It is often suggested that benefit *and* detriment are not essential, i.e., if either is present, the "value" element of consideration is present. It is not difficult to suggest examples where there is no discernible "benefit" to the promisor but where the "detriment" to the promisee is clear. If Ames seeks to borrow money from the bank but her credit rating is poor, the bank will not make a loan to Ames on Ames' credit alone. Ames may call her brother-in-law, Barnes, and request that Barnes become secondarily liable on Ames' debt to the bank. If Barnes has a good credit rating and agrees to become surety for Ames on Ames' obligation to the bank, is Barnes' promise enforceable, i.e., is it supported by consideration? There is no discernible benefit to the promisor, Barnes. He may have become surety for Ames only because he is related to Ames, and may have undertaken this secondary obligation to the bank grudgingly. Though the benefit to Barnes is speculative, there is no question about the detriment to the bank. The bank would not have lent the money to Ames on her credit, alone. When Barnes agreed to pay the bank if Ames failed to pay, the bank was willing to make the loan to Ames. The detriment suffered by the bank can be described as parting with its money in exchange for two promises: the promise of Ames to repay the debt with interest, and the promise of Barnes to pay the same amount if Ames fails to perform her promise to repay the loan. Again, however, Barnes has received no discernible benefit for his promise — there is no "benefit to the promisor."[8] It is, however, clear that courts will not require a showing of any discernible benefit to the promisor if the promisee has suffered a detriment induced by the other party's promise.[9] The classic case is *Hamer v. Sidway*[10] where an uncle promised his nephew $5000 on his twenty-first birthday in consideration of the nephew's refraining from drinking, smoking, swearing and gambling until he reached that age. The benefit to the uncle (promisor) is not discernible. We can speculate that he wanted to avoid the worry and concern that would attend unhealthy habits of his nephew. The promisor may have been interested in preserving his reputation by inducing

---

[8] It is plausible to consider various motivations of promisors who appear to receive no discernible benefit. In one sense, if the promisor induces the promisee to suffer a detriment, the promisor receives the benefit of that detriment, i.e., why the promisor sought the particular detriment is her own affair. In such situations, therefore, it is desirable to suggest that there is no "discernible" benefit to the promisor, i.e., whatever benefit the promisor may have received from the detriment suffered by the promisee is speculative.

[9] In Citibank, N. A. v. Bearcat Tire, A. G., 550 F. Supp. 148, 152 (N.D. Ill. 1982), the court states, "First-year law school principles teach us that consideration, ample to support contract liability, may stem from *detriment* to the *promisee* rather than benefit to the promisor."

[10] 124 N.Y. 538, 27 N.E. 256 (1891).

his nephew of the same name to avoid notorious behavior. Whatever the benefit to the promisor, if any, there was a detriment to the promisee.

2. "Legal" Detriment Distinguished.

It may appear unusual to characterize refraining from alcohol, smoking and other arguably unhealthy pursuits as a *detriment* to the nephew. To constitute consideration, a detriment need not constitute any economic or physical loss. From the standpoint of health or finances, the nephew received a benefit. Yet, by abstaining from those substances and practices as required by the promisor, the promisee-nephew surrendered his right, protected by law, to use those substances and engage in the practices his uncle induced him to avoid.[11] The suggestion that we must distinguish economic, health or other detriments from "legal" detriments since only the latter constitute the value element of consideration, has been criticized on the ground that it does not answer the question, how does one differentiate between ordinary detriments and "legal" detriments?[12] While the descriptive adjective, "legal," does not provide any insight into this question, it is no worse a label than that provided for other legal concepts which cannot be understood simply by the description attached to them. The concept of "legal" detriment as contrasted with what one court has termed, "detriment in fact,"[13] can be described as follows: if the promisee has done or forborne something, or promised to do or to forbear doing something, the doing or forbearing of which involves the surrender of a legal right or the circumscribing of his liberty of action, the legal value element of consideration is present.[14] Thus, the nephew-promisee surrendered a legal right to drink, smoke, swear and gamble. In surrendering that right, he suffered a loss — a loss of his freedom of action or a circumscription of his liberty. In this sense, he has suffered a "detriment" which is recognized as the kind of detriment a promisee must suffer if the legal value element of consideration is to be found.

---

[11] "A benefit to the promisor or a detriment to the promisee is a sufficient consideration for a contract. The detriment need not be real; it need not involve actual loss to the promisee. The word, as used in the definition, means legal detriment as distinguished from detriment in fact. It is the giving up by the promisee of a legal right; the refraining from doing what he has a legal right to do, or the doing of what he has the legal right not to do." Phillips, J., in Petroleum Refractionating Corp. v. Kendrick Oil Co., 65 F.2d 997, 998 (10th Cir. 1923). In Harris v. Time, Inc., 237 Cal. Rptr. 584 (1987), the three-year-old son of a prominent attorney received mail addressed to him containing a statement clearly visible from the unopened envelop that the sender would give to the addressee a "new calculator watch free just for opening this envelope...." The boy's mother opened the envelope for her son. The contents revealed that a magazine subcription would have to be purchased to receive the watch. This requirement was not visible simply by reading the terms of the offer on the envelope. One of the issues in the case was whether the act of opening the envelope would constitute consideration for the promise to supply the watch. The court held that even though the opening of the envelope may have been relatively insignificant to the promisee, it was, nonetheless, an act or forbearance sought by the promisor and did constitute consideration. The action had been brought, inter alia, for punitive damages of $15 million. Notwithstanding its holding concerning consideration, the court held for the defendant on the footing that "the law disregards trifles" (*de minimis non curat lex*).

[12] 1 CORBIN § 123.

[13] Harrington v. Harrington, 365 N.W.2d 552, 555 (N.D. 1985).

[14] In *Harrington, id.*, the court describes "legal detriment" as "giving up something which the promisee was privileged to retain, or doing or refraining from doing something which he was privileged not to do, or not to refrain from doing."

3. Absence of Detriment.

It is impossible to conceive of a situation involving a benefit to the promisor with no detriment to the promisee amounting to consideration. If Ames tells Barnes, "I will pay you $100 if you will refrain from driving my (Ames') car tomorrow," there is no detriment to the promisee, Barnes, because he has no right to drive Ames' car absent Ames' permission. Thus, he surrenders no right in forbearing from driving Ames' car. Neither is there a benefit to Ames since she received nothing in exchange for her promise to pay $100 to which she was not previously entitled. Unlike the situation described above where there is a clear detriment to the promisee and no discernible benefit to the promisor though one or more benefits may be imagined, it is not possible to meet the legal value element of consideration absent a detriment to the promisee. Consequently, while the formula for this element of consideration is typically stated as a benefit to the promisor or detriment to the promisee, the emphasis is upon the detriment to the promisee since there will be no benefit to the promisor absent a detriment to the promisee. Again, the student should recall that the typical contract involves benefits and detriments to both parties.

4. Benefit to the Promisee or Detriment to the Promisor.

When the traditional formula of benefit to the promisor or detriment to the promisee is under analysis, students sometimes wonder why the formula cannot be reversed, i.e., why is there no consideration where there is a benefit to the promisee or a detriment to the promisor? If Ames promises to give $10,000 to Barnes and Barnes accepts by saying, "Thank you, very much," there is no consideration for Ames' promise. Ames has made a gratuitous or donative promise which is not enforceable.[15] There is a detriment to the promisor, Ames, and a benefit to the promisee, Barnes. Thus, when the traditional formula for legal value is reversed, it describes an unenforceable gift promise.

5. Benefits or Detriments to or From Third Parties.

In the typical situation, the consideration moves between the promisor and promisee. Thus, where Ames promises to sell her car to Barnes in exchange for Barnes' promise to pay Ames $5000, we have seen that both parties are promisors and promisees and, as such, both receive benefits and suffer detriments in their capacities of promisor and promisee. From the standpoint of Barnes as promisor, he is receiving the benefit of the car. As a promisee, Barnes is surrendering his $5000. Promisor Ames receives the $5000 and promisee Ames surrenders the car. Regardless of which party is viewed as promisor or promisee, there is a benefit to the promisor and a detriment to the promisee with the legal value moving to the promisor and from promisee. While this is the typical situation, it is possible for the consideration to move *to* a party other than the promisor or *from* a party other than the promisee. If, for example, Barnes promises to pay Ames $5000 if Ames will deliver her car

---

[15] For an analysis of donative promises and the bases for the refusal to enforce such promises in our legal system, *see* Eisenberg, *Donative Promises,* 47 U. Chi. L. Rev. 1 (1979).

to Barnes' daughter, Ames' performance (delivering the car to the daughter) is consideration for Barnes' promise which Ames can enforce even though the car was not delivered to Barnes (the promisor) but to a party other than the promisor (Barnes' daughter). Assuming that Barnes' daughter now has the car and Ames wishes to repurchase it, if Ames promised to pay Barnes $5000 if the daughter would deliver the car to Ames, there is consideration for Ames' promise even though the consideration did not move from the promisee, Barnes, but from a party who was not the promisee, Barnes' daughter. The English courts have quite consistently held that the consideration must move from the person who seeks to enforce the promise (the promisee) and that no one, be he promisee or beneficiary, who did not furnish at least some part of the consideration for the promise can have any rights under it.[16] While there was some early support for that view in this country,[17] it has been rejected. It is clear that, "It matters not from whom the consideration moves or to whom it goes."[18]

6. Detriment in Contracts Involving Mutual Promises.

Where the parties form their contract through a mutual exchange of promises, the consideration for either promise is the promise received from the other party to form what is traditionally known as a bilateral contract.[19] This raises the question, is *any* promise sufficient to support a counter-promise? If the response to a promise (offer) is the performance of the act requested by the promisor, the necessary detriment to the promisee is found in the performance of the act as the exchange for the promise.[20] In a bilateral contract, however, a promise is given in exchange for a counter-promise. Since no one is bound to make a promise, it could be argued that it is the making of the promise itself that supplies the necessary detriment to the promisee to evidence consideration.[21] An examination of this proposition, however, immediately suggests that it is unsound. If, for example, Ames promises Barnes $100 in exchange for Barnes' promise to forbear from driving Ames' automobile for twenty-four hours, if Barnes had no prior right to drive Ames' car, Ames is receiving nothing for her promise *except the promise of Barnes*. It is conceivable that Ames simply wanted Barnes to articulate a promise, even though it was a promise to forbear from an act which Barnes had a legal duty to forbear.

---

[16] *See* Dunlap Pneumatic Tire Co. v. Selfridge & Co., A.C. 847 [1915].

[17] *See, e.g.,* Cottage Street M. E. Church v. Kendall, 121 Mass. 528, 531, 23 Am. Rep. 286 (1877).

[18] RESTATEMENT 2d § 71 comment e. *See* Marine Contrs. Co. v. Hurley, 365 Mass. 280, 310 N.E.2d 915, 919 (1974) where the consideration moved to the promisor from a party other than the promisee and the court quoted from Palmer Sav. Bank v. Insurance Co. of N. Am., 166 Mass. 189, 196, 44 N.E. 211, 213 (1896): "[I]t is not in all cases necessary that the consideration should move from the promisee to promisor." *See also* General Bldrs. Supply Co. v. MacArthur, 288 Md. 320, 179 A.2d 868 (1962).

[19] Ebling v. Gove's Cove, Inc., 34 Wash. App. 495, 663 P.2d 132, 134 (1983) ("A bilateral contract is one in which there are reciprocal promises. The promise by one party is consideration for the promise by the other."); Pick Kwik Food Stores, Inc. v. Tenser, 407 So. 2d 216, 218 (Fla. App. 1981) ("In a bilateral contract, the promise of one party constitutes the sole consideration for the promise of the other.").

[20] RESTATEMENT 2d § 72.

[21] *See* Ames, *Two Theories of Consideration,* 12 HARV. L. REV. 515 (1898), 13 HARV. L. REV. 29 (1899).

Absent the most unusual circumstances that would lend credibility to such a desire of Ames, it is clear that the typical promisor does not seek a promise of performance alone, but wants both the promise of performance as well as the performance itself.[22] If the performance, alone, would not be a detriment to the promisee, would a promise of such performance constitute a detriment to the promisee? While courts often speak in terms of a promise exchanged for a counter-promise as consideration, they are quick to qualify that general statement by insisting that the promise must signify an act or forbearance that would, without a promise, constitute a bargained-for detriment to the promisee.[23] A theory suggesting that the detriment to the promisee is to be found in the legal obligation which the promisee's promise imposes upon him[24] has long been discredited as circular reasoning. Consideration is necessary because without it (or another validation device), a promise is not legally binding. To find the required detriment that creates consideration in the legal obligation which results from the presence of consideration is circular reasoning. Rather, the detriment is found in what has, in fact, been undertaken — if the doing of what has been undertaken by the promisee is a legal detriment to the promisee, the promisee's promise is sufficient.[25]

§ 57. Illusory Promises.

A. *Basic Concept — Conditional Promises Where Promisor Does Not Control Condition.*

If Ames promises to purchase a car from Barnes unless Ames changes her mind, the promise of Ames is illusory because Ames has not committed herself to any future action or inaction. As one court suggests, "An illusory contract may be defined as an expression cloaked in promissory terms, but which, upon closer examination, reveals that the promisor has not committed himself in any manner. In other words, an illusory promise is a promise that is not a promise. The promise is an illusion."[26] The student of contract law, however, should not easily arrive at the conclusion that a particular promise is illusory. A promise that may first appear to leave the promisor wholly unconstrained may, upon reflection, reveal a detriment. If we change the example to a prom-

---

[22] *See* 1 CORBIN § 142.

[23] "The general rule is that an executory agreement, by which the plaintiff agrees to do something on the terms that the defendant agrees to do something else, may be enforced, if what the plaintiff has agreed to do is 'either for the benefit of the defendant or to the trouble or prejudice of the plaintiff.'" Bolton v. Maddan, L.R. 9 Q.B. 55, 56 [1873]. "If one party has the unrestricted right to terminate the contract at any time, that party makes no promise at all and there is not sufficient consideration for the promise of the other." Pick Kwik Food Stores, Inc. v. Tenser, 407 So. 2d 216, 218 (Fla. App. 1981). "The Defendant asks this Court to recognize the 'agreement' as an enforceable bilateral contract, where the necessary consideration is the parties' promise of performance.... Generally, the Defendant's promise to forbear from engaging in an activity that she had the legal right to engage in, can provide her necessary consideration for the Plaintiff's return promise.... [A]lthough the Defendant's promise to forbear could constitute consideration, it cannot if it was not sought after by the Plaintiff, and motivated by his request...." Whitten v. Greeley-Shaw, 520 A.2d 1307, 1309-10 (Me. 1987).

[24] *See* Langdell, *Mutual Promises as a Consideration for Each Other,* 14 HARV. L. REV. 496 (1900).

[25] *See* Williston, *Consideration in Bilateral Contracts,* 27 HARV. L. REV. 503 (1913).

[26] Harrington v. Harrington, 365 N.W.2d 553, 555 (N.D. 1985). *See also* Krebs v. Strange, 419 So. 2d 178 (Miss. 1982) and RESTATEMENT 2d § 77 comment a.

ise by Ames to purchase Barnes' car for $5000 if Ames receives a $5000 bequest from her recently deceased uncle's estate (in exchange for Barnes' promise to sell the car on these terms), Ames' promise may appear to leave Ames without detriment since the conditioning event, the receipt of the bequest, may not occur. Unless Ames is aware that the condition cannot occur at the time she makes the agreement with Barnes,[27] however, she has made a commitment which circumscribes her liberty of action. If the conditioning event does not occur, Ames duty will never be activated and she will have no liability to Barnes. The duty, however, existed from the moment the agreement with Barnes was made. The objection may be that this is circular reasoning in that the duty exists only if a contract is made, and a contract exists only if a duty exists. At the moment of the agreement, however, Ames circum- • scribed her liberty of action in promising to purchase the car from Barnes if an event over which she had no control occurred. Her commitment was, therefore, detrimental and constituted consideration to support Barnes' counter promise even though the failure of the condition to occur would result in the discharge of Ames' duty.[28] If Ames had agreed to purchase Barnes' house for $200,000 conditioned upon Ames' ability to procure a mortgage loan of at least $150,000 at a rate no higher than 11 percent, the fact that Ames may be unsuccessful in her attempt to procure the loan does not make her promise illusory. She has committed herself to the purchase of the house though her commitment is conditional. If the condition does not occur, Ames will be discharged from her duty under the contract.[29] The contract, however, existed from the moment the parties exchanged their promises. Ames could not refuse to make application for the loan since that action would prevent the occurrence of the condition.[30] Barnes could not treat Ames' promise as non-detrimental and proceed to sell the house to another before Ames had an opportu-

---

[27] If Ames knew that she would receive nothing from her uncle's estate when she made the agreement with Barnes, she would be promising nothing. RESTATEMENT 2d § 76(1).

[28] See Doughty v. Idaho Frozen Foods Corp., 736 P.2d 460 (Idaho App. 1987) (if less than 10 percent of potatoes were of a desired size, buyer need not accept them — held, not illusory though seller did not have coextensive right to cancel); Charles Hester Enters. v. Illinois Founders Ins. Co., 114 Ill. 2d 278, 499 N.E.2d 1319 (1986) (Dramshop statute limited liability of insured to $15,000. Insurer's promise to pay amounts exceeding statutory limit if statute was amended was detrimental); Hoffman v. Garden State Farms, Inc., 76 N.J. Super. 189, 184 A.2d 4 (1962) (promise to give refunds to milk consumers when state milk control law is repealed or changed. Though the law may never be repealed or changed so as to activate the duty to give refunds, the promise was still detrimental); Rosenberg v. Garfinkel, 294 Mass. 196, 200 N.E. 907 (1936) (promise to guarantee payment of all debts of a corporation though the corporation was solvent and eventually paid all of its debts).

[29] See Lach v. Cahill, 138 Conn. 418, 85 A.2d 481 (1951) (buyer is entitled to recover any deposit when he was unable to obtain the mortgage loan since seller's retention of the deposit would unjustly enrich the seller). In Dibenedetto v. Dirocco, 372 Pa. 302, 93 A.2d 474 (1953), the condition was that if buyer "cannot" make the settlement, he may cancel the agreement. The court held that "cannot" does not mean "will not," i.e., the condition went to the buyer's objective ability to make the settlement rather than his unfettered discretion. The promise was, therefore, detrimental. See, however, Paul v. Rosen, 3 Ill. App. 2d 423, 122 N.E.2d 603 (1954) where the agreement was conditioned upon the buyer obtaining a new lease from the owner for a period of five years from a certain date under a contract to purchase a retail liquor business. The seller refused to perform and the court held for the seller indicating that the conditional promise of the buyer was non-detrimental. This decision and rationale should be disapproved.

[30] Ames would be said to have impliedly promised to make good faith efforts to obtain a suitable mortgage loan.

nity to seek the loan. Innumerable transactions of this nature occur daily, binding the parties to an exchange of promises though one or both promises are conditioned upon an event beyond the control of either party.

B. *Condition Within Control of Promisor.*

If the conditioning event is *within* the control of the promisor, such a promise may appear to be illusory beyond question. Again, however, further reflection suggests that even this type of promise may be detrimental. The classic illustration is found in a well-known case where the defendant, who was contemplating the purchase of a ship, promised to charter the ship to the plaintiff if the defendant purchased the ship. The defendant had not promised to purchase the ship and could, therefore, refrain from purchasing it without violating any duty. His promise was to charter the ship only if he decided, in his sole discretion, to purchase it. To understand why the defendant's promise was held to be detrimental,[31] it is important to consider his status before and after making the promise to charter the ship conditioned upon his purchase of the ship. Before making the promise, the defendant could decide to purchase or not purchase the ship without any restriction upon his subsequent freedom of action. After making the promise, however, while he was still free to purchase or not to purchase the ship, that decision could no longer be made in an unfettered fashion. If he purchased the ship, his duty to charter it to the plaintiff would be activated. That duty could be discharged only if defendant decided against purchasing the ship. The analysis of such cases is often put in terms of alternative performances, i.e., the promisor has a choice of alternative performances. If one of the alternatives is not detrimental, there is no consideration.[32] Thus, again, if Ames agrees to purchase Barnes' car for $5000 unless Ames changes her mind, the alternative of not purchasing the car at the whim or caprice of Ames is non-detrimental. This situation, however, is distinguishable from the promise to charter the ship conditioned on the promisor's purchase of the ship. After making that promise, the promisor must either purchase the ship and charter it to the plaintiff (which is detrimental) or not purchase the ship (which is detrimental).[33]

Other promises that may appear to suggest that a particular performance is within the sole discretion of the promisor and, therefore, illusory, may be construed by modern courts to contain limitations making such promises detrimental. Thus, even though a state official had the discretion to set rates for medical and dental services, a court held that the discretion was not uncon-

---

[31] Scott v. Moragues Lumber Co., 202 Ala. 312, 80 So. 394 (1918).

[32] *See* Dwyer v. Graham, 99 Ill. 2d 205, 457 N.E.2d 1239 (1983) (use of premises as long as desired was non-detrimental); Mastaw v. Naiukow, 105 Mich. App. 25, 306 N.W.2d 378 (1981) (unfettered discretion of counsel to approve or not approve settlement agreement). *See also* RESTATEMENT 2d § 77.

[33] The same analysis would apply even if the conditioning event were fortuitous thereby making the promise an "aleatory" promise. An aleatory promise is one under which the duty of the promisor to perform is conditioned upon a purely fortuitous event. RESTATEMENT 2d § 232 comment c. The classic example is a casualty insurance contract under which the insurer-promisor agrees to pay if the casualty (fire, flood or the like) occurs. If the casualty never occurs, the promisor's duty is never activated. Aleatory promises are not illusory since they are detrimental. *See* RESTATEMENT 2d § 76 comment c.

trolled; it had to reflect the "usual charges" for such services.[34] Even the phrase "sole discretion" may, by implication, impose the duty of good faith and fair dealing upon the promisor in the exercise of that discretion and, thereby, so limit it as to make it detrimental.[35] The limitation of good faith in requirements and output contracts for the sale of goods eliminates any suggestion that such contracts are illusory. The questions surrounding such contracts necessitate a comprehensive exploration which is found in the next section.[36]

C. *Notice as a Detrimental Alternative.*

If Ames promises to purchase Barnes' auto for $5000 or to notify Barnes that she will not purchase it, is the alternative performance of notification detrimental to Ames? It is clear that the alternative performances are both detrimental. Consequently, it may seem that there is no question that consideration is present. Giving notice is not much of a detriment, but courts should not inquire into the adequacy of consideration.[37] The analysis is not quite that simple, however. Consideration requires more than a detriment to the promisee. As will be seen more fully in later sections of this chapter, the detriment to the promisee must be "bargained-for" if consideration is to be found. If Ames may either pay $5000 to Barnes for his auto, or simply notify Barnes that she will not purchase it, it is at least questionable whether Barnes "bargained for" Ames' promise to give notice. Courts that have dealt with this situation have concluded that notice is a detrimental alternative constituting consideration and they have not focused upon the lack of the bargained-for element.[38] If there is a unilateral right to cancel the contract and there is no requirement that notice of cancellation be given, there is no discernible detriment to the promisee in cancelling.[39] It is, however, possible to construe such a right to cancel as requiring the giving of notice, thereby discovering a detrimental alternative to performance of the contract.[40]

---

[34] California Med. Ass'n v. Lackner, 117 Cal. App. 3d 552, 172 Cal. Rptr. 815 (1981).

[35] Omni Group, Inc. v. Seattle-First Nat'l Bank, 32 Wash. App. 22, 645 P.2d 727 (1982). *See also* Wyss v. Inskeep, 73 Or. App. 661, 669 P.2d 1161 (1985) (discretion to fix amounts employees were to receive from bonus plan was not unlimited; it had to be exercised in good faith); Prentice v. Lackner, 117 Cal. App. 3d 552, 172 Cal. Rptr. 815 (1981) (fact that one of the parties has the power to fix the price or other performance does not make his promise illusory if the power is subject to prescribed or implied limitations — with respect to discretion to set prices in contracts for the sale of goods, *see* UCC § 2-305); Ledford v. Wheller, 620 P.2d 903, 906 (Okla. App. 1980) ("Buyer gave an enforceable promise to buy [real property] unless, in good faith, he determined the title was unsatisfactory. This limitation on buyer's freedom is sufficient detriment to supply the needed consideration....").

[36] *See infra* § 58.

[37] *See infra* § 59.

[38] The best known case is Sylvan Crest Sand & Gravel Co. v. United States, 150 F.2d 642 (2d Cir. 1945) where the court interpreted a clause in the contract, "cancellation may be effected at any time" as requiring the government to either take and pay for the trap rock to be used in an airport project, or to notify the supplier of cancellation. *See also* Wilson v. Gifford-Hill & Co., 570 P.2d 624, 626 (Okla. App. 1977): "[W]here notice of cancellation is required the promisor is bound sufficiently so that his promise to buy or give notice of cancellation meets the requirement of consideration."

[39] *See Wilson, ibid.*

[40] *See Sylvan Crest, supra* note 38.

While the RESTATEMENT 2d is in accord with this analysis,[41] it suggests an interesting illustration that deserves comment.[42] A orders goods from B for shipment within three months, reserving the right to cancel the order prior to shipment. B has the goods in stock and accepts the offer. The RESTATEMENT 2d concludes, "A's promise to pay for the goods is consideration for B's promise to ship, since B can prevent cancellation by shipping immediately."[43] Notwithstanding doubt over whether the alternative performance of notice of cancellation was bargained for, the illustration suggests that a contract was formed and will be subject to cancellation upon notice from the buyer, so long as notice occurs prior to shipment by the seller. Since the seller has the power to avoid cancellation by shipping, another analysis of this illustration springs to mind. It could be argued that the seller simply has a power of acceptance which can be exercised by performance and the notice of cancellation could be viewed as a simple revocation of the offer which would be effective upon communication to the seller. If shipment occurs prior to the seller's receipt of such revocation, there is a contract formed by the seller's performance or, in the older terminology, a unilateral contract is formed. The RESTATEMENT 2d, however, finds a contract formed through the exchange of promises. With respect to the buyer's power to cancel the order, the effect would be the same if the cancellation were treated as a mere revocation of the offer. If, however, the seller has a duty created by the exchange of promises requiring the seller to ship within a stated time or within a reasonable time,[44] if no notice of cancellation occurred within that time, the duty of the seller to ship would become absolute. Under the unilateral contract analysis, however, the failure of the seller to ship within a reasonable time would not subject the seller to any liability since no contract would be formed and the seller would have no duty if he chose not to perform the act required by the offer.

D. *Notice of Termination and Good Faith.*

1. Section 2-309 of the Uniform Commercial Code.

If a contract contains no stated duration, it is terminable at will.[45] If the parties agree that one party will supply another with goods but the agreement is indefinite in duration, the UCC prescribes that such a contract is valid for a reasonable time, but, unless otherwise agreed between the parties, either party may terminate the contract at any time.[46] The power to terminate such a contract, however, is circumscribed under the Code. Termination becomes effective only upon the receipt of reasonable notification of such termination, and if the parties' agreement provides that notification is unnecessary, that provision will be deemed invalid if its enforcement would be unconscionable.[47] The requirement of notification under this Code section is designed to effectu-

---

[41] *See* RESTATEMENT 2d § 77.

[42] Ill. 7 to § 77.

[43] *Id.*

[44] This was the fact in the case upon which the illustration is based, Gurfein v. Werbelovsky, 97 Conn. 703, 118 A. 32 (1922).

[45] *See, e.g.,* Brownsboro Road Restaurant v. Jerrico, Inc., 674 S.W.2d 40 (Ky. App. 1984).

[46] UCC § 2-309(2).

[47] UCC § 2-209(3).

ate good faith and commercially reasonable practices. Thus, if a seller has been supplying goods to a buyer under a terminable at will contract, notification of the seller's intention to terminate the agreement should permit the buyer to discover a substitute supplier[48] and the buyer should have a reasonable time to discover the substitute supplier. What is a "reasonable time" will depend upon the particular circumstances — it is a question of fact.[49] No particular form of notice is required,[50] but notice is a requirement for an effective termination and, like the exercise of the power of termination, it must demonstrate good faith.[51] While the parties may provide that notice of termination will not be necessary, such a provision will be a nullity if it is deemed unconscionable.[52] Unconscionability is a concept that will be explored fully later in this volume. It may be summarily described as providing courts with the power to nullify contractual provisions or entire contracts on the ground of unfair surprise or oppression created by a party with superior bargaining power.[53] Finally, it should be emphasized that a *breach* of a terminable at will contract will justify *cancellation* of the contract without any notice[54] since the breach discharges the duty of the aggrieved party.

2. Franchise Contracts.

The common law notion that contracts without a stated duration are terminable at will could have a devastating effect upon a distributor of a manufacturer's products or a franchisee operating a business under the nationally-recognized name of a franchisor. The distributor or franchisee could invest considerable time, effort and money in the development of the business only to be terminated at the will of the manufacturer or franchisor.[55] As seen above, § 2-309 of the UCC can apply to a contract for the resale of the manufacturer's products and require reasonable notice of termination so as to provide the distributor with a reasonable time to seek a substitute arrangement.[56] The Code will not apply to numerous franchise agreements, however. The franchisee does not purchase goods from the franchisor. Rather, the franchisee is licensed to operate a business under the trademark name of the franchisor and must adhere to the requirements set forth in the licensing agreement. To

---

[48] UCC § 2-309 comment 8.

[49] *See, e.g.,* Zeidel Explorations, Inc. v. Conval Int'l, Inc., 719 F.2d 1465 (9th Cir. 1983); Leibel v. Raynor Mfg. Co., 571 S.W.2d 640 (Ky. App. 1978); Superior Foods, Inc. v. Harris-Teeter Super Markets, Inc., 288 N.C. 213, 217 S.E.2d 566 (1975); McGinnis Piano & Organ Co. v. Yamaha Int'l Corp., 480 F.2d 474 (8th Cir. 1973).

[50] *See* Circo v. Spanish Gardens Food Mfg. Co., 643 F. Supp. 51 (W.D. Mo. 1985).

[51] The "good faith" requirement for merchants under the UCC combines honesty-in-fact and commercial reasonableness under § 2-103(1)(b). Non-merchants need only meet the honesty-in-fact standard. § 1-201(19).

[52] UCC § 2-309(3).

[53] The unconscionability provision of the Code is found in § 2-302. *See also* RESTATEMENT 2d § 208. Cases dealing with the alleged unconscionability of clauses making notice of termination unnecessary include Zapatha v. Dairy Mart, Inc., 408 N.E.2d 1370 (1980) and Sinkoff Beverage Co. v. Joseph Schlitz Brewing Co., 51 Misc. 2d 446, 173 N.Y.S.2d 364 (1966).

[54] *See* International Therapeutics, Inc. v. McGraw-Edison, 721 F.2d 1465 (9th Cir. 1983). *See also* comment 9 to UCC § 2-309, and UCC § 2-703(f).

[55] *See* Brownsboro Road Restaurant v. Jerrico, 674 S.W.2d 40 (Ky. App. 1984); Plaskitt v. Black Diamond Trailer Co., 209 Va. 460, 164 S.E.2d 645 (1968).

[56] *See* City Bldrs. Supply Co. v. National Gypsum Co., 39 UCC Rep. Serv. 826 (D.C. Mass. 1984).

avoid injury to franchisees who devote considerable time and effort to the
development of the business but are subject to termination at the whim of the
franchisor, a number of states have enacted statutes prohibiting cancellation
or nonrenewal of franchise agreements except for good cause.[57] These efforts
may be seen as part of the general judicial or statutory developments to avoid
unfairness resulting from terminable at will contracts evidenced in employment contracts with no stated duration.[58]

§ 58. Requirements and Output Contracts — Section 2-306 of the Uniform Commercial Code.

If a buyer promises to purchase from a particular seller all of a particular
product that the buyer "requires," or if a seller promises to sell his entire
output of a particular product to a particular buyer, are such "requirements"
or "output" agreements enforceable? If either type of promise is properly construed as a commitment to deal exclusively with the other party, i.e., if the
buyer may not purchase certain goods from any other supplier or if the seller
may not sell his products to any other buyer, there can be no question that the
promisor suffers a detriment. Therefore, the promise is not illusory. If, however, the promisor may choose to deal with others, there is no restriction upon
his freedom of action and the promise is illusory.[59] This analysis, however,
may be difficult to apply if there is no maximum or minimum limitation on
the quantity of goods which the seller must produce or the buyer must purchase. If, for example, a buyer enters into a requirements contract on a speculative basis, i.e., while promising to purchase all the widgets he requires from
a particular seller, the buyer is a middleman who will purchase large quantities of widgets if the market price exceeds the price in his contract with the
supplier. If the market price is below the contract price, however, he will
purchase no widgets. Such a buyer (or a seller in a comparable output contract
example) appears to be virtually unfettered in his freedom of action leading
some older cases to characterize his promise as illusory.[60] Yet, in terms of a
detriment to the promisee, the buyer suffers a detriment in that he is precluded from contracting with any other supplier of widgets, even at a price
below the market price, to purchase widgets for resale. The fact that it is more
than unlikely that he will do so should not detract from discovering the neces-

---

[57] In Dunkin Donuts of Am. v. Middletown Donut, 100 N.J. 166, 495 A.2d 66 (1985), the Supreme Court of New Jersey analyzes the New Jersey Franchise Practices Act, N.J. STAT. ANN.
§§ 56:10-1 to 10-15 as well as a number of other statutes with similar purposes though the scope
and details of the statutes differ. The opinion represents desirable analysis of the current application of these statutes. The best known federal legislation of this type is the 1956 Congressional
legislation designed to protect automobile dealers from arbitrary termination by the manufacturer. The Automobile Dealer Franchise Act (15 U.S.C. §§ 1221-1225) (sometimes called the
"Auto Dealer's Day in Court Act") imposes a "good faith" standard on the manufacturer who
seeks to terminate, cancel, or refuse to renew a franchise. In general, see Gellhorn, *Limitations on
Contract Termination Rights — Franchise Cancellations,* 1967 DUKE L.J. 465, and Chisum, *State
Regulation of Franchising: The Washington Experience,* 48 WASH. L. REV. 291 (1973).

[58] The extensive judicial development concerning the protection of employees in terminable-at-
will employment contracts was explored in *supra* § 38(B)(4), Chapter 2.

[59] *See, e.g.,* Billings Cottonseed, Inc. v. Albany Oil Mill, Inc., 173 Ga. App. 825, 328 S.E.2d 426
(1985); Harvey v. Farris Wholesale, Inc., 589 F.2d 451 (9th Cir. 1979).

[60] *See e.g.,* Crane v. C. Crane & Co., 105 F. 869 (7th Cir. 1901).

sary detriment to support a counter promise. The problem is not one of discovering a detriment; the judicial problem is one of discovering appropriate terms to be implied where there are no stated estimates, much less "ceiling" or "floor" quantities in the agreement. Where, for example, the buyer has no established business and there are, therefore, no prior requirements upon which to base an estimate of his needs, courts may not discern any detriment to support a counter promise.[61] In another well-known case,[62] however, the buyer agreed to purchase all of the sand that the buyer could resell outside the City of Tulsa, Oklahoma. Though the buyer was an experienced sand salesman, he had no established business. The court found consideration supporting the promise of the buyer since he could either not sell any sand outside Tulsa, or sell sand anywhere in that vast universe outside Tulsa only if he purchased the sand from the defendant.[63] A number of older cases supported this analysis,[64] but there were occasional statements of a contrary view. The contrary view was often the product of confusing the requirement of consideration with the requirement of sufficient definiteness of the terms of the agreement.[65] If the parties agree to a requirements or output agreement without any specification of minimum or maximum levels, if there is no prior business history established to which the court can look for guidance as to the terms of the contract or, even with such a history, drastic changes in requirements or output occur, courts may feel hard-pressed to discover sufficiently definite terms. Even then, however, courts should not conclude that the agreement is unenforceable because there is no consideration which is a totally separate question from the question of sufficient definiteness. Since requirements and output contracts are desirable planning instruments, assuring a continuous

---

[61] See Pessin v. Fox Head Waukeshaw Corp., 230 Wis. 277, 282 N.W. 582 (1938) where the defendant agreed to supply the plaintiff with as much beer as plaintiff would require in becoming the sole distributor of defendant's beer in a certain territory. The court held that in the absence of an established business or known enterprise, there was no measurable obligation on the part of the plaintiff which could constitute a detriment, i.e., the contract lacked "mutuality of obligation." In G. Loewus & Co. v. Vischia, 2 N.J. 54, 65 A.2d 604 (1949), the plaintiff was assured of an ample supply of wine from the defendant. In return, however, plaintiff was required to purchase such wines from defendant that plaintiff might require under labels bearing its brand or trade names, i.e., names owned exclusively by the plaintiff. The trial court found that neither party was in a position to make a reasonable estimate of the wines the plaintiff might require. Since the plaintiff was not required to purchase any wine from the defendant except that which plaintiff would resell in bottles bearing its brand or trade names, the court found no consideration, i.e., a lack of mutuality of obligation, in that plaintiff was not circumscribed in its liberty of action or, perhaps, that it was not sufficiently limited as to its future action. The court, however, appeared to confuse the requirement of consideration with the requirement of sufficient definiteness.

[62] McMichael v. Price, 177 Okla. 186, 58 P.2d 549 (1936).

[63] The court was not as clear and decisive in its rationale as it could have been. Though finding consideration, the court countered the argument that plaintiff could escape liability by going out of the sand business with the statement that, "[I]t was the intent of the parties to enter into a contract which would be mutually binding." Ibid. at 58 P.2d 553. Regardless of the intention of the parties to be mutually bound, if the liberty of one party is not circumscribed, he suffers no detriment and the promise of the other party is not supported by consideration. This is sometimes described by suggesting that there is a lack of "mutuality of obligation," i.e., both parties must be bound or neither is bound. This unfortunate phrase will be explored and, it is hoped, emasculated, later in the discussion of consideration.

[64] See, e.g., T. W. Jenkins & Co. v. Anaheim Sugar Co., 247 F. 958 (9th Cir. 1918) (promise to buy requirements of sugar); Minnesota Lumber Co. v. Whitebreast Coal Co., 160 Ill. 85, 43 N.E. 774 (1895) (promise to buy requirements of anthracite).

[65] See supra note 61.

source of supply at predictable prices or a single customer bound to purchase all that the seller produces at agreed upon prices, many courts were astute to avoid the argument that such contracts were too indefinite to enforce if they could discover some plausible basis for estimating a reasonable quantity.[66] The apparent desirability of output and requirements contracts made it clear that their use would not only continue but increase. The UCC makes a valiant effort to react to this felt commercial need. In § 2-306(1), the Code deals with the problems of consideration and sufficient definiteness.[67] The consideration problem is met by requiring the party who will determine quantity (the seller by output and the purchaser by requirements) "to operate his plant or conduct his business in good faith and according to commercial standards of fair dealing in the trade so that his output or requirements will approximate a reasonably foreseeable figure."[68] The problem of sufficient definiteness is dealt with by defining the quantity under such contracts as "the actual good faith output or requirements of the particular party."[69] The general thrust of the Code provision directed courts to favor the enforceability of requirements and output contracts and to eschew notions of any lack of "mutuality of obligation" (i.e., consideration) or sufficient definiteness unless that were impossible.[70] Yet, these problems were dealt with through the implication of good faith,[71] a rather amorphous standard that required case law elaboration.

"Good faith" cannot be used as a substitute for consideration, i.e., if a buyer is free to purchase his requirements from others, there is no consideration to support the promise of the seller to supply all that the buyer desires to purchase from that seller.[72] With respect to the measurement of quantity, while a comment to § 2-306 indicates that output or requirements contracts will not fail for indefiniteness since the measurement of quantity will be based upon "actual good faith output or requirements of the particular party,"[73] the language of § 2-306(1) refers to "stated estimates" or, in the absence of stated estimates, "to any normal or otherwise prior output or requirements." In an agreement without stated estimates and without any prior business history,

---

[66]See generally 1 WILLISTON § 104A.

[67]"A term which measures the quantity by the output of the seller or the requirements of the buyer means such actual output or requirements as may occur in good faith, except that no quantity unreasonably disproportionate to any stated estimate or in the absence of a stated estimate to any normal or otherwise comparable prior output or requirements may be tendered or demanded." UCC § 2-306(1).

[68]UCC § 2-306 comment 2.

[69]Ibid.

[70]See Sacks v. F & S Petr. Co., 6 Ark. App. 327, 641 S.W.2d 726 (1982).

[71]The UCC definitions of "good faith" are found in § 1-201(19) ("honesty in fact in the conduct of the transaction concerned") which is generally applicable, and the Article 2 "merchant" standard of good faith in § 2-103(1)(b) ("'Good faith' in the case of a merchant means honesty in fact and the observance of reasonable commercial standards of fair dealing in the trade."). The Article 1 definition, not applicable to merchants, may be somewhat facetiously described as the "pure heart/empty head" type of good faith, i.e., the assumption is that one can be honest but unreasonable. Merchants, however, must be both honest in fact and commercially reasonable. See Summers, "Good Faith" In General Contract Law and the Sales Provisions of the Uniform Commercial Code, 54 VA. L. REV. 195 (1968).

[72]In Harvey v. Fearless Farris Whsle., Inc., 589 F.2d 451 (9th Cir. 1979), the court found no consideration where the buyer could purchase from others if their prices were lower. It should be noted, however, that even in such a case, a detriment to the buyer can be shown, i.e., he must purchase from the seller unless he can purchase the same goods at lower prices from others.

[73]UCC § 2-306 comment 2.

how does a court measure "normal" output or requirements? It is possible for a seller to agree to supply the requirements of a new venture where there is little if any predictability to such requirements, i.e., the seller could foresee extreme variations in the buyer's good faith requirements from zero to an unknown level. The risk of the seller would be considerable and it is possible for a seller to assume such a risk. At this time, there is no dispositive interpretation of § 2-306(1) dealing with such an open-ended situation. It is, however, theoretically possible for a court to confront a situation to which the Code applies that is bereft of any "normal" standard to which the court may resort to complete the quantity term in such a contract and where one party is subject to an enormous risk while the other party risks very little.[74] The implication of "good faith" in such an agreement may be insufficient to meet the requirement of sufficient definiteness.

Notwithstanding these possibilities, § 2-306 has been successful in dealing with an increasing number of requirement and output situations. The good faith standard has not proven so amorphous as to be ineffective. Where a buyer increased its demand some sixty-three percent above a contract estimate for a given year, the absence of good faith in this increase was clear from the fact that the buyer decided to pursue new lines of business that were not the basis for the original estimate so as to profit from a fixed price when market prices were increasing rapidly.[75] On the other hand, where a contractor no longer had any requirements for concrete in the building of a state hospital when the state terminated the project, the contractor's reduction of requirements to zero was held to be a good faith reduction.[76] A loss of profit or even no profit on a particular item will not justify a shut down by a seller under an output contract or a buyer under a requirements contract.[77] If a buyer under a requirements contract decides to stockpile or otherwise purchase unneeded goods because the fixed price under the contract is beneficial, such an increase in demand is not in good faith because it is not generated by the purchaser's actual requirements.[78] In precluding the supply or demand of

---

[74] For example, where a middleman may choose to purchase nothing or a very large quantity on the basis of market price, it is conceivable that a court may find such an agreement to be fatally indefinite even under the liberal standards of § 2-306 of the UCC.

[75] Orange & Rockland Utils., Inc. v. Amerada Hess Corp., 59 App. Div. 2d 110, 397 N.Y.S.2d 814 (1977). (Sale of power to a power pool which had not been considered at the time of the original estimate and which permitted plaintiff to profit from its contract to purchase oil at fixed prices when oil and other energy prices were increasing rapidly).

[76] Wilsonville Concrete Prods. v. Todd Bldg. Co., 281 Or. 345, 574 P.2d 1112 (1978).

[77] See Feld v. Henry Levy & Sons, 37 N.Y.2d 466, 335 N.E.2d 320 (1975) and comment 2 to UCC § 2-306: "A shutdown by a requirements buyer for lack of orders might be permissible when a shut-down merely to curtail losses would not." In the Feld case, however, the court suggests that the defendant would be justified in ceasing production if its losses were more than trivial and that would be a question of fact. How much more than "trivial" such losses would have to be to justify cessation of production, however, is made more difficult by other statements in the opinion. The output contract dealt only with one line of defendant's production, the production of bread crumbs. The court indicates that if defendant were facing bankruptcy, i.e., an imperiling of its entire business if forced to continue that line of production, the cessation of production would be warranted. Absent that effect, however, good faith would require a continuation of production even if the bread crumb line produced no profit.

[78] See Homestake Min. Co. v. Washington Public Power Supply Sys., 476 F. Supp. 1162 (D.C. N.D. Cal. 1979), aff'd, 652 F.2d 28 (9th Cir. 1981); Massachusetts Gas & Elec. Light Supply Corp. v. V-M Corp., 387 F.2d 605 (1st Cir. 1967). See also Amerada Hess, supra note 75.

a quantity unreasonably disproportionate to a stated estimate or prior output or requirements, § 2-306(1) provides courts with an articulated standard of good faith.[79] A stated estimate provides a median or center from which variations can be measured to determine whether the output or requirements are unreasonably disproportionate.[80] Absent any estimate, prior output or requirements furnishes a similar basis for determining unreasonably disproportionate increases or decreases.[81] In general, courts have found § 2-306 to be a useful statutory guide in their efforts to determine appropriate quantity standards in output and requirements contracts.[82]

1. Exclusive Dealing Contracts — "Best Efforts."

Section 2-306(2) of the UCC is concerned with the implied obligations of parties to exclusive dealing contracts. If a party agrees to become the exclusive agent of a seller in a given territory, the Code imposes a good faith obligation on the agent to use his best efforts to promote the seller's product in that territory.[83] The classic exposition of this implied obligation is found in the opinion by Judge Cardozo in *Wood v. Lucy, Lady Duff-Gordon*[84] which will be discussed later in this chapter. Though they are found in the same UCC section, the implied obligation of good faith in exclusive dealing contracts is different from the good faith obligation implied in requirements and output contracts. In requirements and output contracts, we have seen an implied obligation to use good faith in measuring output or requirements. In exclusive dealing contracts, however, there is a good faith obligation to use best efforts to supply or promote a product.[85] Doubt has been expressed that § 2-306(2) should include sellers since output contracts merely require sellers to use good faith rather than best efforts.[86] A comment to § 2-306(2), however, suggests that the best efforts of the seller have nothing to do with the supply of the

---

[79] *See* Harry Thuresson, Inc. v. United States, 197 Ct. Cl. 88, 453 F.2d 1278 (1972) (tendered quantity of 1.7% of estimated quantity was "unreasonably disproportionate" in an output contract).

[80] *See* comment 3 to UCC § 2-306: "If an estimate of output or requirements is included in the agreement, no quantity unreasonably disproportionate to it may be tendered or demanded. Any minimum or maximum set by the agreement shows a clear limit on the intended elasticity. In similar fashion, the agreed estimate is to be regarded as a center around which the parties intend the variation to occur." *See also* Shea-Kaiser-Lockhead-Healy v. Department of Water & Power of City of Los Angeles, 73 Cal. App. 3d 679, 140 Cal. Rptr. 884 (1977) which applies this "median" standard.

[81] In Duval & Co. v. H. A. Malcom, 233 Ga. 784, 214 S.E.2d 356 (1975), the seller offered to supply its entire output of cotton from certain acreage to the buyer as it had in the past. In two prior crop years, the acreage had produced 756 bales and 380 bales respectively. When the buyer received the written offer, he added an estimate of 875 bales. The court held that this estimate was a material alteration of the offer since, under § 2-306, the estimate of 875 bales added by the purchaser was unreasonably disproportionate to prior output.

[82] For an analysis of § 2-306, *see* Weistart, *Requirements and Output Contracts: Quantity Variations Under the UCC,* 1973 DUKE L.J. 599.

[83] The "territory," of course, could be the entire world or any part thereof.

[84] 222 N.Y. 88, 118 N.E. 214 (1917).

[85] Kubik v. J & R Foods of Or., Inc., 282 Or. 179, 577 P.2d 518 (1978). *See also* Gestetner Corp. v. Case Equip. Co., 815 F.2d 806 (1st Cir. 1987). See, however, Flynn v. Gold Kist, Inc., 181 Ga. App. 637, 353 S.E.2d 537 (1987) where the court casually suggests that, regardless of whether the good faith requirement of § 2-306(1) or the best efforts requirement of § 2-306(2) applies, the good faith standard applies.

[86] *See* FARNSWORTH, CONTRACTS § 7.17, at 530 n.19 (1982).

seller's entire output. Rather, the seller or principal[87] "is expected under such a contract to refrain from supplying any other dealer or agent within the exclusive territory."[88] An exclusive dealing arrangement may require an agent[89] not to deal in the products of other manufacturers[90] while the supplier agrees to refrain from supplying other distributors within the agent's exclusive territory. If the supplier may not supply others within that territory, the supplier has agreed to supply its agent, exclusively, within that territory. Output is irrelevant in such an arrangement. Rather, the requirements of the buyer in its effort to expand the market for the seller's product within a given territory are relevant. In such a situation, a "best efforts" obligation may be imposed upon the supplier to ascertain that it provides the agent with a sufficient and expeditious supply of the product,[91] again, to permit the agent to use its best efforts in promoting the sale of the product. While it is not inappropriate to speak of the "best efforts" of the supplier, certainly, the implied obligation of "best efforts" is much more obvious in its application to the agent who must use all of his capabilities to foster the marketing of the manufacturer's product.[92] There is no UCC or other satisfactory definition or description of "best efforts."[93] The issue of whether a distributor used best efforts will often arise where the distributor decides to sell another product in competition with the original supplier's product. The sale of a competing product is not, *per se*, a violation of obligation to use best efforts.[94] The particular circumstances will have to be taken into account in any such case.[95] While "best efforts" must always be viewed in the particular circumstances of each

---

[87] The terms "principal" and "agent" are used in this discussion for convenience as they are used in the analysis of exclusive dealing arrangements in Goetz & Scott, *Principles of Relational Contracts,* 67 VA. L. REV. 1089, 1090, n.6 (1981), where the terms are not limited to their technical agency sense, but include franchisees, distributors, and others who are typically independent contractors and not technical agents.

[88] UCC § 2-306 comment 5. *See* Sally Beauty Co. v. Nexxus Prods. Co., 801 F.2d 1001 (7th Cir. 1986).

[89] *See supra* note 87.

[90] *See,* however, Randall v. Peerless Motor Car Co., 212 Mass. 352, 99 N.E. 221 (1912) (dealer required to use "best energies" to promote the sale of manufacturer's product but it was not precluded from selling a line of noncompeting cars.)

[91] *See* Famous Brands, Inc. v. David Sherman Corp., 814 F.2d 517, 521 (8th Cir. 1987) where, after discovering an implied promise by the distributor to promote the products of the supplier, the court indicates that the arrangement could also be regarded as a requirements contract. *See also* Sally Beauty Co. v. Nexxus Prods. Co., 801 F.2d 1001 (7th Cir. 1986).

[92] Bloor v. Falstaff Brewing Corp., 454 F. Supp. 259 (S.D. N.Y. 1978), aff'd, 601 F.2d 609 (2d Cir. 1979).

[93] In Joyce Beverages of N.Y. v. Royal Crown Cola, 555 F. Supp. 271, 277 (S.D. N.Y. 1983), the court indicates that an express best efforts clause should be read in the light of trade practice and usage.

[94] *Ibid.*

[95] In *Joyce, ibid.,* the court concluded that the sale of a competing cola would violate the best efforts obligation, basing that decision upon trade practice and usage. In HML Corp. v. General Foods Corp., 365 F.2d 77 (3d Cir. 1966), the court interpreted the "Supply Agreement" to ascertain primarily that the distributor had a ready source of supply rather than an agreement requiring promotion on the part of the distributor. In Parev Prods. Co. v. I. Rokeach & Sons, 124 F.2d 147 (2d Cir. 1941), the court candidly recognized that the parties had not contemplated certain market changes concerning competing products from other suppliers which required the court to decide the case absent any such intention by the parties. The court permitted the distributor to market a new product, competing with the old product, until the plaintiff could demonstrate that the sale of the new product reduced royalty payments beyond reductions that would have occurred through sales of other manufacturers' products even if the new product had not been marketed.

case, it should be clear that the phrase imports some positive drive beyond the good faith standard of honesty in fact and commercial reasonableness.[96] There is a level of industry and even creativity reasonably assumed under a "best efforts" obligation which would not be appropriate in describing the good faith obligation.[97]

Finally, it should be noted that exclusive dealing arrangements are subject to antitrust laws, i.e., where such arrangements may substantially lessen competition or tend to create a monopoly in any line of commerce, they violate Section 3 of the Clayton Act.[98]

§ 59. Equivalence in Value — "Adequacy" of Consideration — "Sufficient" Consideration.

A. *Actions at Law for Damages.*

One of the shibboleths of the common law is that courts will not generally inquire into the adequacy of consideration.[99] The allocation of the goods and resources of our society occurs through the mechanism of contract, and contracts are made by private parties who are free to place whatever value they wish upon that which they seek in exchange for a promise or performance.[1] Even if that freedom were not considered necessary, it would not be possible for courts to begin to police the bargain of the parties in terms of their estimates of value. A dissatisfied party could always complain that he or she did not receive adequate or "sufficient" consideration, thereby necessitating the otherwise impracticable task of judicial policing of value. Courts have, therefore, studiously avoided questions of the relative values exchanged by the parties except where fraud or similar overreaching can be shown or when a court is asked to decree an equitable remedy.[2] If a promise has some value, that is, if it involves a detriment which the law recognizes, as described earlier,[3] the promise will be binding. The value need not be significant and it need not involve any economic detriment or actual loss. In the sense of a real

---

[96] UCC § 2-103(1)(b).

[97] In their article, *Principles of Relational Contracts,* 67 VA. L. REV. 1089, 1111 (1981), Professors Goetz & Scott suggest that, "[T]he precise legal meaning to be attached to a best efforts requirement is not at all clear, either from a consideration of the case law or from theoretical discussions in standard legal scholarship." They proceed to suggest (1111-26) an analysis of "best efforts" on the basis of an economic model and suggest that best efforts cases "hinge on two factors, strategic adaptation to the conflict of interest between the parties and the problem of managerial incompetence."

[98] 15 U.S.C. § 14. The drafters of § 2-306(2) apparently recognized this possibility since the language of that subsection begins, "A *lawful* agreement ... for exclusive dealing...."

[99] Recent cases attest to the continuing strength of this statement. *See, e.g.,* Carroll v. Lee, 148 Ariz. 10, 712 P.2d 923 (1986); Kristerin Dev. Co. v. Granson Inv., 394 N.W.2d 325 (Iowa 1986); Vogelhut v. Kandel, 308 Md. 183, 517 A.2d 1092 (1986); Haretuer v. Klocke, 709 S.W.2d 138 (Mo. App. 1986); C & D Inv. v. Beaudoin, 364 N.W.2d 850 (Minn. App. 1985). *See also* RESTATEMENT 2d § 79 comment c.

[1] *See* Keith v. Town & Country Act Hardware Store, Inc., 81 N.C. App. 185, 343 S.E.2d 562 (1986); Buckingham v. John C. Wray, II, 19 Neb. 807, 366 N.W.2d 753 (1985).

[2] *See* Bayshore Royal Co. v. Doran Jason Co. of Tampa, Inc., 480 So. 2d 651 (D. Fla. 1986); Harwood v. Randolph Harwood, Inc., 124 Mich. App. 137, 333 N.W.2d 609 (1983). The question of adequacy of consideration where a party seeks an equitable remedy such as specific performance will be explored in part B of this section.

[3] *See supra* § 57.

detriment rather than a "legal" detriment, the RESTATEMENT 2d suggests that, "[T]here is no requirement of detriment."[4] Perhaps the best-known statement of the virtual worthlessness of the detriment is the suggestion that even a "peppercorn" will be sufficient.[5] In *Haigh v. Brooks*,[6] the plaintiff surrendered a document which the parties thought to be a binding guaranty. However, it was claimed that the document was a worthless scrap of paper. The court held that the surrender of this scrap of paper, even if it were worthless, was consideration for a promise to guarantee the payment of $110,000 under the circumstances.[7] A modern example of a trivial detriment is seen in a case involving an offer contained in an envelope addressed to a three-year old containing a statement on the face of the envelope, "I'll give you this versatile new calculator watch free Just for Opening this Envelope Before Feb. 15, 1985." The mother of the child opened the envelope for her son and discovered that it was necessary to subscribe to a magazine in order to procure the watch. The defendant argued that, "the mere act of opening the envelope was valueless and therefore did not constitute adequate consideration" which the court found to be "technically ... incorrect" because "*any* bargained-for act or forbearance will constitute adequate consideration."[8]

It is sometimes suggested that there is an exception to the general proposition that courts will not inquire into the relative values exchanged between the parties to a contract. The so-called exception involves a promise to exchange one sum of money for a different sum. Thus, a promise to pay $200 in exchange for one cent was held not supported by consideration.[9] The refusal of courts to view such promises as supported by consideration is not a reflection on the inadequacy of the value of one cent compared to two hundred dollars. Rather, such an exchange is what the RESTATEMENT 2d calls a "pretended exchange,"[10] i.e., the promisor who undertook to pay $200 in exchange for one cent was not bargaining for one cent. It must not be forgotten that consideration requires more than a detriment to the promisee. The detriment must be bargained-for, i.e., the promise must induce the detriment *and* the detriment must induce the promise.[11] The detriment of one cent can hardly be viewed as

---

[4] RESTATEMENT 2d § 79 comment b.

[5] *See* Whitney v. Stearns, 16 Me. 394, 397 (1837) which can be traced as far as Lord Coke's discussion where, in a rent apportionment situation, he suggested that a "pepper corne" would be sufficient. E. COKE ON LITTLETON 222 (1628). *See also* Hyde v. Shapiro, 216 Neb. 785, 346 N.W.2d 241, 243 (1984): "[E]ven 'a peppercorn' may be sufficient."

[6] 10 A. & E. 309 [1839].

[7] See, however, Newman & Snell's State Bank v. Hunter, 243 Mich. 331, 220 N.W. 665 (1928) where a widow promised (through her own note) to pay the indebtedness of her husband to the bank which surrendered the husband's note. Held: no consideration because the note was a worthless piece of paper. Yet, the widow may have valued what to others was a worthless piece of paper, i.e., it was not worthless to the widow. As suggested in Hyde v. Shapiro, *supra* note 5, at 243-44, "A valuable consideration to support a contract need not be one translatable into dollars and cents; it is sufficient if it consists of the performance, or promise thereof, *which the promisor treats and considers a value to him*," quoting from Asmus v. Longenecker, 131 Neb. 608, 611, 269 N.W. 117, 119 (1936) (emphasis added).

[8] Harris v. Time, Inc., 237 Cal. Rptr. 584, 587 (Cal. App. 1 Dist. 1987).

[9] Schnell v. Nell, 17 Ind. 29, 79 Am. Dec. 453 (1861). *See also* Shepard v. Rhodes, 7 R.I. 470, 84 Am. Dec. 573 (1863).

[10] RESTATEMENT 2d § 79 comment d.

[11] The "bargained-for-exchange" element of consideration will be explored in subsequent sections.

inducing the promise to pay $200. It is, therefore, appropriate to suggest that the refusal to enforce such a promise has nothing to do with "inadequate" consideration. That refusal is properly based on the unwillingness of courts to believe that the transaction evidences a bargained-for-exchange. It should be noted, however, that if the one cent is a rare or sentimental coin, it is quite possible that it was bargained-for and consideration would be found in such a transaction.[12] Similarly, if the parties were buying and selling money as a commodity, i.e., purchasing and selling foreign currency, such a transaction clearly evidences detriments which are the subject of a bargained-for exchange.[13]

The confusion surrounding the phrase "adequacy of consideration" is exacerbated by the use of the term "sufficiency of consideration."[14] To the extent that "sufficiency" is an inquiry into "adequacy," it is generally irrelevant. "Sufficiency," however, is often used as a redundant qualification of the existence of consideration. Consideration either exists or it does not exist, i.e., one cannot find "insufficient" consideration and still have consideration. The RESTATEMENT 2d, therefore, rejects the usage of "sufficient consideration" as redundant.[15]

The view that courts should not inquire into the adequacy of consideration absent a showing of fraud, mistake or overreaching, is the only sensible view that can be supported. There is no standard for measuring the values of detriments exchanged between the parties. Economic values are so variable as to defy equivalence even if courts attempted to discover equivalence. If the promisor is content to make a particular bargain, there is no reason for refusing enforcement of that bargain, again, in the absence of fraud, mistake or overreaching.[16] If inadequacy of consideration is accompanied by evidence of fraud, mistake or overreaching, or if it is so "gross" as to give rise to an inference of fraud,[17] relief may be obtained in an equitable action of rescission or cancellation.[18]

B. Inadequacy of Consideration in Equity — Equitable Unconscionability.

Mere inadequacy of consideration will not prevent a court, sitting as a court of equity, from decreeing specific performance of a contract.[19] If, however, the consideration is grossly inadequate, if the terms of the contract are unfair, if the enforcement of the contract will cause unreasonable hardship or loss to the defendant or third persons or, finally, if the contract was induced by some sharp practice, misrepresentation or mistake, a court may refuse the discre-

---

[12] See Schnell v. Nell, supra note 9.

[13] Cf. The 1972 amendments to Article 9 of the UCC which treats money as the subject of a security interest, permitting a possessory security interest in money with numismatic value. See UCC §§ 9-304 and 9-305.

[14] See, e.g., Berkman v. Commercial Bank of Douglasville, 171 Ga. App. 890, 321 S.E.2d 339 (1984) where the court describes the issue in the case as one of "adequacy," and mentions "sufficiency" where the issue is whether consideration exists.

[15] See RESTATEMENT 2d § 17 comment d.

[16] Cf. Note, The Peppercorn Theory of Consideration and the Doctrine of Fair Exchange in Contract Law, 35 COLUM. L. REV. 1090 (1935).

[17] See, e.g., Dreyer v. Dreyer, 48 Or. App. 801, 617 P.2d 955 (1980).

[18] RESTATEMENT 2d § 79 comment e.

[19] See Seier v. Peek, 456 So. 2d 1079 (Ala. 1974). See also RESTATEMENT 2d § 208 comment c.

tionary remedy of specific performance.[20] The elements just described may appear in varying combinations and the fact situation must, as usual, be considered in context. Thus, a slight inadequacy which, alone, would not prevent the equitable remedy may be sufficient to prevent it in combination with some sharp practice, some severe hardship or other factor.[21] Courts must, however, be careful to determine the adequacy of consideration at the time the contract is formed rather than some later time such as the time of trial when the values exchanged may appear grossly disproportionate.[22]

In the absence of fraud, duress, mistake or misrepresentation, the fact that a contract could be characterized as harsh, oppressive or "unconscionable" was insufficient to make such a contract unenforceable, void or voidable at common law.[23] Yet, the discretionary remedy of specific performance was often denied in such cases.[24] When the remedy is denied, it may be asserted that the plaintiff is not deprived of all remedies but is merely relegated to his action at law for damages. Yet, the denial of the equitable remedy may be a complete denial of remedy in the typical specific performance case, i.e., where the remedy at law is either inadequate or useless.

The use of the amorphous term, "unconscionable" in cases denying the equitable remedy has caused some confusion in relation to the developing doctrine of unconscionability as found in the Uniform Commercial Code.[25] The Code and related concepts of unconscionability evolved from an effort to permit courts to refuse enforcement of contracts or portions of contracts which evidenced certain material, risk-shifting terms — typically found in the printed or "boilerplate" clauses of standardized forms — designed to operate against a party with inferior bargaining power who would have little or no opportunity to understand their import or succeed in negotiating such terms out of the agreement, again, even if he understood their significance.[26] The material term would often be inconspicuously printed and contain language that only lawyers could begin to appreciate.[27] Moreover, even if the disfavored party was totally aware of the ramifications of the clause(s), he was often unable to seek another bargain since he required the goods or services contracted for and would not be able to obtain them elsewhere on less oppressive

---

[20] See Patterson v. Goldsmith, 358 S.E.2d 163 (S.C. App. 1987); Bramson v. Mastroni, 151 Ariz. 194, 726 P.2d 610 (1986); Patterson v. Merchants Truck Line, 448 So. 2d 288 (Miss. 1984). See also RESTATEMENT 2d § 364.

[21] See FIRST RESTATEMENT § 367 comment c.

[22] See Pitts Truck Air, Inc. v. Mack Trucks, Inc., 173 Ga. App. 801, 328 S.E.2d 416 (1985).

[23] See 5A CORBIN § 1164.

[24] See, e.g., Payne v. Simmons, 232 Va. 379, 350 S.E.2d 637 (1987); Pascarella v. Bruck, 190 N.J. Super. 118, 462 A.2d 186 (1983); Smith v. Harrison, 325 N.W.2d 92 (Iowa 1982); Lenawee Cty. Bd. of Health v. Messerly, 98 Mich. App. 478, 295 N.W.2d 903 (1980).

[25] UCC § 2-302. In denying specific performance due to a combination of inadequacy of consideration and other circumstances, a court may resort to the use of "unconscionable." See, e.g., McKinnon v. Benedict, 38 Wis. 2d 607, 157 N.W.2d 665 (1968).

[26] For a case antedating the UCC concept of unconscionability but containing all of the elements just described, see Cutler Corp. v. Latshaw, 374 Pa. 1, 97 A.2d 234 (1953) (confession of judgment clauses printed on reverse sides of standardized forms, the reverse sides deliberately ignored by the plaintiff though fewer sheets could have been used to set forth the specifications).

[27] The classic example is found in Williams v. Walker-Thomas Furn. Co., 121 U.S. App. D.C. 315, 350 F.2d 445 (1965) (An "add-on" clause was part of a "maze" of fine print and subjected the purchaser of an inexpensive stereo set to the loss of all the furniture she had ever purchased from the seller and paid for prior to the purchase).

terms. In this "take-it-or-leave-it"[28] or "contract of adhesion"[29] posture, the signature of the disfavored party on the document did not represent his *genuine* assent to the deal though it suggested his *apparent* assent.[30] The UCC or related concepts of unconscionability[31] now permit courts to refuse enforcement of provisions apparently assented to under such circumstances, whether the court is asked to grant legal or equitable relief. This significant development will be explored in a later section.[32] Because the principles of unconscionability as found in the UCC appeared to some to be as amorphous as earlier equitable statements of unconscionability, it was tempting to suggest that the Code had simply incorporated the earlier concepts. Scholarly explorations, however, have revealed clear differences between the old equity notion of unconscionability and the new concept under the UCC.[33] Beyond the fact that there is no reliance on the old equity concept in the new Code formulation, the equity concept applied to overreaching in individualized bargaining transactions while the Code concept applies to situations involving mass transactions in which the standardized, printed ("pad") contract form is used. The equity doctrine was applied to situations involving inadequacy of consideration or "gross overall imbalance" while the Code and related unconscionable concepts apply to separate, unconscionable clauses in the typical case.[34] Again, the Code concept is predicated upon an inquiry into whether the party against whom the risk-shifting provision is designed to operate apparently assented, i.e., was the clause printed in such a fashion as to be readily readable and understandable to such a party, as well as whether such a party genuinely assented, i.e., did he or she have any reasonable choice in apparently agreeing to a harsh or oppressive provision.[35] While equitable unconscionability often involves one or more of these elements, it may also be used when they are absent but when the *result* of the deal is harsh or oppressive. For all of these reasons, the student of contract law must maintain a clear distinction between the equitable concept of unconscionability — often mentioned in connection with an inquiry into the relative values exchanged (adequacy of consideration) — and the UCC concept which deals with assent to allegedly

---

[28]*See* Henningsen v. Bloomfield Motors, Inc., 32 N.J. 358, 161 A.2d 69 (1960), the landmark case suggesting the unconscionability analysis before the UCC.

[29]The phrase, "contract of adhesion" is usually attributed to Professor Patterson in his article, *The Delivery of a Life Insurance Policy,* 33 HARV. L. REV. 198, 222 (1919). However, the development of the concept is principally attributable to Professor Eherenzweig, *Adhesion Contracts in the Conflict of Laws,* 53 COLUM. L. REV. 1072, 1088-89 (1953) and Professor Kessler, *Contract of Adhesion — Some Thoughts About Freedom of Contract,* 43 COLUM. L. REV. 629 (1943).

[30]In Grady Parton v. Mark Pirtle Oldsmobile-Cadillac-Isuzu, Inc., 730 S.W.2d 634 (Tenn. App. 1987), the court adopts the "genuine assent/apparent assent" analysis, citing the third edition of this book. This analysis will be explored in detail later in this volume with respect to the modern concept of unconscionability. See, however, Cubic Corp. v. Marty, 185 Cal. App. 3d 438, 229 Cal. Rptr. 828 (1986) indicating that a contract of adhesion may be enforced unless the terms are oppressive.

[31]*See, e.g.,* RESTATEMENT 2d § 208.

[32]*See infra* § 96.

[33]See the important article by Professor Leff, *Unconscionability and the Code — The Emperor's New Clause,* 115 U. PA. L. REV. 485, 528-41 (1967).

[34]The Code concept is broad enough to apply to the "gross overall imbalance" situation.

[35]For a listing of unconscionability factors, *see* Doughty v. Idaho Frozen Foods, 736 P.2d 460 (Idaho App. 1987) (one-sided, superior bargaining power).

oppressive or unfairly surprising terms typically found in printed provisions of standardized (form) contracts.

§ 60. Bargained-for-Exchange — Condition of a Gratuitous Promise Distinguished.

A. The Basic Concept.

The fundamental concept which underlies the informal contract is that of bargain or exchange. It is not enough that the promisee suffers a detriment even if that detriment is induced by the making of a promise. Detriment is one of the two necessary elements of consideration. The detriment must be bargained-for and it is not bargained for simply because it was induced by the making of a promise. The classic formula was stated by O. W. Holmes, Jr. "The promise must induce the detriment *and* the detriment must induce the promise."[36] The distinction between a promise inducing a detriment and a detriment inducing a promise can be understood by considering the difference between a gratuitous promise subject to an attached condition and a bargained-for-exchange.

Assume that Ames telephones her son stating, "If you will agree to meet me downtown, I will take you to a store to purchase that new video cassette recorder I know you want so badly." If the son promises to meet his mother, is the mother's promise to purchase the recorder supported by consideration? There is a detriment to the son in traveling downtown. It is also reasonable to assume that the son suffered that detriment because he was induced by his mother's promise. The promise, therefore, induced the detriment. Assuming an amicable relationship between mother and son, however, the detriment did not induce the promise, i.e., the mother did not make the promise because she wanted her son to meet her downtown. Rather, Ames wished to confer a gift upon her son and requested the son's presence downtown at a particular time only as a convenient time and place to purchase the recorder and deliver it, gratuitously, to her son. The fact that the mother's promise was in the form of a condition to her promise — "*If* you will meet me downtown" — does not change the analysis from one of gift to bargained-for-exchange. The detriment to the son, therefore, was a mere condition to the gratuitous promise of Ames. Gratuitous promises are unenforceable because they lack consideration.[37]

---

[36] Wisconsin & Michigan Ry. v. Powers, 191 U.S. 379 (1903). The RESTATEMENT 2d describes the "bargained-for" element as follows: "A performance or return promise is bargained for if it is sought by the promisor in exchange for his promise and is given by the promisee in exchange for that promise." RESTATEMENT 2d § 71(2). Another description of "bargained-for-exchange" provided by Justice Holmes is "reciprocal conventional inducement," as suggested in his famous work, THE COMMON LAW 230 ([1881] Howe ed. 1963). For a suggestion that Holmes created this bargain theory of consideration from whole cloth, *see* G. GILMORE, The Death of Contract 17-21 (1974). For a balanced view in disagreement with Professor Gilmore, *see* Speidel, *An Essay on the Reported Death and Continued Vitality of Contract*, 27 STAN. L. REV. 1161, 1167-71 (1975).

[37] There is no benefit to the gratuitous promisor and no bargained-for detriment to the promisee. In the well-known case of Kirksey v. Kirksey, 8 Ala. 131 (1845), a brother-in-law promised to provide a residence for his sister-in-law and her family upon the death of her husband if she would move from her residence some sixty to seventy miles away. The promisee surrendered her residence and moved to the brother-in-law's property where she was placed in "comfortable houses" and given land to cultivate. Two years later, she was notified to move to an uncomfortable house. Thereafter, she was told to leave even that house. She brought an action claiming

If we change the assumption concerning the amicable relationship between mother and son to one of estrangement, adding the fact that the son has refused, on several occasions, to meet his mother who is eager to remedy their strained relationship, the analysis changes dramatically. As in the earlier analysis, the promise of the mother induced the son to suffer the detriment of meeting the mother downtown. Under the changed facts, however, the same detriment has induced the mother's promise. The mother is primarily interested in having a conference with her son who has refused to meet the mother on several occasions. To achieve that desired result, the mother makes a promise to purchase the video recorder for the son. She does not intend to make a gift to the son regardless of the meeting downtown though she may phrase her promise in gratuitous terms, *e.g.,* "If you meet me downtown, I will *give* you a video recorder." The purpose of her promise is to induce the son to meet her, i.e., to suffer the detriment of meeting the mother. The son has a legal right to refuse a meeting with his mother. By forbearing that legal right and meeting his mother, having been induced to do so by the mother's promise, the son suffers a detriment which is the principal, if not exclusive, reason for the mother's promise.[38] We now have both parts of the bargained-for-exchange requirement of consideration, i.e., the mother's promise induced the detriment of the son *and* the son's detriment induced the mother's promise. In effect, the mother placed a price tag on her promise to purchase the recorder for her son, i.e., the price of the son suffering the detriment of meeting the mother he had been avoiding. The mother wanted that detriment in exchange for her promise. She bargained for it. The mother, incidentally, benefits from this exchange since she meets with her son who had previously refused to meet the mother. The legal value element of consideration is present in the detriment to the promisee-son and benefit to the promisor-mother though it should be remembered that the detriment, alone, would be sufficient. The bargained-for-exchange element of consideration is present because, again, the promise induced the detriment *and* the detriment induced the promise.[39]

---

breach of contract to which the court replied that the promise to her was "a mere gratuity" and no action would lie thereon. Though the promisee suffered a detriment in surrendering her original abode and moving to the promisor's property, and though she was induced to suffer that detriment by the promise thereby fulfilling the requirement of bargained-for-exchange that the promise induce the detriment, the other half of the formula was wanting, i.e., the detriment did not induce the promise. The promisor did not seek the detriment suffered by the promisee as the price of his promise. Rather, it was a necessary condition to the fulfillment of the gratuitous promise. Consequently, the court was correct in finding no consideration because of the lack of a bargained-for-exchange. It should be noted that the same facts would find modern courts enforcing the promise of the brother-in-law on the basis of another validation device to be discussed later in this chapter, i.e., detrimental reliance, known popularly as promissory estoppel. *See also* the famous Williston "tramp" illustration *infra* note 39.

[38] As will be seen in the next section, the motive or purpose of the mother need not be the sole or even principal reason for her promise, so long as it is at least one, even subsidiary, motivation or purpose.

[39] The classic illustration of a gift promise with an attached condition is the Williston "tramp" example. "If a benevolent man says to a tramp, — 'if you go around the corner to the clothing shop there, you may purchase an overcoat on my credit,' no reasonable person would understand that the short walk was requested as the consideration for the promise, but that in the event of the tramp going to the shop, the promisor would make a gift. It is a legal detriment to the tramp to take the walk, and the only reason why the walk is not consideration is because, on a reasonable interpretation, it must be held that the walk was not requested as the price of the promise, but was merely a condition of a gratuitous promise." 1 WILLISTON § 112 (3d ed. 1957).

B. *Determining Whether the Detriment Was Bargained-For — Illustrative Cases.*

It may be difficult to determine whether the detriment to the promisee induced the promise in a given case though it may be clear that the promise induced the detriment. A comparison of two well-known cases is helpful. Where a newspaper advertised a "permanent" position for a news reporter and the plaintiff surrendered his job in a bakery to take the position, it was clear that the promise of the employer induced the plaintiff to suffer the detriment of surrendering his position at the bakery, i.e., the promise induced the detriment. The facts of the case, however, evidenced no particular interest on the part of the promisor in the detriment suffered by the plaintiff. Though the plaintiff could not work at the newspaper and the bakery simultaneously, the promisor was apparently disinterested in the detriment, i.e., the necessity for the plaintiff to surrender his bakery position was simply a necessary condition to his performance at the newspaper. The newspaper did not attempt to entice him away from the bakery job. Thus, the court held that there was no bargained-for-exchange because the detriment did not induce the promise though the promise had induced the detriment.[40] In order for a detriment to induce a promise, the promisor must desire that detriment, i.e., he or she must want the promisee to suffer that detriment as the price of the promisor's promise. If, for example, engineering firm X was desirous of employing an engineer from competing engineering firm Y though the engineer was pleased to be at Y, X could entice the engineer to leave Y and to join X for "permanent" or "lifetime" employment. In such a situation, the promise induces the detriment *and* the detriment induces the promise because X desires that detriment as the necessary price of its promise. The engineer's surrender of the position at Y would not be a mere incident of accepting the position at X as it was in the case of the employee who surrendered his job at the bakery to become a reporter. Rather, it would be a bargained-for detriment.[41] While firm X seeks the ultimate benefit of having the engineer work for X, it must first entice him away from Y. The newspaper did not seek to entice the plaintiff from his bakery position. Therefore, we may view the engineer's detriment of his departure from Y as a detriment that X wanted since the suffering of that detriment was essential to the ultimate benefit to X which desired the detriment as the price of its promise. Similarly, in another well-known case,[42] the defendant was eager to attract potential buyers to an auction of certain residential lots. The advertisement for the sale contained an offer to give potential buyers a chance to win a new Ford automobile. In response to the offer, plaintiff attended the sale, received her chance and won the contest. The defendant refused to provide the prize and defended its action on the ground that there was no consideration to support its promise. The court found consideration since the object of the defendant was to attract persons to the sale and

---

[40]Fisher v. Jackson, 142 Conn. 734, 118 A.2d 316 (1955).

[41]*See* Collins v. Parsons College, 203 N.W.2d 594 (Iowa 1973) where the court held that the surrender of a tenured position at one school was consideration for a promise of tenure at another school where the employment surrendered was permanent (tenured) and the new employer was aware of the facts.

[42]Maughs v. Porter, 157 Va. 415, 161 S.E. 242 (1931).

the plaintiff, among others, suffered the detriment sought by the defendant, i.e., the detriment induced the promise. Since the promise also induced the detriment, the detriment was bargained-for. The ultimate desire of the defendant was to sell lots to those in attendance. To achieve that goal, the defendant had to attract potential buyers to the sale and offered a chance at winning a new automobile in exchange for the detriment suffered by those who were induced to attend by the promise of an opportunity to win the car.

C. *The Purpose of the Promisor.*

The typical contract for the purchase and sale of goods or services presents no obstacle in identifying the bargained-for-exchange. If, for example, Ames agrees to sell her car to Barnes for $5000 in exchange for Barnes' promise to purchase the car at that price, Ames' promise induces Barnes' detriment of parting with $5000 and the surrender of $5000 is clearly what Ames wants in exchange for her promise. Barnes' promise to pay the $5000 induces Ames' promise to transfer ownership of the car and that detriment is clearly sought by Barnes in exchange for his promise to pay $5000. Where the fact situation is not that clear with respect to bargained-for-exchange, the analysis can be assisted by focusing upon the *purpose* of the promisor, i.e., in making the promise, was it the purpose of the promisor to induce the detriment? Did the promisor make the promise because she wanted the promisee to do something which the promisee had a legal right to forbear, or forbear an action that the promisee had the legal right to perform? If the promisor made the promise for the purpose of inducing the detriment, the detriment induced the promise. If, however, the promisor made the promise with no particular interest in the detriment that the promisee had to suffer to take advantage of a promised gift or other benefit, the detriment was incidental or conditional to the promisee's receipt of the benefit.[43] Even though the promisee suffered a detriment induced by the promise, the purpose of the promisor was not to have the promisee suffer the detriment because she did not seek that detriment in exchange for her promise.[44]

---

[43] In Cady v. Coleman, 315 N.W.2d 593, 596 (Minn. 1982), at a golf outing, a lawyer in a firm to which an insurance company referred business purchased drinks for an official of the insurance company. The official became inebriated and crashed his automobile into another car, killing the driver and injuring two passengers. The occupants of the car brought an action against, *inter alia,* the law firm on the footing that the law firm "sold or bartered" rather than gave liquor to the official, making the law firm liable under a Minnesota "dram shop" act. The opinion states, "Consideration requires the voluntary assumption of an obligation by one party *on the condition* of an act or forbearance by the other.... If appellant's (law firm's) purchase of liquor for Coleman (the official) was not on the condition that Coleman send appellant more defense cases, and if Coleman's referring of his company's business to appellant was not on the condition that appellant entertain him, there was no bargained-for consideration and hence no sale or barter."

[44] In Penley v. Penley, 65 N.C. App. 711, 310 S.E.2d 360 (1984), the plaintiff (husband) claimed that he left his tire business and came to the aid of his wife in her franchised business in exchange for his wife's promise to share her business with him. The court held that the husband's purpose in coming to the aid of his ill wife was to aid his wife pursuant to the normal presumption of gratuitous services of husband to wife rather than in exchange for a share of her business. *See also* Baehr v. Penn-O-Tex Oil Co., 258 Minn. 533, 104 N.W.2d 661, 665 (1960) where forbearance in instituting a suit, albeit a detriment, was not bargained-for. The opinion states, "Consideration, as essential evidence of the parties' intent to create a legal obligation, must be something adopted and regarded by the parties as such. Thus, the same thing may be consideration or not, as it is dealt with by the parties."

D. *Aids in Determining the Purpose of the Promisor — Other Favored Policies.*

In determining whether a purpose of the promisor is to have the promisee suffer the detriment or whether the detriment is a mere incident to the completion of a gift or other benefit to the promisee, courts may consider the extent of the detriment to the promisee[45] or the purpose of the promise, i.e., if the purpose of the promise is favored in the eyes of the law, a court will be easily satisfied that the promise was bargained-for even though considerable doubt exists as to whether the promisor sought the detriment in exchange for his or her promise.[46] Similarly, courts may discover a bargained-for-exchange in highly doubtful circumstances if they are eager to modify outmoded or mistaken contract doctrines that may be said to perpetuate injustice. Thus, to modify the traditional "terminable-at-will" doctrine governing employment contracts with no stated duration, a number of courts have discovered a bargained-for-exchange from statements in a manual, handbook or stated policy issued by the employer subsequent to the employment contract which allegedly contain promises by the employer with a purpose of having the employee suffer the detriment of continuing his or her employment, thereby forming a unilateral contract by the employee's continued performance.[47] As will be seen

---

[45] *See, e.g.*, Davies v. Rhonda Dist. Urban Council 87 L. J. (K.B.) (n.s.) 166 [1917] (defendant promised to continue the salary of any teacher who enlisted in the army); Miller v. Bank of Holly Springs, 131 Miss. 55, 95 So. 129, 31 A.L.R. 698 (1923) (bank promised to keep customer's savings stamps in its regular vaults if he could continue to leave them in its care. The bank failed to perform its promise and the stamps were stolen).

[46] The classic example is the celebrated opinion by Judge Cardozo in De Cicco v. Schweizer, 221 N.Y. 431, 117 N.E. 807, 810 (1924) where consideration was found to support a promise of a father to his prospective son-in-law to pay an annuity to his daughter after the marriage even though the parties were affianced at the time of the promise. In a highly creative opinion, Judge Cardozo had to deal with the pre-existing duty rule (to be discussed later in this chapter). He discovered a promise to the daughter as well as the son-in-law on the assumption that the daughter had learned of the father's promise. With two promisees, he then created a forbearance by the promisees to rescind their prior agreement to marry and found that such forbearance was bargained-for by the father, i.e., it was the father's purpose to have the parties suffer the detriment of not rescinding their marriage agreement. At the conclusion of his opinion, however, Judge Cardozo admits that "marriage settlements" are highly favored by the courts and are enforced "where consideration, if present at all, has been dependent upon doubtful inference.... It strains, if need be, to the uttermost interpretation of equivocal words and conduct in the effort to hold men to the honorable fulfillment of engagements designed to influence in their deepest relations the lives of others." A similar Cardozo effort is found in another celebrated opinion, Allegheny College v. National Chautauqua Cty. Bank, 246 N.Y. 369, 159 N.E. 173 (1927) where Judge Cardozo provides a pedagogical analysis of the doctrine of promissory estoppel (detrimental reliance) and proceeds to discover a bargained-for-exchange supporting a charitable subscription promise. Such promises are looked upon with great favor by the courts as will be seen later in this chapter. *See* RESTATEMENT § 90(2) which makes charitable subscription or marriage settlement promises binding without proof of any bargained-for exchange.

[47] *See, e.g.*, Continental Air Lines, Inc. v. Keenan, 731 P.2d 708 (Colo. 1987); Bachelder v. Communications Satellite Corp., 657 F. Supp. 423 (D. Me. 1987); Duldulao v. Saint Mary of Nazareth Hosp., 115 Ill. 2d 482, 505 N.E.2d 314 (1987) and other cases cited in *supra* § 45(C). See, however, Johnson v. National Beef Packing Co., 220 Kan. 52, 551 P.2d 779 (1976) holding that such promises by an employer are not bargained-for. *See also* Matlock v. Data Processing Sec., Inc., 607 S.W.2d 946 (Tex. Civ. App. 1980) holding that a promise not to compete after severance from the employer was supported by the employer's forbearance from discontinuing the employment relationship even though the promise was made after the employment contract was formed. See, however, George W. Kistler, Inc. v. O'Brien, 464 Pa. 475, 347 A.2d 311 (1975) holding that such covenants not to compete made after the employment relationship is already established

in the remainder of our exploration of the concept of consideration, there are other situations in which courts find consideration with little or no discussion of the bargained-for-exchange element. In some of these cases, there is little doubt that courts have unwittingly ignored that element. In others, there is equally little doubt that courts have deliberately ignored it to achieve what they perceive to be just and desirable results.[48]

§ 61. Nominal, Formal, and "Sham" Consideration — Must the Detriment Be a Real Inducement or Motive?

A. *Nominal Consideration — FIRST RESTATEMENT and RESTATEMENT 2d Distinguished.*

If Ames wants to make a legally enforceable gratuitous promise, i.e., a promise to give Barnes, her nephew, land worth $100,000, absent the availability of the seal or a more modern formalistic validation device, Ames confronts a significant problem. She may attempt to make her promise to Barnes enforceable by the creation of a document evidencing a promise to convey the land to Barnes in exchange for one dollar which Barnes promises to pay. If the parties sign this document and Barnes then pays one dollar to Ames, should Ames' promise be binding? It is patently clear that the payment of one dollar, albeit a detriment to Barnes, did not motivate or induce Ames to promise to convey the valuable land.[49] The statement or "recital" of consideration in such a document is a mere formality often called "nominal" consideration and it is so understood by the parties. Since there is no bargained-for-exchange involved in such a transaction, it is impossible to characterize the promise by Ames as supported by consideration. If, however, a court merely requires a formal exchange — a sham bargain — to constitute what it calls consideration without any bargained-for-exchange, the promise will be enforceable. Some decisions cannot easily be explained on any other basis.[50] The FIRST RESTATE-

---

requires new consideration which is not found in the continuation of the employment relationship despite the fact that the employment contract was terminable at will.

[48] When courts "discover" bargained-for-exchange in a situation where it apparently does not exist, the result they seek to achieve is often desirable. In such cases, it would be preferable for courts to dispense with the fiction that bargained-for-exchange and, therefore, consideration exists, and to arrive at the desired result on the basis of sound policy reasons. Such an approach would promote law settlement, i.e., predictability and consistency which are, indeed, high values in any legal system.

[49] It is frequently said that consideration must not be confounded with motive. Thus, in Clayman v. Bibler, 210 Iowa 497, 231 N.W. 334, 336 (1930), the court distinguishes these concepts: "'Motive' and 'consideration' are not identical. The expectation of a definite result is often the motive which prompts the execution of a contract. Such expectation is not, however, binding. Ordinarily, 'consideration' is the price paid for the undertaking of the promisor...." While it is undoubtedly true that a promise is not binding simply because it was made as the result of a worthwhile motive, as Justice Holmes suggests, "[I]t is of the essence of consideration, that by the terms of the agreement, it is given and accepted as the motive or inducement of the promise." O. W. HOLMES, THE COMMON LAW 293 (1881).

[50] The best known example is Thomas v. Thomas, 2 Q.B. 852, 114 Eng. Rep. 330 [1842] in which the brothers of the deceased, in order to carry out his wishes, promised to convey a life estate in certain property in exchange for a promise to pay £1 per year and to keep the premises in good repair. The court found that the promise to pay £1 annually clearly established consideration. There is little question that the brothers were not induced to make their promise to convey the life estate in exchange for the nominal payment or even the promise of good repair, i.e., there was no bargained-for-exchange. The court seems disposed to enforce the promise to carry out the

MENT supports this view.[51] The RESTATEMENT 2d, however, finds no consideration where there is "a mere pretense of bargain ... as where there is a false recital of consideration or where the purported consideration is merely nominal."[52] While the RESTATEMENT 2d insists that mere pretense of a bargain — "sham consideration" — is not consideration, that situation must be distinguished from another involving a combination of bargain and gift in which the dominant motivation of the promisor may be gratuitous.

B. *Bargain and Gift Motivations Combined — Other Motivations.*

If Jane Ames has a house for sale which has a reasonable market value of $100,000, is her agreement to sell that house to her only child for $25,000 supported by consideration? The situation differs markedly from one in which the promisor is willing to part with property worth $100,000 for one dollar since $25,000 is, on its face, more than nominal consideration. Ames would not sell the house for $25,000 to anyone in the world except her only child. Clearly, she is motivated to make a gift to her child. Yet, Ames' promise is supported by consideration. Beyond the fact that $25,000 is clearly more than nominal in this example,[53] courts should find consideration for several reasons. As seen earlier in this chapter,[54] courts will not normally inquire into the adequacy of consideration, i.e., the relative values exchanged by the parties. That rationale, however, misses the mark since the question remains, was the detriment bargained for? Even though Ames appears to be motivated by a desire to make a gift to her child, she also appears to want the payment of $25,000 from her child, i.e., the detriment to the promisee-child is something Ames desires in exchange for her promise. Numerous reasons may be hypothesized for this desire. She may not be able to afford a complete gift of the property, or, perhaps Ames is very wealthy and wants the child to pay $25,000 only for the purpose of ascertaining that the child develop a sense of responsibility in financial matters. Whatever her motivation, the fact that she insists upon the detriment from the child in exchange for the property indicates that the detriment is bargained-for.[55] The fact that the dominant motivation of Ames is gratuitous is also irrelevant. A promisor may have a number of

deathbed wishes of the husband and to regard the payment of £1 annually as consideration because it was a detriment to the promisee, notwithstanding the lack of bargained-for-exchange. Other cases have been collected in 24 COLUM. L. REV. 896 (1924) and 27 MICH. L. REV. (1928).

[51] FIRST RESTATEMENT § 84 ill. 1, suggests that a promise by *A* to convey land worth $5000 to *B* in exchange for one dollar is supported by "sufficient" consideration.

[52] RESTATEMENT 2d § 71 comment b. In ill. 5 to this section of the RESTATEMENT 2d, *A* desires to make a binding promise to give $1000 to *B*. Recognizing the unenforceability of gratuitous promises, *A* offers to purchase a book worth less than $1 from *B* for a price of $1000. "There is no consideration for *A*'s promise to pay $1000." Among the cases supporting this view, *see* Fisher v. Union Trust Co., 138 Mich. 612, 101 N.W. 852 (1904); Shepard v. Rhodes, 7 R.I. 470, 84 Am. Dec. 573 (1863). The RESTATEMENT 2d position, however, should be carefully distinguished from its position with respect to recital clauses in guaranty or option contracts discussed later in subsection (C) of this section.

[53] It is conceivable that $25,000 could be nominal consideration to a multi-billionaire with a millionaire child in the sale of property worth millions of dollars.

[54] *See supra* § 59.

[55] *See* RESTATEMENT 2d § 71 comment c: "Even where both parties know that a transaction is in part a bargain and in part a gift, the element of bargain may nevertheless furnish consideration for the entire transaction."

motivations in her bargain with a promisee including the motivation to make a gift. The principal desire of Ames may be to give the property to her child. If, however, she also wants the $25,000 payment in exchange for her promise, her promise is supported by consideration. As the RESTATEMENT 2d suggests, "Unless both parties know that the purported consideration is mere pretense, it is immaterial that the promisor's desire for the consideration is incidental to other objectives and even that the other party knows this to be so."[56] The motivations other than a desire for the detriment may be of an almost endless variety, i.e., they need not be gratuitous. At this point, one should recall the analogous situation involving the question of the motivation of an offeree who, with knowledge of an offer, performs the act requested in the offer. In the earlier exploration of that concept, we saw that such an offeree accepts the offer by performing the act, notwithstanding evidence that his motivation for performing it was dominantly for reasons other than his desire to accept the offer, so long as he still apparently intended to accept the offer by his performance.[57] Just as mixed motivation does not prevent acceptance of an offer, mixed motivation does not preclude a finding of bargained-for-exchange. Again, however, the detriment must, to some extent, induce the promise if consideration is to be found in support of the promise.

C. Recital of Consideration — Option and Guaranty Contracts.

1. Option Contracts.

The concept of the option contract was explored earlier.[58] The purpose of an option contract is to keep another offer, the main offer, open, i.e., irrevocable, for the time stated in the option contract or, if no time is stated, for a reasonable time. If Ames offers to sell her land to Barnes for $100,000 and Barnes desires to have the offer made irrevocable, the parties may enter into an option contract to achieve that effect. Option contracts often contain "recitals" of consideration, i.e., statements such as, "In consideration of one dollar in hand paid,[59] Ames grants an option to Barnes to purchase Ames' land (described) at a price of $100,000 for ninety days from the date of this option contract." It may be difficult to measure the worth of the right the option holder receives under an option contract. If he has an irrevocable power of acceptance for a lengthy period, however, it is often difficult to believe that the owner of the land surrendered her right to sell that land to any other party during the option period in exchange for a consideration as nominal as one dollar or a slightly higher though still apparently nominal sum. There are numerous cases involving recited consideration of one, five or ten dollars, where the question of whether that nominal amount was bargained for is not explored.[60] It is not a sufficient answer to the question of whether the amount

---

[56] RESTATEMENT 2d § 81 comment b.

[57] See supra § 44(C).

[58] Section 43(B).

[59] At this point, many "recitals" contain the phrase, "receipt whereof is hereby acknowledged."

[60] For example, in Solomon Mier Co. v. Hadden, 148 Mich. 488, 11 N.W. 1040 (1907), the option contract provided the offeree with an irrevocable offer from June, 1906 to November 1, 1906 for a payment of one dollar. There was no discussion of whether the one dollar was bargained-for. A

was bargained-for to suggest that courts do not inquire into the adequacy (relative values) of consideration. While the RESTATEMENT 2d suggests the difficulty of determining the worth of the irrevocability of offers, it clearly admits that gross disproportion between the amount paid by the option holder and the value of the option typically indicates that there was no bargained-for-exchange.[61] Notwithstanding the lack of consideration, the RESTATEMENT 2d suggests that a recital of nominal consideration which is, essentially, a fiction or, more bluntly, a lie, is "sufficient to support a short-time option proposing an exchange on fair terms."[62] The rationale is important: "The fact that the option is an appropriate preliminary step in the conclusion of a socially useful transaction provides sufficient substantive basis for enforcement, and a signed writing taking a form appropriate to a bargain satisfied the desiderata of form."[63] The operative term in this rationale is *form*. The part of the RESTATEMENT 2d in which this rationale appears collects thirteen sections under the caption, "Contracts Without Consideration."[64] It is clear that the RESTATEMENT 2d suggests that recital clauses in option contracts have been and should continue to be regarded as formalistic validation devices which have nothing to do with consideration. Yet, the particular *form* of these validation devices should be a "signed writing taking a form appropriate to a bargain...."[65] By reciting the payment of nominal consideration in a signed writing, therefore, a promise to keep an offer open is made enforceable even though it is clear that there is no consideration in terms of any bargained-for-exchange. The recital of consideration takes on a life of its own, i.e., it has the same effect as the seal (prior to its abolishment or severe modification) or a modern formalistic validation device such as a "firm offer" under the UCC.[66] The paucity of formalistic validation devices created by statute is made emphatically clear by this example of the willingness of courts to ignore the bargained-for-exchange requirement. The recital formalistic device, however, is not a creature of statute; it is judicially created and maintained by deliberately ignoring the bargained-for-exchange requirement.

It should be emphasized that there is no reason why a formalistic validation device cannot be judicially created. The sole difficulty has been the reluctance of courts to admit what they were doing. The RESTATEMENT 2d openly confesses the lack of any consideration and the "socially useful" desirability of recital clauses to make promises enforceable under option contracts. It properly qualifies the strength of this device by insisting that the terms of the main contract, i.e., the land for the price, be fair. What may appear to be a second qualification, however, may be questioned. The RESTATEMENT 2d may be read to suggest that recital device will be effective only for "short-term" options. On its face, this appears to be another fairness safeguard similar to that found in the "firm offer" section of the UCC though, for reasons that

recital clause in a release of liability is often said to "import consideration." *See, e.g.,* Buddy L. Inc. v. General Trailer Co., 672 S.W.2d 541 (Tex. App. 1984).

[61] RESTATEMENT 2d § 87 comment b.
[62] *Ibid.*
[63] *Ibid.*
[64] This is "Topic 2" of the RESTATEMENT 2d which includes §§ 82-94.
[65] RESTATEMENT 2d § 87 comment b.
[66] *See supra* § 43(C).

appear below, it is more than questionable as to whether the RESTATEMENT 2d would insist upon this "short-term" qualification.[67] If safeguards were thought desirable, i.e., if there was concern that the offeror may not recognize that his offer will become irrevocable because of the recital clause in the signed writing, other possible safeguards may be desirable. Recital clauses often appear in printed forms that may not be in conspicuous print[68] and the forms may be supplied by the party who seeks to obtain the option.[69] There is no suggestion that such clauses be made so apparent that they would be understood by a reasonable party under the particular circumstances of the signing. It may be highly desirable to require separate authentication of a recital clause, at least by a party who is not in the practice of signing such documents such as a home owner signing a document containing a recital clause prepared by the prospective buyer.[70] While separate authentication requirements are created by statute, since the recital validation device is a judicial creation, its safeguards could be judicially engrafted. These or other safeguards are not mentioned in the RESTATEMENT 2d. Moreover, it is unlikely that the RESTATEMENT 2d would insist upon the "short-term" qualification.

One illustration in the RESTATEMENT 2d suggests the payment of twenty-five cents for a 120-day option on a tract of land priced at $100,000.[71] Since the terms of the exchange of land for a price of $100,000 are fair, the option is effective making the offer irrevocable for four months.[72] The notion that only "short term" options are made effective through the formalistic recital device is made even more dubious by another illustration[73] in which a ten-year option to take phosphate from land is supported by the payment of one dollar. The terms of the main contract require the taker to pay a royalty of twenty-five cents per ton on phosphate taken from the land. The taker knows that the prevailing royalty exceeds one dollar per ton. The terms of the main exchange, therefore, are not fair and the RESTATEMENT 2d concludes that the offer is not made irrevocable by the one dollar payment for the option.[74] Presumably, had

---

[67] Section 2-205 of the UCC limits the firm (irrevocable) offer to three months. For the other limitations on this formalistic validation device created by statute, see supra § 43(C). RESTATEMENT 2d § 87 comment d refers to § 2-205 of the Code. However, the three-month limitation of that section is not mentioned in the rationale for "short-term" options supported by a recital of nominal consideration in comment b of § 87. The limitation, however, is so obviously similar to the three-month limitation of § 2-205 that it [could be viewed] as a "fairness" safeguard.

[68] Analogously, the UCC requires a particular method of disclaiming implied warranties to be conspicuous if in writing. UCC § 2-316(2). UCC § 1-201(10) defines "conspicuous" to mean "A term or clause [that] is so written that a reasonable person against whom it is to operate ought to have noticed it." The definition appears to relate to physical conspicuousness, i.e., the size or other attention-calling nature of the print. A clause that is capitalized, italicized, printed in bold face, or otherwise attention-calling, however, may still not be comprehensible to a reasonable person who is asked to sign the document containing such clause. It may be suggested that material, risk-shifting clauses ought to be "substantively" as well as physically conspicuous, i.e., they ought to be understandable, to the reasonable person in terms of the risks sought to be imposed upon the signer.

[69] In the UCC firm offer situation, § 2-205 requires a separate authentication of a firm offer clause in a form supplied by the offeree, i.e., the party who will benefit from the firm offer.

[70] Cf. UCC § 2-209(2) which requires the separate signing of no oral modification clauses by non-merchants if such parties are to be bound by such clauses.

[71] RESTATEMENT 2d § 87 ill. 1.

[72] The illustration is based on Marsh v. Lott, 8 Cal. App. 384, 97 P. 1163 (1908).

[73] RESTATEMENT 2d § 87 ill. 2.

[74] The illustration is based on Killebrew v. Murray, 151 Ky. 345, 151 S.W. 662 (1912).

the royalty payment been set at prevailing market rates, the ten-year option in exchange for one dollar would be effective. Consequently, the statement in the RESTATEMENT 2d that a nominal, unbargained-for, consideration recorded in a recital clause "is regularly held sufficient to support a *short-term* option proposing an exchange on fair terms,"[75] simply represents holdings in a number of cases. The RESTATEMENT 2d will insist only that the main exchange is on fair terms, i.e., apparently it will not insist on the "short-term" qualification.

2. Guaranty Contracts.

A guaranty or suretyship contract is one in which the surety or guarantor promises to pay the debt of another (the principal obligor) if the principal fails to pay. A bank or other lender of money or credit may not be willing to suffer a detriment on the promise of the principal, alone. If, however, the principal arranges for a surety (guarantor), the creditor is willing to assume the risk. If a party becomes a surety at the time the credit is extended, there is no consideration problem, i.e., the loan or credit extended is a detriment inducing the promise of the principal debtor and the guarantor. If, however, the creditor and principal debtor have contracted prior to the promise of the surety, the surety's promise must be supported by consideration or another validation device.[76] The RESTATEMENT 2d adopts the position set forth above concerning option contracts with respect to guaranty promises, i.e., if it recites a nominal consideration in writing, it is difficult to determine whether that amount was bargained for. Even if it is shown to have been a mere formality or pretense, the recital clause is effective as a formalistic validation device to support the guarantor's promise.[77]

3. Recited Nominal Consideration in Option or Guaranty Contract Not Paid.

If clauses reciting the payment of one dollar in option or guaranty contracts are to be enforceable though the recited amount was not, in fact, bargained for, the question arises, suppose it can be shown that the recited amount was not paid. Should that fact cause the recital clause to be ineffective as a formalistic validation device? In the well-known case of *Lawrence v. McCalmont*,[78] Mr. Justice Story dealt with a clause reciting the payment of one dollar to a guarantor who had not, in fact, received the dollar.

> "The guarantor acknowledged the receipt of the one dollar and is now estopped to deny it. If she has not received it, she would now be entitled to recover it. A valuable consideration, however small or nominal, if given or stipulated for in good faith, is, in the absence of fraud, sufficient to support an action on any parol contract...."

[75] RESTATEMENT 2d § 87 comment b (emphasis added).

[76] A guaranty promise may also be binding because of the reliance of the creditor, RESTATEMENT 2d § 88(c) and comment d. It may also be statutorily binding, *e.g.*, UCC §§ 3-113 and 3-408 and RESTATEMENT 2d § 88(b). If there is a failure of consideration in the contract between the principal debtor and the creditor, the guarantor may assert that defense when called upon to pay the debt. Jones v. Dixie O'Brien Div., O'Brien Corp., 174 Ga. App. 67, 329 S.E.2d 256 (1985).

[77] RESTATEMENT 2d § 88(a) and comment b.

[78] 43 U.S. (2 How.) 426, 452 (1844).

The RESTATEMENT 2d expressly adopts the view that a clause reciting nominal consideration in either a guaranty or an option contract should operate as a formalistic validation device, supporting the promise in either type of contract, regardless of the fact that the recited amount was never paid:[79]

> The signed writing has vital significance as a formality while the ceremonial manual delivery of a dollar or peppercorn is an inconsequential formality. In view of the dangers of permitting a solemn written agreement to be invalidated by oral testimony which is easily fabricated, therefore, the option [or guaranty] agreement is not invalidated by proof that the recited consideration was not in fact given.[80]

The RESTATEMENT 2d position maintains total consistency with its view that a recital clause should be treated as a formalistic validation device. The guaranty or option contract promise supported by such a device is made enforceable exclusively because of the *form* of the written promise. A formalistic validation device is effective exclusively because it signals the enforceability of a promise by the appearance of the promise, i.e., on its face, it is recognized as an enforceable promise because of the particular form of the promise. There is no consideration in the typical recital clause since the amount recited therein is not bargained for. Under these circumstances, it is irrelevant whether the recited amount has or has not been paid since the payment of a nominal sum is not the inducement for the promise. Notwithstanding the compelling view of the RESTATEMENT 2d, however, most courts will not only permit evidence to the effect that the recited amount has not been paid; upon proof that the recited amount has not, in fact, been paid, they will find that the promise fails for want of consideration.[81] Since the typical recital clause does not evidence consideration even if the nominal amount recited was paid, to suggest that evidence revealing the falsity of the recital converts a promise supported by consideration into one not supported by consideration is analytically unsound. If a court deludes itself into believing that the typical recital clause evidences genuine consideration, i.e., that the one dollar or other nominal sum was bargained for, evidence that the sum was not paid should result in a finding of a *failure* of consideration, i.e., a breach by the party who was to pay the consideration, rather than the absurd notion that the failure to pay converts the option or guaranty promise into one not supported by consideration at the time the promise was made. To address that possibility, courts in Georgia have adopted the view that evidence of failure to pay creates an implied promise to pay the nominal consideration thereby making the promise enforceable.[82] The RESTATEMENT 2d properly rejects this view, again, on the basis that the recited consideration was not bargained for whether it was

---

[79] RESTATEMENT 2d § 87 comment c and § 88 comment b.

[80] RESTATEMENT 2d § 87 comment c. The parol evidence rule would not bar evidence that a fact recited in an integrated agreement is untrue. RESTATEMENT 2d § 218.

[81] *See* Lewis v. Fletcher, 101 Idaho 530, 617 P.2d 834 (1980) and cases cited therein. The best-known case supporting this view is an opinion by Justice Traynor in Bard v. Kent, 19 Cal. 3d 449, 122 P.2d 8 (1942).

[82] *See* Jones v. Smith, 206 Ga. 162, 56 S.E.2d 462 (1949); Smith v. Wheeler, 233 Ga. 166, 210 S.E.2d 702 (1974); Baumer v. United States, 580 F.2d 863 (5th Cir. 1978), *rehearing denied,* 585 F.2d 520 (5th Cir. 1978) (applying Georgia law).

paid, impliedly promised to be paid, or not paid.[83] Even the case law holding that the promisor will be estopped from attempting to prove that the recited amount was not paid, which may appear to support the RESTATEMENT 2d position, is not predicated upon the RESTATEMENT 2d rationale that the recital should operate as a formalistic validation device. Rather, it is based on the notion that, absent fraud, one who acknowledges receipt of consideration should not be heard to deny that which he had previously acknowledged in a written recital.[84] The RESTATEMENT 2d position that forthrightly acknowledges the absence of any consideration in recital clauses and proceeds to strip away any fiction in arriving at a thoroughly consistent position that such clauses should be viewed as judicially created formalistic validation devices regardless of whether the recited amount has been paid, presents a compelling analysis that courts would do well to adopt.

§ 62. Consideration in Charitable Subscription Agreements.

When a promise is made to a charitable institution, e.g., a church, hospital, educational institution or similar institution, is such a promise supported by consideration? In most cases, the truthful answer is, no, because it is clear that the typical promise to a charity is intended to be gratuitous, i.e., it is motivated, not by the desire to receive something in return, but rather by feelings of generosity, duty, the hope of heavenly reward or some other ethereal aspiration which the promisee could not possibly provide. It is, of course, possible that the promisor seeks recognition from his promise of a gift. In a famous opinion, Judge Cardozo reminds us that, "The longing for posthumous remembrance is an emotion not so weak as to justify us in saying that its gratification is a negligible good."[85] A particular promisor may, for example, combine a gratuitous motivation with a genuine desire to have a university building, a university chair or a hospital wing dedicated in his name. It is even possible that another promisor may make a subscription promise with no gratuitous motivation whatsoever, i.e., he or she would be exclusively concerned with a named memorial. If a charity or school promised to name something in exchange for the promise, a detriment is clearly present. Again, however, whether that detriment was bargained for or whether the naming of a building or the like was a mere condition to a gratuitous promise raises questions of interpretation that can be very difficult in a given situation. Courts look upon charities, schools and the like as institutions that perform useful public service. It is, therefore, not remarkable that courts should demonstrate a proclivity to discover a validation device to make the promise of the subscriber enforceable. While English courts took the strictly logical view that such promises are gratuitous and, therefore, unenforceable in the normal case,[86] our courts have managed to discover one or another validation device

[83] RESTATEMENT 2d § 87 comment c.

[84] Real Estate Co. of Pittsburgh v. Rudolph, 301 Pa. 5502, 153 A. 438 (1930) which expressly relies upon Lawrence v. McCalmont, *supra* note 78.

[85] Allegheny College v. National Chautauqua Cty. Bank, 246 N.Y. 369, 159 N.E. 173, 176 (1927).

[86] *See* Governors of Dalhousie College v. Boutilier, 3 D.L.R. 593 [1934]; *In re* Hudson, 54 L.J. Ch. 811 [1885].

to make the promises enforceable.[87] In seeking a device, some courts have stretched to find an implied promise on the part of the charity to continue its humanitarian work[88] or to perpetuate the name of the donor in connection with a memorial fund she promised to establish.[89] Often, a subscription or charity fund drive will identify the purpose of the drive leading some courts to discover an implied promise by the charity to use the funds in accordance with the terms of the subscription.[90] Another imaginative effort is used by some courts which discover consideration in the mutual promises of subscribers, i.e., *A* subscribes in consideration of *B*'s promise which is consideration of *C*'s subscription and the like with the charity receiving the benefit as a donee beneficiary of the contract.[91] Beyond the fact that the typical subscriber is not bargaining for the promises of others, he is not making his promise to other subscribers, i.e., he is making his promise to the charity which is a promisee and not a third party beneficiary of the mutual promises of others.[92] Another judicial initiative is found in those cases which enforce charitable subscription promises on the basis of detrimental reliance (promissory estoppel), i.e., the charity has relied on the promise(s) to its substantial detriment.[93] Whatever the merits of this theory generally, in a given situation it may be more than difficult to discover any substantial change of position on the part of the charity in reliance on one or more subscription promises.[94]

---

[87]"There can be no denying that the strong desire on the part of the American courts to favor charitable institutions has established a doctrine which one would have been looked upon as legal heresy. Doubtless this judicial attitude is largely responsible for the massive machinery of benevolence to be observed on every side. The reasons announced in justification of these holdings, however, have not always been technically satisfying." Danby v. Osteopathic Hosp. Ass'n of Del., 34 Del. Ch. 427, 104 A.2d 903, 907 (1954).

[88]I. & I. Holding Corp. v. Gainsburg, 276 N.Y. 427, 12 N.E.2d 532 (1938).

[89]Allegheny College, *supra* note 85.

[90]*In re* Couch's Estate, 170 Neb. 518, 103 N.W.2d 274 (1960); Central Maine Gen. Hosp. v. Carter, 125 Me. 191, 132 A. 417, 44 A.L.R. 1333 (1926).

[91]*See* Congregation B'nai Sholom v. Martin, 382 Mich. 659, 173 N.W.2d 504 (1969). However, in Jordan v. Mount Sinai Hosp., 276 So. 2d 102 (Dist. App. 1973), aff'd, 290 So. 2d 484 (Fla. 1974), a recital that the promise was in consideration of and to induce the subscriptions of others was held ineffective. The consideration-among-subscribers theory may also be pursued in the "bellweather" situation of a promise by a major contributor whose promise is conditioned upon other subscribers matching the amount promised or reaching some other goal.

[92]Third party beneficiary contracts will be fully explored in a later chapter.

[93]*See* Danby v. Osteopathic Hosp. Ass'n, *supra* note 87; Thompson v. McAllen Federated Woman's Bldg. Corp., 273 S.W.2d 105 (Tex. Civ. App. 1954); Trustees of Baker Univ. v. Clelland, 76 F.2d 14 (8th Cir. 1936); Miller v. Western College, 177 Ill. 280, 52 N.E. 432 (1898). The detrimental reliance (promissory estoppel) validation device will be fully explored later in this chapter.

[94]In the famous *Allegheny College* opinion, *supra* note 85, which undoubtedly prompted subsequent courts to use the detrimental reliance device to support charitable subscription promises, Judge Cardozo provides a *tour de force* of the application of detrimental reliance to such promises. He then finds, however, that there is no need to resort to the detrimental reliance device since the facts can be fitted within the traditional mold of consideration by finding an implied promise on the part of the College to forever promulgate the memorial fund in the name of the donor, Mary Yates Johnson. There is more than a suspicion that Judge Cardozo recognized a problem in the application of the detrimental reliance device to the facts of the case, i.e., that no particular reliance by the College could be shown. This may be said to have forced him to find consideration which he discovers in typical Cardozo fashion, by creatively circumventing any lack of bargained-for-exchange and discovering an implied promise by activating the Cardozo implication machine. Whatever criticisms may be made of this opinion, if forced to use only one judicial opinion to pursue the concepts of consideration, detrimental reliance, and all other actual and possible validation devices, this author, in his capacity as a teacher of contract law, would, without

For many years it has been an open secret that courts will typically discover means to enforce promises which they favor whether they are charitable subscription promises or marriage settlement promises.[95] Instead of resorting to myriad fictions, no matter how creative or entertaining, the high values of predictability and certainty in the law long ago suggested the desirability of a candid recognition that such promises, albeit gratuitous, should be enforceable simply because institutions such as charities, schools and the institution of marriage are socially useful and desirable and that promises made to benefit and help perpetuate them should be enforced. Fortunately, the RESTATEMENT 2d has adopted the candid approach in stating[96] that charitable subscription or marriage settlement promises are enforceable though there is no evidence that they induced any action or forbearance (much less bargained-for action or forbearance) on the part of the promisee.[97] They are enforced simply because it is desirable, as a matter of public policy, to enforce them.

§ 63. Forbearance From Suit as Consideration — The Invalid Claim.

A promise to forbear suit on a valid claim is a detriment that, if bargained-for, clearly constitutes consideration for a counter-promise. If, however, the claim which is surrendered is groundless or invalid, the immediate tendency is to suggest that it cannot constitute consideration because it is a surrender of nothing of value in the eyes of the law. On the other hand, a promise to forego a lawsuit may be viewed as the surrender of a legal right since there are no impediments to the bringing of an action. Yet, examples leap to mind that suggest the folly of this notion. If Ames, knowing that she has no claim whatsoever against Barnes, promises to forego suing Barnes in exchange for Barnes' promise to pay Ames $1000, Barnes may be justifiably concerned that he will be forced to defend against even a groundless claim and may choose to promise Ames $1000. If such promises were enforceable, the knaves of any era would quickly discover a form of legal extortion. A party may have the power to do something which he has no legal right to pursue simply because there is no effective method of prevention. It would hardly be good policy to permit such an action when the party bringing it knows that his claim is groundless. If, however, the claimant honestly believes that his claim is valid, it is at least

---

hesitation, choose the *Allegheny College* opinion. *Inter alia,* the discussion of consideration in this opinion is a premier pedagogical effort.

[95] See the estimable effort by Judge Cardozo in De Cicco v. Schweizer, 221 N.Y. 431, 117 N.E. 807 (1917) where he singlehandedly creates a promisee out of a third party beneficiary, finds that the created promisee impliedly agreed with the real promisee not to rescind their agreement to marry, and discovers that detriment as having induced a marriage settlement promise by the father of the bride to pay an annuity to his married daughter notwithstanding clear evidence of the donative intent of the father-promisor. In the end, however, Judge Cardozo freely admits that he has concocted the whole analysis to ascertain the enforcement of marriage settlement promises which the law clearly favors.

[96] The term "stating" rather than "restating" is used since this concept was not supported by prior case law. It is more than unusual for a "restatement" of the law to assert a totally new concept. Ample precedent existed, however, with respect to the result. The RESTATEMENT 2d simply eschews the fictions typically used by courts to arrive at the result and recognizes the clear judicial proclivity to enforce charitable subscription and marriage settlement promises notwithstanding their gratuitous character.

[97] RESTATEMENT 2d § 90. This approach has been expressly followed in Salsbury v. Northwestern Bell Tel. Co., 221 N.W.2d 609 (Iowa 1974).

arguable that he has a right rather than a mere power to bring the action, whatever the merits of his case may later prove to be. One of the reasons for the existence of our courts is the desideratum of having tribunals with power to determine the justice of claims honestly made. On this view of the matter, it can be persuasively argued that one who honestly believes he has a claim has a legal right to prosecute it and, if he surrenders that right, suffers a legal detriment that, if bargained for, will support a promise to pay for the surrender of that right.

In light of the foregoing discussion, the evolution of the judicial reaction to promises to forbear suit on an invalid claim was not remarkable. There are three discernible stages of that development at common law. In the first stage, courts held that the surrender of a groundless claim could not be consideration under any circumstances.[98] Some time later, the English courts began to hold that, if the surrendered claim was in fact doubtful, i.e., if either the facts or the law were in doubt, then refraining from suit would be consideration for a promise even though it should ultimately appear that the claim was groundless.[99] Then, in the latter part of the nineteenth century, the present rule evolved, i.e., one who surrenders a claim which he honestly believes he may enforce will constitute a bargained-for detriment.[1] Each of these stages in the evolution of the law in England is reflected in American decisions.

A few American cases take the view that the surrender of a groundless claim, regardless of honest belief in the assertion of the claim, cannot constitute consideration.[2] The dominant view, however, is reflected in the FIRST RESTATEMENT of Contracts: forbearance to assert an invalid claim would constitute consideration only if the party asserting the claim had *both* an honest *and* reasonable belief in the possible validity of the claim and this view was widely followed.[3] The party asserting the claim had to be asserting it in good

---

[98] *See* Johnes v. Ashburnham, 4 East 455 [1804]; Loyd v. Lee, 1 Str. 94 [1718]; Barnard v. Simons, 1 Rolle's Abr. 26, pl. 39 [1616].

[99] Longridge v. Dorville, 5 B. & Ald. 117 [1821].

[1] *See* Miles v. New Zealand Alford Estate Co., 32 Ch. D. 266 [1886].

[2] *See* State *ex rel.* Ludwick v. Bryant, 237 Kan. 47, 697 P.2d 858 (1985), suggesting that the issue was not the validity of the debt but the possibility of enforcing it. If there is no possibility of enforcing a claim, both the claim and forbearance to press it are valueless and cannot constitute consideration. The court quotes Professor Corbin at 1 CORBIN § 140, pp. 600-01 for this view. The Corbin statement, however, is merely descriptive of the position taken by some courts and is followed by, "Some of these decisions seem not in harmony with generally prevailing decisions...." (601). Another well-known but much earlier opinion from the Supreme Court of Kansas, Ralston v. Mathew, 173 Kan. 550, 250 P.2d 841 (1952) relies upon even earlier Kansas precedent in suggesting that forbearance to assert a claim that is reasonably doubtful and not obviously invalid, worthless, or frivolous, constitutes consideration. Such a reasonably doubtful but ultimately invalid claim would constitute consideration. In the *Ludwick* case, however, even if a claim were valid, if it were not enforceable, forbearance to assert it could not be consideration. In Orange Cty. Found. v. Irvine Co., 139 Cal. App. 3d 195, 188 Cal. Rptr. 552, 555 (1983), the court states, "Compromise of a wholly invalid claim is inadequate consideration to support a contract." The case, however, dealt with the appropriateness of a summary judgment where the pleadings alleged bad faith. Renney v. Kimberly, 211 Ga. 396, 86 S.E.2d 217 (1955) is the only recent American case clearly holding that forbearance to sue on a groundless claim cannot constitute consideration.

[3] FIRST RESTATEMENT § 76(b). This view finds wide support in the case law. *See, e.g.,* Agristor Credit Corp. v. Unruh, 571 P.2d 1220 (Okla. 1977); Jacobs v. Atlantco Ltd. Pt'ship No. 1, 36 Md. App. 335, 373 A.2d 1255 (1977); Intermodal Transp. Sys. v. Hucks Piggyback Serv., 30 N.C. App. 289, 226 S.E.2d 859 (1976). *See also* Fiege v. Boehm, 210 Md. 316, 123 A.2d 316 (1956) requiring a *bona fide* assertion of a claim that is not obviously unfounded, citing FIRST RESTATEMENT § 76(b).

faith *and* that assertion had to be premised upon a claim that had some merit in fact or in law. While there was no question concerning the requirement of good faith, courts encountered considerable difficulty in articulating the objective standard of merit the claim had to meet. Instead of clinging to the requirement that the claim be "reasonable," courts resorted to negative characterizations such as "not obviously unfounded,"[4] or "not utterly groundless"[5] or not "wholly baseless or utterly unfounded."[6] The most candid judicial recognition of this difficulty is found in an opinion from a Missouri appellate court:

> It is difficult to reconcile the antinomous rules and statements which are applied to the 'doubtful claims' and to find the words which will exactly draw the line between the compromise ... of an honestly disputed claim which has some fair element of doubt and is therefore to be regarded as consideration and ... a claim, though honestly made, which is so lacking in substance and virility as to be entirely baseless.... We think we had best leave definitions alone, confident that, as applied to each individual case, the facts will make the thing apparent. But if we should make further effort to distinguish, we would say that if the claimant, *in good faith,* makes a mountain out of a mole hill the claim is 'doubtful.' But if there is no discernible mole hill in the beginning, then the claim has no substance.[7]

The RESTATEMENT 2d no longer requires a combination of good faith and some objective merit in the claim. Rather, if the claim (or defense) is doubtful in fact or law, *or* if the forbearing or surrendering party believes that the claim or defense may be valid, there is consideration.[8] If the claim was doubtful in fact or in law, there is no need to inquire into the subjective honesty of the forbearing party. If the invalidity of the claim should have been clear at the time it is forborne or surrendered, an honest belief in the claim is still sufficient.[9] Courts have considered the reasonableness of the claim as a significant though not conclusive factor in determining the underlying requirement of good faith.[10] The RESTATEMENT 2d indicates that where the invalidity of the claim is obvious, such evidence may indicate that the party surrendering or forbearing suit on the claim knew that it was invalid and could not, therefore, honestly assert it.[11] Again, however, the significant change in the RESTATEMENT 2d is finding consideration for *either* an objectively (fact or law) doubtful

---

This case is sometimes regarded as the high water mark of the invalid claim cases. The plaintiff promised to forbear a bastardy prosecution in exchange for defendant's promise to pay the expenses of the birth and to provide for the support of a child plaintiff alleged defendant fathered. After making some payments, defendant refused to perform the remainder of his promise because blood tests revealed that he could not have been the father. The plaintiff then instituted bastardy proceedings and the defendant was acquitted because of the blood tests. Plaintiff then sought to enforce the defendant's promise and the court held that his promise was supported by consideration since the forborne claim had been honestly asserted and was not frivolous, baseless, or vexatious.

[4] Bullard v. Curry-Cloogan, 367 A.2d 127, 131 (D.C. App. 1976).
[5] Frasier v. Carter, 92 Idaho 79, 437 P.2d 32, 34 (1968).
[6] Agristor Credit Corp. v. Unruh, 571 P.2d 1220, 1224 (Okla. 1977).
[7] Duncan v. Black, 324 S.W.2d 483, 486 (Mo. App. 1959).
[8] RESTATEMENT 2d § 74(1)(a) and (b).
[9] RESTATEMENT 2d § 74 comment b.
[10] *See, e.g.,* Dick v. Dick, 167 Conn. 210, 355 A.2d 110 (1974).
[11] RESTATEMENT 2d § 74 comment b.

claim *or* an honest belief that it may be determined to be valid without any objective validity in the claim. This view is a recognition of the natural evolution in the case law. Courts appear to focus upon the honesty of the claimant while minimizing the requirement of an objective validity test with respect to the claim itself as manifested by their difficulty in attempting to articulate the standard to be applied to that requirement.[12] The RESTATEMENT 2d test suggests a heightened awareness of the strong policy in favor of compromise and settlement. A requirement that the forborne claim manifest some objective validity wars against that policy by permitting litigation of the compromise.[13] The RESTATEMENT 2d position is a beneficial modification of the earlier test.

It should be noted that some earlier cases took the position that actual forbearance, as contrasted with a promise to forbear, could not constitute consideration for a promise, i.e., it was not possible to have a "unilateral" contract in which the consideration consists of the forbearance itself.[14] The reason for this position is not entirely clear. It probably resulted from a misapprehension as to what, in fact, had been decided in certain cases — cases where the actual forbearance was, for other reasons, not consideration. If, for example, the promisor requests a promise to forbear as the exchange for his promise, it is clear that nothing short of a promise will consummate a contract.[15] Another type of case in which it is suggested that actual forbearance is not consideration occurs where the promisor hopes for forbearance but does not request it in exchange for his promise.[16] In this type of case, no contract results, not because actual forbearance cannot constitute consideration, but because, in this instance, the promise was, in fact, gratuitous. The RESTATEMENT 2d recognizes this difficulty in suggesting that, where the forbearance is temporary and it is contemplated that the claim will be asserted later, there may be a question of whether the forbearance was bargained for.[17] In general, however, there is no reason to question actual forbearance, if bargained for, any more than a promise to forbear as consideration.[18] Finally, in later sections of this chapter we will examine the validation device popularly known as promissory estoppel where promises are enforced because they induce detrimental reliance on the part of the promisee though the reliance does not

---

[12] Church of Bible Understanding v. Bill Swad, 2 Ohio App. 3d 382, 442 N.E.2d 78 (1981).

[13] Dyer v. National By-Products, Inc., 380, N.W.2d 732, 735 (Iowa 1986) adopting the RESTATEMENT 2d position and overruling contrary holdings.

[14] *See, e.g,* Cown v. Browne, 63 Mont. 82, 206 P. 432 (1922); Saunders v. Bank of Mecklenburg, 112 Va. 443, 71 S.E. 714 (1911); Smith v. Bibber, 82 Me. 34, 19 A. 89 (1889).

[15] *See, e.g.,* Lewis v. Siegman, 135 Or. 660, 296 P. 51 (1931); Sellars v. Jones, 164 Ky. 458, 175 S.W. 1002 (1915); Strong v. Sheffield, 144 N.Y. 392, 39 N.E. 330 (1895); Miles v. New Zealand Alford Estate Co., 32 Ch. D. 266 [1886].

[16] "Forbearance, at request, is a valid consideration. Not so in the absence of both request and promise to forbear." Shaw v. Philbrick, 129 Me. 259, 151 A. 423, 424 (1930). *See also* Schroyer v. Thompson, 262 Pa. 282, 105 A. 274, 2 A.L.R. 1567 (1918); J. H. Queal v. Peterson, 138 Iowa 514, 116 N.W. 593 (1908).

[17] RESTATEMENT 2d § 74 comment d.

[18] Thus, in *In re* All Star Feature Corp., 232 F. 1004 (S.D.N.Y. 1916), it is said, "Forbearance, even without an agreement to forbear, will serve as a consideration, if it be completed." *See also* Veilleux v. Merrill Lynch Relocation Mgt., 226 Va. 440, 309 S.E.2d 595 (1983); Ruegg v. Fairfield Sec. Corp., 308 N.Y. 313, 125 N.E.2d 585 (1955); McDonald Bros. Co. v. Koltes, 155 Minn. 24, 192 N.W. 109 (1923); Dillon v. Lineker, 266 F. 688 (9th Cir. 1920); Fullerton v. Provincial Bank of Ireland, A.C. 309 [1903]. RESTATEMENT 2d § 74 comment d.

induce the promise, i.e., there is no consideration because the promise was not bargained for. Even though forbearance is not bargained for in a given situation, a promise inducing such forbearance may be enforceable on the basis of detrimental reliance.[19]

§ 64. The Pre-Existing Duty Rule.

A. *The Basic Doctrine.*

If a party to a contract promises an act or forbearance that he was previously bound to perform under an existing contract, it should be clear that the new promise cannot be consideration for any counter promise because the promisor has a pre-existing duty to perform or forbear what he now promises. If, for example, an employee refuses to perform his contractual duty unless he receives additional compensation, a promise to pay the additional compensation may succeed in inducing the employee to perform his pre-existing legal duty. There may be an economic benefit to the promisor in such a case because he avoids the trouble and expense of litigation. Yet, there can be no benefit to the promisor or detriment to the promisee in the eyes of the law because of the pre-existing duty. Otherwise, anyone who knows that the other party to the contract would face severe practical difficulties if the promisor refused to perform absent additional consideration would be able to exact a promise to pay additional consideration before performing his contractual duty. The pre-existing duty rule, therefore, provides an effective defense against such extorted promises.[20] The rule also protects employers or the public against failures of performance absent additional incentives. Thus, employees of a bank[21] or a police department[22] who provide information requested in a reward offer are performing their pre-existing duties rather than providing consideration for the reward promise.[23] Where a party promises to forbear the assertion of a claim that is not doubtful in fact or in law, there can be no question that there is no consideration to support a counter-promise.[24] Similarly, a promise to perform ordinary marital obligations will not constitute consideration for a

[19] RESTATEMENT 2d § 74 comment d.

[20] Perhaps the best-known case involving the refusal of employees to perform their contractual duties absent additional compensation is Alaska Packers Ass'n v. Domenico, 117 F. 99 (9th Cir. 1902), where employees were hired to fish for salmon and, upon arriving at the fishing location, refused to perform for the compensation to which they had agreed when hired. The employees knew they had leverage since the employer could not practically return to San Francisco to hire substitute fishermen. The court applied the pre-existing duty rule in finding no consideration to support the promise to pay additional compensation. *See also* Argeros & Co. v. Commonwealth Dept. of Transp., 447 A.2d 1065 (Pa. Commw. (1982) (alleged promise to pay painter additional compensation for painting bridge); Palmer v. Safe Auto Sales, Inc., 114 Misc. 2d 694, 452 N.Y.S.2d 995 (1982) (promise to pay additional consideration for a new car was not supported by consideration); Garrett v. Mathews, 474 F. Supp. (N.D. Ala. 1979) (promise of college teacher to do only what he was previously bound to do under his contract was not consideration).

[21] *See* Denney v. Reppert, 432 S.W.2d 647 (Ky. App. 1968).

[22] *See* Slattery v. Wells Fargo Armored Serv. Corp., 366 So. 2d 157 (D. App. Fla. 1979).

[23] A law enforcement officer out of his jurisdiction, however, has no pre-existing duty in another jurisdiction. His performance, therefore, constitutes consideration for the promise. *See* Denney v. Reppert, *supra* note 21.

[24] Agristor Credit Corp. v. Unruh, 571 P.2d 1220 (1977) (promise to forego disruption of a foreclosure sale where promisors had no claim doubtful in fact or in law). RESTATEMENT 2d § 73.

counter-promise.[25] Notwithstanding the continued use of the pre-existing duty rule in such cases, it has been severely criticized for many years as "one of the relics of antique law which should have been discarded long ago."[26] It is important to compare the effect of the rule as a bar to unfair pressure as contrasted with the operation of the rule as a technical constraint to the fulfillment of reasonable expectations.

If a builder threatens to stop construction unless the owner agrees to pay additional compensation, the owner's promise to pay the additional amount will not be enforced and the rationale supporting the holding will be a pure, pre-existing duty rule analysis, i.e., the builder is only promising to do what he had a pre-existing duty to perform. The owner is receiving nothing for his promise, but makes the promise because of the practical problems of delay and litigation he would face in pursuing his legal rights against the builder. The application of the pre-existing duty rule in such a case suggests a desirable purpose, again, the prevention of extorted promises. If, however, the facts are changed to place the builder in a reasonable, good faith posture, the application of the rule is not easily justified. Suppose, for example, the builder encounters what has come to be called an unanticipated difficulty, e.g., an unanticipated subsoil condition will make it impossible for the builder to complete the job without considerable financial hardship. Not only will the builder fail to make a profit on the job; he will lose a considerable sum and the situation does not permit him to be legally excused.[27] If the owner promises to pay additional compensation to the builder under these circumstances and, upon completion of the work, the owner refuses to make that payment, should that promise be enforced? There is no consideration for the subsequent promise of the owner. He is receiving no more than he should have received under the pre-existing contract since the risk of the subsoil condition was on the builder. Yet, when compared with the illustration involving an extorted promise, there is more than a plausible argument that the pre-existing duty rule should not bar enforcement of the owner's promise to pay additional consideration to the builder. There is no unfair pressure or coercion in the second illustration and the objectively demonstrable reason for the owner's promise to pay constitutes a fair and equitable basis for enforcement notwithstanding the lack of consideration.[28] A strict application of the pre-existing duty rule would preclude the enforcement of the promise. Later in this section we will consider how the rule may be avoided in this situation.

Many other situations can be found where the application of the pre-existing duty rule is questionable. For example, if merchants agree upon a modifi-

---

[25] Earp v. Earp, 57 N.C. App. 194, 290 S.E.2d 739 (1982). *See also* Altman v. Munns, 82 N.C. App. 102, 345 S.E.2d 419 (1986) (separation agreement required defendant to pay for his children's college expenses and no distinction was made between private and public college. Therefore, promise to pay private college tuition was not consideration for modification of separation agreement).

[26] Rye v. Phillips, 203 Minn. 567, 282 N.W. 459, 460, 119 A.L.R. 1120 (1938).

[27] Unanticipated difficulty does not excuse a party's performance of his contractual duty. *See* Ramco Roofing & Supply Co., Etc. v. Kaminsky, 156 Ga. App. 708, 275 S.E.2d 764 (1980); Codell Constr. Co. v. Commonwealth of Ky., 566 S.W.2d 161 (Ky. App. 1977). The doctrines of impossibility of performance or commercial impracticability which can excuse performance will be discussed in a subsequent chapter.

[28] *See* RESTATEMENT 2d § 89 comment b.

cation of their contract in good faith and the modification lacks consideration, the refusal to enforce the modification may be viewed as an unnecessary technical bar to an otherwise desirable modification.[29] Another situation involves a promise by a stranger to a pre-existing contract. If, for example, Ames promises to pay $1000 to Barnes if Barnes will perform an act which Barnes is already bound to perform under a contract with Smith, the pre-existing duty rule will prevent the enforcement of Ames' promise since Barnes had a pre-existing duty to perform, albeit that duty was owed to Smith. Yet, there is little probability of coercion or other unfair pressure on the promisor, Ames, in such a case. The application of the rule in these circumstances may also be avoided.[30] The pre-existing duty rule will prevent the enforcement of a promise by a creditor to permit her debtor to pay a matured debt over a period of time or to pay a lesser sum than the amount owed since the creditor is receiving nothing for her promise. Dissatisfaction with the application of the rule in these and other circumstances, however, has led courts to search for some additional detriment, *no matter how slight,* to justify the enforcement of the promise.[31] The fact that the additional detriment was not bargained-for is of little concern to a court seeking to circumvent the pre-existing duty rule to enforce a promise that it believes should be enforced.[32] Other fictions have been employed to circumvent the rule. One of the methods of discharging a contract which will be considered much later in this volume is a contract of rescission where the parties to an executory contract surrender their rights against each other having concluded that they should discharge their prior contract. Some courts have avoided the pre-existing duty rule by finding a simultaneous rescission and modification of the original contract which, as will be seen, is an analytical impossibility.

It is important to consider these and other direct and indirect attacks on the pre-existing duty rule.

---

[29] UCC § 2-209 comment 1.

[30] RESTATEMENT 2d § 73 comment d.

[31] *See* West India Ind. v. Tradex, Tradex Petr. Serv., 664 F.2d 946, 950 (5th Cir. 1981); Howarth v. First Nat'l Bank of Anchorage, 596 P.2d 1164 (Alaska 1979).

[32] This circumvention of the pre-existing duty rule has been an open secret for many years. For example, in Levine v. Blumenthal, 117 N.J.L. 23, 186 A. 457 (1936), the court notes that any consideration for the promise, however insignificant, satisfies the pre-existing duty rule. For example, a promise to pay part of a debt before maturity, to pay the debt at a different place than required by the original contract, to pay in some form of property other than money as required by the original contract, or similar change in the original duty of the promisee would be sufficient. The RESTATEMENT 2d § 73 comment c admits that, "Slight variations of circumstance are commonly held to take a case out of the rule, particularly where the parties have made an equitable adjustment in the course of performance of a continuing contract...." More recent cases indicating that even slight, additional consideration is sufficient to avoid the pre-existing duty rule include Betterton v. First Interstate Bank, 800 F.2d 732 (8th Cir. 1986) (withholding payment from pay check was new consideration though the amount was unchanged); Leone v. Precision Plumbing & Heating, Inc., 121 Ariz. 514, 591 P.2d 1002, 1003 (1979) (any new obligation, "even if the new obligation is almost the same performance as the pre-existing duty," is sufficient).

B. *Payment of Debt as Consideration — Disputed (Unliquidated) Claims and the Application of Uniform Commercial Code Section 1-207.*

1. Liquidated (Undisputed) Debts.

At a very early time it was said that payment of a lesser sum in satisfaction of a greater sum cannot satisfy the entire debt owed.[33] Ever since that time it has been quite uniformly held that if Ames owes Barnes $1000 which is payable at a stated time and, at the time the debt is mature, Barnes agrees to accept $500 in full satisfaction of the undisputed debt of $1000, there is no consideration to support Barnes' promise. This is popularly known as the doctrine of·*Foakes v. Beer.*[34] Whatever criticism that doctrine has engendered,[35] an agreement to discharge a debt is, like any other agreement, in need of a validation device and there is no consideration in such an agreement. Even though it may be necessary to resort to the trouble and expense of litigation to enforce the payment of a debt, it can hardly be admitted that the debtor suffers any detriment that should be recognized as consideration in paying what she already owes, or that the creditor gets any benefit that could be recognized as consideration in being spared the expense and trouble of a lawsuit. While the debtor can, in fact, refuse payment, she has no right to do so and the purported surrender of such an illusory right is a surrender of nothing. There is no benefit to the creditor and no detriment to the debtor.

Notwithstanding the lack of consideration in such agreements, dissatisfaction with the pre-existing duty rule has made courts astute in discovering some additional detriment, no matter how insignificant,[36] beyond that which the debtor was already bound to perform, and to treat that detriment as consideration. If, for example, a debtor pays the debt before it is due,[37] or at a place other than that in which it is in terms payable,[38] or pays in a different medium or provides some insignificant additional performance in addition to the payment of the amount already owed,[39] consideration is usually found to

---

[33] In Pinnel's Case, 5 Coke Rep. 117a, 77 Eng. Rep. 237 [1600], the statement appeared "... that payment of a lesser sum on the day in satisfaction of a greater, cannot be any satisfaction for the whole, because it appears to the judges that by no possibility a lesser sum can be a satisfaction to the plaintiff for a greater sum." It may be doubted, however, whether Pinnel's case intended to raise or decide any question of consideration, although it has generally been so interpreted by later authorities. *See* Gold, *The Present Status of the Rule in Pinnel's Case*, 30 Ky. L.J. 72 and 187 (1941).

[34] 9 App. Cas. 605 [1884].

[35] *See, e.g.,* Ferson, *The Rule in Foakes v. Beer*, 31 YALE L.J. 15 (1921). A few cases repudiate the doctrine. *See* Winter Wolff & Co. v. Co-Op Lead & Chem. Co., 216 Minn. 199, 111 N.W.2d 461, 465-67 (1961) influenced by the dictum in Rye v. Phillips, 203 Minn. 567, 569, 282 N.W. 459, 460, 119 A.L.R. 1120 (1938). *See also* Watkins & Son v. Carrig, 91 N.H. 459, 21 A.2d 591, 138 A.L.R. 131 (1941).

[36] *See* cases cited *supra* note 31.

[37] Codner v. Siegel, 246 Ga. 368, 271 S.E.2d 465 (1980); Princeton Coal Co. v. Dorth, 191 Ind. 615, 133 N.E. 386 (1921); Sonnenberg v. Riedel, 16 Minn. 83 (1870).

[38] Jones v. Perkins, 29 Miss. 139, 64 Am. Dec. 136 (1855); Harper v. Graham, 20 Ohio 105 (1851). See, however, Foster Cty. State Bank v. Lammers, 117 Minn. 94, 134 N.W. 501 (1912) where the court held that if a debt is not paid at maturity, the creditor has a legal right to collect it wherever he can find the debtor regardless of the place stipulated for payment in the contract. *See also* Vanbergen v. St. Edmonds Properties Ltd., 2 K.B. 223 [1933] holding that payment at a different place was merely a favor, i.e., the different place of payment had not been bargained-for as the price of the promise and did not, therefore, constitute consideration.

[39] Betterton v. First Interstate Bank, 800 F.2d 732 (8th Cir. 1986) (payments deducted from pay check was enough to support the promise); Raedele v. Gibraltar S & L Ass'n., 111 Cal. Rptr. 693,

exist. While a "legal" detriment can be found in such cases, it is often inserted not as a bargained-for exchange but as a formality designed to make the promise binding.[40] If the new performance is bargained-for, consideration is clearly present.[41]

2. Unliquidated (Disputed) Claims.

Where the debt is unliquidated, i.e., where the amount involved has not been agreed upon or where it cannot be precisely determined, or where the debt is disputed in good faith by the debtor, a different analysis is appropriate. Consideration can be found in these cases in the payment of part or all that is claimed by the creditor. Where an honest dispute exists in regard to the amount owed,[42] the liability itself,[43] or even the method of payment,[44] no legal duty arises until the question of amount, liability or method has been determined. If, for example, services have been performed or goods have been delivered with no prior agreement as to price and the parties have an honest dispute over the amount owed, if the debtor pays a definite amount, she is surrendering her right to pay a lesser amount if the matter had been adjudicated. The creditor may be receiving more than he would have received after adjudication. Whether either party actually received more or less than he or she would have received had the matter been adjudicated will never be known. The mutual surrender of rights to receive more or pay less, however, are detriments which constitute consideration for the mutual promises of the parties to pay and receive the "settled" amount.[45]

698, 517 P.2d 1157, 1162 (1974) (promise to find suitable buyer). In a number of cases, the debtor has given a check or note for part of the debt. In American Seeding Mach. Co. v. Baker, 55 Ind. App. 624, 104 N.E. 524 (1914) and Goddard v. O'Brien, 9 Q.B.D. 37 [1882], giving a check for part of the debt was held to be consideration. However, in Shanley v. Koehler, 80 A.D. 566, 80 N.Y.S. 679 (1903), aff'd, 178 N.Y. 446, 70 N.E. 1109 (1904), the debtor's note for part of the debt was not consideration. In Vaughn v. Robbins, 254 Mass. 35, 149 N.E. 677, 41 A.L.R. 1488 (1925), the debtor gave the check of a firm of which he was a member for part of the debt which the court upheld as consideration. In Jaffray v. Davis, 124 N.Y. 164, 26 N.E. 351 (1891), the giving of a note and chattel mortgage as security for part of the debt was upheld as consideration. UCC § 3-408 indicates that "... no consideration is necessary for an instrument or obligation thereon given in payment or as security for an antecedent obligation of any kind."

[40] The RESTATEMENT 2d would characterize such arrangements as "pretense" since they are not bargained-for, (§ 71 comment b). It later suggests that "Any payment ... at an earlier time, or in a different medium from that required by the duty, is consideration ... if the difference in performance is part of what is requested and given in exchange for the promise." See § 73 comment c ill. 7. Statements in the case law to the effect that anything new, no matter how slight, will operate as consideration, seem to ignore the bargained-for element. See cases cited supra.

[41] If the creditor agrees to extend the maturity of the debt with the understanding that interest will continue during the extension, consideration is present since the creditor bargains for the additional interest that he would not have received had the debt been paid at the original maturity date. See Adamson v. Bosick, 82 Colo. 309, 259 P. 513 (1927).

[42] See Nowicki Constr. Co. v. Panar Corp., N. V., 342 Pa. Super. 8, 492 A.2d 36 (1985); Air Power, Inc. v. Omega Equip. Corp., 54 Md. App. 534, 459 A.2d 1120 (1983); Ruble Forest Prods., Inc. v. Lancer Mobile Homes of Or., Inc., 99 Or. 895, 524 P.2d 1204 (1974).

[43] See Koedding v. N. B. West Contr'g Co., 596 S.W.2d 744 (1980).

[44] Gottlieb v. Charles Scribner's Sons, 232 Ala. 33, 166 So. 685 (1936).

[45] See RESTATEMENT 2d § 74 comment c. Where part of a claim is undisputed and the other part is disputed, payment by the debtor of the undisputed part is generally held to be consideration for the creditor's promise to release the debtor as to the balance. See RESTATEMENT 2d § 74 ill. 6. Where there are two distinct claims, although both arise from a single contract and one is liquidated, its payment is not consideration to support a discharge of the other, unliquidated,

3. "Payment in Full": Accord and Satisfaction — Uniform Commercial Code
   Section 1-207.

Debtors often attempt to settle good faith, disputed claims by tendering a
check in an amount the debtor believes he owes, marking the check "payment
in full" or similar phrase. Such a tender constitutes an offer by the debtor to
settle the disputed claim with the intention of putting the creditor to the
choice of returning, destroying or cashing the check. If the creditor cashes the
check, the common law treated this act as an acceptance of the debtor's offer.
The resulting contract is called an "accord and satisfaction" which is a contract under which an obligee agrees to accept a stated performance in satisfaction of the obligor's existing duty.[46] An agreement to settle a prior unliquidated or disputed obligation is an accord. The "satisfaction" is merely the
performance of the accord. When the creditor cashes a check marked "payment in full" tendered by a debtor where the obligation is unliquidated or
honestly disputed, the accord and satisfaction occur simultaneously and the
duty of the debtor is discharged.[47] Again, the consideration is found in the
debtor's payment of a sum which may or may not be owed and the creditor's
surrender of a claim which may be greater than the debt. If the amount owed
is neither unliquidated nor honestly disputed, there could be no consideration
for the payment of a lesser sum than the definite amount owed. Thus, if the
creditor cashed a check for an amount less than a liquidated, undisputed debt,
though the check was marked "payment in full," the debtor's duty to pay the
remainder of the liquidated or undisputed obligation would not be discharged.
    Creditors are rarely pleased to receive a check in an amount less than that
which they believe they are owed marked "payment in full." Their desire to
receive the proceeds of the check is strong, but they also wish to preserve what
they perceive to be their right to collect a greater sum from the debtor. To
avoid the Hobson's choice of not cashing the check or taking less than the
creditor believes he is owed, a creditor may resort to such tactics as deleting
the phrase, "payment in full" (or similar phrase). The erasure or deletion of
the phrase will not affect the legal characterization of the transaction, i.e., the
cashing of the check after the deletion of the phrase will still constitute an
accord and satisfaction — the underlying obligation will be discharged.[48] A
more recent tactic by creditors was prompted by the enactment of the Uniform
Commercial Code throughout the country. Section 1-207 of the UCC may
appear to provide creditors with a method of avoiding the Hobson's choice:

---

claim. Lippard v. Dupont Garage Co., 71 F.2d 350 (D.C. Cir. 1934); Jefferson Standard Life Ins.
Co. v. Lightsey, 49 F.2d 586 (4th Cir. 1931); Commercial Union Assur. Co. of London, England v.
Creek Cotton Oil Co., 96 Okla. 189, 221 P. 499 (1923). The RESTATEMENT 2d is in accord with this
position but adds that where there are no circumstances of unfair pressure or economic coercion
and the disputed item is closely related to an undisputed item, the two should be treated as
constituting a single, unliquidated claim permitting payment of the amount admittedly due to
constitute consideration for a promise to surrender the entire claim. RESTATEMENT 2d § 74 comment c.
    [46]RESTATEMENT 2d § 281(1). See Cook & Franke, S. C. v. Meilman, 136 Wis. 2d 434, 402 N.W.2d
361 (1987); Duke Indus. v. Waldrop, 16 Ark. App. 125, 697 S.W.2d 936 (1985); Charleston Urban
Renewal Auth., Etc. v. Spyros Stanley, 346 S.E.2d 740 (W. Va. App. 1985).
    [47]See RESTATEMENT 2d § 281 ill. 6.
    [48]See Wong v. Paisner, 14 Mass. App. 923, 436 N.E.2d 990 (1982).

A party who with explicit reservation of rights performs or promises performance or assents to performance in a manner demanded or offered by the other party does not thereby prejudice the rights reserved. Such words as "without prejudice," "under protest" or the like are sufficient.

Suppose that a creditor receives a check from an honest debtor marked "payment in full." The claim is honestly disputed or unliquidated. Armed with § 1-207 of the UCC, may the creditor reserve his rights against the debtor for what the creditor deems to be the full amount and still cash the check by simple insertion of the phrase, "without prejudice" or "under protest" written above his indorsement of the check before cashing it? To phrase the question more abstractly, was § 1-207 designed, *inter alia,* to change the common law of accord and satisfaction with respect to checks marked "payment in full"? There has been considerable debate concerning this question among the courts and the legal scholars. The conflicting views are well-stated in two cases which deserve analysis.

In *Horn Waterproofing v. Bushwick Iron,*[49] the defendant disputed the amount of a bill submitted by the plaintiff for certain roofing work causing the plaintiff to lower the amount of the bill. Still unsatisfied, the defendant submitted a check for less than half the revised amount and the check contained the following notation: "This check is accepted in full payment, settlement, satisfaction, release and discharge of any and all claims and/or demands of whatsoever kind or nature." Plaintiff received this check containing the notation and, directly under it, printed the words, "Under Protest," before cashing the check. Plaintiff then instituted an action to recover the balance of the amount he claimed from the defendant. The New York Court of Appeals recognized the conflict among courts and scholars concerning the application of § 1-207 of the UCC. The court also recognized that most of the courts that have adjudicated this issue have held that § 1-207 should not affect the common law rule that a check tendered in "full payment" of a disputed debt is an accord and satisfaction that discharges the original claim of the creditor precluding the creditor from recovering any alleged balance due.[50] The court was mindful of the policy of the law in favoring settlements. After considering the conflicting constructions of § 1-207, however, the court held that § 1-207 changes the common law rule so as to permit the creditor to cash the check and still maintain an action for the balance after if he had noted his "protest" on the check. The court was moved to that holding because, "the common law doctrine of accord and satisfaction creates a cruel dilemma for the good-faith creditor of a full payment check. Under that rule, the creditor would have no

---

[49] 66 N.Y.2d 321, 488 N.E.2d 56 (1985).

[50] *Ibid.* at note 1, the court listed numerous books and articles taking different positions on this issue, *inter alia,* 1 ANDERSON, UNIFORM COMMERCIAL CODE § 1-207:7, §§ 3-408:54 — 3-408:57 (3d ed.) to the effect that the better rule is that § 1-207 does not apply to the "full payment" check. *Accord,* 6 CORBIN ON CONTRACTS § 1279 (2d ed. 1984 Supp.). J. WHITE & R. SUMMERS, UNIFORM COMMERCIAL CODE § 13-21 (2d ed.), however, believe that § 1-207 permits a debtor such as the plaintiff in the instant case to accept with explicit protest and still claim the balance due him. In note 2, the court lists New York case law holding that § 1-207 permits the creditor to sue for the balance due. In note 3, the court lists cases in other jurisdictions in agreement with that position before listing "an admittedly larger number of jurisdictions [that] have held the common law rule is not affected...."

other choice but to surrender the partial payment or forfeit his right to the remainder."[51] Critics of this view often point to comment 1 to § 1-207 which does not specifically address the question of accord and satisfaction.[52] They see comment 1 as an elaboration of the concept of "performance" found in the statutory language of the section. They conclude that the section was designed to permit an aggrieved party to reserve its rights where that party does not wish to terminate the contract.[53] Under this view, § 1-207 was not designed to alter the common law doctrine of accord and satisfaction as applied to "full payment" checks. The court, however, was unpersuaded by this interpretation of § 1-207. While the comment to the section does not deal with accord and satisfaction specifically, the court suggests that it is "fairly subject to a wide variety of interpretations as to the purpose of section 1-207."[54] The court also pointed to a report of the New York Law Revision Commission[55] which supports the view that § 1-207 alters the common law concept.[56]

The other view, currently accepted as prevailing, is found most effectively in a decision of the Supreme Court of Connecticut.[57] In a scholarly opinion by Chief Justice Peters,[58] the court addressed the same question where the debtor disputed the amount claimed by the creditor and submitted a check for a lesser amount marked "Final payment" and contained the notation, "By its endorsement, the payee accepts this check in full satisfaction of all claims against the C. F. Wooding Co. arising out of or relating to the Uphon Project under Purchase Order #3302, dated 11/17/81." The plaintiff crossed out the conditional language on the check and added, "This check is accepted under protest and with full reservation of rights to collect the unpaid balance for which this check is offered in settlement." The plaintiff cashed the check and then sought to recover the balance it claimed was still due. The Court thought it important to reconcile § 1-207 with provisions found in other articles of the UCC. It first reconciled the section with provisions in Article 3 of the Code dealing with checks and other negotiable instruments.[59] This analysis led the

---

[51] 488 N.E.2d 56, 59 (1985).

[52] "This section provides machinery for the continuation of performance along the lines contemplated by the contract despite a pending dispute, by adopting the mercantile device of going ahead with delivery, acceptance or payment 'without prejudice,' 'under protest,' 'under reserve,' 'with reservation of all our rights,' and the like. All of these phrases completely reserve all rights within the meaning of this section. The section therefore contemplates that limited as well as general reservations and acceptance by a party may be made 'subject to satisfaction of our purchaser,' 'subject to acceptance by our customers,' or the like." UCC § 1-207 comment 1.

[53] *See, e.g.,* Rosenthal, *Discord and Satisfaction: Section 1-207 of the Uniform Commercial Code,* 78 COLUM. L. REV. 48, 63 (1978).

[54] 488 N.E.2d 56, 60 (1985).

[55] REPORT OF COMM'N ON UNIFORM STATE LAWS TO LEGISLATURE, 19-20 (1961).

[56] Another problem in the case was that the underlying obligation was created by a contract for services rather than a contract for the sale of goods, thereby raising the argument that the Code did not apply to this transaction. The court concludes, however, that the transaction was "Code-covered" because the tender of a check brought it within Article 3 of the UCC which deals with negotiable instruments. See, however, RMP Indus. v. Linen Center, 386 N.W.2d 523 (Iowa App. 1986) which rejects the argument that § 1-207 should apply through Article 3 to a transaction to which Article 2 does not apply.

[57] County Fire Door Corp. v. C. F. Wooding Co., 202 Conn. 277, 520 A.2d 1028 (1977).

[58] Prior to her judicial appointment, Chief Justice Peters was a Professor of Law at the Yale Law School where she distinguished herself as a teacher and scholar, particularly with respect to the law of commercial transactions.

[59] The court noted that § 3-112(1)(f) preserves the negotiability of a check that includes a notation of full satisfaction of the drawer's obligation and points out that there is no such validation

court to the strong view that relevant provisions of Article 3 of the UCC would be undermined if § 1-207 were construed as permitting alteration of the common law concept of accord and satisfaction as applied to checks marked "payment in full" in disputed debt situations.[60] Recognizing that § 1-207 does not fit easily within Article 3 of the Code, the court found harmony between § 1-207 and the provisions of Article 2.[61] This analysis demonstrated a fundamental purpose of Article 2 in urging contracting parties to engage in a continuing dialogue about acceptable performance of their contract. That purpose is "entirely consistent" with the purpose of § 1-207 which is particularly manifested in comment 1 to § 1-207 as suggested earlier.[62] Under this analysis, the conclusion is inevitable that "§ 1-207 was not intended to empower a seller, as payee of a negotiable instrument, to alter that instrument by adding words of protest to a check tendered by a buyer on condition that it be accepted in full satisfaction of an unliquidated debt."[63]

As a matter of statutory construction, the evidence is compelling that § 1-207 was not designed to alter the common law view of accord and satisfaction as applied to "full payment" checks. From the perspective of fairness to the parties where the debtor, in good faith, disputes the debt and submits such a check to the creditor, the notion that the creditor is subject to a harsh or cruel choice in either cashing the check, thereby relinquishing any remaining claim, or returning the check, thereby maintaining his claim for the alleged balance due, often seems to assume, unwittingly, that the creditor is owed some additional amount and is forced to surrender it in order to reap the proceeds of only part of what he is owed. If the practice of settling disputed claims is not only permissible but desirable, that policy, alone, suggests that the common law concept be retained, intact. The safeguard of that concept, i.e., that the claim be honestly asserted, should effectively prevent overreach-

---

anywhere in Article 3 for a term on the check negating such a condition placed thereon by a drawer. In fact, § 3-407 frowns upon any unauthorized alteration of the instrument. The court also notes that § 3-802(1)(b) provides a presumption that the taking of the instrument suspends the underlying obligation until the instrument is due and that discharge of the obligor on the instrument also discharges the obligor on the underlying obligation. Finally, § 3-603(1) discharges a drawer from liability on an instrument "to the extent of his payment or satisfaction."

[60] 520 A.2d 1028, 1032-33 (1987).

[61] The court emphasizes the fact that Article 2 "recurrently draws inferences from acquiescence in, or objection to, the performance tendered by one of the parties." 520 A.2d 1028, 1033 (1987). Thus, § 2-208 deals with the parties' course of performance which helps determine the meaning of their contract. With respect to proposals for additional terms, if a merchant submits a timely notification of objection, such terms do not become part of the contract under § 2-207(2)(c). A buyer must seasonably object to a defective tender of goods or lose his right of rejection pursuant to §§ 2-602(1), 2-605, 2-606(1) and 2-607(2). [Another section not mentioned in the opinion that appears highly relevant to this analysis is § 2-607(3)(a) requiring notification of defects in accepted goods within a reasonable time after the buyer discovered or should have discovered the defect. Absent such notification, the buyer is barred from any remedy. This section has been interpreted to emphasize the importance of maintaining the contract by permitting settlement of disputes between the parties. The leading case is Eastern Airlines, Inc. v. McDonnell-Douglas Corp., 532 F.2d 957 (5th Cir. 1976).] In installment contracts, a buyer who accepts a nonconforming installment without seasonably notifying the seller of cancellation reinstates the contract under § 2-612(3), and a buyer who fails to offer reasonable alternatives for modification or termination of a contract after a seller's notification that performance has become impracticable will cause the contract to lapse under § 2-616(1) and (2).

[62] 520 A.2d 1028, 1034-35 (1987). See discussion of comment 1 to § 1-207 in the text supra notes 52-54.

[63] 520 A.2d 1028, 1035 (1987).

ing by debtors seeking to avoid full payment. An interpretation of § 1-207 that would, in effect, emasculate this practice is not supported by the underlying purposes of Article 2 or other provisions in the Code. Moreover, to indulge in an artistic reading of § 1-207 to accomplish this purpose serves no particular value in our legal system. Rather, it undermines the value of finality for reasons that are hardly plausible. The prevailing view should now find even greater favor in future cases.[64]

C. Rescission — Two Parties and Three Parties.

On the basis of what has already been stated in this section, it should be clear beyond peradventure that a promise to pay additional compensation to a party who agrees not to breach the contract is not supported by consideration. If, for example, an employee provides highly valuable service in a particular job at a particular time, his threat to breach may induce the promise of additional compensation by the employer. The employer may have weighed the advantages and disadvantages of this commitment. The employee may have been underpaid and the additional compensation may equal fair compensation for his or her valuable services. The continuation of the employment may, from the employer's perspective, be an efficient use of resources. Regardless of these justifications, they do not import consideration to support the employer's new promise. The inescapable fact remains that the new promise is not induced by any detriment that could possibly be called the surrender of a legal right because the law must regard the employee's continued performance of his contract, albeit, perhaps, undersalaried in terms of the market value of his service, as a duty. The employee has no more "right" to breach that duty than he does to commit a tort. The promise to perform that duty is the quintessential illustration of the promise to perform a pre-existing duty. Throughout this section, we have explored efforts to circumvent that rule and that exploration continues.

To permit the enforcement of the agreement modifying the salary of the employee without any modification of his duties, a few courts have suggested that it is possible to view the pre-existing duty as consideration for the new agreement so as to encourage the enforcement of modifications.[65] It would have been preferable if these courts had simply found the modifying promise enforceable without consideration. The fiction is absurd.

Another method is much more imaginative but equally flawed. Before this device can be seen for what it is, it is important to understand the concept of rescission. "Rescission" is a term that is so widely used that it is subject to considerable ambiguity. It should be relegated to one use, i.e., rescission is a

---

[64] *Accord,* RESTATEMENT 2d § 278 comment a and § 281 comment d. The cases adopting the prevailing view that § 1-207 does not alter the common law accord and satisfaction applied to "full payment" checks include Cass Constr. Co. v. Brennan, 222 Neb. 69, 382 N.W.2d 313 (1986); Stultz Elec. Works v. Marine Hydraulic Eng'g Co., 484 A.2d 1008 (Me. 1984); R. A. Reither Constr. v. Wheatland Rural Elec. Ass'n., 680 P.2d 1342 (Colo. App. 1984); Air Van Lines, Inc. v. Buster, 673 P.2d 774 (Alaska 1983). Other cases adopting this view may be found at 520 A.2d 1028, 1035 (1987).

[65] This is sometimes called the "Wisconsin fiction." *See* Mid-Century Ltd. of Am. v. United Cigar-Whelan Stores Corp., 109 F. Supp. 433 (D.D.C. 1953); Holly v. First Nat'l Bank, 218 Wis. 259, 260 N.W. 429 (1935). *See* criticism of this position in Note, 39 CORNELL L.Q. 114 (1953).

contract between parties who are already bound to an executory contract, and who agree to surrender their rights against each other with the purpose of discharging their unperformed obligations under the existing contract. A rescission is like any other contract, i.e., it must be supported by a validation device. If A and B have an unperformed (executory) contract and decide that it would be in their mutual interest to discharge that contract, they each suffer a detriment and each receive a benefit that is bargained for in their release of each other from the duties of their contract.[66] Parties to a contract may agree to rescind that contract and then, free from any obligations to each other, they may enter into another contract on any terms they choose. It should be emphasized that this scenario includes three separate contracts — the first contract that is still executory, the second contract of rescission which discharges the first contract,[67] and the third contract. If Barnes has agreed to work for Ames at $1000 per week and is grumbling about his salary, the parties could enter into a contract of rescission under which Ames releases Barnes from his duties and Barnes does the same for Ames. The parties are now entirely free from any legal duties toward each other. Since Barnes has no legal duty to work for Ames, Ames could promise to pay Barnes $2000 per week under a new contract and, if Barnes accepted the offer, there is consideration to support both promises. Similarly, Ames could offer Barnes $500 per week and, if Barnes accepted, the new (third) contract would evidence consideration. While there is nothing in these arrangements violating any prescript of consideration, another arrangement that may appear to be identical is fatally flawed.

If Ames and Barnes conclude a rescission contract and *simultaneously* enter into the new contract on terms different from the terms of the first (original) contract of employment, it is impossible to discover consideration to support Ames' promise to pay more ($2000 per week) or Barnes' promise to accept less ($500 per week). Cases validating simultaneous rescissions and new agreements modifying the original agreement appear to have little or no understanding of the concept of consideration.[68] In our example, if Ames was never free of her duty to Barnes, Barnes was never free of his duty to Ames. There must be some period of time, perhaps only a moment, between the formation of the rescission contract and the formation of the third contract. If there never was a mutual release of duties, the parties were never free to enter into a new contract since they were still bound by the original contract. There would be no third contract in this situation. The second contract of rescission and simultaneous modification would lack consideration. Contrary reasoning is necessarily circular and is seen as such by other courts.[69]

---

[66] For a general discussion of contracts of rescission, *see* Lemlich v. Board of Trustees of Harford Comm., 385 A.2d 1185 (Md. App. 1978). The concept of rescission will be discussed further in the last chapter of this volume dealing with discharge.

[67] A contract of rescission is interesting in that it not only discharges the original contract but discharges itself upon formation. It is, therefore, not only self-destructive upon formation, but it destroys the original contract simultaneously.

[68] The classic illustration is Schwartzreich v. Bauman-Basch, Inc., 231 N.Y. 196, 131 N.E. 887 (1921). As early as 1895, another court concluded that such an analysis indulges the worst kind of fiction since it invites parties to repudiate their contractual obligations whenever they perceive a gain thereby. King v. Duluth, M. & N. Ry., 61 Minn. 482, 63 N.W. 1105, 1106 (1895).

[69] *See* Recker v. Gustafson, 279 N.W.2d 744, 758 (Iowa 1979). RESTATEMENT 2d § 89 comment b rejects the simultaneous rescission and new agreement concept as "fictitious."

If the promise of additional consideration is not made by one of the parties to the contract but by a third party stranger to the contract, the situation becomes more complex. One of the best-known cases in this area involved a driver who had a contractual duty with the owner of a horse to drive in a particular trotting race. A stranger to the contract promised the driver $1000 if he won the race. The driver "won" the race.[70] The stranger was particularly desirous that the horse being driven would win since he owned the dam of the entered horse and stood to win $300 if the driven horse was victorious. Since the driver had a pre-existing duty to use his best efforts to win the race under his contract with the owner of the horse, the question arose, was the promise of the stranger supported by consideration? The court accepted the traditional view that there was no consideration to support the promise since there was no detriment to the promisee-driver.[71]

The FIRST and RESTATEMENT 2d take a contrary position.[72] It is possible to construct consideration by finding a benefit to the third party. Even though the driver owed a pre-existing duty to the owner, he owed no duty to the stranger. Thus, when the driver performs the act requested by the stranger, the stranger receives a benefit. Though there is no detriment to the promisee-driver, the classic consideration formula is satisfied, i.e., there must be *either* a benefit to the promisor *or* a detriment to the promisee.[73] This theory collapses, however, when applied to the facts of the driving case because the argument is circular. One can be entitled to a performance by another only if the other has a legal duty to perform and that duty must rest upon some contractual theory. If there is a contract, there is a duty on the part of the promisee-driver to the stranger. In order to find this contractual duty, however, consideration must exist. Though the driver may have felt an extra incentive because of the stranger's promise, he was still required, under his pre-existing duty to the owner, to use his best efforts. No greater effort could be judicially recognized. Thus, the driver could not be induced to win the race by the stranger's promise. The theory suggesting that a benefit to the stranger suffices necessarily eliminates the requirement that the detriment induce the promise, i.e., that the promise of the stranger must be bargained for. The stranger's promise could not be induced by the detriment since the driver, necessarily, suffered no detriment. Notwithstanding this analysis, both RE-STATEMENTS insist that the promise is enforceable. The RESTATEMENT 2d appears to recognize that such promises by third parties are not enforceable because they are supported by consideration. Rather, they are enforceable because "there is less likelihood of economic coercion or other unfair pressure" in making a promise by a stranger enforceable than there would be if the promise had been made by one of the parties to the original contract.[74] Unfor-

---

[70] One should not forget the efforts of the horse.

[71] McDevitt v. Stokes, 174 Ky. 515, 192 S.W. 681 (1917).

[72] FIRST RESTATEMENT § 84(d); RESTATEMENT 2d § 73 comment d.

[73] *See* Briskin v. Packard Motor Car Co., 269 Mass. 394, 169 N.E. 148 (1929); Shadwell v. Shadwell, 30 L. J. C. P. 145, 9 C. B. (n. s.) 159 [1860]. *See also* Morgan, *Benefit to the Promisor as Consideration for a Second Promise for the Same Act,* 1 MINN. L. REV. 383 (1915); SELECTED READINGS ON CONTRACTS 491 (1931); FIRST RESTATEMENT § 84(d), approved in Willard v. Hobby, 134 F. Supp. 66 (E.D. Pa. 1955).

[74] RESTATEMENT 2d § 73 comment d.

tunately, the analysis proceeds to suggest that, "the tendency of the law has been simply to hold that performance of contractual duty can be consideration if the duty is not owed to the promisor."[75] Here, "consideration" appears to be used as a synonym for suggesting that the promise is enforceable rather than any strong assertion that the technical requirements of consideration are present.[76]

Another circumvention device is suggested by one of the best-known cases in the literature of contract law. In *DeCicco v. Schweizer,*[77] the father of the prospective bride promised her fiance that he would pay an annuity to the daughter during her lifetime. Since the couple had previously agreed to marry, there was no readily observable detriment to the promisee (fiance) in proceeding with the marriage. In an imaginative opinion by Judge Cardozo, however, the court held that the father's promise induced the parties to refrain from rescinding their marriage contract and the forbearance from rescission induced the father's promise. To accomplish this feat, Judge Cardozo had to characterize the daughter as a promisee though the promise was apparently made exclusively to the fiance. He creates that fact by assuming that the daughter had learned of the promise prior to the marriage though the record was devoid of supporting evidence to this effect. Having transformed the daughter from a third party (donee) beneficiary to a promisee, the stage was set to discover another implied fact, i.e., that the fiance and daughter refrained from rescinding their agreement and did so in exchange for the father's promise. Judge Cardozo was faced with precedent indicating that a promise to one party to a contract seeking forbearance from rescission was valueless since it takes two to rescind. Absent that precedent, it is possible to discover consideration by the forbearance of one party *offering* a rescission to the other party. This would be particularly true in a marriage agreement where emotions play a greater role than commercial contracts. Thus, if it could be demonstrated that the father promised an annuity to the daughter *in exchange* for the fiance's promise to forbear offering a rescission of the marriage contract to the daughter, there would be consideration for the father's promise. The facts of the case, however, show little justification for any bargained-for exchange or forbearance from rescission. Notwithstanding the use of the term, "consideration" in the father's written promise, there is no evidence that it was anything other than a gift promise conditioned only upon the occurrence of the marriage. After this remarkable effort in discovering consideration, Judge Cardozo admits the strong policy of the law in favor of

---

[75] *Ibid.* Ill. 12 to § 73 is based upon the race horse case and concludes that the driving of the race is consideration for the promise of the stranger. Under agency law principles, however, the illustration suggests that, while the stranger owes the promised amount to the driver, but the owner of the horse may be entitled to that amount, citing RESTATEMENT 2d AGENCY §§ 313, 388.

[76] In comment b to § 73, the RESTATEMENT 2d finds no consideration in a promise to a public official to perform his public duty. The policy reasons for this result are sound, i.e., public officials may threaten to withhold the performance of their duties which threaten public and private interests. Yet, from the standpoint of consideration, if there is consideration in the promise of a stranger to a driver of a trotting horse, a third-party promise to a public official such as a police officer might also admit of consideration. Again, the determination of whether such promises by strangers should be enforced is properly placed on policy grounds rather than a technical consideration construct.

[77] 221 N.Y. 431, 117 N.E. 807 (1917).

marriage settlements and the willingness of courts to construct consideration, if need be, to make such promises enforceable. While the RESTATEMENT 2d mentions the possibility of discovering a mutual forbearance to rescind or the forbearance of an offer to rescind as consideration for a third-party promise, it appears to dismiss that rationale as less than persuasive.[78] While some support can be discovered for the approach of the RESTATEMENTS,[79] there is insufficient case law to assume that the pre-existing duty rule has been totally overcome with respect to promises by third parties.

D. *Modifications Without Consideration Enforced Because of Unanticipated Difficulties.*

Where a promisee begins to perform his contractual duty and encounters unanticipated difficulties, he may not abandon his contract because of such difficulties.[80] If, however, the promisor agrees to pay additional compensation because of the unanticipated difficulties, there is authority for holding the modification enforceable albeit there is no consideration for the new promise.[81] The RESTATEMENT 2d adopts this position with no suggestion that it amounts to consideration.[82] A modification based upon unanticipated difficulty is typically devoid of unfair pressure or economic coercion which may be said to justify the continuation of the pre-existing duty rule where a promisee demands additional payment only because he is in a position to place unfair pressure upon the promisor.[83] It is important to distinguish "unanticipated" difficulty which may be remotely foreseeable from "unforeseeable" contingencies which more than materially change the nature of the bargain and may be sufficient to excuse the promisee from performing.[84] The modification must be

---

[78] RESTATEMENT 2d § 73 comment d.

[79] *See, e.g.,* Perry M. Alexander Constr. Co. v. Burbank, 350 S.E.2d 877 (N.C. App. 1986) (promise to third party to perform demolition where the demolition duty was already owed to another — applying FIRST RESTATEMENT § 84(d)). *See also* Burton v. Kenyon, 46 N.C. App. 309, 264 S.E.2d 808 (1980) (applying FIRST RESTATEMENT § 84(d) and Morrison Flying Serv. v. Denning Nat'l Bank, 404 F.2d 856 (10th Cir. 1968), *cert. denied,* 393 U.S. 1020 (1969) (applying FIRST RESTATEMENT § 84(d)). The position is also supported by Professor Corbin in 1 CORBIN ON CONTRACTS § 176 (1950).

[80] *See, e.g.,* Ramco Roofing & Supply Co., Etc. v. Kaminsky, 156 Ga. App. 708, 275 S.E.2d 764 (1980); Codell Constr. Co. v. Commonwealth of Ky., 566 S.W.2d 161 (Ky. App. 1977). If, however, the promisee relied upon an estimate of the promisor as to the amount of work to be done, the promisee is free to abandon the remainder of the work absent assurances of additional compensation and, as to any additional work already performed, he may recover in quantum meruit for the reasonable value of the additional work, i.e., a restitutionary recovery to prevent the unjust enrichment of the promisor. *See* Murdock-Bryant Constr. Co. v. Taylor Pearson Constr. Co., 146 Ariz. 57, 703 P.2d 1206 (1984).

[81] *See, e.g.,* Angel v. Murray, 113 R.I. 482, 322 A.2d 630 (1974) (city promised to pay trash collector $10,000 per year more on contract to collect all trash because of unanticipated increase of dwelling units within city). Pittsburgh Testing Lab. v. Farnsworth & Chambers Co., 251 F.2d 77 (10th Cir. 1958) supporting this concept though holding that a promise to pay additional compensation was based on settlement of a bona fide dispute. *See also* Lichtenstein v. Watt, 684 F.2d (D.C. Cir. 1982) which discusses the unanticipated difficulty concept and Watkins & Son v. Carrig, 91 N.H. 459, 21 A.2d 591, 138 A.L.R. 131 (1941).

[82] RESTATEMENT 2d § 89(a). This is one of the sections in Topic 2 of the RESTATEMENT 2d (§§ 82-94) captioned, "Contracts Without Consideration."

[83] RESTATEMENT 2d § 89 comment b.

[84] Impossibility of performance, impracticability of performance and frustration of purpose permit the promisee to be legally excused from performing. RESTATEMENT 2d §§ 261-272 and UNI-

fair and equitable under circumstances that were not anticipated at the time of contract formation.[85] It is important to consider any evidence of pressure or imposition on the promisor which would suggest a rejuvenation of the pre-existing duty analysis. Among other circumstances, the relative bargaining power of the parties and the extent of performance under the new promise should be considered. Absent bad faith on the part of the promisee and assuming a voluntary commitment by the promisor, the modification should be enforced with a candid recognition that the basis for enforcement is the effectuation of good faith adjustments in on-going transactions rather than any fictitious notion of consideration or other traditional validation device.

E. *Modifications Under the Uniform Commercial Code Section 2-209.*

1. Section 2-209(1): Changing the Pre-Existing Duty Rule.

The Uniform Commercial Code governs contracts for the sale of goods. Under the Code, good faith modifications of such contracts need no consideration to be binding.[86] In light of prolonged criticism of the pre-existing duty rule prior to Code, it is not remarkable that the Code would include a section dispensing with the need for consideration or any other validation device. While the earlier criticism facilitated the inclusion of this concept, it is at least arguable that it would have been included absent that criticism. The "father" of the Code and principal draftsman of Article 2, Professor Karl Llewellyn, was more than insistent that technical barriers to good faith and commercially reasonable practices be removed.[87] Permitting the parties to a contract for the sale of goods to make modifications without the technical constraint of consideration is a clear illustration of the underlying philosophy of Article 2 of the Code which seeks to identify the factual bargain of the parties.[88]

Section 2-209(1) may be criticized because it does not expressly require modifications to be made in good faith though the good faith standard[89] should

---

FORM COMMERCIAL CODE, §§ 2-614 and 2-615. Unanticipated difficulty does not excuse the promisee. *See* RESTATEMENT 2d § 89 comment b.

[85] RESTATEMENT 2d § 89(a).

[86] "An agreement modifying a contract with this Article needs no consideration to be binding." UCC § 2-209(1).

[87] Comment 1 to UCC § 2-209 illustrates the anti-technical nature of Article 2 with respect to modifications: "This section seeks to protect and make effective all necessary and desirable modifications of sales contracts without regard to the technicalities which at present hamper such adjustments." Other illustrations of the anti-technical nature of Article 2 include § 2-204(3) (contract does not fail for indefiniteness notwithstanding absence of one or more terms, if parties intended to form a contract and there is a basis for an appropriate remedy); § 2-206 comment 1 ("[f]ormer technical rules as to acceptance . . . are rejected"). In Columbia Nitrogen Corp. v. Royster Co., 451 F.2d 3, 10 (4th Cir. 1971), the court speaks of "the overly legalistic interpretations which the Code seeks to abolish."

[88] The factual bargain analysis is predicated upon the definition of "contract" in UCC § 1-201(11) which defines contract in terms of effect, i.e., "the total legal obligation which results from the parties' agreement...." "Agreement" is defined in § 1-201(3) as "the bargain of the parties in fact as found in their language or by implication from other circumstances including course of dealing or usage or trade or course of performance...." For a more complete statement of the factual bargain analysis *see* Murray, *The Article 2 Prism: The Underlying Philosophy of Article 2 of the Uniform Commercial Code*, 21 WASHBURN L.J. 1 (1981). *See also* Murray, *The Chaos of the "Battle of the Forms": Solutions*, 39 VAND. L. REV. 1307 (1986).

[89] Section 2-103(1)(b) defines good faith in the case of a merchant as "honesty in fact and the observance of reasonable commercial standards of fair dealing in the trade." The general (non-

be implied and a comment clearly limits enforceable modifications without consideration to those made in good faith.[90] The same comment suggests the possibility that such modifications require a "legitimate commercial reason" or "an objectively demonstrable reason" for seeking modification.[91] Unforeseen difficulty that would provide a legal excuse[92] is not necessary. If, however, the requirements of § 2-209(1) were compared to the "unanticipated difficulty" concept of the RESTATEMENT 2d discussed *supra*,[93] there is no unanticipated difficulty requirement in § 2-209(1) though the existence of such a difficulty or other sound commercial reason for the modification would provide evidence of the essential requirement of good faith.[94] Courts have evidenced very few problems in the application of § 2-209(1), i.e., the UCC change in the pre-existing duty rule. Problems have arisen, however, with respect to the remaining four subsections of § 2-209.

2. Section 2-209(2): No Oral Modification Clauses.

The parties to a written contract may decide that any changes or modifications of their contract will not be enforceable unless they are evidenced by writing. These "no oral modification" (NOM) clauses were not favored at common law because of the principle that parties to a contract should not be deterred from changing their minds.[95] A New York statute made such clauses

---

merchant) definition is found in § 1-201(19): "honesty in fact in the conduct or transaction concerned."

[90] Comment 2 to § 2-209.

[91] *Ibid.*

[92] *See* UCC §§ 2-614 and 2-615.

[93] RESTATEMENT 2d § 89(a).

[94] In Gross Valentino Printing Co. v. Clarke, 120 Ill. App. 3d 907, 458 N.E.2d 1027 (1983), the plaintiff informed the defendant that the job of printing a magazine would cost more than the original price quotation. Defendant did not object at that time, nor did he object after receiving a confirming letter to that effect and an invoice reflecting the price increase. Only after receiving the entire shipment did defendant object. The court applied § 2-209(1) enforcing the modification. *See also* A & G Constr. Co. v. Reid Bros. Logging Co., 547 P.2d 254 (Alaska 1976). In Bone Int'l, Inc. v. Johnson, 329 S.E.2d 714 (N.C. App. 1985), the defendant purchased two used trucks without warranties. Later, plaintiff agreed to perform major engine repairs without charge and the court held the subsequent modification enforceable without consideration under § 2-209(1). One of the better-known cases construing § 2-209(1) is Skinner v. Tober Foreign Motors, Inc., 345 Mass. 429, 187 N.E.2d 669 (1963) where the buyer of an airplane agreed to pay the purchase price in installments, both parties contemplating that the installment payments would be made out of future earnings. When the engine developed problems not covered by the warranty, the buyer could not afford to maintain the monthly payments and pay for the repairs. He sought to return the plane in exchange for a release. The parties agreed to modify the contract to permit the buyer to make reduced payments and to extend the obligation. The modification was viewed as one made in good faith and was upheld notwithstanding the lack of consideration.

[95] Professor Corbin suggests, "Any written contract ... can be rescinded or varied at will by the oral agreement of the parties; and this is held to be true, except as otherwise provided by statute, even of a written agreement that the contract shall not be orally varied or rescinded." CORBIN, 6 CORBIN ON CONTRACTS § 1295, at 206 and n.32. Judge Cardozo suggested, "Those who make a contract may unmake it. The clause which forbids a change may be changed like any other." Beatty v. Guggenheim Exploration Co., 225 N.Y. 380, 387, 122 N.E. 378, 381 (1919). Justice Musmanno of the Supreme Court of Pennsylvania stated that even "[t]he most ironclad written contract can always be cut into by the acetylene torch of parol modification supported by adequate proof. ... Even where the contract specifically states that no non-written modification will be recognized, the parties may yet alter their agreement by parol negotiation. The hand that pens a writing may not gag the mouths of the assenting parties. The pen may be more precise in permanently recording what is to be done, but it may not still the tongues which bespeak an

enforceable and, to avoid circumvention of the statute through oral discharges, it was amended to prohibit terminations as well as modifications.[96] Section 2-209(2) of the UCC is fashioned after the New York statute. It makes clauses excluding modifications or rescissions except by a signed writing enforceable and adds a safeguard to protect non-merchants against such clauses on forms supplied by merchants by requiring the clause to be separately signed by the non-merchant.[97] When parties include an NOM clause in their original contract, it is sometimes referred to as a "private" statute of frauds clause as contrasted with the "public" statute of frauds which we will now explore.

3. Section 2-209(3): The Contract as Modified — Statute of Frauds.

Section 2-209(3) of the UCC deals with a problem that was well-known prior to the Code. To prevent false allegations that particular parties had made promises or contracts when they had not, a statute of frauds was enacted in England in 1677 to prevent fraud and perjury. Under this statute, certain types of contracts were required to be evidenced by a writing to be enforceable. Promises by sureties, executors or administrators to answer for the debt of another, contracts for the sale of land, contracts in consideration of marriage, contracts not to be performed within one year from their making, and contracts for the sale of goods were within the original statute of frauds.[98] Modern versions of the statute in the United States rarely omit one of these categories and often include others such as promises to pay debts previously discharged in bankruptcy, arbitration agreements and promises to pay commissions to real estate brokers.[99] The statute of frauds will be explored fully later in this volume. At this point, however, it is necessary to deal with the satisfaction of the statute with respect to modifications of contracts.

If Ames and Barnes formed an oral contract which could not be performed within one year from its making, the contract would be unenforceable under the typical statute of frauds. If, however, the parties later modified their oral agreement with another oral agreement that permitted the contract to be performed within one year from the making of the modification, the *contract as modified* was enforceable without a writing.[1] A modification agreement involves two analytically distinct operative effects: (1) the termination or rescission of the original contract, and (2) the creation of a new contract. The typical modification incorporates both effects simultaneously in an entire (in-

---

improvement in or modification of what has been written." Wagner v. Graziano Constr. Co., 390 Pa. 445, 558, 136 A.2d 83-84 (1957). *See also* RESTATEMENT 2d § 148 comment b which suggests that § 2-209(2) negates the rule stated in § 148 where the Code applies, i.e., to contracts for the sale of goods.

[96] McKinney's N.Y. GEN. OBLIG. LAW § 15-301. For a statement of the history of the New York statute, see the analysis of Professor Edwin Patterson of the Columbia Law School, 1 N.Y. Law Rev. Comm'n, STUDY OF THE UNIFORM COMMERCIAL CODE 307-08 (1955).

[97] UCC § 2-209(2): "A signed agreement which excludes modification or rescission except by a signed writing cannot be otherwise modified or rescinded, but except as between merchants such a requirement on a form supplied by the merchant must be separately signed by the other party."

[98] Stat. 29 Car. II, c. 3 (1677).

[99] *See* Statutory Note dealing with the Statute of Frauds at the beginning of Chapter 5, prior to § 110 of the RESTATEMENT 2d.

[1] *See* Flowood Corp. v. Chain, 247 Miss. 443, 152 So. 2d 915 (1963).

divisible) contract so that the resulting (second) contract contains part of the terms of the original contract and the new terms.[2] There has never been any question that "the new contract is viewed as a whole,"[3] i.e., "the contract as modified."[4] Section 2-209(3) applies only to modifications of contracts for the sale of goods since Article 2 is relegated to such contracts. Section 2-201 of the UCC requires contracts for the sale of goods with a price of $500 to be evidenced by a writing to be enforceable. The writing, however, may be frugal. It need only contain the identity of the contracting parties,[5] a sufficient description of the goods to be purchased and sold and the quantity term.[6] "The price, time and place of payment or delivery, the general quality of the goods, or any particular warranties may be omitted."[7] The UCC statute of frauds also contains a number of satisfaction devices apart from a writing signed by both parties. Thus, in a contract between merchants,[8] if one merchant sends a written confirmation of the prior oral contract to the other merchant, the confirmation is effective against the non-signing merchant if he does not object to it within ten days after it is received.[9] If goods are to be specially manufactured and are not suitable for sale to others in the ordinary course of the seller's business, an oral contract for such goods will be enforceable if the seller has made a substantial beginning of their manufacture or commitments for their procurement.[10] If an oral contract was made and the party against whom enforcement is sought admits, in his pleading, testimony or otherwise in court, that he made the contract, the contract becomes enforceable through the admission.[11] Finally, if the seller has received and accepted payment for goods, or the buyer has received and accepted goods pursuant to an oral contract, the contract is enforceable without any writing to the extent of the part of the goods received and accepted or the part of the payment received and accepted.[12] In addition to these alternate satisfaction devices, i.e., devices other than a satisfactory writing evidencing the contract, some courts have begun to view detrimental reliance as a general satisfaction device. Thus, an oral contract that does not satisfy the requirements of § 2-201, according to these courts, will be enforceable if the party seeking to enforce it has justifiably relied upon the oral promise of the other party.[13]

[2] See RESTATEMENT 2d § 149 and Murray, *The Modification Mystery: Section 2-209 of the Uniform Commercial Code*, 32 VILL. L. REV. 1, 21 (1987).
[3] RESTATEMENT 2d § 149 comment a.
[4] 2 CORBIN ON CONTRACTS § 304, at 97 suggests: "The second agreement is within the statute if these two parts, taken together, make a contract that would be within the statute if it had been the only executory contract that the parties had made, otherwise not."
[5] The parties need not be identified specifically as buyer or seller, i.e., the identification of the parties is sufficient.
[6] The quantity term in a requirements or output contract necessarily depends upon the needs of the buyer or the output of the seller. While the quantity term in such contracts is not determined at the time of contract formation, it is determinable and will be determined at the end of the contract period. Therefore, such contracts contain a quantity term.
[7] UCC § 2-201 comment 1.
[8] See UCC § 2-104 for definitions of "merchant." For the purposes of the statute of frauds section, § 2-201, "merchant" is defined broadly and would include anyone in business.
[9] UCC § 2-201(2).
[10] UCC § 2-201(3)(a).
[11] UCC § 2-201(3)(b).
[12] UCC § 2-201(3)(c).
[13] There is a split of authority in this area. Courts finding a general reliance satisfaction device include Potter v. Hatter Farms, 56 Or. 254, 641 P.2d 628 (1982); Warder & Lee Elevator Co. v.

Section 2-209(3) merely requires the "contract as modified" to meet the requirements of the statute of frauds as contained in § 2-201.[14] The conventional wisdom concerning the scope of § 2- 209(3), however, recognizes five possibilities:[15] (1) if the original contract is within § 2-201, *any* modification must be evidenced by a writing. One case supports this view and suggests that a modification permitting the buyer to extend the time for payment had to be in writing.[16] Since the time, amount or place of payment do not have to be in writing to satisfy § 2-201, and § 2- 209(3) merely requires satisfaction of § 2-201 with respect to the contract as modified, the construction of § 2-209(3) is silly. (2) If the changed term in the modification agreement brings the contract within § 2-201 for the first time, the modification must be evidenced by a writing. Thus, a contract for the sale of goods with a price less than $500 need not be evidenced by a writing under § 2-201(1). If the parties modify their agreement by raising the price to $500 or more, a writing would be required for the contract as modified. (3) The modification must be in writing if the quantity term is changed. If the quantity were established at 1000 units in the original written contract and the modification changed the quantity to more or fewer units, the modification agreement would require written evidence. Section 2-201 limits enforcement of the contract to the quantity term stated in the writing.[17] If, therefore, the only writing were the original writing stating 1000 units, the enforcement of the modified contract would be limited to that quantity term since no other written quantity term exists. (4) A modification must be in writing if the modification, itself, is within § 2-201. If a contract for services not required to be evidenced by a writing were modified to include goods priced at $500 or more, the modification, itself, would subject the contract as modified to the requirement of a writing under § 2-201. (5) Some combination of the foregoing may very well require the contract, as modified, to be evidenced by a writing to satisfy the requirement of the "public" statute of frauds, § 2-201.

Unfortunately, the case law construing § 2-209(3) often fails to address the question of scope. Where the parties formed a contract for the sale of a certain quantity of sweaters at a certain price subject to a power of cancellation in the seller, an oral modification eliminated the cancellation term and provided the buyer with a right to purchase if its sealed bid were no lower than the highest sealed bid. The court assumed that the modification had to be evidenced by a writing though none of the critical terms required to be in writing under § 2-201 were modified.[18] Similarly, in a case involving the purchase and sale of

Britten, 274 N.W.2d 339 (Iowa 1979); Robert Johnson Grain Co. v. Chemical Interchange Co., 541 F.2d 207 (8th Cir. 1976); R. S. Bennett & Co. v. Economy Mech. Indus., 606 F.2d 182 (7th Cir. 1979). Cases rejecting the application of detrimental reliance to satisfy the requirements of § 2-201 include McDabco v. Chet Adams Co., 548 F. Supp. 456 (D. S.C. 1982); Ivey's Plumbing & Elec. Co. v. Petrochem Main., 463 F. Supp. 543 (N.D. Miss. 1978); Cox v. Cox, 292 Ala. 106, 289 So. 2d 609 (1974).

[14] "The requirements of the statute of frauds section of this Article (§ 2-201) must be satisfied if the contract as modified is within its provisions." UCC § 2-209(3).

[15] These possibilities are identified in J. WHITE & R. SUMMERS, HANDBOOK OF THE LAW UNDER THE UNIFORM COMMERCIAL CODE § 1-5, at 42-43 (2d ed. 1980).

[16] Asco Mining Co. v. Gross Contr'g Co., 3 U.C.C. Rep. 293 (Pa. C. P. 1965).

[17] UCC § 2-201 comment 1.

[18] *See* Double-E Sportswear v. Girard Trust Bank, 488 F.2d 292 (3d Cir. 1973).

wheat, the plaintiff alleged an oral modification extending the delivery date and the court found that this modification had to be evidenced by a writing though, again, § 2-201 would not require such a term in the original contract.[19] The failure of courts to address the fundamental problem of the scope of § 2-209(3) has created considerable confusion in the application of that subsection as well as the remaining subsections of § 2-209.[20]

4. Sections 2-209(4) and (5): Waivers and Retractions.

Section 209(4) suggests that an attempt at modification which does not satisfy subsection (2) (NOM clauses) or (3) (§ 2-201 as applied to the contract as modified) "can operate as a waiver."[21] Like other parts of § 2-209, this subsection is an effort to codify pre-Code law.[22] The term, "waiver", has always been troublesome because it is used to describe a variety of events.[23] The most common definition is "a voluntary relinquishment of a known right."[24] Unfortunately, this definition is misleading.[25] It implies that one can termi-

---

[19] See Farmers Elevator Co. of Reserve v. Anderson, 170 Mont. 175, 552 P.2d 63 (1976). The original contract was not evidenced by a writing. However, the defendant admitted that contract was made, thereby satisfying § 2-201 through the process of admission in § 2-201 (3)(b). The original contract was evidenced by the admission just as if it had been evidenced by a writing. Since § 2-201 does not require delivery dates to be in writing, there would seem to be no reason for requiring the "contract as modified" to evidence such a term in writing.

[20] In Bone Int'l, Inc. v. Johnson, 74 N.C. App. 703, 329 S.E.2d 714 (1985), the issue was whether an oral modification of a disclaimer of warranty clause in the original contract should be enforceable. While the statute of frauds was not raised, the court stated that, had it been raised, modification would have been enforceable because of defendant's reliance thereon. The court did not discuss whether an oral modification concerning a warranty term must satisfy § 2-201. In Ruble Forest Prods., Inc. v. Lancer Mobile Homes of Or., Inc., 269 Or. 315, 524 P.2d 1204 (1974), the court found statute of frauds satisfaction for an oral modification changing a payment term in a letter by plaintiff's president. There was no direct discussion of whether such a modification was within § 2-201 as incorporated in § 2-209(3). The most myopic judicial effort is found in Symbol Techs. v. Sunoco, Inc., 36 UCC Rep. Serv. 497 (E.D. Pa. 1983) where the court concluded that the evidence of an alleged oral modification was inadmissible because (1) the parol evidence rule barred it, though the court understood the modification to be a *subsequent* agreement and, as will be seen later in this volume, the parol evidence rule is not applicable to such agreements; (2) there was no consideration alleged for the modification (the court did not discuss the § 2-209(1) negation of the consideration requirement in good faith modifications); (3) the modification violated the statute of frauds. In granting summary judgment, the court failed to consider Pennsylvania precedent holding the statute of frauds to be an affirmative defense forcing either an admission or denial of the existence of the contract. See Duffee v. Judson, 251 Pa. Super. 406, 380 A.2d 843 (1977).

[21] UCC § 2-209(4).

[22] For an exploration of the pre-UCC history of §§ 2-209(4) and (5), see Murray, *The Modification Mystery: Section 2-209 of the Uniform Commercial Code*, 32 VILL. L. REV. 1, 33-44 (1987).

[23] Meanings of the term were the subject of study in the early part of the century. See J. EWART, WAIVER DISTRIBUTED AMONG THE DEPARTMENTS: ELECTION, ESTOPPEL, CONTRACT, RELEASE (1917). Professor Corbin states that the term "has been given various definitions; the fact is that it is used under many varying circumstances." 3A CORBIN ON CONTRACTS § 752, at 478.

[24] See e.g., Van Der Broeke v. Bellanca Aircraft Corp., 576 F.2d 582 (5th Cir. 1978); Farmers Elev. Co. of Reserve v. Anderson, 170 Mont. 175, 552 P.2d 63 (1976); Clark v. West, 193 N.Y. 349, 86 N.E. 1 (1908), aff'd, 201 N.Y. 569, 95 N.E. 1125 (1911).

[25] The definition is misleading because it suggests that one can simply "waive" a right unilaterally as contrasted with waiving a condition to a duty, and it is also misleading in that it may suggest that the promisor must "know" the legal effect of his promise as contrasted with simply knowing the essential facts. See RESTATEMENT 2d § 84 comment b. See also Rubin v. Los Angeles Fed. Sav. & Loan, 205 Cal. Rptr. 455, 459 (Cal. App. 1984): "Although waiver is frequently said to be the intentional relinquishment of a known right, waiver may also result from conduct 'which,

nate or discharge a right by "waiving" it. It is possible to relinquish a known right voluntarily in numerous ways including gratuitous termination. Such a relinquishment, however, is not a waiver even though the correlative duty is discharged.[26] It would have been desirable to restrict the use of the term "waiver" to those situations to which it clearly applies, i.e., the elimination of a condition (express, implied or constructive) to the duty to which it is attached. As will be seen in the exploration of conditions in the law of contracts in a subsequent chapter, a condition attached to a contractual duty must occur to activate that duty. A party may choose to perform a conditional duty even though the condition has not occurred. If, for example, a seller was not to deliver goods until a payment was made by the prospective buyer, the failure of the buyer to make the payment would be a breach of his contractual duty. At the same time, it would constitute a failure of a constructive condition to the duty of the seller. The seller could choose to perform notwithstanding the failure of pre-payment. Moreover, the seller could inform the buyer that he need not make the pre-payment as required under the contract. This unilateral announcement would be a promise or representation by the seller that he will not insist upon the occurrence of the condition of pre-payment to his duty. If this announcement caused the buyer to change his position, i.e., to rely on the seller's statement, the seller should later be precluded from asserting this failure of condition as a basis for the seller's refusal to deliver the goods. It could be said that the seller is "estopped" from asserting the failure of the condition or that the condition has been "waived." "Estoppel" and "waiver," however, are mere conclusions. It is the justifiable reliance on the part of the buyer that eliminates the condition to the seller's duty. If the buyer has not relied, the condition could be reinstated if the seller notified the buyer within a reasonable time to make the pre-payment. If the parties *agreed* to modify the requirement of an early payment and the buyer relied on this agreement, such a modification could be characterized as a "waiver" that would be irrevocable because of the buyer's reliance.

The curiosity of this analysis is that no validation device such as consideration or detrimental reliance is necessary to make a modification enforceable under § 2-209(1). The curiosity is removed, however, if we remember that *modifications* are enforceable without a validation device; *waivers*, however, require a validation device. The absence of a validation device will not preclude enforcement of a modification. The statute of frauds (§ 2-201) or an NOM clause, however, *will* preclude the enforcement of a modification that does not satisfy those requirements. If a modification is so precluded, *as a modification* it is unenforceable. An unenforceable modification, however, "can operate as a waiver."[27] Waivers are not irrevocable absent a validation device unless the time for the occurrence of the condition has passed and the term waived is not a material part of the agreed exchange.[28] There is nothing

---

according to its natural import, is so inconsistent with the intent to enforce the right in question as to induce a reasonable belief that such right has been relinquished.'"

[26] *Ibid.*

[27] UCC § 2-209(4).

[28] RESTATEMENT 2d § 84. This section of the RESTATEMENT 2d deals with waiver in terms of the elimination of conditions. If a waiver of a condition occurs prior to the time for its occurrence,

in the Uniform Commercial Code suggesting any change in the pre-Code or extra-Code law governing waivers, including waivers arising from modification agreements. Comment 4 to § 2-209 indicates the drafters' intention to avoid any interference with that pre-Code law so as to give "legal effect [to] the parties' later conduct." When subsection (5) of § 2-209 is added to this analysis, the UCC purpose to codify pre-Code concepts is complete. § 2-209(5) permits the reinstatement of the "waived" requirement through reasonable notification that strict performance of the waived term will be required if there has been no material change of position in reliance on the waiver.[29]

It is important to note that there is no possibility of enforcing an otherwise unenforceable oral modification simply by calling it a "waiver" under § 2-209(4) that has been made irrevocable through reliance under § 2-209(5). In a contract for the sale of goods, if a buyer requests a seller to delay shipment and the seller complies with that request, it would be horrendous to permit the buyer to defend a later action by the seller on the basis of a failed tender to deliver in accordance with the precise time of delivery. Absent evidence that the seller could not have delivered at the original time for other reasons, the situation screams for the elimination of the original delivery term.[30] If, however, the parties had agreed orally to change the subject matter of the contract or to change the quantity term of the original contract, such an oral modification could not be made enforceable by calling it a "waiver."[31]

It is important to emphasize the very narrow application of §§ 2-209(4) and (5) of the UCC. These subsections become operative only if the oral modification fails to meet the requirements of the "public" (§ 2-201) or "private" (§ 2-209(2)) statute of frauds. While the § 2-209(2) NOM requirement does not expressly state that it will be satisfied by alternate satisfaction devices under § 2-201, the purposes of Article 2 would be frustrated if such devices were not effective. Consider, for example, an oral modification that violates the parties'

---

absent consideration or reliance, it may be reinstated if notice is given and there is a reasonable time for the conditioning event to occur.

[29] UCC § 2-209(5): "A party who has made a waiver affecting an executory portion of the contract may retract the waiver by reasonable notification received by the other party that strict performance will be required of any term waived, unless the retraction would be unjust in view of a material change of position in reliance on the waiver."

[30] In Gold Kist, Inc. v. Pillow, 582 S.W.2d 77 (Tenn. App. 1977), a buyer of soybeans formed several contracts with the seller at prices varying from $5.95 per bushel to $7.22 per bushel. The contracts contained NOM clauses and stipulated that the delivery of the soybeans would be applied first to the contract with the earliest date until delivery of that contract amount was completed, and then to subsequent contracts in chronological order. The earliest contracts called for the lowest prices. The plaintiff-buyer alleged an oral modification prompted by seller's request that his deliveries be applied to the later, higher-priced contract because he needed the money. The buyer agreed and paid the higher prices on earlier deliveries. The seller then resued for performance of the remaining contract calling for lower prices. The court stated that it would be "repulsive" to permit a party to request a change in terms of payment and then to escape liability because the other party had, in good faith, granted the request. The conduct of the defendant in this case cries out for an application of the waiver/estoppel analysis. It should also be noted, however, that when the plaintiff made and defendant accepted payments in excess of the terms of the writing, there was reliable course of performance evidence that could be viewed as an alternate satisfaction device, i.e., other than a writing, making the oral modification enforceable.

[31] Comment 5 to UCC § 2-209 states: "Subsection (5) allows retraction of a waiver with reference to the future, subject always to the qualification of reasonable notice and other avoidance of injustice. To limit this estoppel phase to its proper purpose, this Article gives preference in any case of doubt to the 'waiver' construction as against that of unauthenticated 'modification.'"

NOM clause and also violates § 2-209(3). If the party against whom enforcement of the oral modification is sought admits in her pleading, testimony or otherwise in court that she agreed to the modification, § 2-209(3) would be satisfied since that subsection, again, only requires that the modified contract satisfy § 2-201.[32] If the NOM clause were not satisfied through such an admission, a party could use the NOM clause as a technical shield while admitting she made the modification. That would subvert a specific purpose of Article 2[33] as well as the essential philosophy of Article 2.[34] Any device, apart from a writing, that satisfies the requirements of § 2-201 should serve to satisfy the parties' own NOM requirement.[35] As suggested earlier, a number of courts have also permitted satisfaction of the public statute of frauds if reliance on an oral promise is shown.[36] If any of these satisfaction devices is present, there is no need to resort to the "waiver" concept of § 2-209(4) since the writing requirement has been met through an alternate satisfaction device.[37]

A recent judicial analysis involving two former academic lawyers who now serve on the same United States Court of Appeals reveals the current confusion in this area. In *Wisconsin Knife Works v. National Metal Corporation*,[38] a purchase order contained an NOM clause[39] and the supplier of goods sought to be excused from original delivery dates in the contract through an oral modification. As to the possibility that the oral modification could be said to operate as a waiver under § 2-209(4), the majority opinion suggests that an attempt at modification may operate as a waiver only if it is accompanied by reliance.[40] The dissenting opinion suggests that this interpretation effectively

---

[32] UCC § 2-201(3)(b) permits enforcement of an oral contract through an admission in court (including depositions) that the party against whom enforcement is sought has made the contract.

[33] *Ibid.*

[34] *See supra* note 87.

[35] Section 2-201 of the UCC permits satisfaction through a writing signed by the party to be charged, a confirmation between merchants sent by the other party, specific reliance by a seller in beginning to manufacture specially-manufactured goods or making commitments for their procurement, admission of the oral contract or performance under the oral contract to the extent of such performance. The New York statute upon which § 2-209(2) was based is N.Y. GEN. OBLIG. LAW § 15-301 (McKinney). In a recent case, the written agreement evidencing a shareholder's agreement required that amendments or modifications be signed by *all* of the parties to the original agreement. The modification was not signed by all of the parties, but it was signed by the party to be charged. The court affirmed a denial of a motion to dismiss on the ground that the statute did not require precise compliance with the terms of the NOM clause, but only that the evidence show that the modification was authentic or was otherwise ratified by the parties' conduct. Landau v. Salzman, 514 N.Y.S.2d 767 (A.D. Dept. 1987).

[36] It should be remembered that the general reliance satisfaction of the statute of frauds requirement is not expressed in §§ 2-201 or 2-209(2) or (3). Rather, it has been judicially engrafted. If that device had been generally effective at the time these UCC sections were drafted, it is quite possible that there would have been little need for §§ 2-209(4) and (5).

[37] Another peculiarity is inspired by § 2-209(5). If, for example, the parties modified their contract orally in contravention of §§ 2-209(4) and (5), and prior to reliance one of the parties notified the other, in writing, that the oral modification they had made is to be withdrawn, such written notice may unwittingly satisfy the writing requirement of the public statute of frauds (§ 2-201) or the NOM requirement of § 2-209(3) thereby making any further discussion of "waiver" or "retraction of waiver" irrelevant.

[38] 781 F.2d 1280 (7th Cir. 1986).

[39] "No modification of this contract shall be binding upon Buyer unless made in writing and signed by Buyer's authorized representative...."

[40] *Id.* at 1287. The majority opinion was written by Judge Posner, well-known in academic circles for his work in law and economics.

eliminates subsection (4) of § 2-209.[41] It should be recalled that § 2-209(4) indicates that an attempt at modification that does not satisfy § 2-209(2) or (3) (such an "attempt" must be an oral modification) *can* operate as a waiver. This language reflects the careful approach of Professor Corbin who criticizes courts which "content themselves with saying that the written contract cannot be modified by oral agreement, without considering whether or not there was any basis for an estoppel" (reliance).[42] Corbin suggests that courts should not "refuse a remedy by merely denying the possibility of an oral variation"[43] though he admits that such cases can often be justified on the footing that there was no basis for an estoppel. Absent any reliance, the "waiver" created by an otherwise unenforceable oral modification under § 2-209(4) may be retracted under § 2-209(5). The dissenting opinion in *Wisconsin Knife* suggests the preferable analysis of these subsections.[44]

5. Summary of Section 2-209.

It is important to summarize the foregoing analysis of UCC § 2-209. Section 2-209(1) has worked very well as a significant but relatively unremarkable revision of the pre-existing duty rule. Section 2-209(2) permits the parties to restrict their future action in modifying their contract by requiring any such modification to be evidenced by a writing. Any satisfaction device recognized under § 2-201 should be effective to satisfy the parties' "private" statute of frauds just as it would satisfy a requirement of the "public" statute of frauds. Section 2-209(3) should receive the traditional interpretation so forcefully suggested by Professor Corbin and others: treat the "contract as modified" as the only contract. If there is an original writing containing the essential terms of the contract as modified, that writing should be sufficient evidence of the contract as modified though it contains other terms such as price, time of delivery or other non-essential memorandum terms that have been orally modified. The recognition of the scope of § 2-209(3) will eliminate much of the disconcertion in the extant case law. Section 2-209(4) should be limited to the traditional waiver/estoppel situations upon which it was modeled. If a party

---

[41] "Under the majority's reading, however, ... [n]o waiver is effective without detrimental reliance. It is as if the majority has eliminated § 2-209(4) from the UCC and rewritten § 2-209(5) to begin: 'A party who has made [an ineffectual attempt at modification] affecting [any] portion of the contract may retract....'" 781 F.2d at 1291. The dissenting opinion was written by Judge Easterbrook who was a colleague of the majority opinion writer, Judge Posner, when both served on the faculty at the University of Chicago School of Law. *See also* Rubin v. Los Angeles Fed. Sav. & Loan, 205 Cal. Rptr. 455, 459 (Cal. App. 1984): "Los Angeles Federal asserts that its failure to foreclose earlier did not induce Rubin to change his position or act otherwise than he did. However, detrimental reliance is not a necessary element of waiver, only of estoppel."

[42] 2 CORBIN ON CONTRACTS § 310, at 116.

[43] *Ibid.*

[44] The majority opinion suggests that § 2-209(5) "is not limited to attempted modifications invalid under subsection (2) or (3); it applies, for example, to an express written and signed waiver, provided only that the contract is still executory." The opinion suggests that subsection (4) qualifies subsection (2); but subsection (5) does not qualify subsection (2). 781 F.2d 1287. The dissenting opinion finds that the majority has twisted the proper construction of the two subsections. "This distinction implies that subsection (4) applies to a subset of the subjects of subsection (5). Things are the other way around. Subsection (4) says that an attempt at modification may be a 'waiver,' and subsection (5) qualifies the effectiveness of 'waivers' in the absence of reliance." 781 F.2d at 1291.

pleads an oral modification, he or she should have the opportunity to prove that a condition to the duty of the other party was eliminated through the oral modification. Typically, such evidence will demonstrate reliance. Section 2-209(5) permits the waiving party to retract the waiver by reasonable and timely notice. If such notice satisfies the memorandum requirement of either § 2-209(2) or § 2-209(3), however, §§ 2-209(4) and (5) are inapplicable because the writing requirement has been satisfied and the question of waiver is then moot.

Notwithstanding the developing case law concerning § 2-209, many of these questions have not been addressed by the courts. If courts focus upon the purpose of each part of the section, an effective construction is more than likely. While Article 2 contains many radical innovations in classical contract law, it should be remembered that apart from an unremarkable change in the pre-existing duty rule (in § 2-209(1)), the remainder of the section was designed to codify well-known pre-Code concepts.[45]

§ 65. Mutuality of Obligation.

The so-called "doctrine" of mutuality of obligation is capable of causing considerable confusion. The conventional wisdom suggests that the "doctrine" originated in the early case of *Harrison v. Cage* involving an exchange of promises to marry. In response to the argument that the man's promise was not consideration for the woman's promise, but the woman's promise was consideration for the man's promise, the court felt compelled to suggest that either both promises are binding or neither is binding: "[E]ither all is a nudum pactum, or else one promise is as good as the other."[46] This dictum has been repeated in scores of cases.[47] The dictum, like the "doctrine," is devoid of any substance. It is either meaningless or, again, confusing. If the statement means that a promise that is not legally binding cannot constitute consideration, it is a tautology. Earlier in this chapter, illusory promises were explored. An illusory promise promises nothing, *e.g.,* "I promise to sell you my car unless I choose not to sell you my car." Such a promise cannot support a counter promise to purchase the car for a certain sum because the buyer-promisor is receiving nothing for his promise. There is no consideration for the buyer's promise. To suggest that such an agreement lacks "mutuality of obligation" adds absolutely nothing to the analysis. A number of courts have recognized the superfluousness of this "doctrine".[48]

---

[45] For a more comprehensive analysis, *see* Murray, *The Modification Mystery: Section 2-209 of the Uniform Commercial Code,* 32 VILL. L. REV. 1 (1987).

[46] 5 Mod. 411 [1698]. The "doctrine" of mutuality of obligation must be distinguished from another doctrine of mutuality — sometimes characterized as mutuality of remedy — developed in courts of equity to the effect that specific performance cannot be had of the defendant's promise unless the contract is one which could have been specifically enforced against the plaintiff. *See* Ames, *Mutuality in Specific Performances,* 3 COLUM. L. REV. 1 (1903); Stone, *The Mutuality Rule in New York,* 16 COLUM. L. REV. 443 (1916). For a case that mentions both types of mutuality and refers to both as necessary in a suit for specific performance, *see* Madaio v. McCarthy, 199 N.J. Super. 430, 489 A.2d 1197 (1985).

[47] A recent repetition occurred in De Witt Cty. Pub. Bldg. Comm'n v. County of De Witt, 128 Ill. App. 3d 11, 469 N.E.2d 689 (1984): "In its most elemental sense, the doctrine of mutuality of obligation means that unless both parties to a contract are bound by its terms, neither is bound."

[48] For example, in Zamore v. Whitten, 395 A.2d 435, 443, n.3 (Me. 1978), the court states: "The phrase 'mutuality of obligation' has caused much confusion to courts and commentators over the

The "doctrine" is capable of creating confusion in a number of ways. It may be confused with an equitable doctrine often called "mutuality of remedy"[49] or with "adequacy of consideration," i.e., the relative values promised by each party.[50] Another problem occurs with respect to unenforceable promises that will, nonetheless, constitute consideration. A promise voidable because of the infancy or insanity of the promisor, or because of fraud, duress or illegality, can constitute consideration to make a counter promise enforceable by a party who has no power of avoidance or disaffirmance.[51] Voidable promises are enforceable until the party with the power of avoidance or disaffirmance chooses to disaffirm. Thus, there is consideration even though one party is given a power to disaffirm because of incapacity. A promise that is unenforceable because it does not satisfy the statute of frauds will constitute consideration.[52] The statute of frauds imposes an evidentiary requirement on an otherwise enforceable promise, i.e., it has nothing to do with the general requirement that promises must be supported by consideration or another validation device. In light of these holdings, it appears futile to argue that a nonbinding promise can never constitute consideration.

One of the classic cases in this area which troubles law students is *Hay v. Fortier*.[53] The defendant became surety on a bond, i.e., she promised to pay if the principal debtor failed to pay. When the principal debtor did not pay, the surety was called upon to perform her promise. She sought an extension of time, i.e., she promised to pay the entire amount then due in installment payments over a stated period of time. It is important to recognize that, when the surety made this promise, she promised nothing more than the amount already due, i.e., she did not even promise to pay additional interest on the debt during the extension period. In exchange for this promise, which was a promise to do nothing beyond her present duty, she sought forbearance from suit on the principal obligation (the bond) by the creditor. The creditor's promise to forbear, however, was not supported by consideration because the

---

years.... In fact, mutuality embodies a particularized application of the consideration doctrine in the context of formation of a bilateral contract. In a bilateral contract, one promise is good consideration for another. If the promisee fails to give the required return promise, mutual obligations are not, in fact, created. It is less confusing, and equally accurate, however, to conclude that no contract exists due to the promisee's failure to give legally sufficient consideration." (Citing 1 WILLISTON ON CONTRACTS § 105A (3d ed. 1957)). In Riedman Corp. v. Jarosh, 289 S.C. 191, 345 S.E.2d 732 (1986), the court notes that "consideration" and "mutuality of obligation" are sometimes confused. Consideration is essential; mutuality of obligation is not. The doctrine of mutuality of obligation is simply a statement of the rule that mutual promises constitute considerations for each other. The RESTATEMENT 2d in § 79 comment f, criticizes the doctrine: "'Both parties must be bound or neither is bound.' That statement is obviously erroneous as applied to an exchange of promise for performance; [It is generally suggested that the "doctrine" does not apply to unilateral contracts since there is no unilateral contract until the promisee completely performs the act required by the offeror.] it is equally inapplicable to contracts governed by §§ 82-94 and to contracts enforceable by virtue or their formal characteristics under § 6."

[49] *See supra* note 46.

[50] The "adequacy of consideration" doctrine was explored *supra*. For a case in which this confusion is discussed, *see* Hillsman v. Sutter Community Hosps. of Sacramento, 153 Cal. App. 3d 743, 200 Cal. Rptr. 605 (1984). *See also* Zamore v. Whitten, 395 A.2d 435, 443 n.3 (Me. 1978), where the court mentions Professor Corbin's criticism of the expression, "mutuality of obligation," for its tendency to connote a need for obligations equivalent in terms of detriment and value.

[51] RESTATEMENT 2d § 78 comment b.

[52] RESTATEMENT 2d § 78 comment c.

[53] 116 Me. 455, 102 A. 294 (1917).

surety, again, had promised nothing. The creditor was receiving no legal value for his promise. If, immediately after promising, the creditor had brought an action on the bond, he would have breached no contract since he could not be said to be bound to any contract with the surety. While this situation appears to be a perfect manifestation of the requirement that either both parties are bound by their promises or neither is bound, to clutter the analysis with conclusory labels such as a lack of "mutuality of obligation" adds nothing to the analysis. Again, the creditor's promise is not binding because it is not supported by consideration. Notwithstanding the lack of consideration to support the plaintiff's promise to forbear, the plaintiff did, in fact, forbear for a period exceeding the promised duration of forbearance. The defendant-surety failed to perform her subsequent promise to pay the debt in installments and the creditor brought an action on the subsequent promise rather than the original debt evidenced by the bond.[54] The defendant argued that there was no consideration for her promise since the plaintiff's promise was unenforceable because it was not supported by consideration. There should be no confusion about this analysis. If the transaction is viewed at the moment the promises were exchanged, there was no consideration. Defendant could not enforce the plaintiff's promise because plaintiff could demonstrate no consideration for that promise. Since the defendant could not enforce that promise, she received nothing for her promise. Thus, her promise was unenforceable. When, however, the plaintiff performed its unenforceable promise, the defendant received a forbearance for which she had bargained. When viewed from the perspective of an executory bilateral contract, therefore, the agreement lacked consideration. However, once the plaintiff performed the act sought by the defendant, query, should the plaintiff be able to enforce the defendant's promise? The court held the defendant's promise enforceable:

> Having enjoyed the forbearance of the plaintiff from bringing the action against her on the bond for the full period agreed upon, the defendant is now estopped from refusing performance on her part on the ground that the contract was not originally binding on the plaintiff, who did, nevertheless, perform it and she received the benefit thereof.[55]

It is unfortunate that the court resorted to the conclusory label of estoppel. Precisely why was the defendant estopped from refusing the performance or her promise to pay in installments? The simple but sound analysis is that, upon completion of the forbearance by the plaintiff, a unilateral contract was formed with one right in the plaintiff who had already suffered a detriment in performing the requested act, and one correlative duty in the defendant who had received the benefit of the performance. There was no executory bilateral contract because the exchange of promises lacked consideration, but there was a unilateral contract in which the defendant's promise was supported by consideration.[56] The FIRST RESTATEMENT refused to adopt this or any other analy-

---

[54] The plaintiff had brought an action on the bond but that action was "discontinued without costs and without prejudice."

[55] 102 A. at 295.

[56] See First Wis. Nat'l Bank of Milwaukee v. Oby, 52 Wis. 2d 1, 188 N.W.2d 454, 458-59 (1971): "Though at its inception the agreement lacked mutuality of obligation since plaintiff was not bound to make any loans whatsoever, the real question is whether at the time this action was

sis that would make the defendant's promise enforceable.[57] The RESTATEMENT 2d, however, disagrees and finds the promise enforceable conditioned on the performance of the act, i.e., the plaintiff's forbearance.[58] The formulation in the RESTATEMENT 2d is devoid of any useful rationale[59] and the unilateral contract analysis is highly preferable. In any case, the "doctrine" of mutuality of obligation provides no assistance in the development of a sound analysis. The "doctrine" has outlived any possible usefulness and should be frankly disavowed in those jurisdictions where its tautological nature has yet to be discerned.

§ 66. Detrimental Reliance — "Promissory Estoppel."

A. *The Doctrine and Its Antecedents — The Lack of Bargained-For Exchange.*

The purpose of contract law is often stated as the fulfillment of those expectations induced by the making of a promise.[60] While the expectation interest has been recognized as the normal interest protected by contract law, it cannot be gainsaid that the reliance interest presents a greater claim to protection.[61] If a party has reasonably relied to his detriment on the promise of another, he has suffered a loss which is properly characterized as an out-of-pocket or minus quantity.[62] If a bilateral, executory contract has been breached, however, no reliance or out-of-pocket loss need be shown to permit the aggrieved party a remedy for the disappointment of his expectations. That disappointment is his loss and the law will intervene to place him in the

brought the plaintiff had fully or partially executed the act which formed the basis for defendant's promise. Clearly it had.... It is sufficient that something of value flows from the promisee, or that it performed any act or suffered any inconvenience which it was not obligated to, and that it relied upon the strength of the promise as the inducement for such act. Therefore, to the extent that plaintiff's promise no longer remained executory and illusory, but was executed, sufficient consideration ... was given in reliance upon the promises of defendant and her husband to support her promise, and to allow enforcement of the contract against defendant."

[57] FIRST RESTATEMENT § 78 ill. 4.

[58] RESTATEMENT 2d § 75 ill. 4. *See* Ward v. Goodrich, 34 Colo. 369, 372, 82 P. 701 (1905): "While it is settled that the promising to do, or the doing of, that which the promisor is already legally bound to do, does not, as a rule, constitute consideration for a reciprocal promise, or support a reciprocal undertaking given by the promisee, it by no means follows that such promise may not be enforced against such promisor by the promisee, although its enforcement compels the performance of that which was already a legal obligation."

[59] Illustration 4 to § 75 is based on the facts, but not the rationale, of Hay v. Fortier. "A promises to forbear suit against B in exchange for B's promise to pay a liquidated and undisputed debt to A. A's promise is not binding because B's promise is not consideration ... but A's promise is nevertheless consideration for B's.... B's promise is conditional on A's forbearance and can be enforced only if the condition is met." Having suggested that A's promise is not binding because B's promise is not consideration, it is difficult to understand how "A's *promise* is nevertheless consideration for B's" promise. It is submitted that A's promise is never consideration for B's *promise*. Rather, A's promise becomes enforceable in exchange for B's act of forbearance.

[60] 1 CORBIN ON CONTRACTS § 1. "[C]ontract law provided a framework of reasonably assured expectations with which men might plan and venture." J. HURST, LAW AND ECONOMIC GROWTH: THE LEGAL HISTORY OF THE LUMBER INDUSTRY IN WISCONSIN 1836-1915, at 297 (1964). *See also* Straup v. Times Herald, 423 A.2d 713, 719 (Pa. Super. 1980): "The purpose of contract law may be stated as the fulfillment of expectations induced by the making of a promise," citing the second edition of this book at p. 195.

[61] Fuller & Perdue, *The Reliance Interest in Contract Damages* (pts. 1 & 2), 46 YALE L.J. 52, 373 (1936).

[62] *See* discussion of the reliance interest as well as the expectation and restitution interests *infra* Chapter 9.

position he would have been in had the contract not been broken. That remedy relieves his disappointment. The relying promisee, however, is more obviously injured since he has already suffered a measurable loss when the promisor refuses to perform. The injured promisee presents a compelling argument to be compensated, at least to the extent of restoring him to status quo ante, i.e., the position he was in before he justifiably relied, by permitting him to recover the amount of his minus quantity.

There is reason to believe that the original enforcement of informal contracts was based on the reasonable reliance of the promisee.[63] The concept of reliance antedates the concept of protected expectations.[64] With the development of consideration, however, there was a tendency to ignore the protection of the reliance interest. Where a promise induces reliance, the promisee has suffered a detriment. Yet, as we have seen in the exploration of the bargained-for-exchange element of consideration, if the detriment did not induce the promise, consideration is lacking. For those who thought of consideration as the apotheosis of validating promises, a promise that merely induced a detriment where the detriment did not also induce the promise was unenforceable. There was a great fear that reliance would make gratuitous promises enforceable and the doctrine of consideration would be emasculated.[65] That fear has been overcome because of the manifest injustice in refusing to recognize that certain promises induce a substantial change of position in reasonable promisees.[66] Unfortunately, general recognition of detrimental reliance as a validation device is a product of twentieth-century contract law. It was given limited recognition in Section 90 of the FIRST RESTATEMENT, and that recognition has been augmented substantially in Section 90 of the RESTATEMENT 2d. Notwithstanding its relatively recent discovery as a general validation device, the doctrine has clearly identifiable antecedents. Family promises, gratuitous promises to convey land, gratuitous bailments and charitable subscription promises clearly recognized the vitality of detrimental reliance before its recognition as a general validation device.[67] It is important to consider these antecedents.

1. Promises Within the Family — Equitable Estoppel to "Promissory Estoppel."

A promise made by one member of a family to another member was enforceable even without consideration if the promisee reasonably relied upon the promise. Some courts would find consideration to support such promises notwithstanding the lack of a bargained-for-exchange.[68] Other courts candidly

---

[63] Fuller & Perdue, *supra* note 61, at 68.

[64] *See* Loranger Constr. Corp. v. E. F. Hauserman Co., 376 Mass. 757, 384 N.E.2d 176, 179 (1978) where Justice Braucher, former Reporter of the RESTATEMENT 2d so states relying, in part, on RESTATEMENT 2d § 90 comment a.

[65] "It would cut up the doctrine of consideration by the roots, if a promisee could make a gratuitous promise binding by subsequently acting in reliance on it." O. W. Holmes, Jr. in Commonwealth v. Scituate Sav. Bank, 137 Mass. 301, 302 (1884).

[66] *See* Minor v. Sully Buttes Sch. Dist. No. 58-2, 345 S.W.2d 48 (S.D. 1984) citing the 2d edition of this book at § 91.

[67] *See* Overlock v. Central Vermont Pub. Serv. Corp., 126 Vt. 549, 237 A.2d 356 (1967).

[68] *See, e.g.*, Devecmon v. Shaw, 69 Md. 199, 14 A. 464 (1888) where an uncle promised to reimburse a nephew for his expenses if he would take a trip to Europe. The court found the

recognized the lack of consideration but found the promise enforceable because of detrimental reliance. The best known case is *Ricketts v. Scothorn*[69] where a grandfather delivered a written promise in the form of a note in the amount of $2000 with interest to his granddaughter to permit her to leave her employment. The granddaughter left the employment. At the time of his death, the grandfather had not paid the note, though he had paid some of the interest thereon. The granddaughter brought an action against the executor of the estate to recover the total amount due. The court recognized that there was no consideration to support the promise since the grandfather required no detriment from the promisee. The evidence indicated that his purpose was to permit her to be independent, i.e., to either work or remain idle, but to require nothing from her. Yet, the promisee suffered a detriment and, though her detriment had not induced her grandfather's promise, his promise has induced her detriment. Moreover, the grandfather certainly contemplated that she would rely on his promise by suffering the detriment of surrendering her employment. The court found an "equitable estoppel" which precluded the defendant from showing that the note lacked one of the essential elements of a contract, i.e., consideration. The application of an equitable estoppel theory to the facts of the case is misleading. Normally, equitable estoppel occurs where a party makes a false representation to, or knowingly conceals material facts from, another party with the intention that the innocent party should act upon the false representation or concealment.[70] Liability attached if the innocent party so acted to his detriment. There was no false representation in the *Ricketts* case. Rather, the grandfather made a *promise,* apparently in good faith. The notion that the promise is enforceable notwithstanding the lack of consideration because the promisor is *estopped* to deny consideration is nothing more than a conclusion. The promise was enforceable because the promisee changed her position to her detriment in the reasonable belief that the promise would be performed. The court's use of equitable estoppel to make the promise enforceable because of reliance may be laid to the felt necessity of the court to discover an extant doctrine in support of the result the court sought to reach. Subsequently, it became clear that *equitable estoppel* was much too narrow a ground to support the enforcement of promises which had induced reasonable detrimental reliance. Though not inevitable, it was predictable that, instead of rejecting the estoppel notion and developing the doctrine in accordance with its substantive basis, detrimental reliance, courts and

---

promise to be enforceable as supported by consideration though the facts and the rationale of the court clearly indicate that the basis for enforcing the promise was detrimental reliance notwithstanding the lack of any bargained-for-exchange.

[69] 57 Neb. 51, 77 N.W. 365 (1898).

[70] This sentence appeared in § 91 of the second edition of this book and is quoted by the court in Valley Bank v. Dowdy, 337 N.W.2d 164, 165 (S.D. 1983). Equitable estoppel, or estoppel *in pais,* is frequently defined as, "The species of estoppel which equity puts upon a person who has made a false representation or a concealment of material facts, with knowledge of the facts, to a party ignorant of the truth of the matter, with the intention that the other party should act upon it, and with the result that such party is actually induced to act upon it to his damage." Henderson, *Promissory Estoppel and Traditional Contract Doctrine,* 78 YALE L.J. 343, 376 n.182 (1969). For a recent case providing an analysis and comparison of equitable estoppel and promissory estoppel, *see* Reeve v. Georgia-Pacific Corp., 510 N.E.2d 1378 (Ind. App. 1987). *See also* Straup v. Times Herald, 423 A.2d 713, 720 (Pa. Super. 1980).

scholars would permit the doctrinal antecedents to persist in modified fashion. The modern doctrine, therefore, is known as "promissory estoppel."[71] The fact that "estoppel" has nothing to do with the enforcement of the promise and the continuation of that term can be misleading has not deterred the use of the label, "promissory estoppel."[72] The student, however, should remember that the essence of the doctrine is justifiable detrimental reliance which makes the promise enforceable or, in the language of its caption, "estops" the promisor from denying the enforcement of the promise.

2. Gratuitous Promises to Convey Land.

Like other gratuitous promises, a gratuitous promise to convey land is unenforceable because it lacks consideration. If, however, the promisee takes possession of the land and makes valuable improvements, the promisee will succeed in a suit for specific performance of the promise to convey the land.[73] A gratuitous license to use the land has been held to be specifically enforceable where the licensee has incurred substantial outlays in reliance on the promise.[74] While some courts felt compelled to discover "consideration" in such cases because of the reliance of the promisee,[75] it is clear that the overwhelming majority of decisions in this area are based upon detrimental reliance.[76]

---

[71] The label, "promissory estoppel" is attributed to Professor Williston at 1 WILLISTON ON CONTRACTS § 139 (1st ed. 1920) in Boyer, *Promissory Estoppel: Requirements and Limitations of the Doctrine,* 98 U. PA. L. REV. 459 (1950). In Valley Bank v. Dowdy, 337 N.W.2d 164, 165 (S.D. 1983), the court cites § 91 of the second edition of this book in explaining, "When cases first appeared involving agreements lacking the element of consideration and the promisee reasonably relied upon a promise to his detriment, courts held the detrimental reliance substituted for the consideration and enforced the contract under equitable estoppel.... Courts then subsequently developed the broader theory of detrimental reliance, which is usually referred to as the doctrine of promissory estoppel."

[72] *See* Loranger Constr. Corp. v. E.F. Hauserman Co., 376 Mass. 757, 384 N.E.2d 176, 179 (1978) where the opinion by Justice Braucher suggests that "the expression, 'promissory estoppel' tends to confusion rather than clarity." Prior to his judicial career, Justice Braucher was a member of the Harvard Law Faculty and served as Reporter for the RESTATEMENT 2d. When he joined the Supreme Judicial Court of Massachusetts, he was replaced as Reporter by Professor Alan Farnsworth of the Columbia University School of Law. In light of Justice Braucher's criticism of the label "promissory estoppel," it is not remarkable that the RESTATEMENT 2d does not employ that terminology though it is mentioned in comment a to § 90. The Chief Reporter of the FIRST RESTATEMENT, Professor Williston, avoided the use of the phrase in the original § 90.

[73] Seavey v. Drake, 62 N.H. 393 (1882). *See also* Miller v. Lawlor, 245 Iowa 1144, 66 N.W.2d 267, 48 A.L.R. 2d 1058 (1954).

[74] Lembke v. Lembke, 196 Iowa 136, 194 N.W. 367 (1923).

[75] *See, e.g.,* Lindell v. Lindell, 135 Minn. 368, 160 N.W. 1031 (1917).

[76] Greiner v. Greiner, 131 Kan. 760, 293 P. 759 (1930) upon which ill. 16 to RESTATEMENT 2d § 90 is based: *A* orally promises to give her son *B* a tract of land to live on. As *A* intended, *B* gives up a homestead elsewhere, takes possession of the land, lives there for a year and makes substantial improvements. *A*'s promise is binding." While enforcement of a promise based upon detrimental reliance should certainly protect at least the reliance interest, at first blush there would seem to be little possibility of protecting the restitution interest which requires a showing of benefit to the promisor, i.e., an unjust enrichment, while the essence of detrimental reliance is a minus quantity, i.e., an out-of-pocket loss to the promisee. Where a promise induces the promisee to make valuable improvements to land, however, if the promise is not specifically enforceable, the restitution interest of the relying promisee may be protected through a judicial declaration that the promisor holds the land as a constructive trustee for the relying promisee. A constructive trust is a trust created by the court to prevent unjust enrichment, i.e., to protect the restitution

3. Gratuitous Bailments — Gratuitous Agency.

Perhaps the oldest antecedents of the modern doctrine of detrimental reliance (promissory estoppel) are those involving gratuitous bailments. From a very early day it has been held that a promise by a gratuitous bailee made before the goods were delivered to him was enforceable if it was relied upon by a bailor who suffered a serious loss because the bailee failed to perform his promise. Where, for example, prior to the delivery of goods, a gratuitous bailee promised that he would have them insured but failed to do so after they were delivered to him, he was held liable for the loss when the goods were destroyed. It was held that the delivery of the goods to the bailee was the "consideration" for the promise to insure.[77] This is patently unsound since it is clear that the parties had not bargained for anything in this situation. The promise of the bailee to procure insurance was gratuitous and the bailor-promisee relied on that promise by not procuring insurance. It seems clear that the bailee should be liable for his dereliction, but it is impossible to discover a basis for that liability on any theory of consideration. The basis of liability in this type of case can be traced to the earliest notions of assumpsit as an action sounding in tort (*ex delicto*), i.e., when one who undertook to do something performed *badly,* he *misfeased* and was liable under the writ of assumpsit.[78] In a gratuitous bailment situation, if a party promises to become a bailee but does not enter upon the performance of the bailment, the promisor will be guilty of *nonfeasance* and no liability is imposed when the promisor fails to perform the bailment at all. If, however, the promisor begins to perform as a bailee and then breaches his promise, he is guilty of *misfeasance* and is liable under this line of cases.[79]

Though no bailment was involved, the distinction between misfeasance and nonfeasance was evident in some cases. Thus, in a classic case, an unperformed promise to procure insurance was not enforceable[80] whereas some older cases held such a promisor liable if he procured insurance and the insurance was ineffective.[81] These cases involved gratuitous agencies and modern courts no longer permit liability to depend upon misfeasance vs. nonfeasance in such cases. Rather, they recognize an agent's promise as one that may cause justifiable detrimental reliance whether or not the agent has begun to

interest. The best-known case of this type is Monarco v. Lo Greco, and opinion by Justice Traynor, at 35 Cal. 2d 621, 220 P.2d 737 (1950).

[77] Siegel v. Spear & Co., 234 N.Y. 479, 138 N.E. 414 (1923). *See* comments on this case in 22 MICH. L. REV. 64 (1923), 23 COLUM. L. REV. 573 (1923), 32 YALE L.J. 609 (1923). The classic case is Coggs v. Bernard, 92 Eng. Rep. 107 (K.B. 1703).

[78] *See* 3 HOLDSWORTH, HISTORY OF ENGLISH LAW 336 (1909).

[79] *See* Tomko v. Sharp, 87 N.J.L. 385, 94 A. 793 (1915). *See also* Coggs v. Bernard, 92 Eng. Rep. 107, 114 (K.B. 1703).

[80] Thorne v. Deas, 4 Johns 84 (N.Y. 1809). *See also,* Comfort v. McCorkle, 149 Misc. 826, 268 N.Y.S. 192 (1933).

[81] In Barile v. Wright, 256 N.Y. 1, 175 N.E. 351 (1931), the defendant promised to obtain insurance and did so. However, the policy he procured contained a clause to the effect that the insurer would not be liable if there was any other policy covering the insured property. There was such a policy as the defendant well knew. By failing to obtain a waiver or consent concerning the clause, the defendant failed to exercise reasonable diligence and was held liable to the mortgagor for the face amount of the policy. *See also* Elam v. Smithdeal Realty & Ins. Co., 182 N.C. 599, 109 S.E. 631 (1921).

perform.[82] The promise may involve liability that is quite substantial, particularly with respect to gratuitous promises to procure insurance. In light of the risk allocated to the promisor in such cases, evidence of the fact of reliance and the justifiable nature of the reliance under the circumstances should be clear.[83] While the misfeasance/nonfeasance distinction is emasculated in gratuitous agency situations, it remains in the gratuitous bailment cases though the justification for the distinction in such cases is purely historical.

4. Charitable Subscriptions.

An earlier exploration of promises made to charities demonstrated the proclivity of courts to discover one or more validation devices, including detrimental reliance, to make such promises enforceable.[84] At this point, it is appropriate to emphasize the use of the detrimental reliance device in charitable subscription cases that long antedated the recognition of detrimental reliance as a general validation device. A relatively recent case, for example, has traced the use of detrimental reliance to a case in the middle of the nineteenth century.[85] Later, in the famous opinion by Judge Cardozo in *Allegheny College v. National Chautauqua Bank,* we are told that, "[T]here has grown up of recent days a doctrine that a substitute for consideration or an exception to its ordinary requirements can be found in what is styled 'a promissory estoppel'"[86] which could be applied to charitable subscriptions. Judge Cardozo, however, found consideration to support a promise to the charity and there is reason to believe he did so because it would have been difficult for the charity

---

[82] *See, e.g.,* Franklin Inv. Co. v. Huffman, 393 A.2d 119 (D.C. App. 1978); Estes v. Lloyd Hammerstad, Inc., 8 Wash. App. 22, 503 P.2d 1149 (1972); Spiegel v. Metro. Life Ins. Co., 6 N.Y.2d 91, 188 N.Y.S.2d 486, 160 N.E.2d 40 (1959); Graddon v. Knight, 138 Cal. App. 2d 577, 292 P.2d 632 (1956); East Providence Credit Union v. Geremia, 103 R.I. 597, 239 A.2d 725 (1968). *See* RESTATEMENT 2d AGENCY § 378 which is an application of the detrimental reliance concept to gratuitous promises by agents. *See also* RESTATEMENT 2d TORTS § 323 which makes one who undertakes, gratuitously or for consideration, to render services to another which the promisor should recognize as necessary for the protection of the other person or things, liable for failure to exercise reasonable care if such failure increases the risk of harm or the harm is suffered due to the other's reliance upon the undertaking. *See also* Wangerin, *Damages for Reliance Across the Spectrum of Law: Of Blind Men and Legal Elephants,* 72 IOWA L. REV. 47 (1986) in which the author traces the reliance concept to five different areas, i.e., contracts, agency, torts, insurance, and constructive trusts (restitution), concluding that legal scholars have failed to expose overlaps among these areas concerning the reliance interest and the possibilities of different remedies depending upon which substantive analysis is chosen as the vehicle to protect the relying promisee.

[83] RESTATEMENT 2d § 90 comment e.

[84] *See supra* § 62.

[85] In Maryland Nat'l Bank v. United Jewish Appeal, 286 Md. 274, 407 A.2d 1130 (1979) the court finds the detrimental reliance concept as a validation device for promises to charities espoused in Gittings v. Mayhew, 6 Md. 113 (1854). Though the statement of the law in *Gittings* was dictum, there is no question that the court was stating what it believed to be a principle that should be generally recognized. At p. 131-132 of the *Gittings* opinion, the court makes this point with unquestioned clarity: "In whatever uncertainty the law concerning voluntary subscriptions of this character may be at this time, in consequence of the numerous decisions pronounced upon the subject, it appears to be settled, that where advances have been made, or expenses or liabilities incurred by others, in consequence of such subscriptions, before notice of withdrawal, this should, on general principles, be deemed sufficient to make them obligatory, provided the advances were authorized by a fair and reasonable dependence on the subscription.... The doctrine is not only reasonable and just, but consistent with the analogies of the law."

[86] 246 N.Y. 369, 159 N.E. 173, 175 (1927).

to prove a critical element of promissory estoppel, i.e., that the charity had actually relied upon the promise.[87] More recent cases suggest the same infirmity.[88] Whatever problems are inspired by the use of the detrimental reliance theory to enforce charitable subscriptions, however, it is clear that the expanded use of detrimental reliance which pervades modern case law is due in no small measure to the success of the doctrine in charitable subscription cases. While a few courts recognize other antecedents of the modern doctrine,[89] the typical judicial inquiry into the history of detrimental reliance will focus upon the use of the device in charitable subscription cases.[90]

B. *Section 90 of the* Restatements.

The inclusion of the detrimental reliance device in the First Restatement promulgated in 1933 was the catalyst for the expansion of the doctrine which continues to the present time. There is some evidence that its inclusion was grudgingly accepted since consideration was, without doubt, the dominant validation device.[91] A new version of § 90 appears in the Restatement 2d and it is important to compare the two versions. The First Restatement reads as follows:

§ 90. Promises Reasonably Inducing Definite and Substantial Action.

A promise which the promisor should reasonably expect to induce action or forbearance of a definite and substantial character on the part of the promisee and which does induce such action or forbearance is binding if injustice can be avoided only by enforcement of the promise.

Section 90 of the Restatement 2d contains two subsections. § 90(2) emphasizes the fact that our courts have shown high favor for charitable subscriptions and marriage settlements. It therefore allows such promises to be binding "without proof that the promise induced action or forbearance."[92] The comment to this section candidly recognizes the judicial discovery of consideration in such cases though the element of bargained-for-exchange was doubtful or nonexistent. It further recognizes that when recovery is rested upon reliance in such cases, "a probability of reliance is enough...."[93] Section 90(1) modifies the language of § 90 of the First Restatement. In the following quotation of the new § 90(1), the language deleted from the First Restatement is in brackets, and the language added by the Restatement 2d is italicized.

---

[87] *See* § 62 at *supra* note 94.

[88] *See* Maryland Nat'l Bank v. United Jewish Appeal, 286 Md. 274, 407 A.2d 1130 (1979); Jordan v. Mount Sinai Hosp. 290 So. 2d 484 (Fla. 1974).

[89] *See, e.g.,* Overlock v. Central Vermont Pub. Serv. Corp., 126 Vt. 549, 237 A.2d 356 (1967).

[90] *See, e.g.,* Alix v. Alix, 497 A.2d 18 (R.I. 1985).

[91] "Only the scholarly counterattack by Professor Corbin prevented the complete ascendancy of consideration by confronting the *Restatement* drafters with a multitude of reliance decisions. Corbin succeeded in carving out a place for promissory estoppel as an instance of the *Restatement's* residual category of 'Informal Contracts Without Assent or Consideration.'" Feinman, *Promissory Estoppel and Judicial Method,* 97 Harv. L. Rev. 678-680 (1984), citing G. Gilmore, The Death of Contract 62-64 (1974).

[92] Restatement 2d § 90(2). *See supra* § 62.

[93] Restatement 2d § 90 comment f.

§ 90. Promise Reasonably Inducing [Definite and Substantial] Action or Forbearance.

(1) A promise which the promisor should reasonably expect to induce action or forbearance [of a definite and substantial character] on the part of the promisee *or a third person* and which does induce such action or forbearance is binding only if injustice can be avoided by enforcement of the promise. *The remedy granted for breach may be limited as justice requires.*

The two versions of § 90 are very similar. Under both versions, there must be a promise[94] which the promisor must reasonably expect to induce reliance, i.e., the promisor must foresee such reliance,[95] and the promisee (or third party under the RESTATEMENT 2d version) must actually rely.[96] Both versions suggest a condition to the enforcement of the promise if all elements are met, i.e., that *injustice* can be avoided only by enforcing the promise.[97] Among the distinctions between the two versions, the reference to "forbearance" in the caption to the RESTATEMENT 2d version is merely stylistic. Since the FIRST RESTATEMENT contemplated forbearance as well as action, however, the addition of "forbearance" suggests no substantive difference. There are, however, three significant changes in the RESTATEMENT 2d version, (1) the deletion of the requirement that reliance be "of a definite and substantial character," (2) the addition permitting protection of "a third person" who relies upon the

---

[94] There are numerous cases holding that it is impossible to apply the doctrine of promissory estoppel absent a promise. *See, e.g.,* B. M. L. Corp. v. Greater Providence Corp., 495 A.2d 675 (R.I. 1985); McCroskey v. State, 8 Ohio St. 3d 29, 456 N.E.2d 1204 (1983); Keil v. Glacier Park, Inc., 188 Mont. 455, 614 P.2d 502 (1980). Some courts insist that the promise be clear, definite, and unambiguous as to essential terms. *See, e.g.,* Lohse v. Atlantic Richfield Co., 389 N.W.2d 352 (N.D. 1986); Neeley v. Bankers Trust Co. of Tex., 757 F.2d 621 (5th Cir. 1985); Jungmann v. St. Regis Paper Co., 682 F.2d 195 (8th Cir. 1982). Other courts, however, are willing to apply the doctrine where the promise and the details of the arrangement are not sufficiently clear or definite to be enforced if consideration existed. *See* Janke Constr. Co. v. Vulcan Materials Co., 386 F. Supp. 687 (W.D. Wis. 1974), *aff'd,* 527 F.2d 772 (7th Cir. 1976); Kiley v. St. Germain, 670 P.2d 764 (Colo. 1983); Hoffman v. Red Owl Stores, Inc., 26 Wis. 2d 683, 133 N.W.2d 267 (1965).

[95] *See, e.g.,* Gerson Elec. Constr. Co. v. Honeywell, Inc., 117 Ill. App. 3d 309, 453 N.E.2d 726, 728 (1983); Farm Crop Energy v. Old Nat'l Bank of Wash., 38 Wash. App. 50, 685 P.2d 1097 (1984); Berryman v. Kmoch, 221 Kan. 304, 559 P.2d 790 (1977).

[96] *See, e.g.,* Landes v. Borden, Inc., 667 F.2d 628 (7th Cir. 1981). However, *see* Farber & Matheson, *Beyond Promissory Estoppel: Contract Law and the 'Invisible Handshake,'* 52 U. CHI. L. REV. 903 (1985), in which the authors deal with cases applying promissory estoppel where the actual reliance is at least doubtful, *e.g.,* Vastoler v. American Can Co., 700 F.2d 916 (3d Cir. 1983) and Oates v. Teamsters Affiliates Pension Plan, 482 F. Supp. 481 (D.D.C. 1979). They suggest the enforceability of promises where commitments are made in furtherance of economic activity, notwithstanding the lack of a bargained-for-exchange.

[97] There is very little discussion of this requirement in the case law. It appears conclusory once it is shown that a party justifiably relied on a promise and the promisor reasonably expected such reliance. One court has suggested that the "injustice" requirement is a matter of "law" while the other elements constitute questions of fact. R. S. Bennett & Co. v. Economy Mech. Indus., 606 F.2d 182 (7th Cir. 1979). In Hoffman v. Red Owl Stores, Inc., 26 Wis. 2d 683, 698, 133 N.W.2d 267, 275 (1965), the court suggests that the "injustice" requirement "involves a policy decision by the court" and that it "embraces an element of discretion." It may be suggested that insubstantial reliance need not be remedied since the requirement that injustice be avoided is not met in such a case. Yet, any requirement concerning the extent of reliance is dealt with by the "substantial" requirement in the original § 90, while the new § 90 permits partial enforcement to alleviate the difficulty of determining whether particular reliance was substantial. This distinction between the two versions of § 90 is explored *infra.*

promise, and (3) the addition of a flexible remedy standard, i.e., the remedy "may be limited as justice requires."[98]

1. Reliance of a "Definite and Substantial Character."

The deletion of the requirement that the reliance be "of a definite and substantial character" is related to the third change, i.e., the flexible remedy. If the remedy may be limited as justice requires, a court may decide upon partial enforcement of the promise rather than refusing to enforce the promise at all because the requirement of reliance of a definite and substantial character has not been met in a particular case.[99] Under the FIRST RESTATEMENT version of § 90, controversy arose as to whether the substantial change of position on the part of the promisee had to result in serious economic loss.[1] This problem is alleviated through the deletion of the definite and substantial requirement in the RESTATEMENT 2d. This change in the new version of § 90, however, may present other troublesome questions. If reliance need no longer be either definite or substantial, should a court enforce a promise which has been relied upon in an indefinite and insubstantial fashion? The new Section 90 continues to condition the enforceability of the promise on the avoidance of injustice. If the reliance is neither definite nor substantial, a court may be hard pressed to discover sufficient injustice to meet that requirement. Moreover, comment b to the new § 90 indicates that one of the factors to be considered in determining whether injustice can be avoided is "the definite and substantial character" of the reliance.[2] Unfortunately, ambiguity in the new version of § 90 is not relegated to this change.

2. Detrimental Reliance by Third Persons.

The change providing protection to a relying third person as well as the promisee is clear in the case of what are known as "intended beneficiaries."[3] If Ames makes a promise to Barnes for the benefit of Charles and Ames' promise is supported by consideration (e.g., a payment from Barnes), Charles is an intended beneficiary who may bring an action against the promisor, Ames. If,

---

[98] See Valley Bank v. Dowdy, 337 N.W.2d 164 (S.D. 1983) suggesting the differences between the two versions of § 90 and citing the second edition of this book at § 91.

[99] See Reporter's Note to RESTATEMENT 2d § 90.

[1] In the earliest major article on the original § 90, Dean Benjamin Boyer suggested that there was no reason to insist upon relegating the loss to those of an economic nature. Boyer, *Promissory Estoppel: Requirements and Limitations of the Doctrine,* 98 U. PA. L. REV. 459, 478 (1950). *See also* Boyer, *Promissory Estoppel: Principle From Precedents,* 50 MICH. L. REV. 639, 873 (1952).

[2] The splendid analysis of Dean Knapp suggests this problem and further suggests that the deletion of the "definite and substantial" test may be traceable to an earlier draft that attempted to deal with charitable subscriptions cases only in a comment. With the addition of subsection (2) to the new § 90, however, it is clear that the "definite and substantial" test would not apply to such cases since subsection (2) even removes any requirement that the promise induced the action or forbearance. Knapp, *Reliance in the Revised Restatement: The Proliferation of Promissory Estoppel,* 81 COLUM. L. REV. 52, 59 (1981). Dean Knapp is supported in this analysis by language in the final version of comment b to § 90: "[R]eliance need not be of substantial character in charitable subscription cases, but must in cases of firm offers and guaranties.... §§ 87, 88." Sections 87 and 88 are special cases of reliance supported promises that will be discussed later in this section. Dean Knapp refers to these and two other reliance sections of the RESTATEMENT 2d · (§§ 89 and 150) as "satellite promissory estoppel sections." *Id.* at 59.

[3] Third party "intended" beneficiaries is a topic that will be explored fully in a later chapter.

however, Ames makes the same promise that is not supported by consideration, there would be no recovery under classical contract law even though Charles justifiably relied upon the promise to his detriment. To permit a promisee to recover on the basis of detrimental reliance but to preclude a recovery for a third party who is equally justified in relying upon the promise is unsound. Reliance by such an intended beneficiary should, therefore, provide a basis for recovery.[4] The RESTATEMENT 2d version of § 90, however, would also permit a recovery by a third party who justifiably relies even though such party is not an intended beneficiary.[5] To this point, the RESTATEMENT 2d has enjoyed only limited success.[6]

3. Flexible Remedy of New Section 90 — Partial Enforcement.

The third change in new § 90, the creation of a flexible remedy that would permit either full or partial enforcement of the promise, was clearly designed as the principal change.[7] The change was fostered by the scholarship of Professor Corbin who emphasizes the origin of the action in assumpsit where damages were measured by the extent of reliance injury rather than by the value of the promised performance[8] and by the monumental article by Fuller and Perdue.[9] The classic illustration was one of the highlights in the discussion of the original § 90 in 1926. The Chief Reporter, Professor Williston, was presented with a hypothetical of an uncle promising $1000 to a nephew who reasonably relied upon the promise by purchasing an automobile for $500. Under the original § 90, Professor Williston was asked, is the uncle liable for $500 or $1000? Professor Williston left no doubt about the clear answer: the uncle would be liable for $1000. "Either the promise is binding or it is not. If the promise is binding it has to be enforced as it is made."[10] The RESTATEMENT 2d, however, does not embrace this all-or-nothing approach. It provides courts

---

[4]RESTATEMENT 2d § 90 comment c.

[5]See Hoffman v. Red Owl Stores, Inc., 26 Wis. 2d 683, 133 N.W.2d 267 (1965).

[6]See Aronowicz v. Nalley's, Inc., 30 Cal. App. 3d 27, 106 Cal. Rptr. 424 (1972); Lear v. Bishop, 86 Nev. 709, 476 P.2d 18 (1970). See, however, Lee v. Paragon Group Contrs., 78 N.C. App. 334, 337 S.E.2d 132 (1985) which refused to apply the doctrine to a third party beneficiary. See also Bolden v. General Acc. Fire & Life Assur., 119 Ill. App. 3d 263, 456 N.E.2d 306, 309 (1983), where the court refused to apply the RESTATEMENT 2d protection to third persons because it was not clear whether an agreement existed between the parties and the plaintiffs failed to adequately allege the requisite detriment, i.e., a definite and substantial action or forbearance. Thus, this case "would not provide the best vehicle for effectuating a change in Illinois law, *even if desirable....*" (emphasis added). Also, in C. R. Fedrick, Inc. v. Sterling-Salem Corp., 507 F.2d 319 (9th Cir. 1974), the plaintiff was denied recovery where defendant quoted a price to its customer who was plaintiff's supplier. The price was different from the price quoted by the supplier to plaintiff. Plaintiff claimed reliance upon defendant's price and the court found that the defendant did not reasonably expect the plaintiff (third party) to rely upon the price defendant quoted to its customer. The court, however, also expressed reservations about the application of new § 90 to protect third parties. At the very least, these cases suggest the necessity of clear, justifiable, reliance by the third party. This is, however, not inconsistent with language in comment c to new § 90 which suggests that, "Justifiable reliance by third persons who are not intended beneficiaries is less likely...."

[7]See Reporter's Note to RESTATEMENT 2d § 90.

[8]1 CORBIN ON CONTRACTS § 205 at 238-40.

[9]Fuller & Perdue, *The Reliance Interest in Contract Damages:* 46 YALE L.J. 52, 63-65 (1935); *id.*: 46 YALE L.J. 373, 401-06 (1937).

[10]4 ALI Proceedings, Appendix at 103-04 (1926).

with discretion to determine the remedy "as justice requires."[11] Since "justice" is a fine aspiration but a Delphic guide, users of the RESTATEMENT 2d may rush to the relevant comment to § 90. The comment, however, does not provide substantial assistance: "The same factors which bear on whether any relief should be granted also bear on the character and extent of the remedy."[12] The factors suggested to determine whether any relief should be granted begin with the well-known requirement that the promisor must foresee the reliance and enforcement must be necessary to avoid injustice.[13] More specific factors are the reasonableness of the promisee's reliance, its definite and substantial character in relation to the remedy sought, the formality with which the promise was made, whether evidentiary, cautionary, deterrent and channeling functions are met in the context in which the promise was made, and whether the enforcement of bargains and the prevention of unjust enrichment have any bearing on the enforcement of the promise.[14] The illustrations supporting this analysis begin with one based upon a well-known case where the court limited recovery to reliance or out-of-pocket losses rather than protecting the promisee's expectation interest by also granting recovery for lost profits.[15] The second illustration merely changes the promise to a misrepresentation. Presumably because of the bad faith of the promisor, the promise is enforced completely, i.e., the promisee recovers his lost profits or expectation interest.[16] On the basis of these two illustrations, it would seem that the remedy is normally limited to the reliance interest but can be expanded to the expectation interest if the promise is made in good faith. Yet, another comment preceding these illustrations suggests that "full-scale enforcement by normal remedies is often appropriate."[17] The next illustration provides further disconcertion. It is based on what has become the most famous promissory estoppel case in dealing with the issue of flexible remedies as well as extensions of the application of the doctrine which will be pursued later in this section. The plaintiff owned and operated a bakery business but was eager to enter the grocery business. He received various assurances from the defendant, a franchisor of supermarkets, that he could enter the grocery business for a limited sum. On defendant's advice, plaintiff sold his bakery business and purchased a small grocery to gain experience. He further followed

[11] RESTATEMENT 2d § 90(1).

[12] RESTATEMENT 2d § 90 comment d.

[13] RESTATEMENT 2d § 90 comment b.

[14] Ibid.

[15] Illustration 8 to RESTATEMENT 2d § 90 is based upon Goodman v. Dicker, 169 F.2d 684 (D.C. Cir. 1948). Professor Wangerin suggests that Goodman v. Dicker "had nothing to do with the idea of flexible damages in contract law reliance situations. Rather, Goodman represented nothing more than routine application of a somewhat obscure principle in the common law of agency, a principle named the 'Missouri Rule.'" Wangerin, Damages for Reliance Across the Spectrum of Law: Of Blind Men and Legal Elephants, 72 IOWA L. REV. 47, 55 (1986). Professor Wangerin suggests that the "Missouri Rule" emanated from Beebe v. Columbia Axle Co., 233 Mo. App. 212, 117 S.W.2d 624 (1938) where a distributorship was terminated and the court held the distributor could not collect lost profits but was awarded out-of-pocket expenditures. Professor Wangerin relies, in part, on the scholarship of Professor Gellhorn, Limitations on Contract Termination Rights — Franchise Cancellations, 1967 DUKE L.J. 465, 479-80.

[16] Illustration 9 to RESTATEMENT 2d § 90 is based on Chrysler Corp. v. Quimby, 51 Del. 254, 144 A.2d 123, 885 (1958). For a discussion of reliance recovery through tort misrepresentation theories, see Wangerin, supra note 15, at 58-69.

[17] RESTATEMENT 2d comment d.

the advice of defendant by selling the grocery and took other actions in reliance on defendant's assurances. Subsequently, defendant informed plaintiff that the original sum required to become a franchisee of defendant's supermarket chain would have to be increased substantially. At this point, the negotiations collapsed and plaintiff brought an action based on promissory estoppel. The court limited the plaintiff's recovery to his actual losses, i.e., the reliance interest.[18] The RESTATEMENT 2d illustration adopts that conclusion because "the proposed agreement was never made."[19] If this meager rationale were based upon the lack of certainty or foreseeability of the damages to a party such as the plaintiff, it would be understandable since certainty and foreseeability limit the recovery of damages even where an agreement is complete and the defendant's promise is supported by consideration.[20] Absent further explanation, however, the Restatement, Second, illustration could be interpreted as requiring only reliance damages whenever the agreement is incomplete regardless of the foreseeability or certainty of expectation damages.[21] Again, however, the suggestion that "full-scale enforcement by normal remedies is often appropriate"[22] belies this analysis.

The uncertainties suggested by the flexible remedy in the new § 90 have not been addressed by the overwhelming majority of courts.[23] The typical reaction among those that have addressed the issue is to eschew a "mechanical" approach to damages in order to fashion a "discretionary"[24] or "equitable"[25] remedy. Whether particular courts have or have not confronted the flexible remedy issue, it is clear that the typical recovery protects the expectation interest, i.e., full enforcement of the promise, rather than partial enforcement by protecting the reliance interest.[26] If the promise is enforceable through detrimental reliance, undoubtedly some courts will protect the interest they have always protected regardless of the validation device, i.e., the expectation interest. If the plaintiff cannot prove expectation damages with reasonable certainty or, if they were unforeseeable at the time of the promise (the promisor must foresee reliance but will not be liable beyond foreseeable damages), a

---

[18] Hoffman v. Red Owl Stores, Inc., 26 Wis. 683, 133 N.W.2d 267 (1965).

[19] RESTATEMENT 2d § 90 ill. 10.

[20] See Royal Am. Dev., Inc. v. City of Jacksonville, 508 So. 2d 528 (Fla. App. 1987) where the court permitted recovery of preconstruction expenditures on assurances of municipality and did not discuss any possibility of expectation recovery). The certainty and foreseeability limitations as well as other limitations on contract damages will be fully explored in a subsequent chapter dealing with contract remedies.

[21] See Knapp, supra note 2 at 57-58.

[22] RESTATEMENT 2d § 90 comment d.

[23] Professor Wangerin suggests that over forty jurisdictions, virtually all of which readily accept the general concept of detrimental reliance, "have avoided the issue of flexibility." Wangerin, Damages for Reliance Across the Spectrum of Law: Of Blind Men and Legal Elephants, 72 IOWA L. REV. 47, 94 (1986). Another study identified 222 cases over the decade 1975-1985 which applied either version of § 90 of the RESTATEMENTS. Only 72 of these cases addressed the issue of the extent of recovery. Farber & Matheson, Beyond Promissory Estoppel: Contract Law and the 'Invisible Handshake,' 52 U. CHI. L. REV. 903 n.14, 907, 909 n.24 (1985).

[24] See Gerson Elec. Constr. Co. v. Honeywell, Inc., 117 Ill. App. 3d 309, 453 N.E.2d 726 (1983) (lost profits allowed).

[25] See Farm Crop Energy v. Old Nat'l Bank of Wash., 38 Wash. App. 50, 685 P.2d 1097 (1984) (lost profits allowed).

[26] See Farber & Matheson, supra note 23, who further suggest at 909 n.24, that of the 72 cases of 222 that apply § 90, only one-sixth of those 72 cases explicitly limit recovery to reliance damages. Full expectation recovery was granted in the remaining five-sixths of the cases.

court could not award expectation damages any more than it could do so if the promise had been supported by consideration. In such a situation, the reliance interest — the minus quantity or out-of-pocket loss — should be awarded to restore the relying promisee to *status quo ante*. If, however, the expectation damages can be shown and there is doubt concerning the proper measurement of reliance damages, "injustice" may be avoided only by enforcing the promise. If the expectation interest is protected, the reliance interest is normally protected and it is preferable to enforce the promisee's expectation to ascertain protection of the reliance interest. If reliance and expectation damages are provable with mathematical certainty, which interest should be protected? It is at least plausible to permit the remedy to be co-extensive with the validation device. Thus, absent detrimental reliance, the promise would not be enforceable unless, of course, consideration or another validation device was present. If the sole reason for enforcing the promise is the detrimental reliance of the promisee and justice requires that reliance to be compensated, it may appear that there is precious little reason for awarding expectation damages, *e.g.*, lost profits. Yet, when the concept is applied in a commercial context, reliance may result not only in actual out-of-pocket losses; there are lost opportunities which are usually impossible to measure. The unmeasurable lost opportunity damages returns the analysis to the situation where expectation damages are reasonably certain and foreseeable while the reliance interest is either extremely difficult or impossible to measure. As suggested earlier, the RESTATEMENT 2d indicates the possibility of a deterrence factor with respect to the bad faith of the promisor. That factor is usually very difficult to prove. More important, absent bad faith, the foregoing suggests the general desirability of full enforcement of the promise to protect the expectation interest.

C. *Application and Expansion of Detrimental Reliance.*

As suggested earlier, there was great concern about the use of a new validation device that might interfere with the purity of consideration in all of its bargained-for-exchange glory.[27] It was clear that the new device would not compete with consideration as a general validation device. Rather, it would be relegated to the gratuitous promise which was justifiably relied upon such as the family cases suggested earlier in this section. The thinking was that the application of detrimental reliance in bargaining situations would be absurd. Under this view, an offeree would have no right to rely upon the offer; he has a power of acceptance but he has no right to rely so as to make the offer irrevocable. While this may be a desirable position with respect to typical offers, there are offers that appear to invite reliance before the offers are accepted.

Where a subcontractor submits a bid to a general contractor who is seeking the award of the contract for the entire project, the subcontractor contemplates the use of his bid by the general and understands that the general may rely upon the bid of that subcontractor as well as the bids of other subcontractors in computing the general bid. There is no contract between the general

---

[27] *See supra* text at note 65.

and sub since the general may not be awarded the contract. The sub's bid, therefore, is merely an offer. Since offers are generally revocable, the sub may revoke his offer. If the general is awarded the contract and, before he can accept the sub's offer, the subcontractor revokes that offer, the general may suffer a substantial loss after justifiably relying upon the sub's promise. Should detrimental reliance operate to make the subcontractor's offer irrevocable for a reasonable time after the general is awarded the main contract?

This question has been explored earlier in this volume.[28] At this point, it is mentioned only to focus upon the initial concept of the original version of Restatement, § 90. Judge Hand distinguished gratuitous or donative promises from promises intending a bargained-for-exchange. He saw the doctrine of "promissory estoppel" as designed to avoid the harsh results of permitting a promisor to repudiate a promisor which a promisee had relied upon. In a bargain context, however, Hand could not conceive of the doctrine applying since he felt an offeror should be bound only upon receiving that for which he had bargained. The conclusion was inescapable: "There is no room in such a situation for the doctrine of 'promissory estoppel.'"[29] Another judicial giant, Justice Roger Traynor of the Supreme Court of California, disagreed. In a similar case, Justice Traynor emphasized the clear and justifiable reliance of the general contractor in such a situation. Moreover, he suggested that subcontractors who make such offers not only reasonably expect or foresee reliance by general contractors; they desire such reliance since they are hoping that the general is awarded the contract so that they, the subs, will get the subcontract.[30] Justice Traynor was not concerned about the application of the reliance concept beyond the confines of gratuitous promises. In this contest between judicial luminaries, there is no longer any doubt about the victor. There have been many similar cases before a large number of courts and the Traynor analysis has prevailed.[31]

While reliance has a long history in the validation of certain types of promises, as suggested much earlier in this section, the Traynor opinion was, to some extent, a catalyst for courts to cast aside artificial barriers surrounding the scope of the independent validation device known as detrimental reliance. While it is still possible to discover a judicial utterance of the absurd notion that detrimental reliance is a "substitute for consideration,"[32] courts are be-

---

[28] See § 43(E) supra Chapter Two.

[29] James Baird Co. v. Gimbel Bros., 64 F.2d 344, 346 (2d Cir. 1933).

[30] Drennan v. Star Paving Co., 51 Cal. 2d 409, 333 P.2d 757 (1958). The Traynor opinion relies upon comment b to § 45 in the FIRST RESTATEMENT: "[M]erely acting in justifiable reliance on an offer may in some cases serve as sufficient reason for making a promise binding." (See § 90.)

[31] See, e.g., Arango Constr. Co. v. Success Roofing, Inc., 46 Wash. App. 314, 730 P.2d 720 (1986); Tolboe Constr. Co. v. Staker Paving & Constr. Co., 682 P.2d 843 (Utah, 1984); Powers Constr. Co. v. Salem Carpets, Inc., 283 S.C. 302, 322 S.E.2d 30 (1984); Alaska Bussell Elec. Co. v. Hickel Constr. Co., 688 P.2d 576 (Alaska 1984); Haselden-Langley Constr., Inc. v. D. E. Farr & Assocs., 676 P.2d 709 (1983); Montgomery Indus. Int'l, Inc. v. Thomas Constr. Co., 620 F.2d 91 (5th Cir. 1980); Janke Constr. Co. v. Vulcan Materials Co., 386 F. Supp. 687 (W.D. Wis. 1974), aff'd, 527 F.2d 772 (7th Cir. 1976). See also RESTATEMENT 2d § 87(2) which applies § 90 reliance concepts specifically to the unaccepted offer.

[32] See, e.g., Middle East Banking Co. v. Citibank, N. A. 897, 907 (2d Cir. 1987). The court cites the opinion by Judge Cardozo in Allegheny College v. National Chautauqua Cty. Bank, 246 N.Y. 369, 159 N.E. 173 (1927) which, indeed, did contain the phrase "substitute for consideration." The continuation of the error a half century later, however, hardly seems necessary.

ginning to view detrimental reliance for what it is, i.e., an independent validation device that should not be pursued only after a court concludes that an
agreement lacks consideration.[33] The device will not be limited to particular
fact situations though the typical offer is revocable and does not engender
justifiable reliance to make it irrevocable. In addition to the subcontractor
bidding cases, the device can be found in myriad cases such as promises by
employers[34] or franchisors,[35] as well as cases involving leases,[36] stock acquisi-
tions[37] and sundry other matters.[38] The most controversial applications, however, have occurred in cases where it may be said that no "offer" occurred, or
where the promise was not clear and definite, or where the terms of the
arrangement were so indefinite that there would have been no enforceable
agreement had consideration been present, i.e., there would have been a mere
"agreement to agree."

Certainly, the two best-known "extensions" of the "promissory estoppel"
doctrine where the terms were indefinite are *Hoffman v. Red Owl Stores,
Inc.*,[39] discussed earlier in this section with respect to the flexible remedy of
the RESTATEMENT 2d version of § 90,[40] and another case handed down the same
year, *Wheeler v. White.*[41] *Hoffman* was in a bargain context but no bargain
was made. There were promises, i.e., several assurances, by authorized agents
of the defendant, but it was clear that the plaintiffs, husband and wife, had
relied on preliminary assurances. The contract to which these preliminary,
relied-upon assurances was supposed to lead was never formed. Another court
has recently referred to the *Hoffman* case as the classic case of a promisor
"stringing along" a promisee.[42] The *Hoffman* court, however, was not dis-
suaded by the fact that the parties ultimately envisioned a bargain but never
achieved one, or because the preliminary negotiations had not achieved an
adequate level of definiteness to constitute an offer, much less a contract. The
court saw the need to avoid manifest injustice caused by detrimental reliance
which the promisors not only foresaw but urged upon the promisees. In
Wheeler, the defendant promised to procure construction financing for the
plaintiff's shopping center and, failing that, to furnish such financing himself.
In justifiable reliance upon that promise, the plaintiff proceeded to reconstruct

---

[33] *See* Metzger & Phillips, *The Emergence of Promissory Estoppel as an Independent Theory of
Recovery,* 35 RUTGERS L. REV. 472 (1983). *See also* Farber & Matheson, *supra* note 23, at 908 and,
in particular, n. 19.

[34] *See, e.g.,* D'Ulisse-Cupo v. Board of Dirs., 503 A.2d 1192 (Conn. App. 1986); Perlin v. Board of
Educ., 86 Ill. App. 36, 108, 407 N.E.2d 792 (1980); Division of Labor Law Enforcement v.
Transpacific Transp. Co., 69 Cal. App. 3d 268, 137 Cal. Rptr. 855 (1977). *See also* Feinberg v.
Pfeiffer Co., 322 S.W.2d 163 (Mo. App. 1959) (promise to pay pension to long-time employee
whenever she decided to retire).

[35] *See, e.g.,* Hoffman v. Red Owl Stores, Inc., 26 Wis. 2d 683, 133 N.W.2d 267 (1965).

[36] Kramer v. Alpine Valley Resort, Inc., 108 Wis. 2d 417, 321 N.W.2d 293 (1982) (lease terms
not a defense to promissory estoppel claim).

[37] *See, e.g.,* Gruen Indus. v. Biller, 608 F.2d 274 (7th Cir. 1982) (promissory estoppel rejected not
because the doctrine was inapplicable but because the reliance was unreasonable).

[38] *See, e.g.,* Reeve v. Georgia-Pacific Corp., 510 N.E.2d 1378 (Ind. App. 1987) (workmen's compensation benefits via equitable estoppel or promissory estoppel); Mesa Petr. Co. v. Coniglio, 629
F.2d 1022 (5th Cir. 1980) (promissory estoppel theory permitted recovery on a promissory note).

[39] 26 Wis. 2d 683, 133 N.W.2d 267 (1965).

[40] *See supra* text prior to note 18.

[41] 398 S.W.2d 93 (Tex. 1965).

[42] *See* Pappas Indus. Parks, Inc. v. Psarros, 24 Mass. App. 596, 511 N.E.2d 621 (1987).

the site for the new center by, *inter alia*, tearing down existing structures. When the defendant did not perform, the plaintiff sought damages on the basis of the agreement evidenced by a writing which an intermediate appellate court found too indefinite to enforce. The Supreme Court of Texas held the agreement to be fatally indefinite as a traditional contract but felt compelled to protect the reliance interest of the plaintiff who had justifiably relied on the defendant's assurances. The Court explained its holding that damages should be limited to the reliance interest by placing "partial" responsibility on the plaintiff who failed to bind the promisor to a legally sufficient contract. With respect to such a plaintiff, the court concluded that justice required only that the plaintiff be placed in the position he would have been in had he not acted in reliance on the promise. Thus, *Wheeler* is one of the relatively few cases to the present time limiting recovery to the reliance interest.

The *Hoffman* and *Wheeler* cases suggested a movement toward the recognition of promissory estoppel to situations where even consideration would have been ineffective as a validation device. Other courts have not been willing to move that far. They insist "that the promise or agreement must be clear, definite and unambiguous as to essential terms."[43] There can be no question that detrimental reliance as an independent validation device that is not limited to certain fact situations has been generally accepted. The continued growth and application of the doctrine will be subject to the inevitable judicial tensions over its parameters. The reliance principle is so broad as to invite its application in myriad cases at least as another argument in support of a particular result. As suggested earlier, however, the rationale relying entirely or primarily on detrimental reliance is no longer remarkable.

D. RESTATEMENT 2d "Satellite" Sections — Detrimental Reliance.

The detrimental reliance concept is not relegated to § 90 of the RESTATEMENT 2d. With respect to reliance by a general contractor on a bid from a subcontractor discussed earlier, the RESTATEMENT 2d deals with offers made irrevocable through reliance in a separate section.[44] Similarly, any offer which the offeror expects to induce and does induce substantial[45] reliance is made irrevocable through such reliance. Thus, an option contract for the purchase and sale of land may be binding because of detrimental reliance.[46] Another RESTATEMENT 2d section applies the detrimental reliance analysis to promises by sureties which induce reliance of a substantial character.[47] A third section applies the § 90 analysis to promises modifying duties under executory contracts. Such promises are made enforceable where the promisee changes his

---

[43] *See* Lohse v. Atlantic Richfield Co., 389 N.W.2d 352, 357 (N.D. 1986) and cases cited therein.

[44] *See* RESTATEMENT 2d § 87(2).

[45] The "satellite" sections of RESTATEMENT 2d § 90, i.e., §§ 87(2), 88(c), 89(c), and 150, require either a reliance of substantial character, or a material change of position in reliance on the promise.

[46] *See* Berryman v. Kmoch, 221 Kan. 304, 559 P.2d 790 (1977) where the court discusses the elements of promissory estoppel in such a case but concludes that the elements are not found in the case before the court. *See* RESTATEMENT 2d § 87, ill. 4.

[47] RESTATEMENT 2d § 88(c). Suretyship contracts will be considered in the next chapter, the Statute of Frauds, where oral promises by sureties will be examined.

position materially in reliance on the promise.[48] A RESTATEMENT 2d section addresses problems of reliance on oral promises which are unenforceable because of the statute of frauds.[49] Still another section concentrates on problems of reliance on oral modifications, i.e., the "waiver" of the statute of frauds and the irrevocability of such waivers because of reliance.[50] This section attempts to set forth the analysis found in §§ 2-209(4) and (5) of the Uniform Commercial Code which was explored earlier in this chapter.[51] While Section 90 of the RESTATEMENT 2d could be applied in each of these and other situations, the drafters of the RESTATEMENT 2d felt compelled to devote separate sections to these particular situations to complement § 90 and to emphasize the wide application of the reliance concept by leaving no doubt that courts should continue to apply it in particular situations.

§ 67. Promises Enforceable Through Moral Obligation.

A. *Past Acts and Precedent Debts as "Consideration."*

Promises not supported by consideration, detrimental reliance or a formalistic validation device are generally unenforceable in our law. There are, however, exceptions to this general rule. Certain types of promises have always been enforced without any evidence of traditional validation devices simply because of a conviction that such promises should be enforced. Three products of the common law must be explored to understand these otherwise irrational notions: (1) the idea that a past act done at request should operate as consideration for a subsequent promise; (2) the doctrine that a precedent debt is consideration for a promise to pay that debt; and (3) the doctrine that a moral obligation is consideration for a promise to perform that obligation.

1. Past Acts As Consideration.

A "past consideration" — some act or forbearance done or suffered in the past — cannot support a later promise. If certain work is performed and the beneficiary later promises to pay for the completed work, there is no benefit to the promisor since he had received the benefit prior to making his promise, and there is no detriment to the promisee since he had suffered the detriment prior to becoming a promisee. The promise induced no detriment and the detriment induced no promise. Consequently, "past consideration" is "no consideration."

Notwithstanding the unassailable nature of the foregoing analysis, at the end of the sixteenth century, where a past act was done at the request of the promisor, it was held that a later promise was made enforceable by the doing of the past act.[52] At the time these cases were decided, the action was brought in assumpsit and assumpsit would lie only upon a promise expressed in lan-

---

[48]RESTATEMENT 2d § 89(c). *See also* § 2-209 of the UCC which is explored in detail *supra* § 64.
[49]*See* RESTATEMENT 2d § 139. This concept will be explored more fully in the next chapter dealing with the Statute of Frauds.
[50]RESTATEMENT 2d § 150.
[51]*See supra* § 64(E)(4).
[52]*See, e.g.,* Riggs v. Bullingham, Cro. Eliz. 715, 78 Eng. Rep. 949 [1599]; Hunt v. Bate, 3 Dyer, 272 (a), 73 Eng. Rep. 605 [1568].

guage.[53] Under modern contract law, if one requests another to perform valuable services, an inference of an enforceable promise to pay for them is drawn without difficulty. The early limitations on the action of assumpsit precluded such an obvious inference. To overcome this injustice, courts decided to enforce a promise expressed after receipt of the services by carrying over the prior services to support the later promise. These holdings were later broadened to permit the enforcement of a subsequent promise for a past act that was originally requested as a favor.[54]

By the nineteenth century, we find English courts repudiating the broad doctrine of the earlier cases and holding that a past act, though done at request, will not support a subsequent promise.[55] There are American cases taking the modern English view,[56] but a number of older cases applied the old rule quite broadly.[57] Whether or not such cases have been expressly overruled, it is more than doubtful that they would be followed today.

2. Precedent Debt as "Consideration."

Another well-settled rule of sixteenth century common law was that a precedent debt was consideration for a subsequent promise to pay that debt.[58] At early common law, if the writ of *debt* would lie, the action of assumpsit could not be employed to enforce the obligation. Earlier in this volume the severe limitations on the action of debt were explored.[59] Inasmuch as assumpsit was a much more advantageous remedy than debt, it was inevitable that courts would eventually discover a way to circumvent the limitations required by the action in debt. That effort culminated in *Slade's Case*[60] after which the writ of assumpsit became the dominant cause of action for the enforcement of informal promises.

3. Moral Obligation.

The doctrine that a moral obligation is a sufficient reason to make a promise enforceable was a product of Lord Mansfield, Chief Justice of King's Bench in England from 1756 to 1788. The Chief Justice was trained in the civil law which made him impatient with some of the more technical rules of the common law, in particular the requirement of consideration. In 1782, he authored an opinion involving a promise by an executrix to pay a legacy which promise

---

[53] *See* Ames, *The History of Assumpsit*, 2 HARV. L. REV. 1, 53 (1888).

[54] *See* Bosden v. Thinne, Yelv. 40, 80 Eng. Rep. 29 [1603].

[55] "In *Lampleigh v. Braithwait* (Hobard, 105), it was assumed that the journeys which the plaintiff performed at the request of the defendant, and the other services he rendered, would have been sufficient to make any promise binding if it had been connected therewith in one contract; the peculiarity of the decision lies in connecting a subsequent promise with a prior consideration after it had been executed. Probably at the present day, such service on such request would have raised a promise by implication to pay what it was worth; and the subsequent promise of a sum certain would have been evidence for the jury to fix the amount." Kennedy v. Broun, 13 Q.B. (n.s.) 677, 740 [1863]. *See also* Roscorla v. Thomas, 3 Q.B. 234 [1842].

[56] *See, e.g.*, Conant v. Evans, 202 Mass. 34, 84 N.E. 438 (1909).

[57] *See, e.g.*, Friedman v. Suttle, 10 Ariz. 57, 85 P. 726 (1906); Montgomery v. Downey, 116 Iowa 632, 88 N.W. 810 (1902); Stuht v. Sweesy, 48 Neb. 767, 67 N.W. 748 (1896).

[58] Ames, *The History of Assumpsit,* 2 HARV. L. REV. 53 (1888).

[59] *See* Chapter 1, § 2.

[60] 4 Coke 92(b) [1602].

was not supported by consideration. He clearly stated that moral obligation constitutes consideration.[61] The same ground was relied upon to uphold a promise by an overseer of the poor to pay an apothecary who had, in an emergency, rendered medical aid to a pauper without first consulting the overseer.[62] A debtor's promise to pay the lawful part of a usurious debt[63] and a widow's promise to repay money loaned at her request[64] were enforced absent consideration. While these cases illustrate the moral obligation doctrine, the promises were not gratuitous but were unenforceable because of existing procedural requirements, the choice of the wrong court, or because of a technical rule of law such as that which made it impossible for a married woman to bind herself by contract.

Since each case clearly demonstrated a duty to perform that which had been promised, there was a strong urge to brush aside technical problems to make the promises enforceable. While the doctrine of moral obligation survived for a time after Lord Mansfield's death, it was accepted by the courts with some misgivings.[65] Finally, in 1840, it was repudiated in England.[66] The rationale for the repudiation of the doctrine is the same rationale found in modern cases that repudiate moral obligation as a general validation device. In 1840, the court felt that no satisfactory limits to the doctrine could be fixed. Therefore, the doctrine of consideration would be emasculated since the mere fact that a promise has been given creates a moral obligation to perform it. The identical objection can be found in modern cases. In 1961, an American court expressed its objection to moral obligation as a general validation device in the following terms:

> The difficulty we see with the doctrine is that if a mere moral, as distinguished from a legal, obligation were recognized as a valid consideration for a contract, that would practically erode to the vanishing point the necessity for finding a consideration. This is so, first because in nearly all circumstances where a promise is made there is some moral aspect of the situation which provides the motivation for making the promise even if it is to make an outright gift. And second, if we are dealing with the moral concepts, the making of a promise itself creates a moral obligation to perform it. It seems obvious that if a contract to be legally enforceable need be anything other than a naked promise, something more than mere moral consideration is necessary. The principle that in order for a contract to be valid and binding, each party must be bound to give some legal consideration to the other by conferring a benefit upon him or suffering a legal detriment at his request is firmly implanted in the roots of our law.[67]

---

[61] "Where a man is under a moral obligation which no Court of Law or Equity can enforce, and promises, the honesty and rectitude of the thing is a consideration." Hawkes v. Saunders, 1 Cowper 289, 290, 98 Eng. Rep. 1091 [K.B. 1782]. See also Atkins v. Hill, Cowper 284 [1775].

[62] Watson v. Turner, Buller's N.B. 129 [1767].

[63] Barnes v. Hedley, 2 Taunt. 184 [1809].

[64] Lee v. Muggeridge, 5 Taunt. 36 [1813].

[65] See Littlefield v. Shee, 2 B. & Ad. 811 [1831], where Lord Tenderten said, "I must also observe that the doctrine that a moral obligation is a sufficient consideration for a subsequent promise is one which should be received with some limitation."

[66] Eastwood v. Kenyon, 11 A. & E. 438 [1840].

[67] Manwill v. Oyler, 11 Utah 2d 433, 361 P.2d 177, 178 (1961).

The above statement suggests two major problems in the recognition of moral obligation as a validation device. The first problem is one of uncertainty, i.e., if moral obligation is recognized, would every promise then become enforceable on the footing that there is a moral obligation to perform one's promises (*pacta sunt servanda* — promises must be kept)? If not, which moral obligations would be sufficient to support a promise? The classic response to this concern is provided by Professor Fuller who suggests that the threat to certainty suggested by the recognition of moral obligation is not solved by simply rejecting the doctrine out of hand. Rather, the solution lies in "taming it" through the process of judicial inclusion and exclusion which is certainly not foreign to the common law methodology.[68] The second problem suggested in the quoted statement rejecting moral obligation is the notion that consideration is threatened and that consideration is the only sound validation device. We have already seen other validation devices, particularly detrimental reliance, that operate at least as effectively as consideration. Indeed, many scholars believe that consideration is so riddled with exceptions and has been modified by statute and the courts in so many ways that it has proven to be "a rather awkward tool."[69] There is no justifiable rationale for a failure to develop a moral obligation validation device through judicial purification of myriad fact situations. That process has begun and its continuation appears assured as we validate more and more promises with neither consideration nor the other major validation device, detrimental reliance.[70]

B. *Contract Without Consideration or Detrimental Reliance in Modern Contract Law — Moral Obligation.*

While the three historical doctrines discussed above have been repudiated, for the most part, by modern courts, there are certain kinds of promises which are enforced though they evidence no consideration, detrimental reliance or formalistic validation device. These promises are enforced because courts have decided there is sufficient reason for enforcing them without any of the other devices. It is difficult to categorize these promises. Some are widely enforced; others have only limited judicial support. Notwithstanding difficulties of categorization, there are three classifications of promises that come within the ambit of promises enforceable without consideration, detrimental reliance or an otherwise operative formalistic device: (1) situations in which a legal duty created by a promise is subject to an absolute defense because of a more or less arbitrary rule and a new promise is made to perform that duty; (2) cases in which the promisor had promised to perform but his duty was voidable under a rule designed to protect him and he makes a new promise to perform; (3) cases in which the promisor has received substantial economic benefits for which he should make restitution although the law furnishes no remedy to compel him to do so and he promises to pay for those benefits;

---

[68] Fuller, *Consideration and Form*, 41 COLUM. L. REV. 799, 821-22 (1941).

[69] C. FRIED, CONTRACT AS PROMISE 39 (1981) (Professor Fried is here paraphrasing some of the views of Professor Lon L. Fuller).

[70] *See* C. FRIED, *ibid.*

1. Promise to Perform a Prior Legal Duty Discharged by Operation of Law —
Statute of Limitations and Bankruptcy Discharges.

a. Statute of Limitations.

A promise to pay a debt barred by the statute of limitations is enforceable
without consideration or detrimental reliance. Moral obligation is sufficient to
sustain the new promise.[71] Courts are adamant in refusing to recognize moral
obligation as a general validation device[72] though they are in agreement that
moral obligation can be used as such a device when the promisor is simply
promising to perform a duty which had been enforceable but became unenforceable because of the statute of limitations.[73] Thus, courts are confident in
characterizing a moral obligation as enforceable if it once was enforceable at
law but are more than reluctant to discover an original moral obligation
which they are willing to view as sufficient to validate a promise. There are, of
course, a number of situations that may be said to create moral obligations of
greater significance than ordinary debts barred by the statute of limitations.[74]
If there had been no antecedent legal obligation which was technically barred,
however, there would be no basis upon which to discover an enforceable moral
obligation. In effect, courts use the prior, albeit currently unenforceable, legal
obligation as a condition to the recognition of a validating moral obligation
since they have discovered no other effective means of limiting moral obligation. This limited use of moral obligation is "safe" since it is merely resurrect-
ing a prior legal obligation.

A promise to pay a debt barred by the statute of limitations may be inferred
from a mere acknowledgment admitting the present existence of the antecedent debt.[75] A promise not to plead the statute of limitations will amount to a
promise to pay an antecedent debt.[76] Even a part payment of the old debt
amounts to a promise to pay it.[77] In many states, an express or implied prom-

---

[71] Young v. Pileggi, 455 A.2d 1228 (Pa. Super. 1983); Kopp v. Fink, 204 Okla. 570, 232 P.2d 161
(1951). RESTATEMENT 2d § 82.

[72] Schoenfeld v. Ochsenhaut, 114 Misc. 2d 585, 452 N.Y.S.2d 173, 174-75 (N.Y. City Civ. 1982).

[73] See Stone v. Lynch, 315 S.E.2d 350, 354 (N.C. App. 1984); International Aircraft Sales v.
Betancourt, 582 S.W.2d 632, 636 (Tex. Civ. App. 1979).

[74] See, e.g., Harrington v. Taylor, 225 N.C. 690, 36 S.E.2d 227 (1945), where a neighbor inter-
vened to save a husband from an axe-wielding wife. The neighbor was seriously injured and the
husband promised to pay her damages. After paying a small sum, he refused to complete payment. The court held his promise unenforceable because it lacked consideration, notwithstanding
the fact that the defendant should have been impelled by common gratitude to alleviate the
plaintiff's misfortune.

[75] RESTATEMENT 2d § 82(2)(a).

[76] RESTATEMENT 2d § 82(2)(c). It is generally held that a promise to "waive" or not to plead the
statute of limitations as part of the original promise is invalid. If the promise is made after the
maturity of the debt, however, it can be treated as a new promise or acknowledgment of the debt
and will be valid. If, however, it is properly interpreted as a new promise not to plead the statute
of limitations but to retain all other possible defenses, a new consideration will be required to
support that promise. See RESTATEMENT 2d § 82, comment f and ill. 16. Section 2-725(1) of the
UCC permits the parties to reduce the period of limitation to not less than one year in their
original agreement. The parties may not, however, extend the period of limitation, which is four
years, commencing from the time of delivery of the goods, regardless of the aggrieved party's lack
of knowledge of the breach at time of delivery. The purpose of this four-year statute of limitations
for contracts for the sale of goods was to eliminate jurisdictional variations which had hampered
interstate sellers prior to the UCC.

[77] RESTATEMENT 2d § 82(2)(b).

ise to pay such an antecedent debt must be evidenced by a writing.[78] Statutes requiring a writing, however, do not apply to promises implied from part payment of the debt.[79] It must be emphasized that a promise to perform an obligation arising from a tort that has become barred by the statute of limitations is not enforceable absent new consideration or detrimental reliance.[80] The prior indebteness must be either contractual or quasi contractual.

b. Debts Discharged in Bankruptcy — Bankruptcy Reform Act Changes.

Prior to the Bankruptcy Reform Act of 1978,[81] the analysis of promises to pay debts barred by the statute of limitations which we have just explored was essentially the same analysis as that applied to promises to pay debts discharged in bankruptcy. Courts had no difficulty in discovering a moral obligation as a validation device for such promises since the debt had been legally enforceable and was barred by a discharge in bankruptcy.[82] The differences between the two analyses were minor. We saw that an acknowledgment or part payment could operate as a promise to pay a debt barred by the statute of limitations. With respect to a debt discharged in bankruptcy, however, an express promise to pay that debt was essential.[83] While an express or implied promise to pay a debt barred by the statute of limitations was typically subject to a statutory writing requirement, promises to pay debts discharged in bankruptcy were required to be in writing in only a few states.[84] A promise to pay a debt discharged by a voluntary composition among creditors was enforceable without a new validation device if the composition occurred pursuant to the Bankruptcy Act. A promise to pay a debt discharged outside of bankruptcy through a voluntary composition of creditors, however, required a new validation device.[85]

The entire common law structure concerning promises to pay debts discharged in bankruptcy was changed dramatically by the new Federal Bankruptcy Code.[86] Under § 524(c) of the new Code, an agreement between a holder of a claim and the debtor, "the consideration for which, in whole or in part, is based on a debt" dischargeable in bankruptcy is enforceable only if certain conditions are met: (1) the agreement was made *before* the granting of the discharge in bankruptcy; (2) the agreement contains a clear and conspicuous statement advising the debtor that the agreement may be rescinded at any time prior to discharge or within sixty days after such agreement is filed with the court — whichever occurs later — through notice of rescission to the

---

[78] RESTATEMENT 2d § 82 comment a. This requirement is traceable to Lord Tenderten's Act, Geo. 4, c. 14 (1828), which is now the Limitation Act, 2 & 3 Geo. 6 c. 21, § 24 (1939) in England. The purpose of the original Act was to avoid disputes as to whether a subsequent promise was made.

[79] RESTATEMENT 2d § 110(4).

[80] See RESTATEMENT 2d § 82 comment b.

[81] The Bankruptcy Reform Act is found in Title 11 of the U.S.C.

[82] See Super Chief Credit Union v. McCoy, 3 Kan. App. 2d 25, 595 P.2d 346 (1978); Stanek v. White, 172 Minn. 390, 215 N.W. 784 (1927); Herrington v. Davitt, 220 N.Y. 162, 115 N.E. 476 (1917). See also RESTATEMENT 2d § 83.

[83] See, e.g., Gillingham v. Brown, 178 Mass. 417, 60 N.E. 122 (1901) (part payment); Spencer v. Hemmerde, 2 A.C. 507 [1922] (acknowledgment). RESTATEMENT 2d § 83.

[84] RESTATEMENT 2d § 83 comment a.

[85] See RESTATEMENT 2d § 83 comment b.

[86] Most of the Bankruptcy Reform Act (Title 11 U.S.C.) became effective on October 1, 1979.

holder of the claim; (3) the agreement has been filed with the court and is accompanied by a declaration or affidavit of the debtor's attorney stating that the agreement (a) represents a fully informed and voluntary agreement of the debtor, and (b) does not impose undue hardship on the debtor or a dependent of the debtor; (4) the debtor has not rescinded the agreement within the sixty-day period of condition (2) above; (5) any hearing required by subsection (d) of § 524 has been complied with; (6) where an individual was not represented by an attorney while the agreement was negotiated, the court must approve the agreement as not imposing undue hardship on the debtor or a dependent of the debtor, and as one which is in the best interest of the debtor.[87]

The typical promise to pay a debt already discharged in bankruptcy will not be enforceable under this preempting federal statute if the "consideration" for such a promise is, "in whole or in part" based on the debt discharged in bankruptcy. It is clear that the drafters of the Bankruptcy Code were particularly concerned about serious abuses of debtors discharged in bankruptcy by their creditors who applied undue pressure to have unsophisticated debtors sign writings (reaffirmation agreements) promising to pay debts discharged in bankruptcy. The most fundamental concept of bankruptcy law is to provide the discharged debtor with a "fresh start." If the discharged debtor signed a reaffirmation agreement without full knowledge of his rights under the bankruptcy discharge or without awareness of the significance of the reaffirmation agreement, he could be placed back on the road to bankruptcy as soon as his fresh start was supposed to begin. To avoid undermining the "fresh start" policy, some legislators sought to place a blanket prohibition on *all* reaffirmation agreements.[88] That position was rejected, however, in favor of the compromise now found in Section 524(c) which does permit the enforcement of such promises under court supervision if they meet the tests set forth in that section.[89] Prior to 1984, the agreement would be enforceable if the court discerned that it was either a good faith settlement *or* was in the best interest of the debtor and would not cause undue hardship.[90] Under a 1984 amendment to § 524(c), however, the good faith settlement alternative was deleted. The reaffirmation agreement must now be in the best interest of the debtor and not cause the debtor undue hardship. A creditor's demonstration that the agreement was a good faith settlement is irrelevant.[91]

The ramifications of this statutory change are at least very interesting. Consider a debtor who was discharged in bankruptcy and who is a sophisticated merchant. Some years after his discharge, he has attained great success in the business world and, without a scintilla of coercion from any former creditor, promises to pay an unsophisticated creditor $5000, the amount of the debt discharged in bankruptcy. The language of § 524(c) would preclude the enforcement of the promise though the situation is one at which the statute is not aimed. Query: should the statute be interpreted to operate in *per se* fash-

---

[87] 11 U.S.C. § 524(c). Section 524(c)(6)(B) exempts § 524(c)(6)(A) (court approval of agreement as one not imposing undue hardship and one in best interest of debtor) with respect to a consumer debt secured by real property. *See In re* Malagesi, 39 B.R. 629 (Bankr. 1984).

[88] *See In re* Roth, 38 B.R. 531, 535 (Bankr. 1984).

[89] *In re* Farmer, 13 B.R. 319 (Bankr. 1981).

[90] *See* former 11 U.S.C. § 524(c)(4)(B) (1982).

[91] *In re* Hirte, 71 B.R. 249 (Bankr. 1986).

ion, i.e., should it be applied regardless of its purpose? One response to this query is found in § 524(f) which permits a debtor to repay his debt voluntarily, i.e., § 524(c) merely prohibits the enforcement of a reaffirmation agreement except those that comply with the rather stringent provisions of § 524(c). The debtor may, after discharge, simply pay the creditor the amount of the debt discharged in bankruptcy. Yet, other situations may create significant problems of interpretation. If the discharged debtor's promise is, again, voluntary and the creditor provides consideration or detrimentally relies upon the promise, the promise is still unenforceable if *part* of the "consideration" is the discharged debt under the language of § 524(c).[92] If the debtor draws a check to the order of the creditor but stops payment on the check before it is accepted or paid by the drawee, is the drawer/debtor liable on the negotiable instrument? Suppose the creditor has negotiated the check to a holder in due course (i.e., a party who has taken the check for value, in good faith and without notice of any claims or defenses to the instrument); would such a holder prevail against the drawer/debtor? These and other questions concerning the proper interpretation and construction of § 524(c) will occupy the attention of courts.

2. Promise to Perform Previous Undertaking Subject to Defenses.

Certain executory promises are said to be voidable at the election of the promisor because of a rule of law designed to protect the promisor. For example, we have explored promises made by infants and other incapacitated parties[93] who are given a power of avoidance or disaffirmance because the law seeks to protect such persons against their own improvidence. Similarly, promises induced by fraud or duress provide the promisor with a power of avoidance. If the promisor freely makes a new promise to perform his previously voidable promise, he ratifies the original undertaking and the new promise is binding without consideration or any other validation device.[94] This assumes, of course, that the new promise is not subject to the same defense which made the original promise voidable.

Some courts have held a promise to perform an undertaking that is void rather than merely voidable to be enforceable. Thus, a subsequent promise to perform an undertaking that was void because of a usury statute[95] or a Sunday statute[96] is binding without consideration. Other courts, however, reached contrary conclusions on the ground that a subsequent promise is effective without consideration only when the original undertaking was voidable as distinguished from void.[97] Since a power of ratification applies to a

---

[92] The term "consideration", as used in § 524(c), appears to deal with the purpose or motive of the promisor. The student should recall the "mixed motivation" situations explored in *supra* § 61 C., which concluded that the promisor may have many motivations or reasons for seeking the promisee's detriment, including gratuitous motivations. If, however, the promisor seeks the detriment, even as a quite subsidiary purpose of his promise, consideration is present. RESTATEMENT 2d § 81(1) indicates that the detriment need not be the sole inducement for the promise.

[93] *See* Chapter 1, *supra* § 21 *et seq.*

[94] RESTATEMENT 2d § 85.

[95] Barnes v. Hedley, 2 Taunt 184, 127 Eng. Rep. 1047 [1809].

[96] Rosenblum v. Schachner, 84 N.J.L. 525, 87 A. 99 (1913).

[97] *See, e.g.,* Stout v. Humphrey, 69 N.J.L. 436, 55 A. 281 (1903); Holloway's Assignee v. Rudy, 22 Ky. L. Rep. 1406, 60 S.W. 650 (1901).

voidable contract,[98] a new promise to perform a voidable duty may be viewed as an exercise of that power or conversely as a waiver of a defense such as infancy, fraud or the like. This analysis presents no conflict with the doctrine of consideration. Where, however, the original undertaking was void, the only basis for the new obligation is the new promise which appears to require consideration or another effective validation device. Notwithstanding this analytical distinction, where the rule of law that relieves the obligor from performing is more or less arbitrary, there is good reason for holding that a subsequent promise should be enforceable since that promise is made at a time when the circumstances which made the rule of law operative no longer exist.

3. Promise to Pay for Benefits Previously Received.

Where one person confers benefits upon another under circumstances negating a gratuitous intention, the recipient of those benefits may be under no legal duty to pay for them. If the benefits have been conferred because of a mistake or in an emergency, quasi contractual relief may be available to prevent unjust enrichment.[99] If the recipient of the benefits requested them and should have expected to pay for them, a real contract can be discovered though it may be characterized as an "implied-in-fact" contract.[1] If, however, benefits are conferred voluntarily without prior request, mistake or emergency, neither contractual nor quasi contractual relief may be available. Under these circumstances, the recipient of the benefits who had no legal duty to pay for them may decide to promise payment for the past benefits received. Under these circumstances, a few courts have enforced the promise because "... the moral obligation to make recompense for pecuniary benefit received will sustain a subsequent promise to pay for the benefit."[2] The prevailing view is clearly contrary.[3]

Notwithstanding the prevailing case law, the RESTATEMENT 2d adopts the view that a promise made in recognition of received benefits from the promisee should be enforceable to the extent necessary to prevent injustice.[4] Among the illustrations in this section, two are based upon well-known cases which apply what is often called the "material benefit" rule.

Where a rescuer suffered permanent disability in saving the life of his employer who subsequently promised to pay the rescuer $15.00 every two

---

[98] RESTATEMENT 2d § 85 comment a.

[99] The concept of the restitution interest for which the quasi contract device is used will be discussed subsequently in this volume.

[1] A so-called "implied-in-fact" contract is one where the manifested intention of the parties to be bound to each other is found in their conduct rather than language. In the sense of expressing mutual assent, it is as much an express contract as one manifested in the words, written or spoken, of the parties.

[2] Holland v. Martinson, 119 Kan. 43, 237 P. 902, 903 (1925). See also Kaiser v. Fadem, 280 P.2d 728 (1955) (subsequent promise to pay commission to finder of property desired by promisor); Edson v. Poppe, 24 S.D. 466, 124 N.W. 441 (1910) (tenant dug well on landlord's property without the knowledge of the landlord, who later promised to pay). See also cases discussed later in this section.

[3] See, e.g., Stone v. Lynch, 315 S.E.2d 350 (N.C. App. 1984); Miller v. Miller, 664 P.2d 39 (Wyo. 1983); Schoenfeld v. Ochsenhaut, 114 Misc. 2d 585, 452 N.Y.S.2d 173 (1982); International Aircraft Sales, Inc. v. Betancourt, 582 S.W.2d 632 (Tex. Civ. App. 1979).

[4] RESTATEMENT 2d § 86(1).

weeks for the rest of his life, the court enforced the promise even though the benefit was conferred without the request of the promisor. The court reasoned that the emergency nature of the rescue precluded the possibility of a request from the employer but such a request would have occurred had there been time. The court concluded that a moral obligation is "a sufficient consideration" to support a subsequent promise even though the promise was not one to pay for a voidable or barred legal obligation. Rather, since the employer received a "material benefit," moral obligation was sufficient to support the promise.[5] The RESTATEMENT 2d indicates that a promise for benefits previously received is not binding if the promisee had conferred the benefit as a gift *or* if the promisor had not been unjustly enriched for other reasons. There would be no cause of action in quasi contract (i.e., for unjust enrichment) by the rescuer. His emergency action would be presumed gratuitous. Yet, the RESTATEMENT 2d suggests that the subsequent promise "may remove doubt as to the reality of the benefit and as to its value, and may negate any danger of imposition of a false claim. A positive showing that payment was expected is not then required. An intention to make a gift must be shown to defeat restitution."[6] Thus, because the recipient of the benefit has made a promise to pay for the benefit, the RESTATEMENT 2d removes the normal requirement of the rescuer's expectation of payment and places the burden of establishing a gratuitous intention on the promisor.

The second illustration is based upon *In re Hatten's Estate*,[7] where a millionaire bachelor was provided with innumerable meals, companionship and other services including transportation by the promisee and her son over a number of years. The bachelor subsequently promised to pay an amount that was considerably greater than the value of the services received. The promise was contained in a negotiable instrument which provided the court with a traditional basis for enforcing the promise, i.e., there is a presumption of consideration in negotiable instruments. The court, however, chose to suggest the Wisconsin "liberal" view that moral obligation is an effective validation device when the promisor has received an actual benefit sufficient to arouse a moral, as contrasted with a legal, "consideration." The fact that the value of the bachelor's promise was disproportionate to the benefit he received would appear to make the promise unenforceable under the RESTATEMENT 2d view which suggests that such a promise is not binding "to the extent that its value is disproportionate to the benefit."[8] Yet, the illustration based on these facts concludes that a promise to pay $25,000 for a benefit valued at no more than $6,000 is binding.[9] The next illustration is based on the same facts except that the bachelor makes an oral promise to leave his *entire estate* to the promisee.[10] The illustration concludes that the promise is binding only to the extent

---

[5] Webb v. McGowin, 27 Ala. App. 82, 168 So. 196 (1935). Illustration 7 to RESTATEMENT 2d § 86 is based on the facts of Webb v. McGowin. *Contra* Harrington v. Taylor, 225 N.C. 690, 36 S.E.2d 227 (1945).

[6] RESTATEMENT 2d § 86 comment d.

[7] 233 Wis. 199, 288 N.W. 278 (1939). Illustration 12 to RESTATEMENT 2d § 86 is based on the facts of this case.

[8] RESTATEMENT 2d § 86(2)(b).

[9] Illustration 12 to RESTATEMENT 2d § 86.

[10] RESTATEMENT 2d § 86 ill. 13.

of the reasonable value of the benefit conferred, i.e., the restitution interest. One of the differences between the illustrations is that one promise is in writing and the other is oral. Presumably, a written promise is sufficient to ward off the dangers of false claims[11] whereas an oral promise may not be sufficient. The major difference, however, appears to be the gross disproportion between a $6,000 benefit and the entire estate valued in the millions as contrasted with a promise to pay $25,000 for a $6,000 benefit. Notwithstanding this explanation, the comment language is still difficult to reconcile with the illustration.[12] As the Reporter for this section indicated, however, the section "bristles with nonspecific concepts."[13] It will continue to present a significant challenge to courts.

In general, the "material benefit" rule, supported by the RESTATEMENT 2d though not yet generally accepted by our courts, has much to commend it. As the RESTATEMENT 2d insists, there is little danger of false claims since benefits have been received and the subsequent promise to pay for the benefits fulfills an evidentiary function.[14] There may, however, be a problem in the lack of what Professor Fuller would call the "cautionary" function, i.e., the immediate and overwhelming sense of gratitude on the part of the recipient of the benefit, particularly in extreme situations, could induce an impulsive promise. Notwithstanding this danger, if the promise is not excessive in relation to the benefit received, there would appear to be little risk in enforcing it where the benefit received is substantial. The usual arguments against enforcing such promises on the ground of uncertainty should not prevail. Modern courts opposing the "material benefit rule" or more general notions of moral obligation suggest little more than the fact that contract law has not enforced such promises in the past.[15] Surely this is an insufficient basis for opposing an otherwise desirable extension of the validation concept.

---

[11] This is the rationale stated in support of ill. 7 involving the promise to pay the disabled rescuer. Restatement § 86 however, does not require the promise to be evidenced by a writing.

[12] "Where the value of the benefit is uncertain, a promise to pay the value is binding and a promise to pay a liquidated sum may serve to fix the amount due if in all the circumstances it is not disproportionate to the benefit." RESTATEMENT 2d § 86 comment i.

[13] See 42 ALI Proceedings 274 (1965). See also Braucher, *Freedom of Contract and the Second Restatement,* 78 YALE L.J. 598, 605 (1969). The nonspecific concepts include "injustice," "unjust enrichment," and "gift."

[14] A New York statute makes promises for past benefits binding if the promise is in a signed writing, is proved to have been given or performed and would have been a valid consideration except for the time it was given. N.Y. GEN. OBLIG. LAW § 5-1105. See also CAL. CIV. CODE § 1606 and Henderson, *Promises Grounded in the Past: The Idea of Unjust Enrichment and the Law of Contracts,* 57 VA. L. REV. 1115 (1971).

[15] See, e.g., Manwill v. Oyler, 11 Utah 2d 433, 361 P.2d 177 (1961).

Chapter 4

THE STATUTE OF FRAUDS

§ 68. Origin of the Statute of Frauds — Repeal of the English Statute.

Except for formal contracts, i.e., contracts under seal, the common law does not require contracts to be evidenced by a writing. A promise is legally binding though expressed orally or by conduct if the other essentials for contract formation exist. Any requirement that a contract be evidenced by a writing is a statutory requirement. In practically every state,[1] certain types of contracts are required to be evidenced by a writing as a matter of enforceability, proof, or validity.[2] Generally, these statutes emulate certain sections of the "Statute of Frauds" which was enacted by the English Parliament during the reign of Charles II in 1677, and they are commonly indexed under that caption in the statute books. The original Statute of Frauds contained twenty-five sections. Only two are important for our purposes, Sections 4 and 17, though Section 4

---

[1] In New Mexico, the English Statute of Frauds was adopted as part of New Mexico common law. *See* Whelan v. New Mexico W. Oil & Gas Co., 226 F.2d 156, 160 (10th Cir. 1955). In Maryland, the statute is in effect as part of the Maryland Declaration of Rights, Md. Const. art. 5. All other states except Louisiana have statutes similar to the original English Statute of Frauds of 1677.

[2] *See infra* § 79, dealing with the effect of noncompliance with the statute of frauds.

contains six subsections designating five types of contracts that must be evidenced by a writing. The original Sections 4 and 17 are worth considering:

"Sec. 4. And be it further enacted by the authority aforesaid. That from and after the said four and twentieth day of June no action shall be brought (1) whereby to charge any executor or administrator upon any special promise, to answer damages out of his own estate; (2) or whereby to charge the defendant upon any special promise to answer for the debt, default, or miscarriages of another person; (3) or to charge any person upon any agreement made upon consideration of marriage; (4) or upon any contract or sale of lands, tenements, or hereditaments, or any interest in or concerning them; (5) or one year from the making thereof; (6) unless the agreement upon which such action shall be brought, or some memorandum or note thereof, shall be in writing, and signed by the party to be charged therewith, or some other person thereunto by him lawfully authorized."

"Sec. 17. And be it further enacted by the authority aforesaid. That from and after the said four and twentieth day of June no contract for the sale of any goods, wares and merchandises, for the price of ten pounds sterling or upwards, shall be allowed to be good, except the buyer shall accept part of the goods so sold, and actually receive the same, or give something in earnest to bind the bargain, or in part of payment, or that some note of memorandum in writing of the said bargain be made and signed by the parties to be charged by such contract, or their agents thereunto lawfully authorized."

In 1677, the essentially medieval trial by jury left much to be desired. Not only was there little or no control over jury verdicts, but the jurors were free to decide the facts on their own knowledge, disregarding the evidence. The parties to the contract were precluded from testifying on their own behalf, and the general history of the period lent itself to "fraudulent practices which are commonly endeavoured to be upheld by perjury and subornation."[3] One of the puzzling aspects of the Statute was the choice of six types of contracts made subject to its requirements. There is little doubt that an earlier draft covered all contracts. Historians have discovered earlier parallels on the Continent which lend support to the notion that the reasons behind the Statute were much broader than fear of perjury and subornation.[4]

American versions of the English Statute reveal minor differences in terminology among the different states to which attention will be directed as this exploration proceeds. Modern versions of the statute will often include types of contracts not covered by the original Statute.[5] Thus, promises to pay a commission to a real estate broker or contracts to leave property by will are often included.[6] The student of contract law should also recall that a promise to pay a debt barred by the statute of limitations is typically required to be evidenced by a writing though this requirement emanates from a nineteenth century English statute.[7] The modern version of Section 17 of the original

---

[3] This is the preamble to the bill which was finally enacted. The principal author of the original Statute of Frauds was Lord Fincy, later Lord Nottingham, who was chancellor (1673-1682) under Charles II. In general, see 6 HOLDSWORTH, HISTORY OF ENGLISH LAW 379-97 (1924).

[4] See Rabel, *The Statute of Frauds and Comparative Legal History,* 63 LAW Q. REV. 174 (1947).

[5] See RESTATEMENT 2d Ch. 5, Statutory Note, "Other Similar Statutes."

[6] *Ibid.*

[7] Lord Tenderten's Act, 9 Geo. IV, c. 14, sometimes referred to as the Statute of Frauds Amendment Act, enacted in England in 1828. See RESTATEMENT 2d Ch. 5, Statutory Note which quotes this Act.

Statute dealing with contracts for the sale of goods is now found in the Uniform Commercial Code.[8] The UCC, however, requires other types of promises to be evidenced by a writing.[9] The main features of the original Statute of Frauds have been copied with remarkable unanimity.[10]

Having spawned the Statute of Frauds, England repealed it, except for two sections, by the Law Reform Act of 1954.[11] This action was based on a report of the English Law Revision Committee in 1937.[12] After indicating that contemporary opinion is almost unanimous in condemning the statute and favoring its amendment or repeal, the report suggests that the conditions which gave rise to the statute have long passed away. At a time when the parties themselves could not give evidence and the jury was entitled to act on its own knowledge of the facts in dispute, there may have been some reason for the statute. There can be no quarrel with the report in this regard, i.e., these conditions no longer exist. The report further suggests that the statute promotes more fraud than it prevents. While it shuts out perjury, it also more frequently shuts out the truth since it strikes impartially at the perjurer and the honest man who has omitted a precaution, "sealing the lips of both." The classes of contracts covered by the statute appear to have been arbitrarily selected and to exhibit no common quality. The report insists that the statute operates in a partial manner. Thus, when A and B contract and A has signed a sufficient memorandum and B has not, B can enforce the contract against A, but A cannot enforce the contract against B who has signed no writing. (Later, we will see how the UCC deals with this situation in requiring a signed writing to evidence a contract for the sale of goods priced at $500 or more.) The report also suggests that the statute is obscure and ill-drafted, making it the subject of considerable litigation.

A number of American scholars have been critical of the statute. One of the true giants of American contract law, Arthur Linton Corbin, suggests that, if the statute were repealed in the United States, he would suffer only to the extent that one volume of his treatise would no longer be sold.[13] Professor Corbin, however, expressed grave doubt that the statute would be repealed in the United States since, unlike England, each of our states would have to repeal the statute. Corbin's prophecy has proven accurate for many years.

Another giant of American law, Karl Llewellyn, best known as the "father" of the UCC, was one of the rare defenders of the statute:

That statute is an amazing product. In it de Leon might have found his secret of perpetual youth. After two and one half centuries the statute

---

[8] UCC § 2-201.

[9] See, e.g., UCC § 8-319 (sale of investment securities); § 9-203 (security agreement); § 1-206 (property not otherwise covered such as the sale of contract rights, royalty rights, patent rights, and rights to copyright. See also § 2-205 (firm offer must be in writing); § 2-209(2) (enforcing no oral modification clauses which require any modifications to be in writing).

[10] See RESTATEMENT 2d, Statutory Note at the beginning of Chapter 5.

[11] Act, 1954, 2 & 3 Eliz. 2, ch. 34. The two exceptions are contracts to answer for the debt of another (the suretyship provision) and contracts for the sale of land. For comments on the Acts of 1954, see Note, 70 LAW Q. REV. 441 (1954) and 17 MOD. L. REV. 451 (1954).

[12] English Law Revision Committee (Sixth Interim Report) (1937), the full text of which can be found in 15 CAN. B. REV. 585 (1937).

[13] 2 CORBIN ON CONTRACTS § 275.

stands, in essence better adapted to our needs than when it first was passed. By 1676 literacy (which need imply no great consistency in spelling) may well have been expected in England of such classes as would be concerned in the transactions covered by the statute's terms. Certainly, however, we had our period here in which that would hardly hold — we counted our men of affairs who signed by mark in plenty. But schooling has done its work. The idea, which must in good part derive from the statute, that contracts at large will do well to be in writing, is fairly well established in the land. "His word is as good as his bond" contains a hinting innuendo preaching caution. Meantime the modern developments of business — large units, requiring internal written records if files are to be kept straight, and officers informed, and departments coordinated, and the work of shifting personnel kept track of; the practice of confirming oral deals in writing; the use of typewriters, of forms — all these confirm the policy of the statute; all these reduce the price in disappointments exacted for its benefits.[14]

Notwithstanding Llewellyn's defense of the statute, as will be seen later in this chapter, his version of the statute in relation to contracts for the sale of goods in the UCC contains a number of modifications designed to overcome some justified criticism of the treatment of such contracts in the original Statute and its progeny. There is little question that current versions of the statute are often applied narrowly by our courts which manifest an understanding, though a somewhat myopic understanding, of its irrationality in certain situations. The judicial recognition of reliance in lieu of a writing as a method or device to satisfy the statute may be said to indicate erosion of the statute, at least in its original form.

The student of contract law must be aware of judicial trends in the application of the statute. These trends will be examined in the exploration which follows. They can be understood, however, only if three basic questions are thoroughly pursued: (1) What contracts are embraced within the terms of the statute? (2) What are the requirements of the statute in relation to contracts within its scope? (3) What is the effect of failing to fulfill the requirements of the statute?

§ 69. Suretyship Promises — Contracts of Executors and Administrators.

A. *The Basic Concept of Suretyship — Two Types of Suretyship Promises.*

To understand the operation of "suretyship" provisions of the statute of frauds, it is essential to understand the fundamental concept of suretyship. Suretyship involves three parties, the *principal debtor or obligor* (*D*) who is obligated to a *creditor or obligee* (*C*) and a *surety, S,* who promises to pay *C* if *D* fails to pay. If, for example, *D* seeks goods, services or a loan from *C*, *C* may be unwilling to extend credit to *D* because *D* has a poor credit rating. *C* may agree to perform in accordance with *D*'s request only if *D* and a third party, *S,* agree to repay *C*. If the agreement contemplates that *S* will pay only if *D* fails

---

[14]Llewellyn, *What Price Contract? — An Essay in Perspective,* 40 YALE L.J. 704, 747 (1931).

to pay, and if *C* either knows or has reason to know of this relation, the promise of *S* is a suretyship promise *within*[15] the statute of frauds, i.e., *S*'s promise must be evidenced by a writing. *D* and *S* are both liable for the full amount of the obligation though *C* is entitled to only one satisfaction. As between *D* and *S*, *D* should perform because *D* is the principal debtor and *S* is surety who has undertaken to pay *C* only if *D* does not pay. *S* is *promising to answer for the debt of another*, i.e., *S*'s promise is "collateral" to the promise of the principal debtor. Therefore, *S*'s promise is within the statute of frauds. It is important to emphasize that the relation between the two obligors (*D* and *S*) as one of principal and surety *must be known to the Creditor, C.* If goods are delivered or services are rendered to *D* with the understanding that they are to be charged to *S alone*, i.e., *C* is not extending any credit to *D* but is relying solely upon *S* to pay, *S*'s promise is not that of a surety, i.e., it is not a "collateral" promise. Rather, it is an "original" or "primary" promise that is without the statute of frauds.[16]

The inclusion of suretyship promises within the statute of frauds is clearly designed to serve the same function as that served by requiring other types of promises to be in writing, i.e., an evidentiary function.[17] The original Statute of Frauds was captioned, "An Act for the Prevention of Frauds and Perjuries"[18] and suretyship promises were included because they appeared to be particularly inviting targets for inspiring false allegations. If a principal debtor fails to pay and is judgment proof, the creditor may be inclined to seek another source of payment. Requiring written evidence of the surety's promise provides a threshold safeguard against such false allegations. In addition to the evidentiary function, however, the requirement of a writing for promises of suretyship also serves a cautionary function, i.e., "guarding the promisor against ill-considered action."[19]

The first and second clauses of the original Statute of Frauds are directed at suretyship promises. It is important to consider each clause to determine the relationship between them.

1. Contracts of Executors and Administrators.

The language used in the first clause of the original Statute of Frauds concerning promises of executors or administrators is clearly limited to contracts made in relation to the affairs of the deceased *only* when the contract requires a performance by the executor or administrator in his personal rather than his representative capacity. The statute has no application to a contract by an executor or administrator concerning his personal affairs, nor does it apply to a contract to be performed only out of the assets of the estate.[20]

---

[15] A promise *within* the statute of frauds is one that is covered by the statute of frauds and must be evidenced by a writing. A promise *without* the statute of frauds does not require a writing and may be enforced as an oral promise.

[16] *See* J.J. Brooksbank Co. v. American Motors Corp., 289 Minn. 404, 184 N.W.2d 796 (1971).

[17] "In general the primary purpose of the Statute of Frauds is assumed to be evidentiary." RESTATEMENT 2d § 112 comment a.

[18] 29 Car. II, ch. 3.

[19] RESTATEMENT 2d § 112 comment a.

[20] *See* Mann v. Rudder, 225 Ala. 540, 244 So. 13 (1932); Hannan v. Dreckman, 182 Ill. App. 146 (1913).

If there was no debt chargeable to the estate at the time of the promise of the executor or administrator, the promise is obviously not one to pay a debt of the estate from the personal assets of the executor or administrator.[21]

The question arises, what is the difference between the "special promise" of an executor or administrator in the first clause of the statute, and the "special promise" of any other promisor to answer for the debt of another in the second clause of the statute? The answer is found in the apparent purpose of Parliament to single out the executor or administrator for special mention. Courts have taken the position that the promise of an executor or administrator to answer for the debts of the estate is merely a species of the general requirement that the promise of any surety be evidenced by a writing.[22] The classic exposition of this explanation is found in *Bellows v. Sowles*:[23]

> The promise must be "to answer damages out of his own estate." This phraseology clearly implies an obligation, duty, or liability on the part of the testator's estate, for which the executor promises to pay damages out of his own estate. The statute was enacted to prevent executors or administrators from being fraudulently held for the debts or liabilities of the estates upon which they were called to administer. In this view of the case this clause of the statute is closely allied, if not identical, in principle, with the following clause: "No action, etc., upon a special promise to answer for the debt, default or misdoings of another." And so Judge Royce, in delivering the opinion of the court in *Harrington v. Rich,* 6 Vt. 666, declares these two classes of undertaking to be "very nearly allied," and considers them together. This seems to us to be the true idea of this clause of the statute — that the undertaking contemplated by it, like that contemplated by the next clause, is in the manner of a guaranty; and that the reasoning applicable to the latter is equally applicable to the former.

In light of this rationale which has been generally accepted, it is appropriate to proceed with the discussion of the requirement that any suretyship promise, including that of executors and administrators, must be evidenced by a writing.

2. Promises to Answer for the Debt of Another — Determining Whether the Surety's Promise Is Within or Without the Statute of Frauds.

At the beginning of this section we explored the basic concept of suretyship and the application of the statute of frauds to promises of sureties. In essence, we emphasized the fact that there must be a relationship between the two obligors (*S* and *D*) whereby *D*, the principal debtor, should pay and *S*, the surety, should pay only if *D* does not pay. We also emphasized the requirement that the creditor, *C*, must be aware of this relationship. We distinguished "original" from "collateral" promises, i.e., if the understanding is that the promisor is solely liable, the promise is "original." If, however, the promisor is to pay only if the principal debtor does not pay, the promise is "collateral." "Original" and "collateral" are, therefore, conclusions which can be arrived at only through an analysis of the particular fact situations under

---

[21] *See, e.g.,* Schneider v. Bytner, 105 A.D.2d 498, 481 N.Y.S.2d 777 (A.D. 3 Dept. 1984).

[22] *See* RESTATEMENT 2d § 11 comment a.

[23] 57 Vt. 164, 52 Am. Rep. 118, 119 (1884).

which the promises are made. A number of problems arise in making this determination. We will now consider those problems.

a. Was the Promise "Original" or "Collateral?"

In a given fact situation, it may be difficult to determine whether the promise is a suretyship ("collateral") promise or an "original" (sometimes called "primary" or "direct") promise. It is a question of interpretation.[24] One of the better known cases presenting this problem involved a promise by a daughter to a physician who answered an emergency call to provide services to her father. The father was unconscious and the daughter directed the physician to "do everything under the sun to see this man is taken care of." A witness testified that the daughter also said, "I want my father taken care of, and give him the best care you can give him, and what the charges are ... I will pay for it." The court viewed the daughter's promise as "original" in *form,* i.e., on its face, it was not a promise to answer for the debt of another. Rather, it appeared to be a primary, direct or, again, "original" promise which would make only the daughter liable. Thus, on the basis of the *form* of the promise, it was not within the statute of frauds. The court, however, also properly considered the reaction of the plaintiff-physician to the statement of the daughter. The plaintiff sought to recover from the injured party and, failing that, from the estate of the injured party. When payment was not forthcoming from the estate, the plaintiff sent bills to the injured party's widow. Only after failing to collect the amount due from these other sources did the plaintiff finally seek his recovery from the daughter, i.e., the conduct of the plaintiff raised an inference that he understood the daughter's promise as a suretyship promise, regardless of its form. While the plaintiff's earlier attempts to collect were not conclusive evidence of his understanding of the daughter's promise, he offered no explanation to rebut the inference that he regarded the daughter's promise as a suretyship or "collateral" promise. The court, therefore, interpreted the daughter's promise as a suretyship promise which was *within* the statute of frauds and was, therefore, unenforceable because it was not evidenced by a writing.[25] To determine the proper characterization of the promise, it is not enough to consider merely the form of the promise. As in other questions of interpretation, all of the relevant circumstances must be considered.

b. Joint Obligors.

If two parties make oral promises for the same consideration, a question of suretyship may arise. Thus, if *D* and *S* both orally promise to pay for goods

---

[24] There are, of course, some relatively easy fact situations. For example, in Johnson Co. v. City Cafe, 100 S.W.2d 740 (Tex. 1936), the foreman of the Johnson Construction Company had been obtaining meals on credit from the City Cafe located where the company was performing construction work. When the foreman's account was in arrears, the owner of the cafe approached the owner of the company, who provided a check to the cafe in the full amount of the debt owed by the foreman. Later, when the foreman was again in arrears, the company owner told the cafe owner to "Go ahead and let him continue to have meals and I will pay for it if he doesn't." The cafe continued to supply meals to the foreman. *Inter alia,* the owner of the cafe testified, "I would not have advanced that line of credit if Mr. Johnson (the owner of the company) had not promised to pay it." Johnson's promise was clearly *within* the suretyship provision of the statute of frauds.

[25] Lawrence v. Anderson, 108 Vt. 176, 184 A. 689 (1936).

from C, S's promise will be a suretyship promise *only* on the following conditions: (1) as between S and D, the parties understand that S will be a surety, (2) the promisee, C, knows or has reason to know that the goods will be delivered and used exclusively by D, i.e., no benefit will inure to S,[26] and (3) the promises are *joint* and do not create *several* duties or *joint and several* duties.[27] With respect to the first element, if there is no suretyship relation between the parties, S cannot be said to have made a suretyship promise. As to the second element, it is not enough that S and D intended only D to benefit from C's performance. As suggested earlier, there is the general requirement that C, the creditor, know or have reason to know that S is promising as a surety. To understand the third element requires a basic understanding of the distinction between joint liability as contrasted with several or joint and several liability. Joint promisors were historically viewed as a unit, i.e., the obligation of one of the joint promisors could not viewed as that of "another" for the purposes of the suretyship provision of the statute of frauds because there was only one obligation owed by both promisors and that obligation must, therefore, be "original" rather than "collateral." If the promisors were under joint liability, the promisee could not bring an action against one of the joint promisors without joining all other living joint promisors. If, however, the promisors undertook "joint and several" or simply "several" liability, the promisee avoided this disadvantage. Joint and several liability or just several liability involves more than one obligation. Therefore, a joint and several or several promise could be a promise to answer for the debt of another. The archaic rules of multiple promisors have been significantly changed by statute in most jurisdictions. These statutes indicate that, although the express terms of the contract provide for joint liability, the duties of the parties are treated as joint and several.[28] Thus, if such a statute were operative, a joint promise would create joint and several liability and the third element for the application of the suretyship provision of the statute of frauds would be met. Where the distinction between joint and several duties is retained, however, the suretyship provision does not apply if the obligation is expressed as joint rather than joint and several or several.

c. Primary Obligation Must Exist at Time "Special" Promise Is Performed.

Since the suretyship provision requires a promise "to answer for the debt ... of another," it is universally agreed that the primary obligation of a third party (D) must be in existence at the time the "special" promise is to be performed.[29] Thus, if the third person for whose supposed debt the promisor

---

[26] *See* Burrillville Lumber Co. v. Rawson, 68 R.I. 1, 26 A.2d 110 (1942); Boyce v. Murphy, 91 Ind. 1, 46 Am. Rep. 567 (1883).

[27] *See* Doodlesack v. Superfine Coal & Ice Corp., 292 Mass. 424, 198 N.E. 773 (1925). With respect to all three elements, *see* RESTATEMENT 2d § 113.

[28] *See* RESTATEMENT 2d Ch. 13.

[29] "It is essential that a primary obligation of some kind be incurred in order to bring the case within the statute.... A promise is not within this clause of the statute unless there is an obligation of some third person to the promisee. The third person must at some time be under a legal duty of performance to the promisee, a duty that will be discharged by the performance of the new promisor...." Gen. Elec. Co. v. Hans, 242 Miss. 119, 133 So. 2d 275, 276 (1961). *See also* Schneider v. Bytner, 105 A.D.2d 498, 481 N.Y.S.2d 777 (A.D. Dept. 1984).

has agreed to be answerable, is not liable, either because he never actually made an undertaking,[30] or because he lacked even voidable capacity to bind himself,[31] or for any other reason, the statute is not applicable.[32]

d. Novation.

A novation is a tripartite arrangement whereby a creditor releases the debtor in exchange for a new debtor in substitution for the original debtor. By agreement of all three parties to a contract, a novation discharges one of the original parties to the contract and substitutes a new one. Since the debt of the original obligor is discharged as soon as the contract is made between the substitute debtor and the creditor, there is no "debt of another" in existence as of the moment the new promise is made. Therefore, the new promise cannot be a suretyship promise and it is not within the statute of frauds.[33] The original creditor need not know that the debt is discharged at the moment the contract between the creditor and substitute debtor is formed.[34] If the original debtor is not released at the time the new debtor's promise is made, the new promise is within the suretyship provision because the original obligation would then be in existence after the new promise is made.

e. Promise Made to the Debtor Rather than the Creditor.

There is universal agreement among our courts that the promise to answer for the debt of "another" should be interpreted as a promise to the creditor of the "other" rather than to the debtor, himself. The purpose of the suretyship

---

[30] See, e.g., Duca v. Lord, 331 Mass. 51, 117 N.E.2d 145 (1954) (decedent promised orally to pay for repairs to property if trustees did not pay. The oral promise was not within the statute because there was no obligation on the part of the trustee to which decedent's promise could be secondary); Mease v. Wagner, 1 McCord 395 (S.C. 1821) (promise to pay for goods furnished for a friend of the promisor if the nephew of the deceased did not pay. The nephew had made no promise and later refused to pay).

[31] If the claim asserted against the principal debtor is void, e.g., a claim against a party suffering from mental illness or other incapacity who has been adjudicated incompetent and a guardian has been appointed, a promise by a purported surety would not be within the statute because there is no debt of another. If, however, there is an obligation of another, albeit a voidable or unenforceable obligation, the promise of the surety is within the statute of frauds. Thus, a promise to answer for the debt of an infant is within the statute of frauds even though the infant's obligation is voidable. Similarly, a promise to pay the debt of another who may avoid enforcement of the debt on the grounds of fraud or duress is also a promise within the statute of frauds. If the debtor's obligation, itself, is within the statute of frauds, a promise to pay that debt if the debtor fails to pay is within the statute of frauds even though the principal obligation may be said to be unenforceable because of the statute of frauds. See 2 CORBIN ON CONTRACTS § 356.

[32] If the performance of a promise involves only the performance of a duty which the promisor is bound to perform because of a duty other than that imposed by the promisee (e.g., a trust relationship), the promise is not within the suretyship provision. Whenever a promisor, albeit a surety, promises to answer for his own obligation as well as that of another, his promise is not within the suretyship provision. See RESTATEMENT 2d § 114.

[33] See Klag v. Home Ins. Co., 116 Ga. App. 678, 158 S.E.2d 444 (1967); Blaylock v. Stephens, 36 Tenn. App. 464, 258 S.W.2d 779 (1953); LaDuke v. John T. Barbee & Co., 198 Ala. 234, 73 So. 472 (1916); Wilhelm v. Voss, 118 Mich. 106, 76 N.W. 308 (1898). See also RESTATEMENT 2d § 115.

[34] While concurrence by the original debtor is normal, there are decisions holding that concurrence is not necessary. The "consent" of the original debtor is usually not stressed. Some courts suggest a presumption of such consent though the original debtor would have the right to disclaim the benefit of having his obligation satisfied. See Greenwood Leflore Hosp. Comm'n v. Turner, 213 Miss. 200, 56 So. 2d 496 (1952).

provision was to preclude false claims by creditors who, not having been paid by their debtors, might be inclined to allege that a promise to pay the debt had been made by another. Thus, even though the statutory language could be construed to bring within its ambit promises to debtors as well as creditors, it has not been so construed.[35]

f. Contract to Purchase the Creditor's Right.

A party in the business of debt collection may promise the creditor to purchase the right of the creditor against the debtor. If the right is assigned at the moment the promise is made, there is a mere substitution of a new creditor for the original creditor and the suretyship provision of the statute of frauds is not involved. If, however, the creditor agrees to assign the right sometime after the promise to pay the creditor consideration (typically less than the amount of the debt because there may be some obstacles in collecting the debt), it is possible to stretch the language of the suretyship provision to bring this situation within its scope. Such a promise is not, however, within the suretyship provision of the statute of frauds for the obvious reason that no suretyship was intended.[36]

g. The Four-Party Indemnity Situation.

Though the word "indemnity" is often misused,[37] it should be relegated to those situations where a promise is made to a debtor or obligor to save him harmless from loss or liability. If, therefore, A promises to save B from loss if B will purchase goods from C, the promise is made to a debtor and, as we have seen,[38] A's promise is without the statute of frauds. Another situation involving four parties, however, creates additional problems.

Suppose that A says to B, "If you (B) will become a surety on C's loan to D, I (A) will save you harmless from loss." Is A's promise to indemnify a surety within the statute of frauds? The judicial analysis of this question focuses upon the proper characterization of the promisee (B). B may be characterized as an obligor (debtor) because, in relation to C, he will be liable as a surety on C's loan to D. B, however, may also be characterized as a creditor because, in relation to D, B will be entitled to reimbursement or exoneration from D, the principal debtor, if B must pay C after D fails to pay. The prevailing view is to treat B as a debtor whose promise is, therefore, without the statute of frauds.[39]

---

[35] See Farmers State Bank v. Conrardy, 215 Kan. 334, 524 P.2d 690 (1974); Danby v. Osteopathic Hosp. Ass'n, 34 Del. 427, 104 A.2d 903 (1954); Clack v. Rico Exploration Co., 23 Ariz. 385, 204 P. 137 (1922); Eastwood v. Kenyon, 11 A. & E. 438 [1840].

[36] RESTATEMENT 2d § 122. While a promise to purchase a right is not within the suretyship provision of the statute of frauds, it may be within other statutory provisions. See, e.g., UCC §§ 1-206, 8-319, and 9-203.

[37] Sometimes the word "indemnity" is used to mean guaranty or surety. Generally, indemnity contracts are those in which the promisee is a debtor (obligor) whereas in suretyship or guaranty contracts, the promisee is an obligee (creditor). The RESTATEMENT 2d distinguishes "non-surety" indemnitors from surety indemnitors. See RESTATEMENT 2d § 118 comments a and b.

[38] See supra Subsection (2)(e).

[39] See Biestek v. Varrichhio, 34 Conn. Super. 620, 380 A.2d 1351 (1977); Thomas v. Williams, 173 Okla. 601, 49 P.2d 557 (1935); Newbern v. Fisher, 198 N.C. 385, 151 S.E. 875 (1930); Tighe v. Morrison, 116 N.Y. 263, 22 N.E. 164 (1889). Accord RESTATEMENT 2d § 118 differing from the FIRST RESTATEMENT § 186. Cases holding that the promise of an indemnitor to a surety is a

The justification for the prevailing view is best suggested by Professor Corbin who believes there is no harm in distinguishing this type of situation from ordinary suretyship cases that fall within the statute of frauds.[40] It should also be noted that modern courts are not persuaded that the statute of frauds is as necessary as it may have been in the seventeenth century. Thus, when confronted with a situation that may or may not require the statute to be applied, courts are inclined to avoid the statute if only technical purity rather than necessary protection of a promisor is served by its application.

h. The Main Purpose or Leading Object Rule — Assignors and *Del Credere* Agents.

Certain types of transactions, though falling within the literal language of the suretyship provision, are excluded from its operation because they do not present the dangers which the statute sought to avoid and are not, therefore, within its spirit or purpose. One of the better statements of the purpose of the suretyship provision is found in the opinion of Justice Brewer in the leading case of *Davis v. Patrick*:[41]

> There is ... a temptation for a promisee, in a case where the real debtor has proved insolvent or unable to pay, to enlarge the scope of the promise, or to torture mere words of encouragement and confidence into an absolute promise; and it is so obviously just that a promisor receiving no benefits should be bound only by the exact terms of his promise, that this statute requiring a memorandum in writing was enacted. Therefore, whenever the alleged promisor is an absolute stranger to the transaction, and without interest in it, courts strictly uphold the obligations of this statute. But cases sometimes arise in which, though a third party is the original obligor, the primary debtor, the promisor, has a personal, immediate and pecuniary interest in the transaction and is therefore himself a party to be benefited by the performance of the promisee. In such cases the reason which underlies and prompted this statutory provision fails, and the courts will give effect to the promise.

The portion of this quotation suggesting that, if a promisor has an immediate pecuniary interest either in the creation or payment of the third person's debt, the promise is outside the statute, is often called the *main purpose* or *leading object* rule.[42] In any of the various forms in which the rule has been stated, the purpose of the rule is to recognize a distinction between promises which are made principally for the promisor's benefit and promises which are made for the benefit of another. This distinction is deeply entrenched in our law. Innumerable cases have taken promises out of the suretyship provision of the statute on the basis of this distiction though, superficially, the promise appears to be within the provision.[43] The difficult question has been, and

---

promise to a creditor and, therefore, within the statute of frauds include Wilder v. Clark, 263 Ala. 55, 81 So. 2d 273 (1955) and Nugent v. Wolfe, 11 Pa. 471, 4 A. 15, 56 Am. Rep. 291 (1886).

[40] 2 CORBIN ON CONTRACTS § 386.

[41] 141 U.S. 479, 487-88 (1891).

[42] For a general discussion of the "main purpose" or "leading object" rule, *see* Contractor's Crane Serv. v. Vermont Whey Abatement Auth., 519 A.2d 1166 (Vt. 1986). *See also* Morrison-Knudsen Co. v. Hite Crane & Rigging, Inc., 36 Wash. App. 860, 678 P.2d 346 (1984); Gulf Liquid Fertilizer Co. v. Titus, 163 Tex. 260, 354 S.W.2d 378 (1962); RESTATEMENT 2d § 116.

[43] Statutes in several western states set forth a "main purpose" exception to the statute of frauds. *See, e.g.,* CAL. CIV. CODE § 2794 (1974); MONT. CODE ANN. tit. 30, § 105 (1961); N.D. CENT. CODE § 22-01-05 (1978); UTAH CODE ANN. § 25-5-6 (1976).

continues to be, what is the test for determining when the promisor's purpose is basically or essentially to benefit himself, rather than to benefit and accommodate another?

The formulations found in the case law are invariably insufficient.[44] Where, for example, the promise is characterized as "original" rather than "collateral," the courts are stating conclusions rather than supplying workable tests.[45] The reason for the lack of success in formulating a workable test is that the question to be answered relates to the purpose, motive, object or desire of the promisor. That question can be answered only by analyzing the complex objective manifestations surrounding the making of the promise.[46] One of the important factors to be addressed in this analysis is the consideration received by the promisor. The discovery of consideration to support such a promise, however, should not lead a court to conclude that the main purpose or leading object of the promisor was to benefit himself rather than the principal debtor. Some judicial opinions clearly manifest this confusion.[47] Even though the promisor received an economic benefit for his promise, his promise may still be a promise within the suretyship provision.[48] If, however, the benefit to the promisor is of substantial pecuniary value, this fact will be strong evidence that his promise, though in the form of a suretyship promise, was designed to benefit himself and should, therefore, be taken out of the suretyship provision of the statute. The substantial benefit received by the promisor provides an evidentiary substitute for written evidence of the promise.[49]

The difficulties encountered in discovering a sufficient articulation of the "main purpose" or "leading object" rule suggest a brief consideration of certain clusters of cases that illustrate its use. Where a subcontractor refused to continue supplying labor and materials because the general contractor failed to pay, the owner orally promised to pay the subcontractor to induce the completion of performance. Clearly, the owner's promise is, in form, a suretyship promise within the statute. Yet, it is equally clear that the owner seeks to benefit himself substantially, i.e., he has no particular interest in benefit-

---

[44] See Contractor's Crane Serv. v. Vermont Whey Abatement Auth., 519 A.2d 1166 (Vt. 1986).

[45] See Henry C. Beck Co. v. Fort Wayne Structural Steel Co., 701 F.2d 1221 (7th Cir. 1983) which cites the second edition of this book for this proposition.

[46] See Thomas A. Armbruster, Inc. v. Barron, 341 Pa. Super. 409, 491 A.2d 882 (1985) quoting from the second edition of this book. See also First Nat'l Bank in Clarksville v. Moore, 628 S.W.2d 488 (Tex. App. 1982) holding that promisee's failure to secure a jury finding that the main purpose of the promisor was to obtain a benefit to himself resulted in the promise remaining within the suretyship provision of the statute of frauds.

[47] In 1811, Chancellor Kent suggested that a promise to pay the debt of another arising from some new and original consideration takes the promise out of the suretyship provision. Leonard v. Vredenburgh, 8 Johns. 29, 5 Am. Dec. 317 (N.Y. 1811). For a modern manifestation of this confusion of thought, see Gulf Liquid Fertilizer Co. v. Titus, 162 Tex. 260, 354 S.W.2d 378 (1962). These opinions overlook the fact that any promise needs consideration or an alternate validation device to support it. Thus, to say that the promise is supported by consideration does not, in itself, provide any assistance in the determination of whether the promisor made the promise essentially to benefit himself.

[48] See First Nat'l Bank in Clarksville v. Moore, 628 S.W.2d 488 (Tex. App. 1982); Colpitts v. L. C. Fisher Co., 289 Mass. 232, 293 N.E. 833 (1935); Knight v. Kiser, 271 F. 869 (4th Cir. 1921); Wells & Morris v. Brown, 67 Wash. 351, 121 P. 828 (1912); Templeton v. Bascom, 33 Vt. 132 (1860).

[49] See RESTATEMENT 2d § 116 comments a and b.

ing the general contractor for whom he may even feel some hostility, but he has an overriding desire to see the completion of the building and he makes the promise to pay the subcontractor to serve that main purpose or leading object. Such a promise is taken out of the suretyship provision of the statute even though the effect of the promise is to pay the debt of another.[50]

Another group of cases applying the main purpose rule are those where the promisor has an interest in certain property on which the promisee either has a lien or has the power to create a lien as security for a debt of another. If the promisor agrees to discharge the debt of another in exchange for the promisee's forbearance to enforce the lien or to create one, courts have found the main purpose of the promisor was to avoid the lien on his property rather than to benefit the debtor.[51]

Promises by stockholders of corporations to pay corporate bills if promisees continue to supply goods or services to the corporation may appear to suggest another application of the main purpose or leading object rule since the promises are often motivated by the stockholder's own interests and their leading object is to protect the value of their stock. Yet, such promises are usually held to remain within the suretyship provision of the statute unless the benefit to the promisor can be shown to be *special, direct* and/or *immediate*.[52] A stockholder's promise to answer for the debt of the corporation normally provides no more than a remote and indirect benefit to the promisor.[53] A promise made merely to protect the value of one's shares does not activate the main purpose rule.[54] If the promisor seeks to protect his personal financial interests beyond the value of his shares, however, a special, direct or immediate benefit may be shown as sufficient to apply the main purpose rule.[55]

---

[50]Fairview Lumber Co. v. Makos, 44 Wash. 2d 131, 265 P.2d 837 (1954) (house builder was in arrears to a materials supplier and the land owner promised to pay the past debt and future charges if the promisee would continue to supply materials). This is, essentially, the fact situation of ill. 3 of RESTATEMENT 2d § 116. In Morrison-Knudsen Co. v. Hite Crane & Rigging, 36 Wash. App. 860, 678 P.2d 346 (1984), a general contractor promised to pay the debt of a subcontractor to a supplier of crane services and the court held that the promise was made to assure the completion of the contract on schedule. *See also* Wilson Floors Co. v. Sciota Park, 54 Ohio St. 2d 451, 377 N.E.2d 514 (1978) where a bank's promise to a subcontractor to ascertain continuation of payments was held to be for the interest of the bank in reducing the costs of completing the project.

[51]*See* Grammar v. Builders Brick & Stone Co., 277 S.W.2d 185 (Tex. Civ. App. 1955); Miller v. Hanna-Logan, Inc., 95 Colo. 464, 37 P.2d 393 (1934).

[52]*See* Armbruster v. Barron, 341 Pa. Super. 409, 491 A.2d 882, 886 (1985) which quotes this portion of the second edition of this book.

[53]Martin Roofing, Inc. v. Goldstein, 60 N.Y.2d 262, 457 N.E.2d 700, 702 (1983).

[54]*See* 2 CORBIN ON CONTRACTS § 372.

[55]*See* Armbruster v. Barron, *supra* note 52, where the promise was held to go beyond the purpose of protecting the value of shares, i.e., it was made to insure the financial success of a new enterprise. In Merdes v. Underwood, 742 P.2d 245 (Alaska 1987) the promise was held to be outside the statute because it was made to serve the promisor's own business advantage in forestalling litigation against a corporation in which the promisor initially had an 80% interest and later a 100% interest. The promise also served to benefit his credit reputation. *See also* Mid-Atlantic Appliances, Inc. v. Morgan, 194 Va. 324, 73 S.E.2d 385, 35 A.L.R. 2d 899 (1952). *Cf.* Contractor's Crane Serv. v. Vermont Whey Abatement Auth., 519 A.2d 1166 (1986) where the court held that a group of producers of cheese who formed a joint venture to dispose of liquid whey, a by-product of cheese, were liable on their promise to pay for the debt of the joint venture concerning the hauling of the whey because their main purpose was to enable them, as cheese producers, to continue disposing of their whey.

Contracts of guaranty insurance are excluded from the "main purpose" exception regardless of whether the promisor is in the regular business of providing such insurance. RESTATEMENT 2d § 116 comment c.

Where the holder of a contract right (assignor) assigns that right to an assignee, the assignor may promise that the obligor (the party who has the correlative duty) will perform his duty. Though the promise may appear to be within the suretyship provision, it is typically made for the benefit of the assignor who is eager to effectuate the assignment. It falls, therefore, within the rationale of the "main purpose" exception.[56] Similarly, a promise of a *del credere* agent is not within the suretyship provision of the statute of frauds. A *del credere* agent is one who takes possession of the creditor's goods and earns a commission in reselling them. A promise by such an agent to the creditor which guarantees the accounts of customers who purchase the goods is not within the statute because, typically, the agent seeks only to advance his own interest. Therefore, such a promise falls within the rationale of the "main purpose" exception.[57]

Any criticism of the "main purpose" rule is drowned in the sea of cases that have found it useful in removing certain promises from the suretyship provision of the statute of frauds. With the exception of New York, the "main purpose" rule is recognized throughout the country.[58] The difficulties encountered in formulating a precise guide to its application should not suggest the rejection of the rule. Rather, we should recognize that the concept presents difficult questions of fact as to the purpose of the promisor. As in other areas of our law, solutions should be derived through typical case-by-case adjudication.

§ 70. Agreements Made in Consideration of Marriage.

The language of the original Statute of Frauds provides that "[N]o action shall be brought ... to charge any person upon any agreement made in consideration of marriage." The all-inclusive phrase, "any agreement," would, if read literally, include even mutual promises to marry. There is reason to believe that even the drafters of the original Statute, however, did not intend it to apply to such promises.[59] Early decisions made it clear that courts would not apply this provision of the Statute to mutual promises to marry which are typically exchanged in an ambience that does not admit of a writing require-

---

[56] RESTATEMENT 2d § 121(1).

[57] RESTATEMENT 2d § 121(2).

[58] The unusual New York approach is traceable to nineteenth century cases. In White v. Rentoul, 108 N.Y. 222, 15 N.E. 318 (1888), the court dealt with the main purpose rule in accordance with its understanding of New York precedent. It suggested three necessary elements: (a) there must be consideration to support the promise of the surety; (b) the consideration must benefit the promisor; (c) the promisor must come under an independent duty of payment regardless of the liability of the principal debtor. The third element has been more recently interpreted as to require a manifested intention by the parties that the promisor become a principal debtor, primarily liable. Martin Roofing v. Goldstein, 60 N.Y.2d 262, 469 N.Y.S.2d 595, 457 N.E.2d 700 (1983), cert. denied, 466 U.S. 905 (1984). Unless the third element is satisfied, the court may not treat the promise as having been taken out of the suretyship provision. Thus, a suretyship promise that would be removed from the statute in other jurisdictions will remain subject to the statute in New York. See Capital Knitting Mills, Inc. v. Duofold, Inc., 519 N.Y.S.2d 968 (A.D. 1st Dept. 1987). This opinion contains a splendid analysis of the treatment of the main purpose rule in New York as well as a suggestion that the New York Court of Appeals might be receptive to reconsidering the unique New York approach so as to have New York recognize the main purpose concept in accordance with other jurisdictions.

[59] RESTATEMENT 2d § 124 comment a.

ment.[60] Modern courts continue this policy decision though, in a number of jurisdictions, judicial exclusion was unnecessary because mutual promises to marry were legislatively excluded from the marriage provision of statute.[61] The marriage provision applies to a promise to surrender any property right in consideration of marriage.[62] Thus, an antenuptial agreement concerning the disposition of property is within the marriage provision of the statute.[63] A promise by a third party, X, to pay a sum to A, if she will marry B, is within the marriage provision.[64] Agreements to adopt children[65] or to permit a spouse's parent to live with the couple[66] have been held to be within the marriage provision of the statute. If, however, the marriage is merely the occasion for making the contract or if the contract is made merely in contemplation of marriage where the promises are supported by other consideration, the contract is not within the statute.[67] Similarly, if the marriage is merely a condition of a promise which is supported wholly by some other consideration, the contract is not within the statute.[68] The case law suggests that courts are often astute to find that a contract is outside the operation of the statute for one or another of these reasons.

It is, however, generally held that the occurrence of the marriage in reliance upon an oral agreement within the marriage provision is not sufficient part performance to take the contract out of the statute.[69]

Elsewhere in this volume, we explore the relatively new problem confronting courts of contracts between unmarried cohabitants. Contracts between the cohabitants are often not reduced to written form.[70] While the possibility of fraudulent claims may suggest a greater need for the application of the mar-

---

[60] See, e.g., Short v. Stotts, 58 Ind. 29 (1877); Withers v. Richardson, 21 Ky. (5 T. B. Mon.) 94, 17 Am. Dec. 44 (1827). It was also early held, however, that mutual promises to marry can be within the provision of the statute requiring promises not to be performed within one year from the making. See Derby v. Phelps, 2 N.H. 515 (1823).

[61] See, e.g., Tice v. Tice, 672 P.2d 1168, 1170 (Okla. 1983) which mentions Title 15 OKLA. STAT. 1981, § 136(3). See also HAW. REV. STAT. § 656-1(3) (1976).

[62] See, e.g., Byers v. Byers, 618 P.2d 930 (Okla. 1980) where the court held that the situation of a wife who promised to marry only because her husband agreed to support a child fathered by another prior to the marriage, was within the statute of frauds. See also Stevens v. Niblack's Adm'r, 256 Ky. 255, 75 S.W.2d 770 (1934) where a promise of the father, made to the mother of an illegitimate child, to leave the father's estate to the child in consideration of the mother's promise to marry was within the statute of frauds. If the performance of the contract involves the transfer of an interest in land, it should be remembered that it will fall within the land clause of the statute, which will be explored later in this section. See Rainbolt v. East, 56 Ind. 538, 26 Am. Rep. 40 (1877).

[63] See, e.g., Rossiter v. Rossiter, 666 P.2d 617 (Haw. App. 1983) (alleged oral antenuptial agreement that wife would never force the sale of marital residence).

[64] RESTATEMENT 2d § 124 ill. 4.

[65] Maddox v. Maddox, 224 Ga. 313, 161 S.E.2d 870 (1968).

[66] Koch v. Koch, 95 N.J. Super. 546, 232 A.2d 157 (1967).

[67] Riley v. Riley, 25 Conn. 154 (1856) (promise to prospective bridegroom that note held by fiancee should be paid out of his estate, made in consideration of forbearance, on the eve of marriage).

[68] Bader v. Hiscox, 188 Iowa 986, 174 N.W. 565, 10 A.L.R. 316 (1920) (promise of father to convey land to woman seduced by his son, if she would drop civil and criminal bastardy proceedings).

[69] Rossiter v. Rossiter, 666 P.2d 617 (Haw. App. 1983). RESTATEMENT 2d § 124 comment d.

[70] The alleged contract may not even have been expressed orally and the action is based on an implied-in-fact contract. See Marvin v. Marvin, 18 Cal. 3d 660, 134 Cal. Rptr. 815, 557 P.2d 106 (1976).

riage provision of the statute of frauds to these contracts than to a marriage contract, at the time of this writing, the marriage provision has been held inapplicable to such contracts.[71] Though the marriage provision does not apply to such contracts, other provisions of the statute of frauds such as those applicable to a contract to transfer an interest in real estate, or a contract that cannot be performed within one year from the making thereof, will apply to such contracts if the contract involves the subject matter of other provisions of the statute of frauds.[72]

§ 71. Contracts for the Sale of Land.

A. *History — Distinguishing Contracts and Conveyances.*

One of the types of contracts covered by the original Statute of Frauds was a contract for the conveyance of an interest in land. The purpose of the land contract provision is the same as the purpose underlying the other provisions of the Statute dealing with other types of contracts, i.e., to protect an owner or purchaser of real estate from fraudulent claims that he or his agent have agreed to sell or buy an interest in real estate.[73]

It is important to distinguish between that section of the statute of frauds requiring written evidence of an executory contract to transfer an interest in land and another section of the statute dealing with the conveyance or present transfer of an interest in land. A conveyance is an executed transaction and the requirements for its validity are commonly prescribed by separate statutes beyond the scope of this book. The situation is made somewhat confusing by the fact that the English version of the land contract clause of the Statute of Frauds uses the language, "contract or sale" which would appear to cover both a contract to convey as well as the conveyance itself. In view of the fact, however, that other sections of the original Statute cover the subject of conveyances more directly and comprehensively,[74] the land contract clause of the fourth section has commonly been viewed as if it only contained the words, "contract for the sale of...." Most of the American versions of the land contract clause are worded in this fashion.

While there is no doubt that the statute applies to any promise to transfer an interest in land, there has been some question as to whether a promise to *buy* an interest in land is also within the statute. The prevailing view is that such promises are covered by the statute[75] and even payment of the price, itself, will not satisfy the statute.[76] If the owner of the land tenders a deed to the buyer who accepts the deed, however, the buyer's oral promise to pay is taken out of the statute and becomes enforceable unless the "price" which the

---

[71] *See, e.g.,* Morone v. Morone, 50 N.Y.2d 481, 429 N.Y.S.2d 592, 413 N.E.2d 1154 (1980).

[72] *See, e.g.,* Baron v. Jeffer, 515 N.Y.S.2d 857 (A.D. 2 Dept. 1987) where the contract between unmarried cohabitants did not require a writing because of the marriage provision, but did require a writing because of the one year provision (*see infra* § 72) and the provision concerning contracts for the sale of land (*see infra* § 71).

[73] Wiggins v. Barrett & Assocs., 295 Or. 679, 669 P.2d 1132 (1983).

[74] *See* 29 Car. 2, ch. 3, § 1. *See also* RESTATEMENT OF PROPERTY §§ 467, 522.

[75] RESTATEMENT 2d § 125 comment d.

[76] RESTATEMENT 2d § 129.

buyer promised to pay was, in whole or in part, itself an interest in land.[77] Presumably, the evidentiary formalities of the statute are satisfied by an executed conveyance but they are not satisfied by performance of a promise to pay.

B. *What Is an "Interest in Land"?*

One of the fundamental questions concerning this section of the statute is, what is an interest in land? In general, the section encompasses any contract the performance of which involves the transfer or creation of what, historically, is known as a property interest in real estate.[78] The real estate interest promised may be legal or equitable.[79] The statute, therefore, applies not only to a promise to transfer a legal estate in lands,[80] or to create or transfer an easement,[81] or profit,[82] or rent,[83] or other similar legal property interest, but also an agreement to rescind,[84] or to assign,[85] a land contract, or to create or assign a beneficiary's interest in land held in trust,[86] or an equitable lien by mortgage,[87] or restriction on land.[88]

---

[77] RESTATEMENT 2d § 125(3) and comment e thereto.

[78] The words "lands, tenements and hereditaments" of the original Statute have not been accorded individual meanings. It has been assumed that they are synonymous with the phrase, "real estate." *See* RESTATEMENT 2d § 127.

[79] *See* Shalimar Ass'n v. D. O. C. Enters., 142 Ariz. 36, 688 P.2d 682 (1984) (implied restriction limiting use of property to a golf course was an equitable restriction generally considered to be an interest in land within the statute of frauds).

[80] *See, e.g.,* Carley v. Carley, 705 S.W.2d 371 (Tex. Civ. App. 1986) (life estate is an interest in land within the statute). *See also* Moloney v. Weingarten, 118 A.D.2d 836, 500 N.Y.S.2d 320 (1986) (statute applicable to a contract purporting to create or convey an interest in a cooperative apartment); Del Rio Land, Inc. v. Haumont, 118 Ariz. 1, 574 P.2d 469 (1977) (sale of real property at auction is within the statute). If the price for the land is something other than money, the statute applies: Sealock v. Krug-Robinson Auto Co., 110 Kan. 302, 203 P. 728 (1922) (promise to convey land in exchange for automobiles); Baxter v. Kitch, 37 Ind. 554 (1871) (promise to convey land for services rendered); Purcell v. Coleman, 71 U.S. (4 Wall.) 513 (1866) (agreement to exchange lands). A unilateral contract to purchase land at the owner's option is within the statute: Alamoe Realty Co. v. Mutual Trust Life Ins. Co., 202 Minn. 457, 278 N.W. 902 (1938). A contract to convey or purchase land owned by a third person is within the statute, Wright v. Green, 67 Ind. App. 433, 119 N.E. 379 (1918). Most courts hold an agreement conferring an "option" on lands to be within the land contract clause of the statute, Rooney v. Dayton-Hudson Corp., 310 Minn. 256, 246 N.W.2d 170 (1976).

[81] Bob Daniels & Sons v. Weaver, 681 P.2d 1010 (Idaho 1984) (easement); Wiggins v. Barrett & Assocs., 669 P.2d 1132 (Or. 1983) (easement); Estabrook v. Wilcox, 226 Mass. 156, 115 N.E. 233 (1917) (right of way). *See also* Silva v. McGuinness, 615 P.2d 879 (1980) (agreement to change exit of road involves an interest in land subject to the statute of frauds).

[82] Riddle v. Brown, 20 Ala. 412, 56 Am. Dec. 202 (1852) (promise to give the right to dig and carry away ore).

[83] Brown v. Brown, 33 N.J. Eq. 650 (1881). *But see* Note, *Statute of Frauds, Unaccrued Rents as Interest Within,* 20 CORNELL L.Q. 131 (1934).

[84] *See* Annotation, 38 A.L.R. 294 (1925). *Cf.* Nicholson v. Nicholson, 199 N.J. Super. 525, 489 A.2d 1247 (1985), where the parties entered into a reconciliation agreement in which the wife agreed to resume cohabitation with the husband and to abandon her plan to divorce him on ground of adultery in exchange for husband's promise to convey his interest in the marital home. The court held that, since the agreement involved real estate, compliance with the statute of frauds was essential.

[85] *See* Esslinger v. Pascoe, 219 Iowa 86, 105 N.W. 362 (1905).

[86] Holmes v. Holmes, 86 N.C. 205 (1882). *See* Annotation, 173 A.L.R. 281 (1948).

[87] *See, e.g.,* Lambert v. Home Fed. Sav. & Loan Ass'n, 481 S.W.2d 770 (Tenn. 1972) and

---

[88] Ham v. Massasoit Real Estate Co., 42 R.I. 293, 107 A. 205 (1919). *Contra* Thornton v. Schobe, 79 Colo. 25, 243 P. 617 (1925) *noted,* 24 MICH. L. REV. 854 (1926). No attempt has been made to catalog the myriad kinds of rights in relation to land that are classified as property interests.

Under the English Statute, leases (which are both contracts and conveyances) were excepted from the Statute if they did not exceed three years "from the making thereof." Today, most of the American statutes make an exception for short term leases for a term up to one year, and the year is typically not measured from the time the contract is made.[89] It is equally well settled that the statute does not affect a contract merely because the performance of it relates to land or the use of land, so long as the transfer of what is known as a "property interest" or "right in rem" as distinguished from a "contract right" or "right in personam," is not involved. Consequently, a promise to construct a building on land,[90] or to do work on land,[91] or give another a mere license to go on land for some purpose,[92] is not within the land provision of the statute. Moreover, if an actual conveyance as contrasted with a promise to convey has occurred, a promise to pay the agreed price in consideration of the actual conveyance of an estate or interest in land is not within the land contract provision of the statute.[93] A majority of courts hold that a contract creating a partnership is not within the statute though the transaction includes an understanding that the partnership shall own lands or deal in lands to be held in the name of one or less than all of the partners.[94] Similarly, an agreement to divide profits on the intended sale of real property is not within the statute.[95]

C. *Purchases and Sales by Agents.*

Another situation that deserves special mention is one involving a contract appointing an agent to purchase or sell real estate. A number of jurisdictions have added a provision to their statutes of frauds requiring a contract to pay a

---

Hatlestad v. Mutual Trust Life Ins. Co., 197 Minn. 640, 268 N.W. 665 (1936). *Contra* Martyn v. First Fed. Sav. & Loan Ass'n, 257 So. 2d 576 (Fla. Dist. App.) *cert. denied,* 262 So. 2d 446 (Fla. 1972) (limiting land contract provision to transfers of title and holding a mortgage is not within the statute if state law treats it only as a lien). *See* Douglas Co. v. Gatts, 456 N.E.2d 841 (Ohio App. 1982), holding that an oral agreement to release or discharge a mortgage is within the land contract provision of the statute because a mortgage is an interest in land. *Contra* Riley v. Atherton, 185 Ark. 425, 47 S.W.2d 568 (1932).

[89] The short term lease is excepted from both the land contract and one year provisions of the statute of frauds. RESTATEMENT 2d § 125(4). As will be seen in the exploration of the one year clause in the next section, the measurement of one year begins with the making of the contract. A literal application of that clause of the statute to a one year lease would measure the year from the time the oral contract of lease was made. If the lease term is not to commence until some time after the making of the contract, the contract would be within the one year provision. The typical exception in American statutes for short term leases, however, does not measure the year from the time of contract formation. Thus, whether a short term lease contract is within the one year provision depends upon the duration of the lease itself, regardless of the time the lease contract was formed.

[90] Smith v. Hudson, 48 N.C. App. 347, 269 S.E.2d 172 (1980); Scales v. Wiley, 68 Vt. 39, 33 A. 771 (1895).

[91] Plunkett v. Meredith, 72 Ark. 3, 77 S.W. 600 (1903); Haight v. Conners, 149 Pa. 297, 24 A. 302 (1892).

[92] *See* Moon v. Central Bldrs. Inc., 65 N.C. App. 793, 310 S.E.2d 390 (1984) (promise to permit use of road during construction work); Burgess v. Swetnam, 257 Ky. 64, 77 S.W.2d 385 (1934) (promise to permit neighbor to use gas from well on property); Johnson v. Wilkinson, 139 Mass. 3, 29 N.E. 62 (1885) (promise to permit use of hall for entertainment purposes). *Accord,* RESTATEMENT 2d § 127 comment b. *See also* RESTATEMENT OF PROPERTY § 514.

[93] Pettett v. Cooper, 62 Ohio App. 377, 24 N.E.2d 299 (1939).

[94] *See* J. Crane & A. Bromberg, The Law of Partnership § 39 (1968).

[95] Bowart v. Bowart, 128 Ariz. 331, 625 P.2d 920 (1980).

commission to a real estate broker to be evidenced by a writing.[96] In the absence of such a statutory provision, however, a contract defining the terms under which an agent undertakes merely to negotiate on behalf of his principal for the purchase or sale of land is not with the land contract provision of the statute.[97] If the agent agrees, however, to purchase the land in his own name and later to convey it to the principal, or if the agent, though he is to take title in the name of the principal, is to pay for the land out of his own pocket in the first instance so that he becomes the beneficiary of a resulting trust,[98] of if he contracts to cause the land to be conveyed to his principal,[99] the contract is within the statute.

D. *Minerals, Timber, and Growing Crops — Uniform Commercial Code.*

Prior to the UCC, courts were confronted with the proper characterization of minerals such as coal, timber, growing crops and other products attached to the land. Should such products of the land be characterized as "land", so as to bring a contract for their sale within the land contract provision, or should they be characterized as goods, placing contracts for their sale outside the land contract provision?[1] There was little disconcertion about growing crops, i.e., annual crops grown with the assistance of man, known as *fructus industriales,* such as wheat and corn. Growing crops were considered chattels, i.e., goods, even if the contract to sell such crops was formed prior to their severance. Thus, the land contract provision did not apply to growing crops even prior to the UCC.[2] Contracts for the purchase and sale of timber, minerals and the like, i.e., products which grew or developed spontaneously without the aid of man, created considerable confusion among the courts as to whether they were within the land contract provision of the statute. Some courts adopted an arbitrary rule with respect to such products. The decision was said to depend upon whether the parties to the contract dealt with the subject matter as land or chattels.[3] Other courts held that the proper charac-

---

[96] *See, e.g.,* CAL. CIV. CODE § 1624(d) as discussed in Phillippe v. Shapell Indus., 43 Cal. 3d 1247, 241 Cal. Rptr. 22, 743 P.2d 1279 (1987); N.J.S.A. 25:1-9 as discussed in Joseph Hilton & Assocs. v. Evans, 201 N.J. Super. 156, 492 A.2d 1062 (1985); IND. CODE § 32-2-2-1 as discussed in Shrum v. Dalton, 442 N.E.2d 366 (Ind. 1982). *See also* MONT. CODE ANN. § 37-51-401 and WASH. REV. CODE § 19.36.010(5).

[97] *See* Murphy v. Nolte & Co., 226 Va. 76, 307 S.E.2d 242 (1983) in which the court recites the holding in Reich v. Kimnach, 216 Va. 109, 216 S.E.2d 58 (1975) which held that the statute of frauds did not apply to an oral listing agreement between a seller and a broker because it was a contract for services and not a contract for the sale of real estate. In 1976, however, Virginia added a brokerage provision to its statute of frauds (§ 11-2 (6a)) which brought such contracts within the statute. *See also* Roberts v. Ross, 344 F.2d 747 (3d Cir. 1965). Even without a provision dealing with brokerage commissions, however, where the consideration for the broker's services is, itself, an interest in real estate, the contract is within the statute. *See* Smith v. Gilbraltar Oil Co., 254 F.2d 518 (10th Cir. 1958).

[98] McDonald v. Conway, 254 Mass. 429, 150 N.E. 200 (1926); Houston v. Farley, 146 Ga. 822, 92 S.E. 635 (1917).

[99] Allen v. Richard, 83 Mo. 55 (1884).

[1] The characterization of goods as land would place the contract within the statute of frauds. As will be seen, however, there are significant differences in the satisfaction of the land contract provision versus the provision dealing with contracts for the sale of goods.

[2] *See* Shedaker v. James, 154 A. 394, 107 N.J.L. 400 (1931); Marshall v. Ferguson, 23 Cal. 65 (1863).

[3] *See, e.g.,* Home Owners' Loan Corp. v. Gotwals, 67 S.D. 579, 297 N.W. 36 (1941); Leonard v. Medford, 85 Md. 666, 37 A. 365 (1897); Long v. White, 42 Ohio St. 59 (1884).

terization of the products depended upon whether the thing agreed to be sold was to be removed promptly, i.e., if it was to be left as part of the land for a considerable time, the contract was for an interest in land to which the land contract provision applied. If the products were to be severed promptly, however, the contract was one for the sale of chattels.[4] Still other courts adopted a more persuasive analysis. They suggested that the answer depended upon when the purchaser was to become the owner of the product. If it were contemplated that the buyer was to become the owner before the product was severed from the land, he would then acquire title while it was still land and the contract was one for the transfer of an interest in land. On the other hand, if the buyer were not to become the owner of the timber, coal or other minerals until after it was severed from the land, he was agreeing to purchase goods. In that situation, the only right the buyer would receive in relation to the land would be a license to enter and to sever the product. We have already seen that a license is not regarded as an interest in land within the meaning of the statute.[5] Several courts adopted this analysis.[6]

Under the 1962 version of the UCC, the problem was resolved by adopting an analysis similar to the last position described. As to standing timber, minerals, structures attached to the land or the like, the contract was for the sale of *goods* if the contract required or authorized the seller to sever them, i.e., the seller would be selling severed products — goods. If the understanding was that the buyer was to sever such products, the contract was characterized as one for the sale of an interest in land.[7] The land contract provision of the statute would, therefore, apply to such a contract. A contract for the sale of growing crops or other things attached to realty and capable of severance without material harm to the realty continued to be characterized as a contract for the sale of goods under the Code, regardless of which party was to sever them.[8] The 1972 version of the UCC modified the earlier version by placing timber in the same classification as growing crops, i.e., a contract for the sale of timber is now regarded as a contract for the sale of goods regardless of which party is to sever the timber.[9] This change was designed to reflect the same change that had been effected earlier in several timber-growing states. The change was, therefore, in keeping with the basic UCC philosophy of reflecting commercial practices in accordance with the normal intention of

---

[4] *See, e.g.,* Marshall v. Green, L.R. 1 C.P.D. 35 [1875].

[5] *See supra* note 92 and accompanying text.

[6] *See* Baird v. Elliott, 63 N.D. 738, 249 N.W. 894 (1933); Rosenstein v. Gottfried, 145 Minn. 243, 176 N.W. 844 (1920); Wetkopsky v. New Haven Gas Light Co., 88 Conn. 1, 90 A. 30 (1914).

[7] UCC § 2-107(1), 1962 Official Text: "A contract for the sale of timber, minerals or the like or a structure or its materials to be removed from realty is a contract for the sale of goods within this Article if they are to be severed by the seller but until severance a purported present sale thereof which is not effective as a transfer of an interest in land is effective only as a contract to sell."

[8] UCC § 2-107(2).

[9] UCC § 2-107(2) (1972 Official Text). It should be noted that, even under this modified version, the buyer may not acquire a property interest in the timber (though the timber is goods) until "identification" occurs, UCC § 2-501. If a buyer agrees to purchase an entire stand of timber, identification would occur when the contract is formed. If, however, the intention of the parties is that the buyer will pay only for the timber cut and payment is due after severance, the parties may be said to have intended that the buyer would have a property interest only in cut timber. In one case, this distinction led to a devisee rather than residuary legatees taking the proceeds of a timber contract. *See* Fisher v. Elmore, 610 F. Supp. 123 (E.D.N.C. 1985).

parties engaged in making particular types of contracts.[10] With respect to the classification of minerals or the like, the 1972 version clarified the earlier version by expressly including oil and gas as products that would be characterized as land if they were to be severed by the purchaser.[11]

§ 72. Contract Not Performable Within One Year From Formation.

A. *Origins — Narrow Application — Possibility of Performance — Measurement of One Year.*

The fifth section of the original Statute of Frauds required written evidence of "an agreement that is not to be performed within the space of one year from the making thereof." In construing this provision, courts have generally paid little attention to its original purpose and have applied it in such a fashion as to narrow its scope as much as possible.[12] Accordingly, it is universally agreed that the one-year clause includes only those contracts whose terms are such *that performance cannot be completed within a year from the time they are made.* Thus, an oral contract of employment for one year will be within this provision of the statute if performance is not to begin until some time after formation.[13] Performance must be capable of being *completed* within one year from formation and the performance of such an employment contract could not possibly be completed within one year from formation. The one year duration commences on the date of formation, i.e., with the acceptance of the offer, and ends on midnight of the anniversary of the day on which the contract was formed.[14] Courts have consistently emphasized the mere *possibility* of performance within one year, i.e., regardless of how unlikely it is that performance will be completed within a year from the date of formation, if it is merely *possible* that the performance of both promises will be completed within a year, the oral contract is outside the statute and is, therefore, enforceable.[15] This is so even though performance has, in fact, extended beyond the year,[16]

---

[10] UCC § 1-102(2)(b).

[11] UCC § 2-107(1) (1972 Official Text).

[12] The one year provision was designed to avoid trusting the memory of witnesses for longer than one year, but the language was not effective to ascertain that purpose. The courts have, therefore, narrowed its application. *See* RESTATEMENT 2d § 130 comment a.

[13] *See, e.g.,* Kass v. Ronnie Jewelry, 118 R.I. 100, 371 A.2d 1060 (1977) where a one year employment contract was held to be within the statute since the employee would not begin performance until four days after contract formation.

[14] Fractions of a day are disregarded. *See* RESTATEMENT 2d § 130 comment c.

[15] *See* Griffith v. One Inv. Plaza Assoc., 62 Md. App. 1, 488 A.2d 182, 184 (1985) where the court suggests two sets of circumstances under which the one-year clause of the statute will bar a claim. (1) where the parties expressly and specifically agree that their oral contracts were not to be performed within a year; (2) where it is impossible, by the terms of the contract, for it to be performed within one year. The court relies, *inter alia,* upon an 1853 Maryland case which suggested that, "the statute will not apply where the contract can, *by any possibility,* be fulfilled or completed in the space of a year, *although the parties may have intended its operation should extend through a much longer period.* Ellicott v. Peterson, 4 Md. 476, 488 (1853).

[16] City of Clewiston v. B & B Cash Grocery Stores, Inc., 445 So. 2d 1038 (Fla. Dist. App. 1984). In Aldape v. State, 98 Idaho 912, 575 P.2d 891 (1978), a lease terminable at will was held not to be within the one year provision since it was possible that the contract would be performed within one year. In Nickerson v. Harvard College, 298 Mass. 484, 11 N.E.2d 444, 114 A.L.R. 414 (1937), an agreement to work for one year, the employment to begin whenever the employer should elect, was held outside the statute since it was possible that the employment could begin on the date of

and even though this likelihood was contemplated when the contract was formed. Thus, a leading case held that a contract to furnish a right-of-way "so long as the promisee needed it" was not within the one year provision because it was possible that the contract would be completed within one year, although, at the time the contract was formed, it was assumed that performance would continue for 20 or 30 years, and it had, in fact, continued for 13 years prior to the alleged breach.[17]

B. *"Lifetime" and "Permanent" Employment — "Reasonable Time."*

It has been held that an agreement to work for, employ, or to support another for life is not within the one year provision of the statute.[18] Since the term of the contract is "life," it is completely performable within one year from the making.[19] A "permanent" employment contract may be completely performed within one year from its making since the employee may die within that time.[20] If there is no stated duration in the contract, the court will imply a "reasonable time." Whether a contract performable within a reasonable time is one that can be performed within one year from its making is a question of fact, i.e., the factual determination will indicate whether the reasonable time exceeds one year from formation, thus bringing the contract within the one year provision.[21]

C. *Alternative Performances — Excuse — Termination — Renewal.*

If the parties agree that performance will be complete upon the performance of either of two acts, only one of which is capable of being performed within a year from formation, the contract is not within the one year provision since the contract may be completely performed within a year if that alternative is chosen.[22] When applied to certain situations, however, this principle becomes

---

formation. The fact that the employment contract is not performed within one year is irrelevant since it was *possible* that it would be performed within a year from the time of formation.

[17] Warner v. Texas & Pac. Ry., 164 U.S. 418 (1896). *See also* Freedman v. Chemical Constr. Corp., 42 N.Y.2d 260, 372 N.E. 12 (1977) (agreement to procure a contract and to construct a chemical plant in Saudi Arabia which required three years to procure the contract and six years to construct the plant. Held: contract was still performable within one year from the making).

[18] *See* Thurston v. Nutter, 125 Me. 411, 134 A. 506 (1926) (agreement to support for life); Pierson v. Kingman Milling Co., 91 Kan. 775, 139 P. 394 (1914) (agreement to employ for life). In City of New York v. Heller, 487 N.Y.S.2d 288, 290 (N.Y. Civ. Ct. 1985), the court held that an oral agreement for a tenancy measured by the life of the tenant was not within the one year provision since "a lifetime can be shorter than a year."

[19] Some states have added a "lifetime" provision to their statutes of frauds. Such a provision brings the lifetime contract within the statute. *See* N.Y. GEN. OBLIG. LAW § 5-701(1); CAL. CIV. CODE § 1624(6).

[20] *See* Bussard v. College of St. Thomas, 294 Minn. 215, 200 N.W.2d 155 (1972). See, however, Benoit v. Polysar Gulf Coast, Inc., 728 S.W.2d 403 (Tex. App. 1987) where the court held a promise of "lifetime" or "permanent" employment to be within the one year provision over a dissenting opinion relying on Kelley v. Apache Prods., Inc., 709 S.W.2d 772 (Tex. App. 1986) which held that a contract of employment for an indefinite duration is not in violation of the one year provision of the statute.

[21] *See* Mercer v. C. A. Roberts Co., 570 F.2d 232 (5th Cir. 1978); Apache Trailer Sales, Inc. v. Redman Indus., 117 Ariz. 504, 573 P.2d 904 (1977).

[22] North Shore Bottling Co. v. C. Schmidt & Sons, 22 N.Y.2d 171, 292 N.Y.S.2d 86, 239 N.E.2d 189 (1968) (defendant orally agreed to make plaintiff the exclusive wholesale distributor of defendant's beer in Queens County as long as defendant sold beer in the New York metropolitan area.

murky. Where, for example, the contract contains a promise not to compete for a period exceeding one year, some courts have held that the promise is not within the one year provision because the implied alternative of death of the promisor within a year from formation would assure the completion of performance since competition after death is impossible.[23] Other courts view the possibility of the promisor's death within a year as excusable nonperformance or justifiable termination of the contract, i.e., death is not an alternative performance.[24] The split of authority on this question is found in other contexts. Perhaps the best known case in which the question was raised is *Hopper v. Lennen & Mitchell, Inc.,*[25] where the plaintiff agreed to perform radio programs for the defendant for a total period of five years divided into twenty-six week segments. This unusually detailed oral contract specified an increase in the plaintiff's salary for each segment after the first twenty-six weeks and defendant's power to terminate the agreement by giving notice one month before the end of any segment. If the agreement was interpreted to permit alternative *performances,* one of which could be completed within a year from formation, the contract was not within the statute. If, however, the contract was construed to allow either *performance* requiring more than a year (five years) or *termination* by the defendant within a year, the contract would be within the statute of frauds because the only *performance* could not be completed within a year, i.e., *termination* is not an alternative mode of *performance.* The *Hopper* court, relying in part on a New York case,[26] applied California law and held that the defendant's promise was outside the one year provision of the statute.[27] The majority of courts, however, would place the promise within the one year provision because the exercise of a power of termination is not performance.[28] Similarly, if a party who fails to perform a contract requiring more than one year to perform is legally excused from

---

The court held that the distributorship could have continued (1) indefinitely, or (2) until defendant stopped selling beer in the New York metropolitan area. Since the second alternative permitted the possibility of performance within one year, the contract was not within the statute. In D & N Boening, Inc. v. Kirsch Beverages, Inc., 471 N.Y.S.2d 299 (A.D. 2 Dept. 1984), the court recognized the distinction in *North Shore,* but distinguished it from the case before it, which provided that a distributorship would continue so long as plaintiff satisfactorily distributed the product. If the distributor had not performed satisfactorily during the first year of the contract, the unsatisfactory performance would not have constituted a contemplated alternative mode of performance. Rather, it would have been a breach of the agreement. If fulfillment of an alternative is not contemplated except in the case of a breach of the main promise, the contingency is not a true alternative but, rather, a breach of the agreement. In this regard, *see* Radio Corp. v. Cable Radio Tube Corp., 66 F.2d 778 (2d Cir. 1933).

[23] The leading case is Doyle v. Dixon, 97 Mass. 208 (1867). *Accord,* Decker v. West, 273 Ill. App. 532 (1934); Sauser v. Kearney, 147 Iowa 335, 126 N.W. 322 (1910); Erwin v. Hayden, 43 S.W. 610 (Tex. Civ. App. 1897). The RESTATEMENT 2d § 130 takes this position.

[24] *See, e. g.,* Collection & Investigation Bur. v. Linsley, 37 Md. App. 66, 375 A.2d 47 (1977); Higgins v. Gager, 65 Ark. 604, 47 S.W. 848 (1898).

[25] 146 F.2d 364 (9th Cir. 1944).

[26] Blake v. Voigt, 134 N.Y. 69, 31 N.E. 256 (1892).

[27] Subsequent California opinions have reaffirmed this view. *See* White Lightning v. Wolfson, 68 Cal. 2d 336, 66 Cal. Rptr. 697, 438 P.2d 345 (1968). A more recent California opinion contains a complete analysis of this view which, like the *Hopper* opinion, it characterizes as the "minority" position and further suggests the "compelling logic" of the other view, i.e., the "majority" position. Plumlee v. Poag, 198 Cal. Rptr. 66 (Cal. App. 1984).

[28] Deevy v. Porter, 11 N.J. 594, 95 A.2d 596 (1953); Blue Valley Creamery Co. v. Consolidated Prods. Co., 81 F.2d 182 (8th Cir. 1936); Hanau v. Ehrlich, 37 A.C. 39 [1911].

completing performance, the promise is within the statute. If, for example, *A* orally promises to work for *B* for a period of five years, *A* may die within a year of formation. *A*'s death, however, is not an alternative performance; it is excusable nonperformance. To complete the performance of this promise would require a period of five years and that is impossible if *A* is dead. *A*'s promise, therefore, is within the one year provision.[29] If the contract expressly states that it will be terminated upon the death of the employee, the same result should follow.[30] On the other hand, if *A* orally promises to work for *B* for a period of five years if *A* lives that long, courts may be willing to view that promise as providing alternative performances, one of which is, in effect, a promise to work for life, not exceeding five years, which could be performed within a year.[31]

The different views on performance versus termination or excusable non-performance were not confined to case law. The two giants of contract law, Professor Williston and Professor Corbin, disagreed.[32] The more traditional view was Williston's, i.e., a contract with a stated duration exceeding one year which provided one or both parties with a power of termination is within the one year provision because such a contract cannot be *performed* within one year. Professor Corbin championed the view that such a contract should fall within the rules of conditional promises and alternative performances, i.e., the party with the power and privilege to terminate has a choice between performing for the entire duration (beyond one year), or for less than one year. The duty to work for the entire period is expressly conditioned upon the absence of termination before that time. With the split in the case law and the differences between the giants of contract law, the stage was set for a resolution of the problem in the RESTATEMENT 2d.

The RESTATEMENT 2d provides a disappointing reaction to the conflict. A comment to the RESTATEMENT 2d suggests, "This distinction between performance and excuse for nonperformance is sometimes tenuous; it depends on the terms and the circumstances, particularly on whether the essential purposes of the parties will be attained."[33] This directive is of little assistance and one hurries to the illustrations following it to overcome the confusion. Unfortunately, two of the illustrations exacerbate the confusion. Both proceed on a hypothetical oral contract of employment between A and B with a stated term of five years. One illustration assumes that a provision of the contract permits either party to terminate by giving 30 days notice at any time. On these facts, the illustration concludes, "The agreement is one of uncertain duration and is not with the one year provision of the Statute."[34] The next illustration changes the provision in the contract to one that permits one of the parties to quit at any time. This contract is within the one year provision.[35] The first

[29] *See e.g.,* Dickens v. Tennesee Elec. Power Co., 175 Tenn. 654, 137 S.W.2d 273 (1940); Bristol v. Sutton, 115 Mich. 365, 73 N.W. 424 (1897).

[30] *See* Gilliam v. Kouchoucos, 161 Tex. 299, 340 S.W.2d 27 (1960) where the court held that an express termination upon death provision did not alter the analysis.

[31] *See* Silverman v. Bernot, 218 Va. 650, 239 S.E.2d 118 (1977).

[32] 3 Williston §§ 498A, 498B; 2 Corbin § 449.

[33] RESTATEMENT 2d § 130 comment b.

[34] RESTATEMENT 2d § 130 ill. 6.

[35] RESTATEMENT 2d § 130 ill. 7.

illustration is said to be based on a well-known New York case[36] recognized as the landmark opinion of the "minority" view. The second hypothetical is based upon the leading case for the "majority" view.[37] The RESTATEMENT 2d, therefore, appears to have "resolved" the conflict by including both positions. The aforementioned comment language,[38] however, appears to suggest an emphasis upon the manifested purpose of the parties, i.e., did the parties intend a contract of uncertain duration with a ceiling of five years (without the one year provision), or was the overriding purpose of the parties to have a contract for five years permitting termination by notice within a year (within the one year provision). If the drafters of the RESTATEMENT 2d intended this analysis, it would have been desirable to provide a clear and emphatic statement of it rather than the pusillanimous language of the comment.

Another situation with a similar split of authority occurs where the parties form an oral contract that can be performed within a year from formation but which includes an option for renewal or extension.[39] Still another is found where the contract cannot be performed in the manner contemplated by the parties, but can be performed within a year in some other fashion, without violating the literal terms of the contract.[40]

D. *Performance on One Side — Unilateral Contracts.*

An oral contract which is executory on both sides is within the one year provision unless *both* promises can be performed within a year from the making of the contract.[41] Yet, an overwhelming majority of the decided cases have held that the provision is not applicable if the contract is one that can be, and in fact has been, completely (fully) performed *on one side,* whatever may be true with regard to the time required for the other party's performance.[42] This concept, which is difficult to justify in view of the language of the statute, first appeared in an early English case[43] which simply stated a conclusion that the

---

[36] Blake v. Voigt, 134 N.Y. 69, 31 N.E. 256 (1892).

[37] Deevy v. Porter, 11 N.J. 594, 95 A.2d 596 (1953).

[38] *See supra* note 22 and accompanying text.

[39] *See* Hand v. Osgood, 107 Mich. 55, 64 N.W. 867 (1895) (within the statute) and Ward v. Hasbrouch, 169 N.Y. 407, 62 N.E. 434 (1902) (without the statute). *See also* Conger Life Ins. Co. v. Deimel, 441 So. 2d 904 (Fla. App. 1983) holding an oral renewal of a one year oral contract of employment, performance of which was to commence on the day the renewal was entered into, is not within the one year provision of the statute. Professor Corbin suggests that, since the option may never be exercised, complete performance could occur within one year. 2 Corbin on Contracts § 450.

[40] Cumberland & Manchester R.R. v. Posey, 196 Ky. 379, 244 S.W. 770 (1922) (promise to pay a bonus upon completion of a railroad) and White v. Fitts, 102 Me. 240, 66 A. 533 (1906) (contract to log a tract of land as fast as timber was needed by the owner's mill) hold such contracts to be within the statute. *Contra* McClanahan v. Otto-Marmet Coal & Mining Co., 74 W. Va. 543, 82 S.E. 752 (1914) (agreement to cut and deliver all the mine props on a large tract of land).

[41] RESTATEMENT 2d § 130(2).

[42] *See* Lamboustis v. Johnston, 657 P.2d 358 (Wyo. 1983); Glass v. Minnesota Protective Life Ins. Co., 314 N.W.2d 393 (Iowa 1982); Nesson v. Moes, 215 Cal. App. 2d 655, 30 Cal. Rptr. 428 (1963). The cases are collected in Annotation, 6 A.L.R.2d 1053, 1111 (1949). A notable exception is New York which requires full performance on *both* sides to take a contract out of the one year provision. *See* Montgomery v. Futuristic Foods, Inc., 66 A.D.2d 64, 411 N.Y.S.2d 371 (1978). *See also* Ordon v. Johnson, 346 Mich. 38, 77 N.W.2d 377 (1956); *In re* Hippe's Estate, 200 Wis. 373, 228 N.W. 552 (1930). Some jurisdictions adopting the majority view qualify it be requiring the full performance on one side to be completed within one year from the time of formation.

[43] Donnellan v. Read, 3 B & Ad. 899 [1832], followed in Cherry v. Heming, 4 Exch. 631 [1849].

statute should not apply to such a case. Presumably, the court reached this conclusion because of the supposed unfairness of permitting a defendant who had received full performance from the other party to rely on the statute as a defense.[44] While this reasoning may justify a quasi contractual recovery by a plaintiff who has performed to the benefit of the defendant, it is difficult to see how it justifies enforcing the defendant's oral promise, contrary to the apparent meaning of the statutory language. If, however, full performance on one side should satisfy the evidentiary function of the statute's one year provision, there would seem to be little reason for refusing to enforce the other (executory) promise. Moreover, it should make no difference whether the executed promise was performed within a year, or whether its performance required more than a year.[45] This view would make the one year provision inapplicable to contracts which are originally "unilateral" or those which have become, in effect, "unilateral" by full performance on one side within a year.[46]

E. Application of One Year Provision Where Other Provisions Apply.

It should be emphasized that, unlike the other provisions of the statute of frauds, the one year provision cuts across the whole field of contracts and embraces all kinds, regardless of their subject matter, and whether or not they are included within another clause of the statute. Thus, a contract to provide services not within another provision of the statute would still be subject to the one year provision. Absent statutory modification, a promise of suretyship, a promise in consideration of marriage, a promise to buy or sell land[47] or a promise within any other section of the statute must meet the requirements of those sections and, if it is also a promise not to be performed within one year from the making thereof, it is subject to the one year requirement. Concentration upon the satisfaction of another section of the statute may result in the failure to recall the requirement of the one year provision. Thus, if an oral suretyship promise was taken out of the suretyship provision through the "main purpose" exception, but the same promise was not performable within a year of formation, the promise would remain unenforceable because it failed to meet the requirement for the one year provision though the suretyship requirement had been satisfied. The identical caveat applies to contracts in consideration of marriage or contracts for the sale of land or goods.[48]

---

[44] The court suggested, "[A]nd surely the law would not sanction a defense on that ground, when the buyer had the full benefit of the goods on his part."

[45] This is the position of the RESTATEMENT 2d § 130 comment d.

[46] See Mapes v. Kalva Corp., 60 Ill. App. 3d 654, 386 N.E.2d 148 (1979).

[47] In most jurisdictions, statutes except from the one year provision leases of land for one year, though the lease term will not begin until a future date. The one year provision will also not prevent specific performance of a contract to transfer an interest in land if there has been sufficient reliance on the contract as suggested in RESTATEMENT 2d § 129.

[48] RESTATEMENT 2d § 110 comment b.

§ 73. Contracts for the Sale of Goods — Uniform Commercial Code.

A. *History — Price Versus Value.*

Section 17 of the original Statute of Frauds required any contract for the sale of goods for the *price* of ten pounds sterling or more to be evidenced by a writing. Section 4 of the Uniform Sales Act, widely enacted in the United States, required that any contract for the sale of goods with a *value* of $500 or more be evidenced by a writing. The current statute of frauds provision for sale-of-goods contracts is § 2-201 of the UCC,[49] which requires any contract for the sale of goods with a *price* of $500 or more to be evidenced by a writing.[50] The return to a *price* minimum rather than a *value* minimum is desirable to avoid inevitable controversies over the proper value of goods. If, however, the parties agree to exchange goods for other goods, the statute will apply if the value of the exchange meets the minimum of $500.[51] The modification of price for value under the old Sales Act is only one of many changes in this provision of the statute of frauds effected by the UCC. Moreover, the other changes are much more significant. In this section and the sections that follow, all of these modifications will be considered in terms of their purpose as well as their current interpretation by our courts.

---

[49] The only U. S. jurisdiction that has not enacted Article 2 of the UCC at the time of this writing is Louisiana.

[50] UCC § 2-201 provides:

(1) Except as otherwise provided in this section a contract for the sale of goods for the price of $500 or more is not enforceable by way of action or defense unless there is some writing sufficient to indicate that a contract for sale has been made between the parties and signed by the party against whom enforcement is sought or by his authorized agent or broker. A writing is not insufficient because it omits or incorrectly states a term agreed upon but the contract is not enforceable under this paragraph beyond the quantity of goods shown in such writing.

(2) Between merchants if within a reasonable time a writing in confirmation of the contract and sufficient against the sender is received and the party receiving it has reason to know its contents, it satisfies the requirements of subsection (1) against such party unless written notice of objection to its contents is given within ten days after it is received.

(3) A contract which does not satisfy the requirements of subsection (1) but which is valid in other respects is enforceable:

(a) if the goods are to be specially manufactured for the buyer and are not suitable for sale to others in the ordinary course of the seller's business and the seller, before notice of repudiation is received and under circumstances which reasonably indicate that the goods are for the buyer has made either a substantial beginning of their manufacture or commitments for their procurement; or

(b) if the party against whom enforcement is sought admits in his pleading, testimony or otherwise in court that a contract for sale was made, but the contract is not enforceable under this provision beyond the quantity of goods admitted; or

(c) with respect to goods for which payment has been made and accepted or which have been received and accepted (Sec. 2-606).

[51] Section 2-304(1) of the UCC permits the "price" to be payable either in money "or otherwise." When the price is payable in goods, each party is a "seller" with respect to the goods he is to transfer. Thus, when a purchaser of a new car pays for the car in part with a trade of his old car, he is a "seller" of the old car. *See* Martin v. Melland's, Inc., 283 N.W.2d 76 (N.D. 1979) (purchase of truck and haystack mover for a total price of $35,389 with purchaser being allowed $17,389 on his old unit as a trade-in allowance. Buyer was a "seller" of his old unit and, therefore, the risk of loss had not passed to the "buyer" (dealer) of the old unit when it was destroyed while still in the possession of the original owner).

B. *Goods — Present versus Future Sale — Distinguishing Land and Labor and Materials — Specially Manufactured Goods.*

One of the problems that arose under the original Statute was whether the sale of goods section should include a contract to transfer ownership of goods in the future as well as a contract to effect a present transfer of ownership. Prior to the UCC, it had become well settled that both kinds of transactions were covered[52] and the UCC now expressly provides for "both a present sale of goods and a contract to sell goods at a future time."[53]

We have already explored some of the problems generated by the proper characterization of a contract for the sale of land versus a contract for the sale of goods and the UCC solution to those problems.[54] Where, however, the contract requires a transfer of both real estate and goods in exchange for money and there is no sound basis for allocating the consideration between the real and personal property, the land contract provision of the statute of frauds will apply.[55] If the monetary consideration can be allocated between the real estate and the goods intended to be transferred, the "goods" portion of the transaction can be made subject to the provisions of the Code.[56] If the real estate portion of the transaction is relatively minor in relation to the goods component, the contract may be viewed as dominantly one for the sale of goods and the UCC may apply exclusively.[57] As will be seen, this analysis has been applied to contracts involving a combination of goods and services.

Other difficulties beset courts confronted with the proper characterization of a contract involving the sale of goods connected with the sale of labor and materials. The language of the statute, either in its original or more modern forms, has never, in terms, included a contract to furnish labor (services), i.e., it covers only contracts for the sale of goods. Often, however, the subject matter of the contract is a mixture of labor and materials. Prior to the Code, a contract to furnish labor and materials in the erection of a building or other fixture on land, or to repair an automobile, in the absence of a manifested intention to transfer ownership of the materials prior to annexation, was typically held to be outside the statute, although the value of the material to be furnished exceeded the statutory minimum amount.[58] Courts facing similar problems under the Code have settled upon the analysis already suggested with respect to contracts involving land and goods, i.e., if the dominant or

---

[52]*See, e.g.,* Russell v. Bettes, 107 Ark. 629, 156 S.W. 457 (1913).

[53]UCC § 2-106(1). *See also* UCC § 2-102 where Article 2 of the Code is said to apply to "transactions in goods" whether it is a "contract to sell or present sale."

[54]*See supra* § 71(D). Where the parties agree that part of the "price" will be paid by transferring an interest in land in exchange for goods, the transfer of the goods and the seller's obligations concerning the goods are governed by Article 2 of the UCC. The Code, however, does not apply to the transfer of the interest in realty or the transferor's obligations in connection with that transfer. UCC § 2-304(2).

[55]*See* Beaulieu of Am. Inc. v. Coronet Indus., 173 Ga. App. 556, 327 S.E.2d 508 (1985).

[56]*See* Foster v. Colorado Radio Corp., 381 F.2d 222 (10th Cir. 1967).

[57]*See* Dehahn v. Innes, 356 A.2d 711 (Me. 1976).

[58]*See, e.g.,* Frederick Raff Co. v. Murphy, 110 Conn. 234, 147 A. 709 (1929) (contract to supply and install plumbing fixtures); Underfeed Stoker Co. v. Detroit Salt Co., 135 Mich. 431, 97 N.W. 959 (1904) (contract to furnish and install stoker); Scales v. Wiley, 68 Vt. 39, 33 A. 771 (1895) (contract to furnish labor and materials in erecting a building on land).

primary purpose of the contract is the sale of goods, the contract will be subject to § 2-201 of the Code.[59]

1. Specially Manufactured Goods.

Where the parties agree to buy and sell chattels that are to be specially manufactured by the seller, three exclusive rules evolved prior to the UCC to determine the applicability of the sale of goods provision of the statute of frauds. The English courts adopted the view that the statute would apply if the performance of the contract would ultimately result in the transfer of title to a chattel.[60] This perfectly logical rule had little following in this country. Prior to the adoption of the Uniform Sale Act, New York took the view that the statute would apply to such goods only if they were in existence at the time of formation in substantially the same form in which they were to be sold and delivered.[61] On the other hand, Massachusetts early adopted the rule that, if the goods were in existence at the time of contract formation, or if they were such as the seller in the ordinary course of his business would manufacture or procure for the general market, the statute applied to the contract; otherwise, it was a contract for labor and materials and enforceable, though oral.[62] This rule was adopted by the Uniform Sale Act and followed by the greater number of courts in this country.[63]

The UCC has adopted the position of the Sales Act in requiring the goods to be "specially manufactured ... not suitable for sale to others in the ordinary course of the seller's business."[64] The Code, however, in one sense enlarged

---

[59] *See, e.g.,* Colorado Carpet Installation, Inc. v. Palermo, 668 P.2d 1384, 45 A.L.R.4th 1113 (Colo. 1983) (suggesting that factors to be considered are whether the contract included an overall price for goods and labor as contrasted with separate billings for each, the ratio of the cost of goods to the total contract price, and whether a reasonable buyer would be particularly interested in acquiring a property interest in the goods); Glover School & Office Equip. Co. v. Dave Hall, Inc., 372 A.2d 221 (Del. Super. 1977) (where a mixed contract (sale of goods and services) is concerned, the court must consider all of the surrounding circumstances to determine whether the contemplated performance of the contract was predominantly one for the sale of goods or services).

It should be noted that numerous consequences beyond the application of the UCC statute of frauds provision (§ 2-201) attend a determination of whether the contract is one for goods, services, or land. Thus, whether the warranty protection of the UCC is available will depend upon whether the contract is one for goods or one for services. A well-known case confronting this issue is Newmark v. Gimbel's, Inc., 54 N.J. 585, 258 A.2d 697 (1969) where the New Jersey Supreme Court, in an opinion by Justice Francis, found that the UCC applied where the plaintiff received a permanent wave and suffered severe hair loss and scalp problems allegedly due to a product used by the provider of the wave even though the price for the product was not separated from the total price of the wave. The court described the transaction as a hybrid involving incidents of sale and service but applied the UCC on the basis that there is no sound reason for restricting implied warranties such as found in §§ 2-314 and 2-315 of the UCC to "conventional sales of goods."

[60] Lee v. Griffin, 1 B. & S. 272 [1861] (contract to make a set of false teeth); *but cf.* Robinson v. Graves, 1 K.B. 579 [1935] (contract to paint a protrait held one for work and labor and thus outside the statute).

[61] Parsons v. Loucks, 48 N.Y. 17, 8 Am. Rep. 112 (1871). This rule had limited following. *See, e.g.,* Wallace v. Dowling, 86 S.C. 307, 68 S.E. 571 (1910).

[62] *See, e.g.,* Goddard v. Binney, 115 Mass. 450, 15 Am. Rep. 112 (1874) (contract to manufacture a carriage on special order held to be a contract for labor and materials).

[63] *See, e.g.,* Bond v. Bourk, 54 Colo. 51, 129 P. 223 (1912).

[64] In Impossible Elec. Techniques, Inc. v. Wackenhut Protective Sys., 669 F.2d 1026 (5th Cir. 1982) the court elaborates this requirement. Where a seller has commenced or completed manufacture of goods conforming to the special needs of a particular buyer, thereby rendering the goods unsuitable for sale to others, the nature of the goods provides an alternative evidentiary function.

but otherwise placed restrictions on the use of this "exception."[65] Under the Sales Act,[66] the exception applied only where the seller was the manufacturer of the specially manufactured goods. Under the UCC, however, there is no requirement that the seller, himself, be the manufacturer of the goods. This is clear from the language of the Code which permits the exception to apply where the seller "has made ... commitments for their procurement" from another manufacturer. Having enlarged the exception to this extent, the Code then proceeds to place new requirements on its application. First, the seller must have either made a substantial beginning of the manufacture of the special goods or, again, commitments for their procurement.[67] Second, the circumstances surrounding the transaction must be such as to reasonably indicate that the goods are for the buyer.[68] The second requirement is not entirely clear. It appears to be no more than a requirement that the seller must prove, as part of its *prima facie* case, that one in the position of the buyer would naturally and normally agree to purchase the specially manufactured or procured goods in question.

C. *Other Forms of Personal Property.*

Since the statute of frauds section of the Uniform Sales Act had been interpreted to include all forms of personal property, it was reasonably expected that interpretation of the UCC would be the same. The original version of the Code in 1952 contained statute of frauds provisions applying to the sale of goods,[69] the sale of investment securities,[70] and to secured transactions.[71] There were, however, other forms of personality not covered by the 1952 official text of the UCC, apparently due to inadvertence.[72] Thus, as of the 1957

The likelihood of a perjured claim of a contract is diminished and denying enforcement of such a contract would impose a substantial hardship on the seller. The court also notes that "specially manufactured goods" as used in UCC § 2-201(3)(a) includes goods that the seller may be in the business of making, i.e., they need not be goods unusual to the seller's normal manufacturing process. The crucial inquiry is whether the goods could be sold to others in the ordinary course of business. If they could be sold with only slight alterations, they are not "specially manufactured" goods. If, however, major changes would be required to make the goods marketable to others, they are "specially manufactured" goods.

[65] It has become common to view the specially manufactured goods section of the UCC statute of frauds, § 2-201(3)(a), as one of several "exceptions" to the normal requirements of a writing to evidence a contract for the sale of goods.

[66] Uniform Sales Act, § 4.

[67] *See, e.g.,* Frank Adams & Co., Inc. v. Baker, 1 Ohio App. 3d 137, 439 N.E.2d 953 (1981); LTV Aerospace Corp. v. Bateman, 492 S.W.2d 703 (Tex. Civ. App. 1973). As to what constitutes a "substantial beginning of performance," *see* Perlmuter Printing Co. v. Strome, Inc., 436 F. Supp. 409 (N.D. Ohio 1976) (contract for advertising flyers where 62 percent of the 17,000,000 flyers ordered were printed which was considerably more than a "substantial beginning"); Epprecht v. I.B.M. Corp., 36 U.C.C. Rep. 391 (E.D. Pa. 1983) (production of 7000 parts fell within the "specially manufactured" goods exception, but there was no evidence to suggest that this production was a "substantial beginning" of an alleged remaining 43,000 parts).

[68] An obvious application of this requirement is found in Flowers Baking Co. of Lynchburg v. R-P Packaging, Inc., 329 S.E.2d 462 (Va. 1985) where cellophane wrapping material was manufactured to the size required by the buyer's containers and was imprinted with the buyer's name and unique artwork.

[69] UCC § 2-201.

[70] UCC § 3-819. *See* Conaway v. 20th Century Corp., 420 A.2d 405 (Pa. 1980).

[71] UCC § 9-203.

[72] Some of the more common "general intangibles" not covered were the transfer of rights and duties under executory contracts and the sale of royalties, patents, and copyrights.

version, a new section was added providing for the application of the statute of frauds to property "not otherwise covered."[73] The limited case law construing this section manifests few problems in determining whether this section of the statute, another section of the statute or no section of the statute of frauds applies to the transaction before the court.[74]

D. *Other Changes Under the Uniform Commercial Code.*

Other changes of the Uniform Sales Act effected by the UCC are, indeed, substantial. In summary, those changes include permitting a memorandum signed by a merchant to be effective against another merchant if the latter does not object within ten days of its receipt,[75] permitting enforcement of an oral contract to the extent that it is admitted by the party to be charged in his or her pleadings, testimony or other evidence before the court,[76] and permitting enforcement of an oral contract for the sale of goods to the extent of receipt and acceptance of the goods, or receipt and acceptance of payment for the goods.[77] These modifications of pre-Code law will be explored in the appropriate sections dealing with the requirements of signed memoranda, admissions and performance exceptions to the requirement of a writing.

§ 74. Satisfaction of the Statute — Memorandum.

A signed writing is the specified mode for satisfying the requirements of the statute of frauds with respect to any type of contract within its provisions. The essential questions concerning the writing (memorandum) deal with its *form,* its *content,* the requirement that it be *signed,* and questions concerning the *time of its making* and the effect of *destruction* of a satisfactory memorandum. These questions will now be explored.

A. *Form of Memorandum.*

The typical American statute of frauds does not require the writing evidencing the contract to be intended by the parties as their complete and/or final statement of the contract. A memorandum of the contract will be sufficient.[78]

---

[73] UCC § 1-206. The minimum statutory amount for this section is $5000 rather than the $500 required under § 2-201. The comment to this section indicates that its purpose is to "fill the gap left by" other UCC statute of frauds provisions. "The Uniform Sales Act covered the sale of 'choses in action'; the principal gap relates to sale of the 'general intangibles' ... Typical are the sale of bilateral contracts, royalty rights or the like . . ." *See* Federal Deposit Ins. Corp. v. Herald Square Fabrics Corp., 81 App. Div. 2d 168, 439 N.Y.S.2d 944 (1981) (applying § 1-206 to a sale of chattel paper, albeit intended as security, rather than § 9-203).

[74] *See, e.g.,* Greyhound Lines, Inc. v. Superior Ct., 98 Cal. App. 3d 604, 159 Cal. Rptr. 657 (1979), the court held § 1-206 inapplicable to an oral agreement to compromise and settle a lawsuit since there was no sale of a chose in action involved. In Olympic Junior, Inc. v. David Crystal, Inc., 463 F.2d 1141 (3rd Cir. 1972), an oral agreement to include the plaintiff who was a contractor for the tailoring of suits marketed by defendant in the defendant's sale of the business was held subject to § 1-206 since it was not a contract for the sale of goods or the sale of investment securities, but was a form of personal property included within § 1-206.

[75] UCC § 2-201(2).

[76] UCC § 2-201(3)(b).

[77] UCC § 2-201(3)(c).

[78] RESTATEMENT 2d § 131. If, however, a particular statute of frauds requires the "contract" to be in writing, a mere memorandum will not be sufficient. *See, e.g.,* Halsell v. Renfrow, 202 U.S. 287

It is important to emphasize the requirement that the writing evidence a *contract* rather than a mere offer or preliminary negotiation.[79] It is clear that a writing evidencing a contract will satisfy the statute even though it was not dealt with by the parties as the final embodiment of the terms of their agreement.[80] It is of utmost importance, however, to recognize the distinction between the satisfaction of the statute of frauds and the burden on the plaintiff to establish that a contract has been made. A memorandum that would be sufficient to satisfy the statute does not, in itself, establish that a contract was made.[81] If, however, a contract was in fact made and the writing sets forth the terms thereof, the statute of frauds is satisfied. The fact that the writing was made for some other purpose, or that it also contains extraneous matter not related to the contract, is not material.[82] A memorandum intended as a repudiation of an oral contract will be a sufficient writing to satisfy the statute of frauds, provided it contains the necessary terms.[83] The requirement may be satisfied by a writing even though it is undelivered and never intended to be delivered to the other contracting party.[84] The writing may be in the form of a

(1906); Zimmerman v. Zehender, 164 Ind. 466, 73 N.E. 920 (1905). *See also* RESTATEMENT 2d § 131 comment a.

[79] *See* W.H. Barber Co. v. McNamara-Vivan Contr'g Co., 293 N.W.2d 351 (Minn. 1979); Maderas Tropicales S. de R. L. de C. V. v. Southern Crate & Veneer Co., 588 F.2d 971 (5th Cir. 1979); Derden v. Morris, 247 So. 2d 838 (Miss. 1971); Arcuri v. Weiss, 198 Pa. Super. 506, 184 A.2d 24 (1962).

[80] As will be seen in the next chapter, if the parties intend their writing to be the final embodiment of their contract, evidence of prior understandings will not be admissible under the "parol evidence rule." The curiosity is that, where the parties evidence their contract by a mere memorandum which is not intended to be final and/or complete (fully or partially "integrated"), extrinsic evidence of their oral agreement is admissible. If the admissible evidence contradicts a term of the writing, the writing may be destroyed as evidence of the contract sufficient to satisfy the statute of frauds. A recent judicial recognition of the distinction between the parol evidence rule and the statute of frauds is found in Wemhoff v. Investors Mgt. Corp. of Am., 528 A.2d 1205 (D.C. App. 1987) where, after suggesting the different purposes of the parol evidence rule and the statute of frauds, the court concludes that the statute of frauds does not require an exhaustive, integrated, statement of the agreement, but only a sufficient writing to establish that there was an agreement to which the party to be charged should be bound.

[81] *See* Lorenz Supply Co. v. American Std., Inc., 419 Mich. 610, 358 N.W.2d 845 (1984); C. Itoh & Co. v. Jordan Int'l Co., 552 F.2d 1228 (7th Cir. 1977) chiding certain courts for their fundamental misconception of the purpose and effect of the statute of frauds, relying upon comment 3 to § 2-201 of the UCC: "The only effect is to take away ... the defense of the statute of frauds; the burden of persuading the trier of fact that a contract was in fact made orally prior to the [writing] is unaffected." *See also* Spinnerin Yarn Co. v. Apparel Retail Corp., 614 F. Supp. 1174 (S.D.N.Y. 1985).

[82] *See* Bicknell v. Joyce Sportswear Co., 173 Ga. App. 897, 328 S.E.2d 564 (1985) where invoices were held to be sufficient writings between merchant parties. *See also* Azevedo v. Minister, 86 Nev. 576, 471 P.2d 661 (1970) where periodic accountings were held sufficient confirmations of the oral agreement between the merchant parties. *See* RESTATEMENT 2d § 133. An exception is made, however, with respect to contracts in consideration of marriage since the marriage provision performs a cautionary as well as an evidentiary function. *See* RESTATEMENT 2d § 124 comment d and RESTATEMENT 2d § 133 comment a.

[83] RESTATEMENT 2d § 133 comment c. In Atlas Road Constr. Co. v. Commercial Stone Co., 41 U.C.C. Rep. 1186 (Pa. Comm. Pl. 1984), the court held that a letter sent by plaintiff's attorney containing the terms of an oral agreement alleging a breach thereof constituted a sufficient memorandum to satisfy the statute of frauds.

[84] *See, e.g.,* Smith v. McClam, 287 S.C. 452, 346 S.E.2d 720 (1986) where the court found a memorandum to be sufficient even though it was not delivered to the other contracting party, nor intended for, nor known to him, if it otherwise evidences the contract of the parties and its contents are disclosed for that purpose. *See* UCC § 2-201 comment 6: "It is not necessary that the writing be delivered to anybody."

letter, even if the letter is addressed to a third person.[85] It may be in the form of a telegram,[86] a check,[87] an invoice,[88] corporate minutes,[89] a pencilled note on a scratch pad,[90] a diary entry,[91] a petition filed in a court proceeding relating to some other transaction,[92] a contract with another party,[93] or even a will.[94]

1. Several Writings.

If a writing is incomplete, the issue arises of whether other writings relating to the same transaction may be considered in overcoming the deficiency. There is no doubt that the memorandum required to satisfy the statute of frauds may be found in more than one writing.[95] A signed offer and a signed acceptance will constitute a sufficient memorandum if they contain the essential terms of the agreement and manifestly refer to each other.[96] Any number of separate pieces of paper may be joined to constitute a sufficient memorandum so long as one of the writings is signed and they manifestly relate to the same transaction. If the writings are physically attached and, together, constitute a sufficient memorandum, the statute of frauds is satisfied.[97] The questions surrounding the requirement that a memorandum be *signed* will be explored later in this section. The problem with a memorandum evidenced by several writings relates to the signature requirement, i.e., if one (incomplete) writing is signed and others that clearly relate to it are unsigned, must the signed writing expressly refer to the unsigned writings, or is it enough that there is clear and convincing evidence that the unsigned writings refer to the same agreement between the parties?

A well-known case took the position that the signed writing need not expressly refer to the unsigned writings where the writings all referred to the same transaction.[98] Oral evidence was admissible to demonstrate the connection among the writings. While the RESTATEMENT 2d adopts this view,[99] a

---

[85] *See, e.g.,* Boswell v. Rio De Oro Uranium Mines, Inc., 68 N.M. 457, 362 P.2d 991 (1961); Dennison v. Hildt, 180 Okla. 399, 70 P.2d 56 (1937).

[86] Hansen v. Hill, 215 Neb. 573, 340 N.W.2d 8 (1983); Hillstrom v. Gosnay, 188 Mont. 388, 614 P.2d 466 (1980).

[87] *See* A. B. C. Auto Parts v. Moran, 359 Mass. 327, 268 N.E.2d 844 (1971).

[88] Bicknell v. Joyce Sportswear Co., 173 Ga. App. 897, 328 S.E.2d 564 (1985).

[89] *See, e.g.,* Jennings v. Rudoso Racing Ass'n, 79 N.M. 144, 441 P.2d 42 (1968).

[90] UCC § 2-201 comment 1.

[91] *See* RESTATEMENT 2d § 133 comment b.

[92] McCall v. Lee, 182 N.C. 114, 108 S.E. 390 (1921).

[93] *See* Morris Cohon & Co. v. Russell, 23 N.Y.2d 569, 245 N.E.2d 712 (1969).

[94] Annotation, 94 A.L.R.2d 921 (1964).

[95] Evco Distrib., Inc. v. Commercial Credit Equip. Corp., 627 P.2d 374 (Kan. 1981); Alaska Indep. Fishermen's Mktg. Ass'n v. New England Fish Co., 15 Wash. App. 154, 548 P.2d 348 (1976); Marks v. Cowdin, 226 N.Y. 138, 123 N.E. 139 (1919).

[96] *See* Huntington Beach Union High Sch. Dist. v. Continental Information Sys. Corp., 621 F.2d 353 (9th Cir. 1980) where the court treated a statute of frauds argument as "meritless" under these circumstances.

[97] The RESTATEMENT 2d suggests that if the party to be charged physically attaches the writings or places them in the same envelope, the writings may be considered together in determining the sufficiency of the memorandum. RESTATEMENT 2d § 132 comment c.

[98] Crabtree v. Elizabeth Arden Sales Corp., 305 N.Y. 48, 110 N.E.2d 551 (1953). *See also* Stahlman v. Nat'l Lead Co., 318 F.2d 388, 395 (5th Cir. 1963).

[99] RESTATEMENT 2d § 132 comment c states that "It is sufficient that the signed writing refers to the unsigned writing explicitly or by implication."

number of courts insist upon an explicit reference in the signed writing to the unsigned writing.[1]

2. Tape Recordings — Electronic Files.

It is clear from the foregoing that no particular form is essential to meet the requirements of a sufficient writing to satisfy the statute. Even if the evidence takes a form other than paper, it may be considered effective. Thus, a tape recording of the parties' agreement may be sufficient.[2] With the increased use of computerized purchasing and selling of goods, an electronic file may be sufficient evidence of a contract for the sale of goods under § 2-201 of the UCC. Similarly, an electronic file containing letters or other memoranda evidencing any type of contract within the statute of frauds should be effective to satisfy the statute whether such letters were ever sent or delivered. Cases involving such issues are inevitable, and courts should be prepared to deal with them. There is a clear trend in the case law, emphasized by the UCC with respect to contracts for the sale of goods, that the purpose of the statute of frauds is evidentiary. If, therefore, there is sufficient evidence of such a contract in a form other than a writing, but in a form that is intended to be relatively permanent and generally considered to be reasonable, the purpose of the statute to prevent fraud is served by treating such reliable evidence as sufficient to meet the statutory requirement.[3] While this view may be seen as an extension of satisfying the writing requirement under other provisions of the statute of frauds, it is mandated by the UCC which requires courts to liberally construe its provisions so as to permit the expansion of commercial practices.[4]

---

[1] *See, e.g.,* Hoffman v. S V Co., 102 Idaho 187, 190, 628 P.2d 218, 221 (1981): "[A]n unsigned writing may be considered as part of the memorandum only where express reference is made to it in a signed writing." Module Mobile, Inc. v. Fulton Nat'l Bank, 150 Ga. App. 808, 258 S.E.2d 614, 616 (1979): "If the writing in question refers to other writings which can be identified by this reference without the aid of parol evidence, then the two writings can constitute compliance with the statute." Alaska Indep. Fishermen's Mktg. Ass'n v. New England Fish Co., 15 Wash. App. 154, 548 P.2d 348, 351-52 (1976): "[T]he signed writing [must] expressly refer to the unsigned writing."

[2] There is a split of authority concerning the effectiveness of tape recordings to meet the writing requirement of the statute of frauds. In Ellis Canning Co. v. Bernstein, 348 F. Supp. 1212 (D. Colo. 1972), the court held that a tape recording which the parties had agreed to would satisfy the requirement of UCC § 8-319, i.e., the UCC statute of frauds relating to the sale of securities. The court relied upon the broad definition of a "writing" in UCC § 1-201(46) which includes "any intentional reduction to tangible form." In Londono v. City of Gainesville, 768 F.2d 1223 (11th Cir. 1985), the court held that a tape recording satisfied the provision of the Florida Statute of Frauds dealing with contracts for the sale of land. However, in Swink & Co. v. Carroll McEntee & McGinley, 266 Ark. 279, 584 S.W.2d 393 (1979), the court stated that, even assuming the tape recording can be characterized as a "writing," it fails because it was not "signed." In Sonders v. Roosevelt, 64 N.Y.2d 869, 487 N.Y.S.2d 551, 476 N.E.2d 996 (1985), the New York Court of Appeals held that a tape recording is not a memorandum in writing subscribed by the defendant as required by N.Y. GEN. OBLIG. LAW § 5.081[a].

[3] There is some recognition that the suretyship and marriage provisions of the statute of frauds serve a cautionary as well as an evidentiary function, and the land contract provision serves a channeling as well as evidentiary function. Recognizing these additional functions with respect to these types of contracts, the Second Restatement, nonetheless, suggests, "Even where these provisions are involved, however, there is no evidence of statutory purpose to facilitate repudiation of firm oral agreements fairly made, to protect a promisor from a temptation to perjure himself by false denial of the promise, or to reward a candid contract-breaker by denying enforcement." RESTATEMENT 2d § 131 comment c.

[4] UCC § 1-201(1)(b).

B. *Content of Memorandum — Relaxation of Requirements Under the Uniform Commercial Code.*

When it comes to the requirements of a writing that is sufficient to satisfy the statute of frauds, the UCC has gone far in relaxing earlier requirements. We will, therefore, deal with the UCC requirements after considering the content requirements in general.

In general, a memorandum will be sufficient to satisfy the statute if it reasonably identifies the subject matter of the contract, indicates that a contract with respect to that subject matter has been made between certain parties, and sets forth the essential terms of the contract with reasonable certainty.[5] If the memorandum contains an unambiguous statement of all of the terms agreed upon by the parties in relation to their bargain, including the consideration for any promise made, so that one can determine from an inspection of the document what obligations were assumed and by whom they were assumed, the memorandum will be sufficient even though it also contains extraneous matter. The only questions of doubt are raised in determining what, if anything less than this, will satisfy the statutory requirements.

1. Must the Consideration Be Expressed in the Writing?

One issue is whether the memorandum must state the consideration that supports a promise contained in the writing. An early English case emphasized the term "agreement" in the original Statute[6] and held that everything agreed upon by the parties that is material to the transaction, including the consideration, must be found in the writing.[7] The case, however, involved a suretyship promise where the writing failed to state the consideration which had been completely executed. Most of our courts distinguish executory contracts from those which have been executed on one side. If the contract is executory, our courts will insist that the memorandum indicate any implied or constructive conditions which qualify the defendant's undertaking.[8] Therefore, in the case of an executory bilateral contract, it is necessary to set forth in the memorandum that which constitutes the agreed exchange for the defendant's performance. If, however, the contract is executed on one side, the memorandum need not express the consideration that has already been performed. Thus, in a contract for the sale of land, if the price has already been paid, the memorandum need not contain the price. If the price has not been paid, however, the memorandum must contain the price to be a sufficient memorandum under this provision of the statute.[9] The question of the expres-

---

[5] *See* North Coast Cookies, Inc. v. Sweet Temptations, 16 Ohio App. 3d 342, 476 N.E.2d 388 (1984); Brechman v. Adamar of N.J., Inc., 182 N.J. Super. 259, 440 A.2d 480 (1981). *See* RESTATEMENT 2d § 131.

[6] The original Statute also contains the term "promise" which is used several times, and the term "contract."

[7] Wain v. Warlters, 5 East 10 [1804], followed in Saunders v. Wakefield, 4 B. & Ald. 595 [1821]. This view was changed in England by the Mercantile Law Amendment Act, 19 & 20 Vict. c. 97, § 3 [1856].

[8] *See, e.g.,* Standard Oil Co. v. Koch, 260 N.Y. 150, 183 N.E. 278 (1932); Reid v. Diamond Plate-Glass Co., 85 F. 193 (6th Cir. 1898). *Contra* Ruzicka v. Hotovy, 72 Neb. 589, 101 N.W. 328 (1904); Hayes v. Jackson, 159 Mass. 451, 34 N.E. 683 (1893).

[9] RESTATEMENT 2d § 131 comment h.

sion of consideration may, of course, be controlled by statute. Some statutes of frauds require the consideration to be expressed in the memorandum[10] or a court may interpret a particular statute as requiring the consideration to be expressed in the writing.[11] There are also statutes that expressly negate any requirement of stating the consideration in the memorandum.[12]

2. Resort to Oral Evidence to Overcome Deficiencies in the Memorandum.

Questions concerning the use of oral or parol evidence to supply deficiencies in the memorandum have created some disconcertion among the courts. The general rule is that the memorandum must contain, within itself, all of the contract terms though, as we have seen earlier in this section, the writing need not be intended as a complete statement of the parties' agreement or as a writing to satisfy the statute. Any writing, however, must be interpreted. In a well-known opinion by Judge Cardozo,[13] an employment contract formed orally in January was evidenced by a memorandum signed the following December. The memorandum described a continuing employment but failed to describe the position. The plaintiff had been performing the services of sales manager and the defendant attempted to change the plaintiff's duties materially. Plaintiff claimed that he was entitled to continue in his sales manager position. The court admitted evidence to identify the position described in the writing and described the process as one of turning signs and symbols into their equivalent realities, a process which must always occur regardless of the number of identifying tokens in the writing. Earlier signed writings described the role of the plaintiff and the court adopted the accepted view that more than one writing can be used to create the memorandum.[14] It insisted, however, that the writings, considered together, must contain all of the material terms of the agreement, and held: "[W]e exclude the writing that refers us to spoken words of promise. We admit the one that bids us ascertain a place or a relation by comparison of the description with some 'manifest, external and continuing fact.'"[15] The plaintiff did not require one spoken word of promise to identify his position. The identification emanated exclusively from the writings.

The general rule, therefore, permits oral or parol evidence to be used for the purpose of making the indefinite definite, i.e., interpreting or translating the words or symbols in the writing without, under any circumstances, enlarging the obligations manifested by the writing. The only situation suggesting a relatively liberal use of oral evidence occurs where an agent uses her own name in the writing. Courts will permit parol evidence that the name was used as a pseudonym for the name of the principal. The memorandum, there-

---

[10] See, e.g., MINN. STAT. § 513.01; N.Y. GEN. OBLIG. LAW § 5-703; OR. REV. STAT. § 41.580; NEV. REV. STAT. § 111.210.

[11] See, e.g., the interpretation of § 9-505 of the Idaho Code in Hoffman v. S V Co., 102 Idaho 187, 190, 628 P.2d 218, 221 (1981).

[12] See, e.g., the Virginia Statute of Frauds, § 11-2 concerning the sale of real estate where the statute states, ". . . but the consideration need not be set forth or expressed in writing . . ." as applied in Drake v. Livesay, 341 S.E.2d 186, 188 (Va. 1986). See also KY. REV. STAT. § 371.010.

[13] Marks v. Cowdin, 226 N.Y. 138, 123 N.E. 139 (1919).

[14] See supra subsection (A)(1).

[15] 123 N.E. 139, 141 (1919).

fore, would be sufficient to make the principal a party to the contract, though she is not identified in the writing by her own name or by any other form of description peculiarly appropriate to the purpose.[16]

3. Uniform Commercial Code Relaxation of Memorandum Requirements Concerning Content.

The UCC effected a major change with respect to the contents of the memorandum necessary to satisfy the requirement of a writing in a contract for the sale of·goods. The language of the statute itself is quite instructive since it only requires "some writing sufficient to indicate that a contract for sale has been made between the parties and signed...."[17] It would, therefore, be incorrect to suggest that the UCC statute of frauds provision requires a contract for the sale of goods with a price of $500 or more to be "in writing." Rather, an oral contract for the sale of goods with a price of $500 or more will be enforceable if *some* signed writing indicating a contract for the sale of goods between the parties can be produced.[18] The contents of the writing may be frugal, indeed. It should be emphasized, however, that it is too facile to suggest that the only required term is the *quantity* term. The general requirements of contract formation under the UCC should be recalled, i.e., numerous terms may be missing from the contract between the parties, but a contract will be recognized if (a) the parties manifestly intended to form a contract, and (b) there is a reasonably certain basis for a court to fashion a remedy.[19] Some operative quantity term must be available to a court if it is to fashion an appropriate remedy. Thus, a comment to the statute of frauds section suggests, "The only term which must appear is the quantity term which need not be accurately stated but recovery is limited to the amount stated."[20] This portion of the comment, however, must be read in the context of those "terms" which need not be contained in the writing, i.e., "The price, time and place of payment or delivery, the general quality of the goods, or any particular warranties may all be omitted"[21] without affecting the viability of the memorandum. It should, however, be clear that the goods must be sufficiently identified though, again, their quality need not be mentioned in the writing. The general principle of the UCC memorandum requirement "is that the writing afford a basis for believing that the offered oral evidence rests on a real transaction."[22] A real transaction, however, is for identified goods of a definite quantity. Even the quantity may be indefinite at the time of contract formation so long as it will become definite by the end of the contract term as in the

---

[16] *See* Looman Realty Corp. v. Broad Street Nat'l Bank, 32 N.J. 461, 161 A.2d 247, 253 (1960). (While the case involved signatures by the agents who informed the seller that they were acting for an unnamed company that they owned, the case suggests that parol evidence would have been admissible had the agents not mentioned the existence of an unnamed principal). Cases are collected in Annotations, 23 A.L.R. 939-43 (1923); 138 A.L.R. 330-36 (1942).

[17] UCC § 2-201(1).

[18] *See* Impossible Elec. Techniques, Inc. v. Wackenhut Protective Sys., 669 F.2d 1026 (5th Cir. 1982).

[19] UCC § 2-204(3).

[20] UCC § 2-201 comment 1.

[21] *Ibid.*

[22] *Id.*

case of output or requirements contracts.[23] If the goods are sufficiently identified and the quantity term is present, the remaining requirement is that the memorandum identify the parties to the contract and that the writing is signed. We will deal with the "signed" requirement in the next section. The UCC comment elaborating the memorandum requirements suggests that the buyer and seller be identified though, "It need not indicate which party is the buyer and which the seller."[24]

While the UCC substantially relaxes the requirements for a sufficient memorandum, the requirement that the writing evidence a *contract* rather than a mere offer or preliminary negotiation is maintained.[25] It is also clear that a sufficient writing merely satisfies the statute of frauds under the Code, i.e., it does not, in itself, prove the terms of the contract.[26] Neither does the Code affect the case law concerning a memorandum composed of more than one writing, i.e., a court is just as likely to require the signed writing to refer expressly to the unsigned writings as it would if the contract had been within another provision of the statute of frauds rather than the sale-of-goods provision of the UCC.[27] The UCC modification of the memorandum requirements relate exclusively to content, i.e., "The required writing need not contain all the material terms of the contract and such material terms as are stated need not be precisely stated. All that is required is that the writing afford a basis for believing that the offered oral evidence rests on a real transaction."[28] This is completely consistent with the underlying philosophy of contract law under the Code, i.e., the effectuation of the factual bargain of the parties[29] and the pervasive anti-technical nature of Article 2 of the Code.[30] Other changes in

---

[23]*See, e.g.,* Seaman's Direct Buying Serv. v. Standard Oil of Cal., 36 Cal. 3d 752, 206 Cal. Rptr. 354, 686 P.2d 1158 (1984) (requirements contract); R. L. Kimsey Cotton Co. v. Ferguson, 233 Ga. 962, 214 S.E.2d 360 (1975) (output contract). *But see* Cavalier Mobile Homes, Inc. v. Liberty Homes, Inc., 53 Md. App. 367, 454 A.2d 367 (1983) where three writings did not establish a quantity term and the arrangement was not a requirements contract. Output and requirements contracts are generally favored under the UCC, i.e., they are not fatally indefinite. *See* UCC § 2-306.

[24]UCC § 2-201 comment 1.

[25]*See, e.g.,* R. S. Bennett & Co. v. Economy Mech. Indus., 606 F.2d 182 (7th Cir. 1979) (writings evidence offer rather than contract); Conaway v. 20th Century Corp., 420 A.2d 405 (Pa. 1980) (construing the statute of frauds under § 8-319 (investment securities) suggesting that the relaxation of the memorandum requirements of § 2-201 does not evidence an intention to relax the requirement that the writing must indicate that a contract for sale has been made); Derden v. Morris, 247 So. 2d 838 (Miss. 1971) (letter indicated parties were still negotiating); Arcuri v. Weiss, 198 Pa. Super. 506, 184 A.2d 24 (1962) (check with notation, "tentative deposit on tentative purchase" did not evidence parties' intention to close a contract).

[26]Lorenz Supply Co. v. American Std., Inc., 419 Mich. 610, 358 N.W.2d 845 (1984).

[27]*See, e.g.,* Alaska Indep. Fishermen's Mktg. Ass'n v. New England Fish Co., 15 Wash. App. 154, 548 P.2d 348 (1976).

[28]UCC § 2-201 comment 1.

[29]"Contract" is defined in the UCC as "the total legal obligation which results from the parties' agreement as affected by this Act and any other applicable rules of law. (Compare 'Agreement')" UCC § 1-201(11). The more fundamental definition is that of "Agreement": '... the bargain of the parties *in fact* as found in their language or by implication from other circumstances including course of dealing or usage of trade or course of performance....' UCC § 1-201(3). For an elaboration of the "factual bargain" concept, *see* Murray, *The Article 2 Prism: The Underlying Philosophy of Article 2 of the Uniform Commercial Code,* 21 WASHBURN L.J. 1 (1981).

[30]*See, e.g.,* § 2-204(3) of the UCC which precludes the necessity for completeness of terms if the parties intended to make a contract and there is a reasonable basis for affording a remedy. Other Article 2 sections of the Code which manifest this anti-technical nature include § 2-206 which, as comment 1 to this section indicates, rejects formal "technical" rules of contract formation;

the statute of frauds for the sale of goods under the Code will be explored in the sections which follow.

C. *The Memorandum Must Be Signed.*

1. Form of Signature.

The usual requirement of the statute of frauds is that the memorandum be signed "by the party to be charged or his agent." As early as 1814, Lord Ellenborough removed any doubt that "signed" as used in the original Statute did not require a handwritten signature.[31] No particular form or kind of signature is essential.[32] It may be printed or typewritten,[33] made with a rubber stamp,[34] or a pencil[35] as well as with pen and ink. An existing symbol on paper may be adopted by the party as his signature as in the case of a billhead or letterhead.[36] Initials, a mark, or even a thumbprint may be sufficient.[37] The essential question has little to do with the particular symbol used or adopted. Rather, the question is, did the party execute or adopt the symbol with a present intention, actual or apparent, to authenticate the writing as the signer of the writing?[38]

2. Placement of Signature.

The original Statute of Frauds did not require the signature to be at a particular place on the writing, e.g., it did not require signing at the end of the document. Some statutes, however, are drafted with the term "subscribed" which can mean at the end or foot though it can also be viewed as a loose synonym for "signed."[39] Whether a court construing a statute using "subscribed" will require the document to be signed at the end or will accept a signature elsewhere on the document will depend upon the court's construction of "subscribed."[40]

---

§ 2-209(1) comment 1, suggests that this section makes good faith modifications enforceable "without regard to the technicalities which at present hamper such adjustments." *See also* §§ 2-305 and 2-202 and their comments.

[31] Schneider & Another v. Norris, 2 M. & S. 286, 105 Eng. Rep. 388 (1814).

[32] RESTATEMENT 2d § 134.

[33] Hansen v. Hill, 215 Neb. 573, 340 N.W.2d 8 (1983) (printed); Prairie State Grain & Elevator Co. v. Wrede, 217 Ill. App. 407 (1920) (printed); Hillstrom v. Gosnay, 188 Mont. 388, 614 P.2d 466 (1980) (typewritten); Garton Toy Co. v. Buswell Lumber & Mfg. Co., 150 Wis. 341, 136 N.W. 147 (1912) (typewritten).

[34] *In re* Deep River Nat'l Bank, 73 Conn. 341, 47 A. 675 (1900).

[35] Kleine v. Kleine, 281 Mo. 317, 219 S.W. 610 (1920).

[36] *See* Associated Hardware Supply Co. v. Big Wheel Distrib. Co., 355 F.2d 114 (3d Cir. 1966) (letterhead). UCC § 1-201(39) comment 39 suggests that the signature may be on the document and may be found in a billhead or letterhead.

[37] Stephens v. Perkins, 209 Ky. 651, 273 S.W. 545 (1925) (mark); Salmon Falls Mfg. Co. v. Goddard, 55 U.S. (14 How.) 446 (1852) (initials). UCC § 1-201(39) comment 39 (thumbprint or initials).

[38] The language of RESTATEMENT 2d § 134 and UCC § 1-201(39) is quite similar. The language used in the text is a combined paraphrase of the RESTATEMENT 2d and Code language.

[39] RESTATEMENT 2d § 134 comment b.

[40] *See, e.g.,* Commercial Credit Corp. v. Marden, 155 Or. 29, 62 P.2d 573, 112 A.L.R. 931 (1936), Annotation, 112 A.L.R. 937-40 (1938), where the Oregon court construed "subscribed" as interchangeable with "signed" and did not, therefore, require the writing to be signed at the end thereof. If the statute has been changed from "signed" to "subscribed," however, a court may feel

Where the memorandum is written on more than one piece of paper, the placement of the signature(s) can be troublesome. If the defendant has signed each piece of paper which manifests a clear relation to the transaction in question, there is no difficulty.[41] If the defendant has not signed each paper, however, the placement of the signature will depend upon the degree of relation between or among the documents giving rise to an analysis that is indistinguishable from the earlier analysis in this section dealing with the form of the memorandum where there are several writings. Thus, if the writings are physically attached at the time of signing, the attached parts will be considered as a single document and a signature on any part should authenticate the whole,[42] absent a statute requiring a "subscribed" signature which courts interpret as requiring a signature at the end of the document.[43] If the defendant has signed one writing which expressly refers to unsigned writings, it is assumed that he has incorporated the contents of the unsigned writings into the signed paper and has, therefore, authenticated the whole.[44]

3. Who Must Sign the Memorandum?

As suggested earlier, the usual requirement is that the memorandum be signed "by the party to be charged or by his or her agent." The curiosity, of course, is that if only one of the parties has signed the memorandum, that party can be charged while the other, non-signing, party cannot be charged. This appears to suggest a lack of mutuality of obligation since, again, one party can be sued while the other cannot be sued. The apparent inequity is solved by some courts who suggest that, when the non-signing party brings suit on the contract, he binds himself to the contract, thereby rendering it mutual.[45] While the overwhelming majority of our courts do not require both parties to sign, there are occasional decisions that mutuality of obligation requires the signature of both parties.[46] With respect to contracts for the sale of land, some states require the vendor to sign regardless of whether he is the

---

compelled to require the signature at the end of the document. *See, e.g.,* 300 West End Ave. Corp. v. Warner, 250 N.Y. 221, 165 N.E. 271 (1929).

[41] *See, e.g.,* Forman v. Gadouas, 247 Mass. 207, 142 N.E. 87 (1924); Thayer v. Luce, 22 Ohio St. 62 (1871).

[42] The case law has been liberal in finding sufficient physical attachment for this purpose. *See, e.g.,* Hopkins v. Walker, 144 Okla. 254, 291 P. 70 (1930) (draft and lease together forwarded by mail — in this connection see RESTATEMENT 2d § 132 comment c which suggests that if writings are enclosed in the same envelope, they should be regarded as attached); Schlotz v. Philbin, 157 Md. 196, 145 A. 487 (1929) (auctioneer's memo and copy of advertisement "affixed" to it); Tallman v. Franklin, 14 N.Y. 584 (1856) (papers pinned together); Pearce v. Gardner, 1 Q.B. 688 [1897] (letter and envelope); Jones Bros. v. Joyner, 82 L.T. (n.s.) 768 (cover of loose leaf memorandum book used with pages in book).

[43] In this situation, a signature at the end of the last writing should meet the "subscribed" signature requirement. *See, e.g.,* Seidman v. Dean Witter & Co., 70 App. Div. 2d 845, 418 N.Y.S.2d 6 (1979).

[44] Alaska Indep. Fishermen's Mktg. Ass'n v. New England Fish Co., 15 Wash. App. 154, 548 P.2d 348 (1976); Wagner-White Co. v. Holland Co-op Ass'n, 222 Mich. 58, 192 N.W. 552 (1923).

[45] Cottom v. Kennedy, 140 Ill. App. 3d 290, 488 N.E.2d 682 (1986). That this analysis does not provide a complete solution to the problem will become apparent in the discussion of the UCC change in the statute concerning confirmations between merchants which is explored in the next subsection.

[46] *See, e.g.,* Houser v. Hobart, 22 Idaho 735, 127 P. 997 (1912); Wilkinson v. Heavenrich, 58 Mich. 574, 26 N.W. 139 (1886).

party to be charged.[47] This view creates a problem for unwitting vendees. If a vendor decides to sue a vendee on a land contract, the vendor has the power to sign a memorandum evidencing an alleged contract with the non-signing vendee just before the vendor brings his action. To defeat this possibility, most courts will require the memorandum signed by the vendor to be delivered to and accepted by the vendee, i.e., the vendee's signature is not necessary, but his act of accepting the memorandum signed by the vendor is essential to remove the statute of frauds bar to enforcement of the contract.[48]

A party may appoint an agent to sign and the agent's signature will have the same effect as if the party (principal) himself had signed. Only a small minority of states have statutes requiring a writing to evidence the conferral of agency authority to sign for a principal. Many more, however, require such written authority with respect to land contracts.[49]

D. *Uniform Commercial Code — Confirmation Writing Between Merchants.*

1. An Overview of Uniform Commercial Code Section 2-201(2) — "Merchants."

Under the old Uniform Sales Act and prior versions of the statute of frauds provision for contracts for the sale of goods, a typical business transaction could result in manifest unfairness to one of the parties. If Ames met Barnes with an eye towards forming a contract for the sale of goods and the parties succeeded in forming an oral contract, it was and is common practice for one or both parties to send written confirmations of the already formed contract. If the parties sent accurate confirmations, or if one party sent an accurate confirmation that the other signed and returned, there was no potential unfairness. If, however, Ames sent a confirmation to Barnes who received it but did not sign it or return his own confirmation to Ames, Barnes could speculate at the expense of Ames. Since Barnes had signed no memorandum, he could raise the statute of frauds as an effective bar to any action by Ames. If Barnes chose to enforce the contract against Ames, however, Ames' signed confirmation deprived Ames of the same defense. The situation appeared to be one lacking mutuality of obligation in the sense that one party could enforce the contract while the other could not.[50] If, therefore, at the time the contract was to be performed, Barnes decided that the contract was beneficial to him, he could enforce the contract. If, however, the contract was beneficial to Ames and not to Barnes, Barnes could preclude the enforcement of the contract.

To overcome the manifest injustice of this situation, the UCC includes a provision which appears radical but, upon further reflection, overcomes the

---

[47] Case are collected in Palmer v. Wheeler, 258 Or. 41, 481 P.2d 68 (1971) (applying California law). For a dubious holding that the "party to be charged" is necessarily the vendor in land contract cases, *see* Murray v. Crawford, 138 Ky. 25, 127 S.W. 494 (1910).

[48] Schwinn v. Griffith, 303 N.W.2d 258 (Minn. 1981); Simpson v. Dyer, 268 Mich. 328, 256 N.W. 341 (1934); National Bank v. Louisville Trust Co., 67 F.2d 97 (6th Cir. 1933).

[49] RESTATEMENT 2d § 135 comment b.

[50] It should be emphasized that there is no lack of mutuality of obligation as that doctrine was described in the last chapter dealing with the validation process, i.e., there is no lack of consideration to support either promise by Ames or Barnes. Rather, there is a practical bar to any action by Ames (the statute of frauds bar), while Barnes would not be precluded by the statute.

injustice. If both parties are "merchants" as defined in the UCC,[51] a written confirmation sent within a reasonable time by one merchant to the other satisfies the statute with respect to the non-signing recipient of that confirmation if the confirmation is "sufficient against the sender," the recipient has reason to know its contents, and the recipient does not give notice of objection to the sender within ten days from receipt.[52] The provision appears radical since a non-signing party can be bound by the writing signed by the other party. The non-signing recipient can, however, avoid this possibility by simply sending[53] timely notice of objection. Such a notice of objection effectively destroys the confirmation as a memorandum in satisfaction of the statute.

2. Recipients of Memorandum.

While this UCC provision appears to provide a solution to the evil it sought to eradicate, it is not without its problems. If a confirmation of a fictitious contract is received by a merchant, he may no longer ignore it with impunity. If he fails to object to the confirmation within ten days from receipt, he loses the statute of frauds as a defense. Though the other merchant would still have the burden of proving the contract, she would not have to overcome the threshhold defense of the statute of frauds. Thus, the merchant-recipient of a confirmation should be advised to send timely notice of objection to any confirmation evidencing a contract the recipient has not made.

---

[51] For the definition of "merchant," see UCC § 2-104(1). While the statutory definition is helpful, it is important to consider comment 2 to this section which identifies three types of merchants. In essence, however, there are only two types of merchants which may be generally characterized as "broad" or "narrow" merchants. Certain sections of article 2 apply to the broad definition of merchant who is anyone in business. Thus, a bank purchasing crystal which it intends to provide to its customers as incentives to open accounts would be a merchant. A University purchasing necessary supplies would be a merchant. Section 2-201 of the Code (the statute of frauds) applies to such merchants as do §§ 2-205, 2-207 and 2-209. A "narrow" merchant, however, is a merchant with respect to goods of that kind. Thus, a merchant who regularly sells appliances or other goods would sell such goods with an implied warranty of merchantability (§ 2-314) attached to them because he is a merchant who regularly sells goods of that kind. A bank providing crystal as a "premium" to entice customers to open accounts would not be engaged in selling such goods on a regular basis. Similarly, if a corporation found that it had purchased an excess number of personal computers and sold some to another company, the seller would not be a narrow merchant because it does not regularly sell such goods. Thus, it would not make the implied warranty of merchantability.

Section 2-104(3) defines "Between merchants" as a transaction to which both parties are chargeable with the knowledge and skill of merchants. The determination of whether a particular party is a "merchant" for the purposes of § 2-201(2) can be troublesome in certain cases. Farmers may or may not be viewed as "merchants" with respect to § 2-201(2). Circumstances may suggest that a particular farmer should not be characterized as a merchant in a given transaction. See, e.g., Terminal Grain Corp. v. Freeman, 270 N.W.2d 806 (S.D. 1978) (the farmer had no experience with respect to future commodity contracts); Loeb & Co. v. Schreiner, 321 So. 2d 199 (Ala. 1975) (cotton farmer who allegedly promised to sell cotton to a corporation engaged in the business of selling cotton was not a merchant); Sebasty v. Perschke, 404 N.E.2d 1200 (Ind. App. 1980) (farmer was a merchant in a grain transaction); Currituck Grain, Inc. v. Powell, 38 N.C. App. 7, 246 S.E.2d 853 (1978) (farmer raising corn and soybeans was a merchant). See also Cudahy Foods Co. v. Holloway, 55 N.C. App. 626, 286 S.E.2d 606 (1982) (real estate broker purchasing cheese was not a merchant).

[52] UCC § 2-201(2).

[53] Since § 2-201(2) requires the recipient to "give notice." § 1-201(26) indicates that such a recipient would "give" notice "by taking such steps as may be reasonably required to inform the other in ordinary course whether or not such other actually comes to know of it." Thus, if the recipient simply mails a notice of objection within ten days from the date he receives the confirmation, such notice is effectively "given."

3. Sending Memorandum — Within a Reasonable Time.

The language of the provision creates other problems. The confirmation must be sent "within a reasonable time."[54] Courts are generally agreed that this phrase is not very helpful since it raises a question of fact. They have been less than clear in deciding whether a particular period between the formation of the oral contract and the sending of the confirmation is reasonable.[55] Trade usage[56] and the fluctuation of price concerning the subject matter of the contract would certainly have a bearing on the determination of a reasonable time as it would in any other context of the determination of a reasonable time.

4. Sufficient Against Sender.

The confirming writing sent by one merchant to the other must be sufficient against the sender, i.e., it must be a writing that meets the requirements of UCC § 2-201 and would be effective to satisfy the statute if an action were brought by the non-signing merchant against the merchant who sent it.[57] There is, therefore, no particular form required of this writing any more than there would be if the writing was not a confirmation but one that had been executed prior to or contemporaneously with the formation of the contract. While the term "confirmation" need not be used,[58] the writing must evidence a contract between the parties rather than a mere offer or other preliminary negotiation. Thus, if a buyer sends its purchase order as a confirmation, it may be insufficient because it could be construed to evidence a mere offer rather than a confirmation of a contract.[59] Even if the writing is captioned "letter of confirmation," but its contents indicate that the other party must submit a written acceptance of such a "letter," the writing will fail as a confirmation of the contract.[60] As usual, the caption atop the document does not provide a conclusive characterization.

5. Recipient Must Have Reason to Know Contents of Confirmation.

The requirement that the recipient of the confirmation have reason to know its contents could raise a question concerning the recipient of a confirmation

---

[54] UCC § 2-201(2).

[55] See, e.g., Atlas Road Constr. Co. v. Commercial Stone Co., 33 D & C 3d 477 (Pa. Ct. Comm. Pl. 1984) (3½ months was within a reasonable time where defendant did not show it was prejudiced thereby); Serna, Inc. v. Harman, 742 F.2d 186 (5th Cir. 1984) (3½ months was not unreasonable where the parties were in communication with each other and the price of the cattle to be purchased and sold did not fluctuate during this period); Azevedo v. Minister, 471 P.2d 661 (Nev. 1970) (ten weeks is not unreasonable as a matter of law).

[56] See Rockland Indus. v. Frank Kasmir Assocs., 470 F. Supp. 1176 (N.D. Tex. 1979).

[57] See R. S. Bennett & Co. v. Economy Mech. Indus., 606 F.2d 182 (7th Cir. 1979).

[58] Perdue Farms, Inc. v. Motts, Inc. of Miss., 459 F. Supp. 7 (N.D. Miss. 1978).

[59] See Trilco Terminal v. Prebilt Corp., 167 N.J. Super. 449, 400 A.2d 1237 (1979) (purchase orders did not refer to any previous contract). See also Harry Bubin & Sons, Inc. v. Consolidated Pipe Co., 396 Pa. 506, 153 A.2d 472 (1955) where the court indicated doubt that the purchase order, alone, would constitute a confirmation of the contract. However, when combined with a letter, the writings were sufficient to evidence a confirmation. See also Dura-Wood Treating Co. v. Century Forest Indus., 675 F.2d 745 (5th Cir. 1982) where the court recognized that an order for goods, alone, often evidences only an offer but can, in a given case, constitute sufficient evidence of confirmation of a contract.

[60] Great Western Sugar Co. v. Lone Star Donut Co., 721 F.2d 510 (5th Cir. 1983).

who never made a contract with the sender. In such a situation, does the recipient have reason to know the contents of the memorandum? This question has not been litigated. Another question which has been litigated concerns the addressee of the confirmation. Where the oral contract was made through a specific agent of a corporation, but the confirmation was not addressed to that particular individual but to the company, the court held the confirmation effective, i.e., it construed the language of § 2-201(2) that the recipient have reason to know the contents of the confirmation as not requiring the confirmation to be received by any particular person.[61] The case law construing this language of § 2-201(2) typically deals with questions of *receipt* of the confirmation. Thus, the sender is entitled to the presumption that a properly addressed, stamped and mailed writing was received.[62]

E. *Time of Making and Destruction of Memorandum.*

1. Time of Making.

Statutes of fraud, as they are commonly worded, do not purport to fix the time when the memorandum must be made with relation to the time the contract was formed. Neither does the English version of the fourth section of the Statute, which has often been copied literally in this country, purport to invalidate the contract if no memorandum is made. Rather, it provides that "no action shall be brought" on the contract, unless a memorandum is made.[63] The traditional view, therefore, is that the statute is satisfied if the memorandum evidencing the contract comes into existence at any time before the action in which it is sought to be used, regardless of when the contract came into being.[64] The RESTATEMENT 2d, however, goes further in permitting the memorandum to be made even after the action is begun.[65] It is conceivable that a written pleading would be a sufficient memorandum.[66] There would seem to be no reason in any of the statutory language or in the history of the statute to insist that the memorandum exist prior to the filing of a lawsuit in which it would be used. Moreover, as will be seen in the next section, if a party admits in her pleadings, testimony or otherwise in court that she made the contract, she may not use the statute as a shield. If an admission in court will be sufficient to satisfy the statute, a memorandum created after the action has begun, whether or not in the form of a court document, should be admitted as written evidence of the contract.

---

[61] Thompson Printing Mach. Co. v. B. F. Goodrich Co., 714 F.2d 744 (7th Cir. 1983).

[62] Sebasty v. Perschke, 404 N.E.2d 1200 (Ind. App. 1980); Tabor & Co. v. Gorenz, 43 Ill. App. 3d 124, 356 N.E.2d 1150 (1976); Perdue Farms, Inc. v. Motts, Inc. of Miss., 459 F. Supp. 7 (N.D. Miss. 1978). *See also* Pillsbury Co. v. Buchanan, 37 Ill. App. 3d 876, 346 N.E.2d 386 (1976) where the confirmation was improperly addressed, thereby negating the presumption. However, the trial court's finding of receipt was supported by evidence that the letter had not been returned and by defendant's admission that he was known in the small town to which the letter had been sent.

[63] The statute of frauds section of the predecessor of the UCC, the Uniform Sales Act, uses the language, "shall not be enforceable by action," which is deemed to be the equivalent of the original fourth section of the English Statute. UCC § 2-201 states, "... a contract ... is not enforceable by way of defense unless there is some writing...."

[64] *See* Watson v. McCabe, 527 F.2d 286 (6th Cir. 1975); Gaines v. McAdam, 79 Ill. App. 201 (1898). This was the view set forth in the FIRST RESTATEMENT § 215.

[65] RESTATEMENT 2d § 136 comment b.

[66] *See* RESTATEMENT 2d § 133 comment d.

2. Destruction of Memorandum.

It is quite clear that the loss or destruction of the memorandum is not fatal to the party who seeks to enforce a contract within the statute of frauds.[67] The statute of frauds is not a rule of evidence though its purpose is evidentiary. If, therefore, the writing does not exist at the time the action is brought, the plaintiff is entitled to prove that the writing did in fact exist and oral evidence of its contents is admissible.[68]

§ 75. Admissions — Uniform Commercial Code.

Assume that Ames and Barnes have made an oral contract within one or more provisions of the applicable statute of frauds. Before any performance has occurred, Barnes announces that he will not perform his duties under the contract, i.e., he commits an anticipatory repudiation which Ames treats as a breach. Ames brings an action against Barnes. In his answer to Ames' complaint, Barnes raises the statute of frauds as a defense but also admits that he made the contract. The question before the court is: Should a party who admits in his pleading, testimony or otherwise in court that he made the contract, nonetheless, be permitted to use the statute of frauds as an effective bar to the enforcement of a contract which he has admittedly made? If the question were one of first impression, it would seem that it scarcely survives its statement. If a defendant admits that he made the contract upon which the action against him is brought, there is no possibility that the plaintiff is asserting a false claim. Any requirement of a sufficient writing to evidence the admitted contract becomes superfluous after such an admission. Indeed, "[F]or more than one hundred years after the passage of the [original] Statute of Frauds, there continued to be expressions of belief in the principle that the statute was not intended to be used to defeat performance of an admitted oral agreement."[69] By the close of the eighteenth century, however, this view was reversed for reasons which now appear fatally flawed. The rationale may be stated as follows: If a defendant who made an oral contract were forced to admit or deny that he made the alleged oral contract, he has two choices: (a) to admit he made the contract thereby losing the statute of frauds as a defense, or (b) commit perjury by denying he made the contract. In such a situation, the inducement to make a perjured denial is a great temptation. To remove that temptation, the defendant will be able to admit he made the contract and still use the statute of frauds as an effective bar to the enforcement of the

---

[67] RESTATEMENT 2d § 137.

[68] See Combs v. Lufkin, 123 Ariz. 210, 598 P.2d 1029, 1032-33 (1979); Computer Servicenters, Inc. v. Beacon Mfg. Co., 328 F. Supp. 653 (D.S.C. 1970), aff'd, 443 F.2d 906 (4th Cir. 1971); Joseph E. Seagram & Sons v. Shaffer, 310 F.2d 668, 675 (10th Cir. 1962) (dictum). See also Fed. R. Evid. 1001-04.

[69] Stevens, Ethics and the Statute of Frauds, 37 CORNELL L.Q. 355, 367 (1952). The Stevens article is the seminal piece concerning the use of the statute of frauds by a defendant who admits the making of the oral contract. Professor Stevens points to Child v. Godolphin, 1 Dickens 39 (Ch. 1723) as the leading, early case from which he provides the following quotation (at 42): "His Lordship said, the plea insisting on the statute was proper, but then the defendant ought by answer to deny the agreement; for if she confessed the agreement, the Court would decree a performance notwithstanding the statute, for such confession would not be looked upon as perjury, or intended to be prevented by the statute." (emphasis added).

contract. The modern reaction to this "rationale" is effectively suggested by one court, "However, apart from creating obvious ethical problems this approach is in obvious contradiction to the rationale of other recognized exceptions to the Statute."[70]

Notwithstanding the absurdity of this rationale, American courts adopted it so that the prevailing view continued in this country permitted an admission of the contract and an effective use of the statute of frauds. In the first half of this century, only a few American courts came to insist upon the sound analysis that had prevailed in England for a century after the passage of the original Statute.[71] We will explore more recent developments in American jurisdictions. First, however, it is important to consider the significant change concerning judicial admissions effected by the UCC.

A. The Uniform Commercial Code Admissions Exception.

As one of several alternate satisfaction devices, the UCC provides that if a party admits in his pleadings, testimony or otherwise in court, that a contract for sale has been made, the admitted contract is enforceable to the extent of the quantity of goods admitted.[72] A comment to this Code section states that it is no longer possible to admit the contract in court and still treat the statute of frauds as a defense whether the admission occurs in a pleading, by stipulation or by oral statement before the court.[73] Neither the statutory language nor the comment, however, provides answers to other questions which necessarily arise from this provision. The fundamental question left unanswered was whether the party seeking to enforce the oral agreement could compel the other party to admit or deny the making of the contract.[74]

If the party against whom enforcement of an oral contract is sought may avoid either admitting or denying the making of a contract through a pleading device such as a demurrer or a motion to dismiss the complaint on the ground that the complaint does not allege any written evidence of the contract and is, therefore, unenforceable under the statute of frauds, the effect will be to emasculate the admissions exception to the UCC statute of frauds. A technical admission made in connection with a motion to dismiss or a demurrer has been held not to be the kind of "admission" to which the Code provision refers.[75] Such holdings, however, do not address the fundamental question of

---

[70] Wolf v. Crosby, 377 A.2d 22, 26 (Del. Ch. 1977).

[71] See Shedd, *Statute of Frauds: Judicial Admission Exception — Where Has It Gone? Is It Coming Back?*, 6 WHITTIER L. REV. 1 (1984). Professor Shedd cites Hagedorn v. Hagedorn, 194 Iowa 172, 188 N.W. 980 (1922), Degheri v. Carobine, 100 N.J.Eq. 493, 135 A. 518 (N.J. Ch. 1927) and Trossbach v. Trossbach, 185 Md. 47, 42 A.2d 905 as important early cases in this century recognizing the judicial admission exception as precluding the effective use of the statute of frauds.

[72] UCC § 2-201(3)(b).

[73] UCC § 2-201 comment 7.

[74] "The Comment does not indicate that such was intended, but it is not clearly foreclosed by the language of the section." 1 REPORT OF N.Y. LAW REVISION COMM'N, STUDY OF THE UNIFORM COMMERCIAL CODE 372 (1955).

[75] See Anthony v. Tidwell, 560 S.W.2d 908 (Tenn. 1977) (motion to dismiss was granted and upheld where the complaint alleged an oral contract for the sale of goods within the UCC statute of frauds and court states that "technical admissions of this nature, made solely in connection with a motion to dismiss, do not necessarily constitute admissions chargeable to the party for the purposes of the litigation as a whole); Beter v. Helman, 7 W.J.L. Vol. XLI (Pa. C. P. Westmore-

whether these procedural niceties permit the effective use of the statute of frauds and simultaneously preclude any possibility of the kind of "admission" to which the Code provision refers. Some courts have confronted this question and have concluded that permitting the statute to be raised in this manner would effectively negate the Code provision. In these jurisdictions, the statute may not be raised in this manner. Rather, the defendant is forced to admit or deny the making of the contract in a responsive pleading, pre-trial discovery or during the trial.[76] Other jurisdictions continue to permit the use of a motion to dismiss or the like to establish the statute of frauds as a bar to the enforcement of the alleged oral contract.[77]

If a defendant is forced to admit or deny the existence of the contract in order to raise the statute of frauds as a defense, other questions arise. If such a defendant denies that she made the alleged contract in her answer to the complaint, should the statute then operate to permit a successful motion for summary judgment, or should the court deny such a motion to provide the plaintiff an opportunity to elicit an admission? A defendant may, in good faith, deny the existence of a contract because that is her subjective view of the facts. If, however, she is forced to do more than simply deny the existence of the contract, i.e., she is forced either to submit to a deposition or to testify at trial, her testimony may reveal that she did make the contract, notwithstanding her good faith but erroneous legal conclusion that she had not formed the contract.[78] Forcing a continuation of proceedings in terms of a trial with respect to a defendant who has not, in fact, made a contract, however, may be said to permit judicial harrassment of the defendant and to ignore the value of judicial economy.[79] One solution to this dilemma is to permit the plaintiff to depose the defendant. If the deposition does not evidence the making of a contract as alleged, a motion for summary judgment could then be granted.

Other issues arising under the UCC admissions exception have not caused great difficulty for the courts. Thus, it is clear that a contract made enforceable by an admission rather than a writing is enforceable only to the extent of the admission.[80] Since a contract evidenced by a writing is only enforceable to the extent of the writing under the UCC statute of frauds,[81] admission evidence should rise no higher than written evidence to satisfy the statute. It is abundantly clear that admissions in depositions fall within the statutory requirement of admissions made in pleadings, testimony or otherwise in court

land Cty. 1958) held that demurrer was not the type of "admission" referred to in § 2-201(3)(b) of the UCC.

[76] See M & W Farm Serv. Co. v. Callison, 285 N.W.2d 271 (Iowa 1979); Duffee v. Judson, 251 Pa. Super. 406, 380 A.2d 843 (1977); Garrison v. Piatt, 113 Ga. App. 94, 147 S.E.2d 374 (1966).

[77] Boylan v. G. L. Morrow Co., 63 N.Y.2d 616, 479 N.Y.S.2d 499, 468 N.E.2d 681 (1984) (two judges vigorously dissented, concluding, "If a prepleading motion to dismiss is permitted to defeat a cause of action on an oral sales contract before plaintiff has had an opportunity to elicit from defendant a statement in court of any kind, only malpractice by defendant's attorney would subject the defendant to the statute's ameliorative purpose." 468 N.E. at 682); International Plastics Dev., Inc. v. Monsanto Co., 433 S.W.2d 291 (Mo. 1968); Anthony v. Tidwell, supra note 75.

[78] See, e.g., Lewis v. Hughes, 276 Md. 247, 346 A.2d 231 (1975).

[79] See Weiskopf, In-Court Admissions of Sales Contracts and the Statute of Frauds, 19 U.C.C. L.J. 195, 217 (1987).

[80] See Barton v. Tra-Mo, Inc., 73 Or. App. 804, 699 P.2d 1182 (1985).

[81] UCC § 2-201 comment 1.

whether such admissions are voluntary or involuntary,[82] just as involuntary admissions made by a party as an adverse witness under direct examination constitute admissions within the contemplation of the statute.[83] The statute provides, however, that the admission must be made by the party against whom enforcement is sought. While an agent of the party can make such an admission,[84] it has been held that an admission by a former agent or employee of the party to be charged cannot bind the former employer without authorization from the employer.[85]

B. *Extension of Judicial Admission Exception Beyond the Uniform Commercial Code.*

The satisfaction of the statute of frauds through judicial admissions for contracts other than UCC sale-of-goods contracts can be found in several jurisdictions.[86] The applicable statute of frauds may contain such an exception.[87] Without any statutory change, some courts have returned to the basic view of the English courts in the first century after the enactment of the original Statute, i.e., the purpose of the statute is to prevent fraud, not to perpetuate fraud.[88] Other courts have recognized that fundamental concept and they have also been influenced by the Uniform Commercial Code provision in engrafting the admissions exception on all contracts within the statute of frauds.[89] In addition to the merit of the admissions exception, there is something to be said for uniformity and consistency in the treatment of all provisions of the statute of frauds to the extent permissible under the statutory language. Absent a negation of the admissions exception by the legislature, courts should not feel precluded from recognizing this exception with respect to any provision of their statutes of fraud. The only possible preclusion is found in antiquated and flawed precedent that should not be followed.[90]

---

[82] *See* Babst v. FMC Corp., 661 F. Supp. (S.D. Miss. 1986); Roth Steel Prods. v. Sharon Steel Corp., 705 F.2d 134 (6th Cir. 1983); Usra Farmers Coop. Co. v. Trent, 58 Ill. App. 3d 930, 374 N.E.2d 1123 (1978).

[83] *See* Bahnsen v. Rabe, 276 N.W.2d 413 (Iowa, 1979).

[84] *See, e.g.,* Oskey Gasoline & Oil Co. v. Continental Oil, 534 F.2d 1281 (8th Cir. 1976).

[85] Miller v. Sirloin Stockade, 224 Kan. 32, 578 P.2d 247 (1978). If otherwise proper admissions in depositions were not properly filed with the court, such admissions are not properly before the court. Lippold v. Beanblossom, 23 Ill. App. 3d 595, 319 N.E.2d 548.

[86] In the earlier cited article by Professor Shedd, *supra* note 71 at 26-27, the author concludes that as of the time of that article (1984), there are nine U.S. jurisdictions that prevent the defendant from asserting the statute of frauds if he has admitted in the pleadings, during discovery, or in court, than the oral contract exists.

[87] *See* IOWA CODE ANN. § 622.34; ALASKA STAT. § 09.25.020.

[88] *See, e.g.,* Power v. Hastings, 20 Wash. App. 873, 582 P.2d 897 (1978), *aff'd,* 93 Wash. 2d 709, 612 P.2d 371 (1980).

[89] *See, e.g.,* Hackney v. Morelite Constr., 418 A.2d 1062, 1066-67 (D.C. App. 1980).

[90] In Pierce v. Gaddy, 42 N.C. App. 622, 257 S.E.2d 459, 462 (1979), the court rejects the admissions exception out of hand, citing two nineteenth century North Carolina cases.

§ 76. Performance Satisfying the Statute of Frauds.

A. *Effect of Part Performance in General.*

Parties to a contract within one or more provision of the statute of frauds may, of course, perform their contract and, once performed, it is an executed contract to which the statute of frauds has no application.[91] If, however, the contract is not fully performed, the issue arises of whether part performance will remove the contract from the enforcement bar of the statute of frauds? Only three types of contracts within the statute of frauds admit of a part performance satisfaction: (i) contracts that cannot be performed within one year from their making; (ii) contracts for the sale of land; (iii) contracts for the sale of goods. Otherwise, it is the general rule that part performance will not make a contract enforceable where it would otherwise be unenforceable. We have already examined the part performance exception with respect to contracts that cannot be performed within one year from formation.[92] We will now examine the cases allowing part performance in the other two classifications.

B. *Part Performance — Contracts for the Sale of Land.*

Soon after the original Statute of Frauds was enacted, English courts of equity permitted part performance of a land contract such as payment of the purchase price or the transfer of possession of the land to the grantee[93] to satisfy the statute of frauds notwithstanding contrary language in the statute. Today, it is clear that once a transfer of an interest in land has been completed, the promise to pay the price will be enforceable notwithstanding the lack of any writing to evidence the contract unless the price, itself, is wholly or partially an interest in land.[94] If, however, only the price has been paid by the prospective buyer, it is now generally held that the buyer may not obtain specific performance of the contract since he may be restored to status quo through the remedy of restitution.[95] Some performance beyond payment of the price will be required to allow a buyer to avoid the application of the statute. It is often suggested that whatever the performance, it must be "unequivocally referable" to the alleged oral agreement.[96] The extent of the part performance that will suffice has not been determined precisely by the courts over the years. It has been held that where the buyer pays all or part of the purchase price and the seller gives possession of the land to the buyer, the oral

---

[91] *See* Alexander v. Holmberg, 410 N.W.2d 900 (Minn. App. 1987).

[92] *See supra* § 72(D).

[93] *See* Butcher v. Stapley, 1 Vern. 363, 23 Eng. Rep. 524 (Ch. 1685).

[94] RESTATEMENT 2d § 125(3).

[95] *See* Pugh v. Gilbreath, 571 P.2d 1241 (Okla. App. 1977). *Contra* Hamilton v. Traub, 20 Del. Ch. 475, 51 A.2d 581 (1947).

[96] The most famous statement of this requirement is found in the opinion by Judge Cardozo in Burns v. McCormick, 233 N.Y. 230, 232, 135 N.E. 273, 273 (1922) which emphasizes that the performance "must itself supply the key to what is promised. It is not enough that what is promised may give significance to what is done." The performance, therefore, must be the dominant manifestation of intention since such conduct will be the evidentiary substitute for the writing. To permit the alleged oral promise to be the dominant evidence contradicts the purpose of the land contract provision of the statute of frauds.

contract will be enforced.[97] Other courts have found satisfaction of the statute in possession plus the making of valuable improvements to the land.[98] The making of valuable improvements, however, cannot properly be characterized as part performance where the oral contract for the sale of land does not purport to include terms dealing with the taking of possession and making improvements.[99] Yet, the making of valuable improvements is often viewed as having special significance in terms of part performance.[1] Where specific performance of an oral contract for the sale of land is granted on the basis of such acts, the decision is based on a combination of the fulfillment of the evidentiary function of the statute through the conduct of the parties and the detrimental reliance of the buyer which should not go unremedied.[2] As will be seen in the next section, detrimental reliance (promissory estoppel) sufficient to remove a contract from the statute of frauds may be discovered in acts other than the taking of possession and the making of valuable improvements to the land.[3] There can be no doubt that courts are primarily concerned with the protection of promisees who justifiably rely upon oral promises though they may resort to a less than precise "part performance" characterization rather than a direct application of detrimental reliance.[4]

C. *Part Performance of Contracts for the Sale of Goods — Uniform Commercial Code.*

Section 17 of the original Statute of Frauds required contracts for the sale of goods for the price of ten pounds sterling or more to be evidenced by a writing *unless* the buyer received and accepted *part* of the goods or gave "something in earnest to bind the bargain, or in *part* of payment...."[5] Thus, part performance in terms of receipt and acceptance of the goods or in the form of part payment or giving something in earnest would allow a court to enforce an oral contract for the sale of goods. As to the latter exception, Professor Corbin

---

[97] *See* Darby v. Johnson, 477 So. 2d 322 (Ala. 1985); Smith v. Cox, 247 Ga. 563, 277 S.E.2d 512 (1981); Shaughnessy v. Eidsmo, 222 Minn. 141, 23 N.W.2d 362 (1946).

[98] Seavey v. Drake, 62 N.H. 393 (1882). This case is generally viewed as an antecedent of the modern doctrine of detrimental reliance (promissory estoppel). Detrimental reliance is not only an effective validation device. As this case suggests, it may also be an effective device to satisfy the statute of frauds. Subsequent discussion will demonstrate this to be so.

[99] RESTATEMENT 2d § 129 comment a.

[1] *See* Breen v. Phelps, 186 Conn. 86, 439 A.2d 1066, 1073 (1982).

[2] RESTATEMENT 2d § 129 comment b.

[3] *See* Chapman v. Boman, 381 A.2d 1123 (Me. 1978) where the court held that a promise to make a memorandum sufficient to satisfy the land contract provision of the statute of frauds may, if relied upon, create a promissory estoppel to bar the assertion of the statute.

[4] *See* RESTATEMENT 2d § 129 which "restates what is widely known as the 'part performance doctrine'" (comment a) into a reliance doctrine which is more precise since acts such as taking possession and making valuable improvements when the contract does not provide for such conduct is not "part performance." Thus, *reliance* is a more accurate rationale for these holdings. *See also* Dunham v. Dunham, 204 Conn. 303, 528 A.2d 1123, 1130 (1987) where the court suggests the possibility of a "part performance" satisfaction of the statute of frauds one year provision through plaintiff's "part performance" in making valuable improvements to certain property though in the case before the court, there was no evidence of an oral agreement and, even if an oral agreement had been proven, the trial court found that the acts undertaken by the plaintiff were insufficient to satisfy the part performance exception. The court emphasizes the RESTATEMENT 2d § 129 requirement of "reasonable reliance *on the contract.*"

[5] 29 Car. II, ch. 3 [1677] (emphasis added).

emphasizes the difference between giving "something in earnest to bind the bargain" and "part of payment," i.e., the former is not part of the purchase price as is the latter. Rather, giving something in earnest to bind the bargain may refer to the payment of a token sum, apart from the purchase price, or the delivery of a chattel of some value, either of which would serve an evidentiary function so as to permit a court or jury to find that an alleged oral contract was made.[6] Whether the payment of money in a given situation was intended as giving something in earnest or payment of part of the purchase price would be determined by oral testimony. The Uniform Sales Act, which was widely enacted throughout the United States, continued the part performance exceptions to the writing requirement for a sale-of-goods contract.[7] They have been substantially modified, however, under the UCC.[8] The dominant UCC modification is the change from enforcement of the entire contract through part performance to enforcement of the oral contract only to the extent of part performance.[9] The Code views receipt and acceptance of the goods or the price of the goods as "unambiguous overt admission[s] by both parties that a contract actually exists."[10] But, "'[p]artial performance' as a substitute for the required memorandum can validate the contract only for the goods which have been accepted or for which payment has been made and accepted."[11] While the Code has generally liberalized the statute of frauds, the part performance exception has been tightened to reflect consistency with other provisions throughout § 2-201. Thus, if there is a writing evidencing the parties' contract for the sale of goods, the necessary quantity "need not be accurately stated but recovery is limited to the amount stated."[12] Similarly, if there is no writing but the party sought to be charged admits in his pleading, testimony or otherwise in court that he made the contract alleged by the plaintiff, the contract is enforceable only to the extent of the admission.[13] There is simply no evidentiary basis for enforcing an oral agreement beyond the quantity admitted, what was stated in the memorandum, what was received and accepted, or that for which payment has been made and accepted. Unlike part performance of a contract for the sale of land, however, there is no requirement that the performance be "unequivocally referable" to the oral agreement.[14] An understanding of this part performance concept under the UCC is

---

[6] "The legislature did not mean to require great formality in the sale transactions of everday business; it meant only to require some objective evidential factor to supplement oral testimony...." 2 CORBIN § 494 at 662-63.

[7] Uniform Sales Act § 4.

[8] See In re Augustin Bros. Co., 460 F.2d 376 (8th Cir. 1972); Cohn v. Fisher, 118 N.J. Super. 286, 287 A.2d 222 (1972).

[9] UCC § 2-201(3)(c).

[10] UCC § 2-201 comment 2. See Wire Prods., Inc. v. Marketing Techniques, Inc., 99 Ill. App. 3d 29, 424 N.E.2d 1288 (1981).

[11] Id. See Del Hayes & Sons v. Mitchell, 230 N.W.2d 588 (Mich. 1976) and Bagby Land & Cattle Co. v. California Livestock Com. Co., 439 F.2d 314 (5th Cir. 1971) (enforceability only with respect to goods received and accepted); In re Augustin Bros. Co., 460 F.2d 376 (8th Cir. 1972) (enforcement only to the extent of part payment).

[12] UCC § 2-201 comment 1.

[13] UCC § 2-201(3)(b) states that, in the case of such an admission, "the contract is not enforceable ... beyond the quantity of goods admitted...."

[14] See Hoffman v. Stoller, 320 N.W.2d 786 (N.D. 1982); West Cent. Packing, Inc. v. A. F. Murch Co., 109 Mich. App. 493, 311 N.W.2d 404 (1981).

aided by separate exploration of receipt and acceptance of *goods* followed by an exploration of receipt and acceptance of *payment.*

1. Receipt and Acceptance of Goods — Revocation of Acceptance.

Prior to the UCC, it was generally agreed that "receipt" dealt with possession of the goods whereas "acceptance" related to title to the goods.[15] While the concept of "receipt" has remained virtually unchanged under the UCC, one of the radical changes in Sales law effected by the Code was the emasculation of "title" as an analytical tool.[16] Thus, as will be seen later in this subsection, the concept of "acceptance" under the Code has undergone a considerable change and is no longer related to "title." We begin our exploration with the concept of "receipt."

Courts have dealt with the concept of "receipt" in essentially the same fashion before and after the enactment of the UCC. The goods must have been "actually received" in the sense that actual possession, or the immediate right to possession, of part or all of the goods, with the seller's consent, must have occurred.[17] Moreover, the buyer need not have received the goods himself, i.e., if they have been delivered to a third party at the direction of the buyer, the buyer will be said to have received them.[18] Receipt alone, however, without acceptance is insufficient.[19]

---

[15]*See* United States Rubber Co. v. Bercher's Royal Tire Serv., 205 F. Supp. 308 (W.D. Ark. 1962); Gordy v. Leonard, 113 Conn. 760, 155 A. 67 (1931).

[16]Sales law under the UCC is essentially contract law rather than property law relying heavily upon the title concept. A cogent example is the allocation of risk of loss for goods to be delivered by an independent carrier lost or damaged during transit. UCC § 2-509(1)(a) and (b) allocate the risk between buyer and seller on the basis of the contract term, i.e., either an FOB "shipment" or "destination" contract. The UCC philosophy with respect to the title concept is best expressed in a comment to § 2-101: "The arrangement of the present Article [2] is in terms of *contract for sale* and the various steps of its performance. The legal consequences are stated as following directly *from the contract* and action taken under it *without resorting to the idea of when property or title passed or was to pass as being the determining factor.* The purpose is to avoid making practical issues between practical men turn upon the location of an intangible something, the passing of which no man can prove by evidence and to substitute for such abstractions proof of words and actions of a tangible character" (emphasis supplied). *See also* Martin v. Melland's, Inc., 283 N.W.2d 76 (N.D. 1979) where the court indicates that the risk of loss is determined not by title but by contract. The court also refers to § 2-401 of the Code which does provide rules for the passage of title. That section is not designed as an analytical tool for Article 2 of the Code, however. Rather, it was inserted to deal with extra-Code issues involving criminal law, taxation, and public regulation as well as questions of "ownership" which may arise beyond the Code in such matters as liability insurance coverage.

[17]In Hoffman v. Stoller, 320 N.W.2d 786 (N.D. 1982), the court suggests that "receipt" requires the goods to change possession, while "acceptance" contemplates unilateral action on the part of the buyer. *See* the discussion of "acceptance" later in this subsection. UCC § 2-103(1)(c) defines "receipt" of goods as taking physical possession of them.

[18]Pre-Code cases include Houghton & Dutton Co. v. Journal Engraving Co., 241 Mass. 541, 135 N.E. 688 (1922); Cuask v. Robinson, 1 B. & S. 209 [1861]. UCC cases include Allied Wire Prods., Inc. v. Marketing Techniques, Inc., 99 Ill. App. 3d 29, 424 N.E.2d 1288 (1981); Jim & Slim's Tool Supply, Inc. v. Metro Commun. Corp., 328 So. 2d 213 (Fla. App. 1976); Double R Enters. v. Sappie, 11 Pa. D & C 3d 56 (Pa. Comm. Pl. 1978). Under the pre-Code law, courts would not recognize the "receipt and acceptance" exception to the normal requirement of a writing if the seller retained a lien on the goods. *See, e.g.,* Clark & Co. v. D. & C. E. Scribner Co., 122 Me. 418, 120 A. 609 (1923). This was so even though legal title to the goods had already vested in the buyer. Rodgers v. Jones, 129 Mass. 420 (1880). Under the UCC, however, there is no preclusion of the "receipt and acceptance" exception of § 2-201(3)(c) simply because the seller or another has retained a security

---

[19]Estate of Nelsen, 209 Neb. 730, 311 N.W.2d 508 (1981).

There are three ways in which goods will be said to have been accepted under the UCC. The most interesting of the three may occur through inaction and silence by a purchaser who is in possession of the seller's goods. With certain exceptions,[20] a buyer may reject goods for *any* nonconformity of the goods or their tender.[21] The buyer, however, must have a reasonable opportunity to inspect the goods before deciding upon acceptance or rejection.[22] If the buyer chooses to ignore the right to inspect and simply permits the goods to remain in his possession beyond the reasonable time for inspection, the buyer will be said to have accepted the goods.[23] If the buyer's attempt at rejection is ineffective, it will be treated in the same fashion, i.e., as if he had made no rejection with the reasonable time permitted for rejection.[24] Again, the failure to make an effective rejection constitutes acceptance and, together with the prior receipt of the goods, will serve to satisfy the statute of frauds with respect to the goods received and accepted.[25] Another method of acceptance under the UCC is the buyer's conduct with respect to the goods, i.e., treating the goods in a fashion inconsistent with the seller's ownership.[26] If a buyer has received the goods and begins to use them in this fashion, the statute of frauds will be satisfied with respect to the goods which the buyer has, in effect, treated as his own since he will be said to have accepted such goods.[27] The third and most obvious method of acceptance is relatively rare in the case law compared to the methods just explored. If the buyer receives the goods and, after a reasonable opportunity to inspect, "signifies" to the seller that the goods are conforming or that he, the buyer, will retain them despite their nonconformity, this manifestation of the buyer's intention constitutes acceptance.[28] If the buyer has not only received and accepted goods shipped by the

---

interest in the goods under Article 9 of the Code. It is conceivable that a seller would have an attached security interest in goods which, except for possessory security interests, requires a written security agreement, § 9-203(1)(a), that would not satisfy the memorandum requirement of § 2-201 because, *e.g.*, it failed to state a quantity term. Thus, an Article 2 statute of frauds issue could be raised. If all or a portion of the goods were received and accepted by the purchaser or a third party at his direction, however, § 2-201(3)(c) would remove the statute of frauds as a bar to enforcement to the extent of the goods received and accepted.

[20] Contrary agreement by the parties or installment contracts (UCC § 2-612).

[21] UCC § 2-601.

[22] The buyer's right to inspection is found in UCC § 2-513(1) which states in pertinent part, "... the buyer has a right before payment or acceptance to inspect them...." Even this right is subject to contrary agreement because the subsection begins, "Unless otherwise agreed...." One of the examples of parties agreeing that the buyer will pay the price before acceptance is the "C. O. D." (cash on delivery) contract recognized expressly in § 2-513(3)(a).

[23] UCC § 2-606(1)(b).

[24] UCC § 2-606(1)(b). Typically, a rejection is ineffective because it fails to meet the requirements of § 2-602, requiring the rejection to be within a reasonable time and also requiring the buyer to "seasonably notify" the seller. Since the buyer is only required to notify the seller, i.e., there is no requirement that the seller receive the notice, pursuant to the definition of "notifies" in § 1-201(26), the notice need only be sent through a proper medium for which the proper fee (*e.g.*, postage) is paid, and the correct address should appear. The risk of transmission is on the seller with respect to the rejection notice.

[25] *See, e.g.*, Alarm Device Mfg. Co. v. Arnold Indus., 65 Ohio App. 2d 256, 417 N.E.2d 1284 (1979).

[26] UCC § 2-606(1)(c).

[27] *See, e.g.*, Johnson v. Holdrege Coop. Equity Exch., 293 N.W.2d 863 (Neb. 1980) (commingling seller's goods with buyer's own goods).

[28] UCC § 2-606(1)(a). It is important to note comment 3 to § 2-606 which emphasizes that the act of "payment" after tender of the goods is "one circumstance tending to signify acceptance of the

seller but has also paid the seller who has accepted the payment, the conduct of the parties has provided ample evidence of the contract and no writing is needed to make it enforceable.[29]

One of the interesting questions about which § 201 of the UCC is silent concerns the right of a buyer to revoke acceptance of the goods. Under appropriate circumstances, a buyer is permitted to revoke acceptance of the goods[30] and an effective revocation places the buyer in the same position as he would have been in had he rejected the goods.[31] This situation, then, raises the possibility that a buyer could have received and accepted goods but, after discovering a sufficient non-conformity and otherwise complying with the requirement for an effective revocation of acceptance, would be said to have withdrawn the acceptance. Would the initial satisfaction of the statute of frauds under § 2-201(3)(c) then be said to have been withdrawn along with the withdrawal of the buyer's acceptance? In the absence of clear UCC directives to the contrary, a revocation of acceptance should have no effect on the satisfaction of the § 2-201 statute of frauds through the alternative satisfaction device of receipt and acceptance of the goods. Upon such receipt and acceptance, the evidentiary function of the statute has been fulfilled and the buyer should be precluded thereafter from raising the statute of frauds as a defense to a contract he intended to make as manifested by his receipt and acceptance of the goods. To permit the buyer to raise the defense simply because he has exercised his right to revoke acceptance of the goods based on a non-conformity of the goods would be to allow the statute to be used as a technical defense and would contradict another policy of the statute, i.e., to preclude the use of the defense when the defendant has admitted he made the contract.[32]

As a practical matter, this situation would arise where a buyer, under an oral contract, has effectively revoked acceptance of the goods and now seeks one of the available UCC remedies.[33] The statute of frauds argument would be raised by the seller, i.e., by the effective revocation, the buyer has withdrawn his acceptance thereby negating the receipt and acceptance satisfaction device under the UCC. Again, that argument should fail. If the buyer seeks no remedy for the seller's breach, except in the rare situation in which the buyer, for other reasons, desires an adjudication that he had made a contract with the seller, a buyer who can effectively revoke his acceptance of the goods but seeks only to avoid any contractual liability achieves that result through his

---

goods but it itself can never be more than one circumstance and is not conclusive. Also, a conditional communication of acceptance always remains subject to its expressed conditions."

[29] See TCP Indus. v. Uniroyal, 661 F.2d 542 (6th Cir. 1981); Alabama Great S. Ry. Co. v. McVay, 381 So. 2d 607 (Miss. 1980).

[30] UCC § 2-608 permits a buyer to revoke acceptance if he has accepted goods (a) on the reasonable assumption that a non-conformity which the buyer had discovered would be cured and it is not cured, or (b) without discovery of the non-conformity if the buyer's acceptance was reasonably induced by the difficulty of discovery before acceptance or by the seller's assurances that the non-conformity would be cured, and, in either case, the non-conformity "substantially impairs the value of the goods to him [the buyer]...."

[31] UCC § 2-608(3).

[32] See UCC § 2-201(3)(b).

[33] The buyer's remedies under the UCC are listed in § 2-711 which permits the buyer to pursue any of the listed remedies where, inter alia, the buyer has rightfully revoked acceptance of the goods.

revocation of acceptance. He has no need to avoid any contractual liability through the statute of frauds defense.

2. Receipt and Acceptance of Payment — the Indivisible Unit.

Prior to the UCC, questions as to what constituted part payment to satisfy the statute of frauds as it related to a contract for the sale of goods were not particularly troublesome. The payment need not have been made in money, i.e., the delivery of anything of value as part of the agreed price or exchange for the goods would suffice. Thus, in a contract for the sale of corn, the buyer's delivery and seller's acceptance of sacks in which the corn was to be put and which the parties had agreed would constitute part of the price was held to be sufficient to satisfy the statute if the allegation could be established by the evidence.[34] Where the buyer of hay baled the hay at his own expense pursuant to the agreement with the seller, the buyer's work was considered to be part payment which satisfied the statute of frauds to make the agreement for the purchase and sale of hay enforceable.[35] It must be remembered that part performance under the pre-UCC statute of frauds took the entire contract out of the statute rather than making the contract enforceable only to the extent of the part performance as the UCC directs for reasons explored earlier in this section. Pre-Code cases also required the actual transfer of something of value to the seller. Thus, a surrender of a job, though a bargained-for detriment, was insufficient part performance to make the contract enforceable.[36]

Other questions concerning part performance by payment were somewhat troublesome to pre-Code courts. Thus, whether the taking of a check, before it was cashed, was sufficient to satisfy the statute was a question to which the courts did not provide uniform answers.[37] Another issue was whether the buyer's agreement to accept goods in complete or partial satisfaction of an existing obligation owed by the seller to the buyer constituted "payment." An older English case, obiter, said that it did,[38] i.e., if the buyer had accepted the promise to deliver goods as a present discharge of the pre-existing obligation (an accord and satisfaction). There was support for this view by some American courts,[39] though others concluded that such evidence was precisely the

---

[34] Weir v. Hudnut, 115 Ind. 525, 18 N.E. 24 (1888).

[35] Conway v. Mrachowsky, 260 Wis. 540, 55 N.W.2d 909 (1952). *See also* Driggs v. Bush, 152 Mich. 53, 115 N.W. 985 (1908).

[36] Patterson v. Beard, 227 Iowa 401, 288 N.W. 414 (1939). Annotation, 125 A.L.R. 399 (1940).

[37] Some courts suggested that, if the check were accepted as a present discharge of the seller's claim for the price of the goods or some part thereof, the statute was satisfied. *See, e.g.,* Dutton v. Bennett, 256 Mass. 397, 152 N.E. 621 (1926); Coffman v. Fleming, 301 Mo. 313, 256 S.W. 731 (1923); Summers v. Wood, 131 Ark. 345, 198 S. W. 692 (1917). If, however, there was no affirmative evidence to establish such an understanding, the usual presumption applied, i.e., that the claim for the price was not discharged until the check had been cashed. Thus, a number of courts provided the logical and technically correct position, i.e., that "payment" had not occurred. *See, e.g.,* Gay v. Sundquist, 42 S.D. 327, 175 N.W. 190 (1919); Bates v. Dwinell, 101 Neb. 712, 164 N.W. 722 (1917). A few courts, however, took the position that the statute should be satisfied by giving a check. *See, e.g.,* Logan v. Carroll, 72 Mo. App. 613 (1897); McClure v. Sherman, 70 F. 190 (D. Mont. 1895).

[38] Walker v. Nussey, 16 M. & W. 302 [1847].

[39] *See, e.g.,* Roberts v. Williams, 6 Wash. 2d 599, 108 P.2d 334 (1940) (buyer's deposit of money with seller in connection with an offer later withdrawn constituted payment and acceptance with

kind of "say-so" evidence of the parties that the statute was designed to prevent.[40] Another problem was the timing of the part payment, i.e., was it sufficient if the payment was received and accepted at any time prior to the commencement of litigation as some courts held,[41] or did the statute specify that the payment must be made at the time of the formation of the oral contract? Some statutes were so drafted prior to the adoption of the predecessor to the Code, the Uniform Sales Act, and under such statutes, payment at a time later than the time of contract formation would not suffice.[42]

Against this background, the major UCC change is, again, the limitation of enforceability to the extent of the part payment.[43] A comment to this section suggests that with respect to receipt and acceptance of goods or receipt and acceptance of payment for goods, a court must be able to make a just apportionment of the agreed price of any good actually delivered or "an apportionable part of the goods" with respect to the part payment made and accepted.[44] If part payment is to make a contract enforceable only to the extent of an apportionable part of the goods, what is to be done in the case of an indivisible item, such as an automobile, for which the buyer has made and seller has accepted a part payment? A strict reading of the Code section precludes enforcement of the contract to any extent and an early trial court so concluded: "The Code ... makes an important change by denying the enforcement of the contract where in the case of a single object the payment made is less than the full amount."[45] There is no longer any doubt that this initial interpretation was unduly restrictive as evidenced by the holdings of numerous courts that the oversight by the Code drafters would be resolved in favor of a liberal interpretation where the goods could not be apportioned as, again, in the example of the automobile.[46] If apportionment is possible, however, the part payment continues to take the contract out of the statute of frauds only to the extent of the part payment.[47] The part payment must not only be made, it must be accepted.[48] In the case of payment by check, the check must be cashed.[49] If, however, the check has been presented to the drawee for payment and the drawee honors a stop payment order, the payment has been accepted since the seller has manifested its intention to accept the payment by presenting the check for payment by the drawee.[50] Payment may also be in the form

respect to a new agreement where the parties understood the money in seller's possession to apply to the purchase price). *See also* Dow v. Worthen, 37 Vt. 108 (1864).

[40] *See* Scott v. Mundy & Scott, 193 Iowa 1360, 188 N.W. 972 (1922).

[41] *See, e.g.,* United States Rubber Co. v. Bercher's Royal Tire Serv., 205 F. Supp. 368 (W.D. Ark. 1962); Dean v. W. S. Given Co., 123 Me. 90, 121 A. 644 (1923).

[42] *See, e.g.,* Jackson v. Tupper, 101 N.Y. 515, 5 N.E. 65 (1886).

[43] UCC § 2-201(3)(c).

[44] UCC § 2-201 comment 2.

[45] Williamson v. Martz, 29 Northum L.J. 32, 11 Pa. D. & C. 2d 33, 35 (Pa. Comm. Pl. 1956).

[46] *See, e.g.,* The Press, Inc. v. Fins & Feathers Pub'g Co., 361 N.W.2d 171 (Minn. App. 1985); Morris v. Perkins Chevrolet, Inc., 663 S.W.2d 785 (Mo. App. 1984); Paloukos v. Intermountain Chevrolet Co., 99 Idaho 740, 588 P.2d 939 (1978); Thomaier v. Hoffman Chevrolet, Inc., 64 App. Div. 2d 492, 410 N.Y.S.2d 645 (1978); Lockwood v. Smigel, 18 Cal. 3d 800, 96 Cal. Rptr. 289 (1971).

[47] *See, e.g.,* In re Augustin Bros. Co., 460 F.2d 376 (8th Cir. 1972).

[48] UCC § 2-201 comment 2.

[49] *See* Nelson v. Hy-Grade Constr. & Materials, Inc., 215 Kan. 631, 527 P.2d 1059 (1974).

[50] *See* Miller v. Wooters, 131 Ill. App. 3d 682, 476 N.E.2d 11 (1985).

of goods or services which must not only be received but accepted to satisfy the statute of frauds.[51]

§ 77. Enforcement of Part of the Contract — Multiple Promises.

Where the contract contains one or more promises within the statute of frauds and one or more without the statute and the statute has not been satisfied, it has generally been held that the whole contract is unenforceable under the statute.[52] While there is nothing in the statute to require this conclusion, any other result would be unjust in the normal case. The parties formed the contract on the assumption that all promises would be performed. It would, therefore, be unfair to enforce some of the promises if others are unenforceable since there is always the possibility that the promises that are outside the statute would not have been made if the promisor(s) understood that the remainder of the contract would not be enforced. The same analysis applies even though the contract is divisible, i.e., portions of the performances on each side are the agreed equivalents of performances on the other side,[53] and divisible portions of the performance on both sides are outside the statute.[54] Some courts have enforced divisible portions of contracts within the one year provision of the statute, however, though their analyses contain no suggestion that they could not be extended to other types of contracts within the statute.[55] It is at least plausible to suggest that these courts see no distinction between a contract that is divisible into agreed equivalents and separate contracts. If the parties have, in fact, made separate contracts, the statute of frauds does not prevent a court from enforcing the contract(s) that are outside the statute while refusing to enforce those within the statute. Whether the parties have, in a given situation, made one divisible contract or separate contracts, however, can be a difficult question of interpretation.[56]

Another distinction must be made with respect to a contract that permits alternative performances. If, for example, a promisor may completely fulfill his contractual duty by either conveying real property or paying a sum of money, the promise to pay money is enforceable since it is outside the statute

---

[51] UCC § 2-201 comment 2.

[52] *See* RESTATEMENT 2d § 147(3). *See also* Fuller v. Apco Mfg. Co., 51 R.I. 378, 155 A. 351 (1931). *Contra* White Lightning v. Wolfson, 68 Cal. 2d 336, 438 P.2d 345 (1968).

[53] *See supra* § 76.

[54] *See* Hornady v. Plaza Realty Co., 437 So. 2d 591 (Ala. App. 1983).

[55] *See* Vanston v. Connecticut Gen. Life Ins. Co., 482 F.2d 337, 342 (5th Cir. 1973): "If the contract is severable — that is, susceptible of division and apportionment, having two or more parts not necessarily dependent on each other — the fact that one obligation is unenforceable does not prevent a recovery as to the other." *See also* Dickenson v. Dickenson Agency, Inc., 512 N.Y.S.2d 952 (A.D. 4 Dept. 1987); Buttorf v. United Elec. Labs., 450 S.W.2d 581 (Ky. 1970) and Blue Valley Creamery Co. v. Consolidated Prods. Co., 81 F.2d 182 (8th Cir. 1936).

[56] The RESTATEMENT 2d suggests the following guide: "Whether an agreement creates a single contract or more than one for the present purpose, depends primarily on the terms of the agreement, the interdependence of its parts, and the possibility of apportioning the consideration on one side among several promises on the other without doing violence to the expectation of the parties." RESTATEMENT 2d § 147 comment c. It is interesting to compare this statement with the quotation from the *Vanston* case in the preceding note. The consideration in a divisible contract must be capable of being apportioned without doing violence to the expectation of the parties. Unlike separate contracts, however, an assumption that the parts of a divisible contract are not interdependent is typically unwarranted.

and, if performed, will discharge the duty of the promisor.[57] This distinction should be viewed in the context of a broader principle recognized by the RESTATEMENT 2d, i.e., where part of a contract within the statute of frauds is exclusively beneficial to the party seeking enforcement, he may enforce that part if he agrees to forego the remainder of the contract.[58] Thus, a party may insist upon an alternative performance without the statute of frauds if he foregoes the alternative performance within the statute. Even where the performances are not alternative, however, the party seeking enforcement exclusively beneficial to himself may enforce the part without the statute while foregoing the part within the statute.[59]

Finally, if the promises within the statute of frauds have become enforceable or are discharged because they have been completely performed or legally excused, there is no harm in enforcing any unperformed promises outside the statute of frauds, i.e., they may be treated as if they were separate contracts.[60]

§ 78. Reliance to Avoid the Statute of Frauds — Estoppel.

A. *Equitable Estoppel.*

It has long been recognized that a party may be estopped from relying on the statute of frauds as a defense if the other party has reasonably and substantially relied on a misrepresentation or concealment of material facts. A so-called equitable estoppel arises where one party misrepresents or conceals material facts with the knowledge that her representations are untrue and where the other party is unaware of the misrepresentation or concealment and relies thereon to his detriment.[61] Thus, if a party misrepresents that she has signed a satisfactory memorandum evidencing an oral contract within the statute, she will be estopped to assert the statute as a defense.[62] Similarly, if a party misrepresents his intention to sign a memorandum satisfying the statute of frauds he will be estopped from asserting the statute.[63] Absent evidence of such misrepresentation, however, the doctrine of equitable estoppel would not apply, regardless of substantial detrimental reliance by a promisee.[64] The application of the doctrine almost invariably compels a court to inveigh against the use of the statute of frauds to protect a fraud rather than prevent

---

[57] *See* Chandler v. Doran Co., 44 Wash. 2d 396, 267 P.2d 907 (1954); Ward v. Ward, 94 Colo. 275, 30 P.2d 853 (1934); Welsh v. Welsh's Estate, 148 Minn. 235, 181 N.W. 356 (1921).

[58] RESTATEMENT 2d § 147(1). This subsection is expressly inapplicable to contracts for the transfer of property on the promisor's death on the footing that it would be contrary to the Statute of Wills and because of the availability of the remedy of restitution.

[59] In ill. 2 to § 147 the RESTATEMENT 2d suggests a promise by A to insure a shipment of B's goods against casualty and to answer for certain defaults of the carrier. B pays a single premium in exchange for A's promises. When the goods are damaged by fire, B may enforce the insurance coverage promise. The illustration is based on Mobile Marine D. & M. Ins. Co. v. McMillan & Sons, 31 Ala. 711 (1858).

[60] RESTATEMENT 2d § 147(2).

[61] *See* Frantz v. Parke, 729 P.2d 1068, 1073 (Idaho App. 1986). *See also* Ozier v. Haines, 411 Ill. 160, 103 N.E.2d 485 (1952) (suggesting that deceit on the part of the defendant must be shown).

[62] *See* FIRST RESTATEMENT § 178 comment f.

[63] Seymour v. Oelrichs, 156 Cal. 782, 106 P. 88 (1909).

[64] Ozier v. Haines, 411 Ill. 160, 103 N.E.2d 485 (1952).

a fraud or similar exhortation.[65] As we noted in our exploration of "promissory estoppel," however,[66] the suggestion that a party is "estopped" is hopelessly conclusory. The reason that one party is estopped is justifiable reliance by the other party. Just as the restrictions of equitable estoppel were removed to allow promissory estoppel to operate as a validation device in lieu of consideration, the development of promissory estoppel as a device to satisfy the statute of frauds proceeds apace. It is not difficult to discover a modern case treating equitable and promissory estoppel interchangeably to avoid the statute of frauds.[67] It is, however, more than premature to suggest the general acceptance of promissory estoppel as an alternate device to satisfy the statute.[68] As in other developing areas of our law, it is important to trace this development to the present time and to perceive the nature of the trend so as to provide a reliable forecast of its future application.

B. *The Shift to Promissory Estoppel.*

A landmark opinion written by Justice Roger Traynor for the Supreme Court of California provided the catalyst for the current development of reliance as a judicially engrafted device to satisfy the statute of frauds. In *Monarco v. LoGreco,*[69] the court confronted a situation which seemed to compel relief from a technical application of the statute of frauds. When he was 18 years old, Christie LoGreco decided to leave the home of his mother and stepfather in quest of an independent living. They persuaded him to remain and participate in the family farm enterprise which was then valued at $4,000. They orally promised Christie that, if he stayed and worked, they would keep the property in joint tenancy so that it would pass to the survivor who would then leave it to Christie by will. Christie remained and worked diligently in the family venture and surrendered any opportunity for further education or other opportunity to accumulate his own property. He received only lodging and spending money. When he married, his mother told him that his wife should move in with the family. Mother then repeated the original promise that Christie would receive the property when she and her husband died. In two decades from the time of the original promise to Christie, the value of the farm had increased to $100,000. Shortly before the stepfather died, he arranged conveyances to terminate the joint tenancy and executed a will leaving all his property to a grandson who received the property after probate and brought an action for partition, relying on the statute of frauds to defeat the oral promise on which Christie had relied for twenty years. Since no assurance had been made to Christie that he would be protected from the statute of frauds, the plaintiff argued that the doctrine of equitable estoppel

---

[65]*See, e.g.,* Lunning v. Land O'Lakes, 303 N.W.2d 452, 457 (1980), "Where an application of the Statute will protect, rather than prevent, a fraud, equity requires that the doctrine of equitable estoppel be applied." The most familiar suggestion is, "The purpose and intent of the Statute of Frauds is to prevent fraud and not to aid in its perpetration." Dean v. Myers, 466 So. 2d 952, 955 (Ala. 1985) quoting from 73 Am. Jur. 2d *Statute of Frauds* § 562 (1974).

[66]*See supra* § 66.

[67]*See, e.g.,* Nygard v. Nygard, 156 Mich. App. 94, 401 N.W.2d 323 (1986).

[68]*See, e.g.,* Florida Power & Light Co. v. American Ltd., 511 So. 2d 1103 (Fla. App. 1987) stating that promissory estoppel is not a valid bar to the statute of frauds.

[69]35 Cal. 2d 621, 220 P.2d 737 (1950).

should not apply. Writing for the Court, Justice Traynor emphasized precedent which applied the doctrine of estoppel to prevent fraud that would result from the refusal to enforce oral contracts in circumstances involving unconscionable injury to a relying promisee or unjust enrichment of the promisor. The critical component of the opinion, however, was the rejection of the notion that estoppel can be based only on representations by a party that he will not rely upon the statute of frauds as a defense, or that he will execute a writing to satisfy the statute, or that a writing is not necessary. Justice Traynor read the precedent mentioning such traditional requirements as really focusing upon unconscionable injury or unjust enrichment where the remedy of restitution would not be adequate as in the case of Christie LoGreco.[70] Where such injury or unjust enrichment was present, Traynor suggested that the representation requirements were ignored. Moreover, the opinion clearly suggests that the focus should not be on representations concerning the formal requirements of the statute. Rather, courts should focus upon the promise and the substantial reliance on that promise by the other party. Though the *Monarco* opinion clearly invited the application of a reliance device without the shackles of the traditional representation requirements of equitable estoppel, its emphasis upon unconscionable injury or unjust enrichment which could not be adequately remedied through restitution continues to operate as an effective deterrent to a general application of reliance as a satisfaction device.[71]

The next major initiative toward the recognition of promissory estoppel rather than equitable estoppel to satisfy the statute of frauds appeared four years after *Monarco*. In *Alaska Airlines v. Stephenson*,[72] the plaintiff was permitted to take a leave of absence from his employment at Western Airlines without prejudice to his tenure. Plaintiff took the leave to become general manager of the defendant, a new airline. When the six month leave was about to expire, the parties orally agreed that plaintiff would have a two year contract and that defendant would execute a writing evidencing the contract as soon as it obtained a certificate to operate the airline between Seattle and Alaska. Plaintiff had moved his family to Alaska and had relied by surrendering his tenure at Western. Though it obtained the certificate, defendant discharged the plaintiff. In holding the oral promise to be enforceable, the court was heavily influenced by a comment in the FIRST RESTATEMENT: "... [A] promise to make a memorandum, if similarly relied on, may give rise to an effective promissory estoppel if the Statute would otherwise operate to defraud."[73] Thus, the combination of a traditional element of equitable estoppel — an unperformed promise to make a memorandum — and the elements of

---

[70] There is considerable difficulty in measuring the benefit conferred by a member of the family who has devoted himself to an enterprise over a long period such as two decades. Recognizing that the work performed by someone in the position of Christie LoGreco was not in exchange for any wage but was, rather, a lifetime commitment to an enterprise he assumed he would own, the impossibility of adequately compensating such a person by way of restitutionary damages becomes clear.

[71] *See, e.g.,* Phillippe v. Shapell Indus., 43 Cal. 3d 1247, 743 P.2d 1279 (1987).

[72] 217 F.2d 295 (9th Cir. 1954).

[73] FIRST RESTATEMENT § 178 comment f.

promissory estoppel permitted enforcement of a contract violating the one-year provision of the statute of frauds.

There were those who believed that these cases augured the application of a virtually unfettered promissory estoppel concept as a statute of frauds satisfaction device. The RESTATEMENT 2d confirmed that prophecy in a section which is virtually identical to the promissory estoppel section, § 90, except that it makes promises "enforceable notwithstanding the Statute of Frauds" rather than simply making them "binding" in the absence of other validation devices.[74] There is no requirement of unconscionable injury, unjust enrichment or an unperformed promise to execute a writing to satisfy the statute of frauds. There is, however, a separate subsection listing five "circumstances" that are "significant" in deciding whether injustice can be avoided only by enforcing the oral promise notwithstanding the statute.[75] Even in tentative draft form, this creation of the RESTATEMENT 2d found support[76] and there is no question that it will continue to influence courts that have yet to address the argument.[77] Yet, there is considerable tenacity in the analysis suggested almost three decades ago by Justice Traynor.[78] Thus, a recent opinion refused to adopt the RESTATEMENT 2d position and, instead, adhered to the requirement of "an unjust and unconscionable injury and loss."[79] Another suggests that, a party seeking to take a contract out of the statute of frauds through the estoppel doctrine "must demonstrate that the circumstances are such as to render it unconscionable to deny the oral promise...."[80] Still other jurisdic-

---

[74] RESTATEMENT 2d § 139(1) substitues "enforceable notwithstanding the Statute of Frauds" for "binding" in § 90. The only other change is in the last sentence of both sections. Section 90 reads, "The remedy granted for breach *may be* limited as justice requires," while § 139(1) reads, "The remedy granted for breach *is to be* limited as justice requires." (emphasis added). The difference may appear to permit judicial discretion in § 90 as to an expectation or reliance interest remedy while § 139(1), on its face, may suggest that courts should be more willing to limit relief to the reliance interest. Comment d to § 139, however, belies this notion by suggesting, "In some cases, it may be appropriate to measure relief by the extent of the promisee's reliance rather than by the terms of the promise. *See* § 90 comment e and illustrations." Since comment e to § 90 deals with gratuitous promises to procure insurance, the § 139 comment reference is undoubtedly to comment d of § 90 which deals with partial enforcement.

It should also be recalled that RESTATEMENT 2d § 129 provides for specific performance of an oral contract for the sale of land on a reliance basis. This is the modern form of the "part performance" doctrine discussed earlier in § 76 B. *See also* RESTATEMENT 2d § 128 involving "part performance" in boundary and partition agreements. Comment a to § 139 suggests that §§ 128 and 129 are particular applications of the reliance principle to land contracts.

[75] RESTATEMENT 2d § 139(2) lists "(a) the availability and adequacy of other remedies, particularly cancellation and restitution; (b) the definite and substantial character of the action or forbearance in relation to the remedy sought; (c) the extent to which the action or forbearance corroborates evidence of the making and terms of the promise, or the making and terms are otherwise established by clear and convincing evidence; (d) the reasonableness of the action or forbearance; (e) the extent to which the action or forbearance was foreseeable by the promisor."

[76] *See, e.g.,* Warder & Lee Elevator Co. v. Britten, 274 N.W.2d 339 (Iowa 1979); Walker v. Ireton, 221 Kan. 314, 559 P.2d 340 (1977); McIntosh v. Murphy, 52 Haw. 29, 469 P.2d 177 (1970). *But see* Tannenbaum v. Biscayne Osteopathic Hosp., 190 So. 2d 777 (Fla. 1966) for an early rejection of this view.

[77] A recent case adopting RESTATEMENT 2d § 139 is Cooper v. Re-Max Wyandotte Cty. Real Estate, Inc., 241 Kan. 281, 736 P.2d 900 (1987).

[78] Where a contractor relied on the oral bid of subcontractor, the defendant was permitted to plead the statute of frauds since he was not unjustly enriched. *See* C. R. Fedrick, Inc. v. Borg-Warner Corp., 552 F.2d 852 (9th Cir. 1977).

[79] Whiteco Indus. v. Kopani, 514 N.E.2d 840, 845 (Ind. App. 3 Dist. 1987).

[80] Greenbaum v. Weinstein, 131 A.D.2d 430, 515 N.Y.S.2d 866, 868 (1987).

tions expressly admit that they are "unsettled" as to whether promissory estoppel absent the other elements should operate to make a promise within the statute of frauds enforceable[81] though cognitive dissonance may be a more realistic characterization than the euphemistic "unsettled." The sale-of-goods section of the statute contained in the UCC has not escaped the development of the reliance device. It is important to explore that line of cases.

C. *Reliance Satisfying the Uniform Commercial Code Statute of Frauds — Specially Manufactured Goods.*

1. Uniform Commercial Code Specially Manufactured Goods Exception.

The UCC statute of frauds expressly recognizes reliance as an alternate satisfaction device in a very narrow situation. If the parties contract orally to purchase and sell goods which are to be specially manufactured for the buyer and are not suitable for sale to others in the seller's ordinary course of business, and the seller, before receiving notice of repudiation and under circumstances reasonably indicating that the goods are for the buyer, has made either (a) a substantial beginning of their manufacture, or (b) commitments for their procurement, the oral contract becomes enforceable.[82] This Code provision modifies its predecessor which only required the goods to be manufactured for the buyer if such goods were not suitable for sale to others in the seller's ordinary course of business.[83] While that exception applied only to the manufacturer of the goods, the Code enlarges the exception to apply even where the seller is not the manufacturer. The Code provision, however, also restricts the exception by adding a reliance requirement, i.e., that the seller/manufacturer has made a substantial beginning in manufacturing these "custom" goods, or that a seller who is not the manufacturer has made commitments for the procurement of the goods. To this point, the limited case law construing the "specially manufactured goods" exception to the UCC writing requirement has concentrated largely on the question of whether the goods were not only to be specially manufactured,[84] but were also unsuitable for sale in the seller's ordinary course of business. Thus, specially manufactured goods may still be suitable for sale to others and the exception would not apply.[85] If the goods are custom made and cannot be made suitable for sale to others except with major alterations, the exception will apply if a substantial beginning of their manufacture by the seller has occurred or the seller has made commitments for the procurement of such goods.[86] An obvious example

---

[81] *See* Phillips v. Phillips, 162 Ill. App. 3d 774 (1987) relying upon Goldstick v. ICM Realty, 788 F.2d 456, 465-66 (7th Cir. 1986).

[82] UCC § 2-201(3)(c).

[83] Uniform Sales Act § 4.

[84] *See* Colorado Carpet Installation, Inc. v. Palermo, 647 P.2d 686 (1982) (carpeting which was a standard item taken from a full roll and not specially cut to fit defendant's rooms was not a specially manufactured good).

[85] *See* Impossible Elec. Techniques, Inc. v. Wackenhut Protective Sys., 669 F.2d 1026 (5th Cir. 1982) (just because seller makes goods which are custom designed, such goods may still be suitable for sale to others); Maderas Tropicales S. de R. L. de C. V. v. Southern Crate & Veneer Co., 588 F.2d 971 (5th Cir. 1979) (cleats suitable for sale to others).

[86] *See, e.g.,* S. C. Gray, Inc. v. Ford Motor Co., 92 Mich. App. 789, 286 N.W.2d 34 (1979) (equipment not suitable for sale to others); Walter Balfour & Sons v. Lizza & Sons, 6 U.C.C. Rep. 649 (N.Y. Super. 1969) (rolling steel garage doors for buyer's building).

occurs where advertising flyers or other materials are imprinted with the buyer's name.[87] Where the substantial beginning of manufacture occurs only with respect to a portion of a contract alleged for a larger quantity, one court has held that the exception should apply only with respect to those goods as to which a substantial beginning has occurred.[88] This view is consistent with other provisions of the UCC statute of frauds, i.e., the contract is enforceable only to the extent of the quantity stated in the writing or, in the absence of a writing, only to the extent of the quantity admitted, or only to the extent of the goods received and accepted or the apportionment of the goods represented by payment received and accepted. On the other hand, if the seller/ manufacturer has purchased materals, plant equipment and facilities as well as employed workers to manufacture special goods not suitable for sale to others, sufficient reliance may be shown to make the contract enforceable for the entire quantity alleged in the oral contract.[89]

2. General Reliance Exception Added to the Code Provision by the Courts.

Should a court permit detrimental reliance to serve as a satisfaction device where the subject matter of the alleged oral contract is goods suitable for sale to others or not of special manufacture? As a matter of statutory construction, there are two substantial arguments precluding such a judicially engrafted alternate satisfaction device. The Code drafters were certainly aware of the use of reliance as a device to satisfy the statute of frauds in lieu of a writing. By using reliance exclusively in the specially manufactured goods context, they evidenced an intention, presumably ratified by the legislatures enacting the Code, that reliance was to be so limited as a statute of frauds satisfaction device. Moreover, the opening phrase of § 2-201 of the Code, "Except as otherwise provided in this section ...," clearly suggests that the intention was to limit any exceptions to the writing requirement to stated exceptions. Recognizing the considerable liberalization of prior statute of frauds requirements effected by the Code[90] and the normal constraints of statutory construction just explored, restricting the exceptions to those stated in § 2-201 seems neither harsh nor unduly conservative. The argument in favor of permitting a general reliance exception to be judicially engrafted is based on the UCC directive that principles of law not displaced by particular provisions of the Code shall supplement its provisions.[91] A number of courts have addressed

---

[87] See, e.g., Flowers Baking Co. of Lynchburg v. R-P Packaging, 329 S.E.2d 462 (Va. 1985); Perlmuter Printing Co. v. Strome, Inc., 436 F. Supp. 409 (D.C.N.D. Ohio 1976).

[88] Epprecht v. I.B.M. Corp., 36 U.C.C. Rep. 391 (E.D. Pa. 1983) (manufacture begun of 7000 specially manufactured parts in a contract alleged to be for 50,000 parts).

[89] LTV Aerospace Corp. v. Bateman, 492 S.W.2d 703 (Tex. Civ. App. 1973).

[90] The relaxation of pre-Code requirements include (1) the recognition of a frugal writing that only has to evidence an intention to make a contract, identify the parties (and not as buyer and seller), the goods, and the quantity term, (2) the effectiveness of a confirmation against a non-signing party in a deal between merchants, and (3) the admissions exception which makes a contract enforceable to the extent of an admission made in pleadings, testimony, or otherwise in court. UCC §§ 2-201(1), (2), and (3)(b). As suggested earlier in this subsection, the specially manufactured goods exception has been enlarged to include non-manufacturer sellers but tightened to require reliance in § 2-201(3)(a), and the part performance exception in § 2-201(3)(c) has been limited to make the contract enforceable only to the extent of the part performance.

[91] UCC § 1-103. The illustrative list of acceptable supplementary principles expressly mentions "estoppel."

this question and they are not in agreement. The courts refusing to add a general reliance exception typically emphasize the statutory construction arguments addressed above.[92] The larger number of courts accepting general reliance as an additional satisfaction device are not persuaded by the arguments of statutory construction and also seem to be heavily influenced by the need to recognize a promissory estoppel theory to satisfy the statute of frauds.[93] If a general reliance theory is to be accepted, the narrow reliance exception concerning specially manufactured goods tends to be superfluous. Thus, if a seller has relied to his substantial detriment in manufacturing custom goods, a court accepting the general reliance device would hold the contract to be enforceable even though the goods are still suitable for sale to others in the seller's ordinary course of business. Similarly, if a general reliance device is judicially added to § 2-201, the concept of irrevocable waivers through oral modifications under UCC §§ 2-209(4) and 2-209(5) may be superfluous.[94] These concerns are, however, only parts of the many general concerns as to whether the reliance development will undermine the statute of frauds.

D. *The Future of the Statute of Frauds and Reliance.*

Notwithstanding the reservations of courts which reject the reliance concept as an alternate satisfaction device because the statutory language does not easily admit such judicial modifications or because there is a commitment to the continuation of a strong statute of frauds for myriad reasons, the developments traced in this section augur a continuous evolution of detrimental reliance as a device that will avoid the statute of frauds. In the garb of "part performance" and "equitable estoppel," reliance has always been recognized as a significant reason for refusing to permit the statute to bar the enforcement of an oral contract. The recognition of promissory estoppel as a validation device at least equal to consideration suggested the strong concern for the protection of relying promisees. If such reliance can overcome technical constraints of classical contract law with respect to the validation of a promise, it should not seem remarkable that the same concept would be viewed as equally deserving of protection to overcome what, to an increasing number of courts and lawyers, appears to be an even more technical constraint — one that has been, for the most part, repealed in the country of its origin. The protection of a relying promisee to avoid injustice may even be seen as such an overriding value that it is in a separate dimension from questions of enforcea-

---

[92] See McDabco v. Chet Adams Co., 548 F. Supp. 456 (D.S.C. 1982); Ivey's Plumbing & Elec. Co. v. Petrochem Main., 463 F. Supp. 543 (N.D. Miss. 1978); Cox v. Cox, 292 Ala. 106, 289 So. 2d 609 (1974).

[93] See Potter v. Hatter Farms, 56 Or. App. 254, 641 P.2d 628 (1982); Warder & Lee Elev. Co. v. Britten, 274 N.W.2d 339 (Iowa 1979); R. S. Bennett & Co. v. Economy Mech. Indus., 606 F.2d 182 (7th Cir. 1979); Robert Johnson Grain Co. v. Chemical Interchange Co., 541 F.2d 207 (8th Cir. 1976).

[94] See Murray, *The Modification Mystery: Section 2-209 of the Uniform Commercial Code*, 32 VILL. L. REV. 1, 42 (1987): "Thus, assuming the addition of a general reliance satisfaction device to § 2-201, the possibility of waiver under § 2-209(4) and (5) becomes academic." This thesis is based on the assumption that § 2-201 satisfaction devices would be effective in satisfying the requirements of § 2-209(2) involving no oral modification (NOM) clauses. *See supra* § 64(E)(2).

bility of oral contracts within the statute of frauds.[95] The accretion of case law adoptions of a general reliance device in the form of a barely modified promissory estoppel concept such as that found in the RESTATEMENT 2d appears inevitable.[96] The effect on the statute of frauds will be significant in that only executory contracts within the statute where there has been no substantial reliance will be denied enforcement. Difficult technical questions currently confronted in determining whether part performance or equitable estoppel have been established will be gradually overcome. The statute of frauds will not disappear during the lifetimes of those reading these words. The most conservative prediction, however, is that its significance will be materially diminished.

§ 79. Effect of Failing to Comply With the Statute of Frauds.

A. *Legal Operation of Statute — Language of the Statute — "Void," "Voidable," and "Unenforceable."*

If an oral agreement is within one of the provisions of the statute of frauds, what effect does the statute have on that agreement? Does the statute preclude the agreement from recognition as a contract? If it is a contract, is it "void," "invalid," "voidable" or "unenforceable"? These and related questions have been confronted since the original Statute of Frauds was enacted. Unfortunately, the language of the various statutes of fraud does not necessarily provide ready solutions. The fourth section of the original Statute states that "no action shall be brought" against the promisor absent a signed memorandum. Query, does this mean that any attempt to bring such an action will be regarded as a nullity? The seventeenth section (sale of goods) of the original Statute uses the words, "no contract shall be allowed to be good...." Does this language suggest that there is or was a contract but it will prevented from being valid or enforceable? Some statutes specificy that a contract must fulfill the requirements of the statute to be "valid," i.e., if it fails to meet those requirements, it is "invalid." Still others prescribe that contracts failing to meet the statutory requirements "shall be void" or "are void." UCC § 2-201(1) states that a contract failing to comply with the statute of frauds provision "is not enforceable by way of action or defense." It is possible to discover different effect language attached to different provisions of a single statute of frauds.

It is important to recognize the significant differences that could flow from particular language in the statute. A so-called "void contract" is a contradiction, i.e., it has no legal effect whatsoever. If a contract is "voidable," one party has a legal power — a power of avoidance or disaffirmance.[97] While it is possible that only one party to an oral contract has signed a sufficient memorandum which becomes enforceable against him though he cannot enforce the

---

[95] For example, in Janke Constr. Co. v. Vulcan Materials Co., 386 F. Supp. 687, 697 (W.D. Wis. 1974), aff'd, 527 F.2d 772 (7th Cir. 1976), the court reasoned, "The statute of frauds relates to the enforceability of *contract;* promissory estoppel relates to *promises* which have no contractual basis and are enforced only when necessary to avoid injustice.... Accordingly, I find the statute is not applicable in an action based on promissory estoppel."

[96] RESTATEMENT 2d § 139.

[97] *See supra* § 17.

contract against the non-signing party, it is less than accurate to suggest that the non-signer has a power of avoidance or disaffirmance. The non-signer need not bring an action on the contract, but if she does bring an action against the signer of the memorandum, the signer may raise any available defense on the contract though he could not have enforced the contract.[98] This is only one of many illustrations of the operative effect of a contract that will not be enforced because it is within the statute of frauds. Thus, even where a contract is unenforceable between the parties to it, a third party who allegedly induced one of the parties to breach the unenforceable contract may still be held liable by either party to the contract for tortious interference with that contract.[99] Where benefits have been conferred through the performance of one party to a contract within the statute of frauds, though the contract is unenforceable, it may be admitted as evidence of the understanding that the party conferring the benefit expected compensation as well as evidence of the value of the services.[1] There is considerable doubt that the drafters of the various statutes of fraud were interested in suggesting effects different from the original Statute. Apparently, they were attempting to duplicate the original Statute. The divergences in language have typically been glossed over and minimized by the courts.[2] If, for example, a particular statute states that a contract failing to comply with its requirements will be "void," courts have generally displayed little difficulty in reading "void" as "unenforceable"[3] or at least "voidable."[4] There is little precision among courts and lawyers in using the precise statutory term. In particular, the terms "void" and "unenforceable" are often used interchangeably. American statutes of frauds are generally interpreted to mean that a contract failing to comply with its provisions is "unenforceable."[5] Under this interpretation, it is clear that a contract which can be effective for many other purposes exists though it cannot be enforced by one or both parties to the contract.

---

[98] See Johnson v. Holiday Inns, 565 F.2d 790 (1st Cir. 1977). See also RESTATEMENT 2d § 140. There are a few decisions that would prevent the non-signer from successfully bringing an action against the signer on the footing that the signer received nothing in exchange for his signed promise, i.e., there would be no "mutuality of obligation." See Burg v. Betty Gay, Inc., 423 Pa. 485, 225 A.2d 85 (1966). This view is not generally accepted, however. Another court has held that an agreement to forego one's rights under an oral contract within the statute does not constitute consideration to support a counter promise. Fuller v. Apco Mfg. Co., 51 R.I. 378, 155 A. 351 (1931). This view is unsound since even forbearance to sue on an invalid claim constitutes consideration.

[99] Daugherty v. Kessler, 264 Md. 281, 286 A.2d 95 (1972). See also RESTATEMENT 2d § 144. Section 142 of the RESTATEMENT 2d illustrates how an unenforceable contract may include authority or consent to perform acts which would otherwise be tortious. Thus, an oral contract for the sale of land may include an understanding that the buyer would have an immediate license to enter the land. If the buyer went on the land, the contract would remain unenforceable but the buyer would have a defense to the seller's action for trespass.

[1] See Rice v. Insurance & Bonds, Inc., 366 So. 2d 85 (Fla. App. 1979). RESTATEMENT 2d § 143.

[2] See Svoboda v. De Wald, 159 Neb. 594, 68 N.W.2d 178 (1955); Herring v. Volume Merchandise, Inc., 249 N.C. 221, 106 S.E.2d 197, 78 A.L.R.2d 927 (1958).

[3] See, e.g., Country Corner Food & Drug, Inc. v. Reiss, 22 Ark. App. 222, 737 S.W.2d 672 (1987) (equating "void" with "unenforceable"). See also Montanaro Bros., Bldrs. v. Snow, 4 Conn. App. 46, 492 A.2d 233 (1985).

[4] Korff v. Pica Graphics, Inc., 121 A.D.2d 511, 504 N.Y.S.2d 17 (1986).

[5] RESTATEMENT 2d § 138.

B. *Pleading the Statute as a Defense.*

If the statute of frauds is viewed as a defense to an otherwise enforceable contract and the defendant does not raise the statute as a defense, a contract that is otherwise established by the plaintiff should be enforceable. Thus, the statute must be pleaded as an affirmative defense and failure to do so will constitute a waiver of the defense.[6] Such pleading is required even where the applicable statutory language indicates that a contract failing to comply with the statute shall be "void." This is simply another indication that courts do not view contracts that fail to meet the statutory requirements as void. Again, such contracts are unenforceable. Older cases that permitted the statute to be raised by a general denial were simply reflecting the outmoded view that a failure to meet the requirements of the statute compels the holding that no contract ever existed, i.e., the so-called contract was void *ab initio*.[7] Since the statute is an affirmative defense it will not be permitted to be raised for the first time on appeal.[8] Notwithstanding the usual requirement that the statute must be pleaded affirmatively at trial, if the complaint alleges an oral contract, it may be subject to a demurrer or motion to dismiss. To the extent that the defendant's judicial *admission* of the contract will satisfy the statute in lieu of a writing, however, courts should not permit the statute to be raised in this fashion since it effectively avoids the necessity for the defendant to admit or deny the existence of the contract. The impetus for judicial reconsideration of the scandalous practice of permitting a party to admit the existence of the contract and still plead the statute of frauds was the UCC.[9] Courts have begun to recognize that permitting the statute to be raised by demurrer or motion to dismiss emasculates that statutory prescription.[10] Moreover, as courts begin to apply the admissions exception to provisions of the statute of frauds beyond the sale-of-goods section of the UCC, the use of demurrers or motions to dismiss should erode further. It may eventually become impossible to raise the statute of frauds in this technical fashion to avoid the necessity of admitting or denying the existence of the contract, regardless of the type of contract within the statute before the court.

---

[6] *See, e.g.,* Majewski v. Cantrell, 293 Ark. 360, 737 S.W.2d 649 (1987); Hubbard v. Peairs, 24 Mass. App. 372, 509 N.E.2d 41 (1987); Brown v. Brown, 744 P.2d 333 (Utah 1987); Good v. Hansen, 110 Idaho 953, 719 P.2d 1213 (1986); McCracken v. Olson Cos., 149 Ill. App. 3d 104, 500 N.E.2d 487 (1986); Marcoux v. Marcoux, 123 A.D.2d 844, 507 N.Y.S.2d 458 (2 Dept. 1986); Altomare v. Altomare, 355 Pa. Super. 391, 513 A.2d 486 (1986); Baudanza v. Mood, 496 A.2d 310 (Me. 1985).

[7] *See, e.g.,* Bruder v. Wolpert, 178 Minn. 330, 227 N.W. 46 (1929); Jordan v. Greensboro Furnace Co., 126 N.C. 143, 35 S.E. 247 (1900).

[8] *See* cases cited *supra* note 7.

[9] *See* the exploration of UCC § 2-201(3)(b) and related matters concerning admission and their effect on pleading *supra* § 75.

[10] *Ibid.*

§ 80. Restitution in Unenforceable Contracts.

A. *The Concept of Restitution — Applied to Part Performance Under a Contract Unenforceable Because of the Statute of Frauds.*

The interest normally protected in the law of contracts is the expectation interest so as to place the injured party in the position he would have been in had the contract been performed. Two other interests are also recognized: the reliance interest to compensate the injured party for his loss or minus quantity suffered in reliance on a promise, and the restitution interest which compensates the injured party for losses sustained through the unjust enrichment of another. Both restitution and reliance differ from the expectation interest in that they seek to restore the injured party to *status quo ante,* i.e., the position he was in before the reliance or unjust enrichment as contrasted with placing the injured party in the *future* position he would have been in had his expectation been fulfilled. Restitution differs from reliance in that the former is concerned with a plus quantity (the unjust enrichment or benefit conferred upon the other party) at the expense of the party conferring the benefit (the minus quantity) whereas reliance is concerned only with the minus quantity, i.e., the loss suffered by the relying party. We will explore all of these interests in a subsequent chapter dealing with contract remedies[11] and we have already explored the reliance interest in connection with promissory estoppel in a prior chapter.[12] As will be seen in our exploration of remedies, the restitution interest may be protected in lieu of the expectation or reliance interest where the defendant has breached the contract.[13] The restitution interest, however, may also be protected where no contract exists, i.e., the plaintiff may recover the amount of the unjust enrichment in quasi contract. It is not remarkable that our courts would look quite favorably upon the avoidance of unjust enrichment since it suggests a stronger claim to protection that either the expectation or reliance interest.[14]

With this brief background, it is appropriate to consider the plight of a party who has conferred a benefit upon another party by performing part of a contract that is unenforceable because of the statute of frauds. On the assumption that the contract is not enforceable even to the extent of part performance,[15] should the unjust enrichment of one party at the expense of the other

---

[11] *See infra* Chapter 9.

[12] *See supra* § 78.

[13] For example, where a building contractor underbids a particular job and is proceeding to perform with the expectation of suffering a loss, if the owner breaches the contract, the builder may choose to recover his restitution interest which may be considerably greater than his expectation interest. *See, e.g.,* Boomer v. Muir, 24 P.2d 570 (Cal. App. 1933) where the contractor recovered an amount $230,000 in excess of the contract price. This concept will be explored *infra* Chapter 9.

[14] The expectation interest may be protected absent any out-of-pocket loss by the plaintiff. While the reliance interest protects such a loss, the restitution interest protects against a loss to the plaintiff and a commensurate gain to the unjustly enriched party. For a complete analysis of the three interests and the greater claim suggested by the restitution interest, see the classic article by Fuller and Perdue, *The Reliance Interest in Contract Damages,* 46 YALE L.J. 52, 373 (1936).

[15] If an oral contract for the sale of goods is partly performed through receipt and acceptance of part of the goods, or receipt and acceptance of part payment which can be related to a portion of

party go unremedied? The question scarcely survives its statement. In general, our courts have taken the position that the statute of frauds is not undermined by permitting restitution of the benefits conferred under a contract that cannot be enforced because of the statute of frauds.[16] Thus, if parties have made an oral contract for the purchase and sale of land and the buyer has made a down payment, the unenforceability of the contract will not prevent the buyer's recovery of his down payment so as to avoid the unjust enrichment of the owner.[17] Where services are rendered in exchange for a promise that is unenforceable under the statute, the party who has rendered the services may recover their reasonable value in a quasi contract action to protect her restitution interest.[18]

B. *The Measure of Restitutionary Recovery.*

There is no difficulty in measuring the restitution interest where money has been paid in part performance of an unenforceable contract. The recipient of the money is unjustly enriched to the extent of the payment and by returning that amount to the other party, the injured party is restored to status quo.[19] Where the benefit is in the form of services rendered, the recovery is normally the reasonable value of the services.[20] While it is traditional to characterize the measure of restitutionary recovery as the amount of the "benefit conferred" on the unjustly enriched party, it is possible for a party to perform services pursuant to an unenforceable contract that confer no benefit upon the other party in terms of enhancing that party's economic position. Yet, if the performance has been received in accordance with the unenforceable contract, it will be viewed as a benefit, notwithstanding the lack of any discernible economic benefit to the recipient.[21] If the plaintiff's acts are merely preparatory to performing the contract, however, it is usually suggested that no action in restitution will lie since no performance has been received.[22] In such a situation, the plaintiff would be relegated to an attempt to recover his reliance interest.[23] In jurisdictions recognizing promissory estoppel as a method of satisfying the statute of frauds, the plaintiff's reliance interest would be protected notwithstanding the fact that the contract was within the statute of frauds.[24]

C. *Limitations on Restitutionary Recovery.*

As suggested earlier, restitutionary recovery is not generally seen as undermining the statute of frauds because such recovery does not amount to enforc-

---

the goods, the contract becomes enforceable to that extent. UCC § 2-201(3)(c). *See supra* § 76(C). for a discussion of this concept.

[16] RESTATEMENT 2d § 375.

[17] *See, e.g.,* Gilton v. Chapman, 217 Ark. 390, 230 S.W.2d 37 (1950). *See also* Jeanblanc, *Restitution Under the Statute of Frauds: What Constitutes a Legal Benefit,* 26 IND. L.J. 1, 8-9 (1950).

[18] *See, e.g.,* Peters v. Morse, 96 A.D. 662, 466 N.Y.S.2d 504 (1983) (nurse renders medical services to an elderly couple in exchange for the couple's unenforceable oral promises to convey their farm to the nurse upon their death).

[19] *See supra* note 17. *See also* RESTATEMENT 2d § 375 ill. 2.

[20] *See supra* note 18. *See also* RESTATEMENT 2d § 375 ill. 1.

[21] *See* Farash v. Sykes Datatronics, Inc., 59 N.Y.2d 500, 452 N.E. 1245 (1983).

[22] RESTATEMENT 2d § 370.

[23] RESTATEMENT 2d § 349.

[24] *See* RESTATEMENT 2d § 139. This concept is explored *supra* § 78(B).

ing the contract; it simply prevents the unjust enrichment of one party who has received the performance of the other. Yet, a particular statute of frauds could expressly preclude such recovery and a court would have no discretion in granting it in such a situation. Even where the statute does not expressly prevent such recovery, a court may perceive the purpose of a particular provision of the statute of frauds as preventing such recovering, i.e., unjust enrichment would be tolerated to effectuate an overriding statute of frauds purpose. The principal illustration of this situation occurs with respect to statutes of frauds in numerous jurisdictions that prevent the recovery of a real estate broker's commission unless there is a written memorandum of the contract. Real estate brokers are subject to statutory licensing requirements and are typically licensed only after having demonstrated their knowledge of laws relating to real estate transactions, including the statute of frauds with respect to their commissions. To permit such a licensed broker to recover in restitution would frustrate the purpose of the statute.[25]

If a party seeking restitution for performance under an unenforceable contract is himself in breach of the contract, the older view that there could be no recovery by such a contract breaker appears to be giving way to the view that a defaulting plaintiff should recover that amount over and above the loss to the defendant caused by the plaintiff's breach.[26] If, therefore, such a recovery were permissible in general, it should be permitted though the contract is unenforceable under the statute of frauds.

The RESTATEMENT 2d takes the position that specific restitution or, in the older terminology, restitution *in specie* is also permitted (though not for a breaching plaintiff) where monetary restitution is permitted if, in the court's discretion, such a remedy would not unduly interfere with the certainty of title to land or otherwise cause injustice.[27] This view is considerably more liberal than older views which restricted such relief to cases involving fiduciary relationships[28] or to the creation of constructive trusts which required a showing of fraud, mistake, misrepresentation, duress or undue influence, or a fiduciary relationship.[29] One of the interesting carry-overs from the FIRST RESTATEMENT[30] appears at this point. If the plaintiff claims restitutionary damages and the defendant tenders what has been received, i.e., the defendant provides specific restitution, the RESTATEMENT 2d adheres to its predecessor's view (notwithstanding a dearth of authority) that the defendant can discharge his duty by tendering such restitution, with or without a sum of

---

[25] *See* Phillippe v. Shapell Indus., 43 Cal. 3d 1247, 241 Cal. Rptr. 22, 743 P.2d 1279 (1987) where the court provides the policy rationale for a rigorous application of the statute of frauds to *licensed* real estate brokers and holds that even equitable estoppel will not apply to such brokers except where the real estate broker cancelled a contract with the sellers of the property in reliance on the buyer's oral promise to pay the broker's commission, or where the broker's principal represented to the broker that his authorization was in writing when in fact it was not. *See also* Louisville Trust Co. v. Monsky, 444 S.W.2d 120 (Ky. 1969) and RESTATEMENT 2d § 375 ill. 3.

[26] The classic case, albeit not a statute of frauds case, is Britton v. Turner, 6 N.H. 481 (1834). *See also* RESTATEMENT 2d § 374. This concept will be explored thoroughly *infra* Chapter 6.

[27] RESTATEMENT 2d § 372(1).

[28] *See* RESTATEMENT OF RESTITUTION § 182.

[29] A constructive trust could also be created where the transfer of land was made exclusively as security. *See* Straight v. Hill, 622 P.2d 425 (Alaska 1981).

[30] FIRST RESTATEMENT § 355.

money in addition to the particular benefit tendered, if the plaintiff will be placed in substantially the same position he would have been in through restitution in money.[31]

---

[31] RESTATEMENT 2d § 372(3).

Chapter 5

OPERATIVE EXPRESSIONS OF ASSENT

(Parol Evidence, Interpretation and Mistake)

371

§ 81. Introduction.

Once it has been determined that parties having legal capacity have formed a contract, the next step is to determine, as precisely as possible, the duties that they have undertaken to perform and their correlative rights. The simplistic notion that parties exercise their volition by committing themselves to future action or inaction, and that the law protects their circle of assent with the status of a private law, is fundamental to any discussion of contracts. The expressions of the parties through language and conduct must initially manifest assent to some kind of agreement. Once it is determined that they apparently intended to conclude an agreement, the process of determining the terms of their agreement begins, i.e., the parameters of their assent must be established. We know that the expressions of assent must be viewed objectively, i.e., we can only determine their agreement from outward manifestations since a subjective approach is unworkable.[1] Yet, some of their outward manifestations will be denied operative effect. In the last Chapter, we recognized that certain oral expressions of the parties would be denied such effect for the reasons associated with the statute of frauds.[2] In the next Chapter, we will see that certain expressions, oral or written, will be denied effect because the bargain struck by the parties is illegal or because all or part of their agreement is unconscionable. In the present Chapter, we will explore difficult questions which courts must confront at the earliest stages of defining the agreement of the parties, i.e., questions dealing with the parol evidence rule, interpretation and mistake.

If the parties take the time and trouble to express their agreement in writing, the question arises, should that writing be treated as their sole and exclusive manifestation of agreement, i.e., should evidence of prior understandings of the parties not be given operative effect? The so-called *parol evidence rule* may preclude the admission of such evidence. The basic question is whether the parties intend their writing as the final or complete expression of their agreement? That question of *fact* will be decided by a court rather than a jury because jurors may not give the unchanged, written record of the parties' agreement greater weight it deserves as compared to the less reliable recollection of the parties' intention at the time of contract formation.

Upon completion of the parol evidence process, the court has accomplished only one part of the process of determining the operative expression of assent. Whether the writing of the parties constitutes that expression, or whether the prior understanding and the writing are both operative, the court must still consider the preferred meaning of all of the expressions, i.e., the court must pursue the process of *interpretation*. The language and conduct manifesting agreement is typically imprecise. Language or conduct may superficially appear to be so clear and unambiguous that it requires no interpretation. Professor Corbin provided the consummate rejection of this view:

> It is sometimes said, in a case in which the written words seem plain and clear and unambiguous, that the words are not subject to interpretation or construction. One who makes this statement has of necessity already given the words an interpretation — the one that is to him plain and clear; and in making the statement he is asserting that any different interpretation is "perverted" and untrue.[3]

Where a defendant agreed to harvest a crop grown by the plaintiff, a clause in the contract excused the defendant from harvesting under "adverse weather conditions." Unusually good weather conditions prevailed causing the crops to mature almost simultaneously, thereby placing a considerable strain on the ability of the defendant to harvest all of the crop. He was forced to bypass certain acreage. The court was, therefore, confronted with the proper interpretation of the phrase, "adverse weather conditions" which may

---

[1] *See supra* Chapter 2, § 30.
[2] *See supra* Chapter 4.
[3] Corbin, *The Interpretation of Words and the Parol Evidence Rule,* 50 CORNELL L.Q. 161, 171-72 (1965). *See also* Farnsworth, *"Meaning" in the Law of Contracts,* 76 YALE L.J. 939 (1967).

have been contemplated as an excuse for poor weather conditions but may also be legitimately activated because of unusually good weather conditions.[4] Trade usage may dictate an interpretation which differs from the dictionary definition of a term in the agreement. Thus, "fifty percent" may be shown to mean less than fifty percent to the members of a particular trade.[5] The expression of the parties may also be affected by their prior course of dealing, in effect a private trade usage, which should be viewed as more important evidence of the meaning of their expressions than the general usage of trade.[6] If the parties have begun to perform their contract, their course of performance will constitute the strongest evidence of the meaning of their written expression[7] or of a modification of their express terms.[8] There may be inconsistencies or contradictions between or among different manifestations of agreement and the courts will have to choose that which they believe best effectuates the intention of the parties, i.e., which of the expressions should be accorded operative effect? Statutory[9] and common law guidelines[10] are of limited aid to courts in this process. Their use, however, must be explored.

If the parties have not manifested any intention concerning an unforeseeable event and such unforeseeable event changes their agreement dramatically, courts may be faced with a problem that can hardly be called one of interpretation since there is nothing to interpret. If the event does not amount to a legal excuse for a continuation of performance by one of the parties,[11] courts may be confronted with the necessity of "making a contract" for the parties in terms that appear fair under the changed circumstances.[12]

If questions of parol evidence and interpretation are answered, the facts may reveal that the parties have made a contract which one or both may later seek to avoid on the ground of *mistake*. The various types of unilateral mistake must be explored, i.e., mistake of identity, mistake of subject matter, mistake of computation or mistake of value. Both parties may make a basic assumption at the time of contract formation that is not in accord with the facts. Relief may be available under the doctrine of mutual mistake. The

---

[4] Stender v. Twin City Foods, Inc., 82 Wash. 2d 250, 510 P.2d 221 (1973). While the parties may not have consciously adverted to the possibility of unusually good weather conditions, if their purpose was to permit additional time if the harvesting process was delayed because of weather conditions, the fact that the conditions were unusually good rather than unusually bad should not deter a court from applying the clause in terms of its underlying purpose.

[5] Hurst v. W.J. Lake & Co., 141 Or. 306, 16 P.2d 627, 89 A.L.R. 1222 (1932).

[6] UCC §§ 1-205(1) and (3). *See also* Columbia Nitrogen Corp. v. Royster Co., 451 F.2d 3 (4th Cir. 1971).

[7] *See* UCC § 2-208(2).

[8] UCC § 2-208(3).

[9] *See, e.g.,* UCC §§ 1-205(4) and 2-208(3). A similar problem occurs where there is a conflict of warranties, i.e., express warranties (§ 2-313), the implied warranty of merchantability (§ 2-314) and the implied warranty of fitness for a particular purpose (§ 2-315), which is dealt with in § 2-317.

[10] Courts often use maxims (or canons) of construction or interpretation which are nothing more than common sense guidelines to assist in these matters. The maxims are criticized because there is, arguably, a counter-maxim for every maxim. *See* Llewellyn, *Remarks on the Theory of Appellate Decision and the Rules or Canons About How Statutes Are to Be Construed,* 3 VAND. L. REV. 395 (1950). While the canons, rules, or maxims are discussed in the context of statutory interpretation, they are also applied to the interpretation of contracts.

[11] Questions of excusing performance will be explored *infra* Chapter 8.

[12] *See* Parev Prods. Co. v. I. Rokeach & Sons, 124 F.2d 147 (2d Cir. 1941).

parties may have a mutual misunderstanding based on a latent ambiguity so that they each attach a different meaning to a term of their contract. Here, courts must deal with the issue of whose meaning prevails. Neither party may have made a mistake but the intermediary chosen to deliver a message may have mistakenly transmitted it or otherwise caused a reasonable recipient to believe something other than that intended by a reasonable sender. Resolution of problems created by an intermediary's mistake must be examined.

Unlike the common law principles relating to mistake, the parol evidence rule and the concept of interpretation have been significantly affected by the UCC and concomitantly by the RESTATEMENT 2d. Those modifications will also be explored in this chapter before the current judicial reaction to mistake in its various guises in the law of contracts is considered.

§ 82. The Parol Evidence Rule.

A. *Prevalence of Subsequent Expression Over Antecedent Expression.*

If parties express agreement and subsequently express another agreement, intending the subsequent agreement to prevail over their antecedent expression, their final expression will prevail. This is not a statement of the parol evidence rule. It is a much broader statement because it is accurate in the following situations:

(a) Both expressions of agreement are oral;
(b) the first expression is written and the second is oral;
(c) both expressions are written;
(d) the first expression is oral and the second is written.

The parol evidence process may become operative only in situations (c) and (d) where the second expression is evidenced by a *writing*. Yet, the general principle that the subsequent expression prevails over the antecedent expression is true in all of the foregoing situations where the parties intend the second expression to be the only operative expression of assent.[13] Where the second agreement is evidenced by a writing, the parol evidence process *may* become operative whether the prior agreement was oral or written. If one of the parties alleges that the subsequent written agreement was intended to be the final and/or complete expression of the parties' agreement, thereby discharging any prior agreement, the parol evidence process is activated. It then becomes necessary to decide a question of intention, i.e., whether the parties intended their written expression of agreement to become their final and/or complete or "integrated" expression, or, whether they intended to be bound by their prior (oral or written) agreements as well as the agreement manifested in their last writing. This is the only situation in which the parol evidence rule is invoked.[14] If the parties disagree as to the *meaning* of their manifesta-

---

[13] Professor Corbin insists that a written integration should have no greater effect upon antecedent agreements than a "parol integration" since, in both cases, the later agreement discharges the antecedent ones in so far as it contradicts or is inconsistent with the earlier ones. 3 CORBIN ON CONTRACTS § 573, at 369.

[14] *See* Murray, *The Parol Evidence Rule: A Clarification,* 4 DUQ. L. REV. 337 (1966) as cited in the leading case of Masterson v. Sine, 65 Cal. Rptr. 545, 436 P.2d 361 (1968).

tions of intention, the parol evidence rule will not resolve that disagreement since the question is one of interpretation. The parol evidence rule "defines the subject matter of interpretation"[15] but it has nothing to do with the determination of the meaning of the subject matter so defined. If one of the parties alleges that the writing does not state the true intention of the parties, the remedy of reformation may be granted on clear and convincing evidence of the mistake in the writing. Again, the parol evidence rule is not involved.

B. *The Parol Evidence Rationale — Preference for Written Evidence and Controlling Juries — Substantive Rather than Evidentiary — Procedural Function.*

Why has the relatively simple matter, the determination of the intention of the parties with respect to the finality or completeness of their last written manifestation of agreement, been described as a legal concept whose mysteries are familiar to many but fathomed by few?[16] In the first and second situations (a) and (b), *supra,* the question is simply whether the parties intended the second (last) expression to control their earlier expression of agreement and courts would determine that question in the usual fashion of determining the total agreement of the parties. In (c) and (d), however, where the last expression is written, the same question invokes the parol evidence machinery because courts have traditionally followed a policy of affording special protection to written evidence of agreements. Memories of oral understandings are fallible and are, therefore, subject to favorable or unfavorable (conscious or unconscious) recollection.[17] The written evidence of the parties' intention, on the other hand, is a permanent record of their intention, not subject to the vagaries of memory. To provide the written evidence with the strength that courts felt it deserved, they created a rule which sounded very much like a rule of evidence. The shibboleth was often stated as the inadmissibility of evidence that would "vary or contradict the terms of the writing."[18] Because judges assumed that juries would lack the necessary sophistication to provide the written evidence of the contract with the preference such evidence

---

[15]RESTATEMENT 2d § 213 comment a. This concept appears to suggest that the parol evidence application must precede the process of interpretation. If, however, a party claims that certain evidence of agreement prior to the final writing contradicts that writing, it will be necessary to interpret the writing before deciding the parol evidence question since, "No parol evidence that is offered can be said to *contradict* a writing until, by process of interpretation, it is determined what the writing means." Tigg Corp. v. Dow Corning Corp., 822 F.2d 358, 362 (3d Cir. 1987).

[16]This phrase is quoted from the first edition of this book in Astor v. Boulos Co., 451 A.2d 903 (Me. 1982). In his Preliminary Treatise on Evidence at the Common Law (1898), James Bradley Thayer starts his discussion of the parol evidence rule with the statement, "Few things are darker than this or fuller of subtle difficulties."

[17]*See* Luria Bros. & Co. v. Pielet Bros. Scrap Iron, 600 F.2d 193, 110, n.5 (7th Cir. 1979).

[18]*See* Federal Deposit Ins. Corp. v. First Mtg. Inv., 76 Wis. 2d 151, 250 N.W.2d 362 (1977); Bruce v. Blalock, 241 S.C. 155, 127 S.E.2d 439, 442, 63 A.L.R.2d 1337 (1962). A modern restatement is found in Kruse Classic Auction v. Aetna Cas. & Sur., 511 N.E.2d 326, 329 (Ind. App. 1987): Parol or extrinsic evidence is inadmissible to expand, vary, or explain the instrument unless there has been a showing of fraud, ambiguity, illegality, duress or undue influence." The court in MacLeod v. Chalet Susse Int'l, Inc., 401 A.2d 205, 208 (N.H. 1979) suggested the illusory character of such statements: "Nevertheless the apparent neatness of the stated rule is misleading; for whether extrinsic evidence is offered to 'interpret' rather than to 'vary' the terms of the writing, or whether the writing is indeed the 'complete and accurate integration' of the agreement rather than a partial or incomplete integration are, in may cases, questions not easily answered."

deserved over the relatively unreliable prior oral expressions, the judges re-served to themselves the determination of the admissibility of the prior evidence. They did so even though the question was clearly one of fact,[19] i.e., was there an oral agreement and, if so, did the parties intend to abandon that agreement when they expressed themselves in writing? This *procedural* function of the parol evidence rule,[20] however, is undermined by the fact that parol evidenced is deemed inadmissible whether the evidence of the prior agreement is *oral or written*. A more comprehensive statement of the rule may be stated as follows:

If the parties to a transaction have embodied that transaction in whole or in part in a single memorial such as a writing or writings, and if they regard that memorial as the final expression of their intention as a whole, or of a part thereof, then all other prior or contemporaneous utterances by the parties in connection with that transaction, whether oral or written, are inoperative for the purpose of ascertaining the terms of their contract, or at least so much of it as it embodied in the memorial.[21]

The fact that this rule is one of substantive law rather than a rule of evidence has been amply demonstrated for many years by scholars[22] and courts.[23] Thus, even if a party failed at trial to object to the admission of evidence violating the rule, the evidence would not be considered operative on appeal.[24] Similarly, a Federal court required to apply state law under the familiar doctrine of *Erie R.R. v. Tompkins*[25] would apply the state parol evidence rule because it is a rule of substantive law rather than a rule of evidence.[26] Thus, the purpose of the rule is much broader than one of keeping oral

---

[19] Courts characterize the question as one of fact. *See* Luria Bros. & Co. v. Pielet Bros. Scrap Iron, 600 F.2d 103 (7th Cir. 1979); Peter Pan Seafoods, Inc. v. Olympic Foundry Co., 17 Wash. App. 761, 565 F.2d 819 (1977). A few courts have held that such a question of fact may be submitted to the jury. *See, e.g.,* Associated Hardware Supply Co. v. Big Wheel Distrib. Co., 355 F.2d 114 (3d Cir. 1966).

[20] The procedural function of the parol evidence rule is related to rules of evidence insofar as the origin for both is common, i.e., the distrust of juries. Professor McCormick presents a very clear picture of this functions and its origins in Chapter 24 of his book. *See,* in particular, C. McCormick, Handbook on the Law of Evidence § 214 (1954).

[21] This statement is quoted, in the slightly different form in which it appeared in the second edition of this book, in Friestad v. Travelers Indem. Co., 260 Pa. Super. 178, 393 A.2d 1212 (1978). In Corn Exch. Nat'l Bank & Trust Co. v. Taubel, 113 N.J.L. 605, 175 A. 55, 58 (1934), the court states, "[W]here, as here, the parties have made a memorial of their bargain, or a writing is required by law, their actual intent unless expressed in some way in the writing is ineffective, except when it may, in accordance with established principles, afford the basis for a reformation of the writing. While the intention of the parties is sought, it can be found only in their expression in the writing. In effect, it is not the real intent but the intent expressed or apparent in the writing that controls.... Otherwise, there would be a disregard of the well-settled rule forbidding the introduction of parol evidence to contradict the terms of the written contract."

[22] The scholars dealing with the law of Evidence include: J. Wigmore, Evidence § 2400 (3d ed. 1940); J. Thayer, Preliminary Treatise on Evidence at the Common Law, 390, 397 (1898). The two giants of contract law concur: 4 Williston § 631, and 3 Corbin § 573.

[23] *See* Lower Kuskokwim Sch. Dist. v. Alaska Diversified Contrs., 734 P.2d 62 (Alaska 1987); Franklin v. White, 493 N.E.2d 161 (Ind. 1986); Peter Pan Seafoods, Inc. v. Olympic Foundry Co., 17 Wash. App. 761, 565 P.2d 819 (1977); Farmers Mut. Hail Ins. Co. v. Fox Turkey Farms, Inc., 301 F.2d 697 (8th Cir. 1962).

[24] *See* Lower Kuskokwim Sch. Dist. v. Alaska Diversified Contrs., 734 P.2d 62 (Alaska 1987); Tuttle v. Simpson, 735 S.W.2d 539 (Tex. Ct. App. 1987); First Tennessee Bank Nat'l Ass'n v. Wilson, 713 S.W.2d 907 (Tenn. App. 1985).

[25] 304 U.S. 64 (1938).

[26] Beta Labs. v. Hines, 647 F.2d 402 (3d Cir. 1981).

evidence from juries who might give such evidence undue significance when comparing it with a later written statement of the parties' agreement. It is important to consider the justifiable purpose of the parol evidence rule.

C. *The Justifiable Purpose of the Parol Evidence Rule — The Corbin View.*

The most important critic of the parol evidence rule is Professor Corbin, who suggests that the parol evidence rule and the statute of frauds have a similar purpose, i.e., the prevention of successful fraud and perjury, and each of the rules only haltingly attains its purpose.[27] He suggests that both the statute and the rule may have caused more litigation and harm than they have prevented and that both are attempts to determine justice and truth by a mechanistic device evidencing a distrust of the capacity of courts and juries to weigh human credibility.[28] Other critics of the parol evidence rule point to its complexity as suggested by the numerous tests applied by courts in efforts to apply the rule.[29] The suggestions of Professor Corbin should never be dismissed lightly, and there is no doubt that courts have engaged in a number of intellectually untidy exercises in attempts to apply the parol evidence rule. There is, however, a single justification for the rule that should be emphasized.

Even Professor Corbin would insist that any contract, regardless of how it is made or evidenced, can be discharged or modified by a subsequent agreement of the parties. In his refreshing and illuminating fashion, Corbin states the proposition very simply: "Today may control the effect of what happened yesterday; but what happened yesterday cannot change the effect of what happens today. This, it is believed, is the substance of what has been unfortunately called the 'parol evidence rule.'"[30] If the parties have made certain agreements and subsequently intend to discharge or modify them, or if they have had preliminary discussions and then form a contract with the intention of being bound solely and exclusively by the terms of a final and complete writing, there is no reason to preclude their intention to be bound only by what appears in their final expression of agreement. Ordinarily, that final and complete expression of agreement is in the form of a writing, signed by both parties. It need not be in that form[31] though no court would characterize a complete and final *oral* integration of the parties' agreement as the type of final expression giving rise to the application of the parol evidence rule. Here lies Professor Corbin's basic quarrel with the parol evidence rule. He suggests that the parties' final expression of agreement should control, but, "This is the ordinary substantive law of contracts; it is not a rule of evidence and is not stated in the language of evidence, parol or otherwise."[32] Corbin would, therefore, eliminate much if not all of the complexity currently attending the appli-

---

[27] 3 CORBIN § 575.

[28] *Ibid.*

[29] *See, e.g.,* Sweet, *Contract Making and Parol Evidence: Diagnosis and Treatment of a Sick Rule,* 53 CORNELL L.Q. 1036 (1968).

[30] 3 CORBIN § 574 at 372.

[31] "Indeed, the parties to an oral agreement may choose their words with such explicit precision and completeness that the same legal consequences follows as where there is a completely integrated agreement." RESTATEMENT 2d § 209 (comment b.).

[32] 3 CORBIN § 574 at 375.

cation of the rule and criticized by others. Certainly, he identifies the basic justification for a rule of law that would fulfill the intention of the parties who seek to be bound exclusively by the terms of the final expression of their agreement. Indeed, this section began with an emphasis upon the basic rule of substantive contract law that the last expression of agreement, whether oral or written, should be the controlling expression if that is the parties' intention. Thus, Corbin does not disagree with what may be called the sole justification for the parol evidence rule. Rather, he convincingly suggests that the purpose of the parol evidence rule can and should be attained without regard to whether the final expression is written or oral and that we can properly avoid any discussion of "parol" or "evidence." It should be recalled that there is no doubt among those courts applying the "parol" evidence rule that it applies to oral or written evidence of agreement prior to the final writing. Notwithstanding his monumental contributions to twentieth century contract law, Corbin's penetrating view of the parol evidence process has not been accepted by the courts nor by the RESTATEMENT 2d though, as will be seen in a later section, the RESTATEMENT 2d was influenced by his views. It is, therefore, essential to consider the parol evidence rule as applied by the courts in all of its sometimes Byzantine complexity which may make the rule appear to be one whose mysteries are familiar to many but fathomed by few.

§ 83. The Parol Evidence Rule — "Inconsistent" and "Contradictory" — Form of Writing — The Meaning of "Integration."

A. *The Possible Intention of the Parties.*

The parties to a contract may express their assent in oral or written language or by their conduct. The terms of their agreement may be discovered in any combination of such manifestations of assent. When the parties take the time and trouble to express their agreement in writing or writings, three possibilities arise: (1) they do not intend their written expression to preclude evidence of other expressions of agreement; (2) they intend their writing to be final as to any matters contained in the writing, but they also intend to be bound to other manifestations of agreement not contained in the writing; (3) the parties not only intend their writing to be the final expression of their agreement with respect to the matters set forth in the writing; they also intend their writing to be the *complete* and *exclusive* manifestation of their agreement, i.e., they do not intend *any* other manifestation of their agreement prior to the writing to be operative. In the last section, we saw the question of intention as one of fact though it will be decided by judges rather than jurors. If the parties clearly express their intention as to whether their writing is final, complete, or neither, there will be no question as to the effect of their written expression of agreement since they have consciously adverted to the question and directed that their writing have one or another effect. A common method for achieving a manifestation of intention in the writing that the writing is complete and final is a clause that is often called a "merger" clause which simply expresses the parties' intention that their writing was intended to be complete and final.[33] The same clause may also be called an "integration" clause or even a "zipper" clause which is discussed in a subsequent section. If the parties do not expressly indicate their intention as to the character of their writing, i.e., either final, complete or neither, a court will then decide which of the three possibilities is more likely under all of the relevant circumstances.

B. *The Unlikely First Possibility.*

Absent countervailing evidence, the first possibility — that the parties did not intend their writing to eclipse any prior manifestations of agreement — is unlikely. If the parties have taken the time and trouble to express themselves in writing, certainly evidence of prior *contradictory* agreements would appear to be less credible than the subsequent written agreement. Assuming the prior agreement was made, if the parties later executed a written agreement containing contradictory terms, the later expression of agreement should prevail on the rudimentary principle of contract law that the parties may always agree today to rescind or modify their agreement of yesterday.[34] Thus, where there is a final writing, an extrinsic term (prior to the writing) which is *inconsistent* with the terms of the writing, in the sense that it contradicts or negates a written term,[35] will not be operative since this is the apparent intention of the parties.

C. *The Form of the Writing.*

The written expression of the parties need not be in any particular form. It may be in one document, or it may appear in more than one informal writings such as letters, telegrams or the like.[36]

---

[33] A clause stating the parties' intention that the writing supersede all prior agreements and that it constitute the entire contract of the parties helps to resolve the question of the parties' intent concerning the effect of their written expression of agreement. It does not, however, conclusively establish the parties' intention, i.e., the extrinsic matter must still be examined to determine whether the parties intended it to be a part of their operative bargain. *See* Gerdlund v. Electronic Dispenser Int'l, 190 Cal. App. 3d 263, 235 Cal. Rptr. 279 (1987).

[34] *See* the previous discussion of the Corbin analysis *supra* § 82(C).

[35] The prior term may be characterized as "inconsistent" with the terms of the subsequent writing. In Hatley v. Stafford, 284 Or. 523, 588 P.2d 603 (1978), the court quotes Hunt Foods & Indus. v. Doliner, 26 App. Div. 41, 270 N.Y.S.2d 937, 940 (1966) as follows: "In a sense any oral provision which would prevent the ripening of the obligations of a writing is inconsistent with the writing. But that obviously is not the sense in which the word is used.... To be inconsistent the term must contradict or negate a term of the writing." In § 213 comment b., the RESTATEMENT 2d suggests, "Whether a binding agreement is completely integrated or partially integrated, it supersedes inconsistent terms of prior agreements." (The distinction between "partially integrated" and "fully integrated" is explored later in this section.) Again, in comment b to § 215, the RESTATEMENT 2d suggests, "Whether there is a contradiction depends, as is stated in § 213, on whether the two are consistent or inconsistent." Thus, the RESTATEMENT 2d may be said to equate "inconsistent" with "contradictory." In Michigan Nat'l Bank v. Holland-Dozier-Holland, Etc., 73 Mich. App. 12, 250 N.W.2d 532 (1976), the court adopted this construction citing Murray, *The Parol Evidence Process and Standardized Agreements Under the Restatement (Second) of Contracts,* 123 U. PA. L. REV. 1342, 1362 (1975).

[36] RESTATEMENT 2d § 209 comment b. A question arose concerning the UCC statement of the parol evidence rule which refers to "confirmatory memoranda" in § 2-202. In the last edition of this book, it was suggested that the UCC version would permit either a single confirmatory memorandum or more than one writing to operate as an "integration" because § 2-202 also refers to "a writing." *See* CALAMARI & PERILLO, CONTRACTS at 151-52 (1986): "Another interesting

D. *The Second and Third Possibilities — The* RESTATEMENT *2d and "Integration."*

Having decided that prior inconsistent statements of the parties will be inoperative, a court will likely decide that the second possibility is the appropriate interpretation of the parties' intention, i.e., that the parties intended their writing to be final as to any matters set forth in the writing. The parties, however, may have also intended their writing to be not only final as to the matters set forth therein; they may have intended the writing to be their complete and exclusive manifestation of agreement, i.e., the third possibility. In this situation, evidence of *any* prior agreement between the parties — even consistent (non-contradictory) agreements — would be excluded since the parties intended to be bound only by the terms of the writing which they viewed as the *exclusive* repository of their agreement. Whether the parties intended their writing to be complete as well as final is the most difficult question of intention for courts to decide. In a subsequent section certain tests used by courts to provide guidance with respect to this question of intention will be explored. At this point, it is of critical importance that the student concentrate on the threshold question in the application of the parol evidence rule: *Did the parties intend their writing to be final at least as to the matters expressed therein, or did they intend their writing to be both final and complete so that no prior expression of agreement of any kind will be operative?*

E. *The Meaning of "Integrated" — "Fully" and "Partially" Integrated.*

If a court determines that the parties intended their writing to be *final and complete,* the writing is said to be "fully integrated." If, however, the parties intended their writing to be only *final* as to the matters expressed therein but not complete as to any consistent extrinsic matter, the writing is said to be "partially integrated."[37] Unfortunately, considerable emphasis has been placed on the term "integrated" as if it were an effective analytical tool. The RESTATEMENT 2d uses the phrase "parol evidence rule" in connection with a section captioned, "Effect of Integrated Agreement on Prior Agreements."[38] Subsections (1) and (2) of this section have the qualities of truisms: (1) a binding integrated agreement has the effect of discharging prior agreements to the extent that they are inconsistent with the 'integrated' writing;[39] (2) a

---

question is whether it is possible under the Code to have a total integration based upon a single confirmatory memorandum. It has been argued that this result may no longer obtain because of the use of the words 'confirmatory memoranda.' [citing Album Graphics, Inc. v. Beatrice Foods Co., 87 Ill. App. 3d 338, 41 Ill. Dec. 332, 408 N.E.2d 1041 (1980).] Professor Murray disagrees and argues that a single confirmatory memorandum may still operate as [a] total integration under the Code and Professor Farnsworth agrees with him."

[37] The UCC does not use the phrases, "partially integrated" or "fully integrated." Rather, it uses the terms, "final expression" which is comparable to "partially integrated" and "complete and exclusive statement" which is comparable to "fully integrated." *See* UCC § 2-202.

[38] RESTATEMENT 2d § 213.

[39] The RESTATEMENT 2d uses the phrase "integrated agreement" rather than the phrase "integrated writing." This phraseology is confusing because it does not emphasize the important distinction between the two terms. Any written expression of the agreement is nothing more than the manifestation of agreement. It is not the agreement. "Two forms of intention must be distinguished if any attempt to understand the parol evidence process is to be successful. In order to have any binding agreement, the parties must intend to be bound to certain obligations they have

binding *completely* integrated agreement discharges prior agreements to the extent that they are within the scope of the completed integrated writing.[40] Recognizing that the term "integrated" is not very useful, the RESTATEMENT 2d Reporter could discover no better term.[41] The term "integrated" states a conclusion rather than a test. Only a comment to this RESTATEMENT 2d section begins to reveal the underlying problem:

> Whether a binding agreement is completely integrated or partially integrated, it supersedes inconsistent terms of prior agreements. To apply this rule, the court must make preliminary determinations that there is an integrated agreement and that it is inconsistent with the term in question.[42]

The essence of the so-called parol evidence rule is found in the *process* used by courts to make these "preliminary determinations." How does a court go about deciding whether the parties intended their written expression to be the final or final and complete statement of their agreement, i.e., how does a court decide whether the writing is "partially integrated" (or to use the terminology of the UCC, a "final expression") or "fully integrated" ("complete and exclusive statement" in UCC terminology)?[43] This is not only the threshhold question — it is the *only* question which must be pursued to understand the "parol evidence rule." There are many facets to this question and several accepted guides which courts use in their efforts to arrive at the conclusion of partial or complete integration. It is, therefore, highly preferable to view this judicial effort as a process rather than the application of a mechanical rule. This process will be explored in detail.

---

voluntarily undertaken.... The parol evidence process, on the other hand, is concerned with a different intention, the intention to be bound exclusively to those undertakings evidenced by a writing or writings." Murray, *The Parol Evidence Process and Standardized Agreements Under the Restatement (Second) of Contracts,* 125 U. PA. L. REV. 1342, 1353-54 (1975).

[40] *Id.* Courts are not always precise in their use of the terms, "partially integrated" or "fully" or "completely" integrated. For example, in South Side Plumbing Co. v. Tigges, 525 S.W.2d 583, 588 (Mo. App. 1975), the court suggests that prior or contemporaneous agreements which vary or contradict the terms of a written instrument are not admissible if the instrument "is a complete integration of the parties' agreement...." Later, the court suggests that, "Testimony concerning a prior or contemporaneous agreement, if consistent with the writing, may supplement a writing incomplete on its face, but should not be permitted to vary or contradict the writing." If, however, the writing is "a complete integration," even consistent prior terms should not be admissible. If by the phrase "incomplete on its face" the court meant to suggest that the writing would not be a "complete integration" but would only be a "partial integration," its statement is reconcilable with generally accepted distinctions between "partial" and "complete" integrations. Since the court was dealing with what it viewed as a "complete integration" because of a "merger" or "integration" clause in the writing, however, it is difficult to assure such a reconciliation.

[41] 68 ALI Proceedings 446 (1971).

[42] RESTATEMENT 2d § 213 comment b. *See also* McGuire v. Schneider, Inc., 534 A.2d 115 (Pa. Super. 1987); City of Warwick v. Boeing Corp., 111 Idaho 68, 720 P.2d 1033 (1986); Chain Inv. Co. v. Cohen, 15 Mass. App. 4, 443 N.E.2d 126 (1982).

[43] *See supra* note 37.

§ 84. The Parol Evidence Process — Tests.

Once it is recognized that the critical question in the parol evidence process is how a judge determines whether the writing is integrated, and then, whether it is partially ("finally") or fully ("completely") integrated, a significant amount of the mystery surrounding the parol evidence rule is removed. The response to the critical question is, however, the subject of considerable controversy. At first glance, the question appears quite simple, i.e., did the parties intend the writing to be their final and/or complete statement of agreement? In determining precisely how the judge proceeds to deal with that question, however, the courts and scholars have devised various tests and the UCC has added its own. The RESTATEMENT 2d has attempted to incorporate all of the tests as well as the conflicting views of the giants of Contract law, Professor Williston and Professor Corbin. Unfortunately, the result has been to add to the confusion surrounding the parol evidence rule. This section provides a critical analysis of each of the tests. To avoid unnecessary confusion, certain preliminary questions will be examined before each of the tests is explored.

A. "Prior" Versus "Contemporaneous" Statements.

The FIRST RESTATEMENT made any oral or written agreements prior to a written integration inoperative, and it also made "all contemporaneous oral agreements relating to the same subject matter" inoperative.[44] If the contemporaneous agreement was in writing, however, it became part of the integration.[45] The rationale for the exclusion of oral agreements contemporaneous with an integration was based on the definition of "integration." "An integration by definition contains what the parties agreed upon as a complete statement of their promises."[46] If, therefore, the parties have agreed that their writing contains a complete statement of their undertakings, they do not intend to be bound by any contemporaneous oral agreements. Professor Corbin found error in this view. If "contemporaneous" meant "simultaneous," Corbin could not understand how the parties could have assented to a complete and final writing and, at the same time, assented to the oral addition evidenced by the contemporaneous oral agreement. If the parties had assented to both the terms of the writing and a contemporaneous (simultaneous) oral agreement, unassailable logic compelled the conclusion that the writing was not a complete integration because, "One cannot express simultaneous assent to two things and at the same instant agree that one of them supplants the other."[47] Once the parties are found to have assented to a complete integration, Corbin suggested that there is no simultaneous oral addition.[48] If "contemporaneous" does not mean "simultaneous," the oral agreement was either before or after the integration. The parol evidence rule would apply to such an

---

[44] FIRST RESTATEMENT § 237.

[45] FIRST RESTATEMENT § 237 comment a. See McDonald's Corp. v. Butler Co., 158 Ill. App. 3d 902, 511 N.E.2d 912 (1987) in which the court states that the parol evidence rule does not bar contemporaneous written documents from being admitted.

[46] FIRST RESTATEMENT § 237 comment b.

[47] 3 CORBIN § 577 at 401.

[48] Ibid.

agreement made before a valid integration, and would have no applicability to an agreement made after the integration since the rule does not affect subsequent modifications.[49]

The use or nonuse of "contemporaneous" along with "prior" in statements of the parol evidence rule provides one of several sterling examples of the RESTATEMENT 2d effort to be all things to all persons and, in particular, to reconcile the Williston/First Restatement analysis of the rule with the perceptions of Professor Corbin. In one of the critical sections of the parol evidence analysis, the RESTATEMENT 2d conspicuously avoids the use of "contemporaneous"[50] but adds the term in the next section.[51] The explanation admits that the Reporter was torn between the logic of Corbin and the pull of tradition.[52] Elsewhere, this author suggested that the RESTATEMENT 2d permits "the grotesque possibility ... that prior, but not contemporaneous, inconsistent agreements will be superseded by binding integrated agreements, while both prior and contemporaneous agreements or negotiations will be inadmissible to contradict the terms of a binding integrated agreement."[53] One court has reacted to this concern by holding that the parol evidence rule applies to both prior and contemporaneous agreements.[54] The typical judicial statement of the parol evidence rule continues to preclude "contemporaneous" as well as prior understandings[55] and the UCC version of the parol evidence rule also precludes "contemporaneous" as well as prior agreements.[56]

B. *Admissibility of Evidence Concerning Intention to Integrate.*

Unless the parties intend their writing to be an integrated writing, the parol evidence rule is inapplicable. Thus, the preliminary determination for a court is to determine whether the parties intended their writing to be a final or final and complete statement of the terms of their contract. Only after determining that the writing is integrated should the parol evidence rule apply to preclude evidence of prior or contemporaneous agreements. This preliminary determination permits admission of all relevant evidence, i.e., there is no question of exclusion of evidence until it is determined that the parol

---

[49] *Ibid.* "The swath of the parol evidence rule is not so broad as to prevent a showing of subsequent oral modifications." Michigan Nat'l Bank v. Holland-Dozier-Holland, Etc., 73 Mich. App. 12, 250 N.W.2d 532, 533 (1976).

[50] RESTATEMENT 2d § 213.

[51] RESTATEMENT 2d § 214.

[52] The Reporter included "contemporaneous" in the subsequent section (§ 214) at the suggestion of an unidentified member of the American Law Institute, explaining the omission in § 213 as follows: "I left out the 'or contemporaneous' partly because Professor Corbin was so opposed to the idea, and partly because I don't know that anything is ever contemporaneous with anything else really, it either comes before or after. But it can be relatively contemporaneous, and I think what we say here is that evidence of prior or contemporaneous agreements or negotiations is not admissible in evidence to contradict the term of the writing, that is to say, show a different agreement from the one that the writing would show." 48 ALI Proceedings 449 (1971).

[53] Murray, *The Parol Evidence Process and Standardized Agreements under the Restatement (Second) of Contracts,* 123 U. PA. L. REV. 1342, 1363 (1975).

[54] Michigan Nat'l Bank v. Holland-Dozier-Holland, Etc., 73 Mich. App. 12, 250 N.W.2d 532, 534, n.1 (1975) where the court quotes material appearing in the text at the preceding note (53).

[55] For a recent illustration, *see* Marani v. Jackson, 183 Cal. App. 3d 695, 228 Cal. Rptr. 518 (1986).

[56] UCC § 2-202.

evidence rule is operative, and the rule becomes operative only after it is determined that the parties intended to adopt their writing as a final (partially integrated) or complete and exclusive (fully integrated) writing. It would be difficult to discover any modern case law in disagreement with this view.[57]

C. Tests Used in the Application of the Parol Evidence Rule.

A trial judge is confronted with the application of the parol evidence rule, and must decide whether to admit or exclude evidence of agreements or negotiations occurring prior to (or contemporaneously with) the writing. In a jury trial, the judge must ascertain that the jury is unaware of the evidence extrinsic to the writing unless and until he decides to admit it. In a nonjury trial, the judge finds the facts and also applies the law. In that situation, as will be seen, he may consider extrinsic evidence for the purpose of determining its admissibility and later decide that it should be excluded. Then, as the fact finder, he must not consider the evidence which he earlier excluded. It is important to have a precise understanding of the various tests that have been created by courts to guide the trial judge in these determinations. We will now examine each of these tests.

1. The "Appearance" or "Four Corners" Test.

As suggested earlier, the question before the court is one of intention, i.e., did the parties intend their writing(s) to be the final (partially integrated) or complete and exclusive (fully integrated) memorial of their agreement? The first step in this process is for the judge to examine the writing. It is possible to discover cases holding that the entire parol evidence process is contained in this examination. Thus, if the judge simply examines the writing and, from its appearance alone, determines that it is "complete," he will refuse to admit any evidence of prior understandings.[58] Under this test, the writing is the sole criterion of its own completeness. Such a rule borders on the absurd. As Dean Wigmore suggested long ago, "The conception of a writing as wholly and intrinsically self-determinative of the parties' intent to make it a sole memorial of one or seven or twenty-seven subjects of negotiation is an impossible one."[59] The critical question is whether the writing was intended to cover certain subjects of negotiation, and that cannot be known until the writing is *compared* with the extrinsic matter. The judge admits the evidence provisionally, out of the earshot of the jury in a jury trial, to determine whether he will subsequently admit or exclude the evidence.[60] The RESTATEMENT 2d suggests

---

[57] Among the cases supporting this proposition, *see* Schultz v. Delta-Rail Corp., 156 Ill. App. 3d 1, 108 Ill. Dec. 566, 508 N.E.2d 1143 (1987); Marani v. Jackson, 183 Cal. App. 3d 695, 228 Cal. Rptr. 518 (1986); Union Bank v. Swenson, 707 P.2d 663 (Utah 1985); J. W. Burge v. Frey, 545 F. Supp. 1160 (D. Kan. 1982); Federal Deposit Ins. Corp. v. First Mtg. Inv., 76 Wis. 2d 151, 250 N.W.2d 362 (1977); Rempel v. Nationwide Life Ins. Co., 471 Pa. 404, 370 A.2d 366 (1977). *See also* RESTATEMENT 2d § 214(a) and (b).

[58] *See, e.g.,* Seitz v. Brewers' Refrig. Mach. Co., 141 U.S. 510, 517 (1891); Eighmie v. Taylor, 98 N.Y. 288 (1885).

[59] 9 WIGMORE, EVIDENCE § 2431, at 103 (3d ed. 1940).

[60] *Id.* § 2430(2) at 98.

the viability of the "appearance" test in one section[61] but apparently returns to a sound analysis in the next section.[62] The RESTATEMENT 2d is anything but clear with respect to the appearance test and this typifies its approach throughout its analysis of the parol evidence process, i.e., attempting to be all tests to all courts.[63] It is, however, reasonably safe to interpret the RESTATE- MENT 2d as refusing to adopt the outmoded notion of permitting a writing to be the sole source of proving its own completeness. The "appearance" test has been expressly rejected in a number of cases including the landmark opinion by Justice Traynor in *Masterson v. Sine*.[64] In other opinions, it may be men- tioned along with other tests, but it is usually ignored as one or more of the other tests is set forth as the basis for the decision.[65]

2. Merger Clause Test.

If the central question in determining the completeness of the writing is one of the intention of the parties, should a clear statement of that intention in the parties' writing conclusively establish the writing as a complete and exclusive statement of their intention so as to require a court to refuse to admit any evidence of prior understandings, simply because of the statement in the writing? The parties may include a "merger" ("integration" or "zipper") clause in their writing stating that the writing constitutes the sole and exclusive repository of the parties' agreement and somewhat redundantly adding that they do not intend to be bound by any other agreement, understanding or negotiation of whatsoever kind or nature.[66] Professor Corbin and Professor Williston suggest that such a merger clause should have conclusive effect in determining an integration unless the writing was obviously incomplete, the clause was inserted as a result of fraud or mistake, or there are grounds to set aside the contract.[67] Corbin is careful to point out that such a clause does not prove that the writing itself was ever assented to or became operative as a

---

[61] "Where the parties reduce an agreement to a writing which in view of its completeness and specificity reasonably appears to be a complete agreement, it is taken to be an integrated agree- ment unless it is established by other evidence that the writing did not constitute a final expres- sion." RESTATEMENT 2d § 209(3). This section is relied upon in United Artists Commun., Inc. v. Corporate Prop. Investors, 410 N.W.2d 39 (Minn. App. 1987).

[62] "A document in the form of a written contract, signed by both parties and apparently com- plete on its face, may be decisive of the issue [of the intention of the parties to adopt the writing as a completely integrated agreement] in the absence of credible contrary evidence. *But a writing cannot of itself prove its own completeness, and wide latitude must be allowed for inquiry into circumstances bearing on the intention of the parties.*" RESTATEMENT 2d § 210 comment b (em- phasis added).

[63] For a complete analysis of the RESTATEMENT 2d parol evidence analysis, *see* Murray, *The Parol Evidence Process and Standardized Agreements Under the Restatement (Second) of Con- tracts*, 123 U. PA. L. REV. 1342 (1975) as cited in the Reporter's Note after the introduction to Topic 3. Effect of Adoption of a Writing to the Second Restatement, §§ 209-18.

[64] 65 Cal. Rptr. 545, 436 P.2d 561 (1968).

[65] *See, e.g.,* the well-known case of Gianni v. Russel & Co., 281 Pa. 320, 126 A. 791 (1924). For a more modern illustration, *see* Traudt v. Nebraska Pub. Power Dist., 197 Neb. 765, 251 N.W.2d 148 (1977).

[66] In Betz Labs. v. Hines, 647 F.2d 402, 403 (3d Cir. 1981) the following merger clause appeared in the writing: "This agreement contains the whole agreement between the Seller and Buyer and there are no other terms, obligations, covenants, representations, statements or conditions, oral or otherwise, of any kind whatsoever."

[67] 4 WILLISTON § 633; 3 CORBIN § 578.

contract.[68] The RESTATEMENT 2d suggests that a merger clause *"if agreed to"* is likely to conclude the issue whether the agreement is completely integrated."[69] The phrase, "if agreed to," is later amplified with the Corbin influence, "But such a clause does not control the question whether the writing was assented to as an integrated agreement...."[70] Another possible interpretation of "if agreed to" and the attendant requirement of "assent," may suggest a distinction between a printed merger clause in a standard form and a negotiated merger clause which the parties have apparently consciously considered. The problem with printed clauses in standardized agreements will be considered later in this volume. For now, it is appropriate to suggest that serious questions attend their enforceability. Absent evidence that the parties have consciously considered and assented to a printed merger clause, it should not be afforded conclusive effect with respect to the question of integration.[71]

The RESTATEMENT 2d refuses to give conclusive effect to a merger clause. Though admitting that such a clause "is likely to conclude" the question of integration,[72] it insists that "such a declaration may not be conclusive."[73] Several cases have also shown reluctance in affording conclusive effect to such clauses, i.e., a judge may not ignore the collateral evidence simply because the writing contains a merger clause.[74] A number of other courts, however, follow the path created by Williston[75] in holding such clauses conclusive absent fraud, mistake, or another reason for setting aside the contract.[76] There can be

---

[68] *See* CORBIN § 578 at 405.

[69] RESTATEMENT 2d § 216 comment e (emphasis added).

[70] *Id.*

[71] *See* Levien Leasing Co. v. Dickey Co., 380 N.W.2d 748 (Iowa App. 1985) where the court distinguishes a prior holding involving a negotiated ("handcrafted") contract in Montgomery Props. Corp. v. Economy Forms Corp., 305 N.W.2d 470 (Iowa 1981) from the "boilerplate motor vehicle lease" containing a printed merger clause which did not convince the court that the parties intended the lease to be a complete expression of the parties' agreement. Jordan v. Doonan Truck & Equip., Inc., 220 Kan. 431, 552 P.2d 881 (1976) where the court held that a printed merger clause in a purchase order was effective to preclude parol evidence may appear to be contra. It is important to note, however, that the undisputed evidence revealed that the appellant read the entire purchase order contract and saw a handwritten warranty disclaimer that the truck was "Sold as is, where is, no warranty." In Zinn v. Walker, 87 N.C. App. 325, 361 S.E.2d 314 (1987), the court refused to give effect to a preprinted merger clause where the parties manifested their intention to include collateral agreements in their contract. On the general problem of standardized printed forms and the parol evidence rule, *see* Darner Motor Sales v. Universal Underwriters, 140 Ariz. 383, 682 P.2d 388 (1984). *See also* Broude, *The Consumer and the Parol Evidence Rule: Section 2-202 of the Uniform Commercial Code,* 1970 DUKE L.J. 881, 889 where the author directs attention to language in comment 3 to an early version of UCC § 2-202 which was later deleted: "[B]oth parties must have intended the writing to be a complete and exclusive statement of the terms agreed upon." The author suggests that the deletion is "perhaps explainable on the ground that it merely restated what was already set out in section 2-202(b) and was thereby excised as redundant."

[72] RESTATEMENT 2d § 216 comment e.

[73] RESTATEMENT 2d § 209 comment b.

[74] *See, e.g.,* Gerdlund v. Electronic Dispenser Int'l, 190 Cal. App. 3d 263, 235 Cal. Rptr. 279, 282 (1987) (Our Supreme Court held in *Masterson v. Sine* that such a clause, while it certainly helps to resolve the issue, does not of itself establish an integration; the collateral agreement itself must be examined in order to determine whether the parties intended it to be part of their bargain." To the same effect, *see* Matthews v. Drew Chem. Corp., 475 F.2d 146 (5th Cir. 1973) and Anderson & Nafziger v. G. T. Newcomb, Inc., 100 Idaho 175, 595 P.2d 709 (1979).

[75] *See supra* text at note 67.

[76] *See, e.g.,* Colafrancesco v. Crown Pontiac-GMC, Inc., 485 So. 2d 1131 (Ala. 1986); FMC Corp. v. Seal Tape Ltd., 90 Misc. 2d 1043, 396 N.Y.S.2d 993 (1977). *See also* Jordan v. Doonan Truck & Equip., Inc., *supra* note 71.

no question that evidence of fraud, mistake or other invalidating causes cannot be precluded by a merger clause.[77] In the absence of such invalidating clauses, if the parties have assented to a negotiated merger clause, why should a court even consider extrinsic evidence of a prior agreement? One possible answer is found in a case where a writing containing a merger clause did not mention the principal inducement for the plaintiff's execution of the writing. The court held that the merger clause stating that the writing contained the entire agreement "means that the writing contains the entire agreement as to its limited subject matter alone."[78] Thus, an agreement may be "partially integrated" and the writing evidencing that agreement will not contain evidence of other, non-contradictory agreements between the parties. Thus, if the parties intended to be bound only by the terms of the writing with respect to the subject matter of the writing, such evidence may be admissible even in the face of a merger clause in the partially integrated agreement. A carefully drafted merger clause, however, could avoid such a holding if it was assented to and there was no evidence of fraud or the like.

3. The Natural Inclusion Test — Williston/Corbin — *Gianni v. Russel* — *Mitchill v. Lath* — *Masterson v. Sine.*

If the writing of the parties appears to be complete though it contains no merger clause, the court must decide the question of integration. If the question of whether the extrinsic (prior) agreement is to be operative is determined on the usual basis of the intention of the parties, Professor Williston is concerned that the parol evidence rule would be destroyed.[79] Consider, for example, the facts of a well-known case.[80] Gianni leased space in an office building conducting a business which included selling tobacco, fruit, candy and soft drinks. Russel acquired the property and negotiated a new lease with Gianni which contained a provision that the lessee would thereafter sell only fruit, candy, soda water and the like, but that he would not sell tobacco in any form. The lease was carefully read to Gianni by his daughter. Shortly after this lease was signed, Russel leased the adjoining room in the building to a pharmacy that began to sell soda water and soft drinks. Gianni contended that two days before signing the lease, he had been assured that he had the exclusive right to sell these products and that he had surrendered his right to

---

[77]*See* Betz Labs. v. Hines, 647 F.2d 402 (3d Cir. 1981) which relies upon the second edition of this book as authority for the proposition that an "integration" (merger) clause is part of the contract and if fraud taints the relationship between the parties, the integration clause is, itself, struck down. RESTATEMENT 2d § 214(d) which lists evidence of illegality, fraud, duress, mistake, lack of consideration, or other invalidating causes as not being barred by the parol evidence rule even in the face of a merger clause. *See* GTE Automatic Elec. Inc. v. Martin's Inc., 127 A.D.2d 545, 512 N.Y.S.2d 107 (1987) (evidence of fraudulent misrepresentations are not barred by the parol evidence rule); Franklin v. White, 493 N.E.2d 161 (Ind. 1986) (parol evidence rule does not bar evidence of mistake); City of Warwick v. Boeing Corp., 472 A.2d 1214 (R.I. 1984) (parol evidence rule does not bar evidence of lack of consideration). A contrary view which should be rejected is found in Danann Realty Corp. v. Harris, 5 N.Y.2d 317, 157 N.E.2d 597 (1959).

[78]Gem Corrugated Box Corp. v. National Kraft Container Corp., 427 F. Supp. 499, 503 (1970) (principal inducement for plaintiff to purchase its requirements of boxes was stock purchase plan not mentioned in the writing).

[79]4 WILLISTON § 633.

[80]Gianni v. Russel & Co., 281 Pa. 320, 126 A. 791 (1924).

sell tobacco in exchange for the exclusive right. The court held this evidence inadmissible because the writing was "integrated."

Professor Williston was concerned that if someone such as Mr. Gianni could prove by a mere preponderance of the evidence that the oral agreement concerning Gianni's exclusive right to sell soda water and soft drinks had actually been made, and if this proof would be sufficient to make the extrinsic agreement operative as part of the overall agreement, there would be no need for the parol evidence rule, and the special status afforded final written evidence of an agreement would be emasculated. Williston believe that the test had to focus *not* on whether the extrinsic agreement had, in fact, been made, but *whether reasonable parties, situated as were the parties to this contract, would have naturally and normally included the extrinsic matter in the writing.* If parties might naturally form a separate agreement as to such extrinsic matter, the writing was not integrated as to that matter.[81] While this test preserves the sacredness of the writing as superior evidence of the parties' agreement, it deliberately ignores the actual intention of the parties, i.e., it creates a fictitious intention which may or may not coincide with the actual intention of the parties. Professor Corbin was not pleased with this test.

Corbin insisted on a test which would have the trial judge (in most cases) consider the extrinsic evidence for two purposes: (a) to determine whether there existed "respectable" evidence to show that the antecedent agreement was made, and (b) to determine whether such an antecedent agreement had been discharged by the subsequent writing which one of the parties relied upon as the sole repository of the agreement.[82] The Corbin position is simple: Either the parties assented to the writing as an integrated agreement or they did not, and all "respectable" evidence should be considered to determine this critical question. This position is completely consistent with the basic Corbin view that courts must determine whether the parties have agreed today to nullify their agreement of yesterday and that there is no need to call upon some "parol evidence rule" to prove this.[83] It is generally assumed that the Corbin position would virtually emasculate the parol evidence rule.[84]

In terms of the recorded American cases, it is clear that the Williston test which was, not remarkably, replicated in the FIRST RESTATEMENT,[85] is the dominant, common law[86] test in American case law. Even though other tests are often mentioned, the overwhelming majority of courts apply the Williston test. Thus, in the *Gianni* case, though the court mentions other tests, it suggests that the extrinsic (oral) agreement between Gianni and Russel had to be compared with the written lease to determine "whether parties situated as were the ones to the contract would naturally and normally include the one in the other *if it were made.*"[87] The court is not to determine whether the alleged extrinsic agreement was, in fact, made. Rather, on the assumption that it was

---

[81] 4 WILLISTON §§ 638-639.

[82] 3 CORBIN § 582.

[83] *Id.* at 457.

[84] *See* ALI Proceedings at 442 (1971).

[85] FIRST RESTATEMENT § 240(1)(b). Professor Williston was the Reporter for the FIRST RESTATEMENT.

[86] The UCC test which will be considered later modifies the Williston test.

[87] 126 A. 791, 792. (emphasis added).

made, was it the kind of agreement, in light of the subject matter of the
writing when compared to the subject matter of the extrinsic agreement, that
would ordinarily (naturally and normally) be executed at the same time and
placed in the writing? The question is to be determined by the court and, in
this case, the court found no difficulty in holding that the extrinsic agreement,
concerning the *exclusive* right to sell soda water and soft drinks, was clearly
the kind of agreement that reasonable parties would naturally and normally
include in a writing which was a lease of premises to be used for the purpose of
selling, *inter alia,* soda water and soft drinks.

   Mitchill v. Lath[88] involved the sale of a farm. The sellers also owned an
unsightly icehouse on land owned by another across from the farm. Prior to
the execution of the writing for the sale and conveyance of the farm, the
parties allegedly agreed that the sellers would remove the unsightly icehouse.
When they failed to perform, the buyer brought an action and sought to
introduce evidence of the icehouse removal agreement. While it suggested
other tests which will be discussed subsequently in this section, the majority
of the court applied the Williston test, i.e., whether the extrinsic agreement
concerning the icehouse was the kind of agreement that the parties would not
ordinarily be expected to be embodied in a writing such as the one before the
court for the purchase and sale of the farm. The majority refused to admit the
evidence though it could have been established by the overwhelming weight
of the evidence. A dissenting opinion quarreled not with the test used but the
application thereof.[89]

   Four decades later, Justice Traynor wrote the opinion for the court in
Masterson v. Sine[90] where a grant deed reserved an option in the grantors to
repurchase the property for the same consideration as that received by the
grantors with a depreciation allowance. The property was a ranch owned by
the brother of one of the grantees. Upon the bankruptcy of the grantor, the
trustee in bankruptcy sought to enforce the option. The defendants sought to
introduce evidence that the parties intended the option to be exercised only by
a member of the family because the parties wanted the property kept in the
family though there was no such provision in the writing. In a pedagogical
opinion, Justice Traynor relied upon the Williston test, i.e., was the extrinsic
agreement the kind of agreement that might naturally be made as a separate
agreement by parties situated as were the parties to the written contract?[91]
The opinion focuses upon *these* parties, i.e., the parties to this contract, and
concludes that there was nothing in the record to indicate that these parties to
this *family* transaction, inexperienced in land transactions, had any awareness of the disadvantages of failing to include the entire agreement in this
kind of writing — a deed. Thus, parties situated as were these parties, would
not naturally include a provision restricting the exercise of the option to a
family member in the deed. The evidence was admissible.

---

[88] 247 N.Y. 377, 160 N.E. 646, 68 A.L.R. 239 (1928).

[89] Judge Lehman's dissent clearly reveals his disagreement based on his view that parties such
as the parties in this case would naturally and normally omit an agreement to remove the
icehouse from the kind of writing involved. The writing was for the conveyance of land and the
promise to remove the icehouse was not related to that subject matter.

[90] 65 Cal. Rptr. 545, 436 P.2d 561 (1968).

[91] Justice Traynor quoted the language from § 240(1)(b) of the FIRST RESTATEMENT.

There is no dearth of additional case law applying the Williston/First Restatement test.[92] It must be emphasized, however, that the test, like other legal tests, cannot be applied with mathematical precision. As suggested earlier with respect to the case involving the extrinsic agreement for the removal of the icehouse, the application of the same test can lead to different conclusions. It is not remarkable that, on the same facts, some judges would decide that the extrinsic agreement is the type that would have been naturally and normally included in the writing under the particular circumstances of the parties and their document, while other judges would decide the opposite. It is a question not unlike that of what reasonable persons, situated as were these persons, would do under the circumstances. Moreover, there is no merit in characterizing the agreement as "partially integrated" when the evidence is admissible (because such parties would not naturally include such an extrinsic agreement in the writing) or "fully or completely integrated" (because such parties would naturally include such extrinsic matter in the writing). "Partial" or "full" integration simply adds a conclusory label to the analysis and is, otherwise, unhelpful. The Williston test has withstood the test of time in myriad cases and, except where it is statutorily preempted by the UCC in contracts for the sale of goods, it appears to be well ensconced for future application.

4. The RESTATEMENT 2d Analysis: "Natural Omission," "Separate Consideration," and "Scope" Tests.

The RESTATEMENT 2d includes the Williston test, among others, calling it the "natural omission" test: "An agreement is not completely integrated if the writing omits a consistent additional agreed term which is ... such a term as in the circumstances might naturally be omitted from the writing."[93] The change from the FIRST RESTATEMENT is essentially one of terminology and not concept, i.e., it is arguably more accurate to call the Williston test a "natural inclusion" rather than "natural omission" test.[94] What may appear to be another RESTATEMENT 2d test is a carry-over from the FIRST RESTATEMENT.[95] If the extrinsic agreement is one that has been made for a "separate consideration," evidence of that agreement is admissible. Certainly, if the parties made separate contracts supported by separate considerations, the last contract does not supersede the earlier contract. Even if the parties have made only one contract, however, a consistent additional (prior) term supported by a separate consideration is not excluded under this test. As the RESTATEMENT 2d admits, however, the "separate consideration" test is nothing more than a particular

---

[92] See, e.g., Lee v. Joseph E. Seagram & Sons, 552 F.2d 447 (2d Cir. 1977); Traudt v. Nebraska Pub. Power Dist., 197 Neb. 765, 251 N.W.2d 148 (1977); De Vore v. Weyerhauser Co., 508 P.2d 220 (Or. 1973).

[93] RESTATEMENT 2d § 216(2)(b). Comment d to this section suggests that this test would be particularly applicable to contracts evidenced by standard, printed forms which often do not allow space for additional terms. The comment is careful to emphasize that these examples are not exclusive.

[94] FIRST RESTATEMENT § 240(1)(b) uses language more consistent with the original Williston concept, i.e., "as might naturally be made as a separate agreement by parties situated as were the parties to the written contract."

[95] See FIRST RESTATEMENT § 240(1)(a).

application or species of the "natural omission" test.[96] The illustration supporting the "separate consideration" test in the RESTATEMENT 2d clearly supports this conclusion. Where A and B have signed an integrated writing for the purchase and sale of an automobile and, as part of their transaction, the parties have orally agreed that B may keep the auto in A's garage for one year for $15 per month, evidence of the oral agreement is admissible.[97] The evidence is admissible either because the parties have agreed upon a "separate consideration" in the garage part of the transaction, or because parties, situated as were these parties to this agreement, would not naturally and normally include the garage rental agreement in their writing for the purchase and sale of the car. The fact that the parties have agreed upon a separate consideration for the garage rental reinforces their manifestation of intention that the garage rental agreement was not intended to be merged into their writing concerning the purchase and sale of the car.

Another discernible test in the RESTATEMENT 2d may be called the "scope" test, the description of which is, unfortunately, rather complicated. Because the RESTATEMENT 2d is obsessed with the notion of "integration," it places this test in a section captioned, "Effect of Integrated Agreement on Prior Agreements (Parol Evidence Rule)."[98] This caption is revealing in that it focuses upon integration and suggests that when the integration question is resolved, the application of the parol evidence rule will follow without difficulty. As suggested throughout the foregoing analysis of the parol evidence rule, the critical question is whether the parties intended their writing to be a final or both final and complete statement of their agreement. *How* a court goes about answering that question in a given situation is the heart of the parol evidence process, i.e., what tests or guidelines do courts utilize in that effort. Little is to be gained from suggesting a test such as that found in the RESTATEMENT 2d section which includes the "scope" test. We are first informed that, "A binding integrated agreement discharges prior agreements to the extent that it is inconsistent with them."[99] Again, the critical question is whether there is a "binding integrated agreement" and, more particularly, how does a court decide that question. The next subsection adds to the confusion: "A binding completely integrated agreement discharges prior agreements to the extent that they are within its scope."[1] In a prior section, one finds the RESTATEMENT 2d definition of "a completely integrated agreement," i.e., "an integrated agreement adopted by the parties as a complete and exclusive statement of the terms of the agreement."[2] A comment to that section distinguishes partially integrated from completely integrated agreements. A partially integrated agreement is one which the parties intend to be final on some matters but did not intend to preclude consistent additional terms. A fully integrated agreement, however, was intended to be the complete statement of the terms of agreement between the parties. If that was the intention, "evidence of the

---

[96] RESTATEMENT 2d § 216 comment c.
[97] RESTATEMENT 2d § 216 ill. 3.
[98] RESTATEMENT 2d § 213.
[99] RESTATEMENT 2d § 213(1).
[1] RESTATEMENT 2d § 213(2).
[2] RESTATEMENT 2d § 210(1).

alleged making of consistent additional terms must be kept from the trier of fact."[3] This is a clear and effective statement of the effect of a completely integrated agreement which is restated in a separate section.[4] In yet another section, however, we are told that such a completely integrated agreement discharges prior agreements only "to the extent that they are within its scope."[5] The inevitable question arises, if an agreement is completely integrated, what kind of prior agreements are not within its scope? The two RESTATEMENT 2d illustrations following this analysis are anything but helpful. In the first, the parties orally agree on repair services to certain property to be completed by October 1. They then execute a memorandum of their agreement which is complete in all respects except that it is silent on the time for performance. The conclusion is hardly satisfying: "If the memorandum is a binding completely integrated agreement, the agreement to finish by October 1 is discharged, and the repairs are to be finished within a reasonable time."[6] There is a question as to whether a memorandum which is silent on the time for performance is a completely integrated agreement. Professor Corbin suggests that judicial gap-fillers such as "a reasonable time" do not constitute any part of the "integration" that is protected by the parol evidence rule. Moreover, he suggests that his view is supported by the weight of authority.[7] Thus, the writing in the illustration may be said to have been only partially integrated. If it *had* been completely integrated, just as night follows day, the effect would be to exclude evidence of the prior agreement that the repairs would be finished by October 1. The RESTATEMENT 2d fails to address the question of how such an agreement could be said to be completely integrated. The second and last illustration of the "scope" test is even more curious. The parties made an agreement for the purchase and sale of land with a hotel thereon together with the hotel furniture. They employed a lawyer to draft the writing evidencing the contract and the writing contained no mention of the furniture. The inescapable conclusion is, "The agreement as to furniture is discharged if there is a binding completely integrated agreement covering the entire transaction, but not if only the part of the agreement relating to real property is integrated."[8] The case upon which this illustration is based relied upon Dean Wigmore's analysis of the parol evidence process (to be discussed later in this section) and found that the agreement was not completely integrated, thereby admitting the evidence as to the furniture.[9] Like the previous illustration, this illustration suggests that *if* the agreement is completely integrated, the extrinsic evidence is not admissible; if it is not completely integrated, the evidence is admissible. Unfortunately, the scope test amounts to nothing more than this, i.e., the scope test is a snare and a delusion since it is unnecessary to allow for the truism concerning the effect of completely versus partially integrated agreements. It leaves the question of how a court

---

[3] RESTATEMENT 2d § 210 comment a.
[4] RESTATEMENT 2d § 216(1).
[5] RESTATEMENT 2d § 213(2).
[6] RESTATEMENT 2d § 213 ill. 3. The illustration is based on Hayden v. Hoadley, 94 Vt. 345, 111 A. 343 (1920).
[7] 3 CORBIN § 593, at 556-57.
[8] RESTATEMENT 2d § 213 ill. 4.
[9] Brown v. Oliver, 123 Kan. 711, 256 P. 1008 (1927).

decides whether a writing is completely integrated or integrated at all unanswered.

The essential problem with the "scope" test section is that it assumes a completely integrated agreement and further assumes that there may also be a prior agreement beyond the scope of the completely integrated agreement. There is no suggestion of what kind of extrinsic agreement may fit that description. The conceptual fallacy of this approach is to assume a completely integrated agreement before considering the proferred extrinsic matter. The scope test is not another version of the appearance test since it contemplates the possibility that an extrinsic agreement not within the scope of the writing was made. The determination of whether a particular writing is completely integrated requires a comparison of the writing with the alleged extrinsic agreement. The only test in the RESTATEMENT 2d which assists courts in that process is the "natural omission" (Williston) test explored earlier.

The inescapable conclusion is that the RESTATEMENT 2d speaks of four tests and contains only one. The "appearance" test in the RESTATEMENT 2d self destructs.[10] The "separate consideration" test is an admitted species of the "natural omission" test, and the "scope" test is a truism that requires the support of the only viable test in the RESTATEMENT 2d to determine whether a writing is completely integrated, again, the "natural omission" test. In a number of areas, the RESTATEMENT 2d makes valuable contributions to the analysis of contract law. Unfortunately, its treatment of the parol evidence process is not numbered among them.[11]

5. The Uniform Commercial Code Parol Evidence Rule.

Unlike the RESTATEMENT 2d analysis of the parol evidence rule, the UCC provides a significant improvement over prior attempts to restate the concept. In one tightly drafted section, the UCC version manages to overcome the confusion of the past and provides a highly effective guide to courts confronted with a parol evidence issue in a contract for the sale of goods. Section 2-202 of the Code avoids a basic flaw found in the RESTATEMENT 2d by captioning its parol evidence section, "Final Written *Expression:* Parol or Extrinsic Evidence." The RESTATEMENT 2d insisted on the term *"agreement"* rather than "expression," thereby failing to distinguish between the "agreement" and the writing expressing the agreement. The UCC also avoids the unfortunate, conclusory term, "integration" and the necessity of distinguishing between a "partial" and "full" or "complete" integration. Rather, it characterizes writings as either "final" (comparable to "partial integration") or "complete and exclusive" (comparable to "full" or "complete" integrations). In just about a dozen lines, the UCC section manages to set forth clearly the following principles: (1) if the parties intend their written expression of agreement to be merely *final,* the terms of that final agreement may not be *contradicted* by any prior or contemporaneous oral agreement. (2) Such terms in a final writ-

---

[10] *See supra* text at notes 61 and 62.

[11] For a complete analysis of the RESTATEMENT 2d parol evidence rule analysis, *see* Murray, *The Parol Evidence Process and Standardized Agreements Under the Restatement (Second) of Contracts,* 123 U. PA. L. REV. 1342 (1975).

ing may, however, be explained or supplemented by evidence of consistent additional terms or by evidence of course of dealing, usage of trade or course of performance. (3) If the parties intended their writing to be not merely *final* but also a *complete and exclusive* statement of the terms of their agreement, evidence of consistent additional terms is excluded, but even with respect to such a complete and exclusive expression of agreement, evidence of trade usage, course of dealing, and course of performance is admissible.[12] There is, therefore, no presumption that the writing is the complete and exclusive expression of the parties' agreement. Rather, the opposite is assumed, i.e., the writing will not be viewed as complete and exclusive unless the court finds that the parties intended it to be complete and exclusive.[13]

If there is a flaw in the UCC version of the parol evidence rule, it is the failure to state *in the language of the section* the test to be used to determine whether the writing is complete and exclusive (in the older and RESTATEMENT 2d terminology, "completely integrated"). The test is found, however, in a comment: "If the additional terms are such that, if agreed upon, they *would certainly* have been included in the document in the view of the court, then evidence of their alleged making must be kept from the trier of fact."[14] This is a modified Williston test. Under the Williston test ("natural inclusion" or "natural omission"), if parties situated as were the parties to the contract would have naturally (normally or ordinarily) included the alleged extrinsic matter in the kind of writing they executed, the evidence is excluded. Under the UCC test, only if such parties *would certainly* have included such extrinsic terms in their writing is the evidence excluded. Thus, less evidence of extrinsic agreements is excludable (or more evidence is admissible) under the UCC test than the Williston test.[15]

The benefits of the UCC formulation have not been lost in our courts. There is a clear repudiation of the notion that the writing will be regarded as complete and final if it merely *appears* to be complete and final.[16] There is a much improved judicial understanding of why trade usage, course of dealing and course of performance evidence is admissible regardless of the fact that the parties intended their writing to be the complete expression of their agreement, i.e., in the language of a comment to the UCC section, the section

---

[12]UCC § 2-202: Final Written Expression: Parol or Extrinsic Evidence.

Terms with respect to which the confirmatory memoranda of the parties agree or which are otherwise set forth in a writing intended by the parties as a final expression of their agreement with respect to such terms as are included therein may not be contradicted by evidence of any prior agreement or a contemporaneous oral agreement but may be explained or supplemented

(a) by course of dealing or usage of trade (Section 1- 205) or by course of performance (Section 2-208); and

(b) by evidence of consistent additional terms unless the court finds the writing to have been intended also as a complete and exclusive statement of the terms of the agreement.

[13]*See* Killion v. Buran Equip. Co., 27 UCC Rep. 970, 972 (Cal. App. 1979).

[14]UCC § 2-202 comment 3 (emphasis added).

[15]The earliest judicial manifestation of this distinction is found in the opinion of Justice Traynor in Masterson v. Sine, 65 Cal. Rptr. 545, 436 P.2d 561, 564 (1968): "The draftsmen of the Uniform Commercial Code would exclude evidence in still fewer instances...." *See also* Cosmopolitan Fin. Corp. v. Runnels, 625 P.2d 390 (Haw. App. 1981).

[16]*See, e.g.,* Anderson & Nafziger v. G. T. Newcomb, Inc., 595 P.2d 709 (Idaho 1979); S. M. Wilson & Co. v. Smith Int'l, Inc., 587 F.2d 1363 (9th Cir. 1978); Killion v. Buran Equip. Co., 27 UCC Rep. 970 (Cal. App. 1979).

makes admissible evidence of course of dealing, usage of trade and course of performance *to explain or supplement any writing stating the agreement of the parties in order that the true understanding of the parties as to the agreement may be reached.*[17] The emphasis upon the importance of trade usage, course of dealing and course of performance evidence is consistent with the basic UCC definition of "contract" which is "the total legal obligation which results from the parties' *agreement ....*"[18] and the definition of "agreement" which is "the bargain of the parties in fact as found in their language or by implication from other circumstances including *course of dealing or usage or trade or course of performance....*"[19] Thus, even a complete written expression of agreement may be *supplemented* by such terms because they are automatically terms of the contract, and the written terms may also be *explained* or *interpreted* by usage of trade, course of dealing and course of performance.[20] Again, it must be remembered that interpretation is essential regardless of the completeness of the writing since the parol evidence rule merely defines the subject matter of that interpretation. While merger (integration) clauses are effective to manifest the intention of the parties that their written expression is complete,[21] evidence of trade usage, course of dealing and course of performance will be admissible even if the writing contains a merger clause indicating that the parties intended their writing to be the complete and sole repository of their agreement whether the merger clause is a printed clause ("boilerplate")[22] or a negotiated clause.[23] The only route to the excision of such supplementary terms is through their express negation, and a merger clause will be insufficient for that purpose.[24]

The UCC parol evidence concept, like other UCC sections, is not designed to replace all of the common law that preceded it. Unless displaced by the provisions of the Code, the principles of the common law are operative.[25] Therefore, parol evidence concepts developed at common law remain effective unless they are displaced by the UCC section on parol evidence.[26] Parol evidence may be introduced to show fraud[27] even in the face of a merger clause.[28] As in other

---

[17] UCC § 2-202 comment 2. *See* Ralph's Distrib. Co. v. AMF, Inc., 667 F.2d 670 (8th Cir. 1981); Jenks-White Seed Co. v. Riddell, 47 Or. App. 573, 614 P.2d 1221 (1980): Brunswick Box Co. v. Coutinho, Caro & Co., 617 F.2d 335 (4th Cir. 1980); Michigan Bean Co. v. Senn, 93 Mich. App. 440, 287 N.W.2d 257 (1979); Campbell v. Hostetter Farms, Inc., 251 Pa. Super. 232, 380 A.2d 463 (1977); Columbia Nitrogen Corp. v. Royster Co., 451 F.2d 3 (4th Cir. 1971).

[18] UCC § 1-201(11) (emphasis added).

[19] UCC § 1-201(3) (emphasis added).

[20] *See* UCC §§ 1-205 and 2-208. *See also* Trans World Metals, Inc. v. Southwire Co., 769 F.2d 902 (2d Cir. 1985) permitting trade usage to explain or supplement the contract terms.

[21] *See* Earman Oil Co. v. Burroughs Corp., 625 F.2d 1291 (5th Cir. 1980).

[22] *See* Nanakuli Paving & Rock Co. v. Shell Oil Co., 664 F.2d 772 (9th Cir. 1981).

[23] *See* Columbia Nitrogen Corp. v. Royster Co., 451 F.2d 3 (4th Cir. 1971).

[24] *See* UCC § 2-202 comment 2 requiring "careful negation" of trade usage and prior course of dealing. As to course of performance, such evidence is typically subsequent to the writing and, though the strongest source of interpretation of the writing among the three aids to interpretation (UCC § 2-208(2)), as a subsequent manifestation it could operate as a modification of the express terms of the writing (§§ 2-208(3) and 2-209(1)) which would not be affected by the parol evidence rule. *See* Lease Fin. Inc. v. Burger, 575 P.2d 857 (Colo. App. 1977).

[25] UCC § 1-103.

[26] *See* Glenn Dick Equip. Co. v. Galey Constr., Inc., 541 P.2d 1184 (Idaho 1975).

[27] Cone Mills Corp. v. A. G. Estes, Inc., 377 F. Supp. 222 (N.D. Ga. 1974). *See also* Universal Drilling Co. v. Camay Drilling Co., (10th Cir. 1984) where fraud in the inducement could not be proven but court would allow such evidence notwithstanding the parol evidence rule.

[28] City Dodge, Inc. v. Gardner, 232 Ga. 766, 208 So. 2d 794 (1974).

applications of the parol evidence rule, the court decides the question of the intention of the parties to have a final or complete expression of agreement.[29] Even if the UCC is not technically applicable to a particular transaction, some courts have applied the Code parol evidence provision by analogy.[30] In sum, the UCC version of the parol evidence rule is a significant improvement over its predecessors. The RESTATEMENT 2d recognizes the UCC version in its effort to restate the concept, but any Code influence was lost in the maze of language attempting to provide something to support any view of the rule. It is unfortunate that the RESTATEMENT 2d did not simply use the UCC version as the basic model which could have been elaborated into a highly effective analysis.

6. The Wigmore Aid and the "Collateral Agreement" Test.

a. Wigmore.

Dean Wigmore early on suggested a cogent analysis of the parol evidence process which was designed to overcome any reliance on the "appearance" or "four corners" test. As suggested earlier,[31] Wigmore thought it impossible to determine what the writing of the parties was intended to cover until it is known what there was to cover. Thus, he insisted that the extrinsic matter be received provisionally by the judge to be compared to the writing so as to permit the judge to determine whether the writing was intended to cover the extrinsic matter.[32] The Wigmore test, however, is admittedly quite modest:

> In deciding upon this intent, the chief and most satisfactory index for the judge is found in the circumstance whether or not the particular element of the alleged extrinsic negotiation is dealt with at all in the writing. If it is mentioned, covered, or dealt with in the writing, then presumably the writing was meant to represent all of the transaction on that element; if it is not, then probably the writing was not intended to embody that element.[33]

As such, this test could preclude evidence of consistent additional terms simply because the writing mentioned the subject matter of such extrinsic terms. If the extrinsic terms contradicted the terms of the subsequent writing, the evidence would be excluded under any test, including the Wigmore test. As stated, however, the test suggests an intention to have a complete and exclusive writing with respect to any matter mentioned or dealt with at all in the writing since it would, again, preclude evidence of consistent (non-contradictory) terms dealing with that subject matter. It may also be interpreted to permit evidence of extrinsic agreements which would normally be included in the writing simply because the writing does not mention the particular extrinsic matter. Since Wigmore did not suggest the test as anything more than

[29] Peoria Harbor Marina v. McGlasson, 105 Ill. App. 3d 723, 434 N.E.2d 786 (1982).

[30] See Interstate Indus. Uniform Rental Serv. v. F. R. Lepage Bakery, Inc., 413 A.2d 516 (Me. 1980) (uniform rentals) (the article 1A (leases) provision is also § 202 and is identical to § 2-202); Conran v. Yager, 263 S.C. 417, 211 S.E.2d 228 (1975) (sale of real estate).

[31] See the discussion of the "Appearance" or "Four Corners" test supra text at note 58.

[32] 9 WIGMORE ON EVIDENCE (3d ed.) § 2430.

[33] Ibid., § 2430(3) at 98.

an aid to a judge, he apparently recognized that its utility was limited. The test appears, along with others, in various cases when it can serve as a bulwark to a decision reached on the basis of other tests, usually the Williston ("natural inclusion") test.[34] It is not viewed as a dispositive test in the extant case law.

b. The "Collateral Agreement" Test.

The well-known case of *Mitchill v. Lath* [35] *was explored earlier* [36] *as an* illustration of the "natural inclusion" test created by Professor Williston. Like many other cases confronting a parol evidence issue, that opinion suggested other "tests" though the majority and dissenting opinions appeared to rely on the "natural inclusion" test for their opposed results. The majority opinion suggested that, before any evidence of a prior oral agreement which is not supported by a separate consideration could be admitted, three conditions had to be met: (1) the agreement must in form be a *collateral* one, (2) the extrinsic evidence must not contradict express or implied provisions of the "written contract," and (3) it must be one which the parties would not ordinarily (naturally) be expected to embody in the writing. The third condition is clearly the Williston test and, again, it appeared to be the basic analysis leading the court to hold that the extrinsic evidence was not admissible. The second condition is a truism and would apply even if the writing were "final" ("partially integrated") rather than complete. The first condition — that the agreement must appear to be a "collateral" one provides no analytical basis for a court to decide the question of admissibility. The *Mitchill* majority concluded, "Were such an agreement [the extrinsic agreement concerning removal of an icehouse] made it would seem most natural that the inquirer should find it in the contract [for the purchase and sale of the farm]."[37] Having concluded that parties situated as were the parties to this contract would have naturally included the extrinsic matter in the writing, it is quite superfluous to suggest that the agreement concerning the icehouse removal is not admissible because it is not a "collateral" agreement. If the evidence were admissible because parties would not have included such extrinsic matter in the writing, it is equally superfluous to suggest that the extrinsic agreement *was* "collateral." A recent application of the three conditions in *Mitchill v. Lath* reveals the conclusory nature of the "collateral agreement" requirement. The plaintiffs contended that an insurance agent had agreed to supply a homeowner's policy and a workmen's compensation policy to cover casualty to a home which was to be constructed and liability coverage for any workman injured on the premises during the construction. The writing dealt exclusively with homeowner's coverage and the plaintiffs sought to introduce evidence concerning the negotiations for the workmen's compensation coverage. The trial court admitted

---

[34] *See, e.g.,* Traudy v. Nebraska Pub. Power Dist., 197 Neb. 765, 251 N.W.2d 148 (1977); Gianni v. Russel & Co., 281 Pa. 320, 126 A.2d 791 (1924).

[35] 247 N.Y. 377, 160 N.E. 646, 68 A.L.R. 239 (1928).

[36] *See supra* text following note 88.

[37] 247 N.Y. at 381-82, 160 N.E. at 647. This is the "natural inclusion" test of Williston which, again, was the basis for the decision. The RESTATEMENT 2d mentions the case only with respect to the natural omission test, i.e., "[P]rior oral agreement discharged if parties would 'ordinarily be expected to embody' it in the writing." RESTATEMENT 2d § 213, Reporter's Note to comment c.

the evidence over defendant's objections that it violated the parol evidence rule. On appeal, the Supreme Court of Alabama applied the three condition test of *Mitchill v. Lath*. As to the first condition, i.e., that the agreement must in form be a collateral one, the court concluded that, "any agreement to provide workmen's compensation coverage would have been collateral to the agreement to issue a homeowner's policy."[38] The basis for the court's conclusion was quoted testimony by the parties. The court found the second condition satisfied, i.e., that the homeowner's policy, while stating that workmen's compensation benefits would not be paid pursuant to the homeowner's policy, did not prevent a compensation policy from being in effect simultaneously. Therefore, there was no contradiction between the alleged prior agreement and the writing.[39] The third condition was also satisfied: "A reasonable person would not ordinarily expect workmen's compensation coverage to be included in the same writing as homeowner's coverage."[40] Comparing the third and first conditions as applied by this court, it clearly appears that the court's determination that parties, situated as were these parties, would not naturally include workmen's compensation coverage in a writing evidencing homeowner's coverage, is the sole and exclusive rationale for the court's earlier holding that the prior workmen's compensation was "collateral." Thus, to determine whether a particular extrinsic agreement was a collateral agreement, it is necessary to determine whether the parties would ordinarily (naturally and normally) include such coverage in the particular writing expressing their agreement. If they would have naturally included such a matter in the writing, the extrinsic agreement is not called "collateral" and the evidence is excluded. If, however, they would not have naturally included such a matter in the writing, the extrinsic agreement is called "collateral" and the evidence is admitted. Again, however, the question of admissibility is determined by the "natural inclusion" or "natural omission" test — not by the label attached to the extrinsic agreement. The so-called "collateral agreement" test is not a test; it is a conclusory label attached after the critical test — the Williston test — has already been applied and the court has already determined whether the evidence should be admitted.

§ 85. Situations to Which the Parol Evidence Rule Does Not Apply.

A. *Integration, Interpretation, Invalidating Causes — Consideration.*

The most significant test of one's understanding of the parol evidence process may be the ability to distinguish it from situations to which it does not apply. Some of these distinctions have already been suggested. Thus, we have seen that the parol evidence rule does not preclude evidence to determine the preliminary question of integration, i.e., whether the parties intended their writing to be the final (partially integrated) or complete and exclusive (fully or completely integrated) statement of their agreement.[41] Another critical

---

[38] Alabama Farm Bur. Mut. Cas. Ins. Co. v. Haynes, 497 So. 2d 82, 85 (Ala. 1986).
[39] *Id.*
[40] *Id.*
[41] *See supra* § 84(B). In addition to these authorities, *see* Clark v. Di Pietro, 525 A.2d 623 (Me. 1987); Burge v. Frey, 545 F. Supp. 1160 (D. Kan. 1982).

process that must be distinguished from the parol evidence process is interpretation, which will be explored in sections to follow. Throughout our prior discussion of the parol evidence concept, we have distinguished the intepretation process[42] and emphasized the admissibility of trade usage, course of dealing, and course of performance evidence regardless of how complete the final writing of the parties.[43] We have also focused upon the admissibility of evidence that would lead a court to hold a contract void, voidable, or unenforceable regardless of the parol evidence process. Thus, evidence of fraud, misrepresentation, duress, mistake, or other invalidating cause such as the lack of consideration is admissible.[44] The parties may have included a clause reciting that consideration has been received by one of the parties who later attempts to introduce evidence to show that the recital is false. The RESTATEMENT 2d indicates that such evidence is admissible.[45] This view, however, should be compared with the RESTATEMENT 2d analysis explored earlier as to the effect of recital clauses in the discussion of consideration.[46]

Beyond these situations to which the parol evidence process does not apply, there are two others that are worthy of separate consideration: (1) the admissibility of evidence that the *writing* of the parties is mistaken, i.e., that it fails

---

[42] *See, e.g.,* § 82, particularly the text at note 15.

[43] *See supra* § 84(C)(5). *See also* Phillips Oil Co. v. OKC Corp., 812 F.2d 265 (5th Cir. 1987) (testimony of accounting experts did not violate parol evidence rule). *See also* Maritime Overseas Corp. v. Puerto Rico Drydock & Marine Terminals, Inc., 391 F.2d 1010 (1968); Martindell v. Lake Shore Nat'l Bank, 15 Ill. 2d 272, 154 N.E.2d 683 (1958).

[44] *See* § 84(C)(2), notes 76 and 77, and (C)(5), notes 27 and 28. In addition to these authorities, *see* Reimann v. Saturday Evening Post Co., 464 F. Supp. 214 (S.D.N.Y. 1979); Iafolla v. Douglas Pocahontas Coal Corp., 250 S.E.2d 128 (W. Va. 1979); National Bldg. Leasing, Inc. v. Byler, 252 Pa. Super. 370, 381 A.2d 963, 965 (1977) citing second edition of this book for the following proposition: "If the bargain between the parties is illegal or induced by fraud or duress, or if there is no validation device, evidence of these and other invalidating causes is admissible with no concern for the parol evidence rule." *See also* RESTATEMENT 2d § 214(d). If a promise is made with a preconceived intention of not performing it, the fraud or misrepresentation is called "promissory fraud." *See* Walker v. Woodall, 288 Ala. 510, 262 So. 2d 756 (1972); Entron v. General Cablevision of Palatka, 435 F.2d 995 (5th Cir. 1970). Promissory fraud is treated like other types of fraud by most courts which permit such evidence notwithstanding the parol evidence rule. *See, e.g.,* Abbott v. Abbott, 188 Neb. 61, 195 N.W.2d 204 (1972). It is important to distinguish this situation from proper applications of UCC § 2-316(1) which clearly indicates that evidence of express warranties made by oral or written statements prior to the execution of an integrated writing will be inadmissible because of the § 2-202 parol evidence rule. It is not uncommon for salespersons to make statements about goods which amount to express warranties prior to the execution of a writing which may be final or complete and exclusive. Should the parol evidence be inadmissible under proper application of the § 2-202 standard, the statement will not be operative. The UCC is silent with respect to evidence of fraud in such matters. Pre-Code standards pursuant to § 1-103 are then applied. *See* Associated Hardware Supply Co. v. Big Wheel Distrib. Co., 335 F.2d 114 (3d Cir. 1965). If the proponent of the evidence could establish that the seller had no intention of warranting the goods when the statement was made, promissory fraud could be shown and the evidence would be admissible regardless of § 2-202. As to the minority of courts holding that evidence of promissory fraud is barred by the parol evidence rule, see the criticism of these cases in Sweet, *Promissory Fraud and the Parol Evidence Rule,* 49 CALIF. L. REV. 877 (1961).

[45] RESTATEMENT 2d § 218(1).

[46] *See supra* Chapter 3, § 61(C). In that discussion, we explored the Restatement distinction between recital clauses in guaranty and option contracts. As to recital clauses in option contracts, the RESTATEMENT 2d adopts a formalistic validation device view, i.e., that the recital, even if untrue, satisfies the requirements of "form," and expressly rejects the view that the promisor's acceptance of delivery of a written instrument falsely reciting the promisor's receipt of consideration should imply a promise to furnish the recited consideration. Though rejecting this view in § 87, in § 218a comment e, the RESTATEMENT 2d recognizes that, "In some such cases the recital may imply a promise not explicitly stated." This is a disconcerting suggestion.

to state the true intention of the parties, and one of the parties is seeking *reformation* of the writing, and (2) the admissibility of evidence that the parties did not intend their writing, which may appear to evidence a contract between them, to operate as such evidence until a certain event has occurred, i.e., the parties did not intend to be bound to *any* contract until a *condition precedent to contract formation* occurred. We will now explore these situations.

B. *Reformation and the Parol Evidence Rule.*

The parties may have entered into an agreement about which they are not mistaken, i.e., they may have a clear understanding of all of the terms of their agreement. The written expression of that agreement, however, may be mistaken in any one of several ways: (1) the expression may contain terms which the parties never intended; (2) it may fail to express terms to which the parties actually agreed; (3) the written expression may contain the terms the parties intended, but the legal effect of those terms may be inconsistent with the actual intention of the parties. In each of these cases, there is a mistake in *expression,* i.e., the written evidence of the agreement does not comport with the true intention of the parties. It is important to contrast a mistake in *expression* from the mutual mistake of the parties themselves. In any agreement, the parties make certain basic, factual assumptions. A buyer of timber, for example, may agree to purchase a tract of land because of the valuable timber thereon. At the moment of contracting, unknown to either party, a fire has destroyed the timber.[47] In such cases, there has been a material effect on the agreed exchange of the parties because of their mistake of fact which was a basic assumption of their agreement and the buyer of the timber can avoid the contract.[48] Suppose, however, the parties agreed to buy and sell a tract of land which they understand to be "Blueacre." When their agreement is reduced to writing by a third party, the land is mistakenly identified as "Greenacre" which, coincidentally, is a tract owned by the same seller. Here, the parties made no mistake in their actual agreement. The mistake was one of expression, i.e., what was known at the early common law as a "scrivener's" error or mistake. The actual intention of the parties (as objectively manifested dehors the writing) was to purchase and sell Blueacre. Under proper evidentiary safeguards, a court, sitting as a court of equity, may *reform* the writing to state the true intention of the parties.[49] To do so, a court must receive the prior evidence of the parties intention, and such evidence will be admissible notwithstanding the parol evidence rule.[50] If parol evidence were not admissible in such a case, the parol evidence rule would become an instrument of the very fraud it was designed to prevent.[51] On the other hand, where there is no mistake in expression but the parties have, themselves, made a mutual mis-

---

[47] *See* Restatement 2d § 152 ill. 1.
[48] Restatement 2d § 152. This type of mistake as well as other types will be discussed later in this chapter.
[49] *See* Davenport v. Beck, 576 P.2d 1199 (Okla. App. 1977). *See also* Restatement 2d § 155.
[50] Weil Bros. Cotton, Inc. v. T. E. A., Inc., 181 Ga. App. 122, 351 S.E.2d 670 (1986). *See also* Chimart Assocs. v. Paul, 66 N.Y.2d 570, 498 N.Y.S.2d 314, 489 N.E.2d 231 (1986).
[51] Alabama Farm Bureau Ins. Co. v. Hunt, 525 So. 2d 415 (Ala. 1987).

take, reformation is not an available remedy because there is no true intention to which the written expression can be reformed. Thus, where the parties agreed to buy and sell the tract containing timber, their written expression was precisely in accordance with their actual agreement. The mistaken basic assumption (that the timber continued to exist at the time of the agreement) occurred prior to their actual agreement. Therefore, where the parties are mutually mistaken, the mistake is antecedent to the actual agreement, while in reformation cases, the mistake occurs after the actual agreement, i.e., it occurs in the reduction of the actual agreement to written form.

The classic reformation case is the one already hypothesized, i.e., the mistake by a third party in reducing the agreement to written form.[52] As suggested earlier, reformation is also available where there is an omission in the writing[53] as well as a mistake as to the legal effect of the expression of agreement.[54] In one fascinating case, a party sought a particular interpretation of a clause and, having failed in that effort, convinced another court that the writing was correctly interpreted by the first court but was in need of reformation since it mistakenly failed to state the actual intention of the parties.[55]

Courts are generally agreed that reformation will not be granted unless the plaintiff can prove the actual agreement of the parties by more than the usual preponderance of the evidence. The usual statement is that, for reformation purposes, the evidence must be "clear and convincing"[56] but a number of other phrases may be found in the case law such as "clear, cogent and convincing,"[57] or a "high order" of evidence required to overcome the presumption that the deliberately prepared writing manifests the true intention of the parties,[58] or in various other phrases similar to "clear and convincing."[59] It is important to emphasize that the remedy of reformation, like other equitable remedies, will depend heavily upon the facts of the case and, in particular, the inherent credibility of the evidence.[60]

Where a party seeking reformation has failed to read the document which allegedly fails to state the true intention of the parties, the defendant often argues that reformation should be denied because of the negligence of the plaintiff in failing to read. Some older cases accepted this view, particularly in

---

[52] See, e.g., Olds v. Jamison, 195 Neb. 388, 238 N.W.2d 459 (1976) ("lessor" should have read "lessee").

[53] See, e.g., Parrish v. City of Carbondale, 61 Ill. App. 3d 500, 378 N.E.2d 243 (1978) (omission of rights of plaintiffs to use city water and sanitary facilities at the same rates as users within the city limits); Bollinger v. Central Pa. Quarry Strip & Constr. Co., 425 Pa. 430, 229 A.2d 741 (1967) (omission of understanding that defendant would remove topsoil and place refuse between topsoil and bare earth. The facts of this case may also suggest that the parties had modified their written expression through course of performance, or such course of performance may have been strong evidence of the proper interpretation of the writing. Neither of these views, however, is found in the opinion).

[54] Ralph v. McGowan, 20 Wash. App. 251, 579 P.2d 1011 (1978) (legal effect of "subject to").

[55] See Sadowski v. General Disct. Corp., 295 Mich. 340, 294 N.W. 703 (1940) and General Disct. Corp. v. Sadowski, 183 F.2d 542, 546-47 (6th Cir. 1950).

[56] See Parrish v. City of Carbondale, supra note 53.

[57] Ralph v. McGowan, supra note 54 at 1014.

[58] Chimart Assocs. v. Paul, supra note 50.

[59] See Retenbach Eng'g Co. v. General Realty Ltd., 707 S.W.2d 524 (Tenn. App. 1985) where the court rehearses numerous phrases similar to "clear and convincing" used by prior Tennessee courts.

[60] RESTATEMENT 2d § 155 comment c.

cases of reformation because of mistake rather than fraud, though some refused the remedy even where fraud was shown.[61] Other older cases, however, recognized that the failure to read amounts to a bar to the remedy of reformation only if the negligence was "gross."[62] More recent cases either agree that ordinary negligence should not bar reformation[63] or that only "reasonable diligence" is required, and the innocent failure to read the formal document is not a departure from the standard of "reasonable diligence."[64]

Finally, it should be noted that reformation may be granted at the request of any party to the contract including a third party beneficiary, or the right of a successor in interest. It may be granted to a party whose performance would have been unenforceable or voidable absent reformation.[65]

C. Condition Precedent to Formation — RESTATEMENT 2d Analysis.

As suggested earlier,[66] the parol evidence rule does not affect questions concerning the formation, validity or enforceability of a contract. If, therefore, the parties do not intend their contract to come into existence until a certain event occurs, evidence of such intention does not vary, add to, or contradict the terms of their writing. Rather, such evidence goes to the question of whether there is any contract. Innumerable cases have held such evidence admissible, notwithstanding the parol evidence rule.[67] As will be seen in a subsequent chapter dealing with conditions, however, the typical condition is

---

[61] See, e.g., Knight & Bostwick v. Moore, 203 Wis. 540, 234 N.W. 902 (1931).

[62] See, e.g., Kroschel v. Martineau Hotels, Inc., 142 Or. 31, 18 P.2d 818, 823 (1933).

[63] See, e.g., Anderson, Clayton & Co. v. Farmers Nat'l Bank, 624 F.2d 818 (10th Cir. 1980).

[64] See Akkerman v. Gersema, 260 Iowa 432, 149 N.W.2d 856 (1967).

[65] RESTATEMENT 2d § 155 comment e.

[66] See supra subsection (A).

[67] See Palatine Nat'l Bank v. Olson, 366 N.W.2d 726, 730 (Minn. App. 1985) (written release indicated no condition and letter stated that party was discharged from loan, but testimony was admissible parol evidence that the release was subject to the condition precedent of bringing the loans to a successful conclusion) quoting from Jansen v. Herman, 304 Minn. 572, 575-76, 230 N.W.2d 460, 463-64 (1975): "In every instance where the parol evidence rule is sought to be applied, however, a threshold question must be asked: Is the contract valid and operative? If the contract was to be binding only upon performance of an agreed-upon condition precedent, then the contract goes into force only upon the performance of that condition. Thus, parol evidence may be admissible to show that, notwithstanding the existence of a written contract, it was the intention of the parties that the contract should not become operative except upon the happening of some future event.... In Minnesota we have repeatedly held that parol evidence is admissible to show that, notwithstanding the delivery of an instrument, the intention of the parties was that it should not become operative as a binding contract except upon the happening of a future contingent event.... Whether or not a certain oral agreement constituted a condition precedent for a subsequent contract is a factual determination to be decided by the trier of fact." See also Matter of Prior Bros., 29 Wash. App. 905, 632 P.2d 522 (1981) (§ 2-202 of the UCC does not address this matter and, therefore, pre-Code law must apply); Hunt Foods & Indus. v. Doliner, 26 App. Div. 2d 41, 270 N.Y.S.2d 937 (1966) (condition to formation was "consistent" and, therefore, not barred by § 2-202 of the UCC); White Showers, Inc. v. Fischer, 278 Mich. 32, 270 N.W. 205 (1936) (evidence admissible that contract for irrigation system was not to become effective until prior contract was cancelled); Hicks v. Bush, 10 N.Y.2d 488, 255 N.Y.S.2d 34, 180 N.E.2d 425, 427 (1962): "Parol testimony is admissible to prove a condition precedent to the legal effectiveness of a written agreement...."; Blackstad Mercantile Co. v. Parker & Glover, 163 N.C. 275, 79 S.E. 606 (1913) (sales order containing merger clause did not prevent evidence that the signed order was not to be "sent in" until defendant gave a further direction to that effect). See also Brummet v. Pope, 685 S.W.2d 238 (Mo. App. 1985); Rincones v. Windberg, 705 S.W.2d 846 (Tex. App. 1986); The classic case is Pym v. Campbell, 6 El. & Bl. 370 (Q.B. 1856) (buyer of invention permitted to show that his purchase was conditioned on approval of invention by a particular engineer).

one that merely postpones the activation of a duty, i.e., the contract is formed and the existing duty of one or both parties remains in a state of quiescence until a particular event has occurred. If, therefore, one of the parties attempts to introduce evidence of a typical condition to an existing duty under a formed contract where the writing evidencing that contract is integrated and does not mention the condition, the parol evidence rule is applicable and such evidence will be subjected to the usual tests of admissibility.[68]

Though the case law is clear that there is no reason to apply the parol evidence rule where the question is whether any enforceable agreement exists, the RESTATEMENT 2d rejects this view and substitutes a different rationale. It suggests that, where the written agreement is subject to the occurrence of a stated condition, the agreement is not integrated with respect to the oral condition.[69] A comment explains, "If the parties orally agreed that performance of the written agreement was subject to a condition, either the writing is not an integrated agreement or the agreement is only partially integrated until the condition occurs."[70] This is followed by the curious suggestion that even a merger clause which explicitly negates oral terms does not control the question of whether the agreement is integrated.[71] Certainly, a writing may appear to be a complete and exclusive statement of the parties' intention and it may contain a well-drafted merger clause to strengthen that effect. Yet, the most complete and exclusive statement of agreement may not be intended as legally binding until a conditioning event has occurred. In addition to the obsession of the RESTATEMENT 2d with the notion of "integration" in its treatment of the parol evidence process, an explanation may be found in a Reporter's note to this section which refers the user to a comment in another section defining conditions.[72] That comment and the Reporter's note explaining it are critical of the use of the term "condition" to describe an event upon which the *existence* of a contract is dependent. The definition of "condition" in the RESTATEMENT 2d is relegated to an event upon which the *performance* of a duty under an existing contract is dependent, i.e., the typical use of the term "condition" as described above. Yet, the RESTATEMENT 2d explanation suggests, "[T]here is no great substantive disparity between the terminology used in this [Restatement Second] Comment and descriptions of such events as conditions to the existence of a contract."[73] Notwithstanding the lack of "great substantive disparity," the RESTATEMENT 2d appears to reject the generally accepted rationale or conditions precedent to the *existence* of a contract only because of its preferred (narrower) description of "condition." Ambiguity in the use of the term "condition" can be avoided by identifying that to which the condition is attached, again, to the *existence* of a contract or to a *duty* under an existing contract. Indeed, as will be seen in the later discussion of

---

[68] *See* Hong Kong Deposit & Guar. Co. v. Hibdon, 611 F. Supp. 224 (S.D.N.Y. 1985) and Schacht v. Beacon Ins. Co., 742 F.2d 386 (7th Cir. 1984) where the courts refused to apply the condition precedent to formation exception to the parol evidence rule because the conditions sought to be proven were "subsequent", i.e., they were attached to existing contractual duties.

[69] RESTATEMENT 2d § 217.

[70] RESTATEMENT 2d § 217 comment b.

[71] *Ibid.*

[72] RESTATEMENT 2d § 224 comment c.

[73] RESTATEMENT 2d § 224 Reporter's Note.

conditions, when conditions are described as either "precedent" or "subsequent," ambiguity in the use of these descriptive terms (which are no longer used in the RESTATEMENT 2d) can be avoided by identifying the referent point, i.e., "precedent" or "subsequent" to what? The case law permitting evidence of a condition to the existence of a contract almost invariably identifies the condition as "precedent" to such *existence*. Thus, the RESTATEMENT 2d rejection of the case law and its substitution of a puzzling, alternative rationale lacks any apparent justification.

§ 86. Interpretation, Construction and "Plain Meaning."

A. *The Process of Interpretation — Who Decides? — Construction.*

The parties to a contract may have manifested their agreement by words (oral or written), or by conduct. Whatever the expression of agreement, the *meaning* of that expression must be ascertained, and the process of ascertaining the meaning of such expression is the process of interpretation.[74] This description of the process of interpretation immediately raises numerous questions. Who shall decide the meaning of the parties' expression of agreement, i.e., shall it be the judge or jury? Is it a question of *law* the judge will decide, or a question of *fact* that the jury should decide? The notion that questions of fact are for the jury while questions of law are for the judge is a tautology. It is an open secret that certain questions of fact are decided by the court and characterized as questions of "law" because the court chooses to decide them.[75] Since interpretation deals with the meaning of language, it is clearly a question of fact.[76] Earlier courts, however, distrusted jurors, some of whom were illiterate, and even modern courts recognize the desirability of characterizing certain question of interpretation as question of law to preserve judicial review which would be lost if the question were characterized as one of fact.[77] Where the evidence is so clear that reasonable parties would not disagree on the meaning of certain manifestations of intention, the question of interpretation is for the court.[78] If, however, the interpretation depends upon extrinsic evidence or a choice among reasonable inferences to be drawn from

---

[74] *See* RESTATEMENT 2d § 200: "Interpretation of a promise or agreement or a term thereof is the ascertainment of its meaning."

[75] For a superb analysis of the "law"/"fact" dichotomy, *see* HART & SACKS, THE LEGAL PROCESS: BASIC PROBLEMS IN THE MAKING AND APPLICATION OF LAW 369 *et seq.* (Cambridge, tentative ed. 1958).

[76] Chief Justice Traynor candidly recognized the question of interpretation as a question of fact but still insisted that interpretation "is essentially a judicial function to be exercised according to the generally accepted canons of interpretation." Parsons v. Bristol Dev. Co., 62 Cal. 2d 861, 865, 402 P.2d 839, 842 (1965).

[77] *See* RESTATEMENT 2d § 212 comment d which suggests that appellate review of such questions may contribute to stability and predictability, particularly in cases involving standardized printed forms. *See also* the opinion by Traynor in Parsons v. Bristol Dev. Co., *id.*, where it is suggested that appellate courts are not bound by a construction of the contract based solely on the terms of the writing.

[78] *See* American Med. Intern v. Scheller, 462 So. 2d 1, 7 (Fla. App. 1984) where the court held that the trial court had improperly shifted to the jury the burden of initially construing the contract.

that evidence, the trier of fact (jury or judge sitting without a jury) will perform that task.[79]

If the question is one of the legal *effect* of the parties' expression rather than their meaning, this process has often been called *construction* rather than interpretation.[80] The process of interpretation — the determination of meaning — must precede the process of construction — the determination of legal effect. Though this distinction is sound, the untidy fashion in which courts sometimes use the term "construction" to mean "interpretation" affects the utility of the distinction.[81]

B. *Whose Meaning Should Prevail? — "Plain Meaning" Standard.*

Once the issue of *who* is to decide is resolved, the next question is, *whose meaning should prevail?* This is a complicated question to be explored in the sections that follow. The test or standard of interpretation is critical in dealing with this question. The meaning which a reasonable (hypothetical) third party may attach to certain expressions of intention may be different from the meaning which one or both parties attach. If the standard is that of the reasonable third party and a court refuses to consider evidence of particular meanings attached by the contracting parties, the court may discover a contract which neither party intended. If the parties have attached different individual meanings, which of these meanings should prevail? Should there be a contract at all if neither party knew of the other's meaning, or if both knew of the other's meaning? Issues of ambiguity (double meanings or equivocal meanings) or vagueness (a spectrum of meanings) arise. It is questionable whether there is any word or phrase which may be accurately described as having an ideal meaning, apart from any particular usage. There is a "plain meaning" school of interpretation which would ascribe singular meanings to any written words. Professor Corbin exquisitely emasculates this view:

> It is sometimes said, in a case in which the written words seem plain and clear and unambiguous, that the words are not subject to interpretation or construction. One who makes this statement has of necessity already given the words an interpretation — the one that is to him plain and clear; and in making the statement he is asserting that any different interpretation is "perverted" and untrue.[82]

The view that words do have an ideal meaning and that parties would be held to that meaning regardless of how far it may differ from their intention is traceable to an earlier period in our law. Fortunately, we have seen much progress in this area. "The history of the law of interpretation is the history of a progress from a stiff and superstitious formalism to a flexible rationalism."[83]

---

[79] RESTATEMENT 2d § 212 comment e; C. & J. Fertilizer, Inc. v. Allied Mut. Ins. Co., 227 N.W.2d 169 (Iowa 1975); Meyers v. Selznick Co., 373 F.2d 218 (2d Cir. 1966).

[80] *See* 3 CORBIN ON CONTRACTS § 534; 4 WILLISTON ON CONTRACTS § 602; RESTATEMENT 2d § 201 comment c. *See* Farm Bur. Mut. Ins. Co. v. Sandbutte, 302 N.W.2d 104 (Iowa 1981) ("Construction" of a contract is the process of determining its legal effect and is always a matter for the court.).

[81] *See* American Med. Intern v. Scheller, 462 So. 2d 1, 7 (Fla. App. 1984) where the court uses the term "construction" meaning "interpretation."

[82] Corbin, *The Interpretation of Words and the Parol Evidence Rule,* 50 CORNELL L.Q. 161, 171-72 (1965).

[83] 9 WIGMORE, EVIDENCE § 2461 (3d ed. 1940).

The earlier point of view is frequently expressed in the supposed rule that you cannot depart from "the strict, plain, common meaning of the words themselves."[84] That such a rule is unsound is amply demonstrated by Wigmore:

> The fallacy consists in assuming there is or ever can be *some one real* or absolute meaning. Certainly, it should be made prohibitively difficult for an unscrupulous party to establish a meaning foreign to what was in fact understood by the parties at the time of contract formation. However, this result can be accomplished without the aid of an inflexible rule. The so-called rule should be viewed "not so much as a canon of construction as a counsel of caution."[85]

While the interpretation process should begin with the usual and ordinary meaning of the words in a contract, courts should be willing to admit evidence that would supercede the usual meaning, e.g., evidence of trade usage.[86] A famous remark by O. W. Holmes, Jr. suggests a liberal view that would reject the "plain meaning" standard: "A word is not a crystal, transparent and unchanged; it is the skin of a living thought and may vary greatly in color and content according to the circumstances and the time in which it is used."[87] Holmes, however, balked at the use of private conventions or codes between the parties. Thus, "five hundred feet ... should not mean one hundred inches."[88] Modern courts which emphatically reject the view that a judge may determine whether a writing is ambiguous by simply reading it (sometimes called the "four corners" approach) and insist that the court must allow the parties to present evidence to determine whether the terms are susceptible to different meanings may still refuse to permit the objective trade meaning of a term to be overcome by evidence of a special agreement between the parties.[89] There is also a question of whether words must appear to be ambiguous on their face before any evidence may be admitted to explain their meaning. The question should scarcely survive its statement.

---

[84] "[T]he general rule I take to be, that where the words of any written instrument are free from ambiguity in themselves, and where external circumstances do not create any doubt or difficulty as to the proper application of those words to claimants under the instrument, or the subject matter to which the instrument relates, such instrument is always to be construed according to the strict, plain, common meaning of the words themselves; and that, in such case, evidence 'dehors' the instrument, for the purpose of explaining it according to the surmised or alleged intention of the parties to the instrument, is utterly inadmissible." Tindal, C. J., in Attorney-General v. Shore, 11 Sim. 592, 615 [1833-34]. *See also* Young v. Hornbrook, Inc., 153 Me. 412, 140 A.2d 493 (1958); Goode v. Riley, 153 Mass. 585, 28 N.E. 228 (1891).

[85] 9 WIGMORE, EVIDENCE § 2462.

[86] *See, e.g.,* Fryar v. Currin, 312 S.E.2d 16 (S.C. App. 1984) which quotes the second edition of this book to this effect.

[87] Towne v. Eisner, 245 U.S. 418, 425 (1918).

[88] Holmes, *The Theory of Legal Interpretation*, 12 HARV. L. REV. 417, 420 (1899) based upon his famous opinion in Goode v. Riley, 153 Mass. 585, 586, 28 N.E. 228 (1891).

[89] In Mellon Bank, N.A. v. Aetna Bus. Credit, Inc., 619 F.2d 1001 (3d Cir. 1980), the court recognizes that certain terms may appear unambiguous but prior dealings or trade usage may reveal that the terms are more than susceptible to a meaning which differs from the uninformed interpretation of the judge. Thus, where parties contract for 100 ounces of platinum at a price of $100,000, there may be a consistent course of dealing in Canadian dollars and a trade usage measuring platinum in troy ounce (12 rather than 16 ounces to the pound). A "pound of caviar" is fourteen ounces. (When one goes to a lumber yard and asks for a "two by four," he does not receive wood two inches thick and four inches wide. In fact, if he did receive wood measuring two by four, he would not have received what he bargained for.) While the court would permit, *e.g.,* evidence that "ten dollars" meant "ten Canadian dollars," it would not permit the parties to show that "ten dollars" meant "twenty dollars."

"If a judge simply applied his own linguistic background and experience to the words of a contract, contracting parties would live in a most uncertain environment.... A court must have a reference point to determine if words may reasonably admit of different meanings. Under a 'four corners' approach a judge sits in chambers and determines from his point of view whether the words before him are ambiguous. An alternative approach is for the judge to hear the proffer of the parties and determine if there is objective indicia that, from the linguistic reference point of the parties, the terms of the contract are susceptible of different meanings. We believe the latter approach to be the correct approach.... If a *reasonable* alternative interpretation is suggested, even though it may be alien to the judge's linguistic experience, objective evidence in support of that interpretation should be considered by the fact finder."[90]

Notwithstanding the progress made in rejecting the "plain meaning" rule,[91] it is still possible to discover modern cases supporting this unfortunate notion.[92] The RESTATEMENT 2d and the UCC, however, join in rejecting the myth that language can have a singular, unalterable meaning. They insist that meaning can only be discerned in context.[93]

§ 87. Standards of Interpretation — Mutual Misunderstanding — Mistake in Expression.

A. *FIRST RESTATEMENT — Williston/Corbin.*

The FIRST RESTATEMENT listed six possible "standards"[94] of interpretation:[95]

(1) General Usage: what the hypothetical average person in the community or nation as a whole would understand the expression to mean. This is sometimes called the "popular" standard.

(2) Limited Usage: This is a constriction of (1), differing only in degree. Here, the test is the meaning which would be given to the expression in a particular locality, trade or profession.

(3) Mutual Standard: The meaning that conforms to the intention of the parties to the contract, even if such meaning violates common and other usages.

(4) Individual Standard: The meaning intended by the expressing party *or* the understanding of the party to whom the expression was directed.

---

[90] Mellon Bank, N.A. v. Aetna Bus. Credit, Inc., 619 F.2d 1001, 1010, 1011 (3d Cir. 1980). *See also* Sawyer v. Arum, 690 F.2d 590 (6th Cir. 1982) holding that Michigan law rejects any requirement that facial ambiguity must be discovered to permit the consideration of interpretation evidence. UCC § 2-202 comment 1(c): "This section definitely rejects... [t]he requirement that a condition precedent to the admissibility of the type of [interpretation evidence] is an original determination by the court that the language used is ambiguous."

[91] *See, e.g.,* Tigg Corp. v. Dow Corning Corp., 822 F.2d 358 (3d Cir. 1987).

[92] *See, e.g.,* First Union Real Estate Equity v. Crown Am., 639 F. Supp. 838 (M.D. Pa. 1986).

[93] UCC § 2-202 comment 1(b); RESTATEMENT 2d § 212 comment b. *See also* Anderson v. Kammeier, 262 N.W.2d 366 (Minn. 1978); Columbia Nitrogen Corp. v. Royster Co., 451 F.2d 3 (4th Cir. 1971); Michael Schiavone & Sons v. Securralloy, Inc., 312 F. Supp. 801 (D. Conn. 1970); Hurst v. W. J. Lake & Co., 141 Or. 306, 12 P.2d 627 (1932).

[94] Professor Corbin disliked the term "standard" and suggested that, if it is to be used at all, he preferred to say that "standards are the evidential tests by which to determine whether a man's mode of expression and understanding have been prudent and reasonable." 3 CORBIN § 560 at n.22.

[95] FIRST RESTATEMENT § 227 comment a.

(5) Reasonable Expectation: The meaning which the expressing party should reasonably expect the expression would convey to the other party.

(6) Reasonable Understanding: The meaning which the party to whom the manifestations are addressed would reasonably give to such expressions.

The FIRST RESTATEMENT characterized standards (1), (2), (5), and (6) as *objective,* and 3 and 4 as *subjective* since (3) and (4) are based upon the actual intention of the parties regardless of the reasonableness of such intention.[96] While these characterizations are generally accepted, it should be noted that, in the use of either "subjective" standard of interpretation (3) or (4), the actual intention would be evidenced by outward manifestations, i.e., the evidence of such intention would still be "objective." The test, however, would be the actual intention of the party or parties rather than the standard of the hypothetical reasonable person in the nation or locality or, the expectation or understanding of a reasonable person (standards (1), (2), (5), and (6)).

The FIRST RESTATEMENT applied different standards of interepretation depending upon the question of *integration,* i.e., whether the parties adopted a writing as the final and complete expression of agreement.[97] The standard of interpretation applied to an integration was the second, i.e., limited usage, as viewed by an objective third (reasonable) person. Thus, the test was the meaning to be attached by a reasonably intelligent person acquainted with all operative usages and knowing all of the circumstances prior to and contemporaneous with the integration *other than statements by the parties of what they actually intended the final and complete writing to mean.*[98] There is considerable case law support for this test.[99] The exclusion of statements by the parties as to their actual intention is important. A comment emphasizes the exclusion of "oral statements by the parties of what they intended the written language to mean ... though these statements might show the parties gave their words a meaning that would not otherwise be apparent. Such a common understanding may justify reformation, but cannot be the basis of intepretation of an integration."[1] A justification is found in the next comment[2] which suggests that, where parties contract without an integrated writing, they are not focusing upon the symbols of their agreement, i.e., their oral or written expressions. Rather, they are concentrating on the things for which the symbols stand. Where, however, they reduce their agreement to an integrated writing, they are concentrating on the symbols themselves.[3] Thus, where the agreement is evidenced by an integrated writing, "the terms of the writing are conclusive, *and a contract may have a meaning different from that which either party supposed it to have.*"[4]

---

[96] FIRST RESTATEMENT § 227 comment b.

[97] FIRST RESTATEMENT § 228.

[98] FIRST RESTATEMENT § 230.

[99] *See, e.g.,* Smith v. Liberty Mut. Ins. Co., 536 A.2d 164 (N.H. 1987); State Auto. Ins. Ass'n v. Anderson, 365 Pa. Super. 85, 528 A.2d 1374 (1987); Soliva v. Shand, Morahan & Co., 345 S.E. 33 (W. Va. 1986); Sherman v. Ward, 68 Md. App. 212, 511 A.2d 64 (1986); Roth v. Farmers Mut. Ins. Co. of Neb., 220 Neb. 612, 371 N.W.2d 289 (1985); Howard Univ. v. Best, 484 A.2d 958 (D.C. App. 1984).

[1] FIRST RESTATEMENT § 230 comment a.

[2] FIRST RESTATEMENT § 230 comment b.

[3] *Ibid.* Williston, of course, agrees in 4 WILLISTON § 606 at 84.

[4] FIRST RESTATEMENT § 230 comment b, (emphasis added).

Professor Corbin "flatly disapproved" of this view.[5] He vigorously asserted that, "No contract should ever be interpreted and enforced with a meaning that neither party gave it."[6] His persuasive support for this position includes an example of A intending to sell Blackacre and B intending to purchase Whiteacre. The final writing of the parties, however, evidences a contract between them (intepreted according to the understanding of a reasonable third party) as one for the purchase and sale of Greenacre. Corbin believed that enforcement of a contract for the purchase and sale of Greenacre under these circumstances would be "to hold justice up to ridicule."[7]

It is important to emphasize a limitation on the First Restatement (Williston) position. If an integration is interpreted according to the First Restatement test described above, but that intepretation produces an uncertain or ambiguous result, a different "standard" applies, i.e., the test applicable to unintegrated agreements.[8] The test applicable to unintegrated agreements is standard (5), i.e., the standard of the reasonable expectation of the party manifesting assent of the meaning his words or other manifestations would convey to the other party.[9] Again, however, the application of this standard to an integrated writing is contingent upon the application of "standard" (2) to such writing and the production of an uncertain or ambiguous result in that process. Illustrations provide some clarification of this analysis.

One illustration suggests that parties A and B have agreed that in any future stock transactions, the term "abracadabra" shall mean "Northern Pacific." This code term is used to conceal the nature of the dealings. Subsequently, a writing evidences a contract for the purchase of 100 shares of "abracadabra." If the writing was integrated, the application of standard (2) would produce an uncertain result since the meaning of "abracadabra" is uncertain. Thus, the oral understanding of the parties as to the meaning of "abracadabra" can be shown in this situation.[10]

Another illustration has a seller agreeing to sell "my horse" though he owns two horses. "My horse" is, therefore, ambiguous.[11] If, however, the evidence discloses the actual intention of the parties relates to the same horse, such evidence would be admissible to show that "my horse" meant the same horse to both parties.[12]

A third illustration is more troublesome. A and B wish to buy and sell stock but they also wish to conceal the nature of the dealing. They orally agree that, in any future deals, the word "buy" shall mean "sell" and "sell" shall mean "buy." Assuming a subsequent integrated writing evidences an offer from A to "sell" stock to B, the evidence of their private understanding (the "subjective" third standard, the "mutual standard" of intepretation) would not be admissi-

---

[5] 3 CORBIN § 539 at n.61.5.
[6] 3 CORBIN § 572 B (1971 Supp.).
[7] 3 CORBIN § 539 at 81.
[8] FIRST RESTATEMENT § 231.
[9] FIRST RESTATEMENT § 227 comment a.
[10] FIRST RESTATEMENT § 231 ill. 1.
[11] The situation creates a latent ambiguity requiring extrinsic evidence for interpretation between two possible meanings. See Crown Mgt. Corp. v. Goodman, 452 So. 2d 49 (Fla. App. 1984); Hamada v. Valley Nat'l Bank of Ariz., 27 Ariz. App. 433, 555 P.2d 1121 (1976).
[12] FIRST RESTATEMENT § 231 ill. 3.

ble to make "sell" mean "buy."[13] This conclusion is consistent with the view that the application of the normal standard to integrated writings (the reasonable person standard) will not be changed unless that process produces uncertain or ambiguous results. Unlike the "abracadabra" illustration, if the term "sell" is interpreted by an objective third person who is not acquainted with the actual intention of the parties, "sell" is neither uncertain nor ambiguous and will not, therefore, permit a different test (standard) of interpretation. The illustration goes on to suggest, however, that B can recover through reformation, assuming the clear and convincing evidence standard is met. Professor Corbin is particularly critical of this illustration and his criticism provides an excellent view of his position.

First, Corbin wonders whether the analysis would change if the private understanding of the parties was written rather than oral. Second, he suggests that if the parties had agreed that a word such as "run" would be understood as "buy" rather than "sell" meaning "buy," presumably the application of the normal standard applied to an integrated writing would not have produced a certain or unambiguous result. Thus, the standard for unintegrated writings would be applied permitting evidence of the mutual understanding that "run" means "buy." Yet, just as "sell" does not mean "buy" according to the dictionary, neither does "run" mean "buy" in the dictionary. The third Corbin criticism is the most devastating. Recall that the illustration suggested that one of the parties may be able to secure a decree for reformation, thereby giving effect to the private understanding of the parties. Yet, there is not antecedent agreement to buy or sell anything, i.e., there is no "true intention" of the parties to which the writing may be reformed. The prior agreement of the parties dealt exclusive with their understanding of a certain word and its meaning. Earlier we saw that reformation is granted on the basis of fraud or mistake. There is neither fraud nor mistake in the illustration. The writing is not mistaken. It is an accurate expression of the parties' intention as to the symbols they sought to use. Reformation, therefore, should not be an available remedy and B can only recover if a court permits an interpretation of the parties' symbols in accordance with the "mutual standard" or actual intention of the parties.[14]

The RESTATEMENT 2d has been influenced by the Corbin analysis. It is now appropriate to explore the RESTATEMENT 2d analysis.

B. *Restatement 2d Analysis — Parties Attach Materially Different Meanings to Their Expressions — "Chicken" and "Peerless."*

It is too facile to suggest that contract language should be interpreted according to a standard of reasonableness without regard for the meaning of the language attached by the parties at the time of contract formation.[15] When the

---

[13] FIRST RESTATEMENT § 231 ill. 2.

[14] *See* this analysis in 3 CORBIN § 540 at 93-94.

[15] Judge Learned Hand made several statements to the effect that the actual intention of the parties is irrelevant. *See, e.g.,* Eustis Mining Co. v. Beer, Sondheimer & Co., 239 F.2d 976, 985 (S.D.N.Y. 1917): "[I]f both parties severally declared that their meaning had been other than the natural meaning, and each declaration was similar, it would be irrelevant, saving some mutual agreement between them to that effect." In New York Trust Co. v. Island Oil & Transp. Corp., 34

parties dispute the meaning of the terms of their agreement, they are attaching different meaning to those terms. Courts must attempt to determine the meaning attached by the parties at the time of formation since they obviously disagree on the proper interpretation of their mutual manifestations at the time of trial. It must, however, be recognized that parties may have given little or no thought to the particular language which they assumed was an accurate reflection of their intentions. There are many reformation cases where an unread or barely considered writing fails to reflect the true intention of the parties. An even more compelling example of this phenomena occurs in the massive use of standardized, printed forms which evidence most of the contracts in our society.[16] It is an open secret that parties to such contracts do not read, understand or otherwise consciously advert to much of the "boilerplate" language in such forms. If parties enter into a long term contract, though it is evidenced by a negotiated (non-printed form) writing, their lack of omniscience will become clear with respect to situations that were unanticipated at the time of contract formation. While it is common for courts to continue to speak in terms of the "intention of the parties" in such cases, judicial candor, though rarely articulated, may require recognition of the fact that there may be no discoverable intention of the parties under the circumstances.[17] As will be seen in a later section, in such cases a court must supply a term which is reasonable in the circumstances.[18]

There are numerous rules which are more aptly described as common sense guides to interpretation available to courts in their quest for the meaning of the expressions or manifestations of the parties, viewing the parties as reasonable parties under all of the circumstances. We will discuss these rules in the next section. For now, it is important to emphasize how courts must *begin* their search for the meaning of the outward manifestations of the parties. Evidence of particular meanings attached by one or both parties to the contract may not be ignored. Following a Corbin approach, the RESTATEMENT 2d begins its treatment of interpretation by making it clear "that the primary search is for a common meaning of the parties, not a meaning imposed on

---

F.2d 655, 656 (2d Cir. 1929) he wrote, "[C]ontracts depend upon the meaning which the law imputes to the utterances, not upon what the parties actually intended...." Finally, in Hotchkiss v. National City Bank, 200 F. 287, 293 (S.D.N.Y. 1911), he suggested, "A contract has, strictly speaking, nothing to do with the personal or individual intent of the parties." Later, however, he added, "Of course, if it appear by other words, or acts, of the parties, that they attribute a peculiar meaning to such words as they use in the contract, that meaning will prevail, but only by virtue of the other words, and not because of their unexpressed intent." Judge Hand is usually regarded as one of the leading spokespersons of the objectivists who reject a standard of mutual understanding of the language of an agreement if that understanding differs from the understanding of a reasonable person. As can be seen from these quotations, however, even Judge Hand would permit evidence of a mutual understanding of unusual meaning to attach to certain expressions of agreement if such understanding was manifested and the parties had agreed to that understanding.

[16] *See* Murray, *The Standardized Agreement Phenomena in the Restatement (Second) of Contracts,* 67 CORNELL L. REV. 735 (1982); Slawson, *Standard Form Contracts and Democratic Control of Lawmaking Power,* 84 HARV. L. REV. 529 (1971).

[17] The classic illustration of judicial candor is found in the opinion by Judge Clark in Parev Prods. Co. v. I. Rokeach & Sons, 124 F.2d 147 (2d Cir. 1941).

[18] *See* RESTATEMENT 2d § 204.

them by law."[19] Thus, the caption of this primary section on interpretation in the RESTATEMENT 2d is, "Whose Meaning Prevails."[20]

1. "Chicken" — Frigaliment Importing Co. v. B.N.S. International Sales Corp.[21]

It is desirable to begin with an analysis of a celebrated case where the issue was, "What is chicken"? The buyer argued that "chicken" meant only "young" chicken suitable for broiling or frying as contrasted with stewing chicken or fowl. The seller argued that "chicken" includes stewing chicken and, therefore, when it shipped such chicken, plaintiff had no basis for damages as to the chicken it had accepted. Nothing in the written expressions of the parties mentioned types of chicken. The parties had used the same term to describe the subject matter of the contract, i.e., "chicken." They operated in good faith in later asserting their different interpretations of that term. The parties had both "said" the same word but they assumed that "chicken" communicated different thoughts to the other.[22] Each party presented evidence of the trade usage in the business of buying and selling chickens as to what members of the trade would understand from the term, "chicken." Much of the plaintiff-buyer's evidence from experts in the trade was, however, unpersuasive.[23] When the plaintiff argued that the contract price was closer to the market price of "young" chicken than stewing chicken, the court appeared unmoved since the buyer's argument failed to recognize the necessity for the seller to make a profit on the transaction. References to dictionary definitions and U. S. Department of Agriculture definitions of "chicken" were inconclusive. The buyer's argument that by "chicken" it did not mean *that* kind of chicken (i.e., fowl) was highly reminiscent of a classical illustration by Wittgenstein dealing with the intention of a speaker to exclude certain consequences of his statement. "Someone says to me: 'Show the children a game.' I teach them gaming with dice, and the other says, 'I didn't mean that sort of game.' Must the exclusion of the game with dice have come before his mind when he gave me the order?"[24] In his cogent analysis of this case, Professor Corbin argued that "chicken" has more than one *objective* meaning and the problem before the court was how the term was used in this context by the parties. Since the buyer sued for damages, the buyer had the burden of showing that the seller either knew or had reason to know that the buyer intended to purchase only broilers or fryers rather than fowl. It failed to sustain that burden and this is

---

[19] RESTATEMENT 2d § 201 comment c. In Klair v. Reese, 531 A.2d 219, 223 (Del. Super. 1987), the court expressly adopts this position.

[20] RESTATEMENT 2d § 201.

[21] 190 F. Supp. 116 (C.D.N.Y. 1960).

[22] *See* the Corbin criticism in 3 CORBIN § 543 B (1971 Supp.) of the court's acceptance of the famous remark by O. W. Holmes, Jr. (THE PATH OF THE LAW, COLLECTED LEGAL PAPERS at 178) "[T]he making of a contract depends not on the agreement of two sets of external signs — not on the parties having meant the same thing but on their having *said* the same thing."

[23] Thus, when one witness testified that he would understand "chicken" to mean young chicken, i.e., in accordance with the plaintiff-buyer's position, he also testified that in his own transactions he was careful to distinguish types of chicken. This led the court to recall the remark of Lord Mansfield in Edie v. East India Co., 2 Burr. 1216, 1222 (1761) that no credit should be given "witnesses to usage, who could not adduce instances in verification."

[24] *See* M. WHITE, THE AGE OF ANALYSIS 233 (1955).

why the buyer lost the case, i.e., the buyer did not lose because it failed to show that *an* objective meaning of the term "chicken" was limited to young chicken.[25]

The RESTATEMENT 2d bases one of its illustrations on this case but changes the facts by having the buyer reject the shipment of chicken. Each party then seeks damages from the other. Both parties acted in good faith, and neither had reason to know of the difference in the meaning of "chicken" attributed by the other. Under these facts, the RESTATEMENT 2d suggests that both claims fail.[26] The analysis is based on the notion that, had the seller brought the action for the buyer's refusal to accept the chicken, the seller may not have been able to show that the buyer had reason to know of the meaning attributed by the seller. One should not, however, easily arrive at this conclusion. "Chicken" should be viewed in a generic sense as comprising both types of chicken. Absent sufficient evidence of prior course of dealing, trade usage or other specification of "young" chicken by the purchaser, the seller's shipment of stewing chicken is justified as performance within the range of meaning embraced by the term, "chicken."[27]

2. *"Peerless" — Raffles v. Wichelhaus.*[28]

The term "chicken" may be viewed as vague, i.e., as one having a "spectrum of applications."[29] Vagueness may be remedied, at least sufficiently for judicial applications, by defining a term more precisely.[30] Had the parties precisely defined the type of "chicken" they intended to buy and sell, any vagueness in their contract term could have been cured. "Chicken" could also be viewed as an equivocal term, i.e., one with a double meaning, if it may be treated as meaning one type or chicken ("young") or the other ("fowl").[31] The classic case of equivocation is *Raffles v. Wichelhaus*[32] which is often characterized as a case involving "latent ambiguity" rather than equivocation.[33] The

---

[25] 3 CORBIN § 543 B (1971 Supp.).

[26] RESTATEMENT 2d § 201 ill. 4.

[27] *See* Young, *Equivocation in the Making of Agreements,* 64 COLUM. L. REV. 619, 629 (1964) where the author analyzes a case involving "egg coal," Indiana Fuel Supply Co. v. Indianapolis Basket Co., 41 Ind. App. 658, 84 N.E. 776 (1908). The seller tendered "steam egg coal" and the buyer asserted a right to the more expensive "domestic egg coal." The buyer prevailed because of evidence of prior dealings. Professor Young suggests that, absent such evidence, the seller should have prevailed for the reasons set forth in the text. *See also* Mellon Bank, N.A. v. Aetna Bus. Credit, Inc., 619 F.2d 1001 (3d Cir. 1980) which permitted evidence that the parties had used the term "insolvency" in a narrower sense than its usual meaning as a legal term of art, but held that the evidence was insufficient to persuade the court that the parties had understood the term to be used in the narrower sense.

[28] 2 Hurl. & C. 906, 159 Eng. Rep. 375 (Ex. 1864).

[29] *See* Young, *supra* note 27, at 627.

[30] *See, e.g.,* WAISMANN, VERIFIABILITY, IN LOGIC AND LANGUAGE 117, 120 (1st ser. Flew ed. 1951).

[31] Dean Wigmore viewed equivocation as "a term which, upon application to external objects, is found to fit two or more of them equally." 9 WIGMORE EVIDENCE § 2472 (3d ed. 1940). In the example of "egg coal," *supra* note 27, Professor Young describes the term as "equivocal" in the sense that the coal must have been one ("steam") or the other ("domestic"). He argues, however, that contract rules dealing with ambiguous (equivocal) manifestations of agreement should not apply to this case. *See* Young, *supra* note 27, at 626.

[32] 2 Hurl. & C. 906, 159 Eng. Rep. 375 (Ex. 1864).

[33] For a criticism of the term "ambiguity" as applied to this case, see Young, *supra* note 27, at 626. Recent cases suggesting that "latent ambiguity" refers to a situation where the language

parties agreed upon the purchase and sale of cotton from a ship named *Peerless* which was to depart from Bombay. Subsequent evidence revealed two ships named *Peerless,* both of which departed from Bombay albeit, at different times, i.e., one in October and the other in December. The buyer claimed that the contract should be interpreted to mean the October *Peerless,* while the seller claimed that it should be interpreted to mean the December *Peerless.* The seller alleged that he had tendered the cotton from the December *Peerless* but the buyer had refused the tender. The buyer did not deny these allegations but proceeded to urge its interpretation of the contract language. The facts of the case do not reveal how the buyer may have been affected by a delivery from the December *Peerless* rather than the October *Peerless.* Presumably, the buyer's concern for delivery from the October *Peerless* was based on the precipitous decline in the price of cotton.[34] The court simply treated the contract as one in which the particular ship carrying the cotton was of material importance to the parties. Thus, if the buyer "meant" the October *Peerless* while the seller "meant" the December *Peerless,* there was no "consensus ad idem" and no binding contract.[35]

There is more than a strong suspicion that the *Peerless* case was decided by a court that was committed to the *subjective* theory of contract formation.[36] In any event, the case is often regarded as the singular exception to the objectivist theory of contract formation. The only evidence before the court was the statements of the parties *at the time of dispute.* These statements disagreed as to what each party *meant* by the term *Peerless* in their manifestation of agreement. There was no evidence of any prior understanding, prior course of dealing or trade usage which was available to assist the court in making a determination that, for example, a reasonable person in the position of one or both parties would have understood the agreement to refer to the earlier or later *Peerless.* In the absence of such evidence, there is no *objective* basis to prefer one interpretation over another. The case, therefore, is viewed as one of an innocent, mutual misunderstanding of a term which is ambiguous, and the buyer's asserted interpretation is equal to the asserted interpretation of the seller.

---

employed by the parties is clear and suggests a single meaning, but extraneous evidence creates the necessity for choosing among two or more possible meanings, include Crown Mgt. Corp. v. Goodman, 452 So. 2d 49 (Fla. App. 1984) and Hamada v. Valley Nat'l Bank, 27 Ariz. App. 433, 555 P.2d 1121 (1976).

[34] Professor Gilmore suggests that after the contract had been formed, the Union army had captured the port of New Orleans, a critical cotton port which the Union had previously blockaded, and the price of cotton was declining steeply. G. GILMORE, THE DEATH OF CONTRACT at 37, n.87 (1974).

[35] "The straightforward point is that the two parties, though they seemed to have agreed, had not agreed in fact.... There is just no agreement as to what is or turns out to be an important aspect of the arrangement. In *Raffles* there was agreement to purchase cotton from India on a ship named *Peerless.* As it turned out, there was no agreement at all on the crucial issue of which ship *Peerless....* The one basis on which these cases cannot be resolved is on the basis of the agreement — that is, contract as promise. The court cannot enforce the will of the parties because there are no concordant wills. Judgment must therefore be based on principles external to the will of the parties." C. FRIED, CONTRACT AS PROMISE, 59-60 (1981).

[36] *See* Gilmore, *supra* note 34, at 39. *See also* LANGDELL, A SUMMARY OF THE LAW OF CONTRACTS, § 148 (2d ed. 1880): "... a want of mutual consent...."

3. The Analyses of the RESTATEMENT — The Effect of Misunderstanding on Mutual Assent and Interpretation Compared — Ramifications.

Both the FIRST RESTATEMENT and RESTATEMENT 2d provide an analysis of the *Peerless* situation.[37] The following analysis is based on the RESTATEMENT 2d version. There are essentially four categories to be considered in a purported contract between parties who attach materially different meanings to their manifestations of agreement.

(1) If neither party knows or has reason to know the meaning attached by the other, there is no mutual assent and no contract.

(2) If both parties know or have reason to know the meaning attached by the other, there is no mutual assent and no contract.

(3) If one party knows the meaning attached by the other and the other party does not know of any different meaning (though such party *may* have reason to know of a different meaning), there is a contract according to the intention of the party who does not know of the different meaning.

(4) If one party has reason to know of the meaning attached by the other and the other has no reason to know of any different meaning, and neither party knows of the meaning attached by the other, there is a contract according to the intention of the party who had no reason to know of any different meaning.

This section of the RESTATEMENT 2d (§ 20) is found in the chapter dealing with formation of contracts as it relates to mutual assent and the *effect* of misunderstanding on mutual assent and formation. Since the Second Restatement is committed to the view that the primary concern in interpretation is the search for the common meaning of the parties rather than the meaning imposed on the parties by law,[38] the first substantive section of the topic of interpretation is the section captioned, "Whose Meaning Prevails."[39] That section is drafted in accordance with the underlying concept and terminology of § 20. Thus, (1) if the parties have attached the same meaning to the terms of their contract, that meaning will prevail; (2) if the parties have attached different meanings and one party either knows or has reason to know of any different meaning attached by the other, the meaning attached by the party who neither knows nor has reason to know (the innocent party) will prevail; (3) if neither party knows nor has reason to know the meaning attached by the other, and each party has attached a different meaning to the expression, neither is bound by the meaning attached by the other, notwithstanding a failure of mutual assent.[40] It is important to consider the ramifications of this approach.

If the parties to a contract attach the same meaning to their expression, it should prevail over the meaning which a hypothetical reasonable party would attach. Thus, to return to the case involving the meaning of "chicken," if the

---

[37] FIRST RESTATEMENT § 71; RESTATEMENT 2d § 20.

[38] *See* RESTATEMENT 2d § 201 comment c.

[39] RESTATEMENT 2d § 201.

[40] *See* Merced Cty. Sheriff's Emps. Ass'n v. County of Merced, 188 Cal. App. 3d 662, 233 Cal. Rptr. 819 (Cal. App. 1987) (suggesting that the basic principle governing material misunderstanding is that no contract is formed if neither party is at fault or if both parties are equally at fault and citing RESTATEMENT 2d § 20).

buyer and seller attached the meaning of "young chicken" to the word "chicken" as used in their manifestation of agreement, a court should provide an interpretation in accordance with the meaning of both parties even if a reasonable interpretation by an objective third party would lead to a different meaning of "chicken."[41] If both parties in the *Peerless* case had intended the December *Peerless,* that meaning should prevail even in the face of trade usage or other objective evidence that such parties would have normally attached an October meaning to the term *Peerless.* If one party in either the "chicken" or *Peerless* situation either knew or had reason to know of a meaning attached by the other party, the meaning attached by the innocent party should prevail and there is a contract according to that interpretation.[42] It is important to recognize that this analysis is predicated upon a *fault* concept. If one party knows the meaning attached by the other (innocent) party, the first party may be guilty of misrepresentation which would provide the innocent party a power of avoidance.[43] Whether that power is exercised, as in the situation involving mere reason to know rather than actual knowledge, the contract expression will be construed against the party at fault and in favor of the innocent party.[44] In the *Peerless* case, there was no evidence that either party knew or had reason to know the meaning of the term attached by the other. In the "chicken" case, however, had the action been brought by the seller after the buyer rejected the shipment of chickens, a court may have found that the buyer had reason to know that a reasonable seller of chicken might attach the meaning of stewing chicken to the contract term "chicken," notwithstanding the truth of the buyer's assertion that he attached the narrower meaning of "young" chicken to the contract expression. Thus, where the parties attach different meanings to one or more words in their agreement, one should not easily conclude that there is no contract for lack of mutual assent. If one of the meanings is reasonable and the other unreasonable under the circumstances, the parties will be bound in accordance with the reasonable meaning.[45] If, however, both parties know or have reason to know the meaning attached by the other, neither party is bound to the meaning attached by the other[46] since both parties are at fault, and no contract is formed.[47]

C. *Misunderstanding, Misrepresentation and Mistake.*

Though misrepresentation and mistake are explored in a later section, it is important to distinguish and compare the effects of misunderstanding, mis-

---

[41] *See* Sunbury Textile Mills v. Commissioner of Internal Revenue, 585 F.2d 1190 (3d Cir. 1978) (conclusive meaning given to the words as both parties intended them).

[42] In relation to actual knowledge, *see, e.g.,* Hamann v. Crouch, 211 Kan. 852, 508 P.2d 968 (1973); Jet Forwarding v. United States, 437 F.2d 987, (Ct. Cl. 1971). In relation to "reason to know," *see, e.g.,* United States *ex rel.* Union Bldg. Materials v. Haas & Haynie Corp., 577 F.2d 568 (9th Cir. 1978); Emor Inc. v. Cyprus Mines Corp., 467 F.2d 770 (3d Cir. 1972).

[43] *See* RESTATEMENT 2d § 164. Misrepresentation and related matters will be discussed later in this section.

[44] RESTATEMENT 2d § 20 comment d.

[45] *See, e.g.,* Sunshine v. M. R. Mansfield Realty, Inc., 194 Colo. 95, 575 P.2d 847 (1978) where the court upheld the "reasonable" meaning after finding that the parties had ascribed different meanings to a clause in their agreement.

[46] RESTATEMENT 2d § 201(3).

[47] RESTATEMENT 2d § 20 comment d.

representation, and mistake in relation to whose meaning prevails. The RE-
STATEMENT 2d does not define "misunderstanding." In dealing with the question of the belief of one party as to the understanding of a contract expression
by the other party, however, it prefers the term "misunderstanding"[48] rather
than "mistake" which it does define as "a *belief* that is not in accord with the
facts."[49] It also defines "misrepresentation": "an *assertion* that is not in accord
with the facts."[50] A misrepresentation may be fraudulent or non-fraudulent
though a "truthful" (non-fraudulent) misrepresentation will have no operative
effect unless it is material.[51] It is possible to consider certain facets of the
Peerless illustration under the rubrics of mistake or misrepresentation.

The actual *Peerless* case illustrates the lack of knowledge or reason to know
on the part of either party leading to the conventional wisdom that there was
simply no mutual assent. Yet, the parties in *Peerless* could be said to have
been mistaken in the sense that A not only intended Peerless No. 1, but also
mistakenly believed that B also intended No. 1 while B was similarly mistaken as to A's intention as to Peerless No. 2 which B intended. Both parties
could also be said to have been mistaken as to the "basic assumption" underlying their contract, i.e., that there was only one ship named *Peerless*.[52]

If both parties were aware of the existence of two ships named *Peerless*,
they were equally at fault in failing to clarify the particular ship each had in
mind. There is no mistake and, perhaps, no misrepresentation in such a case.
If, however, A knows that B means Peerless No. 1, but A means No. 2 and B is
unaware that there are two ships, A — the knowing party — is not mistaken.
B — the innocent party — is mistaken and would certainly be able to avoid
the contract with respect to No. 2. Moreover, even with respect to the contract
concerning ship No. 1 which the innocent party (B) had in mind, if the knowing party (A) made the contract with the undisclosed intention of not performing it, even that contract is voidable by B because of A's misrepresentation.[53]
If one party (A) merely has reason to know that the other (B) means Peerless
No. 1 and A means No. 2, the formula result is a contract for the goods to be
sold from No. 1, i.e., the intention of the innocent party prevails. It is impossible to bind the innocent party (B) to a contract for goods from No. 2 since B
was not at fault. If A attempted to enforce the No. 2 contract, B could exercise
a power of avoidance because he cannot be bound to a contract where the other
party (A) had reason to know that B was making a mistake in assuming that
there was only one Peerless, i.e., No. 1.[54]

D. *Mistake in Expression.*

There is one other type of mistake which should be considered in relation to
misunderstanding between the parties. The FIRST RESTATEMENT and RESTATE-
MENT 2d include the same illustration but reach different conclusions.

---

[48] RESTATEMENT 2d § 20 and § 201.

[49] RESTATEMENT 2d § 151 (emphasis supplied).

[50] RESTATEMENT 2d § 159 (emphasis supplied).

[51] RESTATEMENT 2d § 159 comment a.

[52] As will be seen in a subsequent section, the power of avoidance based on mistake may be
exercised only where the mistake went to a "basic assumption" of the contract. *See* RESTATEMENT
2d §§ 152 and 153.

[53] *See* RESTATEMENT 2d § 20 and §§ 159-164 (misrepresentation).

[54] *See* RESTATEMENT 2d § 153 comment e.

"*A* says to *B*, 'I offer to sell you my horse for $100.' *B* knowing that *A* intends to offer to sell his cow for that price, not his horse, and that the word 'horse' is a slip of the tongue, replies, 'I accept.'"

The FIRST RESTATEMENT found no contract for the sale of the horse or the cow.[55] The RESTATEMENT 2d finds no contract for the sale of the horse, but *does* find a contract for the sale of the cow.[56] As to the sale of the horse, there is no question that the offeree, *B*, may not "snap up the offer" because he knew or had reason to know of the mistake by *A*.[57] The problem arises with respect to the contract for the sale of the cow. The RESTATEMENT 2d result is consistent with the principle that there is a contract for the sale of the cow because the innocent party, *A*, had the cow in mind and *B* knew that *A* intended to offer to sell the cow. No explanation is offered in the FIRST RESTATEMENT for its conclusion that there is no contract for the sale of the cow. A critic of the RESTATEMENT 2d view, however, provides the rationale: "When the words are unambiguous neither of the generally accepted bases of contract formation is present. There has been neither actual agreement nor expression of agreement for the sale of the cow."[58] The criticism is that suggested earlier concerning the "mutual" standard of interpretation to integrated agreements.[59] In the illustration, if *B* knows that *A* intends to offer to sell his cow for $100 notwithstanding *A*'s use of the term "horse," there must be objective evidence to support a finding that *B* knows. The evidence that *B* knows of *A*'s mistake in expression and of *A*'s intent to offer the cow for sale is sufficient in both RESTATEMENTS to preclude a contract for the sale of the horse. If the standard of interpretation applied were exclusively that of an objective third person with no knowledge of prior dealings or other evidence to support *B*'s knowledge, there should be a contract for the sale of the horse. If *B* knew that *A* did not intend to sell the horse but did not know that *A* *did* intend to sell the cow, there should be no contract for the sale of the cow. The illustration, however, indicates that *B* knew both, i.e., that *A* did not intend to sell the horse but did intend to sell the cow. If *A* and *B* had a prior understanding that a code term, "gork," meant "cow," even under the FIRST RESTATEMENT, the evidence of their mutual understanding of the term "gork" would be admissible to assist a court to discover a contract for the cow. Critics of the RESTATEMENT 2d would admit such evidence because the term "gork" is ambiguous or uncertain. Their criticism of the RESTATEMENT 2d change in result in the horse/cow illustration is, therefore, predicated upon the use of an *unambiguous* term, i.e., "horse" which, to them, simply cannot mean "cow." Yet, no word is totally certain or unambiguous. The contextual evidence of a transaction can certainly lead to an irrefutable finding that parties meant "cow" when they said "horse," or "buy" when they meant "sell," or "black" when they meant "white."

---

[55] FIRST RESTATEMENT § 71 ill. 2.

[56] RESTATEMENT 2d § 20 ill. 5.

[57] *See* RESTATEMENT 2d § 153. Tyra v. Cheney, 129 Minn. 428, 430, 152 N.W. 835 (1915): "One cannot snap up an offer knowing that it was made in mistake." For a "reason to know" example, *see* Geremia v. Boyarsky, 107 Conn. 387, 140 A. 749 (1928).

[58] Palmer, *The Effect of Misunderstanding on Contract Formation and Reformation under the Restatement of Contracts, Second,* 65 MICH. L. REV. 33, 48 (1965).

[59] *See supra* subsection (A).

There are, however, certain ramifications that could lead to unjust results. Critics point to the possibility that A's offer to sell the cow may have been for $600 where the cow is worth only $300 and the horse is worth $1000. To hold B to the cow contract at a price that is double the value of the cow would, according to the criticism, inflict "a punishment on B that does not fit the wrong."[60] The RESTATEMENT 2d avoids this problem in the illustration by adding a fact not contained in the original illustration, i.e. that $100 is a fair price for either the horse or cow.[61] In apparent reaction to the criticism and the possibility that the price of the cow would be excessive, the Reporter's Note to this section suggests that, in such a case, the court may refuse to enforce the contract against B ($600 for the cow worth only $300) "on grounds analogous to those applicable in a suit for reformation."[62] Presumably, the "analogous" application of reformation concepts suggests that a court may use discretion in either recognizing or refusing to recognize a contract for the cow. This is a peculiar suggestion. Another analysis that arrives at the RESTATEMENT 2d result is possible.

Where A makes the offer to sell the "horse" and B accepts, the objective manifestations suggest a contract for the sale of the horse. A, however, will be permitted to show a "subjective" standard in that B knew that A misspoke and intended to say "cow." When B said, "I accept," the evidence indicates that B understood his power of acceptance to be limited to the purchase of the cow. He manifested an intention to purchase the cow though he sought to take advantage of A's mistake. In an action by A for B's refusal to perform the contract for the cow, it is anything but punitive to apply an interpretation standard that would permit A to show B's state of mind, but to apply a different standard to B to preclude him from showing his state of mind in uttering the words, "I accept." Where misrepresentation is shown, the contract is voidable by the innocent party. It would be absurd to permit the party making the misrepresentation to suggest that there either is no contract[63] or that he has a power to avoid the contract because of his misrepresentation. Once the contract for the cow is established according to the objective standard of B's manifestation of acceptance, it does not punish B to hold him to a contract for the sale of the cow even though the price exceeds market value. Evidence that the price is grossly disproportionate to market value may suggest that A was not entirely innocent. Moreover, if A knows that B may intend the horse when B "accepts" the stated offer though B also knows that A intended to say "cow," both parties are *at fault* and there is no contract for the sale of the cow.

---

[60] *See* Palmer, *supra* note 58, at 49.
[61] RESTATEMENT 2d § 20 ill. 5.
[62] *See* RESTATEMENT 2d § 20 Reporter's Note, referring to § 166 comment a.
[63] *See* RESTATEMENT 2d § 163.

§ 88. Rules of Interpretation.

A number of rules or guides to interpretation have been developed by courts over the years. It should be emphasized that they are mere aids, developed in a common sense fashion for determining the meaning to be attributed to the expressions of the parties to the contract and are not to be applied with conclusive effect. These aids will now be explored.

A. *Surrounding Circumstances — Context.*

If a court seeks to determine the meaning attributed by the parties to their expressions of agreement, it is important for the court to place itself in the position of the parties at the time of contract formation.[64] It must take into account all of the surrounding circumstances prior to and contemporanous with the making of the contract so as to more precisely identify the sense of the expressions in questions as apparently understood by the parties.[65] The same thought may be expressed by suggesting that the expressions of the parties depends upon the *context* in which they are manifested.[66] Interpretation according to all of the surrounding circumstances or context was not always the guideline. The tendency of earlier authorities, when all contracts were in writing and under seal, was to suggest that the document must "speak" for itself, and that all aids to a determination of the sense of the expressions must be found within that document.[67] This arbitrary view has long since been abandoned.

B. *The General and Specific Purpose of the Parties — Preambles (Recitals) ("Whereas" Clauses).*

The expressions of the parties are typically words written on paper though the parties may, of course, manifest their intention by conduct. To make sense of these expressions, one of the more helpful guides to interpretation is to discover the apparent *purpose* of the parties. The search for purpose can be traced to the sixteenth century in *Heydon's Case*[68] though that case dealt with statutory interpretation rather than contract interpretation. While there are differences between statutory and contract intepretation, since contract interpretation requires courts to consider manifestations by two or more parties while legislative intent may appear to be a unilateral manifestation of intention,[69] courts are, nonetheless, quite willing to apply similar, if not identical interpretation guidelines to both types of interpretation.[70]

---

[64] RESTATEMENT 2d § 202 comment b.

[65] Recent judicial expressions of this guide to interpretation include Merdes v. Underwood, 742 P.2d 245 (Alaska 1987); Koontz v. Lee, 737 S.W.2d 766 (Mo. App. 1987); Cunha v. Ward Foods, Inc., 804 F.2d 1418 (9th Cir. 1986); Goodstein Constr. Corp. v. Gliedman, 117 A.D.2d 170, 502 N.Y.S.2d 136 (1986). *See also* Standard Land Corp. of Ind. v. Bogardus, 289 N.E.2d 803 (Ind. App. 1972); Murphy Slough Ass'n v. Avila, 27 Cal. App. 3d 649, 104 Cal. Rptr. 136 (1972).

[66] *See* Estate of Johnson v. Carr, 288 Ark. 461, 706 S.W.2d 388 (1986). *See also* RESTATEMENT 2d § 202 comment b.

[67] *See* 9 WIGMORE, EVIDENCE § 2470 (3d ed. 1940).

[68] 30 Co. 7a, 76 Eng. Rep. 637 Exchequer [1584].

[69] It should be noted, however, that legislative history may reveal differences in views or approaches by numerous members of the legislature who were involved with the particular statute.

[70] *See, e.g.,* Pritchard v. Wick, 406 Pa. 598, 178 A.2d 725 (1962) which mentions a number of guidelines and suggests that their application in a contract interpretation also complies with the

Courts will often suggest that the parties' expression should give effect to their "general purpose." This rule, guide, or aid to interpretation, however, is invariably couched in terms of the next guide to be discussed, i.e., the requirement that the expression of the parties be read as a whole.[71] The determination of the purpose of particular language in the contract can be significant where the language is vague or ambiguous. Thus, where a clause excused a party because of "adverse weather conditions," the purpose of the parties was helpful in deciding whether unusually good weather was contemplated within that clause.[72] Similarly, where a contract permitted an extension of time for performance "in the event of high water" and the purchaser was to sever the timber, the court viewed the purpose of the clause as providing additional time if the purchaser was prevented from exercising his rights rather than the incidental occurrence of high water at some point during the original severance period.[73] Where a party feigned suicide, and left his wife and attempted to marry another woman, then took out an insurance policy naming his "wife" as beneficiary, his purpose was important in determining the meaning of the term, "wife."[74] Courts invariably seek the intention of the parties. In large measure, they are seeking the purpose of the parties in making the contract.

If the principal purpose of the parties is ascertainable, it is given great weight by the courts and further interpretation of the contract is guided by it.[75] Parties sometimes seek to emphasize their purpose(s) by inserting a *preamble* ("recital" or "whereas") clause in the written expression of their agreement which typically appears at the inception of the writing. These clauses are viewed as persuasive but not controlling in determining the intention or purpose of the parties.[76] Where there is ambiguity or inconsistency between the preamble and the remainder of the writing, the following construction has been accepted: (a) where the preamble (recital or whereas clause) is clear and the remainder of the writing is ambiguous, the preamble will control; (b) where the preamble is ambiguous and the remainder clear, the remainder will control; (c) where the preamble and remainder are both clear but inconsistent with each other, the remainder of the writing will control.[77] These guides are in the same vein as common sense directives that a particular manifestation will control a general expression, or a more recent or more detailed manifestation of the parties' intention should prevail over earlier inconsistent or more general statements. These aids will be considered later in this section.

---

same guidelines as found in the Pennsylvania Statutory Construction Act. For a pristine analysis of various views of statutory interpretation and the problems raised by different approaches, *see* H. HART & A. SACKS, THE LEGAL PROCESS: BASIC PROBLEMS IN THE MAKING AND APPLICATION OF LAW, ch. VII at 1144 *et seq.* (tent. ed. 1958).

[71] *See, e.g.,* Rosebud Sioux Tribe v. A & P Steel, Inc., 733 F.2d 509 (8th Cir. 1984).

[72] Stender v. Twin City Foods, Inc., 82 Wash. 2d 250, 510 P.2d 221 (1973).

[73] Lawson v. Martin Timber Co., 238 La. 467, 115 So. 2d 821 (1959).

[74] *In re* Soper's Estate, 196 Minn. 60, 246 N.W. 427 (1935).

[75] Alvin, Ltd. v. United States Postal Serv., 816 F.2d 1562 (Fed. Cir. 1987); Crestview Bowl, Inc. v. Womer Constr. Co., 225 Kan. 335, 592 P.2d 74 (1979); Hanson v. Stern, 102 Ga. App. 341, 116 S.E. 2d 237, 239 (1960). RESTATEMENT 2d § 202 comment c.

[76] *See* State of Alaska v. Fairbanks North Star Borough Sch. Dist., 621 P.2d 1329 (Alaska 1981).

[77] *See* Stech v. The Panel Mart, 434 N.E.2d 97 (Ind. App. 1982) relying on Maddux & Sons v. Trustees of Ariz. Laborers, 125 Ariz. 475, 478-479, 610 P.2d 477 at 480-81 (1980) which quotes Williams v. Barkley, 165 N.Y. 48 at 57, 58 N.E. 765 at 767 (1900). Both of the cases relied upon quote the originator of this concept, i.e., Lord Esher in Ex parte Dawes, 17 Q.B.D. 275, 286 (1886).

C. *The Transaction Must Be Viewed as a Whole.*

Numerous cases indicate that all of the different parts of an agreement must be viewed together, i.e., as a whole, and each part interpreted in the light of all of the other parts.[78] As suggested earlier,[79] this guide is often found in statements suggesting that courts must be concerned about the "general purpose" of the parties to the contract and that purpose can be discovered only by interpretation of the whole agreement of the parties. Similarly, the requirement that interpretation occur in *context* is another illustration of this guide since only by a contextual determination is the general purpose of the parties discernible and, again, that purpose is discernible only by considering the entire expression of the parties. As the RESTATEMENT 2d suggests, "A word changes meaning when it becomes part of a sentence, the sentence when it becomes part of a paragraph."[80] Thus, an interpretation which gives meaning to every part of the expression will be preferred to one that gives no effect to one or more parts.[81] If this is not reasonably possible, the expression should be interpreted to give effect to the apparent principal purpose of the parties.[82] A corollary to the rule that the contract should be interpreted as a whole is that all of the different writings relating to the same transaction should be interpreted together, whether or not they form a single contract.[83]

D. *A Reasonable, Lawful, or Effective Interpretation Is Preferred.*

It is a general rule of interpretation that a reasonable interpretation of an expression is preferred to one that is literal, unusual, absurd, or of no effect.[84] Thus, it has been held that an interpretation permitting a professional guide not only to be a contestant in a bass fishing tournament but allowing him to fish the tournament waters prior to the tournament would be an absurd interpretation which is not permitted.[85] Similarly, an interpretation that would allow a $7,000 forfeit for an uncompleted repair costing $50 was rejected as absurd.[86] An interpretation that will make the transaction a lawful and effective contract is preferred to one that will make it illegal[87] or ineffective.[88]

---

[78] *See* Elliot Leases Cars, Inc. v. Quigley, 118 R.I. 321, 373 A.2d 810 (1972); Pritchard v. Wick, 406 Pa. 598, 178 A.2d 725 (1962) (also stating other guides to interpretation). RESTATEMENT 2d § 202(2) and comment d.

[79] *See supra* text at note 71.

[80] RESTATEMENT 2d § 202 comment d.

[81] Intertherm, Inc. v. Coronte Imperial Corp., 558 S.W.2d 344, 351-52 (Mo. App. 1977); Central Ga. Elec. Membership Corp. v. Georgia Power Co., 217 Ga. 171, 121 S.E.2d 644, 646 (1961). RESTATEMENT 2d § 203(a) and comment a.

[82] *See supra* subsection (B).

[83] *See* Paisner v. Renaud, 102 N.H. 27, 149 A.2d 867 (1959) and RESTATEMENT 2d § 202(2).

[84] "[W]here one construction would make a contract unusual and extraordinary while another equally consistent with the language used would make it reasonable, just and fair, the latter must prevail." Bank of Cashton v. La Crosse Cty. Scandinavian Town Mut. Ins. Co., 216 Wis. 513, 518, 257 N.W. 451 (1934). *See also* Soliva v. Shand, Morahan & Co., 345 S.E.2d 33 (W. Va. 1986); Harper v. Gibson, 284 S.C. 274, 325 S.E.2d 586 (1985); Rosebud Sioux Tribe v. A & P Steel, Inc., 733 F.2d 509 (8th Cir. 1984); City of Baltimore v. Industrial Elecs., Inc., 230 Md. 224, 186 A.2d 469 (1962). RESTATEMENT 2d § 203(a).

[85] Newmac/Bud Light Team Bass Circuit, Inc. v. Adams, 486 So. 2d 255 (La. App. 1986).

[86] Brown v. Hotard, 428 So. 2d 505 (La. App. 1983).

[87] *See* Service Emp. Int'l Union Local 18 AFL-CIO v. American Bldg. Main. Co., 29 Cal. App. 3d 356, 105 Cal. Rptr. 564 (1972); Central Ga. Elec. Membership Corp. v. Georgia Power Co., 217 Ga. 171, 121 S.E.2d 644 (1961). RESTATEMENT 2d § 203(a) and comment c.

[88] *See* Explosive Corp. of Am. v. Garlam Enters. Corp., 817 F.2d 894 (1st Cir. 1987); Sletten

E. *Public Interest Favored.*

If the transaction in question affects the public interest, it is often stated that an interpretation will be preferred that is most favorable to the public interest.[89] This rule is one of "construction" rather than interpretation, i.e., the theory is not that it aids in determining the intention of the parties; rather, it is based on the policy that it is desirable to favor the public interest where there is doubt as to the intended meaning. It finds its most frequent applications in contracts made by public utilities[90] or by contracts in which one of the parties is a governmental unit.[91]

F. *Subsequent Conduct of the Parties (Course of Performance) as an Interpretation Aid.*

If the parties to a contract have started to perform the contract and their performance manifests a common manifestation of their understanding of the prior expression of agreement, this evidence will be given great weight in determining the meaning attributed to their expressions.[92] As will be seen in the next section dealing with trade usage, course of dealing, and course of performance under the UCC, course of performance evidence is the strongest evidence of the parties' intention except for their express terms, and even their express terms can be overcome by course of performance evidence on the footing that it constitutes a subsequent modification of their prior expression of agreement. It is not remarkable that course of performance evidence has been elevated to this premier position since it is the most recent and most specific manifestation by the parties themselves as to the meaning of their contract.

Constr. Co. v. Audit Servs., 619 P.2d 177 (Mont. 1980); H. P. Hood & Sons v. Heins, 124 Vt. 331, 205 A.2d 561 (1964).

[89] "[A] sound public policy favors the free and unrestricted use of land by the legal holder, and therefore alleged restrictive covenants should be construed strictly against the establishment and effect of such covenants, and liberally in support of the free use of the land." Ferguson v. Beth Mary Steel Corp., 166 Md. 666, 172 A. 238 (1934); Seman v. First State Bank of Eden Prarie, 394 N.W.2d 557 (Minn. App. 1986) (public interest in preserving integrity of cashier's checks); *See also* Houk v. Ross, 34 Ohio St. 2d 77, 296 N.E.2d 266 (1973); De Long Corp. v. Lucas, 176 F. Supp. 104 (S.D.N.Y. 1959), *aff'd,* 278 F.2d 804 (2d Cir. 1960), *cert. denied,* 364 U.S. 833 (1960). *See also* RESTATEMENT 2d § 207.

[90] In a contract between two utilities, however, the public utilities commission will not intervene unless the contract is adverse to the public interest. *See* Lemhi Tel. Co. v. Mountain States Telephone and Telegraph Co., 98 Idaho 692, 571 P.2d 753 (1977).

[91] *See* Codell Constr. Co. v. Commonwealth of Ky., 566 S.W.2d 161 (1977) (rule in construing contracts to which government is a party is to resolve ambiguities in its favor because an interpretation is preferred which favors the public).

[92] "It is quite the universal holding that, where the interpretation of a contract is fairly debatable, the court will adopt the practical construction which the parties to the contract have heretofore adopted, whether by conduct or otherwise." Fort Dodge Co-op Dairy Mktg. Ass'n v. Ainsworth, 217 Iowa 712, 716, 251 N.W. 85 (1935). RESTATEMENT 2d § 202(4) and comment g. *See also* Hamblen Cty. v. City of Morristown, 656 S.W.2d 331 (Tenn. 1983).

G. Construction Against Drafter — "Contra Proferentem."

It is a general rule of interpretation that an expression is to be interpreted most strongly against the party responsible for its drafting.[93] The rule is particularly applicable if it has been embodied in a writing prepared by the skilled adviser of one of the parties, or if the person who drew it had special competence in such matters. The rule finds frequent application in cases dealing with insurance contracts or other contracts containing standardized (printed) terms.[94] The common sense basis for the rule is that, where the language may be reasonably interpreted in a way that favors the drafter or in a way that favors the non-drafter, the latter interpretation will be preferred since the drafter had control over the language and may even have left the language less than clear so as not to alert the other party to certain troublesome possibilities of which the drafter now seeks a favorable interpretation.[95] Since the drafter is responsible for the unclear language, it should be interpreted against him even if he intended no advantage to himself in drafting it.

H. Expressio Unius Est Exclusio Alterius — The Enumeration of Some Excludes Others.

Parties to a contract may specify certain items in detail in their contract. When this occurs, a rule of interpretation is invoked which suggests that the specification of such items impliedly excludes other items relating to the same general matter, i.e., the expression in the contract of one or more things of a class implies exclusion of all not expressed, or, *expressio unius est exclusio alterius*.[96] Like other guides to interpretation, this rule is not conclusive[97] and may give way to superior rules of interpretation.[98]

I. Ejusdem Generis.

Where the language of a contract is uncertain, another canon of construction or interpretation to which courts sometimes resort is the rule of *ejusdem generis* which applies where general language in the contract is followed by

---

[93] *See* Z. R. L. Corp. v. Great Central Ins. Co., 156 Ill. App. 3d 856, 510 N.E.2d 102 (1987) (citing the second edition of this work for this proposition). *See also* United States v. Turner Constr. Co., 819 F.2d 283 (Fed. Cir. 1987); Pappas v. Bever, 219 N.W.2d 720 (Iowa 1979).

[94] *See, e.g.,* National Ins. Underwriters v. Carter, 17 Cal. 3d 380, 131 Cal. Rptr. 42, 551 P.2d 362 (1976) in which the court finds this rule to be much more significant than other "maxims" of interpretation or construction because the rule of resolving ambiguities against the insurer rests upon basic considerations of policy.

[95] RESTATEMENT 2d § 206 and comment a.

[96] *See* Eden Music Corp. v. Times Square Music Publications Co., 127 A.D.2d 161, 514 N.Y.S.2d 3 (1987); Sonneman v. Blue Cross & Blue Shield of Minn., 403 N.W.2d 701 (Minn. App. 1987); United States v. First Nat'l Bank of Crestview, 513 So. 2d 179 (Fla. App. 1987); Park View Manor v. Housing Auth., 300 N.W.2d 218 (N.D. 1980).

[97] CKB & Assoc., Inc. v. Moore McCormack Petr., Inc., 734 S.W.2d 653 (Texas 1987). *See also* Rad-Razorback Ltd. Pt'ship v. B. G. Coney, 289 Ark. 550, 713 S.W.2d 462 (rule is not dispositive) and Kaiser Motors Corp. v. Savage, 229 F.2d 525, 533-34 (8th Cir. 1956) where the court indicates that the doctrine is an aid in construction which would not apply where there are clearer indications of the parties' intentions.

[98] National Ins. Underwriters v. Carter, 17 Cal. 3d 380, 131 Cal. Rptr. 42, 551 P.2d 362 (1976) (the "expressio unius" maxim cannot defeat the rule of "contra proferentem" in insurance contracts which rests on basic considerations of policy).

enumerated specific terms relating to the same subject matter. The meaning of the general language is said to be limited to matters similar in kind or classification to the enumerated specific terms.[99] Thus, where a lease contract could be terminated "for good cause" and this general language was followed by enumerated items such as nonpayment of rent, serious or repeated damage to the premises, or the creation of physical hazards, the general phrase, "for good cause" did not include other violations of the lease such as maintaining a dog.[1] The rule of *ejusdem generis* may be avoided by including language indicating that the general language includes but is not limited to the specific, enumerated items following it.[2]

J. Presumptions About Interpretation — Ordinary Meaning, Technical Meaning, Legal Meaning, and Trade Usage.

As we have seen, no single standard of interpretation is necessarily applied in determining the meaning of the contracting parties' expressions. Certain presumptions, however, reappear in the case law and should be considered.

1. The ordinary or popular sense of words as used throughout the country is preferred in the absence of circumstances indicating a contrary understanding.[3]

2. Technical terms and words or art are to be given their technical meaning unless the circumstances indicate a contrary understanding.[4]

3. Where words have come to have an established meaning in the law, that meaning will be adopted, in the absence of competent affirmative evidence of a contrary understanding.[5] If mutual understanding is overcome by statute or administrative regulation, the obligation results from the governmental regulation rather than interpretation.

4. The usage of a trade, locality, profession or the like will supersede the ordinary or popular sense of words where the situation justifies the assumption that these usages would more nearly approximate the understanding of the parties.[6] If the usage is, in fact, the settled habit of expression of the group in question and not merely the expression of a few persons, and if the parties to the contract are members of the group, the special usage will always pre-

---

[99] *See* General Elec. Credit Corp. of Tenn. v. Larson, 387 N.W.2d 734 (N.D. 1986); Propis v. Fireman's Fund Ins. Co., 112 A.D.2d 734, 492 N.Y.S.2d 228 (1985); United Cal. Bank v. Prudential Ins. Co. of Am., 140 Ariz. 238, 681 P.2d 390 (1984).

[1] Housing Auth. of Mansfield, Mo. v. Rovig, 676 S.W.2d 314 (Mo. App. 1984).

[2] *See* Eastern Air Lines v. McDonnell Douglas Corp., 532 F.2d 957 (5th Cir. 1976) (delays in performance due to causes beyond seller's control, including but not limited to, enumerated events).

[3] *See* Fryar v. Currin, 280 S.C. 241, 312 S.E.2d 16 (1984) citing the second edition of this book for this proposition. *See also* I. J. Scott, Jr. v. East Ala. Educ. Found., Inc., 417 So. 2d 572 (Ala. 1982). *See also* RESTATEMENT 2d § 202(3)(a).

[4] *See* Kleiner v. First Nat'l Bank of Atlanta, 97 F.R.D. (N.D. Ga. 1983); RESTATEMENT 2d § 202(3)(b).

[5] *See, e.g.,* Mellon Bank, N.A. v. Aetna Bus. Credit Inc., 619 F.2d 1100 (3d Cir. 1980) (legal term of art, "insolvent," interpreted in accordance with technical meaning where defendant failed to sustain burden of showing different meaning attached by the parties). *See also* Robin v. Sun Oil Co., 548 F.2d 554, 558 (5th Cir. 1977).

[6] *See* Stewart v. Brennan, 748 P.2d 816 (Haw. App. 1988); Bischoff v. Quong-Watkins Props., 748 P.2d 410 (Idaho App. 1987); Hurst v. W. J. Lake & Co., 141 Or. 306, 16 P.2d 627 (1932). *See* RESTATEMENT 2d § 202(5).

vail in the absence of competent evidence that the parties understood that some other meaning was to be attributed to the language in question. The UCC has emphasized the importance of trade usage, course of dealing, and course of performance as evidence of the factual bargain of the parties. The UCC treatment of these concepts will be explored in the next section.

K. *Interpretation of Inconsistent Expressions.*

Generally accepted rules are found in the case law to avoid apparent inconsistencies in the parties' expression of their contract.

1. Specific terms will usually be held to qualify general terms since parties are more likely to advert consciously to specific rather than general terms and the specific terms, therefore, normally suggest a more precise identification of the parties' intentions.[7]

2. A word or phrase used more than once is to be interpreted in the same sense throughout the contract absent a clear indication of contrary intention.[8]

3. Obvious mistakes of grammar or punctuation will usually be corrected or they will be disregarded to the extent that they conflict with a clear intention expressed in the contract.[9]

4. Where there is a conflict between printed and written provisions, the preferred interpretation will give effect to the written provisions as superior evidence of the parties' intentions.[10] Similarly, separately negotiated terms will be preferred over standardized printed terms which have not been separately negotiated.[11]

5. Where one clause of the contract suggests one intention and another clause of the same contract suggests an inconsistent intention, the intention manifested in the principal or more important clause should be preferred.[12]

L. *Inconsistent Warranties — Uniform Commercial Code.*

The UCC requires courts to strive to construe express and implied warranties as consistent with each other.[13] Where such construction is unreasonable, however, the UCC suggests rules of construction that are in keeping with common law notions that more particular or detailed statements of warranty are preferred over more general warranty statements, and the parties' expressions prevail over any warranties implied by law. Thus, exact or technical

---

[7] *See, e.g.*, Enchanted World Doll Museum v. Buskohl, 398 N.W.2d 149 (S.D. 1986); Royal Ins. Co. (U. K.) Ltd. v. Ideal Mut. Ins. Co., 649 F. Supp. 130 (E.D. Pa. 1986); Auto Numerics, Inc. v. Bayer Indus., Inc., 144 Ariz. 181, 696 P.2d 1330 (1984). *See also* RESTATEMENT 2d § 203(c).

[8] Jordan v. Smith, 596 F. Supp. 1295 (D.C. Ga. 1984); Miller Cattle Co. v. Mattice, 38 Ariz. 180, 298 P. 640 (1931).

[9] Ultimate Computer Servs. v. Biltmore Realty Co., 186 N.J. Super. 144, 443 A.2d 713 (1982); Vogt v. Calvary Lutheran Univ. Missionary Soc'y, 213 Wis. 380, 251 N.W. 239 (1933).

[10] Wood River Pipeline Co. v. Will Bros. Energy Serv. Co., 738 P.2d 866 (Kan. 1987); Tuzman v. Leventhal, 174 Ga. App. 299, 329 S.E.2d 610 (1985). *Cf.* UCC § 3-118(b) and (c) with respect to negotiable instruments such as checks: handwritten terms control typewritten and printed terms, and typewritten control printed; words control figures except that if the words are ambiguous, figures control.

[11] RESTATEMENT 2d § 203(d).

[12] Joseph Cumacho Assocs. v. Millard, 169 Ga. App. 937, 315 S.E.2d 478 (1984); Union Water Power Co. v. Inhabitants of Lewiston, 101 Me. 564, 65 A. 67 (1906).

[13] Gable v. Silver, 258 So. 2d 11 (Fla. App. 1972).

specifications which constitute express warranties are preferred over more general express warranties such as those created by sample, model or general language of description.[14] A warranty created by taking a sample from an existing bulk of goods displaces inconsistent general language of description,[15] and express warranties prevail over inconsistent implied warranties of merchantability[16] but not over implied warranties of fitness for a particular purpose[17] since the latter are created through the buyer's reasonable reliance on the seller's exercise of skill or judgment.[18]

Like other rules or aids to interpretation, these UCC rules "are designed to ascertain the intention of the parties by reference to the factor which probably claimed the attention of the parties in the first instance."[19] They are not, however, absolute rules[20] and may be varied if the circumstances indicate that their application would preclude the effectuation of the dominant intention of the parties.[21]

§ 89. Custom as a Standard — Trade Usage, Course of Dealing, Course of Performance — Uniform Commercial Code.

A. *Custom as Standard — Definitions.*

In a given trade, profession, or calling, parties may adhere to certain practices to such an extent that the practices may appear to be the "standard" within that industry or vocation. There may be a temptation to treat the customary practices as the legal standard. The well-known Judge Learned Hand reminded us some time ago, however, that the determination of the legal standard of reasonable conduct still lies with courts, regardless of how well-established a particular practice may be.[22] If, however, a court is attempting to discern the intention of the parties to a contract, in the absence of express terms to the contrary, it is reasonable to assume that the parties have contracted in the context of any applicable trade usage.[23] *Trade usage* is defined in the UCC as "any practice or method of dealing having such regularity of observance in a place, vocation or trade as to justify an expectation that it will be observed with respect to the transaction in question."[24] Parties may

---

[14] UCC § 2-317(a).

[15] UCC § 2-317(b).

[16] The implied warranty of merchantability is described in UCC § 2-314.

[17] The implied warranty of fitness for a particular purpose is found in UCC § 2-315.

[18] UCC § 2-317(c). *See* Singer Co. v. E. I. du Pont de Nemours & Co., 579 F.2d 433 (8th Cir. 1978) and Morrison v. Devore Trucking, Inc., 68 Ohio App. 2d 140, 428 N.E.2d 438 (1980) (dealing with the conflict between express warranties and the implied warranty of fitness for a particular purpose.)

[19] UCC § 2-317 comment 3.

[20] *Ibid.*

[21] *See, e.g.,* Stewart-Decatur Sec. Sys. v. Vone Weise Gear Co., 517 F.2d 1136 (8th Cir. 1975) where an exact or technical specification was inconsistent with a model, but the evidence clearly indicated that the parties intended to contract with reference to the model rather than the specification. Thus, the rule of interpretation in UCC § 2-317(a) that exact or technical specifications displace inconsistent express warranties by sample or model was inapplicable.

[22] The T. J. Hooper v. Northern Barge Co., 60 F.2d 737 (2d Cir. 1932).

[23] RESTATEMENT 2d § 220(1) suggests that an agreement is to be interepreted in accordance with a relevant usage if each party either knew or had reason to know of the usage, and neither knew nor had reason to know that the meaning attached by the other was inconsistent with the usage.

[24] UCC § 1-205(2). *Accord,* RESTATEMENT 2d § 222. *See* Heggblade-Marguleas-Tenneco, Inc. v. Sunshine Biscuit, Inc., 59 Cal. App. 3d 948, 131 Cal. Rptr. 183 (1976).

have dealt with each other in the past. If their prior *course of dealing* constituted "a sequence of previous conduct ... which is fairly to be regarded as establishing a common basis of understanding for interpreting their expressions and other conduct,"[25] it would be foolhardy for a court to ignore such course of dealing in determining the intention of the parties in a given transaction.[26] After forming a contract, the parties may have begun to perform it. If their *course of performance* involved "repeated occasions for performance ... with knowledge of the nature of the performance and opportunity for objection to it by the other, any course of performance accepted or acquiesced in without objection [should] be relevant to determine the meaning of the agreement."[27]

B. *Hierarchy — Modifications Through Course of Performance.*

Among the three concepts of trade usage, course of dealing, and course of performance, trade usage is the most general since it covers all who deal in a particular trade. Course of dealing is much more specific since it relates only to the parties to the transaction, and course of performance is just as specific as course of dealing. In addition, however, course of performance is a more recent or immediate manifestation of the parties' intentions. Where it is not possible to treat the three concepts as consistent with each other in a given situation, therefore, course of performance will control course of dealing, and course of dealing will control trade usage.[28] Express terms of the parties' agreement are typically viewed as dominant over all three.[29] Since course of performance is subsequent to the express terms of the contract, however, course of performance may be viewed as a modification of the contract by conduct, i.e., in this light, course of performance will be superior to even the express terms of the contract.[30]

C. *Custom Versus Trade Usage — Existence, Scope, and Meaning of Trade Usage.*

The UCC is very clear in its departure from common law notions of "custom." Common law tests which required custom to be "ancient," "immemorial," "universal," "notorious" or the like have been abandoned by the Code.[31]

---

[25] UCC § 1-205(1). *Accord,* RESTATEMENT 2d § 223.

[26] It should be noted that the UCC descriptions of trade usage and course of dealing appear in Article 1 of the Code and are, therefore, applicable to all Articles of the Code rather than just Article 2.

[27] UCC § 2-208(1). *Accord,* RESTATEMENT 2d § 202(4).

[28] UCC §§ 1-205(4) and 2-208(2). *Accord,* RESTATEMENT 2d § 203(b). *See* Delano Growers' Coop. Winery v. Supreme Wine Co., 393 Mass. 666, 473 N.E.2d 1066 (1985) (course of dealing controls usage of trade); R. G. Le Tourneau, Inc. v. Quinn Equip. Co., 131 Ill. App. 2d 295, 266 N.E.2d 151 (1970) (course of performance controls course of dealing and usage of trade).

[29] *Ibid.*

[30] UCC § 2-208(3) referring to UCC § 2-209 dealing with modifications which, it should be recalled, require no consideration to be binding if made in good faith. *See* T. J. Stevenson & Co. v. 81,193 Bags of Flour, 629 F.2d 338 (5th Cir. 1980) (failure to object to buyer's failure to comply with contract provisions concerning notice of breach constituted a modification of the notice requirement); Owens v. Harnett Transfer, Inc., 42 N.C. App. 532, 257 S.E.2d 136 (1979) (for five consecutive months, defendant took payment from plaintiff's monthly share of freight charges. Contract was modified as to the method of payment, and plaintiff's subsequent failure to make payments for two months was not a breach).

[31] UCC § 1-205 comment 5. *See also* Threadgill v. Peabody Coal Co., 34 Colo. App. 203, 526 P.2d 676 (1974).

New and current usages observed by the great majority of dealers in the trade will be observed.[32] Moreover, there is no requirement that trade usage be certain or precise in the sense that "custom" had to be certain or precise.[33] The existence and scope of trade usage are questions of fact,[34] but if the trade usage is found in a written code or similar document, the interpretation of the document is a question for the court and, as such, it is a question of "law."[35] There may be a specific usage of trade in a locality to which the parties are bound that differs from the general usage of trade.[36] Industry standards may be explained by trade usage.[37] Parties who are engaged in a trade are subject to the trade usage even if they are newcomers to the trade.[38] In general, courts have applied the standard of trade usage to parties who either know or have reason to know the usage.[39] There is no requirement that the trade usage be consistent with the meaning of the agreement apart from trade usage nor that the agreement be ambiguous before evidence of trade usage will be admitted.[40] As will be seen later in this section, trade usage may be used by courts to interpret the expression of the parties, or it may be seen as supplying terms in the agreement of the parties.

---

[32] RESTATEMENT 2d § 222 comment b, supports this position.

[33] See Nanakuli Paving & Rock Co. v. Shell Oil Co., 664 F.2d 772 (9th Cir. 1981). See also Levie, Trade Usage and Custom under the Common Law and the Uniform Commercial Code, 40 N.Y.U. L. REV. 1101 (1965).

[34] UCC § 1-205(2). See also Nanakuli Paving & Rock Co. v. Shell Oil Co., supra note 33; Federal Express Corp. v. Pan Am. World Airways, Inc., 623 F.2d 1297 (8th Cir. 1980); Mieske v. Bartell Drug Co., 92 Wash. 2d 40, 593 P.2d 1308 (1979).

[35] RESTATEMENT 2d § 222(2). See supra § 86, text prior to note 75, where the tautology of questions of "fact" versus questions of "law" was considered.

[36] See Nanakuli Paving & Rock Co. v. Shell Oil Co., supra note 33.

[37] Craig Food Indus. v. Weihing, 746 P.2d 279 (Utah App. 1987). In Action Time Carpets, Inc. v. Midwest Carpet Brokers, Inc., 271 N.W.2d 36 (Minn. 1978), evidence that "at once" as used in a purchase order was understood in the carpet industry to mean "as soon as possible." See also Hurst v. W. J. Lake & Co., 141 Or. 306, 16 P.2d 627, 89 A.L.R. 1222 (1932) where the question of the meaning of "minimum 50 per cent protein" was explained as permitting a protein content of not less than 49.5 percent. Inter alia, the court also suggests the following industry or trade standards: in the bricklaying trade, a contract fixing the bricklayer's compensation at "$5.25 per thousand" does not contemplate that he will lay 1000 bricks but that he will build a wall of a certain size; in the lumber industry, a contract requiring the delivery of 4000 shingles will be fulfilled by the delivery of only 2500 because the trade usage regards two packs of a certain size as 1,000 shingles and delivery of eight packs fulfills the contract though they actually contain only 2500.

[38] UCC § 1-205(3). See also United States ex rel. Union Bldg. Materials Corp. v. Haas & Haynie Corp., 577 F.2d 568 (9th Cir. 1978). But see Foxco Indus. v. Fabric World, 595 F.2d 976 (5th Cir. 1979) applying trade usage of a trade association to a party who was not a member of the association and was unaware of usage).

[39] RESTATEMENT 2d § 222(3). See also Mieske v. Bartell Drug Co., 92 Wash. 2d 40, 593 P.2d 1308 (1979) (consumer who supplied home movies for splicing on large reels was not bound by trade usage concerning exclusionary clause though film processors would be bound by such usage). L. F. Pace & Sons v. Travelers Indem. Co., 9 Conn. App. 30, 38-39, 514 A.2d 766, 771 (1986) ("In its instructions, the court also cautioned the jury that custom and usage would not be the basis for the defendant's obligation if the plaintiff knew or had reason to know that the defendant had an intention inconsistent with such usage. The trial court's instructions were correct in law....").

[40] RESTATEMENT 2d § 222 comment b. See American Mach. & Tool Co. v. Strite-Anderson Mfg. Co., 353 N.W.2d 592 (Minn. App. 1984) and Camargo Cadillac Co. v. Garfield Enters., 3 Ohio App. 3d 435, 438, 445 N.E.2d 1141, 1145 (1982) (a showing of ambiguity need not be made before evidence of trade usage may be introduced).

D. *Existence, Scope, and Meaning of "Course of Dealing."*

As suggested earlier, "course of dealing" is defined in the UCC as "a sequence of previous conduct between the parties to a particular transaction which is fairly to be regarded as establishing a common basis of understanding for interpreting their expressions or other conduct."[41] A *sequence of previous conduct* is not defined in the Code in terms of the number of transactions that must occur before a course of dealing may be said to be established. A *sequence* would suggest a number of prior transactions. Yet, the number of transactions alone would not necessarily determine the existence of a course of dealing. Parties may have dealt with each other on several occasions in the past, but their prior dealings could be insufficiently similar to a current transaction. Thus, the Code adds the requirement that the "sequence of previous conduct" must be "fairly to be regarded as establishing a common basis of understanding for interpreting their expressions and other conduct." Thus, one, relatively small, bank transaction did not constitute course of dealing for a larger transaction.[42] Even where a single prior transaction is identical or sufficiently similar to the present transaction, it hardly constitutes a sequence of prior events necessary to establish a course of dealing between the parties.[43] On the other hand, a continuous relationship for the purchase and sale of goods in a consistent fashion over a period of five years obviously establishes a course of dealing between the parties.[44]

As in the case of trade usage, there is no necessity to establish ambiguity in the contract before evidence of course of dealing is admissible,[45] and the course of dealing evidence may be inconsistent with the meaning of the agreement apart from the course of dealing.[46] Again, as in the case of trade usage, course of dealing evidence may be used to interpret the parties' expression of agreement, or it may be used to evidence a term of the agreement as will be seen later in this section.

E. *Existence, Scope, and Meaning of "Course of Performance."*

Course of performance relates to conduct after the formation of the contract, i.e., the parties conduct in performing the previously made contract. The UCC does not parrot the language used to define course of dealing (prior to formation conduct), i.e., a sequence of conduct. Rather, course of performance requires "repeated *occasions* for performance ... with knowledge of the nature of the performance and opportunity for objection to it by the other [party]" that would indicate acceptance of or acquiescence in such performance.[47] While one instance of performance could not qualify as "repeated occasions" constituting a course of performance,[48] as few as two instances could qualify where there

---

[41] UCC § 1-201(1).
[42] Atlanta Corp. v. Ohio Valley Provision Co., 414 A.2d 123 (Pa. 1980).
[43] International Therapeutics, Inc. v. McGraw-Edison Co., 721 F.2d 488 (5th Cir. 1983).
[44] Delano Growers' Coop. Winery v. Supreme Wine Co., 393 Mass. 666, 473 N.E.2d 1066 (1985).
[45] Columbia Nitrogen Corp. v. Royster Co., 451 F.2d 3 (4th Cir. 1971) relying on UCC § 2-202 comment 1(c).
[46] RESTATEMENT 2d § 223 comment b.
[47] UCC § 2-208(1). (emphasis added).
[48] Prewitt v. Numismatic Funding Corp., 745 F.2d 1175 (8th Cir. 1984).

were only two possible occasions to demonstrate adherence to a particular mode of performance.[49] Where there are "repeated occasions" for performance by one party with knowledge and opportunity for objection by the other party who does not object, there is no question that a course of performance has been established.[50] Like trade usage and course of dealing, course of performance evidence is admissible to interpret the expressions of the parties.[51] Moreover, it is the strongest evidence of that meaning.[52] While the express terms of the contract are said to be superior to course of performance evidence concerning the meaning of the agreement,[53] as suggested earlier,[54] course of performance which is inconsistent with the express terms of the contract and, therefore, not admissible as interpretation evidence, may constitute a modification of the contract.[55] If the parties have knowingly engaged in repeated occasions of performance which are inconsistent with the express terms of the contract, they have manifested their intention to modify their contract.[56] It is difficult to conceive of a court refusing to regard such conduct as a subsequent modification of the contract. In this subsequent modification sense, therefore, course of performance becomes superior to the express terms of the contract. Thus, as will be seen below, just as trade usage and course of dealing may *supply* terms to the original contract which precede express terms (as well as providing assistance in determining the meaning of terms expressed in the contract), course of performance may provide *new* terms, i.e., terms that modify the prior, express terms of the contract.

Unlike the definitions of trade usage and course of dealing which appear in Article 1 of the UCC and thereby apply to all commercial contracts including, but not limited to, contracts for the sale of goods, the definition of course of performance appears in Article 2 which is relegated to contracts for the sale of goods. This placement has caused some courts to insist that the operation of course of performance is limited to contracts for the sale of goods as contrasted, for example, with security agreements governed by Article 9 of the UCC.[57] Other courts emphasize the basic definition of "agreement" in Article

---

[49] Nanakuli Paving & Rock Co. v. Shell Oil Co., 664 F.2d 772 (9th Cir. 1981).

[50] Blue Rock Indus. v. Raymond Int'l, Inc., 325 A.2d 66 (Me. 1974); Oskey Gasoline & Oil Co. v. OKC Ref. Inc., 364 F. Supp. 1137 (D.C. Minn. 1973).

[51] *See, e.g.,* National Heater Co. v. Corrigan Co. Mech. Contrs., 482 F.2d 87 (8th Cir. 1973).

[52] *See* Nanakuli Paving & Rock Co. v. Shell Oil Co., 664 F.2d 772 (9th Cir. 1981).

[53] UCC § 2-208(2).

[54] *See supra* text preceding note 30.

[55] *See supra* note 30.

[56] *See* Westinghouse Credit Corp. v. Shelton, 645 F.2d 869 (10th Cir. 1981) (course of performance was sufficient not only to waive express term requiring installment payments when due, but was also sufficient to waive express "anti-waiver" clause which read, "The waiver or indulgence of any default by the Buyer of any provision of this Agreement or any promissory note which it secures shall not operate as a waiver of any subsequent default by the Buyer of such provision or as a waiver of any of the other rights of [Westinghouse] herein. Time shall be deemed the essence of this Agreement."). *See also* Oregon Bank v. Nautilus Crane & Equip. Corp., 28 Or. App. 131, 683 P.2d 95 (1984) (which suggests that not only anti-waiver clauses may be waived by course of performance, but, pursuant to UCC § 2-316(3)(c), implied warranties may be excluded or modified by either trade usage or course of performance).

[57] *See* Cox v. Bancoklahoma Agri-Serv. Corp., 641 S.W.2d 400 (Tex. App. 1982); United Am. State Bank & Trust Co. v. Wild West Chrysler Plymouth, Inc., 561 P.2d 792 (Kan. 1977); Universal C. I. T. Credit Corp. v. Middlesboro Motor Sales, Inc., 424 S.W.2d 409 (Ky. 1968). UCC § 9-105(1)(l) defines a security agreement as "an agreement which creates or provides for a security

1 of the Code, and that definition includes "course of performance."[58] Thus, they conclude that course of performance is not limited to contracts for the sale of goods.[59]

F. Supplying Contract Terms Through Trade Usage, Course of Dealing, or Course of Performance — The "Consistency" Mystery.

It is important to emphasize the basic concept of "agreement" as found in the UCC.[60] The agreement of the parties is not limited to their words. The "bargain of the parties in fact" may be discovered in circumstances other than language, i.e., trade usage, course of dealing, or course of performance. Perhaps the most significant judicial manifestation of this view is found in a well-known case, *Columbia Nitrogen Corp. v. Royster Co.*[61] Royster had been a major purchaser of products from Columbia for a number of years. After constructing a phosphate producing facility, however, Royster had excess phosphate and agreed to sell large quantities to Columbia over a three year term. The contract was evidenced by what appeared to be a complete writing (integrated writing) which included a price escalation clause. Soon after the contract was formed, the market price of phosphate plunged precipitously and Columbia, unable to resell the phosphate at competitive prices, ordered only part of the annual scheduled tonnage of 31,000 tons it was required to purchase from Royster. At Columbia's request, Royster agreed to lower the price for three months of the first year of the contract, insisting that the price would thereafter be elevated to the contract price. This concession left Royster's price well above market levels and Columbia ordered less than one tenth the amount it was scheduled to receive during the first contract year. Columbia offered to perform the contract at market prices, but Royster refused. When Columbia refused delivery at the contract price, Royster resold the unaccepted phosphate at prices substantially below market prices. Columbia attempted to introduce evidence of trade usage to the effect that uncertain crop and weather conditions, farming practices and government agricultural programs created an understanding of all dealers in the trade that contracts for products such as phosphate in the mixed fertilizer industries were not viewed as legally binding arrangements, i.e., they were mere projections to be adjusted according to market forces. Columbia also sought to introduce evidence of its long relationship with Royster demonstrating a pattern of repeated and substantial deviation from contract prices and four instances where Royster (then a buyer rather than a seller) had taken none of the goods contracted for, resulting in a total variance of a half million dollars in reduced sales to Columbia. The trial court refused to admit the evidence on the ground that it contradicted the plain language of the contract. In a sophisticated opinion that was

---

interest," and "security interest" is defined in § 1-201(37) as "an interest in personal property or fixtures which secures payment or performance of an obligation...."

[58] UCC § 1-201(3) defines agreement as "the bargain of the parties in fact as found in their language or by implication from other circumstances including course of dealing or usage of trade or *course of performance as provided in this Act*...." (emphasis added).

[59] *See* Westinghouse Credit Corp. v. Shelton, *supra* note 56; National Livestock Credit Corp. v. Schultz, 653 P.2d 1243 (Okla. App. 1982).

[60] UCC § 1-201(3).

[61] 451 F.2d 3 (4th Cir. 1971).

almost precocious for its time, the United States Court of Appeals for the Fourth Circuit reversed.

Relying heavily upon the UCC parol evidence section, § 2-202(a) which appears to permit evidence of course of dealing, usage of trade, or course of performance regardless of how complete and final (fully integrated) the written expression of the parties' contract may be, the court focused upon the critical question of whether the trade usage and course of dealing evidence was inconsistent with the express terms of the writing since UCC § 1-205(4) states the hierarchy mentioned earlier in this discussion, i.e., express terms control course of dealing and trade usage.[62] The court found no inconsistency in the express terms of the contract which was silent concerning price adjustments to reflect declining markets.[63] Moreover, the court emphasized the UCC directive that course of dealing and usage of trade would "supplement" the written terms unless they were "carefully negated."[64] While other cases suggest similar holdings,[65] no opinon appears to recognize the underlying philosophy of the UCC with respect to the factual bargain of the parties as effectively as *Columbia Nitrogen.* Though, like other courts, it suggests that trade usage and course of dealing may *supplement* the express terms of the contract, it emphasizes the critical importance of identifying the "agreement" of the parties by considering express terms as well as trade usage, course of dealing, and course of performance.[66]

1. The "Consistency" Mystery.

It may appear difficult to reconcile UCC language concerning the admission of trade usage and course of dealing evidence. Section 2-202 clearly permits the introduction of trade usage and course of dealing evidence even where the writing is complete and final or fully integrated, i.e., such evidence would be permitted even in the face of a negotiated merger clause. Moreover, such course of dealing or usage of trade need not be consistent with the express terms of the writing since the subsection dealing with course of dealing and usage of trade conspicuously avoids any qualification concerning "consistent"

---

[62] It will be recalled that course of performance is preferred over course of dealing and course of dealing controls trade usage, but express terms are superior to all three as a matter of interpretation. UCC § 2-208(2).

[63] As suggested in Carter Baron Drilling v. Badger Oil Corp., 581 F. Supp. 582 (D. Colo. 1984), there is some dispute among the courts as to what constitutes "consistent" trade usage or course of performance. The court points to Columbia Nitrogen Corp., *supra* note 61, Chase Manhattan Bank v. Marion Bank, 437 F.2d 1040 (5th Cir. 1971) and Nanakuli Paving & Rock Co. v. Shell Oil Co., 664 F.2d 772 (9th Cir. 1981) as suggesting liberal interpretations of "consistent" while other courts such as Southern Concrete Servs., 407 F. Supp. 581 (N.D. Ga. 1975) *aff'd per curiam,* 569 F.2d 1154 (5th Cir. 1978) and Luria Bros. & Co. v. Pielet Bros. Scrap Iron, 600 F.2d 103 (7th Cir. 1979) "are less generous" in their interpretations of "consistent." The *Carter Baron* court decided to adopt the liberal position on the footing that this was the result desired by the drafters of the UCC and admission of such evidence does pose the risks against which the parol evidence rule was designed.

[64] UCC § 2-202 comment 2.

[65] *See, e.g.,* Carter Baron Drilling v. Badger Oil Corp., 581 F. Supp. 582 (D. Colo. 1984); Ralph's Distrib. Co. v. AMF, Inc., 667 F.2d 670 (8th Cir. 1981); Heggblade-Marguleas-Tenneco, Inc. v. Sunshine Biscuit, Inc., 59 Cal. App. 3d 948, 131 Cal. Rptr. 183 (1976).

[66] The court does so by relying exclusively on UCC §§ 1-205(4) and 2-202. Unfortunately, it fails to mention the section defining "agreement," § 1-201(3).

terms which the next subsection conspicuously includes.[67] (The UCC also permits course of performance evidence to be introduced regardless of the completeness of the writing, but this is quite unremarkable since the UCC follows the usual view that subsequent modifications are not affected by the parol evidence rule.) The problem is exacerbated by the UCC directive in Article 1 whereby express terms "control" course of dealing and usage of trade, i.e., where it is not possible for express terms to be construed consistently with either trade usage or course of dealing, express terms shall "control."[68] There has been no judicial or scholarly reconciliation of these sections to this time. The following, however, is submitted.

UCC § 2-202 dealing with the parol evidence rule precludes the admission of even "consistent" *additional* terms if the writing evidencing the contract is final and complete. Why does it not preclude trade usage and course of dealing evidence where the writing is final and complete? The answer to this part of the puzzle is reasonably clear. The Code does not view trade usage or course of dealing evidence as *additional* terms. In the basic UCC definition of *"agreement,"*[69] trade usage and course of dealing are emphasized as manifestations of the parties' factual bargain along with the language used by the parties. Trade usage and course of dealing are *not,* therefore, *added* to the agreement of the parties; rather, they pre-exist the agreement of the parties. The writings of the parties, albeit complete and final, "are to be read on the assumption that the course of prior dealings between the parties and the usages of trade were taken for granted when the document was phrased."[70] Thus, course of dealing and usage of trade evidence do not "supplement" the terms of the agreement as if added judicially after the writing existed. Rather, the evidence of course of dealing and usage of trade, though judicially discovered after the writing, *preceded* the writing, no matter how final and complete, and must be viewed as the background against which the written terms are interpreted. It is, therefore, admissible on this basis. If prior course of dealing or trade usage evidence does not contradict the express terms of the writing, there is no question that the evidence should be admitted as a term of the contract.[71] The difficult question, however, is whether such evidence can overcome inconsistent express terms of the agreement.

The parties may choose to overcome trade usage or prior course of dealing by the express terms of their agreement. Trade usage or course of dealing which the parties intend to be overcome by the *negotiated* express terms of their contract should be rejected on the footing that the parties have expressly addressed the particular matter which would otherwise be controlled by trade usage or course of dealing and intended their express terms to control.[72] Parties may always change their prior agreement manifested by either language

---

[67]*See* UCC §§ 2-202(a) and (b).

[68]UCC § 1-205(4).

[69]UCC § 1-201(3).

[70]UCC § 2-202 comment 2.

[71]*See, e.g.,* Budget Sys. v. Seofert Pontiac, Inc., 40 Colo. App. 406, 579 P.2d 87 (1978) (course of dealing concerning mileage limitation admissible where such evidence did not contradict language of writing).

[72]State *ex rel.* Conley Lott Nichols Mach. Co. v. Safeco Ins. Co. of Am., 671 P.2d 1151 (N.M. App. 1983).

on the one hand or trade usage or course of dealing on the other. For example, if the trade usage or prior course of dealing indicated that the time for performance should be thirty days, a negotiated express term requiring performance in a shorter time or allowing a greater time for performance should control if that is the intention of the parties. In such a situation, the course of dealing could be viewed as having been "carefully negated." If, however, the parties have used standardized (printed) forms in the past that set forth a time for performance or other term which the parties have contradicted by their course of performance on repeated occasions, such course of performance evidence as to past transactions could be viewed as a course of dealing with respect to a new, identical transaction that is inconsistent with one or more express terms of the printed form evidencing their agreement. In this situation, the course of dealing indicates that the parties have ignored the relevant printed terms of the documents evidencing their past transactions and have substituted a different understanding of such terms.[73] The objective of the court is to discover "the true understanding of the parties"[74] or their "bargain in fact."[75] Courts must be careful, however, to admit trade usage or course of dealing evidence to make such determinations because they are questions of fact. Thus, where the express terms of the writing required shipment of limestone at 1500 tons per day, course of dealing evidence clearly indicated that the 1500 ton figure was a goal rather than a requirement, and that the buyer did not reasonably expect the seller to meet that goal under the circumstances.[76]

2. Warranty Disclaimer and Other Limitations.

The UCC implies certain warranties of quality in contracts for the sale of goods, i.e., the implied warranty of merchantability[77] and the implied warranty of fitness for a particular purpose.[78] Another Code section sets forth the ways in which such warranties may be disclaimed.[79] One of the methods of disclaiming such warranties is through trade usage, course of dealing and course of performance[80] and courts have properly adhered to this provision in finding such warranties disclaimed.[81] Another method of disclaimer of the implied warranty of merchantability authorized by the UCC is effective if the language mentions the term, "merchantability," and, if the disclaimer is writ-

---

[73] See, however, Lockhee Elecs. Co. v. Keronix, Inc., 114 Cal. App. 3d 304, 170 Cal. Rptr. 591 (1981) in which the court suggested that seller's contention that previous dealings in which the same form of offer had been used and seller's acceptance had stated additional and different terms constituted a prior course of dealing or course of performance that would negate the buyer's limitation of the terms of its offer was without merit.

[74] See UCC § 2-202 comment 2.

[75] UCC § 1-201(3).

[76] Luedtke Eng'g Co. v. Indiana Limestone Co., 740 F.2d 598 (7th Cir. 1984).

[77] UCC § 2-314.

[78] UCC § 2-315. This warranty, however, is implied only where the seller has reason to know of the buyer's particular purpose and the buyer has relied on the seller's skill and judgment in choosing a product fit for that particular purpose.

[79] UCC § 2-316.

[80] UCC § 2-316(3)(c).

[81] See, e.g., Kincheloe v. Geldmeier, 619 S.W.2d 272 (Tx. App. 1981) (trade usage); Agricultural Servs. Ass'n v. Ferry-Morse Seed Co., 551 F.2d 1057 (6th Cir. 1977) (course of dealing); Gulash v. Stylarama, Inc., 364 A.2d 1221 (Conn. 1975) (course of performance).

ten, the language is "conspicuous."[82] If a seller attempts to disclaim the implied warranty of merchantability in this fashion but fails to mention "merchantability" or fails to insert the written disclaimer in conspicuous fashion, he may still prove an effective disclaimer through the mutual exclusive method of trade usage, course of dealing or course of performance.[83] The normal remedies set forth in the UCC may also be limited through the agreement of the parties.[84] Since the definition of "agreement" includes trade usage, course of dealing and course of performance, courts have held that such remedies may be limited through these non-language manifestations of agreement.[85] Other limitations through trade usage, course of dealing or course of performance include the necessity of notice under certain circumstances[86] or the necessity to seek a particular remedy within a certain time.[87]

§ 90. Omitted Terms.

In an earlier chapter,[88] the implication of various terms where parties failed to mention them such as a reasonable time for performance, a reasonable price and many other "gap-filling" terms was explored. The modern trend permitting courts to supply such omitted terms and rejecting the notion that such indefiniteness is fatal was heralded by the UCC which permits numerous terms to be omitted from the expression of agreement if (a) the parties manifest an intention to be bound and (b) there is a reasonable basis for a court to fashion a remedy.[89] When an omitted term is supplied by a court, it is not *interpreting* the contract, i.e., it is not discovering such a term by discerning the meaning of the parties' expression of agreement. Before a court may supply such an omitted term, it must first interpret the expression of agreement to determine whether such implication is necessary. If the manifestations of the parties provide such a term, the court may not overcome that manifested intention. If, however, there is a dispute over the proper interpretation of a contract and neither party's suggested interpretation is acceptable, the court must then supply the omitted term.[90]

---

[82] UCC § 2-316(2). "Conspicuous" is defined as "so written that a reasonable person against whom it is to operate ought to have notice of it." § 1-201(10).

[83] *See, e.g.,* South Carolina Elec. & Gas Co. v. Combustion Eng'g, Inc., 322 S.E.2d 453 (S.C. App. 1984); Basic Adhesives, Inc. v. Robert Matzkin Co., 420 N.Y.S.2d 983 (N.Y. Civ. 1979).

[84] UCC § 2-719.

[85] *See, e.g.,* Transamerica Oil Co. v. Lynes, Inc., 723 F.2d 758 (10th Cir. 1983); Kunstoffwerk Alfred Huber v. R. J. Dick, Inc., 621 F.2d 560 (3rd Cir. 1980).

[86] *See* Provident Tradesmens Bank & Trust Co. v. Pemberton, 196 Pa. Super. 180, 173 A.2d 780 (1961).

[87] *See* Valley Nat'l Bank v. Babylon Chrysler-Plymouth, Inc., 53 Misc. 2d 1029, 280 N.Y.S.2d 786 (Sup. Ct.), *aff'd,* 28 A.D.2d 284, 284 N.Y.S.2d 849 (1967).

[88] Chapter 2, *supra* § 38.

[89] UCC § 2-204(3).

[90] *See* Haines v. City of N.Y., 41 N.Y.2d 769, 364 N.E.2d 820 (1977) (city agreed to construct, operate, and maintain a sewage system for two communities so as to prevent untreated sewage from entering a stream feeding the city's water supply. Years later, a state environmental control law prohibited the discharge of untreated sewage into the stream and, after a half century when the system reached full capacity, the city refused to expand the disposal plant or otherwise meet the demand of the communities. The city argued that the contract should be interpreted to be "terminable at will," while the communities argued that it should be interpreted to bind the city in perpetuity. The court rejected both suggested interpretations.

The parties may fail to include a term because they did not foresee a particular situation which later causes a dispute between them, or they may have
failed to manifest their intention with respect to a foreseeable situation, or,
they may have deliberately avoided manifesting any intention with respect to
a foreseeable situation because it could have hampered negotiations or simply
because they considered the matter not worth mentioning.[91] Even where the
situation was not foreseen and the parties, therefore, had no intention whatsoever concerning it, courts will often supply the missing term under the guise
of "interpretation," i.e., discovering the "intention of the parties."[92] In one
well-known case, however, the court candidly admitted that it was not interpreting any manifestation of the parties but was supplying an omitted term.
The case is instructive, generally, concerning the judicial implication of an
omitted term. We will now consider that case and others involving the judicial
reaction to requests to supply omitted terms.

A. *Some Examples: Parev Products Co. v. I. Rokeach & Sons*[93] *and Warner-
Lambert Pharmaceutical Co. v. John J. Reynolds.*[94]

Rokeach obtained the exclusive use of a secret formula for the manufacture
and sale of a cooking oil (which it called Nyafat) that was usable without
violation of the Jewish dietary laws, from Parev, who was to receive royalties
from the sale of the oil for a term of twenty-five years with an option to renew
for another twenty-five years. For the first fifteen years, royalties in the
amount of some $135,000 were paid to Parev. Shortly thereafter, Rokeach
began marketing another (semisolid) cooking oil usable under the Jewish
dietary laws manufactured from different raw material and according to a
different formula. Rokeach asserted that it began marketing the new product
(Kea) to compete with new products — Crisco and Spry — which had begun to
cut into the Nyafat market. Kea competed with Nyafat but Rokeach argued
that it required a product that could compete more effectively with Crisco and
Spry. Parev claimed that Rokeach sought to reduce its royalty obligation on
Nyafat sales through the marketing of Kea and sought an injunction against

[91] RESTATEMENT 2d § 204 comment b.

[92] In Lake LBJ Mun. Util. Dist. v. Coulson, 692 S.W.2d 897, 906 (Tex. App. 1985), the court
found no express provision in the contract dealing with the dispute. Citing § 204 of RESTATEMENT
2d, the opinion states that courts must supply a term in this situation which is reasonable in the
circumstances. It then states, "This is often done by 'interpretation,' and chiefly by 'implication.'
But these words may obscure the fact that the court is really supplying an omitted term necessary
to effectuate the purposes of the contract in circumstances where, for a variety of reasons, the
parties failed to make express provision about an event that did occur to affect their rights and
obligations." *See also* Williams, *Language and the Law* (Pt. IV), 61 LAW Q. REV. 384, 401 (1945),
the author suggests that judges are accustomed to reading into documents and transactions many
terms that are not logically implied in them. He suggests three kinds of non-logical implication:
(1) terms that the parties probably had in mind but did not trouble to express (here, the judicial
effort is one of arriving at actual intention); (2) terms that the parties, whether or not they
actually had them in mind, would probably have expressed if the question had been brought to
their attention (here the effort is to arrive at hypothetical or condition intention, i.e., the intention the parties would have had if they had foreseen the problem); (3) terms that the parties,
whether or not they had them in mind or would have expressed them had they foreseen the
problem, are implied by courts on fairness or policy grounds or in consequence of rules of law (this
effort is not concerned with the intention of the parties).

[93] 124 F.2d 147 (2d Cir. 1941).

[94] 178 F. Supp. 655 (S.D.N.Y. 1959), *aff'd*, 280 F.2d 197 (2d Cir. 1960).

any further sales of Kea by the defendant, Rokeach, through the implication of a negative covenant in the contract that defendant would not compete with sales of Nyafat. The court attacked the notion that its task was to determine the intention of the parties in candidly stating that the contract simply did not deal with an unforeseen situation — there was no intention of the parties as to this development fifteen years after contract formation. It then recognized the reasonable protection required by Parev, i.e., the continuation of Nyafat sales without interference by Kea so as to insure maximum royalties. On the other hand, Rokeach had to compete effectively with the new products that had not been contemplated fifteen years earlier. The court unveiled the equitable solution of permitting Rokeach to continue to sell Kea so long as it did not invade the Nyafat market, a point the court felt capable of proof. While refusing to grant an injunction that would be vague and meaningless, it invited the plaintiff, Parev, to return with proof that sales of Nyafat had been lost to sales of Kea rather than to sales of the competing products, Crisco and Spry.

It is anything but remarkable to discover an unforeseen situation arising in a long term contract many years after contract formation. Another well-known illustration is the famous "Listerine" case. After devising a secret formula for an antiseptic liquid compound called "Listerine," in 1881 Dr. Lawrence formed a contract with Lambert, the predecessor of the Warner-Lambert Company, whereby Lawrence and his heirs, executors, and assigns would receive royalty payments on the sale of the product. No later than 1949, the trade secret formula was known to the public as it was published in the Journal of the American Medical Association, the U.S. Pharmacopoeia and other publications. The royalty payments had risen to one and one-half million dollars annually. Warner-Lambert sought a declaratory judgment that it was no longer liable to pay royalties to the heirs of Dr. Lawrence on the ground that a term should be implied in the contract that royalty payments could be terminated when the secret formula became public knowledge. The court refused to imply the term, clinging to what it saw as the "plain and unambiguous"[95] agreement of the parties that the royalties would be paid "as long as this preparation is manufactured and sold by Lambert and his successors"[96] regardless of the disclosure of the secret formula.

B. *"Best Efforts" and "Good Faith."*

While courts manifest little difficulty in cases supplying a "reasonable time" for the duration or performance of a contract, a reasonable price for goods or services where such terms are omitted,[97] or other terms where an inartfully drawn clause would be unintelligible or purposeless absent the implication of a word,[98] they are quite reluctant to imply negative covenants. Thus, where the owner of a franchised motel sought an implied negative

---

[95] 178 F. Supp. 655, 660.

[96] *Ibid.*

[97] *See, e.g.,* Lake LBJ Mun. Util. Dist. v. Coulson, 692 S.W.2d 897, 906 (Tex. App. 1985) where the court suggests that the supply of such terms is "well-settled" (citing Texas authorities).

[98] Chemetron Corp. v. McLouth Steel Corp., 522 F.2d 469 (7th Cir. 1975) (clause required either "and" or "or" to make it intelligible and purposeful).

covenant that the franchisor would not permit another franchised motel in the same territory, the court refused to supply the covenant. Since territorial exclusivity had been discussed before the contract was formed,[99] the contract failed to include such a clause, and the contract also contained a merger clause, such a covenant would not have been reasonable under the circumstances. In the same case, however, the court was willing to imply a duty to operate the business in a manner consistent with the standard of other business carrying the franchised name based upon a standard of fair dealing which the court was willing to imply in any contract where the fruits of a contract of one party depend upon the efforts of another.[1] Similarly, in exclusive agency contexts, courts are willing to supply clauses requiring the agent to use best efforts in the promotion of the principal's name or product.[2] In addition, the pervasive duty of good faith and fair dealing is implied in every contract though the definition of "good faith" is amorphous even within the UCC which contains two definitions depending upon the particular party and type of transaction involved.[3]

C. *Defining the Standard for Supplying Omitted Terms.*

The generalizations surrounding the decisions of courts to supply or not to supply omitted terms does not suggest anything resembling a precise set of guidelines for that process. The best the RESTATEMENT 2d can suggest is that, where the parties have omitted a term "essential to a determination of their rights and duties, *a term which is reasonable in the circumstances is supplied by the court.*"[4] Notwithstanding this amorphous standard, certain comments to the section are helpful. The RESTATEMENT 2d suggests, for example, that the notion that the parties would have included a particular term had they thought of it may be a factor in determining what term may be reasonable

---

[99]It should be noted that the omission of an essential term may indicate, for purposes of the parol evidence rule, that the writing of the parties is not integrated or that it is merely partially integrated (final) rather than fully integrated (final and complete). Such omission, however, is not conclusive concerning the question of integration. If there is a complete and final writing, evidence of prior negotiations may not be admitted to supply the omitted term. Such evidence may be admissible, however, to determine what would be reasonable under the circumstances. *See* RESTATEMENT 2d § 204 comment e.

[1]Snyder v. Howard Johnson's Motor Lodges, Inc., 412 F. Supp. 724 (S.D. Ill. 1976).

[2]The classic case is Wood v. Lucy, Lady Duff-Gordon, 222 N.Y. 88, 118 N.E. 214 (1917), opinion by J. Cardozo. *See also Parev Products, supra* note 93, and UCC § 2-306(2). For a case construing a "best efforts" clause, *see* Bloor v. Falstaff Brewing Corp., 454 F. Supp. 259 (S.D.N.Y. 1978).

[3]*See* RESTATEMENT 2d § 205 which suggests, in comment a, "The phrase 'good faith' is used in a variety of contexts, and its meaning varies somewhat with the context." *See also* UCC § 1-201(19) defining "good faith" as honesty in fact and § 2-103(1)(b), applicable to merchants (defined in § 2-104), defining "good faith" as honesty in fact *and* the observance of reasonable commercial standards of fair dealing in the trade. In Zapatha v. Dairy Mart, Inc., 381 Mass. 284, 408 N.E.2d 1370 (1980), the court indicates that the Article 2 definition applicable to merchants includes a higher standard of conduct through the addition of the observance of reasonable commercial standards of fair dealing in the trade. In Martin Marietta Corp. v. New Jersey Nat'l Bank, 612 F.2d 745 (3d Cir. 1979), the court distinguishes the Article 1 standard as "subjective" and the Article 2 standard as "objective." In Mattex v. Malofsky, 42 Wis. 2d 16, 165 N.W.2d 406 (1969), the court suggests that the Article 1 standard applies only to members of the consuming public as contrasted with merchants to which the Article 2 standard applies. A number of cases have held that the Article 2 standard does not apply to Article 9 transactions involving merchants. *See, e.g.,* Sea Harvest, Inc. v. Rig & Crane Equip. Corp., 181 N.J. Super. 41, 436 A.2d 553 (1981).

[4]RESTATEMENT 2d § 204 (emphasis added). For a helpful analysis concerning omitted terms, *see* Farnsworth, *Disputes Over Omission in Contracts,* 68 COLUM. L. REV. 860 (1968).

under certain circumstances, but, in the absence of agreement, courts "should supply a term which comports with community standards of fairness and policy rather than analyze a hypothetical model of the bargaining process."[5] There is simply no escape from such judicial intervention where the courts are, necessarily, "making" a contract for the parties.

§ 91. Mistake.

A. *Definition — Poor Judgment and Prediction Distinguished — Mistake of "Law" Versus "Fact."*

The FIRST RESTATEMENT defined "mistake" as "a state of mind that is not in accord with the facts."[6] The RESTATEMENT 2d definition is similar: "A mistake is a belief that is not in accord with the facts,"[7] i.e., "an erroneous belief."[8] The RESTATEMENT 2d is careful to restrict its use of "mistake" to facts existing at the time of contract formation, i.e., it is not used to refer to an "improvident act" such as assuming a risk that the facts will remain as they are at the time of contract formation.[9] Moreover, "mistake" does not refer to a prediction or exercise of judgment that a particular situation will exist in the future. Thus, in the sale of a business, both buyer and seller may believe that the business will earn a certain amount in the ensuing year and that judgment may be the basis for a reasonable prediction. If, however, the economy or other events do not permit that judgment or prediction to prove true, neither party has made a "mistake" as defined in the RESTATEMENT 2d, i.e., an erroneous belief of fact existing at the time the contract is formed.[10] The erroneous belief of a fact existing at the moment of contract formation may be articulated or unarticulated, and it may be a mistake as to the contents or legal effect of an expression of agreement i.e., a so-called mistake of law is, itself, a fact which can be the basis for an erroneous belief.[11]

When action or inaction has been induced by a mistake, what is the effect of such mistake? The question is monumental when considered in relation to the law, in general. Mistake can have a significant impact in criminal law, tort law, contract law and other areas. We will, of course, focus upon mistake in contract law so as to permit a manageable analysis.

---

[5] *See* RESTATEMENT 2d § 204 comment d.

[6] FIRST RESTATEMENT § 500.

[7] RESTATEMENT 2d § 151.

[8] *Id.* at comment a.

[9] Illustration 1 to § 151 defining "mistake" deals with the facts of Wills v. Shockley, 52 Del. 295, 157 A.2d 252 (Super. 1960), where A contracted to raise and float B's boat which had run aground on a reef. A believed that the sea would remain calm until the work was completed but a sudden storm caused the boat to fall into deep water making it much more difficult to raise. The Restatement suggests that A's poor judgment was not a "mistake" as it defines the term.

[10] *See* RESTATEMENT 2d § 151 ill. 2, based on Leasco Corp. v. Taussig, 473 F.2d 777 (2d Cir. 1972), where the buyer of a business argued that the parties assumed that they were dealing with a corporation that would earn $200,000 in a given year and the company lost $12,000 instead. The court viewed the assumption as nothing more than a poor prediction rather than a mistake that would have permitted the buyer to avoid the contract.

[11] The RESTATEMENT 2d suggests the possibility of mistake based on an assumption of a party who is unaware of alternatives. It also rejects earlier distinctions between mistakes of "fact" versus mistakes of "law" since the law existing at the time of contract formation is a fact at that time. An erroneous belief as to the law, regardless of its basis in a statute, judicial decision, or otherwise, is, therefore, a mistake. RESTATEMENT 2d § 151 comment a.

B. *Types of Mistake and Related Matters to Be Explored.*

We have already explored some of the kinds of mistake and its effects in the law of contracts. Thus, we have considered *mistakes in expression* such as a slip of the tongue.[12] We have explored the problems surrounding *mutual misunderstanding* as suggested in the famous case involving two ships named *Peerless*[13] where mistake and equivocal meanings, particularly those involving latent ambiguity, overlap. We have analyzed the problems of a *mistake in the writing* where, for example, a scrivener fails to set forth the true intention of the parties in the document evidencing their contract giving rise to the possible remedy of reformation.[14] It is now important to explore the other types of mistake. In this section we will consider *mistake of identity*, i.e., where a party has an erroneous belief as to the party with whom he is dealing, *mistake of subject matter*, where one or both parties entertain erroneous beliefs concerning the subject matter of the contract, *computation mistake* where one of the parties has made what amounts to a clerical error, *mistake of value* where the parties may have entertained an erroneous belief as to the value of the subject matter *at the time of contract formation* as contrasted with the predicted value,[15] *mistake by the intermediary* where neither party to the contract has made any mistake but the intermediary responsible for communication between or among the parties has made a mistake and, finally, *releases* of claims where, *e.g.*, a personal injury claimant who has signed a release of her claim may later seek to attack it on the ground that she was, at the time of the release, unaware of the full extent of her injury.

It will be necessary to consider the difference between unilateral and mutual mistake and their legal effects as well as other factors which will govern the legal effect of mistake including: (a) the importance of the mistake, (b) the actual or presumed knowledge of the mistake by either or both parties, (c) the negligence of the mistaken party, (d) the reliance by the nonmistaken party, (e) any manifestation of risk assumption by either party and (f) the possible remedies a court may grant to balance the conflicting interests under all of the circumstances, including the circumstance of mistake, itself.

Before considering the various types of mistake and their legal effects, certain preliminary questions will now be explored to avoid later confusion.

C. *Offeree's Knowledge of Mistake — Failure to Read — Misrepresentation.*

In an earlier analysis of mistake of expression,[16] we saw that an offeree "cannot snap up an offer"[17] if he knows[18] or reasonably should know[19] that the

---

[12] *See supra* § 87(D).

[13] *See supra* § 87(B)(2), (3) and (C).

[14] *See supra* § 85(B).

[15] *See supra* text at note 9.

[16] *See supra* § 87(D).

[17] *See* Tyra v. Cheney, 129 Minn. 428, 152 N.W. 835 (1915). A more recent statement of the

---

[18] Where one party has actual knowledge of a mistake by the other as to a basic assumption on

---

[19] Where one party makes a mistake and the other party had reason to know of the mistake, the contract is voidable under § 153(b) of the RESTATEMENT 2d.

offeror is making a mistake. That concept is applicable to any type of mistake, i.e., a mistake in identity of the other party to the contract, a mistake in subject matter, an error in computation or any other type of mistake to be considered later in this section. On the other hand, where an offeree appears to assent to an offer, *e.g.,* by signing a writing containing the terms of the proposed contract, he will be bound to the terms of that contract even though he failed to read it or understand it, providing the offeror was not aware of the offeree's misconception [20] and provided that the contract is otherwise not susceptible to claims of unconscionability [21] or other grounds of avoidance. [22] Such a rule is obviously proper since one who has negligently induced an offeror to believe that the offer has been accepted is hardly in a position to ask for relief because he, the offeree, did not take the time or trouble to inform himself of the contents of the writing he signed. [23] A party's failure to read a particular contract document however, notwithstanding that party's lack of diligence which some courts may choose to call negligence of "contributory negligence,"

---

same concept is found in Howell v. Waters, 347 S.E.2d 65, 69 (N.C. App. 1986) and Risher v. Stolaruk Corp., 110 F.R.D. 74 (E.D. Mich. 1986) (rescission is justified where offeree who snaps up an offer refuses to permit the mistake to be corrected when discovered by the offeror). *See also* Galloway v. Russ, 175 Ark. 659, 300 S.W. 390 (1927) (seller knew that buyer thought he was buying a different make of machine than that called for by the writing which buyer signed); Bell v. Carroll, 212 Ky. 231, 278 S.W. 541 (1925) (seller of stock offered to sell at "par" which he thought meant market price and buyer, who knew market price was much above "par" accepted at "par"); Hardman Lumber Co. v. Keystone Mfg. Co., 86 W. Va. 404, 103 S.E. 282 (1920) (offeree snapped up offer which he had reason to know was erroneous).

---

which the other is making the contract, and the first party deliberately fails to disclose that information, such non-disclosure amounts to an assertion that the fact does not exist. *See* RESTATEMENT 2d § 161.

[20] *See, e.g.,* Quinn v. Briggs, 172 Mont. 468, 565 P.2d 297 (1977).

[21] Unconscionability and related concepts will be explored in the next chapter.

[22] *See* G & R Trie Distribs., Inc. v. Allstate Ins. Co., 177 Conn. 58, 411 A.2d 31 (1979) (following charge by trial court was not erroneous: "[the] general rule is that where a person of mature years who can read and write signs or accepts a formal written contract affecting his pecuniary interests, it is his duty to read it, and notice of its contents will be imputed to him if he negligently fails to do so; but this rule is subject to qualifications including the intervention of fraud or artifice, or mistake not due to his negligence, and applies only if nothing has been said or done to mislead the person sought to be charged or to put a man of reasonable business prudence off his guard in this matter." A "bad bargain" does not provide any basis for relief for a party who has signed a release without reading it. Sanger v. Yellow Cab Co., 486 S.W.2d 477 (Mo. 1972). *See also* § 3-305(2)(c) of the UCC which permits a defense by a party to a negotiable instrument where there is "such misrepresentation as has induced the party to sign the instrument with neither knowledge nor reasonable opportunity to obtain knowledge of its character or its essential terms...." Comment 7 to this section suggests that this type of misrepresentation is sometimes called "real" or "essential" fraud or "fraud in the factum" involving trick or artifice in having someone sign a negotiable instrument in the belief that it is merely a receipt or some other document. If a party cannot read or understand a document, he must seek assistance in having the writing read or explained to him. Absent fraud, he will not be able to avoid his obligation under the instrument simply because he failed to understand it. *See* Standard Fin. Co. v. Ellis, 657 P.2d 1056 (Haw. App. 1983); State Bank of Albany v. Roarke, 91 A.D.2d 1093, 458 N.Y.S.2d 300 (1983).

[23] "[I]n the absence of fraud or misrepresentation, a party is charged with knowing the legal effect of a contract voluntarily made.... To state the rule differently, absent fraud, a party to a contract who has access to the full information of its contents cannot avoid it on the ground of his own neglect in failing to read it." Reynolds-Penland Co. v. Hexter & Lobello, 567 S.W.2d 237, 240 (Tex. App. 1978). *See also* RESTATEMENT 2d § 157 comment b.

does not necessarily preclude a remedy for that party, even an equitable remedy such as reformation.[24]

Where the offeror has misrepresented the contents of the writing and the offeree relies upon the misrepresentation without reading the document before signing it, courts are confronted with the fraud of one party versus the negligence of the other. While some older cases may be found holding the offeree negligent notwithstanding the fraud of the offeror,[25] the clearly prevailing position is effectively suggested by a Kentucky court: "Is it better to encourage negligence in the foolish, or fraud in the deceitful? Either course has obvious dangers. But judicial experience exemplifies that the former is the least objectionable, and least hampers the administration of pure justice."[26]

Courts must balance the conflicting policies of deterring fraud on the one hand and discouraging inattention to the obligations in a written instrument on the other. They should, however, be reluctant to deny relief on the footing that, had one party been more attentive and carefully read the document, the fraud of the other would have been ineffective.[27] Whether the party who failed to read the document was reasonable in relying on the misrepresentation by the other party is a question of fact.[28]

D. Mistake in Formation, Integration, or Performance — The Anatomy of Mistake — "Basic Assumption," "Material Effect," and Risk Allocation.

Before considering different types of mistakes such as those relating to identity, subject matter, value, or the like, it is important to recognize that the parties to a contract can make mistakes at different stages of the contract. They can hold an erroneous belief as to the facts at the time of formation, i.e., they assume a past or existing fact and their belief is erroneous at the moment of formation. If the parties make no mistake at the time of formation, they may fail to insert an agreed term in the writing memorializing their agreement, i.e., a mistake in integration. Assuming no mistake at formation or with respect to integration, the parties may make a mistake in the performance of the contract where, for example, one party overpays or underpays

---

[24] See, e.g., Wehner v. Schroeder, 354 N.W.2d 674 (N.D. 1984) (the negligent failure of a party to read an instrument before signing it does not, in itself, bar reformation — citing RESTATEMENT 2d § 157 comment b); Accord Northwestern Bank v. Roseman, 81 N.C. App. 228, 344 S.E.2d 120 (1986). See also Floral Consultants, Ltd. v. Hanover Ins. Co., 128 Ill. App. 3d 173, 473 N.E.2d 527 (1984) (while insured's failure to read policy may amount to contributory negligence, it does not operate as a bar to relief as a matter of law); Precision Castparts Corp. v. Johnson & Higgins of Or., Inc., 44 Or. App. 739, 607 P.2d 763 (1979) (failure to read insurance policy does not excuse defendant upon whom plaintiff was entitled to rely in securing the appropriate policy); Brewer v. Vanguard Ins. Co., 614 S.W.2d 360 (Tenn. App. 1981) (failure to read insurance policy, especially a renewal policy, is not such negligence as will defeat insured's right to reform the policy).

[25] See, e.g., Mutual Benefit Health & Acc. Ass'n v. Ferrell, 42 Ariz. 477, 27 P.2d 519 (1933); Crum v. McCollum, 211 Iowa 319, 233 N.W. 678 (1930); J. B. Colt Co. v. Thompson, 114 Okla. 61, 242 P. 1030 (1926).

[26] Western Mfg. Co. v. Cotton & Long, 126 Ky. 749, 104 S.W. 758, 760 (1907). So also in the law of torts, it is generally held that the negligence of the plaintiff is not a defense to an action based upon the defendant's intentional misrepresentation. W. PROSSER & R. KEETON, TORTS 750 (5th ed. 1984).

[27] Northwestern Bank v. Roseman, 81 N.C. App. 228, 344 S.E.2d 120, 124 (1986).

[28] Ibid.

the other.[29] A mistake as to integration may lead to difficulties under the parol evidence rule or, in a situation where the omission in the writing causes the writing to state an intention different from the true intention of the parties, reformation may be appropriate. Where a party underpays the other during the performance stage of the contract, the other has a claim for full payment. A party who overpays will have a claim for restitution to avoid the unjust enrichment of the other.[30] If a party seeks to *avoid* the contract, however, the only type of mistake that will permit avoidance is the first type of mistake, i.e., a mistake in the *formation* stage of the contract.

A mistake at the formation stage must be foundational to the contract,[31] the mistake must relate to a past or existing fact which is material where the risk of mistake should not be allocated to one of the parties. In the language of the RESTATEMENT 2d, the mistake must constitute a basic assumption on which the contract was made, it must have a material effect on the agreed exchange of performances, and the otherwise adversely affected party must not bear the risk of the mistake.[32]

1. "Basic Assumption" on Which Contract Was Made.

The phrase, "basic assumption" is taken from the UCC.[33] There is no UCC or Restatement definition of "basic assumption" though the phrase suggests that for an assumption to be "basic," it must be foundational to the contract or, in the language of one court, the *sine qua non* or *efficient cause* of the contract.[34] Thus, there must be an erroneous belief as to an existing or past fact at the time of contract formation without which fact one or both parties would not have made the contract. If the parties merely disagreed as to the interpretation of their contract, they are not mistaken as to an existing material fact.[35] If one of the parties suffers disappointed expectations concerning the value or profit from the contract, there is no mistake as to basic assumptions.[36] As suggested earlier,[37] that situation is one of poor judgment or prediction. Neither party is justified in assuming that market conditions or its own financial situation may not change,[38] i.e., the opposite prediction is more reasonable. If, however, the parties have attempted to limit future risks in mar-

---

[29] *See* Pathology Consultants v. Gratton, 343 N.W.2d 428, 437 (Iowa 1984).

[30] *See* Frank Sharp, III v. Bowling, 511 So. 2d 363 (Fla. App. 1987). *See also* RESTATEMENT OF RESTITUTION § 20.

[31] *See* Howell v. Waters, 82 N.C. App. 481, 347 S.E.2d 65, 69 (1986) ([I]n order to affect the binding force of a contract, the mistake must be of an existing or past fact which is material; it must be as to a fact which enters into and forms the basis of the contract, or in other words it must be of the essence of the agreement, the *sine qua non*, or, as is sometimes said, the efficient cause of the agreement, and must be such that it animates and controls the conduct of the parties.") quoting from MacKay v. McIntosh, 270 N.C. 69, 73-74, 153 S.E.2d 800, 804 (1967).

[32] RESTATEMENT 2d §§ 152(1) and 153. The RESTATEMENT 2d would add that the mistaken party must not bear the risk of the mistake. *See* § 153 comment b.

[33] This phrase is used in the UCC section dealing with commercial impracticability, § 2-615, and is used in that connection by the RESTATEMENT 2d (§§ 261 and 266(1)) as well as in the section dealing with the related doctrine of frustration of purpose (§§ 265 and 266(2)).

[34] *See* Howell v. Waters, *supra* note 31.

[35] Creative Commun. Consultants, Inc. v. Gaylord, 403 N.W.2d 654 (Minn. App. 1987).

[36] *See* Diedrich v. Northern Ill. Pub'g Co., 39 Ill. App. 3d 851, 350 N.E.2d 857, 862 (1976).

[37] *See supra* text at note 10.

[38] RESTATEMENT 2d § 152 comment b.

ket changes and have employed a particular formula for that purpose, their basic assumption concerning the formula may be mistaken at the time of contract formation. If that mistake has a material effect on the agreed exchange, the contract may be avoided.[39]

2. Material Effect on Agreed Exchange.

The RESTATEMENT 2d suggests a stark illustration of a mistake as to a basic assumption which has a material effect on the agreed exchange. *A* purchases an annuity from *B*, an insurance company, on the life of *C*. Both *A* and *B* believe at the time of contract formation that *C* is alive but their beliefs are erroneous since *C* is dead. Thus, there was a mistake as to a basic assumption at the time of contract formation which had a material effect upon the agreed exchange. The contract is voidable by the purchaser.[40] Where parties entered a contract on the basic assumption that they were buying and selling rental income property and later learned that the property had no value because it has been condemned as unfit for human habitation, their erroneous belief with respect to the basic assumption had a material effect upon their agreed exchange.[41] Beyond the situation where the parties share the same erroneous belief as to a particular vital fact, the parties may have *different* erroneous beliefs as to the same basic fact as where a buyer believed it was purchasing an apartment building equipped with sewer facilities and the seller believed that it was agreeing to sell the building without such facilities.[42] There is still a material effect upon the agreed exchange of performances which makes the contract voidable.

Even though a party establishes a shared mistake as to a basic assumption which was the efficient cause for his entering the contract, unless he can also demonstrate that the effect on the agreed exchange is such that he should not be called upon to perform, he has not established the critical element of material effect upon the agreed exchange.[43] If the discovered mistake reveals an

---

[39] *See* Aluminum Co. of Am. v. Essex Group, 499 F. Supp. 53 (W.D. Pa. 1980) (price formula in long term aluminum conversion contract held mistaken from the moment of contract formation — "a present actuarial error" — and the court reformed the contract to its interpretation of the true intention of the parties though it curiously suggests that reformation was not an available remedy). *See also* Mastroni v. Mastroni, 151 Ariz. 194, 726 P.2d 610 (1986) (parties agreed on an escalation clause based on the rate of inflation and the attorney (scrivener) inserted a term, "cost of living index for the City of Phoenix prepared by the Bureau of Labor Statistics." No such cost of living index existed. The parties mistakenly believed they had a workable formula at the time of contract formation.).

[40] *See* RESTATEMENT 2d § 152 ill. 6. The same illustration is mentioned in comment b to this section.

[41] *See* Lenawee Cty. Bd. of Health v. Messerly, 295 N.W.2d 903 (Mich. App. 1980). *See also* Winter v. Skoglund, 404 N.W.2d 786 (Minn. 1987) (mistake about a basic assumption that there was no risk that certain trusts were not bound affecting Minnesota Vikings football team that had material effect upon agreed exchange); Dover Pool & Racquet Club v. Brooking, 366 Mass. 629, 322 N.E.2d 168 (1975) (erroneous basic assumption at the time of formation concerning zoning laws which had a material effect upon the operation of a pool and racquet club. As suggested earlier (text *supra* at note 11), mistakes of "law" are erroneous factual assumptions).

[42] Ouellette v. Bolduc, 440 A.2d 1042 (Me. 1982). In such a situation, the mistake is still a "mutual" mistake (to be discussed in the next subsection). If, however, the parties have different basic assumptions, i.e., as to different vital facts, which are erroneous, each has committed a "unilateral" mistake. *See* RESTATEMENT 2d § 152 comment h.

[43] RESTATEMENT 2d § 152 comment c.

exchange that is not only substantially less desirable for one party, but substantially more desirable for the other, a court will be more amenable to granting relief than if there is merely a loss to one party without a corresponding gain to the other.[44] A combination of gain to one party and a corresponding loss to the other party — the protection of the restitution interest or prevention of unjust enrichment — was long ago identified as more deserving of legal protection than other, commonly protected interests in contract law, i.e., the expectation or reliance interests.[45] The standard of materiality is the usual standard, i.e., one that must be considered in light of all the circumstances. If the mistake does not relate to a material aspect of the bargain but only to a collateral matter, there is no material effect upon the agreed exchange and no relief for such a mistake is available.[46]

3. Risk Allocation.

If the parties have allocated the risk of mistake by their agreement, the party to whom the risk has been allocated is precluded from later alleging the mistake as a ground for avoidance.[47] Thus, if the parties contemplated certain risks and assumed such risks, neither party could later raise such risks as the basis of either avoidance or reformation.[48] Where the parties have not expressly agreed to allocate certain risks, they may have contracted with complete awareness of their lack of knowledge concerning potential risks. It is sometimes suggested that where a party has contracted with knowledge that he is unaware of certain facts or has only limited knowledge of certain facts, he has not agreed to assume the risk that underlies that lack of knowledge or information. His "conscious ignorance," however, is then said to be the basis for allocating the risk to him.[49] While the risk should be allocated to him, the analysis is unfortunate. If the evidence is clear that a party formed an agreement on certain terms with knowledge that he was unaware of certain critical facts, to suggest that such party has not agreed to bear potential risks relating to consciously unknown facts misconceives the concept of agreement. In a

---

[44] In Aluminum Co. of Am. v. Essex Group, *supra* note 39 for example, the projected loss to Alcoa was $60 million with a substantial gain to Essex.

[45] "The 'restitution interest,' involving a combination of unjust impoverishment with unjust gain, presents the strongest case for relief. If, following Aristotle, we regard the purpose of justice as the maintenance of an equilibrium of goods among members of society, the restitution interest presents twice as strong a claim to judicial intervention as the reliance interest, since if *A* not only causes *B* to lose one unit but appropriates that unit to himself, the resulting discrepancy between *A* and *B* is not one unit but two." Fuller & Perdue, *The Reliance Interest in Contract Damages*, 46 YALE L.J. 52, 56 (1936), as quoted in United States v. Algernon Blair, Inc., 479 F.2d 638, 641 (1973).

[46] *See* Horner v. Bourland, 724 F.2d 1142, 1145 (5th Cir. 1984) (mistaken assumption that FHA loan could be recast was not material); Interstate Indus. Uniform Rental Serv. v. Couri Pontiac, Inc., 355 A.2d 913, 918 (Me. 1976) (mistake related to collateral issue of wisdom of entering into bargain and did not touch the subject matter of the bargain). *See also* Perry v. Stewart Title Co., 756 F.2d 1197, 1205-06 (5th Cir. 1985) (alleged mistake concerning land survey did not relate to a material aspect of the bargain but merely to a collateral matter).

[47] *See* RESTATEMENT 2d § 154(a) and particularly comment b.

[48] *See* Beecher v. Able, 575 F.2d 1010 (2d Cir. 1978). *See also* RESTATEMENT OF RESTITUTION § 11(1) comment d.

[49] RESTATEMENT 2d § 154(b) and particularly comment c. *See also* PUD 1 v. WPPSS, 104 Wash. 2d 353, 705 P.2d 1195, 713 P.2d 1109 (1985).

well-known case,[50] the plaintiff found a stone and, not knowing what it was, offered it to the defendant who was also unaware of its identity or value. The defendant offered one dollar for the stone and the plaintiff chose not to sell it. At a later time, still ignorant of its identity or value, the plaintiff agreed to sell the stone to the defendant who was equally unaware of the stone's value. Subsequently, the value of the stone was established at $700 and the defendant sought its return by tendering $1.10. The plaintiff refused the tender and the court held that the risk of value had been assumed by the plaintiff-seller. Clearly, the seller had assumed the risk that the value of the stone would be much greater than the amount received from the buyer since the seller chose to sell the stone with full consciousness that she was unaware of its value. Moreover, the seller had *agreed* to assume that risk by agreeing to sell the stone with such consciousness, i.e., the seller said, in effect, I hereby part with my ownership of this "thing," regardless of its worth, for one dollar, and I assume all risks of value in relation to this transaction. To require the parties to express a specific agreement concerning risk allocation in such a setting in order to find that they had agreed upon such allocation is excessively formalistic. The factual bargain of the parties clearly manifests that both parties assumed all risks of value.

The RESTATEMENT 2d also suggests that the risk of a mistake should be borne by one of the parties where the court decides that it is reasonable to allocate it to that party.[51] This situation, again, assumes that the parties have made no agreement concerning the allocation of risk. The RESTATEMENT 2d suggests an illustration, however, that is similar to the case involving the sale of the stone for one dollar. If a seller of farm land seeks to avoid the contract on the ground that valuable mineral rights have been newly found on the land, the court will allocate that risk to the seller.[52] The seller may not be said to have been "consciously ignorant" of the value of the land in this case as was the seller of the stone who had consciously adverted to the fact that she was unaware of what the stone was or its value. The seller of the farm land may have never consciously considered the possibility that valuable minerals were part of the land. Yet, when one is parting with the ownership of any property, real or personal, it would be unreasonable for that seller to assume that he or she reserves the right to reclaim it should it prove to be more valuable. In such cases, courts are faced with the necessity of supplying an omitted term.[53] That process includes an examination of the parties' manifestations to determine whether (as suggested in the case involving the sale of the stone) they have manifested an intention as to risk allocation. If a court cannot discover such a manifestation, it must proceed to a consideration of the apparent purposes of the parties in making the contract and the court's empathy for parties in that position.[54] In this sense, the court will supply the omitted risk allocation term.

---

[50] Wood v. Boyton, 64 Wis. 265, 25 N.W. 42 (1885).

[51] RESTATEMENT 2d § 154(c) and particularly comment d. *See* Chemical Bank v. WPPSS, 102 Wash. 2d 874, 691 P.2d 524 (1984).

[52] *See* RESTATEMENT 2d § 154 comments a and d.

[53] *See supra* § 90.

[54] The RESTATEMENT 2d suggests this concept in somewhat different language: "[T]he court will consider the purposes of the parties and will have recourse to its own general knowledge of human behavior in bargain transactions...." RESTATEMENT 2d § 154 comment d.

E. *Unilateral Versus Mutual Mistake — Remedies.*

What has been said to this point concerning the concept of mistake applies to either of two traditional categories of mistake, i.e., *unilateral* mistake and *mutual* mistake. *Unilateral* mistake occurs where only one of the parties has an erroneous belief at the time of formation as to a basic assumption on which he made the contract which will have a material effect on the agreed exchange that is adverse to him.[55] A *mutual* mistake is found where both parties have an erroneous belief as to a basic assumption of the contract at the time of formation which will have a material effect on the agreed exchange as to either party.[56] There is a significant problem in permitting a contract to be avoided on the ground of unilateral as contrasted with mutual mistake. If only one party is mistaken, the other party is innocent, i.e., if the other party is unaware of the mistake of the first party, though she may be said to be "mistaken" in that sense, she is entirely without fault and has a great claim to the protection of her expectations under the contract. Thus, it is not difficult to discover case law that permits reformation of a contract only on the basis of mutual mistake, i.e., absent fraud or inequitable conduct, unilateral mistake will not be an acceptable basis for reformation.[57] More generally, courts are likely to suggest that unilateral mistake is "not ordinarily" a basis for relief.[58] As suggested earlier in this section, there has never been any doubt that an offeree who knows or should know that the offeror is making a mistake may not "snap up the offer."[59] This situation involves a kind of misrpresensation, however, and there has always been relief available for the mistaken party in such situations, even in the form of reformation.[60] Absent knowledge of mistake by the non-mistaken party or some other form of misrepresentation or fraud inducing the mistake, courts have tended to relegate relief for unilateral mistakes to cases involving the excusable negligence found in clerical errors by bidders in construction cases if other elements are present.[61] There is, however, a movement toward expanding the availability of relief for unilateral mistake in other types of cases. Thus, where the purchasers of a house discovered that the house was not suitable for year-round living, the court granted rescission of the contract where the buyers were neither neligent nor imprudent, the mistake had such a material effect upon the agreed exchange that the consequences would work an unconscionable hardship on the buyers, and the seller could be restored to *status quo*.[62] The RESTATEMENT 2d has

---

[55] RESTATEMENT 2d § 154.

[56] RESTATEMENT 2d § 152.

[57] *See, e.g.,* A. J. Concrete Pumping, Inc. v. Richard O'Brien Equip. Sales, Inc., 256 Ga. 795, 353 S.E.2d 496 (1987).

[58] *See, e.g.,* Mutual of Enumclaw Ins. Co. v. Wood By-Products, Inc., 107 Idaho 1024, 695 P.2d 409 (1984).

[59] *See supra* text at notes 16 and 17.

[60] "As for reformation, the Court of Chancery observed that such relief is granted in the absence of fraud or misrepresentation only where it is demonstrated that there was a mutual mistake, or a unilateral mistake coupled with knowing silence...." Hanby v. Alymont Fire Co. No. 1, 528 A.2d 1196, 1198 (Del. 1987).

[61] These cases will be discussed *infra*.

[62] Cummings v. Dusenbury, 129 Ill. App. 3d 338, 472 N.E.2d 575 (1984). Other courts have suggested relief for unilateral mistake in other types of contracts. *See, e.g.,* Gamewell Mfg., Inc. v.

operated as a catalyst for this expansion of the application of unilateral mistake as a ground for contract avoidance.[63] This expansion is, however, much
less significant than it may appear to be. The mistaken party must not only
show a mistake at contract formation which has a material effect on the
agreed exchange that is adverse to him; he must also bear "the substantial
burden of establishing unconscionability and must ordinarily show not only
the position he would have been in had the facts been as he believed them to
be but also the position in which he finds himself as a result of the mistake."[64]
The rather amorphous concept of unconscionability[65] which suggests "unfair
surprise" and "oppression"[66] can be extremely difficult to establish even if the
mistaken party can surmount the other hurdles to establish a unilateral mistake to make the contract voidable. The RESTATEMENT 2d should be commended for creating an analysis that allows for relief caused by unilateral
mistake in situations other than computation errors. If all of the elements can
be established, there is no reason to limit the relief to that isolated type of
contract.

If the relief sought is not contract avoidance but reformation, that remedy is
only available when both parties shared a mistake with respect to the written
expression of agreement.[67] Whether the mistake is mutual or unilateral, however, a court may, in addition to permitting avoidance of the contract, provide
additional relief in the form of restitution (to prevent unjust enrichment
where it is not possible to return benefits conferred) or it may protect the
reliance interest where avoidance of the contract fails to protect that interest
sufficiently.[68]

F. Mistake of Identity.

Mistakes of identity of the other party are unilateral mistakes. A mistake of
identity provides a significant illustration of why relief for unilateral mistake
should be granted only to avoid an unconscionable result. Assume that Ames
offers to sell goods to Barnes thinking Barnes is a particular Barnes with
whom Ames would like to develop a continuous contractual relationship.
Barnes, however, is a different Barnes who does nothing to induce Ames to
make the mistake and is reasonably unaware that Ames is making a mistake.
Barnes accepts the offer and, when Ames discovers her mistake, she seeks to
avoid the contract. There is every reason to enforce this contract against Ames
in favor of Barnes who is totally innocent and should not be deprived of his
expectation interest.[69] The only escape from this analysis may be found in

---

HVAC Supply, Inc., 715 F.2d 112 (4th Cir. 1983) (settlement agreement); Zapatero v. Canales,
730 S.W.2d 111 (Tex. App. 1987).

[63] RESTATEMENT 2d § 153.

[64] RESTATEMENT 2d § 153 comment c.

[65] The developing concept of unconscionability will be thoroughly explored in the next chapter.

[66] These terms are found in a comment to the UCC version of unconscionability, § 2-302 comment 1. *See also* RESTATEMENT 2d § 208.

[67] RESTATEMENT 2d § 155 comment b.

[68] *See* RESTATEMENT 2d § 158.

[69] In a well-known case, the court adopts this analysis on the basis of § 503 of the FIRST RESTATE-
MENT (ill. 2) but then finds a "solvent," i.e., that an offer can be accepted only by the party to
whom it is made. *See* Nutmeg State Mach. Corp. v. Shuford, 129 Conn. 659, 30 A.2d 911 (1943).
While it cannot be gainsaid that an offer can be accepted only by the party to whom it is made

situations where compelling Ames to perform would be unconscionable as in situations where Barnes would be an insolvent buyer and where Ames is likely to lose the goods shipped to such a buyer.[70] The RESTATEMENT 2d would permit relief for Ames where unconscionability is shown.[71] If, however, a buyer is insolvent, query, does such a buyer have reason to believe that a party agreeing to sell to such a buyer on credit is mistaken as to the buyer's ability to pay? There is, at least, a plausible argument to this effect and it may provide relief for a seller such as Ames on the usual footing that buyer Barnes, having reason to know of such a mistake, may not "snap up the offer." If, therefore, this situation can be fitted into that generally accepted analysis, the possibility of relief for a unilateral mistake of identity where the buyer neither knows nor has reason to know of any mistake appears even more remote.

G. *Mistake of Subject Matter.*

Among the numerous cases involving a mistake of subject matter are those in which the buyer makes a unilateral mistake and the seller neither knows nor has reason to know of the mistake. Thus, where a buyer sent its agent to inspect a used dredge and then decided to purchase it, the buyer could not avoid the contract when it later determined that the dredge was not suited to its needs.[72] Since law students and some lawyers may have difficulty envisioning the operation of a dredge, a simple illustration may be even more compelling. If a buyer tells a store clerk that the buyer wishes to purchase a displayed item, the clerk will typically provide the purchaser with the same item in a sealed container rather than the sample on display. If the purchaser returns within a few days announcing that the product "doesn't work," and responds to the clerk's inquiry of the nature of the defect with, "I don't know what's wrong with it — I plug it in, press the buttons and talk into it but it doesn't record," the buyer may be startled to hear the clerk's retort: "That's because it's a typewriter." If the reasonable buyer should have known that the displayed item was a typewriter and not a tape recorder because it had all of the normal appearance of a typewriter, he has made a unilateral mistake of subject matter for which relief should not be granted.[73] Similarly, where the seller thought it was selling 21 or 22 acres of land but agreed upon the inser-

---

(because the offeror is master of the offer), if offeror Ames reasonably appears to make an offer to offeree Barnes, Barnes has a power of acceptance, i.e., he would not have such a power only if he knew or had reason to know that he was not an offeree. *See* RESTATEMENT 2d § 52 comment b. *See also* Boulton v. Jones, 2 H. & N. 564 (Ex. 1857) and In re Gendron, 13 F.2d 263 (D. Mass. 1926). *See also* Williams, *Mistake as to Party in the Law of Contracts, (Pt. II)*, 23 CAN. B. REV. 380, 383-97 (1945).

[70] As to the seller's difficulty of an action in reclamation in such a case, *see* In re Samuels & Co., 510 F.2d 139, *rev'd en banc*, 526 F.2d 1238 (5th Cir. 1976), *cert. denied*, 429 U.S. 834 (1976).

[71] RESTATEMENT 2d § 153.

[72] Anderson Bros. v. O'Meara, 306 F.2d 672 (5th Cir. 1962).

[73] There is nothing unconscionable about compelling the buyer to pay for the typewriter. On the other hand, a store may have a policy of returning the purchase price in such a transaction notwithstanding no legal compulsion to do so. Of course, if the policy creates a course of dealing, the store may be legally compelled to return the purchase price regardless of the lack of any defect in the product sold. It should also be recognized that with the advent of word processing devices which are unfamiliar in appearance, a buyer of such a product may be justified in assuming that it is a different product.

tion of a clause as to another tract of land as part of the sale and later learned that the contract required the conveyance of some thirty-five acres, relief on the basis of unilateral mistake of the subject matter was denied because the mistake was not sufficiently grave as to cause an unconscionable result.[74]

If the mistake as to subject matter is mutual, courts are much more willing to grant relief since the mistake, albeit as to a basic assumption made at the time of contract formation, need only have a material effect upon the agreed exchange, i.e., an unconscionable effect absent relief need not be shown. Thus, as suggested earlier,[75] where the parties agreed to buy and sell property which they later discover cannot be used for the purpose both intended because of a mutual mistake as to a basic assumption at the time of contract formation which has a material effect upon the agreed exchange, the contract is voidable.

H. *Computation Mistakes — Erroneous Bids.*

In making an offer to supply a number of items or different services, a party may make a mistake in the computation of the total price or in omitting an item that should have been included in the computation. If the offeree neither knows nor has reason to know that the total price is predicated upon a faulty computation and accepts at the stated price, should the offeror be bound to a contract at that price, notwithstanding the relatively innocent computation error? It is important to emphasize the fact that the offeror *intended* to make the offer at the price stated, i.e., his mistake was not one of expressing a price he did not intend. Rather, his mistake was antecedent to the making of the offer. Thus, the acceptance of the offer should be said to form a contract. The only question is whether relief will be granted because of the unilateral mistake of the offeror in miscomputing or omitting an item in totaling the offer before it was made.

The situation typically arises in submitting bids in construction contracts. A bidder on such a project is typically required to submit a bid bond which promises to pay the difference between its bid and the next higher bid should the bidder refuse to perform the contract with the owner. Since the mistake involved in such cases is unilateral, relief will be granted only if (a) the mistake is material, (b) enforcement of the contract pursuant to the erroneous bid would be unconscionable, (c) the mistake was the type of mistake that a reasonable person would make rather than "culpable negligence," (d) the non-mistaken party will not be prejudiced by granting relief, and (e) prompt notice of the mistake is given.[76] As in other questions concerning the element of materiality, there is no specific number or percentage that can be provided as a litmus test. Cases dealing with this question have found the computation or omission mistake to be material where the percentage of total bid affected by the mistake is as low as three and one-half percent.[77] Normally, however, the

---

[74] Montgomery v. Strickland, 384 So. 2d 1085 (Ala. 1980).

[75] *See supra* text at notes 41 and 42.

[76] These are the elements set forth in Boise Junior College Dist. v. Mattefs Constr. Co., 92 Idaho 757, 450 P.2d 604 (1969).

[77] *See* Smith & Love Constr. Co. v. Herrera, 79 N.M. 239, 442 P.2d 197 (1968).

percentage has to be considerably higher.[78] A relatively small percentage of a very large total bid may still result in the bidder losing a substantial amount of money.[79] The amount to be lost by the bidder goes to the element of unconscionability. Thus, if a bidder omits a $25,000 item in a $100,000 bid, it may appear to be a material mistake. If, however, the bid included a $50,000 profit the only hardship on the bidder would be a reduction in its profit to $25,000 and there would be no unconscionability in the enforcement of the contract.[80] Assuming a material effect upon the agreed exchange that would be adverse to the bidder and assuming considerable hardship upon the bidder fulfilling the unconscionability requirement, the mistake will not serve as the basis for contract avoidance if the bidder is careless in his creation of the bid. On the other hand, extraordinary meticulousness is not required, i.e., the bidder may be said to operate within the zone of reasonableness of similar businesses which, on occasion, suffer computation mistakes.[81] If the foregoing three elements are met, there is concern for the possible hardship to the other party to the contract. If the only complaint from the owner is that it will not gain the advantage of what appears to be a bargain that would be inequitable to the bidder, the contract may be avoided by the bidder.[82] If, on the other hand, the owner has justifiably and substantially relied on the mistaken bid and will suffer a significant loss if the contract is not performed at the mistaken price, as between the mistaken bidder and the innocent owner, the owner should prevail. To preclude such reliance, courts may add a requirement of prompt notification of the mistake to the owner. This, however, is not a separate requirement since prompt notice is a factor with respect to the fourth criterion of damage to the offeree-owner.[83] The question of prompt notice, however, may be seen as a manifestation of diligence by the bidder to overcome the effect of his mistake at the earliest opportunity.[84]

I. Mistake of Value — Rose 2d of Aberlone.

A purchaser of stock may hope that the value of the security will increase. If it does, she reaps the benefits of her wise purchase; if it decreases, she has assumed the risk of devalue and suffers the loss. A seller of land may be distressed to learn that the new owner has discovered valuable mineral de-

---

[78] See Alaska Int'l Constr., Inc. v. Earth Movers of Fairbanks, Inc., 697 P.2d 626, 630 (Alaska 1985), where the court held that two and one-half percent of the total bid was insufficient to meet the materiality requirement, setting forth (note 8) a comprehensive list of cases where the percentages were deemed material.

[79] City of Devil's Lake v. St. Paul Fire & Marine Ins. Co., 497 F. Supp. 595 (D. N.D. 1980) (4½% error where bidder would lose a considerable sum was deemed material).

[80] This is the example suggested in the Boise case, supra note 76. See also RESTATEMENT 2d § 153 ills. 1 and 2.

[81] See M. F. Kemper Constr. Co. v. City of Los Angeles, 37 Cal. 2d 696, 235 P.2d 7 (1951). See also Regional Sch. Dist. No. 4 v. United Pac. Ins., 4 Conn. App. 175, 493 A.2d 895, 897 (1985), where the court rejects the suggestion that there must be an absence of negligence in order to permit rescission of the contract due to the bidder's error. Rather, the court suggests that the true criterion is the achievement of equity under all of the circumstances.

[82] See Florsheim Co. v. Miller, 575 F. Supp. 84, 85 (E.D. Tex. 1983) (suggesting that rescission of the contract will be granted if the parties can be returned to status quo ante, i.e., defendant will not be prejudiced except by loss of its bargain — applying Texas law).

[83] See Boise, supra note 76.

[84] See Regional Sch. Dist. No. 4 v. United Pac. Ins., supra note 81.

posits. A buyer of goods agrees to pay what appears to be a low price until the buyer discovers that the market price has fallen. Any number of other illustrations could be provided to support the generally accepted view that, in the absence of fraud, misrepresentation or actual or presumed knowledge of the mistake on the part of the non-mistaken party, or contrary agreement between the parties, including any course of dealing or trade usage, *risks of value are normally assumed by the parties to the contract.* Any other rule would be entirely unworkable. Courts would be besieged by petitions for relief from contracts that proved less valuable than the prediction of one of the parties. Much earlier we saw that predictions are necessarily fraught with peril and our law takes the position that contracting parties ought to be aware of that peril and the genuine possibility of a change in circumstances that will reduce the value of their bargains. We also saw that courts will allocate the risk of a mistake to a party who should have assumed that risk, as in the case involving the purchase and sale of a stone, the value of which was consciously unknown by either party.[85] The best known case dealing with mistake of value involves a contract for the sale of a cow named Rose 2d of Aberlone.[86]

Walker was a breeder of cattle and sold Rose 2d of Aberlone to Sherwood, a banker. The court found that both parties believed that Rose was sterile and the purchase price of $80 reflected that belief. When Walker discovered that Rose was fertile, he refused to deliver her because she was worth some $750. Sherwood brought an action to replevy Rose and the court held for Walker on the curious ground that Rose was not in fact the animal, or the kind of animal, that Walker intended to sell or Sherwood intended to buy since a breeding cow is a substantially different creature from a barren cow. This is a rather metaphysical explanation which fails as a reliable analysis. The RESTATEMENT 2d provides little additional assistance. It mentions the famous case involving Rose as an analogy relating to an illustration where *A* agrees to assign to *B* for $100 a $10,000 debt owed to *A* by *C* who is insolvent. *A* and *B* believe the debt to be unsecured and, therefore, worthless. In fact it is secured by stock worth some $5000. The illustration concludes that the contract is voidable by *A*.[87] It is difficult to understand why the contract should be voidable by *A* in this illustration any more than the holding that Walker need not surrender Rose. Rose was the same cow that the parties had in mind. The mistake was as to a quality of the cow.[88] In the case involving the sale of a stone that turned out to be an uncut diamond, the same analysis may appear to apply.[89] In the stone case, however, there was a conscious assumption of the risk of value, i.e., both parties expressed their ignorance as to the value of the stone. Thus, whatever its real value, the risk was assumed. In the case of Rose 2d of

---

[85]*See supra* text at note 50.

[86]Sherwood v. Walker, 66 Mich. 568, 33 N.W. 919 (1887). Professor Brainerd Currie created a ballad concerning Rose of Aberlone which appeared in the Harvard Law School Record, March 4, 1954.

[87]RESTATEMENT 2d § 152 ill. 5. The other relevant RESTATEMENT 2d concept is that which has already been explored, i.e., the necessity for courts on occasion to allocate the risk of mistake in a manner reasonable under the circumstances. *See* RESTATEMENT 2d § 154(c) discussed at text, *supra* note 51 *et seq.*

[88]*See* Hecht v. Batcheller, 147 Mass. 335, 17 N.E. 651 (1888) (parties made no mistake as to subject matter but rather its quality).

[89]*See* Wood v. Boyton, 64 Wis. 265, 25 N.W. 42 (1885), discussed at text, *supra* note 50.

Aberlone, on the other hand, the parties believed that the value was exclusively the value of a barren cow. The result in that case may, therefore, be justified on the basis that the parties either manifested an intention to bear no risk beyond the risk that the value of the cow would be that of a barren cow, or, in the absence of such manifested intention, the circumstances made it reasonable for a court to conclude that the seller should not bear that risk. Professor Corbin reminds us that the court's judgment is a judgment on a matter of fact, not a judgment as to law. Thus, "No rule of thumb should be constructed for cases of this kind."[90]

J. Mistake in Transmission — Intermediary.

Where an offer is transmitted through an intermediary such as the telegraph and the message received by the offeree is not the message sent, but the offeree has no reason to believe a mistake has occurred and purports to accept the offer, is a contract formed? If the offer is sent at $10 million but transmitted at $9 million which the offeree may assume is a reasonable and not mistaken amount, if a court finds a contract between the parties, what is the critical price term, $9 million or $10 million? The case law is neither voluminous nor recent but does suggest several views. First, there is a fictitious agency view which binds the offeror because its agent, the telegraph company, made the mistake in transmission and the principal is liable for the mistakes of its agent.[91] An even worse fiction is that the telegraph company is a special agent which has exceeded its authority in transmitting an incorrect message and the offeree deals with a special agent at the offeree's peril.[92] A third view, represented by the best-known case in this area,[93] is much more sensible in that it recognizes the innocence of both offeror and offeree and does not resort to the absurdity of treating the telegraph or other intermediary as an agent. As between these two innocent parties, the court chooses the party who selected the telegraph as the means of communication as the party to bear the loss.[94] The problem with this view is that the party who chose the means of transmission may have done so casually and reasonably. Moreover, though the court uses the term "first proposer" to characterize the party who will bear the risk of transmission,[95] it is not clear that the court necessarily means "offeror" by "proposer." Suppose one party (a future offeree) chooses the telegraph medium to inquire as to price or other information concerning a potential contract. The response is an offer which is incorrectly transmitted but innocently accepted by the offeree. Is the offeree the "proposer" since he hap-

---

[90] 3 CORBIN § 605 at 643.

[91] See Des Arc Oil Mill v. Western Union Tel. Co., 132 Ark. 335, 201 S.W. 273, 6 A.L.R. 1081 (1918). The same analysis has been applied for a mistake by an interpreter, Bonelli v. Burton, 61 Or. 429, 123 P. 37 (1912).

[92] See Postal Tel. Cable Co. v. Schaefer, 110 Ky. 907, 62 S.W. 1119 (1901); Henkel v. Pape, L.R. 6 Ex. 7 [1870].

[93] Ayer v. Western Union Tel. Co., 79 Me. 493, 10 A. 495 (1887).

[94] "The first proposer can select one of many modes of communication, both for the proposal and the answer. The receiver has no such choice, except as to his answer. If he cannot safely act upon the message he receives through the agency selected by the proposer, business must be seriously hampered and delayed." Id. at 497.

[95] See the quotation supra note 94.

pened to select the telegram as the medium of communication, or is the offeror the "proposer" since only offers create legal powers and the offer was the first incorrectly transmitted message? The notion that the party who chooses the medium must bear the risk is a slender reed. As between the two innocent parties, it makes much more sense to recognize that there is a complete albeit innocent absence of mutual assent. If an offeror seeks to contract at a price ($10 million) which the offeree may or may not have found acceptable, the offeree has not assented to that price if he can demonstrate conclusively that he agreed to purchase only at $9 million. It is preferable to find no contract in these circumstances.[96] As for the liability of the intermediary, if it is viewed as a public utility such as telephone or telegraph, it is surrounded by tariffs or other federal or state regulations limiting its liability, typically to an amount which casts more than serious doubt on a decision to litigate.[97]

K. Releases — "Unknown Injury" Rule.

If a party has a claim against another party, he may agree to release that claim in exchange for certain consideration. In an earlier chapter concerning the validation process, we noted how strongly our courts have favored settlements of such claims, even to the point of treating forbearance to sue on an invalid claim as consideration to support the promise received in exchange for such forbearance.[98] In agreeing to such a settlement, the claimant often signs a *release* designed to protect the other party from any and all claims which might have otherwise been asserted against him by the claimant. Subsequently, the former claimant may discover a claim that was unknown at the time he signed the release, or he may discover that the nature or extent of his claim was unknown at the time he signed the release. He may, therefore, seek rescission or avoidance of the release agreement on the basis of mistake. While the problems in this area may involve any kind of claim, they are particularly significant with respect to personal injury claims and the courts have not been consistent in their approach to these problems.

If a claimant signs a release at a time when he assumes that he suffers from a particular injury and later discovers that the nature or extent of the same injury is greater than he had originally assumed, most of our courts will not permit him to avoid the release on the basis of his mistake.[99] If, however, the very injury discovered after the execution of the release was unknown as contrasted with the discovery of unknown consequences of injuries known at the time of the release, the overwhelming majority of our courts apply what has become known as the "unknown injury" rule which permits avoidance of the release on the basis of this kind of mistake.[1] The form of the release signed by the claimant will have an effect on this analysis. Thus, some courts will refuse to permit a release agreement to be avoided or rescinded if the release document clearly and explicitly discharges liability for both known and un-

---

[96] *See, e.g.,* Murray Oil Prods. Co. v. Poons Co., 190 Misc. 110, 74 N.Y.S.2d 814 (1947); Holtz v. Western Union Tel Co., 294 Mass. 543, 3 N.E.2d 180 (1936).

[97] *See, e.g.,* Crowley Indus. Bag Co. v. Western Union Co., 204 So. 2d 725 (La. App. 1967).

[98] *See* RESTATEMENT 2d § 74 and the treatment of this concept *supra* Chapter 3.

[99] *See, e.g.,* Dustin v. Union Pac. R.R. 109 Idaho 361, 707 P.2d 472 (1985).

[1] *See* LaFleur v. C. C. Pierce Co., 398 Mass. 254, 496 N.E.2d 827 (1986), and cases cited therein.

known injuries.[2] Other courts have held that such clear and explicit language does not necessarily preclude avoidance of a release because such all-inclusive langauge is often standardized and may not be consciously adverted to by the claimant.[3] This is another manifestation of courts disregarding certain printed form (boilerplate) language in agreements as conclusive. One court has declined to follow either of these approaches and adopted the view that it must consider the intent of the parties to be inferred from all of the circumstances of the agreement including but not limited to the language of the release.[4] There is no parol evidence bar to the admission of such evidence.[5] If a claimant signed a release when he was consciously ignorant of his injuries, the risk of exacerbation of those injuries or even unknown injuries (where the release contemplated unknown injuries) will be allocated to the claimant.[6] The RESTATEMENT 2d focuses upon the basic assumptions of the parties at the time of the release and, in particular, suggests that the following circumstances be considered: the fair amount required to compensate the claimant for his known injuries, the probability that the other party would be liable on such a claim, the amount actually received by the claimant under the release, and the relationship between the known and unknown injuries.[7] The RESTATEMENT 2d properly suggests that express provisions in releases that are all inclusive concerning known and unknown injuries may be judicially disregarded as unconscionable if that langauage appears inconsistent with the basic assumption of the parties at the time of the release.[8]

---

[2] See, e.g., Hybarger v. American States Ins. Co., 498 N.E.2d 1015 (Ind. App. 1986) (holding agreement not voidable where the release document was captioned, "Full and Final Release" and by its terms released the defendant from all claims and causes of action and all other loss and damage of every kind and nature caused by or resulted or hereafter resulting to the claimant from a particular accident, even though the release did not specifiy "unknown" or "unforeseen" injuries). See also Gecy v. Prudential Ins. Co., 257 S.E.2d 709, 712 (S.C. 1979) (release included subsequently discovered unknown injuries).

[3] See, e.g., Mangini v. McClurg, 24 N.Y.2d 556, 564 (1969).

[4] See LaFleur v. C. C. Pierce Co., supra note 1.

[5] For this proposition, the court in LaFleur cites Micelson v. Barnet, 390 Mass. 786, 792 (1984).

[6] See Hoggatt v. Jorgensen, 43 Wash. App. 782, 719 P.2d 602 (1986) (petition for review granted).

[7] RESTATEMENT 2d § 152 comment f.

[8] Id.

Chapter 6

ABUSE OF BARGAIN, UNCONSCIONABILITY, GOOD FAITH, AND ILLEGALITY

§ 92. Introduction — Relation Among Concepts Evidencing an Abuse of the Bargaining Process.

The last chapter was concerned with those expressions of assent that were "operative" as contrasted with those that were not legally recognized, i.e., those that were "inoperative." We considered certain expressions prior to the execution of the writing evidencing the parties' agreement which would be inoperative if the parties intended their written expression of agreement as the final and complete expression, i.e., we were concerned about compliance with the *parol evidence rule.* We examined the operative effect given to various expressions of agreement, i.e., the *meaning* of the terms used by the parties under the rubric of *interpretation.* We then examined the expressions of the parties where one or both later alleged that such expressions were mistaken to determine whether courts should afford operative effect to the expressions as normally interpreted, or whether evidence of mistake was sufficient to justify giving operative effect to other manifestations of intention, i.e., the true intention of the parties. In an earlier chapter, we examined the operative effect of oral expressions of agreement with respect to certain kinds of contracts that, as a general rule, must be evidenced by a sufficient writing. There, we directed our attention to the satisfaction of the *statute of frauds.* The concepts to be examined in this chapter could also be grouped under the generic caption "operative expressions of assent," since we will explore the ways in which courts decide that certain expressions of agreement will not be legally recognized. The focus, however, will be different because we will be particularly concerned about abuses of the bargaining process which may have the effect of treating certain apparent manifestations of agreement as inoperative.

We will first consider abuses of the bargaining process where courts will either give no credence at all to the alleged contract, or they will permit the abused party to avoid what otherwise appears to be an enforceable contract, i.e., the courts will treat such manifestations of agreement as inoperative. We will consider these abuses from the most egregious to the more subtle. The compelling example of the most egregious abuse of the barganing process is a manifestation of assent induced by physical compulsion such as a writing signed by a party at the point of a gun or other physical compulsion. The circumstances under which such a writing is signed belies the apparent manifestation of assent by the victim of the *duress.* It is the antithesis of volition and assent. Courts have no difficulty in treating such cases as involving no contract at all, i.e., there is no need for the abused party to exercise a power of avoidance or disaffirmance to avoid the contract. There was no contract *ab initio.* Lesser forms of duress involve improper threats that are sufficiently grave to induce assent by the victim of the threat. Here, courts will permit the victim to avoid or disaffirm the contract, thereby rendering it inoperative. In the absence of duress, one party may induce the assent of another by misleading the other. Such *misrepresentation* permits the other party to avoid or disaffirm the contract, again making the apparent manifestation of agreement inoperative. Where neither duress nor misrepresentation can be shown, one party may exert *undue influence* upon another, thereby inducing assent to an unfair transaction where the adversely affected party, though not lacking capacity to contract, falls victim to the improper persuasion of the other. The victim may avoid the contract. Though duress, misrepresentation or undue influence cannot be established, if a court deems a contract or particular terms thereof to be *unconscionable,* it will refuse operative effect to that contract or certain terms of the contract. The concept of unconscionability is amorphous. It has all of the qualities of the even broader concept of "justice." It is often suggested that "justice" does not admit of anything resembling a precise definition.[1] On the other hand, manifest injustice can often be discerned, sometimes quite easily. Similarly, unconscionability may be detected in a given situation though the court may be less than pleased with its inability to suggest the parameters of the concept.[2] A concept that may prove to be even more elusive than unconscionability is the pervasive concept of *good faith.*[3] Where there is no duress, misrepresentation, undue influence or unconscionability, the absence of good faith will permit a court to refuse to enforce all or part of a contract, i.e., a court will deem the parties' expression of agreement to be inoperative because one of the parties has not performed in good faith. Two definitions of "good faith" are provided by the UCC and those concepts must be explored in light of case law interpretations. Finally, even where there is no lack of good faith and no evidence of duress, misrepresentation, undue influence, or unconscionability, certain agreements of the parties may be deemed unenforceable because they violate an elusive standard called *"public policy."* The nebulous nature of "public policy" has long been recog-

---

[1] A classic definition is the product of Ulpian who suggested that justice means to render to each his due. This and similar efforts to define "justice" typically suggest a tautology.

[2] *See, e.g.,* Jones v. Star Credit Corp., 59 Misc. 2d 189, 298 N.Y.S.2d 264 (1969), where the court suggests that deciding that unconscionability exists in a given situation is substantially easier than explaining it.

[3] For a courageous effort to analyze the concept of good faith, *see* Summers, *"Good Faith" in General Contract Law and the Sales Provisions of the Uniform Commercial Code,* 54 Va. L. Rev. 195 (1968).

nized.[4] Yet, courts have confronted the necessity of deciding whether a particular agreement exceeds the bounds of public policy by, for example, violating a statutory or common law standard. Courts may refuse to enforce the entire bargain between the parties, or may decide that the agreement may be enforced after surgically removing the portion of the agreement that violates a pervasive standard in society. In either event, the court is, again, deciding which manifestations of agreement shall or shall not be operative. These and related problems will be explored in the portion of this chapter dealing with *"illegal bargains."*

§ 93. Duress.

A. *Duress by Physical Compulsion — "Void" Contract.*

If a party is compelled to manifest assent by physical force where, for example, his hand is physically forced to sign a document or where he signs at gunpoint, it is clear that the signature is no manifestation of assent since the signer had no intention of performing the act. The phrase often quoted is that the compelled party is "a mere mechanical instrument"[5] operating as a robot controlled by physical means. Since such a signature is not an effective manifestation of assent, there is no assent and there is no contract. It is often suggested that such physical compulsion creates a "void contract" rather than a voidable contract. A "void contract" is a contradiction since there is no assent and no contract ever existed. A voidable contract, however, is perfectly valid though the party with the power of avoidance or disaffirmance may exercise that power to avoid it. If a check is signed at gunpoint, the check is void, i.e., the party signing the check (the drawer) will have a defense even against a subsequent party who takes the check in good faith, for value and without notice of any defenses to the instrument.[6] If, however, the duress is lesser in degree as where an instrument is signed under a threat to prosecute a relative of the signer for theft, the instrument may be merely voidable.[7]

Whether duress by physical compulsion is exercised by another party to the purported contract or by a third person, the effect is the same, i.e., there is no contract.[8] It is also important to note that a party who appears to manifest assent will not be held to have manifested an operative (legally effective) assent if such a manifestation has been induced by sufficient control over his consciousness. Thus, one who is hypnotized or under the influence of a mind

---

[4] "I, for one, protest ... against arguing too strongly upon public policy: — it is a very unruly horse, and when once you get astride it you never know where it will carry you. It may lead you from the sound law. It is never argued at all but when other points fail." Justice Burrough in Richardson v. Mellish, 2 Bing. 229, 252 (C.P. 1824). On the general subject, *see* Percy H. Winfield, *Public Policy in the English Common Law,* 42 Harv. L. Rev. 76 (1928).

[5] *See* Restatement 2d § 174 comment a.

[6] UCC § 3-305(2)(b). The defense is often characterized as a "real" defense which is available even against a holder in due course, defined in the UCC at § 3-302(1) as one who takes the instrument for value, in good faith and without notice that it is overdue or has been dishonored or of any defense against or claim to it on the part of any person.

[7] *See* UCC § 3-305 comment 6 which suggests this example and concludes that, if the instrument is merely voidable, the defense would not be available against the holder in due course described in the preceding note.

[8] Restatement 2d § 174 comment b.

controlling drug may not be responsible for a manifestation of assent, i.e., though his conduct appears to suggest assent, he does not voluntarily create that impression of assent.[9]

B. *Duress by Threat — Improper Threat in General.*

A threat is an expression of intention to injure another.[10] The expression may be by words or conduct. If one person commits a battery against another or imprisons another, the victim's fear of further blows or imprisonment will constitute duress.[11] Promises induced by threats of violence must be unenforceable so as to discourage such threats.[12] On the other hand, if Ames is desirous of purchasing an automobile from Barnes and Barnes will not sell unless Ames pays what Ames views as an excessive price, Ames may characterize Barnes' demand as a threat. Any offer could be viewed as a threat not to make a contract unless the offeree acquiesces in the terms of the offer.[13] "Driving a hard bargain" is commonplace in numerous negotiations.[14] Even if such a demand could be called a "threat," it certainly does not amount to duress. As is so often the case, the question becomes, at what point does a party step over the line separating the legitimate, though perhaps harsh, demand from the demand which should be viewed as illegitimate? The line is not bright; in fact, it is wavering and blurred. The ancient common law view relegated the type of threat necessary to show duress to loss of life, loss of a member, mayhem or imprisonment.[15] The modern position has greatly enlarged the categories of threats that may cause duress. The difficulty of providing an appropriate characterization of the type of threat that modern courts regard as a sine qua non to a finding of duress is implicit in the current characterization that the threat must be *improper*.[16] Thus, the Second Restatement suggests that a contract is voidable by a victim whose manifestation of assent has been induced by an improper threat if the victim has no reasonable alternative.[17] If only *improper* threats are sufficient to cause duress, it is essential to distinguish between proper and improper threats. Those who seek a litmus test to distinguish proper from improper threats will be

---

[9] *See* RESTATEMENT 2d § 19(2) and comment c thereto suggesting that a manifestation of assent is not the mere appearance of assent if the party is not responsible for that appearance. "There must be conduct and a conscious will to engage in that conduct."

[10] In Zardies v. Zardies, 64 Cal. App. 3d 11, 134 Cal. Rptr. 181 (1976), the court repeated a definition of "threat" as found in WEBSTER'S THIRD NEW INTERNATIONAL DICTIONARY (1966): "expression of an intention to inflict evil, injury or damage on another, usually as retribution or punishment" and an "expression of intention to inflict loss or harm on another by illegal means and especially by means involving coercion or duress of the person threatened."

[11] *See* RESTATEMENT 2d § 175 comment a. *See also* Polito v. Polito, 121 A.D.2d 614, 503 N.Y.S.2d 867 (1986) where a former wife had been battered by her former husband on many occasions and was in fear of further physical abuse when she succumbed and signed a release.

[12] *See* Selmer Co. v. Blakeslee-Midwest Co., 704 F.2d 924, 927 (7th Cir. 1983).

[13] RESTATEMENT 2d § 176 comment a.

[14] "Hard bargaining . . . [is] acceptable . . . in our economic system." Rich & Whillock, Inc. v. Ashton Dev., Inc., 157 Cal. App. 3d 1159, 204 Cal. Rptr. 86, 89 (1984).

[15] *See* E. COKE, SECOND INSTITUTE, 482-83 (1642). *See also* Rubenstein v. Rubenstein, 20 N.J. 359, 120 A.2d 11, 14 (1956).

[16] A similar characterization is "wrongful." *See, e.g.,* Jones v. Jones, 276 Or. 1125, 557 P.2d 239 (1976).

[17] RESTATEMENT 2d § 175(1). *See, e.g.,* Penn v. Transportation Lease Haw., Ltd., 2 Haw. App. 272, 275, 630 P.2d 646, 649 (1981) which adopts the RESTATEMENT 2d definition of duress.

disappointed since no such test exists. Since the generic subject of this volume is law and not physics, however, students of the law should not be disappointed. As usual, we must examine clusters of cases to determine how courts have made the distinction.

C. *Improper Threats Not Causing Duress.*

If the threatened act would be a crime or a tort, the threat is improper. Thus, threats of gangster violence and arsenic poisoning are improper threats.[18] It should be emphasized that, even if the threat is a technical crime or tort and is, therefore, improper, there may be no duress because other elements of duress are absent. Thus, if the improper threat failed to induce the assent of the victim or if the victim of the threat had a reasonable alternative to succumbing to the threat, duress will not be found notwithstanding the improper threat. These other elements will be discussed later in this section.

D. *Threatened Act Is Proper But Threat Is Improper.*

The threatened act may not be wrongful, but the threat, itself, may be wrongful. Thus, where a wife claimed that she signed a settlement agreement with her husband because she feared that he might carry out his threat to inform the Internal Revenue Service of her failure to report income from her business, the court found duress.[19] The court recognized the right of the husband to turn his wife in to the IRS His *threat* to do so for his own pecuniary advantage, however, constituted extortion under the law of that state.[20]

E. *Threat to Do That Which One Has Legal Right to Do — Threat of Criminal Prosecution.*

A threat may be neither tortious nor criminal. One of the axiomatic statements found in numerous cases is that it is never duress to threaten to do that which one has a legal right to do.[21] Like so many maxims in our law, however, this one is misleading — even more misleading than the typical maxim. Thus, a threat of criminal prosecution, whether against the other party to the agreement or a third person, is an improper threat even if the party making the threat honestly believes the threatened party to be guilty of a crime, and even if such party is guilty of the crime.[22] The honest belief (good faith) of the party making the threat is irrelevant since he is misusing, for personal gain, a power designed for other proper ends.[23] Modern courts have, therefore, modified the maxim that it is never improper to threaten to do that which one has

---

[18] *See* Rubenstein v. Rubenstein, *supra* note 15.

[19] Berger v. Berger, 466 So. 2d 1149 (Fla. App. 1985).

[20] FLA. STAT. § 836.05.

[21] *See, e.g.,* Red-Samm Mining Co. v. The Port of Seattle, 8 Wash. App. 610, 508 P.2d 175 (1973) suggesting that a threat of litigation by one who has a legal right to sue is not duress.

[22] RESTATEMENT 2d § 176 comment c. Moreover, as suggested in *Berger v. Berger, supra* note 19, the threat, itself, may constitute a crime.

[23] *See,* however, Pleuss v. City of Seattle, 8 Wash. App. 133, 504 P.2d 1191 (1972) where the court suggests that a threat to exercise a right in good faith, i.e., in the honest belief that valid grounds exist to justify the threatened action, cannot be the basis for duress or conversion.

a legal right to do, by carefully excepting threats of criminal prosecution and even suggesting the possibility of other exceptions.[24]

F. *Threat of Civil Process.*

It is difficult to characterize a threat to institute a civil action as improper in our legal system which prides itself on free access to that system. Recall that even the assertion of claims that turn out to be invalid constitute consideration to support a promise if the assertion was made in good faith.[25] The emphasis, however, is upon the good faith assertion of such claims. Thus, if a threat is made to institute a civil action in bad faith, i.e., the party making the assertion did not believe that he had a reasonable foundation to assert the claim, the threat would be improper.[26] Similarly, if the threat to institute legal proceedings is done with an intent to coerce a grossly unfair contract not related to the proceedings, the threat is improper.[27] Again, even if the threat to institute civil proceedings is improper, it will often not amount to duress because the recipient of the threat will have the reasonable alternative of defending in the threatened action.[28] The alternative of defending the threatened action, however, may not be a reasonable alternative as will be seen later in this section.

G. *Economic Duress — Business Compulsion — Threat to Breach a Contract — Modifications Induced by Threat — Uniform Commercial Code.*

A party to a contract may threaten to breach it unless it is modified. In response to a claim asserted by one party, the other may threaten to pay nothing unless the first party agrees to accept only half or less of the claimed amount in settlement of the claim. Freedom of contract is favored in our society as is the desirability of settling disputes without litigation. These values have traditionally made courts reluctant to interfere with modifications or settlements and releases of claims, even those induced by a threatened breach.[29] Suing for an admittedly due debt was considered a reasonable alternative even if the plaintiff was in financial difficulty and could not practically await judicial relief.[30] Modern courts, however, recognize that there is

---

[24] *See, e.g.,* Eggleston v. Humble Pipe Line Co., 482 S.W.2d 909 (Tex. Civ. App. 1972) where the court repeats the "general" rule that a threat to do that which an individual has a legal right to do will not constitute duress but adds the exception for threats of criminal prosecution and also suggests that the rule may otherwise be subject to "a most limited possible modification."

[25] *See* discussion of the assertion of such invalid claims *supra* § 63, Chapter 3.

[26] *See, e.g.,* Leepter v. Beltrami, 53 Cal. 2d 195, 347 P.2d 12 (1959) (extortion of funds through mortgage foreclosure).

[27] *See* Link v. Link, 278 N.C. 181, 179 S.E.2d 697 (1971) (wife confessed adultery and husband threatened to take children away unless wife transferred valuable stocks to him). The RESTATEMENT 2d would characterize such a demand as "exorbitant" and would call the threat improper because it was made in bad faith. RESTATEMENT 2d § 176 comment d.

[28] *See* RESTATEMENT 2d § 175 comment b and ill. 1.

[29] *See* the well-known case of Hackley v. Headly, 45 Mich. 569, 8 N.W. 511 (1881) where the defendant knew he owed the plaintiff $4,260 but also knew that the plaintiff would face financial ruin if he did not receive payment quickly. The defendant offered the plaintiff $4,000 on a take-it-or-leave-it basis and the plaintiff signed the release required by the defendant. The plaintiff then sought to avoid the release on the basis of duress and the court held that no duress had been shown.

[30] If the contract was with the government, it was early recognized that there may be no remedy since the government could raise the sovereign immunity defense. That defense, however, has

no freedom of contract between bargaining unequals. They are much more reluctant to enforce agreements made under economically coercive circumstances.[31] For a number of years, courts have recognized a form of duress that is not dependent upon showing that the threat is tortious or criminal. A party may not avoid a contract simply because he can demonstrate that he agreed to a modification or a settlement and release because his financial situation was necessitous.[32] If, however, the financial distress was caused by the other party's conduct, duress may be shown.[33] Even where the financial distress was not caused by the other party, duress may be shown under certain circumstances. If Ames knows that she owes Barnes $157,000 and she also knows that unless Barnes receives at least $5,000 immediately, Barnes will lose certain valuable property through foreclosure proceedings, Ames knows that she has Barnes "over a barrel." Barnes cannot afford to await a judicial remedy to recover the acknowledged amount due. Thus, Ames offers Barnes $5,000 and demands an immediate release with the threat to pay Barnes nothing and force him to sue unless he signs the release. Barnes' signature on such a release is the antithesis of freedom of contract. The agreement is inherently coercive because Barnes was forced to accept a sum grossly disproportionate to the amount owed (there was no honest dispute about the amount owed) under circumstances where the debtor took advantage of the immediate financial necessity of the creditor. It is not remarkable that courts find duress in such cases.[34] This type of duress is not physical compulsion nor is the threat involved a tort or a crime. Yet, it is now viewed as duress and often characterized as *economic duress* or *business compulsion.* "Business compulsion" should not be viewed as a concept distinct from economic duress.[35]

It is often suggested that a threat to breach a contract is not, in itself, improper.[36] Yet, if such a threat constitutes a breach of the duty of good faith and fair dealing which every contract imposes, it is improper and can, therefore, constitute the basis of avoidance for duress.[37] The classic illustration of such a breach occurred in the well-known case, *Alaska Packers' Ass'n v. Domenico* [38] where sailors and fishermen had agreed to work for the defendant at a stated compensation in distant waters during a short fishing season. The plaintiffs knew that the defendant had a significant investment in the opera-

---

been in a state of decline for a number of years. Courts also recognized that contracts with public utilities or common carriers were one-sided in that the utilities and carriers had a lawful monopoly. Thus, if a utility or a carrier induced an oppressive bargain, the other party had no reasonable alternative but to succumb.

[31] *See* Totem Marine T. & B. v. Alyeska Pipeline, 584 P.2d 15, 21 (Alaska 1978).

[32] *See* Selmer Co. v. Blakeslee-Midwest Co., 704 F.2d 924, 928 (7th Cir. 1983).

[33] "The mere stress of business conditions will not constitute duress where the defendant was not responsible for the conditions." Johnson, Drake & Piper, Inc. v. United States, 531 F.2d 1037, 1042 (Ct. Cl. 1976).

[34] The figures and other circumstances in the example are identical to those found in Capps v. Georgia Pac. Corp., 253 Or. 248, 453 P.2d 935 (1969) where the court found duress and permitted the release to be avoided. For a similar fact situation and holding, *see* Rich & Willock, Inc. v. Ashton Dev., Inc., 157 Cal. App. 3d 1154, 204 Cal. Rptr. 86 (1984) ($72,286.45 admittedly due and debtor insisted that creditor sign a release in exchange for $50,000 knowing that creditor was in dire need of funds). *See also* Totem Marine T. & B. v. Alyeska Pipeline, *supra* note 31.

[35] *See* Dalzell, *Duress by Economic Pressure, I, II,* 20 N.C.L. REV. 237, 341 (1942).

[36] *See* RESTATEMENT 2d § 176 comment e.

[37] RESTATEMENT 2d § 176(1)(d). *See also* § 205.

[38] 117 F. 99 (9th Cir. 1902).

tion and, upon arrival at the distant location, they refused to perform their contract unless the defendant agreed to a modification through which they would receive additional compensation. The defendant agreed to the modification but refused to perform it. When plaintiffs sued for breach of the modified contract, the court held for the defendant on the basis of a lack of consideration, i.e., the pre-existing duty rule provided a technical basis for refusing to enforce the modification. There is, however, no question that the court was concerned about the coercive nature of the modification. As one court recently suggested:

> *Alaska Packers Ass'n* shows that because the legal remedies for breach of contract are not always adequate, a refusal to honor a contract may force the other party to the contract to surrender his rights.... It undermines the institution of contract to allow a contract party to use the threat of breach to get the contract modified in his favor not because anything has happened to require modification in the mutual interest of the parties but simply because the other party, unless he knuckles under to the threat, will incur costs for which he will have no adequate remedy.[39]

As we have seen earlier in this volume, the UCC permits contract modifications without consideration if such modifications are made in good faith.[40] A comment to this section makes clear that extortionate "modifications" to escape performance of the original contract are barred since they are, necessarily, bad faith modifications. Moreover, even a technical consideration will not support a bad faith modification.[41] The question remains, however, where is the line between good faith and bad faith modifications? One court suggests that this question requires two distinct inquiries: (1) whether the party inducing the modification has acted in accordance with reasonable commercial standards and fair dealing in the trade, and (2) whether the parties were in fact motivated to seek modification by an honest desire to compensate for commercial exigencies.[42] The first inquiry requires that the party asserting the modification demonstrate that the decision to seek a modification was the result of a factor (e.g., increased costs) which would cause an ordinary merchant to seek a modification. The second inquiry is less clear since it requires the party asserting the modification to demonstrate that he was, in fact, motivated by a sound commercial reason and that he did not offer such a reason as mere pretext to induce additional compensation. The court adds that "[T]he trier of fact must determine whether the means used to obtain the modification are an impermissible attempt to obtain a modification by extortion or overreaching."[43]

The RESTATEMENT 2d provides a striking illustration of the difficulty in drawing the distinction between a modification induced by bad faith and one induced by good faith. *A* contracts to excavate *B*'s cellar for a stated price and

---

[39] Opinion by Posner, J. in Selmer Co. v. Blakeslee-Midwest Co., 704 F.2d 924, 927 (7th Cir. 1983).

[40] UCC § 2-209(1). *See supra* § 64(E), Chapter 3.

[41] UCC § 2-209 comment 2.

[42] Roth Steel Prods. v. Sharon Steel Corp., 705 F.2d 134, 146 (6th Cir. 1983).

[43] *Ibid.* As the court suggests in a footnote to this sentence (note 24), this question might be more properly analyzed in terms of procedural unconscionability, which will be discussed in a subsequent section.

encounters solid rock during the excavation. He threatens not to complete performance unless *B* agrees to a modification which will increase the price nine times the original price. *B* has no reasonable alternative and agrees to the modification, induced by *A*'s threat. The new price is reasonable in light of the unanticipated difficulty. The RESTATEMENT 2d concludes that there is no duress because *A* is not violating his duty of good faith and fair dealing.[44] The illustration is similar to that found in another RESTATEMENT 2d section dealing with fair and equitable modifications in light of unanticipated circumstances[45] except for the presence of a "threat" by *A*. If *A*'s "threat" is based upon *A*'s good faith but erroneous belief that he is excused from performing because of the unanticipated solid rock, it is difficult to discover any duress.[46] If, however, *A* is fully aware of his contractual responsibility but threatens to breach because he knows of *B*'s critical need to have the work performed without delay, the situation appears quite similar to cases discussed earlier involving coerced settlements.[47] Certainly, the threat in such a case is not made in good faith and as such, it should be deemed improper.[48] The only consistent conclusion, therefore, is that the RESTATEMENT 2d illustration assumes *A*'s good faith in "threatening" to cease his performance.

H. *Threats Resulting in Unfair Exchanges — RESTATEMENT 2d.*

The RESTATEMENT 2d divides improper threats into two categories. The first category includes the kinds of threats already discussed, i.e., threats amounting to crimes or torts, threats of criminal prosecutions, threats to use the civil process in bad faith, and threats amounting to breaches of the duties of good faith and fair dealing.[49] The second category deals with threats that become improper if the resulting exchange is not on fair terms.[50] Thus, if a former employer threatens to prevent a former employee from obtaining other employment unless the employee agrees to a release of his claim against the employer, the threatened act would harm the employee but would not benefit the employer, i.e., the act would be malicious or vindictive. The resulting exchange is unfair and is voidable by the employee.[51] Similarly, while a threat to refuse to deal with a particular buyer is normally not improper, if a supplier of goods induces a customer to believe that he will supply such goods in the future causing the buyer to rely upon that assurance until the goods are unavailable elsewhere, the supplier's subsequent threat to refuse to deal with that buyer except at an extortionate price is improper.[52] A threat to breach a

---

[44] RESTATEMENT 2d § 176 ill. 8.

[45] *See* RESTATEMENT 2d § 89(a) and ill. 1 thereto.

[46] *Cf.* Pittsburgh Testing Lab. v. Farnsworth & Chambers Co., 251 F.2d 77 (1958) where the court focused upon the question of consideration and discovered a solution through the settlement of a bona fide dispute and further suggested the possibility of using the doctrine of good faith modifications in light of unanticipated circumstances.

[47] For example, where the threatening party knows that the other party needs cash immediately and offers a lesser amount than the liquidated debt which is not honestly disputed.

[48] RESTATEMENT 2d § 176(1)(d).

[49] RESTATEMENT 2d § 176(1).

[50] RESTATEMENT 2d § 176(2).

[51] *See* Perkins Oil v. Fitzgerald, 197 Ark. 14, 121 S.W.2d 877 (1938). *See also* RESTATEMENT 2d § 176(2)(a).

[52] *See* Hocman v. Ziegler's, Inc., 139 N.J. Eq. 139, 50 A.2d 97 (1946).

contract, itself not improper, can become improper because of prior unfair dealing by the threatening party which places the recipient of the threat in a position of having no reasonable alternative but to succumb to the threat. An agreement inducing the victim to appear to assent under these circumstances should be voidable because of duress.[53] A threat to use a power for illegitimate ends resulting in an unfair exchange is also an improper threat. Thus, if a party threatens to refuse delivery of goods unless another party pays an amount owed to the threatening party by a third party, a court could conclude that this constitutes use of a power for illegitimate ends.[54]

Again, the line between hard bargaining and illegitimate use of power resulting in an unfair exchange may be very difficult to draw in a given situation. It is important for the student of contract law to recognize the willingness of modern courts to find duress where that line has been crossed.

I. *Causation — Overcoming the Will of a Person of Ordinary Firmness — Depriving a Party of Free Will — No Reasonable Alternative — Objective Versus Subjective.*

We have seen that the threat inducing action or forebearance by the recipient of the threat must be *improper* in order for the contract to be avoided. It is important to emphasize the requirement that the threat *cause* or *induce* a manifestation of assent by the recipient.[55] Causation must be a fact question requiring an analysis of all the surrounding circumstances to determine whether the threat, in fact, induced or caused apparent assent. The causation element has not been very troublesome with respect to duress. Courts, however, have spent considerable energy dealing with a related question, i.e., what is the test to determine whether the recipient of the threat was justified in succumbing to the threat?

The early judicial standard used to deal with this question shifted from an objective standard employed at early common law requiring evidence that a "resolute" person or person of "ordinary firmness" would have bowed to the threat under the circumstances[56] to a subjective standard that the recipient

---

[53] *See, e.g.,* Litten v. Johnathan Logan, Inc., 220 Pa. Super. 274, 286 A.2d 913 (1971) (pursuant to an oral agreement, plaintiffs transferred all of the stock of two corporations to defendant in exchange for defendant's promise to pay corporate loans, pay the excess to plaintiffs, employ plaintiffs for one year, and give one of the plaintiffs an option to purchase stock. Defendant failed to perform even the first promise of paying creditors and, when plaintiffs were threatened with bankruptcy proceedings, defendant presented plaintiffs with a written agreement which was different from the oral agreement but which defendant insisted plaintiff sign the same day with the threat that the creditors would not be paid unless plaintiff signed. After resisting, plaintiff signed with manifestations of protest.). *See also* RESTATEMENT 2d § 176(2)(b).

[54] *See* the discussion of ill. 15 of the FIRST RESTATEMENT § 318(2) (which illustration is repeated as ill. 15 in RESTATEMENT 2d § 176) in Eckstein v. Eckstein, 38 Md. App. 506, 379 A.2d 757, 762 (1978). *See also* RESTATEMENT 2d § 176(2)(c).

[55] There is no special rule for causation of duress found in the RESTATEMENT 2d. Rather, it is suggested that the same standard be used as found in the section dealing with the causation of misrepresentation, i.e., § 167, which suggests that "[a] misrepresentation induces a party's manifestation of assent if it substantially contributes to his decision to manifest assent." *See also* Wilson v. Wilson, 642 S.W.2d 132 (Mo. App. 1982) where the court found no duress because the demand for the agreement to which Mr. Wilson agreed was not made by Mrs. Wilson. Rather, the idea was Mr. Wilson's who apparently felt a need to motivate Mrs. Wilson to alter her behavior.

[56] *See* 2 H. BRACTON, ON THE LAW AND CUSTOMS OF ENGLAND 65 (Thorne Tr. 1968).

was deprived of free will, a standard still found in modern cases.[57] The RE-STATEMENT 2d rejects both the "ordinary firmness" and deprivation of "free will" tests because of their "vagueness and impracticability" and substitutes a test that requires the victim to show that he had "no reasonable alternative" to manifesting assent to the improper threat.[58] As we will see later in this subsection, the objective or subjective nature of this test can cause confusion. Earlier we saw that a threat to institute a civil action is ordinarily not duress because the aggrieved party typically has the reasonable alternative of asserting his rights in that action. Yet, the circumstances may suggest that such an alternative may not be reasonable under the circumstances. For example, where Ames leaves a piece of equipment for repair with Barnes and, though Ames has paid for the repairs, Barnes refuses to deliver the equipment unless Ames either pays an additional amount or agrees to have Barnes do additional work. While Ames has a cause of action in replevin for her equipment, her immediate need for the equipment may cause the remedy to be inadequate.[59] Similarly, where a party threatens to breach a contract unless the victim manifests assent to a modification, the circumstances may suggest that an exercise of the victim's right to bring an action for breach may prove inadequate, thereby leaving him no reasonable alternative but to succumb to the threat by manifesting assent to the modification.[60]

The RESTATEMENT 2d standard may create confusion as to whether it is objective or subjective because it requires two elements: (1) the victim's manifestation of assent must be induced by an improper threat and (2) the induced assent must leave the victim no reasonable alternative to manifesting assent to the threat.[61] As to the first element, the RESTATEMENT 2d clearly intends a subjective standard which would consider age, background and the relationship between the parties.[62] The focus is upon *causation*, i.e., if the threat *in fact* caused the manifestation of assent because the victim was an infant, timid, or otherwise easily frightened, where the same threat would have been ignored by a reasonable person, duress is shown.[63] The second element, i.e., whether the victim had a reasonable alternative, is irrelevant in such a case since such a victim would not consider any reasonable alternative, having been induced by a threat which, itself, would not induce a reasonable person

---

[57] *See, e.g.,* Peter Matthews, Ltd. v. Robert Mabey, Inc., 117 A.D.2d 943, 499 N.Y.S.2d 254, 255 (1986); Raymundo v. Hammond Clinic Ass'n, 449 N.E.2d 276, 283 (Ind. 1983); Food Fair Stores, Inc. v. Joy, 283 Md. 205, 389 A.2d 874 (1978) (mentioning different RESTATEMENT 2d test — discussed, *infra,* this subsection, and suggested that application of the new RESTATEMENT test would only serve to attenuate the claim of duress in this case).

[58] RESTATEMENT 2d § 175(1) and, particularly, comment b thereto. *See* Penn v. Transportation Lease Haw., Ltd., 2 Haw. App. 272, 275, 630 P.2d 646, 649 (1981) and *In re* Marriage of Hitchcock, 265 N.W.2d 599 (Iowa 1978) which adopts this test.

[59] *See* S. P. Dunham & Co. v. Kudra, 44 N.J. Super. 565, 131 A.2d 166 (1959) and Murphy v. Brilliant Co., 323 Mass. 526, 83 N.E.2d 166 (1948). The earlier common law version of this type of duress was characterized as "duress of goods." *See* Astley v. Reynolds, 2 Strange 915, 93 Eng. Rep. (K.B. 1732) (where pawned goods were threatened to be detained absent payment of excessive interest).

[60] *See* the discussion of the classic case of Alaska Packers' Ass'n v. Domenico, 117 F. 99 (9th Cir. 1902) in Selmer Co. v. Blakeslee-Midwest Co., 704 F.2d 924, 927 (7th Cir. 1983).

[61] RESTATEMENT 2d § 175(1).

[62] RESTATEMENT 2d § 175 comment c.

[63] *See* ills. 8 and 9 to RESTATEMENT 2d § 175.

to manifest assent. The maker of the threat to such a victim should not escape a finding of duress on the ground that the victim was unreasonable in taking the threat seriously. The requirement that there be no reasonable alternative, by its very characterization, suggests an objective standard and is imposed only upon a reasonable person. Such a person may have been reasonable in taking the threat seriously. If, however, he had a reasonable alternative to manifesting assent induced by the threat, he would not be able to establish duress.

J. Remedies for Duress.

As we have seen, an agreement induced by physical compulsion is not a contract though it is sometimes inartfully called a "void contract."[64] Where an agreement is induced by an improper threat leaving the victim no reasonable alternative, the resulting contract is "voidable," i.e., the victim has the power to disaffirm the contract either by defending or instituting a cause of action. A delay in disaffirming after the threat has ceased will result in the affirmance of the contract[65] as will conduct by the former victim after the threat is extinguished. If an agreement is *void ab initio* or if the victim has exercised the power of disaffirmance with respect to a voidable contract, the victim is entitled to have returned any benefit the victim had conferred upon the threatening party to avoid unjust enrichment. Similarly, the victim must return any benefit received under the disaffirmed contract. The relief is designed to protect the restitution interest, i.e., to restore the parties to *status quo ante*. If specific restitution can occur, it will be ordered. If a sum of money is paid under duress, an action in quasi contract will lie to provide restitution to the victim.[66] Often, the benefits cannot be returned and an action in quasi contract for the reasonable value of goods or services supplied under a voidable contract will be appropriate.[67] If the benefit conferred has enhanced the property of the defendant, the victim may be able to have a constructive trust or equitable lien decreed which, again, protects the restitution interest.[68]

§ 94. Undue Influence.

Whereas duress involves an improper threat, undue influence involves improper or *unfair persuasion*.[69] Unfair persuasion may result from the domination of the party exercising the persuasion resulting from a confidential relationship between the parties where the party reposing the trust is not on guard, i.e., he is exposed and relies on the other because he is justified in assuming that the other will act in a manner consistent with his welfare.[70] A

---

[64] *See supra* subsection (A) of this section.

[65] *See, e.g.,* Austin Instrument Co. v. Loral Corp., 29 N.Y.2d 124, 272 N.E.2d 533 (1971).

[66] *See, e.g.,* Stroop v. Rutherford Cty., 567 S.W.2d 753 (Tenn. 1978).

[67] *See, e.g.,* Jurgensmeyer v. Boone Hosp. Center, 727 S.W.2d 441 (Mo. App. 1987); First Nat'l Bank of Cincinnati v. Pepper, 454 F.2d 626 (2d Cir. 1972).

[68] *See, e.g.,* Balish v. Farnham, 92 Nev. 133, 546 P.2d 1297 (1976) (discussing constructive trust remedy for duress); Worley v. Ehret, 36 Ill. App. 3d 48, 343 N.E.2d 237 (1976) (discussing equitable lien remedy for duress).

[69] *See* Kazaras v. Manufacturers Trust Co., 4 A.D.2d 227, 164 N.Y.S.2d 211 (1957).

[70] *See* First Nat'l Bank in Sioux City v. Curran, 206 N.W.2d 317, 322 (Iowa 1973). *See also* RESTATEMENT 2d § 177.

confidential relationship shifts the burden of proof to the party seeking to uphold the validity of the transaction to establish that the transaction was fair and voluntarily concluded by the other. Thus, one who has the advantage of such a relationship and who profits at the expense of the other may not claim an arm's length transaction, i.e., the transaction is presumptively void-able.[71] The relationship is often one between spouses, parent and child, physician and patient, or clergyman and parishioner.[72] Numerous other relationships may be confidential as well. Thus, a bank and its depositor/debtor[73] or a teacher and his principal[74] may manifest such a relationship. A confidential relationship alone, however, is insufficient to constitute undue influence. The dominant party must have used unfair persuasion over the servient person.[75] The determination of whether the persuasion was "unfair" is, as usual, a fact question. The test has been stated as overcoming the will of the servient person,[76] or "the exercise of an improper influence over the mind and will of another to such an extent that the action is not that of a free agent,"[77] or whether the victim has been deprived of "the free and competent exercise of judgment,"[78] or similar language. In determining whether the victim has been deprived of the free and competent exercise of his judgment, courts will consider whether he had independent advice or whether the other party urged him to act immediately without such advice.[79] Courts will also consider the unfairness of the bargain struck by the influenced party and his susceptibility to persuasion under the circumstances.[80] A contract induced by undue influence is voidable by the victim.[81] If the undue influence emanates from a third party, the victim may still avoid the contract unless the other party to the contract had no reason to know of the undue influence and, in good faith, gave value or relied materially on the contract.[82]

---

[71] Peoples Bank & Trust Co. v. Lala, 392 N.W.2d 179 (Iowa App. 1986).

[72] See RESTATEMENT 2d § 177 comment a.

[73] See Peoples Bank & Trust Co. v. Lala, 392 N.W.2d 179 (Iowa App. 1986).

[74] Odorizzi v. Bloomfield Sch. Dist., 246 Cal. App. 2d 123, 54 Cal. Rptr. 533 (1966).

[75] Matter of Cheryl E., 161 Cal. App. 3d 601, 207 Cal. Rptr. 728, 737 (1984) "Undue influence consists of the use of excessive pressure by a dominant person over a servient person...."

[76] "Excessive pressure ... resulting in the apparent will of the servient person being in fact the will of the dominant person." Id.

[77] See Curl v. Key, 316 S.E.2d 272, 276 (N.C. 1984).

[78] RESTATEMENT 2d § 177 comment b. See Gerimonte v. Case, 42 Wash. App. 611, 712 P.2d 876 (1986) which adopts this view.

[79] See Odorizzi, supra note 74, where the principal and school district superintendent urged the victim to resign immediately because he did not have time to consult an attorney.

[80] See RESTATEMENT 2d § 177 comment b.

[81] RESTATEMENT 2d § 177(2).

[82] RESTATEMENT 2d § 177(3). See also Kennedy v. Thomsen, 320 N.W.2d 657, 659 (Iowa App. 1982).

§ 95. Misrepresentation.

A. *Definition — Concealment and Non-Disclosure Distinguished.*

Misrepresentation is typically defined as "an assertion that is not in accord with the facts."[83] Such an assertion is usually spoken or written, but it may be inferred from conduct. *Concealment* does not involve language, but it is an affirmative act designed to prevent another from learning the fact. Thus, where a builder knew of a defect in the floor of a basement and covered the defect with tile to conceal it, this was a conduct assertion not in accordance with the facts.[84] There is an element of non-disclosure in such a case. Concealment, however, involves an affirmative act to prevent the other party from learning the facts. *Non-disclosure,* on the other hand, involves no affirmative act. Moreover, the notion that one party has a duty to disclose relevant information to the other party who has equal access to such information appeared antithetical to courts holding traditional views of individuality and bargaining. None other than Chief Justice John Marshall could not assimilate a concept of a duty to communicate where a party purchased a large quantity of tobacco with private knowledge that the Treaty of Ghent had been signed, ending the war of 1812, resulting in a more than substantial increase in the price of tobacco through the removal of the British blockade of New Orleans.[85] Yet, modern courts recognize the fact that non-disclosure may have the same effect as an assertion not in accord with the facts. There have, for example, been a number of cases involving the sale of a residence known to the seller to be infested with termites. Modern courts hold that the vendor has a duty to disclose such a material fact.[86] Similarly, when a seller of property failed to disclose a flooding incident when asked a relevant question about a sump hole, the court held that the seller had a duty to speak when asked that question, and its failure to disclose the incident amounted to fraudulent non-disclosure.[87]

The fact situations requiring disclosure of a material fact are myriad. Thus, if a party knows that the drawer of a check is stopping payment on a check but arranges to have the check cashed, he knows that the other party would not cash the check if the information concerning the stop payment process were disclosed. This failure to act in good faith to correct the mistake of the other as to an assumption that is basic to the transaction is the equivalent of an assertion not in accordance with the facts.[88] Similarly, a half-truth will operate as a misrepresentation as where an airline fails to inform a passenger that a "confirmed reservation" is subject to deliberate overbooking.[89] Even where

---

[83] RESTATEMENT 2d § 159.

[84] Jenkins v. McCormick, 184 Kan. 842, 339 P.2d 8 (1959). *See* RESTATEMENT 2d § 160.

[85] *See* Ladilaw v. Organ, 15 U.S. (2 Wheat.) 178 (1817).

[86] The most recent case at the time of this writing is Hill v. Jones, 151 Ariz. 81, 725 P.2d 1115 (1986). *See also* Johnson v. Davis, 480 So. 2d 625 (Fla. 1985); Mercer v. Woodard, 166 Ga. App. 119, 303 S.E.2d 475 (1983); Lynn v. Taylor, 7 Kan. App. 2d 369, 642 P.2d 131 (1982); Obde v. Schlemeyer, 56 Wash. 2d 449, 353 P.2d 672 (1960). *See also* Annotation, 22 A.L.R. 3d 972 (1968).

[87] Marchand v. Presutti, 7 Conn. App. 643, 509 A.2d 1092 (1986).

[88] Bossuyt v. Osage Farmers Nat'l Bank, 360 N.W.2d 769 (Iowa 1985). *See also,* Allstate Redev. v. Summit Assoc., 206 N.J. Super. 318, 502 A.2d 1137 (1985) (question of disclosure of state's riparian claim prior to execution of lease) and RESTATEMENT 2d § 161, cited in both cases.

[89] *See* Nader v. Allegheny Airlines, 445 F. Supp. 168, 175-76 (D.D.C. 1978).

the statement was completely true when made, if subsequent conditions make the statement false and the maker fails to disclose the change to the other party who is assuming the truth of the original statement, this failure to correct the original statement can amount to a misrepresentation.[90] If one party knows that a writing evidencing a contract does not contain a term which the other party thinks it contains, non-disclosure of the second party's mistake, notwithstanding his failure to read, may amount to a misrepresentation under the circumstances.[91] Similarly, the relation between the parties, even though it may not constitute a fiduciary relationship, may be one of such trust and confidence as to create an expectation of disclosure.[92]

B. *Fraudulent or Material.*

A statement not in accord with the facts may amount to a misrepresentation even though it is not fraudulent.[93] "A contract will be voidable if a party's assent is induced by either a fraudulent or material misrepresentation by the other party, and is an assertion on which the recipient is justified in relying."[94] A misrepresentation is *fraudulent* where the maker knows or believes the assertion to be false and intends to mislead the other party. This type of misrepresentation involves *scienter,* i.e., the maker knows or believes what he is asserting is untrue. Even if the maker does not know or believe his assertion is untrue, if he makes the assertion with confidence, though he does not have such confidence, his statement is reckless. Here, the maker is lying about the basis for his assertion and the assertion is a fraudulent misrepresentation. Similarly, where he implies certain knowledge in the assertion, though he does not have a basis for the assertion, the making of the assertion in this fashion with the intention of inducing assent is a fraudulent misrepresentation.[95] A misrepresentation is *material* if it would be likely to induce a *reasonable* party to manifest assent,[96] or if the maker knows that, because of

---

[90] RESTATEMENT 2d § 161(b). *See also* Bursey v. Blement, 118 N.H. 412, 387 A.2d 346 (1978) (failure to correct original statement concerning certain legislation).

[91] *See* Skagit State Bank v. Rasmussen, 716 P.2d 314 (Wash. App. 1986) (While failing to read a document before signing it is not condoned, where a former business partner brought the document to the signer while the latter was in the midst of planting cauliflower and the signer spoke only briefly with his friend before signing, signing under these circumstances was not negligence). *See* RESTATEMENT 2d § 161(c).

[92] *See* Shaffer v. Terrydale Mgt. Corp., 648 S.W.2d 595, n.8 at 607 (Mo. 1983) where the court suggests that even the rule that one able to read and understand is bound by his signature regardless of whether he read the document "is tempered where the relation of trust and confidence subsists between the drafter and signatory," citing RESTATEMENT 2d § 161(d) and comment f thereto. *See also* Nie v. Galena State Bank & Trust Co., 387 N.W.2d 373 (Iowa 1986).

[93] That the doctrine of "innocent misrepresentation," first enunciated in Michigan in 1866 in Converse v. Blumrich, 14 Mich. 109, 123, 90 Am. Dec. 230 (1866) still prevails in Michigan is the holding of United States Fid. & Guar. Co. v. Black, 412 Mich. 99, 313 N.W.2d 77, 83 (1981).

[94] Carpenter v. Vreeman, 409 N.W.2d 258, 260-61 (Minn. App. 1987) citing RESTATEMENT 2d § 164(1) in support.

[95] In general, *see* Carpenter v. Vreeman, *Ibid. See also* RESTATEMENT 2d § 162(1).

[96] *Id. See* Skagit State Bank, supra note 91 at 317. *See also* Cousineau v. Walker, 613 P.2d 608, 613 (Alaska 1980) (was the assertion one to which a reasonable person might be expected to attach importance in making a choice of action?) *See* Hampton v. Sabin, 49 Or. App. 1041, 621 P.2d 1202, 1207 (1980) (A representation is material if "it would be likely to affect the conduct of a reasonable man with reference to a transaction with another person," quoting from Millikin v. Green, 283 Or. 283, 285, 583 P.2d 548 (1978)).

special reasons, it would be likely to induce a *particular* party to assent, though it would not induce such assent by a reasonable party.[97] If the misrepresentation is nonfraudulent, it must be material to be actionable.[98] The interesting question is, why should an immaterial but fraudulent misrepresentation create a power of avoidance or disaffirmance in the recipient?

If a misrepresentation is *not* likely to induce a reasonable party to manifest assent, or if the maker does *not* know of any special reasons making it likely to induce assent by a particular person where a reasonable person would not be induced by the assertion, it is still possible for an assertion to induce assent in an unwise or foolish person. If such an assertion is fraudulent, the recipient should have a power of avoidance notwithstanding the immateriality of the assertion because it did, in fact, induce assent. The dearth of case law involving fraudulent albeit immaterial assertions does not detract from the universal view that a misrepresentation can be the basis for avoidance of the resulting agreement if it is either fraudulent or material.[99] The conclusion is, however, inescapable that this revered view is based on dicta.

C. *Inducement — Fraud in the Inducement Versus Fraud in the Execution or Factum.*

The misrepresentation need not be the sole or dominant factor influencing the conduct of the other party. It is sufficient if the assertion substantially contributed to that conduct.[1] Normally, misrepresentation only *induces* the conduct or assent of the other party who may then exercise a power of avoidance or disaffirmance. It is possible, however, for the misrepresentation to go to the *execution* or *factum,* thereby creating a different legal effect. Suppose, for example, Ames returns from a visit to the ophthalmologist and cannot read a document presented by Barnes, her confidant. Barnes falsely tells Ames that the document is a rent receipt which Ames should sign. Ames signs, not knowing that the document is a contract which will have an unfair effect upon Ames. Here, Ames was unaware of the true character of the document she signed and was induced to sign by the misrepresentation of a party in whom Ames legitimately reposed trust and confidence. The misrepresentation or "fraud" is so foundational in this case as to go to the very execution of the writing and results in no contract being formed or, as some courts unfortunately suggest, a "void contract" as contrasted with a voidable contract.[2] The principal significance of this distinction relates to the rights of third parties such as holders in due course of negotiable instruments and good faith purchasers of goods. With respect to holders in due course, negotiable instru-

---

[97] *See* RESTATEMENT 2d § 162(2) and comment c. A maker may know of particular idiosyncrasies of the recipient and, while the assertion may not induce a reasonable person to assent, the maker may know that the assertion is likely to induce this person. *See* RESTATEMENT OF TORTS 2d § 526(2)(b).

[98] *See* Hendren v. Allstate Ins. Co., 100 N.M. 506, 672 P.2d 1137, 1140 (1983) (if misrepresentations are material, it makes no difference whether the maker acted fraudulently, negligently, or innocently). *See also* Guardian Life Ins. Co. v. Tillinghast, 512 A.2d 855 (R.I. 1986).

[99] *See also* RESTATEMENT 2d § 161 comment b which suggests that "[t]here is ... no requirement of materiality if it can be shown that the non-disclosure was actually fraudulent."

[1] RESTATEMENT 2d § 167 and, in particular, comment a thereto.

[2] *See* RESTATEMENT 2d § 163.

ments law has traditionally distinguished between "fraud in the inducement" as contrasted with "fraud in the execution or factum" which is also sometimes known as "real fraud" or "fraud in the essence." Where the maker of a note or other party signing a negotiable instrument is tricked into signing it having been told that it is a mere receipt, the signature is ineffective since he did not intend to sign such an instrument at all.[3] This is a classic illustration of a "misrepresentation as has induced the party to sign the instrument with neither knowledge nor reasonable opportunity to obtain knowledge of its character or essential terms...."[4] This type of misrepresentation will be an effective defense even against a holder in due course, i.e., a party who takes the check from the misrepresenting party for value, in good faith, and without notice that it is overdue or has been dishonored or of any other defense against it.[5] If, however, the misrepresentation simply induces a party to make a note or draw a check and the maker or drawer knows what he or she is signing, such misrepresentation will not be a defense against a holder in due course.[6] Analogously, if a party procures goods through misrepresentation, that party has voidable title and a good faith purchaser from such a party will prevail over the true owner.[7] On the other hand, if goods are stolen, the thief has no power to transfer ownership to even a good faith purchaser for value since no "transaction of purchase" has occurred.[8]

D. *Reliance by the Induced Party.*

To this point, we have analyzed the elements necessary to permit a contract to be avoided for misrepresentation, save one. We have defined "misrepresentation" and insisted that it be either fraudulent or material. We then added the causation element, i.e., the victim's manifestation of assent must have been "induced" by that assertion. The last principal element is the requirement that the victim be justified in relying on the misrepresentation.[9] This element may be viewed as simply another perspective of the "inducement" element, i.e., a misrepresentation cannot be a substantial factor in the victim's manifestation of assent unless the victim relied on the misrepresentation.[10] Whether a party is justified in relying upon certain representations is a

---

[3] UCC § 3-305 comment 7.

[4] UCC § 3-305(2)(c). *See* United Bank & Trust Co. of Md. v. Schaeffer, 370 A.2d 1138 (Md. 1977) (signer who was unable to read was told he was signing a character reference). *See also* Odessa v. Fazzari, 223 N.Y.S.2d 483, 179 N.E.2d 493 (1961) (party unable to read or write English was induced to sign a promissory note upon the misrepresentation that it was a statement of wages).

[5] UCC § 3-302(1).

[6] *See* Standard Fin. Co. v. Ellis, 3 Haw. App. 614, 657 P.2d 1056 (1983). It should be noted that the misrepresentation in such a case would allow the maker or drawer to avoid the underlying obligation against the original party to the contract. Again, however, it would not be a defense against a holder in due course of the instrument, i.e., a third party who has, in good faith and without notice of any defenses to the instrument, exchanged value for the instrument.

[7] UCC § 2-403(1).

[8] UCC § 2-403(1) requires a "transaction of purchase" to create voidable title in a party who has, *e.g.,* misrepresented his identity or otherwise procured goods through misrepresentation. "Purchase" is defined in UCC § 1-201(32) which lists various methods of "taking" goods, all of which are "voluntary transactions creating an interest in property." There is no such voluntary transaction where goods are stolen.

[9] *See* RESTATEMENT 2d § 164(1).

[10] RESTATEMENT 2d § 167 comment a. *See* Barrer v. Women's Nat'l Bank, 761 F.2d 752, 759 (D.C. Cir. 1985) ("Inducement, as comment a explains, is shown through actual reliance."). *Cf.*

question of fact to be determined by the trial court.[11] There are a number of issues surrounding the general question, what constitutes justifiable reliance?

1. Victim's Failure to Investigate or Read.

Is reliance upon a misrepresentation (fraudulent or innocent) justifiable if the relying party is at fault in failing to make a reasonable investigation which would have exposed the misrepresentation? The answer is yes, unless the fault amounts to a failure to act in good faith or in accordance with reasonable standards of fair dealing.[12] As suggested by one court, "[T]he purchaser of business property is entitled to rely on the truth of the seller's representations even though the falsity could have been ascertained had the buyer made an investigation — unless the latter *knew* the representations to be false, or the falsity was *obvious* to him — if the seller, as owner of the property, had *superior knowledge* of its size, condition and income."[13] Any duty to investigate will be absolved where deliberate misrepresentations have lulled the recipient into a false sense of security.[14] Courts are more than reluctant to permit the maker of a misrepresentation to escape the victim's power of avoidance on the footing that the victim was negligent or credulous.[15] While the failure to read a legible document that need not be signed immediately is not consonant with justifiable reliance,[16] we have seen that other circumstances such as a relation of trust and confidence between the parties will overcome even this kind of "fault" by the victim.[17]

2. Opinion — Fact Versus Knowledge — Reliance on Opinion — Value, Quality, Quantity, Price — Matters of Law.

A distinction is often suggested between statements of fact which may induce justifiable reliance and statements of opinion which should not induce such reliance.[18] The distinction has been criticized on the footing that state-

---

Sessa v. Riegle, 427 F. Supp. 760 (E.D. Pa. 1977) where the seller of a race horse made the statement, "This horse is sound," and the court held it not to be an express warranty under § 2-313 of the UCC because the buyer did not rely upon that statement in purchasing the horse but, rather, relied upon statements by his own agent. There is considerable confusion in the case law concerning the question of whether reliance is necessary to establish an express warranty. *See,* in general, Murray, *"Basis of the Bargain": Transcending Classical Concepts,* 66 MINN. L. REV. 283 (1982) suggesting that reliance is not necessary.

[11]*See* Carpenter v. Vreeman, 409 N.W.2d 258, 261 (Minn. App. 1987).

[12]*See* Barrer v. Women's Nat'l Bank, *supra* note 10. *See also* First Nat'l Bank & Trust Co. v. Notte, 97 Wis. 2d 207, 293 N.W.2d 530 (1980) and RESTATEMENT 2d § 172.

[13]*See* Besett v. Basnett, 389 So. 2d 995, 998 (Fla. 1980). *See also* Yost v. Rieve Enters., 461 So. 2d 178, 182 (Fla. App. 1984) which relies upon this quotation for its holding. In Bodenheimer v. Patterson, 278 Or. 367, 370, 563 P.2d 1212, 1216 (1977) the court suggests, "[A] purchaser who has, in fact, been induced to enter a contract by an intentional misrepresentation may rescind the contract even though his reliance may have been negligent."

[14]*See* Marino v. United Bank, 484 N.E.2d 935, 938 (Ill. App. 1985). *See also* West v. Western Cas. & Sur. Co., 846 F.2d 387 (7th Cir. 1988).

[15]*See* Negyessy v. Strong, 136 Vt. 193, 388 A.2d 383 (1978). *See also* James & Gray, *Misrepresentation — Part II,* 37 MD. L. REV. 488, 511 (1978). Part I of this article appears at 37 MD. L. REV. 286 (1977).

[16]*See, e.g.,* Maw v. McAlister, 252 S.C. 280, 166 S.E.2d 203 (1969) (failure to read release).

[17]*See* cases cited *supra* note 92.

[18]For example, in Woodling v. Garrett Corp., 813 F.2d 543, 552 (2d Cir. 1987), the court suggests that to constitute a misrepresentation, a statement must falsely assert fact rather than

ments of opinion are, themselves, statements of fact, i.e., if a person states an opinion, he is stating his particular state of mind which is a fact.[19] Such statements imply that the person making the statement does not have sufficient knowledge to assert the statement as fact as contrasted with belief. At most, it suggests that he is unaware of facts that are incompatible with his belief. The true distinction, therefore, should be between assertions of *knowledge* (rather than facts) and assertions of opinion.[20] If a person says, "This computer is compatible with an IBM personal computer," he asserts his *knowledge*. If, on the other hand, he says, "I believe this computer is compatible with an IBM personal computer, but I can't be sure," he is clearly stating an opinion. Normally, reliance on statements of opinion is not justified for the obvious reason that the statement is couched in terms that suggest the party making the statement may be wrong.[21] Under certain circumstances, however, the recipient may be justified in relying on a statement of opinion.

One court states the test as whether, "under the circumstances surrounding the statement, the representation was intended and understood as one of fact as distinguished from one of opinion."[22] Thus, where a builder asserted there was "nothing wrong" with a house, it could have been reasonably understood to be an assertion based on sufficient information to justify the builder's opinion and, as such, reliance on such a statement could be justifiable.[23] Where there is a relationship of trust and confidence between the parties, the recipient may be reasonable in relying upon a statement of opinion.[24] If the recipient is reasonable in believing that the person making the statement of opinion has particular skill or judgment with respect to the subject matter of the statement, the recipient may be justified in relying thereon. This is particularly true in cases involving statements about artistic ability or talent. Thus, if a violin teacher would inform a prospective pupil or the parent of the pupil that the pupil has great potential as a violinist even though the teacher knows that the pupil demonstrates little or no aptitude as a violinist and is making the statement merely to encourage payment for lessons, reliance on the teacher's statement is justified and the contract would be voidable.[25] The recipient of statement of opinion may be particularly gullible through lack of intelligence, immaturity or similar reasons. Reliance on the statement of opinion by such a person may also be justifiable.[26]

---

opinion. In West v. Western Cas. & Sur. Co., 846 F.2d 387 (7th Cir. 1988), the court suggests that a statement merely expressing an opinion or relating to future or contingent events rather than past or present facts does not constitute an actionable misrepresentation. In Barnes v. Barnes, 207 Va. 114, 148 S.E.2d 789, 795 (1966) the court suggests that, for a statement to amount to fraud, it must be a positive statement of fact and not a mere expression of opinion.

[19] RESTATEMENT 2d § 168 comment a.

[20] *Ibid.*

[21] The famous statement of Chancellor Kent is worth remembering: "Every person reposes at his peril in the opinion of others, when he has equal opportunity to form and exercise his own judgment." J. KENT, COMMENTARIES ON AMERICAN LAW 381 (1st ed. 1827).

[22] Crowther v. Guidone, 183 Conn. 464, 441 A.2d 11, 13 (1981).

[23] Johnson v. Healy, 176 Conn. 97, 101, 405 A.2d 54, 57 (1978).

[24] See DSK Enters. v. United Jersey Bank, 189 N.J. Super. 242, 459 A.2d 1201 (1983). *See also* RESTATEMENT 2d § 169(a).

[25] See Vokes v. Arthur Murray, Inc., 212 So. 2d 906 (Fla. Dist. App. 1968) (dance lessons). *See also* RESTATEMENT 2d § 169(b).

[26] See *DSK Enters., supra* note 24. *See also* RESTATEMENT 2d § 169(c).

Statements of value or quality are typically statements of opinion because reasonable parties should expect different opinions on such matters and seller's "puff" as to value or quality is part of common experience.[27] Statements of quantity, however, or statements of the price which something had previously brought, are not statements of opinion.[28]

Notwithstanding the outmoded suggestion that everyone is presumed to know the law,[29] assertions of legal conclusions are generally regarded as statements of opinion.[30] Yet, such assertions are treated like other assertions. If, for example, there is an assertion that a particular statute has been enacted or repealed or a certain court has rendered a decision, it is an assertion that may induce justifiable reliance.[31] As suggested earlier, a party may justifiably rely upon an assertion of opinion if the statement is made by one with special knowledge. Thus, an opinion by a lawyer may permit justifiable reliance,[32] though a statement by a lawyer concerning the possible outcome of litigation or how a court might rule on a particular issue would typically be viewed as a statement of opinion.[33] If the maker of the statement is not a lawyer but has other special competence, her statement may be viewed as an opinion upon which the other party may justifiably rely.[34]

E. Effects of Misrepresentation — Remedies for Misrepresentation.

Except for those rare situations where misrepresentation goes to the execution of a document and no contract results,[35] misrepresentation which *induces* a contract makes the contract *voidable*.[36] Thus, the victim may exercise a power of avoidance or disaffirmance[37] though courts often characterize this

---

[27] *See* Page Inv. Co. v. Staley, 105 Ariz. 562, 468 P.2d 589 (1970) (statement that land worth only $4000 per acre was worth $7500 per acre was mere opinion). *See also* RESTATEMENT 2d § 168 comment c. It is important to compare the distinction between mere statements of value or commendation versus express warranties under the UCC. Section 2-313(2) of the Code suggests, "but an affirmation merely of the value of the goods or a statement purporting to be merely the seller's opinion or commendation of the goods does not create a warranty." Yet, in Keith v. Buchanan, 220 Cal. Rptr. 392, 42 UCC Rep. 386, 390 (1985), the court suggests, "Recent decisions have evidenced a trend toward narrowing the scope of representations which are considered opinion, sometimes referred to as "puffing" or "sales talk," resulting in an expansion of the liability that flows from broad statements of manufacturers or retailers as to the quality of their products" (holding statement of "seaworthiness" to be an express warranty). *See also* Ewers v. Eisenzopf, 88 Wis. 2d 482, 276 N.W.2d 802 (1979) (when sales clerk was asked whether certain sea shells, coral, and driftwood were suitable for placement in a salt water aquarium and clerk responded that they would be suitable for such an aquarium if they were rinsed, the court held the clerk's statement to be an express warranty).

[28] RESTATEMENT 2d § 168 comment c.

[29] *See* Platt v. Scott, 6 Black 389, 390 (Ind. 1843) ("It is considered that every person is acquainted with the law....").

[30] *See* Pennsylvania Life Ins. Co. v. Bumbrey, 665 F. Supp. 1190, 1201 (E.D. Va. 1987) ("Generally, statements regarding legal conclusions have been held to be mere expressions of opinion.").

[31] RESTATEMENT 2d § 170 comment a.

[32] Woodling v. Garrett Corp., 813 F.2d 543, 553 (2d Cir. 1987). RESTATEMENT 2d § 170 comment b.

[33] *See* Piedmont Trust Bank v. Aetna Cas. & Sur. Co., 210 Va. 396, 171 S.E.2d 264, 267 (1969). *See also* RESTATEMENT 2d § 170 comment b.

[34] *See, e.g.,* Hendren v. Allstate Ins. Co., 672 P.2d 1137 (N.M. App. 1983) (statement of insurance claims adjuster concerning uninsured motorist coverage).

[35] *See supra* § 95(C).

[36] *See* RESTATEMENT 2d § 164(1).

[37] *See, e.g.,* Carpenter v. Vreeman, 409 N.W.2d 258, 260 (Minn. App. 1987) ("A contract is voidable if a party's assent is induced by either a fraudulent or a material misrepresentation by

effect as providing the victim a ground for rescission of the contract.[38] The victim may lose his power of avoidance by affirming the contract. Such affirmance occurs through a manifestation of his intention to affirm, or acts inconsistent with disaffirmance, after the circumstances permitting avoidance have stopped, or after the victim has reason to know of a non-fraudulent misrepresentation or knows of a fraudulent misrepresentation.[39] The victim should not be permitted to disaffirm "beyond a reasonable" time after he discovers or should have discovered the misrepresentation, or use the property of the other party (except for perservation) and inconsistently exercise the power of disaffirmance.[40] Further, if the misrepresentation is "cured" before the victim exercises his power of disaffirmance and the victim has suffered no injury, the contract should no longer be voidable.[41] It should be emphasized, however, that a victim should not be precluded from bringing a tort action for deceit (if the elements of that tort are established) and avoiding the contract, so long as the circumstances do not render such remedies incompatible.[42] Unless the contract is divisible, however, the contract cannot be avoided only in part.[43]

Where the power of avoidance is effectively exercised, courts seek to restore the parties to *status quo ante,* i.e., the position they were in before the voidable contract was made. Thus, courts seek to protect the restitution interest. The victim who seeks restitution must return or offer to return any benefit he has received under the contract.[44] Where, however, the product the victim has

---

the other party and is an assertion on which the recipient is justified in relying," citing RESTATEMENT 2d § 164(1)).

[38] *See, e.g.,* Held v. Trafford Realty Co., 414 So. 2d 631, 632 (Fla. App. 1982) ("Whether made innocently or knowingly, misrepresentation of a material fact acted on by the other party to his detriment is a ground for rescission of a contract.").

[39] RESTATEMENT 2d § 380(1) and (2).

[40] *See, e.g.,* Hampton v. Sabin, 49 Or. App. 1041, 621 P.2d 1202, 1208 (1980) ("The law is well settled that upon discovery of fraud one who desires to rescind a contract must act promptly.... The question, however, is whether they should be held to constructive notice of fraud sooner. If they are, rescission would be barred by their delay and their actions which were inconsistent with their intent to rescind, such as continuing to operate the property and putting the property up for sale."). *Cf.* Under the UCC, a buyer must revoke acceptance of goods within a reasonable time after he discovers or should have discovered the basis for such revocation. UCC § 2-608(2). UCC § 2-606(1)(c) states that any act inconsistent with the seller's ownership constitutes acceptance of the goods, thereby depriving the buyer of his right to reject under § 2-601.

[41] *See* RESTATEMENT 2d § 165.

[42] If, for example, the victim sues in tort for deceit but is precluded from recovery in that action because the statute of limitations has run, he is not precluded from subsequently avoiding the contract. *See* Schenck v. State Line Tel. Co., 238 N.Y. 308, 344 N.E. 592 (1924). *Accord,* UCC § 2-721 and RESTATEMENT 2d § 380 ill. 4. The contrary view is predicated on an antiquated "election of remedies" notion which suggests that a party injured by fraud may elect to accept the situation and recover damages or repudiate the transaction and seek restoration of the status quo, but he cannot do both. Albin v. Isotron Corp., 421 S.W.2d 739, 744 (Tex. Civ. App. 1967). This opinion is expressly rejected by the RESTATEMENT 2d: *see* Reporter's Notes to § 380.

[43] RESTATEMENT 2d § 383. A party may not, for example, affirm a desirable part of the contract while disaffirming the undesirable part. If, however, the contract is divisible (severable), and the victim discovers the misrepresentation after performing a divisible portion thereof, he may avoid the remainder of the contract. This is equitable in that the portion of the contract already performed consisted of agreed equivalents so that the portion remaining to be performed is, by definition, not the undesirable portion of the contract.

[44] *See* the general discussion of this requirement in Wade & Kamenshine, *Restitution for Defrauded Consumers: Making the Remedy Effective Through Suit by Government Agencies,* 37 GEO. WASH. L. REV. 1031, 1041-42 (1969). *See also* RESTATEMENT 2d § 384. An earlier distinction between law and equity concerning the victim's offer to return any benefit received saw courts, sitting as courts of law, insisting upon an offer to return such benefits as a condition to an action

received is expected to be consumed, this requirement is relaxed.[45] Where the property is not expected to be consumed but cannot be returned, courts will achieve a return to *status quo* through an award of damages.[46] If the property restored to the victim has been improved, the victim will be liable for any increase in value.[47] Equitable remedies protecting the restitution interest such as a constructive trust or an equitable lien are also available to the victim. Under the UCC, the victim has a security interest in goods in his possession for any payments made on their price as well as any expenses incurred in receiving or possessing such goods.[48]

§ 96. Unconscionability.

A. *Freedom of Contract — Unconscionability in Equity.*

The indispensable tool in the operation of a free enterprise society is contract. The essence of contract is volition, that free exercise of will by parties who are on a relatively equal economic footing and who are brought together in the dynamic market place by their needs and desires.[49] This natural process through which each individual pursues his own, perhaps selfish, interests was deeply imbedded in the thinking of Americans in the late 18th and 19th Centuries. The dominant belief was that a *laissez faire* system would permit the greatest possible individual contributions that would combine automatically to achieve the best interests of the community. "Freedom of contract" was an oft-repeated phrase of that time. There was a strong belief that the free enterprise system itself was automatically regulated through competition, the mechanics of which were supplied by the social institution of contract. In the great growth period of American law, the 19th Century, competition, like contract, was considered a natural self-regulating mechanism. Competition continuously accommodated the production of goods to the changing demand for them.[50] Thus, competition and the mechanism upon which it depended, contract, were dominated by a notion of economic Darwinism. It soon became apparent, however, that the economic survivors were not always the fittest. Business entities often found it more advantageous to agree than to compete, and there was no freedom of contract in the equal treatment of

---

for rescission of the contract. Courts of equity, however, did not require such an offer because the equitable decree could be conditioned on such an offer. The merger of law and equity has made this distinction untenable. Therefore, the RESTATEMENT 2d takes the position that a party will be granted restitution either upon his offer to return any interest in property received or upon the court's assurance of such return. § 384(1)(a) and (b).

[45] See Consumer Protection v. Consumer Pub'g, 304 Md. 731, 501 A.2d 48, 72 (1985) (misrepresentation concerning diet pills which were consumed).

[46] See Neidermeyer v. Latimer, 79 Or. App. 116, 717 P.2d 1265, 1267 (1986) (dry rot discovered in cabin, causing buyer to hire contractor whose efforts resulted in making cabin uninhabitable).

[47] See Walker v. Galt, 171 F.2d 613 (5th Cir.), *cert. denied,* 336 U.S. 925 (1948).

[48] UCC § 2-711(3). This remedy applies to any buyer who rightfully rejects or justifiably revokes acceptance of the goods whether or not a misrepresentation has induced the contract. The buyer may resell such goods as if he is an aggrieved seller under § 2-706.

[49] This statement is quoted from the second edition of this book in Brokers Title Co. v. St. Paul F. & M. Ins. Co., 610 F.2d 1174, 1179 (3d Cir. 1979). The basis for many of the thoughts suggested in this section is found in the classic introduction, *Contract as a Principle of Order,* in F. KESSLER & M. SHARP, CASES AND MATERIALS ON CONTRACTS (1953).

[50] See Hamilton, *An Analysis of Competition,* 4 ENCYCLOPEDIA OF SOCIAL SCIENCE, 141-47 (1931).

unequals. It became clear that unrestrained competition results in economic control by industrial empires. It also became clear that unrestrained freedom of contract permits one party with an enormous bargaining advantage to dictate the terms of the contract to the weaker party, thereby undermining the essence of contract, volition.

To maintain competition, Congress enacted antitrust laws.[51] The need for legislation to maintain freedom of contract became clear in certain areas of widespread significance such as labor contracts, insurance contracts, and contracts with public utilities, among others. Absent such legislative prescription, however, the courts upheld freedom of contract notwithstanding those "legitimate inequalities of fortune"[52] which inevitably exist between and among the parties to a contract. Rarely did a court recognize the fact that there could be little or no freedom of contract where the bargaining inequality between the parties was great.[53] In a court of law, absent fraud or the like, a contract was neither illegal nor unenforceable because it was oppressive or contained harsh provisions.

Unlike courts of law, courts of equity had a long history of refusing to enforce oppressive provisions of contracts dating back to "equity of redemption" days.[54] Absent fraud or the like, common law courts would not refuse to enforce a contract merely because it was oppressive or contained harsh provisions. Courts of equity, however, have traditionally refused to grant injunctions where the hardships clearly outweigh the benefits, and they have refused to grant specific performance where enforcement would be oppressive or cause disproportionate hardship to the defendant.[55] In a well-known case, a farmer agreed to supply carrots to a canner under a contract containing provisions that were obviously harsh to the farmer. When the type of carrots to be supplied were in short supply, causing a more than substantial increase in the market price, the farmer began selling them elsewhere. The canner sought to enjoin such sales and also sought specific performance of the contract. The lower court circumvented the issue of the harsh provisions by holding that the subject matter of the contract was not unique, thereby precluding the remedy sought by the canner.[56] The appellate court affirmed, but on the forthright ground that the provisions of the contract were so harsh or oppressive to the farmer that they were unconscionable, concluding, "That equity does not en-

---

[51] A brief survey of these statutes is found in the subsequent discussion of illegal bargains *infra* § 98.

[52] Pitney, J. in Coppage v. Kansas, 236 U.S. 1, 17 (1914).

[53] One of the rare recognitions is that of Chief Justice Hughes in his dissenting opinion in Morehead v. New York *ex rel.* Tipaldo, 298 U.S. 587, 627 (1936): "We have had frequent occasion to consider the limitations of liberty of contract. While it is highly important to preserve that liberty from arbitrary and capricious interference, it is also necessary to prevent its abuse, as otherwise it could be used to override all public interests and thus in the end destroy the very freedom of opportunity which it is designed to safeguard."

[54] Notwithstanding the express terms of the contract, equity permitted the mortgagor to redeem the estate after it had been forfeited at law, i.e., after "law day."

[55] *See* McKinnon v. Benedict, 38 Wis. 2d 607, 157 N.W.2d 665 (1968) relying on the First Restatement, § 367(b) and refusing to grant specific performance of a contract involving harsh restrictions on the use of land in exchange for a $5000 interest-free loan which interest would have amounted to only $145.

[56] Campbell Soup Co. v. Wentz, 75 F. Supp. 952 (E.D. Pa. 1948).

force unconscionable bargains is too well established to require elaborate citation."[57]

The type of contract used in this case was a standardized mass contract, a printed form or "pad" contract. The growth of a complex, industrialized society has carried with it the inevitable development of such printed forms for the sake of efficiency. These "pad contracts" are used by the large enterprise in all of its orthodox dealings and the printed provisions of such "contracts," the "boilerplate," are typically duplicated in the form contracts used by competitors of the large enterprise. Standardized forms have probably decreased distribution costs and thereby lessened prices to some degree. But this benefit has been more than offset by the inclusion of oppressive, risk-exclusion or risk-limitation provisions for the benefit of the large firm with immensely greater bargaining power than the party with whom it deals. The individual is typically the weaker party to the contract and he must *adhere* to the dictated terms of the printed form if he wants the goods or services at all. It will do him no good to deal with a competitor of the large firm which uses a printed form containing clauses indistinguishable from the clauses the individual sought to escape in refusing to contract with the original, large enterprise.

1. Precocious Views of Unconscionability — No Choice.

These standardized contracts, these contracts of *adhesion*,[58] contain oppressive provisions which are imposed on the individual who may not even be cognizant of their existence. A good illustration of the contract of adhesion occurred in a well-known case[59] where the buyer contracted to purchase a new automobile. The contract contained an express warranty from the manufacturer for the replacement of defective parts. That express warranty provision, however, included a disclaimer of all other warranties, express or implied. The buyer brought an action for breach of the implied warranty of merchantability and the seller defended on the basis of the disclaimer of that warranty in the contract signed by the buyer, i.e., the buyer should be bound by what he signs, whether or not he read the terms of the document he signed. The court agreed that the defendant had stated a general rule which it normally followed, but quickly added that such general rules should not be applied on a

---

[57] Campbell Soup Co. v. Wentz, 172 F.2d 80, 83 (3rd Cir. 1948), citing (in n.12) POMEROY, EQUITY JURISPRUDENCE § 1405a (5th ed. 1941) and 5 S. WILLISTON, CONTRACTS § 1425 (rev. ed. 1937).

[58] The phrase, "contract of adhesion," is usually attributed to Professor Patterson, *The Delivery of a Life Insurance Policy*, 33 HARV. L. REV. 198, 222 (1919). The development of the concept, however, is principally attributable to Professor Ehrenzweig, *Adhesion Contracts in the Conflict of Laws*, 53 COLUM. L. REV. 1072, 1088-89 (1953) and Professor Kessler, *Contracts of Adhesion — Some Thoughts About Freedom of Contract*, 43 COLUM. L. REV. 629 (1943). In Jones v. Dressel, 623 P.2d 370, 374 (Colo. 1981) the court suggests that a contract of adhesion is one that is "drafted unilaterally by a business enterprise and enforced upon an unwilling and often unknowing public for services that cannot readily be obtained elsewhere. An adhesion contract is generally not bargained for but is imposed on the public for a necessary service on a take-it-or-leave-it basis." A recent comprehensive discussion of contracts of adhesion is Rakoff, *Contracts of Adhesion: An Essay in Reconstruction*, 96 HARV. L. REV. 1173 (1983).

[59] Henningsen v. Bloomfield Motors, Inc., 32 N.J. 358, 161 A.2d 69, 75 (1960).

"strict doctrinal basis."[60] The court recognized the development of contracts of adhesion and proceeded to illuminate this development:

> The warranty before us is a standardized form designed for mass use. It is imposed upon the automobile consumer. He takes it or leaves it, and he must take it to buy an automobile. No bargaining is engaged in with respect to it.... The form warranty is not only standard with Chrysler but ... it is the uniform warranty of the Automobile Manufacturers Association.... [Here, the court noted that the membership of the Association included virtually all American manufacturers.]
>
> The gross inequality of bargaining position occupied by the consumer in the automobile industry is thus apparent. There is no competition among the car makers in the area of express warranty. Where can the buyer go to negotiate for better protection? Such control and limitation of his remedies are inimical to the public welfare, and, at the very least, call for great care by the courts to avoid injustice through the application of strict common-law principles of freedom of contract.[61]

In this portion of the opinion, the court focused upon the lack of any meaningful choice by the typical automobile consumer-buyer since he had to choose between signing a contract taking away fundamental protection accompanying the purchase of any product[62] or not receiving the product. Thus, such a buyer has no reasonable choice.[63] The fact is, however, that the typical buyer of an automobile or innumerable other products or services is typically unaware of such risk-shifting provisions in the fine print clauses of the printed form he signs. Such a buyer does not read such provisions and, even for the rare buyer who does read them, there is more than considerable doubt that he understands what he read. Thus, the paradigm of the consumer buyer who is aware of material, risk-shifting provisions over which he has no bargaining power is extremely rare. The sad reality is that the typical consumer does not have the foggiest notion of such provisions but signs what the salesperson refers to as the "standard form" though the salesperson is equally ignorant of the import of the boilerplate provisions.[64] This reality raises the confrontation between the requirement that one must be bound by what he signs, whether or not he reads or understands it, to insure the stability of

---

[60] Id. at 84.

[61] Id. at 87.

[62] There is no more fundamental protection than that afforded by the implied warranty of merchantability found in UCC § 2-314. Such protection, inter alia, assures goods that are fit for ordinary purposes, § 2-314(2)(c).

[63] If the product is not necessary to the physical or economic well-being of the buyer, arguably he does not require or need the product and, therefore, the seller may impose otherwise harsh provisions on the buyer. This argument, however, suggests a difficult if not impossible distinction, i.e., the distinction between goods that are "necessaries" and those that are not, a distinction that has not proven analytically effective in other contexts. Products that may at first appear to be "luxuries" or non-necessaries may quickly take on the characteristics of necessaries. Thus, an automobile may have appeared to be something of a luxury earlier in this century. Today, however, it would be difficult to characterize it as anything other than a necessary except in rare situations. Though the distinction may be possible in rare contexts, e.g., a custom-made sports car purchased for pleasure and not racing, it does not suggest significant illumination in the analysis of unconscionability. For further discussion suggesting that, in a given situation, even where the subject matter of the contract is a "frill," unconscionability may be found, see Murray, Unconscionability: Unconscionability, 31 U. Pitt. L. Rev. 1, 29-30 (1969).

[64] "[C]an it be said that an ordinary layman would realize what he was relinquishing?" Henningsen v. Bloomfield Motors, 32 N.J. 358, 161 A.2d 69, 92 (1960).

contracts, and the reality that innumerable consumer buyers (and, if the truth be known, merchant buyers, as well) are apparently assenting to the deprivation of fundamental protection by unwittingly signing documents containing clauses disclaiming basic warranties and excluding fundamental remedies. It was inevitable that courts would confront this paradox by searching for common law devices to avoid injustice to the unknowing buyer while paying lip service to the preservation of that citadel of stability, i.e., one is bound by what he signs, regardless of his failure to read or understand it.

2. Precocious Views of Unconscionability — Covert Tools.

It is one thing to suggest that a party is not excused from the terms of a writing on the footing that he neither read nor understood it.[65] It is quite another to bind a party to a contract when the writing allegedly representing that contract is not reasonably viewed as evidence of a contract. Thus, where a package is left in a parcel room and the owner is handed a small, cardboard check, is he unreasonable if he views that pasteboard merely as a means of identifying his parcel at the time of retrieval rather than evidence of a special contract limiting the liability of the parcel room? A number of courts have said, no, i.e., the owner is not bound by unread material on such a claim check because, as a reasonable person, he would not view the check as evidence of any special contract. Thus, he did not assent to such a contract.[66] Here, courts circumvent the terms of a writing simply by denying that any assent to the writing or a particular provision ever occurred. Similarly, where a material, risk-shifting clause appears inconspicuously on the writing, courts did not shirk from holding such provisions inoperative, albeit the writing otherwise evidenced a contract. Thus, where a particularly oppressive provision was printed on the reverse side of a writing calling for the buyer's signature on the face of the writing, the clause was held unenforceable because the clause was not even remotely contemplated.[67]

---

[65] See Independent Directory Corp v. Vanderbrock, 94 N.E.2d 229, 230 (Ohio App. 1950): "It is somewhat unusual that a court at this late day should have to repeat, that one who signs a contract without first making a reasonable effort to learn what is in it may not in the absence of fraud, or mutual mistake, avoid the effect of such a contract ... 'It will not do for a man to enter into a contract and, when called upon to respond to its obligations, to say that he did not read it when he signed it, or did not know what it contained. If this were permitted, contracts would not be worth the paper on which they are written; but such is not the law. A contractor must stand by the words of his contract; and, if he will not read what he signs, he alone is responsible for his omission....'"

[66] See Klar v. H. & N. Parcel Room, Inc., 270 App. Div. 538, 61 N.Y.S.2d 285 (1946). See also Lachs v. Fidelity & Cas. Co., 306 N.Y. 357, 117 N.E.2d 555 (1954) (decedent procured airline insurance from a vending machine at the airport and a clause in the policy restricted coverage to scheduled airline flights. The majority of the court held the clause inoperative because it provided insufficient notice).

[67] Cutler Corp. v. Latshaw, 374 Pa. 1, 97 A.2d 234, 237 (1953) where Justice Musmanno, in typically florid language, suggested, "One of the most hateful acts of the ill-famed Roman tyrant Caligula was that of having the laws inscribed on pillars so high that the people could not read them. Although the warranty of attorney in the numerous sheets of the contract at bar was within the vision of the defendant, it was so placed [on the reverse side where her signature was not required] as to be completely beyond her contemplation of its purport. An inconspicuously printed legend on a contract form or letterhead which is obviously fortuitous, irrelevant, or superfluous is no more part of the agreement entered into than the advertisements on the walls of the room in which the contract is signed."

Unfortunately, these and other devices[68] to avoid oppression of the party against whom they are designed to operate may appear curable through re-drafting the document. Thus, for example, placing the nefarious provision on the side of the document where the signature appears may make it enforce-able.[69] Yet, the physical placement of such a clause hardly insures the cogni-zance of its victim.[70] The drafter has often taken the document "to the abso-lute limit of what the law can conceivably bear."[71] Even if the language is excruciatingly clear, courts were willing to suggest that such "unbelievable" provisions could have been made clearer.[72] Thus, courts used "covert tools" to achieve just ends giving rise to the famous dictum of Karl Llewellyn, "Covert tools are never reliable tools."[73] What was needed was a device to bring this judicial process "out into the open," i.e., a device that would permit courts to say what they were doing — a device that in essence would have courts state, "[W]hen it gets too stiff to make sense, then the court may knock it over."[74] That device is now found in § 2-302 of the UCC, the famous — or infamous — section on unconscionability.

B. *The Meaning of Unconscionability.*

1. Vague Definitions — Uniform Commercial Code — Llewellyn's Purpose — RESTATEMENT 2d.

It is almost mandatory to begin an exploration of the meaning of unconscio-nability with the quotation from an eighteenth century English case, i.e., an unconscionable agreement is one "such as no man in his senses and not under delusion would make on the one hand, and as no honest and fair man would accept on the other."[75] This statement has no more utility than those found in many opinions by courts of equity. We certainly are aware that one's conduct should be "conscionable," or, that "unconscionable" conduct is one of the law's

---

[68] Still another device to avoid oppressive clauses is the strict construction of clauses against the drafter, *e.g.,* Galligan v. Arovitch, 421 Pa. 301, 219 A.2d 463 (1966) (construing clause exculpat-ing the lessor from liability strictly as not involving "lawns" where clause mentioned sidewalks and other places of injury).

[69] *See* L. B. Foster Co. v. Tri-W Constr. Co., 409 Pa. 318, 186 A.2d 18 (1962) which can be read to suggest that confession of judgment clauses become enforceable if they appear on the same side of the document as the signature.

[70] There was early recognition that extremely complicated, fine-print clauses of casualty insur-ance policies were virtually impossible for the insured to understand. *See* De Lancey v. Rocking-ham Farmers' Mut. Fire Ins. Co., 52 N.H. 581 (1873).

[71] Statement of Karl Llewellyn in 1 State of New York 1954 Law Revision Commission Report, Hearings on the Uniform Commercial Code, at 113.

[72] "The clause is perfectly clear and the court said, 'Had it been desired to provide such an unbelievable thing, surely language could have been made clearer.' Then counsel redrafts, and they not only say it twice as well, but they wind up saying, 'And we really mean it,' and the court looks at it a second time and says, 'Had it been the kind of thing really intended to go into an agreement, surely language could have been found....'" K. Llewellyn, *id.* at 114.

[73] "The net effect is unnecessary confusion and unpredictability, together with inadequate rem-edy, and evil persisting that calls for remedy. Covert tools are never reliable tools." Llewellyn, Book Review, 52 HARV. L. REV. 700, 703 (1939) (reviewing O. PRAUSNITZ, THE STANDARDIZATION OF COMMERCIAL CONTRACTS IN ENGLISH AND CONTINENTAL LAW (1937)).

[74] K. Llewellyn, *supra* note 71, at 114.

[75] Hume v. United States, 132 U.S. 406, 10 S. Ct. 134 (1889) quoting from Earl of Chesterfield v. Janssen, 2 Ves. Sen. 125, 155, 28 Eng. Rep. 82, 100 (Ch. 1750).

great frowns. Unfortunately, it cannot be said that the Llewellyn solution in the UCC is even a limited improvement:

"If the court as a matter of law finds the contract or any clause of the contract to have been unconscionable at the time it was made the court may refuse to enforce the contract, or it may enforce the remainder of the contract without the unconscionable clause as to avoid any unconscionable result."[76]

The harshest criticism of this statement of unconscionability is that it amounts to no more than "an emotionally satisfying incantation" which clearly indicates that "it is easy to say nothing with words."[77] Yet, Professor Llewellyn regarded this section "as perhaps the most valuable section in the entire Code."[78] He certainly did not believe that the section itself would provide the necessary certainty, stability, and predictability that "covert tools" failed to provide. Rather, courts had to confront questions of unfairness in the bargaining process without the aid of covert tools. The statute, itself, would not be effective because, "an approach by statute [is] dubious, uncertain and likely to be both awkward in manner and deficient and spotty in scope."[79] The first part of § 2-302, therefore, simply commands *courts* to confront these questions which are necessarily factual questions, though they will be decided exclusively by courts.[80] The result of these confrontations will be "precedent."

---

[76] UCC § 2-302(1). Courts have recognized that the UCC does not attempt to define unconscionability. *See, e.g.,* Fotomat Corp. of Fla. v. Chanda, 464 So. 2d 626 (Fla. App. 1985). In Bishop v. Washington, 331 Pa. Super. 387, 399, 480 A.2d 1088, 1094 (1984), the court suggests, "It is impossible to formulate a precise definition of the unconscionability concept."

[77] Leff, *Unconscionability and the Code — The Emperor's New Clause,* 115 U. PA. L. REV. 485, 558-59 (1967). Professor Leff's article was the first major analysis of the concept to be followed by a plethora of law review articles on the subject. Professor Leff describes his work as "a study in statutory pathology, an examination in some depth of the misdrafting of one section of a massive, codifying statute and the misinterpretations which came to surround it." *Id.* at 485. Another analysis, critical of the Leff approach, is Murray, *Unconscionability: Unconscionability,* 31 U. PITT. L. REV. 1 (1969). This article was submitted to three scholars for their comments and reactions which appeared in a subsequent issue of U. PITT. L. REV.; Braucher, *The Unconscionable Contract or Term,* 31 U. PITT. L. REV. 337 (1970); Speidel, *Unconscionability, Assent and Consumer Protection,* 31 U. PITT. L. REV. 359 (1970); Leff, *Unconscionability and the Crowd — Consumers and the Common Law Tradition,* 31 U. PITT. L. REV. 349 (1970). In commenting on all of these articles, one text writer suggested that the academic effort to afford meaning to the concept of unconscionability has become embroiled in concepts that might be justly called elusive, though the debaters are about as elusive as the concepts. D. DOBBS, HANDBOOK ON THE LAW OF REMEDIES 708 n.12 (1973). Among the numerous additional articles, the following deserve mention: Ellinghaus, *In Defense of Unconscionability,* 78 YALE L.J. 757 (1969); Spanogle, *Analyzing Unconscionability Problems,* 117 U. PA. L. REV. 931 (1969); Epstein, *Unconscionability: A Critical Reappraisal,* 18 J.L. & ECON. 293 (1975); Schwartz, *A Reexamination of Nonsubstantive Unconscionability,* 63 VA. L. REV. 1053 (1977); Hillman, *Debunking Some Myths About Unconscionability: A New Framework for UCC § 2-302,* 67 CORNELL L. REV. 1 (1981).

[78] K. Llewellyn, *supra* note 71, at 57.

[79] K. LLEWELLYN, THE COMMON LAW TRADITION: DECIDING APPEALS 370 (1960).

[80] Section 2-302(1) restricts questions of unconscionability to courts rather than juries. *See* Northwest Acceptance Corp. v. Almost Gravel, Inc., 162 Mich. App. 294, 412 N.W.2d 719 (1987); Frank's Main. & Eng'g, Inc. v. C. A. Roberts Co., 86 Ill. App. 3d 980, 408 N.E.2d 403 (1980); Industralease Automated & Scientific Equip. Corp. v. R. M. E. Enters., 58 A.D.2d 482, 396 N.Y.S.2d 427 (1977). In Mullan v. Quickie Aircraft Corp., 797 F.2d 845 (10th Cir. 1986), the court suggests that, while a finding of unconscionability is a question of law, when such a finding is made upon the presentation of evidence, the finding becomes a mixed question of law and fact. If what must be decided in the mixed question involves primarily a consideration of legal principles, the appellate court reviews *de novo* (citing Allis-Chalmers Credit Corp. v. Tri-State Equip., 792 F.2d 967 (10th Cir. 1986)).

To restrain "the untutored imagination of courts,"[81] the second part of the section permits "all kinds of [business] background to be presented to instruct the court."[82] The overall effect of the section will be to "greatly advance certainty in a ... most baffling, most troubling, and almost unreckonable situation."[83] Thus, Llewellyn unequivocally presented the challenge of adumbrating the concept of unconscionability to the courts.

The lack of guidance in the language of § 2-302 invites the use of the comments to the section. In keeping with the purpose of Llewellyn, the first comment unequivocally indicates the intention of the drafters to permit courts "to police explicitly against the contracts or clauses which they find to be unconscionable ...," and to avoid past judicial efforts to accomplish this effect through "adverse construction of language, by manipulation of the rules of offer and acceptance or by determinations that the clause is contrary to public policy or to the dominant purpose of the contract."[84] As to the judicial test to be applied, the comment suggests:

"The basic test is whether, in the light of the general commercial background and the commercial needs of the particular trade or case, the clauses involved are so one-sided as to be unconscionable under the circumstances existing at the time of the making of the contract.... The principle is one of the prevention of oppression and unfair surprise ... and not of disturbance of the allocation of risks because of superior bargaining power."[85]

Notwithstanding sixteen years of experience under the UCC version of unconscionability,[86] the RESTATEMENT 2d version of the concept replicates the Code statement, i.e., it makes no attempt to set forth a workable statement of unconscionability but merely indicates what a court may do once it finds that a contract or clause of a contract is unconscionable.[87] The accompanying com-

---

[81] K. Llewellyn, *supra* note 71.

[82] *Id.* UCC § 2-302(2): "When it is claimed or appears to the court that the contract or any clause thereof may be unconscionable the parties shall be afforded a reasonable opportunity to present evidence as to its commercial setting, purpose and effect to aid the court in making the determination." *See* Capital Assocs. v. Hudgens, 455 So. 2d 651 (Fla. App. 1984); Luick v. Graybar Elec. Co., 473 F.2d 1360 (8th Cir. 1973); Beckman v. Vassall-Dillworth Lincoln-Mercury, Inc., 321 Pa. Super. 428, 468 A.2d 784 (1983) (full evidentiary hearing not required as long as no issue of material fact exists). *See also* Lindemann v. Eli Lilly & Co., 816 F.2d 199 (5th Cir. 1987) (district court raised issue of unconscionability *sua sponte* — held: trial court's procedure fundamentally disadvantaged appellant and deprived it of defense since the court must have evidence of unconscionability before it can support any finding on that issue and a defendant is entitled to fair notice that a portion of its contract will be challenged for unconscionability.

[83] K. Llewellyn, *supra* note 71.

[84] UCC § 2-302 comment 1.

[85] *Id. See* Resource Mgt. Co. v. Weston Ranch, 706 P.2d 1028, 1041 (Utah 1985) suggesting that § 2-302 does not define unconscionability but the quoted comment provides a test. There has been considerable confusion concerning the last portion of the quoted comment, i.e., that risks should not be disturbed simply because of the appearance of superior bargaining power. The statement may be read to suggest that the mere existence of superior bargaining power does not give rise to declaring a contract or clause unconscionable. Rather, it is the use of such power — the oppressive use — which should alert courts to the application of the judicial power to strike down a contract or clause.

[86] The first jurisdiction to enact the Code was Pennsylvania where it became effective in 1954. The preliminary draft of the RESTATEMENT 2d section on unconscionability appeared in 1970.

[87] "If a contract or term thereof is unconscionable at the time the contract is made, a court may refuse to enforce the contract, or may enforce the remainder of the contract without the unconscionable term, or may so limit the application of any unconscionable term as to avoid any unconscionable result." RESTATEMENT 2d § 208. Courts recognize that this is not "an attempt to

ment suggests that unconscionability must be determined in the light of its setting, and, "Relevant factors include weaknesses in the contracting process."[88] Moreover, while inadequacy of consideration, itself, would not signal unconscionability, "gross disparity in the values exchanged [overall imbalance] may be an important factor in a determination that a contract is unconscionable...."[89]

Notwithstanding the comment language of either the UCC or the RESTATE-MENT 2d, it is clear that both direct courts to adumbrate the concept of unconscionability on a common law, case-by-case basis.

2. The Meaning of Unconscionability in the Courts.

a. Scope.

While the UCC is a statutory prescription requiring courts sitting as courts of law to police contracts for unconscionability, the use of the doctrine has not been relegated to contracts for the sale of goods though the Code is technically applicable only to such contracts. "Many courts have applied the UCC approach to cases not strictly governed by the Code."[90] Thus, the doctrine has been held applicable to cases involving oil and gas royalty rights,[91] an equipment lease,[92] a ground lease of condominium property,[93] rental agreements for mobile home lots,[94] a judgment note,[95] failure to list the plaintiff's business in a telephone directory,[96] a bank signature card,[97] a contract to promote a concert tour,[98] and numerous other cases not involving a sale-of-goods contract. With the incorporation of the concept in the RESTATEMENT 2d[99] and the inclusion of similar concepts in various consumer protection statutes,[1] there is no doubt that the doctrine may be applied to any type of contract whether through use of the RESTATEMENT 2d provision, a specialized statute, or through analogous application of the UCC provision where the Code does not otherwise apply.

---

define unconscionability in a black letter rule of law." Steinhardt v. Rudolph, 422 So. 2d 884, 890 (Fla. App. 1982).

[88] RESTATEMENT 2d § 208 comment a.

[89] RESTATEMENT 2d § 208 comment c.

[90] Resource Mgt. Co. v. Weston Ranch, *supra* note 85.

[91] *Id.*

[92] John Deere Leasing Co. v. Blubaugh, 636 F. Supp. 1569 (D. Kan. 1986). *See* UCC Article 2A (promulgated in 1987), § 108, which applies the unconscionability concept to personal property leases.

[93] Steihardt v. Rudolph, 422 So. 2d 884 (Fla. App. 1982).

[94] Garrett v. Janiewski, 480 So. 2d 1324 (Fla. App. 1986).

[95] Germantown Mfg. Co. v. Rawlinson, 491 A.2d 138 (Pa. Super. 1985).

[96] Rozenboom v. Northwestern Bell Tel. Co., 358 N.W.2d 241 (S.D. 1984).

[97] Perdue v. Crocker Nat'l Bank, 190 Cal. Rptr. 205 (1983).

[98] Graham v. Scissor-Tail, 28 Cal. 3d 807, 623 P.2d 165 (1981).

[99] RESTATEMENT 2d § 208.

[1] *See, e.g.,* John Deere Leasing Co. v. Blubaugh, 636 F. Supp. 1569, 1572 (D. Kan. 1986) where the court states that unconscionability came into the law of Kansas through the UCC along with the Consumer Credit Code (KAN. STAT. ANN. § 16a-5-108), the Consumer Protection Act (KAN. STAT. ANN. § 50-627) and the Residential Landlord and Tenant Act (KAN. STAT. ANN. § 58-2544). *See also* Uniform Consumer Sales Practices Act of 1970 and Uniform Consumer Credit Code of 1974 which contain provisions dealing with unconscionability though neither has been enacted in a large number of jurisdictions as of the date of this writing. UCC § 2A-108(2) is modeled on the Uniform Consumer Credit Code, § 5.108, 7A U.L.A. 167-69 (1974).

b. Tests of Unconscionability in the Courts — "Procedural — Substantive" *et al.*

Notwithstanding the plethora of case law dealing with the concept of unconscionability, there is no single description of the concept to which all courts subscribe. Courts emphasize the "flexibility" of the concept depending upon the facts.[2] Generally, the time for determining whether a contract or clause thereof is unconscionable is the time the contract was made.[3] Numerous cases contain the historic definition of unconscionability as a contract or clause that no person in his right senses would make.[4] Modern judicial statements of unconscionability, however, never end with this definition. They may include quotations or paraphrases from the UCC comments, i.e., "The principle is one of the prevention of oppression and unfair surprise."[5] Among the various expressions attempting to define the concept, a statement from a well-known opinion appears to be more popular than others:

"Unconscionability has generally been recognized to include an absence of meaningful choice on the part of one of the parties together with contract terms which are unreasonably favorable to the other party."[6]

"Oppression" and "unfair surprise" are two discernible elements which may have some utility in the process of determining whether a contract or term, thereof, is unconscionable. Similarly, the "absence of meaningful choice" and "unreasonably favorable terms" are two discernible elements which may provide some solace to courts searching for a workable statement of unconscionability. One of the earliest analyses of unconscionability divided the concept into two types which may be seen as equivalent to these elements.[7] The author viewed defects in the bargaining process as *procedural* unconscionability ("bargaining naughtiness"), i.e., the manner in which the contract was negotiated under the circumstances.[8] *Substantive* unconscionability, on the other

---

[2] *See, e.g.,* Perdue v. Crocker Nat'l Bank, 190 Cal. Rptr. 205, 209 (1983); A & M Produce Co. v. FMC Corp., 135 Cal. App. 3d 486, 186 Cal. Rptr. 114, 121 (1982); Hollywood Leasing Corp. v. Rosenblum, 100 Misc. 2d 120, 418 N.Y.S.2d 887, 889 (1979).

[3] *See* Resource Mgt. Co. v. Weston Ranch, 706 P.2d 1028, 1043 (Utah 1985): "Generally, the critical juncture for determining whether a contract is unconscionable is the moment when it is entered into by both parties ... To judge the substantive fairness of contracts at a date subsequent to their making could nullify many contracts entailing a speculative element."

[4] *See* the full text of the quote at text, *supra* note 75.

[5] UCC § 2-302 comment 1. Concepts of oppression and unfair surprise as found in this comment are mentioned in numerous unconscionability cases. *See, e.g.,* Resource Mgt. Co. v. Weston Ranch, 706 P.2d 1028, 1041 (Utah 1985); A & M Produce Co. v. FMC Corp., 135 Cal. App. 3d 486, 186 Cal. Rptr. 114, 121-22 (1982); Kerr-McGee Corp. v. Northern Utils., Inc., 673 F.2d 323 (10th Cir. 1982); W. L. May Co. v. Philco-Ford Corp., 273 Or. 701, 543 P.2d 283 (1975).

[6] This statement is from the opinion of Judge Skelly Wright in the well-known case, Williams v. Walker-Thomas Furn. Co., 350 F.2d 445, 449 (D.C. Cir. 1965) which is introduced in Snyder v. Rogers, 499 A.2d 1369, 1371 (Pa. Super. 1985) with the statement, "As other courts have done, ... we turn to Judge Skelly Wright's definition...." *See also* Municipality of Anchorage v. Locker, 723 P.2d 1261 (Alaska 1986); A & M Produce Co. v. FMC Corp., 135 Cal. App. 3d 486, 186 Cal. Rptr. 114 (1982).

[7] Leff, *supra* note 77 at 487.

[8] One court has suggested the following indices of *procedural* unconscionability: "'[t]he use of printed form or boilerplate contract drawn skillfully by the party in the strongest economic position' generally offered on a take-it-or-leave-it basis, ... phrasing contractual terms 'in language that is incomprehensible to a layman or that divert[s] his attention from the problems raised by them or the rights given up through them,' ... hiding key contractual provisions in a maze of fine print, ... or in an inconspicuous part of the document, ... minimizing key contractual

hand, is concerned with whether the obligations assumed are unreasonably favorable to one of the parties, i.e., whether a term of the contract is particularly one-sided or lopsided or manifests an outrageous degree of unfairness.[9] For the sake of symmetry, it would be at least emotionally satisfying if it could be said that courts would view "unfair surprise" and the "absence of meaningful choice" as grist for the mill of *procedural* unconscionability, while they would regard "oppression" and "unreasonably favorable" (or unfavorable) terms as the subject matter of *substantive* unconscionability. Unfortunately, there is confusion in the use of these terms. Thus, one court suggests that "Substantive unconscionability is indicated by 'contract terms so one-sided as to oppress or unfairly surprise an innocent party,'"[10] which would place the concepts of "oppression" and "unfair surprise" from the UCC comment under the *substantive* rubric. Another court, however, suggests that, the *procedural* element encompasses the two factors of oppression and surprise.[11] Still another court suggests that clauses of an oppressive character suggest *substantive* unconscionability, while *procedural* unconscionability is either (1) lack of knowledge ("unfair surprise") or (2) lack of voluntariness (*e.g.*, a contract of adhesion).[12] While the last analysis appears preferable, the lack of precision in the use of these labels raises doubts as to whether it is the "oppression" and "unfair surprise" notions, the *procedural* and *substantive* labels or both that lack utility.[13] There is also a lack of clarity as to whether one form of unconscionability (procedural or substantive) is sufficient without the other.[14] We are, of course, still left with the "absence of meaningful choice"

---

provisions by deceptive sales practices, ... 'lack of opportunity for meaningful negotiation,' ... whether the aggrieved party was compelled to accept the terms, ... an 'exploitation of the underprivileged, unsophisticated and illiterate. ...' " Resource Mgt. Co. v. Weston Ranch, 706 P.2d 1028, 1042 (Utah 1985).

[9] "Substantive unconscionability requires proving that the terms of the contract are unreasonable and unfair ... it requires a showing of commercial unreasonableness ... the terms must be unreasonably favorable to one party." Garrett v. Janiewski, 480 So. 2d 1324, 1326 (Fla. App. 1985).

[10] Resource Mgt. Co. v. Weston Ranch, 706 P.2d 1028, 1041 (Utah 1985), relying on Bekins Bar V Ranch v. Huth, 664 P.2d 455, 462 (Utah 1983).

[11] A & M Produce Co. v. FMC Corp., 135 Cal. App. 3d 486, 186 Cal. Rptr. 114, 121 (1982), (emphasis added).

[12] Bank of Indiana, N. A. v. Holyfield, 476 F. Supp. 104 (S.D. Miss. 1979).

[13] A number of courts suggest the *procedural/substantive* distinction. In addition to the cases cited *supra* notes 8 and 9, *see* Steinhardt v. Rudolph, 422 So. 2d 884, 889 (Fla. App. 1982). The court, however, suggests that the "procedural-substantive analysis is ... only a general approach to the unconscionability questions and is not a rule of law. For example, the Florida decisions concerning unconscionability as applied to a mortgage foreclosure case are directly devoid of this analysis." *Id.*

[14] One court suggests, "Gross disparity in terms, absent evidence of procedural unconscionability, can support a finding of unconscionability.... While it is conceivable that a contract might be unconscionable on the theory of unfair surprise without any substantive imbalance in the obligations of the parties to the contract, that would be rare." Resource Mgt. Co. v. Weston Ranch, 706 P.2d 1028, 1043 (Utah 1985). RESTATEMENT 2d § 208 comment c suggests, "Theoretically, it is possible for a contract to be oppressive taken as a whole, even though there is no weakness in the bargaining process and no single term which is in itself unconscionable. Ordinarily, however, an unconscionable contract involves other factors as well as overall imbalance." One of the often cited articles in this area suggests that unbargained-for terms should be denied enforcement only when they are substantively unreasonable, and where a bargain has been achieved through complete and free assent, it would be at least rare to strike down such a bargain. Ellinghaus, *In Defense of Unconscionability,* 78 YALE L.J. 757, 766-67, 775 (1969). Typically, courts discover both procedural and substantive unconscionability, *see* A & M Produce v. FMC Corp., 135 Cal. App. 3d 489, 186 Cal.

and "unreasonably favorable" terms dichotomy. Again, however, these phrases are barren of meaning absent an application to given fact situations.

More elaborate efforts to suggest the elements of unconscionability have been less than successful. Thus, one court suggests seven elements[15] while another finds ten elements[16] to consider in applying the unconscionability standard. These are blunderbuss efforts that repeat factors found in various cases or in other treatments of unconscionability. In a word, they are of limited utility because they fail to provide a meaningful, workable analysis of the concept.

c. Risk Allocation and Lack of Assent — "Apparent" and "Genuine" Assent — "Unexpected" and "No Choice" Unconscionability — A Suggested Analysis.

The difficult modern concept of unconscionability cannot be effectively analyzed absent an appreciation of the underlying philosophy of Article 2 of the UCC from whence it came. Article 2 of the UCC made radical changes in contract law and its related predecessor statute.[17] The essential change was to overcome the technical and monistic notions of classical contract law in order to effectuate the factual bargain of the parties.[18] The agreement-in-fact of the parties,[19] however, should include only those terms to which the parties actually or presumably assent. The situation is complicated because of the widespread use of printed forms which go unread by almost all who look upon them as evidence of their agreement.[20] The fundamental concept of contract law is

---

Rptr. 114 (1982), and some expressly require a finding of both types, *see* Garrett v. Janiewski, 480 So. 2d 1324, 1326 (Fla. App. 1985): "[T]his court has held that there must be a coalescing of the two elements, procedural and substantive unconscionability, before a case of unconscionability is made out."

[15]Mullan v. Quickie Aircraft Corp., 797 F.2d 845, 850 (10th Cir. 1986): (1) a standardized agreement executed by parties of unequal bargaining power; (2) a lack of opportunity to read or become familiar with the document before signing it; (3) use of fine print in the portion of the contract containing the disputed provision; (4) absence of evidence that the provision was commercially reasonable or should have been reasonably anticipated; (5) whether the terms of the contract are substantively unfair; (6) the relationship of the parties including factors of assent, unfair surprise and notice; and (7) all the circumstances surrounding the formation of the contract, including its commercial setting and purpose.

[16]Wille v. Southwestern Bell Tel. Co., 219 Kan. 755, 549 P.2d 903, 906-07 (1976): (1) the use of printed forms by the economically superior party involving adhesive provisions; (2) a significant cost-price disparity or excessive price; (3) a denial of basic rights and remedies to a consumer buyer; (4) the inclusion of penalty clauses; (5) the circumstances surrounding the formation of the contract, i.e., commercial setting, purpose and effect; (6) inconspicuous clauses; (7) phrasing clauses in a manner that is not understandable to the other party; (8) overall imbalance in rights and obligations; (9) exploitation of the underprivileged, unsophisticated, uneducated and illiterate; and (10) inequality of bargaining power.

[17]Professor Llewellyn, the "Father" of the UCC and principal draftsman of Article 2, was particularly annoyed at suggestions that Article 2 did not purport to change the prior law in a material fashion since he was committed to the view that Article 2 made changes that were "deep, wide [and] vital." 1 State of New York Law Revision Commission Report, Hearings on the Uniform Commercial Code 49 (1954).

[18]*See* Murray, *The Article 2 Prism: The Underlying Philosophy of Article 2 of the Uniform Commercial Code,* 21 WASHBURN L.J. 1 (1981). *See also,* Murray, *The Chaos of the Battle of the Forms: Solutions,* 39 VAND. L. REV. 1307, 1311-15 (1986).

[19]*See* the UCC definition of "agreement" in § 1-201(3).

[20]*See* Murray, *The Chaos of the Battle of the Forms: Solutions, supra* note 18, at 1317 and, in particular, n.47. *See also* the next section of this book dealing with standardized agreements.

the concept of assent. The basic idea that parties exercise their volition by committing themselves to future action and that the law provides their *circle of assent* with the status of a private law is fundamental to any discussion of contracts.[21] As for those boilerplate, printed terms that go unread, the parties should be said to have assented to those which are reasonable, fair, expected, or, to use the term chosen by Professor Llewellyn, "not indecent."[22] Whether a term is reasonable, fair, expected or not indecent must depend upon the particular circumstances. Certainly, a clause simply repeating the automatic warranty protection a buyer would receive under the UCC would be a decent or reasonable as well as expected term. On the other hand, a more realistic scenario finds a disclaimer of basic warranty protection, e.g., a disclaimer of the implied warranty of merchantability or a limitation of its duration, in a printed form.[23] This is a deviation from the standard term of a contract for the sale of goods.[24] Similarly, it is normal for a buyer to expect to be compensated for consequential damages caused by a seller's breach.[25] A typical printed form will exclude such damages. Apart from its unconscionability provision, the UCC places threshold safeguards on the disclaimer of implied warranties. Thus, where the implied warranty of merchantability is disclaimed in writing and no trade expressions are used,[26] to help insure at least *apparent* assent by the purchaser to such a disclaimer, the Code requires the written disclaimer to be *conspicuous*[27] and to mention the term, "merchantability."[28] While no

---

[21] Quoted with approval from the second edition of this work in A & M Produce Co. v. FMC Corp., 135 Cal. App. 3d 473, 186 Cal. Rptr. 114, 122, n.11 (1982) and Perdue v. Crocker Nat'l Bank, 141 Cal. App. 3d 200, 190 Cal. Rptr. 204 (1983).

[22] "Instead of thinking about 'assent' to boilerplate clauses, we can recognize that so far as concerns the specific, there is no assent at all. What has in fact been assented to, specifically, are the few dickered terms, and the broad type of the transaction, and but one more. That one more is a blanket assent (not a specific assent) to any not unreasonable or indecent terms the seller may have on his form, which do not alter or eviscerate the reasonable meaning of the dickered terms. The fine print which has not been read has no business to cut under the reasonable meaning of those dickered terms which constitute the dominant and only real expression of agreement, but much of it commonly belongs in." K. LLEWELLYN, THE COMMON LAW TRADITION: DECIDING APPEALS 370 (1960).

[23] The UCC permits implied warranties to be disclaimed under § 2-316(2) and (3), subject to certain safeguards. These safeguards will be discussed, *infra*. The Magnuson-Moss Warranty Act, 15 U.S.C. § 2308(a) and (b) (§ 108(a) and (b)) precludes the disclaimer of implied warranties in relation to *consumer* goods, but permits the warranty to be *limited in duration*.

[24] See Rakoff, *Contracts of Adhesion: An Essay in Reconstruction*, 96 HARV. L. REV. 1173, 1182 (1983) who suggests that Article 2 of the Code "is in large part a catalogue of the implied terms of contracts of sale," i.e., the standardized terms of sales, and any deviation from such terms are deviations from the parties' normal expectations and are frowned upon. There is no need for clauses of a contract to deal with warranties at all since they are implied under §§ 2-314 and 2-315 of the Code, or expressed through descriptions, affirmations of fact, promises, samples, or models pursuant to UCC § 2-313. Thus, when parties deal with warranties in one or more printed clauses, they are engaging in an exercise of "specifying deviation from the standardized plan rather than in defining the obligation *ab initio.*" *Id. See also* Hartwig Farms, Inc. v. Pacific Gamble Robinson Co., 28 Wash. App. 539, 544, 625 P.2d 171, 174 (1981): "The code does not imply disclaimers; in fact, disclaimers are not favored by the law."

[25] Consequential damages are defined in UCC § 2-715 and are recoverable by the purchaser in proper circumstances along with the buyer's direct damages such as contract price/market price differential (§ 2-713) or the remedy of "cover," § 2-712.

[26] UCC § 2-316(3)(a) permits implied warranties to be disclaimed by trade expressions like "as is" or "with all faults."

[27] UCC § 1-201(10) sets forth the test for conspicuousness: "[W]hen it is so written that a reasonable person against whom it is to operate ought to have noticed it."

[28] UCC § 2-316(2).

similar requirement is expressly set forth to exclude consequential damages,[29]
a court may require such an exclusionary clause to be conspicuous.[30] Requirements such as conspicuousness, however, are physical requirements, e.g.,
placing the clause on the front of a printed form in larger or darker print.
Most buyers, consumers and merchants alike, are, however, unaware of the
drastic nature of such a disclaimer or exclusionary clause. Thus, while a
physically conspicuous clause may assure *apparent* assent, it does not assure
genuine assent. If, therefore, the clause is physically conspicuous but incomprehensible to a reasonable buyer regardless of its print size or placement on
the printed form, should the disclaimer be effective?

An even more compelling argument can be found in the situation of one who
reads and understands a clause that would shift a material risk to him. Understanding the legal effect of a particular clause and signing the form containing that clause may still not manifest assent to the clause if the clause is
presented as a contract of adhesion, i.e., a take-it-or-leave-it contract. Again,
such an arrangement is the antithesis of volition and factual agreement of the
parties — there is no bargain-in-fact in such a case. While the signing of such
a document may, again, manifest *apparent* assent, it does not manifest *genuine* or *real* assent. The parties are certainly free to reallocate normal risks in
their agreement and, if both *apparent* and *genuine* assent are present, such a
reallocation is within their circle of assent.[31] Yet, a party should not be bound
to a material, risk-shifting, inconspicuous provision in a standard form.[32] At a
minimum, the reallocation must be physically conspicuous and it should be
substantively conspicuous, i.e., understandable to a reasonable buyer. Moreover, the party against whom it is designed to operate should have had a
reasonable choice in relation to such reallocation of normal risks at the time
the contract was formed.[33]

On the basis of the foregoing, unconscionability may be seen as falling
within either of two categories involving material, risk-shifting terms: (a)
where such terms are unexpected by the party against whom they will operate, or (b) where such terms, though known and, therefore, not unexpected,
are dictated by the party with superior bargaining power since the other party
has no reasonable choice. "Unexpected" unconscionability is equivalent to
"unfair surprise," i.e., the terms are such that they are not expected by the

---

[29] *See* UCC § 2-719(3).

[30] *See, e.g.,* Insurance Corp. of N. Am. v. Automatic Sprinkler Corp. of Am., 67 Ohio 2d 91, 423
N.E.2d 151 (1981). The prevailing view, however, is otherwise. *See supra* note 68.

[31] Even here, if the reallocation of risks eventually leaves the buyer remediless because, *e.g.,*
there is an express warranty of repair or replacement and that warranty is breached, the remedy
in the contract "fails of its essential purpose" and the buyer is entitled to normal remedies under
the Code notwithstanding the document that excludes such remedies. UCC § 2-719(2).

[32] "The most detailed and specific commentaries observe that a contract is largely an allocation
of risks between the parties, and therefore that a contractual term is substantively suspect if it
reallocates the risks of the bargain in an objectively unreasonable or unexpected manner." Perdue v. Crocker Nat'l Bank, 190 Cal. Rptr. 205, 210 (1983) relying on Murray, *Unconscionability:
Unconscionability,* 31 U. PITT. L. REV. 1, 12-23 (1969).

[33] The "circle of assent" analysis is adopted in Parton v. Pirtle Oldsmobile-Cadillac-Isuzu, 730
S.W.2d 634, 637 (Tenn. App. 1987), quoting from the 2d edition of this book, and followed in
Board of Dirs. Harriman Sch. Sw. Dist. v. Petroleum Corp., 757 S.W.2d 669 (Tenn. App. 1988).
See also Germantown Mfg. Co. v. Rawlinson, 341 Pa. Super. 42, 491 A.2d 138, 146 (1985) which
also adopts this analysis.

party who is asked to assent to them. Such a clause often appears in the "boilerplate" of a seller's form. It is not, however, unconscionable simply because it appears in the fine print. The clause must be a material, risk-shifting clause that the party would not expect to find therein.[34] The other type of unconscionability which may be captioned, "no choice," is equivalent to "oppression" since it involves a party who requires certain goods or services that are necessary to his physical or economic well-being and who signs the dictated terms of the seller's form because he has no reasonable alternative. This is the classic contract of adhesion.[35] This analysis suggests greater utility than others because it emphasizes the two dominant themes found in the unconscionability case law. It avoids the illusion of certainty created by a procedural/substantive dichotomy and requires courts to apply these two pervasive concepts to the huge tapestry of fact situations which continue to unfold. It seems preferable to avoid a laundry list of elements which are often redundant and may refer to certain elements which are typically present in unconscionability cases but cannot be classified as necessary.[36] It has been wisely suggested that, "[V]iable law on an issue of this kind must, inherently, be worked out on a case by case basis."[37]

d. The Analysis Applied — A Survey of the Unconscionability Case Law — Consumers, Merchants, Excessive Price.

In the exploration of unconscionability to this point, we have considered certain statements from the case law that attempt to define or describe the concept of unconscionability. It is appropriate to consider some of the more significant cases in light of the foregoing analysis since, again, it is the application of these concepts to diverse fact situations that will continue to occupy the courts in their future attempts to use the concept. It is difficult to find a more instructive opinion dealing with unconscionability than *Henningsen v. Bloomfield Motors, Inc.*,[38] despite its age and the fact that it does not mention the term, "unconscionability," or deal with the UCC formulation. As suggested earlier,[39] that case dealt with a clause disclaiming the implied war-

---

[34] This "expectation" test is particularly well developed with respect to clauses in insurance contracts. *See, e.g.,* Darner Motor Sales, Inc. v. Universal Underwriters Ins. Co., 140 Ariz. 383, 682 P.2d 388 (1984).

[35] The foregoing analysis involving "unexpected" and "no choice" unconscionability is adopted in Germantown Mfg. Co. v. Rawlinson, 341 Pa. Super. 42, 491 A.2d 138, 146-48 (1985) and is based on Murray, *The Standardized Agreement Phenomenon in the Restatement (Second) of Contracts,* 67 CORNELL L. REV. 735, 776-77 (1982). *See also* McGinnis v. Cayton, 312 S.E.2d 765, 777 (W. Va. 1984) where the concurring opinion by Justice Harshbarger analyzes the author's analysis in three steps: "Risks that have been allocated by the parties — expected or at least not unexpected — are not usually unconscionable. If the risk allocation was inconspicuous or if there was no allocation because the risk was unexpected, the contract may be unconscionable if the risk was material. If the risk was unexpected but was immaterial, a contract affected by it is not unconscionable."

[36] Thus, courts that list numerous elements often include standardized (printed) forms. *See* the cases and lists of elements *supra* notes 15 and 16. While the printed form is typically present in unconscionability cases, it is not essential, i.e., a negotiated document may contain unconscionable provisions or it may be evidence of an unconscionable contract.

[37] R. SPEIDEL, R. SUMMERS & J. WHITE, COMMERCIAL AND CONSUMER LAW 662 (3d ed. 1981).

[38] 32 N.J. 358, 161 A.2d 69 (1960).

[39] *See* text *supra* note 59 *et seq.*

ranty of merchantability in a contract between an auto dealer and a consumer buyer. The court emphasized the two central themes of unconscionability in dealing with the buyer's awareness of the disclaimer and whether the buyer had any reasonable choice in light of the use of the same clause by other sellers of automobiles.[40] An equally well-known case is *Williams v. Walker-Thomas Furniture Co.*,[41] where a poor consumer purchaser of a stereo set signed a form contract containing an "add-on" clause that permitted the seller, upon the buyer's default, to repossess all items which the buyer had purchased from that seller over a five year period though she had paid for the prior items except for a relatively small balance. The clause was oppressive as well as obscure.[42] The court emphasized the lack of either apparent assent (unexpected terms or "unfair surprise") or genuine assent (no choice or oppression), though it commingled the concepts:[43]

> Ordinarily, one who signs an agreement without full knowledge of its terms might be held to assume the risk that he has entered a one-sided bargain. But when a party of little barganing power, and hence any real choice, signs a commercially unreasonable contract with little or no knowledge of its terms, it is hardly likely that his consent, or even an objective manifestation of his consent, was ever given to all the terms. In such a case the usual rule that the terms of the agreement are not to be questioned should be abandoned and the court should consider whether the terms of the contract are so unfair that enforcement should be withheld.[44]

In this portion of the opinion as well as elsewhere in the opinion, the court emphatically suggests that a party with no choice (lack of genuine assent) who is reasonably unaware of a material provision which attempts to allocate an unexpected risk to that party (lack of apparent assent) is not bound by such a provision. In determining the lack of apparent assent, the particular circumstances of the buyer must be considered. Thus, the court emphasized the buyer's general lack of education as well as her failure to read or understand the fine print provision.[45]

Another court suggests: "High pressure sales tactics, failure to disclose terms of the contract ... refusal to bargain on certain crucial terms, clauses

---

[40] *See also* Gladden v. Cadillac Motor Car Div., 83 N.J. 320, 416 A.2d 394, 402 (1980): "The purchaser of a mass-produced consumer article with a standard warranty form or booklet, as in this case, has no opportunity to bargain over its terms."

[41] 350 F.2d 445 (D.C. Cir. 1965) Though this litigation antedated the enactment of the UCC in the District of Columbia, the Court decided the case as if § 2-302 of the Code applied by suggesting that the pre-Code common law of unconscionability in the District was essentially identical to that set forth in the Code section.

[42] The court states, "The effect of this rather obscure provision was to keep a balance due on every item purchased until the balance due on all items, whenever purchased, was liquidated. As a result, the debt incurred at the time of purchase or each item was secured by the right to repossess all the items previously purchased by the same purchaser, and each new item purchased automatically became subject to a security interest arising out of previous dealings." 350 F.2d at 448.

[43] "In many cases the meaningfulness of the choice is negated by a gross inequality of bargaining power. The manner in which the contract was entered is also relevant to this consideration." *Id.* at 449.

[44] *Id.*

[45] *Id.* Other cases considering a party's lack of education include Wille v. Southwestern Bell Tel. Co., 219 Kan. 755, 549 P.2d 903 (1976); Johnson v. Mobil Oil Corp., 415 F. Supp. 264 (E.D. Mich. 1976); Weaver v. American Oil Co., 276 N.E.2d 144 (Ind. 1971).

hidden in fine print and unequal bargaining power aggravated by the fact that the consumer, in many cases, cannot speak English, have been recognized as procedurally unconscionable."[46]

Again, the central themes of unconscionability are commingled in one statement. High pressure sales tactics undermine choice, consent, or assent. A refusal to bargain on certain crucial terms suggests a gross disparity of bargaining power — no choice unconscionability or a lack of genuine assent. Clauses hidden in fine print return to the lack of apparent assent or unexpected terms which are unconscionable. The inability of the buyer to speak English is also a manifestation of the lack of apparent assent, i.e., such a person could easily be "unfairly surprised" at what he had signed. Similarly, where a Spanish-speaking buyer had agreed to pay over $1100 for a freezer which had a wholesale cost of less than $350, the court was influenced by the buyer's apparent lack of understanding of the transaction that was aggravated by the salesman's representation that the freezer would cost nothing since the buyer would receive a $25 commission on every sale made to friends.[47] Even where the buyer is capable of understanding the writing, if the risk-shifting provision is in light-colored print, buried in the fine print or indecipherable, the buyer may be said to lack even apparent assent to such a clause.[48] It cannot be gainsaid that such a clause is unexpected. A clause that is highly legible and understandable, on the other hand, cannot be characterized as unexpected. If, however, the clause shifts a material risk to the buyer and the seller has a monopoly on an important product or service, or if all sellers use essentially the same printed form containing such a clause, the buyer literally has no choice but to sign the contract containing the oppressive provision and, for that reason alone, the oppressive clause should be deemed unconscionable.[49] While the typical unconscionability case manifests both the unexpected and no choice evils of unconscionability,[50] it is important to distinguish them so as to provide a meaningful analysis.

---

[46] Hollywood Leasing Corp. v. Rosenblum, 100 Misc. 2d 120, 418 N.Y.S.2d 887, 889 (1979).

[47] Frostifresh Corp. v. Reynoso, 52 Misc. 2d 26, 274 N.Y.S.2d 757 (1966).

[48] In John Deere Leasing Co. v. Blubaugh, 636 F. Supp. 1569 (D. Kan. 1986), the lease agreement contained a default provision making the lessee liable for the purchase price. The clause was on the back of the form and written in such fine, light print as to be nearly illegible. Neither party was able to obtain a photocopy because the print was so light. Thus, the court did not read the lease until it received the original and then had to use a magnifying glass to read the reverse side.

[49] See Rozenboom v. Northwestern Bell Tel. Co., 358 S.W.2d 241 (1984) (contract between telephone company and merchant containing clause exculpating the telephone company for any liability beyond the amount of advertising charges for failure to publish the plaintiff's business in the yellow pages of the new directory).

[50] See, e.g., Steinhardt v. Rudolph, 422 So. 2d 884, 894 (Fla. App. 1982) (rent escalation clause in condominium ground lease placed excessive burdens on tenants making them liable for the entire 99-year lease at an annual rental which escalates as the Consumer Price Index rises but does not decrease when the Index falls and further escalates upon devaluation of the dollar. The lease was made a precondition of the sale of individual units creating an adhesive choice and the entire transaction "was hidden, in part, under a smoke screen wherein the developer successfully urged the unit owners not to obtain lawyers to protect their rights in their respective closings, withheld in part the legal papers associated with the transaction, and had a lawyer at the individual closings who represented solely the developer's own interests. It is difficult ... to imagine a lease with more procedural and substantive indicia of unconscionability than the lease we examine in the instant case."

Among the increasing number of unconscionability cases, courts have been concerned about cases involving disparity between the price and value of the product or service. Courts have traditionally avoided any inquiry into the so-called "adequacy of consideration" or, better put, the relative values exchanged, except where they sit as courts of equity and the values are grossly disproportionate. As a practical matter, courts cannot afford to deal with the plethora of claims that would be assessed because of an alleged unfair bargain, and the problems of determining whether a particular price was "excessive" may appear overwhelming. Sharp increases in price, alone, will not permit a court to condemn a contract or clause as unconscionable since these risks are obviously assumed at the time the contract is formed.[51] Yet, where there is a gross disproportion between price and value accompanied by some manifestation of overreaching,[52] particularly where the buyer is at a bargaining disadvantage because of illiteracy, unfamiliarity with the language or sharp practices by the seller's representative, courts have found such contracts unconscionable.[53]

The successful use of unconscionability to strike down a contract or clause typically involves a consumer buyer. The consumer is obviously unaware of the legal effect of clauses disclaiming warranties or limiting remedies and, therefore, almost invariably lacks apparent assent. The analysis of a typical consumer case may justifiably end at this point, i.e., there is no need to pursue the lack of genuine assent on the basis that the consumer also had no choice. Courts, however, almost invariably proceed to consider the no choice element as well.[54] With respect to merchants, it is more than difficult to establish the lack of apparent assent, i.e., the element of "unfair surprise." If, for example, a public utility agrees to purchase a generator and signs the manufacturer's contract containing a clause excluding consequential damages, the parties will be viewed as sophisticated corporations who were fully aware of the terms of the agreement.[55] Even if the buyer is relatively small, if he is knowledgeable about business and the law, courts will be loathe to find any unfair

---

[51] See Kerr-McGee Corp. v. Northern Utils., Inc., 673 F.2d 323 (10th Cir. 1982).

[52] In Davis v. Kolb, 263 Ark. 158, 563 S.W.2d 438 (1978), the contract price obtained by the buyer was based on a valuation less than half of the real value and there was evidence that the buyer misrepresented his experience and knowledge, invested no capital and assumed no risk, the court set aside the deed as unconscionable.

[53] See Frostifresh Corp. v. Reynoso, supra note 47; Kugler v. Romain, 58 N.J. 522, 279 A.2d 640 (1971); American Home Imp., Inc. v. MacIver, 105 N.H. 435, 201 A.2d 886 (1964); Jones v. Star Credit Corp., 59 Misc. 2d 189, 298 N.Y.S.2d 264 (1969); Central Budget Corp. v. Sanchez, 53 Misc. 2d 620, 279 N.Y.S.2d 391 (1967); Toker v. Westerman, 113 N.J. Super. 452, 274 A.2d 78 (1970).

[54] The classic illustration is the famous Williams case, supra note 41. Mrs. Williams was obviously unaware of the drastic "add-on" provision in the writing and would be "unfairly surprised" by such a clause.

[55] Potomac Elec. Power Co. v. Westinghouse Elec. Corp., 385 F. Supp. 572 (D. D.C. 1974). See also FMC Fin. Corp. v. Murphee, 632 F.2d 413 (5th Cir. 1980); Geldermann & Co. v. Lane Processing, Inc., 527 F.2d 571 (8th Cir. 1975); Royal Indem. Co. v. Westinghouse Elec. Corp., 385 F. Supp. 520 (S.D.N.Y. 1974); W. L. May Co. v. Philco-Ford Corp., 273 Or. 701, 543 P.2d 283 (1975). See, however, Salt River Project Agrl. Dist. v. Westinghouse Elec. Corp., 143 Ariz. 368, 694 P.2d 198, 214 (1984): "There is no doubt that SRP and Westinghouse are both commercial 'giants' and bargained for the LMC in a commercial setting. However, comparability of size among corporations does not mean, as a matter of law, that in a particular transaction a corporation has bargaining strength relatively equal to all other corporations of similar size. Much depends on the nature of the transaction, the nature of the product, the relative knowledge of the parties concerning the product and the availability of other products to fit the needs of the purchaser."

surprise.[56] Where, however, the buyer is a technical merchant because he is in business, but his business and educational background is no greater than that of a consumer and the seller knows or reasonably should be aware of that fact, courts treat such a buyer, in effect, as a consumer and are willing to find a lack of apparent assent.[57] The lack of genuine assent, however, is, at least, a theoretical basis for a finding of unconscionability even in the case of knowledgeable and experienced merchants. The few merchant cases holding a clause to be unconscionable on the basis of no choice involve franchisees where courts have been willing to discover unconscionability on the footing that the dealer has no choice but to sign a renewal contract containing an unfair clause.[58] These cases are based on the inherent unfairness of such clauses and the obvious lack of any bargaining power on the part of the dealer. Where a buyer is a substantial corporation, however, it is difficult for courts to believe that such a buyer is in a substantially inferior bargaining position.[59] For such a buyer to establish that it had no choice but to assent to a material, risk shifting clause, it would have to demonstrate that it could not purchase the product elsewhere absent such a clause or that the seller was the sole supplier of such a product. Moreover, the buyer would have to produce evidence that it made significant efforts to have the clause removed from the writing before it was executed. With such evidence, it is conceivable that a court would find the provision unconscionable. The fact is, however, that corporate buyers may see no point in such negotiations or attempts to purchase the product elsewhere without such a clause because such efforts may appear to be useless gestures.[60] It would require considerable foresight and care to pursue such negotiations. The possibility exists, however, that courts would consider such evidence as sufficient to discover no choice unconscionability if the evidence were clear and convincing.

e. Unconscionability Notwithstanding Adherence to Uniform Commercial Code Formulas — "Failure of Essential Purpose."

One of the intriguing questions causing controversy among scholars and courts is whether a clause that meets the requirements of the UCC to disclaim warranties or limit or exclude certain remedies may still be declared uncon-

---

[56] K & C Inc. v. Westinghouse Elec. Corp., 437 Pa. 303, 263 A.2d 390 (1970) (clause excluding consequential damages where the buyers were an attorney and experienced business man).

[57] See, e.g., Johnson v. Mobil Oil Corp., 415 F. Supp. 264 (E.D. Mich. 1976); Weaver v. American Oil Co., 276 N.E.2d 144 (Ind. 1971).

[58] See, e.g., Shell Oil Co. v. Marinello, 63 N.J. 402, 307 A.2d 598 (1973), cert. denied, 415 U.S. 920 (1974) (clause giving Shell absolute right to terminate on ten days notice was unenforceable). Accord Ashland Oil v. Donahue, 223 S.E.2d 433 (W. Va. 1976). Other courts, however, have been unsympathetic to this view. See, e.g., Zapatha v. Dairy Mart, Inc., 408 N.E.2d 1370 (Mass. 1980); Corenswet, Inc. v. Amana Refrig., 594 F.2d 129 (5th Cir. 1979).

[59] See, however, the quotation from the Salt River Project case supra note 55.

[60] In Potomac Elec. Power Co. v. Westinghouse Elec. Corp., 385 F. Supp. 572, 579 (D.D.C. 1974), the court states that the buyer failed to show that it was precluded from contracting with a competing domestic manufacturer or a foreign manufacturer. Nor did the buyer show that it was a reluctant or unwilling purchaser forced to yield to the seller's allegedly onerous terms. If such a buyer had made efforts to have one or more clauses removed from the seller's draft and had also attempted to contract with other manufacturers whose documents contained similar or identical clauses, the court appears to suggest that it would consider such evidence as evidence of the lack of genuine assent, i.e., no choice unconscionability.

scionable. The Code insists upon certain safeguards as prerequisites to an effective disclaimer of implied warranties. Thus, a written disclaimer must be conspicuous and, with respect to the implied warranty of merchantability must include the term, "merchantability,"[61] or use language that would clearly indicate the disclaimer like "as is" or "with all faults."[62] If a seller's clause adheres to these formalistic requirements, can such a disclaimer still be attacked on the ground of unconscionability? The scholarly debate considers the language of the UCC disclaimer of warranty section and other sections as well as comments and cross references to the unconscionability section. The prevailing scholarly view is that a disclaimer that meets UCC requirements may still be unconscionable[63] and a growing body of case law supports this view.[64] To strip a contract of the basic protection provided by the implied warranty of merchantability which essentially requires only that the goods be fit for the ordinary purposes of such goods[65] is a major deviation from the presumed factual bargain of the parties. Thus, the drafters of the section disclaiming such warranties were eager to assure threshold safeguards of a formalistic nature. If these safeguards are not met, it might safely be suggested that the disclaimer is unconscionable *per se* because it does not allow for minimal apparent assent. A comment to the UCC disclaimer section suggests its purpose:

"It seeks to protect a buyer from unexpected and unbargained language by denying effect to such language ... and permitting the exclusion of implied warranties only by conspicuous language or other circumstances which protect the buyer from surprise."[66]

The purpose is clearly one of preserving apparent assent. If, however, the buyer is aware of disclaimer language at the time he manifests assent, he may still have no choice but to agree to this language. Thus, to preclude the possibility of finding such a clause unconscionable simply because it meets formalistic safeguards would excise the possibility of discovering unconscionability on one of its two principal bases, i.e., the contract of adhesion or no choice

---

[61] UCC § 2-316(2).

[62] UCC § 2-316(3)(a). Implied warranties may also be disclaimed through pre-contract inspections of the product or refusals to inspect under § 2-316(3)(b), and trade usage or prior course of dealing under § 2-316(3)(c).

[63] Professor Leff was the principal advocate for the view that a disclaimer meeting UCC requirements could not be attacked on the footing that it was unconscionable. Leff, *Unconscionability and the Code: the Emperor's New Clause*, 115 U. PA. L. REV. 485, 523-24 (1967). In response, *see* Murray, *Unconscionability: Unconscionability*, 31 U. PITT. L. REV. 1, 45-49 (1969) suggesting the contrary view. In general, other scholars reach the same conclusion as Murray. *See, e.g.,* Ellinghaus, *In Defense of Unconscionability*, 78 YALE L.J. 757, 798-803 (1969); R. DUESENBERG & L. KING, SALES AND BULK TRANSFERS UNDER THE U.C.C., § 7.03[2] (1980). In their well-known treatise, THE UNIFORM COMMERCIAL CODE § 12-11 (2d ed. 1980), Professors White & Summers disagree. Professor White believes that a disclaimer clause adhering to UCC requirements should not be susceptible to a finding of unconscionability, while Professor Summers takes the opposite view. Professor Farnsworth concludes that the view permitting an unconscionability attack on a clause meeting UCC requirements is "sounder." E.A. FARNSWORTH, CONTRACTS § 429 (1982).

[64] *See, e.g.,* Martin v. Joseph Harris Co., 767 F.2d 296 (6th Cir. 1985); Barco Auto Leasing Corp. v. PSI Cosmetics, Inc., 125 Misc. 2d 68, 478 N.Y.S.2d 505 (1984); A & M Produce Co. v. FMC Corp., 135 Cal. App. 3d 472, 186 Cal. Rptr. 114 (1982); Hahn v. Ford Motor Co., 434 N.E.2d 943 (Ind. App. 1982). *See also* Schroeder v. Faegol Motors, Inc., 80 Wash. 2d 256, 544 P.2d 20 (1975).

[65] UCC § 2-314(2)(c) which is one of six descriptive criteria of the implied warranty of merchantability though it is often viewed as the fundamental criterion.

[66] UCC § 2-316 comment 1.

unconscionability precluding genuine assent. Moreover, there is still the question of whether a reasonable buyer would have understood the import of a clause disclaiming implied warranties even though the clause met the threshold safeguards of the Code. Thus, even apparent assent may be absent, notwithstanding compliance with the safeguards.

The Code expressly permits the parties to agree that the seller will not be held liable for consequential damages in the event of a breach. This section, however, expressly precludes enforcement of such clauses if they are unconscionable and, with respect to consequential damages for personal injury, such a clause is prima facie unconscionable.[67] There is no express requirement that such clauses be conspicuous and most courts have read the statute literally.[68] Conspicuousness, however, may be a factor in determining whether an exclusionary clause is unconscionable.[69] There is also no question that such clauses are necessarily subject to the overriding requirement that they be conscionable,[70] and unconscionability may be found even though the loss suffered is not a bodily injury.[71]

The UCC expressly permits parties to limit remedies under their contract for the sale of goods to repair or replacement of defective parts, but this limitation is subject to the section limiting consequential damages exculpation to those which are conscionable.[72] If there is no unconscionability in such a clause at the time of contract formation, subsequent events may still leave the buyer remediless. Thus, if the seller fails to perform its warranty of repair or replacement,[73] fails to perform within a reasonable time,[74] or will not or cannot repair the product,[75] the repair and replacement remedy which substitutes for the buyer's normal UCC remedies is worthless. In this situation, another UCC provision becomes operative:

"Where circumstances cause an exclusive or limited remedy to fail of its essential purpose, remedy may be had as provided in this Act."[76]

While "failure of essential purpose" is distinct from unconscionability since it deals with events arising after contract formation where the contract, as formed, was conscionable, a court may fail to make this distinction in deciding that the remedy fails of its essential purpose as of the moment of formation.[77]

---

[67] UCC § 2-719(3).

[68] Cases holding that no conspicuous requirement be read into UCC § 2-719 include Xerox Corp. v. Hawkes, 124 N.H. 610, 475 A.2d 7, 11 (1984); Flinkote Co. v. W.W. Wilkinson, Inc., 220 Va. 571, 260 S.E.2d 229 (1979); Collins Radio Co. of Dallas v. Bell, 623 P.2d 1039 (Okla. App. 1980). For a contrary view, see Avenell v. Westinghouse Elec. Corp., 41 Ohio App. 2d 150, 324 N.E.2d 583 (1974).

[69] See Schroeder v. Faegol Motors, Inc., 86 Wash. 2d 256, 544 P.2d 20, 23-24 (1975).

[70] See, e.g., A & M Produce Co. v. FMC Corp., 135 Cal. App. 3d 473, 186 Cal. Rptr. 114 (1982).

[71] Gladden v. Cadillac Motor Car Div., 83 N.J. 320, 416 A.2d 394 (1980).

[72] UCC § 2-719(1)(a).

[73] See Waters v. Massey-Ferguson, Inc., 775 F.2d 587 (4th Cir. 1985); Adams v. J. I. Case Co., 125 Ill. App. 2d 388, 261 N.E.2d 1 (1970).

[74] See Jones & McKnight Corp. v. Birdsboro Corp., 320 F. Supp. 39 (N.D. Ill. 1970).

[75] See Clark v. International Harvester Co., 99 Idaho 321, 581 P.2d 784 (1978); S. M. Wilson & Co. v. Smith Int'l, Inc., 587 F.2d 1363 (9th Cir. 1978).

[76] UCC § 2-719(2). For an analysis of this concept, see Eddy, On the "Essential" Purposes of Limited Remedies: The Metaphysics of U.C.C. Section 2-719(2), 65 CALIF. L. REV. 28 (1977). See also Anderson, Failure of Essential Purpose and Essential Failure of Purpose: A Look at Section 2-719 of the Uniform Commercial Code, 31 SW. L.J. 759 (1977).

[77] Wilson Trading Corp. v. David Ferguson, Ltd., 297 N.Y.S.2d 108, 244 N.E.2d 685 (1968) (clause stated that seller would not be liable for any claims relating to the quality or shade of

The analysis is unsound. If a court believes that the exclusive remedy is virtually worthless *ab initio,* i.e., at the time the contract is formed, the appropriate analysis might involve unconscionability or another UCC concept.[78]

Another problem of overlap between "failure of essential purpose" and unconscionability is also evident in the case law. As the "failure of essential purpose" section of the Code suggests, where the exclusive remedy fails, other Code remedies then become available.[79] The application of this device raises the question of whether *all* such Code remedies then become available, i.e., whether consequential damages as well as direct damages become available, or whether the failure of the exclusive remedy leaves the exclusion of consequential damages provision intact while providing the buyer with direct damages for breach of warranty,[80] cover,[81] or the difference between the contract price and market price at the time the buyer learned of the breach.[82] If failure of essential purpose and unconscionability are considered mutually exclusive, once failure of essential purpose is discovered, the exclusive remedy provision of the contract, including the exclusion of consequential damages, may be viewed as totally inoperative and the buyer may recover consequential damages.[83] On the other hand, where failure of essential purpose is found, if the clause excluding consequential damages is not unconscionable, a court may find that portion of the exclusive remedy clause retains is operative effect.[84] Even where a court allows consequential damages after finding failure of essential purpose, that determination may suggest the flavor of unconscionability, i.e., the court may have been influenced by a significant disparity in bargaining power between the parties.[85]

§ 97. Standardized Agreements (Printed Forms).

A. *The Basic Problem and* RESTATEMENT *2d Approach.*

No set of problems in modern contract law may be more perplexing than those associated with the massive use of standardized, printed ("pad") forms to evidence the contract.[86] One authority suggests that standard forms are prob-

---

yarn made after processing or more than ten days after receipt of the yarn by the purchaser. The buyer alleged a defect that could not have been discovered until after processing and washing. *Held:* the time provision eliminated all remedy for defects not discoverable before processing and the remedy, therefore, failed of its essential purpose).

[78] In Clark v. Int'l Harvester, *supra* note 75, the court suggests that it agreed with the concurring opinion in *Wilson, id.,* to the effect that the analysis should have been predicated on whether the time limitation in that contract was manifestly unreasonable under UCC § 1-204. The court also suggests agreement with J. WHITE & R. SUMMERS, THE UNIFORM COMMERCIAL CODE § 12-10 at 381 who suggest the possibility of an unconscionability analysis.

[79] UCC § 2-719(2).

[80] *See* UCC § 2-714 which measures the damages by the difference in the value received and the value that should have been received.

[81] UCC § 2-712, i.e., the difference between the contract price and the substitute purchase price.

[82] UCC § 2-713.

[83] *See* Caterpillar Tractor Co. v. Waterson, 13 Ark. App. 77, 679 S.W.2d 814 (1984).

[84] *See, e.g.,* Carboline Co. v. Oxmoor Center, 40 UCC Rep. 1728 (Ky. App. 1985); American Elec. Power Co. v. Westinghouse Corp., 418 F. Supp. 435 (S.D.N.Y. 1976).

[85] *See* Clark v. International Harvester, *supra* note 75, (contract between a custom farmer and large corporation).

[86] This section is based upon Murray, *The Standardized Agreement Phenomena in the Restatement (Second) of Contracts,* 67 CORNELL L. REV. 735 (1982) (hereinafter *Standardized Agreement.*)

ably the evidence of the contract in up to ninety-nine percent of all contracts.[87] Among the plethora of problems associated with the use of standard forms, the basic problem may be stated rather simply: Since virtually no one (consumer or merchant) bothers to read the printed clauses of forms in regular use, is the non-drafting party bound by all of the terms contained in the form? One response to this question is predicated on the stability and security of transactions, i.e., one is bound by the terms of the form whether he reads it or not. This may be called the "flagellant" view, i.e., a party who later complains that he failed to read the form is told to live with the consequences of that failure in the hope that he will never sin again. This view is unrealistic as demonstrated by the continuing failure of consumers and merchants to read the boilerplate provisions of standardized forms. There have always been exceptions to the prescription that one is bound to a particular document whether he reads it or not. One of the obvious exceptions is found in holdings that some documents cannot reasonably be viewed as contractual, *e.g.*, receipts, parcel checks, invoices, and the like.[88] Another exception occurs when the printed form is signed by a party under duress or misrepresentation as discussed in the previous section of this book.[89] In another section, we also saw numerous cases holding printed clauses unconscionable.[90] There are so many unconscionability cases involving printed forms that some courts mistakenly list the printed form as one of the prerequisites to a finding of unconscionability.[91] There can be no question of the substantial intersection between the problem of whether one is bound by particular printed clauses and the concept of unconscionability. Much earlier in this volume we explored the maze of problems connected with the exchange of printed forms that do not match, the "battle of the forms."[92] The fundamental tenet of that radical UCC solution to the "battle of the forms" is that merchants do not read or understand their own printed forms, much less those received from the other party.[93] Certain provisions in such forms are not binding because they would result in "surprise or hardship" to the party against whom they are designed to operate.[94] The critical comment to the unconscionability section of the Code speaks in

---

[87] Slawson, *Standard Form Contracts and Democratic Control of Lawmaking Power*, 84 HARV. L. REV. 529 (1971).

[88] Culbreth v. Simone, 511 F. Supp. 906 (E.D. Pa. 1981) (condition on money order did not become part of the contract); Birmingham T.V. Corp. v. Water Works, 292 Ala. 147, 290 So. 2d 636 (1974) (term on back of warehouse receipt not part of contract); Goldstein v. Harris, 24 Ala. App. 3, 130 So. 313 (term on storage receipt for coat not binding on bailor); Iowa-Missouri Walnut Co. v. Grahl, 237 Mo. App. 1093, 170 S.W.2d 437 (1943) (term on back of check did not become part of contract); Charles v. Charles, 478 S.W.2d 133 (Tex. 1972) (written statement on back of promissory note not part of contract); Green's Ex'rs v. Smith, 146 Va. 442, 131 S.E. 846 (1926) (terms on circulars enclosed with monthly bills under the contract did not become part of contract).

[89] *See, e.g.*, United States v. 1,557.28 Acres of Land, 486 F.2d 445 (10th Cir. 1973); Laemmar v. J. Walter Thompson Co., 435 F.2d 680 (7th Cir. 1970); College Watercolor Group, Inc. v. William H. Newbauer, Inc., 468 Pa. 103, 360 A.2d 200 (1976); Allen-Parker Co. v. Lollis, 257 S.C. 266, 185 S.E.2d 739 (1971).

[90] *See supra* § 96.

[91] *See* § 96(B)(2)(b), *supra* note 16.

[92] *See* the discussion of the "Battle of the Forms" *supra* Chapter 2, §§ 49 and 50.

[93] *See* Murray, *The Chaos of the Battle of the Forms: Solutions*, 39 VAND. L. REV. 1307, 1317 at note 47. *See also Standardized Agreement, supra* note 86, at 778-79, n.207.

[94] *See* UCC § 2-207 comment 4.

terms of avoiding "oppression" and "unfair surprise."[95] The relationship between these sections may be seen as the "battle of the forms" section, 2-207, precluding certain printed provisions from becoming operative, *ab initio*, while the unconscionability section, 2-302, is designed to permit courts to exercise certain terms that manifest apparent assent. Thus, § 2-207 may be seen as a form of unconscionability, i.e., "incipient unconscionability."[96] If there is no exchange of forms and, therefore, no "battle of the forms" because only one form is signed or adopted as evidence of the contract by both parties, the problem of the enforceability of unread, printed, provisions remains. The UCC did not address this problem directly. The FIRST RESTATEMENT had ignored it,[97] but the RESTATEMENT 2d confronted it. Unfortunately, the results of that confrontation are less than satisfactory.

The new section on Standardized Agreements is disconcertingly included in that part of the RESTATEMENT 2d captioned, "Effects of Adopting a Writing,"[98] which deals with integrated agreements and other parol evidence rule problems. The first subsection of the new section is faithful to the FIRST RESTATEMENT view that one is bound by what he signs or adopts as evidence of the contract:

> Except as stated in Subsection (3), where a party to an agreement signs or otherwise manifests assent to a writing and has reason to believe that like writings are regularly used to embody terms of agreements of the same type, he adopts the writing as an integrated agreement with respect to the terms included in the writing.[99]

The Reporter intended this subsection to do nothing more than restate the obvious.[1] If the intention was to bind a party to the terms of a standardized writing to which he assented but did not read, that intention is faithful to the same concept in the FIRST RESTATEMENT[2] which did not refer to "integration." The new section need not have referred to integration to make this point since the central problem is not whether a standardized document is the final or complete manifestation of agreement. The problem is whether all of the printed terms contained in such a document are operative and, if not, what is the test to determine whether one or more printed terms shall be inoperative? Since § 211(1) is expressly subject to subsection (3), it is important to consider that subsection: "Where the other party has reason to believe that the party manifesting such assent would not do so if he knew that the writing contained a particular term, the term is not part of the agreement."[3]

---

[95] UCC § 2-302 comment 1.

[96] *See* Murray, *Section 2-207 of the Uniform Commercial Code: Another Word About Incipient Unconscionability*, 39 U. PITT. L. REV. 597 (1978).

[97] The FIRST RESTATEMENT § 70, took the uncompromising position that, absent fraud, duress, or mistake, one is bound by what he signs or adopts as the written evidence of the contract although he is ignorant of the terms of the writing or the proper interpretation of those terms.

[98] Chapter 9, Topic 3 of the RESTATEMENT 2d.

[99] RESTATEMENT 2d § 211(1).

[1] "I stated first a rather reactionary proposition, which is subsection (1); that is, that when you agree to a standard agreement, you agree to it, and that means everything that's in it, subject, of course, to qualifying terms." This statement of the original Reporter of the RESTATEMENT 2d, Robert Braucher, is found in 47 ALI Proceedings 524 (1970).

[2] FIRST RESTATEMENT § 70.

[3] RESTATEMENT 2d § 211(3).

When should a party have "reason to believe" that the other party would not have manifested assent if he knew that the writing contained a particular term? The response to this question is found in a comment to the section which states that "reason to believe" may be inferred from the fact that a particular term in the writing is "bizarre or oppressive, from the fact that it eviscerates the non-standard terms explicitly agreed to, or from the fact that it eliminates the dominant purpose of the transaction."[4] If the term is illegible or otherwise hidden, or if the "adhering party" had no opportunity to read the term, the inference is reinforced.[5] The language is more than reminiscent of an unconscionability analysis. Under this RESTATEMENT 2d section, a party should not be bound by a term in a printed form that "unfairly surprises" him. A "bizarre" or oppressive term would be unexpected. The drafters, however, were insistent upon maintaining some loyalty to the fundamental notion that one is bound by what he signs. Thus, if a term is perfectly legible, it cannot be unexpected. If that legible term is allegedly oppressive in some way, the drafters suggest that the question is not within § 211. Rather, it must be considered under the unconscionability section, § 208.[6] It is important to refer, again, to the comment explaining the situations under which a party would have "reason to believe" the other party would not assent to a particular term. The list includes bizarre or oppressive terms as well as terms that "eviscerate the non-standard terms explicitly agreed to" or terms that eliminate "the dominant purpose of the transaction."[7] Certainly the latter terms are necessarily "oppressive." The comment does not suggest that "reason to believe" is predicated upon such terms being illegible or otherwise hidden. Rather, it suggests that the inference is *reinforced* if the terms are hidden or if the *adhering* party never had an opportunity to read them.[8] Thus, the comment would suggest that a bizarre or oppressive term may be deemed inoperative because one party had reason to believe that the other party would not assent to such term, and if such term were hidden, etc., it is more likely that such term will be deemed inoperative. The comment, therefore, is indistinguishable from an unconscionability analysis, i.e., an oppressive term, even if known at the time of formation by the party against whom it is to operate, may be unconscionable because the *adhering* party had no choice. If the oppressive term is also illegible or otherwise hidden, *a fortiori,* it is unconscionable. But again, the drafters, though recognizing a significant relationship between the unconscionability section and the standardized agreement section, intended to limit the scope of the latter to terms that were not only oppressive but were also hidden, i.e., they emphasize unfair surprise. This irreconcilability as well as other confusion[9] does not augur an effective judi-

---

[4] RESTATEMENT 2d § 211 comment f.

[5] *Id.*

[6] *See Standardized Agreement, supra* note 86, at 766-67.

[7] RESTATEMENT 2d § 211 comment f.

[8] *Id.*

[9] RESTATEMENT 2d § 211(2) states that a standardized writing "is interpreted wherever reasonable as treating alike all those similarly situated, without regard to their knowledge or understanding of the standard terms of the writing." The standard is explained as treating the party who signs or otherwise assents to the printed document as "the average member of the community who is likely to use this kind of agreement." 47 ALI Proceedings 524-25 (1970). As suggested in *Standardized Agreement, supra* note 86 at 774: "This immediately raises the question: Should

cial analysis based upon the new section on standardized agreements. The *seeds* of an effective analysis, however, are discoverable in the new RESTATE-MENT effort.

B. *The "Reasonable Expectation" Test.*

Certain comment language accompanying new § 211 is particularly significant: "Although customers typically adhere to standardized agreements and are bound by them without even appearing to know the standard terms in detail, they are not bound to unknown terms which are beyond the range of *reasonable expectation.*"[10]

If the drafters had concentrated on this underlying principle rather than simply having it appear in a comment, it would have heralded a significant development in the analysis of the legal effect of standardized agreements. If only one printed form serves as the evidence of the actual or purported assent of the parties, the principle may be elaborated as follows: The parties are bound by those terms in a printed form that they reasonably expect that form to contain, regardless of what the form contains. Thus, if the form contains unexpected, materially risk-shifting terms, the signing party is not bound to such terms. If the form does not contain expected terms, the party is bound to such expected terms that do not appear in the form.[11] This concept may be called the "reasonable expectation" test which had its origins in a line of insurance cases. Since the modern judicial notion of a "contract of adhesion" was first detected in cases involving insurance contracts which may be viewed as the quintessence of "take-it-or-leave-it" contracts,[12] it is anything but remarkable that the "reasonable expectation" concept would appear initially in

---

one's education, experience, or particular knowledge of the printed form be a factor in determining the operative effect of one or more printed terms? In dealing with the meaning of "reason to believe" in subsection (3), the Reporter emphasized that it is an objective standard requiring the exercise of reasonable judgment in light of the facts available to the party whose "reason to believe" is at issue. If a seller submits a printed form to a customer who is knowledgeable and sophisticated regarding such forms, the seller may very well have reason to believe that such a customer is aware of certain clauses in the form. If that customer assents with presumed knowledge of these clauses, the seller would then have reason to believe that the buyer intended to assent to them. Yet, the comment attempting to explain section 211(2) states: '[C]ourts in construing and applying a standardized contract seek to effectuate the reasonable expectations of the average member of the public who accepts it. The result may be to give the advantage of a restrictive reading to some sophisticated customers who contracted with knowledge of the ambiguity or dispute.'" [§ 211, comment e.]

[10] RESTATEMENT 2d § 211 comment f. (emphasis added).

[11] In the discussion of RESTATEMENT 2d § 211 by members of the American Law Institute, this concept is developed in the following colloquy:

Judge Conford [N.J.]: I'm not sure whether the formulation by Mr. Willard [who was one of the principals involved in formulating the language of § 211] would cover both the situations of the signing party or the assenting party assuming that a provision was in as well as an assumption that the assenting party assumed that a provision was out. In other words, would it cover both? I think it should cover both.

Professor Braucher: I think I need Mr. Willard's help on this. I think we mean to cover both, but I think the language does not quite cover both.

Mr. Willard: I think that's correct, Mr. Reporter, and if a form of words can be found to say it both ways, that seems to me to be appropriate. 47 ALI Proceedings 526 (1970).

[12] *See* Patterson, *The Delivery of a Life Insurance Policy,* 33 HARV. L. REV. 198, 222 (1919).

such cases.[13] The most recent comprehensive application of this concept in an insurance policy context is from the Supreme Court of Arizona which relies upon the reasonable expectation test as well as the new RESTATEMENT section.[14] Though judicial applications are typically found in insurance contract contexts, as Professor W. David Slawson suggests, it is now found in other contexts as well.[15]

A reasonable expectation test is a logical extension of the underlying philosophy of the UCC which insists on an identification of the "bargain-in-fact" of the parties.[16] The operative agreement should not be the document with unread printed terms unless those terms are in accordance with the reasonable expectations of the parties. Such reasonably expected terms should become the terms of the contract because they are reasonably expected, not because they are part of the unread boilerplate. The use of the test in traditional contracting could be the basis for achieving the goal of Article 2 of the Code, i.e., a more precise and fair identification of the actual or presumed assent of the parties, a goal that can be deciphered from the vagaries of at least comment language in the Second Restatement as well. With the development of electronic message systems,[17] difficult questions arise concerning fun-

---

[13] See Keeton, *Insurance Law Rights at Variance with Policy Provisions,* 83 HARV. L. REV. 961 (1970) where Professor (now Judge) Keeton suggested that eight jurisdictions adopted the "reasonable expectation" concept with regard to insurance contracts. In his treatise on Insurance Law, the same author suggests that the doctrine of reasonable expectations finds courts refusing to enforce insurance policies to the extent that they conflict with the reasonable expectations of the insured unless such conflicting terms are clear and conspicuous. *See* KEETON, BASIC TEXT ON INSURANCE LAW 350-61 (1971).

[14] Darner Motor Sales, Inc. v. Universal Underwriters Ins. Co., 682 P.2d 388 (Ariz. 1984) (policy limited coverage to $15,000 on an auto liability claim though insurer had created reasonable expectations of coverage of $100,000).

[15] Slawson, *The New Meaning of Contract: The Transformation of Contracts Law by Standard Forms,* 46 U. PITT. L. REV. 21 (1984). Professor Slawson is the dominant scholarly influence suggesting the development of the "reasonable expectation" test beyond insurance contracts. He points out that it was proposed by three of the nine members of the Iowa Supreme Court in C & J Fertilizer Inc. v. Allied Mut. Ins. Co., 227 N.W.2d 169, 182 (Iowa 1975), a majority of the Rhode Island Supreme Court adopted it in Elliot Leases Cars, Inc v. Quigley, 373 A.2d 810, 811 (R.I. 1977), and then a majority of the Iowa court accepted it in Farm Bur. Mut. Ins. Co. v. Sandbutte, 302 N.W.2d 104 (Iowa 1981). Beyond these supreme court adoptions, he suggests that, "[A]nywhere from four to twelve state courts, depending upon how their decisions are interpreted, have accepted a new version of the reasonable-expectations doctrine, which is tantamount to the new meaning of contract, except that it applies only to insurance. In addition, the new meaning has been effectively adopted by several state and federal courts as an interpretation of Section 2-207 ... of the Uniform Commercial Code. I say 'effectively adopted' because the new meaning of contract and only the new meaning of contract provides a logical rationale for what these courts have done. The opinions, however, deal only with the provisions of the Code. The Restatement (Second) of Contracts published in 1981 evidences no awareness of the new meaning." *Id.* at 30-31. Professor Slawson apparently sees no merit in the RESTATEMENT 2d comment language quoted in the text at *supra* note 10. That language does suggest some awareness of the reasonable expectation concept though, again, its appearance only in a comment is more than unfortunate since it states the only meaningful analysis of standardized agreements. *See Standardized Agreement, supra* note 86, at 780-81: "If a principle underlies the plethora of problems involving the standardized printed form, that principle is scattered throughout the *Restatement Second....* [T]he most important statement in section 211 is the statement in the comment that a party should not be bound "to unknown terms which are beyond the range of reasonable expectation."

[16] "Agreement" is defined in terms of the factual bargain of the parties in § 1-201(3) of the UCC. For an elaboration of this view, see *Standardized Agreement, supra* note 86, at 741-44.

[17] Electronic message systems are computer-based telecommunications systems that incorporate various technologies, *e.g.,* electronic mail (Email), electronic mailbox (Emailbox), electronic data interchange (EDI, which is a computer application of inter-company electronic interchange

damental contracts concepts including the identification and operative effect of the "standard" terms of the deal. The accelerated evolution of the reasonable expectation test could provide a basis for solving numerous problems which the new technology will inevitably bring.

§ 98. Contracts Against Public Policy — "Illegal Bargains."

A. *General Principles.*

Like any other freedom, freedom of contract is circumscribed by overriding policies. If a statute or other governmental regulation prohibits the enforcement of an agreement, courts will not enforce it, notwithstanding the presence of all the requirements for an enforceable agreement. Even if a statutory policy or judicially created policy is silent with respect to agreements violating that policy, courts will refuse to lend aid to their enforcement. If a court discovers an overriding interest of society that is incongruous with the enforcement of an agreement, it will refuse to enforce it. There are two fundamental reasons for such court action: (a) deterrence of undesirable conduct and (b) the great reluctance of courts to become involved in suggesting any justification for an unsavory transaction.[18] If an agreement is prohibited by statute, there is considerable certainty as to the policy reason for refusing its enforcement. Considerable uncertainty, however, may attend a decision to refuse enforcement because the agreement is contrary to "public policy." The "unruly horse"[19] called "public policy" is difficult to describe, much less define. Certain types of conduct are so outrageous that they may be viewed as contrary to public policy, *per se.* Thus, an agreement to commit a crime[20] or a tort[21] as well as a promise to breach a fiduciary duty[22] has no redeeming virtue and is obviously contrary to public policy. Where, however, the agreement does not involve a commitment to pursue such outrageous conduct, the lines become wavering and blurred. This is because the very idea of "public policy" is predicated upon a "community common sense and common conscience ... applied ... to matters of public morals, public health, public safety, public welfare, and the like. It is that general and well-settled public opinion relating to man's plain, palpable duty to his fellow men, having due regard to

---

of business transactions such as purchase orders, invoices, shipping documents, etc.), Facsimile (FAX, which is a real time "instantaneous" system for transmission of text and graphical hard copy), telex, voice mail, and other devices.

[18] *See* RESTATEMENT 2d, Introductory Note to Chapter 8, Unenforceability on Grounds of Public Policy, §§ 178-199.

[19] *See* the famous dictum of Judge Burrough in Richardson v. Mellish, 2 Bing. 229, 252, 130 Eng. Rep. 294, 303 (1824) where the opinion suggests that public policy is "a very unruly horse, and when once you get astride it you never know where it will carry you. It may lead you from the sound law. It is never argued at all but when other points fail."

[20] *See, e.g.,* State v. Grimes, 85 Or. App. 159, 735 P.2d 1277, 1278 (1987) (Or. Rev. Stat. § 167.007(1)(a) makes it a Class A misdemeanor to engage in sexual conduct for a fee. An agreement to do so would on its face be an illegal contract and would, therefore, be unenforceable.). An agreement immunizing a party from criminal prosecution in exchange for cooperation with authorities, is, however, enforceable. *See, e.g.,* Zani v. State, 657 S.W.2d 196 (Tex. App. 1983) (agreement that would have been enforceable was unenforceable because defendant lied).

[21] *See* RESTATEMENT 2d § 192.

[22] *See* RESTATEMENT 2d § 193.

all the circumstances of each particular relation and situation."[23] In an era of relativism where any notion of objective moral standards is often viewed with disdain, it may be particularly difficult for a court to provide a satisfactory basis for its holding that a certain agreement is contrary to "public morals" or that it is in accordance with "well-settled public opinion" which is often anything but well-settled. We have also known for a considerable time that these standards are not only difficult to identify in general, but change over time.[24] In what may be characterized as a "future shock" society, such changes often occur at a highly accelerated pace. Judges of the past would undoubtedly be surprised, if not shocked, by decisions we will explore later in this section. Thus, we will see decisions upholding agreements between unmarried cohabitants, decisions enforcing wagering contracts, decisions upholding clauses exculpating a party from his own negligence and numerous other changes in precedent that allegedly reflect the changing mores of our society.

Complete volumes can be devoted to the great spectrum of problems found in agreements allegedly violating one or more standards of public policy. Within the space constraints of this volume, we will focus upon those clusters of cases that have dealt with particular problems in this area over many years — problems that continue to inspire litigation. An exploration of these cases will not only provide necessary comprehension of these developed areas; it will also provide a sense of how courts attempt to deal with the necessary flexibility of an amorphous concept.

It has become common to characterize the problems in this area as problems of "illegal bargains." While a particular bargain or agreement may be illegal, in large measure the kinds of agreements dealt with by courts under the rubric, "illegal bargains," are not technically illegal, i.e., courts will simply refuse to enforce them because they violate one or more standards of public policy rather than any statute containing criminal sanctions. For the most part, therefore, we will avoid the use of the phrase, "illegal bargain" except when it is accurately used, for example, as in a conspiracy under a criminal statute that would be an illegal bargain between or among the conspirators.

B. *Agreements Exculpating a Party From Tort Liability — Indemnity — Strict Liability.*

Standards of conduct requiring all members of society to avoid creation of unreasonable risks are imposed under the law of torts. Agreements to exempt a party from creating such a risk, i.e., to exempt him from tort liability, are not enforceable for intentional or reckless torts.[25] If, however, the tort liability arises from negligence, absent statutory prohibitions,[26] the modern view suggests that a clause exempting the tortfeasor from such liability will be enforceable unless its purpose is to exempt an employer from liability to an

---

[23] McCardie, J. in Naylor, Benzon & Co. v. Krainische Industrie Gesellschaft, 1 K.B. 331 [1881].

[24] "The standard of such policy is not absolutely invariable or fixed, since contracts which at one stage of our civilization may seem to conflict with public interests, at more advanced stages are treated as legal and binding." Brown, J. in Pope Mfg. Co. v. Gormully, 144 U.S. 224, 233 (1892).

[25] *See* RESTATEMENT 2d OF TORTS § 500 and RESTATEMENT 2d § 195(1).

[26] *See, e.g.,* Illinois statutes voiding exculpatory clauses in leases of real property (Ill. Rev. Stat. ch. 80, para. 91 (1985)), construction contracts (para. 61), and bailment agreements (para. 7-204).

employee, or to exculpate one charged with a public service duty (*e.g.,* a common carrier) to one protected by that duty.[27] A related issue concerns indemnity clauses ("hold harmless" clauses) which seek to indemnify a tortfeasor against his own negligence.[28] A majority of courts have rejected the older view that such contracts violate public policy.[29] The widespread use of insurance against such risks is largely responsible for the repudiation of the older view.[30] Again, however, the general rule is subject to the exception that the indemnity clause must not promote a breach of a public duty[31] or breach of a statutory proscription.[32] As in the case of exculpatory clauses generally, an indemnification agreement purporting to indemnify the tortfeasor against intentional torts is against public policy since it can be effective only with respect to unintentional torts and when the agreement is made without any unlawful design.[33] Courts are particularly insistent that any exculpatory clause be clearly stated.[34] Moreover, they will be construed strictly "since they are not favorites of the law."[35]

---

[27]*See* Lohman v. Morris, 146 Ill. App. 3d 457, 497 N.E.2d 143 (1986) (suggesting the general rule that such exculpatory contracts are valid as long as they do not involve a unique relationship such as those between common carrier and passenger or those between employers and employees). *See also* RESTATEMENT 2d § 195(2). *See* Gardner v. Downtown Porsche, 180 Cal. App. 3d 713, 225 Cal. Rptr. 757 (1986), suggesting compliance of California case law with this position but emphasizing that no public interest may be involved nor may any statute expressly prohibit such a clause. Thus, under CAL. CIV. CODE § 1668, an automobile repair garage may not exempt itself from liability, even for ordinary negligence if it provides a service involving the public interest. The court proceeds to suggest six characteristics of the public interest from the opinion in Tunkl v. Regents of Univ. of Cal., 60 Cal. 2d 92, 383 P.2d 441 (1963): (1) it concerns a business of a type generally thought suitable for public regulation; (2) the party seeking exculpation is engaged in performing a service of great importance to the public (as in the *Tunkl* case which struck down exculpatory clauses in hospital admission forms); (3) the party holds himself out as ready to serve any member of the public seeking the service; (4) the party seeking exculpation has a decisive advantage in bargaining power because of the essential nature of the service (again, the hospital); (5) in pursuing that bargaining advantage, the service provider presents the other party with a contract of adhesion; (6) as a result of the service provided, the other party is placed under the control of the provider, subject to the risk of carelessness. The court emphasized the fact that the contract could involve a public service even though every one of these six criteria was not met.
    While exculpatory clauses will not be enforceable in contracts involving common carriers or public utilities, they may be able to limit their liability. For example, *see* the Carmack Amendment, 49 U.S.C. § 20(11), permitting common carriers to limit their liability.

[28]An indemnity clause generally creates an obligation by one party to pay for loss or damage another party has incurred. Rossmoor San., Inc. v. Pylon, Inc., 119 Cal. Rptr. 449, 532 P.2d 97 (1975). A recent illustration is found in Morton Thiokol, Inc. v. Metal Bldg. Alteration Co., 193 Cal. App. 3d 1025, 238 Cal. Rptr. 722 (1987): "Metal Building ... agrees to indemnify and hold harmless the Owner and its agents and employees from any and all liability, loss, damage, cost and expense (including attorney's fees) sustained by reason of Contractor's breach of warranty, breach of contract, misrepresentation or false certification, or failure to exercise due care."

[29]*See* Kuhn v. State of Alaska, 692 P.2d 261 (Alaska 1984).

[30]Manson-Osberg Co. v. State, 552 P.2d 654 (Alaska 1976).

[31]*See, e.g.,* Northwest Airlines, Inc. v. Alaska Airlines, Inc., 351 F.2d 253 (9th Cir. 1965).

[32]*See, e.g.,* GA. CODE ANN. § 13-8-2(b) proscribing indemnification of the promisee against his own negligence in a construction contract as against public policy.

[33]Jacksonville State Bank v. Barnwell, 481 So. 2d 863 (Ala. 1985). *See also* RESTATEMENT 2d § 192 comment.

[34]*See* Singleton v. Crown Central Petr. Corp., 713 S.W.2d 115 (Tex. App. 1986) setting forth a clear and unequivocal test to be applied to an indemnity provision which seeks to absolve the indemnitee from its own negligence. *See also* Pittsburgh S. Co. v. Patterson-Emerson-Comstock, Inc., 171 A.2d 185 (Pa. Super. 1961).

[35]*See* Richard's 5 & 10 v. Brooks Harvey Realty Inv., 399 A.2d 1103, 1105 (Pa. Super. 1979). *See also* Osgood v. Medical Inc., 415 N.W.2d 896 (Minn. App. 1987) (while "negligence" need not be mentioned in an indemnity provision exculpating the indemnitee from his own negligence, the

Strict liability in tort is imposed on sellers of products for defects causing personal injury or economic loss without personal injury.[36] Before this theory saw the light of day, warranty theory was used to provide a strict liability basis for recovery.[37] The case law is scant and unclear as to whether parties may agree to exempt the seller of a defective product for such strict liability. A comment to the products liability section of the RESTATEMENT 2d OF TORTS has been construed by one court to preclude the enforcement of such an exempting clause where the injury was to the product itself and there were no personal injuries.[38] In indistinguishable fact situations, two other courts suggest that such clauses exempting the seller from strict tort liability for injury to the product itself are enforceable where the buyer and seller are business entities of relatively equal bargaining strength.[39] The RESTATEMENT 2d treats such exemption clauses as generally unenforceable, but would permit an exception in the case of a contract between business entities if there were no taint of unconscionability in such an agreement.[40]

C. Contracts in Restraint of Trade.

In a very broad sense, every contract concerning trade is a contract in restraint of trade since the parties to the contract necessarily restrict themselves from future dealings with other parties with respect to the subject matter of the contract.[41] It would, therefore, be absurd to suggest that Anglo-American law ever recognized a principle that *all* contracts in restraint of trade, in the literal sense, were illegal bargains. In the early, immobile society

---

language must otherwise be sufficiently clear to permit that interpretation.) In Morton Thiokol, Inc. v. Metal Bldg. Alteration Co., 193 Cal. App. 3d 1025, 238 Cal. Rptr. 722 (1987) the court distinguished "general" indemnity clauses which do not address themselves to the indemnitee's own neligence and those that provide for such indemnity which must be "clear and explicit."

[36] See RESTATEMENT 2d OF TORTS § 402A.

[37] See the warranties of quality under UCC §§ 2-313, 2-314 and 2-315, the allowance for third party recovery in § 2-318 and the recognition of consequential damage recovery for injury to person or property in § 2-715(2)(b). See the history of products liability as found in PROSSER & KEETON, THE LAW OF TORTS § 97 (1984) and the classic exposition of this development in Seely v. White Motor Co., 45 Cal. Rptr. 17, 403 P.2d 145 (1965).

[38] Sterner Aero AB v. Page Airmotive, Inc., 499 F.2d 709, 713 (10th Cir. 1974) ("We construe [Oklahoma law] as precluding the defendants from asserting the existence of a contractual disclaimer provision as a valid defense to liability," quoting comment m to § 402A of the RESTATEMENT 2d OF TORTS. The court proceeds, however, to suggest that it would be possible for the parties to agree that the seller would be exempt from negligence liability, though an effective disclaimer of warranty liability under the UCC would not be sufficient for this purpose.

[39] See Keystone Aeronautics Corp. v. R. J. Enstrom Corp., 499 F.2d 146 (3d Cir. 1974) which construes comment m to § 402A of the RESTATEMENT 2d OF TORTS as relegated to the typical consumer situation since the comment is concerned with consumer buyers. The opinion, however, finds the clause in question unenforceable because it merely disclaimed warranties as provided by the UCC. Since such an effective warranty disclaimer would not be an effective clause exempting negligence liability, it was not effective to exempt the seller from strict liability under § 402A. See also Delta Air Lines, Inc. v. McDonnell-Douglas Corp., 503 F.2d 239 (5th Cir. 1974) which upholds a clause that is broad enough to exempt the seller from negligence liability or strict liability with no reference to § 402A or its comments.

[40] See RESTATEMENT 2d § 195(3) and comment c, which further suggest that the exempting clause would not affect the rights of third parties. The exception is expressly predicated upon *Keystone Aeronautics Corp., id. See* Reporter's Note, comment c, which mistakenly refers to subsection (2) of § 195 rather than subsection (3).

[41] See the classic exposition of this concept by Justice Brandeis in Chicago Bd. of Trade v. United States, 246 U.S. 231 (1918).

of the guilds, however, contracts which adversely affected the opportunity of a person to earn a livelihood or engage in a trade or business were viewed with deep suspicion. When a promisor undertook to refrain from engaging in a particular occupation, trade or business, the contract was viewed as inimical to the public interest and was, therefore, illegal because it was a contract in restraint of trade. Yet, other types of promises or covenants in restraint of trade would simply have to be enforced.

1. Covenants Not to Compete — Sale of a Business.

If a person had established a trade or business and was desirous of selling it so as to benefit from the good will his work and labor had developed over a period of time, a prospective buyer would be wary of buying the business if the seller were not prohibited from establishing a competing business in the same territory. The protection required by such a purchaser would necessarily prevent the seller from establishing the competing business and thus deprive the buyer of the patronage for which he had paid. The only suitable protection was a promise by the seller that he would not engage in that business within the relevant geographic market of the buyer, at least for a period of time that permitted the buyer to cement the relationships with customers that he had gained by purchasing the good will. To protect such buyers and to permit sellers to dispose of their good will for a fair consideration, it was necessary for courts to distinguish enforceable and unenforceable covenants in restraint of trade. Courts began to develop these distinctions between covenants in restraint of trade that were subsidiary (ancillary or indirect) to a legitimate purpose such as the sale of a business, and those that were naked covenants not to compete (direct or non-ancillary restraints) whose purpose was to permit monopolistic control of a trade or business in a given territory.[42] Thus, the classic example of a direct, non-ancillary contract in restraint of trade that has no redeeming virtue is an agreement among competitors to fix prices or to divide markets. While there is considerable diversity of opinion as to how non-ancillary restraints were viewed at common law,[43] the better view is that most American courts treated them as illegal *per se*.[44] Again, however, ancillary restraints were upheld if they were partial rather than general.

If a hair stylist wishes to sell his or her business, often the only valuable asset is the good will of the business, i.e., the premises and equipment may be leased and even the incidental sales of products may be on a consignment basis. The good will, however, may be valuable and may constitute the only asset of significant value that the efforts of the stylist have created at that site over a period of time. To facilitate the legitimate purpose of the stylist to sell that good will, courts must be willing to enforce a promise by the stylist that

---

[42] The distinction between ancillary and non-ancillary restraints is found in the classic exposition by Justice Taft in United States v. Addyston Pipe & Steel Co., 85 F.2d 271 (6th Cir. 1898).

[43] *See* Dewey, *The Common Law Background of Antitrust Policy,* 41 Va. L. Rev. 759 (1955); Letwin, *The English Common Law Concerning Monopolies,* 21 U. Chi. L. Rev. 355 (1954); Peppin, *Price Fixing Agreements Under the Sherman Antitrust Law,* 28 Calif. L. Rev. 297, 677 (1940).

[44] *See* M. Handler, A Study of the Construction and Enforcement of The Federal Antitrust Laws (4-5 TNEC Monograph No. 38, 1941).

she will not compete with the buyer in the same territory, at least for a period necessary to permit the new owner to reestablish relationships with the customers of that business. Absent such willingness on the part of courts, the stylist will not be able to sell his or her only valuable asset. The resulting restraint of trade is ancillary to a legitimate purpose and is, therefore, enforceable if it is reasonable.[45] The difficulty, of course, is in the application of the "reasonableness" test to myriad fact situations.

Over the years, the courts have developed certain guidelines to provide some predictability in the application of the test. Thus, it is generally agreed that the restraint of trade is unreasonable if it is greater than required for the protection of the party for whose benefit it is imposed.[46] Other factors include the degree of hardship imposed upon the restricted party, possible injury to the public, and the tendency of the restraint to create a monopoly or to unreasonably restrict the alienation of property.[47] If the restraint is not ancillary to a contract for the sale of a business or other legitimate purpose, it will be viewed as unreasonable absent statutory authorization or overriding social or economic justification.[48] The operation of these general criteria will depend upon all of the surrounding circumstances. The case law in this area is typically concerned with two basic situations: (1) the sale of a business under a contract containing a restrictive covenant such as those illustrated earlier, and (2) employment contracts containing a promise or covenant by the employee not to compete after leaving the employment. We will now consider how the courts apply, interpret, and construe such covenants.

D. *The Protection of Good Will and Employer's Rights.*

There is a tendency to place all types of restraints of trade into one category and then to focus upon the problem of distinguishing the reasonable and unreasonable restraints. It is, however, important to consider the purpose of the restraint in each situation since purposes will differ from one situation to

---

[45] *See* Mattis v. Lally, 138 Conn. 51, 82 A.2d 1155 (1951) (sale of barbering business where seller agreed not to engage in the barbering business in the city where the business was located for a period of five years was not against public policy). *See also* RESTATEMENT 2d § 188(2)(a). In the well-known case of Mitchell v. Reynolds, 1 P. Williams 181, 24 Eng. Rep. 347 (1711), a lease of a messuage and bakehouse was assigned to the plaintiff. An ancillary covenant to this assignment made the defendant liable to the plaintiff in the sum of fifty pounds if the defendant exercised his trade as a baker in a certain area during a five-year period. The ancillary covenant in restraint of trade was upheld because it was reasonably limited in time and geographical area. The opinion, however, suggested that all general restraints, i.e., those unlimited in time or space, were invalid, *per se.* This view was changed by the middle of the 19th Century [*see* Hitchcock v. Coker, 6 A. & E. 438, 112 Eng. Rep. 167 [1837] — covenant not to carry on the trade of chemist or druggist within the town of Taunton, in the county of Somerset, or within three miles thereof, unlimited as to time]. By the end of that century, the House of Lords stated the broad test to be one of reasonableness as suggested in the opinion by Lord M'Naghten in Nordenfelt v. Maxim Nordenfelt Guns & Ammunition Co., A.C. 535, 565 [1894]: "It is a sufficient justification, and indeed it is the only justification, if the restriction is reasonable — reasonable, that is, in reference to the interests of the public so framed and so guarded as to afford adequate protection to the party in whose favour it is imposed, while at the same time it is in no way injurious to the public." The "reasonableness" test prevails at this time. *See* RESTATEMENT 2d §§ 186-188.

[46] *See* RESTATEMENT 2d § 188(1)(a).

[47] *See* RESTATEMENT 2d 188(1)(b) and RESTATEMENT OF PROPERTY § 406(c) (restraint on alienation of property).

[48] *See* RESTATEMENT 2d § 187.

another, and the determination of purpose will assist courts and lawyers to analyze each situation more effectively. We have seen that the good will of a business in the hands of the new buyer must be protected since the essential value of many businesses is found only in their good will.[49] The purpose of another type of ancillary restraint, however, is quite different. Employers often require new employees to agree that they will not compete with their employer's business when the employee leaves the job. The purpose of these types of post-employment restraints is typically to protect the employer against the use of certain information (*e.g.,* trade secrets, secret processes, and customer lists) which the employee has acquired during employment. The sale of a business where good will is the dominant part of the agreed exchange requires protection against the seller's competition so that the very consideration moving to the buyer will not be diminished in value. In postemployment restraints, however, the employee who has rendered full services during the term of employment is not providing the essential consideration for his or her wages when refraining from using certain information or from soliciting certain customers after the employment is completed. The main purpose of the employment was fulfilled through the services rendered during that term. It has, therefore, been aptly suggested that, "courts properly should, and do, look more critically to the circumstances of the origin of post-employment restraints than to circumstances of other classes of restraint."[50]

With respect to the sale of a business or postemployment restraints, courts generally agree that restrictive covenants must be (a) necessary to protect the legitimate interest of the buyer of the business or interests of the employer, (b) reasonable with respect to territory and time, (c) not unduly harsh or oppressive on the seller or employee, and (d) not injurious to the public.[51] Although the requirement that the restraint must not be unduly harsh or oppressive to the seller may be stated separately,[52] it actually relates to the

---

[49] *See supra* text preceding note 45. Professor Corbin suggests that, when the good will of a business forms part of the consideration and there is *no* restrictive covenant, though the seller may open a new business in competition with the purchaser, he may not solicit former customers or otherwise deprive the purchaser of the good will so purchased. 6 CORBIN ON CONTRACTS § 1386.

[50] *See* Blake, *Employee Agreements Not to Compete,* 73 HARV. L. REV. 625, 647 (1960). The author suggests that a court may discover that the parties were of unequal bargaining power and, therefore, the covenant was not really bargained for, or the court may determine that the employee was improvident in surrendering his only significant asset, i.e., proficiency in a given occupation or profession. Moreover, such covenants may unfairly reduce the mobility or bargaining power of the employee during his employment. For these reasons, courts are more prone to declare such restraints unreasonable or, at least, to limit the protection afforded the employer. *See* Amex Distrib. Co. v. Mascari, 150 Ariz. 510, 724 P.2d 596, 600, 604 (1986) (restrictive covenants tending to prevent employee from pursuing a similar vocation after termination of employment are disfavored and where such a noncompetition covenant seeks to eliminate competition *per se* and has no valid interest in protecting the employer is unenforceable). *See also* Grant v. Carotex, 737 F.2d 410, 411-12 (4th Cir. 1984) and Columbia Ribbon & Carbon Mfg. Co. v. A-1A Corp., 398 N.Y.S.2d 1004, 369 N.E.2d 4, 6 (1977).

[51] *See* Fine Foods, Inc. v. Dahlin, 523 A.2d 1228 (Vt. 1987) (sale of business); Compton v. Joseph Lepak, D.D.S., P.C., 397 N.W.2d 311 (Mich. App. 1986) (post-employment); Boisen v. Petersen Flying Serv., 222 Neb. 239, 383 N.W.2d 29 (1986) (post-employment); Knight Vale and Gregory v. McDaniel, 37 Wash. App. 366, 680 P.2d 448 (1984) (post-employment); Jewel Box Stores Corp. v. Morrow, 272 N.C. 659, 158 S.E.2d 840 (1968) (sale of business); Montgomery v. Getty, 284 S.W.2d 313 (Mo. 1955) (sale of business). *See also* RESTATEMENT 2d § 188.

[52] *See, e.g.,* McCook Window Co. v. Hardwood Door Corp., 52 Ill. App. 2d 278, 202 N.E.2d 36 (1964).

relative degree of restraint necessary to protect the buyer. Thus, if the restraint is necessary to protect the buyer, presumably it is not oppressive to the seller. As to the requirement that the restraint not be injurious to the public, this element is typically explored in cases involving post-employment restraints such as professional practices in which a young physician is employed by a doctor with an established practice or a partnership arrangement between the old and new physicians. Thus, in one case, the question arose as to whether the reduction of 70 doctors by one in the territory would cause such injury to the public as to justify the court in refusing to enforce the restrictive covenant.[53] Post-employment restraints cases emphasize the reasonableness of the territorial limitation but are not concerned if the covenant fails to limit the restraint in time since a reasonable time can be implied.[54] This should not suggest, however, that the duration of the restraint is irrelevant. Thus, many cases involving postemployment restraints regard the duration of the restraint and the reasonableness of the territorial limitation as equally important.[55]

In light of the different purpose normally associated with post-employment restraints and the consequent refusal of courts to limit the former employee's activity beyond the point of necessary protection for his or her former employer,[56] courts must carefully explore all of the circumstances surrounding such restraints.[57] Since the protection of the employer's customer relationships is typically involved in such restraints, it is important to consider certain critical factors in relation to that purpose. These factors include (1) the number of contracts between the employee and customers; (2) the exclusiveness of such contracts, i.e., whether these are the only contracts between the business and the customer; (3) the place of the contracts, i.e., either at the situs of the business or at the customer's home or place of business; (4) the kind of functions performed by the employee, i.e., routine and mechanical functions versus functions requiring a high degree of skill which may make the customer more conscious of the efforts of the particular employee.[58] Post-

---

[53] See Bauer v. Sawyer, 8 Ill. 2d 351, 134 N.E.2d 329 (1956) (finding that restraint would not injure the public).

[54] See Compton v. Joseph Lepak, D.D.S., P.C., *supra* note 51; Karpinski v. Ingrasci, 28 N.Y.2d 45, 268 N.E.2d 751 (1971).

[55] See, e.g., Briggs v. R. R. Donnelley & Sons, 589 F.2d 39 (1st Cir. 1978) (suggesting that the temporal duration and geographical extent of the commitment not to compete are two important factors in determining the enforceability of the covenant. *See also* Fidelity Union Life Ins. Co. v. Protective Life Ins. Co., 356 F. Supp. 1199 (N.D. Tex. 1972).

[56] See, e.g., Howard Schultz & Assocs. v. Broniec, 239 Ga. 181, 236 S.E.2d 265 (1977) (employee's covenant not to accept employment "in any capacity" imposed a greater limitation upon the employee than was necessary to protect the employer).

[57] See, e.g., Philip G. Johnson & Co. v. Salmen, 211 Neb. 123, 317 N.W.2d 900, 904 (1982), where the court suggested the following factors: the degree of inequality of bargaining power, the risk of the employer losing customers, the extent of respective participation by the parties in securing and retaining customers, the good faith of the employer, the existence of sources or general knowledge pertaining to the identity of customers; the nature and extent of the business position held by the employee, the employee's training, health, and education and needs of his family, the current conditions of employment, the necessity of the employee changing his calling or residence, and the correspondence of the restraint with the need for protecting the legitimate interest of the employer. The covenant in this case was too broad since it sought to prohibit the employee from earning fees from clients or former clients of the accounting firm, or from such clients' officers and agents, no matter where they may be.

[58] See Blake, *supra* note 50, at 659-65.

employment restraints designed to prevent the divulging of confidential information (as contrasted with preserving customer relationships) must also be explored critically. The two basic inquiries will center around the nature of the confidential information (*e.g.*, a trade secret which is clearly valuable in the industry is entitled to substantial protection, particularly if it is the result of the employer's investment of time, money and effort) and the efforts of the employer to protect the confidentiality of the information.[59]

E. *The Severance Rule — "Blue Pencil" Rule.*

If the restrictive covenant attached to the sale of a business or former employment is too broad in geography or too long in duration, courts are often asked to enforce the covenant in terms of a lesser area or shorter duration if such a modification would make the restraint reasonable. While there appears to be little reason for precluding a court from such judicial modification, the concept of "divisibility" or "severance" created problems as early as 1843. In *Mallan v. May*,[60] the court created what came to be known as the "blue pencil" rule. If the restrictive covenant was drafted so that certain portions could be deleted leaving the remaining portion intact and enforceable as a reasonable restraint, the covenant, so modified, became enforceable. Thus, if a seller of the good will of a business promised not to compete for a certain duration "in Los Angeles or elsewhere in California," it would be possible to blue pencil "or elsewhere in California." If the restraint were reasonable where the territory was confined to Los Angeles, it could be enforced since the court merely had to delete a phrase and did not have to otherwise modify the covenant. This approach, however, was mechnical and could be used only where the parties happened to include an overly broad clause in a form that was subject to such deletion or blue pencilling.[61] The "blue pencil" approach has not been followed in modern cases, which appear quite willing to enforce restrictive covenants for smaller areas or shorter durations, though no mechanical division of the language is possible.[62] One of the criticisms of the severability concept, whether in its more modern or mechanical "blue pencil" form, is that it may lead to the inclusion of an overly broad clause which, if successfully attacked on that basis, will still be enforced in modified form.[63] Modern courts, however, will refuse to enforce only that portion of a covenant that is opposed to

---

[59] *Id.* at 671-74.

[60] 11 M. & W. 653 [1843].

[61] For an opinion criticizing the "blue pencil" rule on the footing that it elevates form over substance, *see* the dissent of Judge Bobbit in Welcome Wagon Int'l, Inc. v. Pender, 255 N.C. 244, 120 S.E.2d 739 (1961).

[62] *See* Karpinski v. Ingrasci, 320 N.Y.S.2d 1, 268 N.E.2d 751 (1971); Redd Pest Control Co. v. Heatherly, 248 Miss. 34, 157 So. 2d 133 (1963); Fullerton Lumber Co. v. Torborg, 270 Wis. 133, 70 N.W.2d 585 (1955). *See also* RESTATEMENT 2d § 184 which rejects the "blue pencil" approach.

[63] *See* Howard Schultz & Assocs. v. Broniec, 239 Ga. 181, 136 S.E.2d 265 (1977), in which the court refused to apply the "blue pencil" rule to a post-employment restrictive covenant that was overly broad. The court seemed, not remarkably, particularly concerned about applying the concept or a modern severability concept to such a covenant. A Georgia court has, however, more recently applied the modern severability concept to a covenant not to compete ancillary to the sale of a business, Jenkins v. Jenkins Irrig., 244 Ga. 95, 259 S.E.2d 47 (1979). Other courts have applied the severance concept to post-employment restraints, *e.g.*, Sidco Paper Co. v. Aaron, 465 Pa. 587, 351 A.2d 250 (1976).

public policy if the enforceable portion has been obtained in good faith and in accordance with standards of fair dealing.[64]

F. *Antitrust Statutes — Non-ancillary Restraints — Naked Covenants Against Competition.*

As a practical matter, much of the law dealing with non-ancillary restraints is now governed by statute. On the federal level, the antitrust laws began with the "charter of economic freedom" known as the Sherman Act of 1890.[65] Major additions occurred in 1914 with the enactment of the Clayton[66] and Federal Trade Commission Acts,[67] in 1936 with the Robinson-Patman amendment to the Clayton Act concerning price discrimination,[68] and in 1950 with the Celler-Kefauver amendment[69] to the Clayton Act in relation to mergers. The states have also enacted laws against naked contracts in restraint of trade and monopolizing which often contain proscriptions similar to the federal statutes.[70] While the statutes now govern, antitrust law, analytically, remains a "common law" area requiring extensive judicial elaboration because the statutes are typicaly drafted in broad language designed to permit courts to cope with myriad types of anticompetitive behavior. Under the basic Federal statute, the Sherman Act, with the exception of certain blatant manifestations of anticompetitive behavior which suggest no redeeming virtue and are, therefore, viewed as *per se* illegal,[71] courts apply a "rule of reason" requiring a definite factual showing of illegality to determine whether the conduct in question has the actual or probable effect of injuring competition.[72] Later antitrust statutes such as the Clayton Act and Robinson-Patman amendment to the Clayton Act require a showing of actual or probable substantial lessen-

---

[64] RESTATEMENT 2d § 184(2). Comment b to this section emphasizes the fact that the power of a court to enforce part of such a restrictive covenant is not a power of reformation, i.e., the court will not increase the scope of the term in any fashion.

[65] 15 U.S.C. §§ 1-7.

[66] 15 U.S.C. §§ 12-27.

[67] 15 U.S.C. §§ 41-45.

[68] 15 U.S.C. § 13.

[69] 15 U.S.C. § 18.

[70] *See, e.g.,* section 2 of the Michigan Antitrust Reform Act (MARA), MICH. COMP. LAWS § 445.772; MICH. STAT. ANN. § 28.70(2) which is identical to the same provision in the Uniform State Antitrust Act (USAA) promulgated by the National Conference on Uniform State Laws in 1973: "A contract, combination or conspiracy between 2 or more persons in restraint of trade, or to monopolize trade or commerce in a relevant market is unlawful." The language is similar to §§ 1 and 2 of the Sherman Antitrust Law of 1890 as amended.

[71] A recent U.S. Supreme Court opinion dealing with *per se* violations is Arizona v. Maricopa Cty. Med. Soc'y, 457 U.S. 332 (1982) where the majority opinion by Justice Stevens deals with the classic *per se* categories of price fixing, division of markets, group boycotts (collective refusals to deal) and tying arrangements; citing Northern Pac. R.R. v. United States, 356 U.S. 1 (1958), and suggests the rationale for *per se* illegality, i.e., the elaborate inquiry into the reasonableness of such a restraint is costly and the litigation of the effect or purpose of the restraint is often excessive, complex, and often wholly fruitless. Moreover, even though it is conceivable that cases not fitting the generalization of *per se* illegality may arise, they are not sufficiently common or significant to justify the time and expense necessary to identify them. United States v. Topco Assocs., 405 U.S. 596 (1972).

[72] The "rule of reason" approach requiring an inquiry into the purpose of the restraint, the market power of the parties involved, and the actual or probable effects of the restraint was created in the opinion by Justice Brandeis in Chicago Bd. of Trade v. United States, 246 U.S. 231 (1918).

ing of competition. The statutory language is, at best, only a point of departure in such an inquiry with the overwhelming effort devoted to a study of the precedent and its application to the actual or probable economic effect in the case *sub judice.* Further exploration of antitrust law must be left for courses in that area and the extensive antitrust literature.

G. *Wagers and Gambling Contracts — "Futures" — Aleatory Contracts — "Futures."*

There was no policy condemning wagers and gaming contracts in English common law. Such agreements were regarded as illegal only if the subject matter of the particular transaction was deemed to be inconsistent with the public welfare. As time went on, however, English judges became astute in finding reasons for refusing to sanction such agreements,[73] and in 1845 a statute was enacted which made all wagering and gambling contracts unenforceable.[74] American courts, however, clung to the view that such bargains were *per se* contrary to public policy because of their tendency to induce shiftlessness, poverty, and immorality.[75] Eventually, statutes were enacted in practically every jurisdiction prohibiting lotteries as well as all other gaming and wagering transactions. As will be seen below, the mores of our society have changed dramatically with respect to wagers, lotteries, and gaming contracts and, to some extent, the law reflects such changes.

Among the problems courts have confronted with such contracts is the necessity of determining the kind of transaction falling within the ban. Certain contracts may be called "aleatory," i.e., an aleatory promise is conditional on the happening of a fortuitous event, i.e., an event of chance.[76] The classic example is the fire insurance contract where the insurance company agrees to indemnify the owner against loss of property in exchange for the payment of a premium by the owner. Casualty to the property is a fortuitous event that the insured hopes will not occur. This is not a wagering contract because the owner has an interest in the contingency (the property loss) prior to the formation of the contract. On the other hand, if the insurer promises to pay a definite sum, contingent upon the occurrence of a fire at a particular house in which the insured has *no* interest, the promise is a wager and unenforceable since the only interest that either party has in the contingency (the fire) is to determine whether the insurer must pay the amount of the policy. Absent an insurable interest on the part of the insured, the typical casualty insurance policy becomes an "illegal bargain." Similarly, in any game of chance in which a party promises to pay a certain sum with the hope of receiving some multiple of that sum which the other party has promised to pay upon a chance event such as a drawing of a lottery ticket, neither party has an interest in the occurrence of the contingency other than as a determinant of the enforceabil-

---

[73] *See* Thackoorseydass v. Dhondmull, 6 Moore, P.C. 300, 13 Eng. Rep. 699 [1848].

[74] 8 & 9 VICT., c. 109, § 18. *See* Hampden v. Walsh, 1 Q.B.D. 189 [1876]. For a brief summary of the history of wagering contracts in English law, *see* PATTERSON, CASES ON INSURANCE 103-06 (1932).

[75] The early American cases are collected in 37 AM. ST. REP. 697 (1894).

[76] *See* RESTATEMENT 2d § 379 comment a. "Aleatory" is derived from the Latin, "alea," meaning dice.

ity of the promise to pay. Such a bargain is not an enforceable aleatory promise. It is a wagering bargain and, therefore, unenforceable.

It is generally agreed that a bargain is a wager if the promisor is required to pay upon the happening of an uncertain event and will not have received anything of commensurate value with the payment he makes, and the promisee will have suffered no detriment commensurate with the promisor's payment.[77] The mere fact that a promisee has a conditional right to receive a benefit upon the occurrence of a fortuitous event, however, does not necessarily make the transaction objectionable. Where, for example, a purchaser of land upon which cotton was grown agreed to pay a higher or a lower price for the land depending upon the future price of cotton, it was held that the contract was lawful since the price of cotton had a direct relation to the value of the land, i.e., the buyer's interest in the land was directly affected by the fortuitous market value of cotton.[78]

The determination of whether a contract dependent upon a fortuitous event is enforceable is typically involved in contests with money or valuable prizes held out as awards to the winner. If the cash or other valuable prize is to be awarded on the basis of mere chance and each of the contestants has paid to enter the contest, the transaction amounts to a lottery and is illegal on that ground.[79] If mental or physical prowess or other skill is involved, however, the agreement is not illegal, provided the prize is not furnished as a result of the contributions of one or more of the contestants.[80] Even if the contestants are required to pay an entry fee, the transaction is not invalidated unless the collected fees are the sole or primary source of the prize.[81] A modern, complex, and insidious version of a prize from the contestants' entry fees may be seen in various kinds of "chain letter" and "pyramiding" schemes involving multilevel membership recruitments with the payment of finder's fees for membership recruitment and advancemenet within the various levels of such a plan. Notwithstanding their complexity, courts will penetrate the veneer of legitimacy and discover an illegal lottery.[82] Even though a lottery is an illegal activity, however, the voluntary delivery of a prize awarded in such a lottery is not prohibited. A plaintiff won a new car as a prize in a lottery and delivered the winning ticket to the defendant who agreed to pick up the car for the benefit of the plaintiff. The defendant subsequently refused to return the car to the plaintiff on the footing that the car had been received through an illegal lottery. The court held that the plaintiff was entitled to the car since the only party who could successfully assert the defense of an illegal lottery was the

---

[77] See Chenard v. Marcel Motors, 387 A.2d 596, 600 (Me. 1978). See also FIRST RESTATEMENT § 520.

[78] Ferguson v. Coleman, 3 Rich. L. 99, 45 Am. Dec. 761 (S.C. 1846).

[79] See Youngblood v. Bailey, 459 So. 2d 855 (Ala. 1984) suggesting three elements are required to constitute a lottery violative of Article IV, § 65 of the Alabama Constitution: (a) a prize, (b) awarded by chance, (c) for a consideration.

[80] See Brenard Mfg. Co. v. Jessup & Barrett Co., 186 Iowa 872, 173 N.W. 101 (1919).

[81] See Chenard v. Marcel Motors, 387 A.2d 596 (1978) (prize of new car for any golfer who shot a hole in one was not violative of gambling and lottery laws where the payment of entrance fees do not make up the purse). See also Toomey v. Penwell, 76 Mont. 166, 245 P. 943 (1926).

[82] See Frye v. Taylor, 264 So. 2d 835 (Fla. App. 1972).

conductor of the lottery, i.e., that defense is available only as between the immediate parties to the contract.[83]

Another common transaction in which it is difficult to distinguish between lawful agreements and unlawful wagers involves an agreement for the sale of goods for future delivery. It is clear that such a transaction is not *per se* unenforceable. Yet, such a transaction may be nothing more than a mere cover for a wager relating to the future price of the goods involved. When this is the true character of the arrangement, it is unenforceable. If the parties to the agreement contemplate that the goods agreed to be sold are not to be received or delivered, but the transaction will be liquidated by the payment of the difference between the market price of the goods and the contract price, it is generally held that such an agreement is a wager and unenforceable.[84] While it is usually suggested that the wrongful intent must be shared by both parties to the transaction to make the contract unenforceable,[85] it has been held that if one party alone harbors such an intent, he will not be permitted to enforce the contract although the other party, having no such intent, could successfully bring an action upon it.[86] If both parties intend at the time of formation that delivery of the goods shall be made and received but later agree that there will be a settlement of their difference rather than a delivery, the transaction is unobjectionable.[87] A related problem dealing with off-setting contracts must be distinguished. Under the mechanism of a commodity exchange involving "futures" contracts, it is possible to avoid taking delivery of goods purchased by making off-setting contracts. Such transactions appear to be indistinguishable from gaming contracts since no delivery of the commodities is contemplated. Rather, the parties appear to be wagering on the future of the price of certain commodities, i.e., as the price of the commodity changes, offsetting contracts will be made since the parties are dealing simply for a margin. Even though the parties intended to settle on the margin and intended no delivery of the goods, if they have effected a bona fide buy and sell transaction on a recognized board of trade or commodity exchange, the transaction will be lawful and "delivery" can be accomplished by offset.[88] It is important to note that statutes governing dealing in futures have been enacted in virtually every state as well as by the Congress of the United States and such statutes should be consulted.[89]

---

[83] Matta v. Katsoulas, 192 Wis. 212, 212 N.W. 261 (1927). Even if the taint of illegality has been removed from a particular activity, however, an agreement between the operator of the activity and a contestant may not be enforceable. For example, in Kennedy v. Annandale Boys Club, Inc., 272 S.E.2d 38 (Va. 1980), the court refused to enforce an agreement by the winner of $6000 in a bingo game even though the legislature had legalized bingo in the sense of precluding criminal prosecutions for those conducting or playing the game. In removing the criminal sanctions, the legislature did not render valid and enforceable agreements between the operators of the game and those who play. Such agreements under Virginia law are "utterly void."

[84] See, e.g., Rohrer v. Traina, 35 Ill. App. 36, 342 N.E.2d 390 (1976).

[85] See Browne v. Thorn, 260 U.S. 137 (1922); Benson-Stabeck Co. v. Reservation Farmers' Grain Co., 62 Mont. 254, 205 P. 651 (1922).

[86] Nash-Wright Co. v. Wright, 165 Ill. App. 243 (1910); Higgins v. McCrea, 116 U.S. 671 (1886) (*semble*).

[87] See T. Barbour Brown & Co. v. Canty, 115 Conn. 226, 161 A. 91 (1932); Gettys v. Newburger, 272 F. 209 (8th Cir. 1921).

[88] See Merrill Lynch, Pierce, Etc. v. Schriver, 541 S.W.2d 799 (Tenn. App. 1976).

[89] See, e.g., TENN. CODE ANN. § 39-2028 which withdraws from all gaming and wagering laws all transactions executed up and in accordance with the rules and regulations of a legitimate produce, stock, or cotton exchange or board of trade.

At the beginning of this discussion concerning wagering and gaming contracts, it was suggested that the mores of society have changed rather dramatically concerning such agreements in recent years due, in some measure, to legislation condoning or inviting various forms of wagering. It is, therefore, sometimes difficult for courts to assess the strength of precedent decided prior to these legislative developments. Thus, as one court suggests:

> A significant difference, however, is that when [certain cases] were decided there were no exceptions to the lottery and gambling laws. Subsequent to these opinions, the Legislature has legalized pari-mutuel betting at harness and running horse racetracks, licensed bingo games and gambling conducted by nonprofit organizations, and a state-operated lottery. These exceptions have riddled the gambling and lottery statutes to the point where it can no longer be said that it is "the intention of the legislature to prohibit every pecuniary transaction in which pure chance has any place."[90]

If a state legislature has authorized various forms of gambling and is, itself, conducting a statewide lottery which it solicits citizens to pursue, it is impossible to suggest that the public policy of that state is contrary to gambling. If a state permits casino gambling in a given part of the state, it is facilitating and legitimizing a gambling industry.[91] Whatever the merits or faults of such a determination by a given jurisdiction, the older public policy against wagering or gaming and its attendant evils is significantly modified. While a private wager on a sporting event between two or more individuals is still an illegal bargain in these jurisdictions, the moral force of the arguments against gambling which had been available to support such holdings is significantly diminished since the state can no longer be said to take a policy position against gambling. Rather, it merely requires gambling to be conducted in various ways authorized by the state. While the state may justify its position by pointing to the regulation of gambling and consequent fairness to the participants through these authorized means, the dominant motivation for legalization is more than clear, i.e., the raising of additional revenue.

H. Contracts Adversely Affecting the Administration of Justice, Champerty, and Maintenance — Arbitration.

Common law courts viewed with disfavor any contract which had a tendency to stir up unnecessary litigation or to interfere with the proper administration of justice. The early law took a particularly severe view of "maintenance" and "champerty."[92] Maintenance was the assisting of another in litigation where the party furnishing the assistance had no personal interest in the litigation. The transaction was champertous if it was accompanied by an agreement that the party furnishing assistance should receive part of the proceeds of the litigation, i.e., what is now called a contingent fee arrangement.[93] Today, however, it is generally agreed that a contract to assist another

[90] Chenard v. Marcel Motors, 387 A.2d 596, 599-600 (Me. 1978).

[91] See N.J. STAT. ANN. § 5.12 which authorizes casino gambling in Atlantic City, New Jersey.

[92] See Winfield, The History of Maintenance and Champerty, 35 L.Q. REV. 50 (1919).

[93] See Kenrich Corp. v. Miller, 377 F.2d 312 (3d Cir. 1967); Fordson Coal Co. v. Garrard, 277 Ky. 218, 125 S.W.2d 977 (1939); Hutley v. Hutley, L.R. 8 Q.B. 112 [1873].

in litigation is lawful if it is actuated by charitable motives or by an intention
to secure a decision on a question affecting the interest of a party and not
merely by a desire to promote litigation for ulterior purposes.[94] An attorney in
a criminal[95] or divorce[96] proceeding, however, may not recover on a contingent fee agreement. Legal services in criminal cases do not provide a fund
from which the fee may be paid. Even more important is the possible conflict
of interest for a lawyer who may be influenced to advise against a favorable
plea bargain.[97] Similarly, in divorce proceedings, if the lawyer will receive
payment on the contingency that the divorce is decreed, such an attorney may
be influenced to avoid a reconciliation between the spouses, and the law favors
reconciliation.[98] Even if an agreement is champertous as, for example, where
an attorney agrees to be paid contingent on the successful outcome of a criminal proceeding, the contingent fee agreement is unenforceable, but courts may
permit an attorney to recover in quasi contract for the reasonable value of
services rendered.[99] There is some authority for the view that a contract for a
contingent fee that would otherwise be lawful is unenforceable if it contains a
provision that the client shall not compromise or settle his claim since the law
favors settlements.[1]

Notwithstanding the decline of maintenance and champerty, an agreement
that has an undue tendency to promote litigation for the benefit of the promoter rather than the litigant, or which is oppressive to the litigant, or which
involves an abuse of legal proceedings, is more than likely to be deemed
unenforceable.[2]

Similarly, any agreement that tends to interfere with the proper functioning of the judicial machinery is unenforceable. The following agreements have
been held unenforceable on this ground: a contract to pay another a contingent fee for procuring evidence to be used in a lawsuit,[3] a contract to pay a
physician for treatment and testimony in a personal injury action with an
understanding that part of the physician's fee would emanate from the personal injury recovery,[4] an agreement to pay a witness who is amenable to
process a fee, contingent or fixed, in addition to that he is entitled to by law,[5]

---

[94] *See* Reed v. Chase, 238 Mass. 83, 139 N.E. 257 (1921); Johnson v. Great Northern Ry., 128
Minn. 365, 151 N.W. 125 (1915).

[95] *See* O'Donnell v. Bane, 385 Mass. 114, 431 N.E.2d 190 (1982). *See* FIRST RESTATEMENT § 502.
See, in general, RESTATEMENT 2d § 178.

[96] *See* Shanks v. Kilgore, 589 S.W.2d 318 (Mo. App. 1979).

[97] *See* ABA Annotation, Code of Professional Responsibility 108 (1979).

[98] *See* Burns v. Stewart, 290 Minn. 289, 188 N.W.2d 760 (1971).

[99] *See* Genins v. Geiger, 144 Ga. App. 244, 240 S.E.2d 745 (1977) (contract providing for payment of $25,000 contingent on a disposition of criminal charge is against public policy but this
does not preclude recovery on a quantum meruit (quasi contract) basis). *See also* Ownby v.
Prisock, 243 Miss. 203, 238 So. 2d 279 (1962); Kamerman v. United States, 278 F.2d 411 (2d Cir.
1960).

[1] *See* Davy v. Fidelity & Cas. Ins. Co., 78 Ohio St. 256, 85 N.E. 504 (1908).

[2] *See, e.g.,* Ellis v. Frawley, 165 Wis. 381, 161 N.W. 364 (1917) (agreement between lawyers to
discover persons having claims against a power company and to induce them to permit the
lawyers to prosecute the claims on a contingent fee basis); Gammons v. Johnson, 76 Minn. 76, 78
N.W. 1035 (1899) (scheme of attorney to employ a layman to hunt up claims against a railroad to
be prosecuted by the attorney for a share of the proceeds).

[3] Duteau v. Dresbach, 113 Wash. 545, 194 P. 547 (1920).

[4] Weinberg v. Magid, 285 Mass. 237, 189 N.E. 110 (1934).

[5] Dodge v. Stiles, 26 Conn. 463 (1857). If, however, the witness is rendering an expert opinion,
particularly where he will have to inform himself of the facts prior to trial, the witness may be

an agreement to pay a witness for testimony, the content of which is specified in the bargain,[6] a contract having for its purpose the concealment or compounding of a crime or suspicion of crime,[7] an agreement calling for the use of personal influence to induce a court or prosecuting officer to discharge or to be lenient with a criminal,[8] an agreement by a law enforcement official not to disclose relevant and pertinent information to a judge,[9] an agreement prescribing certain rules of evidence to be applied if a lawsuit should arise out of the contract[10] or providing that a statutory presumption shall not apply,[11] an agreement involving a lawyer who was incorporated to practice law and conducted another business in the same office,[12] and an agreement containing an unreasonable limitation on the time permitted to commence an action or extending the period of time beyond that permitted by the relevant statute of limitations.[13]

Courts are jealous of their jurisdiction and have, therefore, been inclined to condemn as illegal any agreement tending to oust them from their jurisdiction. It has been held, for example, that an agreement specifying that any suit that is brought shall be brought only in a particular tribunal, or in the courts of a certain jurisdiction, is unenforceable.[14] Earlier decisions also held that an agreement to arbitrate, whether in the form of a promise or a condition, was unenforceable, particularly if the agreement contemplated arbitration of all matters including the existence of a cause of action and not merely a fact

---

paid an additional fee. See Lincoln Mt. Gold Mining Co. v. Williams, 37 Colo. 193, 85 P. 844 (1906).

[6] Griffith v. Harris, 17 Wis. 2d 255, 116 N.W.2d 133 (1962), cert. denied, 373 U.S. 927 (1963).

[7] See Good Hope State Bank v. Kline, 303 Ill. App. 381, 25 N.E.2d 425 (1940); Farmers' Nat'l Bank v. Tartar, 256 Ky. 70, 75 S.W.2d 758 (1934); Union Exch. Nat'l Bank v. Joseph, 231 N.Y. 250, 131 N.E. 905 (1921). A party injured by the commission of a crime may agree to settle his claim for his injury, and such an agreement is enforceable unless part of the consideration consists of an express or implied promise to refrain from instituting criminal proceedings. The mere fact that a criminal prosecution does not occur is not, of itself, material. See Wilhelm v. King Auto Fin. Co., 259 Mich. 463, 244 N.W. 130 (1932); Blair Milling Co. v. Fruitiger, 113 Kan. 432, 215 P. 286 (1923). See also O'Neil v. Dux, 257 Minn. 383, 101 N.W.2d 588 (1960) where the injured party agreed not to present the matter to the county attorney. The court enforced the agreement because no prosecution had been threatened.

[8] Liberty Mut. Ins. Co. v. Gilreath, 191 S.C. 244, 4 S.E.2d 126 (1939); Aycock v. Gill, 183 N.C. 271, 111 S.E. 342 (1922).

[9] Grant v. State, 73 Wis. 2d 441, 243 N.W.2d 186 (1976).

[10] Fidelity & Deposit Co. v. Davis, 129 Kan. 790, 284 P. 430 (1930) (provision in indemnity contract that certain prescribed evidence shall be conclusive of the liability of the principal obligor).

[11] Modern Woodmen of Am. v. Michelin, 101 Okla. 217, 225 P. 163 (1924) (agreement that the statutory presumption of death arising from seven years of absence shall not apply).

[12] Marvin N. Benn & Assocs. v. Nelsen Steel & Wire, Inc., 107 Ill. App. 3d 442, 437 N.E.2d 900 (1982) (the conduct of another business in the same office from which the attorney conducts his legal practice is a form of solicitation or recommendation which violates the code of professional responsibility).

[13] See Page Cty. v. Fidelity & Deposit Co., 205 Iowa 798, 216 N.W. 957 (1927) (agreement limiting the time to 90 days after default); Burlew v. Fidelity & Cas. Co., 276 Ky. 132, 122 S.W.2d 990 (1938) (agreement extending time for bringing suit). UCC § 2-725 establishes a four year statute of limitations in contracts for the sale of goods, the four years to commence from the time of delivery of the goods, regardless of the aggrieved party's knowledge of the breach. Section 2-725(1) permits the parties to agree to reduce the period to not less than one year, but precludes any agreement to extend the period.

[14] See Huntley v. Alejandre, 139 So. 2d 911 (Fla. 1962). See Annotation, 56 A.L.R.2d 306 (1957).

question.[15] That view has undergone a marked change so that arbitration agreements are now viewed as enforceable.[16]

I. *Contracts Tending to Corrupt or Cause a Neglect of Duty — Lobbying.*

A contract which has a tendency to corrupt a public official or cause neglect of duty, is contrary to public policy and, therefore, unenforceable.[17] Blatant forms of this activity such as bribing a public officer are such obvious violations that the dearth of case law illustrating actions brought to recover unpaid bribes is not remarkable. Almost as obvious is a bargain contemplating personal influence or that other improper means shall be used to induce a public official.[18] While it is perfectly lawful for one person to employ another, for a consideration, to present the merits of a particular proposition to a public official, courts are astute in scrutinizing such agreements to ascertain that the use of personal influence is not contemplated, before a contract will be upheld. Nevertheless, where a lawyer was hired to represent a trucking company and it was clear that the only reason for this contract was the lawyer's personal relation with the President of the United States, the court upheld the contract on the footing that one may employ an agent or attorney to use his influence to gain access to a public official as long as the case is presented on its merits after access is gained.[19] A statute, however, may preclude payment under a contract to a person whose exclusive use is one of influence to public officials.[20] This entire area of agreements to assist in bringing about desired action by one or more public official are well-known under the caption, "lobbying contract," and there is a host of federal and state statutes, executive orders and administrative regulations in this area which go well beyond the scope of this section or volume. Since the earlier cases in particular tended to frown on contingent fee contracts, it is not remarkable that some courts took the position that any agreement based on the contingency that an agent would succeed in persuading a public official to a particular action or vote was illegal *per se.*[21] The better view, however, is that such contracts are not auto-

---

[15] *See* W. H. Blodgett Co. v. Bebe Co., 190 Cal. 665, 214 P. 38 (1923).

[16] *See* Pettinaro Constr. Co. v. Harry C. Partridge, Etc., 408 A.2d 957, 961 (Del. Ch. 1979): "It is no longer of any consequence that a court, otherwise competent to hear the dispute, is ousted of its jurisdiction by the arbitration process." The modern view is often based on a statutory requirement. The Uniform Arbitration Act (a product of the National Conference of Commissioners on Uniform State laws) has been adopted by at least almost half the states and suggests that litigation should be discouraged and specialized forums reflecting the particular trade practices and needs of the parties should be encouraged to provide results that are speedier, less expensive, and, in some cases, based on greater expertise.

[17] *See, e.g.,* Anderson v. Branstrom, 173 Mich. 157, 139 N.W. 40 (1912) (agreement between prosecuting attorney and his law partner to divide his salary).

[18] *See, e.g.,* Ewing v. National Airport Corp., 115 F.2d 859 (4th Cir. 1940).

[19] Troutman v. Southern Ry., 441 F.2d 586 (5th Cir. 1971). The court suggested that decisions in these cases will necessarily depend largely on the particular facts in each case. The burden of proving illegality is upon the party asserting it.

[20] *See, e.g.,* Samuel J. Plumeri Realty v. Capital Place, 101 N.J. 13, 499 A.2d 1356 (1985) construing New Jersey statute proscribing retaining persons on a commission basis to obtain state contracts unless such persons are bona fide employees or bona fide established commercial or selling agencies maintained by the contractor for the purpose of securing business. Since the broker in this case could not demonstrate continuity in the relationship with the contractor, the contract violated this statute, N.J. STAT. ANN. § 52:34-15.

[21] *See, e.g.,* Trist v. Child, 88 U.S. (21 Wall) 441 (1875). *See also* Chambers v. Coates, 176 Okla. 416, 55 P.2d 986 (1936); Noonan v. Gilbert, 68 F.2d 775 (D.C. Cir. 1934); *In re* Crook's Estate, 316 Pa. 285, 175 A. 410 (1934).

matically invalid; rather, the contingent fee arrangement is simply a factor to be considered.[22] If a person hires a lawyer to prosecute a claim against the government and the only feasible remedy to compensate that person is private legislation, a contingent fee contract in such circumstances would be upheld.[23] There can be no doubt, however, that a contingent fee contract in relation to securing a particular result from one or more public officials will be viewed with some initial suspicion.

It is not only agreements which tend to corrupt public officials or to induce violations of their duties that are illegal; any bargain which has a tendency to cause a person who is subject to a private duty to violate that duty is equally obnoxious in the eyes of the law, whether he is an agent, trustee, corporate stockholder, officer or director, or one who has assumed to act on another's behalf.[24]

J. Contracts Concerning Marriage — Changing Mores — Cohabitation Agreements.

Our courts have always viewed the marriage relationship as the foundation stone of the social order. It is, therefore, not difficult to discover numerous cases suggesting that any agreement which tends to prevent marriage or to disrupt a marriage already consummated has been traditionally viewed with disfavor.[25] These expressions are found in recent cases, notwithstanding what some may view as their startling conclusions, which will be discussed later in this section. The older cases pursued this position to its logical extension in holding that *any* bargain that had a tendency to prevent or restrain a first marriage, even though the restraint would be operative for only a limited time, was illegal.[26] Subsequent cases were not as rigid. One of the earliest manifestations of flexibility came from a Texas court:

> [T]he term "general restraint" as used in the rule should be construed to mean restraint which binds a competent person not to marry any one at any time, and that the validity of a contract, where the restraint it imposes is only against marrying a particular person, or a person of a particular class, or within a specified limited time, should be determined

---

[22] "The payment of contingent fees in public contracts is not illegal *per se.*" State Kugler v. Arnold Constable Corp., 138 N.J. 551, 351 A.2d 771, 778 (1976).

[23] *See* Gesellschaft Fur Drahtlose Telegraphie M.B.H. v. Brown, 78 F.2d 410, 413-14 (D.C. Cir. 1935).

[24] *See, e.g.,* McQuade v. Stoneham, 263 N.Y. 323, 189 N.E. 234 (1934) (agreement between stockholders to elect themselves as directors and then to elect particular individuals as officers at named salaries); Y. & M.V.R. Co. v. Whittington, 191 Miss. 776, 4 So. 2d 343 (1941) (father who was operating as guardian of his child received certain payments for agreeing to approve a settlement of the child's personal injury claim); King v. Raleigh & P. S. R.R., 147 N.C. 263, 60 S.E. 1133 (1908) (railroad's payment to newspaper editor for favorable editorials); Pike v. Pike, 266 Mass. 186, 165 N.E. 5 (1929) (agreement to make payment in return for advising another to refrain from making a certain will).

[25] *See, e.g.,* Note, *Marriage Contracts and Public Policy,* 54 HARV. L. REV. 473 (1941).

[26] *See* McCoy v. Flynn, 169 Iowa 622, 151 N.W. 465 (1915) (promise to pay $3000 if promisee should be unmarried after three years — promise made in connection with an agreement to settle a claim for breach of promise to marry); Sterling v. Sinnickson, 5 N.J.L. 756 (1820) (promise to pay $1000 if promisee should remain unmarried for six months).

with reference to the reasonableness of such restraint under the circumstances of the particular case.[27]

For reasons that are not entirely clear, contracts restraining second marriages are generally upheld, particularly where there are children of the first marriage, or if the other spouse has made financial provision for the promisor.[28] Promises to marry made while the promisor is already married are unenforceable even though the promisor has separated from the other spouse and is in the process of securing a divorce.[29] So also any contract tending to encourage or facilitate separation or divorce, or to diminish the reciprocal rights and duties which the law attaches to the marital relationship — whether made before marriage as part or all of an antenuptial (prenuptial) agreement or during marriage where the spouses are living in amity — is unenforceable.[30] Thus, where a husband and wife agree that the husband will not have to support the wife as provided by law either during or after marriage, such agreements are clearly unenforceable.[31] However, once the parties have separated or, contemporaneously with a separation, have agreed upon a property settlement, such agreements are enforceable if adequate provision is made for the support of the wife[32] and, where the agreement deals with the custody of any children, the disposition of custody is consistent with the best interests of the children.[33]

Without any doubt, the most significant development in this area in recent years deals with cohabitation agreements, i.e., express or implied agreements between unmarried cohabitants who choose to live together in a fashion identical or very similar to husband and wife, perhaps holding themselves out as husband and wife in the community, though they do not marry. In the celebrated case of *Marvin v. Marvin*,[34] the plaintiff averred that she and the well-known actor, Lee Marvin, entered into an oral agreement that, while living together, they would combine their efforts and earnings and would share equally all accumulated property. Plaintiff agreed to render her services as companion, homemaker, housekeeper, and cook to the defendant. Plaintiff surrendered "her lucrative career as an entertainer" to devote her full time to the defendant. The defendant argued that the alleged contract was of an "immoral" character and, therefore, violative of public policy. The court recognized "radical" changes in the mores of society regarding marriage though it

---

[27]Barnes v. Hobson, 250 S.W. 238, 242-43 (Tex. Civ. App. 1923) (promise of 16-year-old girl to her uncle upon whom she was dependent that she would not marry until she was 22 years old). *See also,* RESTATEMENT 2d § 189: "A promise is unenforceable on grounds of public policy if it is unreasonably in restraint of marriage."

[28]*See* Cowan v. Cowan, 247 Iowa 729, 75 N.W.2d 920 (1956); Nunn v. Justice, 278 Ky. 2, 129 S.W.2d 564 (1939); Lewis v. Johnson, 212 Mo. App. 19, 251 S.W. 136 (1923).

[29]Beach v. Arblaster, 194 Cal. App. 2d 145, 14 Cal. Rptr. 854 (1961); Jones v. Sovereign Camp, 35 F.2d 345 (5th Cir. 1929).

[30]*See* RESTATEMENT 2d § 190.

[31]*See* Cord v. Neuhoff, 94 Nev. 21, 573 P.2d 1170 (1978) (agreement limiting the husband's duty to support wife during marriage and after any termination thereof); Werlein v. Werlein, 27 Wis. 2d 237, 133 N.W.2d 820 (1965) (antenuptial agreement limiting husband's liability to wife in the event of separation or divorce).

[32]Gallemore v. Gallemore, 94 Fla. 516, 114 So. 371 (1927).

[33]*See In re* Custody of Neal, 260 Pa. Super. 151, 393 A.2d 1057 (1978). *See also* RESTATEMENT 2d § 191.

[34]134 Cal. Rptr. 815, 557 P.2d 106 (1976).

reiterated the long-held belief that societal structure depends largely on the institution of marriage. Yet, the court felt that it could not ignore the increasing number of nonmarital relationships and concluded that unmarried cohabitants could enter into an enforceable contract unless their contract was *explicitly* based upon "the immoral and illicit consideration of meretricious sexual services." This approach has spawned considerable litigation and has been generally accepted in other jurisdictions.[35] The contrary view rejects the notion that the policy of maintaining and enhancing the institution of marriage can be achieved while recognizing agreements between unmarried cohabitants:

> We cannot confidently say that judicial recognition of property rights between unmarried cohabitants will not make that alternative to marriage more attractive by allowing the parties to engage in such relationships with greater security [than the marriage relationship].... In thus potentially enhancing the attractiveness of a private arrangement over marriage, we believe that the appellate court decision in this case contravenes the [legislative] policy of strengthening and preserving the integrity of marriage.[36]

In what appears to be an effort to restrict the *Marvin* rationale to its facts, subsequent courts have reemphasized the strong public policy favoring marriage and have sought to avoid any misconceptions concerning the holding in *Marvin* by emphasizing the narrowness of that holding, i.e., it "simply established the right of unmarried cohabitants to enter into a valid contractual obligation of support to the extent that the agreement does not rest upon illicit meretricious consideration."[37] An agreement based on the performance of sexual acts is obviously unenforceable.[38] If, however, "homemaking" and other legal purposes can be severed from a meretricious relationship, the agreement can be enforceable.[39] In a number of jurisdictions, fornication or cohabitation are still criminal offenses. Such statutes, however, have not persuaded courts to view cohabitation agreements as unenforceable if the relationship resembles a normal family relationship.[40] On the other hand, actions based upon the *Marvin* rationale are relegated to express or implied contracts between the parties. They are not "family law" matters, i.e., the unmarried partners are not protected by legislation designed for the marital relation-

---

[35] *See* Boland v. Catalano, 202 Conn. 333, 521 A.2d 142 (1987) which cites cases from seventeen other jurisdictions adopting the *Marvin* rationale. *See also* Carroll v. Lee, 148 Ariz. 10, 712 P.2d 923 (1986) which suggests agreement with the *Marvin* approach in a case involving the partition of property where the title was in the names of unmarried cohabitants. In general, *see* M. GLENDON, THE NEW FAMILY AND THE NEW PROPERTY (1981).

[36] Hewitt v. Hewitt, 77 Ill. 2d 49, 394 N.E.2d 1024, 1209 (1979). Other courts reflect the same concern: Rehak v. Mathis, 239 Ga. 541, 238 S.E.2d 81 (1977); Schwegmann v. Schwegmann, 441 So. 2d 316 (La. App. 1983), *cert. denied,* 104 S. Ct. 2389 (1984). Other courts have mentioned the *Hewitt* rationale favorably: Grishman v. Grishman, 407 A.2d 9, 12 (Me. 1979); Merrill v. Davis, 673 P.2d 1285, 1287 (N.M. 1983). Another court suggests that cohabitation agreements would contravene the public policy in favor of de jure marriage. Slocum v. Hammond, 346 N.W.2d 485, 491 (Iowa 1984).

[37] Gonzales v. Hudson, 200 Cal. App. 3d 45, 245 Cal. Rptr. 753, n.3 (1988).

[38] *See* State v. Grimes, 85 Or. App. 159, 735 P.2d 1277 (1987); Hill v. Estate of Westbrook, 95 Cal. App. 2d 599, 213 P.2d 727 (1950).

[39] Carroll v. Lee, 148 Ariz. 10, 712 P.2d 923 (1986).

[40] *See* Estate of Steffes, 95 Wis. 2d 490, 290 N.W.2d 697 (1980); Tyranski v. Piggins, 44 Mich. App. 570, 205 N.W.2d 595 (1973).

ship.[41] Moreover, an unmarried cohabitant has no cause of action for loss of consortium which would be available to a married spouse.[42] Since unmarried cohabitants are relegated to protection via their contract, they are well advised to set forth their agreement in a detailed writing so as to avoid problems of proving the existence and terms of their contract.

K. *Contracts Facilitating an Illegal Purpose.*

A contract that appears to be perfectly legal may be held illegal because it is made in aid of the accomplishment of an illegal purpose by one of the parties. Thus, while a contract for the purchase and sale of a gun is not illegal absent statutory restrictions, if the seller knows that the buyer intends to use the gun to commit homicide, such an agreement would be unenforceable since the harm to society is so grievous. On the other hand, where the social harm is not so grievous, mere knowledge that the other party may use the property for some illegal purpose does not make the contract unenforceable where the seller is indifferent to the buyer's use of the property.[43] If the seller made the contract with the purpose and intent of enabling the other party to carry out his wrongful purpose, however, such a seller is not simply indifferent to the use of the property by the purchaser and he may not enforce the contract.[44] Again, if the contemplated wrongful act involves the commission of a serious crime, a seller should not be able to claim indifference as to the buyer's use of the property.[45]

L. *Statutory Prohibitions on Contracting — Sunday, Usury, Licensing, and Other Statutes.*

Where a statute expressly or by implication prohibits the making of a certain kind of contract, it is clear that any agreement in violation of that statute is unenforceable. It is, however, important to consider legislative intention in such cases because that intention may suggest, *e.g.,* that a contract in contravention of the statute is voidable and not void, thereby permitting an action in restitution to avoid a forfeiture.[46] Among the common illustrations of statutes that expressly or impliedly prohibit the making of certain kinds of contracts are Sunday ("Sabbath-breaking") laws which prohibit the making of contracts

---

[41] *See* Schafer v. Superior Ct. of San Diego Cty., 180 Cal. App. 3d 305, 225 Cal. Rptr. 513 (1986).

[42] *See* Gonzales v. Hudson, 200 Cal. App. 3d 45, 245 Cal. Rptr. 753 (1986).

[43] *See* Potomac Leasing Co. v. Vitality Centers, Inc., 290 Ark. 265, 718 S.W.2d 928 (1986) (otherwise lawful lease of equipment that lessee intended to use for an unlawful purpose); Carroll v. Beardon, 142 Mont. 40, 381 P.2d 295 (1963) (sale of real property to be used as house of prostitution); Graves v. Johnson, 179 Mass. 53, 60 N.E. 383 (1901) (sale of liquor to be resold in another jurisdiction contrary to its laws).

[44] Advance Whip & Novelty Co. v. Benevolent P.O. of Elks, 106 Vt. 72, 170 A. 95 (1934) (contract to supply merchandise and games of chance to be used for gambling purposes). *See also* RESTATEMENT 2d § 182(a).

[45] *See* Hanauer v. Doane, 79 U.S. (12 Wall) 342 (1871) (consequence of seller's acts are too serious and enormous to permit the seller to plead that, although he knew of the buyer's purpose, he did not sell the goods for that purpose). *See also* Tracy v. Talmage, 14 N.Y. 162, 67 Am. Dec. 132 (1856) and RESTATEMENT 2d § 182(b).

[46] Yank v. Juhrend, 151 Ariz. 587, 729 P.2d 941 (1986) permitting restitution in accordance with RESTATEMENT 2d § 197 comment b.

on Sunday,[47] and usury statutes which prohibit the lender of money from charging more than a specified maximum rate of interest.[48]

Where a statute prohibits the performance of certain acts, a contract to engage in that activity is illegal, not because the statute makes it so, but because enforcing the contract would encourage a violation of the statute. Thus, enforcement of the contract is against public policy. Where, for example, a Sunday law prohibits doing work or carrying on a business on Sunday, a contract requiring performance on a Sunday, though made on a weekday, is unenforceable.[49]

Though there is no common law restriction on the rate of interest charged for the loan of money, statutes commonly provide for maximum rates. The scope of a usury statute must be carefully considered since certain types of loans may not be violative of the statute.[50] The typical usury statute only applies to the loan of money as contrasted with a sale of goods on credit. Thus, even though the credit price in such a transaction exceeds the cash price by more than the amount of interest permitted under the applicable usury statute, there is no violation of the statute.[51] If the contract provides for acceleration of the loan upon default of the debtor, i.e., the entire principal and interest becomes due upon such default, such clauses are not violative of usury statutes.[52] When an agreement is held to violate the applicable usury statute, three different effects are discernible: (a) the contract is void and is, therefore, unenforceable in its entirety;[53] (b) the usurious contract is voidable as to the interest specified beyond the lawful rate;[54] (c) the contract is not only unenforceable as to the usurious portion, but a penalty is recoverable by the injured party.[55]

There are numerous statutes prohibiting a party from engaging in a particular line of business or a profession without a license. Thus, statutes require real estate brokers, milk dealers, pawn brokers, lawyers, dentists, physicians, and many others to secure a license to conduct their businesses or practice their professions. Whether contracts made in pursuance of such businesses or

---

[47] There is considerable variation in the types of transactions prohibited by such statutes. *See* Denton v. Winner Commun., Inc., 726 P.2d 911 (Okla. App. 1986) (Sunday statute prohibited only public selling or offering or exposing for sale certain commodities; therefore, contract for stallion's stud services was not within the scope of the statute). *See also* Sauls v. Stone, 286 Ala. 461, 241 So. 2d 836 (1970) (agreement for sale of business violated Sunday statute). There is no common law restriction on making contracts on Sunday. Rodman v. Robinson, 134 N.C. 503, 47 S.E. 19 (1904); Ward v. Ward, 75 Minn. 269, 77 N.W. 965 (1899); Richmond v. Moore, 107 Ill. 429, 47 Am. Rep. 445 (1883). Therefore, absent a statutory proscription, contracts made on Sunday are enforceable.

[48] *See, e.g.,* Metro Hauling, Inc. v. Daffern, 44 Wash. App. 719, 723 P.2d 32 (1986).

[49] *See, e.g.,* Jacobs v. Clark, 112 Vt. 484, 28 A.2d 369 (1942); Ewing v. Halsey, 127 Kan. 86, 272 P. 187 (1928).

[50] *See* 6 CORBIN ON CONTRACTS, § 1499.

[51] *See, e.g.,* Lundstrom v. Radio Corp. of Am., 17 Utah 2d 114, 405 P.2d 339 (1965).

[52] *See, e.g.,* Campbell v. Werner, 232 So. 2d 252 (Fla. App. 1970).

[53] *See* Beneficial Fin. Co. v. Administrator of Loan Laws, 260 Md. 430, 272 A.2d 649 (1971). *See also* Yakutsk v. Alfino, 43 App. Div. 2d 552, 349 N.Y.S.2d 718 (1973).

[54] *See* Mulcahy v. Loftus, 439 Pa. 111, 267 A.2d 872 (1970).

[55] *See* Cerasoli v. Schneider, 311 A.2d 880 (Del. Super. 1973); White v. Seitzman, 230 Cal. App. 2d 756, 41 Cal. Rptr. 359 (1964) (treble damage recovery under usury statute not recoverable where plaintiff had not only knowingly initiated and consented to the transaction, but had been the "guiding hand" and "had originated the scheme or device to evade the usury law.").

professions without a license are unenforceable is a question of sound public policy since these statutes often do not expressly deal with that question. The purpose of the statute must be the decisive judicial guide in such cases. Where the dominant purpose of the statute is clearly one of raising revenue, a contract made by an unlicensed party should not be unenforceable because the penalties which the statute imposes are deemed adequate to insure its observance.[56] If, however, the licensing statute has a regulatory purpose designed for the protection of third parties, it is generally held that a contract made in violation thereof is illegal and unenforceable by the person who has violated the statute.[57] Even if the statute has a regulatory purpose, however, a technical violation where the purpose of the statute has been met should not preclude enforcement of a contract.[58] Moreover, if a party has performed a contract and "denial or relief is wholly out of proportion to the requirements of public policy or appropriate individual punishment," the contract will be enforced despite the violation of the statute.[59] In such cases, courts must balance the regulatory purpose of the statute and the public policy supporting it against the forfeiture to the performing party and the consequent unjust enrichment of the other party.[60] It is, however, important to note that courts will tolerate forfeiture where the statutory mandate is clear and the act involves moral turpitude. Thus, where a buyer received goods pursuant to a contract obtained by bribing the store's agent, the court refused to enforce the promise to pay for the goods.[61]

M. *Effect of Agreements Contravening Public Policy.*

The manner in which common law courts have dealt with agreements contravening public policy has often left something to be desired. While it is frequently asserted that such a bargain is "void," thereby indicating that the situation is as if no contract had been made, this is not the effect found in many cases. In the absence of a statute specifying otherwise, common law courts have taken the position that the judicial machinery is not available to one who has participated in a transaction violating public policy, i.e., "No court will lend its aid to a man who founds his cause of action upon an immoral or an illegal act."[62] The parties to an illegal transaction are left where they find themselves, not because the court seeks to protect the defendant, but because it will not lend its aid to the plaintiff.[63] No aid will be extended to a party to enforce the illegal bargain which he has made, or to

---

[56]*See, e.g.,* Howard v. Lebby, 197 Ky. 324, 246 S.W. 328 (1923).

[57]*See* Cashin v. Pliter, 168 Mich. 386, 134 N.W. 482 (1912) (violation of statute prohibiting carrying on a business under an assumed name without complying with prescribed requirements). *See also* RESTATEMENT 2d § 181(a).

[58]*See* H. O. Meyer Drilling Co. v. Alton V. Phillips Co., 2 Wash. App. 600, 468 P.2d 1008 (1970) (failure to obtain renewal certificate and pay $20 fee deprived no class of beneficiaries of the protection intended by the statute).

[59]John E. Rosasco Creameries v. Cohen, 276 N.Y. 274, 11 N.E.2d 908 (1937).

[60]RESTATEMENT 2d § 181(b).

[61]*See* Sirkin v. Fourteenth St. Store, 124 App. Div. 384, 108 N.Y.S. 830 (1908). *See also* McConnell v. Commonwealth Pictures Corp., 7 N.Y.2d 465, 166 N.E.2d 494 (1960).

[62]Lord Mansfield in Holman v. Johnson, 1 Cowper 341 [1875].

[63]*Id. See also* Goldberg v. Sanglier, 96 Wash. 2d 874, 639 P.2d 1347 (1982); Rose v. Vulcan Materials Co., 15 N.C. App. 695, 190 S.E.2d 719 (1972).

restore what he has parted with in performing, unless the result of refusing aid would be to defeat the purpose sought to be accomplished in condemning the transaction. If, for example, a transaction is outlawed for the protection of one of the parties, the party who is supposed to be protected may enforce the contract. Thus, where an innocent party deals with an unlicensed architect or contractor who fails to perform in a reasonable fashion, the innocent party who was unaware of the license deficiency may bring an action on the contract.[64] Where, however, the court takes the usual path and refuses to aid either party, the result may be that one wrongdoer is enriched at the expense of another. No doubt the theory supporting this conclusion is that the refusal to aid has a deterrent effect. Whatever the merit of this rationale, its effect in a given case may be to encourage the defendant to find another person whom he can dupe.

For many years, courts have taken the position that illegality need not be pleaded by the defendant, i.e., a court will, on its own motion, deny relief to a plaintiff whose cause of action appears from his own presentation to emanate from an illegal bargain.[65] It is, however, dangerous to place excessive reliance on this supposition, particularly in cases where the illegality does not involve moral turpitude. Where no moral turpitude is involved, a court may choose the view expressed by a Massachusetts court:

> It is believed that in actions at law like the one at bar, in which the defence of illegality has not been set up, the court will recognize no absolute duty to interfere and of its own mere motion to sustain a defence not set up by the party, and generally will not so interfere, unless, first, the plaintiff declaration shows that he relies upon an illegal agreement or violation of law, or secondly, unless he has been obliged to show his own guilt in fully proving his case.[66]

N. *Effect of Partial Contravention of Public Policy.*

Where a contract only partially contravenes public policy, a court may enforce the other part of the contract if that part is not an essential part of the agreed exchange and if the party seeking enforcement of that part operated in good faith and fairly and did not engage in serious misconduct.[67] If there is a serious contravention of public policy so that a considerable degree of moral turpitude attaches to it, courts generally refuse to enforce any part of the agreement.[68] If, however, the violation of public policy is not of so serious a character, the contract may be divisible in the technical sense of certain per-

---

[64] *See* Hedla v. McCool, 476 F.2d 1223 (9th Cir. 1973) (architect); Cohen v. Mayflower Corp., 196 Va. 1153, 86 S.E.2d 860 (1955) (contractor).

[65] *See* Oscanyan v. Winchester Repeating Arms Co., 103 U.S. 261 (1881).

[66] O'Brien v. Shea, 208 Mass. 528, 535, 95 N.E. 99, 101 (1911). *See also* O'Donnell v. Bane, 385 Mass. 114, 431 N.E.2d 190 (1982) (unless the evidence shows a contract which is inherently wrongful, such as a contingent fee arrangement with an attorney in a criminal matter, a claim of illegality not presented on the pleadings will not be considered).

[67] RESTATEMENT 2d § 184.

[68] *See, e.g.,* cases involving bribery, such as McConnell v. Commonwealth Pictures Corp., 7 N.Y.2d 465, 166 N.E.2d 494 (1960) and Sirkin v. Fourteenth St. Store, 124 App. Div. 384, 108 N.Y.S. 830 (1908). *See also* Smilansky v. Mandel Bros., 254 Mich. 575, 236 N.W. 866 (1931) (original contract against public policy where foreign corporation was unauthorized to do business taints new promise to perform the same contract pursuant to settlement of litigation).

formances being the agreed equivalents of counter performances. If such divisible parts, standing alone, would not contravene public policy, they may be enforced while the other parts of the contract would remain unenforceable.[69] Notwithstanding a willingness to apply this principle, courts are precluded from applying it where the contract is simply not divisible.[70] Even where the contract is technically entire, if the lawful part of the defendant's promise is separable and the entire consideration furnished by the plaintiff is lawful and he is prepared to perform the whole of it, the promise will be enforced.[71] On the other hand, if any part of the consideration offends public policy, no part of the defendant's promises will be enforced, though all of his promises are, in themselves, in accordance with public policy.[72]

The decisions concerning partial "illegality" often appear to be technical or arbitrary though there is an underlying manifestation of judicial effort to avoid forfeitures where the violation of public policy is not sufficiently serious to justify a penalty.[73]

O. *Mitigating Doctrines — Pari Delicto and Locus Pœnitentiae — Restitution.*

The maxim, *In pari delicto, potior est conditio defendentis* (in case of equal fault, the condition of the party defending is the stronger) is found in many cases involving contracts violating public policy. Like other maxims, however, this one does not offer an automatic solution to the myriad problems involved in such contracts.[74] If, however, a party to a bargain violating public policy has conferred a benefit upon the other party and then seeks restitution, he may be successful if he was not in pari delicto, i.e., "not equally in the wrong"[75] with the other. Moreover, even if he was in pari delicto he may have "repented" and chosen to withdraw from the agreement prior to the attainment of its "unlawful" purpose.[76] If his withdrawal is timely, he is said to have done so within his "locus pœnitentiae," literally a place for repentance,

---

[69] *See* Jones v. Brantley, 121 Miss. 721, 83 So. 802 (1920) (part of contract performable on Sunday).

[70] *See, e.g.*, Starr v. Robinson, 181 Ga. App. 9, 351 S.E.2d 238 (1986) (attorney sued to recover lump sum fee in exchange for handling all matters connected with sale including services as a real estate broker and attorney was not licensed as broker. The fee was not apportioned with respect to different services and the court, therefore, could not enforce any part of the contract); Slusher v. Greenfield, 488 So. 2d 579 (Fla. App. 1986) (physicians who were junior shareholders of professional corporation could not prevent voiding of entire contract where illegal provisions for senior shareholders were indivisible).

[71] *See* Illinois Bankers Life Assur. Co. v. Brydia, 180 Okla. 436, 70 P.2d 73 (1937); Poultry Producers v. Barlow, 189 Cal. 278, 208 P. 93 (1922); McCall Co. v. Hughes, 102 Miss. 375, 59 So. 794 (1912).

[72] Kukla v. Perry, 361 Mich. 311, 105 N.W.2d 176 (1960); Johnson v. McMillion, 178 Ky. 707, 199 S.W. 1070 (1918). *See also* Schara v. Thiede, 58 Wis. 2d 489, 206 N.W.2d 129 (1973) where a one-year lease was expressly conditioned upon the faithful performance of an illegal agreement and the court held that the contract was so permeated by illegality that it left the parties where it found them.

[73] *See generally* Comment, *The Effect of Partial Illegality*, 33 MICH. L, REV. 278-87 (1934).

[74] *See* Lissenden v. C. A. V. Bosch, Ltd., A.C. 412, 435 [1940] as quoted in Grodecki, *In pari Delicto Potior Est Conditio Defendentis*, 71 LAW Q. REV. 254 (1955).

[75] *See* RESTATEMENT 2d 198(b).

[76] Actual repentance is unnecessary, i.e., it is enough that the party withdrew. *See* Aikman v. City of Wheeling, 120 W. Va. 46, 195 S.E. 667 (1938).

though it is used to mean simply an opportunity for withdrawal prior to the fulfillment of the improper purpose.

There are numerous statements in the case law to the effect that a party who was not in pari delicto may recover the value of any performance he has rendered if he was not, in the language of the FIRST RESTATEMENT, guilty of serious moral turpitude.[77] The RESTATEMENT 2d prefers more neutral language in suggesting that such a party need only be "not equally in the wrong with the promisor."[78] One of the better-known cases involved the delivery of $28,000 worth of jewelry to the defendant in exchange for defendant's promise to obtain visas for the plaintiff and his family by bribing a public official. The defendant absconded with the jewelry and did not perform his promise. When the plaintiff much later sought restitution of his money, the court recognized plaintiff's actions as attempting to save himself and his family from the Nazi army and held that the plaintiff was not in pari delicto with the defendant.[79] Though bribing a public official would normally be characterized as a serious wrong or, in the older usage, "serious moral turpitude," the circumstances of this case clearly precluded that characterization.

Where the parties are not in pari delicto, the plaintiff may be a member of a class designed to be protected by the public policy standard. Thus, if a party were prevented from recovering usurious interest, the purpose of the usury statute would be defeated because the aggrieved party has typically acquiesced in the terms of the contract because of his inferior bargaining power.[80] Courts do not deem contracts made with an unlicensed party void. Since the innocent party is one of the persons the licensing statute is designed to protect, he is not in pari delicto with the unlicensed party.[81] The purpose of a particular statute is a critical determinant in these cases. Thus, where a plaintiff sought treble damages under an antitrust statute for a violation of the antitrust laws, the defense argued that the plaintiff had enjoyed the benefits of the unlawful agreements and should be precluded from recovery because he was in pari delicto. The United States Supreme Court refused to recognize the "complex" defense of pari delicto in such an action, though it suggested that complete and voluntary participation in an antitrust offense could bar a plaintiff's recovery.[82] Similarly, where a court finds that a gambling statute is designed to curb organized gambling, a party to a wager is not in pari delicto with a professional bookmaker.[83]

Where the parties are in pari delicto, a court may still grant restitution to encourage withdrawal (if not repentance) from the improper agreement. Where, for example, a party incurred a gambling debt and pledged a bond with a market value more than double the debt as security, the pledgee con-

---

[77] FIRST RESTATEMENT § 604. See also Wade, Restitution of Benefits Acquired Through Illegal Transactions, 95 U. PA. L. REV. 261 (1947).

[78] RESTATEMENT 2d § 198(b).

[79] Liebman v. Rosenthal, 185 Misc. 837, 57 N.Y.S.2d 875, aff'd, 269 App. Div. 1062, 59 N.Y.S.2d 148 (1945).

[80] See Glyco v. Schultz, 62 Ohio Ops. 2d 459, 289 N.E.2d 919 (1972).

[81] See Southern States Life Ins. Co. v. McCauley, 81 N.M. 114, 464 P.2d 404 (1970); Cohen v. Mayflower Corp., 196 Va. 1153, 86 S.E.2d 860 (1955).

[82] Perma Life Mufflers, Inc. v. International Parts Corp., 392 U.S. 134 (1968).

[83] Watts v. Malatesta, 262 N.Y. 80, 186 N.E. 210 (1933).

fessed that he had sold the bond when the pledgor tendered the amount of the bet. In an action by the pledgor for the market value of the bond, the court recognized the doctrine of pari delicto which would leave these parties where they were. However, the court superimposed the concept that one has a right to withdraw from such an improper agreement to either retain or recover his property or money before it goes into the hands of the winner. Thus, where money or property is placed with a third party (stakeholder) from which it can be withdrawn, the loser can always recover from the stakeholder. Even though the bond in this case had been delivered to the winner, it had been delivered as security for the debt and ownership of the bond remained in the loser. Therefore, it could be recovered.[84] It is important to recognize the two requirements for the application of the *locus pœnitentia* concept: (1) the improper ("illegal") purpose has not been attained and restitution will avoid such attainment;[85] (2) the illegality did not involve "moral turpitude"[86] or, as the RESTATEMENT 2d suggests, the party claiming restitution "did not engage in serious misconduct."[87]

P. *Mitigating Doctrines — Ignorance of Facts.*

Sometimes a bargain that is proper on its face is contrary to public policy because of extrinsic facts known only to one of the parties. Courts generally permit the innocent party who is justifiably ignorant to recover damages as if the contract were proper if the facts or legislation violated are of a relatively minor character.[88] An excusably ignorant party may also be entitled to restitution.[89] These principles may be viewed as a species of the general concept protecting a party not in equal fault (in pari delicto) with the other party.

Q. *Effect of Substituted Contract in Discharge of Bargain.*

It is often suggested that a transaction growing out of an "illegal" bargain is, itself, unenforceable though it may be intrinsically "lawful."[90] Some courts, however, have taken a different view where the impropriety is not particularly serious. They have held that when the illegal contract has been discharged by an unperformed substituted contract, which is not in and of itself unlawful in character, the latter contract may be enforced. Thus, where a

---

[84] Gehres v. Ater, 148 Ohio St. 89, 73 N.E.2d 513 (1947). *See also* RESTATEMENT 2d § 199(a).

[85] *See* Woel v. Griffith, 253 Md. 451, 253 A.2d 353 (1969) and RESTATEMENT 2d § 199(b).

[86] *See* Williams v. Brown, 362 S.W.2d 177 (Tex. App. 1962). *But see* Town of Meredith v. Fullerton, 83 N.H. 124, 139 A. 359, 365 (1927).

[87] RESTATEMENT 2d § 199.

[88] Weinsklar Realty Co. v. Dooley, 200 Wis. 412, 228 N.W. 515 (1930) (contract executed on Sunday by one of the parties without knowledge by the other). *See* RESTATEMENT 2d § 180.

[89] RESTATEMENT 2d § 198(a).

[90] In Smilansky v. Mandel Bros., 254 Mich. 575, 236 N.W. 866, 867 (1931), the court quotes from an early American case, Comstock v. Draper, 53 Am. Dec. 78: "It is a well settled doctrine in the English and American books, that an illegal transaction cannot constitute a good consideration for a promise. If the connection between the original illegal transaction and the new promise can be traced, if the latter is connected with and grows out of the former, no matter how many times and in how may different forms it may be renewed, it cannot form the basis of a recovery, for repeating a void promise cannot give it validity." Here, the court held that settlement of litigation, though normally sufficient consideration for a new promise, is insufficient consideration where it will have the effect of enforcing an illegal promise.

lottery resulting in an accounting showing money due the plaintiff which defendant promised to pay, the court held that the plaintiff could enforce the promise. Though it recognized that other courts would refuse to enforce such a promise where the original bargain was tainted with illegality, this court suggested: "[T]his court long ago committed itself to a contrary doctrine, and has established the rule that, where an illegal contract has been fully performed, the illegality is no defense to an action brought upon a subsequent promise to pay over the balance in the hands of one of the parties to the original contract."[91]

R. *Effect of Change in Law.*

It is generally held that a contract that is contrary to public policy when made does not become enforceable if the law is changed to validate such agreements before an action on the agreement is brought.[92] The rule is sometimes justified on the ground that the contract was originally void and therefore could gain no validity from the subsequent change in the law.[93] This view is, however, less than persuasive since contracts violating public policy are not void absent an express statutory directive to that effect.[94] If the contract is unenforceable at the time of formation because of *facts* of which both parties were unaware, a change of those facts should make the contract enforceable.[95] The only justification for the rule involving a change in law validating such transactions is that parties who made the contract when it violated some statute or other legal standard cannot be absolved from their wrongdoing simply because the law has changed. Yet, if legislation is changed because the legislature decides that the underlying rationale of the statute is either wrong or no longer appropriate, there would seem to be little reason for refusing to enforce the contract that was invalid when originally made.

S. *Enforcement of "Illegal" Bargains That Are "Legal" Where Made.*

A contract may be enforceable under the public policy of the jurisdiction where it was made or performed but not under the public policy of the jurisdiction where enforcement is sought. One of the repeated maxims of contract law is that a contract valid under its governing law is valid everywhere.[96] Courts hasten to add, however, that there is an exception to this general rule in that where the enforcement would violate the fixed, settled, or strong public policy of the state in which the action is brought, it will not be enforced.[97] Where the

---

[91] Central Labor Council v. Young, 136 Wash. 550, 240 P. 919, 920 (1925). *Accord, In re* Lowe's Estate, 104 Neb. 147, 175 N.W. 1015 (1920).

[92] *See* Interinsurance Exchange of Auto. Club v. Ohio Cas. Ins. Co., 58 Cal. 2d 142, 23 Cal. Rptr. 592, 373 P.2d 640, 642 (1962): "Whether it be the rule in this state that an unlawful contract is void ... or only unenforceable, ... the law here is, and should be, that a contract or provision in a contract which contravenes public policy when made is not validated by a later statutory change in that public policy."

[93] *See* McClain v. Oklahoma Cotton Growers' Ass'n, 125 Okla. 264, 258 P. 269 (1927).

[94] *See* American Sav. Life Ins. Co. v. Financial Affairs Mgt. Co., 20 Ariz. App. 479, 513 P.2d 1362 (1973).

[95] *See* First Restatement § 609.

[96] *See* Continental Mtg. Inv. v. Sailboat Key, Inc., 354 So. 2d 67, 71 (1978).

[97] *Id.*

winner of a gambling debt enforceable in one jurisdiction sought to enforce it in a jurisdiction where such an agreement contravened public policy, the court enforced the agreement since it did not contravene the strong public policy of its jurisdiction.[98] Similarly, where a restrictive covenant is enforceable in one jurisdiction, another jurisdiction will refuse to enforce it if it violates the strong public policy of the second jurisdiction.[99]

---

[98] Intercontinental Hotels Corp. (P.R.) v. Golden, 15 N.Y.2d 9, 203 N.E.2d 210 (1964) (gambling agreement did not contravene the law of Puerto Rico and court held that such arrangements did not contravene the strong public policy of New York which had by that time legalized pari-mutuel betting and the operation of bingo games and were considering off-track betting. *See,* however, Ciampittiello v. Campitello, 134 Conn. 51, 54 A.2d 669 (1947).

[99] *See* Hollingsworth Solderless Terminal Co. v. Turley, 622 F.2d 1324 (9th Cir. 1980).

Chapter 7

CONDITIONS

§ 99. Meaning and Nature of Condition.

A. *Common Usage.*

A common dictionary definition of "condition" suggests that some event — any event — must occur before something is completed or effective, i.e., some operative fact must happen before a subsequent situation can exist. Used in this broad, non-technical fashion, a conditioning event may be *any* event. For example, before a contract may be said to exist, an offer and an acceptance must occur and a validation device (*e.g.,* consideration) must be present. In the broad sense of the term, each of these events is a condition to the formation of a contract. More specifically, the power of acceptance may be said to be "conditioned" upon an offer since the power will not exist unless an offer has occurred. In other contractual contexts, it may be suggested that when Ames promises to pay Barnes $1000 thirty days from the date of the promise (in exchange for something of value), the mere lapse of thirty days or whatever period of time the parties establish in their agreement is a condition to Ames' promise to pay $1000. Innumerable other examples of the broad use of the term "condition" may be found. In various legal relationships evidenced by a writing, such as contracts, trusts, wills, and the like, there may be qualifying clauses indicating that certain events must occur before certain legal relationships will become operative or effective. These written words, themselves, may be viewed as conditions. Such a use of the term is similar to the use of the term "contract" to refer to the writing or document evidencing the legal relationship of the parties. All of these and other layperson uses of the term "condition," however, must be rejected if the concept of condition as used technically in the law of contracts is to be understood.

B. *"Condition" as Used in Contract Law.*

In contract law, the use of the term "condition" is confined to an event, other than the mere lapse of time, that is not certain to occur but which must occur (unless the condition is excused) in order to *activate* an existing contractual duty.[1] The fact or event properly called a condition occurs during the *performance* stage of a contract, i.e., after the contract is formed and prior to its discharge. When the essential requisites for contract formation have been fulfilled, i.e., offer, acceptance, and validation devices between or among parties with capacity to contract, there is a contractual relationship between the parties. The parties are bound by their duties and each of the duties has correlative rights. These rights and duties, however, may not be immediately active duties or immediately enforceable rights. They are often subject to some fact or event that must occur to activate the duties, thereby making the rights immediately enforceable. Insurance contracts invariably contain conditions such as a fire or other casualty loss which must occur to activate the

---

[1]This description of a condition is similar to the RESTATEMENT 2d definition in § 224: "A condition is an event, not certain to occur, which must occur, unless its non-occurrence is excused, before performance under a contract becomes due." Numerous cases have adopted this definition. *See, e.g.,* Seman v. First State Bank of Eden Prairie, 394 N.W.2d 557 (Minn. App. 1986); Village of Cairo, Mo. v. Bodine Contr'g Co., 685 S.W.2d 253 (Mo. App. 1985); Cambria Sav. & Loan Ass'n v. Estate of Gross, 294 Pa. Super. 351, 439 A.2d 1236 (1982).

duty of the insurer to pay the amount of the policy. In one of the more common transactions occurring innumerable times each day, parties agree upon the purchase and sale of real estate where the agreement recites the requirement that a certain fact or event occur before the buyer's duty to pay the purchase price becomes activated and the seller's correlative right to receive the purchase price becomes enforceable. Typically, that fact or event is the buyer's success in obtaining suitable financing secured through a real estate mortgage to pay a large portion of the purchase price. The buyer's duty to pay the purchase price is, therefore, *conditioned* on the occurrence of that fact or event. It is sometimes forgotten that the parties are bound to each other at the moment their real estate contract is formed, i.e., before the occurrence of the conditioning event. At the moment the contract is formed, the seller may not agree to sell the property to another and the buyer may not refuse to perform his obligation by, for example, failing to make a reasonable effort to obtain financing. The contract obligation is created at the moment of formation. The performance of that obligation is subject to the occurrence of the condition of financing. If the financing cannot be obtained through reasonable efforts, the condition has not occurred, and the buyer's duty is not activated and the seller's right is not enforceable. Once it is clear that the condition will not occur, since the duty to which it attached will never become activated, the duty is discharged and the correlative right can never be enforced. Only at that time are the parties free from each other. Contract obligation must not be confused with contract performance.[2]

Students of contract law will recall another illustration found in the classic *Carbolic Smoke Ball*[3] case discussed earlier in relation to the agreement process.[4] The advertisement offered $100 to any person using the smoke ball in accordance with directions who thereafter contracted influenza, presumably within the "flu season." The acceptance of that offer occurred through the use of the smoke ball in accordance with directions. At that moment, a contract between the defendant company and any such user was formed. It was a contract involving only one right and one duty, in traditional contract law terms, a "unilateral" contract, since the user had performed the act of acceptance required by the offer of using the ball in accordance with directions, thereby creating a right in the user and a correlative duty in the manufacturer of the ball. The duty, however, was conditioned upon the user contracting influenza. The occurrence of that operative fact or event would *activate* the *existing* duty of the manufacturer.[5] As will be seen in the pages that follow, the typical contract containing a condition may be analyzed in this fashion. It is important to consider what kind of fact or event may constitute a condition.

---

[2] For a clear exposition of this analysis in a real estate contract setting, *see* Highland Inns Corp. v. American Landmark Corp., 650 S.W.2d 667 (Mo. App. 1983).

[3] Carlill v. Carbolic Smoke Ball Co., 1 Q.B. 256 (1893).

[4] *See supra* Chapter 2.

[5] In the analysis of conditions, much of the terminology employed is suggested by the classic analysis of Professor Corbin in his article, *Conditions in the Law of Contract*, 28 YALE L.J. 739 (1919).

C. *Nature of the Fact or Event Constituting a Condition.*

Virtually any act or event may constitute a condition.[6] The event may be an act to be performed or forborne by one of the parties to the contract, an act to be performed or forborne by a third party, or some fact or event over which neither party, or any other party, has any control. Moreover, the event constituting the condition need not be a significant or material event, i.e., the parties may agree upon an event that does not apear to be either important or reasonable even where a forfeiture would result where the condition does not occur. Yet, modern courts are loathe to permit the nonoccurrence of an insignificant condition to result in a forfeiture. Thus, as will be seen later in this section, courts will resort to interpretation[7] or other devices and, on rare occasion, simply refuse to give effect to the condition where manifest injustice would otherwise result.[8]

If the contract requires a particular event to occur and no party to that contract has *promised* that it will occur, the occurrence of the event can only be construed as a condition that qualifies one or more duties of the parties. If, however, one of the parties has *promised* that a particular event will occur while the other party's duty is qualified by the identical event, the event is a promise by one party creating a duty in that party and the same event is a condition that must occur to activate the duty of the other party. Thus, where a seller of goods promises to ship the goods to a destination named by the buyer conditioned upon the buyer's providing notice of that destination by a certain date, and the buyer also promises to provide that notice by a certain date, the giving of notice is a promised duty of the buyer while the same event is a condition to the seller's duty to perform.[9] Where the same event is both a promise and a condition, it has been labeled a *promissory condition.*

Events constituting conditions are typically events that will or will not occur in the future. This tends to obscure the fact that such events may be past, present, or future. A policy of marine insurance may be issued after the loss has occurred without the knowledge of the parties, i.e., the effect of a promise must be judged on the basis of what the parties themselves apparently know. If the parties are unaware of a past or present fact as to these parties, it is an uncertain fact and may operate as a condition.[10] If, however, one or both parties are aware of the occurrence of a particular event, the promise cannot be characterized as conditional, i.e., it is either an absolute promise or a nullity.

D. *Differences Between a Promise and a Condition.*

The concept of condition can be greatly illuminated through a comparison of the legal effects of a promise, versus a condition, as suggested in the classic

---

[6] *See* K & K Pharmacy, Inc. v. Barta, 222 Neb. 215, 382 N.W.2d 363 (1986) (conditioning event was the ability of buyer to obtain a new lease satisfactory to buyer).

[7] *See, e.g.,* United Plate Glass Co. v. Metal Trims Indus., 106 Pa. Commw. 22, 525 A.2d 468 (1987). *See also* RESTATEMENT 2d § 227(1).

[8] *See* Jackson v. Richards 5 & 10, Inc., 286 Pa. Super. 445, 433 A.2d 888 (1981) (refusal to effectuate immaterial conditions where forfeiture would otherwise result).

[9] *See* Internatio-Rotterdam, Inc. v. River Brand Rice Mills, Inc., 259 F.2d 137 (2d Cir. 1958).

[10] *See* RESTATEMENT 2d § 224 comment b. *See also* Seward & Scales v. Mitchell, 41 Tenn. (1 Cold.) 87 (1860); Ollive v. Booker, 1 Ex. 416 [1847].

analysis of Professor Corbin where he presents four essential differences: [11] (1) a promise is always made by one of the parties to the contract, whereas an event operates as a condition only where the parties agree that it shall operate as such, except where conditions are created by the court; (2) a promise creates a duty in the promisor, whereas the purpose of a condition is to postpone a duty in the promisor; (3) when a promise is performed, the duty is discharged, but where a condition occurs, the quiescent duty is activated; (4) where a promise is not performed, a breach of contract occurs and the promisee has a remedial right to damages or other relief, but the failure of a condition to occur leaves the duty in its dormant state, i.e., it is simply not activated and, unless the condition is excused, it will be discharged but does not give rise to any remedial relief.[12] Earlier we explored the possibility that the same event is a promised duty of one party and a condition to the duty of the other party, i.e., a promissory condition.[13] When characterized as a promise, the failure of that event to occur would be a breach by the party who promised that it would occur. As to the other party, however, the non-occurrence of the event would leave that party's duty asleep and, if the condition could not occur, the duty would die in its sleep since only the occurrence of the condition could awaken it.[14]

§ 100. Warranties — Uniform Commercial Code — Conditions Distinguished.

A. *The Concept of "Warranty" — "Title" and "Quality."*

The term "warranty" has been used in several distinct senses over the years. Article 2 of the UCC contains four different warranties in relation to a contract for the sale of goods. Beyond a warranty of title or ownership of the goods and related warranties,[15] there are three warranties of quality that will

---

[11] *See* Corbin, *Conditions in the Law of Contracts,* 28 YALE L.J. 739, 745 (1919).

[12] *See* RESTATEMENT 2d § 225.

[13] *See supra* text at note 9.

[14] It is important for students of contract law to appreciate the significance of the same event being a promise and a condition. If, for example, one party promises to give notice by a certain time and fails to do so, he has breached his promise. If that failure, however, is not a material breach (materiality of breach will be explored later in this chapter), the duty of the non-breaching party is not discharged though that party will have a cause of action for any loss occasioned by such an immaterial breach. If the same event — giving notice — is also a condition to the other party's duty to perform, however, then the non-occurrence of the condition has the effect of leaving the other party's duty in a state of quiescence and that duty will be discharged if the condition can never occur. Thus, the non-occurrence of a condition can have a drastic effect on the rights and duties of the parties whereas a breach may have a much less significant effect.

[15] *See* UCC § 2-312(1)(a) and (b) which contain the basic warranty of the seller that the title conveyed by him is good and its transfer rightful and that the goods shall be delivered free from any security interest or other lien or encumbrance of which the buyer at the time of contracting has no knowledge. Also under this section, in § 2-312(3), a seller who is a merchant with respect to goods of the kind sold also warrants that the goods will be delivered free from the rightful claim of any third party by way of patent infringement or the like, though it places a duty on the buyer who furnishes specifications to indemnify the seller against any claim arising out of the buyer's specifications. While the "warranty of title" in this section is not expressly referred to as an "implied" warranty, it *is* implied since no expression of this warranty is necessary for it to exist in a given sale of goods. The reason this warranty is not captioned "implied" is that it contains its own method of disclaimer in § 2-312(2) which requires extremely clear language or other circumstances to evidence the intention of the parties that they contracted without this fundamental

be discussed later in this section, i.e., express warranties,[16] the implied warranty of merchantability,[17] and the implied warranty of fitness for a particular purpose.[18] We will see that even as used in the UCC, the concept of "warranty" is subject to considerable confusion. As to the basic concept of warranty, the principal draftsman of Article 2, Karl Llewellyn, was anything but fond of the term or the confusing set of ideas it suggested.[19] Llewellyn, Corbin,[20] and others encountered difficulty in determining whether a warranty is a promise, a condition, or both. For example, in a simple contract to buy and sell a new lawnmower, if the seller tells the buyer that the mower will operate effectively in cutting a normal, flat lawn, the seller's promise may be viewed as a promise of indemnification, i.e., a promise by the seller to save the buyer harmless if the mower does not operate effectively. If the mower does not operate effectively, the seller will perform his promise of indemnity by taking the mower back and replacing it with one that works, or by returning the purchase price, or, if the purchase price has not yet been paid, by cancelling the debt. If, however, the statement by the seller is not a promise but only a representation of fact, if that representation turns out to be false, it may be said that a condition precedent to the buyer's duty to pay for the mower has not occurred. The buyer's duty, therefore, would not be activated and the duty is discharged.[21]

The characterization of warranties as promises or conditions, however, is no longer significant. They have taken on a life of their own. The warranties of quality that we will examine in this section raise three distinct questions: (1) does the seller in a given sales transaction have any obligation as to the quality of the goods? (2) if the seller does have an obligation as to quality, what kind of goods must he deliver to meet that obligation? (3) if the seller fails to meet his obligation as to quality, what are the buyer's remedies? We will explore the first and second questions in this section and leave the third question for exploration in a later chapter under the topic of remedies for breach of contract.[22]

---

warranty. *See* Sunseri v. RKO-Stanley Warner Theatres, Inc., 248 Pa. Super. 111, 374 A.2d 1342 (1977). Other UCC warranties dealing with the quality of goods, i.e., the implied warranty of merchantability in § 2-314 and the implied warranty of fitness for a particular purpose in § 2-315, both of which are discussed later in this section, are captioned "implied" and they must be disclaimed according to the formulas in § 2-316(2) of the Code. To avoid the application of § 2-316(2) to warranties of title, the warranty of title section is not designated as an "implied" warranty though, again, it is certainly "implied." *See* comment 6 to § 2-312. In fact, it is in one sense *more* implied than the other implied warranties since it is more difficult to disclaim than the other implied warranties. Again, this is the essential reason for ascertaining that the more liberal disclaimer provisions of § 2-316(2) do not apply to "implied" warranties of title.

[16] UCC § 2-313.

[17] UCC § 2-314.

[18] UCC § 2-315.

[19] "To say 'warranty' is to say nothing definite as to legal effect.... [T]he sane course is to discard the word from one's thinking." K. LLEWELLYN, CASES AND MATERIALS ON THE LAW OF SALES 210 (1930). As to why Professor Llewellyn agreed to retain the term "warranty" in the UCC, its retention was simply one of innumerable compromises he made to ascertain the enactment of the new Code throughout the country. A new commercial code dehors the traditional term "warranty" would have appeared radical, indeed.

[20] *See* 1 CORBIN § 14.

[21] As it appeared in the second edition of this book, this analysis is cited in Langley v. FDIC, Justice Scalia, 108 S. Ct. 396 (1987).

[22] *See infra* Chapter 9.

B. *Express Warranties — "Basis of the Bargain."*

The UCC recognizes the creation of express warranties by (a) statements of fact or promises by the seller relating to the goods which become *part of the basis of the bargain;* (b) descriptions of the goods which become *part of the basis of the bargain;* (c) samples or models of the goods which are made *part of the basis of the bargain.*[23] No particular form of language is necessary to create an express warranty, *e.g.*, the term "warranty" or "guarantee" need not be used, but the statement must be a statement of *fact* as contrasted with a statement of the seller's opinion or commendation of the goods.[24] If a seller refers to an automobile as "great" or "wonderful" or other commendatory term, it is obviously not an express warranty since buyers should be aware of the tendency of sellers to "puff" their products. If, however, a seller indicates that the car has not been driven more than 200 miles or that the brake linings have been replaced within the last fifty miles or other statement of fact, an express warranty has been created. Whether a particular statement is one of commendation or opinion as contrasted with a statement of fact is, itself, a question of fact.[25]

A statement, description, model, or sample will not become an express warranty under the Code unless it becomes part of the *basis of the bargain.*[26] The "basis of the bargain" requirement has given rise to considerable consternation.[27] Pre-Code tests to determine the existence of an express warranty generally did not require buyers to demonstrate that they actually relied upon a seller's statement as to the quality of the goods. Rather, courts adhered to the Williston view that the buyer need only show that the seller's statements were of a kind which would naturally induce a buyer to purchase the goods and that the buyer actually purchased the goods.[28] Controversy under the Code has centered on whether the "basis of the bargain" requirement is simply a restatement of the pre-Code "natural inducement" test. UCC comments to the express warranty section suggest that the old test has been rejected since they expressly reject any requirement of a showing of "particular reliance" and presume that any statement of fact by the seller constitutes an express warranty.[29] Moreover, another comment to the express warranty sec-

---

[23] UCC § 2-313(1)(a), (b), and (c).

[24] UCC § 2-313(2).

[25] *See, e.g.*, Autzen v. John C. Taylor Lumber Sales, Inc., 280 Or. 783, 572 P.2d 1322 (1977) where the court managed to avoid determining whether the phrase "A-1 condition" constituted an express warranty. *See also* Ewers v. Eisenzopf, 88 Wis. 2d 482, 276 N.W.2d 802 (1979) where the buyer of certain sea shells, a piece of coral, and a driftwood branch asked a clerk in a store selling such items among sundry items whether these particular goods were "suitable for placement in a salt water aquarium" to which the clerk responded that they had come from salt water and were suitable for salt water aquariums if they were rinsed. Though the buyer rinsed the items in a normal fashion, his fish died. Experts testified that the items would have been suitable if they had been subjected to a week-long cleansing process consisting of soaking the items in boiling water. The majority held that an express warranty had been created by the clerk's statement and that warranty had been breached.

[26] This phrase is used with respect to any type of express warranty listed in § 2-313(1).

[27] The analysis which follows is based essentially on Murray, *"Basis of the Bargain": Transcending Classical Concepts,* 66 MINN. L. REV. 283 (1982).

[28] *See* Uniform Sales Act § 12 and 1 WILLISTON ON CONTRACTS § 206.

[29] *See* Murray, *supra* note 27, at 287-91, analyzing these comments and related sections of the UCC.

tion suggests the possibility of a post-formation warranty, i.e., an express warranty created for the first time *after* the contract for the sale of the goods was formed.[30] The drafting history and language of the comments in particular suggest the distinct probability that Professor Llewellyn and his friends were not thinking in terms of the classical "bargained-for-exchange" in using the phrase, "basis of the bargain." Rather, they were pursuing a bargain continuum which is a bargaining process extending beyond the moment in time when the contract of sale was made.[31] The extrapolation of this concept is that "basis of the bargain," as found in the UCC express warranty sections, seeks to protect the reasonable expectations of the buyer, i.e., such expectations are not relegated to those induced by the seller's statements, nor to those upon which the buyer relied in making the purchase. Rather, the buyer's reasonable expectations are those which are "created by all of the 'affirmations of fact made by the seller about the goods during a bargain.'"[32] Even where the buyer was totally unaware of a particular statement of fact about the goods made by the seller prior to purchasing the goods, that statement should become part of the basis of the bargain. Thus, if a buyer purchases a new car and later discovers that his car is the only car of that model and year without a particular feature that was advertised by the seller as "standard" on that model and year, the buyer is justified in expecting his car to contain that feature together with all other standard features though he was unaware of that feature and, therefore, did not rely upon it as an inducement for the purchase of the car. Modern buyers reasonably expect to find all standard features on goods they purchase though they were unaware of each and every feature prior to the purchase.

The case law in this area continues in a state of confusion under the Code. Some courts suggest that reliance is necessary and proceed to suggest that it can be presumed, though they also suggest that it must actually induce the purchase.[33] A number of courts appear to suggest that the UCC test did not change the pre-Code test.[34] Other courts suggest that reliance is not the test under the Code, but they proceed to suggest that "lack of reliance" is the test.[35] Courts which are convinced that the UCC rejected any version of the old reliance test have not, unfortunately, created a workable test.[36] In general,

---

[30] Comment 7 to § 2-313 states, "The precise time when words of description or affirmation are made or samples are shown is not material. The sole question is whether the language or samples or models are to be regarded as part of the contract. If language is used after the closing of the deal (as when the buyer when taking delivery asks and receives an additional assurance) the warranty becomes a modification and need not be supported by consideration if it is otherwise reasonable and in order (§ 2-209)."

[31] See R. Nordstrom, Law of Sales 206 (1970) which is a basic concept found in the Murray analysis, *supra* note 27. Comment 7 to § 2-313 of the UCC states: "The precise time when words of description or affirmation are made or samples are shown is not material. The sole question is whether the language or samples or models are fairly to be regarded as part of the contract."

[32] Murray, *supra* note 27, at 318, citing UCC § 2-313, comment 3.

[33] See, e.g., Sessa v. Riegle, 427 F. Supp. 760 (E.D. Pa. 1977) aff'd, 568 F.2d 770 (3d Cir. 1978).

[34] See, e.g., Millbank Mut. Ins. Co. v. Proksch, 309 Minn. 106, 244 N.W.2d 105 (1976); General Supply & Equip. Co. v. Phillips, 490 S.W.2d 913 (Tex. Civ. App. 1973); Hagenbauch v. Snap-On Tools, 339 F. Supp. 676 (D.N.H. 1972).

[35] See, e.g., Indust-Ri-Chem Lab. v. Par-Pak Co., 602 S.W.2d 282 (Tex. App. 1980).

[36] See, e.g., Autzen v. John C. Taylor Lumber Sales, Inc., 280 Or. 783, 572 P.2d 1322, 1326 (1977) where the court suggests, "The basis of the bargain requirement ... does not mean that a

the case law continues to suggest some kind of reliance or lack of reliance requirement if only because no other workable test springs to the judicial mind. Courts seem bound to continue the pursuit of a reliance factor unless and until they begin to recognize that "bargain" in "basis of the bargain" has nothing to do with the classical notion of "bargained-for-exchange."

C. Implied Warranty of Merchantability.

The basic and most important warranty protection afforded by the UCC is provided through the implied warranty of merchantability.[37] In any contract for the sale of goods[38] by a seller who deals in goods of that kind,[39] a warranty that the goods "are fit for the ordinary purposes for which such goods are used"[40] is implied. Under this warranty, the buyer is entitled to receive non-defective goods, goods which are of fair or average quality, and goods that perform in accordance with reasonable standards of performance — not the highest quality of such goods, but of good, reasonable quality. If trade usage or prior course of dealing suggest a certain margin of allowable imperfection such as a certain percentage of defective goods in a total shipment, and if the percentage of defective goods does not exceed that percentage, the buyer has received merchantable goods.[41] The standard of "fair, average quality" or "fitness for ordinary purposes," like other legal standards, cannot be applied in algebraic fashion. As usual, the question is one of fact. For example, in a contract for commercial steel, the buyer was entitled to steel that did not crack when welded on to railroad cars.[42] No breach of the implied warranty of merchantability was found where a twenty-month old automobile, subjected to at least the wear and tear of a car of that vintage, developed rust around

---

description by the seller must be bargained for. Instead, the description must go to the essence of the contract."

[37] UCC § 2-314.

[38] There must be a contract for the sale of goods for the implied warranty of merchantability to attach, § 2-314(1). This requirement has given rise to questions of contract formation in self-service store situations. See Barker v. Allied Supermarket, 596 P.2d 870 (Okla. 1979) and Sheeskin v. Giant Food, Inc., 20 Md. App. 611, 318 A.2d 874 (1974) holding that a contract for the sale of goods occurs prior to a customer presenting the goods for purchase at the checkout area in a supermarket, thereby permitting the court to find an implied warranty of merchantability in "exploding bottle" cases.

[39] The implied warranty of merchantability does not attach to goods sold by a seller who normally does not deal in such goods. Therefore, a casual sale by a party who has ordered too many computers, for example, would not carry the implied warranty of merchantability because the seller is not a merchant with respect to goods of that kind. See UCC § 2-314(1) and § 2-104 comment 2.

[40] Section 2-314(2)(c). This is one (usually considered the most essential) of six descriptions of the implied warranty of merchantability in subsection (2) of § 2-314. The others are: "(a) pass without objection in the trade under the contract description; and (b) in the case of fungible goods, are of fair average quality within the description; and ... (d) run within the variations permitted by the agreement, of even kind, quality and quantity within each unit and among all units involved; and (e) are adquately contained, packaged and labeled as the agreement may require; and (f) conform to the promises or affirmations of fact made on the container or label if any."

[41] See, e.g., Agoos Kid Co. v. Blumenthal Import Corp., 282 Mass 1, 184 N.E. 279 (1932) (certain percentage of rotted goat skins allowable according to trade usage). The UCC continues this position through § 2-314(2)(a) (pass without objection in the trade under the contract description) and § 2-314(2)(d) (run, within the variations permitted by the agreement....), and "agreement" is defined in § 1-201(3) as including prior course of dealing and usage of trade.

[42] See Ambassador Steel Co. v. Ewald Steel Co., 33 Mich App. 495, 190 N.W.2d 275 (1971).

the taillights.[43] On the other hand, where linoleum yellowed shortly after installation, the court had no difficulty in finding such a product unmerchantable.[44] While no automobile is accident-proof, any new automobile must meet an ordinary standard of "crashworthiness" or reasonable safety.[45] Whether food served in a restaurant is merchantable has given rise to two tests, i.e., a "natural/normal" test which would find a breach of the implied warranty of merchantability whenever any food contained an unnatural ingredient, and the more sensible and apparently prevailing "reasonable expectation" test which would find a breach even where a natural but unexpected ingredient caused injury.[46] It is not only the product, itself, which must be merchantable; the container, package, or label must also be adequate. Thus, selling a quart of milk in a porous paper bag is ridiculous. A seller of drinks is also liable when the glass containing the otherwise merchantable beverage breaks in the hand of a patron who is using the glass in a normal fashion.[47] An overlap with express warranties is found in that portion of the implied warranty of merchantability description which requires the product to conform to any promises or affirmations of fact made on the container or label such as the statement on a golfing game, "Completely safe. Ball will not hit player."[48] It is important to remember the existence of an express warranty in such a case since, as we will see later in this section, implied warranties may be disclaimed but express warranties may not be disclaimed. Overlaps between express warranties and another implied warranty, the implied warranty of fitness for a particular purpose, are also not uncommon.

D. Implied Warranty of Fitness for a Particular Purpose.

If goods are merchantable and all express warranties are fulfilled, the seller may still be liable for breach of the third warranty of quality, the implied warranty of fitness for a particular purpose.[49] A product may be suitable for ordinary purposes but unsuitable for the special or particular purpose of the buyer. If the seller is unaware of the special or particular purpose for which the buyer seeks to use the goods, it would be absurd to hold a seller to a quality standard higher than merchantability. If, however, the seller is aware of the particular purpose of the buyer *and* the seller is aware that the buyer *relies* on the seller's skill and judgment in choosing a product for that purpose, the reliance of the buyer justifies the imposition of a higher quality standard.

---

[43] See Taterka v. Ford Motor Co., 86 Wis. 2d 140, 271 N.W.2d 653 (1978).

[44] Mindell v. Raleigh Rug Co., 14 U.C.C. Rptr. 1124 (Mass. Housing Ct. 1974).

[45] See Smith v. Fiat-Roosevelt Motors, Inc., 556 F.2d 728 (5th Cir. 1977); Frericks v. General Motors Corp., 274 Md. 288, 336 A.2d 118 (1975).

[46] See Hoshberg v. O'Donnell's Restaurant, Inc., 272 A.2d 846 (D.C. App. 1971) (apparently pitted olive in martini contained an olive pit causing plaintiff to break a tooth). See UCC § 2-314(1) which, in the last sentence, deals specifically with the problem of whether food served in a restaurant is a sale of goods rather than a service. The section resolves the problem by calling food or drink served a sale of goods whether it is consumed on the seller's premises or elsewhere.

[47] See Shaffer v. Victoria Station, Inc., 91 Wash. 2d 295, 588 P.2d 233 (1978) (wine glass broke in plaintiff's hand).

[48] Hauter v. Zogarts, 14 Cal. 3d 104, 120 Cal. Rptr. 681, 534 P.2d 377 (1975) where the court found a breach of the implied warranty of merchantability, *inter alia,* via § 2-314(2)(f) dealing with statements on the container or label.

[49] UCC § 2-315.

Where, for example, an operator of a mill purchased hydraulic equipment and asked his regular supplier of lubricants for a proper lubricant to be used in this equipment, the seller knew or had reason to know the particular purpose of the buyer. The seller also knew that the buyer was relying on the seller's skill and judgment in choosing the product that would suit the particular purpose of the buyer. The buyer then purchased the product recommended by the seller which was a lubricant containing a detergent. Serious loss occurred when the equipment malfunctioned and much of it had to be replaced. The problem was eventually traced to the lubricant recommended by the seller. When a non-detergent lubricant was substituted, the equipment problems disappeared. There is no reason to doubt that the recommended lubricant was merchantable, i.e., fit for *ordinary* purposes. There is no reason to question the fulfillment of any express warranty with respect to statements on the container or other express warranties concerning the original lubricant. Notwithstanding the lack of any breach of express or merchantability warranties, the case is a classic illustration of the breach of the implied warranty of fitness for a particular purpose.[50]

Where a manufacturer encountered difficulty in painting the chassis of its products, it relied upon the skill and judgment of a supplier of paint to provide the paint and process necessary to correct the problem. When the process failed to produce the results sought by the purchaser, there was no breach of the implied warranty of merchantability or any express warranties. In fact, the seller argued that its compliance with all express warranties made any action for breach of warranty impossible because express warranties should displace any inconsistent implied warranties. Yet, the UCC is clear that express warranties displace inconsistent implied warranties of merchantability, but they do not displace implied warranties of fitness for a particular purpose.[51] There is no inconsistency between such warranties since a product may meet all express warranties and still not be fit for the particular purpose for which it was purchased. The court found the elements of seller's knowledge of

---

[50] Lewis v. Mobil Oil Corp., 438 F.2d 500 (8th Cir. 1971).

[51] UCC § 2-317(c). This section sets forth a hierarchy of rules to deal with inconsistent manifestations of warranty. Thus, in § 2-317(a), exact or technical specifications displace inconsistent samples or models or general language of description (which is nothing more than the usual rule of construction that the particular normally controls the general). Section 2-317(b) is another illustration of the same concept, i.e., a sample from an existing bulk displaces inconsistent language of description. Then subsection (c) has express warranties displacing inconsistent implied warranties, but not the implied warranty of fitness for a particular purpose. It is, however, important to note that this section is "designed to ascertain the intention of the parties by reference to the factor which *probably* claimed the attention of the parties in the first instance." Comment 3 to § 2-317 (emphasis added). The comment then emphasizes the fact that such rules are only rules of construction, i.e., they are not absolute, and "may be changed" by showing that the construction called for by the rules is unreasonable. For a splendid example, *see* Stewart-Decatur Sec. Sys., Inc. v. Von Weise Gear Co., 517 F.2d 1136 (8th Cir. 1975) where the defendant seller submitted a prototype geared motor which the buyer tested. Satisfied with the test, the buyer ordered 1560 motors by purchase order which provided that the motors were to be as "per prototype" and to have input speeds of 1590 r.p.m. The seller delivered motors precisely in conformity with the prototype but with input speeds of 3200 r.p.m. Section 2-317(a) suggests that exact or technical specifications displace an inconsistent model. Yet, the court recognized that § 2-317 is nothing more that a list of guides to assist courts to ascertain the probable intention of the parties. When, as here, the parties clearly intended to buy and sell motors of the prototype, that dominant intention should prevail and the court so held.

the buyer's particular purpose, seller's awareness that the buyer was relying on the seller to choose the product and process involved, and the actual reliance on the seller through the purchase of the products and process. There was an implied warranty of fitness for a particular purpose which the seller breached even though its products met all express warranty standards and, again, presumably, the goods were suitable for ordinary purposes, thus satisfying the merchantability standard.[52]

It should be noted that courts are sometimes confused in their determination of which warranty may exist or has been breached. For example, in a case involving an eye injury cased by the shattering of the lens of sunglasses that were advertised as "baseball" sunglasses, fit for any number of different athletic activities not limited to baseball, the court found a breach of the implied warranty of fitness for a particular purpose rather than breach of the implied warranty of merchantability.[53] Yet, baseball sunglasses are *ordinarily* used in playing baseball with all of the attendant risks. Consider a buyer of ordinary shoes or boots. Such a buyer is not entitled to shoes or boots suitable for mountain climbing. If, however, boots are described as designed for mountain climbing, they must meet the ordinary purposes of such goods. Thus, a claim against the manufacturer of mountain climbing boots for defects in the product should be brought on the basis of the implied warranty of merchantability rather than fitness for a particular purpose just as a buyer of baseball sunglasses should be able to demonstrate a breach of the implied warranty of merchantability when the baseball sunglasses shatter when hit by a baseball.[54]

Finally, it should be noted that since the buyer must demonstrate actual reliance on the seller's skill or judgment to establish the implied warranty of fitness for a particular purpose, the drafters of the Code clearly understood how to insert an express reliance element into a particular warranty section of the UCC. Because they deliberately chose to do so with respect to this warranty while deliberately avoiding the insertion of a similar or identical requirement in the express warranty section,[55] we see another reason why the earlier argument against requiring any showing of reliance with respect to express warranties appears sound.[56]

E. *Warranty Disclaimers and Remedy Limitations Under the Uniform Commercial Code.*

1. Warranty Disclaimers.

While the warranty of title may be disclaimed, we saw earlier that such a disclaimer must meet an extraordinarily high standard of clarity in the disclaimer language.[57] A separate section of Article 2 of the Code is devoted to

---

[52] Singer Co. v. E. I. du Pont de Nemours & Co., 579 F.2d 433 (8th Cir. 1978).

[53] *See* Filler v. Rayex Corp., 435 F.2d 336 (7th Cir. 1970).

[54] *See* McCugh v. Carlton, 369 F. Supp. 1271 (D.C. S.C. 1974) where the court held that an action based on the implied warranty of fitness for a particular puprose did not state a claim upon which relief could be granted.

[55] § 2-313.

[56] *See supra* subsection (B).

[57] See the explanation *supra* note 15.

safeguards against warranty disclaimers in relation to the implied warranty of merchantability and the implied warranty of fitness for a particular purpose. Before considering Code requirements for the disclaimer of such warranties, it is important to consider the question of whether express warranties may be disclaimed.

In the section of the UCC captioned "Exclusion or Modification of Warranties," the first subsection[58] suggests that contract language or conduct creating express warranties and language or conduct negating or limiting such warranties is inoperative unless it is reasonable to construe such language or conduct as consistent. A buyer of goods should not be held to "unexpected and unbargained language of disclaimer."[59] It would, for example, be ludicrous to honor a clause generally disclaiming all express warranties. If given literal effect, such a clause would effectively disclaim even the express warranty arising from a description of the goods. In a contract for the sale of an automobile the seller could tender a cardboard box without breaching an express warranty. If, therefore, an express warranty is found to exist, it may not be *disclaimed.*

The UCC, however, carefully distinguishes the impossibility of disclaiming express warranties from the loss of such warranties pursuant to the parol evidence rule.[60] A statement amounting to an express warranty will be inadmissible if the writing of the parties is so final and complete that reasonable parties would certainly include such a statement of fact about the goods in such a writing.[61]

While express warranties may not be disclaimed, implied warranties are subject to disclaimer. The typical disclaimer of implied warranties is often contained in what may appear to be protection for the buyer through an express warranty. Thus, the garden variety clause will warrant goods against defects in materials and workmanship for some relatively short period, *e.g.,* 90 days. This express warranty would be superfluous except for the typical statement following it which may be phrased in any number of ways but invariably looks something like the following: "SELLER MAKES NO [OTHER] WARRANTIES INCLUDING ANY WARRANTIES AS TO MERCHANTABILITY OR FITNESS EITHER EXPRESS OR IMPLIED WITH RESPECT TO THE PROPERTY."[62] This disclaimer illustrates *one* method of effectively disclaiming the implied warranties under the UCC[63] absent a showing of unconscionability.[64] Where the parties agree that such implied warranties will be disclaimed in writing under this methodology, there are safeguards built into such disclaimers: written disclaimers of either type of

---

[58] § 2-316(1).

[59] UCC § 2-316 comment 1.

[60] In § 2-316(1), the Code carefully conditions its directive: "but subject to the provisions of the Article on parol or extrinsic evidence (Section 2-202)...."

[61] This is the essential UCC parol evidence rule test as found in comment 3 to § 2-202.

[62] This disclaimer is essentially that found in Hunt v. Perkins Mach. Co., 352 Mass. 535, 226 N.E.2d 228 (1967).

[63] UCC § 2-316(2).

[64] In the discussion of unconscionability, *supra* § 96, we saw that the fulfillment of the UCC formula for a warranty disclaimer would not preclude an overriding determination that such a clause was unconscionable, *e.g.,* a contract of adhesion or "no choice" unconscionability.

implied warranty must be "conspicuous"[65] and, for the implied warranty of merchantability, the term "merchantability" must be stated.[66] Thus, disclaimer language is often found in print that is large, boldface, italicized, or some combination of these, and it invariably includes the term, "merchantability."

Three additional methods of disclaiming implied warranties, recognized by the UCC, must be considered. The use of "language which, in common understanding, calls the buyer's attention to the exclusion of warranties and makes plain that there is no implied warranty" is illustrated in the Code by the phrases "as is" or "with all faults."[67] While other phrases may be adequate substitutes, it is folly to use them instead of "as is" or "with all faults" which constitute officially approved UCC language.[68] There is no express requirement that such phrases be written or conspicuous, though the section language indicating that the purpose is to call the buyer's attention to the warranty exclusions and to "make plain" the fact that no implied warranties exist may easily suggest the requirement of conspicuousness.[69]

The "as is" or "with all faults" method of disclaiming implied warranties may be seen as a species of another method, i.e., the disclaimer of implied warranties by usage of trade, course of dealing, or course of performance.[70] It is important to emphasize the concepts of usage of trade,[71] course of dealing,[72] and course of performance[73] which were discussed in a prior chapter dealing with interpretation.[74] If any of these concepts is established as constituting a term of the agreement disclaiming implied warranties, there is no reason why such disclaimers should not be effective through this method since it is the very agreement of the parties that establishes the disclaimer.[75] In fact, this method is less likely to permit unconscionability or other overreaching.

---

[65] UCC § 1-201(10), which defines "conspicuous" as requiring a clause to be so written that a reasonable person against whom it is to operate ought to have noticed it.

[66] UCC § 2-316(2).

[67] See UCC § 2-316(3)(a).

[68] Other language may be interpreted to be sufficient to disclaim implied warranties under this section. For example, "I accept the car in its present condition" was the equivalent of an "as is" disclaimer in Joseph Charles Parrish, Inc. v. Hill, 173 Ga. App. 97, 325 S.E.2d 595 (1984).

[69] See Woodruff v. Clark Cty. Farm Bur. Coop. Ass'n, 286 N.E.2d 188, (Ind. App. 1972): "The close interrelation of these two subsections [§ 2-316(2) and (3)] is manifested by their like intent to call the buyer's attention to the exclusion of implied warranties and it would do violence to their stated purpose to do otherwise than imply that excluding expressions like 'as is' must be conspicuous. This interpretation harmonizes with the basic purpose of the UCC which is designed to protect purchasers from surprise." Accord White v. First Fed. Sav. & Loan Ass'n of Atlanta, 158 Ga. App. 373, 280 S.E.2d 398 (1981); Fairchild Indus. v. Maritime Air Servs., 274 Md. 181, 333 A.2d 313 (1975). Osborne v. Genevie, 289 So. 2d 21 (Fla. App. 1974). See, however, Gilliam v. Indiana State Bank, 337 So. 2d 352 (Ala. App. 1976), holding that such disclaimers need not be conspicuous.

[70] UCC § 2-316(3)(c) and comment 7 suggesting the relationship between this subsection and § 2-316(3)(a).

[71] UCC § 1-205(2).

[72] UCC § 1-205(1).

[73] UCC § 2-208(1).

[74] See supra Chapter 5.

[75] See Standard Structural Steel Co. v. Bethlehem Steel Corp., 597 F. Supp. 164 (D. Conn. 1984) (course of dealing for 62 years effectively disclaimed implied warranties); Oregon Bank v. Nautilus Crane & Equip. Corp., 69 Or. App. 131, 683 P.2d 95 (1984) (course of performance may effectively disclaim implied warranties); R. D. Lowrance, Inc. v. Peterson, 185 Neb. 679, 178 N.W.2d 277 (1970) (implied warranties may be disclaimed by trade usage).

The final method recognized by the Code for effectively disclaiming implied warranties is essentially a risk allocation based upon the fault of the buyer. If a buyer examines goods before purchasing them, he should have seen whatever defects were observable by a reasonable party in his position. He will, therefore, be responsible for those defects, i.e., no action for breach of implied warranty will be permitted with respect to non-conformities which the buyer ought to have observed.[76] In one sense, it is not accurate to speak of non-conformities under these circumstances since the buyer has, presumably, decided to purchase with an actual or presumed awareness of what he is purchasing. Thus, there is no non-conformity except one later alleged by the purchaser. The same analysis applies where the buyer has unreasonably refused to examine the goods prior to purchasing them. Here, the buyer has consciously assumed the risk of what would otherwise be one or more breaches of implied warranties by refusing to examine the goods. He, therefore, assumes the risks of any defects which such an examination would have revealed to a reasonable buyer.[77] If a risk has been assumed, there is no warranty as to that risk. To suggest, therefore, that a warranty has been disclaimed through assumption of risk may be seen as inaccurate because the warranty never arose concerning that risk. Nonetheless, it is common to characterize such risk assumption as another method of "disclaiming" or "excluding" implied warranties.

2. Limitation of Remedies.

It must be emphasized that, even if the buyer retains all warranties under the sales contract, they will be of little use if the parties have agreed to limit the buyer's remedies where the buyer's damages suffered by a breach of warranty far exceed the limitation in the contract. The UCC, for example, permits the parties to agree to limit the buyer's remedies to a return of the goods and repayment of the price, or to the replacement of nonconforming goods and parts.[78] Moreover, the Code permits the limitation or exclusion of consequential damages unless the limitation or exclusion is unconscionable,[79] or if exclusive remedies in substitution of normal Code remedies "fail of their essential

---

[76] UCC § 2-316(3)(b). *See* Hall Truck Sales, Inc. v. Wilder Mobile Homes, Inc., 202 So. 2d 1299 (Fla. App. 1981). Implied warranties, however, are not disclaimed if the defect could be revealed only by unreasonably stringent tests. *See* Henry Heide, Inc. v. WRH Prods. Co., 766 F.2d 105 (3d Cir. 1985). It should also be noted that the successful use of this method of disclaiming implied warranties has typically occurred with respect to used goods.

[77] *See* Richards v. Goerg Boat & Motors, Inc., 384 N.E.2d 1084 (Ind. App. 1979).

[78] UCC § 2-719(1)(a). *See* Frick Forest Prods., Inc. v. International Hardwoods, Inc., 161 Ga. App. 359, 288 S.E.2d 625 (1982); Mostek Corp. v. Chemetron Corp., 642 S.W.2d 20 (Tex. App. 1982); Potomac Elec. Power Co. v. Westinghouse Elec. Corp., 385 F. Supp. 572 (D.D.C. 1974).

[79] UCC § 2-719(3). Limitation of consequential damages for personal injury is deemed prima facie unconscionable under this section. As suggested in the earlier section dealing with unconscionability, *supra* § 96, unconscionability in this context will typically fail where the parties are commercially sophisticated. *See* AMF Inc. v. Computer Automation, Inc., 573 F. Supp. 924 (S.D. Ohio 1983). If, however, there is a non-negotiable, material, risk-shifting term on a printed form supplied by a large corporate seller to a small, inexperienced buyer, unconscionability may be an effective deterrent to the enforceability of a clause excluding remedies. *See* A & M Produce Co. v. FMC Corp., 135 Cal. App. 3d 473, 186 Cal. Rptr. 114 (1982).

purpose."[80] These matters have already been considered in the earlier exploration of unconscionability.[81]

§ 101. Classification of Conditions.

A. *Overview.*

Conditions in contract law are classified in various ways. As to the effect of their operation, they are said to be either *precedent* or *subsequent,* though this classification is rejected by the RESTATEMENT 2d.[82] We will examine the case law in this area and the RESTATEMENT 2d analysis. As to how conditions are created, they are often classified as either *express, implied,* or *constructive.* We will explore each of these concepts in this section.

B. *Conditions Precedent Distinguished From Conditions Subsequent.*

1. The Fallacy of the Distinction — Form Over Substance.

There has been considerable confusion created by the classification of conditions into those which are "precedent" as contrasted with those which are "subsequent." The typical description of a condition is that which has been stated earlier in this section, i.e., a condition is an event that must occur in order to activate the contractual duty to which it is attached. In this sense, all conditions are *precedent* to the critical activation of the duty since they must occur *before* the duty is activated. When stating a condition to a duty under their contract, however, parties may choose language that creates the faulty impression that the condition is "subsequent." In the well-known case of *Gray v. Gardner,*[83] the parties agreed to buy and sell a quantity of oil and executed two writings evidencing the buyer's agreement to pay for the oil. One of these obligations stated the price at eighty-five cents per gallon but added a condition stating that, if a greater quantity of oil should arrive at a certain destination between certain periods of time than arrived at that destination between such periods during the previous year, "this obligation to be void." Another note was executed at the same time providing an absolute obligation to pay for the oil at sixty cents per gallon. The purpose of the parties was clear, i.e., the price of the oil would depend upon the amount of supply available since the greater the supply the lower the price. The seller sought to enforce the first note at the higher price and the enforcement of that note depended upon the occurrence of the condition. If there is no difficulty in proving the occurrence or non-occurrence of a condition, either party can sustain the burden of proof. In this case, however, there was considerable difficulty attached to proving whether a greater quantity of oil had or had not arrived due to the problem of determining whether a particular ship containing oil had arrived by a certain time. The court allocated the virtually impossible burden of proof to the defendant simply because the parties happened to state the condition in the *form* of a condition "subsequent," i.e., the parties had written the condi-

---

[80] UCC § 2-719(2).
[81] See, in particular, *supra* § 96(B)(2)(e).
[82] RESTATEMENT 2d § 224 comment e; § 227 comment e.
[83] 17 Mass. 188 (1821).

tion as if it defeated an already activated duty. The writing containing the promise to pay eighty-five cents per gallon was a simple promise to pay that amount *followed* by the statement that if a certain event occurred (more oil arriving than the previous year), the promise was void. The parties could have just as easily structured the writing by placing the condition *before* the duty, *e.g.,* "If a greater quantity of oil does not arrive than the amount arriving last year, the buyer will pay eighty-five cents per gallon." If their writing had been in this *form,* the condition would be *precedent* in form and the court would have allocated the burden of proving the occurrence of the conditioning event (a greater quantity did not arrive by a certain time) on the seller.

Any condition may be stated either in the *form* of a condition precedent or condition subsequent. Thus, in the purchase and sale of real property, the condition of obtaining the mortgage loan may be stated as (1) "If the buyer obtains financing of eighty percent of the purchase price no later than March 1, 1988, the buyer promises to purchase the described property for the purchase price of $100,000" (precedent); (2) "The buyer promises to pay $100,000 as the full purchase price for the described property. If, however, the buyer is unable to secure mortgage financing for eighty percent of the purchase price no later than March 1, 1988, this promise shall be null and void" (subsequent). The *form* of the condition depends upon the stage of the transaction to which it is related. The question must always be asked, precedent or subsequent to what? There must be a reference point in the transaction to which the condition is related.[84] Since a condition can be stated in either form, it is of critical importance to determine the status of a condition as a matter of *substance.* If an existing contractual duty cannot possibly be activated unless a condition has occurred, the condition, as a matter of *substance,* must be *precedent.* In the case of the purchase and sale of oil, the duty of the buyer to pay the higher price of eighty-five cents per gallon could not possibly be activated until it was determined whether a greater quantity of oil arrived by the deadline established in the contract. If a greater quantity did not arrive by that time, the condition had occurred and the duty was activated because the substantive effect of the condition was to activate the duty to pay the higher price only if a greater quantity did not arrive in time. If it did arrive by that time, the condition did not occur and the duty was not and never could be activated so that the duty to pay eighty-five cents per gallon was discharged, leaving only the other obligation intact, i.e., the absolute duty to pay sixty cents per gallon. In the example of the mortgage loan, the identical analysis applies, i.e., the duty of the buyer to pay the purchase price could not possibly be activated until after March 1, 1988 if the mortgage loan for eighty percent of the purchase price had been arranged. Thus, *regardless of the form of the conditions, both conditions were, in substance, conditions precedent.*[85]

---

[84] *See* Harnett & Thornton, *The Insurance Condition Subsequent: A Needle in a Semantic Haystack,* 7 FORDHAM L. REV. 220 (1948).

[85] *See* RESTATEMENT 2d § 227 comment e: "Circumstances may show that the parties intended to make an event a condition of an obligor's duty even though their language appears to make the non-occurrence of the event a ground for discharge of his duty after performance has become due.... The language, in spite of its form, is interpreted so that the failure of that thing to happen is a condition of the obligor's duty. Unless that condition occurs, no performance is due." In the following cases, substantive conditions precedent were held to be subsequent because of the form

2. Burden of Pleading and Proof.

Again, if there is no difficulty in sustaining the burden of proving the occurrence or non-occurrence of a condition, neither party will suffer by the characterization of the condition as precedent or subsequent in form. In the rare case where such a burden cannot be sustained by either party, however, the party upon whom that burden is cast will necessarily lose. To allocate the burden of proving the occurrence or non-occurrence of a condition on the accidental basis of its form as precedent or subsequent has never made any sense. Yet, many courts continue this absurdity.[86] While the burden of pleading has been alleviated by permitting a general averment that conditions have been performed,[87] the burden of proof should be allocated on a more rational basis, particularly the basis of which party is in a better position to sustain the burden. Thus, where a duty was conditioned upon the obtaining of a new lease satisfactory to the defendant, the court mechanically allocated the burden of proving such satisfaction to the plaintiff simply because the condition was a condition precedent.[88] Ordinarily the defendant is in a much better position to prove a lack of satisfaction in such a case.

3. A "True" Condition Subsequent.

It is possible to argue plausibly that what may be called a true or substantive condition subsequent exists in a rare case. The typical example is a fire insurance policy which, like all such policies, is necessarily conditioned on the occurrence of a fire damaging the insured premises. The fire and consequent loss is a condition precedent. Such a policy, however, may contain a clause stating that no action of any kind may be brought against the insurer unless such action shall be commenced within twelve months after the loss.[89] Upon the occurrence of the fire, the condition precedent to the duty of the insurer to pay has occurred, activating that duty. When the insurer refuses to perform

---

of expression used: Horn v. Brand, 133 Ark. 567, 203 S.W. 5 (1918); Root v. Childs, 69 Minn. 142, 70 N.W. 1087 (1897); Gray v. Gardner, 17 Mass. 188 (1821). *See also* FIRST RESTATEMENT § 259 comment b.

[86] *See, e.g.,* Lerner v. Gudelsky Co., 334 S.E.2d 579, 584 (Va. 1985); Schmidt v. J. C. Robinson Seed Co., 220 Neb. 344, 370 N.W.2d 103 (1985) (using RESTATEMENT 2d analysis but clinging to the precedent/subsequent distinction); Smith v. Government Emps. Ins. Co., 558 P.2d 1160 (Okla. 1976). The determination of a condition as "precedent" is almost always substantively correct. The mechanical allocation of the burden of pleading and proof on this basis alone, however, is unsound. *See also* Stephens v. Fire Ass'n, 139 Mo. App. 369, 123 S.W. 63 (1909) where a fire insurance policy exempted the insurer from liability for damage caused by an explosion which was not preceded by a fire. *Held:* the fact of the explosion preceding the fire was a condition subsequent and since the fact was uncertain, the insurer could not sustain the burden of proving the condition and was liable for the loss. *See,* however, Harris-Teeter Supermarkets, Inc. v. Hampton, 334 S.E.2d 81, 83 (N.C. App. 1985): "[W]hether conditions are conditions precedent or conditions subsequent depends entirely upon the intention of the parties shown by the contract as construed in the light of the circumstances of the case, the nature of the contract, the relation of the parties thereto, and other evidence admissible to aid the court in determining the intention of the parties."

[87] *See* Trevino v. Allstate Ins. Co., 651 S.W.2d 8 (Tex. App. 1983) (where plaintiff avers generally that all conditions have been performed, he is then required to prove the performance of only those conditions specifically denied by the defendant. Thus, the rule operates to shift the burden of pleading to the defendant but not the burden of proof.). *See also* Fed. R. Civ. P. 19.

[88] K & K Pharmacy, Inc. v. Barta, 222 Neb. 215, 382 N.W.2d 363 (1986).

[89] *See, e.g.,* Northwestern Nat'l Life Ins. Co. v. Ward, 56 Okla. 188, 155 P. 524 (1916).

that activated duty, the insured's cause of action is said to be conditioned upon bringing that action within twelve months from the time of the loss. The failure of that condition to occur may be said to discharge the previously activated duty of the insurer and, in that sense, it may be termed a condition subsequent. Yet, even this condition may be seen as a condition precedent, i.e., precedent to the secondary or remedial right of the insured to be paid for the loss when the insurer failed to perform its primary duty to pay after the fire. Even if the characterization of this condition as subsequent is accepted, the allocation of the burden of pleading and proving the occurrence of the condition should not automatically follow. Again, the characterization of conditions as precedent or subsequent presents only a question of pleading and proof. Moreover, even if a "true" condition subsequent can be discovered, that discovery provides no justification for those cases which have chosen to characterize true conditions precedent as subsequent simply because of the form in which they are stated.[90]

4. RESTATEMENT 2d Analysis.

The RESTATEMENT 2d seeks to avoid these characterization problems by dispensing with the "precedent" and "subsequent" labels.[91] It insists that the only true condition is a condition precedent and since all conditions are precedent, it eliminates the characterization by simply calling them "conditions," all of which must occur (unless excused) before performance under a contract becomes due, i.e., before the duty to which the condition is attached is activated. If the parties provide that the occurrence of an event will extinguish an activated duty (using the example above of the failure to commence an action within a prescribed time), the RESTATEMENT 2d rejects the appellation, "condition subsequent," since such an event is not a condition at all; rather, it is an event that terminates a duty.[92] If the event occurs, the formerly activated duty is discharged. The rule, however, is subject to certain exceptions. Thus, if the event occurs because the obligor breached his general obligation of good faith or fair dealing, or if the event could not have been prevented because of impracticability and the obligor is not subjected to a materially increased burden because of the continuance of the duty,[93] or, finally, if the obligor promises to perform his duty even if the event occurs and does not revoke that promise before the obligee materially changes his position in reliance on the promise,[94] the duty of the obligor is not discharged even though the event

---

[90] *See also* Rutherford v. John O'Lexey's Boat & Yacht Ins., 576 P.2d 1380, 1382 (Ariz. App. 1978) where an insurer promised temporary coverage on condition that the insured submit a completed application by a certain date and the court construed the condition as a condition subsequent because "completion of the application by Monday was a condition that had to be performed before [the insurer] had any duty to perform." Presumably the court was suggesting that the condition had to occur before the duty of the insurer was activated. It clearly appears that the duty of the insurer under an existing contract of insurance was conditioned on the submission of a completed application. Therefore, it was a condition precedent and the court's own language suggests the legal effect of a condition precedent. Yet, it characterizes the condition as a condition subsequent, citing the FIRST RESTATEMENT § 250.

[91] *See* RESTATEMENT 2d § 224 comment e.

[92] RESTATEMENT 2d § 230.

[93] RESTATEMENT 2d § 230(2).

[94] RESTATEMENT 2d § 230(3).

occurs. In a case applying this new RESTATEMENT analysis,[95] a homeowner signed a contract with an aluminum siding contractor promising to pay for the new siding subject to the following condition: "This contract null and void if customer cannot get disability and death and sickness insurance." The homeowner was recuperating at home and anticipating a return to work when the contract was signed. Shortly after it was signed, the contractor arrived to perform the work but was told by the homeowner not to commence the work. The contractor reappeared to commence the work and the homeowner again refused to permit the work to begin. Conversations then occurred between the contractor's workmen and the agent who had procured the contract as well as an insurance agent resulting in the homeowner permitting the work to be done. The homeowner returned to his job but became disabled again after only ten days. He then discovered that he was unable to procure disability insurance. The work had been completed and the contractor sought payment. The homeowner claimed that his inability to procure disability insurance discharged his obligation under the contract. Notwithstanding its scrupulous effort to apply the RESTATEMENT 2d analysis, the court concluded that the disability insurance clause that had been inserted by the homeowner was a condition because it referred to an event not certain to occur.[96] Yet, the event set forth in the clause was a "negative condition," i.e., "an Event that Terminates a Duty, formerly a 'Condition Subsequent.'"[97] The court found that no waiver of the clause had been made, the contractor had performed with full knowledge of the clause, it was not impracticable to await performance until the determination of the procuring of disability insurance could be made, the homeowner operated in good faith, and the obligor never promised to pay if he did not receive the insurance. Therefore, the event (not procuring the insurance) had occurred. Thus, the duty of the homeowner to pay was terminated. The contractor has simply made a "poor" bargain and was not even entitled to quasi-contractual relief. Since there was no difficulty in proving the occurrence of the event, burden of pleading and proof issues were not raised in this case. If they had been raised, no guidance from the RESTATEMENT 2d would have been available. Moreover, it is particularly interesting to note that in this early application of the new analysis under the RESTATEMENT 2d, the court clings to the characterization of the event as a "condition" and seems to suggest that it is really a "condition subsequent." At the same time, the court recognizes the RESTATEMENT 2d preference that it no longer be so characterized. The court, therefore, dutifully follows the guidance of the RESTATEMENT 2d by eventually characterizing the condition as an "event terminating a duty." This conscious effort to apply the RESTATEMENT 2d analysis does not augur greater stability and certainty than we have enjoyed to this time. The failure of the RESTATEMENT 2d to deal clearly with the only significant question in the "precedent"/"subsequent" dilemma, i.e., the procedural question of the burden of pleading and proof, is simply disconcerting.

---

[95] Cambria Sav. & Loan v. Estate of Gross, 294 Pa. Super. 351, 439 A.2d 1236 (1982).
[96] 439 A.2d at 1239, citing RESTATEMENT 2d § 224.
[97] *Id.*

C. *Express, Implied, and Constructive Conditions Distinguished.*

A condition is created by either of two methods: (1) the parties have manifested an intention (by words or conduct) that the duty to render a promised performance shall be subject to the occurrence of some fact or event other than a mere lapse of time; (2) a court, in the interests of equity and justice, determines that a contractual duty should be subject to a condition even though the parties have manifested no such intention. Where a condition is created by the first method, the manifested intention of the parties, they are called *express* conditions.[98] They are "real" conditions established by the agreement of the parties and the agreement may be manifested in words or by conduct. Where the parties manifest their intention by conduct to create a condition, it is sometimes called an "implied in fact" condition which may be a confusing term. Where a condition is created under the second method, i.e., by a court reading conditions into a contract for reasons of its own, notwithstanding the lack of any manifestation (words or conduct) of the parties to that effect, such a condition is called a *constructive* condition (sometimes, unfortunately, referred to as an "implied in law" condition).[99]

Since express conditions result from a manifestation of intention, it is clear that the only difficulty likely to arise in determining their existence and operation is one of interpretation. On the other hand, the problem of determining the existence of a constructive condition is wholly different. It is not a question of interpretation; rather, it is a question of whether the court should add to the terms of the contract in order to achieve equity and justice in a situation not foreseen and not provided for by the parties.

While these two kinds of conditions are distinct in theory, in practice it is not always easy to distinguish them. First, the manifestations of intention in a particular case are frequently so uncertain that it is difficult to determine whether a court may justifiably find that the parties intended a condition though it may be clear that finding a condition would be desirable regardless of the manifested intention. In this situation, the discovery of a condition can be justified on either of two theories (express or constructive) and the court is

---

[98] *See* RESTATEMENT 2d § 226 comment a.

[99] *See* RESTATEMENT 2d § 226 comment c. *See also* Holloway v. Jackson, 412 So. 2d 774 (Ala. 1982) quoting the FIRST RESTATEMENT § 253: "[A] 'constructive condition' is a condition that is such because of a rule of law, and is not based on interpretation of a promise or agreement."

The classification and nomenclature of conditions set forth in this section have not been uniformly accepted. Some courts and writers insist on a classification including express conditions, by which they mean conditions created by the *words* of the parties, implied-in-fact conditions, meaning conditions created by the manifested *conduct* of the parties, and implied-in-law conditions, meaning conditions created by courts to achieve just results. *See* G. COSTIGAN, THE PERFORMANCE OF CONTRACTS 7 (2d ed. 1927). This classification is objectionable because it may lead to confusion in distinguishing so-called implied-in-fact from implied-in-law conditions. Moreover, there is no utility in distinguishing express and implied-in-fact conditions since both have their basis in the manifested intention of the parties, the only difference growing out of the manner in which that manifestation occurs. Whether expressed in words or through other conduct, the condition can properly be called "express." The only significant distinction, therefore, is the distinction between those conditions that are manifested by words or conduct and those which are added by the court. Thus, the distinction set forth in the text between express and constructive conditions is not only more simple, it is more accurate and clear. For a case adopting this analysis as it appeared in the second edition of this book, *see* Dorn v. Stanhope Steel, Inc., 534 A.2d 798 (Pa. Super. 1987).

likely to ignore the distinction in discovering a condition. Second, earlier courts were not willing to admit that they could "make a contract" for the parties though they frequently did so, disguising their operation under the fiction of interpretation. Modern courts, however, are much more willing to admit that conditions may be found to exist, notwithstanding the manifested intention of the parties.[1] Yet, it is still not always clear whether the court has discovered a condition from the intention of the parties or from the necessity of a just and equitable result. Thus, a franchise agreement provided that the agreement could be terminated if the franchisee was in breach, but was silent as to whether it could be terminated by the franchisee where the franchisor had breached. The franchisor had committed many breaches but the franchisee could not establish damages. The court held that the failures of the franchisor to perform were not only breaches of its duties, but failure of conditions precedent to the activation of the franchisee's duties. Otherwise, the franchisee would be left remediless.[2] This judicial effort suggests a combination of discovering a condition which may have been part of the contemplation of the parties at the time of contract formation and establishing the condition to avoid manifest injustice to the franchisee.

§ 102. Interpretation — Promise Versus Condition.

To determine whether a particular provision in a contract is an express condition, i.e., one intended by the parties to qualify a duty rather than a promise to create a duty, it is necessary to interpret the expression of the parties, and the usual guides to interpretation prevail.[3] There are, however, certain policy considerations that influence the interpretation of the parties' expressions which have given rise to what the RESTATEMENT 2d calls "Standards of Preference with Regard to Conditions."[4] It is important to consider clusters of cases which illustrate the judicial effort to interpret expressions as conditions or promises with regard to these preferences.

A. *The Avoidance of Forfeiture.*

One of the maxims of our law that is often repeated in contract law is that the law abhors forfeitures.[5] Forfeiture suggests a penalty and, normally, contract law is not interested in penalizing any party; it is concerned with compensating aggrieved parties. Conditions may be viewed as drastic devices

---

[1] *See, e.g.,* Seman v. First State Bank of Eden Prairie, 394 N.W.2d 557 (Minn. App. 1986) (court found bank's duty to stop payment on a cashier's check subject to condition implied by the court that the purchaser provide a legally sufficient reason to the bank for stopping payment because of the nature of a cashier's check, i.e., it is viewed as more trustworthy than a personal check).

[2] United Campgrounds, U.S.A. v. Stevenson, 175 Mont. 17, 571 P.2d 1161 (1977).

[3] *See supra* Chapter 5 §§ 86-90.

[4] RESTATEMENT 2d § 227.

[5] *See, e.g.,* Stevenson v. Parker, 25 Wash. App. 639, 608 P.2d 1263, 1267-68 (1980): "This court has held the general doctrine that forfeitures are not favored in the law, and that courts should promptly seize upon any circumstances arising out of the contract or relation of the parties that would indicate an election or an agreement to waive the harsh, and at times unjust, remedy of forfeiture, a remedy which is oftentimes too freely granted by those who have taken no account of the misfortunes and disappointments which conditions, unforeseen and beyond a party's control, have raised as a bar to performance, however honest may be his intent...." quoting from Spedden v. Sykes, 51 Wash. 267, 272, 98 P. 752, 754 (1908).

because their non-occurrence may result in a forfeiture of a right a party has earned by reliance or performance. Thus, where a contractor completed performance, the owner's duty to pay for the work was not activated because of a failure of condition.[6] Parties are free to make that kind of conditional contract within broad limits, and such agreements will be enforced regardless of forfeiture.[7] Yet, the abhorrence of forfeitures creates a proclivity in courts to avoid them through interpretation of the parties' expressions and, as will be seen in a subsequent section, courts will simply excuse conditions under certain circumstances. If the expression of the parties is phrased in unmistakable language of condition, courts will not be able to circumvent the operative effect of the condition through interpretation. There are, however, myriad cases where the language of the parties does not rise to that level of clarity. While courts approach the interpretation process in these cases under the traditional rubric of ascertaining the intention of the parties,[8] the overriding concern for the avoidance of forfeitures is invariably present.[9] In the exploration that follows, it is important to remember this overriding concern.

B. *Form of Expression — Favors and Frowns to Avoid Forfeiture — Preference for Promise.*

There is no particular form of expression required to create a condition, but the form of the parties' expression remains a significant factor in determining whether they intended to create a condition or a promise. Certainly, an expression such as "The parties hereby agree that the duty is subject to the following express condition precedent...," though redundant, would create an insuperable obstacle for a court seeking to avoid construing such language as a condition. Again, however, even where parties intend to create a condition, their language may lack clarity. One court suggests that terms or phrases used to signify conditions include "on condition," "provided that," "when," "so that," "while," "as soon as," and "after."[10] Another court was absolutely con-

---

[6] *See* Cambria Sav. & Loan v. Estate of Gross, 294 Pa. Super. 351, 439 A.2d 1236 (1982), discussed *infra* § 101, text at notes 95 and 96.

[7] *See* A. A. Conte v. Campbell-Lowrie-Lautermilch, 132 Ill. App. 3d 325, 477 N.E.2d 30, 33 (1985) where the court found language in a contract between a general contractor and subcontractor making the general's duty to pay contingent upon the general receiving payment unambiguous and, though recognizing that "courts will not construe stipulations to be a condition precedent when such a construction would result in forfeiture, ... plain, unambiguous language contained in the contract binds the parties to a condition precedent." *See also* RESTATEMENT 2d § 227 comment b and § 229 comment a.

[8] "The parties to a contract are at liberty to agree upon a condition precedent upon which liability shall depend. Whether the doing of an act is a condition precedent depends, not on any hard and fast rule, but on the intention of the parties as deduced from the whole instrument." Partlow v. Mathews, 43 Wash. 2d 398, 261 P.2d 394, 398 (1953). "Whether a provision in a contract is a condition, the nonfulfillment of which excuses performance, depends upon the intent of the parties, to be ascertained from a fair and reasonable construction of the language used in the light of all the surrounding circumstances." Ross v. Harding, 64 Wash. 2d 231, 391 P.2d 526, 531 (1964).

[9] *See, e.g.,* United Plate Glass Co. v. Metal Trims Indus., 525 A.2d 468, 470 (Pa. Commw. 1987); Rohauer v. Little, 736 P.2d 403, 409 (Colo. 1987); Wemhoff v. Investors Mgt. Corp. of Am., 528 A.2d 105, 109 (D.C. App. 1987); Jones Assocs. v. Eastside Props., Inc., 704 P.2d 681, 686 (Wash. App. 1985).

[10] *See* Vogt v. Hovander, 27 Wash. App. 168, 616 P.2d 660 (1979).

vinced that a condition was present where the phrase used was "subject to."[11] It would, however, be foolish to seek a particular word or phrase as conclusive evidence of the parties' intention to create a condition.[12] Thus, if several clauses of a document begin with the phrase, "provided that" or "provided further," which may be viewed typically as language of condition, but some of these clauses reflect the parties' intention to create duties and, therefore, suggest that the language should be construed as language of promise, the overuse of conditional phraseology will cause a court to reject the conditional.[13] Such drafting provides the court with a basis for doubt in the interpretation of the language. With some doubt established, a court may proceed to a rule of construction, i.e., where it is doubtful whether language creates a promise or a condition, the language will be construed as creating a promise.[14] This "rule" is simply a species of the general abhorrence of forfeitures.[15] If the language is construed as a condition, the failure of the condition to occur may cause a forfeiture. If, however, it is construed as a promise and the promise is breached, the promisor is liable in damages but will not suffer a forfeiture. A corollary of the "rule" that a construction resulting in a promise rather than a condition will be preferred is another "well settled rule of contract interpretation that conditions are disfavored and will not be found in the absence of unambiguous language to create a conditional obligation."[16] Again, this "rule" is simply another species of the policy against forfeitures. It is clear beyond peradventure that courts frown upon the construction of language as conditional and favor the construction of the same language as promissory to avoid forfeitures.

In keeping with this strong preference, courts are quick to seize upon promissory language. Thus, where the expression states that certain documents "shall be furnished the purchaser,"[17] or that certain parties "will furnish evidence" of a certain fact,[18] or that title to certain equipment "shall pass to lessor upon installation,"[19] courts are pleased to announce their interpretation of such language as promissory.

C. *Performance Due After an Event Has Occurred — Time of Performance.*

A number of cases have dealt with the construction of language where performance is said to be due only at a time after a particular event has occurred. Terms such as "when," "as soon as," "after," or the like are often used to indicate *when* performance (typically payment) is due. The language

---

[11] Ross v. Harding, 64 Wash. 2d 231, 391 P.2d 526 (1964).

[12] As will be seen in the next subsection, terms or phrases such as "when" or "as soon as" are typically construed not to create conditions.

[13] *See* Southern Sur. Co. v. McMillan Co., 58 F.2d 541 (10th Cir. 1932).

[14] *See, e.g.,* Howard v. Federal Crop Ins. Corp., 540 F.2d 695 (4th Cir. 1976).

[15] *See* Rohauer v. Little, 736 P.2d 403, 409 (Colo. 1987) ("Where, however, there is doubt as to whether a contractual provision is intended as a promise or a condition, it is preferable to construe the provision as a promise, thereby avoiding the potentially harsh effects of a forfeiture that can result in some cases by a contrary construction.").

[16] Logghe v. Jasmer, 686 P.2d 694, 698 (Alaska 1984). *See also* Lockwood v. Wolf Corp., 629 F.2d 603, 610 (9th Cir. 1980).

[17] Rohauer v. Little, 736 P.2d 403 (Colo. 1987).

[18] *See* Mellon Bank, N.A. v. Aetna Bus. Credit, Inc., 619 F.2d 1001 (3d Cir. 1980).

[19] Southland Corp. v. Emerald Oil Co., 789 F.2d 1441 (9th Cir. 1986).

appears to be conditional. Yet, a contextual interpretation may reveal that the parties intended nothing more than to measure the time for performance, i.e., they did not intend to suggest that if a certain event never occurred, the promisor's duty would not be activated. Thus, where a party received valuable services for which he promised to pay "as soon as the crop can be sold or the money raised from any other source," the court held the money was payable within a reasonable time from the date of the promise though neither of the events in the promise had occurred.[20] This interpretation was made much more certain by the last phrase, "or the money raised from any other source," which manifested the promisor's intent to make an absolute promise to pay, merely postponing the time for performance to a later or more convenient time, without any intention to make the duty to pay conditional upon the occurrence of either event. Less clear was a promise to pay an engineer for his services "as soon as the plant [where the engineer had provided his services] is in successful operation," followed by a clause explaining that, because of the expenditures in placing the plant in operation, disbursements had to be delayed until the plant produced income. A construction of this promise as conditional upon the successful operation of the plant on the basis of the language, alone, would not have been untoward. The court, however, considered the original offer by the engineer which contained a fee for his services that was not conditional. Since he agreed to a counter offer at the same fee, the court suggested that it was unlikely he would have done so if the parties intended a genuine contingent fee arrangement.[21] This rationale may be viewed as a valiant effort by this court to achieve the overriding goal of avoiding a forfeiture that would have resulted if it had construed the language as conditional since the engineer had completely performed the promised services.[22]

A number of cases have dealt with the same issue in contracts between general contractors and subcontractors where the contract indicates that the subcontractor will be paid when, or within a certain time after, the general contractor is paid. Almost invariably, courts reason that the subcontractor did not assume the risk that the general contractor would not be paid and conclude that the language in the contract merely established a definite and convenient time for payment rather than a condition upon which any payment depended.[23] The rare exceptions to these holdings appear to be based on

---

[20] Nunez v. Dautel, 86 U.S. (19 Wall.) 560 (1873).

[21] North Am. Graphite Corp v. Allan, 184 F.2d 387 (D.C. Cir. 1950). See also Hood v. Gordy Homes, 267 F.2d 882 (4th Cir. 1959) where the court volunteers the view that a subsequent agreement to pay a pre-existing debt upon the occurrence of an event is payable within a reasonable time if the event does not occur.

[22] See also Wagner v. Kincaid, 291 Mich. 262, 289 N.W. 154 (1939) (promise to pay a debt on sale of a land contract); Glazer v. Klughaupt, 116 N.J.L. 507, 185 A. 8 (1936) (promise to pay upon marriage of parties); American Metal Prods. Co. v. A. Geo. Schultz Co., 221 Wis. 291, 267 N.W. 19 (1936) (promise to build a side track for plaintiff's use "at such time as it [defendant] will begin building operations" on its land); Pegg v. Olson, 31 Wyo. 96, 223 P. 223 (1924) (promise to pay for land "as soon as ... can get a loan through from the government"); Lewis v. Tipton, 10 Ohio St. 88, 75 Am. Dec. 498 (1859) (promise to pay when convenient).

[23] See Peacock Constr. Co. v. Modern Air Conditioning, 353 So. 2d 840 (Fla. 1977) and cases cited therein (payment due five days after owner pays general contractor). See also Sturdy Concrete Corp. v. NAB Constr. Corp., 65 A.D.2d 262, 411 N.Y.S.2d 637, appeal dismissed, 415 N.Y.S.2d 212, 388 N.E.2d 349 (1979); Elk & Jacobs Drywall v. Town Contrs., 267 S.C. 412, 229 S.E.2d 260 (1976); Mignot v. Parkhill, 237 Or. 450, 391 P.2d 755 (1964).

either an appellate court's reluctance to disturb a finding of fact by a trial court,[24] or a court's adherence to the fallacious plain meaning rule of interpretation, i.e., discovering "unambiguous" language of condition.[25]

The RESTATEMENT 2d explains the prevailing view in forfeiture avoidance language, i.e., where the event will occur *before* either party has relied, the obligee risks only the loss of his expectation interest and the language may be construed as an express condition. Where, however, the event will occur only *after* the obligee has performed or relied by preparing to perform, he risks forfeiture and is likely to have assumed that risk only if the event is within his control. Under those circumstances, it is doubtful that he assumed the risk and the event should not be treated as a condition barring the activation of the obligor's duty.[26] Notwithstanding some protestation following this analysis that the rule "is not directed at the avoidance of actual forfeiture and unjust enrichment,"[27] the thrust of the RESTATEMENT 2d analysis appears clearly and pervasively directed toward that goal.

§ 103. Conditions of Satisfaction.

A. *The Meaning of "Satisfaction."*

The parties may agree that one or both performances under the contract must be "satisfactory" so that "satisfaction" or "approval" becomes a condition to one or both duties under the contract. The essential problem with conditions of satisfaction or approval is the determination of whether the promisor has to be personally (subjectively) satisfied, regardless of whether a reasonable party in his or her position would be satisfied, or whether satisfaction as used by the parties was intended to mean objective satisfaction, i.e., would a reasonable party be satisfied regardless of whether the promisor was actually satisfied.[28] Courts have viewed the problem as one of interpretation with a strong infusion of the avoidance of forfeitures.

If the language of the contract clearly and convincingly states that the duty of one of the parties is conditioned on the subjective satisfaction of that party, courts will apply the subjective test because that is the announced intention of

---

[24] *See* Mascioni v. I. B. Miller, Inc., 261 N.Y. 1, 184 N.E. 473 (1933) (where the trial court found that the parties intended that the subcontractor would assume the risk where the language indicated that the sub would receive payments after the general received payments).

[25] A. A. Conte v. Campbell-Lowrie-Lautermilch, 132 Ill. App. 3d 325, 477 N.E.2d 30 (1985) (where the phrases included, "if payment for invoiced material has been received by" the general contractor, and "if payment for such labor and material so invoiced has been received" by the general contractor. A spirited dissent points out that the first illustration under RESTATEMENT 2d § 227 clearly suggests the prevailing view. 477 N.E.2d at 34.

[26] RESTATEMENT 2d § 227 comment b.

[27] *Id.* The explanation is that the intentions of the parties must be viewed as of the time of contract formation, i.e., the test is whether a particular interpretation would have avoided the risk of forfeiture at that time and not whether such an interpretation would avoid actual forfeiture in a dispute arising later.

[28] Recent elaborations of this distinction are found in Kennedy Assocs. v. Fischer, 667 P.2d 174 (Alaska 1983) and Guntert v. City of Stockton, 43 Cal. App. 3d 203, 117 Cal. Rptr. 601 (1974). In *Guntert,* the court suggests that "reasonableness" is discoverable by reference to the facts and a lack of reasonableness is equated with arbitrariness which is found not only where an act is capricious, but where it lacks substantial support in the evidence. "Good faith," however, suggests a moral quality; its absence is equated with dishonesty, deceit, or unfaithfulness.

the parties.[29] When a promisor's duty is so conditioned, the promisee assumes a substantial risk. An artist who creates a painting under a contract subject to such a condition is assuming the risk that the prospective buyer will like the painting. If the buyer does not like the painting though the painting is heralded by connoisseurs as a magnificent work of art, the condition has not occurred and the buyer's duty is not activated. This result may be viewed as a forfeiture of the artist's expectation interest. Yet, by assuming the risk that the buyer would like the painting, the reasonable expectation of the artist includes that risk. The artist did not agree merely to produce a painting that would meet workmanlike standards. Rather, the artist agreed to produce a painting that would meet the subjective satisfaction of the buyer. When that satisfaction standard is not met, the buyer's duty under the contract is not activated.[30]

Where the subject matter of the contract is art or another performance that necessarily involves personal taste or judgment, the inclusion of a condition of personal satisfaction, notwithstanding the possibility of forfeiture, is more than plausible. Whether a particular artistic performance is "satisfactory" does not lend itself to an objective test. Hence, the RESTATEMENT 2d permits the application of a subjective standard since an objective test is not practicable.[31] Where, however, the subject matter is normally viewed in terms of commercial value, mechanical utility, or operative fitness, rather than aesthetic qualities, courts are much less inclined to apply the subjective standard simply because the language of the contract speaks in terms of "satisfaction." The strong policy against forfeitures compels courts to interpret such general "satisfaction" language as requiring the application of an objective (reasonable person) standard.[32] Yet, apt and convincing language may lead a court to

[29] "If the agreement leaves no doubt that it is only honest satisfaction that is meant and no more, it will be so interpreted, and the condition does not occur if the obligor is honestly, even though unreasonably, dissatisfied." RESTATEMENT 2d § 228 comment a.

[30] In Gibson v. Cranage, 39 Mich. 49, 33 Am. Rep. 351 (1878), the plaintiff was to make an enlarged picture of defendant's deceased daughter that the defendant "would like" and would be "perfectly satisfactory" to the defendant. The defendant did not like the picture and refused to take it or pay for it. The court suggested that, although the picture may have been excellent and the defendant ought to have been satisfied, under the agreement the defendant, alone, had the right to decide this question.

[31] See RESTATEMENT 2d § 228 ill. 5.

[32] In Kennedy, supra note 28, a clause permitted termination according to the approval of the lender's representatives and the court applied the objective test because the matter was one of commercial value. In Guntert, supra note 28, a commercial lease could be terminated at the sole discretion of city council and the court applied the objective test for the same reason. See also Meredith Corp. v. Design & Lithography Center, Inc., 614 P.2d 414, 416 (Idaho 1980) (contract for printing advertising sheets was to be determined by an objective standard since idiosyncratic preferences are generally irrelevant between commercial parties); Hall v. W. Brady Invs., Inc., 684 S.W.2d 379 (Mo. App. 1984) (economic value of structure as security for a loan involved commercial value and objective test applies). The RESTATEMENT 2d § 228 prefers the objective test where it is "practicable to determine whether a person in the position of the obligor would be satisfied." The FIRST RESTATEMENT § 265, suggested the same preference as noted in Aztec Film Prods. v. Prescott Valley, Inc., 626 P.2d 132 (Ariz. 1981). See, however, Mattei v. Hopper, 51 Cal. 2d 119, 330 P.2d 625 (1958) involving an executory contract for the sale of land for a shopping center providing that the buyer's obligation to consummate the deal was subject to the procurement of leases satisfactory to the purchaser. The court applied the subjective (honest satisfaction) test because of the multiplicity of factors which must be considered in evaluating a lease. See also Aster v. BP Oil Corp., 412 F. Supp. 179 (M.D. Pa. 1976) (satisfaction clause applied to sewage system held to require subjective (good faith) approval).

conclude that the subjective standard must be applied even in a case that may be said to involve a performance that is normally subject to a reasonableness standard.[33] Absent clear language to the contrary, except where the subject matter involves aesthetic qualities, it is assumed that "satisfaction" or "approval" means satisfaction of a reasonable person in the position of the obligor rather than the subjective satisfaction of the actual obligor.[34] This preference is predicated upon the avoidance of forfeiture to the obligee and the consequent unjust enrichment of the obligor. It is, however, conceivable that a contract to perform an ordinary task such as house painting, cement work, or carpentry could produce a performance that an honest obligor would find unsatisfactory. While the ordinary individual may see little or no difference in how a door is hung or a wall painted, the trained eye of a retired carpenter or painter who had promised to pay for such services only if he were satisfied with them could discern defects in the performance leading to his honest dissatisfaction. If the language of personal satisfaction in the contract is sufficiently clear, courts should not avoid an interpretation of subjective (actual) satisfaction in such a case though protection of the performer's restitution interest in an appropriate case may be in order.

B. *Subjective Satisfaction — Consideration — The Good Faith Standard.*

Where the condition of satisfaction is interpreted as requiring the personal satisfaction of the obligor, a question may arise as to whether there is any consideration moving from the obligor. After all, if the obligor may simply state his dissatisfaction and thereby escape the bargain, was he ever bound to any duty? While it is possible to discover case law finding promises conditioned on the personal satisfaction of the promisor illusory,[35] there is ample case law holding such promises to be supported by consideration on the footing that the promisor is committing himself to perform if he is, in fact, honestly satisfied with the performance.[36] Thus, in cases of the subjective satisfaction of the obligor, the question will often be whether the obligor was, in fact, honestly satisfied with the performance, i.e., did the obligor operate in good faith in stating his dissatisfaction.

If a defendant announces that he is not satisfied with the performance and will not pay for it, how does a plaintiff prove that the defendant is operating in bad faith?[37] While it is possible to discover statements of the defendant that

---

[33]*See* Ard Dr. Pepper Bottling Co. v. Dr. Pepper Co., 202 F.2d 372 (5th Cir. 1953) where the language indicated that the licensor's judgment (in good faith) would be sole, exclusive, and final. *See,* however, *Guntert, supra* note 28, holding that clause resting "sole discretion" in city council does not necessarily require the use of the subjective standard.

[34]RESTATEMENT 2d § 228. While the RESTATEMENT 2d prefers this objective standard, in matters of personal taste or aesthetic qualities such as art, it would apply the subjective test because it is not practicable to apply an objective test.

[35]*See* E. I. DuPont de Nemours & Co. v. Claiborne Reno Co., 64 F.2d 224 (8th Cir.), *cert. denied,* 290 U.S. 646 (1933). *See also* Gibson v. Cranage, *supra* note 30, where the court expresses some doubt as to whether a contract exists because of the satisfaction clause, but proceeds to hold that it did exist.

[36]*See, e.g., Kennedy, supra* note 28; Black Lake Pipe Line Co. v. Union Constr. Co., 538 S.W.2d 80 (Tex. 1976); Mattei v. Hopper, 51 Cal. 2d 119, 330 P.2d 625 (1958).

[37]The plaintiff has the burden of establishing the defendant's dissatisfaction. *See* Hortis v. Madison Golf Club, Inc., 92 A.D.2d 713, 461 N.Y.S.2d 116 (1983) (a condition of personal satisfac-

he is, in fact, satisfied with the performance but will lie about his satisfaction because he is not satisfied with the bargain he made,[38] such evidence is rarely available. If the defendant has simply failed to examine the work, the condition of personal satisfaction should be excused because the defendant prevented its occurrence.[39] If the obligor has made statements to others that he is, in fact, satisfied with the performance, this evidence is admissible concerning his state of mind to establish bad faith.[40] Bad faith may also be established if the obligor states dissatisfaction for reasons that were known at the time of contract formation.[41] Some courts will permit evidence of unreasonableness as an inference of bad faith.[42] If such evidence is admitted, however, there may be a tendency by the finder of fact to find bad faith simply because the decision of the obligor appears unreasonable.[43] Though the mere statement of the obligor that he is dissatisfied will not be conclusive,[44] absent evidence of the kind suggested, it will be particularly difficult for a party to prove bad faith where the subject matter is aesthetic and the other party, after examining the work, simply announces that it does not satisfy him.

C. *Third Party Satisfaction — Architects and Others.*

Many construction contracts require the satisfaction of a third party expert, such as an architect or engineer, rather than the owner. Where a particular individual is named as the third party to be satisfied, the condition can only be met if that named individual is honestly satisfied, i.e., the court may not substitute its judgment for the good faith judgment of the third party expert.[45] Though there is a risk of forfeiture to the obligee where a third party must be satisfied with the obligor's performance, the preference for an interpretation to avoid the risk of forfeiture does not apply.[46] If, for example, a named architect refuses to grant a certificate because of honest dissatisfaction with the contractor's performance, the contractor cannot recover on the contract even though he can produce testimony from other architects that the work has been

---

tion in an employment contract is generally interpreted to vest discretion in the honest, good faith judgment of the employer).

[38] *See* the statement of Judge Learned Hand in Thompson-Starrett Co. v. La Belle Iron Works, 17 F.2d 536, 541 (2d Cir. 1927), *cert. denied,* 274 U.S. 748 (1927), "The promisor may in fact be satisfied with the performance, but not with the bargain." *See also* RESTATEMENT 2d § 228 comment.

[39] *See* Hartford Elec. Applicators of Thermaluz, Inc. v. Alden, 169 Conn. 177, 363 A.2d 135 (1975) where the condition of personal satisfaction rested with a third party (architect) who refused to examine repaired work and the condition was excused.

[40] *See* FIRST RESTATEMENT § 265 ill. 1.

[41] *See* Western Hills v. Pfau, 265 Or. 137, 508 P.2d 201 (1973).

[42] *See, e.g.,* Volos Ltd. v. Sotera, 264 Md. 155, 286 A.2d 101 (1972) (dissatisfaction with employee where contract required performance to be subject to employer's satisfaction).

[43] Compare the distinction between the general definition of good faith and the "merchant" definition of good faith in the UCC. Section 1-201(19) contains the general definition of good faith which is defined as "honesty in fact in the conduct or transaction concerned." Section 2-103(1)(b) defines good faith "in the case of a merchant [as] honesty in fact and the observance of reasonable commercial standards of fair dealing in the trade."

[44] *See* RESTATEMENT 2d § 228 comment a.

[45] This view is widely accepted. *See, e.g.,* James Julian, Inc. v. State Hwy. Admin., 63 Md. App. 74, 492 A.2d 308 (1985); Elec-Trol, Inc. v. C. J. Kern Contrs., 54 N.C. App. 626, 284 S.E.2d 119 (1981); Brezina Constr. Co. v. South Dakota Dept. of Transp., 297 N.W.2d 168 (1980).

[46] *See* RESTATEMENT 2d § 227 comment c and ill. 5.

substantially performed.[47] If, however, the architect's refusal is based on the fraud or bad faith of the architect,[48] or gross mistake amounting to bad faith,[49] the condition would be excused.[50] The failure of the architect or other third party expert to examine the work would amount to bad faith and the condition would be excused.[51]

Even if the third party expert is operating in good faith but either grants approval of the work or refuses to issue a certificate for reasons *beyond the scope* of his expertise, the condition will be excused. Thus, where an engineer granted his approval of defective work in a school building because he was motivated to permit the children to get to school on time,[52] the condition was excused. Similarly, where an architect refused to grant a certificate because he did not want to appear to be issuing it as a prelude to litigation, the condition was excused.[53] Unfortunately, the courts in these cases felt compelled to resort to traditional categories in holding the condition excused. Thus, in the school case, the court stated that the engineer had either failed to make an honest judgment or his judgment was based on a gross mistake. Neither rationale is correct. The engineer decided to operate as a school authority, which was clearly beyond his engineering expertise. Similarly, where the architect refused to issue the certificate because he did not want to appear to be issuing it "for a case," the court resorted to a finding of "constructive fraud."[54] This is another analytical failure since, again, the third party was basing his judgment on the desirability of avoiding litigation which was beyond the scope of his expertise.

If the architect or other expert dies or becomes incapacitated to such an extent that he or she cannot make an honest judgment about the performance, the condition will be excused and a standard of reasonableness will be substituted.[55] If, however, the named third party is supposed to make a judgment of value concerning a work of art or other aesthetic quality for which there is no market price, the death or other unavailability of that trusted person may justify a court in finding both parties excused since their bargain was based on the judgment of that particular expert and no other expert will do.[56] Absent abundantly clear language in a construction contract, a court should not find both parties excused where an architect or other expert becomes unavailable. This is particularly true where the performance has conferred a benefit upon

---

[47] Moreover, an architect is not liable for directing an owner to terminate a contract unless the architect operates in bad faith. *See* Dehnert v. Arrow Sprinklers, Inc., 705 P.2d 846 (Wyo. 1985).

[48] *See* Austin Bridge Co. v. State of Texas, 550 S.W.2d 155 (Tex. App. 1977).

[49] *See* City of Mound Bayou v. Ray Collins Constr. Co., 499 So. 2d 1354 (1986); Arena Constr. Co. v. Town of Harrison, 71 A.D.2d 647, 418 N.Y.S.2d 3 (1979).

[50] *See* First Restatement § 303.

[51] *See Hartford Electric, supra* note 39.

[52] *See* James I. Barnes Constr. Co. v. Washington Twp., 134 Ind. App. 461, 184 N.E.2d 763 (1962).

[53] *See* Rizzolo v. Poysher, 89 N.J.L. 618, 99 A. 390 (1916).

[54] *See* Anthony P. Miller, Inc. v. Wilmington Hous. Auth., 179 F. Supp. 109 (D. Del. 1959) which expressly regrets the using of "constructive fraud" on this ground.

[55] *See* Grenier v. Compratt Constr. Co., 189 Conn. 144, 454 A.2d 1289 (1983).

[56] *See* UCC § 2-205 comment 4, which distinguishes the trusted expert valuing a work of art and a named expert with respect to a commodity with a market price. The unavailability of the latter expert may not destroy the contract while the unavailability of the former may destroy the contract.

the owner or where the contractor can be said to have justifiably relied upon a performance that may not have conferred such a benefit. Again, the strong policy against forfeiture should continue to influence courts in their determination of when a condition is properly excused.

Exceptions to the prevailing view that the test is good faith or honest satisfaction of the third party are limited to a few older cases where the court failed to perceive the difference between the standards of good faith and reasonableness. An old New York case held the condition of architect's approval excused simply because the architect was unreasonable.[57] The case was subsequently explained as an attempt to avoid forfeiture by a New York court that refused to apply the "reasonableness" standard to a condition of third party approval in a case involving the sale of goods.[58] The explanation is unsatisfactory since the enforcement of any condition of personal satisfaction may involve forfeiture. Rather, the case manifests a court rewriting the parties' contract to achieve what the court perceives to be a just result.

D. *Uniform Commercial Code — "Sale on Approval" — "Sale or Return."*

The UCC recognizes contracts that permit a proposed buyer to receive goods and examine or test them before committing to accept the goods.[59] A buyer may not be willing to commit to a purchase of goods before testing or examining them to determine whether they meet satisfaction or approval. Typically, all of the terms of the contract have been agreed to, but the buyer's duty is conditioned on his or her approval. Even though the goods meet all warranty standards, the buyer has the power to return them if they do not meet his or her approval.[60] Unfortunately, certain UCC comment language connected to the "sale on approval" concept may be misleading. While the language is clear with respect to the "particular business risk" undertaken by the seller "to satisfy his prospective buyer with the appearance or performance of the goods...,"[61] the same comment suggests, "The buyer's willingness to receive and test the goods is the consideration for the seller's engagement to deliver and sell."[62] The statement is misleading in two respects. First, a buyer may condition approval merely on the appearance of the goods, i.e., there may be no testing involved. This criticism may suggest that the comment language is simply infelicitous since the earlier language clearly indicates that approval may be based on appearance alone. The second concern is much more significant. If a buyer simply receives and examines or tests the goods, has she fulfilled her entire obligation, i.e., may the buyer notify the seller that she is returning the goods regardless of her approval of the goods? Would such a buyer, for example, be permitted to return the goods though they met her

---

[57]*See* Nolan v. Whitney, 88 N.Y. 648 (1892). *Accord* Coplew v. Durland, 153 Cal. 278, 95 P. 38 (1908).

[58]Van Iderstine Co. v. Barnet Leather Co., 242 N.Y. 425, 152 N.E. 250, 46 A.L.R. 858 (1926). *See* Annotation, 46 A.L.R. 864 (1927).

[59]*See* UCC §§ 2-326(1)(a) and 2-327(1).

[60]*See* UCC § 2-326 comment 1: "The present section is not concerned with remedies for breach of contract. It deals instead with a power given by the contract to turn back the goods even though they are as warranted."

[61]UCC § 2-326 comment 1.

[62]*Ibid.*

approval because she sought to take advantage of a better price from another supplier who appeared after the buyer made the original contract to buy on approval? The question scarcely survives its statement. The UCC imposes a good faith obligation in every contract.[63] This or any other type of bad faith would be antithetical to this pervasive norm.

There can be no question that the UCC recognizes the subjective satisfaction or approval of the buyer.[64] It does not, however, provide guidance as to whether the parties have contracted on the basis of the buyer's satisfaction. That question is left to common law principles.[65] Similarly, once it is determined that the parties have agreed to a contract of sale on approval, whether the parties have agreed to a subjective or objective standard is, again, a question of interpretation for which the UCC provides no guidance. As suggested earlier,[66] where the parties merely use the term "satisfaction," courts will be inclined to apply an objective test rather than a subjective test to avoid forfeiture. A comment indicates that the Code "takes no position" on this point.[67] As in other matters where the Code does not expressly displace prior law, general principles of law apply.[68] Thus, the interpretation of "satisfaction" would presumably be "reasonable satisfaction," i.e., the objective test.[69]

While the UCC recognition of the condition of personal satisfaction is reasonably clear in its "sale on approval" analysis, it is also clear that no sale of goods has occurred until the buyer accepts the goods, i.e., receipt and examination or testing of the goods does not complete the sale. "Acceptance" of the goods must be distinguished from mere "receipt" of goods.[70] The buyer's approval, however, may be inferred from conduct inconsistent with nonapproval, and if the contract states a time for approval, failure to notify the seller of nonapproval prior to the expiration of that period constitutes approval.[71] Even though the goods are in the possession of the buyer under a contract for sale on approval, until the buyer accepts the goods, the risk of loss remains on the seller.[72] It is also important to distinguish a "sale on approval" from a "sale or return" contract. The difference is essentially in the intended purpose of the buyer. If the buyer intends to *use* the goods but contracts with the understanding that he has the power to return them if he disapproves of them, the contract is a "sale on approval" contract.[73] If, however, the buyer intends to

---

[63] UCC § 1-203.

[64] *See supra* note 60.

[65] This analysis is suggested in U.S. Nemrod, Inc. v. Wheel House Dive Shop, Inc., 120 Misc. 2d 156, 465 N.Y.S.2d 674 (1983). *See also* Prior Bros., Inc. v. Bank of Cal., 29 Wash. App. 905, 632 P.2d 522 (1981) (whether the contract was intended to be a sale on approval was a question of fact for the trial court).

[66] *See supra* text preceding note 32.

[67] UCC § 2-316 comment 1.

[68] UCC § 1-103.

[69] *See* Empire South, Inc. v. Repp, 51 Wash. App. 868, 756 P.2d 745 (1988).

[70] UCC § 2-606 deals with the three methods of accepting goods. These methods will be discussed later in this Chapter at § 108(D).

[71] Mahler v. Allied Marine, 513 So. 2d 677 (Fla. App. 1987).

[72] UCC § 2-327(1)(b). Normally, the risk of loss will pass to the buyer no later than the time the buyer receives the goods and, if the contract term so specifies, even earlier, *e.g.*, at the time of delivery of the goods to the carrier under an FOB "shipment" contract.

[73] UCC § 2-326(1)(a).

resell the goods and contracts on the footing that he has the power to return any unsold goods, the contract is viewed as a "sale or return" contract.[74]

§ 104. Nonperformance and Constructive Conditions.

A. *Nature of the Problem.*

Where parties exchange promises of performances, they typically focus upon the extent of the promised performances and fail to consider the effects of nonperformance. In particular, there are three situations which the parties may not consciously consider: (1) the order in which their respective promises must be performed; (2) what effect a partial failure to perform a promise in the required order, or a delay in the performance, will have upon the rights and duties of the other party; and (3) what effect the prospective inability or unwillingness of one party to perform his promise, in whole or in part, shall have on the rights and duties of the other party. A simple illustration helps to clarify these questions.

Suppose *A* contracts to work for *B* for one year at a salary of $30,000, nothing being said as to when, or in what amounts, the salary should be paid to *A*. In what order must *A* and *B* respectively perform, i.e., should *A* perform the work before receiving payment, should *B* pay in advance for *A*'s labor, and, in either event, should *A* work for the entire year before being paid, should *B* pay the entire $30,000 in advance of any work by *A* or should some other arrangement be legally effectuated? If *A* fails to work, may he nevertheless recover the agreed salary? If *A* should be ill for a month and unable to work, what effect should this nonperformance have upon the rights and duties of the parties? If *B* should become insolvent, would *A* be excused from further performance? These and other questions are not to be answered through an interpretation of the manifested intention of the parties because the parties, in their words or conduct, have expressed nothing about them. The parties have not stated, either expressly or impliedly, what relationship was intended to exist between their promised performances. This relationship, however, must be determined before any satisfactory analysis of the parties' rights and duties can be made where a dispute arises concerning performances under their contract.

Since the parties have not provided an express or implied basis to guide courts in determining the relationship that should exist between their performances, it is necessary for courts to *construct* such a basis. Notwithstanding contrary protestations, in constructing such a process, courts are "making a contract for the parties" and thereby departing from the almost sacred principle that courts are only supposed to effectuate the manifested intention of the parties. If courts refrained from such construction, there would be no effective method to determine the rights and duties of the parties.

The process of construction used by courts is typically one of common sense. Thus, in a contract to install a guardrail in connection with a highway project, the guardrail installer agreed to a price based on a price quoted by a supplier with a time limitation similar to the time the highway was to be completed.

---

[74] UCC § 2-326(1)(b).

When the highway contractor delayed completion by some nine months, the installer insisted upon a higher price since it could no longer procure the guardrail at the earlier quoted price. When the contractor refused to agree to the higher price, the installer refused to perform. In an action by the contractor, the court held for the installer. Because it was perfectly obvious that the guardrail could not be installed until the site was ready for such installation, the court constructed a condition that such site would be available at the time for installation contemplated by the parties.[75] The condition was "constructed" rather than implied from the parties' expression of agreement through their words or conduct. Though the court refers to the condition as "implied," it must be taken to mean "implied" or created by law as contrasted with an implied-in-fact condition from the parties' manifested intention.[76] It is desirable to characterize such judicially created conditions as "constructed" since it avoids confusion with implied-in-fact conditions which are just as real as express conditions.[77]

In the sections that follow, we will see how courts have used constructive conditions to resolve numerous questions that are otherwise unanswerable through the manifested intention of the parties to the contract.[78] Before we explore how modern courts have constructed solutions to the kinds of nonperformance questions which parties typically fail to consider at the time of contract formation, however, it is important to examine how earlier courts dealt with these matters. After all, the kinds of questions to which these constructed solutions apply are fundamental to a determination of the rights and duties of the parties and must have occurred in the earliest contract cases. Moreover, as suggested with respect to numerous contract concepts already explored, an historical perspective is essential for reasons other than an understanding of antiquity. Unless the student of contract law understands this perspective, he will find it impossible to understand the modern solutions afforded by contemporary courts because he will not understand the purpose of such doctrines as constructive conditions of exchange.

B. *The Origins of Constructive Conditions — Independent Covenants.*

The early law had a very simple solution for the problems suggested above. It took the view that the performances were *independent* unless the parties in express terms indicated that performance by one was in some specified way *dependent* upon performance by the other. This meant that each party to a contract of exchanged promises was under a duty to perform his or her own undertaking, regardless of whether the other performed or offered to perform, unless performance on one side was expressly made dependent or conditional upon performance on the other side. Thus where *A* promised to work for *B* for

---

[75] R. G. Pope Constr. Co. v. Guard Rail of Roanoke, Inc., 219 Va. 111, 244 S.E.2d 744 (1974).

[76] *See* Holloway v. Jackson, 412 So. 2d 774 (Ala. 1982) quoting FIRST RESTATEMENT § 253 the effect that a constructive condition is not based upon an interpretation of the agreement.

[77] *See* RESTATEMENT 2d § 226 comment c.

[78] *See* Onderdonk v. Presbyterian Homes of N.J., 85 N.J. 171, 425 A.2d 1057 (1981) suggesting that constructive conditions may be imposed where fairness and justice so require. *See,* however, United Cal. Bank v. Prudential Ins. Co. of Am., 140 Ariz. 238, 681 P.2d 390 (1984) suggesting that courts should not read a term into a contract which would materially alter the obligations of the parties.

one year and, in return, *B* promised to pay him 20 pounds, it was said that *A* could sue for and recover the stipulated salary, even though he never did any work.[79] Likewise where *A* promised to sell a cow to *B,* and *B* promised to pay fifty shillings therefor, both promises being absolute in terms, it was held that *A* could sue for and recover the fifty shillings without showing that she had even so much as offered to deliver the cow.[80] Presumably also *B* could sue for and recover the value of the cow without paying or offering to pay the fifty shillings. Thus, for the purpose of enforcement, the law treated the two exchanged promises like two separate and distinct contracts. They were *independent* promises (covenants) bearing no relationship (dependency) to each other. Such a solution is absurd. It is part and parcel of the primitive notion that the language of a transaction must be enforced literally in all cases. The absurdity of this literalism becomes evident on the slightest reflection. In the first place, the solution may result in two lawsuits, when one ought to be sufficient to settle almost any controversy that is likely to arise in connection with such a transaction. In the second place, it takes no account of the essential nature and purpose of a contract of exchanged promises which are obviously dependent on each other.

When two people exchange promises, these promises are the consideration for each other and comprise the contract. It is not, however, in the exchange of the promises that the parties are primarily interested. Their main interest in making the contract is to assure themselves that they will exchange performances. It is perfectly evident that the purpose of the usual "bilateral" contract is to bring about the future exchange of promised performances which are the agreed equivalent for each other. That is to say, in the normal case, the performance or performances promised by the one party are the agreed equivalent or exchange for the performance or performances promised by the other. The primary aim of the legal concepts which deal with this problem should be to bring about the contemplated exchange, and to do it in such a way as to reduce to a minimum the possibility that either party will get an unfair advantage. When this primary aim cannot be achieved through an interpretation of the parties' expressions of agreement, an equitable adjustment should be discovered under rules which prevent unnecessary litigation. The early law wholly ignored these objectives and proceeded entirely on the basis of the literal language of the contract. It overlooked the pertinent fact that the language in which the contract was expressed was not always, or even usually, chosen advisedly with reference to the contingencies that might arise during the course of contract performance.

In the course of time the courts began to realize that their simple solution of the problem was not a sensible one. Not being willing, at first, to overrule the old cases outright, they nevertheless took a step forward by finding some word or phrase linking the two promises in the contract, which could, with some

---

[79] Anonymous [1500], Y.B. 15 Henry VII, folio 10b, placitum 7; LANGDELL, SELECTED CASES ON CONTRACTS 461 (1879). Actually, this case, which dealt with an exchange of sealed promises, antedates the problems of nonperformance which became evident with the enforcement of executory bilateral contracts toward the end of the sixteenth century through the development of the writ of assumpsit. For an historical sketch of this development, *see supra* Chapter 1 at § 3.

[80] Nichols v. Raynbred, Hobert 88 [1615]. *See also* Pordage v. Cole, 1 Williams' Saunders 319 [1669].

show of plausibility, be said to make the one performance expressly *dependent* upon the other.[81] The language most commonly seized upon for this purpose was the word "for" and the phrase "in consideration of." If the performance was, by the express terms of the contract, said to be "for" or "in consideration of" the other, the court might hold that the one was an express condition of the other. Elaborate rules with many fine distinctions were developed for determining just when, in a given case, this language had the effect indicated.[82]

It remained, however, for Lord Mansfield to take the first real step in the direction of putting the whole matter on a reasonably satisfactory basis. The case of *Kingston v. Preston*,[83] decided in 1773, seems to be the first reported case in which a court held that performance of one promise in a bilateral contract might be *dependent* upon the performance of the other promise, even though there were no words in the contract which could be said to justify that result. It is worthy of note that Lord Mansfield apparently justified his decision, in that case, on the ground that it accorded with the manifested intention of the parties. The case departed from prior holdings only in its admission that an apparent intention, though not expressed in words, to have one performance depend upon the other, might be given effect. Once this step was taken, it was but a short additional step to the view that such a condition might be read into the contract in the interests of justice,[84] even though it might be clear that the parties themselves had no actual intention whatsoever in regard to the matter, and consequently had manifested none. This was in fact the ultimate development. The modern law has come to take the view that the performances in a bilateral contract are dependent, except in certain special cases which do not concern us now. Our problem is to discover the nature of that dependency.

Courts, however, frequently hesitate to admit that conditions are being read into the contract. The tendency is to conceal the true nature of the process under the cloak of a spurious interpretation — a tendency which unfortunately obscures the real nature of the problem and its solution.[85] This reluc-

---

[81] "But I expressed my dislike of those cases, though they are too many to be now overruled, where it is determined that the breach of one covenant, though plainly relative to the other, cannot be pleaded in bar to an action brought for the breach of the other; as where there are two covenants in a deed, the one for repairing and the other for finding timber for reparations; this notion plainly tending to make two actions instead of one, and to a circuity of action and multiplying actions, both which the law so much abhors. If therefore this were a new point, I should be inclined to be of opinion that, though where there are mutual covenants relative to one another in the same deed a plaintiff is not obliged in an action brought for the breach of them to aver the performance of the covenant which is to be performed on his part, yet that the defendant in such action may in his plea insist on the nonperformance of the covenant to be performed on the part of the plaintiff; but this has been so often determined otherwise, that it is too late now to alter the law in this respect. But where the words make a condition precedent or a qualification of a covenant, as the present case plainly is, all the cases agree that the plaintiff in his declaration must aver the performance of such condition or qualification." Willes, C.J., in Thomas V. Cadwallader, Willes 469, 499 (1744).

[82] *See* Thorp v. Thorp, 12 Mod. 455 [1702].

[83] 2 Doug. 689.

[84] *See* the concurring opinion by Beatty, J. in Homa-Goff Interiors, Inc. v. Cowden, 350 So. 2d 1035 (Ala. 1977) suggesting that the doctrine of *Kingston v. Preston* is designed to avoid unjust results otherwise reached through literalism.

[85] Thus, in Corn Exch. Nat'l Bank & Trust Co. v. Taubel, 113 N.J.L. 605, 616, 175 A. 55 (1934), it is said, "The tendency of modern decisions is to hold promises mutually dependent. The order in

tance undoubtedly grows out of the historic view that a court must not "make a contract" for the parties in any respect — a view which cannot be supported on any rational basis if we are to have a workable law of contracts. As an original matter it would probably have been wiser had the courts, instead of dealing with the problem through the medium of so-called implied condition,[86] frankly admitted that they were confronting a situation calling for an equitable adjustment of the rights and duties of the parties under circumstances they had not addressed. Such a realistic approach would have facilitated the desired result and avoided the fictions and confusion which are all too evident in many of the cases dealing with these questions.

The way having been paved by Lord Mansfield's decision in *Kingston v. Preston*, modern courts developed various rules and principles of more or less general application for determining the relationship of the performances in bilateral contracts. These rules and principles will now be set forth. As suggested earlier,[87] there are three major questions involved in determining the relationship of performances where the parties have exchanged promises, i.e., the required order of performance, the effect of a failure or delay of performance upon the rights and duties of the other party, and the effect of a prospective failure or unwillingness to perform on the rights and duties of the other party. Very often in the solution of a given case, however, only one of these questions needs to be answered. Which of these questions is involved in the decision of a particular case will depend largely upon the point in the life of the contract at which the dispute arose. We will first consider those rules and principles by which the legally required order of performance in a bilateral transaction is to be determined followed by a discussion of the rules and principles by which we can ascertain the effect of a partial failure of performance, or of a delay in the performance, by one of the parties. We will then

---

which the things are to be done, it would seem, is now a significant, if not the controlling, factor. While the 'older cases lean to construe covenants of this sort to be independent, contrary to the real sense of the parties and the true justice of the case,' the interpretation of such promises now rests upon 'the good sense of the case and the order in which the things are to be done.' The underlying test is the intention of the parties."

So also in R.C.A. Photophone Co. v. Sinnott, 146 Or. 456, 459, 30 P.2d 761 (1934), the court, in holding that a promise that was in terms absolute was nevertheless dependent, said, "Plaintiff relied upon the theory of independent covenant to pay. In determining whether covenants in a contract are dependent or independent, the intention of the parties must govern and this intention must be ascertained from the contract itself where the language is plain and unambiguous."

Compare Cotillo, J., in Lion Brewery v. Loughran, 131 Misc. 331, 226 N.Y.S. 656 (1928), *rev'd,* 223 A.D. 623, 229 N.Y.S. 216 (1928), where he said, "As I understand it, the doctrine of implied conditions in contract law is a creation of the courts, by way of judicial fiction, in order to give the defendant an advantage which logically and equitably should be given to him by way of defense. The doctrine of conditions implied in law dates back to the decision of Lord Mansfield in 1773, sitting on the King's Bench, in the case of Kingston v. Preston, cited in 2 Doug. 689. It is a creation of the courts in order to overcome the hardships of the strict enforcement of the letter of contract law. An express condition is, of course, a real condition actually created by the parties and intended by them, whereas the condition implied in law is an invention of the courts, created by the law in an endeavor to do justice by the parties. In other words, where an unforeseeable and unforeseen contingency arises which the parties, naturally enough, failed to provide for or to contemplate, the law in such an event will think for them along equitable lines, and will imply such conditions as would have been in the minds of the parties, had they thought of them." *See* Jacob & Young's, Inc. v. Kent, 230 N.Y. 239, 129 N.E. 889 (1921).

[86] *See* Excalibur Auto. Corp. v. Roosevelt, 859 F.2d 454 (7th Cir. 1988) quoting 3 CORBIN § 632 to the effect that constructive conditions are neither express nor implied conditions.

[87] *See supra* subsection (A).

consider the effect of a prospective inability or unwillingness of one party to perform, either in whole or in part on the rights and duties of the other party.

A word of caution in regard to these rules and principles seems appropriate. First, the three sets of rules and principles mentioned are not mutually exclusive. They deal with different aspects of what is essentially one problem, and may frequently be employed interchangeably. Second, it must not be forgotten that the problem involved is one of bringing about an equitable adjustment between conflicting interests after a dispute has arisen regarding a matter not provided for in the contract. This being so, all the surrounding circumstances of the particular case must be taken into account. It is, of course, evident that no generalized principle can take into account all of the circumstances of every possible case. From this fact it would seem to follow that the rules and principles laid down should be regarded merely as tentative hypotheses, which are controlling only if the result they produce is equitable. It is more important that the result be just than a particular rule be applied. A careful study of the decided cases suggests that this is the attitude and practice of the courts.

§ 105. Determining When Performances Are Exchanged Under an Exchange of Promises — Lease, Aleatory, and Divisible Contracts.

A. *The Essential Test.*

The rules and principles which we will explore are applicable to all bargains in which promises are exchanged for an exchange of performances, i.e., each promise and each performance is at least part of the consideration for the other.[88] It does not matter whether the particular bargain is expressed formally or informally, or whether it is expressed in one writing or in a number of separate writings. If the promises are exchanged as part of a single contract, the rules and principles apply. It is not always clear whether there is one contract or separate contracts when each party gives more than one promise or gives some performance in addition to a promise as part of the bargain. However, if every promise by one party is at least part of the consideration for every promise by the other party, there is only one, single exchange in which all of the promises on each side are exchanged for all of the promises on the other side. To determine whether there is a single contract or separate contracts, the court must consider the actual bargain of the parties rather than the form of the agreement.[89] There are cases involving two writings in which the courts have decided that there are two contracts notwithstanding the fact that the transaction was essentially a unit and bilateral in nature.[90] This view has been clearly abandoned. Currently, whether there is one writing or several, whether separate performances are the subject of only one promise or separate promises, or whether the agreement of the parties is entirely or partially written or oral, the form itself will not be conclusive. The test is whether the parties exchanged promises contemplating an exchange of perfor-

---

[88] *See* RESTATEMENT 2d § 231. *See also* 3 CORBIN §§ 637, 653-60, 696.
[89] RESTATEMENT 2d § 231 comment d.
[90] *See, e.g.,* Przyblyski v. Pellowski, 141 Minn. 193, 169 N.W. 707 (1918).

mances in which each promise and each performance was contemplated as at least part of the consideration for the other.

Consider a fact situation in which X owns a viable business but is considering its sale. X is healthy and active and does not wish to retire, notwithstanding the sale of his business. He agrees to sell the business to Y for a consideration equal to the value of the business, which sale is evidenced by a writing. Moments later, X and Y execute a separate writing in which X agrees to work for Y for a specific term at a specific salary. When Y unjustifiably discharges X within one month, may X refuse to complete the transfer of the business to Y?[91] The determination of whether there is one contract or two contracts is highly significant. If there are two contracts, Y has breached the employment contract and X has breached the sales contract. However, if there is only one contract, Y has breached the single contract and X has not breached since X was excused from any further performance of his duties to complete the transfer of the business upon the breach of duty by Y. To determine whether the bargain of the parties manifests two contracts or only a single contract, the test suggested above is applied: was each promise and each performance contemplated as at least part of the consideration for the other? If the parties understood that X would not have sold his business to Y (notwithstanding receipt of fair market value for that business as evidenced in the separate writing) unless Y also agreed to employ X in the business for a certain term at a certain salary, the parties then contemplated each promise and each performance as at least part of the consideration for the other and there is one contract. However, if the promise of X to work for Y was no part of the consideration for Y's promise to purchase the business, and the promise of Y to employ X was no part of the consideration for X's promise to sell the business, there are two contracts since this is the bargain contemplated by the parties.[92] There are situations in which there is an exchange of promises where the parties do not contemplate an exchange of performances in the ordinary sense. It is important to consider these exceptions to the general rule that promises are exchanged for an exchange of performances. We will now consider three exceptional situations where the old concept of independent covenants reappears. The first situation, covenants or promises in leases, is predicated on historic accident. The second situation, "aleatory" promises, is an analytical exception to the general rule. The third situation, divisible contracts, is based upon the manifested intention of the parties to divide their respective performances into agreed equivalents.

B. *Leases of Real Property — Constructive Eviction — Warranty of Habitability.*

A lease of real property may appear to be an ordinary contract where the lessor promises to provide such property for a certain term in exchange for the lessee's promise to pay a certain rent. If leases were viewed in this fashion,

---

[91] *See* Rudman v. Cowles Commun., Inc., 30 N.Y.2d 1, 280 N.E.2d 867 (1972). *See also* Star Credit Corp. v. Molina, 59 Misc. 2d 290, 298 N.Y.S.2d 570 (1969); Continental Supermarket Food Serv. v. Soboski, 210 Pa. Super. 304, 232 A.2d 216 (1967).

[92] *See* RESTATEMENT 2d § 231 ill. 5.

they would be viewed as other contracts and the promise to pay rent would be dependent upon the performance of the lessor's promise to provide the property. Historically, however, leases were viewed as conveyances rather than contracts, i.e., a lease created an estate or interest in land in the lessee rather than a mere personal right to enforce the lessor's promises. The payment of the rent was regarded as the exchange for the transfer of this interest in land. The lessee, therefore, received the material, agreed equivalent, or exchange for his promise as soon as the lease was executed. If the landlord rented a dwelling place and promised to keep it in good repair and to supply heat, light, and other normal incidents of such property, these promises or covenants, no matter how material, were viewed as mere collateral incidents to the conveyance. They were construed as *independent* covenants or promises. A failure of the lessor to provide heat or light, or other failures to perform his covenants were actionable. While the lessee could sue the lessor for nonperformance of these promises, the lessee was still required to pay the rent because the promise to pay the rent was an independent covenant which bore no relation to any nonperformance by the lessor. The rent was viewed as consideration for a past performance by the lessor (the conveyance of the premises) and not for the performance of any of the lessor's collateral promises. If the lessee stopped paying the rent, he could be evicted from the premises even though he could prove that the lessor failed to perform his promise to keep the premises in good repair[93] or otherwise failed to perform one or more promises set forth in the lease.[94] Unless the lease expressly made such covenants or promises dependent, they were construed as independent.

A typical lessee who rents an apartment or office space where heat and light are not provided, where the roof leaks, or where the failure to otherwise keep the premises in sufficient repair so that the apartment or office becomes uninhabitable may view the law as unjust when he is told that he must continue to pay the rent and his only recourse is to sue the lessor. He will take little solace in the historical explanation that rules in relation to performances in leases became definitely settled at a time when it was also the rule in other types of contract that mutual performances were independent, unless made dependent in express terms, or that leases were always viewed as part of the law of conveyancing dealing with a thing apart from the law of contracts.[95]

Where a problem in society is clearly exposed and the traditional legal reaction is absurd, courts almost invariably find ways to break the historical shackles which have bound them to untenable positions. The most dramatic and conclusive change would have been to treat convenants in leases as promises in any type of contract, i.e., to presume their dependency. Stability and predictability, however, are high values in any legal system and, absent any legislative change, courts are reluctant to overturn long vested concepts. Rather, they resort to covert tools to achieve just results. The first major

---

[93] *See, e.g.,* Duncan Dev. Co. v. Duncan Hardware, 34 N.J. Super. 293, 112 A.2d 274 (1975); Arnold v. Krigbaum, 169 Cal. 143, 146 P. 423 (1915).

[94] *See, e.g.,* P. J. Moodie Lumber Corp. v. A. W. Banister Co., 286 Mass. 424, 190 N.E. 727 (1934) (failure to pay taxes on the premises).

[95] For a recent judicial statement of this history, *see* Davidow v. Inwood North Prof. Group, 747 S.W.2d 373 (Tex. 1988).

fiction used by courts to accomplish this end in lease cases was the concept of "constructive eviction." The single warranty implied in leases at common law was the warranty of "quiet enjoyment." Courts used this concept to develop the principle that, where the continued enjoyment of the premises was so severly impaired as to make them untenable, the lessee could rightfully abandon the premises and stop paying the rent even though no actual eviction had occurred. Thus, where a landlord violates his express covenant to repair or to furnish other necessary services, courts are willing to consider whether such nonperformance is a material failure by the lessor to perform his covenants and, assuming sufficient materiality, the lessee may abandon the premises without liability for rent.[96] It is now clear that the doctrine of "constructive eviction" is merely a device used by courts to achieve fair results.[97]

Another device reacted to the common law rule that, absent an express promise by the lessor, the lessor was not obligated to keep the premises in good repair. Recognizing this antiquarian rule as the product of an agrarian society which does not reflect contemporary housing patterns, courts have begun to imply a *warranty of habitability* in leases.[98] The standards of this implied warranty of habitability may be analogized to the UCC implied warranty of merchantability,[99] or to extant housing codes which landlords are not free to ignore.[1] The warranty of habitability may also be created by statute.[2] Protection of lessees through the "constructive eviction" or implied warranty of habitability devices was facilitated where the lessee was a consumer rather than a commercial tenant. The consumer was often faced with a "take-it-or-leave-it" lease and the obvious inequality of bargaining power raised the specter of unconscionability. A number of courts, however, have been willing to use these devices to protect even commercial tenants who should be in a position to better understand the risks involved.[3] The extension of these devices and other statutory and judicial protection of tenants is simply a manifestation of the basic issue recognized by an increasing number of courts, i.e., that leases should be treated as contracts and the mutual performances under the lease should be viewed as dependent or, in the more modern usage, con-

---

[96] *See, e.g.,* Charlotte Theatres, Inc. v. Gateway Co., 191 F. Supp. 834 (D. Mass. 1961) *rev'd,* 297 F.2d 483 (1st Cir. 1961) where the court viewed the inexcusable failure to provide air conditioning as such a serious or material failure of the lessor to perform that a constructive eviction had occurred.

[97] "There was an ameliorative exception to this otherwse harsh general rule which was known as 'constructive eviction': If the tenant's possession of the rented premises was so disturbed by unprivileged acts of the landlord that the tenant was deprived of their use, occupation, and enjoyment and was forced to abandon them, the tenant was viewed as effectively 'evicted' and his or her obligation to pay rent was discharged." Napolski v. Champney, 295 Or. 408, 667 P.2d 1013, n.10 (1983).

[98] *See* Javins v. First Nat'l Realty Corp., 428 F.2d 1071, (D.C. Cir. 1970). *See also* Lemle v. Breeden, 462 P.2d 470 (Haw. 1969); Pines v. Perssion, 14 Wis. 2d 590, 111 N.W.2d 409 (1961).

[99] UCC § 2-314. For a discussion of this UCC warranty, *see supra* § 100(C).

[1] *See Javins, supra* note 98.

[2] For a discussion of the Oregon statutes requiring landlords to maintain rental properties in habitable condition, *see Napolski, supra* note 97. *See also* MINN. STAT. § 504.18.

[3] *See Davidow, supra* note 95, where the implied warranty of habitability was extended to nonresidential leases. *See also* Reste Realty Corp. v. Cooper, 53 N.J. 444, 251 A.2d 268 (1969) where a lessee of office space was said to have been constructively evicted when the premises were repeatedly flooded with several inches of water.

structive conditions of exchange.[4] Even though judicial holdings clearly repudiating the antiquarian independent covenant analysis of leases may not exist in numerous jurisdictions, there is great doubt whether the old analysis will continue to prevail.[5] It is clear that the antiquarian view of treating performances of covenants in leases as independent, i.e., refusing to regard them as constructive conditions, is well on its way to complete erosion.

C. *Performance in Spite of Nonoccurence of Condition — "Aleatory" Promises.*

To this point, we have seen that, except for the historical aberration of covenants in leases, mutually promised performances are the contemplated equivalent and exchange for each other. Thus, to return to a simple example, where A agrees to work for B in exchange for B's promise to pay A a certain sum at the completion of the work, the mutual promises are *dependent* in that B's performance of payment is dependent upon A's performance of the work. In more modern usage, A's performance is a constructive condition (precedent) to B's duty of payment. If A does not perform, B's duty is not activated. In the sections which follow, we will explore specific rules designed to implement the basic concept of dependent promises or constructive conditions of exchange. Before exploring those specific rules, however, it is important to consider another exception to this general concept, an exception which, unlike the exception for exchanged promises in leases, is not the product of historic accident.

Where B promises to pay A for work performed by A, B's promise is clearly conditioned on A's performance. B may be said to have assumed a risk that A will not perform. Yet, if A fails to perform, B knows that he will be discharged from his duty to pay because he did not assume the risk of paying the amount promised unless A performed. Remember that A's performance was a constructive condition of B's duty to pay. There are, however, two situations where the mutual performances are not the contemplated exchange for each other, i.e., where a promisor assumes the greater risk that he will perform even though a condition does not occur: (1) where the performance on only one side of the contract is made to depend upon some fortuitous event; and (2) where each of the performances is made to depend upon different fortuitous events. The promise made in such cases is often characterized as "aleatory."[6]

---

[4] *See Javins, supra* note 98, at 1075. *See also* Old Town Dev. Co. v. Langford, 349 N.E.2d 744 (Ind. App. 1976) suggesting that reevaluation of the lessor-lessee relationship was inevitable for numerous reason, the most important of which was that leases were essentially contractual in nature. The RESTATEMENT 2d does not deal with leases in its treatment of constructive conditions of exchange. Rather, it refers the user to RESTATEMENT 2d OF PROPERTY § 5.1 comment a, § 7.1 comments a and c, and § 13.1 comment a. The FIRST RESTATEMENT § 290, contains a statement of the traditional rule of independent covenants.

[5] *See, e.g.,* Holmes Realty Trust v. Granite City Storage Co., 25 Mass. App. 272, 517 N.E.2d 502 (1988) expressing great doubt that the independent covenant analysis remains a correct statement of Masschusetts law.

[6] The FIRST RESTATEMENT § 291 defines an aleatory promise as one that is "conditional on the happening of a fortuitous event, or an event supposed by the parties to be fortuitous." The RESTATEMENT 2d § 239(2) describes this situation but mentions the term "aleatory" only in the accompanying comment b, without defining that term. "Aleatory" is derived from the Latin, *alea,*

The typical illustration of the first situation is the fire insurance contract where the insured promises to pay a definite premium in exchange for the insurer's promise to pay a stipulated amount only in the event a specified loss is suffered. Thus, the performance on one side of the contract, the side of the insurer, is made to depend upon the fortuitous event of a fire loss. Clearly, the insurer is not promising to compensate the insured for an actual, expensive loss in exchange for the relatively small, individual premium paid by the insured. Rather, the insurer is assuming the risk that a fire loss may occur in exchange for the premium payment. Moreover, the parties contemplate that the insured will perform his promise to pay premiums even though the condition to the duty of the insured never occurs. In fact, both parties hope that the condition will never occur. This "aleatory" contract wagering is not an illegal bargain since the insured has an interest, an insurable interest, in his property.[7]

The second situation is illustrated by an exchange of guaranty promises. A promises X to guarantee the payment of the debt of B in exchange for X's promise to A to guarantee the payment of the debt of Y. Each of the performances is made to depend upon different fortuitous events. Neither B nor Y may default on his obligation as the principal debtor, i.e., neither fortuitous event may occur and neither A nor X will be required to perform. Both B and Y may default, thereby activating the duties of A and X to perform. If, however, only one of the principal debtors, B or Y, default and the other does not default, the guarantor of that debt (A or X) must perform while the other guarantor has no duty to perform. It is clear that A and X each assumed the unusual risk of performing even though the other party to the contract may not have to perform. X was not promising to pay Y's debt in exchange for A's agreeing to pay B's debt since each party contemplated the possibility that one would have to pay while the other would have no duty to pay. Rather, it was the risk assumed by one party — that the stipulated fortuitous event may occur — that is the agreed exchange for the assumption of a similar risk by the other. Thus, the mutually promised *performances* were not the contemplated equivalent and exchange for each other.

With respect to both situations,[8] courts have long ago settled on the rule that, unless the promised performances are expressly made dependent, i.e.,

---

meaning dice, and aleatory contracts are often characterized as "betting" contracts. *See infra* note 7.

[7] An "aleatory" promise is often characterized as a betting promise. *See, e.g.,* Davidson & Jones, Inc. v. North Carolina Dept. of Admin., 60 N.C. App. 563, 317 S.E.2d 718 (1984) where the court quotes from Professor Corbin's treatise at § 598 in which Corbin suggests, "When a contractual promise is aleatory in character, the performance being expressly conditioned upon an uncertain and hazardous event, the promisee bets that it will happen and the promisor bets that it will not. The consideration exchanged for such a promise varies in proportion to their opinion as to probability. They consciously assume the risk. If the event occurs sooner than the promisor expects, he is the loser; if it fails to occur or occurs later than the promisee expects, it is he who is the loser. The opinion of one of them as to probability is thus shown to have been erroneous; but his mistake is not ground for rescission because he consciously assumed the risk." *See also* Harlan v. Aetna Life Ins. Co., 6 Wash. App. 837, 496 P.2d 532 (1972) where the court characterizes an insurance contract as an aleatory or betting contract.

[8] In Craig Corp. v. Albano, 55 B.R. 363 (Bankr. N.D. Ill. 1985) the court suggests that insurance and guaranty contracts are aleatory, as is a contract to sell something a person does not yet and may never own (*e.g.*, an inheritance). While these types of contracts are the typical illustrations

constructive conditions of the other, they are independent promises and each party may sue the other for a breach without regard to whether or not he himself is in default.[9] This is a fair solution in light of the great disparity between the values of the ultimate performances promised. If they were held to be dependent or constructively conditional, the party with the less burdensome performance, were he in default, would forfeit an amount wholly out of proportion to the loss suffered by the other party to the contract. Since the performances are not the agreed exchange for each other, there is no reason to regard them as dependent or conditional. In this situation, it is not inappropriate to adjust the rights of the parties through cross actions.

D. Divisible ("Severable") Versus Entire Contracts.

The parties to a bilateral contract may divide their respective performances into units on both sides so that a given unit on one side is dealt with as the agreed equivalent for a given unit on the other side. When this is the manifested intention of the parties, their contract is said to be *divisible*.[10] If, however, the whole performance on each side is dealt with as a single unit, the contract is said to be *entire* and this is the case even though one or both performances are to be furnished in installments.[11] The distinguishing charac-

---

of aleatory contracts, the concept can be applied much more generally. Thus, in *Davidson v. Jones, supra* note 7, the issue was whether the contractor could recover for the excavation of a large amount of rock beyond the 800 cubic yards the parties had included in the contract. The court found that the parties were aware of the fact that the amount of rock to be excavated could be greater or lesser than 800 cubic yards and established a unit price on that basis. In this aleatory contract, the contractor "bet" that the amount of rock would be lesser than 800 cubic yards while the promisee "bet" that the amount of rock would exceed the stated estimate. Both parties were aware of and assumed this risk. *See also* N.L.R.B. v. Columbus Printing Pressmen & Assistants' Union No. 252, 543 F.2d 1161 (5th Cir. 1976) where the court distinguishes arbitrable provisions of a labor contract from cost-of-living clauses by, *inter alia,* suggesting that a cost-of-living clause is in the nature of an aleatory contract.

[9] *See* Harlem v. Aetna, *supra* note 7, (health insurance); Panizzi v. State Farm Mut. Auto. Ins. Co., 386 F.2d 600 (3d Cir. 1967) (auto insurance). Older cases include Massachusetts Bonding & Ins. Co. v. State *ex rel.* Black, 76 Ind. App. 16, 127 N.E. 223 (1920) (contractor's surety bond); Cushing v. Williamsburg City Fire Ins. Co., 4 Wash. 538, 30 P. 736 (1892) (fire insurance contract); Dwelling-House Ins. Co. v. Hardie, 37 Kan. 674, 16 P. 92 (1887) (fire insurance contract); Trade Ins. Co. v. Barracliff, 45 N.J.L. 543, 46 Am. Rep. 792 (1883) (fire insurance contract). *See also* FIRST RESTATEMENT § 293.

[10] *See, e.g.,* Slater v. Westland, 27 Ariz. App. 227, 553 P.2d 1212 (1976) (performance of each severable part by one party is the agreed exchange for a corresponding part by the other party). *See also* RESTATEMENT 2d § 240. Comment b to this section suggests that such contracts are "loosely" described as "divisible" or "severable."

[11] It is important to emphasize that a contract is not divisible simply because the parties divide their respective performances on both sides. Unless each performance on each side is the agreed eqvuialent for the other, the contract is not divisible, i.e., it is entire. In construction contracts, for example, it is common for the parties to agree upon a schedule of progress payments to be paid at intervals as the work progresses. Though the owner makes such payments at stated intervals for each part of the work completed, the parties typically are not treating each payment for each part of the construction performance as the agreed equivalents of each other. Thus, a progress payment may be due when the contractor completes the initial excavation of the building site. The parties are not treating that progress payment as the agreed equivalent for the hole dug in the ground. *See, e.g.,* Lagrange Constr., Inc. v. Kent Corp., 83 Nev. 277, 429 P.2d 58 (1967). Similarly, where a corporation entered into an industrial preparedness contract with the Army Signal Corps, the corporation was to receive payments at the completion of four "steps" under the contract. Each of the first three steps was designed to move the corporation to a level of preparedness to be able to supply volume production of certain devices in the event of war. Except for a small payment, the corporation was paid for steps I, II and III. When it could not perform step IV,

teristic of a divisible contract is that the parties have dealt with a part of the performance on one side as the contemplated equivalent or agreed exchange for a corresponding part of the performance on the other side. Whether the parties have manifested that intention is a question of interpretation.[12] Thus, in a classic case involving a single contract for the purchase and sale of dressed hogs at a stated price per pound to be delivered immediately, and live hogs at a different price per pound to be delivered later, the court held the contract to be divisible.[13] Not only was it possible to apportion the parties' performances into corresponding pairs of performance; it was also possible to regard each pair as the agreed equivalent of the corresponding pair.[14] Unless the parties have apportioned the performances and have dealt with the separate portions as equivalents, a court would not be justified in determining for the parties how much of the performance on one side should be regarded as the equivalent for a stated portion of the performance on the other side. It must, however, be recognized that courts have frequently gone far in finding an agreed equivalence between portions of the promised performances where it may be doubted whether the parties contemplated partial exchanges.[15] By treating a contract as divisible, a court may avoid forfeiture because of the *effect* flowing from such a characterization. It is, therefore, vitally important to understand the difference between the characterization of a contract as either divisible or entire.

1. The Effect of Nonperformance in a Divisible Contract.

Consider the following case. The defendant had agreed to supply seven outdoor display signs for the plaintiff in exchange for a total payment of $95

---

it sought to recover the balance due for the three steps it had completed on the footing that the contract was divisible and it should be paid for each of the agreed equivalents it had performed even though it could not perform the last step. The court held the contract to be entire rather than divisible since the Signal Corps had agreed to make payments to achieve the purpose of step IV, i.e., it had not agreed to pay for each of the first three steps as agreed equivalents. Pennsylvania Exch. Bank v. United States, 170 F. Supp. 629 (Ct. Cl. 1959).

[12] Courts will typically consider whether the parties assented to all promises as a single whole, whether there was a single consideration rather than consideration for each part, and whether the performances were divided into parts. *See* Ellison v. Tubb, 295 Ark. 312, 749 S.W.2d 650 (1988); Big River Hills Ass'n v. Altmann, 747 S.W.2d 738 (Mo. App. 1988); Stratemeyer v. West, 136 Ill. App. 3d 1095, 484 N.E.2d 389 (1985); Cahn v. Antioch Univ., 482 A.2d 120 (D.C. App. 1984); Wilderness Country Club v. Downing, 458 So. 2d 769 (Fla. App. 1984); Woodger v. Woodger Dev., Inc., 106 Idaho 199, 677 P.2d 512 (1984). The basic test may be viewed as whether the parties would have agreed on less than the whole performance promised or would have insisted upon the entire consideration exchanged. Jalasko Assocs. v. Development Assocs., 617 P.2d 406, 408 (Utah, 1980). The intention of the parties is dominant, however. Though a contract may be severable by its terms, it will be construed as entire if that appears as the intention of the parties. Stika v. Albion, 150 Ariz. 521, 724 P.2d 607 (1986).

[13] *See* Tipton v. Feitner, 20 N.Y. 423 (1859).

[14] These are the two elements suggested by the RESTATEMENT 2d at § 240.

[15] *See* RESTATEMENT 2d § 240 comment e. This was particularly true in cases involving salary or wages. If an employee performed for less than the entire term of contract, a construction that the contract was divisible permitted the employee to recover payment for work done even though he would still be liable for breach of the remainder of the contract. If the contract were construed as entire and the employee's breach considered material, the employee would recover nothing. Thus, a forfeiture was avoided through the "divisible" contract construction. The problem has been largely overcome by state legislation mandating the payment of wages on a reasonable, periodic basis. *See* McGowan, *The Divisibility of Employment Contracts,* 21 IOWA L. REV. 50 (1935).

per month for three years and the contract specified the payment for each of the signs. The defendant failed to perform with respect to two of the seven signs even though the plaintiff had made payments for all of the signs. When the plaintiff sought to recover for defendant's breach, the court found the contract to be divisible so that the defendant was entitled to retain the payments for the five signs he had installed properly and had to return only that portion of the payments for the two signs that had not been properly installed. Had the court found the contract to have been entire rather than divisible, the plaintiff could have recovered the total payment because of the defendant's breach.[16]

This is because, in general, the *effect* of breaching an entire contract (assuming a *material* breach)[17] is to discharge the innocent party from his duty to perform. If, however, the contract is divisible, the failure to perform a distinct part does not discharge the other party from paying for the severable or divisible parts performed by the breaching party.[18] In this sense, therefore, each divisible agreed exchange of a contract is viewed as independent of other divisible parts of the contract, i.e., the performance of one divisible part is not a constructive condition of the performance of different divisible parts, though the performance of one divisible part by one party is a constructive condition of the corresponding divisible part to be performed by the other party.[19] If the nonperformance of a divisible part is not a constructive condition to the performance of other divisible parts of the contract, can such nonperformance have *any* effect on the other divisible parts, i.e., can each divisible part of a single contract always be treated as if it were a separate contract, or, are there circumstances where the failure to perform an earlier divisible part justifies the other party in refusing to perform the remainder of the contract?

---

[16] John v. United Adv., Inc., 165 Colo. 193, 439 P.2d 53 (1968).

[17] The concept of material breach and related doctrines such as substantial performance are explored *infra* §§ 107-108.

[18] *See* National Consultants, Inc. v. Burt, 186 Ga. App. 27, 366 S.E.2d 344 (1988).

[19] It should be noted that the respective performances for each divisible part are viewed as dependent or constructively conditional on the performance of *that* divisible part. Any material failure or performance by one party of his side of a given division of a divisble contract excuses the other party from performing his side of that division, regardless of what may be the rights and duties of the parties with respect to the other divisions of the contract. Thus, in the case involving the signs, the parties had agreed that proper installation and maintenance of the largest sign was the agreed equivalent for the plaintiff's promise to pay $35 per month. Had that sign not been properly installed and maintained, the plaintiff's duty to pay $35 per month would not have been activated because the constructive condition of exchange (proper installation and maintenance of the sign) had not occurred. This would, however, have no effect on other divisible parts of the contract fully performed by the defendant. *See also* Gill v. Johnstown Lumber Co., 151 Pa. 534, 25 A. 120 (1892) where the parties agreed that Gill would drive certain logs of different types and cross ties down a river to particular locations. The contract specified different prices for different types of logs and cross ties to different locations. While Gill succeeded in driving some of the logs and ties to the specified locations, the Johnstown flood swept other logs and ties beyond the locations. The court held the contract to be divisible and permitted the plaintiff to recover for each of the logs and ties transported to the prescribed locations at the prices specified in the contract. However, plaintiff could not recover for logs or ties transported only part of the way since the court treated each of the severable parts of the contract as a contract for transportation of each described good all the way to the prescribed location. *See also* Sherrill-Russell Lumber Co. v. Krug Lumber Co., 216 Mo. App. 1, 267 S.W. 14 (1924); Portfolio v. Rubin, 233 N.Y. 439, 135 N.E. 843 (1922); Jackson v. Rotax Motor & Cycle Co., 2 K.B. 937 [1910].

2. Material Nonperformance in a Divisible Contract — Installment Contracts — Uniform Commercial Code.

Even though a divisible contract is one contract, a single unit of performance on one side with its corresponding equivalent on the other side may be viewed as if it were a separate and distinct contract because, by hypothesis, each portion of the performance on one side is the full, agreed exchange for the corresponding portion on the other side. If divisible parts were always viewed as separate contracts, nonperformance of a divisible part would never have an effect on duties to perform other divisible parts. This may appear highly desirable since the parties apportion the consideration in divisible contracts and there is no apparent unfairness in making a party pay for what he has received when he has promised to pay that amount for a divisible portion of the contract. Again, if that party were permitted to refuse payment, the party who had performed the divisible portion would suffer a forfeiture. Yet, a divisible contract is not a series of separate contracts; it is one contract. Since all of its divisions are part of one contract, it is possible that the parties would not have contracted with regard to one or more portions of the agreed performances without the others. Each portion is, after all, but a part of a larger whole. Nonperformance of one divisible part may not appear to be significant, but it could be a part which the other party views as a critical part. Suppose there is nonperformance of more than one divisible part. Does the other party have to await performance of the remaining parts even after repeated failures of performance as to earlier installments? If there is nonperformance of one part and good reason to believe that other divisible parts will not be performed, should the other party be able to treat the whole contract as breached? Earlier courts confronted these problems with some difficulty traceable to nineteenth century English cases that were not entirely clear and were subject to misinterpretation in later cases.[20] With respect to contracts for the sale of goods, however, the matter was effectively dealt with under the old Uniform Sales Act[21] and is currently governed by similar concepts under the UCC.[22]

The UCC does not present an analysis in terms of divisible versus entire contracts. Where a contract either requires or authorizes goods to be delivered

---

[20] In Withers v. Reynolds, 2 B. & Ad. 882 [1831], a buyer failed to pay for a delivered installment of goods and said that he would not pay for any further installments at the time of delivery, but would always keep one installment in arrears. The court engaged in dictum suggesting that the refusal to pay for one installment would not have excused the seller, but the buyer's repudiation of the whole contract excused the seller. In the subsequent case of Hoare v. Rennie, 5 H. & N.19 [1859], where the nonperformance was the seller's failure to deliver the correct quantity of goods on time, the court held the buyer excused from taking later deliveries. Later cases, however, suggested that the failure to perform one installment of a divisible contract excuses the other party only when that failure evinces an intention to repudiate the remainder of the contract. Freeth v. Burr, 9 L R.C.P. 208 [1874]. This view was apparently adopted by the House of Lords in Mersey Steel & Iron Co. v. Naylor, 9 App. Cas. 434 [1884] and was written into the English Sale of Goods Act, St. 56 and 57 Vict. C. 71, § 31, subd. 2. See, however, Maple Flock Co. v. Universal Furn. Prods., Ltd., 1 K.B. 148 [1934] where Lord Hewart suggested that the test should be objective concerning the whole purpose of the contract and should include the ratio quantitatively which the breach bears to the contract as a whole and the degree of probability or improbability that the breach will be repeated. The confusion of the English cases found its way into American cases. See 2 WILLISTON, SALES § 467(c) and (d) (rev. ed. 1948).

[21] USA § 45(2).

[22] UCC § 2-612.

in separate lots to be separately accepted, under the Code such a contract is an "installment contract."[23] Even if the writing evidencing the transaction contains a phrase such as, "each delivery is a separate contract," the contract is still one installment contract.[24] It is clear that a contract will be an installment contract where installment deliveries are tacitly authorized by the circumstances or by the option of either party.[25] Unlike the situation where only one shipment of goods is contemplated by the parties and the buyer may reject the goods for *any* defect,[26] the buyer may reject an installment of goods only where the nonconformity (defect) in such installment substantially impairs its value and cannot be cured.[27] "Substantial impairment of value" is best understood as the UCC version of "material breach."[28] If the nonconformity in one or more installments substantially impairs the whole contract, there is a breach of the whole contract.[29] The determination of when the buyer may have the right to treat the whole contract as discharged because of a nonconformity in one or more installments can be difficult because it is a question of fact.[30] The Code policy is clear in urging a continuation of the installment contract. The test is not whether a nonconformity in a given installment indicates an intent or likelihood that future deliveries will also be defective. Rather, the

---

[23] UCC § 2-612(1). It should be noted that both the UCC, § 2-307, and the RESTATEMENT 2d § 233 set forth the rule that where a complete performance can be provided at one time, the complete performance rather than divisible portions or installments over a period of time is expected. This general rule, however, is almost swallowed by its exceptions. The parties may, of course, expressly agree upon installment deliveries. Installment deliveries may also be inferred from the circumstances such as trade usage (UCC § 1-205(2), RESTATEMENT 2d § 221) or course of dealing (UCC § 1-205(1), RESTATEMENT 2d § 223). Other circumstances may suggest that one delivery is absurd. Thus, if all of the brick necessary for the construction of a large building was delivered at once, construction of the building may be seriously impeded. If installment deliveries are appropriate, the price, if it can be apportioned, must be paid upon the completion of each delivery. RESTATEMENT 2d § 233(2).

[24] *Ibid.*

[25] UCC § 2-612 comment 1.

[26] *See* UCC § 2-601. This Code section is explored subsequently in the section dealing with the "perfect tender" rule, *infra* § 108.

[27] UCC § 2-612(2).

[28] The concept of material breach is fully explored *infra* § 107. "The common law concept of 'material breach' is at least a first cousin to the concept of 'substantial nonconformity,' and it offers a fruitful analogy to one who seeks to determine whether the seller's performance substantially nonconforms." J. WHITE & R. SUMMERS, UNIFORM COMMERCIAL CODE § 8-3, at 305 (1980).

[29] UCC § 2-612(3).

[30] In Cherwell-Ralli, Inc. v. Rytman Grain Co., 180 Conn. 714, 433 A.2d 984 (1980), the buyer was behind in its payments for shipments almost from the inception of the installment contract. The seller repeatedly called for payment while continuing to ship the goods. The buyer sent a check but stopped payment on the check alleging concern that the seller may not continue in business (the court found no valid reason for the buyer's stoppage of payment). The court found the continuous default in payment and the stop payment order to be sufficiently egregious to constitute substantial impairment of the value of the whole contract. In Continental Forest Prods., Inc. v. White Lumber Sales, Inc., 256 Or. 466, 474 P.2d 1 (1970), a 9% variance below grade of one of 20 carloads of lumber provided by contract where a 5% variance was acceptable was held not to be such a substantial nonconformity as to be a breach of the whole contract. *See also* Trunkline LNG Co. v. Trane Thermal Co., 722 S.W.2d 722 (Tex. App. 1987) (the buyer's rejection of only one installment does not establish that the contract was breached); Bodine Sewer, Inc. v. Eastern Ill. Precast, Inc., 143 Ill. App. 3d 920, 493 N.E.2d 705 (1986) (occasional deliveries of defective pipe which were always cured on demand did not constitute nonconformities which substantially impaired the value of the entire contract).

test is whether the non-conformity substantially impairs the value of the whole contract.[31]

§ 106. The Order of Performances in Exchanged Promises.

A. *The General Principle.*

We have criticized the early common law view that treated the performances in a bilateral contract as independent covenants unless they were expressly made dependent by the stated terms of the contract.[32] To avoid the unacceptable consequences of that view and to determine whether a given party is under a present duty of performance, it is necessary to determine the required order of performances in such an exchange of promises.

If the parties have expressed their intention concerning the order of their performances, either in words[33] or through conduct,[34] that intention will control. It is only in those cases where there is no evidence of their intention that a problem arises. It should not be forgotten that the purpose of determining the required order of performances in bilateral contracts is to assure the exchange of mutual performances in a fashion that precludes the possibility that one party will, at any stage of the performance, have an unfair advantage over the other party. To appreciate the common sense guidelines that have been adopted by our courts to avoid any unfair advantage, it is necessary to consider various possibilities of ordering performance and the judicial reaction to them.

B. *Promises Capable of Simultaneous Performances When They Are Agreed Equivalents — Concurrent Conditions — "Tender" and "Offer to Perform."*

If the exchanged promises, by their nature and consistency with the terms of the contract, can be performed simultaneously (concurrently), and if the two promised performances are the agreed equivalents for each other, it is uniformly held that the two performances must be exchanged simultaneously, i.e., the two performances are viewed as constructive concurrent conditions.[35] Where the performances are concurrent conditions and the question arises, which party should perform before the other, the curious answer is "neither" or "either." Consider, for example, a contract for the sale of land where the terms of the contract do not require either party to perform before the other. If *A* simply agrees to sell and *B* to buy *A*'s land for a price of $50,000, the delivery of the deed and payment of the purchase price are concurrent conditions.[36] If *neither* party made an offer to perform or tender,[37] neither party can

---

[31] UCC § 2-612 comment 6.

[32] *See supra* § 104.

[33] *See, e.g.,* Industrial Mercantile Factors Co. v. Daisy Sportswear, Inc., 56 Misc. 2d 104, 288 N.Y.S.2d 109 (1967).

[34] *See, e.g.,* Siple v. Logan, 232 Pa. Super. 322, 355 A.2d 758 (1975) (prior course of dealing can create a constructive condition precedent).

[35] *See* El Dorado Hotel Props., Ltd. v. Mortensen, 136 Ariz. 292, 665 P.2d 1014 (1983); Herring v. Prestwood, 379 So. 2d 548 (Ala. 1979). *See also* RESTATEMENT 2d § 238. The RESTATEMENT 2d avoids the use of the phrase "concurrent condition" which had been used in the FIRST RESTATEMENT § 251 but even there considered an "elliptical expression."

[36] *See* Fogarty v. Saathoff, 128 Cal. App. 3d 780, 180 Cal. Rptr. 484 (1982) (stating the general principle but finding that the obligation to provide a termite clearance and title insurance were not concurrent conditions).

be in default since neither was required to perform before the other.[38] If neither party offers to perform and the time stated in the contract for performance has expired, or where no time is stated, a reasonable time for either party to offer performance has expired, both parties are discharged since the constructive concurrent conditions to their respective performances can no longer occur. Similarly, if *either* party seeks to activate the duty of the other to perform, that party must offer to perform first. If such an offer occurs and the other party fails to perform, the latter is in default because the constructive concurrent condition has occurred thereby activating the latter's duty, and there has been a breach of that duty by failure to perform. The foregoing analysis suggests the rationale for the rule, i.e., neither party is required to risk his own performance without receiving the bargained-for-exchange.

Concurrent conditions are constructed typically in contracts for the conveyance of land and contracts for the sale of goods.[39] Certain acts may be necessary in preparation for an offer to perform or tender. If *A* agrees to sell and deliver coal to *B* at *B*'s residence for which *B* promises to pay a certain amount, and nothing is said as to the time for performance, the transaction involves concurrent conditions though *A* will have to bring the coal to *B*'s house to tender performance.[40] The hauling of the coal is not part of the promised performance. It is an action which *A* must perform in preparation for tender. The law is not concerned with such preparation. Rather, it correctly concerns itself only with the performances which have been expressly undertaken.[41]

Performances under an exchange of promises may be performed simultaneously (concurrently) in four situations: (a) where the same time is set for performance by either party;[42] (b) where the same period of time is fixed for both performances;[43] (c) a time is fixed for the performance of one promise and no time is set for the performance of the other;[44] (d) no time is fixed for the performance of either promise.[45]

---

[37] An "offer of performance" is less exacting than a tender of performance which would involve an actual proffering of the performance, itself, *e.g.*, *B* proffering the $50,000 to *A*. To perform the constructive concurrent condition, *B* would simply have to offer to pay the $50,000 with manifested present ability to make the payment. *See* RESTATEMENT 2d § 238 comment b. Sections 45 and 62 of the RESTATEMENT 2d illustrate the more exacting requirement of a tender of performance. If a tender has occurred where only an offer of performance is required, the tender, of course, more than meets the requirements of an offer to perform. In a contract for the sale of goods, however, the UCC requires tender of delivery as a condition to the buyer's duty to accept the goods and pay for them (UCC § 2-507(1)), or tender of payment as a constructive condition to the seller's duty to tender and complete delivery of the goods (UCC § 2-511(1)).

[38] *See* Century 21 All Western Real Estate v. Webb, 645 P.2d 52 (Utah 1982).

[39] *See, e.g.,* Willener v. Sweeting, 107 Wash. 2d 388, 730 P.2d 45 (1986) (land); Fletcher v. Jones, 314 N.C. 389, 333 S.E.2d 731 (1985) (land); Aurora Aviation v. AAR Western Skyways, 75 Or. App. 598, 707 P.2d 631 (1984) (sale of aircraft).

[40] *See* Morton v. Lamb, 7 Term. Rep. 125 [1797].

[41] *See* Fogarty v. Saathoff, *supra* note 36.

[42] *See* School Dist. No. 2 v. Rogers, 8 Iowa (8 Clarke) 316 (1859). FIRST RESTATEMENT § 267(a); RESTATEMENT 2d § 234(1) and comment b.

[43] Beach v. First Fed. Sav. & Loan Ass'n, 140 Ga. App. 882, 232 S.E.2d 158 (1977); Goodison v. Nunn, 4 Term. Rep. 761 [1792]. *See* FIRST RESTATEMENT § 267 (d); RESTATEMENT 2d § 234(1) and comment b.

[44] *See* Palmer v. Fox, 274 Mich. 252, 264 N.W. 361 (1936); Morton v. Lamb, 7 Term. Rep. 125 [1797]. FIRST RESTATEMENT § 267(b); RESTATEMENT 2d § 234(1) comment b.

[45] *See* Fletcher v. Jones, *supra* note 39; George W. Merrill Furn. Co. v. Hill, 87 Me. 17, 32 A. 712 (1894). FIRST RESTATEMENT § 267(s) and RESTATEMENT 2d § 234(1) and comment b.

C. *Promises Capable of Simultaneous Performances Where They Are Not Agreed Equivalents.*

Where the performance of one or both parties is divided into parts so that one part is not the agreed equivalent of all or a part of the performance of the other party, can some of the performances still be due simultaneously, i.e., may they be concurrently conditional? Suppose that A agrees to convey land to B who agrees to pay a total price of $50,000 in five installments of $10,000, the contract specifying that the land will be conveyed at the same time that the last installment payment is due. It is uniformly held that the conveyance and the last installment payment are concurrently conditional.[46] The rationale for these holdings is obvious. Since the vendor has already received four installments and will receive the remainder of the entire agreed exchange for his conveyance when he receives the last payment, there is no reason for any further credit to be extended by the purchaser before he receives the conveyance. If the parties had agreed that the conveyance would be made at the time of an earlier installment, the payment and that installment would be concurrently conditional.[47] This result simply effectuates the manifested intention of the parties.

Where all or a material part of the performance on one side of the contract can be performed simultaneously with any number of different acts to be performed on the other side, and the parties have *not* specified the times for their respective performances, the whole or material part of the performance on one side is concurrently conditional with the last act to be performed on the other side.[48] If, for example, A promises to convey land to B, no time being set for the conveyance, in return for which B promises to pay a price in specified installments, the conveyance and the last payment are concurrently conditional.

A situation may be supposed where each of the mutual performances in a bilateral contract are to be continuous and will require a period of time for completion during which both performances are to occur. If, for example, A agrees to remodel B's property for which B promises to perform masonry work

---

[46]*See* Kerr v. Reed, 187 Cal. 409, 202 P. 142 (1921); Kane v. Hood, 30 Mass. (13 Pick.) 281 (1832). *See* RESTATEMENT 2d § 234(1) and ill. 6 thereto. *See also* E. E. E., Inc. v. Hanson, 318 N.W.2d 101 (N.D. 1982) where the contract required two installment payments to be made before the delivery of the abstract. Originally, the abstract had to be delivered concurrently with the third installment. That portion of the contract was, however, deleted. Held: the first two installments were required without delivery of the abstract, i.e., they were not concurrently conditional. Citing Professor Corbin's treatise at § 664, the court emphasized that the purchaser had agreed to extend credit to the seller through the first two installment payments. In Ideal Family & Youth Ranch v. Whetsline, 655 P.2d 429 (Colo. App. 1982), the contract required delivery of a deed in escrow prior to any payments. Such delivery was not concurrently conditional with payments; rather, it was a constructive condition precedent to the buyer's obligation to pay.

The language of the contract may specify that the buyer shall first make the payments before the conveyance will be made. Some courts manifest a strong preference for finding simultaneous performance by holding that the last payment is still concurrently conditional with the conveyance. *See, e.g.,* Zintsmaster v. Werner, 41 F.2d 634 (3d Cir. 1930), *aff'd,* 61 F.2d 298 (3d Cir. 1932). *Contra* Walker v. Hewitt, 109 Or. 366, 220 P. 147, 35 A.L.R. 100 (1923), *noted,* 8 Minn. L. Rev. 630 (1923).

[47]Chew v. Egbert, 14 N.J.L. 446 (1834); Green v. Reynolds, 2 Johns. 207 (N.Y. 1807).

[48]*See* El Dorado Hotel Prop. Ltd. v. Mortensen, 136 Ariz. 292, 665 P.2d 1014 (1983). *See also* RESTATEMENT 2d § 234(1), ills. 6 and 12.

for *A* and no time is set for performance, each party must perform within a reasonable time. In such a case, there is no basis for requiring either performance to occur before the other. Neither party, to preserve his rights, should be forced to part with any more of his performance than absolutely necessary without receiving some assurance that he will receive the agreed exchange. The fairest solution is to require the performances to occur concurrently.[49]

D. *Performances Requiring Time Exchanged for Instant Performance.*[50]

Where a material part of the promised performance on one side of a bilateral contract is of a kind that will necessarily extend over a period of time and the performance on the other side can be rendered in an instant, it is uniformly held that the performance that takes time is a constructive condition precedent absent contrary manifestations of contract language or the circumstances.[51] If *A* contracts to construct a building for *B* for which *B* promises to pay a certain price, nothing being said about the time of payment, the building must be completed, at least substantially, before *B*'s duty to pay is activated.[52]

This principle appears to have originated in employment contracts.[53] Since employers as a class were considered more financially responsible than employees, it is not strange that courts elected to adopt a rule compelling the employee to extend credit to the employer, rather than the reverse. The rule seemed particularly appropriate at the time it was established when it was common for the employer to furnish board and lodging to the employee in addition to the stipulated wage. This custom no longer prevails and there are wage statutes in most of the states which largely control the matter.[54] The principle, however, remains and the typical example continues to be building contracts requiring the builder to extend credit to the owner. The builder's risk, however, has been mitigated by the allowance of statutory liens to the extent of the work performed by the builder.

It must be emphasized that the principle requiring the party whose performance takes time to perform first, must always be consistent with the purpose of the contract. If, for example, an owner for whom a building was to be erected agreed to furnish a bond to secure the performance of his payment obligation, and no time was set for furnishing the bond, the owner must furnish the bond as a condition precedent to any duty of performance by the

---

[49] *See* Sutton v. Meyering Land Co., 248 Mich. 601, 227 N.W. 783 (1929); Rosenthal Paper Co. v. National Folding Box & Paper Co., 226 N.Y. 313, 123 N.E. 766 (1919). Ihrke v. Continental Life Ins. & Inv. Co., 91 Wash. 342, 157 P. 866 (1916).

[50] This section is cited in RESTATEMENT 2d § 234, Reporter's Note to comment e.

[51] RESTATEMENT 2d § 234(2) and comment e.

[52] Stewart v. Newbury, 220 N.Y. 379, 115 N.E. 984 (1917). *See* Royal McBee Corp. v. Bryant, 217 A.2d 603 (D.C. App. 1966) (duty to pay rental was constructively conditioned on lessor's duty to keep equipment in good repair). Also, in a divisible contract, if an agreed equivalent on one side requires time for its performance and the corresponding agreed equivalent can be performed instantaneously, the same rule applies. *See* Walsh v. New York & Ky. Co., 88 App. Div. 477, 85 N.Y. Supp. 83 (1903) (contract of employment divisible by months — no recovery for part of a month).

[53] *See* Skagway City Sch. Bd. v. Davis, 543 P.2d 218 (Alaska 1975) (employee's substantial performance is a constructive condition precedent to employer's duty to pay wages).

[54] *See* McGowan, *Divisibility of Employment Contracts,* 21 IOWA L. REV. 50 (1935).

builder.[55] The purpose of a payment bond is to assure the builder of payment for any work performed. The builder should not be required to perform any work until the payment bond is furnished.[56]

E. Performances at Different Times — Condition Precedent — Progress Payments.

Where the exchanged performances under a bilateral contract are expressly due at different times, the performance due first is a constructive condition precedent to the performance due later, provided that the first performance is a material part of the agreed exchange for the later performance.[57] The requirement that the first performance be a material part of the agreed exchange to constitute a constructive condition precedent requires a preview of the concept of materiality of breach. As will be seen in the next section,[58] it is not every failure of performance that excuses the counter performance. A failure of performance may be so insubstantial that the other party must still perform, though there has been a technical failure of performance (breach) for which the first party is liable. If performance that fails is not material, that performance will not be viewed as a constructive condition precedent since the failure of a condition to occur after it can no longer occur has the effect of discharging the duty of the other party.[59] To permit the other party to be discharged from his duty to perform because of an insubstantial failure of performance by the party who was to perform first would result in a forfeiture. If A agrees to sell and deliver an automobile to B on the first day of May for which B promises to pay $10,000 on the following first day of July, a slight delay in the delivery of the automobile beyond May 1 would probably not be a material failure to perform so that the failed performance would not be a constructive condition precedent to B's duty to pay. If the delay in delivery of the auto was so long as to be a material failure under the circumstances, the failed performance would constitute a condition precedent to B's duty to pay the price,[60] and since the condition did not occur and could not occur, B's duty would be discharged. To phrase the same concept in a positive form, the delivery of the automobile without material delay beyond May 1 would be a constructive condition precedent to B's duty to pay the agreed price. It is

---

[55] See Clark v. Gulesian, 197 Mass. 492, 84 N.E. 94 (1908).

[56] Where a seller of whiskey had agreed to furnish advertising, the court held that the furnishing of advertising within a reasonable time was a condition precedent to the duty of the buyer to pay any installments that matured after the lapse of a reasonable time. Rochester Distilling Co. v. Geloso, 92 Conn. 43, 101 A. 500 (1917). See also Lake Dorr Land Co. v. Parker, 104 Fla. 378, 140 So. 635 (1932) (furnishing of abstract within a reasonable time held a condition precedent to duty to pay installments of purchase price maturing thereafter).

[57] RESTATEMENT 2d § 237. The exception to this rule occurs in divisible contracts. Where there are pairs of agreed equivalents, the performance of one part of such a pair is viewed in the same fashion as if that pair of performances were the only pair of performances promised. See RESTATEMENT 2d § 240.

[58] Infra § 107.

[59] See RESTATEMENT 2d § 225(2). The determination of whether a failure of performance is material or immaterial will be explored infra § 107. In general, see RESTATEMENT 2d § 241.

[60] "And it may be laid down as a general rule, where the consideration is to be performed before the day specified for the payment of the money, the performance of the consideration ought to be averred in an action for the money." Bailey v. White, 3 Ala. 330, 332 (1842). Few actual decisions of this kind can be found to support the almost axiomatic statement of the rule.

important to remember that we are discussing "constructive" conditions, i.e., conditions created by the law rather than the parties that are designed to order the performances in bilateral contracts in a fair manner. Where the performance that fails is insubstantial or immaterial, courts will not create such a condition because, again, to view such immaterial performance as a condition precedent will result in a forfeiture.

Constructive conditions will be created not only where the two performances in question are the entire performances mutually promised, but also in cases where the contract is performable in installments on either or both sides. Thus, in a construction contract, it is common to divide the performances into installments to provide the builder with sufficient monies to continue performance.[61] Upon completion of one part of the building, the builder will receive what is typically called a "progress payment." If A promises to construct a building for B in exchange for progress payments at stated intervals during the course of the work, a series of alternate conditions precedent will be constructed. Again, assuming that each part of the respective performances constitutes a material part of the whole, the first stage of the work is a condition precedent to the first progress payment and the first progress payment, in turn, is a condition precedent to the second part of the work. Each successive part of the work and progress payment constitutes a condition precedent to the counter performance that is to follow.[62]

The rule that a material part of the exchange due first is a constructive condition precedent to the duty of the other party is based upon simple fairness to that party. Unless the party whose performance is due later receives substantially what he bargained for as the exchange for his own performance without material delay, he should not have to perform his own promise.[63] By treating the first due material part of the performance as a condition precedent, our law assures this result.

F. *Performances at Different Times — Becoming Concurrent Conditions.*

We have just seen that the performance due first, if material, will be viewed as a condition precedent to the later performance. We have also seen that a material failure of performance due first will discharge the duty of the other party who may bring an action for damages against the breaching party. Suppose, however, the failure of the performance first due is an immaterial delay and the time for the counter performance is now due. Thus, in a contract for the sale of A's auto to B for $10,000, assume that A is supposed to deliver the car on May 1 and B is to pay on May 3. A's failure to deliver the car on May 1 is a failure of performance but, presumably, an immaterial failure so that B is not discharged from his duty. If B waits until May 3 to seek A's

---

[61] Such a contract is not a divisible contract because the pairs of installments are typically not agreed equivalents.

[62] *See* K & G Constr. Co. v. Harris, 223, Md. 305, 164 A.2d 451 (1960); Ringelberg v. Kawa, 242 Mich. 665, 219 N.W. 593 (1928); Guerini Stone Co. v. P. J. Carlin Constr. Co., 248 U.S. 334 (1919). Again, if the part of the performance that is due first is not a material part of the agreed exchange, it will not be a condition precedent. *See, e.g.,* Leiston Gas Co. v. Leiston-Cum-Sizewell Urban Dist. Council, 2 K.B. 428 [1916].

[63] *See* RESTATEMENT 2d § 237 comment b.

performance, the performances due under the contract are now simultaneously due so that each performance becomes a concurrent condition of the other. As seen earlier,[64] to place either party in default, the other will have to tender performance. The same analysis applies even to a material failure of the first due performance if the other party chooses to ignore that failure and wait until his own performance is due.[65]

Where the parties to an entire contract divide their performances into installments on one or both sides, a similar analysis applies. Assume that A contracts to convey land to B, no time being set for conveyance, for which B promises to pay a total of $100,000 in four equal installments. Assume that B pays the first two installments but fails to pay the third until the fourth and final installment is due. If B's failure to pay the third installment on time is a material failure of performance (constructive condition precedent which has not occurred), A is discharged. If, however, that failure is immaterial (and not a condition precedent) or material but ignored by A, the conveyance and the payment of the third and fourth installments are due simultaneously, i.e., they are concurrent conditions.[66]

§ 107. Failure of Performance — Material Breach.

A. *General Principles.*

Where the parties have a bilateral contract and one party fails to perform, our law could have assumed either of the following polar positions:

(1) A party in default should never have the right to insist upon performance by the other. This solution fails to consider the injustice that would often result. The defaulting party, for example, may have performed a substantial part of his promised performance. If that party is not permitted to recover notwithstanding his default, he would suffer a serious forfeiture while the loss sustained by the other party would be relatively insignificant.[67] Even where the defaulting party has not begun to perform, the defects in his tender of performance may be so slight that, as a matter of fairness, he should not be deprived of the benefit of his bargain.

(2) The opposite position which our law could have adopted is that a defect in performance, no matter how substantial, should never prevent an action on the contract by the defaulting plaintiff. Rather, it should only furnish the basis for the defendant's recoupment of the loss suffered by the plaintiff's

---

[64] *See supra* subsection B.

[65] *See* RESTATEMENT 2d § 234 comment d.

[66] RESTATEMENT 2d § 234 comment d and ill. 8. *See also* Henderson v. Morton, 109 Fla. 300, 147 So. 456 (1933); Walsh v. Coghlan, 33 Idaho 115, 190 P. 252 (1920); Underwood v. Tew, 7 Wash. 297, 34 P. 1100 (1893); Beecher v. Conradt, 13 N.Y. (3 Kernan) 108, 64 Am. Dec. 535 (1855). *Cf.* Littlefield v. Brown, 394 A.2d 794 (Me. 1978) (after exercise of option, the arrangement becomes an executory land contract where delivery of payment and conveyance of land become concurrent conditions).

[67] It may be argued that the solution to this problem should be found in permitting the defaulting plaintiff to bring an action in quasi contract, i.e., a restitutionary action to prevent unjust enrichment. *See* Bowen v. Kimbell, 203 Mass. 364, 89 N.E. 542 (1909). This solution, however, would deprive the promisee of the benefits of a profitable bargain when, in many cases, there is little reason for so doing. Moreover, where the performance of the defaulting plaintiff has not conferred any measurable benefit on the other party, no restitutionary remedy would be possible.

failure to perform. This position is reminiscent of the archaic view that all covenants in contracts are independent and multiplicity of litigation is a desirable solution.

Neither of these polar positions has been adopted. Rather, our legal system has developed a principle for distinguishing between cases where the failure to perform does, and those in which it does not, prevent an action on the contract by a party in default. That principle may be stated in relatively simple terms: If the failure of performance is sufficiently serious — if it is substantial or material — the defaulting party should not have the benefit of what might have been a favorable bargain.[68] Having concluded that some failures of performance or breaches of contract may be substantial or material and, therefore, preclude a cause of action by the defaulting party, while others will be insubstantial or immaterial and, therefore, not preclude an action by the defaulting party, a major problem arises: how does a court determine whether a particular failure of performance (breach) is material (substantial) or immaterial (insubstantial)?

B. *Failure of Performance (Material Breach)* — RESTATEMENTS *Compared.*

In searching for an adumbration of the principle that material or substantial breaches preclude an action on the contract while immaterial or insubstantial breaches do not preclude such an action, there has been a great judicial tendency to rely upon the FIRST RESTATEMENT and RESTATEMENT 2d. The difficulty in providing a detailed analysis of this principle, however, has promoted a tendency toward restatements of the principle, itself. Thus, the FIRST RESTATEMENT begins with the statement that, if the failure to perform or delay in performance is so material that it will or may result in the other party not receiving the substantial benefit of his bargain, the duty of the injured party is discharged and he is wholly excused from his undertaking.[69] On the other hand, if the failure to perform or delay in performance is not sufficiently material, the injured party is not discharged or excused, but retains his duty to perform, i.e., there is still a breach of contract but the innocent party must recoup his loss for the immaterial breach while he is still bound to perform.[70] Numerous courts have been prone to state similar generalities.[71] While there is no question that the application of the principle is designed to prevent unreasonable forfeitures to defaulting parties and to

---

[68] In Ott v. Buehler Lumber Co., 541 A.2d 1143 (Pa. Super. 1988), the second edition of this book is cited for the proposition that a party may not insist upon performance if that party has committed a material breach. Where the default is so serious that the defaulter is precluded from recovering on the contract, he may seek a remedy in quasi contract (restitution) to recover the value of any benefits conferred on the other party even though the performance was defective as measured by the contract.

[69] *See* FIRST RESTATEMENT §§ 274, 397.

[70] FIRST RESTATEMENT § 274(1). *See* Millis Constr. Co. v. Sapphire Valley, Inc., 86 N.C. App. 506, 358 S.E.2d 566 (1987); Aldape v. Lubcke, 107 Idaho 316, 688 P.2d 1221 (1984); Jacob & Young's, Inc. v. Kent, 230 N.Y. 239, 129 N.E. 889 (1921); Tichnor Bros. v. Evans, 92 Vt. 278, 102 A. 1031 (1918); Manthey v. Stock, 133 Wis. 107, 113 N.W. 443 (1907).

[71] A recent example is Sohol v. Bruno's, Inc., 527 So. 2d 1245 (Ala. 1988) where the court suggests that a material breach touches the fundamental purpose of the contract and defeats the object of the parties.

assure fairness to innocent parties, there is a serious problem in the application of this principle to myriad fact situations.

1. FIRST RESTATEMENT — Guidelines.

It has become abundantly clear that the determination of whether a particular breach is or is not material is not susceptible to mechanical rules.[72] There was never any doubt in the minds of drafters of either RESTATEMENT that it would be impossible to suggest anything more than guidelines to assist courts in making this distinction. Thus, the FIRST RESTATEMENT listed six "influential circumstances" to assist courts in this effort.[73] These guidelines were designed to expose "the inherent justice of the matter" in answering the basic question, "Will it be more conformable to justice in the particular case to free the injured party, or, on the other hand, to require her to perform her promise, in both cases giving her a right of action if the failure to perform was wrongful?"[74] The FIRST RESTATEMENT recognized the tendency to treat questions of *delay* in performance as different from other types of failure of performance. It devoted a separate section to this question where it listed five "rules" to guide courts in determining whether a delay in performance constituted a material breach.[75]

---

[72] *See* McDuffy, Edwards & Assocs. v. Septews, Inc., 93 Or. App. 226, 762 P.2d 299 (1988).

[73] FIRST RESTATEMENT § 275 provides:

Rules for determining materiality of a failure to perform.
In determining the materiality of a failure fully to perform a promise the following circumstances are influential:
(a) The extent to which the injured party will obtain the substantial benefit which he could have reasonably anticipated;
(b) The extent to which the injured party may be adequately compensated in damages for lack of complete performance;
(c) the extent to which the party failing to perform has already partly performed or made preparations for performance;
(d) The greater or less hardship on the party failing to perform in terminating the contract;
(e) The wilful, negligent or innocent behavior of the party failing to perform;
(f) The greater or less uncertainty that the party failing to perform will perform the remainder of the contract.

Two well-known cases applying these criteria, both concluding that the breach was immaterial, are Walker & Co. v. Harrison, 347 Mich. 630, 81 N.W.2d 352 (1957) (failure to clean sign by lessor of sign was immaterial though annoying) and Continental Grain Co. v. Simpson Feed Co., 102 F. Supp. 354 (E.D. Ark. 1951) which also applies § 276 (immaterial delay in performance).

[74] FIRST RESTATEMENT § 275 comment a.

[75] FIRST RESTATEMENT § 276 begins with the "rule" that, absent an agreement of the parties to make performance on the exact day of "vital importance," failure to perform on that day does not discharge the duty of the other party (§ 276(a)). In mercantile contracts, timely performance is important but a material breach will not be found unless the delay is "considerable" in light of the nature of the transaction and seriousness of the consequences (§ 276(b)). If a party delays before rendering *any* performance, less delay is necessary to constitute a material breach than if the delaying party had begun to perform (§ 276(c)). More delay is necessary in contracts for the sale of land than in mercantile contracts to constitute a material breach (§ 276(d)). Where the suit is for specific performance in a contract for the sale of land, "considerable delay in tendering performance does not preclude enforcement of the contract" where the delay can be compensated unless the contract states that timely performance is essential or the circumstances indicate that enforcement will be unjust (§ 276(e)).

2. RESTATEMENT 2d — Constructive Condition, Cure, Suspension, Termination.

The RESTATEMENT 2d lists guidelines similar to its predecessor but approaches the problem in a significantly different fashion. It begins by characterizing a party's duties under a contract as constructively conditioned upon the lack of any *uncured material* failure by the other party to render any performance due earlier.[76] When a breach is material, the RESTATEMENT 2d views the breaching party's performance as a constructive condition which has not occurred. The nonoccurrence of that condition will prevent the activation of the innocent party's duty, at least temporarily, or it will discharge that duty when the constructive condition can no longer occur.[77] The important difference in the RESTATEMENT 2d treatment of material breach is that it does not simply distinguish between material and immaterial breaches. While it clings to the FIRST RESTATEMENT distinction between material and immaterial failures to perform by suggesting guidelines similar to its predecessor,[78] it treats a material breach as the nonoccurrence of a condition,[79] and it makes a further distinction between *material* breaches which may or may not be "cured." The concept of cure is borrowed from the UCC which permits a seller of goods which have been rejected by the purchaser to notify the buyer of the seller's intention to cure or remedy the nonconformity in the goods and then to make a conforming tender if time for performance remains under the contract.[80] Thus, the RESTATEMENT 2d suggests that where there is a material

---

[76] RESTATEMENT 2d § 237.
[77] RESTATEMENT 2d § 237 comment a.
[78] RESTATEMENT 2d § 241 provides:

In determining whether a failure to perform or to make an offer to perform is material, the following circumstances are significant:
(a) the extent to which the injured party will be deprived of the benefit which he reasonably expected;
(b) the extent to which the injured party can be adequately compensated for the part of that benefit of which he will be deprived;
(c) the extent to which the party failing to perform or to offer to perform will suffer forfeiture;
(d) the likelihood that the party failing to perform or to offer to perform will cure his failure, taking account of all the circumstances including any reasonable assurances;
(e) the extent to which the behavior of the party failing to perform or to offer to perform comports with standards of good faith and fair dealing.

Among the cases relying, to some extent, upon the RESTATEMENT 2d guidelines, are Baillie Commun., Ltd. v. Trend Bus. Sys., 765 P.2d 339, 53 Wash. App. 77 (1988); Miles v. CEC Homes, Inc., 753 P.2d 1021 (Wyo. 1988); Kersh v. Montgomery Dev. Center, 35 Ohio App. 3d 61, 519 N.E.2d 665 (1987); Rohauer v. Little, 736 P.2d 403 (Colo. 1987); Oak Ridge Constr. Co. v. Tolley, 351 Pa. Super. 32, 504 A.2d 1343 (1985); Rose v. Davis, 474 So. 2d 1058 (Ala. 1985); Prudential Ins. Co. of Am. v. Stratton, 14 Ark. App. 145, 685 S.W.2d 818 (1985); Vicenzo v. Cerro, 186 Conn. 612, 442 A.2d 1352 (1982).
[79] An immaterial breach is not treated as the nonoccurrence of a condition because the injured party may not even suspend, much less terminate, his performance in response to such a breach.
[80] UCC § 2-508(1). A simple illustration suggests the reasonableness of this provision. If X has agreed to supply certain goods to Y by the 30th day of the month and delivers nonconforming goods on the 15th of the month which Y rejects, if X notifies Y that he will deliver conforming goods between the 15th and the 30th and does so, Y has received timely delivery of precisely what he ordered. As to whether the repair of goods is a sufficient cure, *see* Zabriskie Chevrolet, Inc. v. Smith, 99 N.J. Super. 441, 240 A.2d 195 (1968) (substitute transmission in automobile) and Wilson v. Scampoli, 228 A.2d 848 (D.C. App. 1967) (new television set required to be returned to shop). Cure is stated in § 2-508 of the Code as available only after the buyer has *rejected* the goods. If

breach, there is a constructive condition to the innocent party's duty to perform that has not occurred. If, however, time remains for that condition to occur, i.e., the breaching party could still perform in a relatively timely fashion, the innocent party may not treat the failure of performance (or nonoccurrence of the condition) as a termination of his duties.[81] Rather, the duties of the innocent party are merely *suspended* because the breaching party may perform or offer to perform in time to *cure* the material breach.[82] Consider, for example, a building contract requiring progress payments as the construction proceeds. The owner may fail to make a progress payment at some stage during the construction. Traditionally, such a failure has been regarded as a material breach by the owner. Absent a progress payment, the builder may not be able to continue the construction because he will be unable to pay subcontractors, material suppliers and the like.[83] If, however, the delay in making the progress payment was only a few hours, the contractor should not be justified in *abandoning* the work.[84] The contractor would be justified in *suspending* performance until sufficient time expired to permit the owner to cure the material breach. Once that time expires, however, the duties of the contract are discharged, i.e., he may treat the contract as terminated.[85] As to the length of time that must expire before the injured party may treat his duties as not simply suspended but discharged, again, the answer depends upon the circumstances. The RESTATEMENT 2d lists certain "significant" cir-

---

the buyer has already accepted the goods and then revokes his acceptance as permitted under UCC § 2-608, the question arises whether cure is still available to the seller if contract time remains. For discussion of this question *see* Asciolla v. Manter Oldsmobile-Pontiac, Inc., 117 N.H. 85, 370 A.2d 270 (1977) and Pavesi v. Ford Motor Co., 155 N.J. Super. 373, 382 A.2d 954 (1978).

It should also be noted that while the typical application of cure under the UCC is one in which contract time remains at the time the goods are rejected, § 2-508(2) suggests the possibility of cure even where no time remains under the contract but the seller has "reasonable grounds to believe" that the goods which were tendered would be acceptable with or without a money allowance. In such a situation, the seller would then have "a further reasonable time to substitute a conforming tender."

The RESTATEMENT 2d suggests a number of inquiries with respect to the application of "cure" which are more than reminiscent of the general guidelines for determining whether a breach is material: (1) To what extent has the reasonable expectation of the injured party already been secured? (2) Does the injured party have security to assure performance by the defaulting party? (3) Did the breaching party submit any reasonable assurances that the breach would be cured? (4) Has the market changed for the goods or services in question so as to make the contract more favorable to the defaulting party? (5) Has the defaulting party breached other contracts or other installments of the contract in question? (6) What is the financial or other condition of the breaching party in relation to his ability to cure? *See* RESTATEMENT 2d § 241 comment c.

[81] In UCC § 2-106(4), "cancellation" is defined as either party putting an end to the contract for breach by the other. This is distinguished from "termination" which is defined in UCC § 2-106(3) as either party putting an end to the contract pursuant to a power conferred by the agreement. "Termination," however, is often used in a fashion synonymous with the concept of "cancellation" under the UCC.

[82] RESTATEMENT 2d § 237 comment b.

[83] *See* Aiello Constr. Co. v. Nationwide Tractor Trailer Training & Placement Corp., 122 R.I. 861, 413 A.2d 85 (1980); Zulla Steel v. A & M Gregos, 174 N.J. Super. 124, 415 A.2d 1183 (1980).

[84] *See* Turner Concrete Steel Co. v. Chester Constr. & Contr'g Co., 271 Pa. 205, 211, 114 A. 780, 782 (1921) where the court states: "[I]t cannot be said that the abandonment of a contract of the magnitude here shown, within a few hours of a large payment, was justifiable." *See also* Underground Constr. Co. v. Sanitary Dist., 367 Ill. 360, 11 N.E.2d 361 (1937).

[85] *See* John Kubinski & Sons v. Dockside Dev. Corp., 33 Ill. App. 3d 1015, 339 N.E.2d 529 (1975). *See also* cases cited *supra* note 84.

cumstances to aid courts in arriving at a satisfactory analysis.[86] The first guideline suggests that courts consider all of the circumstances set forth in the section designed to determine whether a breach is material.[87] The second guideline considers the extent to which the delay may prevent or hinder the injured party in making reasonable substitute arrangements,[88] and the third guideline considers the extent to which the agreement provided for performance without delay.[89] Even here, however, the RESTATEMENT 2d emphasizes that a material failure to perform or offer to perform on a stated day does not, in itself, discharge the other party's duties unless the circumstances indicate that performance or an offer to perform by that day is important. This qualification is a significant illustration of the underlying philosophy of the entire treatment of material breach under the RESTATEMENT 2d. That philosophy harks back to the pervasive concept that forfeitures are to be avoided and the concomitant view that the parties, including even a materially breaching party, are to be treated fairly. Thus, if a breach is immaterial, neither suspension nor termination of the innocent party's duties is permitted. He must continue to perform though he retains a cause of action for any losses he may have sustained.[90] Even where the breach is material, the RESTATEMENT 2d insists upon an allowance for cure of that breach so as to prevent what may amount to a technical claim by the injured party that he has a right to treat his duties as discharged at the moment the material breach occurred. Thus, the RESTATEMENT 2d suggests that, if a material breach can be cured shortly after it occurs, it is highly preferable to view the contract as a continuing obligation. To achieve that goal, the analysis permits the injured party only to suspend his performance to allow for cure and a continuation of the contract. This is the basis for characterizing the situation as one involving constructive conditions. If the material breach is cured, it may be said that the constructive condition has occurred, thereby activating the duty of the formerly injured party.

While the RESTATEMENT 2d is to be commended for its policy of maintaining the contract where possible, one may question whether a "material" breach which has been cured was ever a material breach. Such a breach may appear only to have the potential of becoming a material breach if it is not cured. This

---

[86] RESTATEMENT 2d § 242.

[87] RESTATEMENT 2d § 242(a) referring to the five criteria set forth in § 241 which are quoted *supra* note 78.

[88] RESTATEMENT 2d § 242(b).

[89] RESTATEMENT 2d § 242(c). *See also* June G. Ashton Interiors v. Stark Carpet Corp., 142 Ill. App. 3d 100, 491 N.E.2d 120 (1986) (delay of two to three weeks in delivery of carpeting was a material breach where timely delivery was understood).

[90] UCC § 2-717 permits a party to deduct damages for "partial" breach by deducting the amount of damages from the contract price. It is important to distinguish "partial" breach from "total" breach. An injured party may not suspend or terminate the contract where the breach is immaterial. He may, however, sue for a partial breach that is immaterial even though he is still obligated to perform the contract. Even where the breach is material and the injured party is entitled to suspend his performance, he may choose to continue his performance and sue for partial breach which the RESTATEMENT 2d defines in § 236(2) as "A claim for damages based on only part of the injured party's remaining rights to performance." It is only where the injured party is entitled to terminate the contract, i.e., the breach is material and the time for any cure has expired, that he treats the breach as a "total" breach. "Total" breach is defined in the RESTATEMENT 2d (§ 236(1)) as, "A claim for damages ... based on all of the injured party's remaining rights to performance."

concern, however, is overcome if one recalls that a material breach permits the injured party to *suspend* performance while an immaterial breach does not. Thus, a breach that would be material if uncured permits suspension of the injured party's performance. If cure occurs, the suspension is lifted and the injured party's duties are reactivated. If cure does not occur, the duties of the injured party are discharged, i.e., the contract is terminated. A breach that is immaterial *ab initio* however, does not even permit suspension, i.e., it is not a potentially material breach.

C. *Factors Determining Materiality — In Limine, Wilful, Delay.*

As suggested earlier in this section, the determination of materiality is a question of fact which depends upon the particular circumstances surrounding the contract. This is not at all remarkable since contract law is filled with such questions. The guidelines or "circumstances" provided by the FIRST RESTATEMENT and RESTATEMENT 2d to assist courts in determining questions of materiality have already been mentioned.[91] Here we will consider three circumstances which require further emphasis.

1. Breach at Outset — In Limine.

It is often suggested that a relatively small breach occurring at the outset of the contract is likely to be viewed as material.[92] The rationale is clear: if a party has breached prior to rendering anything other than an insignificant part of his promised performance, he will suffer no substantial forfeiture if the other party is discharged because of the breach. Moreover, when the breach occurs at the earliest stages of the contract, it is difficult to determine the ultimate effect of the breach on the other party were he required to take the performance that is offered or is yet to come. It is fair to resolve the matter in favor of the innocent party. Like other guidelines, the so-called "breach in limine" (at the outset) guideline is not absolute.[93] Although the breach occurs at the outset, it may be so clearly harmless to the defendant that a court would not be justified in denying the plaintiff an action though he would lose nothing more than the value of his bargain if it were denied.

2. Wilful Breach.

Another guideline found in many decisions is the suggestion that a wilful failure to perform is more likely to be regarded as material than a non-wilful breach.[94] Courts typically do not define "wilful" though they appear to be

---

[91] *See supra* notes 73, 75, 78 and text at notes 86, 87, 88, and 89, quoting or discussing §§ 275 and 276 of the FIRST RESTATEMENT and §§ 241 and 242 of the RESTATEMENT 2d.

[92] *See* Leazzo v. Dunham, 95 Ill. App. 3d 847, 420 N.E.2d 851 (1981); Hong v. Independent Sch. Dist. No. 245, 181 Minn. 309, 232 N.W. 329 (1930); Hoare v. Rennie, 5 H. & N. 19 [1859]. FIRST RESTATEMENT § 275(c).

[93] *See* Lutz v. Currence, 91 W. Va. 225, 112 S.E. 506 (1922) (promise to cut and sell logs to be sawed and scaled by a named person held not excused merely because the named person could not be procured by the purchaser to do the work). *See also* Note, *The Breach in Limine Doctrine,* 21 COLUM. L. REV. 358 (1921).

[94] FIRST RESTATEMENT § 275(e) considers whether the conduct of the party failing to perform was wilful, negligent, or innocent. The "wilful" element is stronger than the "negligent" element.

concerned with the motive of the defaulting party. There is judicial support for the view that one whose motive is good should be entitled to greater consideration than one who acts from improper motives.[95] There is, however, considerable difficulty in determining the motivation of a defaulting party in many cases. The principal vice in the use of the "wilful" element is found in cases which hold that a wilful breach is always material in discharging the other party from his duties under the contract even though the breach may be quantitatively and qualitatively slight.[96] The "wilful" element should never be considered anything more than a guideline to aid in the determination of materiality rather than a conclusive test to impose a forfeiture upon the defaulting party. There are preferable decisions supporting this view[97] and the RESTATEMENT 2d substitutes a standard of "good faith and fair dealing" for the "less precise" term "wilful" while emphasizing the inconclusive effect of the new standard.[98]

3. Delay in Performance — "Time of Essence."

Courts have not always dealt effectively with the question of delay in performance. As seen earlier, both RESTATEMENTS deal with delay in sections separate from those setting forth guidelines to determine the question of materiality,[99] and the RESTATEMENT 2d considers delay a significant factor in determining whether an uncured material breach results in the suspension or the discharge of the other party's duty.[1] It is important to consider certain types of cases which have dealt with the problem of delay in performance.

There are cases suggesting that delay in a duty to pay money is usually less material than delay for a similar period in the performance of some other duty.[2] A rationale for this view may be that the promisee can borrow money and then claim easily calculated damages for breach rather than subjecting the delaying party to forfeiture. As usual, however, there may be cases where the failure to pay even a small sum for a relatively short time could be viewed as a material breach. This would be true, for example, where a debtor's solvency is doubtful and there is a justifiable suspicion that he will be unable to make later payments.[3] Moreover, it should be recalled that the failure of an

---

[95] See, e.g., Golwitzer v. Hummel, 201 Iowa 751, 206 N.W. 254 (1925); Rischard v. Miller, 182 Cal. 351, 188 P. 50 (1920); Farmer v. First Trust Co., 246 F. 671 (7th Cir. 1917).

[96] See, e.g., McCormick v. Proprietors of Cem. of Mt. Auburn, 285 Mass. 548, 189 N.E. 585 (1934). See also Bright v. Ganas, 171 Md. 493, 189 A. 427 (1937) and Comment, 50 HARV. L. REV. 1315 (1937) (action by employee against employer to recover for his services where court held it was a complete defense that the employee had, unknown to employer, made improper advances to employer's wife).

[97] See, e.g., Hadden v. Consolidated Edison Co., 34 N.Y.2d 88, 312 N.E.2d 445 (1974) ("wilful" element is not dispositive of materiality—it is only one factor and does not compel a finding of material breach where the value of the performance has not been substantially impaired). See also Mathis v. Thunderbird Village, Inc., 236 Or. 425, 389 P.2d 343 (1964); McNeal-Edwards Co. v. Frank L. Young Co., 51 F.2d 699 (1st Cir. 1931).

[98] RESTATEMENT 2d § 241(e) and comment f.

[99] See supra note 75 and text at notes 87, 88, and 89.

[1] RESTATEMENT 2d § 242.

[2] See Farris v. Ferguson, 146 Tenn. 498, 242 S.W. 873 (1922); Vulcan Trading Corp v. Kokomo Steel & Wire Co., 268 F. 913, 916 (7th Cir. 1920).

[3] See Wolverine Packing Co. v. Hawley, 251 Mich. 215, 231 N.W. 617 (1930) (specific performance refused where plaintiff was one day late in providing payment for cherries); National

owner to make a progress payment to a contractor is considered material in terms of permitting the builder to suspend rather than abandon performance until it is determined whether the breach can be cured.[4]

Delay in the performance of a contract for the sale of goods is treated differently from delay in the performance of a contract for the sale of land. Typically, market prices for goods are subject to much greater fluctuation than contracts for the sale of land, and goods are often purchased for resale so that the buyer is more concerned about time. For many years, therefore, courts have been willing to state that time is of the essence in contracts for the sale of goods.[5] In land contracts, however, most of our courts have refused to imply any understanding that time is of the essence[6] notwithstanding some older cases which have insisted that time should be of the essence in land contracts.[7] The RESTATEMENT 2d suggests that considerable delay will not preclude enforcement of a land contract, absent special circumstances, and assuming the availability of adequate compensatory damages.[8]

The treatment of delay in performance as a unique form of breach is traceable to the statement in older cases that time is of the essence at law. It is highly questionable whether this view was literally accepted even in those nineteenth century cases in which it appeared.[9] It is clear that delay in performance is now considered like any other circumstance in determining the severity of the breach, i.e., it is only one factor to be considered under all of the circumstances.[10]

The parties may include an express provision in the contract that the time for performance is important. Questions of interpretation arise, however, with respect to the language and circumstances of such a provision. If, for example, the contract merely provides for performance on a stated date, failure to perform on that date does not discharge the duty of the injured party. Under an older analysis, the delay would be treated as immaterial and would have to continue for some time to become material when it would discharge the injured party from any further duty. Under the RESTATEMENT 2d, the delay may be viewed as an uncured material breach permitting the other party to suspend performance to determine whether the breach could be cured. If further delay occurred, no cure would be possible and the injured party would be discharged.[11] If the provision in the contract is one that either states or amounts to an agreement that time for performance is of the essence of the

---

Mach. & Tool Co. v. Standard Shoe Mach. Co., 181 Mass. 275, 63 N.E. 900 (1902) (delay of ten days in the payment of a small sum). *Cf.* RESTATEMENT 2d § 241(d).

[4] *See supra* text prior to note 83.

[5] *See* Norrington v. Wright, 115 U.S. 188 (1885). Buyers, however, often receive more tolerant treatment than sellers. Moreover, a court will not treat a buyer's delay as material if there is some suspicion that the seller was eager to discover a breach by the purchaser. *See* Continental Grain v. Simpson Feed Co., 102 F. Supp. 354 (E.D. Ark. 1951).

[6] *See* String v. Steven Dev. Corp., 269 Md. 569, 307 A.2d 713 (1973); McFadden v. Walker, 5 Cal. 3d 811, 488 P.2d 1353 (1971) (even wilful delay was not sufficient to create material breach).

[7] *See* Freeman v. Robinson, 238 Mass. 449, 131 N.E. 75 (1921); Saperstein v. Mechanics' & Farmers' Sav. Bank, 228 N.Y. 257, 126 N.E. 708 (1920).

[8] RESTATEMENT 2d § 242 comment c.

[9] *See* 3 CORBIN § 713.

[10] In some states, statutes provide that time shall not be of the essence unless the terms of the contract expressly so provide. *See, e.g.,* S.D. CODIFIED LAWS ANN. § 53-10-3.

[11] RESTATEMENT 2d § 237 comment b.

contract and there is little or no question that this was the intention of the parties, failure to perform on time will be a material breach discharging the duty of the other party.[12] In this situation, there is no suspension stage. There is no possibility of curing the breach. As usual, the problem is to determine whether the parties genuinely intended time to be of the essence. If the writing is a printed form containing the stock "time is of the essence" clause, it should not necessarily be interpreted as manifesting the intention of the parties.[13] As in other questions of interpretation, all of the surrounding circumstances must be considered.[14]

D. *Erroneous Judgment Concerning Materiality.*

In light of the fact that the determination of materiality is a question of fact and even courts can be disconcerted in applying the various guidelines that have been suggested over the years, an innocent party may find it difficult to determine whether a failure of performance by his counterpart constitutes a material breach discharging the innocent party from further duties under the contract. If the innocent party treats his duties as discharged because he has decided that the other party has materially breached and, as a matter of judicial hindsight, his judgment is wrong, the innocent party is no longer innocent. In a well-known case,[15] the defendant leased a sign which the lessor promised to repair and clean when necessary. On several occasions, the defendant requested that the sign be cleaned but the requests went unheeded. The irritated defendant treated his duties under the contract as discharged. The lessor brought an action under an acceleration clause of the lease/contract and the issue was whether the defendant properly treated his duties as discharged. If the lessor's breach in not cleaning the sign was material, the duties of the defendant were discharged. In deciding that the lessor's breach was immaterial, the court cautioned, "[T]he injured party's determination that there has been a material breach, justifying his own repudiation, is fraught with peril, for should such determination, as viewed by a later court in the calm of its contemplation, be unwarranted, the repudiator himself will have been guilty of material breach and himself have become the aggressor, not an innocent victim."[16] This position appears harsh with respect to an innocent party who is not attempting to escape from his contractual duty. The judgment of the innocent party hinges on his determination of materiality. To permit the other party who has repeatedly refused to perform certain duties, albeit immaterial duties, to treat an innocent though erroneous judgment and action thereon as a material breach which has the effect of discharging the party who first breached suggests the possibility of a forfeiture which should

---

[12]RESTATEMENT 2d § 242(c) and comment d.

[13]*See* Pederson v. McGuire, 333 N.W.2d 823 (S.D. 1983) where the court suggests that whether time is of the essence depends upon the intention of the parties and the purpose of the contract rather than a printed clause in the contract. *See also* RESTATEMENT 2d § 242(c) comment d and ill. 9.

[14]*See* Chariot Holdings, Ltd. v. Eastmet Corp., 153 Ill. App. 3d 50, 505 N.E.2d 1076 (1987) (even where the contract contains a time-of-essence clause, courts will inquire as to whether the delay constitutes a material breach).

[15]Walker & Co. v. Harrison, 347 Mich. 630, 81 N.W.2d 352 (1957).

[16]*Id.*, 347 Mich. at 635, 81 N.W.2d at 355.

be precluded. While another case would not permit such an erroneous judgment by an innocent party to discharge the duties of the party who first breached immaterially,[17] there is a dearth of case law in this area. The holding and rationale in the sign case suggests a mechanical application of the concept of material breach which should be avoided to preclude the possibility of forfeiture. If, however, a party operates in bad faith in judging a breach to be material so as to bring about a discharge of his duties in a bargain he no longer views as beneficial, there should be no judicial concern over his fate.

§ 108. Substantial Performance — Material Breach Compared — "Perfect Tender" Rule.

A. *Material Breach — "Failure of Consideration" — Failure of Performance.*

We have seen the traditional view that whether a breach permits the innocent party to treat her duties as discharged depends upon whether the breach was material. Under the RESTATEMENT 2d, the innocent party would have to show not only a material breach, but the fact that the time for cure of that breach had passed, thereby discharging her duty rather than merely suspending it. Under the traditional view, there was some confusion through the use of the anomalous phrase, "failure of consideration," i.e., the nonperformance of the plaintiff amounted to a "failure of consideration" discharging the defendant. The term "consideration" is used in this context to suggest a failure of performance that is a material failure, but a failure of performance may be either material or immaterial. Moreover, "consideration" is normally used in the context of contract formation. To avoid needless confusion, the RESTATEMENT 2d properly rejects the phrase, "failure of consideration" and substitutes "failure of performance."[18]

B. *Immaterial Failure of Performance — Substantial Performance.*

Courts may treat certain failures of performance by a plaintiff under the doctrine of "substantial performance." For many years, there was a tendency to treat the doctrine of substantial performance as related to but different from the question of materiality of breach. As will be seen, the doctrine of substantial performance is a species of the basic analysis of materiality of breach. That conclusion becomes clear, however, only upon an understanding of the origin of the doctrine of substantial performance.

The story begins with the creation of the doctrine of constructive conditions which was considered earlier in this chapter.[19] In creating the concept of dependent covenants which allowed for the constructive condition analysis,[20] Lord Mansfield made a significant contribution to the common law of contracts.[21] The sensible concept of constructive conditions could, however, lead to

---

[17] *See* Riess v. Murchison, 503 F.2d 999 (9th Cir. 1974), *cert. denied,* 420 U.S. 993 (1975).

[18] RESTATEMENT 2d § 237 comment a.

[19] § 104.

[20] Even modern courts sometimes mention the independent/dependent covenant distinction which is generally articulated in the language of constructive conditions. *See* Hunt v. Salon De Coiffures, 3 Ohio Misc. 2d 5, 444 N.E.2d 488 (1982).

[21] *See* Kingston v. Preston, 2 Doug. 689 [1773].

unjust results in certain cases. Thus, where performance by *A* is a constructive condition to the duty of *B,* a literal or strict application of that concept suggests that *any* failure of performance by *A* is a failure of a constructive condition to *B*'s duty, and *B*'s duty would never be activated. Yet, where a failure of performance is slight and could be easily compensated in damages, *A* should not suffer a forfeiture simply because the last scintilla of his performance has not occurred. Under a different rubric, such a failure of performance would be viewed as an immaterial breach and *B*'s duty would not be discharged. Again, under a strict application of the doctrine of constructive conditions, however, *B*'s duty would never be activated and *B,* in effect, would be discharged from his duty because of an immaterial breach by *A.*

Just four years after he created the doctrine of constructive conditions, Lord Mansfield overcame this defect. In *Boone v. Eyre,*[22] he made it clear that a defendant could not escape his contractual duty by pleading failure of a constructive condition precedent to his duty when the failure was slight. The doctrine of substantial performance was, therefore, designed to mitigate the injustice that could result from a literal or strict application of the doctrine of constructive conditions. The landmark case in the twentieth century elaborating the doctrine is *Jacob & Young's, Inc. v. Kent.*[23] Another judicial giant, Benjamin Nathan Cardozo, wrote the opinion. A building contract included a specification which required all wrought-iron pipe used in the building to be "of Reading manufacture." Through oversight or inattention by a subcontractor, physically identical pipe manufactured by Cohoes was used in the building. The contractor was instructed to replace all of the pipe which was, for the most part, encased in the walls of the building. Replacement of the pipe would have required demolition of large portions of the completed structure resulting in considerable economic waste. When the contractor refused to replace the pipe under these circumstances, the architect refused to issue his certificate which was a condition to the last progress payment due the builder. The builder brought an action to recover this payment. Cardozo recognizes that, while a party to a contract has a duty of full performance as a general rule, a failure of performance, "both trivial and innocent, will sometimes be atoned for by allowance of the resulting damage, and will not always be the breach of a condition to be followed by a forfeiture...."[24] The question in such a case is whether the constructive condition precedent to the owner's duty to make the last progress payment should be excused because the plaintiff has, notwithstanding his default, substantially performed his duties under the contract. Cardozo suggested criteria, virtually indistinguishable from the circumstances courts traditionally consider in determining whether a breach is material, to assist courts in determining whether a particular plaintiff has substantially performed.[25] In essence, the question is whether the builder's failure to perform was a material or immaterial breach.[26] Notwithstanding the

[22] 1 H. Bl. 273 [1777].

[23] 230 N.Y. 239, 129 N.E. 889, 23 A.L.R. 1429 (1921).

[24] *Id.,* 129 N.E. at 890.

[25] "We must weigh the purpose to be served, the desire to be gratified, the excuse for deviation from the letter, the cruelty of enforced adherence." *Id.,* 129 N.E. 893.

[26] The RESTATEMENT 2d recognizes that "[I]t is common to state the issue, not in terms of whether there has been an uncured material failure by the contractor, but in terms of whether

tautological character of the statement, it is not uncommon for modern courts which have been influenced by the RESTATEMENT 2d to suggest that the doctrine of substantial performance does not apply when the party relying on it is "guilty" of an uncured material breach.[27] Courts have begun to slide easily between the "doctrine" of substantial performance and the criteria for determining materiality of breach by using the "circumstances" of materiality as the guidelines for substantial performance.[28] Just as questions of materiality of breach are not reducible to mechanical rules, neither are questions of substantial performance.[29] In the famous *Jacob & Young's* opinion, Cardozo had insisted that the doctrine of substantial performance would not be available to a "wilful" defaulter.[30] Adherence to this view may still be found in modern cases.[31] Yet, just as the RESTATEMENT 2d has modified the "wilful" criterion of material breach to a standard of "good faith and fair dealing" and insisted that neither this criterion of materiality nor others be viewed as conclusive,[32] an identical analysis of this criterion in relation to substantial performance is now more likely in modern cases.[33]

C. *Substantial Performance and Express Conditions.*

In the *Jacob & Young's* opinion, Cardozo took pains to distinguish the situation involving constructive conditions from the situation involving express conditions: "This is not to say that the parties are not free by apt and certain words to effectuate a purpose that performance of every term shall be a condition of recovery. That question is not here."[34] There is no doubt that Cardozo was suggesting that the doctrine of substantial performance was inapplicable to express conditions, i.e., conditions agreed to by the parties as contrasted with those implied or constructed by courts. Thus, if the parties agreed upon an express condition that had to occur to activate a duty, the nonoccurrence of that condition could result in a forfeiture allowed by the courts.[35] The RESTATEMENT 2d recognizes this limitation on the doctrine of substantial performance. It suggests, however, that relief may be had through a section dealing with excuse of condition to avoid extreme forfeiture, unless the occurrence of the condition was a material part of the agreed exchange.[36] An illustration to

---

there has been substantial performance by him. The manner of stating the issue does not change the substance, however, and the rule [concerning material versus immaterial failures of performance] also applies to such cases."

[27] *See* Wilson & Assocs. v. Forty-O-Four Grand Corp., 246 N.W.2d 922 (Iowa 1976).

[28] *See, e.g.,* Prudential Ins. Co. of Am. v. Stratton, 14 Ark. App. 145, 685 S.W.2d 818 (1985); Vincenzi v. Cerro, 186 Conn. 612, 442 A.2d 1352 (1982); Della Ratta, Inc. v. American Better Community Devs., 38 Md. App. 119, 380 A.2d 627 (1977).

[29] Roberts & Co. v. Sergio, 22 Ark. App. 58, 733 S.W.2d 420 (1987).

[30] "The wilful transgressor must accept the penalty of his transgression. For him there is no occasion to mitigate the rigor of implied [constructive] conditions. The transgressor whose default is unintentional and trivial may hope for mercy if he will offer atonement for his wrong." 129 N.E. 893.

[31] *See* Huntsville & Madison Cty. R.R. Auth. v. Alabama Indus. R.R., 505 So. 2d 341 (Ala. 1987).

[32] RESTATEMENT 2d § 241(e).

[33] *See* Vincenzi v. Cerro, 186 Conn. 612, 442 A. 2d 1352 (1982).

[34] 129 N.E. at 891.

[35] *See* Ahrens v. McDaniel, 287 S.C. 63, 336 S.E.2d 505 (1985).

[36] "If, however, the parties have made an event a condition of their agreement, there is no mitigating standard of materiality or substantiality applicable to the non-occurrence of that

that section is based on facts similar to those in *Jacob & Young's*. The specification for the proper brand of pipe, however, is stated as an express condition (in the actual case, the specification was a performance specification amounting only to a constructive condition) and the unpaid balance of the contract price is greater. The illustration concludes that a court may excuse even this *express* condition if it determines that the nonoccurrence of the condition was so relatively unimportant to the owner that the resulting forfeiture to the builder would be extreme.[37] Since the amount of the unpaid balance in the illustration is almost triple the amount in the actual case, the drafters of the RESTATEMENT 2d apparently felt compelled to ascertain that the forfeiture would be "extreme." While the RESTATEMENT 2d effort to overcome extreme forfeitures even in the face of express conditions is commendable, the difficulties in determining whether a particular forfeiture is "extreme" and whether the nonoccurrence of an express condition is relatively unimportant should not be underestimated.[38]

D. *Scope of Substantial Performance — The "Perfect Tender" Rule — Uniform Commercial Code — Rejection, Revocation of Acceptance, Subjective Test, Cure After Revocation of Acceptance.*

While the classic example of substantial performance is the building illustration where the builder has virtually completed the building and would suffer a forfeiture if the constructive condition of absolutely complete performance is not excused, it is clear that the doctrine of substantial performance will be applicable to virtually any other type of contract[39] though it must be remembered that the analysis is really a materiality of breach analysis.[40] The one major exception to the use of the doctrine of substantial performance is found in contracts for the sale of goods.

If the doctrine of substantial performance applied to contracts for the sale of goods and a seller delivered substantially conforming goods (goods with immaterial defects) to the buyer, the seller could recover the contract price minus any loss to the buyer caused by the such defects. Prior to the UCC

---

event. If, therefore, the agreement makes full performance a condition, substantial performance is not sufficient and if relief is to be had under the contract, it must be through excuse of the nonoccurrence of the condition to avoid forfeiture." *See* § 229 and ill. 1 to that section. RESTATEMENT 2d § 237 comment d. *See,* however, Whalen v. Ford Motor Credit Co., 475 F. Supp. 537 (D.C. Md. 1979) which holds that a loan commitment requiring completion of a building is subject to the doctrine of substantial performance to avoid forfeiture. The court suggests that the express condition would have to be clear to the extent of requiring 100 percent performance before any forfeiture should be countenanced.

[37] RESTATEMENT 2d § 229 ill. 1.

[38] A similar suggestion in the second edition of this book is mentioned approvingly in Jackson v. Richards 5 & 10, Inc., 289 Pa. Super. 445, 433 A.2d 888 (1981) which deals with the question of excusing an express condition in the light of substantial performance. Another suggestion to apply the substantial performance doctrine in the face of an express condition is to permit the substantially performing party to recover the contract price minus whatever may be required to comply with the express condition. *See* Della Ratta, Inc. v. American Better Community Devs., 38 Md. App. 119, 380 A.2d 627 (1977).

[39] *See* Prudential Ins. Co. of Am. v. Stratton, 14 Ark. App. 145, 685 S.W.2d 818 (1985).

[40] *See* Hadden v. Consolidated Edison Co., 34 N.Y.2d 88, 312 N.E.2d 445 (1974) where the court applies the doctrine of substantial performance to an employment contract and suggests criteria such as those used for determining materiality of breach.

which now governs contracts for the sale of goods throughout the country, courts refused to apply the doctrine of substantial performance to such contracts.[41] The failure of the seller to deliver the exact quantity or quality of goods in conformity with the contract description of such goods excused the buyer from performing even where the buyer could have been adequately compensated in damages for any loss he may have suffered.[42] How does the current governing statute, the UCC, deal with this question?

At first glance, the UCC appears in compliance with prior law because it suggests what appears to be a buyer's absolute right of rejection. "[I]f the goods or the tender of delivery fail *in any respect* to conform to the contract, the buyer may (a) reject the whole or (b) accept the whole [notwithstanding any nonconformity]; or (c) accept any commercial unit or units and reject the rest."[43] If, for example, the contract called for delivery of 500 expensive wooden cabinets and the seller delivered 498 in perfect condition while two were very slightly scratched, the literal application of the foregoing UCC language would permit the buyer to reject the goods notwithstanding the possibility of easy removal of the scratches in inexpensive fashion. The negative "absolute right to reject" is often seen as the positive requirement that the seller make a perfect tender of perfect goods, the so-called "perfect tender" rule. A literal application of this rule could easily lead to forfeitures. The UCC, however, does not mitigate the potential harshness of this rule through doctrines of immaterial breach or substantial performance. Rather, it surrounds this apparently absolute rule with express and implied qualifications which substantially diminish its thrust.

There are six identifiable qualifications to the buyer's "absolute" right to reject or the correlative duty of the seller to make a "perfect tender."

(1) As in many other sections of Article 2 of the UCC, the buyer's so-called absolute right to reject is qualified by the phrase, "unless otherwise agreed."[44] The parties, therefore, may agree to limit the buyer's apparent absolute right to reject.[45]

(2) The right to reject does not apply to breaches of installment contracts as they are defined in the Code.[46] If the contract is an installment contract, the buyer may reject any nonconforming installment only if the defect "substantially impairs the value of the whole contract and cannot be cured."[47] The "substantial impairment of the value" test is the equivalent of the materiality

---

[41] "There is no room in commercial contracts for the doctrine of substantial performance." L. Hand in Mitsubishi Goshi Kaisha v. J. Aron & Co., 16 F.2d 185, 186 (2d Cir. 1926). For an historical analysis, *see* Ramirez v. Autosport, 88 N.J. 277, 440 A.2d 1345 (1982).

[42] For a collection and discussion of the cases, *see* Note, *Application of the Doctrine of Substantial Performance in the Law of Sales*, 33 COLUM. L. REV. 1021 (1933).

[43] UCC § 2-601 (emphasis added).

[44] UCC § 2-601.

[45] The broad definition of "agreement" under the UCC must also be emphasized: "'Agreement' means the bargain of the parties in fact as found in their language or by implication from other circumstances including course of dealing or usage of trade or course of performance...." UCC § 1-201(3).

[46] "An 'installment contract' is one which requires or authorizes the delivery of goods in separate lots to be separately accepted...."

[47] UCC § 2-612(2).

test. Thus, when the contract is an installment contract, the buyer may not reject for *any* defect; the defect must be material.[48]

(3) Where the contract is an F.O.B. "shipment" contract, i.e., F.O.B. seller's plant,[49] the seller must place the goods in the possession of a reasonable (independent) carrier for transport, obtain and promptly deliver or tender any necessary documents to the buyer, and, finally, promptly notify the buyer of the shipment.[50] Since the rejection section of the UCC permits the buyer to reject not only because of *any* defect in the goods, but also for *any* defect in the *tender* of the goods,[51] it may appear that a failure by a seller either to make a proper contract with a carrier or to notify the buyer of the shipment would create a right of rejection in the buyer. Certainly, either failure would constitute a defective tender. Yet, the UCC section setting forth the seller's duties to make an effective tender indicates that a failure of either of these tender duties "is a ground for rejection only if *material* delay or loss ensues."[52] This is sensible since a failure to notify the buyer or to contract with a proper carrier should not cause a forfeiture to the seller unless there is a substantial loss to the buyer. Thus, the buyer may not reject because of *any* defect in the tender.

(4) If slightly defective goods are shipped to the buyer and the buyer rejects, there may be evidence that the buyer rejected only because he sought to escape his bargain and used the absolute right to reject as an excuse to do so. Such a rejection would not have been made in "good faith," a standard that permeates the entire UCC and particularly Article 2 of the Code dealing with contracts for the sale of goods.[53] An artistic reading of the Code is unnecessary to imply the good faith standard to the section on rejection though evidence of the buyer's bad faith may, as a practical matter, be difficult to discover.

(5) The buyer has only a reasonable time to *reject* the goods.[54] If the buyer fails to reject the goods within a reasonable time, he will be said to have accepted the goods.[55] Once the acceptance stage occurs, the right of rejection is lost. The buyer, however, may still be able to "revoke his acceptance" of the

---

[48] *See* Bodine Sewer, Inc. v. Eastern Ill. Precast, Inc., 143 Ill. App. 3d 920, 493 N.E.2d 705 (1986).

[49] UCC § 2-319(1)(a).

[50] UCC § 2-504.

[51] UCC § 2-601.

[52] UCC § 2-504 (emphasis added). *See also* comment 6 to this section.

[53] *See* Alden Press, Inc. v. Black & Co., 173 Ill. App. 3d 251, 527 N.E.2d 489 (1988) (the question of good faith is one of fact). *See* UCC § 1-201(19) which is the general UCC definition of good faith: "[H]onesty in fact in the conduct of the transaction concerned." UCC § 2-103(1)(b) which defines good faith in the case of a merchant as "honesty in fact and the observance of reasonable commercial standards of fair dealing in the trade." *See also* UCC § 1-102 which precludes the parties to a contract from disclaiming the obligation of good faith.

[54] UCC § 2-602(1) indicates that the rejection of goods must occur within a reasonable time after their delivery or tender. What is a reasonable time is ordinarily a question of fact and will depend upon such factors as whether the goods were perishable, highly fluctuating in price, the nature of the goods, trade usage, the difficulty of determining defects, and any other relevant circumstances. *See* Sherkate Sahami Hass Rapol v. Henry R. Jahn & Son, 35 UCC Rep. Serv. 790 (2d Cir. 1983).

[55] UCC § 606(1)(b). The other methods of "acceptance" of the goods in this section of the Code are found in § 2-606(1)(a) where the buyer signifies to the seller that he will accept the goods, and § 2-606(1)(c) where the buyer performs an act inconsistent with the seller's ownership. *See* Intervale Steel Corp. v. Borg & Beck Div. Borg-Warner Corp., 578 F. Supp. 1081 (E.D. Mich 1984).

goods.[56] Unlike the right of rejection, the right to *revoke acceptance* is expressly qualified under the UCC as requiring substantial impairment of the value of the goods *to the buyer*.[57] On its face, this section may be read as requiring a showing of *subjective* materiality, i.e., if the value of the goods is substantially impaired to the particular buyer even though the value to a reasonable (objective) buyer would not be substantially impaired, the particular buyer may revoke his acceptance.[58] A comment to this UCC section clearly confirms the *subjective* nature of the revocation of acceptance test.[59] Courts are uncomfortable with any subjective test in contract law and they have, therefore, sought to limit the subjective nature of the inquiry.[60] The so-called perfect tender rule or corollary absolute right to reject is, therefore, limited when the goods are accepted since the buyer must prove substantial impairment of the value of the goods to him (the buyer) before he can properly exercise the right to revoke acceptance.

(6) The most significant limitation on the "absolute" right to reject is the UCC concept of *cure* which was discussed earlier.[61] Under this section, the seller has the right to cure (repair or replace) any nonconforming good within "contract time", i.e., the normal time for performing one's contractual duty.[62] Unless the time for performance is clearly bargained not to extend beyond a certain time, it is likely that a court would permit a seller some commercially reasonable time to cure in most cases. Moreover, the UCC, itself, expressly permits cure beyond "contract time" where the seller had reason to believe that the nonconforming goods would be accepted with or without some money allowance.[63] Where the goods have been accepted and the buyer rightfully revokes acceptance, courts are reluctant to permit the seller to cure since the cure section of the Code speaks only in terms of the buyer's rejection of goods.[64]

---

[56] UCC § 2-608. *See* Jensen v. Seigel Motor Homes, 105 Idaho 189, 668 P.2d 65 (1983).

[57] UCC § 2-608(1).

[58] Similarly, if the value to the particular buyer is not substantially impaired though it would have been impaired to a reasonable buyer, the subjective analysis would preclude the exercise of the right to revoke acceptance.

[59] "For this purpose the test is not what the seller had reason to know at the time of contracting; the question is whether the non-conformity is such as will in fact cause a substantial impairment to the buyer though the seller had no advance knowledge as to the buyer's particular circumstances." UCC § 2-608 comment 2.

[60] In Jensen v. Seigel Motor Homes, 105 Idaho 189, 668 P.2d 65, the court suggests that the test is subjective in that it addresses whether the nonconformities substantially impaired the value of the home to the actual buyer rather than the reasonable buyer. However, the actual buyer is to be considered in light of objective evidence of that buyer's purposes and proclivities. *See* Asciolla v. Manter Oldsmobile-Pontiac, Inc., 117 N.H. 85, 370 A.2d 270 (1977) (particularly prudent and painstaking car buyer). *See also* Keen v. Modern Trailer Sales, Inc., 40 Colo. App. 527, 578 P.2d 668 (1978); Jorgensen v. Presnall, 274 Or. 285, 545 P.2d 1382 (1976).

[61] UCC § 2-508. *See supra* § 107(B)(2).

[62] UCC § 2-508(1). *See* Leitchfield Dev. Corp. v. Clark, 757 S.W.2d 207 (Ky. App. 1988); Schiavi Mobile Homes, Inc. v. Gagne, 510 A.2d 236 (Me. 1986).

[63] UCC § 2-508(2) and comment 2.

[64] *See* Fitzner Pontiac-Buick-Cadillac, Inc. v. Smith, 523 So. 2d 324 (Miss. 1988). *See*, however, Werner v. Montana, 378 A.2d 1130 (N.H. 1977) (no right to cure except where buyer accepts with knowledge of defects and seller agrees to repair); Gappelberg v. Landrum, 654 S.W.2d 549 (Tex. App. 1983) (replacement after unsuccessful efforts to cure should be allowed even with respect to revocation of acceptance).

§ 109. Prospective Failure of Performance — Anticipatory Repudiation.

A. *Nature of the Problem.*

Our discussion of failure of performance to this point assumed that the time for performance had arrived and one of the parties had failed to perform, i.e., the constructive condition to the performance of the innocent party had not occurred. There are myriad situations, however, where the time for performance has not arrived and there is very good reason to believe that performance will not occur when it is due. Prior to the time for performance, for example, one party may announce that he will not perform when performance is due. Even without such an announcement, the circumstances may be abundantly clear that one party will be incapable of performance when it is due. In other situations, the circumstances prior to the time for performance may suggest reasonable doubt rather than certainty that one of the parties may not perform when performance is due. These situations give rise to fundamental questions: Should a cause of action *ever* be recognized before the duty of immediate performance is due? If such a cause of action should be recognized, should the recovery be limited to actual rather than prospective losses? Are there situations where a cause of action prior to the time for performance should not be recognized, but one of the parties should, nonetheless, be entitled to suspend performance? These and related questions will now be addressed.

B. *Anticipatory Repudiation — Origin of the Doctrine.*

It is quite clear that the earlier law did not, in general, recognize the possibility of an action based upon the contract where there had not as yet been a breach because the time for performance had not arrived.[65] There are cogent reasons against granting any relief in advance of the date performance is due. Giving a promisee relief at an earlier date is granting him more than he was promised. Damages are measured as of the date of performance.[66] The further in advance of that date they are computed, the more difficult it becomes to approximate the amount to which the promisee would ultimately have been entitled. Yet, in 1853 the leading case of *Hochster v. De La Tour*[67] was decided, in which an employer repudiated his contract to furnish employment in advance of the date the employment was to commence. The English court held that a suit could be brought immediately by the employee before any actual breach of the contract had occurred. It was said that a repudiation by the promisor, in advance of the date, was the equivalent of an actual breach, if the plaintiff elected so to treat it. This has come to be known as the doctrine of *anticipatory repudiation* or, inaccurately, anticipatory breach. Whatever may be the merits of the conclusion reached, it seems clear that the reasons given for its adoption were based upon an unwarranted assumption. The court said that unless the repudiation is treated as a breach giving rise to an immediate

---

[65]*See* Daniels v. Newton, 114 Mass. 530, 19 Am. Rep. 384 (1874).
[66]*See* FIRST RESTATEMENT § 338 comment a(1932).
[67]2 El. & Bl. 678 [1853].

cause of action for damages, the promisee would either have to rescind the contract, giving up all rights under it, or else ignore the repudiation entirely, holding himself in readiness to perform until the date set for performance, and performing all conditions precedent on his part in the meantime. The court apparently assumed that a repudiation by the promisor could give the promisee a choice among only three possible alternative courses of action: (1) to renounce the contract, with the consequence that he would thereafter be limited to the remedy of an action for restitution; (2) to ignore the repudiation entirely; or (3) to treat it as an immediate breach of the contract with all the consequences that ensue from that situation.[68] Positing this dilemma, the court concluded that it was desirable to give him the third suggested alternative to make it unnecessary for him to choose one of the others, neither of which is wholly satisfactory in such a situation. The court did not admit the possibility that the promisee may have a fourth alternative, namely, that of treating the repudiation merely as the basis of an excuse for not performing constructive conditions precedent to the promisor's duty, without thereby losing the right to sue for breach of contract when the time for performance arrives. Once it is admitted that this fourth alternative is open to the promisee, the reason for the holding in *Hochster* obviously loses its force. If the doctrine is to be justified at all, it must be done on the ground of practical convenience, rather than historic precedent or logical necessity.[69] When it becomes clear that the contract will not be performed when the time for performance later arrives, there are practical advantages in dealing with the situation promptly. Whether these advantages outweigh the difficulty involved in estimating the loss that would be properly chargeable to the promisor in advance of the date of performance is doubtful. While the *Hochster* doctrine has been generally accepted both in England and in this country,[70] it is important to understand the unfortunate line of reasoning which apparently motivated its adoption since this reasoning has profoundly influenced its later development and application. Where a new doctrine finds so little sup-

---

[68] The same view is expressed in Frost v. Knight, L.R. 7 Ex. 111 [1872].

[69] For opposing views as to the merits of the anticipatory breach doctrine and the theoretical bases for it, *see* Williston, *Repudiation of Contracts,* 14 HARV. L. REV. 317, 421 (1900), Selected Readings On Contracts 1044 (1931); Ballantine, *Anticipatory Breach and the Enforcement of Contractual Duties,* 22 MICH. L. REV. 329 (1923), Selected Readings On Contracts 1072 (1931); Vold, *The Tort Aspect of Anticipatory Repudiation of Contracts,* 41 HARV. L. REV. 340 (1928), Selected Readings On Contracts 1127 (1931); Limburg, *Anticipatory Repudiation of Contracts,* 10 CORNELL L.Q. 135 (1925), Selected Readings On Contracts 1090 (1931).

[70] It had been thought that only two states, Nebraska and Massachusetts, reject the doctrine. *See, e.g.,* SIMPSON ON CONTRACTS 511, n.45 (1954). After an extensive inquiry into the Nebraska situation, Professor Lawrence Vold concluded: "It is therefore submitted that the doctrine of anticipatory breach generally prevalent throughout the country ... is and always has been also the rule of law on the subject in Nebraska." Vold, *Repudiation of Contracts,* 5 NEB. L. BULL. 269, 301 1927). *See* King v. Waterman, 55 Neb. 324, 75 N.W. 830 (1898) and Carstens v. McDonald, 38 Neb. 858, 57 N.W. 757 (1894), which are the two cases usually cited for the proposition that Nebraska rejects the doctrine. However, Professor Vold points out that statements in both cases rejecting the doctrine are pure dictums. In addition, he cites Hixson Map Co. v. Nebraska Post Co., 5 Neb. 388, 98 N.W. 872 (1904), which is in accord with the great weight of authority. The Massachusetts case which definitely repudiates the doctrine is Daniels v. Newton, 114 Mass. 530, 19 Am. Rep. 384 (1874). However, a more recent Massachusetts case shows some inclination to depart from Daniels v. Newton. *See* Tucker v. Connors, 342 Mass. 376, 173 N.E.2d 619, 623 (1961).

port in historic principles, later courts are apt to view it with varying degrees of favor, particularly when its reasoning is open to question. Consequently, some courts have accepted it wholeheartedly; others, while paying lip service to it, have surrounded it with meaningless distinctions and qualifications which often make prediction as to its application difficult.

C. *What Is an Anticipatory Repudiation?* — *Degree of Definiteness* — RE- STATEMENT *2d, Uniform Commercial Code, Good Faith Denial of Liability.*

In view of the foundation on which the anticipatory repudiation doctrine rests, if it is to have a rational justification, it would seem that it should apply in all cases where it has become reasonably certain that a promisor does not intend to perform his promise substantially. Unfortunately, a few cases arose at a time when the doctrine had not yet become fully established where the promisor, though making it reasonably clear that he would not perform, did not repudiate his promise in absolute terms. It was held that an action for anticipatory repudiation would not lie under these circumstances. Thus, in *Dingley v. Oler*[71] the promisor said that he would not perform unless a speci- fied event should happen when it was reasonably certain the event would not happen. The Supreme Court of the United States held there had been no such repudiation as to justify the application of the doctrine. The court said that this was "very far from being a positive, unconditional, and unequivocal dec- laration of fixed purpose not to perform in any event or at any time." It is quite clear from an examination of this case[72] and similar cases that the decisions were motivated at the time[73] either by the desire to put off the evil day of having to decide whether to accept the doctrine at all, or by a dislike of the doctrine and a desire to limit its application. Largely as a result of these cases, there are a number of subsequent judicial utterances to the effect that nothing short of an absolute and unequivocal renunciation of the contract will suffice for an anticipatory repudiation.[74] The UCC suggests a less stringent test.[75] The RESTATEMENT 2d[76] expressly rejects the holding of *Dingley v. Oler.*

---

[71] 117 U.S. 490 (1886).

[72] *Id.* at 503, the court said: "The construction we place upon what passed between the parties renders it unnecessary for us to discuss or decide whether the doctrine of these authorities can be maintained as applicable to the class of cases to which the present belongs; for, upon that con- struction, this case does not come within the operation of the rule invoked." In the later case of Roehm v. Horst, 178 U.S. 1 (1900), the general doctrine was accepted and applied in the case of an executory contract to sell goods.

[73] *See* Vittum v. Estey, 67 Vt. 158, 31 A. 144 (1894) (vendor said he would not convey unless his father, who refused to do so, should concur); Johnstone v. Milling, 16 Q.B.D. 460 [1886] (landlord stated that he would not be able to perform his promise to rebuild the leased premises).

[74] "'The renunciation must be so distinct that its purpose is manifest, and so absolute that the intention to no longer abide by the terms of the contract is beyond question.'" Wonalancet Co. v. Banfield, 116 Conn. 582, 165 A. 785 (1933). *See also* J.M. Clayton Co. v. Martin, 177 Ga. App. 228, 339 S.E.2d 280 (1985) (absolute refusal to perform and unqualified repudiation of the entire contract is required); Stonecipher v. Pillatsch, 30 Ill. App. 3d 140, 332 N.E.2d 151 (1975) (definite and unequivocal statement of repudiation required). *See also* Diamos v. Hirsch, 91 Ariz. 304, 372 P.2d 76 (1962); McCloskey & Co. v. Minweld Steel Co., 220 F.2d 101 (3d Cir. 1955).

[75] UCC § 2-610 does not attempt to define "repudiation." Even though the section is captioned "Anticipatory Repudiation," the section only sets forth the choices available to an "aggrieved party" (defined in § 1-201(2) as a party entitled to a remedy) where the other party has repudiated in advance of the time for performance. Comment 2, however, suggests: "Repudiation can result

---

[76] RESTATEMENT 2d § 250.

It only requires an expression to be "sufficiently positive to be reasonably interpreted to mean that the party will not or cannot perform."[77] In accordance with the Code, it treats an expression of intention not to perform except on conditions going beyond the contract as a repudiation.[78]

The modern view as to what constitutes a repudiation may be stated as follows: A positive statement by the obligor to the obligee[79] which is reasonably interpreted by the obligee to mean that the obligor will not or cannot perform his contractual duty constitutes a repudiation.[80] Statements of doubt by the obligor as to his ability or willingness to perform are insufficient though such statements may suggest reasonable grounds for insecurity and ultimately constitute a repudiation.[81] Moreover, language which, alone, would not be sufficient to constitute a repudiation, may constitute a repudiation when accompanied by some nonperformance by the obligor.[82] A positive manifestation that the obligor cannot or will not perform need not be expressed in language. It may be inferred from conduct which is wholly inconsistent with an intention to perform.[83] Any voluntary affirmative act which actually or apparently precludes the obligor from performing amounts to a repudiation. Thus, a sale or lease of goods or lands which are necessary to perform a contract, or a contract for their sale or lease prior to the time for performance has been held to furnish a basis for an action for total breach of the contract.[84] It must be emphasized that such actions meet the usual requirement that acts must be voluntary and affirmative to constitute repudiations.[85] Cases suggesting that involuntary financial or other difficulties may give rise to anticipatory repudiation should be rejected.[86]

---

from action which reasonably indicates a rejection of the continuing obligation." Later, the same comment indicates that "a statement of intention not to perform except on conditions which go beyond the contract" is an anticipatory repudiation. As the Reporter's Note to § 250 of the RESTATEMENT 2d suggests, this comment statement is opposed to the holding in *Dingley v. Oler,* *supra* note 71. It should be remembered, however, that the "Official" comments are not part of the enacted law.

[77] RESTATEMENT 2d § 250 comment b.

[78] *See supra* note 75.

[79] The statement must be to an obligee—i.e., a promisee, third party beneficiary, or assignee— not to a stranger. RESTATEMENT 2d § 250 comment b.

[80] Much of the foregoing analysis is discussed in the dissenting opinion in 2401 Pennsylvania Ave. Corp. v. Federation of Jewish Agencies of Greater Philadelphia, 507 Pa. 166, 489 A.2d 733 (1985).

[81] UCC § 2-609; RESTATEMENT 2d § 251. *See* the discussion of prospective inability to perform *infra* subsection (G) of this section.

[82] RESTATEMENT 2d § 250 comment b, referring to RESTATEMENT 2d § 243(2) which states that a partial breach and a repudiation will constitute a total breach. *See* ill. 3 to § 243.

[83] *See* RESTATEMENT 2d § 250 (b); Brady v. Oliver, 125 Tenn. 595, 147 S.W. 1135 (1911); Roehm v. Horst, 178 U.S. 1 (1900).

[84] Pappas v. Crist, 223 N.C. 265, 25 S.E.2d 850 (1943); Crane v. East Side Canal 7 Irrig. Co., 6 Cal. App. 2d 361, 44 P.2d 455 (1935); Suburban Imp. Co. v. Scott Lumber Co., 67 F.2d 335, 90 A.L.R. 330 (4th Cir. 1933) (dictum); Englebrecht v. Herrington, 101 Kan. 720, 172 P. 715 (1917); Synge v. Synge, 1 Q.B. 466 [1894].

[85] *See* RESTATEMENT 2d § 250(b). *See also* Ringel & Meyer v. Falstaff Brewing Corp., 511 F.2d 659 (5th Cir. 1975).

[86] *See, e.g.,* Space Center v. 451 Corp., 298 N.W.2d 443 (Minn. 1980) (loss of title due to a foreclosure constitutes a repudiation); Bonebrake v. Cox, 499 F.2d 951 (8th Cir. 1974) (UCC repudiation where the act was involuntary. Involuntary actions which make future performance highly doubtful should be considered under the analysis of prospective failure of performance in this section at subsection (G).)

Where a statement of future nonperformance is sufficiently positive, or a voluntary and affirmative act will make performance impossible, there can be no question that a repudiation has occurred. Suppose, however, the statement is made or action is taken in a good faith denial of liability. If a party simply does not believe that he has certain duties under a contract,[87] should that party who acts in good faith, albeit mistaken, still be charged with anticipatory repudiation? If the belief of the mistaken party is not only honest but reasonable, there is a more than plausible argument for not subjecting that party to the consequences of an anticipatory repudiation. As will be seen, such a repudiation will have the effect of a material breach which discharges the duties of the other party and places the honest and reasonable repudiator in the position of a contract breaker before the time for performance has arrived.[88] Except for very limited authority,[89] there is no judicial support for this suggestion since a good faith denial of liability is generally considered irrelevant.[90]

D. *Effects of Anticipatory Repudiation — "Election."*

We will see that the obligee may react to an anticipatory repudiation in several ways.[91] Since he need not treat the contract as breached at the moment of the anticipatory repudiation,[92] there is a tendency to treat the anticipatory repudiation as a potential breach rather than a final breach, i.e., there is a pervasive notion that the repudiation must be "accepted" to constitute a breach.[93] There is, however, no requirement of affirmative action by the obligee to convert an anticipatory repudiation into a present breach. An early English case where the court was less than enthusiastic about the doctrine of anticipatory repudiation may have caused this notion.[94] Notwithstanding an

---

[87] For example, a party may interpret the contract in such a fashion that he honestly does not believe that he must perform certain duties under the contract. Another party may honestly believe that he is discharged because his counterpart has repudiated the contract.

[88] As suggested earlier, if *A* mistakenly believes that *B* has committed a material breach and *A*, therefore, refuses to continue his performance, *A's* mistaken judgment is "fraught with peril" in that *A* is now guilty of the only material breach. This is a harsh result for *A* if he is operating in good faith and is not unreasonable in his mistaken judgment. The harshness is intensified where the same result occurs via a good faith and not unreasonable anticipatory repudiation by *A* which is treated as a material breach by *B*.

[89] *See, e.g.,* New York Life Ins. Co. v. Viglas, 297 U.S. 672 (1936) where Justice Cardozo suggests that an insurer apparently operated in good faith to deny a disability claim. *See also* 2401 Pennsylvania Ave. Corp. v. Federation of Jewish Agencies of Greater Philadelphia, 319 Pa. Super. 228, 466 A.2d 132 (1983), note 1, which recognizes this analysis.

[90] *See* REA Express v. Interway Corp., 538 F.2d 953 (2d Cir. 1976).

[91] *See infra* subsection (E).

[92] There may be circumstances where the obligee may not await performance for a reasonable time though that response is typically permissible. *See* Oloffson v. Coomer, 11 Ill. App. 3d 918, 296 N.E.2d 871 (1973) where the court held that the obligee was unreasonable in awaiting performance where such performance would not be possible after the obligor stated that he was not going to plant corn. The obligee should have understood that the obligor would not be able to supply the corn from another source.

[93] In Lumbermen's Mut. Cas. Co. v. Kotz, 251 F.2d 499 (5th Cir. 1958), the court treats an anticipatory repudiation as a "tender of a breach of the entire contract which, on acceptance, permits the other party to obtain damages for a breach." *See also* City of Algona v. City of Pacific, 35 Wash. App. 517, 667 P.2d 1124 (1983); Les Moise, Inc. v. Rossignol Ski Co., 116 Wis. 2d 268, 342 N.W.2d 444 (1983).

[94] Johnstone v. Milling, 16 Q.B.D. 460 [1860].

occasional statement to the contrary, it is now clear that an anticipatory repudiation need not be "accepted" before it can become a breach.[95]

The effects of an anticipatory repudiation may be catalogued as follows: (1) it discharges the duties of the obligee;[96] (2) it permits the obligee to bring an immediate action for total breach of contract;[97] (3) it excuses the nonoccurrence of a condition to the duty of the obligee;[98] (4) if it accompanies nonperformance which would otherwise constitute only a partial breach, the combination of that nonperformance and repudiation will give rise to a total breach.[99] If the repudiation is subsequently nullified as it may be,[1] these consequences are similarly nullified.[2]

Because the obligee need not typically treat the anticipatory repudiation as a present breach, he is sometimes said to have an "election" to treat the repudiation as a breach or to insist upon performance by the obligor. If the analysis suggested in this subsection is kept in mind, there may be no great harm in using the term "election." Since, however, the term is used in other contexts, it seems preferable to characterize the choices available to the obligee in response to an anticipatory repudiation as *permissible responses*. It is important to focus upon these permissible responses.

E. *Permissible Responses to Anticipatory Repudiation.*

A number of questions arise concerning the obligee's response to an anticipatory repudiation which will now be considered.

1. May an Anticipatory Repudiation Be Ignored?

Since an anticipatory repudiation must occur prior to the time for performance, if the obligee simply ignores it, awaits the time for performance, and upon the obligor's present breach then brings an action, is any harm done? While no harm may be done in a given case, the obligee may not recover for any losses that could have been avoided if he had not awaited the time for performance. This is often known as the mitigation principle and it will be discussed in detail in a later chapter of this volume dealing with contract

---

[95] Professor Corbin suggests that a number of well-considered cases now make this point and they should be accepted as having established the law in this area. 4 CORBIN § 981, at 938.

[96] RESTATEMENT 2d § 253(2).

[97] RESTATEMENT 2d § 253(1).

[98] RESTATEMENT 2d § 255. The repudiation, however, must contribute substantially to the nonoccurrence of the condition. Thus, illustration 1 to this section suggests that a condition to a casualty insurance policy requiring written notice of loss would be excused if the insurance company repudiated its obligation following the loss because a useless act need not be performed. Illustration 2, however, involves a condition of obtaining mortgage financing attached to the obligor's duty to purchase property. If the seller anticipatorily repudiated that contract and the bank refused to grant the mortgage loan, the condition would not be excused because the repudiation did not substantially contribute to the nonoccurrence of the condition. A party must be able to demonstrate that he would have been able to perform had the anticipatory repudiation not occurred. *See* Yale Dev. Co. v. Aurora Pizza Hut, 95 Ill. 3d 523, 420 N.E.2d 823 (1981). *See also* RESTATEMENT 2d § 254(1) which discharges the repudiator's duty if it appears that the obligee would not have been able to perform his return promise.

[99] RESTATEMENT 2d § 243.

[1] *See infra* subsection (E).

[2] RESTATEMENT 2d § 256.

remedies.[3] The UCC permits the aggrieved party (the obligee) to await performance only for a commercially reasonable time.[4] While that "reasonable time" may, in many situations, permit the obligee to await performance until the time for performance specified in the contract, there are situations where he should not be permitted to wait that long. Where, for example, a farmer agreed to deliver his corn crop to a grain dealer and, on June 3, the farmer informed the dealer that no crops would be planted, the dealer was not entitled to wait until September — the time for performance under the contract.[5]

2. Must the Obligee Give Notice that He Treats the Anticipatory Repudiation as a Breach?

If the obligee may not ignore the repudiation, must he notify the repudiator that the repudiation will be treated as a breach? It has long been held that the obligee need not "accept" the repudiation by notification to the repudiator. The obligee may simply commence his action for total breach of the contract.[6]

3. Must the Obligee Commence an Action If He Chooses to Treat the Anticipatory Repudiation as a Breach?

If the obligee relies upon the repudiation, that reliance is sufficient evidence of his choice to treat the repudiation as a breach, even though he does not bring his action until later.[7] Moreover, it is not necessary that the obligee notify the repudiator of the obligee's change of position.[8]

4. If the Obligee Does Not Commence an Action or Rely on the Repudiation, May He Still Treat the Repudiation as a Present Breach?

Again, while notice is not essential to treat an anticipatory repudiation as a breach, where the obligee has neither relied nor brought an action for present breach, he may treat the anticipatory repudiation as a breach by simply notifying the repudiator to that effect.[9] An exercise of the obligee's remedial rights under the contract also signifies that he treats the repudiation as a breach.[10]

---

[3] See infra Chapter 9.

[4] UCC § 2-610(a).

[5] Oloffson v. Coomer, 11 Ill. App. 2d 918, 296 N.E. 871 (1973). The dealer could recover the difference between the contract price and the market price as of June 3 rather than the higher market price as of the September date of performance.

[6] See Liberty Life Ins. Co. v. Olive, 180 Ark. 339, 21 S.W.2d 405 (1929); Finch v. Sprague, 117 Wash. 650, 202 P. 257 (1921); Roehm v. Horst, 178 U.S. 1 (1900). RESTATEMENT 2d § 253(1).

[7] Gurrieri v. Severini, 51 Cal. 2d 12, 330 P.2d 635 (1958) (obligee changed his position by purchasing winery to procure necessary wine); Bu-Vi-Bar Petr. Corp. v. Krow, 40 F.2d 488 (10th Cir. 1930) (promisee permitted a lease to lapse, the assignment of which was a condition precedent to the promisor's duty).

[8] Cf. UCC 2-611(1) which suggests that the repudiator may retract the repudiation unless the aggrieved party has materially changed his position "or otherwise indicated that he considers the repudiation final."

[9] In United States v. Seacoast Gas Co., 204 F.2d 709 (5th Cir. 1953), the defendant anticipatorily repudiated the contract and the plaintiff notified the defendant the repudiation would be treated as a breach unless the defendant retracted the repudiation within three days. The defendant failed to retract within three days and the court held the repudiation became a breach, absent any reliance, at the end of the three day period. See also UCC § 2-611(1) which suggests that an anticipatory repudiation can become a breach simply through the obligee's indication that "he considers the repudiation final."

[10] In Gateway Aviation, Inc. v. Cessna Aircraft Co., 577 S.W.2d 860 (Mo. App. 1978), when the

5. May the Obligor Retract the Repudiation?

There is no question that the obligor may retract the repudiation if he does so before the obligee has indicated that he treats the repudiation as a breach or materially changes his position in reliance on the repudiation.[11] No particular method of retraction is required, i.e., it may occur through words or conduct.[12] An effective retraction reinstates the contractual rights and duties of the parties, i.e., the anticipatory repudiation is nullified.[13] It is important to emphasize the effect of the obligee's reliance or simple indication that he treats the repudiation as final, i.e., retraction by the obligor is impossible after either of these events.

6. Suppose the Obligee Provides a *Locus Pœnitentiae.*

An obligee may provide the obligor with a *locus pœnitentiae,* a time for retraction. If the obligee places a time limitation on a *locus pœnitentiae,* the repudiation is final at the conclusion of that period, regardless of any reliance by the obligee.[14] Moreover, even where the obligee has urged the obligor to retract the repudiation and indicated that he would await the obligor's performance, he may commence an action or, in good faith, rely on the repudiation.[15] Thus, if the repudiator is informed that he has a *locus pœnitentiae* of three days, the obligee could change his mind and either commence an action or rely before the end of the three days and either action would treat the repudiation as final. If this is thought to be misleading to the obligor, it must be remembered that the obligor is a repudiator who created the situation.[16]

F. *Anticipatory Repudiation Inapplicable to Unilateral Obligations — Disability Insurance.*

Since the doctrine of anticipatory repudiation is said to have been created in the case of *Hochster v. De La Tour,*[17] it must be recalled that one of the alleged reasons for the doctrine was the notion that it relieved the obligee of main-

---

obligor failed to make payments on an airplane, the obligee repossessed pursuant to a security agreement with the obligor. This act signified the obligee's treatment of the repudiation as a breach and since a repudiation is a material breach, the obligee's duties under the contract were discharged.

[11] UCC § 2-611(1); RESTATEMENT 2d § 256(1). *See* Taylor v. Johnston, 15 Cal. 3d 130, 123 Cal. Rptr. 641, 539 P.2d 425 (1975).

[12] UCC § 2-611(2); RESTATEMENT 2d § 256(2). It may, however, be necessary for the repudiator to provide adequate assurances of performance.

[13] UCC § 2-611(3); RESTATEMENT 2d § 256 comment a.

[14] *See* United States v. Seacoast Gas Co., 204 F.2d 709 (5th Cir.), *cert. denied,* 346 U.S. 866 (1953).

[15] *See* UCC § 2-610(b) and comment 4.

[16] UCC Section 2-610(b) suggests support for this analysis as does comment 4 which suggests that the repudiator should not be considered misled. Comment 4, however, also suggests the possibility of some action by the aggrieved party (obligee) which, in good faith, requires notification to the repudiator. It would seem, however, that the only situation where such notification would be required would occur when the obligee has provided a *locus pœnitentiae* and knows or reasonably should know that the obligor will take action in reliance in such a fashion as to exceed his contractual obligation and suffer losses beyond that obligation. While this situation is conceivable, there is no recorded case suggesting this possibility.

[17] 2 Ellis & Bl. 678 (1853).

taining a state of readiness to perform when the time for performance arrived. To avoid that necessity, the obligee was permitted to commence an action before the time for performance which discharged his duties under the contract.[18] In a unilateral contract or a bilateral contract that has been fully performed on the side of the obligee, the problem of remaining in a state of readiness to perform does not exist. In a unilateral contract, the obligor has received the full exchange promised by the obligee at the time of contract formation. Similarly, if the contract was originally a bilateral contract but the obligee has fully performed, the effect is the same. In such a case, an early court suggested that the reason for the anticipatory repudiation doctrine no longer existed and it was inapplicable.[19] It has generally been held that no action will lie for the anticipatory repudiation of an unconditional, unilateral obligation to pay money or to perform some other act.[20]

A particular type of case has caused consternation in this area. Disability insurance contracts require the insurance company to make disability payments to the insured if the insured can prove disability in accordance with the contract description. The obligation of the insurer, however, is to make such payments only while the insured continues to be disabled. If the company decides that the disability no longer continues, it will cease making payments. The action by the insured may claim not only the payments due to the time of the lawsuit, but damages for total breach which would involve a calculation of the present value of an uncertain number of future installment payments. The insurance company will resist such a lump sum payment as exceeding its present obligation. In support of that argument, the company may point to the traditional rule that an obligation to pay money is a unilateral obligation to which the doctrine of anticipatory repudiation does not apply. Therefore, the company can be liable only for disability payments already due as contrasted with future payments.[21] The insured, however, will argue that he should not be required to litigate continuously to receive his future disability payments. Moreover, he may claim that the obligation of the insurer is not unilateral since the insured is typically required to submit to future medical examinations to provide proof of his continued disability and, therefore, the doctrine of anticipatory repudiation should apply.[22] The analytical confusion in such

---

[18] See supra subsection (B).

[19] This was the view expressed in one of the earliest English cases on the subject where the plaintiff sued for anticipatory repudiation of a covenant to rebuild contained in a lease. Johnstone v. Milling, 16 Q.B.D. 460 [1886]. The opinions were predicated upon the traditional view that covenants in a lease were independent (unless expressly made dependent) so that the covenant to repair appeared to be an independent obligation that was not constructively conditioned upon the performance of the lessee. Consequently, the lessee need not be in a state of readiness to perform since the lessor's performance did not depend upon the lessee's performance. Modern courts, however, recognize that leases should be viewed as contractual obligations which are dependent or constructively conditional. Therefore, the doctrine of anticipatory repudiation would apply to leases at the present time. See Schneitek v. Gordon, 732 P.2d 603 (Colo. 1987).

[20] Roehm v. Horst, 178 U.S. 1 (1900) (in the case of an ordinary monetary obligation such as a promissory note or bond, the consideration has passed, there are no mutual obligations, and such cases, therefore, do not fall within the reason of the doctrine of anticipatory repudiation). See also Harris v. Time, Inc., 191 Cal. App. 3d 465, 236 Cal. Rptr. 471 (1987); Cornett v. Roth, 233 Kan. 936, 666 P.2d 1182 (1983); Davis v. First Nat'l Bank of Ariz., 124 Ariz. 458, 605 P.2d 37 (1979).

[21] See Greguhn v. Mutual of Omaha Ins. Co., 23 Utah 2d 214, 461 P.2d 285 (1969).

[22] This argument was rejected in Cobb v. Pacific Mut. Life Ins. Co., 4 Cal. 2d 565, 51 P.2d 84 (1935) on the footing that such a requirement is so inconsequential that it should not be regarded as an unperformed obligation.

cases is caused by the fact that they involve a partial breach (failure to make certain installment payments) coupled with a repudiation. This is not an anticipatory repudiation.[23] While a present breach by nonperformance accompanied by a repudiation will normally give rise to a claim for total breach,[24] the problem of calculating uncertain future damages remains. The problem has been resolved, not by permitting recovery beyond the installment payments due,[25] but by providing equitable relief to assure future payments,[26] or installment[27] or declaratory[28] judgments that will insure future payments.

G. Prospective Failure of Performance That Is Not a Repudiation — Demanding Adequate Assurances.

1. Demanding Adequate Assurances — Effect.

We have seen that words or conduct must be sufficiently positive to constitute a repudiation. Situations often arise which cause reasonable doubt in the obligee that the obligor will be able to perform when the time for performance arrives. Yet, the obligor cannot be said to have committed an anticipatory repudiation. What is the obligee to do under these circumstances? Both the UCC and the RESTATEMENT 2d permit the obligee to *suspend* performance where he has "reasonable grounds for insecurity" with respect to the obligor's future performance.[29] At this point, the obligee's duties are not discharged but, again, merely suspended. If adequate assurances are not provided within a reasonable time under the RESTATEMENT 2d,[30] or within a reasonable time not exceeding 30 days under the UCC,[31] such a failure will be treated as a repudiation. If an obligee is in doubt as to whether there has been an anticipatory repudiation, he is wise to treat the situation as one permitting a demand for adequate assurances so as to avoid the pitfall of committing an anticipa-

---

[23] In New York Life Ins. Co. v. Viglas, 297 U.S. 672 (1936), Justice Cardozo suggests: "[T]here are times ... when the breach of a present duty, though only partial in its extension, may confer upon the injured party the privilege at his election to deal with the contract as if broken altogether. A loose practice has been growing up whereby the breach on such occasions is spoken of as anticipatory, whereas in truth it is strictly present, though with consequences effective upon performance in the future." This analysis caused Professor Williston to narrow the FIRST RESTATEMENT position on anticipatory repudiation and the American Law Institute adopted the modified version in 1946. *See* FIRST RESTATEMENT § 318 in the 1948 Supplement.

[24] RESTATEMENT 2d § 243(2).

[25] *See* RESTATEMENT 2d § 243(3).

[26] *See* John Hancock Mut. Life Ins. Co. v. Cohen, 254 F.2d 417 (9th Cir. 1958). *See also* Greguhn v. Mutual of Omaha, *supra* note 21, where the majority opinion misanalyzes the application of anticipatory repudiation (as pointed out in the dissent) but does suggest that if the insurance company fails to make future payments requiring the insured to file another action, the court should then fashion relief to compel future performance.

[27] The most satisfactory solution to the problem which insures a minimum of litigation and expense without imposing undue hardship upon an insurance company that denies liability in good faith is to limit the immediate recovery to payments matured at the time, while entering an order providing for the continuance of the case on the court docket and directing the insurance company to pay future installments, if and when they mature. *See* Equitable Life Assur. Soc'y v. Goble, 254 Ky. 614, 72 S.W.2d 35 (1934).

[28] *See* Stephenson v. Equitable Life Assur. Soc'y, 92 F.2d 506 (4th Cir. 1937).

[29] UCC § 2-609(1); RESTATEMENT 2d § 251(1). *See also* Julian v. Montana Univ., 44 Mont. St. Rep. 2046, 747 P.2d 196 (1987) (and cases cited therein); Conference Center, Ltd. v. TRC, 189 Conn. 212, 455 A.2d 857 (1983).

[30] RESTATEMENT 2d § 251(2).

[31] UCC § 2-609(4).

tory repudiation by treating his own duties as discharged only to discover later that his judgment concerning the obligor's "repudiation" was mistaken.[32] Questions concerning the basis for the demand of adequate assurances, the nature of the demand, the form of the demand, and the effect of insolvency have confronted our courts. It is important to address these questions.

2. Basis for the Demand of Adequate Assurances.

An obligee may not demand adequate assurances just because he becomes nervous about the future performance of the obligor.[33] He must have *reasonable* grounds for insecurity. Moreover, such reasonable grounds for insecurity must occur *after* the contract was formed.[34] If the obligee was aware of certain risks at the time of contract formation, he has assumed those risks and may not later invoke them as reasonable grounds for insecurity.[35] Whether an obligee has reasonable grounds for insecurity to support a demand of adequate assurances is a question of fact.[36] Where the obligee has reason to believe that the obligor's performance has become uncertain or where there have been repeated breaches of the contract, a demand for adequate assurances is justified.[37] If an obligor goes out of business, reasonable grounds for insecurity exist.[38] It is impossible to list exhaustively the litany of circumstances that may amount to reasonable grounds for insecurity. The test may be stated as follows: After the contract was formed, was the obligee made aware of substantial risks of nonperformance by the obligor that would lead a reasonable obligee to believe that he would not receive the performance when due?

3. Nature of the Demand of Adequate Assurances.

A demand of adequate assurances must be made in good faith.[39] Certainly, unjustified or repeated demands that harass the obligor are not good faith demands. A demand for assurances that has the effect of forcing a modification of the contract is ineffective.[40] The demand must also be for adequate assurance of *performance*. Thus, a request for a meeting is not a demand for adequate assurance of performance.[41] Neither is a request for information.[42] As to the kind of assurance that will be deemed "adequate," this is a question of fact requiring a consideration of all of the surrounding circumstances in-

---

[32] *See* Ross Cattle Co. v. Lewis, 415 So. 2d 1029 (Miss. 1982).

[33] Cole v. Melvin, 441 F. Supp. 193, 203 (D. S.D. 1977).

[34] UCC § 2-609 comment 1; RESTATEMENT 2d § 251 comment c.

[35] Moreover, even as to events arising after the time of contract formation, if such events arose because of risks assumed by the obligee at the time of formation, they may not be used as reasonable grounds for insecurity. RESTATEMENT 2d § 251 comment c.

[36] *See* SPS Indus. v. Atlantic Steel Co., 186 Ga. App. 94, 366 S.E.2d 410 (1988); AMF, Inc. v. McDonald's Corp., 536 F.2d 1167 (7th Cir. 1976).

[37] USX Corp. v. Union Pac. Resources Co., 753 S.W.2d 845 (Tex. App. 1988).

[38] Smith-Scharff Paper Co. v. Hirsch & Co. Stores, 754 S.W.2d 928 (Mo. App. 1988).

[39] RESTATEMENT 2d § 251 comment d.

[40] Louisiana Power & Light Co. v. Allegheny Ludlum Indus., 517 F. Supp. 1319 (E.D. La. 1981); Pittsburgh Des-Moines Steel v. Brookhaven Manor Water, 532 F.2d 592 (7th Cir. 1976).

[41] Penberthy Electromelt Int'l, Inc. v. United States Gypsum Co., 38 Wash. App. 514, 686 P.2d 1138 (1984).

[42] SPS Indus. v. Atlantic Steel Co., 186 Ga. App. 94, 366 S.E.2d 410 (1988).

cluding prior course of dealing, trade usage, the general reputation of the obligor, the reason for the initial insecurity, and the time for performance.[43]

4. Form of Demand for Adequate Assurances.

The UCC requires the demand for assurances to be evidenced by a writing[44] whereas the RESTATEMENT 2d recognizes the possible effectiveness of an oral demand in certain circumstances though it states a preference for a written demand.[45] While the case law indicates that a written demand is normally required,[46] courts are willing to give effect to oral demands where a pattern of interaction exists demonstrating a clear understanding between the parties that suspension would occur absent assurances.[47]

5. Insolvency as Prospective Failure of Performance.

An obligor who cannot pay his debts in the ordinary course of business or as they mature is insolvent.[48] Insolvency is not a repudiation because the act is not voluntary and affirmative.[49] Moreover, it may not even provide reasonable grounds to believe that the obligor will not perform. For example, in a personal service contract, an employee may become insolvent, but such insolvency may not affect his ability to perform the services for which he has contracted.[50] If, however, the contract is one for sale of goods, the insolvency of the buyer provides reasonable grounds to believe that the buyer will not be able to pay for the goods at the time of performance. Under these circumstances, the UCC permits a seller to refuse delivery except for cash.[51] Unlike the Code, the RESTATEMENT 2d pursues the common law approach in permitting the buyer to either make payment, tender payment, or provide reasonable security to assure his performance.[52] Where insolvency provides reasonable grounds to believe that the obligor will be unable to perform, the obligee has the unqualified power to suspend his own performance.[53] If the obligee

---

[43] UCC § 2-609(2) and comment 4; RESTATEMENT 2d § 251 and comment d.

[44] UCC § 2-609(1).

[45] RESTATEMENT 2d § 251 comment d which allows for an oral demand if time is of particular importance because "the additional time required for a written demand might necessitate an oral one."

[46] See Automated Energy Sys. v. Fibers & Fabrics of Ga., Inc., 164 Ga. App. 772, 298 S.E.2d 328 (1982).

[47] ARB, Inc. v. E-Sys., 663 F.2d 189 (D.C. Cir. 1980). See also Scott v. Crown, 765 P.2d 1043 (Colo. App. 1988) indicating the same analysis but finding no pattern of interaction in the facts of this case to justify an oral demand.

[48] Both the RESTATEMENT 2d (§ 252(2)) and the UCC (§ 1-201(23)) define "insolvency" very broadly: "A person is insolvent who either has ceased to pay his debts in the ordinary course of business or cannot pay his debts as they become due or is insolvent within the meaning of the federal bankruptcy law." The Bankruptcy Code definition of "insolvent" is found in 11 U.S.C. § 101(26).

[49] If an obligor is adjudicated a bankrupt, his contract may be rejected by the trustee representing the estate. Such a rejection has the effect of a repudiation. 11 U.S.C. § 365(g)(1).

[50] See RESTATEMENT 2d § 252 ill. 2.

[51] UCC § 2-702(1) which also requires cash payment for all unpaid goods delivered prior to the insolvency as well as permitting the seller to stop delivery under § 2-705.

[52] RESTATEMENT 2d § 252(1). See Leopold v. Rock-Ola Mfg. Corp., 109 F.2d 611 (5th Cir. 1940); Diem v. Koblitz, 49 Ohio St. 41, 29 N.E. 1124 (1892); Ex parte Chalmers, In re Edwards, L. R. 8 Ch. 289 [1873].

[53] RESTATEMENT 2d § 252 comment a.

wishes to be discharged of his duties, however, he must pursue the process of demanding adequate assurances and await those assurances for a reasonable time.[54] If the obligee merely doubts the solvency of the obligor, again, he must pursue the process of demanding adequate assurances.[55]

§ 110. Splitting a Cause of Action or Claim.

In relation to responses to repudiations or breaches of contract, it is important to mention a particular concept that is more appropriate for the law of judgments than the law of contracts.[56] It has long been the common sense view that a party may not split a single cause of action or claim,[57] thereby prosecuting two or more actions where one would serve the purpose just as well.[58] The underlying principle is the avoidance of unnecessary or vexatious litigation.[59] Consequently, if a promisee sues for breach of contract and he recovers less than he could have claimed in his action, his claim is merged in the judgment and that judgment will bar any further actions for additional breaches on which his action was founded.[60] What may appear to be a sensible policy to avoid unnecessary litigation can pose a dilemma for an aggrieved party. In an old case involving a contract for the delivery of goods in installments, the defendant repudiated after part performance. From our earlier discussion, we know that a partial breach combined with a repudiation gives rise to a claim for total breach.[61] In this case, however, the plaintiff brought an action only for the failure to deliver past installments, i.e., he ignored the repudiation. The court held that the plaintiff cannot split his cause of action by successive actions. He must either recover all of his damages in the first action or wait until the time for delivery of all of the goods has arrived.[62] By bringing an action for only partial breach, the plaintiff is barred from further actions. His claim, therefore, is merged in the judgment for partial breach. The dilemma the plaintiff confronts is that he may bring his action for partial breach immediately after that breach on the assumption that the remainder of the contract will be performed by the obligor. If the partial breach was not an uncured material breach, he is precluded from bringing an action for total breach. Thus, the only cause of action he could have pursued at the time was an action for partial breach.[63] If, instead of performing the remainder of the contract the

---

[54] RESTATEMENT 2d § 251.

[55] Doubts as to solvency may give rise to reasonable grounds to believe that the obligor will breach, and a demand for adequate assurances under § 251 of the RESTATEMENT 2d would be appropriate. Section 252 of the RESTATEMENT 2d applies only to situations where the obligor is, in fact, insolvent. *See* Keppelon v. W.M. Ritter Flooring Corp., 97 N.J.L. 200, 116 A. 491 (1922); Jewett Pub'g Co. v. Butler, 159 Mass. 517, 34 N.E. 1087 (1893).

[56] *See* RESTATEMENT 2d Judgments §§ 24-26.

[57] The situation is referred to in both ways, i.e., splitting a cause of action or splitting a claim and there is no consistency in their use.

[58] In general, *see* Clark, *Joinder and Splitting Causes of Action,* 25 MICH. L. REV. 393 (1926).

[59] *See* Schimmel v. Aetna Cas. & Sur. Co., 506 So. 2d 1162 (Fla. App. 1987).

[60] *See* Reed v. Classified Parking Sys., 324 So. 2d 484 (La. App. 1975).

[61] *See* RESTATEMENT 2d § 243(2).

[62] Pakas v. Hollingshead, 184 N.Y. 211, 77 N.E. 40 (1906).

[63] Notwithstanding this dilemma, Professor Williston insisted that the plaintiff is precluded from bringing a subsequent action because the claim is the same claim pursued in the earlier action for partial breach. 11 WILLISTON, CONTRACTS § 1293. There is, however, considerable difficulty in determining what constitutes a "claim." The RESTATEMENT 2d JUDGMENTS § 24 indicates that the determination of "claim" is a pragmatic judgment.

obligor subsequently repudiates, the plaintiff is deprived of any further damages because he may not split a claim. A number of courts have avoided the dilemma by permitting such a plaintiff to choose between bringing a second action after the repudiation or waiting until the repudiation to bring his only action for total breach.[64] To allow more than one action, however, flies in the face of the policy against splitting a cause of action, which some courts will uphold.[65]

§ 111. Excuse of Condition.

A. *Nature of the Problem.*

Where a contractual duty will not be activated until a condition occurs, circumstances may permit that condition to be excused. The occurrence of a condition may be prevented or hindered through the bad faith of a party to the contract. There may be a subsequent promise to perform notwithstanding the nonoccurrence of the condition, or performance may be accepted even though a condition failed to occur. The conditional duty may be repudiated or the performance of the condition may be impossible or impracticable. In the subsections that follow, we will explore these and related circumstances relating to the excuse of conditions. It should be noted that the problem is analyzed in essentially the same fashion regardless of whether the condition is an express condition or a constructive condition.[66]

B. *Prevention or Hinderance of Condition — Good Faith.*

Where a contractual duty is conditional, there is a generally recognized duty of good faith and fair dealing placed on the promisor[67] to demonstrate reasonable cooperation by either refraining from conduct that would prevent or hinder the occurrence of a condition, or by taking positive steps to cause its performance. A classic example of the *negative* obligation is found in a well-know case[68] where a prenuptial agreement promised a large payment to the wife if she survived her husband. The condition of survival was prevented in

---

[64] *See* Goodwin v. Cabot Amusement Co., 129 Me. 36, 149 A. 574 (1930) (agreement to pay an annuity); Kenworth Sales Co. v. Salantino, 154 Wash. 236, 281 P. 996 (1929) (conditional sales contract containing acceleration provision); Barron G. Collier, Inc. v. Rawson, 202 Iowa 1159, 211 N.W. 704 (1927) (contract to furnish street car advertising space); Gall v. Gall, 126 Wis. 390, 105 N.W. (1905) (contract to furnish support); McMullen v. Dickinson Co., 60 Minn. 156, 62 N.W. 120 (1895) (employment contract). With respect to installment contracts, the UCC indicates that an aggrieved party who brings an action with respect only to past installments simply reinstates the remainder of the contract by waiving his right to cancellation. *See* UCC § 2-612(3) and comment 6.

[65] "An injured party who has a claim for damages for total breach as a result of repudiation, and who asserts a claim merely for damages for partial breach, runs the risk that if he prevails he will be barred under the doctrine of merger from further recovery, even in the event of a subsequent breach because he has 'split a cause of action.'" RESTATEMENT 2d § 243 comment b.

[66] There is, however, one distinction that is important. An express condition may be waived unless it is a material part of the agreed exchange. RESTATEMENT 2d § 84(1)(a). A constructive condition, however, may be waived even if it is a material part of the agreed exchange. RESTATEMENT 2d § 246. The concept of waiver of conditions will be explored later in this section.

[67] Both the UCC and the RESTATEMENT 2d impose these duties on all contractual parties with respect to the performance and enforcement of contracts. UCC § 1-203; RESTATEMENT 2d § 205.

[68] Foreman State Trust & Sav. Bank v. Tauber, 348 Ill. 280, 180 N.E. 827 (1932).

the most direct way by the husband. He shot and killed his wife before committing suicide which may be described euphemistically as a failure to cooperate. The nonoccurrence of the condition was, obviously, excused. A typical example of the *positive* obligation is found in contracts for the purchase and sale of real property where the buyer's duty is conditioned on his ability to obtain adequate financing, i.e., a mortgage loan. A buyer has no duty to obtain the loan under such a contract. He does, however, have a duty of using his best efforts to obtain the loan in accordance with the general principle of good faith and fair dealing, and the specific principle that he should, in such a situation, take positive steps in attempting to secure such a loan. His failure to do so excuses the condition.[69] The justification for the rule making prevention or hindrance a violation of the duty of good faith and fair dealing as well as an excuse of the condition is the fundamental assumption by the parties to the contract that the promisor would not interfere with the occurrence of the condition, or that he would take reasonable steps to ascertain its occurrence.[70]

While there are occasional statements in the case law suggesting that it is necessary to show that the condition would have occurred except for the lack of the promisor's cooperation,[71] it should be sufficient to show that the failure to cooperate has contributed materially to the nonoccurrence of the condition.[72] In the prenuptial agreement case, it would have been impossible to prove that the wife would have survived her husband had he not killed her. Since he destroyed any chance for her to meet the condition of survival, it is eminently fair to conclude that the husband's failure to cooperate contributed substantially to the prevention of the condition, which should be excused. If, however, the *promisor* can show that his lack of cooperation has not materially affected the occurrence of the condition, the condition is not excused.[73]

C. *Condition Excused by Repudiation or Other Inability to Perform — Impossibility, Impracticability.*

If it appears that a promise will not be performed at the time for performance, a condition attached to that promise will generally be excused.[74] Just as the obligor's nonperformance will excuse a condition to his duty, his repudiation will have the same effect since the obligee is entitled to take the obligor at his word.[75] Like excuse of condition for nonperformance,[76] excuse of condi-

---

[69] *See* Bellevue College v. Greater Omaha Realty Co., 217 Neb. 183, 348 S.W.2d 837 (1984). *See also* Lach v. Cahill, 138 Conn. 418, 85 A.2d 481 (1951).

[70] This concept as found in the second edition of this book was relied upon in Barnes v. Atlantic & Pac. Life Ins. Co. of Am., 295 Ala. 149, 325 So. 2d 143 (1975). *See also* Smith v. Morgan Drive Away, 613 S.W.2d 469 (Mo. App. 1981).

[71] *See* Eager Beaver Buick, Inc. v. Burt, 503 So. 2d 819 (1987).

[72] *See* Klondike Indus. v. Gibson, 741 P.2d 1161 (Alaska 1987); Jacobs v. Tenneco West, Inc., 186 Cal. App. 3d 1413, 231 Cal. Rptr. 351 (1986). RESTATEMENT 2d § 245.

[73] It should be emphasized that the burden is on the party in breach to show that the condition would not have occurred notwithstanding his lack of cooperation. RESTATEMENT 2d § 245 comment b.

[74] *See* Champion v. Whaley, 280 S.C. 116, 311 S.E.2d 404 (1984) (condition to brokerage commission that house be sold excused when seller sold house to another); Craddock v. Greenhut Constr. Co., 423 F.2d 11 5th Cir. 1970) (condition of supplying performance bond excused through repudiation). *See also* Chadd v. Franchise Corp., 226 Neb. 502, 412 N.W.2d 453 (1987). *See also* RESTATEMENT 2d § 255.

[75] RESTATEMENT 2d § 255 comment a.

[76] RESTATEMENT 2d § 245.

tion for repudiation depends upon whether the repudiation contributed materially to the nonoccurrence of the condition.[77] If the condition would not occur regardless of the repudiation, both parties are discharged from their duties.[78] If the condition, however, would occur, failing to excuse it in the light of the promisor's repudiation would appear to insist upon a useless requirement. Whether a condition would have occurred absent the repudiation is sometimes a matter of speculation. Thus, where a buyer of a condominium with a boat slip repudiated a contract because he was dissatisfied with the seller's reasonable assurances that the slip would be effective, the buyer sought to be discharged because the seller had failed to arrange proper financing in accordance with the contract. The court held that the financing condition was excused because the seller may have arranged proper financing by the time for performance and the burden of proof was on the buyer to show that the seller would not have arranged such financing.[79] Courts have also demonstrated unwillingness to permit the repudiating party to use the possibility of the nonoccurrence of a condition as a defense to repudiation. A broker brought an action for his commission on the sale of a house pursuant to a contract between the seller and a buyer discovered by the broker. The contract was conditional on the buyer obtaining certain financing. Before the closing date, the seller repudiated by selling the house to a third party. The seller presented evidence that the buyer would not have been able to obtain the required financing in time for the closing. The court held for the broker on the footing that whether the condition would have been met in time was a matter of speculation and the seller should not be discharged from its duty through its own wrongdoing.[80]

Beyond repudiation, the condition may also be excused because performance of the promise may be impossible or impracticable. The concepts of impossibility and impracticability require separate discussion later in this volume.[81] At this point, it is appropriate to recognize that, if the occurrence of a condition becomes impossible or impracticable[82] and the condition is not a material part of the agreed exchange, the condition is excused.[83] A classic example is the condition found in building contracts that the architect must be satisfied with each portion of the work before the owner's duty to make each progress payment is activated. If the architect dies or becomes so incapacitated that he or she is incapable of making the judgment of approval, that condition will be excused.[84] While impossibility or impracticability is nor-

---

[77] RESTATEMENT 2d § 255.

[78] RESTATEMENT 2d § 255 comment a.

[79] Puget Sound Serv. v. Bush, 45 Wash. App. 312, 724 P.2d 1127 (1986). See RESTATEMENT 2d § 245 comment b.

[80] Champion v. Whaley, 280 S.C. 116, 311 S.E.2d 404 (1984).

[81] See infra Chapter 8.

[82] RESTATEMENT 2d § 261 following § 2-615(a) of the UCC states that where a party's performance is made impracticable without his fault by the occurrence of an event the nonoccurrence of which was a basic assumption on which the contract was made, his duty to render that performance is discharged, unless the contract language or circumstances indicated the contrary.

[83] RESTATEMENT 2d § 271.

[84] See Grenier v. Compratt Constr. Co., 189 Conn. 444, 454 A.2d 1289 (1983). See RESTATEMENT 2d § 271 ill. 1. In general, see Multi-Serv. Contrs. v. Town of Vernon, 193, Conn. 446, 477 A.2d 653 (1984). Under the UCC, the parties may enter into a "sale of approval" contract which is some-

mally considered in relation to the performance of the contract, just as performance can be excused on these bases, a condition may also be excused.

D. *Acceptance of Benefits After Nonoccurrence of Condition.*

If a condition does not occur but the promisor nevertheless accepts benefits under the contract which are part of the contemplated exchange for his own conditionally promised performance, it is generally held that the condition is excused. Thus, when a promise to do certain excavating work was conditioned on the work being performed by a specified date, it was held that when the promisor permitted the work to continue after the expiration of that date, the condition was excused.[85] The nonoccurrence of the condition where the promisor knows or has reason to know of such nonoccurrence operates as a promise to perform despite that nonoccurrence.[86] Any other rule could result in a serious forfeiture to the promisee without any equivalent loss to the promisor. Where, however, the defective performance is so attached to the promisor's real or personal property that he cannot avoid availing himself of its use if he is to make any beneficial use of his property, the mere use of the property without knowledge of the nonoccurrence of the condition will not excuse the condition.[87] On the other hand, if the promisor knew or had reason to know of the nonoccurrence of the condition and indicated acceptance of the performance notwithstanding such nonoccurrence, he may not rely upon that nonoccurrence to be discharged from his duty.[88] Under the UCC, acceptance of goods with knowledge of a nonconformity will preclude the buyer from later rejecting the goods or revoking acceptance unless the acceptance was based on the assumption that the nonconformity would be cured.[89] Even the acceptance of

---

times referred to as a sale "on trial" or a sale "on satisfaction." In such a transaction, "the seller undertakes a particular business risk to satisfy his prospective buyer with the appearance or performance of the goods in question." UCC § 2-326(1)(a) and comment 1. Presumably, a condition naming a party to be satisfied in such an agreement could be excused if that party was unavailable or incapable of making a good faith judgment. Another UCC section, § 2-305, deals with a missing price term that will be supplied by a named third party upon whose judgment the parties to the contract have agreed to rely. Comment 4 to that section, however, mentions the special situation where a particular party's judgment is not chosen by the parties merely as a barometer or index of a fair price, but as an essential condition to the parties' intention to make any contract at all. In that situation (*e.g.*, a trusted expert is to "value" a particular painting), the unavailability of such a third party will prevent the formation of the contract.

[85] Dunn v. Steubing, 120 N.Y. 232, 24 N.E. 315 (1890). *See also* Longenecker v. Brommer, 59 Wash. 2d 552, 368 P.2d 900 (1962) (acceptance of timber though not felled and bucked in accordance with regulations required by the contract); Venz v. State Auto Ins. Ass'n, 217 Iowa 662, 251 N.W. 27 (1933) (acceptance of premium by insurer with knowledge of nonoccurrence of condition); Neil v. Kennedy, 319 Ill. 75, 149 N.E. 775 (1925) (vendor's acceptance of overdue installments of price on land contract precludes a termination of the contract to sell though time of payment was of the essence). *See also* RESTATEMENT 2d § 246(1).

[86] *See* RESTATEMENT 2d § 246(1).

[87] Becker Roofing Co. v. Little, 229 Ala. 317, 156 So. 842 (1934); Fitzgerald v. La Porte, 64 Ark. 34, 40 S.W. 261 (1897); Hanley v. Walker, 79 Mich. 607, 45 N.W. 57 (1890). *See also* RESTATEMENT 2d § 246(2) and comment d.

[88] *See* RESTATEMENT 2d § 246 ill. 7.

[89] *See* Courtesy Enters., Inc. v. Richards Labs., 37 UCC Rep. Serv. 765, 768 (Ind. App. 1983) (Even if one were to assume that the [nonconformity existed, the] acceptance of the shipment with knowledge of that tendency precluded its revocation of acceptance." The court cited UCC § 2-607(2) as support for this statement.) On revocation of acceptance, *see* UCC § 2-608(1)(b).

nonconforming goods, however, does not preclude the buyer from recovering damages for such accepted goods.[90]

A promisor sometimes only accepts and retains part of the performance. A number of cases have held that a promisor may not decide to accept part of the entire performance and reject another part[91] even though these cases often dealt with contracts for the sale of goods. Under the UCC, that concept has been modified with respect to sale-of-goods contracts. While the buyer may reject goods under the Code, he also may choose either to accept the whole shipment or accept any "commercial unit or units and reject the rest."[92] In contracts other than those for the sale of goods, the general rule remains that a promisor may not decide to reject part and accept another part of an entire performance.[93] Even under the UCC, if the performance is promised in installments and the nonconformity of one or more past installments gives the buyer the right to treat the whole contract as materially breached, the buyer's subsequent acceptance of another nonconforming installment reinstates the contract absent notification of cancellation because it signals the buyer's intention to continue the contract.[94]

E. *Unjustifiable Basis for Nonperformance as Excuse of Condition.*

If a condition fails to occur and the promisor refuses to perform but states a wholly unjustifiable reason for his refusal rather than the nonoccurrence of the condition, should the condition be excused? Some older cases took the position that the condition must be excused because the promisee has the right to assume that the promisor was relying exclusively on the unjustifiable reason and it would be unjust to permit him later to discover the justifiable reason, i.e., the nonoccurrence of the condition.[95] The corresponding assumption was that, by stating a particular reason for his refusal to perform, the promisor is necessarily indicating satisfaction with all other aspects of the

---

[90] UCC § 2-714(1). *See In re* Precise Tool & Gauge Co., 39 UCC Rep. Serv. 474 (U.S. Bankr. E.D. Tenn. 1984). *See also* RESTATEMENT 2d § 246 comment b.

[91] *See* Loveland v. Aymetts Auto Arcade, Inc., 121 Conn. 231, 184 A. 376 (1936) (buyer of oil burner and tank accepted tank but attempted to return defective burner); Shohfi v. Rice, 241 Mass. 211, 135 N.E. 141 (1922) (buyer of goods under an entire contract who accepted some that conformed to the contract specifications could not reject others that were defective); Pacific Timber Co. v. Iowa Windmill & Pump Co., 135 Iowa 308, 112 N.W. 771 (1907) (buyer of car of lumber could not accept part and reject part that was defective).

[92] UCC § 2-601. "Commercial unit" is defined in § 2-105(6) as "such a unit of goods as by commercial usage is a single whole for purposes of sale and division of which materially impairs its character or value on the market or in use."

[93] RESTATEMENT 2d § 246 comment c.

[94] Similarly, if the buyer brings an action only with respect to past installments or demands future installments, he is indicating his intention that the contract be continued. UCC § 2-612(3). *See* Traynor v. Walters, 345 F. Supp. 455 (M.D. Pa. 1972) (though buyer had the right to treat the whole contract as breached, when the buyer demanded delivery of portion of undelivered goods, the buyer reinstated the contract).

[95] *See* Ginn v. W.C. Clark Coal Co., 143 Mich. 84, 106 N.W. 867, 107 N.W. 904 (1906). *Accord* Cummings v. Connecticut Gen. Life Ins. Co., 102 Vt. 351, 148 A. 484 (1930), *noted,* 39 YALE L.J. 906 (denial of liability under life insurance policy on one ground held to prevent reliance on any other defense); Powers v. Bohuslav, 84 Neb. 179, 120 N.W. 942 (1909) (action for real estate broker's commission); Chevrolet Motor Co. v. Gladding, 42 F.2d 440 (4th Cir. 1930), *noted,* 44 HARV. L. REV. 646 (1930) (unjustified attempt to cancel a contract under one clause prevented treating contract as cancelled under another clause where there was reason to activate that clause).

promisee's performance and a willingness to forego all other possible defenses.[96] Neither of these assumptions is warranted. Where a party rejects a performance, he need not state any reasons for his rejection. A problem may occur, however, if a party decides to particularize the reasons for his rejection and his reasons are not justifiable.

Under the UCC, where the buyer of goods could have stated the justifiable reason for his rejection but, instead, stated an unjustifiable reason, the seller may be misled. If the seller can show that he would have cured[97] the defect if the justifiable reason had been stated within a reasonable time, the nonoccurrence of the condition is excused.[98] The seller has a right to cure under the UCC and, where the Code does not apply, we have seen that even a material breach is subject to cure under the RESTATEMENT 2d. Material interference with the right to cure can, therefore, operate to excuse the condition to the promisor's duty.[99] Since the RESTATEMENT 2d is in conformity with the UCC in the overwhelming majority of instances where the UCC deals with contract law, it is not remarkable that the RESTATEMENT 2d follows the Code in this situation.[1]

F. "Waiver" of Condition — Estoppel and Election.

One of the difficulties encountered in attempts to analyze the case law excusing conditions is the use of the nebulous term "waiver." For many years, writers have criticized the use of the term as one of imprecise and indefinite connotation.[2] It is almost invariably though inexactly defined as the voluntary or intentional relinquishment of a known right.[3] In fact, it deals with excuse of conditions.[4] There is additional confusion as to whether a "waiver" must be supported by consideration or detrimental reliance (promissory estoppel). Thus, one court may suggest that "The essence of waiver is estoppel. Where there is no estoppel, there is no waiver."[5] Another court insists that "While waiver is a member of the family of estoppel, ... an estoppel in pais has connections in no wise akin to waiver."[6] Still another court may state that "A

---

[96] See Oelbermann v. Toyo Kisen Kabushiki Kaisha, 3 F.2d 5 (9th Cir. 1925) (carrier who answers written claim for loss on merits loses right to object to delay in presenting claim).

[97] See UCC § 2-508 and the discussion of "cure" at § 107(B)(2).

[98] See UCC § 2-605. See also Uchitel v. F. R. Tripler & Co., 107 Misc. 2d 310, 434 N.Y.S.2d 77 (1980).

[99] See RESTATEMENT 2d § 245 comment b.

[1] RESTATEMENT 2d § 248. The UCC, of course, preempts with respect to contracts for the sale of goods so that the RESTATEMENT 2d may not differ from the UCC in such cases. In other types of contracts, however, the RESTATEMENT 2d clearly follows the Code with rare exception.

[2] See Ewart, *Professor Williston's Review of Waiver*, 11 MINN. L. REV. 415 (1926). See also Wachovia Bank & Trust Co., N. A. v. Rubish, 306 N.C. 417, 293 S.E.2d 749 (1982) (meaning of "waiver" is at best elusive).

[3] See Penmanta Corp. v. Hollis, 520 N.E.2d 120 (Md. App. 1988); East Larimer City Water Dist. v. Centric Corp., 693 P.2d 1019 (Colo. App. 1984); Hauenstein & Bermeister, Inc. v. Met-Fab Indus., 320 N.W.2d 886 (Minn. 1982); G. Amsinck & Co. v. Springfield Grocer Co., 7 F.2d 855 (8th Cir. 1925). One of the problems with this definition is the inference that the promisor must be aware of his legal rights and intend the legal consequences of his "waiver." Most courts hold that it is enough that he has full knowledge of all the material facts or reason to know such facts. See Garrard v. Lang, 514 So. 2d 933 (Ala. 1987) and RESTATEMENT 2d § 84 comment b.

[4] See RESTATEMENT 2d § 84 and comment b.

[5] Williams v. Neely, 134 F. 1, 10 (8th Cir. 1904).

[6] Quoted with approval in Haynes v. Manning, 263 Mo. 1, 172 S.W. 897, 907 (1914).

waiver, to be operative, must be supported by an agreement founded upon a valuable consideration,"[7] while another tells us that waiver "does not require or depend upon a new contract or a new consideration. Nor does it depend upon estoppel...."[8] Notwithstanding the pervasive confusion in the use of the term, courts continue to use it and it appears in statutes, including the UCC, without definition.[9] Earlier in this volume, the concept of waiver was explored in relation to contract modifications under the UCC[10] where we recognized that the characterization of waiver is more pliable than the concept of modification. Notwithstanding the lack of precision in the use of "waiver," we will explore those situations where the word is used in relation to the excuse of conditions.

By language or conduct,[11] a promisor may manifest his intention[12] to forego the benefit of ("waive") a condition.[13] This manifestation may occur, (1) prior to or at the time of contract formation, (2) after formation but prior to the time for occurrence of the condition, or (3) after formation *and* after the time for occurrence of the condition.

1. "Waiver" at or Prior to Contract Formation.

If a promisor manifests her intention to forego the benefit of a condition prior to the formation of a contract that will be evidenced by a writing containing that condition, there is an obvious parol evidence problem. As suggested earlier in this volume, the parol evidence rule precludes the admissibility of evidence of prior or contemporaneous agreements that will, *inter alia,* contradict or vary the terms of a subsequently formed contract evidenced by a writing. Thus, it would seem that such evidence would not be admissible and the condition would not be excused.[14] In typical cases involving insurance contracts,[15] most of our courts have admitted the evidence and excused the condition, usually on the footing that the promisee has changed her position in reliance upon the promisor's manifestation of intention to forego the benefit of the condition (estoppel).[16] Modern courts may not, however, insist upon a

---

[7]Smith v. Minneapolis Threshing Mach. Co., 89 Okla. 156, 158, 214 P. 178, 180 (1923).

[8]Champion Spark Plug Co. v. Automobile Sundries Co., 273 F. 74, 79 (2d Cir. 1921).

[9]*See, e.g.,* UCC §§ 2-209(4) and 2-605. UCC § 1-107 uses the term "waiver" or "renunciation" in relation to discharging a debt without consideration. RESTATEMENT 2d § 277(1) more properly limits the surrender of a claim to a written "renunciation" which discharges the claim.

[10]*See* Chapter 3, § 64(E).

[11]Pipe Indus. Ins. Fund Trust of Local 41 v. Consolidated Pipe Trades Trust of Mont., 760 P.2d 711 (Mont. 1988).

[12]Whether a waiver has occurred is a question of intention, i.e., a question of fact. *See* East Larimer City Water Dist. v. Centric Corp., 693 P.2d 1019 (Colo. App. 1984).

[13] The burden of proof is on the party asserting the waiver, i.e., the promisee. Pipe Indus. Ins. Fund Trust of Local 41, *supra* note 11.

[14]*See* Lumber Underwriters v. Rife, 237 U.S. 605 (1915); Franklin Fire Ins. Co. v. Martin, 40 N.J.L. (11 Vroom) 568, 29 Am. Rep. 271 (1878).

[15]For a case involving franchising, *see* Ehert Co. v. Eaton, Yale & Towne, Inc., 523 F.2d 280 (7th Cir. 1975), *cert. denied,* 425 U.S. 943 (1976).

[16]*See* Roberts v. Maine Bonding & Cas. Co., 404 A.2d 238 (1979); Kimball Ice Co. v. Springfield Fire & Marine Ins. Co., 100 W. Va. 728, 132 S.E. 714 (1926); Gordon v. St. Paul Fire & Marine Ins. Co., 197 Mich. 226, 163 N.W. 956 (1917); Big Creek Drug Co. v. Stuyvesant Ins. Co., 115 Miss. 561, 76 So. 548 (1917). *See also* Satz v. Massachusetts Bonding & Ins. Co., 243 N.Y. 385, 153 N.E. 844 (1926) (insurance company estopped to show nonperformance of a "condition" where it

showing of estoppel. Thus, where an insurer was constructively aware of the nonoccupancy of a building before issuing a policy containing a condition of occupancy, the court found that a constructive waiver of that condition could be shown without insisting upon a showing of estoppel.[17] This is in keeping with the modern view discussed below that certain conditions may be excused absent any validation device.[18]

2. "Waiver" After Formation and Before Time for Occurrence of Condition.

A post-formation manifestation of intention to forego the benefit of a condition is not affected by the parol evidence rule which applies only to promises made before or at the time of formation. Any promise which is supported by consideration to forego the benefit of a condition is a modification of the contract and is clearly enforceable assuming that any statute of frauds requirement is met. The parties have discharged the old contract and entered the new conditionless contract. Often, however, a promise made after formation but before the time for occurrence of the condition to forego the benefit of a condition is not supported by consideration. Courts have readily moved to enforcement of such promises on the basis of detrimental reliance whether the time for the condition has or has not arrived.[19] The problem arises where there is no consideration, promissory estoppel, or any other validation device.

Where a party manifests an intention to perform his promise notwithstanding the nonoccurrence of a condition to his duty before the time for the condition has arrived, the condition will be excused if it was not a material part of the agreed exchange.[20] Certain conditions are not a material part of the

---

acquiesced in such nonperformance at the time of issuing the policy, but it was not estopped to rely upon breach of "warranty." *See* Note, 75 U. PA. L. REV. 477 (1926).

[17] The court suggested that the line between waiver and estoppel is often blurred, and where an insurer, with knowledge of the facts, performs in a fashion inconsistent with its intention to insist upon a strict compliance with conditions in the contract, the insurer will be treated as having waived their occurrence. Standard Supply Co. v. Reliance Ins. Co., 272 S.E.2d 394 (N.C. App. 1980).

[18] *See* RESTATEMENT 2d § 84(1) and comment d.

[19] *See* Fehl-Haber v. Nordhagen, 59 Wash. 2d 7, 365 P.2d 607 (1961) (by accepting four late monthly payments, conditional vendor "waived" its right to forfeiture which could be reinstated only by giving vendee reasonable opportunity to comply with contract); General Motors Acceptance Corp. v. Hicks, 189 Ark. 62, 70 S.W.2d 509 (1934) (vendor's right to forfeit a conditional sale for default in payments was lost by accepting many other payments late); Hartford Fire Ins. Co. v. Aaron, 226 Ala. 430, 147 So. 628 (1933) (benefit of condition in fire policy stipulating against change in insured's interest in the property lost by failing, after receiving notice of the change of interest, to declare a forfeiture of the policy before a fire after receiving notice of the change of interest). Contracts often contain "anti-waiver" or "nonwaiver" clauses which seek to preserve conditions previously waived. In effect, these clauses are designed to automatically reinstate conditions to future performance even though there have been one or more waivers of such conditions in the earlier performance of the contract. The existence of a nonwaiver clause does not preclude excuse of conditions by manifestation of intention to forego the benefit of one or more conditions. TSS-Seedman's, Inc. v. Elota Realty Co., 72 N.Y.2d 1024, 531 N.E.2d 646 (1988); Carver v. Preferred Acc., Inc., 218 Iowa 873, 256 N.W. 274 (1934); Green v. Minnesota Farmers' Mut. Ins. Co., 190 Minn. 109, 251 N.W. 14 (1933); Ley v. Home Ins. Co., 64 N.D. 200, 251 N.W. 137 (1933). A party may be estopped to assert a nonwaiver clause. *See* Dorn v. Robinson, 762 P.2d 566 (Ariz. App. 1988). If the intention to forego the benefit of the condition is pervasive over a long period, even the nonwaiver clause may be waived. *See* Westinghouse Credit Corp. v. Shelton, 645 F.2d 869, 873-74 (10th Cir. 1981); Willingham Com. Co. v. Spears, 641 P.2d 1, 7-8 (Alaska 1982).

[20] RESTATEMENT 2d § 84(1).

agreed exchange. They are merely technical or procedural such as those requiring proof of loss or notice within a certain time. A promise to forego the benefit of this type of condition is enforceable without any validation device though it subjects the promisor to a new duty. The new duty, however, does not differ significantly from the original duty.[21] If, however, the condition is a material part of the agreed exchange, it will not be "waived." An agreement for the purchase and sale of property contained a condition requiring clear and marketable title. The condition for clear and marketable title was not merely technical or procedural; it was a material part of the agreed exchange and the condition was not excused.[22] An almost absurd example makes the point even more clear. An insurance policy will be paid up to $200,000 on condition that the insured suffers a casualty. If the insurer promises to pay $200,000 to the insured even though no casualty has been suffered, the condition is not excused because it was a material part of the agreed exchange.

Where the "waiver" occurs prior to the time for the occurrence of the condition, it may be possible to reinstate the condition. If, for example, an insurance company promised not to insist upon a condition in the casualty policy requiring notice of loss within 60 days from the time of loss, but, before any loss occurred, notified the insured that it would insist upon such notice should a casualty occur, the insurer's duty would again be subject to the condition, i.e., the excused condition would be reinstated.[23] The condition of notice was within the control of the promisee (insured)[24] and the notification was received while there was still time to cause the condition to occur.[25] Reinstatement of the condition under these circumstances, therefore, is not unjust.[26]

3. "Waiver" After Formation and After Time for Occurrence of Condition — Election.

Where the condition has not occurred after the time for its occurrence, it is impossible to reinstate it. A manifestation of intention to forego the benefit of the condition will certainly excuse the condition if there is reliance upon that manifestation. In the case of a language or conduct promise after the time for occurrence of the condition, that the condition will not be required, reliance is unlikely and some cases have held that the condition is not excused in the absence of reliance (estoppel).[27] More cases, however, hold the condition excused though no reliance has been shown.[28] Both the FIRST RESTATEMENT[29]

---

[21] See RESTATEMENT 2d § 84 comment d.

[22] See Rose v. Mitsubishi Int'l Corp., 423 F. Supp. 1162 (E.D. Pa. 1976).

[23] See RESTATEMENT 2d § 84(2).

[24] It would be sufficient if it were within the control of a beneficiary to the insurance contract. RESTATEMENT 2d § 84(2).

[25] RESTATEMENT 2d § 84(2)(a).

[26] RESTATEMENT 2d § 84(2)(b).

[27] See Coleman Furn. Corp. v. Home Ins. Co., 67 F.2d 347 (4th Cir. 1933); Joye v. South Carolina Mut. Ins. Co., 54 S.C. 371, 32 S.E. 446 (1899).

[28] Whether or not the time for the occurrence of the condition had arrived, in addition to the requirement that the condition not be a material part of the agreed exchange, if the condition is to be excused the risk of uncertainty that the condition would occur must not have induced the formation of the contract. Thus, a fire insurance policy places the risk of the condition of fire on the insurer. A promise to pay regardless of that condition, therefore, materially affects the value received by the promisor. See RESTATEMENT 2d § 84(1)(b) and comment c.

[29] FIRST RESTATEMENT § 88.

and RESTATEMENT 2d[30] arrive at the same conclusion through a different rationale, i.e., as long as the condition was not a material part of the agreed exchange, it may be excused absent reliance or other validation device. The cases supporting the conclusion of the Restatements often characterize the language or (more typically) conduct manifesting an intention to forego the condition as an "election" or "election to waive." For those courts that do not require reliance, the election is absolute. Those requiring reliance, however, permit the promisor to change his mind in the absence of reliance. It cannot be gainsaid that the addition of the less than precise term, "election," to the muddled notion of "waiver" is counterproductive. The fundamental issue is whether a promise by language or conduct to forego the benefit of a condition will be enforced absent any showing of reliance. The Restatements suggest the preferable compromise: If the condition is not a material part of the agreed exchange, the answer is yes; otherwise, no. If there is a promise to surrender a technical or procedural condition, there is little reason to insist upon some validation device to support that promise. This is not to underestimate the difficulty that can be found in determining whether a condition is a material part of the agreed exchange. The question in that context can be as difficult as any question concerning materiality. Yet, materiality is a standard that has proven generally workable, notwithstanding its pliable character. If the terms "waiver" and "election" would fall into disuse, much of the mystery surrounding excuse of conditions would disappear. Unfortunately, the tenacity of those terms, particularly "waiver," suggest their continuation into the next millennium.

---

[30] RESTATEMENT 2d § 84(1).

Chapter 8

RISK ALLOCATION

§ 112. Impossibility and Impracticability of Performance.

A. *History and Nature of the Problem.*

During the course of the life of a contract and before its performance, the surrounding circumstances may change to such an extent as to make performance of the contract, according to its terms, either impossible or something quite different from what was expected by the parties when the contract was made. Death, war, changes in the law or its administration, fires, floods, etc., intervene and give rise to the question of whether the promisor should be required to perform, or to pay damages for nonperformance, in spite of the changed conditions. If the parties had sufficient imagination to foresee the particular contingency which has subsequently arisen, they would not have made the kind of a contract which they did make; but, being typically optimistic, or, of limited foresight, they may have used general language that appears to make the promisor liable although it may be evident that the language was not used advisedly with reference to the situation that has arisen by the time for performance. What is to be done under these circumstances?

It is generally said that the early law of England, which was inclined to enforce a contract in accordance with its literal terms in all cases, took the uncompromising stand that neither impossibility, nor any change of circumstances, however extreme, would excuse performance of a promise. This view is set forth in the case of *Paradine v. Jane*,[1] where it was said that "... when the party by his own contract creates a duty or charge upon himself, he is bound to make it good, if he may, notwithstanding any accident by inevitable necessity, because he might have provided against it by his contract." Such a view, while it may have the merit of being easy of application, obviously takes no account of the fact that human beings are of limited foresight. To hold a promisor to the literal terms of his bargain is frequently to impose a burden upon him which neither he nor the promisee had considered as a possibility. Even the old English courts at the time of this case recognized obvious exceptions to the rigid rule. If a personal service contract could not be performed because the promisor dies, his performance was excused.[2] If performance was prevented by operation of law,[3] or by the destruction of the goods without the fault of the promisor,[4] the performance was held excused. However, the tendency was to deny that there is any general principle, of which these exceptions could be regarded as illustrations, on the basis of which a promisor is to be excused from the performance of his promise because of impossibility or change of circumstances. It is not hard to understand why this should be so. Whenever a promisor is relieved from an obligation which he has apparently assumed, there is always the possibility that he is being relieved of an obligation which he did in fact assume, or which he would have assumed, had the contingency in question been consciously considered at the time of contracting. At best, the tribunal which must decide the case can only speculate as to whether the parties did have it in mind, or, if not, what they would have done, had they thought of it as a possibility. For fear of opening the door too widely to one seeking to escape an obligation which he may have assumed, the ten-

---

[1] Aleyn 26, 82 Eng. Rep. 897 [1647]. The court held that the fact that a lessee had been deprived of the use of leased premises by the king's enemies did not excuse him from paying the rent reserved in the lease. So far as the actual decision is concerned the case would probably be followed today. It should be noted that the promisor's performance, i.e., paying the rent, was not made impossible at all by the supervening event. If he were to be excused from performing, the only basis for such excuse would be frustration of purpose. For a recent case which applies the language of *Paradine v. Jane* literally, *see* Wills v. Shockley, 52 Del. (2 Storey) 295, 157 A.2d 252 (1960).

See also Blackburn Bobbin Co. v. Allen & Sons, 1 K.B. 540, 543 [1918], in which McCardie, J., wrote: "The original rule of the English law was clear in its insistence that where a party by his own contract creates a duty or charge upon himself he is bound to make it good notwithstanding any accident by inevitable necessity, because he might have provided against it by his contract." *But cf.* Page, *The Development of the Doctrine of Impossibility of Performance,* 18 MICH. L. REV. 589 (1919), in which he points out that the early English law frequently did in effect excuse performance under circumstances which today would be dealt with on a theory of excuse because of impossibility of performance.

[2] *See* Hyde v. Dean of Windsor, 78 Eng. Rep. 798 (Q.B. 1597).

[3] Abbot of Westminster v. Clerke, 73 Eng. Rep. 59 (K.B. 1536)

[4] Williams v. Lloyd, 82 Eng. Rep. 95 (K.B. 1629).

dency was to keep the door closed altogether, regardless of the hardship resulting to the promisor. The problem, therefore, was to determine the limited exceptions to the general rule, and the scope of these exceptions.

The modern doctrine of impossibility of performance emerged from the case of *Taylor v. Caldwell*,[5] in 1863. In that case, a music hall, the use of which had been promised to the plaintiff to enable him to give a series of concerts, was destroyed by an accidental fire before the date set for the first concert. In a suit for breach of the contract, it was held that the owner was excused from performing on "... the principle that where, from the nature of the contract, it appears that the parties must from the beginning have known that it could not be fulfilled unless when the time for the fulfillment of the contract arrived some particular specified thing continued to exist, so that, when entering into the contract, they must have contemplated such continuing existence as the foundation of what was to be done; there, in the absence of any express or implied warranty that the thing shall exist, the contract is not to be construed as a positive contract, but as subject to an *implied condition* that the parties shall be excused in case, before breach, performance becomes impossible from the perishing of the thing without default of the contractor."[6]

The statement that the parties "contemplated" the continuing existence of the music hall as the "foundation" of their contract may suggest that they consciously adverted to its continuing existence. On the other hand, the court may have intended to suggest that the parties assumed its continuing existence as the basis of their contract since the contrary assumption would have been absurd. If the court had emphasized the "foundation" of the contract, it would have augured what we now regard as the modern formulation for the impossibility doctrine. Such a concept would have appeared more than radical at that time. It is not remarkable that the court resorted to a fiction — the fiction of an *implied condition*. The notion of an implied condition is unfortunate because it suggests that the contract contains an unstated condition intended by the parties. In fact, the implied condition is a device to permit courts to arrive at results which they deem desirable on policy grounds.[7] Other courts continued the fiction of the implied condition so as to make it appear that they were merely interpreting the contract. Whether the fiction was ever needed, it is generally recognized as undesirable today since there is little doubt as to what the courts are actually doing. When an unforeseen, supervening event changes the circumstances surrounding the contract to such an extent that a greatly increased burden will be imposed upon the promisor, a court must decide whether the promisor must still be liable to perform or whether the promisee will be frustrated in relation to his reasonable expectations. Modern courts now recognize that they are *allocating the risk* of the occurrence of the supervening event to one of the parties when they decide that the promisor is either excused or not excused because of the

---

[5]3B. & S. 826, 32 L.J., Q.B. 164 [1863].

[6]*Id.*, at 833.

[7]Justice Holmes tells us that, "You can always imply a condition in a contract. But why imply it? It is because of some belief as to the practice of the community or of a class, or because of some opinion as to policy, or, in short because of some attitude of [the court] upon a matter not capable of ... founding exact logical conclusions." Holmes, *The Path of the Law*, 10 HARV. L. REV. 457, 466 (1897).

changed circumstances.[8] To place a label of "implied condition" upon this process of risk allocation was unnecessary and dangerous in that it allowed a court to merely state a conclusion with little or no manifestation of its decision-making process. As usual, there is no analysis in labels. The results of these cases, however, clearly indicate a judicial recognition that the task is one of superimposed risk allocation where there is no manifestation of intention concerning supervening events that were not assumed by the parties at the time they made the contract. At times, this process may seem to require the wisdom of Solomon.[9]

We will see that the modern doctrine of impossibility of performance is often referred to as the doctrine of impracticability. Where a contract can be performed, but supervening events have made that performance excessively costly, overtures of the nemesis, *forfeiture,* may suggest that the performance be excused on the footing that the performance, while still possible, has become impracticable and should be excused on that basis. From its inception, the concept of impracticability was treated as extremely dangerous and, as will be seen, the modern judicial reaction clings to that view. To permit a promisor to be excused from performance because the cost of his performance has risen even to extreme levels appeared to threaten the fundamental concept of the social institution of contract. Certainly, any promisor must be said to have anticipated that the contract might prove to be unprofitable, even extremely unprofitable. He should, therefore, be said to have assumed that risk.[10] Occasionally, however, extreme unprofitableness results from factors abnormal and unexpected, and under circumstances which make it unreasonable to suppose that the promisor would have been expected to assume the risk of it, had the possibility been envisaged. In such a case it would seem to be only fair to hold that the promisor is excused. Several courts have reached this conclusion albeit the rationales have not always been totally acceptable. Thus, where a contractor promised to take from a certain tract of land all the gravel that he would need to perform a certain job, and later, after he had taken about half of what he needed, discovered that the rest, while existent, lay below the water level and could be removed and used only at a cost twelve times as great as would otherwise have been the case, it was held that performance was excused.[11] The court justified its decision by saying that the case

---

[8]"It is implicit in the doctrine of impossibility ... that certain risks are so unusual and have such severe consequences that they must have been beyond the scope of the assignment of risks inherent in the contract, that is, beyond the agreement made by the parties." Mishara Constr. Co. v. Transit-Mixed Concrete Corp., 365 Mass. 122, 310 N.E.2d 363, 367 (1974).

[9] *See* American Trading & Prod. Corp. v. Shell Int'l Marine, Ltd., 453 F.2d 939, 946 (5th Cir. 1972), citing 6 Corbin § 1333, at 372 (1962).

[10]*See* Megan v. Updike Grain Corp., 94 F.2d 551 (8th Cir. 1938) (promise to pay rent for grain elevator not excused when unexpected change in rail tariffs caused diversion of so much grain from a certain market as to render leased elevator practically worthless. The court, however, emphasized that the lessee must have been aware of the possibility of the change in tariffs when he took the lease since the I.C.C. had already indicated that it might put such a change into effect); Straus v. Kazemekas, 100 Conn. 581, 124 A. 234 (1924), commented on in 34 Yale L.J. 91 (1924) (contract to purchase Russian rubles to be delivered as soon as possible after the lifting of an existing embargo on their importation not excused when the embargo was continued for about two years although the price of rubles had dropped very materially).

[11]Mineral Park Land Co. v. Howard, 172 Cal. 289, 156 P. 458 (1916). *See also* Fisher v. United States Fid. & Guar. Co., 313 Ill. App. 66, 39 N.E.2d 67 (1942). In Powers v. Siats, 244 Minn. 515,

was not one in which performance was merely more expensive than antici-pated; rather, the case fell within one of the traditional exceptions to the general rule that performance is not excused.[12] The court suggested that, in legal contemplation, the specific gravel contracted for did not exist, thereby placing the facts within the recognized exception — the subject matter did not exist. The court managed this effect by insisting that the special circum-stances made it impracticable for the promisor to remove the gravel and, therefore, the gravel could be said not to exist. The court was attempting to convert the case into a typical one where the general rule disallowing excuse for impossibility was subject to a recognized exception. Though this case is generally recognized as the modern foundation of the doctrine of impractica-bility, had the court not attempted to squeeze the case into one of the recog-nized exceptions, it could have made a more significant contribution to the new concept of impracticability as an excuse for nonperformance. Such a view, however, would have been contrary to the strict position of other courts.[13] Again, the question is one of risk allocation. It was inevitable that the modern doctrine of impracticability would recognize this fundamental principle. It is important to consider the modern doctrine before proceeding to analyze the traditional "exceptions" to the general principle that impossibility/impracti-cability will not excuse nonperformance so that the analysis of those tradi-tional categories can combine the common law perceptions which coexist with the modern perceptions of the doctrine.

B. *The Impracticability Concept — Uniform Commercial Code and Restate-ment 2d.*

The UCC contains a broad concept of excusable nonperformance:

> Except so far as a seller may have assumed a greater obligation ... (a) delay in delivery or non-delivery in whole or in part by a seller ... is not a breach of his duty under a contract for sale if performance as agreed has been made impracticable by the occurrence of a contingency the non-oc-currence of which was a basic assumption on which the contract was made....[14]

The application of this principle to contracts beyond the sale-of-goods cate-gory to which Article 2 of the UCC applies is enhanced by the virtually identical language in the RESTATEMENT 2d which applies to other types of contracts.[15] The Code section is designed to state a general principle of excus-

---

70 N.W.2d 344, 349 (1955), the court states: "A mere difficulty of performance does not ordinarily excuse the promisor, but where a great increase in expense or difficulty is caused by a circum-stance not only unanticipated but inconsistent with the facts which the parties obviously assumed as likely to continue, the basic reason for excusing the promisor from liability may be present." *See* FIRST RESTATEMENT § 454 (1932).

[12] Common law courts insisted on retaining the general principle that performance is not excus-able while they allowed certain exceptions to that rule such as the destruction or unavailability of the subject matter, the death or incapacity of a promisor in a personal service contract, and a supervening act of state where performance became impossible by operation of law. These "excep-tions" are found in modern form in the RESTATEMENT 2d §§ 261-263.

[13] *See infra* § 113.

[14] UCC § 2-615(a).

[15] "Where, after a contract is made, a party's performance is made impracticable without his fault by the occurrence of an event the non-occurrence of which was a basic assumption on which

able nonperformance rather than a rigid principle subject to exceptions,[16] a concept shared by the RESTATEMENT 2d.[17] Both the Code and RESTATEMENT 2d make it clear that the new principle is subject to the assumption of greater liability through the agreement of the parties.[18] Courts have begun to appreciate the change from the narrow defense of impossibility to the broader principle of impracticability.[19] The fiction of the implied condition has been discarded to leave courts unfettered in their efforts to allocate risks that were not anticipated by the parties.[20] Notwithstanding these valiant efforts, it must be reported that the new principle has been anything but an unbridled success.

C. *Conceptual Problems in the New Impracticability Principle.*

1. Angular Phraseology.

Among the problems encountered in the interpretation and construction of the UCC principle, the obvious problem is one of the angular language of the Code section emulated by the RESTATEMENT 2d — "performance ... made impracticable by the occurrence of a contingency the nonoccurrence of which was a basic assumption on which the contract was made." One court suggests, "The latter part of the test seems a somewhat complicated way of putting Professor Corbin's question of how much risk the promisor assumed."[21]

2. Application to Buyers as Well as Sellers.

Another problem in the UCC formulation is that, by its terms, the Code section excuses only sellers whose performance becomes commercially impracticable though a comment suggests the possible application of the section to buyers.[22] The RESTATEMENT 2d section avoids this problem by referring to "a party."[23] Several courts have concluded that the UCC section should apply to

---

the contract was made, his duty to render that performance is discharged, unless the language or the circumstances indicated the contrary." RESTATEMENT 2d § 261.

[16] Comment 2 to § 2-615 insists that the section deliberately refrains from an exhaustive expression of contingencies, i.e., it applies to all cases that can be brought within the scope of the section.

[17] *See* RESTATEMENT 2d § 261 comment a.

[18] UCC § 2-615: "Except so far as a seller may have assumed a greater obligation...." *See also* comment 8 to § 2-615. RESTATEMENT 2d § 261: "[U]nless the language or the circumstances indicate the contrary." *See also* comment c to this section. The RESTATEMENT 2d's expression of "language or circumstances" suggests the broad definition of "agreement" in § 1-201(3) of the UCC which insists that, in addition to language, the "agreement" contains the implication of the parties' intention from all of the relevant circumstances including prior course of dealing, trade usage, and course of performance.

[19] *See, e.g.,* Harper & Assoc. v. Printers, Inc., 46 Wash. App. 417, 730 P.2d 733 (1986) (Narrow defense of impossibility has been subsumed in the more commercially oriented and broader categories of impracticability).

[20] *See* Transatlantic Fin. Corp. v. United States, 363 F.2d 312 (D.C. Cir. 1966) (the doctrine has been freed from the earlier fictional and unrealistic strictures of the implied term).

[21] United States v. Wegematic Corp., 360 F.2d 674, 676 (2d Cir. 1966).

[22] *See* UCC § 2-615 comment 9. The omission of buyers in the section is said to have occurred because the concept of excuse by frustration of purpose (to be discussed later in this section) had been generally accepted as to sellers but the law with respect to buyers in this area was in a state of development. Thus, the Code drafters decided to leave the matter unsettled but "open-ended." 2 G. GILMORE, SECURITY INTERESTS IN PERSONAL PROPERTY § 41.7, at 1105 (1965).

[23] RESTATEMENT 2d § 261.

buyers as well as sellers.[24] The remaining conceptual problems are inherent in the fundamental question, what elements must be shown to allow for the excuse of impracticability?

3. Risk Allocation by Agreement — *Force Majeure.*

In approaching the question of impracticability, courts typically consider whether the parties have allocated the risk either expressly or impliedly by their agreement.[25] Initially, it should be emphasized that both the UCC and the RESTATEMENT 2d allow the parties to allocate risks by their contract in a fashion that differs from the risk allocation formulas that would apply absent such agreements.[26] Parties may, for example, have included a price formula which the court views as the allocation of the risk by agreement.[27] The parties may have included a *force majeure* clause, i.e., a clause listing a series of events such as earthquakes, storms, floods, and other natural disasters ("Acts of God") as well as other kinds of events such as wars and civil strife that the parties have agreed upon as excuses for nonperformance.[28] Since omniscience is reserved for God, no matter how complete such clauses may appear, an unlisted event may occur upon which the promisor may base her claim for excusable nonperformance. A guide to interpretation could play havoc with such a claim if the clause is drafted without deference to that guide.[29] Since contracts for the sale of goods are subject to the automatic protection of the

---

[24]*See, e.g.,* Lawrance v. Elmore Bean Warehouse, 108 Idaho 892, 702 P.2d 930 (1985); Northern Ill. Gas Co. v. Energy Coop., 461 N.E.2d 1049 (Ill. App. 1984).

[25]*See* Martin v. Vector Co., 498 F.2d 16 (1st Cir. 1974).

[26] UCC § 2-615 begins with, "Except so far as a seller may have assumed a greater obligation...." As suggested earlier in this section, courts are willing to apply the section to buyers as well as sellers. The RESTATEMENT 2d (§ 261) conditions its risk allocation formula as follows: "[U]nless the language or the circumstances indicate the contrary." While the UCC language may be seen to suggest that the agreement may permit a party to assume a "greater obligation" but not a lesser obligation than that suggested by the Code formula (*see* Hawkland, *The Energy Crisis and Section 2-615 of the Uniform Commercial Code,* 79 Com. L.J. 75 (1974)), there is language in the UCC at § 2-615 comment 8, suggesting the possibility of "express agreements as to exemptions designed to enlarge upon or supplant the provision of this section...." Moreover, courts have sanctioned agreements enlarging the exemptions, i.e., permitting a lesser obligation than expressed in the Code formula. *See* Interpetrol Bermuda Ltd. v. Kaiser Aluminum Int'l Corp., 719 F.2d 992 (9th Cir. 1983); Eastern Airlines, Inc. v. McDonnell Douglas Corp., 532 F.2d 957 (5th Cir. 1976). The *Interpetrol* case, however, stresses the fact that general language in such clauses ought not to be interpreted as expanding excuses not provided for by the UCC.

[27] Publicker Indus. v. Union Carbide Corp., 17 U.C.C. Rep. 989 (E.D. Pa. 1975) (ceiling provision in price formula was an intentional allocation of risk). *See,* however, Aluminum Co. of Am. v. Essex Groups, Inc., 499 F. Supp. 53 (W.D. Pa. 1980) (price formula did not allocate the risk).

[28] Such clauses may also include strikes or other labor disputes. The RESTATEMENT 2d does not address the effect of a strike on the duty of performance as did the FIRST RESTATEMENT § 461 ill. 7. The RESTATEMENT 2d expressly omits that treatment "because the parties often provide for this eventuality and, where they do not, it is particularly difficult to suggest a proper result without a detailed statement of all of the circumstances." RESTATEMENT 2d Reporter's Note, final paragraph of comment d. *See also* Mishara Constr. Co. v. Transit-Mixed Concrete Corp., 365 Mass. 122, 310 N.E.2d 363, 70 A.L.R.3d 1259 (1974) (issue of impossibility due to labor dispute was properly submitted to jury).

[29] The *ejusdem generis* rule or guide suggests that where general language follows the enumeration of specific items, the general words are to be construed to refer only to items of the same kind or class as those enumerated. It is, therefore, wise to follow the listing of specific items with a phrase such as "including but not limited to" so as to preserve the general protection that would be automatically afforded under a UCC or RESTATEMENT 2d formulation of impracticability. *See* Eastern Air Lines v. McDonnell Douglas Corp., 532 F.2d 957 (5th Cir. 1976).

UCC principle of impracticability, care should be taken to avoid the unwitting effect of diminishing that protection through less than careful drafting.[30] It should also be noted that, even with a properly drafted *force majeure* clause, the excusing event must not be within the reasonable control of the party asserting the excuse.[31] Prior course of dealing, trade usage, or course of performance can also provide a manifestation of the parties' intention to allocate the risk. Absent any manifestation of intention, however, the court is forced to pursue the more difficult process of judicially imposed risk allocation. It must proceed to examine whether there was an unanticipated supervening event that caused the impracticability.

4. Supervening Event — "Unforeseen" or "Unexpected."

The second stage in the process is the discovery of a supervening event, a contingency, that was not anticipated by the parties at the time of contract formation and *caused* the impracticability. It is important to note that impracticability is typically associated with an event that occurs after contract formation — during the performance stage of the contract. As will be seen later in this discussion, impracticability may also exist at the time of contract formation and the analysis applied to existing impracticability is quite similar to that applied to supervening impracticability. At this point, however, it is important to concentrate on supervening or post-formation impracticability. We have said that the supervening impracticability must not have been anticipated at the time of contract formation. An *unanticipated* event may be one that is simply *unexpected,* or it may be one that is *unforeseen.* Comments to the UCC section suggest that the supervening event must be *unforeseen*[32] and some courts cling to that characterization.[33] The RESTATEMENT 2d, however, emphasizes the requirement that the nonoccurrence of the supervening event must be a "basic assumption" of the parties to the contract and concludes, "The fact that the event was foreseeable, or even foreseen, does not necessarily compel a conclusion that its nonoccurrence was not a basic assumption."[34] Perhaps the best known case dealing with the new concept of impracticability substitutes "unexpected" for "unforeseen" and other authorities are in ac-

---

[30] To the extent that courts are influenced by the virtually identical formulation in § 261 of the RESTATEMENT 2d, the same may be said of contracts that are not within the scope of Article 2 of the UCC. *See* Indiana-Kentucky Elec. Co. v. Green, 476 N.E.2d 141 (Ind. App. 1985) (considering whether the phrase "impossible or not impracticable" incorporates the impracticability standard of UCC § 2-615).

[31] *See* Nissho-Iwai Co. v. Occidental Crude Sales, Inc., 729 F.2d 1530 (5th Cir. 1984) where the court, applying California law, suggests that the "reasonable control" limitation has two aspects: (1) a party may not affirmatively cause the event that prevents his performance, and (2) a party may not rely on an excusing event if he could have taken reasonable steps to avoid it because a force majeure event does not prevent performance if that event could have been avoided by the party asserting the excuse.

[32] *See* UCC § 2-615 comment 1: "Unforeseen supervening circumstances not within the contemplation of the parties." *See also* comment 4 referring to an "unforeseen shutdown of major sources of supply or the like."

[33] *See* Waldinger v. C. B. S. Group Eng'rs., Inc., 775 F.2d 781, 786 (7th Cir. 1985); Barbarossa & Sons v. Iten Chevrolet, Inc., 265 N.W.2d 655, 658-61 (Minn. 1978). *See also* Eastern Air Lines, Inc. v. Gulf Oil Corp., 415 F. Supp. 429 (S.D. Fla. 1975).

[34] RESTATEMENT 2d § 261 comment b. *See also* § 265 comment a.

cord.[35] If "foreseeable" is equated with "conceivable," nothing is unforesee-able. An application of the tort standard of foreseeability would be more than confusing.[36] The foreseeability standard in contract remedies which will be considered in the next chapter does not augur success. There is simply no escape from the hard question of risk allocation.[37] If a risk was anticipated or expected, it would be more than difficult to find a basis for excusable nonper-formance. If a risk was foreseeable, it is reasonable to assume that the parties contracted on that basis. That assumption, however, may not be warranted if the foreseeable event was an improbable contingency that reasonable parties may not have expressly or impliedly addressed in their agreement.

5. When Is Performance Impracticable? — Extent of Cost Increase.

Before considering the magnitude of the loss that is necessary to meet the third and final stage of a successful impracticability defense, it must be re-membered that, regardless of the extent of the loss, if that loss was not *caused* by an unforeseeable or unexpected supervening event which changed the ba-sic assumption or foundation of the contract, nonperformance will not be ex-cused. Even if an unforeseen event had occurred and the promisor had suf-fered a loss great enough to suggest commercial impracticability, the inability of the promisor to prove that the loss resulted from the supervening event as contrasted with the promisor's actions would prevent a successful use of the defense.[38] As a comment to the UCC suggests, "Increased cost alone does not excuse performance unless the rise in cost *is due to some unforeseen contin-gency which alters the essential nature of the contract.*" [39]

Assuming the existence of an unforeseen or unexpected supervening event which causes the promisor to suffer "increased cost" or some loss, the question arises, how extensive must a loss be to create a successful impracticability defense? Both the UCC and the RESTATEMENT 2d insist that the increased cost of performance must amount to considerably more than a change in the de-

---

[35] "Foreseeability or even recognition of a risk does not necessarily prove its allocation.... Parties to a contract are not always able to provide for all the possibilities of which they are aware, sometimes because they cannot agree, often simply because they are too busy. Moreover, that some abnormal risk was contemplated is probative but does not necessarily establish an allocation of the risk of the contingency which actually occurs." Transatlantic Fin. Corp. v. United States, 363 F.2d 312, 318 (2d Cir. 1972). This view is expressly adopted in Opera Co. of Boston v. Trap Found. for Performing Arts, 817 F.2d 1094 (4th Cir. 1987) and another well known impracticability case, Aluminum Co. of Am. v. Essex Group, Inc., 499 F. Supp. 53 (1980). The same view is adopted in the RESTATEMENT 2d at § 261 and comments b and c thereto.

[36] *See* Eastern Air Lines v. McDonnell Douglas Corp. 532 F.2d 957, 992, n.97 (5th Cir. 1976).

[37] *See* Posner & Rosenfeld, *Impossibility and Related Doctrines in Contract Law: An Economic Analysis,* 6 J. LEGAL STUD. 83, 98-100 (1977).

[38] *See* Iowa Elec. Light & Power Co. v. Atlas Corp., 467 F. Supp. 129 (N.D. Iowa 1978), *rev'd on other grounds,* 603 F.2d 1308 (8th Cir. 1979). The court found that the loss suffered was insuffi-cient to excuse the defendant's performance but suggested that the defendant had also failed to prove what share of the cost increase was attributable to unforeseen conditions and what share was attributable to its own corporate decisions. *See also* Eastern Air Lines v. Gulf Oil Corp., 415 F. Supp. 419, 441 (S.D. Fla. 1975).

[39] UCC § 2-615 comment 4 (emphasis added). *See* Lawrance v. Elmore Bean Warehouse, 108 Idaho 892, 702 P.2d 930 (1985); Northern Ill. Gas Co. v. Energy Coop., 461, N.E.2d 1049 (Ill. App. 1984); Resources Inv. Corp. v. Enron Corp., 669 F. Supp. 1038 (D. Colo. 1987). *See also* American Trading & Prod. Corp v. Shell Int'l Marine Ltd., 453 F.2d 939, 944 (2d Cir. 1972) citing first edition of this book.

gree of difficulty of performance to constitute impracticability. For example, a shortage of raw materials (caused by an unforeseen or unexpected supervening event such as war) must be a "severe" shortage.[40] Just because performance is made "impractical" does not mean that it is "impracticable."[41] The performance of a supplier of goods or services whose labor, construction, or raw material costs have risen, even substantially, is not impracticable since this is precisely the kind of risk that a fixed price contract is supposed to cover.[42] The First RESTATEMENT suggested that the loss must be "extreme and unreasonable" and, through its illustrations, indicated that tenfold increases or costs multiplied fifty times would constitute such "extreme and unreasonable" burdens.[43] Cases have held that increases of fourteen percent,[44] thirty one and one-half percent,[45] fifty percent,[46] or even a doubling of the cost of performance[47] would be insufficient to meet the requirement of a sufficient increase in cost even if that increase were caused by an unforeseen or unexpected contingency. On the other hand, a ninety-three percent increase,[48] a tenfold increase,[49] and a seventy-five million dollar out-of-pocket loss[50] have been held sufficient.

6. Impracticable Performance Versus Ability to Perform — "Objective" Versus "Subjective" — Burden of Proof.

Related to the size of the loss is the question of the ability or capacity of the promisor to perform as contrasted with the impracticability of performance itself. The ability of a particular promisor to perform would focus upon the particular promisor, sometimes called a "subjective" test, whereas a concern for whether performance, itself, was impracticable would be an "objective" inquiry, regardless of the particular promisor's capacity or resources. It is clear that courts will not excuse a promisor who simply cannot perform even

---

[40] See UCC § 2-615 comment 4; RESTATEMENT 2d § 261 comment d.

[41] RESTATEMENT 2d § 261 comment d.

[42] RESTATEMENT 2d § 261 comment d; UCC § 2-615 comment 4: "Neither is a rise or a collapse in the market in itself a justification, for that is exactly the type of business risk which business contracts made at fixed prices are intended to cover." See Lawrance v. Elmore Bean Warehouse, 108 Idaho 892, 702 P.2d 930 (1985) (market shifts or financial instability do not change one's performance); Maple Farms, Inc. v. City Sch. Dist., 76 Misc. 2d 1080, 1805, 352 N.Y.S.2d 784, 790 (1974) ("There is no precise point, though such could conceivably be reached, at which an increase in price of raw goods above the norm would be so disproportionate to the risk assumed as to amount to [impracticability] in a commercial sense."). See also In re M & M Transp. Co., 13 Bankr. 861, 869 (S.D.N.Y. 1981) citing § 202 of the third edition of this book to this effect.

[43] FIRST RESTATEMENT §§ 454 and 460, ills. 2 and 3. RESTATEMENT 2d § 261 comment d suggests, "Performance may be impracticable because extreme and unreasonable difficulty, expense, injury or loss to one of the parties will be involved."

[44] Transatlantic Fin. Corp. v. United States, 363 F.2d 312 (D.C. Cir. 1966).

[45] American Trading & Prod. Corp. v. Shell Int'l Marine Ltd., 453 F.2d 939 (2d Cir. 1972).

[46] Ocean Tramp Tankers Corp. v. V/O Sovfracht, (The Eugenia), 2 Q.B. 226 [1964].

[47] Tsakiroglou & Co. v. Noblee Thorl G. m. b. H., 2 Q.B. 348 [1960].

[48] Northern Corp. v. Chugach Elec. Ass'n, 518 P.2d 76, modified on other grounds, 523 P.2d 1243 (Alaska 1974). See, however, Publicker Indus. v. Union Carbide Corp., 17 U.C.C. Rep. 989 (E.D. Pa. 1975) (not aware of any cases where something less than 100% cost increase has been held to make a seller's performance impracticable).

[49] Mineral Park Land Co. v. Howard, 172 Cal. 289, 293, 256 P. 458, 460 (1916). This case is often viewed as the modern judicial basis for the recognition of impracticability versus impossibility.

[50] Aluminum Co. of Am. v. Essex Group, Inc., 499 F. Supp. 53 (W.D. Pa. 1980).

though the performance is objectively practicable.[51] Thus, a promisor who becomes insolvent will not be excused because his subjective ability to perform has become impracticable.[52] If, however, the overall resources of the promisor are quite substantial, should such a greater ability to absorb loss be considered in determining the impracticability of the performance, or should the particular transaction at issue be the sole guide? If the overall ability of the promisor to sustain a huge loss were relevant, the standard would be subjective. The better reasoned opinions maintain the consistent standard of refusing to consider such ability just as courts have refused to excuse nonperformance because of subjective inability. Instead, they focus on the reasonableness of the expenditure at issue.[53]

It is clear that courts will place the burden of proving impossibility of performance[54] or impracticability of performance[55] on the party claiming excuse.

7. Implementation of the Impracticability Standard — Illustrative Cases — Energy Cost and "Suez" Cases — Long Term Supply Contracts and Gross Inequity Clauses.

We have examined the three elements essential for the establishment of impracticability which have been repeated since they were initially set forth in *Transatlantic Financing Corp. v. United States* [56]: (1) the occurrence of a contingency, (2) the nonoccurrence of which was a basic assumption upon which the contract was made, and (3) the contingency has caused performance to become impracticable. It has proven at least impracticable to discover these necessary ingredients in virtually any attempted application of the test. Consider, for example, the prototype impracticability case involving a rise in energy prices caused by the OPEC cartel. In the 1960's the Westinghouse Corporation had entered into a number of uranium supply contracts in conjunction with its desire to sell nuclear power plants. While the uranium supply contracts differed from customer to customer, they were typically requirements contracts under which Westinghouse agreed to have uranium supplied

---

[51] *See* Transatlantic Fin. Corp. v. United States, 363 F.2d 312, 319, n.13 (D.C. Cir. 1966) ("The issue of impracticability should no doubt be an objective determination of whether the promise can reasonably be performed rather than a subjective inquiry into the promisor's capability of performing as agreed."). Symposium, *The Uniform Commercial Code and Contract Law: Some Selected Problems*, 105 U. PA. L. REV. 880, 887 (1957). "Dealers should not be excused because of less than normal capabilities. But if both parties are aware of a dealer's limited capabilities, no objective determination would be completed without taking into account this fact." *Accord,* RESTATEMENT 2d § 261 comment e which prefers not to use the terms "subjective" and "objective." Jennie-O-Foods v. United States, 580 F.2d 400 (Ct. Cl. 1978) relies upon this RESTATEMENT 2d section and comment.

[52] *See, e.g.,* Baldi Constr. Eng'g, Inc. v. Wheel Awhile, Inc., 263 Md. 670, 284 A.2d 248 (1971).

[53] *See* Alimenta (U.S.A.), Inc. v. Cargill, Inc., 861 F.2d 650 (11th Cir. 1988); Asphalt Int'l, Inc. v. Enterprise Shipping Corp., 667 F.2d 261 (2d Cir. 1981). *See,* however, Missouri Pub. Serv. Co. v. Peabody Coal Co., 583 S.W.2d 721 (Mo. App. 1979).

[54] Nan Ya Plastics Corp., U.S.A. v. Philip R. DeSantis Nan Ya Plastics Corp., 377 S.E.2d 388 (Va. 1989); Ocean Air Tradeways, Inc. v. Arkay Realty Corp., 480 F.2d 1112 (9th Cir. 1973); Calabrese v. Rexall Drug & Chem. Co., 218 Cal. App. 2d 774, 32 Cal. Rptr. 665 (1963).

[55] Iowa Elec. Light & Power Co. v. Atlas Corp., 467 F. Supp. 129 (N.D. Iowa 1978), *rev'd on other grounds,* 603 F.2d 1301 (8th Cir. 1979).

[56] 363 F.2d 312, 315 (1966).

to its nuclear power plant customers for a fixed period. At that time, utility companies were wary of converting to nuclear power for a number of reasons, including but not limited to their lack of understanding of all of the risks associated with such conversions.[57] When uranium and other energy costs skyrocketed, Westinghouse informed its customers that it was excused in whole or in part from performing the energy supply contracts. The costs to Westinghouse and other energy suppliers in settling these lawsuits were more than substantial.[58] Efforts by energy suppliers to defend their refusal to perform these contracts through the use of the impracticability defense have been notoriously unsuccessful for one or more of the following reasons: (a) the contingency that occurred (OPEC action) was considered foreseeable or not unexpected; (b) even if the contingency had been unforeseen or unexpected, the loss suffered was not sufficient to constitute impracticable performance; (c) the party asserting impracticability failed to show that impracticability was the sole or substantial cause of the increased cost of performance.[59] Similarly, in a series of cases involving the closing of the Suez Canal by the Egyptian Government resulting in numerous actions involving the impracticability excuse,[60] neither the unforeseeability nor sufficient loss factor could be established to demonstrate impracticability.

A number of cases, including some of the energy cases already mentioned, involved long-term supply contracts. In what has become a singular exception to the general refusal of courts to recognize the impracticability defense in such a contract, a court discovered the elements of impracticability where a converter of alumina complained that it would lose in excess of $60 million over the life of the contract because a price formula was based on an assumption that was incorrect.[61] The case is a dubious precedent, however, since it is essentially a mutual mistake case and there is a serious question as to whether the appellate court would have agreed with findings of a lack of foreseeability and sufficient loss to constitute impracticability.[62] Courts ap-

---

[57] See this attitude reflected in Florida Power & Light Co. v. Westinghouse Elec. Corp., 31 U.C.C. Rep. 930 (E.D. Va. 1981).

[58] The October 21, 1976 issue of the Wall Street Journal (page 2, cols. 3 & 4) reports that the Westinghouse Annual Report disclosed settlements of 14 lawsuits exceeding $700 million. A number of other energy supply cases were brought against other suppliers.

[59] Westinghouse Elec. Corp. Uranium Contracts Litig., 517 F. Supp. 440 (E.D. Va. 1981) (not shown that Westinghouse lost money on entire undertaking). See also Missouri Pub. Serv. Co. v. Peabody Coal Co., 583 S.W.2d 721 (Mo. App. 1979) (imposition of the Arab oil embargo was foreseeable and may have contributed to the appreciation in value of promisor's coal reserves); Iowa Elec. Light & Power Co. v. Atlas Corp., 467 F. Supp. 129 (N.D. Iowa 1978), rev'd on other grounds, 603 F.2d 1301 (8th Cir. 1979) (some unforeseen factors but others were foreseeable and some of the increase in cost to Atlas resulted from internal decisions).

[60] See American Trading & Prod. Corp. v. Shell Int'l Marine Ltd., 453 F.2d 939 (2d Cir. 1972); Transatlantic Fin. Corp. v. United States, 363 F.2d 312 (1966); Glidden Co. v. Hellenic Lines, Ltd., 275 F.2d 253 (1960); Ocean Tramp Tankers Corp. v. V/O Sovfracht (The Eugenia), 2 Q.B. 226 [1964]; Tsakiroglou & Co. v. Noblee Thorl G. m. b. H., 2 Q.B. 348 [1960].

[61] Aluminum Co. of Am. v. Essex Group, Inc., 499 F. Supp. 53 (W.D. Pa. 1980).

[62] Compared to other cases, the court applied an extremely liberal concept of "commercial" foreseeability and found that the $60 million loss over 16 years would be sufficient to meet the requirement of a sufficient loss. The opinion must be read in the context of mutual mistake which does not require the same level of loss to permit avoidance of the contract, i.e., mutual mistake only requires a material effect upon performance. See Farnsworth, Brickell & Chawaga, Relief for Mutual Mistake and Impracticability, 1 J.L. & Com. 1, 26-29 (1981). Settlement of this case

pear to be particularly timid about applying the UCC formula in such cases because such contracts are often viewed as carefully negotiated, thereby suggesting that all risks have been assumed. Any suggestion that courts should adjust such a contract creates seemingly insuperable difficulties because courts feel that they lack the information and expertise to make such adjustments.[63] Considerable scholarly effort has been expended on various suggestions for using the impracticability concept in such contracts.[64]

The general refusal of courts to sanction the impracticability defense in long-term supply contracts has led to the inclusion of "gross inequity" clauses, sometimes called "good faith adjustment" clauses.[65] The clauses are designed to prevent hardship to one of the parties due to economic conditions not contemplated by the parties.[66] It is possible to insert a clause that would require renegotiation of the contract where economic conditions cause only a material change in the original agreement, i.e., a change that would not amount to excuse for impracticability but one that would meet the necessary extent of change under a mutual mistake analysis.[67] It is, however, one thing to conceive of such a clause; it may be quite another to convince the other party to the contract to agree to it. At the time of this writing, the use of the impracticability defense in long term supply contracts where a supervening event has changed the risks more than substantially is, at least, impracticable.

D. Existing Impracticability — Mistake Analysis Compared — Effect.

To this point, we have been considering situations where an event which the parties assumed would not occur has occurred *after* the formation of the contract, causing performance to become impracticable. The event or contingency making performance impracticable, however, may exist at the time of contract formation, i.e., it may be a situation of *existing* impracticability rather than supervening impracticability. With only one modification, cases of existing impracticability are analyzed as are cases of supervening impracticability. In a well-known case,[68] a builder agreed to remove an estimated 114,000 cubic yards of gravel from land to construct a bridge. When 50,000 yards were removed, the builder discovered that the remainder was under

occurred after the somewhat unusual request by the United States Court of Appeals for the Third Circuit that the parties negotiate.

[63] *See* Hillman, *Court Adjustment of Long-Term Contracts: An Analysis Under Modern Contract Law,* 1987 DUKE L.J. 1.

[64] *See* Hillman, *ibid.*; Scott, *Conflict and Cooperation in Long-Term Contracts,* 75 CALIF. L. REV. 2005 (1987); Gillette, *Commercial Rationality and the Duty to Adjust Long-Term Contracts,* 69 MINN. L. REV. 521 (1985); Speidel, *Court-Imposed Price Adjustments Under Long-Term Supply Contracts,* 76 Nw. U.L. REV. 369 (1981); Macneil, *Contracts: Adjustment of Long-Term Economic Relations Under Classical, Neo-Classical and Relational Contract Law,* 72 Nw. U.L. REV. 854 (1978).

[65] *See* Consumers Power Co. v. Nuclear Fuel Servs., 509 F. Supp. 201 (W.D.N.Y. 1981).

[66] In Georgia Power Co. v. Cimarron Coal Corp., 526 F.2d 101, 103 (6th Cir.), *cert. denied,* 425 U.S. 952 (1975), the clause read: "Any gross proven inequity that may result in unusual economic conditions not contemplated by the parties at the time of the execution of this Agreement may be corrected by mutual consent. Each party shall in the case of a claim of gross inequity furnish the other with whatever documentary evidence may be necessary to assist in effecting a settlement."

[67] For an example of such a clause see Murray, *Long-Term Supply Contracts: Foreseeing the Unforeseeable,* 2 EASTERN MINERAL LAW FOUND. (1981).

[68] *See* Mineral Park Land Co. v. Howard, 172 Cal. 289, 156 P. 458 (1916).

water and would cost ten times the normal cost of removal. The remainder of the performance was held to be impracticable.[69] The elements of supervening impracticability must be shown. Thus, performance must have been made impracticable because of an unforeseen fact not due to the fault of the party asserting impracticability and not within the risk such party expressly or impliedly assumed. The modification of the analysis relates to the unforeseeability requirement. The party asserting *existing* impracticability must have had no reason to know of the fact causing impracticability at the time of contract formation.[70]

A difficult problem involving existing impracticability occurs where a party undertakes a performance requiring a technological breakthrough. If such a party has reason to know the state of the art at the time of contract formation, he is assuming the risk of such breakthrough and his failure to achieve it will not be excused through impracticability.[71] If, however, a party simply agrees to build a device according to assumptions or plans made by the other party and the builder has no reason to know that it is impossible to comply with such assumptions or plans, existing impracticability will be shown.[72]

The concept of existing impracticability overlaps the mutual mistake analysis. Where, at the time of formation, the parties make a mistake as to a basic assumption on which the contract which made, the contract is voidable by the adversely affected party if he can demonstrate a *material effect on the agreed exchange.*[73] To demonstrate existing impracticability, however, he must meet the more onerous standard of establishing impracticability which, as we have seen, courts are not willing to find simply on the basis of a more onerous burden, even a materially more onerous burden, on the party seeking to be excused from performance.[74]

A final difference between supervening and existing impracticability is found in their effects. If supervening impracticability is found, existing duties of performance are excused. Where existing impracticability is discovered, however, no duty arises under the contract.[75] For example, in the well-known

---

[69] *See* Sunflower Elec. Coop. v. Tomlinson Oil Co., 7 Kan. App. 131, 638 P.2d 963 (1981) (natural gas reserves depleted at time of contract formation). *See also* Faria v. Southwick, 81 Idaho 68, 337 P.2d 374 (1959).

[70] *See* RESTATEMENT 2d § 266(1). *See also* Roy v. Stephen Pontiac-Cadillac, Inc., 15 Conn. App. 101, 543 A.2d 775 (1988) (reason to know at time contract was made that truck would not be manufactured without heavy duty package); Vollmar v. CSX Transp. Co., 705 F. Supp. 1154 (E.D. Va. 1989) (reason to know of foreign exclusion at time of contract formation); *In re* Zellmer's Estate, 1 Wis. 2d 46, 82 N.W.2d 891 (1957) (reason to know that policy had lapsed at time of contract formation).

[71] *See* Aerosonic Instrument Corp., 1959 — 1 Cont. App. Dec. (CCH), Par. 2115 at 9093 (March 12, 1959) (contract to provide three tachometer testers, each tester to weigh no more than thirty pounds, a specification which had not been met to that time. When contractor delivered tachometers, each weighing 51 pounds, the Board stated that where the parties are conscious of existing facts and make their agreement on that assumption, the nonexistence of such facts does not affect the validity of the agreement.).

[72] *See* Wildinger Corp. v. Ashbrook-Simon-Hartley, Inc., 564 F. Supp. 970 (C.D. Ill. 1983) relying on ill. 10 to RESTATEMENT 2d § 266.

[73] RESTATEMENT 2d § 152(1). *See* the analysis of mistake *supra* Chapter 5, § 91.

[74] For a comparison of existing impracticability and mutual mistake, *see* Aluminum Co. of Am. v. Essex Group, Inc., 499 F. Supp. 53 (W.D. Pa. 1980). *See also* National Presto Indus. v. United States, 338 F.2d 99 (Ct. Cl. 1964).

[75] RESTATEMENT 2d § 266(1).

case involving the impracticability of removing gravel discussed above,[76] no duty to remove the remainder of the gravel was found. Where the parties contract to purchase and sell a specific item such as the used automobile owned by the seller, and at the time of formation without the knowledge or fault of either party, that automobile has been destroyed, no duty arises under the contract.[77]

§ 113. Traditional Categories of Impossibility — Impracticability.

A. *The Traditional Categories and the Modern Doctrine.*

We have seen that courts were more than reluctant to grant excuse for nonperformance of a contractual duty. But from the earliest times, they recognized certain obvious exceptions to this general rule. We have also seen that the general rule of the common law was subsumed under the modern concept of impracticability. This evolution, however, did not emasculate the common law exceptions which retain their vitality. Such exceptions as the death or incapacity of the promisor in a personal service contract, the destruction or other unavailability of specific property necessary to carry out performance, or the prevention of performance by operation of law, are now seen as specific applications of the general principle that a supervening event may excuse performance which has become impracticable.[78] The transition from a general rule precluding excuse unless the facts fell within a particular exception, to a general rule of impracticability permitting excusable nonperformance with the former exceptions becoming *applications* of the new general rule, may appear as a dramatic change. Yet, we have also seen that successful illustrations of the new impracticability standard are notoriously few. The change to this point, therefore, may be more apparent than real. The former exceptions which are now applications of the new standard remain intact. It is important to explore these categories which became valid at common law and retain their vitality under a different characterization.

B. *Death, Incapacity, or Threatened Incapacity of a Person.*

The typical contract does not require the continued existence of a particular person. Consequently, the typical contractual obligation survives the death of a party to that contract.[79] Where, however, the existence of a particular person, whether a party to the contract or a third party, is essential to the

---

[76]Mineral Park Land Co. v. Howard, 172 Cal. 289, 156 P. 458 (1916).

[77] The UCC § 2-613 suggests that casualty to *identified* goods (goods which not only exist but have been specifically designated for sale to a particular party — see UCC § 2-501) will avoid the contract if the casualty was suffered without the fault of either party before the risk of their loss passed to the buyer. Comment 2 to this section states: "The section applies whether the goods were already destroyed at the time of contracting with the knowledge of either party...." *See also* ill. 1 to RESTATEMENT 2d § 266.

[78] *See, e.g.,* RESTATEMENT 2d § 262 concerning the traditional exception of death or incapacity of a person necessary for performance which states, in comment a: "This Section states a common specific instance for the application of the rule stated in § 261 [the general principle]." comment a of § 263 concerning the destruction or deterioration of property necessary for performance and comment a of § 264 concerning prevention by governmental regulation or order state identical rationales.

[79]*See* Burka v. Patrick, 34 Md. App. 181, 366 A.2d 1070 (1976).

performance of a contractual duty, the basic assumption of that contract is that death or such incapacity to that person making performance impractical would not occur. If the death or incapacity occurred without the fault of the promisor, the promisor is excused from performance unless the language or the circumstances indicate that the risk of such death or incapacity was assumed by the promisor.[80] If the parties have not expressly indicated whether the continued existence of a particular person is essential under the contract, a court must consider all of the surrounding circumstances to make that determination.[81] Where the parties have named a particular person to establish a price for an item to be sold, they may have named that person as one of a number of reasonable experts who could establish a fair price. In that event, the death of the named person would not excuse the duty of either promisor. If, however, the parties manifest their intention to rely upon a trusted expert to place a value on an item such as a famous painting, a court may hold that the parties did not intend to be contractually bound where such a person is unavailable through death or incapacity.[82]

A reasonable apprehension that performance will result in incapacity or serious injury to the promisor or third persons will also excuse performance. Where, for example, a famous actor took reasonable measures to assure that his throat condition would not worsen, his failure to perform was excused.[83] In another well-known case, the court excused a duty to pay for conducting a baby show where an epidemic of infantile paralysis threatened the children.[84] Clearly, these cases increase the risk of performance beyond a material increase because the risk threatens the life or well-being of a promisor or third parties.

C. *Destruction or Unavailability of Essential Subject Matter — Uniform Commercial Code — "Identification."*

Ever since the famous case of *Taylor v. Caldwell*[85] where the lessor of a music hall was excused from performance upon the destruction of the hall, there has been no doubt that the destruction or unavailability of a specific thing essential to the performance of the contract excuses that performance absent fault or assumption of the risk by the promisor.[86] This was one of the

---

[80] RESTATEMENT 2d §§ 262 and 261. See Dow v. State Bank, 88 Minn. 355, 93 N.W. 121 (1903) (promise to become a member of a partnership excused by death of the promisor); Lacy v. Getman, 119 N.Y. 109, 23 N.E. 452 (1890) (promise to employ a workman who was to work under the immediate direction of his employer was excused by the employer's death); Yerrington v. Greene, 7 R.I. 589, 84 Am. Dec. 578 (1863) (promise by employer to employ a clerk and salesman excused by death of employer); Wolfe v. Howes, 20 N.Y. 197, 75 Am. Dec. 388 (1859) (promise to render personal services excused by death of promisor). If the death or incapacity of an essential person was a fact at the time of contract formation and there was no reason to know of that fact, the same analysis applies under § 266(1).

[81] See Kelly v. Thompson Land Co., 112 W. Va. 454, 164 S.E. 667 (1932) (duty to form corporation where the skill and judgment of the promoter were essential).

[82] UCC § 2-305 comment 4.

[83] Wasserman Theatrical Enters. v. Harris, 137 Conn. 371, 77 A.2d 329 (1950).

[84] Hanford v. Connecticut Fair Ass'n, 92 Conn. 621, 103 A. 838 (1918).

[85] See supra text at note 5.

[86] See Robb v. Parten, 178 Minn. 188, 220 N.W. 610 (1928), rev'd, 226 N.W. 515 (1929) (contract to install plumbing in a building excused by destruction of building); Jones-Gray Constr. Co. v. Stephens, 167 Ky. 765, 181 S.W. 659 (1916) (promise to move barn excused by accidental destruc-

generally recognized common law "exceptions" to the general principle that one must perform his promise regardless of the circumstances. The modern doctrine would suggest that, where the existence of a specific thing is necessary for performance, its failure to come into existence or its destruction or unavailability is an event the nonoccurrence of which was a basic assumption on which the contract was made.[87] Thus, it is simply an application of the general principle of impracticability.[88] Regardless of the characterization, the elements necessary for excusable nonperformance under this "exception" or "application" are unchanged. A modern illustration of the music hall case is found in a promise to provide space on a radio tower for the radio station of a seminary for a period of 99 years. When the tower was destroyed by a windstorm, the court excused the defendant's performance under the authority of the common law rationale as well as the modern rationale.[89]

While the principle finds its most frequent application in cases of contracts to sell or to hire specific property,[90] it is not limited to that type of case. Even though the specific property may be available, its use may be prevented by the nonexistence of a necessary condition to its use. Thus, where lightning caused a severe power outage which could not be remedied in time for a particular performance in an outdoor concert area, and the lack of lighting caused a hazardous condition to thousands of patrons both at the site and on pathways to parking areas, the court held that the promisor could be excused from the duty to pay for the cancelled performance.[91] Moreover, the principle has been applied to cases in which the ability of the promisor to perform depends upon the future existence of specified subject matter which fails to materialize. Where a grower contracted to sell and deliver a definite quantity of potatoes to be grown on a specified tract of land, the Court of Queen's Bench long ago held that the failure of the crop, through no fault of the grower, excused him from performing.[92] This concept has been replicated many times[93] and its principle is found in modern applications of the impracticability standard.[94] It

---

tion of barn); Angus v. Scully, 176 Mass. 357, 57 N.E. 674 (1900) (contract to move and repair a building excused by destruction of the building); Stewart v. Stone, 127 N.Y. 500, 28 N.E. 595 (1891) (contract to manufacture butter and cheese at a certain factory excused when factory was destroyed).

[87] RESTATEMENT 2d § 263.

[88] See RESTATEMENT 2d § 263 comment a. See also Olbum v. Old Home Manor, Inc., 313 Pa. Super. 99, 459 A.2d 757 (1983); Sunflower Elec. Coop. v. Tomlinson Oil Co., 7 Kan. App. 2d 131, 638 P.2d 963 (1981).

[89] Central Baptist Theological Seminary v. Entertainment Commun., Inc., 356 N.W.2d 785 (Minn. App. 1984).

[90] In addition to the cases already discussed, see, e.g., Texas v. Hogarth Shipping Co., 256 U.S. 619 (1921) (promise to furnish a specified ship for a voyage excused when the ship was requisitioned for use by the British Government); Martin Emerich Outfitting Co. v. Siegel, Cooper & Co., 237 Ill. 610, 86 N.E. 1104 (1908) (promise to permit a party to carry on a business in a specified building excused by accidental destruction of the building).

[91] Opera Co. of Boston v. Trap Found. for Performing Arts, 817 F.2d 1094 (4th Cir. 1987) (reversing lower court and remanding the action for findings concerning foreseeability). The court traces the history of impossibility and its evolution to the modern impracticability concept.

[92] Howell v. Coupland, 1 Q.B.D. 258, 46 L.J., Q.B. 147 [1876]. See also International Paper Co. v. Rockefeller, 161 App. Div. 180, 146 N.Y.S. 371 (1914) (contract for the sale of spruce to be cut from a certain tract of land was prevented when a fire destroyed the trees on that tract. Performance was excused.).

[93] See, e.g., Mercantile Co. v. Canning Co., 11 Kan. 68, 206 P. 337 (1922).

[94] See Olbum v. Old Home Manor, Inc., 313 Pa. Super. 99, 459 A.2d 757 (1983) (parties contemplated coal coming from two specific veins of coal); Sunflower Elec. Coop. v. Tomlinson Oil Co., 7

is, however, important to distinguish these cases from those in which the promisor seeks to be excused from its duty because of difficulty in finding a source of supply where the contract does not reveal any basic assumption that the goods will come from a particular source. Even if the seller anticipates a particular source of supply, unless both parties have contemplated that source as the single source from which the goods would be procured, the seller is not excused.[95] This distinction may appear mechanical at first glance. A more careful analysis proves it to be worthwhile as suggested in the UCC.

The Code deals with this concept in a section separate from its general section on impracticability as a species of impracticability which is essentially identical to the common law "exception":

"Where the contract requires for its performance goods identified when the contract is made, and the goods suffer casualty without fault of either party before the risk of losses passes to the buyer..."

"(a) if the loss is total the contract is avoided...."[96]

An understanding of this Code section requires a basic familiarity with the concepts of "identification" and risk of loss. The Code distinguishes "existing" from "identified" goods.[97] A simple illustration aids understanding of this distinction. Assume a seller of refrigerators has hundreds of manufactured refrigerators in his inventory. These refrigerators are "existing" goods because they have already been manufactured. They are not, however, "identified" since no particular refrigerator has been specifically referred to in a contract. A consumer who agrees to buy a refrigerator from a seller who has many refrigerators for sale is not agreeing to purchase an "identified" refrigerator. The consumer only expects to receive a refrigerator as described in the contract of sale and that expectation will be fulfilled if any one of many refrigerators of that model and description are delivered. Thus, the refrigerator was *not* identified at the time the contract was made. If, however, the seller had a floor model which he displayed to the consumer and the parties agreed that they would buy and sell *that particular refrigerator and no other,* the refrigerator would be identified at the time the contract was made. As in the earlier analysis of cases involving crops from a *specified* tract of land, where the item to be bought and sold is a specific item, *e.g.,* the display model refrigerator, the seller's one and only used car, or any unique item such as a famous painting, the parties have contracted for goods identified at the time the contract is made. This is a critical determination because the parties are making a basic assumption that this particular good exists and will be delivered to the buyer. If casualty to such identified goods occurs before the risk of their loss passes to the buyer and without the fault of the seller, the UCC

Kan. App. 2d 131, 638 P.2d 963 (1981) (sale of natural gas limited to a particular well and well was exhausted).

[95] Tomlinson v. Wander Seed & Bulb Co., 177 Cal. App. 2d 462, 2 Cal. Rptr. 310, 314 (1960). *See also* Gulf Oil Corp. v. F.P.C., 563 F.2d 588 (3d Cir. 1977), *cert. denied,* 434 U.S. 1062 (1978).

[96] UCC § 2-613. Subsection (b) indicates that, if the loss is partial either in quantity or quality, the buyer may treat the contract as avoided or accept the goods with due allowance for the difference in quantity or quality without further rights against the seller.

[97] UCC § 2-105. A contract to sell goods that are not both existing and identified is a contract to sell "future" goods. For a helpful case analyzing "existing and identified" goods, *see* Martin Marietta Corp. v. New Jersey Nat'l Bank, 612 F.2d 745 (3d Cir. 1979).

directs that the contract is avoided. Risk of loss will be explored more thoroughly later in this chapter. For now, it is appropriate to suggest the general principle that risk of loss will not pass to the buyer until the seller has delivered the goods to a carrier or tendered or delivered the goods to the buyer.[98] The goods, therefore, remain in the possession and control of the seller. If they are destroyed or damaged without the seller's fault and, again, if they were identified at the time of contract formation, the seller cannot hold the buyer liable because the risk of loss has not yet passed to the buyer. The buyer, however, will confront the seller's power of avoidance since the specific goods which the buyer agreed to purchase have been destroyed without the seller's fault. Since those goods no longer exist, the seller cannot deliver them. He has no duty to deliver similar or identical goods because, again, the parties agreed to purchase and sell only the particular, identified refrigerator, car, etc. If the parties had agreed to purchase and sell any one of hundreds of identical refrigerators and one of those refrigerators was destroyed without the fault of the seller, the seller would not be excused since the parties had not agreed on that specific refrigerator or, in the language of the Code, the refrigerator was not identified at the time the contract was made.[99] While the Code section may appear different from the common law analysis because the Code is structured properly in the form of a statute and uses concepts such as "identification" and risk of loss, it does not differ from the common law analysis in any significant fashion.

The application of these concepts to construction contracts achieves the same result though not without some analytical difficulty. Where a building is partially constructed under a contract and, before completion, it is destroyed without the fault of either party, absent any manifestation of intention as to how the risk should be allocated, the risk of loss will fall on the contractor if he was in complete control of the premises. In such a case, some courts suggest that no specific building was contracted for; rather, the builder was to supply a particular type of building that was not existing, much less identified, at the time the contract was formed.[1] Not only is the duty of the builder not discharged, he is also liable for breach of contract.[2] A preferable rationale would simply allocate the risk to the builder on the footing that the builder would have normally assumed that risk had the parties considered that risk at the time of contract formation. Where the contract is one for repair of an existing building, such a contract assumes the continuing exis-

---

[98] See UCC § 2-509(1) and (3).

[99] See Bunge Corp. v. Becker, 519 F.2d 449 (8th Cir. 1975).

[1] Stees v. Leonard, 20 Minn. 494 (1874); School Dist. No. 1. v. Dauchy, 25 Conn. 530, 68 Am. Dec. 371 (1857).

[2] See United States Fid. & Guar. Co. v. Parsons, 147 Miss. 335, 112 So. 469 (1927). See also RESTATEMENT 2d § 263, ill. 4. The same result will follow even where the owner is to furnish the materials from which the building is to be constructed. Albus v. Ford, 296 S.W. 981 (Tex. Civ. App. 1927); Vogt v. Hecker, 118 Wis. 306, 95 N.W. 90 (1903). A few cases have held that, where the builder and owner are cooperating in the construction, the contract is essentially one for a future, specific, building, presumably to be made of the first combination of assembled materials. Thus, if the structure is destroyed, the contract becomes impossible of performance since no house can be built of that original combination of labor and materials. Helms & Willis v. Unicoi County, 166 Tenn. (2 Beeler) 639, 64 S.W.2d 100 (1933); Butterfield v. Byron, 153 Mass. 517, 27 N.E. 667 (1891).

tence of a specific ("identified") building, and when it is destroyed without the fault of either party, the repair contractor is excused.[3]

Where the contractor promised to construct a building according to certain plans and specifications which proved to be inadequate, a few older cases suggested that the builder assumed the risk that the owner's plans may be defective.[4] The better decided cases, however, have applied a theory of implied warranty. Thus, if the owner rather than the contractor prepared the plans and specifications and they prove to be inadequate, the builder is excused because the party providing them warrants their sufficiency.[5]

D. *Performance Prevented by Operation of Law — Delays — Temporary Impracticability.*

We have seen that a bargain that is contrary to public policy cannot be recognized as a contract.[6] An agreement, however, may be perfectly lawful at the time of formation, but a supervening change in the law may make its performance unlawful. The classical "exception" of a "supervening act of state" excused the performance which had become unlawful as impossible because the contract was subject to the "implied condition" that the law would continue to permit performance.[7] In accordance with the modern treatment of the classical exceptions, a performance prevented by operation of law is now regarded as an application of the generic principle that parties should not be bound where an event has occurred, the nonoccurrence of which was a basic assumption of their contract.[8] As in the other traditional categories, the analysis is unchanged though the characterizations are different. Thus, older cases clung to the implied condition notion[9] while the modern cases arrive at the same result on the footing that the change in the law is an event which the parties assumed would not occur.[10]

---

[3] *See* RESTATEMENT 2d § 263, ill. 3 which is based on FIRST RESTATEMENT § 460, ill. 10.

[4] *See* N. J. Magnan Co. v. Fuller, 222 Mass. 530, 111 N.E. 399 (1916); Board of Educ. v. Empire State Sur. Co., 83 N.J.L. 293, 85 A. 223 (1912).

[5] *See* Chantilly Constr. Corp. v. Department of Hwys. & Transp., 6 Va. App. 282, 369 S.E.2d 438 (1988); Chaney Bldg. Co. v. City of Tuscon, 148 Ariz. 571, 716 P.2d 28 (1986); Gilbert Eng'g Co. v. City of Asheville, 74 N.C. App. 350, 328 S.E.2d 849 (1985); Marine Colloids, Inc. v. M. D. Hardy, Inc. 433 A.2d 402 (Me. 1981); United States v. Spearin, 248 U.S. 132 (1918).

[6] Thus, in RESTATEMENT 2d § 266(1), the effect of existing impracticability differs from supervening impracticability in that existing impracticability results in no duty arising rather than excuse of duty.

[7] Baily v. De Crespigny, L.R. 4 Q.B. 180 [1869] (covenant of landlord to prevent the erection of any buildings on adjoining land excused when the land was taken by a railroad under authority granted by act of Parliament).

[8] RESTATEMENT 2d § 264.

[9] *See, e.g.,* Wischhusen v. American Medicinal Spirits Co., 163 Md. 565, 163 A. 685 (1933) (contract to employ manager of distillery excused when government refused to issue permit to operate distillery unless a different manager was employed); Moore & Tierney, Inc. v. Roxford Knitting Co., 250 F. Supp. 278 (N.D.N.Y. 1918), aff'd, 265 F. 177 (2d Cir. 1920) (contract to manufacture goods excused when the government requisitioned the factory's output); Metropolitan Water Bd. v. Dick, Kerr & Co., A.C. 119 [1918] (contract to build a reservoir excused when the Ministry of Munitions ordered work stopped for an indefinite period).

[10] *See, e.g.,* Landis v. Hodgson, 109 Idaho 252, 706 P.2d 1363 (1985) (assumption that state would continue a lease). Note, however, that a party may assume the risk that the governmental approval necessary for his performance will be denied. *See* RESTATEMENT 2d § 264 comment a.

The change in the law need not be statutory or judicial; a regulation or order will be sufficient.[11] The governmental action, however, must be mandatory, i.e., a mere recommendation will not suffice.[12] The governmental regulation or order, including a municipal ordinance, need not be valid, but a party seeking to be excused because of such governmental intervention must exercise good faith in attempting to avoid its application.[13]

Where the law intervenes to prevent performance because of the fault of the promisor, the promisor is not excused. Thus, where a municipal ordinance prevents the performance of a contract previously made with the same municipality, the municipality is not excused.[14] Where an injunction is issued due to the fault of the promisor, he is not excused.[15]

The question of whether performance prevented by *foreign* governmental regulation is sufficient caused some difficulty in earlier cases which were inclined to seek other traditional "exceptions" to excuse impossibility rather than the "prevention by law" exception.[16] Both the UCC[17] and the RESTATEMENT 2d[18] expressly permit excuse for nonperformance because of either foreign or domestic governmental intervention.

As in all other "applications" of the modern principle, the fundamental requirements remain, i.e., the parties must not have allocated the risk by their agreement, the supervening event must be unforeseen or unexpected, it must not be caused by the fault of the party seeking to be excused, and the event must cause the performance to become impracticable as that term is defined.

Where the performance is merely *delayed* because of governmental action, the question is whether the delay caused performance to become impracticable. If the delay is merely a temporary situation, the impracticability is only *temporary* and the promisor's performance is merely suspended.[19] If the supervening event prevents performance for a sufficiently long time so as to reallocate the risks of the original contract, however, performance may be excused. Where, for example, war prevents the building of a plant in another country

---

[11] *See, e.g.,* McDonnell Douglas Corp. v. Islamic Republic of Iran, 591 F. Supp. 293 (E.D. Mo. 1984) (seller could not ship parts under Iranian Assets Control Regulations). RESTATEMENT 2d § 264 comment b suggests that the regulation or order may emanate from any level of government including municipalities or administrative agencies, i.e., "governmental action" is the generic concept which disregards distinctions between laws, regulations, orders, and the like.

[12] Wien Air Alaska v. Bubbel, 723 P.2d 627 (Alaska 1986).

[13] G. W. Andersen Constr. Co. v. Mars Sales, 164 Cal. App. 3d 326, 210 Cal. Rptr. 409 (1985) relying on RESTATEMENT 2d § 264 comment b.

[14] *See* West Haven Sound Dev. Corp. v. City of West Haven, 201 Conn. 305, 514 A.2d 734 (1986) (city entered into contract which later became impossible when ordinance of same city made the performance illegal). *See also* Elsemore v. Hancock, 137 Me. 243, 18 A.2d 692 (1941).

[15] *See* Peckham v. Indus. Sec. Co., 31 Del. (1 W.W. Harr.) 200, 113 A. 799 (1921) (defendant pleaded injunction secured by third person as an excuse for not performing but did not explain reason for injunction. Held: where the impossibility is due to a judicial order secured by a private litigant, the burden is on defendant to show that the order did not result from his fault). Where, however, performance is prevented by an injunction through no fault of the promisor, he is excused from performing. Kuhl v. School Dist. No. 76, 155 Neb. 357, 51 N.W.2d 746 (1952).

[16] *See, e.g.,* Texas Co. v. Hogarth Shipping Co., 256 U.S. 619 (1921) (act of British Government made performance impossible and court held performance excused on the ground of unavailability of subject matter).

[17] UCC § 2-615(a).

[18] RESTATEMENT 2d § 264

[19] *See* RESTATEMENT 2d § 269.

because of a shortage of materials, or prevents export of goods to another country for the duration of the war, the promise to ship the goods may be excused because of a substantial reallocation of the original risks assumed by the parties.[20] Similarly, a personal service contract interrupted by military service may be excused because of the duration of the war and the consequent change in the rights and duties of the parties that has become so materially burdensome as to reallocate the risks of the original contract.[21]

E. *Failure of Contemplated Mode of Performance — Partial Impracticability.*

Where the performance of the promisor is impracticable only in part, it is possible that such partial impracticability may create such an onerous burden in performing the remainder of her promise that she should be excused entirely from her duty.[22] In the more likely case, however, the partial impracticability is either so insubstantial as to provide no excuse for nonperformance, or the impracticability is substantial but the promisor can render a reasonable substitute performance. Where, for example, a foreseeable conflict closed the Suez Canal, it was possible to deliver the goods to the stated destination by a longer voyage. Even though this route was necessarily more costly, a number of courts refused to excuse the promisors since this alternate mode of performance was a reasonable substitute.[23] Similarly, where a payment was to be made to a governmental authority that later ceased to exist, the lease could be reformed to allow payment to the lessor.[24] Wherever a commercially reasonable alternative performance exists, the impracticability does not excuse substantial performance.[25]

The UCC requires a commercially reasonable substitute method of delivery, transportation, or payment to be tendered and accepted,[26] and the RESTATEMENT 2d requires the promisor to render such a reasonable substitute performance in order to meet his general obligation of good faith under the contract.[27] In effect, the promisor is required to perform if substantial performance can be rendered. Moreover, where substantial performance cannot be

---

[20] *See* Village of Minnesota v. Fairbanks, Morse & Co., 226 Minn. 1, 31 N.W.2d 920 (1948); Heidner v. St. Paul & Tacoma Lumber Co., 124 Wash. 652, 215 P. 1 (1923).

[21] *See* Autry v. Republic Prods., Inc., 30 Cal. 2d 144, 180 P.2d 888 (1947) (plaintiff's artistic career and the quality of artistic performance might be affected by the passage of time).

[22] RESTATEMENT 2d § 270 comment a.

[23] *See* American Trading & Prod. Corp. v. Shell Int'l Marine, Ltd., 453 F.2d 939 (2d Cir. 1972); Transatlantic Fin. Corp. v. United States, 363 F.2d 312 (1966); Glidden Co. v. Hellenic Lines, Ltd., 275 F.2d 253 (1960); Ocean Tramp Tankers Corp. v. V/O Sovfracht (The Eugenia), 2 Q.B. 226 [1964]; Tsakiroglou & Co. v. Noblee Thorl G. m. b. H., 2 Q.B. 348 [1960].

[24] *See* Barnacle Bill's Seafood Galley, Inc. v. Ford, 453 So. 2d 165 (Fla. App. 1984).

[25] *See* United Equities Co. v. First Nat'l City Bank, 52 A.D.2d 154, 383 N.Y.S.2d 6 (1976) (commercially reasonable alternative in yen transaction) relying on UCC § 2-614.

[26] UCC § 2-614. In cases where only a part of the seller's capacity to perform is affected by the impracticability, the seller *must* allocate production and deliveries among his contract customers but may also include regular customers not then under contract as well as his own requirements for further manufacture in that allocation which must always be fair and reasonable. UCC § 2-615(b). *See* Alimenta (U.S.A.), Inc. v. Cargill, Inc., 861 F.2d 650 (11th Cir. 1988) (allocation rule applies absent a provision in the contract that seller will perform even though the contigencies that permit allocation might occur).

[27] RESTATEMENT 2d § 270 comment b, referring to the good faith requirement in § 205. The UCC also contains a general obligation of good faith in § 1-203.

rendered, if the obligee promises to perform in full, the obligor must continue to render performance.[28]

Where a substituted performance will necessarily delay performance, the party who, in good faith, is tendering such substitute performance should not be liable for any reasonable delay. Such a delay may, in fact, be required in order to meet the good faith obligation to render a substitute performance.[29]

§ 114. Frustration of Purpose.

A. History and Nature of Concept.

One of the parties to the contract may wish to receive the literal performance of the other party, not because that performance itself is desired, but because it will enable the first party to accomplish a more remote, specific purpose. A difficult question of contract adjudication is presented when the literal performance is quite capable of being rendered but the more remote purpose which is the chief desire of the promisor becomes meaningless due to supervening events. This question was presented to the English courts in the celebrated "Coronation" cases which arose because the coronation procession of Edward VII was cancelled due to his illness. In one of these cases, a party residing on the proposed line of march made a contract to let his apartment to the defendant to enable him to view the procession. When an action was brought to recover the amount of the rental, the court held that the cancellation of the procession excused the defendant from paying the balance of the agreed price for the use of the apartment.[30] There was no literal impossibility or impracticability of performance since both promises could have been performed without difficulty. The court recognized this fact and proceeded directly to the question of whether the doctrine extended to include situations where the ultimate purpose of one of the parties was frustrated because the existence of a particular state of things (in this case, the procession) which both parties assumed, failed to materialize. The court decided that such an extension was proper when, as in the case before it, the specific state of affairs that is "foundational" to the contract does not exist.[31] Other courts have reached the same conclusion on similar facts.[32]

---

[28] See RESTATEMENT 2d § 270(b), comment c and ill. 4, based on the facts of Van Dusen Aircraft Supplies of New England v. Massachusetts Port Auth., 361 Mass. 131, 279 N.E.2d 717 (1972).

[29] See UCC § 2-615 comment 7: "However, good faith and the reason of the present section and of the preceding one may properly be held to justify and even to require any needed delay involved in a good faith inquiry seeking a readjustment of the contract terms to meet the new conditions."

[30] Krell v. Henry, 2 K.B. 740 [1903]. The defendant had made down payment which he did not seek to recover. This is discussed subsequently in the text of this section.

[31] The court has been criticized for holding that performance of the contract was prevented. See 6 CORBIN § 1355 (1962). While such criticism is correct, the court's opinion can be read as suggesting that performance became impossible in effect, though not literally impossible. It is not strange to find a court taking such a route to a particular result in a case of first impression.

[32] La Cumbre Golf & Country Club v. Santa Barbara Hotel Co., 205 Cal. 422, 271 P. 476 (1928) (contract to pay a monthly fee for the privilege of having hotel guests given membership privileges at a golf club excused when hotel burned); Gulf & S.I.R.R. v. Horn, 135 Miss. 804, 100 So. 381 (1924) (contract to employ one as a claim agent to be trained under a chief about to retire excused when the chief retired immediately); The Stratford, Inc. v. Seattle Brewing & Malting Co., 94 Wash. 125, 162 P. 31 (1916) (lease of premises for saloon purposes only held annulled when prohibition law prevented operation of a saloon); Alfred Marks Realty Co. v. Hotel Hermit-

The basic problem which the courts have had to face in this area is the danger involved in excusing the promisor. After all, the promisee is not concerned with the ultimate purpose of the promisor in making the contract. His sole interest is in obtaining the price for his performance. A purchaser of stock may wish to buy it only because it is reasonably foreseeable that the price of the stock may go up. If that "state of affairs" fails to materialize, the buyer would not be excused from paying the purchase price. This is the usual rule, i.e., supervening disappointments do not excuse the promisor. When, if ever, should such a rule change?

The first criterion suggested by the cases is the extent of the frustration. In the coronation case, the promisor was entitled to view an empty Pall Mall during the period stipulated in the contract, but there could be no real benefit to him in so doing. The cancellation of the procession was virtually a total frustration of the purpose of the rental, a fact that was well known by both parties as attested by the inflated price for the flat and the fact that the period of tenancy was relegated to the approximate time during which the procession was scheduled. In the stock-purchasing case, the fact that there is no rise in the price of the stock may have been disappointing to the purchaser, but he retains a substantial benefit unless the shares have become worthless. Even assuming the stock has become worthless, there is another difference between the two cases which illustrates the second criterion found in the decided cases. In the coronation case, had the parties thought about it, would the promisor have agreed to pay an inflated rental for a brief period whether or not the procession occurred? Or would the parties have agreed on some alternative in the event the procession cancelled? Once again, the question of risk allocation must be faced. In the stock-purchase case, the very nature of the subject matter suggests that the purchaser is assuming all risks in relation to the decline in the stock's value, even to the extent of it becoming worthless. To allocate risks in these cases, the courts must consider the customs and mores of society in relation to the particular circumstances involved. If the circumstances surrounding the making of the contract have been such that there is a probability that the promisor would have been expected to take the risk of what has occurred, he is not excused even though the parties did not anticipate the contingency which has supervened.[33] On the other hand, if the cir-

---

age Co., 170 App. Div. 484, 156 N.Y.S. 179 (1915) (contract to pay for an advertisement to be published in a "souvenir and program" of a yacht race excused when race was cancelled). *Cf.* Retail Merchants' Bus. Expansion Co. v. Randall, 103 Vt. 268, 153 A. 357 (1931), in which it was held that a storekeeper who had contracted for assistance in carrying on an advertising campaign was not excused by the accidental destruction of his store and stock of goods.

[33] Bunting v. Orendorf, 152 Miss. 327, 120 So. 182 (1929), *criticized*, 28 MICH. L. REV. 77 (1929) (duty of lessee to pay rent not discharged by the fact that an unprecedented flood prevented the use of the land); Burgett v. Loeb, 43 Ind. App. 657, 88 N.E. 346 (1909) (duty to pay rent for premises leased for saloon purposes was not discharged when the lessee was denied a license to operate a saloon); London & Northern Estates Co. v. Schlesinger, 1 K.B. 20 [1916] (obligation to pay rent for a flat leased for personal occupancy with right to sub-let on lessor's assent not excused by fact that a later order in council prohibited the lessee, an alien enemy, from residing in the flat); Herne Bay Steam Boat Co. v. Huttone, 2 K.B. 683 [1903] (promise to pay a stipulated sum for the privilege of having a steamer at the promisor's disposal to take passengers to see a naval review not excused when the review was cancelled).

It is on this basis that the cases are justified which hold a school board bound to continue a teacher's salary notwithstanding an epidemic which closes the school. *See* Phelps v. School Dist.

cumstances indicate that the promisor would not have been expected to assume the risk, the courts must decide upon whom the risk must fall as between two innocent parties.

B. *The Modern Doctrine.*

The best-known American case dealing with frustration of purpose is *Lloyd v. Murphy*[34] where a lease stated that the purpose was solely for conducting the business of displaying and selling new automobiles. The court rejected the common law notion that lessees could never be excused because of impossibility or frustration.[35] However, it refused to excuse the duty of the lessee on two fundamental grounds: (1) the restriction on the manufacture of new automobiles due to the war effort was commonly known at the time the lease was executed. Therefore, the lessee certainly should have foreseen the lack of supply. (2) The lack of new automobiles did not prevent the lessee from selling used automobiles which constituted the essential domestic automobile market during World War II. Moreover, since the lessor waived its rights to insist that the premises be used only for the purposes stated in the lease, the defendant could also repair automobiles or even sublease the premises to any responsible tenant. Consequently, the *value* of the lease was not totally destroyed. The opinion of the court, written by one of the more distinguished jurists in America,[36] set a tone for future frustration cases that not only required the particular purpose of the contract to be the dominant or sole purpose, but also required that purpose to be totally frustrated. The RESTATEMENT 2d suggests four elements to establish frustration of purpose, three of which are identical to its test for impracticability. While the first element for supervening impracticability is that performance must have become impracticable,[37] the first element for discharge by supervening frustration requires a party's principal purpose to be substantially frustrated.[38] Otherwise, the elements are identical: the frustration must occur without the fault of the party claiming frustration, the frustration must be caused by an event, the nonoccurrence of which was a basic assumption on which the contract was made, and the party seeking to be excused must not have assumed a greater obligation under the contract to perform in spite of an event that would have allowed for excuse by frustration.[39]

No. 109, 302 Ill. 193, 134 N.E. 312 (1922) (teacher); Montgomery v. Board of Educ., 102 Ohio St. 189, 131 N.E. 497, 15 A.L.R. 715 (1921) (bus driver); Crane v. School Dist. No. 14, 95 Or. 644, 188 P. 712 (1920) (bus driver).

Contra Gregg School Twp., Morgan County v. Hinshaw, 76 Ind. App. 503, 132 N.E. 586, 17 A.L.R. 1222 (1921) (teacher); Sandry v. Brooklyn Sch. Dist. No. 78, 47 N.D. 444, 182 N.W. 689, 15 A.L.R. 719 (1921) (bus driver).

[34] 25 Cal. 2d 48, 153 P.2d 47 (1944).

[35] The common law concept treated a lease as a contract to sell land where the risk of loss passes to the buyer at the time of contract formation since the buyer is then the equitable owner of the land. The modern view, however, recognizes the lease as different from the sale of land, i.e., it is essentially a lease of the buildings on the land rather than any transfer of the land itself. *See* RESTATEMENT 2d PROPERTY § 5.4.

[36] The opinion writer was Justice Roger Traynor.

[37] RESTATEMENT 2d § 261.

[38] RESTATEMENT 2d § 265.

[39] *Ibid.*

As one court suggests, the doctrines of commercial impracticability and frustration should be applied "sparingly."[40] Like commercial impracticability cases, recorded decisions suggest that this may be a euphemistic characterization in frustration of purposes cases. Many cases reflect the virtual impossibility of discovering the necessary combination of elements essential to establish frustration as an excuse. All or some of the elements suggested by the RE-STATEMENT 2d are typically not met.[41] While the fact that the event causing frustration was foreseeable should not, alone, preclude a finding of frustration,[42] foreseeability will still be emphasized where the risk is one that should have been fairly regarded as assumed by the party seeking to be excused.[43] Though other elements are met, the fault of the party seeking to be excused may have contributed to the occurrence of the frustrating event,[44] the counter-performance may retain value notwithstanding the frustration,[45] or the purpose that has been frustrated may not have been the sole purpose of the contract.[46] The occasionally successful use of the frustration doctrine,[47] however, will undoubtedly insure continued attempts to assert it as an excuse for nonperformance.

C. *Existing or Temporary Frustration of Purpose.*

Just as existing as contrasted with supervening impracticability will prevent a duty of performance from arising,[48] existing frustration of purpose has the same effect.[49] Thus, where an existing ordinance prohibited the use of certain premises as a health resort or milk farm, the lessee's duty never arose.[50] Similarly, in one of the Coronation cases, it was discovered that the licensing of a room to view the procession occurred shortly after the decision to perform surgery on the king precluded the procession. Since neither party was aware of the existing frustration at the time the contract was made, no duty of the lessee arose under the contract.[51] As in the case of existing impracticability, existing frustration of purpose must be distinguished from the mutual mistake analysis.[52]

Where frustration of purpose is only temporary, the effect is identical to temporary impracticability, i.e., the duty of performance is, at least, sus-

---

[40] Dorn v. Stanhope Steel, Inc., 368 Pa. Super. 557, 534 A.2d 798 (1988).

[41] *See* National Recruiters, Inc. v. Toro Co., 343 N.W.2d 704 (Minn. App. 1984).

[42] *See* West Los Angeles Inst. for Cancer Research v. Meyer, 366 F.2d 220, 225 (9th Cir. 1966). *See also* RESTATEMENT 2d § 265 comment a. *Contra* Gold v. Salem Lutheran Home Ass'n, 53 Cal. 2d 289, 1 Cal. Rptr. 343, 347 P.2d 687 (1959).

[43] Scullin Steel Co. v. PACCAR, Inc., 708 S.W.2d 756 (Mo. App. 1986); United States Smelting, Ref. & Mining Co. v. Wigger, 684 P.2d 850 (Alaska 1984).

[44] Groseth Int'l, Inc. v. Teneco, Inc., 410 N.W.2d 159 (S.D. 1987).

[45] *See* Bitzes v. Sunset Oaks, Inc., 649 P.2d 66 (Utah 1982).

[46] *See* Beals v. Tri-B Assocs. 644 P.2d 78 (Colo. App. 1982).

[47] *See* Cleasby v. Leo A. Daly Co., 221 Neb. 254, 376 N.W.2d 312 (1985) (termination of two-year employment contract where employee's illness caused absences and employer proved that a knowledgeable manager was required in Saudi Arabia and employee was barred from returning to Saudi Arabia without the consent of a party whose consent could not be obtained before a certain date).

[48] *See supra* § 112(D).

[49] RESTATEMENT 2d § 266(2).

[50] *See* Mariani v. Gold, 13 N.Y.S.2d 365 (1939).

[51] Griffith v. Brymer, 19 T.L.R. 434 (K.B. 1903).

[52] *See supra* § 112(D).

pended, and if the existing or supervening event is of sufficient duration as to increase the burden of performance so materially that the original risks assumed by the parties are reallocated, the duty of performance either never arises or it is discharged.[53]

§ 115. Effects of Impracticability and Frustration of Purpose.

A. *Effect on Excused Party.*

In prior discussion, we have mentioned that the effect of a failure to perform on a party whose performance is excused because of impracticability or frustration of purpose will depend upon whether the excused performance is due to a supervening event or whether the event giving rise to the excuse existed at the time of contract formation. Thus, if the impracticability or frustration occurred because of a supervening event, the existing duty of the excused party is discharged.[54] If, however, the excused party's performance is impracticable or frustrated at the time the contract is made, no duty to render performance for which that party could be held liable ever arose.[55]

While the effect of excusable nonperformance on the excused party is relatively simple, it is essential to consider the effect of that party's excused performance on the other party to the contract.

B. *Effect of Excused Party's Nonperformance on Other Party's Prospective Failure.*

In the earlier discussion of breach of contract, we saw that there is a constructive condition that there be no uncured material breach to any duty to render performance.[56] Where a party's performance has been excused through impracticability or frustration of purpose, that party is not liable for breach of contract. Yet, he has not fulfilled the constructive condition to the other party's performance. Thus, the failure of the excused party to render performance is treated in the same fashion as a breach of contract even though, again, he is not liable for that breach because his performance has been excused.[57] If, for example, the excused party brings an action against the other party, the other party may defend as if the excused party has breached the contract.[58] Certainly, a party should not be required to perform his own duty if it is clear that he will not receive what he bargained for even though the counter-performance is legally excused. The legally excused failure to perform, however, must amount to an uncured material breach to discharge the

---

[53] RESTATEMENT 2d § 269. *See also supra* § 113(D). In the case of existing frustration, the duty would never arise, while supervening frustration would discharge the duty.

[54] RESTATEMENT 2d § 261.

[55] RESTATEMENT 2d § 266. Prior discussion of these concepts is found at § 112(D).

[56] *See* RESTATEMENT 2d §§ 237 and 238.

[57] RESTATEMENT 2d § 267.

[58] *See, e.g.,* Roy's Estate, 278 Mich. 6, 270 N.W. 196 (1936) (payment of note given for promise to marry which was to occur before note was due excused when marriage became impossible due to death of maker); Prescott & Co. v. J. B. Powles & Co., 113 Wash. 177, 193 P. 680 (1920) (buyer of goods excused when seller failed to deliver full quantity under contract though failure was legally excusable).

other party.[59] If the legally excused failure to perform does not amount to an uncured material breach, the other party is not discharged.[60]

The same analysis occurs where the failure to perform is prospective rather than a present failure. It should be recalled that an anticipatory repudiation may be treated as a total breach of contract,[61] and reasonable grounds to believe that the obligor will commit a breach allows the obligee to demand adequate assurances of performance and to suspend his own performance until such assurances are received.[62] Even though the prospective failure of performance may be excused, the other party's performance may be discharged or he may be permitted to suspend performance.[63] As in other cases of prospective failure of performance, however, there is the danger that the other party may mistakenly view his performance as justifiably terminated where only suspension of performance was justifiable. For example, where an artist promised to attend rehearsals for six days prior to a fifteen-week performance contract and, because of illness, could not arrive until two days prior to the first scheduled performance, the termination of the artist's contract was not justified because the artist's delay would not have amounted to a material failure of performance had it not been legally excusable.[64] Suspension of performance would have been justified though termination was not justified. On the other hand, where another artist engaged to perform for three months became ill during rehearsals and could not perform by opening night, the termination of that artist's contract was justified because the artist's inability to perform would have amounted to an uncured material failure of performance had it not been legally excusable.[65]

C. *Relief — Restitution — Divisibility — Reliance — Restatement 2d.*

Where performance is excused due to impracticability or frustration but one party has received a benefit from the part performance by the other, the party receiving the benefit is considered unjustly enriched and, notwithstanding his discharge from contractual duties, he must pay for what he has received.[66] The action is one for restitution of benefits conferred. Where, for example, a carpenter agrees to perform certain work for a homeowner but dies before he completes the work, his duties are discharged under the contract. The value of the benefit conferred upon the homeowner, however, may be recovered by the carpenter's representative to avoid the unjust enrichment of the homeowner. The benefit is usually measured by its reasonable value, i.e., what it would

---

[59] *See, e.g.,* Hong v. Independent Sch. Dist. No. 245, 181 Minn. 309, 232 N.W. 329 (1930) (school teacher absent because of illness during first five weeks of school year); American Mercantile Exch. v. Blunt, 102 Me. 128, 66 A. 212 (1906) (collection agency prevented from performing part of its contract by a supervening statute).

[60] *See, e.g.,* Leiston Gas Co. v. Leiston-Cum-Sizewell Urban Dist. Council, 2 K.B. 428 [1916] (gas company was prohibited from lighting street lights for nine months during war time on a six-year contract).

[61] RESTATEMENT 2d § 253(1). UCC § 2-610.

[62] RESTATEMENT 2d § 251; UCC § 2-609.

[63] RESTATEMENT 2d § 268. *See also* Juarez v. Hamner, 674 S.W.2d 856 (Tex. App. 1984).

[64] Bettini v. Gye, 1 Q.B.D. 183 [1876].

[65] Poussard v. Spiers, 1 A.B.D. 410 [1876].

[66] *See* Frigillana v. Frigillana, 266 Ark. 296, 584 S.W.2d 30 (1979); Quagliana v. Exquisite Home Bldrs., Inc., 538 P.2d 301 (Utah 1975). *See also* RESTATEMENT 2d §§ 272 and 377.

have cost the homeowner to obtain the benefit from a party in the position of the carpenter.[67] Even if the benefit has been destroyed because of the supervening event making performance impracticable, the restitution interest is still protected. Thus, if the carpenter managed part performance before the house was destroyed without the fault of either party, he would still be entitled to his restitution interest[68] though the measure of recovery should be the increased value of the house as contrasted with the reasonable cost of performing the carpentry work.[69] If the part performance rendered prior to impracticability or frustration was a *divisible* portion of the contract,[70] recovery can be had only for that divisible portion.[71]

The coronation cases are well-known as the creators of the doctrine of frustration of purpose. In the principal coronation case,[72] the defendant had agreed to pay £75 to license the flat near the upcoming coronation procession. He paid £25 in advance and refused to pay the balance. The plaintiff brought an action for the remaining £50 for which the defendant was not held liable due to the creation of the frustration of purpose excuse. The defendant did not seek recovery of the £25 paid in advance. In another coronation case, however, the defendant agreed to pay £141 for a desirable vantage point. This contract required the entire amount to be paid immediately after the contract was formed. The defendant paid only £100 and, when the procession was cancelled, he refused to pay the balance and brought an action to recover the £100 payment. The court not only refused to grant restitution of the amount paid; it also held the defendant liable for the £41 not paid on the footing that the defendant's performance was due before the procession was scheduled to occur and, since everything done before the frustrating event was assumed to be validly done, the defendant was liable for the entire contract price.[73] The absurdity of allocating the risks on the sheer accident of when the parties had agreed to perform their promises is clear if one assumes a hypothetical contract where the parties had agreed that the amount would be paid only after the procession. In that case, the defendant would have owed nothing. To the court's credit, it recognized this arbitrary analysis but considered itself in a dilemma and chose what it considered the more desirable horn to adjudicate disputes between two innocent parties. The case was eventually overruled where an advance payment on a contract for machinery was recovered when war prevented performance of the contract.[74] While overcoming the nonsensical precedent, this case found its own dilemma. The seller contended that it

---

[67] *See* Carroll v. Bowersock, 100 Kan. 270, 164 P. 143 (1917); Young v. City of Chicopee, 186 Mass. 518, 72 N.E. 63 (1904). *See also* RESTATEMENT 2d § 371(a).

[68] *See* cases cited *supra* note 66.

[69] *See* RESTATEMENT 2d § 377 comment b and RESTATEMENT 2d § 371(b) which is the restitutionary measure of the increase in value of wealth to the recipient of the benefit as compared to the reasonable cost measure in § 371(a). The two measures are often different. Thus, the cost of a benefit could be greater or less than the value of that benefit to the owner. These matters will be discussed in the next chapter dealing with contract remedies.

[70] The concept of divisible (or severable) versus entire contracts is dealt with *supra* § 105(D).

[71] *See* Mullen v. Wafer, 252 Ark. 541, 480 S.W.2d 332 (1972) (physical assets portion for separate price could be enforced where death excused remaining performance).

[72] Krell v. Henry, 2 K.B. 740 [1903].

[73] Chandler v. Webster, 1 K.B. 493 [1904].

[74] Fibrosa Spolka Akcyjna v. Faribarne Lawson Combe Barbour, Ltd., A.C. 32 [1943].

had performed considerable work on the machines prior to the supervening
event causing impracticability and argued that it should recover the cost of
the work performed. Here, the court was confronted with an argument for the
reliance interest, i.e., the minus quantity or loss suffered by the seller as
contrasted with the restitution interest, the benefit retained by the seller (the
advance payment) at the expense of the buyer. While the restitution interest
generally displays a greater claim to protection because it is not only a loss to
one party but a corresponding gain to the unjustly enriched party, there is no
apparent reason why both interests cannot be considered in such a case. The
court, however, felt that it had achieved all that it could by granting the buyer
restitution of his advance payment, and if other relief were in order, only the
legislature could achieve that goal. Parliament had been hard at work since
the 1930's studying the question of relief for part performance in such cases.
In 1943, it enacted the Frustrated Contract Act[75] which encompasses all contract duties discharged by impracticability or frustration. That act permits a
party such as the machinery buyer to recover his advance payment (restitution), but it also permits a court to decide that the seller can retain all or part
of that payment because of expenses incurred by the seller (reliance). The
curiosity is that the legislation did not deal with the situation where no
benefit was conferred but expenses were incurred, i.e., where there was no
restitution interest but there was a reliance interest. Thus, in the machinery
case, had the buyer made no advance payment but the seller had incurred the
same expenses, the seller would recover nothing because of the accident that
no advance payment was made. Protection of the reliance interest was, therefore, made to depend upon whether there was a restitution interest to protect
in the other party.

Extant authority in American case law would prevent protection of the
reliance interest.[76] Moreover, there is no authority permitting recovery of the
reliance interest even where the other party is entitled to recover the restitution interest. Indeed, the RESTATEMENT 2d insists that one's reliance interest
may not be deducted from the amount of benefit he has received.[77] The illustration supporting this view, however, suggests that the reliance loss may be
"taken into consideration in deciding whether to allow" restitution in the form
of the cost of performance or the increase in value when the former is higher.[78]
This is particularly confusing and may reflect the total absence of case law to
achieve a result desired by the drafters of the RESTATEMENT 2d — a result that
is augured by a general section on relief found in the chapter dealing with
impracticability and frustration.[79] Part of that section suggests that a court
may grant relief to avoid injustice and such relief may include protection of
the reliance interest.[80] Having set the stage in that section, the RESTATEMENT
2d proceeds to deny that recovery in the subsequent section, though its illustration appears deliberately confusing and covert in this regard.[81]

---

[75] 6 & 7 Geo. 6, c. 40.
[76] *See* the cases cited *supra* note 66.
[77] RESTATEMENT 2d § 377 comment b.
[78] RESTATEMENT 2d § 377 ill. 5.
[79] RESTATEMENT 2d Ch. 11.
[80] RESTATEMENT 2d § 272(2).
[81] Illustration 5 to § 377 of the RESTATEMENT 2d suggests a contract to shingle a roof at a price of
$5000. *A,* the contractor, has spent $2000 doing part of the work and has received a progress

§ 116. Risk of Loss — Uniform Commercial Code.

A. *From Property to Contract.*

Among the changes wrought by Article 2 of the UCC, the sections dealing with risk of loss are notable as a prime illustration of the conceptual change in the Code to a contracts orientation from the property orientation of the law the Code replaced. The legal consequences are stated as following directly from the contract and action taken under it without resorting to the idea of when property or title passed or was to pass as being the determining factor.[82]

Risk of loss would not, therefore, be determined on the basis of the "title" or ownership of the goods.[83] Rather, it would be determined by the contract between the parties.[84] Normally, the risk of loss will remain on the seller until the seller delivers the goods to an independent carrier or to the buyer.[85] These normal rules would change where there has been a breach by the seller in not

---

payment of $1800 from *B*. The house is destroyed by fire without the fault of either party. Moreover, $500 worth of shingles placed near the house were also destroyed. The illustration suggests that *A* cannot recover the $500, nor can he deduct it from the $1800 received from *B* which *A* must repay. The prior illustration indicates that *A* is not entitled to restitution in the amount of $2000 because the increase in the value of the house due to the partly completed shingle job was only $1500. When, however, the fact of the $500 loss in shingles is added, the illustration suggests that the court may decide to grant *A* restitution in the amount of $2000 rather than the $1500, i.e., the court may, presumably, consider reliance, not by protecting the reliance interest, but by choosing the higher possible restitution interest. If that choice is made *because* of reliance, however, why should the reliance interest be protected in this awkward fashion, i.e., choosing a higher restitution interest which is necessarily only an accident? This circumvention is apparently due to the lack of any case law support for the protection of the reliance interest. It is a particularly harmful way to restate the law.

[82]UCC § 2-101 comment. *See also* UCC § 2-509 comment 1: "The underlying theory of these sections on risk of loss is adoption of the contractual approach rather than an arbitrary shifting of the risk with the 'property' in the goods." *See also* Martin v. Melland's, Inc., 283 N.W.2d 76 (N.D. 1979); Taylor Martin, Inc. v. Hiland Dairy, 676 S.W.2d 859 (Mo. App. 1984); Hughes v. Al Green, Inc., 65 Ohio St. 2d 110, 418 N.E.2d 1355 (1981).

[83] § 2-401 of the UCC deals with the concept of "title" and the time title passes. It is, however, important to recognize the principal purpose of this section. There are criminal statutes, tax statutes, and governmental regulations beyond the UCC that required the determination of "title." There are also "title" questions in insurance policies concerning the ownership of the property. It is, therefore, essential to have a "title" concept for these extra-code purposes. *See* Martin v. Melland's, Inc., *supra* 82, at n.3. Even though the term "title" is found in other UCC sections, *e.g.,* § 2-327(1)(a) (sale on approval), § 2-312 (warranty of title) and even in the definition of "sale," § 2-106(1), *supra* these uses are traditional and do not require a separate section devoted to the question of when title passes. There is no Article 2 UCC question that depends upon the determination of when title passes.

[84]*See* Russell v. Transamerica Ins. Co., 322 N.W.2d 178 (Mich. App. 1982) (plaintiffs maintained possession of the boat after title passed to buyer and risk of loss was on plaintiffs).

[85]The party in possession should normally bear the risk because that party is in a better position to control and protect the goods. The curiosity is that this was the view of the early law. By the time of Tarling v. Baxter, 6 Barn. & C. 360, 108 Eng. Rep. 484 [1827], however, risk of loss became an incident of title and the question was who had title at the time of loss. The party not in possession may have been "vested" with title and would bear the risk of loss. The "title" approach, however, was an attempt to solve too many problems with a single rule. When faced with criticism of his refusal to adhere to the title concept, Karl Llewellyn provided a classic response: "May I say one other thing in that connection, and say it without any hesitancy for the record? The number of lawyers who have an accurate knowledge of sales law is extremely small in these United States. My brother Bacon has taught sales law for 28 years. When he says it isn't too difficult to determine where the courts will decide the title is or isn't or is going to be or should be, he is speaking a truth within limits for people who have taught sales law for 28 years. I submit to you sir, that there are not many of them." (Statement of K. Llewellyn, 1 Hearings Before the New York Law Revision Commission on the UCC, 96 [160] (1954).)

shipping conforming goods or by the purchaser in not paying for the goods or otherwise repudiating. A comprehensive treatment of risk of loss must be left to treatises on commercial transactions. What follows is a sketch of the UCC treatment of risk of loss.[86]

B. *Risk of Loss in the Absence of Breach.*

Some of the confusion that students develop in dealing with the basic risk of loss section in the UCC, § 2-509, is that the section begins with "shipment" or "destination" contracts, i.e., contracts where the goods will be shipped by an independent carrier rather than the seller's own truck, and where the contract places the risk of loss on the buyer either at the time the goods are delivered to the carrier ("shipment")[87] or at the time they are tendered to the buyer ("destination").[88] The elaboration of "shipment" and "destination" contracts is found in definitions of those terms and the attendant duties of the seller in each. A "shipment" contract is normally identified by the term, "FOB shipment" (or "FOB seller's plant") which requires the seller to bear the risk and expense of putting the goods in the possession of an independent carrier at the seller's location.[89] The seller must choose a reasonable carrier, make a proper contract for the transportation of the goods in relation to the nature of the goods, obtain and promptly deliver any appropriate documents such as bills of lading that the buyer requires to obtain the goods, and promptly notify the buyer of shipment.[90] A "destination" contract is normally identified by the term, "FOB the place of destination" (or "FOB buyer's plant") and requires the seller to transport the goods to that destination at his own expense and risk and tender delivery of the goods to the buyer at that destination.[91] The tender requires the seller to make the goods available at the buyer's disposition at a reasonable hour with proper notice to the buyer to enable him to take delivery.[92]

Once a contract is deemed to be a "shipment" contract, the risk of loss passes to the buyer when the goods are duly delivered to an independent carrier, while in a "destination" contract, the risk passes to the buyer when the goods are duly delivered to the buyer at the buyer's destination.[93] If the contract is silent as to whether the contract is a "shipment" or "destination" contract, the assumption is that the parties intended a "shipment" contract since that is the "normal" one and the destination contract is viewed as a "variant."[94] In addition to identifying a contract as a "shipment" or "destina-

---

[86] In general, *see* Annotation, *Who Bears Risk of Loss of Goods Under UCC 2-509, 2-510?*, 66 A.L.R.3rd 145 (1988).

[87] UCC § 2-509(1)(a).

[88] UCC § 2-509(1)(b).

[89] UCC § 2-319(1)(a).

[90] UCC § 2-504. It should be noted that failure to make a proper contract or to notify the buyer of shipment is a ground for buyer's rejection of the goods only if material delay or loss ensues from such failures.

[91] UCC § 2-319(1)(b).

[92] UCC § 2-503.

[93] UCC §§ 2-509(1)(a) and (1)(b). Thus, where the goods are destroyed prior to shipment, the risk of loss remains on the seller. *See* Silver v. Wycombe, Meyer & Co., 477 N.Y.S.2d 288 (1984).

[94] UCC § 2-503 comment 5.

tion" contract, the FOB term may add "vessel car or other vehicle."[95] This obligates the seller to load the goods on board at the seller's expense and risk. Where the contract also contains a "C.I.F." term (cost, insurance and freight) or "C. & F." term (cost and freight), it is a "shipment" contract and has no effect on the normal allocation of risk. Just because the cost of transportation and/or insurance is included in the price, there is no change in the risk of loss rules.[96]

Millions of dollars worth of goods are stored in warehouses in the possession of a bailee (warehouseman). The owners of such goods often contract to sell them and the buyer takes delivery even though the goods remain where they are, i.e., they simply belong to the buyer. The transaction, therefore, contemplated delivery of the goods without moving them. The UCC contains a risk of loss rule under which the risk passes to the buyer in such a case upon his receipt of a negotiable document of title (a warehouse receipt), or his receipt of a non-negotiable document or other written direction, or, finally, upon the bailee's acknowledgment of the buyer's right to the goods.[97]

The residual subsection deals with cases not involving shipment through independent carriers or delivery of goods without moving them. It deals with a very large number of transactions in goods where, for example, the seller will deliver in his own truck, the buyer will go to the seller's plant to take the goods in the buyer's truck, the consumer takes delivery of a new or used car, and millions of other transactions. This residual section can, therefore, be considered the general rule of risk of loss: the risk passes to the buyer on his receipt of the goods if the seller is a merchant, and it passes on tender of delivery of the goods if the seller is not a merchant.[98] For the purposes of this Code section, a "merchant" would be very broadly defined as anyone in business.[99] While the difference between the buyer's receipt and the seller's tender may be insignificant, it could be controlling in a given case and the Code drafters apparently intended to favor the non-merchant seller at least to the extent of removing the risk from such a seller sooner than it would be removed from a merchant seller. Questions of whether the buyer has "received" the goods[1] or delivery was tendered[2] still arise, though not very often.

In keeping with the freedom of contract philosophy of the UCC in permitting the parties to vary the effect of its provisions,[3] the last subsection expressly permits such variation,[4] i.e., the parties may vary the affect of risk of

---

[95] UCC § 2-319(1)(c).

[96] UCC § 2-320 and comment 1. The FOB term will not be construed as a price term; it is a delivery term. See A. M. Knitwear Corp. v. All Am. Export-Import Corp., 390 N.Y.S.2d 832, 359 N.E.2d 342 (1976).

[97] UCC § 2-509(2). See Whately v. Tetrault, 29 Mass. App. Dec. 112, 5 UCC Rep. 838 (1964) (risk of loss passed on acknowledgment). See also Jason's Foods, Inc. v. Peter Eckrich & Sons 774 F.2d 214 (7th Cir. 1985) (Title is separated from risk of loss under § 2-509(2) and the acknowledgment must be to the buyer rather than the seller. Acknowledgment need not be written but the question of whether acknowledgment means receipt or mailing not decided.).

[98] UCC § 2-509(3).

[99] See UCC § 2-104, last paragraph of comment 2 which will require understanding the remainder of comment 2.

[1] See Ron Mead T.V. & Appliances v. Legendary Homes, Inc., 746 P.2d 1163 (Okla. App. 1987).

[2] See St. Paul Fire & Marine Ins. Co. v. Toman, 351 N.W.2d 146 (S.D. 1984).

[3] UCC § 1-102 comment 2.

[4] UCC § 2-509(4). It also suggests that the provisions of § 2-509 are subject to § 2-327 (sale on approval contracts where the risk of loss does not pass until the buyer accepts the goods

loss rules by their agreement.[5] This section presents uncertainty because it requires interpretation of myriad statements in the agreement which may or may not constitute a § 2-509(4) variation by agreement.[6] Again, however, the UCC prefers the higher value of freedom of contract to the value of certainty.

C. *Risk of Loss Where There Is a Breach.*

If the seller ships goods which are nonconforming, or if the goods are perfect but the *tender* of delivery is nonconforming,[7] the buyer has a *right* of rejection.[8] That right of rejection will reallocate the normal risk of loss rules, i.e., the rules that would apply in the absence of breach. In an FOB shipment contract, the risk would normally pass to the buyer upon delivery of the goods to the carrier. In a destination contract, the risk would normally pass when the goods were tendered to the buyer. When, however, it is discovered that the tender or goods delivered were nonconforming, giving rise to a right of rejection in the buyer, those normal risk of loss rules no longer apply. Instead, the risk of loss remains on the seller until the buyer has accepted the goods,[9] or until the nonconformity is cured.[10]

If the buyer has accepted the goods, she can no longer reject them. She may, however, be able to revoke her acceptance of the goods which will place her in the same position as if she had rejected.[11] If a buyer rightfully revokes her acceptance of the goods, she may treat the risk of loss as remaining on the seller (though, again, normally the risk would be on the buyer) but only to the extent of any deficiency in her insurance coverage.[12] If the buyer has complete coverage, the risk of loss is entirely hers. If she has no coverage, it is entirely on the seller, and if the buyer has incomplete coverage, the risk is on the

---

(§ 2-327(1)(a)), whereas in a "sale or return" contract, the risk remains on the seller throughout the contract. *See* comment 3 to § 2-317. The very concept of "approval" suggests that the buyer is in possession of the goods to determine if he wants to purchase them. In a "sale or return" contract, however, a sale has been made though the buyer may choose to return the goods if he does so seasonably. UCC § 2-327(2)(a). Section 2-509(4) proceeds to suggest that the provisions of § 2-509 are also subject to § 2-510 which deals with risk of loss where there has been a breach of contract and will be discussed in the next subsection.

[5] *See* Forest Nursery Co. v. I.W.S., Inc., 141 Misc. 2d 661, 534 N.Y.S.2d 86 (1988).

[6] *See, e.g.,* Consolidated Bottling Co. v. Jaco Equip. Corp., 442 F.2d 660 (2d Cir. 1971) (holding the "F. O. B. purchaser's truck" was a contrary agreement).

[7] *See* William F. Wilke, Inc. v. Cummins Diesel Engines, Inc., 252 Md. 611, 250 A.2d 886 (1969).

[8] *See* UCC § 2-601.

[9] Acceptance of the goods may occur in any of three ways: (a) the buyer signifies his acceptance, whether or not the goods are conforming, (b) the buyer fails to make an effective rejection under UCC § 2-602 and, thereby, is deemed to have accepted the goods, or (c) the buyer does any act inconsistent with the seller's ownership of the goods such as using the goods unless such use is essential and operates to mitigate damages. UCC § 2-606.

[10] UCC § 2-510(1). *See* Moses v. Newman, 658 S.W.2d 119 (Tenn. App. 1983); Jakowski v. Carole Chevrolet, Inc., 180 N.J. Super. 122, 433 A.2d 841 (1981). Cure (repairing or replacing the good to overcome the nonconformity), is described in UCC § 2-508.

[11] Revocation of acceptance is found in UCC § 2-608 and requires a substantial impairment of the value of the goods which is a much higher standard than the rejection standard of UCC § 2-601 since rejection can occur for any defect including an insubstantial defect. Beyond the "substantial impairment" requirement, the buyer must also show either (1) he accepted the goods on the reasonable assumption that the nonconformity would be cured and it was not cured, or (2) he did not discover the substantial impairment either because (i) it was too difficult to discover, or (ii) he did not discover it because of the seller's assurances.

[12] UCC § 2-510(2).

seller as to the "deficiency" in the buyer's coverage. A moment's thought about this risk of loss rule clearly indicates its anti-subrogation quality, i.e., if the buyer's insurance company must pay for the casualty to the goods, there is no claim to which the insurance company can be subrogated because the insured buyer would have such a claim against the seller only if the buyer's insurance were deficient.

Where the buyer breaches the contract, a similar analysis applies. The situation is fascinating but unlikely as the following example suggests. Buyer and seller form a contract for the sale of equipment. The seller takes conforming equipment from its inventory and marks or otherwise designates it as referring to the buyer, i.e., this particular machine will be sent to the buyer. In so designating this particular one for the buyer, the seller has *identified* the goods to the contract.[13] The contract is an FOB shipment contract. Before the machine is delivered to the carrier, however, the buyer repudiates the contract. Under normal risk of loss rules, the risk of loss has not yet passed to the buyer because, again, the machine has yet to be delivered to the carrier. Shortly after the repudiation, the machine is destroyed without the fault of the seller. If all of these elements are met, i.e., where the goods are conforming and already identified to the contract when the buyer repudiates before the risk of loss would normally pass to the buyer, the seller may, to the extent of any deficiency in its insurance coverage, treat the risk of loss as resting on the buyer for a commercially reasonable time.[14] Again, the provision is clearly an anti-subrogation provision because it precludes recovery by a subrogee insurance company by limiting the seller's claim against the buyer only to that for which the seller is not insured.[15]

The extant case law concerning the UCC risk of loss mechanism suggests no major problems in its operation.

---

[13] *See* UCC § 2-501 and the discussion of "identification," *supra* at § 113(C).

[14] UCC § 2-510(3). For a rare application of this section, *see* Multiplastics, Inc. v. Arch Indus., 166 Conn. 280, 348 A.2d 618 (1974). In Mercanti v. Persson, 160 Conn. 468, 280 A.2d 137 (1971), the court could discover no breach by the buyer. In Poral Galleries, Inc. v. Tomar Prods., Inc., 60 Misc. 2d 523, 302 N.Y.S.2d 871 (1969) more than a "commercially reasonable time" had passed so that the risk no longer rested on the buyer.

[15] Comment 3 to § 2-510 removes the last fig leaf of doubt about the anti-subrogation nature of this section. The father of the UCC, Karl Llewellyn, thought insurance companies ought to pay without being subrogated since they receive premiums to assume such risks.

Chapter 9

REMEDIES FOR BREACH OF CONTRACT

§ 117. Survey — Contract Interests, Compensation, Economics, and Remedies.

A. *The Three Interests.*

The purpose of contract law is often stated as the fulfillment of those expectations which have been induced by the making of a promise. If the promise is breached, the legal system protects the expectations by attempting to place the injured promisee in the position he would have been in had the promise been performed. The promisee has been disappointed in his expectation interest, i.e., whatever he would have gained had the promise been performed.[1] Sometimes this is stated as giving the promisee the "benefit of the bargain." While the expectation interest is paramount in contract remedies, there are two other interests which have strong claims to protection.[2]

A promisee may rely to his detriment and suffer a loss or a minus quantity because of a promise which has been made to him. The same promise may have induced reasonable expectations. Perhaps the expectation interest cannot be protected because it cannot be accurately measured. Or, perhaps there is no reasonable expectation interest. Yet, the promisee has reasonably relied upon the promise and changed his position, thereby incurring a loss. In this situation, the legal system may protect the reliance interest of the promisee.[3] The object is to place the promisee in as good a position as he was in before the promise was made. It is to restore him to his original position by enforcing his claim against the promisor in the amount of loss suffered. Unlike the reliance interest, the expectation interest does not require any showing of loss. The protection of the reliance interest is based upon the loss or minus quantity in the injured promisee.

A third interest protected by the legal system involves both a loss to the injured promisee and a corresponding gain (a plus quantity) or "benefit" to the defaulting promisor. In this situation the injured promisee has relied on the promise and suffered a loss in so doing. Moreover, he not only has incurred a loss but also has conferred gain, i.e., some value, on the defaulting promisor. When the promisor fails to perform, a court may force the promisor to surrender the benefit he has unjustly received from the promisee. The promisor has been unjustly enriched at the expense of the promisee. Here the object is to compel the defaulting promisor to surrender the unjust enrichment (gain) and to restore the injured promisee to his position prior to the making of a promise. By compelling the promisor to return the plus quantity or enrichment to the promisee, the minus quantity in the promisee is cancelled and he is restored to status quo. This is called the restitution interest and is based upon the foundation idea that no one should be enriched at the expense of another.[4]

It is essential to understand each of the three interests set forth — the expectation, reliance, and restitution interests.[5] The analysis which follows

---

[1] RESTATEMENT 2d § 344(a).

[2] The expectation, reliance, and restitution interests are fully explored in the classic two-part article by Fuller and Perdue, *The Reliance Interest in Contract Damages,* 46 YALE L.J. 52, 373 (1936), upon which the discussion in this section is largely based.

[3] RESTATEMENT 2d § 344(b).

[4] RESTATEMENT 2d § 344(c).

[5] For a comprehensive discussion of the three interests, *see* Potter v. Oster, 426 N.W.2d 148 (Iowa 1988).

explores each of these interests in detail. Before proceeding with such analysis, it is essential to understand certain fundamental concepts to avoid needless confusion in the sections which follow.

B. *Compensation.*

The term "compensation" is often used in any discussion of contract remedies. Compensation, however, is a generic term and must always be followed with the question: compensation for what?[6] It is insufficient to answer the question by suggesting that contract remedies deal with compensation for injuries. The exploration must proceed beyond this and answer the question: compensation for injuries to which interest? Whether the legal system is attempting to compensate for injury to disappointed expectations, detrimental reliance, or unjust enrichment, it is attempting to compensate or to provide redress to the injured promisee for the breach of promise. Our legal system does not *compel* the fulfillment of promises. It does not punish contract breakers except in egregious cases. Rather, it provides redress in the form of compensation to injured promisees when a promise is breached.[7] It is conceivable, however, for a legal system to compel the enforcement of promises through its criminal law or at least to allow recoveries to injured promisees which go beyond mere compensation. But the Anglo-American legal system has not chosen this route. It has chosen to attempt to place the injured promisee in the position she would have occupied had the promise been performed (expectation interest) or to restore her to the position she was in before the promise was made (reliance and restitution interests).

C. *Economic Theory.*

In general, it may be said that economic theory supports the protection of the expectation interest through substitutional relief in the form of money damages.[8] At the beginning of this volume, we summarized the economic theory of the social institution of contract, i.e., the allocation of the resources of society through voluntary agreements facilitating future exchanges. Value maximization is effectuated where goods worth $1000 to X are worth $1500 to Y who has $1500 to spend so that the total value is $2500. If the parties agree to an exchange of the goods for $1500, the result is that X now has $1500 and Y has goods worth $1500 for a total of $3000.[9] After making a contract to sell the goods for $1500, X may discover another buyer (Z) who is willing to pay $2200 for them. If X breaches the contract but fully compensates Y to the extent of $500, he is better off because his net return is $1700 after the sale to Z for $2200. Z is pleased because he has received goods worth $2200 to him. This results in economic efficiency but it involves a breach of contract. The protection of the expectation interest through a substitutional money dam-

---

[6]*See* Cooter & Eisenberg, *Damages for Breach of Contract*, 73 CALIF. L. REV. 1432 (1985).
[7]Norman's Heritage Real Estate Co. v. Aetna Cas. & Sur. Co., 727 F.2d 911 (10th Cir. 1984); Quigley v. Pet, Inc., 162 Cal. App. 3d 223, 208 Cal. Rptr. 394 (1984).
[8]*See* Cooter & Eisenberg, *supra* note 6.
[9]"Value" is measured by the value to the individual and the parties' willingness and ability to transfer the goods and to pay. Economic theory does not suggest a preferable measure of value.

ages remedy induces efficient breach.[10] It is important, however, to recognize the limitations of this approach. Even from an economics perspective, it does not consider transaction costs, i.e., those costs associated with the bargaining process and dispute resolution. Nor does it consider non-economic perspectives such as any moral obligation to keep one's promises.[11] Yet, considering contract remedies from the pure economic perspective can be helpful with numerous questions, including whether the remedy of specific performance should be expanded[12] or whether liquidated damage clauses which parties agree to at contract formation should be more available.[13] In general, however, the impact of law and economics scholarship on the law of contracts to this time has been limited to providing economic theory in support of existing structure.[14]

D. *Contract Remedies.*

1. Right to Damages — Nominal Damages.

Any breach of contract, total or partial, provides the aggrieved party with a right to bring an action for damages unless the claim for damages has been suspended or discharged.[15] If the breach of contract causes no loss or where a

---

[10] "The key result is that the expectation remedy is the only remedy that creates efficient incentives with respect to breaches of contracts. This is because the expectation remedy forces the breaching party to pay in damages the value of the good to the breached-against party. If another buyer values the good more than this, then it is efficient for that buyer to have the good. Given the expectation measure of damages, the seller will have an incentive to breach in order to obtain the higher offer.... [I]f damages are below expectation damages an inefficient breach might occur. This is the problem with the reliance remedy, because it leads to a level of damages below the expectation level. The restitution remedy is even worse because it provides less than the reliance measure of damages." A. M. POLINSKY, AN INTRODUCTION TO LAW AND ECONOMICS 33-34 (2d ed. 1989). See, however, Chapter 8 of the same volume which reinforces an earlier conclusion that a breach of contract remedy that is efficient with respect to every consideration does not exist, i.e., while the expectation remedy is preferable with respect to a decision to breach the contract, the restitution remedy is preferable with respect to a reliance decision and a liquidated damage remedy is preferable with respect to risk allocation.

[11] See Introductory Note to Chapter 16, RESTATEMENT 2d.

[12] Specific performance, however, would preclude efficient breach if it were available in the example suggested in the text. For differing views of the expanded availability of specific performance, see Schwartz, *The Case for Specific Performance,* 89 YALE L.J. 271 (1979) as contrasted with Kronman, *Specific Performance,* 45 U. CHI. L. REV. 351 (1978).

[13] See Goetz & Scott, *Liquidated Damages, Penalties, and the Just Compensation Principle: Some Notes on an Enforcement Model and Theory of Efficient Breach,* 77 COLUM. L. REV. 554 (1977).

[14] One writer recently remarked, "At most, the results suggest that 'law and economics' is a source of sometimes useful information for working within already established rules. It does not alter rules nor does it alter the weighing of various judicial interests." Harrison, *Trends and Traces: A Preliminary Evaluation of Economic Analysis in Contract Law,* 1988 ANNUAL SURVEY OF AMERICAN LAW [New York Univ.] 73, 98-99 (1989). Other literature on the economics of contract law includes THE ECONOMICS OF CONTRACT LAW (Kronman & Posner eds. 1979); POSNER, ECONOMIC ANALYSIS OF LAW, ch. 4 (3d ed. 1986); Birmingham, *Breach of Contract, Damage Measures and Economic Efficiency,* 24 RUTGERS L. REV. 273 (1970).

[15] RESTATEMENT 2d § 346(1). The duty to pay damages can be suspended or discharged through the agreement of the parties or otherwise. If the damage claim is discharged, the right to damages is extinguished. If the duty of performance, as contrasted with the duty to pay damages, is suspended or discharged as, for example, when the performance becomes impracticable or the purpose of the performance is frustrated, no breach has occurred. Therefore, there is no right to a damage remedy. For a study of the history of the development of the modern law relating to the recovery of damages in contract actions, see Washington, *Damages in Contract at Common Law,* 47 LAW Q. REV. 345 (1931) and 48 LAW Q. REV. 90 (1932).

purported loss cannot be adequately proven, the breach remains and the aggrieved party has a damage claim to a nominal amount, typically one cent or one dollar, as a manifestation of breach without any provable damage.[16] There may be relatively rare situations where an action for nominal damages will serve, in effect, as a declaratory judgment of the rights and duties of the parties to the contract.

2. Money Damages — Expectation Interest — Reliance Interest.

The usual remedy available to an aggrieved party when a breach of contract has occurred is an action for the recovery of compensation in the form of money damages to protect the expectation interest, i.e, an award that will place the injured promisee in the same position he would have been in had the contract been performed. Where, for example, a buyer agrees to purchase an automobile for $10,000 and the seller breaches that contract, the typical buyer will purchase the car elsewhere. Assuming a reasonable substitute or "cover" purchase price of $11,500, the buyer has been damaged to the extent of the difference between the contract and cover prices and should be awarded $1500 in damages.[17] The court may also award money damages to protect the reliance interest, i.e., the loss caused by the reliance of the promisee to place him in the position he would have occupied had no promise been made to him.[18] Where, for example, a party expends certain sums to start a new business venture relying on a promise that is breached, the promisee's profit expectation may not be provable, but his out-of-pocket loss can be shown. The court should award damages to protect the reliance interest in such a case.

The foregoing illustrations suggest the normal operation of the legal system in protecting the expectation interest or reliance interest of an injured promisee. The party seeking relief brings his action "at law" rather than a "suit in equity" because the relief he seeks is a damage award.

3. Specific Performance or Injunction — Expectation Interest.

What is generally considered an exceptional remedy may also protect the expectation interest. Where the normal remedy of money damages is inadequate to protect the expectation interest, the court may seek to protect that interest by decreeing *specific performance* of the contract, i.e., ordering the promisor to perform or by enjoining (injunction) the non-performance of the contract.[19] The remedy of specific performance does not provide substitutional relief as does the damage remedy. The court simply orders the promisor to perform so as to provide the promisee with the specific or literal performance promised. The most common example of this remedy occurs in contracts for

---

[16]RESTATEMENT 2d § 346(2).

[17]The "cover" remedy is found in UCC § 2-712. It is the counterpart of the seller's "resale" remedy in UCC § 2-706. Where the buyer breaches and the seller finds another buyer, if the reasonable resale price is lower than the contract price, the seller is entitled to the difference between the higher contract price and the lower resale price.

[18]RESTATEMENT 2d § 345(a) and comment b.

[19]*See* RESTATEMENT 2d § 345(b). "[W]e do not grant specific relief ordinarily, but only exceptionally where substituted relief (money damages) is held inadequate." R. POUND, INTRODUCTION TO THE PHILOSOPHY OF LAW 135 (rev. ed. 1954).

the sale of land where the damage remedy is obviously inadequate since any tract of land is unique, at least in terms of its location. Since the buyer cannot purchase that particular land elsewhere as he could purchase an ordinary automobile or other ordinary chattel, the buyer may justifiably claim that the damage remedy would be inadequate. The same analysis would apply to any unique chattel.[20]

The buyer is not compelled to seek specific performance, i.e., he may choose his damage remedy. Again, however, since that remedy is inadequate in the sense that a substitute purchase cannot occur, he is entitled to choose specific performance. Where the remedy of specific performance will not fulfill the total expectation interest of the plaintiff, a court may enforce the promise to the extent possible and also grant damages for that part of the performance that cannot occur.[21]

4. Restoration or Damages — Restitution Interest.

A court can protect the restitution interest (prevention of the enrichment of one party at the expense of another party) either by awarding damages, or, in an appropriate case, by requiring the enriched party to restore a specific thing to the other party (specific restitution).[22] If, for example, a seller is induced to convey land through the misrepresentation of the buyer, the buyer has been enriched at the seller's expense and the seller may have the land restored to him through specific restitution.[23] The seller is then placed in the same position as if the misrepresentation had not occurred.

5. Declaratory Judgment and Arbitration Award.

In addition to the foregoing judicial remedies, courts are also empowered to grant declaratory judgments which determine the legal relations between the parties to a contract without granting damages or other relief. A clarification of the rights and duties of the parties may occur even prior to any breach of contract and can be an effective means to resolve disputes as well as preventing litigation.[24]

A non-judicial remedy is playing an increasingly important role in the resolution of contract disputes. The parties may have agreed at the time of formation that any dispute will be submitted to arbitration, or, absent such an agreement at formation, they may agree to submit a subsequent dispute to arbitration. Statutes regulating the arbitration process have been widely enacted throughout the country and courts typically enforce arbitration awards from one arbitrator or from an arbitration panel where each party is represented. While the dollar amount of disputes submitted to arbitration were originally small, at present it is not uncommon to see multi-million dollar

---

[20] The UCC extends this concept to goods that, in effect, are unique because of scarcity. *See* § 2-716(1) where the remedy of specific performance will be granted where the buyer cannot effect a cover or in other reasonable circumstances.

[21] The other relief may take the form of damages or restitution as well as indemnity against future harm. *See* RESTATEMENT 2d § 358(3) and comment c.

[22] RESTATEMENT 2d § 345(d) (damages) and (c) (specific restitution).

[23] *See* RESTATEMENT 2d § 372(1) and ill. 1.

[24] RESTATEMENT 2d § 345(e).

disputes submitted to the arbitration process rather than the judicial process. The award rendered by the panel of non-judges will typically be transformed into a judgment by a court through summary procedures.[25] Appeals from arbitration awards are normally upheld in the absence of abuse of the arbitrator's discretion. A detailed exploration of the arbitration process is beyond the scope of this volume.

6. Uniform Commercial Code Remedies.

Where the parties form a contract for the sale of goods, the UCC applies. The Code provides remedies protecting the expectation interest for breaches of such contracts. These remedies are a combination of traditional contract remedies and the creativity of the father of the Code, Professor Karl Llewellyn.[26] References to sections of the Code have been included in the discussion of contract remedies to this point, and those references will continue throughout the remaining discussion of traditional contract remedies in this chapter. It is important that the student of contract law recognize the symmetry between Code remedies and traditional contract law remedies. It is also important, however, to provide a summary of UCC remedies in one section of this chapter for convenient reference to those remedies. This section appears at the conclusion of this chapter.

§ 118. The Expectation Interest — Breach by Builder — Cost of Completion Versus Diminution in Value.

A. *The General Concept.*

The expectation interest normally envisions protecting an aggrieved party by placing him in the position he would have occupied had the contract been performed.[27] The protection of that interest will allow recovery for any loss in

---

[25] RESTATEMENT 2d § 345(f).

[26] *See* Peters, *Remedies for Breach of Contracts Relation to the Sale of Goods Under the Uniform Commercial Code,* 73 YALE L.J. 199 (1963).

[27] *See* Vanderpool v. Higgs, 10 Kan. App. 2d 1, 690 P.2d 391 (1984); Thorp Sales Corp. v. Gyuro Grading Co., 111 Wis. 2d 431, 331 N.W.2d 342 (1983); Ford Motor Co. v. Kirkmyer Motor Co., 65 F.2d 1001 (4th Cir. 1933); Frederick Raff Co. v. Murphy, 110 Conn. 234, 147 A. 709 (1929); Smith v. Pallay, 130 Or. 282, 279 P. 279 (1929). *See* RESTATEMENT 2d § 344 and comment b. *See also* UCC § 1-106(1): "The remedies provided by this Act shall be liberally administered to the end that the aggrieved party may be put in as good a position as if the other party had fully performed...." Professors Cooter and Eisenberg in their article, *Damages for Breach of Contract,* 73 CALIF. L. REV. 1432, 1468 (1985), summarize three meanings of "expectation": (1) "expectation principle" which is the usual understanding of placing the injured promisee in the position he would have been in if the contract had been performed, (2) "expectation theory" which bases damages on the measure that parties situated like the contracting parties probably would have agreed to if they had bargained under ideal conditions and addressed the damage issue, and (3) "statistical expectation" where a party makes a number of comparable contracts with a known probable rate of breach in which case he should enjoy the overall profit level he expected to achieve rather that the profit level he would have achieved if the rate of breach were zero. The authors conclude that where the expectation principle and expectation theory diverge, as where a seller has a statistical expectation, the theory rather than the principle should govern. Consequently, where damages would be measured by the seller's lost volume (to be discussed later in this chapter in the exploration of UCC § 2-708(2)), the parties would probably have agreed (expectation theory) to a much smaller measure of damages such as the forfeit of a deposit rather than the seller's profit on the contract of sale which has been breached, had the parties consciously adverted to the damages question.

value to the plaintiff under his particular circumstances[28] as well as any other loss caused by the breach including incidental and consequential damages.[29] This is sometimes stated as allowing compensation for gains prevented as well as losses incurred, i.e., the injured promisee is entitled to recover the economic equivalent of the performance promised at the time and place specified in the contract plus any losses incurred or gains prevented through failure of performance. To accomplish this end, the aggrieved party receives substitutional relief, i.e., compensation in money for defeated expectations in place of the breaching promisor's performance. If, however, a breach occurs prior to the completion of the promisee's performance, he is saved from the time, effort, and expense of completion because of the promisor's breach. Any saved costs or other loss that the promisee has avoided by not having to perform must be deducted from the money damages to which he is otherwise entitled.[30] This is in accordance with the general principle that an aggrieved party may not recover damages that could have been avoided without undue risk, burden or humiliation.[31]

B. Cost of Completion Versus Diminution in Value — Builder's Breach.

The principle that the aggrieved party is entitled to the economic equivalent of the promised performance as well as damages for attendant losses can be easily applied in the garden variety case. If, for example, a builder promises to construct a building and his performance is deficient, it would appear obvious that any additional cost to the owner in having another builder complete the structure would be the measure of damages. Problems arise, however, where the cost of completing performance substantially exceeds the increased value the promisee would have enjoyed had the contract been performed.

In the classic case of *Jacob & Youngs, Inc. v. Kent*,[32] the builder used the wrong brand of galvanized pipe that was physically identical to the specified brand in the construction of a house. The normal measure of damages would have been the cost of replacing all of the pipe encased in the walls throughout the house which would have involved considerable deconstruction and reconstruction of the house at great expense. The defect in the builder's performance was not a structural defect. Had the defect been structural, exposing the owner to a dangerous condition, the cost of replacement (sometimes known as cost of repair) would have been appropriate.[33] Absent any idiosyn-

---

[28] *See* RESTATEMENT 2d § 347(a) and comment b.

[29] RESTATEMENT 2d § 347(b) and comment c describing incidental damages as any reasonable effort to avoid loss, and consequential damages as losses such as injury to person or property resulting from the breach.

[30] *See In re* Kellet Aircraft Corp., 191 F.2d 231, 236 (3d Cir. 1951); Bucholz v. Green Bros., 272 Mass. 49, 172 N.E. 101 (1930). RESTATEMENT 2d § 347(c). If, for example, a builder is not permitted to complete a construction contract through the repudiation of the owner, the saved cost of completion is normally deducted from the contract price to arrive at the builder's measure of expectation damage recovery. This and other formulas will be explored in the next section.

[31] RESTATEMENT 2d § 350. This is often referred to as the mitigation principle or principle of avoidable consequences. It will be explored later in this chapter.

[32] 230 N.Y. 239, 129 N.E. 889 (1921).

[33] *See* Kenney v. Medlin Constr. Co., 68 N.C. App. 339, 315 S.E. 2d 311 (1984). *See also* RESTATEMENT 2d § 348 ill. 3.

cratic reason why the specified brand had to be used,[34] the use of a substitute brand that was physically identical should permit the owner to recover only the diminution in the value of the property caused by the breach where the cost of completion would be grossly disproportionate to the loss in value. In an opinion by Judge Cardozo, the court refused to permit recovery of the cost of replacement and relegated the owner to the difference in value which, it suggested, would be either nominal or nothing in this case. It is fashionable to suggest this result as an avoidance of "economic waste."[35] This is, however, misleading since, if damages were awarded for cost of completion, the typical plaintiff would not destroy the property to replace the existing pipe with identical pipe simply to replace the brand name.[36]

It must be emphasized that the cost of repair or replacement (cost of completion) is the normal remedy since it clearly provides the aggrieved party with his expectation recovery[37] and the cost of completion is typically less than the loss in value.[38] The cost of completion measure, therefore, would be mandated by the principle of avoidable damages, i.e., any losses that can be reasonably avoided should be avoided.[39] The same principle, however, should restrict recovery to the diminished value of the property where awarding cost of completion damages would result in a substantial windfall to the aggrieved party. Where, for example, the cost of repairing defects that were not structural in a $7000 pool amounted to $11,381, the court remanded the case for a determination of diminution in value.[40] But where the cost of completion is not clearly disproportionate to the value expected, courts agree that cost of completion should be the measure.[41] Cost of completion, however, is so ingrained that it may appear as the preferable measure even where it is reasonably clear that the aggrieved party will not use such a damage award to complete the repair.

In a well-known case,[42] the owner operated a gravel excavation plant on certain land which he leased to the defendant for a term of seven years. The lease contained a clause requiring the lessee to leave the property at a uniform grade at the completion of the term. The defendant failed to perform that

---

[34] If the house was to be owned by the president of the company whose brand was specified in the contract, a reason for the use of that brand and no other, including a physically identical product, would be shown. Even in that situation, however, Judge Cardozo apparently would have required that specification to be an express condition precedent to the duty of the owner before deciding that the pipe had to be replaced with all of the attendant costs of that replacement.

[35] See FIRST RESTATEMENT § 346 comment b.

[36] See RESTATEMENT 2d § 348 comment c.

[37] See Gilbert v. City of Caldwell, 112 Idaho 386, 732 P.2d 355 (1987) (comparing § 346(1)(a) of the FIRST RESTATEMENT with § 348(2) of the RESTATEMENT 2d). Under the UCC, § 2-714(2), the measure of damages is the difference at the time and place of acceptance between the value of the goods accepted and the value they would have had if they had been as warranted. Many courts have concluded that a useful application of this measure is found in the cost of repair or replacement. See, e.g., Vista St. Clair, Inc. v. Landry's Com. Furnishings, Inc., 57 Or. App. 254, 643 P.2d 1378 (1982); Winchester v. McCulloch Bros. Garage, Inc., 388 So. 2d 927 (Ala. 1980); S. H. Nevers Corp. v. Husky Hydraulics, Inc., 408 A.2d 676 (Me. 1979); Morrow v. New Homes, Inc., 548 P.2d 279 (Alaska 1976).

[38] RESTATEMENT 2d § 348 comment c.

[39] RESTATEMENT 2d § 350. See also Smart v. Tidwell Indus., 668 S.W.2d 605 (Mo. App. 1984) (wherever evidence shows cost of repair to be less than diminution in value, cost of repair should be the measure whether applied to warranty or other contracts cases).

[40] Mayfield v. Swafford, 106 Ill. App. 3d 610, 435 N.E.2d 953 (1982).

[41] See Eastlake Constr. Co. v. Hess, 102 Wash. 2d 30, 686 P.2d 465 (1980).

[42] Groves v. John Wunder Co., 205 Minn. 163, 286 N.W. 235 (1939).

promise and the plaintiff sought to recover the cost of completion which was found to be approximately $60,000. The diminished value of the premises, however, was only $12,000, i.e., if the $60,000 had been expended to provide the uniform grade required by the lease, the increase in value to this industrial tract would have been only one-fifth the cost of the improvement. Yet, the court held that plaintiff was entitled to the cost of completion. The court emphasized the "wilful" nature of the defendant's breach which is a dubious requirement.[43] It also attempted to distinguish cases involving "economic waste." As suggested earlier,[44] "economic waste" can be misleading in any event because it is more than unlikely that the aggrieved party will spend five times the value of the improvement to complete the contract in accordance with its literal terms.[45] The court failed to inquire into the purpose of the contract, i.e., if the promisee seeks a specific result, even if that result would diminish rather than enhance the value of the property, he is entitled to that result.[46] If, however, the promisee is interested in the net economic gain as where the property is held strictly for investment purposes, a court may properly conclude that the diminution in value standard ought to be applied.[47]

Another manifestation of the purpose of the promisee is found in a well-known case where the defendant agreed to restore the farm on which the plaintiffs lived to an approximation of its original state after completing a strip mining operation. The cost of the restorative work was estimated at $29,000 which would have enhanced the value of the land by only $300 and the total value of the farm was only $5000. It was clear that the plaintiffs were insistent upon the commitment of the defendant to restore the land. The court overturned a $5000 jury verdict because it believed that the plaintiffs were entitled only to diminution in value of $300.[48] The case, however, is similar to the construction of a grotesque structure on the land. The plaintiffs

---

[43] Many courts insist that the diminution in value concept should not apply if the breach is "wilful." Yet, a good faith albeit wilful deviation from construction plans should not be a precluding factor. See Kangas v. Anthony Trust, 110 Ill. App. 3d 876, 441 N.E.2d 1271 (1982) and cases cited therein.

[44] See supra text at note 36.

[45] In this case, in fact, the plaintiff did not spend the settlement which approximated the damage award for this purpose. See J. DAWSON & W. HARVEY, CASES ON CONTRACTS AND CONTRACT REMEDIES 28 (1959).

[46] Assume the extreme hypothetical of a party who desires the erection of a grotesque structure on his property that will actually diminish its value. The contract price is $10,000 and the promisor fails to perform. A reasonable substitute contractor requires $25,000. Should the promisor succeed in his defense that the valuation of the property would have diminished had he performed and, therefore, the plaintiff has suffered no damage? The classic retort is found in an old case: "A man may do what he will with his own, ... and if he chooses to erect a monument to his caprice or folly on his premises, and employs and pays another to do it, it does not lie with the defendant who has been so employed and paid for building it, to say that his own performance would not be beneficial to the plaintiff." Chamberlain v. Parker, 45 N.Y. 569, 572 (1871).

[47] See Advanced, Inc. v. Wilkes, 711 P.2d 524 (Alaska 1985).

[48] Peevyhouse v. Garland Coal & Mining Co., 382 P.2d 109 (Okla. 1962), cert. denied, 375 U.S. 906 (1963). The jury award of $5000 (the value of the farm) appeared to have no basis except sympathy for the plaintiff. In another case, there was testimony that $56,350 would be required to cure defects in an otherwise structurally sound house with a market value of $93,000. Another witness testified that the cost of curing the defects would be $800. Diminution in value estimates ranged from $83,000 to $800. The jury awarded $9000 which the court upheld because the amount was within the outside limits of the testimony. Rands v. Forest Lake Lumber Mart, Inc., 402 N.W.2d 565 (Minn. App. 1987).

were, apparently, untutored and unwise concerning the cost of restoration. They clearly required a result under the contract, i.e., the restoration of their land. Where the property is the dwelling place of a party who insists upon a particular result on that property, the cost of completion appears to be the appropriate measure to protect the expectation interest.[49] Moreover, the result in this case is particularly difficult to accept since it actively encourages nonperformance.[50]

If the diminution in value is difficult to prove with reasonable certainty, the cost of completion measure should apply, even if it appears that the result is something of a windfall for the plaintiff.[51]

§ 119. Expectation, Reliance, and Restitution Interests — Breach.

A. *Introduction.*

As suggested at the start of this chapter, the law may protect three separate interests of the injured promisee, the expectation, reliance, and restitution interests. Normally, an injured promisee will be satisfied to seek his recovery for defeated expectations. However, in certain cases, he may wish to seek protection of his reliance or restitution interests. The operation of the law in protecting each interest will now be explored. Since construction contracts often provide good illustrations of the differences in the protection of each interest, the discussion will focus upon such contracts.[52] However, illustrations involving other types of contracts will also be examined.

B. *Expectation Interest.*

When an owner (*O*) breaches a construction contract with a builder (*B*), the expectation interest of the builder is protected by the simple formula: contract price (or unpaid portion thereof) minus the cost of completion (cost avoided by builder in not having to complete performance).[53] Assume the contract price is $10,000 and the builder has not yet begun performance. If the cost of performing the entire contract is $9,000, the builder expects to receive $1,000 as the benefit of his bargain. The simple formula yields this result: $10,000 minus $9,000 = $1,000. If *B* has begun performance and the cost of the work already done is $5,000, leaving $4,000 as the cost of completion, the simple formula results in a recovery of $6,000, i.e., $10,000 minus $4,000. Here, *B* has been compensated for his loss of bargain (or profit), amounting to $1,000, and he has also been compensated for his cost of reliance, $5,000, which he has expended in performing prior to *O*'s breach. The critical element in this formula

---

[49] *See* Kangas v. Anthony Trust, 110 Ill. App. 3d 876, 441 N.E.2d 1271 (1982).

[50] *See* Vernon, *Expectancy Damages for Breach of Contract: A Primer and Critique,* 1976 WASH. U.L.Q. 179, 228.

[51] *See* RESTATEMENT 2d § 348 comment c.

[52] For an excellent discussion of the measure of damages for breach of construction contracts, *see* Patterson, *Builder's Measure of Recovery for Breach of Contract,* 31 COLUM. L. REV. 1286 (1931).

[53] Millen v. Gulesian, 229 Mass. 27, 118 N.E. 267 (1918). *See also* Guerini Stone Co. v. Carlin Constr. Co., 240 U.S. 264 (1915); Fuller v. United Elec. Co., 70 Nev. 448, 273 P.2d 136 (1954); Hottinger v. Hoffman-Henon Co., 303 Pa. 283, 154 A. 598 (1931); Bergman v. Parker, 216 A.2d 581 (D.C. App. 1966); RESTATEMENT 2d § 348(2)(b).

is the cost of completion which may create difficulties of proof. In the absence of contrary evidence, the builder may succeed in proving this amount ($4,000) by simply subtracting the cost of reliance (the amount already expended, i.e., $5,000) from the total cost of complete performance ($9,000).[54]

C. Reliance Interest — Cost of Completion Cannot Be Shown.

Another formula for recovery by B is stated as follows: The profit upon the contract (contract price less B's cost of construction — both expended and to be expended) plus the cost of work actually performed.[55] Under our illustration, the recovery by B will be identical to that of the first formula: $10,000 - $9,000 + $5,000 = $6,000$. The question arises, why would this second formula be used rather than the first formula which yields the same result and is more simple in application? If the critical element of cost of completion is impossible to prove because B cannot demonstrate that he would have made a profit, the second formula cannot be used in its entirety. However, unlike the first formula, it does express the element of the reliance interest, i.e., the cost of work already performed, and recovery of that portion of the second formula may be permitted. Thus, where B agreed to perform construction work which was somewhat experimental in nature and O breached, the evidence did not indicate whether B would have made any profit or whether a loss would have occurred. In rejecting the argument of O that no recovery should be permitted, the court said:

> It does not lie, however, in the mouth of the party, who has voluntarily and wrongfully put an end to the contract, to say that the party injured has not been damaged at least to the amount of what he has been induced fairly and in good faith to lay out and expend, including his own services, after making allowance for the value of materials on hand; at least it does not lie in the mouth of the party in fault to say this, unless he can show that the expenses of the party injured have been extravagant, and unnecessary for the purpose of carrying out the contract.[56]

It should be noted, however, that if the breaching party (O) can prove that the contract would have resulted in a loss to B, B may not recover his reliance interest.[57] Thus, if the contract price is $10,000, the cost of work performed is $5,000 (reliance), and the cost of completion is $6,000, the result would have been a $1,000 loss to B. B would like to recover his $5,000 reliance interest but, upon proof by O of the cost of completion, B would be relegated to recovering his expectation interest, i.e., $10,000 minus $6,000 = $4,000. The net effect is as follows: if B wishes to recover an amount beyond his reliance interest, the burden of persuasion is upon B to show such profit, which he

---

[54] Since the burden of proof is on the builder, mere speculation as to the cost of completion will not be sufficient to sustain a recovery. *See* Patterson, *Builder's Measure of Recovery for Breach of Contract,* 31 COLUM. L. REV. 1286, 1292-93 (1931).

[55] Warner v. McClay, 92 Conn. 427, 103 A. 113 (1918). *See also* Frank Horton & Co. v. Cook Elec. Co., 356 F.2d 485 (7th Cir. 1966), *cert. denied,* 384 U.S. 952 (1966).

[56] United States v. Behan, 110 U.S. 338 (1884). *See also* RESTATEMENT 2d § 349 ill. 3.

[57] *See* L. Albert & Son v. Armstrong Rubber Co., 178 F.2d 182 (2d Cir. 1949). *See also* Fuller & Perdue, *The Reliance Interest in Contract Damages,* 46 YALE L.J. 52, 75-80 (1936) and RESTATEMENT 2d § 349, ill. 4.

would normally show by evidence of the cost of completion. If he cannot show such profit, he is relegated to his reliance interest. He may recover even less than his reliance interest if *O* can show the cost of completion which would have resulted in a loss to *B*. Here, however, the burden of persuasion as to such loss is upon *O*.

A third formula found in the cases is stated as follows: for work done, such proportion of the contract price as the cost of the work done bears to the entire cost of completing performance, plus, for the remaining portion of the work, the profit that would have been made as to that work.[58] Using our original illustration of a $10,000 contract price, $5,000 cost of work done and $4,000 cost of completion, the formula, again, yields the identical result of the first and second formulae: $5/9$ths of $10,000 + $4/9$ths of ($10,000 − $9,000) = $6,000. Since this formula, like the second, expresses the reliance element, it may be effectively used by *B* to recover at least that portion when the cost of completion cannot be shown. It should be noted that while all three formulae yield the identical result when the proof allows all elements to be shown and the contract will be completed at a profit for *B*, each of the formulae will yield a different result in a situation wherein the contract could be performed only at a loss for *B*.

D. *Reliance — Interest — Other Questions.*

In nonconstruction cases, there is ample authority for recovery of the reliance interest when the direct profit on the contract cannot be shown.[59] Thus, in one well-known case,[60] a manufacturer of a furnace containing a new type of oil and gas burner wished to exhibit the device at a trade convention. The manufacturer contracted with a carrier which agreed to deliver all of the parts of the furnace to the convention. However, the carrier failed to deliver a critical part, thereby preventing display of the device. The manufacturer could show no loss of direct profit. However, it had expended amounts of money for the shipping charges, the expenses of employees, and the cost of renting a booth at the convention. The court protected the reliance interest of the manufacturer in allowing a recovery for all of these expenses.[61]

E. *Restitution Interest — Contract Damages.*

As suggested earlier, when a builder (*B*) has completed part of the performance and the cost of that part performance (the reliance interest) is greater than the recovery *B* would receive if his expectation interest were protected, *B* may not recover the reliance interest because the owner (*O*) can show that the contract, if completed, would have resulted in a loss. *B*, therefore, would usually be relegated to his expectation interest. However, *B* may be able to recover the amount of the value of the labor and materials, i.e., the reasonable

---

[58] Kehoe v. Rutherford, 56 N.J.L. 23, 27 A. 912 (1893). *See also* Chase v. Smith, 35 Wash. 631, 77 P. 1069 (1904).

[59] RESTATEMENT 2d § 349.

[60] Security Stove & Mfg. Co. v. American Ry. Express Co., 227 Mo. App. 175, 51 S.W.2d 572 (1932).

[61] *See also* Reimer v. Badger Wholesale Co., 147 Wis. 2d 389, 433 N.W.2d 592 (1988) (reliance interest protected in at-will employment contract).

value of the benefit conferred on O.[62] This protects B's restitution interest, i.e., it prevents the unjust enrichment of O at the expense of B. Assume that the contract price is $10,000 and B has substantially underbid. Thus, when B completes one-half of the performance, the cost of the work completed is already $15,000 and the cost of completion is another $15,000. If B completes the contract, he will receive the contract price of $10,000 even though it would have cost B $30,000 to complete this losing contract. But assume that O materially breaches the contract when the job is half completed. At such point the reasonable value of the benefit which B has conferred upon O is $15,000. If B seeks his expectation interest, he will recover nothing: $10,000 minus $15,000 (cost of completion) equals a minus quantity. As suggested above, B may not recover his reliance interest since O can show the cost of completion and the fact that the contract would have been completed at a loss. If B elects to recover his restitution interest, however, the value of the benefit conferred on O at the time of the breach is $15,000. B may recover that amount and the contract price of $10,000 does not limit the recovery. Recognition of this kind of protection of the restitution interest is also found in nonconstruction cases.[63] However, one significant limitation has been placed upon an injured party's recovery of his restitution interest. If the plaintiff has completely or substantially performed, there is case law precluding the protection of the restitution interest and relegating the plaintiff to the expectation interest.[64] Thus, in our example, if B had completed performance, assume that the reasonable value of the benefit conferred would have doubled to $30,000. B would have been relegated to his recovery of the contract price (his expectation interest) of $10,000 since he had completed performance. On the other hand, as suggested earlier, if B had completed only half of his performance, he would recover $15,000. The only explanation for the anomalous limitation which precludes the protection of the restitution interest when the plaintiff has completed performance is found in the common-law forms of action.[65] It would appear that there is no reason why this anachronistic shackle should remain. Further discussion of the restitution interest is found in a subsequent section.[66]

§ 120. The Foreseeability Limitation.

A. *History and Rationale.*

If all of the risks of a breach of contract were placed on a defaulting promisor, regardless of the unusual nature of the risks, a crushing burden may be imposed upon him. In the typical case, the promise is made in a time of optimism on the assumption that it will be performed. If the promisor later discovers that he cannot perform the promise or, at least, that it has become highly inexpedient for him to do so, fairness demands that some equitable

---

[62] Hoyt v. Pomeroy, 87 Conn. 41, 86 A. 755 (1913); Clark v. New York, 4 N.Y. (4 Comstock) 338, 53 Am. Dec. 379 (1850); Philadelphia v. Tripple, 230 Pa. 480, 79 A. 703 (1911).

[63] *See* Crofoot Lumber, Inc. v. Thompson, 163 Cal. App. 2d 324, 329 P.2d 302 (1958); RESTATEMENT 2d § 373(1).

[64] *See* Oliver v. Campbell, 43 Cal. 2d 298, 273 P.2d 15 (1954); RESTATEMENT 2d § 373(2).

[65] *See* 5 CORBIN § 1110.

[66] See § 126.

division of the risks of loss flowing from nonperformance occur so that the reasonable expectations of the promisee may be fulfilled without simultaneously placing an undue burden upon the defaulting promisor. After considerable groping,[67] a principle for the accomplishment of this aim was finally evolved and set forth in the leading case of *Hadley v. Baxendale*,[68] decided by the English Court of Exchequer in 1854. In that case the owner of a mill, which was shut down because of a broken shaft, made a contract with the defendant to transport the shaft to another city, where it was to be used as a model for making a new one. When making the contract, the miller notified the carrier that haste in the delivery of the shaft was essential, but did not inform him that the operation of the mill was dependent upon the prompt delivery of the shaft.[69] In a suit by the miller for negligent delay in the delivery, a claim was made for damages for loss of profits from the nonoperation of the mill. On appeal from a verdict for the plaintiff, it was held that the miller should not recover for loss of such profits, since the carrier could not have been expected to anticipate that the operation of the mill would be suspended by the delay in the delivery of the shaft, as no notice to that effect had been given him. The court said that the rule to be applied in measuring the damages in such cases was this:

> Where two parties have made a contract which one of them has broken, the damages which the other party ought to receive in respect of such breach of contract should be such as may fairly and reasonably be considered either arising naturally, i.e., according to the usual course of things, from such breach of contract itself, or such as may reasonably be supposed to have been in the contemplation of both parties, at the time they made the contract, as the probable result of the breach of it. Now, if the special circumstances under which the contract was actually made were communicated by the plaintiffs to the defendants, and thus made known to both parties, the damages resulting from the breach of such a contract, which they would reasonably contemplate, would be the amount of the injury which would ordinarily follow from a breach of contract under these special circumstances so known and communicated. But, on the other hand, if these special circumstances were wholly unknown to the party breaking the contract, he, at the most, could only be supposed to have had in contemplation the amount of injury which would arise generally, and in the great multitude of cases not affected by any special circumstances, from such a breach of contract. For, had the special circumstances been known, the parties might have specially provided for the breach of contract by special terms as to the damages in that case; and of this advantage it would be very unjust to deprive them.

This principle, known popularly as the rule of *Hadley v. Baxendale,* has demonstrated a remarkable record of consistent application since it was first

---

[67] *See* Washington, *Damages in Contract at Common Law,* 47 LAW Q. REV. 345 (1931), and 48 LAW Q. REV. 90 (1932).

[68] 9 Ex. 341, 156 Eng. Rep. 145 [1854].

[69] In the reporter's summation of the facts in this case (9 Ex. 341 at 344), the statement is made that the carrier *was* informed that the mill was stopped because of the broken shaft. This statement is inconsistent with the court's understanding of the fact situation. The reporter's summation was declared erroneous in Victoria Laundry (Windsor), Ltd. v. Newman Indus., 2 K.B. 528, 537, 1 All E.R. 997, 1001 [1949].

announced in 1854. It has been universally accepted by our courts as a correct statement of the principle in accordance with which the extent of the recovery is to be determined in an action for breach of contract.[70] It has been codified in the UCC.[71]

A more recent English case sums up the two rules in *Hadley v. Baxendale* as follows:[72]

> Everyone, as a reasonable person, is taken to know the "ordinary course of things" and consequently what loss is liable to result from a breach of contract in that ordinary course. This is the subject matter of the "first rule" in *Hadley v. Baxendale*. But to this knowledge, which a contract-breaker is assumed to possess whether he actually possesses it or not, there may have to be added in a particular case knowledge which he actually possesses, of special circumstances outside the "ordinary course of things," of such a kind that a breach in those special circumstances would be liable to cause more loss. Such a case attracts the operation of the "second rule" so as to make additional loss also recoverable.

Still another way of stating the test is to look upon the "first rule" of *Hadley v. Baxendale* as imputed foreseeability or contemplation — that which any reasonable person should have foreseen — and the "second rule" as actual foreseeability or contemplation — what the reasonable person with particular knowledge should have foreseen. It is to be noted that the test, as it is usually stated, is objective. The extent of the recovery is to be measured, not by what the defendant actually foresaw when he made the contract, but by what a hypothetical, reasonable person in the position of the defendant, with the defendant's knowledge of the circumstances surrounding the transaction, could reasonably have been expected to foresee, had he directed his attention to a consideration of the matter. If the losses suffered or the gains prevented by the breach are unusual, it becomes necessary to ascertain whether the defendant was made aware of the special circumstances out of which they grew,[73] but, if they are no more than the usual consequence of such a breach as has occurred, then no inquiry as to the state of the defendant's knowledge is necessary.

In summary, it is important to note the following elements of the foreseeability concept: (1) It is a *limitation* on the recovery of plaintiffs. Liability will *not* attach for damages which were not within the contemplation of the parties or brought within such contemplation through special knowledge at the time

---

[70] *See, e.g.,* Florida E. Coast Ry. Co. v. Beaver St. Fisheries, Inc., 537 So. 2d 1065 (Fla. App. 1989); Kenford Co. v. County of Erie, 73 N.Y.2d 312 (1989); Midland Hotel Corp. v. Reuben H. Donnelley Corp., 188 Ill. 2d 306, 515 N.E.2d 61 (1987); Spang Indus. v. Aetna Cas. & Sur. Co., 312 F.2d 363 (2d Cir. 1975). *See also* RESTATEMENT 2d § 351.

[71] *See* UCC § 2-715(2)(a): "Consequential damages resulting from the seller's breach include: (a) any loss resulting from general or particular requirements and needs of which the seller at the time of contracting had reason to know and which could not reasonably be prevented by cover or otherwise...." *See* Cricket Alley Corp. v. Data Term. Sys., 240 Kan. 661, 732 P.2d 719 (1987) (Section 2-715 of the Code simply codifies *Hadely v. Baxendale*). *See also* Troxler Elec. Labs. v. Solitron Devices, Inc., 722 F.2d 81 (4th Cir. 1983); Sun Maid Raisin Growers v. Victor Packing Co., 146 Cal. App. 3d 787, 194 Cal. Rptr. 612 (1983).

[72] Victoria Laundry (Windsor), Ltd. v. Newman Indus., 2 K.B. 528, 1 All E.R. 997 [1949].

[73] *See* Cardozo, C.J., in Kerr S.S. Co. v. Radio Corp. of Am., 245 N.Y. 284, 157 N.E. 140, 142 (1927), in regard to what constitutes knowledge of special circumstances.

the contract was made. (2) Though the opinion of Baron Alderson speaks of "the contemplation of both parties," the modern versions of the rule suggest that only the foreseeability of the breaching party is relevant.[74] (3) The foreseeability of probable consequences must be determined as of the time of contract formation. If additional knowledge comes to the promisor subsequent to that time, it is irrelevant.[75] (4) The objective test is used — the defaulting promisor is liable not only for those consequences which he actually thought were probable but also those which a reasonable person *should* have considered probable.[76]

B. *The "Tacit Agreement" Concept.*

Early in the twentieth century, an attempt was made to modify the principles of *Hadley v. Baxendale.* The question was whether a defaulting promisor should be made liable for "unusual" or "special" damages[77] simply because the promisor was made aware of special circumstances at the time the contract was formed, thus bringing the knowledge of such special circumstances within the circle of foreseeability. Writing for the Supreme Court of the United States, Justice Holmes stated, "It may be said with safety that mere notice to a seller of some interest or probable action of the buyer is not enough necessarily and as a matter of law to charge the seller with special damage on that

---

[74] "[T]he promisor is not required to compensate the injured party for injuries that *he had no reason to foresee* as the probable result of his breach when he made the contract" (emphasis added). Traynor, J., in Coughlin v. Blair, 41 Cal. 2d 587, 262 P.2d 305, 314 (1953). *See also* UCC § 2-715(2)(a); RESTATEMENT 2d § 351.

[75] *See* Hale v. Stoughton Hosp. Ass'n, 126 Wis. 267, 376 N.W.2d 89 (1985) (like tort damages, contract damages compensate the aggrieved party but are limited by foreseeability at the time of contract formation). *See also* Eastern Adv. Co. v. Shapiro, 263 Mass. 228, 161 N.E. 240, 242 (1928) ("The defendant was liable for the consequences of the breach, which were reasonably foreseeable at the time the contract was entered into as probable if the contract were broken."). *See also* Holmes, J. in Globe Ref. Co. v. Landa Cotton Oil Co., 190 U.S. 540, 544 (1903) ("The suggestion thrown out by Bramwell, B., in Gee v. Lancashire & R. R. Co., 6 Hurlst. & N. 211, 218, that perhaps notice after the contract was made and before breach would be enough, is not accepted by later decisions.... The consequences must be contemplated at the time of the making of the contract."). For a comparison of *foreseeable* damages under *Hadley v. Baxendale* with the limitation of *foreseeable liability* in tort law, *see* Evra Corp. v. Swiss Bank Corp., 673 F.2d 951 (7th Cir. 1982).

[76] "The assumption cannot be less than this, that whatever a carrier could ascertain by diligent inquiry as to the nature of the undisclosed transaction, this he should be deemed to have ascertained, and charged with damages accordingly." Cardozo, C.J., in Kerr S.S. Co. v. Radio Corp. of Am., 245 N.Y. 284, 157 N.E. 140, 142 (1927).

[77] The term "unusual" herein is sometimes used synonymously with the term "consequential" or "special." The distinction between general and special damages is often stated as follows: the former arise naturally from the breach and are implied or presumed by the law. The latter do not arise naturally; they are not within the common experience of mankind as arising in the particular situation and, therefore, they are not implied or presumed by the law. Thus, the terms general and special may be used synonymously with the terms natural and unnatural, usual and unusual. The term "consequential," however, does not deserve to be continued, since, literally, it could relate to either type of damage, i.e., general or special, though it is normally considered as synonymous with "special." The term, however, has been continued by courts and its codification in UCC § 2-715 assures its continuation. The RESTATEMENT 2d § 351 comment b suggests, "The damages recoverable for loss that results other than in the ordinary course of events are sometimes called 'special' or 'consequential' damages. These terms are often misleading, however, and it is not necessary to distinguish between 'general' and 'special' or 'consequential' damages for the purposes of the rule stated in this Section."

account if he fails to deliver the goods."[78] Earlier, the Supreme Court of Massachusetts suggested that a defendant could not be held liable for such damages "unless at the time of the sale he, in substance, assented that he would be so held."[79] The suggestion in both cases was that some form of agreement had to be found to make the defaulting promisor liable for special damages rather than considering foreseeability alone. However, the agreement or assent could be presumed. There was no need to prove that an actual agreement existed. Thus, Justice Holmes suggests, "the extent of liability in such cases is likely to be within his [the defendant's] contemplation, and whether it is or not, should be worked out on terms which it fairly may be presumed he would have assented to if they had been presented to mind."[80] This variation of the *Hadley v. Buxendale* concept, which attracted a limited following,[81] appears to be founded upon a mistaken notion of the purpose of the rule. The cases following the Holmes suggestion seem to assume that the purpose of the rule was to afford a basis for the recovery of consequential damages. As suggested earlier, the rule is designed to exclude liability for such damages where it would be unjust to impose such liability. Some courts adopted the variation or qualification of *Hadley v. Buxendale* because the variation appeared to furnish a means of making the application of the original rule even more flexible than it would otherwise be.[82] Through it, unusual damages could readily be ruled out as too remote, even though they were clearly within the terms of the rule as originally formulated, if a court concluded that it was unjust to permit their recovery under the particular circumstances. As one opinion put it:

> [W]here the damages arise from special circumstances, and are so large as to be out of proportion to the consideration agreed to be paid for the services to be rendered under the contract, it raises a doubt at once as to whether the party would have assented to such liability, had it been called to his attention.... To make him liable for the special damages in such a case, there must not only be knowledge of the special circumstances, but such knowledge "must be brought home to the party sought to be charged under such circumstances that he must know that the person he contracts with reasonably believes that he accepts the contract with the special condition attached to it."[83]

---

[78] Globe Ref. Co. v. Landa Cotton Oil Co., 190 U.S. 540, 545 (1903). For critical analyses of this case, *see* 11 WILLISTON § 1357 (3d ed. 1968); 5 CORBIN § 1010 (1951).

[79] Lonergan v. Waldo, 179 Mass. 135, 140, 60 N.E. 479 (1901). *But cf.* Eastern Adv. Co. v. Shapiro, *supra* note 75.

[80] Globe Ref. Co. v. Landa Cotton Oil Co., 190 U.S. 540, 543 (1903). The Massachusetts Court in Lonergan v. Waldo, *supra* note 79, states, "If knowing all the circumstances, the defendant sold the pipe without any protest or statement that he would in no event be liable for a caving of the ditch, he might be found by the jury to have assented to pay damages for its caving if that should be caused by breach of his contract to deliver the pipe."

[81] This rule is sometimes referred to as the requirement of a tacit agreement to assume the particular risk. C. McCORMICK, LAW OF DAMAGES § 141 (1935). Prior to the decision in Erie R.R. v. Tompkins, 304 U.S. 64 (1938), it was generally followed in lower federal courts. Since then, however, there has been a gradual erosion of its popularity. *See, e.g.,* Krauss v. Greenbarg, 137 F.2d 569 (3d Cir. 1943).

[82] See Bauer, *Consequential Damages in Contract,* 80 U. PA. L. REV. 687 (1931), which approves this qualification of the rule because of its added flexibility. The fact of the matter is that the rule, as it is usually stated, has been made very flexible in application by omitting to define too carefully the requirement of "notice." *See* McCormick, *supra* note 81, at 507.

[83] Hooks Smelting Co. v. Planters' Compress Co., 72 Ark. 275, 79 S.W. 1052, 1056 (1904).

Notwithstanding some early support, the "tacit agreement" variation of the basic rule has been expressly rejected by numerous courts,[84] the UCC,[85] and the RESTATEMENT 2d.[86] Though they have rejected the test, courts are loathe to permit clearly foreseeable damages in certain cases. Faced with the determination of "special" ("consequential") damages where the special circumstances were communicated to the promisor at the time of contract formation but where the consideration moving to the promisor is relatively insignificant, courts are likely to find some device to overcome the manifest injustice of holding such a promisor fully liable for all consequential damages.[87] Courts may resort to covert tools by requiring unusually strict applications of the foreseeability or other generally recognized damage limitations.[88] A more candid judicial approach is necessary. There must be a recognition that standards such as foreseeability are nothing more than risk allocation processes. Courts should begin articulating their efforts in this vein. A useful test might be *whether a reasonable person in the position of the defaulting promisor who was made aware of special circumstances at the time of contract formation should be said to have assumed the risk of liability for the special consequences of his breach in light of all of the surrounding circumstances, particularly the consideration he was to receive for performance.* The RESTATEMENT 2d approaches the problem in terms of judicial power, i.e., the court may exclude recovery for loss of profits, allow recovery only for reliance interest damages, "or otherwise if it concludes that in the circumstances justice so requires in order to avoid disproportionate compensation."[89] A combination of the RESTATEMENT 2d conclusion and the suggested test would allow for a workable judicial risk allocation process that could depart from a strict application of the foreseeability standard. It is premature to suggest judicial acceptance of the RESTATEMENT 2d formula.[90] As it stands, the RESTATEMENT 2d

---

[84] See Native Alaskan Reclamation & Pest Control, Inc. v. United Bank of Alaska, 655 P.2d 1211 (Alaska 1984); Krauss v. Greenbarg, 137 F.2d 569 (3d Cir. 1943); McKibben v. Pierce, 190 S.W. 1140 (Tex. Civ. App. 1917).

[85] UCC § 2-715 comment 2, states, "The 'tacit agreement' test for the recovery of consequential damages is rejected."

[86] RESTATEMENT 2d § 351 comment a.

[87] This statement as it appeared in § 225 of the second edition is quoted in A. FARNSWORTH, CONTRACTS § 12.17, at 893 n.10 (1982).

[88] See Kerr S.S. Co. v. Radio Corp. of Am., 245 N.Y. 284, 157 N.E. 140 (1927) which demonstrates the reluctance of courts to apply the usual foreseeability test to public utilities such as the telegraph company. See also RESTATEMENT 2d § 351 comment f which suggests the foreseeability limitation as well as another "covert" limitation, i.e., an unusually strict application of the otherwise normal limitation of certainty which will be explored in the next section.

[89] RESTATEMENT 2d § 351(3). For an interesting application of this concept upon which ill. 19 to this section is based, see Sullivan v. O'Connor, 363 Mass. 579, 296 U.C. 2d 183 (1973) where the court suggested that expectancy recovery in a case involving cosmetic surgery would usually be quite disproportionate to the fee paid to the physician. Reliance damages including pain, suffering, and mental distress for a corrective operation were allowed.

[90] Native Alaskan Reclamation & Pest Control v. United Bank of Alaska, 685 P.2d 1211 (Alaska 1984) (remanding with suggestion that trial court consider § 351(3)); All Points Towing v. City of Glendale, 153 Ariz. 115, 735 P.2d 145 (1987) (principle inapplicable — no disproportion); Kenford Co. v. County of Erie, 108 A.D.2d 132, 489 N.Y.S.2d 939 (1985) (dissenting opinion by Hancock J. suggests application of § 351(3) which majority suggested would not apply because of lack of disproportion even if the court adopted the concept). These cases and other matters involving § 351(3) including its application to general as well as special damages are explored by an author who styles § 351(3) as unconscionability of remedy. See Kniffin, *A Newly Identified Contract Unconscionability: Unconscionability of Remedy*, 63 NOTRE DAME L. REV. 247 (1988).

concept is a desirable addition to assist courts in avoiding covert judicial action and coming to grips with risk allocation. Yet, it appears as amorphous as the unconscionability standard whereas the italicized test, *supra,* suggests a workable standard.

§ 121. The Certainty Limitation.

A. *The Second Limitation.*

We have seen how the foreseeability limitation on the recovery of contract damages was created in the doctrine of *Hadley v. Baxendale.* American courts are often credited with devising another limitation, i.e., the requirement that the proof of contract damages be certain both in terms of the fact of loss and the amount of loss.[91] It is not difficult to find American cases adhering to the view that contract damages must not be speculative or a matter of conjecture or surmise.[92] If this requirement merely required two elements to be shown, i.e., (1) that the damage was caused by the breach, and (2) that the amount of damage claimed was actually suffered, there is no doubt as to its soundness.[93] The concept, however, was designed for a different purpose. It suggested a special requirement as to the quantum and character of proof necessary to establish these two elements. A plaintiff must normally establish his civil case by a *preponderance* of the evidence, i.e., that it is more likely than not that a particular event occurred.[94] The certainty requirement was designed to impose a greater burden on the party claiming damages. Modern cases, however, typically require no more than a preponderance of the evidence because the original certainty requirement has been modified to a requirement of only "reasonable certainty."[95] The cases are legion in which the requirement of "reasonable certainty" is stated as the standard.[96] In some cases, it is abun-

---

[91] Professor McCormick believed that this was a distinctive contribution of American courts. *See* McCormick, *supra* note 81 at 124 (1935). *See,* however, Washington, *supra* note 67, 47 LAW Q. REV. at 363-66 suggesting a similar limitation in English cases. *See* Griffin v. Colver, 16 N.Y. 489, 69 Am. Dec. 718 (1858) (damages must be certain and not speculative or conjectural in either respect); Winston Cigarette Mach. Co. v. Wells-Whitehead Tobacco Co., 141 N.C. 284, 53 S.E. 885 (1906) (damages must be certain in their nature and in respect to their causes). A recent case suggests that the fact of loss as well as the amount of loss must be reasonably certain. Merion Spring Co. v. Muelles Hnos. Garcia Torres, 315 Pa. Super. 469, 462 A.2d 686 (1983).

[92] *See* Matson Plastering Co. v. Plasterers & Shophands Local No. 66, 852 F.2d 1200 (9th Cir. 1988); Triple-A Baseball Club Assoc. v. Northwestern Baseball, Inc., 655 F. Supp. 513 (D. Me. 1987); Schon-Klingstein Meat & Grocery Co. v. Snow, 43 Colo. 538, 96 P. 182 (1908). *See also* Griffin v. Colver, *supra* note 91.

[93] *See* Indiana Bell Tel. Co. v. O'Bryan, 408 N.E.2d 178 (Ind. App. 1980).

[94] *See* Williams v. Superintendent, Clifton T. Perkins Hosp. Center, 43 Md. App. 588, 406 A.2d 1302 (1979) setting forth various definitions of "preponderance" and distinguishing the "preponderance" standard from the "clear and convincing" standard as well as demonstrating the confusion between "clear and convincing" and "beyond a reasonable doubt." *See also In re* Appeal in Maricopa County Juvenile Court, 138 Ariz. 282, 674 P.2d 836 (1983) (preponderance means more probable than not); *In re* David Henry Rogers, 279 N.C. 48, 253 S.E.2d 912 (1979) (preponderance is greater weight of evidence); McCORMICK, HANDBOOK OF THE LAW OF EVIDENCE § 339 at 793 (2d ed. 1972).

[95] *See, e.g.,* Hein v. M & N Feed Yards, Inc., 205 Neb. 691, 289 N.W.2d 756 (1980) (although plaintiff does not have to prove damages to a mathematical certainty, he does have the burden to prove by a preponderance of the evidence the amount of his damages with reasonable certainty).

[96] *See, e.g.,* Spang & Co. v. United States Steel Corp., 519 Pa. 14, 545 A.2d 861 (1988) citing the second edition of this book at § 226 for this proposition. *See also* Clark v. Bank of New York, 687 F. Supp. 863 (S.D.N.Y. 1988) (plaintiff never availed himself of the use of a law library where he

dantly clear that it will be impossible to determine the amount of damage suffered as a result of the breach. Thus, where a publisher breached its contract to publish a book authored by the plaintiff, the amount of royalties to be earned on the unpublished book were impossible of determination.[97] In other cases involving lost profits, the determination of such profits may appear too uncertain to allow a recovery. Courts are loathe, however, to permit a breaching party to escape the consequences of his breach because damages are uncertain. It is generally agreed that doubts will be resolved against the party in breach.[98] It is important to consider how courts have reacted to the antinomies of the requirement of reasonable certainty and the policy of precluding the breaching party from avoidance of his responsibility.

B. *Reasonable Certainty and Lost Profits.*

Where a business has been established and earning profits for some time, there is little difficulty in establishing lost profits for such a business assuming that the prior and subsequent experiences are comparable.[99] Courts have also stretched to admit credible evidence of such profits rather than permit the breaching party to avoid liability on the basis of lack of sufficient certainty.[1] A number of courts, however, have found an insuperable obstacle in

---

would have discovered that only those damages proven with reasonable certainty are recoverable); Native Alaskan Reclamation & Pest Control, Inc. v. United Bank of Alaska, 655 P.2d 1211 (Alaska 1984) (mathematical certainty is unnecessary — only reasonable certainty required); Midwest Sheet Metal Works v. Frank Sullivan Co., 215 F. Supp. 607, 611 (D. Minn. 1963) ("Both parties agree that the measure of damages is loss of anticipated profits, and that such loss must be proved 'with a reasonable degree of certainty and exactness.'... But, 'This rule does not call for absolute certainty.'"); Perfecting Serv. Co. v. Product Dev. & Sales Co., 259 N.C. 400, 131 S.E.2d 9, 22 (1963) ("'Absolute certainty is not required but evidence of damages must be sufficiently specific and complete to permit the jury to arrive at a reasonable conclusion.'"); Tobin v. Union News Co., 18 App. Div. 2d 243, 239 N.Y.S.2d 22, 26 (1963) ("Mathematical certitude is unnecessary. A reasonable basis for the computation of approximate result is the only requisite."). *See also* RESTATEMENT 2d § 352 and UCC § 1-106 comment 1 ("reject any doctrine that damages must be calculable with mathematical accuracy") and § 2-715 comment 4 (as to consequential damages, like the section on the liberal administration of remedies (§ 1-106), this section "rejects any doctrine of certainty which requires almost mathematical precision in the proof of loss.").

[97] Freund v. Washington Square Press, Inc., 34 N.Y.2d 379, 314 N.E.2d 419 (1974). In this case, the court awarded nominal damages (six cents) in the absence of reasonably certain proof of royalty damages. In such a case, the author would be well-advised to insist upon a liquidated damages clause which are designed for situations where actual damages are necessarily fatally uncertain.

[98] *See* Locke v. United States, 283 F.2d 521 (Ct. Cl. 1960) (contract breaker should not profit from his own wrong by insisting on unobtainable proof of damages); Bead Chain Mfg. Co. v. Saxton Prods., 183 Conn. 266, 439 A.2d 314 (1981) (breach made it impossible to go forward with production that would have made historically accurate figures available. Therefore, theoretical cost and price estimates were acceptable.). *See also* S-A-S Dev., Inc. v. Graceland Corp., 537 F. Supp. 549 (D.N.J. 1982); Vitex Mfg. Corp. v. Carbitex Corp., 377 F.2d 795 (3d Cir. 1967); RESTATEMENT 2d § 352 comment a.

[99] *See* Tull v. Gunderson's, Inc., 709 P.2d 940 (Colo. 1985).

[1] *See, e.g.,* Thorp Sales Corp. v. Gyuro Grading Co., 107 Wis. 2d 141, 319 N.W.2d 879 (1981) (15 pieces of equipment had an auction value ranging between $89,600 to $131,000 which court determined was a reasonable range for estimating lost profits with reasonable certainty); Buxbaum v. G. H. P. Cigar Co., 188 Wis. 389, 206 N.W. 59 (1925) (profits allowed on exclusive right to sell a product even though plaintiff had made no profits for a number of years. Evidence was admissible that the new selling agent had made a profit so as to permit a basis for computing profits plaintiff would have made had he been permitted to continue.); Randall v. Peerless Motor Car Co., 212 Mass. 352, 99 N.E. 221 (1912) (profits recoverable for breach of auto sales agency contract though breached during the first month of plaintiff's operation of agency. Evidence was

permitting a "new business" to recover anticipated profits.[2] It is now clear that the "new business" rule has been substantially eroded.[3] While a new business venture necessarily labors under a greater burden than a going concern to prove anticipated profits, there is no *per se* rule precluding such proof so long as reasonably certain data are provided as the basis for recovery.[4] Notwithstanding the difficulty of proof, expert testimony, market analyses and surveys, as well as economic and financial data, including the records of similar businesses, may provide sufficient certainty to permit the recovery of anticipated profits.[5]

C. *Recovery of Conjectural Value — Antitrust Laws.*

In certain types of cases, courts have been willing to stretch the reasonable certainty requirement beyond its limits to permit a recovery. In cases involving aleatory contracts, i.e., contracts where at least one of the parties is under a duty that is conditional on the occurrence of an event that is a matter of chance (a fortuitous event),[6] a breach prior to the occurrence of the fortuitous event will prevent sufficient proof of what would have occurred had there been no breach. Thus, where fifty women were chosen by popular vote in a beauty contest and twelve were to receive prizes based on interviews, the wrongful deprivation of plaintiff's interview was held to permit the recovery of the value of her chance as determined by a jury.[7] There can be no question that

---

admissible to show the number of cars sold by defendant and others in territory as basis for computing anticipated profits.); Lewiston Iron Works v. Vulcan Process Co., 139 Minn. 180, 165 N.W. 1071 (1918) (evidence of profits made by others similarly situated held to furnish basis for allowing recovery of profits).

[2] *See* Evergreen Amusement Corp. v. Milstead, 206 Md. 610, 112 A.2d 901 (1955) (delay by contractor in completing work on new outdoor theatre prevented opening until the middle of August rather than June. Expert evidence of profits of drive-in theatres in the same territory including evidence of population, weather, and other elements of market survey were excluded. Court stated that it was not laying down a "flat rule" that such profits could never be recovered under such circumstances, but no case had permitted profits under such circumstances.). Additional cases are collected in Annotations, 1 A.L.R. 156 (1919); 99 A.L.R. 938 (1935). For a UCC case to this effect, *see* Gerwin v. Southeastern Cal. Ass'n of Seventh Day Adventists, 14 Cal. App. 3d 209, 92 Cal. Rptr. 111 (1971). *See also* Harry Rubin & Sons v. Consolidated Pipe Co., 396 Pa. 506, 153 A.2d 472 (1959).

[3] *See, e.g.,* Drews Co. v. Ledwith Wolfe Assoc., 296 S.C. 207, 371 S.E.2d 532 (1988); Pauline's Chicken Villa, Inc. v. KFC Corp., 701 S.W.2d 399 (Ky. 1986); Merion Spring Co. v. Muelles Hnos. Garcia Torres, 315 Pa. Super. 469, 462 A.2d 686 (1983). *See also* ill. 6 to Restatement 2d § 352 which rejects the holding and rationale in the *Evergreen Amusement* case, *supra* note 2. *See also* UCC § 2-708 comment 2: "It is not necessary to a recovery of 'profit' to show a history of earnings, especially if a new venture is involved." Quoted with approval in Bead Chain Mfg. Co. v. Saxton Prods., 183 Conn. 266, 439 A.2d 314 (1981) (plaintiff's president testified concerning lost profits by setting forth the elements considered in pricing the job. It was not fatal that his cost and price estimates were theoretical.).

[4] Handi Caddy, Inc. v. American Home Prods. Corp., 557 F.2d 136 (8th Cir. 1977) (cornerstone of plaintiff's proof was expert opinion testimony). For a case suggesting lack of certainty, *see* Kenford Co. v. County of Erie, 67 N.Y.2d 257, 493 N.E.2d 234 (1986) (plaintiff not entitled to recover anticipated appreciation in the value of peripheral land when domed stadium contract was breached). The New York Court of Appeals upheld this decision, emphasizing lack of foreseeability, *see* Kenford Co. v. County of Erie, 73 N.Y.2d 312, 537 N.E.2d 176 (1989). *See also* Matson Plastering Co. v. Plasterers & Shophands Local No. 66, 852 F.2d 1200 (9th Cir. 1988) (lost opportunity to bid on subsequent contracts was too speculative and uncertain).

[5] In addition to the cases cited *supra* notes 3 and 4, *see* Restatement 2d § 352 comment b.

[6] *See* Restatement 2d § 379 comment a.

[7] Chaplin v. Hicks, 2 K.B. 786 (1911).

the value of a chance is highly conjectural. Yet, other cases have permitted recovery of the value of a chance.[8] Where the defendant failed to prosecute certain causes of action after promising one-half of the recoveries to the plaintiff, the plaintiff was permitted to go to the jury on the question of the amount that the lawsuits probably would have produced.[9] These departures from the reasonable certainty requirement are explicable only on the basis that courts are simply unwilling to permit a breaching party to avoid liability solely on the basis of the plaintiff's difficulty of proving loss where it was clear at the time of formation that such loss would be impossible to prove with reasonable certainty.

Still another relaxation of the reasonable certainty requirement may occur where a statutory policy conflicts with that requirement. For example, the Federal antitrust laws permit any party who is injured in his business or property through any violation of the antitrust laws to bring an action for threefold the damages sustained, as well as the costs of the lawsuit including a reasonable attorney's fee.[10] This provision was designed to add a significant enforcement dimension to the antitrust arm of the Federal government by inducing private parties to bring their own actions.[11] The recovery of "triple" damages was designed as a deterrent as contrasted with normal compensatory damages for breach of contract. In such a treble damages case, the plaintiff may face difficulty in proving his actual damages (which are to be trebled) with reasonable certainty. To avoid the frustration of antitrust policy in such cases, courts are willing to relax the normal requirements of reasonable certainty.[12]

---

[8] See, e.g., Mange v. Unicorn Press, Inc., 129 F. Supp. 727 (S.D.N.Y. 1955); Wachtel v. National Alfalfa Journal Co., 190 Iowa 1293, 176 N.W. 801 (1920). Accord RESTATEMENT 2d § 348(3) which limits recovery to such contest cases or other fortuitous event cases such as those involving wrongful cancellation of insurance contracts by an insurer such as Commissioner of Ins. v. Massachusetts Acc. Co., 314 Mass. 558, 50 N.E.2d 801 (1943). Cases refusing to permit recovery of the value of a chance include Collatz v. Fox Wis. Amusement Corp., 239 Wis. 156, 300 N.W. 162 (1941) (prize contest), commented on, 1943 Wis. L. Rev. 301; Phillips v. Pantages Theatre Co., 163 Wash. 303, 300 P. 1048 (1931) (damage for breach of prize contest held too speculative on the ground that there was no evidence that plaintiff had a real chance to win).

[9] Jaffe v. Alliance Metal Co., 337 Pa. 449, 12 A.2d 13 (1940). Cf. Herbert Clayton & Jack Waller, Ltd. v. Oliver, A.C. 209 [1930] ($1000 damages allowed for injury to reputation where a theatrical producer breached contract with an actor to give him a leading part in a forthcoming play).

[10] Section 4 of the Clayton Act of 1914, 15 U.S.C., §§ 12-17, permits such an action. The Clayton Act was designed to supplement the basic antitrust statute, the Sherman Act of 1890, 15 U.S.C. §§ 1-7, which had been interpreted in such a fashion as to leave certain restraints in trade without remedy.

[11] A private party was also given the benefit of a prima facie case in its action against a defendant where the United States had brought its action to final judgment or decree. Clayton Act, § 5(a). To further enhance antitrust enforcement, Congress enacted the Federal Trade Commission Act, 15 U.S.C. §§ 41-51, in 1914. This Act created the Federal Trade Commission with power to, inter alia, preclude "unfair" methods of competition. This provision (Section 5 of the FTC Act), is viewed as even broader than the other antitrust laws, i.e., the violation of other antitrust laws constitute a violation of the FTC Act, but the Act may apply to other violations which are not technical violations of the other antitrust laws. Further exploration of the antitrust laws is considered in courses and materials dealing with that area of the law.

[12] See, e.g., Bigelow v. RKO Radio Pictures, 327 U.S. 251, 264 (1946) ("Jury may make a just and reasonable estimate of damage based on relevant data.").

D. *Alternate Bases of Recovery — Reliance and Rental Value.*

If courts cannot overcome the barrier of reasonable certainty, they still permit relief for less than the optimal, measurable damages where possible. This alternative relief typically takes two forms: (i) protection of the reliance interest and (ii) recovery of the rental value of the premises.

1. Reliance Interest Alternative.

We have already considered how courts may resort to a different articulation of the normal formula for builder's damages so as to permit the recovery of the reliance interest where the expectation interest (lost profits) is precluded due to a lack of sufficient certainty in the proof of those damages.[13] In a well-known case, *United States v. Behan*,[14] the experimental nature of the work precluded the normal relief that the contractor expected because he could not sustain the burden of proving lost profits.[15] In response to the government's argument that the failure of the contractor to prove lost profits should result in no recovery, the court was adamant in stating that artificial rules of law should not replace natural justice in permitting the claimant to recover at least his reasonable expenditures (out-of-pocket losses) in a fair effort to perform the contract. Similarly, where the owner expends a certain sum in preparing for the delivery of machinery that never arrives, he may recover his reliance expenditure minus any losses the defendant can prove the owner would have suffered had the contract been performed.[16] Reliance damages may also be shown in other types of cases where lost profits cannot be shown with sufficient certainty.[17] Thus, where the breach precludes an entertainment event, the promoter can recover the reliance expenditures where lost profits would be speculative.[18] One of the interesting questions is whether the reliance recovery can exceed the contract price. The RESTATEMENT 2d insists that the recovery cannot exceed the contract price. The rationale, however, leaves much to be desired. "If the injured party's expenditures exceed the contract price, it is clear that at least to the extent of the excess, there would have been a loss."[19] In a construction contract with a price of $100,000, the builder's reliance expenditures exceeding that price clearly indicate a losing contract. Since a party should never be placed in a *better* position than he would have occupied had the contract been performed, a contract price ceiling

---

[13] *See supra* § 119(C).

[14] 110 U.S. 338 (1884).

[15] The failure to prove lost profits is a result of the inability of the contractor to prove the cost of completion which was true in this case because of the experimental nature of the construction. *See also* Herbert W. Jaeger Assoc. v. Slovak Am. Charitable Ass'n, 156 Ill. App. 3d 106, 507 N.E.2d 863 (1987).

[16] L. Albert & Son v. Armstrong Rubber Co., 178 F.2d 182 (2d Cir. 1949). *See* RESTATEMENT 2d § 349. The reliance interest recovery includes expenses made in preparation for performance such as advertising, hiring personnel, and procuring premises unusable for other purposes, as well as performance itself. Any salvageable expenses will not, of course, be recoverable.

[17] It should also be noted that the plaintiff may simply choose to pursue the recovery of reliance expenditures rather than attempt to prove lost profits. If the defendant cannot establish that plaintiff would have suffered a loss, the reliance expenditures are recoverable. *See* Mistletoe Express Serv. v. Locke, 726 S.W.2d 637 (Tex. App. 1988).

[18] *See, e.g.,* Chicago Coliseum Club v. Dempsey, 265 Ill. App. 542 (1932).

[19] RESTATEMENT 2d § 349 comment a.

on reliance recovery in such a case may be justified.[20] The burden of proving any loss on the part of the relying party, however, is clearly on the defendant. If he cannot prove that the completed contract would result in a loss to the plaintiff, reliance expenditures exceeding the contract price should be recovered. For example, where an actor failed to perform his contract for a leading role in a film for which he would have received £1050, the court permitted a reliance recovery of £2750 for wasted expenditures when the film could not be produced.[21] The profit to be made on the film could not be proven since it was never produced. In such a case, there is no justification for limiting the reliance damages to the contract price since the completion and distribution of the film may well have resulted in an amount that would not only have defrayed the cost of the actor's contract and all reliance expenditures, but also resulted in a profit to the producer.[22]

2. The Rental Value Alternative.

Beyond the reliance alternative, courts may discover a reasonably certain basis for affording a remedy by permitting recovery of the rental value of the property where lost profits would be conjectural. Where, for example, a complete crop failure resulted due to unmerchantable seed wheat, the court permitted recovery of the rental value of the land.[23] It should also be noted that the court also permitted recovery of the expenses of planting the worthless seed. Thus, it permitted both a rental value and reliance recovery. The court did not overcompensate the plaintiff, however, since his gross profit would have enabled him to pay for the cost of planting and would still have permitted a net profit which is simulated by the rental value.[24] Where the construction of a new outdoor theatre was delayed during crucial summer months and the court applied what would now be viewed as a stringent test of certainty, thereby denying lost profits, the court still permitted a recovery of the rental value of the theatre property during the delay plus out-of-pocket (reliance)

---

[20] See L. Albert & Son v. Armstrong Rubber Co., 178 F.2d 182 (2d Cir. 1949). See also H. M. O. Sys. v. Choicecare Health Servs., 655 P.2d 635 (Colo. App. 1983).

[21] Anglia Television Ltd. v. Reed, [1971] 3 All E. R. The court permitted recovery of reliance expenditures before the contract with the actor was made as well as reasonable expenditures incurred after the contract was made since the expenditures prior to contract formation were within the reasonable contemplation of the parties as likely to be wasted if the contract was broken.

[22] See also Security Stove & Mfg. Co. v. American Ry. Express Co., 227 Mo. App. 175, 51 S.W.2d 572 (1932) (contract price of $147 (express charges) and total reliance damages of $801.50 plus interest (total amount of $1000). The $801.50 included the $147 transportation charge which was a wasted expenditure. See also Wartzman v. Hightower Prods., 53 Md. App. 656, 456 A.2d 82 (1983) (failure of law firm to properly incorporate entity created to promote a flagpole sitting stunt where court awarded reliance expenditures presumably much greater than reasonable legal fee).

[23] Moorhead v. Minneapolis Seed Co., 139 Minn. 11, 165 N.W. 484 (1917).

[24] Accord, Paola Gas Co. v. Paola Glass Co., 56 Kan. 614, 44 P. 621 (1891) (recovery of wasted expenditure in attempting to operate plant without gas plus rental value or interest on the value of property). RESTATEMENT 2d § 348(1) permits damages based on rental value of the property or on interest on the value of the property as an alternative to proof of loss of value to the injured party where a breach delays the use of the property. The interest on the value property alternative is viewed as "a last resort" where damages based on a fair rental value cannot be shown with reasonable certainty. See RESTATEMENT 2d § 348 comment a.

costs for that time.[25] Again, the strong judicial policy in favor of compensating the aggrieved party with damages based on some reasonably certain basis and denying the breaching party a technical basis for avoiding liability is revealed.

§ 122. The Mitigation Limitation.

A. *The Third Limitation.*

In addition to the two limitations on recoverable damages already explored, the foreseeability limitation and the certainty limitation, there is a third limitation which may be called the mitigation limitation or the limitation of avoidable losses or avoidable consequences.[26] In the interest of fairness to the defaulting promisor, it is a universally accepted rule that the promisee cannot recover those damages for breach of contract which he could have avoided through the exercise of reasonable diligence if he can do so without incurring undue risk, expense, or humiliation.[27] This rule has both negative and positive dimensions. On the negative side, if an innocent promisee is to be made whole, he is required to refrain from the performance of his own undertakings under the contract, or from any other act which would increase the loss to be paid by the defaulting promisor, unless such refraining would unreasonably prejudice some other interest of the promisee. Thus, where a bridge builder had started to perform and was notified by the county that the contract had been cancelled, the builder could not recover for that portion of the bridge he completed after the notice of cancellation because he could have avoided the cost of completion.[28] On the positive side, the rule requires the injured promisee, *if he is to be made whole,* to take such affirmative steps as may be appropriate and reasonable, in view of the circumstances, to avert losses which would result were he to remain inactive. If he does not take such steps he will, nevertheless, be limited in his recovery to the amount to which his loss would have been reduced had he done so. Suppose, for example, a contract for specially manufactured goods is partially completed by the manufacturer when the buyer breaches. The seller may decide that he should recover the contract price minus any costs saved including any scrap or salvage value the uncompleted goods may bring. If, however, the seller makes a good faith judgment that completion of the manufacture may permit a resale at the contract price or an approximation of the contract price, he may follow this reasonable course of action and complete the manufacture even after the breach. If that reasonable and good faith effort, through no fault of the seller, results in even greater loss than the negative course of stopping manufacture and procuring the salvage value, the seller's reasonable mitigation efforts

---

[25] Evergreen Amusement Corp. v. Milstead, 206 Md. 610, 112 A.2d 901 (1955). For a criticism of this case in terms of denying lost profits, *see supra* text at notes 2 and 3.

[26] The relationship between the concept of avoidable consequences (mitigation principle) in contract or tort law and the foreseeability rule of *Hadley v. Baxendale* is discussed in Evra Corp. v. Swiss Bank Corp., 673 F.2d 951 (7th Cir. 1982).

[27] *See, e.g.,* Grill v. Adams, 123 Ill. App. 3d 913, 463 N.E.2d 896 (1984); Lincoln Nat'l Life Ins. Co. v. NCR Corp., 603 F. Supp. 1393 (N.D. Ill. 1984); Soules v. Independent Sch. Dist. No. 518, 258 N.W.2d 103 (Minn. 1977). *See also* RESTATEMENT 2d § 350(1).

[28] Rockingham Cty. v. Luten Bridge Co., 35 F.2d 301, 66 A.L.R. 735 (4th Cir. 1929).

should be compensated.[29] The same principle requires the injured promisee to exercise reasonable diligence to make the best use of anything left on his hands by reason of the defaulter's breach of contract.

B. *No "Duty" to Mitigate.*

It is important to emphasize that the negative and positive dimensions of the mitigation principle were stated as "requirements" *if the promisee is to be made whole.* Though sometimes stated as a duty, the principle of mitigation or avoidable consequences is not a duty.[30] There was, for example, no *duty* on the builder of the bridge to cease his performance. By continuing his performance after being notified that the completed bridge would be valueless (because it would not connect to any road), he has added losses to the promisor which could have been avoided through reasonable diligence. The mitigation principle simply precludes his recovery of such avoidable losses, i.e., the breaching promisor has no cause of action against the builder for continuing the performance and enhancing damages since, again, the builder had no duty to cease performance. Under the UCC, consequential damages which could have been avoided are not recoverable.[31] Typically, such damages can be avoided by making substitute arrangements. Thus, where a seller fails to deliver certain goods under a contract with a buyer, the buyer will purchase identical or similar goods elsewhere, i.e., the buyer will resort to his remedy of *cover.*[32] This remedy will avoid unnecessary losses for the buyer. Where, for example, a particular device is necessary to conduct the buyer's business and the seller fails to deliver the device as promised, the buyer may not simply allow lost profits to mount up if he could avoid such losses by purchasing a substitute device from another source. The buyer's damages in such a situation would include the difference between the contract price and any reasonably higher (cover) price for the substitute purchase.[33] They would not, however, include any consequential losses that could have been prevented by cover or otherwise. Similarly, if a party who uses a truck in his business loses the use of the truck because of a breach of warranty, he may not recover consequential damages (lost profits) that could have been avoided if he had leased a truck while awaiting the repair of the unmerchantable truck.[34]

The UCC, however, does contain a provision which creates a duty of mitigation. If a merchant buyer rejects goods because they are nonconforming, and if

---

[29] *See* UCC § 2-704(2) which permits the seller to cease manufacture or complete manufacture of the goods if either of these actions is an exercise of reasonable commercial judgment.

[30] *See* Soules v. Independent Sch. Dist. No. 518, *supra* note 27.

[31] UCC § 2-715(2)(a).

[32] UCC § 2-712.

[33] UCC 2-712(2). *See also* Huntington Beach Union High Sch. Dist. v. Continental Information Sys. Corp., 621 F.2d 353 (9th Cir. 1980) (difference between higher cost of substitute computer and contract price).

[34] UCC § 2-714(2) measures damages for breach of warranty as the difference at the time and place of acceptance between the value of the goods as accepted and the value they would have had if they had been as warranted, and § 2-714(3) also permits the recovery of both incidental and consequential damages in a proper case. The typical direct damage will be the repair cost of the accepted goods. Consequential damages, however, may be permitted if lost profits are shown because the goods are not available. Such damages are not recoverable, however, if they could have been avoided by cover or otherwise under UCC § 2-715(2)(a).

the breaching seller has no agent or place of business at the market where the goods have been rejected, the buyer is under a duty to follow reasonable instructions from the seller with respect to such rejected goods.[35] Moreover, if the goods are either perishable or threaten to decline speedily in value, the buyer must make reasonable efforts to resell them if no reasonable instructions from the seller have been received.[36] The buyer is entitled to be reimbursed for any expenses associated with his selling efforts as well as any expenses incurred in caring for the rejected goods.[37] If the goods are neither perishable nor threaten to decline speedily in value, the absence of reasonable instructions from the seller permits the buyer to store the goods for the seller's account, to reship them to the seller or to resell them for the seller's account.[38] In summary, the UCC requires merchants to operate in a commercially reasonable manner which is, essentially, the Code definition of good faith as applied to a merchant.[39]

C. Personal Service Contracts.

In personal service contracts, an employee who is wrongfully discharged cannot sit idly by and recover the promised wages or salary, if it is possible to secure other employment of the same general character and without undue hardship. In such a case the defaulting employer is entitled to deduct from the promised salary whatever the injured employee could have earned in such other employment.[40] If an employee recovered the salary from the breached contract even though he earned a second salary which he could not have earned had the contract not been breached, he would have received a windfall, i.e., he would be placed in a much better position than he would have been in had the contract been performed. His recovery, therefore, should not exceed his expectation interest.[41] An employee, however, need not accept employment that is substantially different from the original employment to mitigate damages.[42] Neither must he seek employment in another locality.[43] The burden of

---

[35] UCC § 2-603(1) states that "a merchant buyer is under a duty after rejection of goods in his possession or control to follow any reasonable instructions received from the seller...."

[36] Id.

[37] UCC § 2-603(2).

[38] UCC § 2-604.

[39] UCC § 2-103(1)(b).

[40] Soules v. Independent Sch. Dist. No. 518, 258 N.W.2d 103 (Minn. 1977) (teacher failed to exert reasonable efforts to pursue or accept other suitable employment despite reduced salary offer). See also Hollwedel v. Duffy-Mott Co., 263 N.Y. 95, 188 N.E. 266 (1933); Harrington v. Empire Cream Separator Co., 120 Me. 388, 115 A. 89 (1921); Ogden-Howard Co. v. Brand, 30 Del. 482, 108 A. 277 (1919).

[41] As to whether the employee's recovery should be diminished by amounts received from other sources such as unemployment compensation, there is a split of authority though the prevailing view appears to indicate that they should not be deducted. See, e.g., Sporn v. Celebrity, Inc., 129 N.J. Super. 449 (1974); Pennington v. Whiting Tubular Prods., Inc., 370 Mich. 590, 122 N.W.2d 692 (1963). Contra, Denhart v. Waukesha Brewing Co., 21 Wis. 2d 583, 124 N.W.2d 664 (1963).

[42] Salem Community Sch. Corp. v. Richman, 406 N.E.2d 269 (Ind. App. 1980) (superintendent of school need not accept position as teacher); Parker v. Twentieth Century Fox Film Corp., 89 Cal. Rptr. 737, 474 P.2d 689 (1970) (Parker (Shirley MacLaine) need not substitute an Australia Western for a musical where she could veto choice of director); Williams v. Robinson, 158 Ark. 327, 250 S.W. 14 (1923) (woman employed to take charge of kitchen need not accept a more menial position); Cooper v. Stronge & Warner Co., 111 Minn. 177, 126 N.W. 541 (1910) (one employed as manager of the millinery department need not accept position as sales clerk).

proof is on the employer to prove both the employee's opportunity to secure comparable employment and the employee's failure to mitigate damages.[44]

D. *Non-Mitigating Value.*

1. The "Lost Volume" Concept.

We have just seen that an employee will not recover damages if he could have secured comparable employment in a convenient location. If the employment is not comparable, the employee need not take the job. If, however, he does accept the new employment, the wages earned in the new employment will be deducted from the damages recovered from the first employer if it was not possible to perform both jobs simultaneously.[45] An employee, however, may be able to perform two jobs. "Moonlighting" is an accepted practice in a free society. If the second employment would be performable without interfering with the breached employment, the value of the second employment is not deducted from the employee's recovery since he would have earned the wages from the second employment whether or not the original contract was breached.[46] While this common sense principle is clear, it can become difficult in cases where there is doubt as to whether the second opportunity could have been pursued along with the breached opportunity.

A supplier of services may be able to convince a court that he would have been able to perform a second opportunity that became available after the original contract was breached. Consider, for example, an individual plumber who never subcontracts his work and who has contracted to perform services that will require a full day's effort. If the owner repudiates that contract and the plumber proceeds to work elsewhere on the day scheduled to perform the original contract, must he deduct his earnings from the second job in mitigation of damages recovered from the breached contract? It is certainly possible that the plumber could have performed the second contract as well as the first if he could have delayed the second job. In the case of enterprises that provide services, courts are inclined to view them as "lost volume" enterprises, i.e., they are entitled to the profits on both contracts because, presumably, they could have performed both contracts and received both profits absent strong

---

[43] *See* Salem Community Sch. Corp. v. Richman, *supra* note 42. *See also* American Trading Co. v. Steele, 274 F. 774 (9th Cir. 1921); James v. County of Allen, 44 Ohio St. 226, 6 N.E. 246 (1886).

[44] *See* Gulf Consol. Int'l, Inc. v. Murphy, 658 S.W.2d 565 (Tex. 1983). In Stewart v. Board of Educ. of Ritenour Consolidated Sch. Dist., 630 S.W.2d 130 (Mo. App. 1982) the court adopted the following statement from Ryan v. Superintendent of Schools of Quincy, 373 N.E.2d 1178, 1181 (Mass. 1978): "A former employer meets its burden of 'mitigation of damages' if the employer proves that (a) one or more discoverable opportunities for comparable employment were available in a location as, or more convenient than, the place of former employment, (b) the improperly discharged employee unreasonably made no attempt to apply for any such job, and (c) it was reasonably likely that the former employee would obtain one of those comparable jobs." *See also* Sayre v. Musicland Group, Inc., 850 F.2d 350 (8th Cir. 1988) holding that the employer must establish such factors as an affirmative defense.

[45] *See* Erler v. Five Points Motors, 249 Cal. App. 2d 560, 57 Cal. Rptr. 516 (1967).

[46] Soules v. Independent Sch. Dist. No. 518, 258 N.W.2d 103 (Minn. 1977) (only earnings from employment which are incompatible with the employee's contractual obligations may be offset as mitigated damages); Dixon v. Volunteer Co-op Bank, 213 Mass. 345, 100 N.E. 655 (1913) (attorney employed to examine land titles for a bank on a fee basis); Nuckolls v. College of Physicians & Surgeons, 7 Cal. App. 233, 94 P. 81 (1907) (dentist employed part-time as teacher).

evidence to the contrary.[47] They have even carried this view to the extreme of allowing recovery of both profits where the second performance is identical to the first. Thus, where a subcontractor was ordered off the job by a defendant contractor when the defendant and owner engaged in controversy, the sub then contracted to do the same work for the owner at a higher contract price than his damages from the defendant. The court rejected defendant's effort to interpose the profit the sub would have made doing the same work in mitigation of damages on the footing that the contract was not a personal service contract.[48] The fact that the services were supplied by an enterprise as contrasted with an individual who could not have made two profits on the identical contract appears as a distinction without a difference. Yet, the strong presumption of virtually unlimited capacity prevailed.

2. "Lost Volume" Seller Under the Uniform Commercial Code.

In contracts for the sale of goods, if a party contracts to sell a unique item and the buyer breaches that contract, the seller's resale to another buyer will produce profit that should be deducted from her damages against the first buyer in mitigation because she could not possibly have made two profits on the only item of its kind, i.e., she can only sell that item once. If, however, the seller is a retailer or manufacturer or jobber who has a virtually inexhaustible supply of goods for sale, the fact that she resells an item to a second buyer after the first buyer breaches the contract should not deprive the seller of profits on both sales. Consider, for example, the seller of automobiles who contracts to sell a typical car to X. X refuses to accept delivery of the auto and the seller resells the car to Y. One of the seller's remedies under the UCC is the remedy of resale which permits the seller to recover the difference be-

---

[47] Kearsarge Computer, Inc. v. Acme Staple Co., 116 N.H. 705, 366 A.2d 467, 86 A.L.R.2d 1081 (1976) (these businesses are expandable and the law presumes that they can accept a virtually unlimited amount of business so that income generated from accounts acquired after breach does not mitigate the plaintiff's damages); Gollaher v. Midwood Constr. Co., 194 Cal. App. 2d 640, 15 Cal. Rptr. 292 (1961) (personal services are not involved in this kind of contract since the contractor is required only to accomplish a specific result which could be achieved by having hired servants perform it and to take as many other contracts elsewhere as the contractor chooses to take). RESTATEMENT 2d § 347 comment f: "Whether a subsequent transaction is a substitute for the broken contract sometimes raises difficult questions of fact. If the injured party could and would have entered into the subsequent contract, even if the contract had not been broken, and could have had the benefit of both, he can be said to have a 'lost volume' and the subsequent transaction is not a substitute for the broken contract.... It is sometimes assumed that [the contractor would have taken the subsequent contract regardless of the breach], but the question is one of fact to be resolved according to the circumstances of each case." In Teradyne, Inc. v. Teledyne Indus., 676 F.2d 865, n.2 (1st Cir. 1982), the court attributes the coinage, "lost volume seller" to Professor Robert J. Harris in his article, A Radical Restatement of the Law of Seller's Damages: Sales Act and Commercial Code Results Compared, 18 STAN. L. REV. 66 (1965) and notes that the phrase has been widely adopted in such cases as Famous Knitwear Corp. v. Drug Fair, Inc., 493 F.2d 251, 254, n.5 (4th Cir. 1974); Snyder v. Herbert Greenbaum & Assoc., 38 Md. App. 144, 157, 380 A.2d 618, 624 (1977); Publicker Indus. v. Roman Ceramics Corp., 652 F.2d 340, 346 (3d Cir. 1981). As seen in the quote above, it has also been adopted by the RESTATEMENT 2d §§ 347 (comment f) and 350 (comment d).

[48] Olds v. Mapes-Reeve Constr. Co., 177 Mass. 41, 58 N.E. 478 (1900). See also Grinnell Co. v. Voorhees, 1 F.2d 693 (3d Cir. 1924) which is a virtually identical case allowing recovery of both profits because the contract was not a personal service contract. See also Gollaher v. Midwood Constr. Co., supra note 47, expressly following Olds v. Mapes-Reeve Constr. Co.

tween the contract price and the resale price as the measure of damages.[49] In a standard-priced item such as a new automobile, that differential will typically be zero since the contract price and the resale price will be identical. Yet, presumably the seller would have made the sale to *Y* regardless of *X*'s breach, i.e., the seller did not search for buyer *Y* because *X* breached — he sought *Y* and as many other customers as he could discover regardless of *X*'s breach. Thus, to characterize the transaction with *Y* exclusively as a resale of the car *X* was supposed to purchase is misleading. In fact, the seller has lost the profit he would have earned on the sale to *X* and the profit earned on the sale to *Y* should not be deducted in mitigation since the seller would have made that profit from the *Y* contract in any event.[50] The UCC recognizes the inadequacy of the remedy of resale or its counterpart, the difference between the contract price and market price at the time and place for tender.[51] Either of these remedies would provide the "lost volume" seller with either no recovery or a recovery that would be substantially lower than the damages necessary to place him in the position he would have occupied had the contract been performed — the standard generally required by the Code.[52] To overcome this inadequacy, the Code includes a provision permitting the seller to recoup his lost profit on the broken contract notwithstanding subsequent sales that would have occurred in any event:

> If the measure of damages provided in subsection (1) is inadequate to put the seller in as good a position as performance would have done then the measure of damages is the profit (including reasonable overhead) which the seller would have made from full performance by the buyer, together with any incidental damages provided in this Article (Section 2-710), due allowance for costs reasonably incurred and due credit for payments or proceeds of resale.[53]

Two major problems have arisen in the interpretation of this section due to infelicitous drafting. The last phrase may literally suggest that the proceeds of resale are to be deducted from the seller's recovery. If the literal interpretation is accepted, it would destroy the concept of permitting the lost profit on the broken contract. Courts have uniformly rejected this literal interpretation because it would undermine the purpose of the statute.[54] The phrase "due

---

[49] UCC § 2-706(1).

[50] This example is essentially that found in Neri v. Retail Marine Corp., 334 N.Y.S.2d 165, 285 N.E.2d 311 (1972) taken from W. Hawkland, Sales and Bulk Sales 153-54 (1958).

[51] UCC § 2-708(1) allows the contract price/market price differential which would be available to a seller who chooses not to resell or who has resold but has not complied with all of the requirements of the resale section, § 2-706, in making the resale in a commercially reasonable manner.

[52] UCC § 1-106(1).

[53] UCC § 2-708(2).

[54] See, e.g., Snyder v. Herbert Greenbaum & Assoc., 38 Md. App. 144, 380 A.2d 618, 625 (1977): "Practically, if the 'due credit' clause is applied to the lost volume seller, his measure of damages is no different from his recovery under § 2-708(1). Under § 2-708(1) he recovers the contract/market differential and the profit he makes on resale. If the 'due credit' provision is applied, the seller recovers only the profit he makes on resale plus the difference between the resale price and the contract price, an almost identical measure to § 2-708(1). If the 'due credit' clause is applied to the lost volume seller, the damage measure of 'lost profits' is rendered nugatory, and he is not put in as good a position as if there had been performance." Accord National Controls, Inc. v. Commodore Bus. Machs., Inc., 163 Cal. App. 3d 688, 209 Cal. Rptr. 636 (1985); Famous Knit-

credit for payments or proceeds of resale" has been interpreted as referring to the privilege of the seller to realize salvage value when he has not completed manufacture of a product and it would be useless to complete the manufacture.[55]

The second major problem in the statutory language is the parenthetical phrase "including reasonable overhead," which is part of the profit the seller has earned. The only inkling of the meaning of "profit" is found in a comment suggesting that profit means "list price less cost to the dealer or list price less manufacturing cost to the manufacturer."[56] When dealing with standard priced goods, the "list price" or "standard price" minus dealer or manufacturer cost can easily be envisioned. If the contract is formed at a price other than "list" or "standard," we may simply use the unpaid contract price from which the cost will be deducted. If we assume a typical transaction involving an automobile with a price of $12,000 and subtract from that the amount the dealer had to pay the manufacturer, e.g., $9,000, plus any expenses including transportation costs, dealer preparation costs and the like which, we will assume, increases the total dealer's cost to $10,000, the seller should recover $2000, i.e., price minus costs. The costs we have considered to this point, however, are *variable* costs, i.e., costs directly related to the sale of this particular automobile. There are, however, other costs which sellers must defray which are *overhead* or *fixed* costs which will remain stable regardless of the number of cars sold.[57] "Profit" may be viewed as "gross profit," i.e., the difference between revenues (price) and variable costs, or "net profit" which is the difference between revenues and a sum representing both variable and fixed costs.[58] Fixed or overhead costs would include such constant costs as utilities, property taxes, rent, and administrative salaries. These costs must be defrayed and they are defrayed by spreading all of them over the total number of sales of automobiles or other products being sold. Each sale must carry its share of the fixed costs which will remain the same regardless of the number of units sold.[59] The total number of sales will not be determined until the end of the fiscal year at which time an accurate measure of overhead or fixed cost per unit of sale may be ascribed. The allocation of overhead cost per unit of sale is, therefore, an accounting construct. Let us assume that, in our automobile example where the price was $12,000 and the variable costs were $10,000, the fixed or overhead allocated cost to that particular sale was $500. One interpretation of the Code language would suggest that it is necessary to subtract from the contract price ($12,000) not only the $10,000 variable costs, but also the accountant's construct of fixed or overhead cost ($500) which

---

wear Corp. v. Drug Fair, Inc., 493 F.2d 251, 254, n.7 (4th Cir. 1974); Neri v. Retail Marine Corp., *supra* note 50.

[55] *See* Neri v. Retail Marine Corp., *supra* note 50, at 314, n.2 which relies upon the 1952 Official Draft of Text and Comments of the UCC [1954] and to commentators who have concluded that the reference in § 2-708(2) is to resale as scrap under § 2-704. The note also finds support in the analysis of the language by Professor Harris in his article cited *supra* note 47, at 104.

[56] UCC § 2-708 comment 2.

[57] *See* David Sloan, Inc. v. Stanley G. House & Assocs., 311 Md. 36, 532 A.2d 694 (1987).

[58] *See* Bead Chain Mfg. Co. v. Saxton Prods., 183 Conn. 266, 439 A.2d 314, n.4 (1981) *citing* Childres & Burgess, *Seller's Remedies: The Primacy of UCC § 2-708(2),* 48 N.Y.U. L. Rev. 833, 846-47 (1973).

[59] *See* Vitex Mfg. Corp. v. Carbitex Corp., 377 F.2d 795, 799 (3d Cir. 1967).

would reveal the *net profit* on one sale to the seller of $1500. The Code, however, expressly permits the recovery of *overhead* ("including reasonable overhead"). Following this circular route, therefore, after having deducted the $500 overhead cost, it would then be added back in to allow a recovery to the seller of $2000. The courts are in agreement that "profit (including reasonable overhead)" means net profit plus overhead, or gross profit including overhead.[60] Recognizing the fact that the determination of reasonable overhead to a particular contract is an accounting construct, it is superfluous to follow the complicated, circuitous route to the proper result. The simple formula of subtracting variable costs from list price (or unpaid contract price) will necessarily include the reasonable overhead which the Code permits the seller to recover.[61]

E. *Expenses or Losses Incurred in Attempts to Mitigate.*

An aggrieved party may incur expenses or losses in his reasonable and good faith efforts to mitigate damages. Since such expenses or losses are occasioned by the breach, it is just that the breaching party bear them. It is, therefore, a generally accepted corollary to the mitigation principle that the innocent promisee may also recover expenses and losses resulting from good-faith attempts to lessen the injury suffered or anticipated from a breach.[62] If the effort to lessen the injury was reasonably warranted by and proportioned to the injury, and if it was conducted with reasonable skill and efficiency, recovery for such expenses and losses may be had although the effort proved futile.[63]

F. *Anticipatory Repudiation and Mitigation — "Learned of the Breach."*

Since an anticipatory repudiation is not, itself, a breach of contract, should a party recover damages that could have been avoided after the repudiation

---

[60] *See* Bead Chain Mfg. Co. v. Saxton Prods., *supra* note 58, *citing* Unique Sys. v. Zotos Int'l, Inc., 622 F.2d 373, 378 (8th Cir. 1980) and Jericho Sash & Door Co. v. Building Erectors, Inc., 362 Mass. 871, 872, 286 N.E.2d 343 (1972) in support. *See* the criticism of RESTATEMENT 2d § 347 comment f (*Lost Volume*) for its suggestion that, "The injured party's damages are then based on the net profit that he has lost as a result of the broken contract," as not recognizing the inclusion of overhead cost, in Teradyne, Inc. v. Teledyne Indus., 676 F.2d 865 (1st Cir. 1982).

[61] *Accord* R. NORDSTROM, HANDBOOK OF THE LAW OF SALES § 177 at 540 (1970).

[62] West Haven Sound Dev. Corp. v. City of West Haven, 201 Conn. 305, 514 A.2d 734 (1986) (bank loans, corporate and individual loans, accounts payable to suppliers, and related costs incurred to remain in business after the breach may be recovered if reasonable); Nunnally Co. v. Bromberg & Co., 217 Ala. 180, 115 So. 230 (1928) (lessee who was given possession of only part of demised premises entitled to recover the extra cost involved in making that part usable); Hoehne Ditch Co. v. John Flood Ditch Co., 76 Colo. 500, 233 P. 167 (1925) (one who had breached contract to carry water in an irrigation ditch held liable for the cost of procuring substitute carrier); Elias v. Wright, 276 F. 908 (2d Cir. 1921) (contractor who broke contract to install glass in building held liable for cost of putting muslin on the windows to protect interior until glass could be installed). *See also* RESTATEMENT 2d § 350 comment h and UCC §§ 2-704(2) and 2-706.

[63] *See* Automated Donut Sys. v. Consolidated Rail Corp., 12 Mass. App. 326, 424 N.E.2d 265 (1981) (even if the costs enhanced the damages, if reasonable they may be recovered); Ninth Ave. & Forty-Second St. Corp. v. Zimmerman, 217 App. Div. 498, 217 N.Y.S. 123 (1926) (where attorney negligently recommended purchase of an unmarketable leasehold, client recovered expense of an unsuccessful suit to clear title). *See also* Casey v. Nampa & Meridian Irrig. Dist., 85 Idaho 299, 379 P.2d 409 (1963) (whether plaintiff's method of minimizing damages due to flooding of his land caused by defendant's negligence was reasonable is a question for the jury under the evidence presented).

but before it became a breach? Older cases eschewed the concept of mitigation in response to an anticipatory repudiation on the footing that the repudiation could be ignored by the innocent party.[64] Prior to the UCC, there was authority supporting the same proposition in contracts for the sale of goods.[65] This view was always difficult to justify. Whatever one may think of the wisdom of requiring the innocent promisee to decide whether to treat the repudiation as an immediate breach or await performance until it is due, there can be little doubt of the injustice in permitting the promisee to fail to take reasonable steps to prevent the accumulation of unnecessary damages where the promisor clearly manifests his intention not to perform the contract. Since it is generally agreed that an anticipatory repudiation excuses the promisee from performing conditions precedent[66] and allows him generally to suspend his performance,[67] requiring reasonable action to avoid unnecessary losses is more than justified. Our courts, therefore, generally hold that the mitigation principle is applicable in such cases, i.e., the innocent promisee cannot recover damages that he could have avoided after the repudiation though he has yet to treat the repudiation as a breach.[68] The UCC has reacted clearly to pre-Code cases that would permit the aggrieved party to ignore the repudiation by allowing him to await the repudiating party's performance only for a commercially reasonable time.[69] Where it was clear that a repudiating party would not perform, a court held that the aggrieved party was unreasonable in failing to take appropriate steps to effectuate a substitute purchase (cover).[70] The court relegated the dealer to the damages measured by the difference between the contract price and the market price at the time the seller learned of the breach which the court concluded was the time the seller learned of the repudiation under these circumstances.[71]

---

[64] See, e.g., Barber Milling Co. v. Leichthammer Baking Co., 273 Pa. 90, 116 A. 677 (1922); John A. Roebling's Sons v. Lock-Stitch Fence Co., 130 Ill. 660, 22 N.E. 518 (1889).

[65] Reliance Cooperage Corp. v. Treat, 195 F.2d 977 (8th Cir. 1952) (the well-known case involving anticipatory repudiation of a contract to deliver barrel staves).

[66] RESTATEMENT 2d § 255.

[67] UCC § 2-610(c).

[68] See, e.g., Rockingham Cty. v. Luten Bridge Co., 35 F.2d 301 (4th Cir. 1929) (bridge construction contract repudiated before completion); Craig v. Higgins, 31 Wyo. 166, 224 P. 668 (1924) (contract to pay for drilling oil well repudiated before completion of well).

[69] UCC § 2-610(a). The aggrieved party also has the choice of resorting to any remedy for breach immediately upon the repudiation. § 2-610(b).

[70] Oloffson v. Coomer, 11 Ill. App. 3d 918, 296 N.E.2d 871 (1973) (farmer informed grain dealer that he would not plant corn because the season had been too wet. The dealer knew or should have known that the farmer would not be able to supply the corn at the time of the farmer's announcement that he would not plant. The court held that it was unreasonable for the dealer to await performance under these circumstances. See also First Nat'l Bank v. Jefferson Mtg. Co., 576 F.2d 479 (3d Cir. 1978).

[71] UCC § 2-713(1) is the source of this remedy. Since the formula in § 2-713(1) deals with the time the buyer "learned of the breach," the question arises whether that time is the time of the repudiation. Since an anticipatory repudiation is not a breach, it is difficult to say that the buyer learned of the breach at the moment of repudiation. UCC § 2-723 may be seen to support this dilemma by treating the time the buyer learned of the repudiation as the time he learned of the breach only in cases where an action based on anticipatory repudiation comes to trial *before* the time for performance. Thus, in a relatively normal situation where the case would not come to trial (in these crowded docket times) until after the time for performance, by negative implication, § 2-723 would suggest that the time the buyer learned of the repudiation is not the time he learned of the breach. Moreover, since § 2-610(a) permits the aggrieved party to await performance for a commercially reasonable time, to suggest that the time the buyer learned of the

§ 123. Emotional Distress Limitation.

In addition to the economic losses caused by a breach of contract, any breach may cause the aggrieved party to suffer mental or emotional distress. It is foreseeable that the aggrieved party will often be at least unhappy after a breach and that the breach may even cause some mental pain and suffering. Notwithstanding such foreseeable results, courts have been particularly reluctant to allow damages for emotional distress in contract actions.[72] Thus, another limitation on contract damages may be seen in the refusal of courts to permit the recovery of such damages. Like all general rules, however, this one is subject to exceptions. There is general agreement that two exceptions exist though there is confusion concerning one of the exceptions.

There is general agreement that where serious emotional disturbance is not only foreseeable but a particularly likely result of a breach, damages for such emotional distress may be recoverable.[73] Contracts for the burial of a spouse or other family member are particularly sensitive. Any funeral director should be aware of the emotional nature of such contracts and that a breach may very well cause emotional distress.[74] Where a telegraph company is made aware of the meaning or import of a death message, it should be aware of the likelihood of emotional distress if it breaches its contract by not delivering the message or delivering it so late that a relative is precluded from attending the funeral.[75] The public humiliation attending the mistreatment or expulsion of guests of hotels,[76] or passengers from public carriers,[77] or ticketholders in places of entertainment or amusement,[78] are traditional categories which courts have regarded as exceptional situations giving rise to recoverable dam-

---

repudiation is the time he learned of the breach would preclude the buyer from this choice. Yet, one case suggests that "learned of the breach" should mean "learned of the repudiation." *See* First Nat'l Bank v. Jefferson Mtg. Co., *supra* note 70. On the other hand, another court has concluded that "learned of the breach" means time of performance. Cargill, Inc. v. Stafford, 553 F.2d 1222 (10th Cir. 1977). Neither interpretation appears sound to this author. While the time the buyer "learned of the breach" would normally be the time for performance, in an anticipatory repudiation situation, the circumstances may suggest a time between repudiation and the time for performance that is the end of the commercially reasonable time the aggrieved party is permitted to wait under § 2-610(a). Thus, such a buyer could await performance for some period after the repudiation and, prior to the time for performance, treat the repudiation as a breach. He would then have "learned of the breach" when he treated the repudiation as a breach, assuming he did so within a commercially reasonable time. If the buyer chose to await performance beyond a commercially reasonable time, he would be deemed to have "learned of the breach" at the end of the commercially reasonable time. While this analysis does not promote the certainty that an all-or-nothing approach (time of performance or time of repudiation) would suggest, it appears to be the only approach consistent with the purposes of the express statutory language. Certainty is a high value in the law, particularly in commercial transactions. It should not, however, become the analytical apotheosis of the UCC which is, at least in its contract sections (Article 2), filled with Llewellynesque leeways.

[72] *See* Buckley v. Trenton Sav. Fund Soc'y, 216 N.J. Super. 705, 524 A.2d 886 (1987); Jankowski v. Mazzotta, 7 Mich. App. 483, 152 N.W.2d 49 (1967). *See also* RESTATEMENT 2d § 353.
[73] RESTATEMENT 2d § 353: "... [T]he contract or the breach is of such a kind that serious emotional disturbance was a particularly likely result."
[74] *See* Lamm v. Shingleton, 231 N.C. 10, 55 S.E.2d 810 (1949); Fitzsimmons v. Olinger Mortuary Ass'n, 91 Colo. 544, 17 P.2d 535 (1932); Renihan v. Wright, 125 Ind. 536, 25 N.E. 822 (1890).
[75] *See* Wadsworth v. Western Union Tel. Co., 86 Tenn. 695, 8 S.W. 574 (1888).
[76] *See* Frewen v. Page, 238 Mass. 499, 131 N.E. 475 (1921).
[77] *See* Gillespie v. Brooklyn Heights R.R., 178 N.Y. 347, 70 N.E. 857 (1904).
[78] *See* Aaron v. Ward, 203 N.Y. 351, 96 N.E. 736 (1911).

ages for emotional distress.[79] One court has permitted recovery of such damages for breach of a contract to perform a surgical operation,[80] while another has gone beyond the pale and permitted such a recovery for breach of warranty of the materials of a roof which leaked.[81]

The second exception is troublesome. The courts are particularly concerned about outrageous conduct accompanying the breach and are typically willing to permit recovery of mental distress damages when such conduct is evident. The problem arises in the characterization of that conduct. The RESTATEMENT 2d insists that this exception be limited to cases in which the breach also caused "bodily harm"[82] and explains that "the action may nearly always be regarded as one in tort."[83] It then suggests, however, that courts generally do not require the plaintiff to specify the nature of the action, i.e., they permit the recovery of emotional distress damages without classifying the wrong.[84] While there are cases indicating that conduct amounting to a tort accompanying a breach of contract will allow such damages,[85] other courts are particularly insistent that it is not necessary to prove a tort to fall within this exception.[86] Rather, wilful, wanton, or insulting conduct, albeit not amounting to a tort, will be sufficient.[87] At least one reason for this confusion may arise from the clear requirement that *punitive* damages, as contrasted with damages for emotional distress, are recoverable only where the conduct constituting the breach amounts to a tort.[88] Courts can become confused concerning the nature of damages for emotional distress. They are generally regarded as sharing the normal purpose of contract damages, i.e., they are designed to have a *compensatory* effect as contrasted with punitive damages which are designed to have a *deterrent* effect.[89]

Notwithstanding judicial insistence that damages for mental suffering are compensatory rather than punitive, they may often be granted more for the

---

[79] *See* FIRST RESTATEMENT § 341 and the elaboration thereof in the concurring opinion of Mr. Justice Musmanno in Gefter v. Rosenthal, 384 Pa. 123, 119 A.2d 250, 251 (1956).

[80] Stewart v. Rudner, 349 Mich. 459, 84 N.W.2d 816 (1957).

[81] F. Becker Asphaltum Roofing Co. v. Murphy, 224 Ala. 655, 141 So. 630 (1932). *See also* Westesen v. Olathe State Bank, 78 Colo. 217, 240 P. 689 (1925) (breach of contract by bank to honor draft drawn by one who was traveling away from home).

[82] RESTATEMENT 2d § 353. *See* Sullivan v. O'Connor, 363 Mass. 579, 296 N.E.2d 183 (1973) where damages for mental distress were allowed from an operation involving cosmetic surgery.

[83] RESTATEMENT 2d § 353 comment a.

[84] *Id.*

[85] *See* Chung v. Kaonohi Center Co., 618 P.2d 283 (Haw. 1980).

[86] *See* Trimble v. City & County of Denver, 697 P.2d 716 (Colo. 1985).

[87] *Id.* It should be noted, however, that third parties may not be entitled to such damages though their emotional distress was clearly foreseeable at the time of contract formation. Thus, where a newborn was kidnapped from a hospital and held for more than four months, the parents were not entitled to recover because they had no cause of action due to a lack of duty on the part of the hospital to the parents. Johnson v. Jamaica Hosp., 478 N.Y.S.2d 838, 467 N.E.2d 502 (1984). Similarly, where a parent suffering from Alzheimer's disease was not properly cared for in a nursing home, the children of the parents had no cause of action. Oresky v. Scharf, 126 A.D.2d 614, 510 N.Y.S.2d 897 (1987).

[88] RESTATEMENT 2d § 355.

[89] *See* Mortgage Fin. Co. v. Podleski, 742 P.2d 900 (Colo. 1987) pointing out the confusion in Denver Pub'g Co. v. Kirk, 729 P.2d 1005 (Colo. App. 1986) in which the court labeled damages for emotional distress as "exemplary" (punitive). *See also* Aaron v. Ward, 203 N.Y. 351, 355, 96 N.E. 736 (1911) ("And it must be borne in mind that a recovery for indignity and wounded feelings is compensatory and does not constitute exemplary damages."). Punitive damages are explored in § 124.

purpose of discouraging the contract breaker through the use of a deterrent rather than attempting to evaluate mental distress on a pecuniary basis. The measurement of such damages is, after all, quite uncertain in a contracts, as contrasted with a tort, context. If, however, courts did not insist on characterizing them as compensatory rather than punitive, their recovery would be significantly restricted since, *inter alia,* there would be a need to demonstrate tortious conduct. The fact is that it is difficult to draw a bright line between compensatory and punitive damages in this context.

§ 124. Damages With Purposes Other Than Compensation.

As we have seen, the normal purpose of contract damages is to *compensate* the aggrieved party, typically by placing that party in the position he would have occupied had the contract been performed, i.e., the protection of his expectation interest.[90] There are, however, two other types of damages which clearly have no *compensatory* purpose. We will now consider *punitive* damages and *nominal* damages.

A. *Punitive (Exemplary) Damages.*

Since the purpose of contract law is to compensate the aggrieved party, damages should not be awarded for the purpose of punishing the contract breaker in an effort to deter similar conduct. On the other hand, in tort actions, particularly outrageous conduct by the tortfeasor will often give rise to punitive damages in addition to compensatory damages for the actual harm suffered. Myriad cases, therefore, support the general rule that punitive or exemplary damages are not recoverable in a contract action unless the breach of contract is also a tort for which punitive damages would be recoverable.[91] A few courts have awarded punitive damages in the absence of a tort where, for example, the conduct is fraudulent though not tortious.[92] More recently, a number of courts have been willing to award punitive damages where there has been a wilful breach of a fiduciary duty such as that owed by a real estate broker to a client[93] or by an insurance company to a client. Where an insurance company wilfully withholds payment of a claim, i.e., where it has no reasonable basis for denying the claim and it knows that it has no basis for denial or recklessly disregards its lack of a reasonable basis for denial, the insurer has not only breached the contract, it has acted in extreme bad faith which, according to a number of courts, amounts to a tort.[94] Other courts have

---

[90] Earlier, we also considered the protection of the reliance and restitution interests which restore the aggrieved party to *status quo ante,* i.e., they place the party in the position it would have occupied had no contract been formed.

[91] *See, e.g.,* Palmer v. Ted Stevens Honda, Inc., 238 Cal. Rptr. 363 (Cal. App. 1987); Wien Air Alaska v. Bubbel, 723 P.2d 627 (Alaska 1986); Morrow v. L. A. Goldschmidt Assoc., 492 N.E.2d 181 (Ill. 1986); Ellmex Constr. Co. v. Republic Ins. Co., 494 A.2d 339 (N.J. Super. 1985); Kamlar Corp. v. Haley, 224 Va. 699, 299 S.E.2d 514 (1983); Z. D. Howard Co. v. Cartwright, 537 P.2d 345 (Okla. 1975). *See also* RESTATEMENT 2d § 355.

[92] In South Carolina, this view was enunciated many years ago in Wellborn v. Dixon, 70 S.C. 108, 49 S.E. 232 (1904). *See also* Boise Dodge, Inc. v. Clark, 92 Idaho 902, 453 P.2d 551 (1969).

[93] *See* Phillips v. Lynch, 101 Nev. 311, 704 P.2d 1083 (1985); Robison v. Katz, 94 N.M. 314, 610 P.2d 201 (1980); Security Corp. v. Lehman Assoc., 108 N.J. Super. 137, 260 A.2d 248 (1970).

[94] *See* White v. Unigard Mut. Ins. Co., 112 Idaho 94, 730 P.2d 1014 (1986); Rawlings v. Apodaca, 151 Ariz. 180, 726 P.2d 596 (1985). *See also* Anderson v. Continental Ins. Co., 85 Wis. 2d 675, 271

rejected this new tort.[95] There is an implied covenant of good faith in every contract and it is possible to construe a wilful violation of that covenant as tortious as well as a breach of contract. While one reading of a particular opinion suggests the application of the concept beyond the special relationship situation in insurance or other special relationship contracts to ordinary commercial contracts,[96] a more recent comprehensive review of this possible extension clearly restricts the earlier holding to its facts and refuses to extend the concept beyond special relationship situations.[97]

Statutes in various jurisdictions are designed to protect the insured against delays in paying insurance claims. These statutes often contain provisions requiring the insurer to pay additional amounts to the insured for such delays as well as reasonable attorney's fees that the insured may be forced to incur to prosecute his claim. Significant questions of statutory interpretation may arise when an insured attempts to recover punitive damages beyond those set forth in the statute. The decisions to this point reject such claims for punitive damages beyond those authorized in the respective statutes.[98]

B. *Nominal Damages.*

Whenever a breach of contract has occurred that was not legally excusable, a cause of action exists regardless of the lack of compensable loss. If the aggrieved party has suffered no compensable loss and is not entitled to exemplary (punitive) damages, she may recover nominal damages.[99] If the aggrieved party cannot establish damages because of a fatal lack of certainty in the proof, she will receive nominal damages.[1] The typical recovery will be a token, such as six cents or one dollar.[2] Where the plaintiff has made a good faith but unsuccessful effort to prove damages, the court may award her court costs.[3]

If a party knows that her recovery will be nominal, she may still bring the action to establish her rights under a continuing contractual relationship or to establish her right because it will bear on other legal relationships. This use

---

N.W.2d 368 (1978); Christian v. American Home Assur. Co., 577 P.2d 899 (Okla. 1978); Gruenberg v. Aetna Ins. Co., 108 Cal. Rptr. 480, 510 P.2d 1032 (1973).

[95] *See* Pillsbury Co. v. National Union Fire Ins. Co., 425 N.W.2d 244 (Minn. App. 1988); Garden State Community Hosp. v. Watson, 191 N.J. Super. 225, 465 A.2d 1225 (1982); Kewin v. Massachusetts Mut. Life Ins. Co., 409 Mich. 401, 295 N.W.2d 50 (1982).

[96] Seaman's Direct Buying Serv. v. Standard Oil of Cal., 206 Cal. Rptr. 354, 686 P.2d 1158 (1984) (egregious breach of the implied covenant of good faith by denial of existence of contract).

[97] Foley v. Interactive Data Corp., 47 Cal. 3d 654, 765 P.2d 373 (1988) (refusal to extend concept to employment contract).

[98] *See* Kaniuk v. Safeco Ins. Co., 142 Ill. App. 3d 1070, 492 N.E.2d 592 (1986) (construing ILL. REV. STAT. 1983 ch. 73 par. 767); Milcarek v. Nationwide Ins. Co., 190 N.J. Super. 358, 463 A.2d 950 (1983) (construing N.J. STAT. ANN. 39: 6A-5); Smith v. Harleysville Ins. Co., 275 Pa. Super. 246, 418 A.2d 705 (1980) (construing 40 PA. CONS. STAT. § 1009.106(a)).

[99] Harper v. Consolidated Bus Lines, 117 W. Va. 228, 285 S.E. 225 (1936); W. H. Kiblinger Co. v. Sauk Bank, 131 Wis. 595, 111 N.W. 709 (1907). RESTATEMENT 2d § 346(2).

[1] *See* Freund v. Washington Square Press, Inc., 34 N.Y.2d 379, 314 N.E.2d 419 (1974) (publisher breached contract to publish book and plaintiff could not establish royalty loss with reasonable certainty so court awarded nominal damages of six cents).

[2] Georgia, however, will award much more significant "nominal" damages, *e.g.,* $1000 or $1500 would not be uncommon. *See* First Fed. S & L Ass'n of Atlanta v. White, 168 Ga. App. 516, 309 S.E.2d 858 (1983).

[3] *See* Fruend v. Washington Square Press, Inc., *supra* note 1.

of actions that are destined to result in nominal damages for this purpose is, however, quite rare since, under current statutes, the troubled party may accomplish the result more effectively in a declaratory judgment action which will establish her rights. In fact, if a trial court erroneously fails to award nominal damages, an appellate court may not bother reversing that judgment. If, however, the lower court commits error and the determination of the rights of the plaintiff is the question before the court, the court will reverse even though only nominal damages are involved.[4]

§ 125. Agreed Damages — Penalties, Liquidated Damages, and Limitations on Liability.

A. *Purposes of Agreed Damages Provisions.*

It is not uncommon for parties who make a contract to agree that a specified amount will be paid to the aggrieved party in the event of a breach instead of having damages assessed in the usual way. The question is whether such a stipulation will be enforced by the courts.

An agreed damages provision may be designed to accomplish any one of at least three distinct purposes. (1) It may be intended to coerce the promisor into performing his contract by fixing a sum to be paid, in case of breach, that far exceeds the probable, actual loss that would result from a breach of the contract. The fear of having to pay an excessive amount could operate *in terrorem* to induce the promisor to carry out his performance, regardless of the circumstances confronting him. (2) The stipulation may be intended merely as a convenient method of determining the amount to be paid in case of breach, i.e., it may be an honest pre-estimate of the probable loss which will be caused by the breach. (3) Such a stipulation may be designed to put a limit on the amount of the loss to be borne by the promisor in case of breach, as where parties fix a sum to be paid which is obviously less than the probable, actual loss that would be suffered by the promisee if a breach should occur. It is clear from the decided cases that if the stipulation calls for the payment of what amounts to a penalty for nonperformance designed to coerce performance, it is unenforceable. While this has not always been so, courts of equity began to relieve against penalties and forfeitures at a very early day. They did so on the ground that it is unconscionable for a private person to exact a penalty or to insist upon a forfeiture because of another's nonperformance of duty, even though the penalty or forfeiture is agreed upon by the parties. They also wished to prevent the collection of usury. Courts of law, partly as the result of statutes, soon adopted the same view of the matter, so that the

---

[4]"The failure to perform a duty required by contract is a legal wrong, independent of actual damage sustained by the party to whom performance is due; and in general, where a contract right is violated, the maxim 'de minimis non curat lex' has no application, and nominal damages will be given. But where a judgment is erroneous only becuase it fails to give nominal damages, it will not be reversed unless nominal damages in the given case would carry costs.... If, however, ... the object of the action is to determine some question of permanent right, the fact that he can only recover nominal damages will not prevent a reversal." Kenyon v. Western Union Tel. Co., 100 Cal. 454, 35 P. 75, 76 (1893). *Accord* Dreelan v. Karon, 191 Minn. 330, 254 N.W. 433 (1934); Elder v. Florsheim Shoe Co., 209 Ky. 509, 273 S.W. 60 (1925).

question is no longer doubtful either at law or in equity.[5] In such a case, the stipulation will be disregarded and the damages will be assessed as if the contract were silent on the question of the amount to be paid in case of breach.[6] On the other hand, it is equally clear that it is perfectly proper for the parties to a contract to pre-estimate the probable loss in case of breach and to stipulate for the payment of the amount so determined to avoid the necessity for the assessment of damages in the usual way. If this is the apparent purpose of the stipulation, the amount agreed to be paid will be called liquidated damages, as distinguished from a penalty, and the promisee will recover the stipulated amount, and only that amount, regardless of whether the actual loss suffered from a breach is greater or less than the stipulated amount.[7] The only question of difficulty encountered in the application of these principles comes in determining whether an agreed damages provision in a given case is to be dealt with as a liquidated damages clause or as a penalty that will not be enforced. It is important to consider the judicial tests used to make this distinction.

B. *Tests to Distinguish Liquidated Damage Clauses From Penalties.*

1. Traditional (Common Law) Test.

Over the years, the courts have developed a test to determine the enforceability of an agreed damages provision that contains three elements regardless of the form of the statement: (1) the parties must have intended to agree upon damages in advance of any breach; (2) the anticipated damages are difficult of ascertainment, i.e., they are uncertain; (3) the amount stipulated was a reasonable forecast of losses that would ensue in the event of a breach, i.e., the amount is not greatly disproportionate to an honest estimate of probable damages.[8] The first element is of highly dubious importance[9] though questions may arise as to whether a given clause should be interpreted as an agreed damages clause at all.[10] The name given to the clause by the parties, i.e.,

---

[5]For the history of the matter, *see* 5 Holdsworth, History of English Law 293 (1924). *See also* Sun Printing & Pub'g Ass'n v. Moore, 183 U.S. 642 (1902); Burnside v. Wand, 170 Mo. 531, 71 S.W. 337 (1902).

[6] *See* RESTATEMENT 2d § 356 comment a referring to § 184(1) which permits a court to enforce the remainder of the agreement where part of the agreement is unenforceable on grounds of public policy.

[7]*See* Monsen Eng'g Co. v. Tami-Gaithens, Inc., 219 N.J. Super. 241, 530 A.2d 313 (1987); Owen v. Christopher, 144 Kan. 765, 62 P.2d 860 (1936); Robbins v. Plant, 174 Ark. 639, 297 S.W. 1027 (1927); Wise v. United States, 249 U.S. 361 (1919); Learned v. Holbrook, 87 Or. 576, 170 P. 530 (1918), *aff'd,* 171 P. 222 (1918).

[8]*See* Yerton v. Bowden, 762 P.2d 786 (Colo. App. 1988); Monsen Eng'g Co. v. Tami-Gaithens, Inc., *supra* note 7; Berger v. Shanahan, 142 Conn. 726, 118 A.2d 311 (1955).

[9]"That their intention as to how the stipulation shall be regarded is immaterial is evidenced from the results reached. It is clear from those results that their intention is important, if at all, only insofar as it relates to the basis on which the sum fixed is determined. It is only the intention to make an honest pre-estimate of the probable loss that counts. Thus, it has been said, 'but agreements to pay fixed sums plainly without reasonable relation to any probable damage which may follow a breach will not be enforced. This circumstance tends to negative any notion that the parties really meant to provide a measure of compensation — to treat the sum named as estimated and ascertained damages.'" Kothe v. R. C. Taylor Trust, 280 U.S. 224, 226 (1930). Another court suggests that "the question is not what the parties intended but 'whether the sum fixed is in fact in the nature of a penalty.'" Central Trust Co. v. Wolf, 255 Mich. 8, 237 N.W. 29 (1931).

[10]The clause may be quite different, *e.g.,* it could be an exculpatory clause or it could be a manifestation of the parties to allow for alternative performances. These issues are discussed later in this section.

either "liquidated damages" or "penalty," will not control[11] though it is inadvisable to draft a clause intended to allow for liquidated damages by characterizing the clause as a "penalty."[12]

The second element is designed to corroborate the parties' assumed intention to honestly forecast damages in the event of a breach. If damages are easily ascertainable, the need for such a clause evaporates and there is some suspicion that the clause was designed for purposes other than the legitimate purpose of honestly forecasting damages. There are situations which are particularly appropriate for agreed damages clauses because actual damages are so uncertain. A contract containing a restrictive covenant not to compete, for example, is an example of precisely the kind promise which, if breached, does not lend itself to easy or accurate measurement of actual loss.[13] One of the most common uses of such a clause is found in highway construction projects where state highway departments will include a clause for a deduction from the contract price for each day of delay.[14] On the other hand, a contract for the sale of ordinary goods with a prevailing market price should leave little room for an agreed damages clause since the actual damages are so readily ascertainable. While there is criticism of the uncertainty requirement[15] and suggestions that the question of enforceability is typically not decided on that basis,[16] the judicial test invariably contains this element and some decisions emphasize its importance.[17] Yet, the third element is unquestionably of paramount concern to courts, i.e., whether the amount fixed in the clause was highly disproportionate to the amount of probable loss in the event of a breach.

It is important to emphasize that the traditional test is applied at the time of contract formation,[18] i.e., did the parties agree upon an amount at the time

---

[11] See In re Lammers, 211 F. Supp. 448 (E.D. Ark. 1962); Independent Sch. Dist. v. Dudley, 195 Iowa 398, 192 N.W. 261 (1923); Horn v. Poindexter, 176 N.C. 620, 97 S.E. 653 (1918); United States v. Bethlehem Steel Co., 205 U.S. 105 (1907).

[12] Such a characterization presents an obstacle, albeit not an insuperable one, to a court in deciding that the clause is an enforceable agreed damages (liquidated damages) clause. There is no point in creating any obstacle to that determination if the intention is to have an enforceable clause.

[13] See Raymundo v. Hammond Clinic Ass'n, 449 N.E.2d 276 (Ind. 1983) (physician worked in a clinic which grossed over 8 million dollars annually. His division produced over $384,000 each year of which he provided over $100,000 in a little more than six months. A liquidated damages provision for breach of a covenant not to compete which required his payment of $25,000 was upheld as clearly not disproportionate to the probable loss of his leaving the clinic.).

[14] See Ledbetter Bros. v. North Carolina Dep't of Transp., 68 N.C. App. 97, 314 S.E.2d 761 (1984); Dave Gustafson & Co. v. State, 83 S.D. 160, 156 N.W.2d 185 (1968). These clauses are typically set forth in prefabricated terms, i.e., there will be a stated amount of liquidated damages per day and that amount may vary with the contract price — the higher the contract price, the larger the amount of daily liquidated damages since delays on larger contracts are typically more costly to the state than delays on smaller projects. The damages are always quite difficult to ascertain. Courts, therefore, concentrate on the amount in the clause as the paramount question. Current practice suggests that it is not uncommon for contractors to agree to such clauses if a corresponding clause granting the contractor a bonus for early completion of projects is included.

[15] See C. McCormick, McCormick on Damages § 148 at 605 (1935) (why not permit parties to relieve the judge or jury of the task of determining damages even if the damages were ascertainable at the time of contract formation?).

[16] Id.

[17] See, e.g., Dave Gustafson & Co. v. State, 83 S.D. 160, 156 N.W.2d 185 (1968).

[18] See Yerton v. Bowden, supra note 8, and Monsen Eng'g Co. v. Tami-Gaithens, Inc., supra note 7.

they formed the contract which, in light of anticipated harm, was an honest and reasonable forecast of actual damages? If the forecast was reasonable at the time of formation, actual damages should be irrelevant.[19] The parties, after all, are substituting their private agreement on damages for the usual judicial assessment process. If they have made an honest forecast of such damages, why should that forecast not control, regardless of the actual losses that may have become ascertainable after the breach but were unascertainable at the time of formation? If actual damages are to be measured, there is no need for an agreed damages clause. Notwithstanding this logic, a problem arises if no actual harm is suffered even though, at the time of formation, actual losses were foreseeable (though uncertain in amount) and the parties made an honest forecast of those losses. We must now consider whether a court should enforce such a clause in light of the absence of any actual loss.

2. The "No Harm" Problem.

Consider the hypothetical of a contract between an upwardly mobile executive with a family and a contractor to construct a house for the executive at the location of his new employment. He has sold his former house and must occupy the new house no later than a certain date. A liquidated damage clause provides a reasonable per diem amount for any delay by the contractor since the executive would then be required to find other housing for himself and his family. The building is delayed but the executive is provided with splendid housing from his immediate superior who will be out of the country for a month. The executive and his family live in splendor for the month at which time the new house is ready for occupancy. The liquidated damage clause appears perfectly enforceable in terms of the anticipated harm, but no harm has resulted — in fact, the executive and family have enjoyed commodious living quarters at no expense. They are, therefore, in a better position than they would have been in had the house been completed on time. Should a court enforce the clause under these circumstances?

An interesting case suggests the problems courts may confront in similar circumstances. A contractor agreed to perform by a certain date under a contract containing an agreed damages provision for $750 per day for each day of delay which was a reasonable amount in the light of anticipated harm. The contractor insisted that his subcontractor agree to a similar clause. The subcontractor failed to complete its work on time as did the contractor. The trial court, however, found that the sub's delay did not cause the contractor's delay. The court struggled to what it deemed a just result, i.e., limit the subcontractor's liability to an amount not greater than the number of days of delay for

---

[19] See Frick Co. v. Rubel Corp., 62 F.2d 765 (1933) where Judge Learned Hand suggests that his brothers on the court think that actual losses are irrelevant where there is an enforceable agreed damages clause because only losses in *contemplation* of breach are relevant to test the validity of such a clause. Learned Hand disagreed. Learned Hand was not entirely alone in his view. In fact, a few courts had even held that it was necessary to determine whether the amount stipulated was reasonable in light of the *actual* loss sustained by the aggrieved party. See Macneil, *Power of Contract and Agreed Remedies,* 47 CORNELL L.Q. 495, 504 (1962).

which the contractor was liable.[20] If, in the example of the house for the executive, the builder was delayed but the executive and his family could not have occupied the house during the delay for personal reasons, he would have suffered no harm because of the delay. Whether there is no actual harm or where the harm is not caused by the breach, courts must choose between the policy in favor of enforcing legitimate agreed damages provisions and the more fundamental policy which precludes windfalls, i.e., damages that place a party in a *better* position than he would have been in had the contract been performed, should not be awarded. A number of courts have chosen the latter policy, at least to the extent of stating that, if there is no harm at all, an otherwise enforceable liquidated damages clause will not be enforced.[21] If more than nominal damages are actually suffered, however, the traditional rule would preclude any further inquiry into the enforceability of the clause since the amount of actual damages beyond zero or nominal damages should be irrelevant.[22] It is important to consider a modification of the traditional test which allows courts to consider actual damages though, as will be seen, it does not affect the foregoing analysis of the "no harm" problem.

3. Uniform Commercial Code and RESTATEMENT 2d Modification.

The UCC makes an important change in the test to be applied to agreed damages provisions[23] and the RESTATEMENT 2d replicates the Code provision.[24] While retaining the uncertainty requirement,[25] the Code and RESTATEMENT 2d provisions state that the amount in the clause must be reasonable "in the light of the anticipated *or* actual harm caused by the breach...."[26] The

---

[20] Mattingly Bridge Co. v. Holloway & Son Constr. Co., 694 S.W.2d 702 (Ky. 1985). The court discovered this solution through a clause in the subcontract indicating that liquidated damages should cease when the work was accepted by the owner.

[21] In relation to the contractor/subcontractor case, *see* Massman Constr. Co. v. City Council of Greenville, 147 F.2d 925 (5th Cir. 1945) which decided that an agreed damages clause was a penalty, *inter alia*, because a delay in the construction of a bridge caused no harm when the road was not connected until 30 days later. *See also* Grand Bissell Towers, Inc. v. John Gagnon Enters., 657 S.W.2d 378 (Mo. App. 1983); Fields Found., Ltd. v. Christensen, 103 Wis. 2d 465, 309 N.W.2d 125 (1981). RESTATEMENT 2d § 356 comment b and ill. 4. *Contra* Southwest Eng'g Co. v. United States, 341 F.2d 998 (8th Cir.), *cert. denied*, 382 U.S. 819 (1965); McCarthy v. Tally, 46 Cal. 2d 577, 297 P.2d 981 (1956).

[22] *See* Comment, *Liquidated Damages and the "No Harm Rule,"* 9 STAN. L. REV. 381, 383-84 (1957) suggesting that holdings in cases to that time suggesting adherence to the "no harm" rule should be limited to the proposition that the plaintiff should not be required to prove the extent of his harm rather than the proposition that the defendant cannot defend against a liquidated damages claim by showing no injury at all.

[23] UCC § 2-718(1).

[24] RESTATEMENT 2d § 356(1). *See* Illingworth v. Bushong, 297 Or. 675, 688 P.2d 379 (1984).

[25] UCC § 2-718(1) suggests that damages may be liquidated "in the light of ... the difficulties of proof of loss and the inconvenience and nonfeasibility of otherwise obtaining an adequate remedy." Notwithstanding this language, it is doubtful that courts will insist upon great uncertainty under this Code provision. For example, with respect to a contract for the purchase of an automobile breached by the buyer, the court suggested that a clause allowing the seller twenty percent of the price as liquidated damages may be reasonable in light of the UCC allowance of lost profit to lost volume sellers under § 2-708(1). The fact that such profits may have been ascertainable at the time of contract formation was not mentioned. *See* Kaiserman v. Martin J. Ain, Ltd., 112 Misc. 2d 768, 450 N.Y.S.2d 135 (1981). Neither the UCC nor the RESTATEMENT 2d bother stating that the parties must have intended to liquidate damages. In light of many years of doubt concerning this "requirement," the absence is not remarkable.

[26] UCC § 2-718(1) (emphasis added). The only change in the RESTATEMENT 2d language is the use of the term "loss" instead of "harm." RESTATEMENT 2d § 356(1).

provision is designed to extend the enforceability of agreed damages clauses by permitting the amount in the clause to be compared with anticipated or actual harm.[27] A recent case may be read to suggest the possibility that a clause will be enforced under the modified test that would have been unenforceable under the traditional test.[28] It is certainly not difficult to conceive a situation where that would be the case. Where, for example, a clause appears clearly disproportionate to anticipated harm and, therefore, appears to be a penalty, actual damages can later be measured in an amount not unreasonably disproportionate to the amount in the clause. The clause would then be enforced under the modified test even though such enforcement would violate two fundamental policies of the common law. First, the court would be enforcing a clause that was intended as a penalty which is antithetical to the compensation concept. Second, since the large actual damages were not anticipated at the time of formation, they were not foreseeable. The enforcement of the clause, therefore, would violate the foreseeability limitation to which the Code and RESTATEMENT 2d adhere and our courts have insisted upon since *Hadley v. Baxendale* in 1854.[29] The possibility that certain sections of Article 2 of the Code may be changed raises the hope that the Code liquidated damage test will be among those changes.

C. *Blunderbuss Clauses.*

Where a liquidated damages clause will, by the terms of the contract, be activated for any one of several possible breaches of that contract, a significant question arises as to whether the clause is an honest forecast of actual loss in the event of a breach. For example, where a lease contained many covenants of varying importance as well as a clause calling for the landlord's retention of a $7,500 security deposit upon the breach of any one of the covenants in the lease, the court recognized the uneven importance of a variety of covenants. The damages for breach of some of the covenants were ascertain-

---

[27] Equitable Lumber Corp. v. IPA Land Dev. Corp., 381 N.Y.S.2d 459, 344 N.E.2d 391 (1976) (decisions which have restricted their analyses of validity of clauses with respect to anticipated harm exclusively have, to this extent, been abrogated by the Code).

[28] *See* Ledbetter Bros. v. North Carolina Dep't of Transp., 68 N.C. App. 97, 314 S.E.2d 761 (1984), the court applied the modified test to a clause in a highway construction project. While the court rejected the argument that the clause may have suffered from lack of specificity in that it applied to breaches of varying significance (the "blunderbuss" clause to be discussed *infra*), the court did not deem it necessary to dwell on that problem because the amount in the clause ($49,500) was not unreasonably disproportionate to the amount of actual damage suffered by the Department of Transportation ($44,837.36).

[29] "It is true that the Code is unusually generous in its appraisal of the amount set by the contracting parties. Even if this amount was entirely unreasonable, as of the time of contract, it can apparently be recovered so long as it turns out, purely as a matter of accident, to approximate the harm actually caused by the buyer's breach." Peters, *Remedies for Breach of Contract Relating to the Sale of Goods Under the Uniform Commercial Code: A Roadmap for Article Two*, 73 YALE L.J. 199, 278 (1963). Prior to the approval of what now appears as RESTATEMENT 2d § 356(1), the author, at the request of the Reporter for the RESTATEMENT 2d, met with the Reporter to suggest changes in certain draft provisions of the RESTATEMENT 2d relating to damages. The Reporter accepted six of seven recommendations. The refused recommendation had suggested that the RESTATEMENT 2d should not follow the UCC section on liquidated damages for the reasons stated in the text. The Reporter conveyed the clear impression that, since the American Law Institute was half responsible for the UCC (i.e., along with the National Conference of Commissioners on Uniform State Laws), it was necessary to follow the Code.

able at the time the contract was made. Others augured actual losses that
were disproportionately smaller than the amount in the clause. The clause
was a "blunderbuss" or "shotgun" clause because it did not discriminate
among possible breaches of different clauses. As to the breaches of some of
these covenants, the clause would clearly have been a penalty. The court felt
compelled to refuse enforcement of the clause because it had to be viewed at
the time the contract was formed and, again, at that time, it would have been
a penalty to at least some of the possible breaches.[30] Other courts have been
willing to assume that the parties intended such a clause to apply only to
major breaches though the parties failed to specify such a restrictive application of the clause.[31] The view espoused by a number of scholars suggests that
the clause should be enforceable if it otherwise would be enforceable with
respect to the breach that actually occurred.[32] This certainly appears to be the
preferable view. In terms of drafting such a contract, however, one should not
rely upon the possibility of a favorable judicial construction since the entire
problem can be avoided by expressly limiting the operation of a liquidated
damages clause to certain breaches.

D. *Liquidated Damages or Alternative Performances.*

Where a contract states that the promisor must either perform a particular
act or pay a stipulated amount, two possible interpretations arise: (1) the
parties intended that the promisor have a real choice between two alternative
performances,[33] or (2) they intended that only the specified act would constitute performance and the stipulated amount is an agreed damages provision.[34]
If the parties intended genuine alternative performances, either performance
of the act *or* payment of the amount would constitute full performance and
would discharge the promisor's duty.[35] If, however, the parties intended that
payment of the amount in the clause should occur only after the promisor
failed to perform the act, the failure to perform should be treated as a breach

---

[30] Seidlitz v. Auerbach, 230 N.Y. 167, 129 N.E. 461 (1920).

[31] *See* Hackenheimer v. Kurtzmann, 235 N.Y. 57, 138 N.E. 235 (1923).

[32] *See* A. CORBIN, CONTRACTS § 1066; C. McCormick, McCORMICK ON DAMAGES § 151, Macneil,
Power of Contract and Agreed Remedies, 47 CORNELL L.Q. 495 (1962).

[33] *See* Western Camps, Inc. v. Riverway Ranch Enters., 70 Cal. App. 3d 714, 138 Cal. Rptr. 918
(1977); Chandler v. Doran Co., 44 Wash. 2d 396, 267 P.2d 907 (1954).

[34] *See* Maybury v. Spinney-Maybury Co., 122 Me. 422, 120 A. 601 (1923) (promise to pay a fixed
sum by a certain date or half that amount at an earlier date); Pennsylvania Re-Treading Tire Co.
v. Goldberg, 305 Ill. 54, 137 N.E. 81 (1922) (promise to deliver stock with a market value of
$120,000 or to pay $50,000 in cash); Goodyear Shoe-Mach. Co. v. Selz, Schwab & Co., 157 Ill. 186,
41 N.E. 625 (1894) (promise to pay a certain amount as royalties if paid by the 15th of the month
or twice that amount if paid thereafter).

[35] Absent an indication in the contract, the promisor may elect between the alternative performances. If she manifests a choice and fails to perform that alternative, she should be liable for
failure to perform the alternative she has selected. Haskins v. Dern, 19 Utah 89, 56 P. 953 (1899)
(promise to return corporate stock which had been delivered to promisor by a certain date or else
to pay a stipulated price. Election manifested by failure to return stock.); Smith v. Bergengren,
153 Mass. 236, 26 N.E. 690 (1891) (promise to refrain from competing or to pay a stipulated sum.
Election manifested by competing with promisee.). Where the promisor makes no choice at all,
most courts hold her liable for damages measured by the value of the less burdensome of the
alternatives on the footing that she would have probably chosen that alternative. Walker v.
Hayes, 100 N.H. 90, 1220 A.2d 140 (1956); Branhill Realty Co. v. Montgomery Ward & Co., 60
F.2d 922 (2d Cir. 1932); Franklin Sugar Ref. Co. v. Howell, 274 Pa. 190, 118 A. 109 (1922).

and the agreed damages clause should become activated only after the breach. In that situation, the promisor's duty would not be discharged by proffering payment of the stipulated amount. It could only be discharged by performing the act. The issue is clearly one of factual interpretation which will not be solved by phrases in the contract referring to "liquidated damages" or "alternative performances."[36] One of the often decisive factors in determining whether a contract is one for alternative performances is the relative value of the alternatives.[37]

A related situation occurs with respect to deposits which the contract indicates shall be forfeited in the event of a breach. The clause allowing for such forfeiture should not be enforced if the amount retained is not a reasonable forecast of actual loss in the event of a breach, i.e., it should not become an enforceable penalty simply because it is captioned "retention of deposit" or similar phrase.[38] Unfortunately, where the contract is one for the sale of land with payments to be made in installments, there has been a tendency to permit the retention of installment payments which are disproportionately greater than the loss suffered by the aggrieved party. There is authority, however, that would require the repayment of any disproportionate sum to avoid the unjust enrichment of the aggrieved party.[39] As to retention of deposits in sale of goods contracts, the UCC has addressed the question which permits restitution to the buyer of any amount by which his payments exceed the amount to which the seller is entitled by virtue of an enforceable agreed damages clause, or, absent such a clause, twenty percent of the value of the total performance for which the buyer is obligated or $500, whichever is smaller.[40]

1. Alternative Remedies: Specific Performance and Liquidated Damages.

Where specific performance or an injunction would otherwise be available to an aggrieved party, does the existence of a liquidated damages clause preclude that remedy? The prevailing view is that specific performance will be available to the aggrieved party unless that remedy is expressly excluded by the contract.[41] Where, however, a plaintiff seeks to enjoin the defendant from competing in a certain profession within a certain geographic area pursuant to a restrictive covenant in the contract, the plaintiff may not enjoy that relief and still expect enforcement of an otherwise valid liquidated damages clause.[42] While specific performance is not precluded because of the presence

[36] See Chandler v. Doran Co., supra note 33 at 910: "It must be solved as a question of factual interpretation, and the form of words used by the parties is not controlling."

[37] See RESTATEMENT 2d § 356 comment c.

[38] See Spivack v. Connecticut Smiles, Inc., 128 Conn. 146, 20 A.2d 731 (1941); Jaeger v. O'Donoghue, 18 F.2d 1013 (D.C. Cir. 1927).

[39] See Schwartz v. Syver, 264 Wis. 526, 59 N.W.2d 489 (1953).

[40] UCC § 2-718(2). See also Feinberg v. J. Gongiovi Contr'g, 110 Misc. 2d 379, 442 N.Y.S.2d 399 (1981).

[41] See Papa Gino's of Am., Inc. v. Plaza & Latham Assoc., 135 A.D. 2d 34, 524 N.Y.S.2d 536 (1988); Southeastern Land Fund, Inc. v. Real Estate World, 237 Ga. 227, 227 S.E.2d 340 (1976). RESTATEMENT 2d § 361.

[42] See Karpinski v. Ingrasci, 320 N.Y.S.2d 1, 268 N.E.2d 751 (1971) where the court held that it would be grossly unfair to grant the injunction and simultaneously enforce a $40,000 liquidated damages clause which the parties intended to apply to a total breach of the covenant since the

of a liquidated damages clause, if payment of the amount in the clause was intended as a true alternative performance and the obligor chooses to pay that price, equitable relief will not be available.[43]

E. *"Underliquidated Damages" — Exculpatory Clauses.*

The typical liquidated damages issue is directed toward determining whether the amount in the clause is disproportionately large in comparison to the amount of anticipated loss. There are situations, however, where the amount appears disproportionately low to the anticipated loss. The typical situation is one involving a contract for security services where the buyer of the services suffers a significant loss and the "liquidated damages" clause provides a nominal amount that is not a reasonable forecast of actual damages.[44] These clauses are, in fact, attempts to disclaim liability disguised as liquidated damages clauses.[45] As such, they are to be tested by the enforceability of exculpatory clauses. Such clauses may be unconscionable and, therefore, unenforceable.[46]

1. Limitation of Remedies Under the Uniform Commercial Code — "Failure of Essential Purpose."

Remedies under the UCC may be limited or altered.[47] If, however, the limited remedy in substitution for normal UCC remedies "fails of its essential purpose," normal Code remedies are restored.[48] Suppose, for example, a seller of equipment provides an exclusive 90 day repair or replacement warranty in place of the normal, more extensive warranty protection provided by the Code and couples that limitation with the typical exclusion of consequential damages. The equipment is delivered and malfunctions causing the buyer not only

---

injunction would hold further violation of the covenant. The liquidated damages provision will not be enforced in these circumstances. Instead, plaintiff will be relegated to showing its actual damages.

[43] *See* RESTATEMENT 2d § 361 comment b and ill. 2.

[44] *See, e.g.,* Better Food Markets, Inc. v. American Dist. Tel. Co., 40 Cal. 2d 179, 253 P.2d 10 (1953) (the clause allowed for the payment of $50 in liquidated damages in a contract for security services where the buyer of the services was a supermarket).

[45] *See* Tessler & Son v. Sonitrol Sec. Sys., 203 N.Y. Super. 477, 497 A.2d 430 (1985) where the court stated that the "real effect" of such clauses is exculpation from liability because they deny liability for all but a nominal amount of damages. Here the amount was $250 which was not an attempt to fairly estimate the plaintiff's likely damage from a break-in since defendant had paid an $800 service cost at the outset of the contract and $600 per year plus telephone charges to the defendant. The clause also contained a statement limiting damages to $250 for the failures of Sonitrol in any respect, even Sonitrol's negligence. While suggesting the possibility that a promise not to sue for simple negligence would be effective, such a promise would not be enforced with respect to an intentional tort or wilful act or gross negligence since the enforcement of such a clause would be contrary to public policy.

[46] *See* UCC § 2-718 comment 1: "An unreasonably small amount ... might be stricken under the section on unconscionable contracts of clauses" [§ 2-302]. Similarly, *see* RESTATEMENT 2d § 356 comment a referring to the RESTATEMENT 2d section on unconscionability, § 208.

[47] UCC § 2-719(1)(a).

[48] UCC § 2-719(2). *See* Ford Motor Co. v. Mayes, 575 S.W.2d 4480 (Ky. App. 1978); Clark v. International Harvester Co., 99 Idaho 326, 581 P.2d 784 (1978). *See also* Eddy, *On the "Essential" Purposes of Limited Remedies: The Metaphysics of U. C. C. Section 2-719(2),* 65 CALIF. L. REV. 28 (1977) and Anderson, *Essential Purpose and Essential Failure of Purpose: A Look at Section 2-719 of the Uniform Commercial Code,* 31 Sw. L.J. 759 (1977).

to lose the use of the equipment but, because he must close his plant awaiting repair or replacement of the equipment, the buyer also loses substantial profits (consequential damages). If the seller fails to meet the warranty obligations under the substituted repair or replacement warranty, the buyer will be able to show that the substituted warranty "failed of its essential purpose." All normal Code remedies would thereby be restored and, in many jurisdictions, the exclusion of consequential damages would also be removed, allowing the buyer to recover his lost profits.

While consequential damages may be limited or excluded under the UCC, such a limitation is unenforceable if it is unconscionable. In the case of injury to the person from consumer goods, the Code expressly states that the limitation of consequential damages is prima facie unconscionable.[49] In effect, this means that it is impossible for a seller of consumer goods to be exculpated from consequential damages in the form of bodily injury.

F. *Attorney's Fees and Bonds.*

American litigation does not permit recovery of attorney's fees by the party awarded judgment. While this policy may allow a party to sue with less risk, it also may be part of the reason for what is typically viewed as a highly litigious society. Since the winner will not be awarded attorney's fees and those fees can be substantial, it is not uncommon to discover a clause in a contract awarding reasonable attorney's fees to the winning party.[50] Under such a clause, the court will award reasonable fees to the attorney for the winning side. Since the court will limit such fees to reasonable levels, there is no violation of policies governing liquidated damages.[51] Where, however, the clause awarding attorney's fees contains a specified amount, that clause is subject to scrutiny as any other agreed damages clause.[52]

Various types of bonds contain clauses for the payment of a specified amount unless a conditioning event occurs. When the condition occurs, the obligation under the bond is discharged. For example, if a distributor of a manufacturer's goods is supposed to account for all monies due the manufacturer, a bond may have been issued to secure that commitment. When the distributor performs properly, the bond obligation is discharged. If the condition does not occur, i.e., the distributor does not account for all of the monies collected for the manufacturer, the stated amount in the bond will not be enforced beyond the loss caused by the failure of the condition.[53] This result is consistent with the underlying concept of the enforcement of agreed damages provisions.

---

[49] UCC § 2-719(3).

[50] Printed form contracts often contain clauses for attorney's fees for collection and related purposes.

[51] *See* Puget Sound Mut. Sav. Bank v. Lillions, 50 Wash. 2d 799, 314 P.2d 935 (1957).

[52] *See* Equitable Lumber Corp. v. IPA Land Dev. Corp., 381 N.Y.S.2d 459, 344 N.E.2d 391 (1976) where the court tested a clause awarding attorney's fees of 30 percent under the UCC test of liquidated damages in UCC § 2-718(1).

[53] RESTATEMENT 2d § 356 comment e.

§ 126. Measure of Recovery for Restitution Interest.

A. *The Restitution Concept.*

The exploration of contract remedies began by distinguishing the three interests that are protected by contract law,[54] the expectation, reliance, and restitution interests. We have discussed the three interests in terms of builder's contracts[55] and other types of contracts. Throughout this volume, we have also dealt with the protection of each of the interests in varying contexts. Our principal concern in this section is to consider the measure of recovery when the restitution interest is protected. At the outset, it is important to recall briefly the concept of restitution, i.e., what is protected by a court when it grants a restitutionary recovery.

The restitution interest is the most deserving of the three interests protected in contract law because it involves the unjust enrichment of one party at the expense of another. The aggrieved party has conferred a benefit upon the unjustly enriched party who is retaining that benefit at the expense of the aggrieved party. Unlike the reliance interest where a party has suffered an out-of-pocket loss and seeks to recover that minus quantity from the party who induced the reliance, the restitution interest represents an exacerbated situation of a minus to the aggrieved party and a plus (benefit or enrichment) to the other party. The purpose of restitution is to restore the aggrieved party to *status quo ante,* i.e., to place him in the position he would have been had he not conferred a benefit upon the enriched party.[56] It may be said that the reliance interest has the same purpose. In restitution, however, the plus or benefit is subtracted from the enriched party and the aggrieved party restored, whereas in reliance, there is no benefit or enrichment to the inducing party. We simply require that party to pay the relying party the reasonable value of his detrimental reliance.[57] Since restitution is designed to prevent unjust enrichment,[58] in this section we will focus upon how the benefit or enrichment is measured so as to restore the aggrieved party to status quo. Before we proceed with that exploration, however, it is important to consider a less than exhaustive list of the circumstances that would lead a reasonable party to choose the protection of the restitution interest rather than the expectation or reliance interest.

B. *Choosing the Restitution Interest as the Interest to Be Protected.*

An aggrieved party who has an action for breach of contract will normally choose to protect her expectation interest because that interest will typically provide the maximum recovery by placing the party in the position she would have occupied had the contract been performed.[59] There are, however, numer-

---

[54] *See supra* § 117.

[55] *See supra* § 119.

[56] *See* Potter v. Oster, 426 N.W.2d 148 (Iowa 1988) (restoring the status quo is the goal of restitution).

[57] The three interests have been explored *supra* § 117.

[58] *See* J. DAWSON, UNJUST ENRICHMENT (1951).

[59] It should be recalled that the expectation interest requires neither a minus (reliance) nor minus and plus (restitution) situation. Rather, this normal contract remedy simply protects the expectation of the aggrieved party.

ous situations in which it would be prudent to choose the restitution interest for protection over the other interests.

1. Quasi Contract.

The obvious situations suggesting the choice of the restitution interest involve those in which the expectation interest cannot be protected. The aggrieved party may have no contractual right at all. Where, for example, a school district refused to perform its statutory duty in providing transportation for certain children and their father transported them to school during the school year, the school district was unjustly enriched at the expense of the father and he was entitled to recover the value of the transportation services since he had performed the legal duty of another at his expense.[60] Where a surgeon performs emergency services for an unconscious patient, no contract can be found but the surgeon should recover the reasonable value of his services since the patient has been unjustly enriched to that extent.[61] In any number of situations where benefits have been conferred under circumstances that suggest unjust enrichment to the recipient of the benefit, the restitution interest is protected though there is no contract. It will be recalled that such actions are characterized as quasi contract actions.

2. Unenforceable Contracts — Fatal Uncertainty.

Where the parties have contracted and there has been an uncured material breach, the aggrieved party may seek protection of the restitution interest rather than the expectation interest because he has no reasonable choice. Where, for example, the contract is unenforceable because it fails to meet the requirements of a particular Statute of Frauds, but the plaintiff has partly performed the contract by conferring a benefit upon the defendant, such as a down payment under a contract for the sale of land or contract for the sale of goods, the restitution interest will be protected. It would be particularly egregious to permit a party to retain money to which he is not entitled simply because he can raise the defense of the Statute of Frauds. Courts, therefore, grant restitution of the benefit conferred in such cases[62] unless the Statute, itself, provides otherwise or the purpose of the Statute would be frustrated by allowing restitution.[63] Similarly, courts grant restitution of benefits conferred under voidable contracts[64] as well as contracts discharged because of non-occurrence of a condition, impracticability, or frustration of purpose.[65]

---

[60] Sommers v. Putnam Cty. Bd. of Educ., 113 Ohio St. 177, 148 N.E. 682 (1925). The duty must be performed by a "proper person" since an officious party will not receive restitution. *See* Greenspan v. Slate, 12 N.J. 426, 87 A.2d 390 (payment to a doctor by friend of minor).

[61] Mathieson v. Smiley, 2 D.L.R. 787 [1932]. Performance of emergency services by a non-professional, however, will not allow for a restitutionary recovery since such services are presumed to have been performed gratuitously.

[62] *See* Montenaro Bros. Bldrs. v. Snow, 190 Conn. 481, 460 A.2d 1297 (1983); Wolf v. Malevania, 343 So. 2d 949 (Fla. App. 1977); Gilton v. Chapman, 217 Ark. 390, 230 S.W.2d 37 (1950).

[63] *See* Phillippe v. Shapell Indus., 43 Cal. App. 3d 1247, 743 P.2d 1279 (1987) (statute required broker's contracts to be evidenced by a writing and a restitutionary (quantum meruit) recovery in such a case would frustrate the purpose of the statute). *See also* RESTATEMENT 2d § 375 ill. 3.

[64] *See* Bowling v. Sperry, 133 Ind. App. 692, 184 N.E.2d 901 (1962). *See also* RESTATEMENT 2d § 376.

[65] RESTATEMENT 2d § 377.

Where the value of the expectation interest is in doubt because damages cannot be shown with reasonable certainty, the aggrieved party may have no adequate expectation remedy but may be able to demonstrate reasonable certainty with respect to the restitution interest.[66] Even if lost profits cannot be shown, the aggrieved party is certainly entitled to recover amounts paid before the breach.[67] This is the most rudimentary form of restitution, i.e., money paid under a contract which has been breached clearly enriches the defendant unjustly.

3. Alternative Remedy — Losing Contracts.

Where the aggrieved party has a cause of action for total breach by the other party who had received a benefit prior to the breach through the performance of the aggrieved party, the aggrieved party may choose to pursue his restitution interest even though he could have chosen either the expectation or reliance interest. Restitution is often called an alternative remedy for breach of contract and it is available to the extent of the benefit conferred on the other party.[68] Why, however, should the aggrieved party choose the restitution interest when the expectation or reliance interest is available? Where a party has entered into a contract that would produce a loss if performed, breach by the other party before performance is completed may produce a considerably larger recovery under the restitution interest than the expectation or reliance interests.[69] If a seller of land materially breached the contract

---

[66] *Id.* Courts will apply a requirement of reasonable certainty to the recovery of restitution interest damages. *See* Lewiston Pre-Mix Concrete, Inc. v. Rhode, 110 Idaho 640, 718 P.2d 551 (Idaho App. 1985).

[67] *See* CBS, Inc. v. Merrick, 716 F.2d 1292 (9th Cir. 1983) (recovery of pre-payments made to David Merrick who breached contract under which he was supposed to allow CBS the use of a book to which he had the rights and he was also supposed to perform as the producer of the film).

[68] *See, e.g.,* McEnroe v. Morgan, 106 Idaho 326, 678 P.2d 595 (Idaho App. 1984). RESTATEMENT 2d §§ 344(c), 370, and 373, particularly comment b thereto.

[69] *See* Harris v. Metropolitan Mall, 112 Wis. 487, 334 N.W.2d 519 (1983) (where profits are uncertain or a losing contract is breached, the plaintiff may have his restitution interest protected). Assume that *A* agrees to build a house for *B* at a contract price of $100,000 and, when it is half completed, *A* has expended $90,000 in labor and materials but has already conferred a benefit upon *B* (in terms of the reasonable value of having another perform the work done to that point) of $90,000. If *A* had completed the house, it can be shown that the cost to *A* would have been $180,000, i.e., a loss of $80,000. When *B* breaches the contract when the house is half completed, the normal expectation recovery for *A* would be contract price minus cost of completion, i.e., $100,000 minus $90,000 or a recovery of $10,000. *A*'s reliance interest would net the same recovery since his $90,000 reliance interest to that point would be reduced by the amount of loss he would have suffered if he had completed the job. L. Albert & Son v. Armstrong Rubber Co., 178 F.2d 182 (1949). If, however, *A* brings an action for his restitution interest, he may be permitted to recover the value of the benefit conferred, i.e., $90,000, with no reduction for the fact that the contract was a losing contract. *See* Southern Painting Co. v. United States, 222 F.2d 431 (10th Cir. 1955) (recovery of $20,000 restitution interest on $10,000 contract). *See also* Boomer v. Muir, 24 P.2d 570 (Cal. App. 1933) (recovery of $230,000 in excess of contract price). In Johnson v. Star Bucket Pump Co., 274 Mo. 414, 202 S.W. 1143, 1153 (1918), the opinion states, "The defendant cannot undertake to limit the recovery by the terms of the contract, because he has breached the contract. To permit him to use his breached contract to limit a recovery against him would be to pay to him a premium for his own wrong. The law does not contemplate such." See, however, Johnson v. Bovee, 40 Colo. App. 317, 574 P.2d 513 (1978) and Wuchter v. Fitzgerald, 83 Or. 672, 163 P. 819 (1917) which preclude restitutionary recovery in excess of the contract price. *See* G. PALMER, LAW OF RESTITUTION § 4.4 (1978) which supports the concept of recovery in excess of the contract price. RESTATEMENT 2d § 373 comment d suggests, "In the case of a contract on which [the

by losing marketable title to the land which has depreciated in value, the recovery of the restitutionary interest will be greater than the expectation interest.[70]

4. Recovery by a Defaulting Plaintiff to Avoid Forfeitures.

Where a party materially breaches a contract after he has partly performed the duties under that contract, he obviously has no cause of action on the contract he breached. Yet, he may have conferred a benefit on the innocent party who would be unjustly enriched if she were allowed to retain that benefit at no cost. Early suggestions that a contract breaker should be able to recover the value of the benefit conferred produced reactions of incredulity.[71] In 1834, however, the opinion in *Britton v. Turner*[72] was announced. The plaintiff agreed to work for one year in exchange for $120 to be paid at the end of the year. He worked for more than nine months and then breached the contract by leaving the employment. He brought an action in quasi contract[73] for the value of the services which conferred a benefit upon the employer. The court permitted a recovery on the logical footing that the longer the plaintiff performed, the more he lost. Had he not commenced working under the contract, his damages would have been insignificant. Thus, unless a recovery was granted, the law would be countenancing a forfeiture which it abhors.[74] This logic has prevailed since that decision though the particular problem to which it was applied (employment contracts) has become virtually moot through the enactment of statutes requiring wage payments to be made at periodic intervals and payment of the appropriate amount to the employee when he terminates the employment.[75] The logic was soon extended, however, to independent contractors providing services,[76] and there has been no doubt of its viabil-

---

injured party] would have sustained a loss instead of having made a profit, however, his restitution interest may give him a larger recovery than would damages on either [expectation or reliance] basis. The right of the injured party under a losing contract to a greater amount in restitution than he could have recovered in damages has engendered much controversy. *The rules stated in this section give him that right.*" (Emphasis added.) The only limitations are (1) the usual limitation that the recovery be limited to the benefit conferred pursuant to § 370, and (2) if the aggrieved party has completed performance and the other party has only the duty to pay the price, the aggrieved party is limited to the contract price (comment b to § 373).

[70] *See* Potter v. Oster, *supra* note 56.

[71] For example, in Stark v. Parker, 19 Mass. (2 Pick.) 267, 13 Am. Dec. 425 (1824), the court wondered why anyone would have any doubt whatsoever about denying relief to a party who breached the contract since, *inter alia,* the ancient maxim should apply, i.e., no man should profit from his own wrong.

[72] 6 N.H. 481, 26 Am. Dec. 713 (1834).

[73] The method of pleading such actions was under the common counts. Thus, in a personal services case, the action would be brought under the common count *quantum meruit* (work and labor done). If the quasi contract action were one to recover money belonging to the plaintiff, the common count used was *money had and received.* If the quasi contract action were for the value of goods delivered to the recipient, the action was often called *quantum valebat* or *quantum valebant* (goods sold and delivered).

[74] For a modern recognition of this analysis, *see* Lancellotti v. Thomas, 341 Pa. Super. 1, 491 A.2d 117 (1987).

[75] *See* Corman, *The Partial Performance Interest of the Defaulting Employee II,* 38 MARQ. L. REV. 139, 162-68 (1955).

[76] *See* Pinches v. Swedish Evangelical Lutheran Church, 55 Conn. 183, 10 A. 264 (1887) (building contract).

ity as applied to any service contract since that time.[77] In contracts for the sale of goods, defaulting sellers were eventually permitted to recover for goods retained by the purchaser under the Uniform Sales Act.[78] Where buyers made down payments that exceeded actual damages suffered by sellers, however, the sellers could retain the excess and be unjustly enriched.[79] The contract would sometimes provide that the deposit would be retained as liquidated damages which courts would enforce though the amounts may have exceeded reasonable forecasts of actual damages. There was considerable creativity which produced judicial devices that were, at least, semi-covert in attempts to reach the logic of *Britton v. Turner* in non-employment cases.[80] The UCC confronted the problem in sale-of-goods cases by simply directing that buyers are entitled to restitution of any amount of their down payment exceeding a valid agreed damages clause.[81] In the absence of such a clause, the Code places a ceiling on the amount the seller may retain.[82] In contracts for the sale of land, there has been a great reluctance on the part of courts to permit a defaulting buyer to recover a down payment ("earnest money") even though it exceeds the actual damages of the vendor.[83] There is, however, a clear trend toward

---

[77] *See* Maxton Bldrs., Inc. v. Lo Galbo, 509 N.Y.S.2d 507, 502 N.E.2d 184 (1986) (In most areas of the law, legislatures and courts have adopted a rule permitting the party in default to recover for part performance of the contract to the extent of the net benefit conferred. However, this is not true with respect to restitution in contracts for the sale of land (discussed in text *infra* note 83 *et seq.*); Lancellotti v. Thomas, *supra* note 74 (adopting the "modern rule" of RESTATEMENT 2d § 374 and setting forth numerous cases under FIRST RESTATEMENT § 357 and RESTATEMENT 2d § 374 to support the view that restitutionary recovery is now allowed generally). As to restitution in land contract situations, see discussion in text *infra* note 83 *et seq.*

[78] U.S.C.A. § 44. The UCC permits a buyer to accept all or any commercial unit of the goods delivered by the seller even though the goods are non-conforming. UCC § 2-601. The buyer is liable for the price of any goods accepted, UCC § 2-709(1)(a), though the buyer has a cause of action for any breach of warranty as to accepted goods, UCC § 2-714.

[79] *See, e.g.,* Atlantic City Tire & Rubber Corp. v. Southwark Foundry & Mach. Co., 389 Pa. 569, 137 A. 807 (1927).

[80] *See, e.g.,* the description of money advanced by a buyer or lessee as mere security rather than a down payment that could be retained upon breach in Amtorg Trading Co. v. Miehle Printing Press & Mfg. Co., 206 F.2d 103 (2d Cir. 1953).

[81] UCC § 2-718(2)(a).

[82] Twenty percent of the value of the total performance for which the buyer is obligated or $500, whichever is smaller. UCC § 2-718(2). *See* the earlier discussion of this concept *supra* § 125.

[83] *See* Annotation, 4 A.L.R.4th 993 (1981). *See also* Maxton Bldrs., Inc. v. Lo Galbo *supra* note 77, which recognizes the modern view in other types of contracts but adheres to the doctrine of Lawrence v. Miller, 86 N.Y. 131 (1881) (precluding restitutionary recovery for a defaulting vendee because allowing such a recovery would be "ill doctrine") particularly if the down payment does not exceed 10 percent of the contract price. The FIRST RESTATEMENT § 357(2) also excepted the payment of "earnest money" from the general rule allowing restitution for defaulting plaintiffs. The RESTATEMENT 2d § 374 comment c, subjects "earnest money" payments to the same reasonableness test applied to liquidated damages. *See also* Lancellotti v. Thomas, *supra* note 74, which adopts RESTATEMENT 2d § 374 as Pennsylvania law and sets forth an excellent detailed analysis of why the "modern" view should be adopted, suggesting that the modern view is now the prevailing view. As to restitution by a defaulting purchaser in contracts for the sale of land, however, the court was constrained by precedent, i.e., Kaufman Hotel & Restaurant Co. v. Thomas, 411 Pa. 87, 190 A.2d 434 (1963) and Luria v. Robbins, 223 Pa. Super. 456, 302 A.2d 361 (1973) which denied restitution. The court suggests that *Luria* is distinguishable because, in land contracts, the seller has several remedies against the buyer, including specific performance, and as long as the seller remains ready, willing, and able to perform, there should be no right to restitution. Other case law certainly supports this qualification — *see, e.g.,* Washington v. Claasen, 218 Kan. 577, 545 P.2d 387 (1976), as does the RESTATEMENT 2d in § 374 comment a. The court in *Lancellotti,* however, justifiably shirks from suggesting whether a defaulting vendee

the avoidance of unjust enrichment in such cases by permitting a recovery of an amount exceeding the loss,[84] particularly in cases where the amount retained grossly exceeds the actual damages of the seller.[85] The influence of the UCC has been felt in such cases[86] and, since the RESTATEMENT 2d adopts this view,[87] it is reasonable to conclude that it will become the prevailing view in contracts for the sale of land as it has with respect to other types of contracts.

5. Limitations on Recovery by Defaulting Plaintiff.

a. Wilful Breaches.

While adopting the view that a defaulting plaintiff should be able to recover the amount of the benefit in excess of the harm that he caused the defendant, the FIRST RESTATEMENT insisted upon an exception for a "wilful and deliberate" breach.[88] The notion that a court will aid a party who wilfully breached a contract to protect that party against the unjust enrichment of the innocent party suggests a contradiction of the equitable influence surrounding actions in restitution. The "wilful" breacher does not have clean hands. If he is the agent of the defendant with all of the fiduciary responsibilities attached to that status, courts will find it particularly difficult to protect his restitution interest.[89] Notwithstanding all of the arguments that can be made against a party who is not a mere contract breaker but a "wilful" contract breaker, very few cases can be found denying restitutionary relief to such a party,[90] while a number can be found stating that a wilful breach is no bar to such recovery.[91] Certainly, courts adopting "the more enlightened approach" of the RESTATEMENT 2d are aware that it does not include the "wilful" exception of the FIRST RESTATEMENT.[92] The only notion of a "wilful" breach in the RESTATEMENT 2d is

---

could recover in restitution after the seller has resold the land because of the Pennsylvania precedent.

[84] For an early case discussing the traditional concept and suggesting the modern trend, see Schwartz v. Syver, 264 Wis. 526, 59 N.W.2d 489 (1953).

[85] See McClendon v. Safe Realty Corp., 401 N.E.2d 80 (Ind. App. 1980); De Leon v. Aldrete, 398 S.W.2d 160 (Tex. App. 1965); Honey v. Henry's Franchise Leasing Corp., 64 Cal. 2d 801, 415 P.2d 833 (1966); Newcomb v. Ray, 99 N.H. 463, 114 A.2d 882 (1955).

[86] See Maxey v. Glindmeyer, 379 So. 2d 297 (Miss. 1980) (suggesting that seller should not retain an amount beyond actual damages, analogizing to UCC § 2-718(2)). See also Lancellotti v. Thomas, supra note 74. It should also be noted that the dominant scholarly influence in the entire movement toward permitting defaulting plaintiffs to recover is generally regarded as the giant of twentieth century contract law, Professor Corbin. See his treatise at §§ 1122-1135. Professor Corbin was particularly influential in the creation of § 357 of the FIRST RESTATEMENT.

[87] RESTATEMENT 2d § 374(2). The comment to this section adds, however, "If the injured party has a right to specific performance and remains willing and able to perform, he may keep what he has received and sue for specific performance."

[88] FIRST RESTATEMENT § 357(1)(a). Comment e to this section distinguishes a "wilful" from a "knowing" breach, i.e., the latter type of breach may occur as a result of negligence or error of judgment or mistake of fact or law; it may be due to hardship, insolvency, or circumstances that tend appreciably toward moral justification. Such a breach is not "wilful."

[89] See, e.g., Fidelity Fund, Inc. v. Di Santo, 347 Pa. Super. 112, 500 A.2d 431 (1985) where the court denied restitution guided, in part, by RESTATEMENT 2d AGENCY § 469 which precludes compensation even for properly performed services of which no compensation has been apportioned if the conduct is wilful.

[90] See, e.g., Harris v. The Cecil N. Bean, 197 F.2d 919 (2d Cir. 1952).

[91] See, e.g., Kitchin v. Mori, 84 Nev. 181, 437 P.2d 865 (1968); Caplan v. Schroeder, 56 Cal. 2d 515, 364 P.2d 321 (1961).

[92] See Lancellotti v. Thomas, supra note 74.

found in a comment suggesting that restitution should not be granted where a party *intentionally*[93] furnishes services or builds a building that is materially different from his promised performance on the ground that he has acted officiously, i.e., he has provided services that were not requested by the innocent party who should not have to pay for them any more than he should have to pay for any other unsolicited benefit.[94] If the deviations were not intentional, the unintentional defaulter could recover for the value of benefits conferred though he would still be liable for his innocent breach. Since the UCC is not affected by the wilful character of the breach,[95] it is not remarkable that the RESTATEMENT 2d would adopt a similar view which coincides with its fundamental approach to contract remedies.[96]

b. Contract Price Limitation, Liquidated Damages, and Specific Performance — Divisible Contracts.

It must be emphasized that a defaulting plaintiff is still a contract breaker and, like any other contract breaker, is liable for any damages that can be established by the innocent party. If the cost of completing the performance is greater than the value of the benefits conferred by the defaulting plaintiff, no restitution will be granted.[97] Thus, the defaulting plaintiff can recover only for the *net* benefit conferred.[98] It is not necessary for the defaulting party to render substantial performance to recover for benefits conferred, but he may not recover for benefits conferred in excess of the contract price or ratable portion thereof.[99] The defendant is innocent and should not be liable for damages exceeding the contract price where the plaintiff is in default. Moreover, the burden of proving the excess of benefits over the loss to the innocent defendant must be borne by the defaulting plaintiff,[1] and if there is any doubt about the measurement of the benefit, the doubt will be resolved against him and he will receive the less generous measure.[2] In a sale of land contract, if

---

[93] The use of the term "intentional" as meaning "wilful" can create confusion. *See* Dodge v. Kimball, 203 Mass. 364, 89 N.E. 542 (1909). An intentional breach may simply be a "knowing" breach which is not "wilful." *See supra* note 88. The RESTATEMENT 2d apparently intends to use "intentional" here to mean "wilful" as contrasted with merely "knowing."

[94] *See* RESTATEMENT 2d § 374 comment b. *See also* RESTATEMENT OF RESTITUTION § 112. In § 113 comment a, the following rationale is presented: "The principle underlying the rule stated in § 112 is that one who officiously intervenes to perform the duty of another is not entitled to compensation...." It should be recalled, however, that one may not avoid the restitutionary duty that will attach if he watches services being performed that will benefit him where the party performing those services apparently assumes he will be compensated. *See* Day v. Caton, 119 Mass. 513, 20 Am. Rep. 347 (1876).

[95] UCC § 2-718(2).

[96] In the Introductory Note to Chapter 16, Remedies, which precedes § 344, the RESTATEMENT 2d emphasizes the underlying theory of compensation to the aggrieved party as contrasted with compulsion of the promisor. *Inter alia*, it suggests that, "'Willful' breaches have not been distinguished from other breaches...."

[97] Denver Ventures, Inc. v. Arlington Lane Corp., 754 P.2d 785 (Colo. App. 1988). A party should recover only the reasonable value of benefits conferred which exceed the loss created by his own breach. Survey Eng'rs, Inc. v. Zoline Found., 190 Colo. 352, 546 P.2d 1257 (1976).

[98] *See* RESTATEMENT 2d § 374.

[99] *See* Boyce Constr. Corp. v. District Bd. of Trustees of Valencia Cty., 414 So. 2d 634 (Fla. App. 1982).

[1] Ben Lomond, Inc. v. Momax, Inc., 758 P.2d 92 (Alaska 1988).

[2] *See* RESTATEMENT 2d § 374 comment b referring to the two measures of benefit set forth in § 371, (a) the reasonable value of the benefit to the other party in terms of what it would have cost

the vendor remains ready, willing, and able to perform and has a right to specific performance, restitution of a down payment for the defaulting vendee will be denied.[3] No restitutionary recovery will be permitted if the amount of the down payment is in an enforceable agreed damages clause even if that clause is in the form of an "earnest money" payment or some other characterization but would have been sustained as a valid clause.[4] Finally, it should be recalled that where the contract is "divisible" or "severable," i.e., where the parties have contracted for performances on each side as agreed equivalents, a defaulting party may recover for the full performance of any divisible portion of the contract and this recovery is one for his expectation interest according to the expressed intentions of the parties rather than his restitution interest.[5]

C. *Measuring the Restitution Interest (Benefit Conferred) — Specific Restitution — Duty to Return Benefit.*

The restitution interest should be measured by the benefit conferred on the unjustly enriched party. Where the plaintiff is merely seeking a return of money paid to that party, the measurement is quite simple.[6] This is a form of specific restitution. Similarly, if the benefit conferred is in a form other than money, the return of that specific benefit will be preferred since there is no question about the measurement of the value of the benefit.[7] In many cases, however, the benefit conferred can be measured in two different ways: (a) by the reasonable value to the enriched party of what it would have cost him to obtain that benefit from someone in the position of the plaintiff, or (b) the extent to which the other party's wealth or property has been increased in value.[8] In a simple case involving the performance of carpentry services, the court remanded the case for a determination of which of these two forms of measurement should control, i.e., what it would have cost the defendant to obtain these services from another carpenter in the position of the plaintiff, or the enhanced value to defendant's property.[9] Where a city contracted with a utility to provide streetlighting services but the contract term expired and the utility continued to supply the services, the court held that the continued service should be measured by the cost to the city of having such services rendered rather than the benefit received in terms of furthering the interests of the city because the latter interest was speculative.[10] Indeed, this measure

---

him to obtain that benefit from a person in his position, or (b) the extent to which his property has been increased in value or his other interests advanced via the benefit conferred.

[3] *See* discussion of Lancellotti v. Thomas *supra* note 83.

[4] RESTATEMENT 2d § 374 comment c.

[5] *See* RESTATEMENT 2d § 240 and the discussion of divisible contracts *supra* § 105.

[6] *See* Harris v. Metropolitan Mall, 112 Wis. 2d 487, 334 N.W.2d 519 (1983) (recovery of amount of investment, $238,100). *See also* CBS v. Merrick, *supra* note 67, involving return of pre-payment.

[7] *See* Lewiston Pre-Mix Concrete v. Rhode, 110 Idaho 64, 718 P.2d 551 (Idaho App. 1985). Where the benefit is land conveyed to the unjustly enriched party, specific restitution will be granted unless it would unduly interfere with title to land or otherwise cause injustice. RESTATEMENT 2d § 372(1)(a). Specific restitution will not be granted to a defaulting plaintiff. RESTATEMENT 2d § 372(1)(b). If a plaintiff has a claim for restitution, the defendant may discharge his duty by tendering specific restitution before suit is brought. RESTATEMENT 2d § 372(3).

[8] RESTATEMENT 2d § 371.

[9] Lee v. Foote, 481 A.2d 484 (D.C. App. 1984).

[10] Lanphier v. Omaha Pub. Dist., 227 Neb. 241, 417 N.W.2d 17 (1987).

(cost to enriched party in obtaining the value of the services elsewhere) is the preferred measure of benefit unless it is unduly difficult to measure because it is speculative.[11] Moreover, a party entitled to restitution should normally receive that measure of benefit because it is typically more generous than the other measure.[12] In situations where the increase in value to the recipient is greater than what it would have cost him to receive the benefit from another party, the latter remains the preferred measure where it would be absurd to grant the increase in value measure. Thus, where emergency surgery is performed which saves the life of the recipient, it is conceivable that the increase in the value of his continued existence could be measured in astronomical sums. He should not be liable for anything more than the reasonable value of the services rendered in terms of what another surgeon in the plaintiff's position would have charged.[13]

1. Duty to Return Benefit.

Since the purpose of restitution is to restore the parties to status quo, if the party seeking restitution has received a benefit, he must return it or offer to return it, conditional on any restitution to himself.[14] If the benefit cannot be returned, as where the buyer of real property seeks restitution of his down payment but has had the benefit of the property, the buyer will be required to account for reasonable rental value.[15] If the plaintiff seeking restitution has received services which cannot be restored in specie, he should offer to compensate the defendant for these services.[16] If, however, property received by the plaintiff is worthless because of defects or if its destruction or loss was caused by the other party, no return or offer to return such property is necessary.[17]

D. Inconsistent Remedies.

At the start of this section, we emphasized the requirement of total breach or uncured material breach for a party seeking restitution. When such a breach occurs, the aggrieved party can choose among the interests to be protected. It would be absurd to permit such a party to recover his restitution interest as well as his expectation interest. For example, in a contract for the purchase and sale of land, if a buyer is granted specific performance of the contract, he must pay for the land, i.e., he may not have the land as well as restitution of the purchase price or whatever portion thereof he has paid. Similarly, if a builder completes a structure and the owner refuses to pay the contract price, it would be absurd to permit the builder to recover the contract

---

[11] Noel v. Cole, 98 Wash. 2d 375, 655 P.2d 245 (1983).

[12] See RESTATEMENT 2d § 371 comment b.

[13] See Cotnam v. Wisdom, 83 Ark. 601, 104 S.W. 164 (1907).

[14] See Puskar v. Hughes, 179 Ill. App. 3d 522, 533 N.E.2d 962 (1989). See also RESTATEMENT 2d § 384.

[15] Williams v. Dunas, 40 Ill. App. 3d 782, 352 N.E.2d 266 (1976); Mahurin v. Schmeck, 95 Ariz. 333, 390 P.2d 576 (1964).

[16] Birggs v. Clinton City Bank & Trust Co., 452 N.E.2d 989 (Ind. App. 1983) (no necessity to tender such compensation here since there was a $9000 C.D. in litigation).

[17] See Kunkle Water & Elec. Inc. v. City of Prescott, 347 N.W.2d 648 (Iowa 1984). See also RESTATEMENT 2d § 384 comment c.

price as well as restitution for benefits conferred (the reasonable value of the structure) or his reliance interest (the cost of the labor and materials). The reliance interest is incorporated in the expectation interest if the builder seeks to protect the expectation interest and the owner is not unjustly enriched if he pays the amount of the contract price in damages. As we have seen, the builder may choose to protect a different interest — either the reliance or restitution interest. Having chosen either of those interests, he is precluded from an expectation interest recovery.[18]

1. Restitution and Reliance.

If, however, a party chooses to protect his restitution interest, he may be able to claim reliance damages as well since they are not necessarily inconsistent. In *CBS v. Merrick*,[19] for example, CBS contracted with David Merrick for the rights to a certain book which Merrick controlled. Merrick also agreed to produce the play for CBS. In exchange for Merrick's commitments, CBS paid Merrick over $916,000. In reliance on Merrick's promises, CBS also paid certain amounts to a director and screenwriter. The trial court allowed only restitution of the $916,000 but refused to allow CBS any damages for its reliance interest. The court of appeals reversed that holding since it saw no inconsistency in permitting a reliance remedy along with a restitutionary remedy. If the reliance interest of CBS were not protected along with its restitution interest, it would not be restored to the position it was in before the contract was made.[20]

§ 127. Specific Performance and Injunctions.

A. *Equitable Remedies and the Common Law.*

The damage remedy for breach of contract which has been explored to this point provides substitutional relief to the aggrieved party rather than the very performance promised. There are situations, however, where a court should provide the specific performance promised.[21] Since the aggrieved party receives exactly what he was promised when he receives specific relief, such a remedy may be preferable.[22] Unlike the civil law system where specific performance is ordered wherever possible, however, the common law system from its inception was based on the notion of substitutional relief. To this day, substitutional relief in money damages is the normal common law remedy for

---

[18] *See* RESTATEMENT 2d § 378.

[19] 716 F.2d 1292 (9th Cir. 1983). *See,* in particular, the concurring opinion by Nelson, J.

[20] *See* RESTATEMENT 2d § 370 comment awhich insists that restitution is available only for benefits conferred upon the other party. It then suggests, "The injured party may, however, have an action for damages, including one for recovery based on his reliance interest." In § 378 comment d, the RESTATEMENT 2d suggests that "a party who seeks restitution may, for example, be entitled to damages to compensate him for costs of transportation of goods that he has incurred." Such damages are reliance damages.

[21] Specific Performance and Injunctions are explored in §§ 357-369 of the RESTATEMENT 2d.

[22] In terms of economic analysis, it may be argued that specific performance neither overcompensates nor undercompensates the aggrieved party's expectation interest and is, therefore, more precise than substitutional damages. *See* Schwartz, *The Case for Specific Performance,* 89 YALE L.J. 271 (1979). *But see* Kronman, *Specific Performance,* 45 U. CHI. L. REV. 351 (1978) suggesting that specific performance may overcompensate the claimant.

breach of contract whereas specific performance, injunctions, and other equitable remedies are extraordinary remedies.

The fascinating story of the development of equity courts is beyond the coverage of this book.[23] It is, however, important to consider some salient background though the treatment is necessarily incomplete. In general terms, common law courts were *property* oriented, i.e., any notion of specific relief came through proprietary actions such as replevin to recover specific property owned by the plaintiff. An action for contract damages was often in the form of the old common law action (writ) of debt based on the half-completed exchange idea, e.g., failure to pay for goods delivered. If the plaintiff prevailed in his debt action, he would be awarded a judgment for the price of the goods. In effect, this provided the seller with specific performance since the seller was receiving exactly what he had bargained for. The early courts, however, did not think in those terms but rather in terms of substitutional relief for breach of contract.

Equity jurisprudence and courts of equity came from another source. Common law writs such as debt and covenant were quite narrow. Until the sixteenth century, there was no writ to enforce what we would now view as the typical modern contract, an exchange of informal promises. Where a party had an otherwise meritorious claim but could find no procrustean common law writ to pursue that claim in a common law court, he may have sought assistance from the Chancellor who was the keeper of the King's conscience, a high official who was supposed to operate *ex aequo et bono,* i.e., in equity and good conscience. Since chancellors were typically clerics, it is not remarkable that canon law influenced their thinking. The Chancellor would not provide relief to someone who acted unreasonably or unconscionably. The classic equitable maxims include the requirement that a party seeking equity must come to the equity court "with clean hands." An equitable remedy is subject to the *discretion* of the court because it developed from the discretion of the chancellor. A party would seek relief from the Chancellor because there was no adequate remedy at law (typically, no proper writ), and when the Chancellor granted a remedy, it was based, in part, on that fact. Thus, the normal remedy was the remedy at law, but if no law remedy was available, one could appeal to the King's conscience through the keeper of that conscience for an extraordinary remedy.

When the Chancellor granted relief, he would do it in the form of a decree, i.e., an order to a person to perform an act or refrain from performing an act. The common law courts were not concerned with ordering anyone to do anything. They were typically concerned with awarding judgments for money and those judgments could be satisfied by having the sheriff seize and sell the defendant's property. Thus, the Chancellor (equity) operated *in personam* — ordering the person, while courts of law operated in rem — against the property of the defendant. Again, however, the *in personam* equitable remedy had been designed to overcome the inadequacies of common law remedies. By the sixteenth century, after assumpsit, equity "followed the law" in requiring the

---

[23] For a more complete analysis, *see* Farnsworth, *Legal Remedies for Breach of Contract,* 70 COLUM. L. REV. 1145, 1149-56 (1970).

same elements to be shown for an enforceable contract as did courts of law. The question then began to turn on the nature of the remedy. The remedy, however, had clearly become the extraordinary remedy. The claimant was supposed to pursue his remedy at law and only if that remedy proved inadequate would the court of equity entertain jurisdiction. If equity granted jurisdiction, again, it would "follow the law" in requiring all other elements of an enforceable contract to be shown. It might, however, withhold equitable relief because, in its discretion, it might conclude that such relief would be too great a hardship on the defendant or that the plaintiff had operated less than fairly or, again, had come to the court of conscience, the court of equity, with unclean hands. The plaintiff may not have been diligent and may, therefore, have lost favor in the eyes of the court of equity because "equity aids the vigilant."

1. Flexible Equitable Relief.

There are no longer any separate courts of equity. Law courts now sit as courts of equity where the relief sought in a given case is specific performance, an injunction, or other form of equitable relief. The court is being asked for discretionary relief which is filled with historic notions of equity and good conscience. The discretion is not unbridled because it must be exercised on the basis of much of the history of the development of equity. The judge in an equity case may still be called "chancellor" for that case.[24] Whatever the judge is called, where equitable relief is sought, the ambience changes. There are no jurors because it is the judge, the successor to the chancellor, who will make the *ex aequo et bono* judgment as to whether the plaintiff is entitled to the extraordinary relief sought.[25] If the court decides to grant relief, it can mold a decree to fit the case precisely, i.e., it need not be concerned with all-or-nothing remedies. Specific performance or an injunction may not be completely effective relief. The court may, therefore, order performance that is not identical to the promised performance.[26] It may also attach money damages to its decree to provide complete relief,[27] or it may condition its order on certain performance by the party seeking equitable relief.[28] We have already seen that specific performance or an injunction may be granted notwithstanding a

[24] *See, e.g.,* McIlwain v. Bank of Harrisburg, 18 Ark. App. 213, 713 S.W.2d 469 (1987).

[25] Equitable matters are triable *de novo* on appeal, i.e., factual issues are tried *de novo* on the record and reach a conclusion independent of the trial court except that where credible evidence is in conflict on a material issue of fact, the appellate court considers and may give weight to the fact that the trial court heard and observed the witnesses and accepted one version of the facts rather than another. Palas v. Black, 226 Neb. 728, 414 N.W.2d 805 (1987).

[26] *See* Chastain v. Schomburg, 258 Ga. 218, 367 S.E.2d 230 (1988) (court cannot decree specific performance of a contract where vendor purports to sell land of another, but it can order specific performance of vendor's own interest in the land).

[27] *See* Tamarind Lithography Workshop v. Sanders, 143 Cal. App. 3d 571, 193 Cal. Rptr. 409 (1983) (injunction to prevent continued distribution of film without screen credits for writer-director-producer — $25,000 damages to time of trial). *See also* Chastain v. Schomburg, *supra* note 26, where court could only order specific performance in part and suggested that damages could be attached for remaining compensation.

[28] *See* Ruth v. Crane, 392 F. Supp. 724, 734, (E.D. Pa. 1975), *aff'd,* 564 F.2d 90 (3d Cir. 1977). *See also* RESTATEMENT 2d § 363.

provision for liquidated damages.[29] "The objective of the court in granting equitable relief is to do complete justice to the extent that this is feasible."[30]

We have seen that the normal substitutional remedy of damages is subject to limitations such as foreseeability, certainty, and mitigation. Since the ordinary remedy is so circumscribed, it is not remarkable that extraordinary equitable remedies contain special limitations. It is important to explore those limitations.

B. *The Inadequacy Limitation.*

Scores of cases state that specific performance or an injunction will not be granted where there is an adequate remedy at law, i.e., where the normal remedy of substitutional damages is adequate to protect the expectation interest of the aggrieved party.[31] The inadequacy limitation may be seen in various situations.

1. The Uncertainty Limitation.

The terms of any contract must be sufficiently certain to allow a court to grant an appropriate remedy.[32] The terms may be sufficiently certain to allow a court to calculate damages, but they may not be certain enough to permit a court to create an order for specific performance or an injunction. In that situation, no equitable remedy is possible.[33] On the other hand, the terms of the contract may be sufficiently certain but the calculation of damages is too speculative. This situation provides one of the illustrations of the inadequacy limitation, i.e., the uncertainty of damages limitation.

It will be recalled that the normal damage remedy is available only if proof of such damage is reasonably certain.[34] Conversely, one of the ways a plaintiff may secure equitable jurisdiction by showing inadequacy of the damage remedy is by establishing that the damages would necessarily be *uncertain.*[35] Though courts are willing to entertain many more actions for damages lacking complete certainty than heretofore, situations remain where the proof is fatally uncertain. Consider, for example, a contract for the sale of an heirloom with dubious market value but great sentimental value to the buyer. There is

---

[29] *See* RESTATEMENT 2d § 361 and the earlier discussion of this concept, *supra* § 125(D)(1). *See also* Fabian v. Sather, 316 N.W.2d 10 (Minn. 1982) suggesting that, when vendors resell land to a third party, they can recover only liquidated damages under their contract with the original breaching buyer rather than actual damages.

[30] RESTATEMENT 2d § 358 comment a.

[31] *See, e.g.,* Abrams v. Rapoport, 163 Ill. App. 3d 748, 516 N.E.2d 943 (1987) (remedy at law adequate and specific performance would require continuous judicial supervision). *See also* RESTATEMENT 2d § 359(1).

[32] *See* RESTATEMENT 2d § 33.

[33] *See* the concurring opinion by Webber, J. in Sinnott Carpentry, Inc. v. Phillips, 110 Ill. App. 3d 632, 443 N.E.2d 597 (1982) (contract stated that plans for addition to house would be attached and no plans were attached — terms insufficient to grant specific performance); Genest v. John Glenn Corp., 298 Or. 723, 696 P.2d 1058 (1985) (uncertainty in terms of option to purchase real property). *See also* RESTATEMENT 2d § 362.

[34] *See supra* § 121.

[35] *See* Cabot Corp. v. Ashland Oil, Inc., 597 F. Supp. 437 (D. Mass. 1984) (damages impossible to calculate); Link v. State of Montana, 180 Mont. 469, 591 P.2d 214 (1979) (refusal to maintain transportation to park made damages to park concessionaire too uncertain).

no possibility of providing sufficiently certain proof of such sentimental value measured in money. Absent specific performance, the aggrieved party would have no remedy. Such a case, therefore, constitutes a classic application of the equitable remedy.[36] In a commercial context, though courts have become much more willing to find ways to allow sufficient proof of lost profits of a new business and, therefore, award damages for breach in such cases,[37] situations remain where such evidence is considered too speculative. In such cases, specific performance may be the only available remedy.[38] Similarly, damages for repudiated output or requirements contracts may be too uncertain and specific performance may be granted.[39]

2. Inadequate Substitute Limitation.

a. Unique Goods — Inability to Cover — Uniform Commercial Code — Insolvency.

Where a promise to deliver an heirloom is breached, not only is proof of damage with reasonable certainty impossible, no damage award will adequately compensate the aggrieved party since he cannot purchase that unique chattel elsewhere. Thus, even if the value of the chattel can be measured with reasonable certainty, such as a famous painting or sculpture, the buyer is entitled to specific performance of the contract on the footing that it will be impossible to purchase an adequate substitute.[40] The UCC has extended the availability of specific performance beyond the classical categories of heirlooms, priceless paintings, and custom-made goods.[41] It continues to authorize specific performance where the goods are unique. The remedy is now available, however, "in other proper circumstances."[42] Such "circumstances" would include output and requirements contracts, typically on the footing that damages are uncertain though the lack of any reliable substitute supplier may constitute an independent rationale.[43] "Other proper circumstances" should not include the bankruptcy of the defendant since granting specific performance in such a case would constitute a preferential transfer that is contrary to Federal bankruptcy policy.[44] Insolvency, however, is viewed as a factor, if

---

[36] See RESTATEMENT 2d § 360 comment b.

[37] See supra § 121(B).

[38] See Hogan v. Norfleet, 113 So. 2d 437 (Fla. App. 1959), aff'd, 143 So. 2d 384 (Fla. 1962).

[39] See Laclede Gas Co. v. Amoco Oil Co., 522 F.2d 33 (8th Cir. 1975) (requirements contract); Eastern Air Lines, Inc. v. Gulf Oil Corp., 415 F. Supp. 429 (S.D. Fla. 1975) (requirements contract); Eastern Rolling Mill Co. v. Micholovitz, 157 Md. 51, 145 A. 378 (1929) (output contract — steel scraps). It should be noted, however, that prior to the UCC, cases such as *Eastern Rolling Mill* were uncommon. See also UCC § 2-716 comment 2: "Output and requirements contracts involving a particular or peculiarly available source or market present today the typical commercial specific performance situation...."

[40] See Fast v. Southern Offshore Yachts, 587 F. Supp. 1354 (D. Conn. 1984) (specific performance of contract to sell custom yacht); Sedmak v. Charlie's Chevrolet, 622 S.W.2d 694 (Mo. App. 1981) (contract to purchase Corvette automobile which was one of a limited number manufactured to commemorate the selection of the Corvette as the pace car for the Indianapolis 500 auto race).

[41] See UCC § 2-716 comment 2.

[42] UCC § 2-716(1).

[43] See supra note 31.

[44] See, however, Proyectos Elecs., S. A. v. Alper, 37 Bankr. 931, 37 UCC 1142 (E.D. Pa. 1983) criticized in J. WHITE & R. SUMMERS, UNIFORM COMMERCIAL CODE § 6-6 at 274 (3rd ed. 1988).

not an exclusive ground, for granting specific performance.[45] Thus, if the contract is fair and remains executory on both sides, specific performance will not cause a preferential transfer because other creditors will be benefited by the consideration received by the party ordered to perform.[46] The fact that damages can be measured with reasonable certainty should not, therefore, preclude specific performance in such cases whether or not they involve the sale of goods.[47] The ground for specific performance in such cases is the prospective inability to collect damages which, alone, is a basis for fulfilling the requirement of inadequacy.

Though the UCC manifests a clear intention to expand the availability of the remedy of specific performance in contracts for the sale of goods, the meaning of "other proper circumstances" is anything but clear, and courts tend to cling to pre-Code analyses of the remedy's availability.[48] Thus, the use of specific performance in a UCC context remains relatively traditional. The UCC also permits the separate remedy of replevin of goods when they have been "identified"[49] to the contract and the seller refuses to deliver.[50]

b. Land — Specific Performance for Buyer.

Courts have always regarded land as unique because any tract of land is necessarily unique in terms of its location. A buyer who desires a particular tract of land should not have to be satisfied with any substitute. If the buyer intends to resell the land and is, therefore, motivated exclusively by the profit he will earn on the resale, it may be argued that he should not be entitled to specific performance because he can be adequately compensated in damages. After all, he had only money in mind and was not concerned with living on the

---

[45] See Milan Steam Mills v. Hickey, 59 N.H. 241 (1879) (no adequate remedy at law because of insolvency); Heilman v. Union Canal Co., 37 Pa. 100 (1860) (insolvency alone is not a ground for equitable remedy), but Estate of Brown, 446 Pa. 401, 289 A.2d 77 (1972) suggests that insolvency supports the granting of specific performance. See also RESTATEMENT 2d § 360 where ill. 9 suggests that insolvency is a factor tending to show that damages are inadequate.

[46] See RESTATEMENT 2d § 360 comment d. See also RESTATEMENT 2d § 365, ill. 4.

[47] See, however, White & Summers, supra note 44, suggesting at 274 that specific performance should not be granted in such cases because damages can be easily measured.

[48] In their well-known book on the UCC, Professors White & Summers (supra note 44) arrive at this conclusion though they mention an occasional case that evidences the expansion of the remedy, e.g., Stephan's Mach. & Tool, Inc. v. D. & H. Mach. Consultants, Inc., 65 Ohio App. 2d 197, 417 N.E.2d 579 (1979) (equipment failed to function and, though damages were clearly measurable and the equipment was not unique since it was available elsewhere, plaintiff could not afford to purchase a replacement and the court granted specific performance).

[49] The concept of identification found in UCC § 2-501 has been explored in Chapter 8 at § 113(C).

[50] Under UCC § 2-502(1), where a buyer has paid all or part of the price for unshipped goods which have been identified in the contract and the seller has become insolvent within ten days after receipt of the first installment payment, the buyer may recover the goods if he makes and keeps good a tender of any unpaid portion of the price. This section is so filled with conditions that its utility is suspect. Failure to meet any of these conditions may relegate the buyer to § 2-716(3) which does not contain all of these conditions but does condition the right of replevin on the identification of the goods, the inability of the buyer to effect cover, or showing that a cover effort would be unavailing, or showing that the goods have been shipped under reservation, and satisfaction of the security interest in the goods has been made or tendered. Except for the showing that the goods have been shipped under reservation, the buyer may find considerable overlap between specific performance in § 2-716(1) and replevin in § 2-716(3) since both are predicated, essentially, on the inability to cover.

land or using for any other special purpose.[51] Yet, the strong policy favoring specific performance for the buyer of land has led to a virtual[52] per se view, and the buyer will still be granted specific performance if he so desires.[53]

c. Land — Specific Performance for Seller — "Mutuality of Remedy" — Adequate Security of Performance.

Where a buyer breaches a contract for the sale of land, the seller is usually entitled to specific performance though there is nothing unique about the performance of the buyer, i.e., the seller receives the contract price.[54] The rationale for this curious result was sometimes based on "mutuality of remedy," i.e., the notion that one party would not be entitled to a remedy if the same remedy would not be available to the other party.[55] The "doctrine" of mutuality of remedy is often traced to a nineteenth century treatise[56] though isolated judicial support for this "doctrine" can still be discovered.[57] The concept underlying "mutuality of remedy" is to assure the party in breach that he will receive the performance due from the aggrieved party after the breaching party performs pursuant to the equity decree. If, for example, a breaching seller of land is ordered to convey the land, he should have reasonable assurance that he will receive the purchase price. This result can be achieved without resorting to the doctrine of mutuality of remedy. The court can, for example, order specific performance conditioned upon the buyer providing adequate security through a mortgage or otherwise.[58] It is not necessary to provide exactly the same remedies for both parties. Mutuality of remedy has been discarded even in jurisdictions which had codified it.[59] If the court cannot

---

[51] See Watkins v. Paul, 95 Idaho 499, 511 P.2d 781 (1973) (buyers had no unique purpose in obtaining the land but simply wanted to resell it for a profit).

[52] Occasionally, a court will insist that the presumption that damages are inadequate for a buyer of land and specific performance, therefore, is required, is only a rebuttable presumption. See Hancock v. Dusenberg, 110 Idaho, 147, 715 P.2d 360 (Idaho App. 1986); Converse v. Fong, 159 Cal. App. 3d 86, 205 Cal. Rptr. 242 (1984). This is, however, contrary to the great weight of authority.

[53] It is sometimes suggested that where the buyer is forced to breach his resale contract because the seller refused to convey the land, the buyer's damages will not be sufficiently certain absent litigation. The notion that uncertainty of damages is a reason for permitting such a buyer to obtain specific performance is a makeweight rationale in many cases. Since courts favor the avoidance of litigation, however, specific performance will accomplish this objective with respect to the resale contract. Again, however, the strong policy in favor of granting specific performance to buyers in land contracts simply does not admit of exceptions in the overwhelming number of jurisdictions. See RESTATEMENT 2d § 360 comment e.

[54] Deans v. Layton, 89 N.C. App. 358, 366 S.E.2d 560 (1988); Kunzman v. Thorsen, 303 Or. 600, 740 P.2d 754 (1987); Palas v. Black, 226 Neb. 728, 414 N.W.2d 805 (1987); Perron v. Hale, 108 Idaho 578, 701 P.2d 198 (1985); Tombari v. Griepp, 350 P.2d 452 (Wash. 1960). RESTATEMENT 2d § 360 comment e.

[55] See Ames, *Mutuality in Specific Performances*, 3 COLUM. L. REV. 1 (1903); Stone, *The Mutuality Rule in New York*, 16 COLUM. L. REV. 443 (1916). Modern authorities, however, suggest another reason for affording the vendor the remedy of specific performance in a land contract, i.e., the difficulty of locating a willing buyer with acceptable credit, particularly if the value of the property is declining. See Deans v. Layton, 89 N.C. App. 358, 366 S.E.2d 560 (1988).

[56] FRY, SPECIFIC PERFORMANCE § 460 (1858).

[57] See, e.g., McIlwain v. Bank of Harrisburg, 18 Ark. App. 213, 713 S.W.2d 460 (1986). For a classic application of mutuality of remedy, see Slip Opinion in Ruhlen v. Columbus First Realty Co., Case No. 6-83-13 (Ohio. App. 1985).

[58] See RESTATEMENT 2d § 363.

[59] For example, California amended CAL. CIV. CODE § 3386 in 1969 to dispense with the requirement of mutuality and to replace it with a flexible concept similar to what now appears in

order adequate security for the specifically performing party, it will refuse to grant an equitable remedy.[60]

d. Essential Equitable Relief.

Situations may occur where it is patently clear that the only effective remedy is an equitable remedy. A cogent example occurs where one's religion may require certain acts on the part of a spouse to obtain a religious divorce. Thus, under traditional Jewish law, a written document of severance of all marital bonds (a "get") is an essential condition to a remarriage by a wife. A "get" can be obtained exclusively by the husband's assertion that it is being sought of his own free will. The parties may have made an agreement that the husband would cooperate in this effort. While courts may feel constrained in such cases because of implied or expressed preclusions of judicial intervention in religious matters, some courts have been willing to grant equitable relief since, in this type of case, any substitute relief is woefully inadequate.[61] Damages in such a case are obviously uncertain. Yet, even if damages were more than reasonably certain, they would be clearly inadequate to provide the aggrieved party with anything resembling effective relief.

C. *The Fairness Limitation.*

It is important to emphasize the discretionary nature of equitable relief. Notwithstanding the fact that an agreement may contain all of the necessary common law elements for enforcement, a court may deny such relief because it concludes that it would be unfair to grant it. "Fairness" includes any number of factors that a court may consider. One of the better examples of such a case is *McKinnon v. Benedict*[62] where prospective buyers of property were in need of financial assistance and agreed to major restrictions on the commercial property they intended to buy in exchange for a loan of $5000 and assistance from the lender in promoting the use of the property. Facing failure in their new venture, the buyers pursued an expansion of the property which violated their contract with the lender who sought to enjoin the buyers from further violations. In denying the plaintiff the equitable remedy of injunction, the court considered the following factors: (1) the gross inadequacy of consideration,[63] (2) the hardship to the defendant as compared with the benefit to the

---

RESTATEMENT 2d § 363. *See* Converse v. Fong, *supra* note 52. *See also* Sablosky v. Edward S. Gordon Co., 538 N.Y.S.2d 513, 535 N.E.2d 643 (1989) (mutuality of remedy has been generally discarded and is not required in arbitration contracts).

[60] *See* RESTATEMENT 2d § 363 indicating that neither specific performance nor an injunction will issue unless the court is satisfied that there is adequate security for the reciprocal performance.

[61] *See* Avitzur v. Avitzur, 459 N.Y.S.2d 572, 446 N.E.2d 136 (1983), *cert. denied,* 464 U.S. 817 (1983); Minkin v. Minkin, 180 N.J. Super. 260, 434 A.2d 665 (1981). These cases and others are discussed in Annotation, 29 A.L.R.4th 746 (1988).

[62] 38 Wis. 2d 607, 157 N.W.2d 665 (1968).

[63] The court computed the value of the loan to the defendants at $145 which was not even an unsecured loan since plaintiffs took a mortgage on other property owned by defendants. Plaintiff had also made general promises to assist the defendants in their enterprise. The plaintiff's performance of those promises was nominal. In exchange for this value, the defendants had surrendered valuable rights in the operation of a recreation facility. Where equitable relief is sought, courts do inquire into the "adequacy of consideration" (relative values exchanged) while

plaintiff,[64] (3) whether the defendant's promise was induced by some sharp practice, misrepresentation or mistake,[65] and (4) the disparity of business background between the parties.[66] The historical concept of unconscionability is a significant factor in the exercise of judicial discretion to determine whether equitable relief should be granted.[67] A court will balance all of these factors in any case where equitable relief is sought.[68] Where the defendant relies upon a term of the agreement to preclude specific performance or an injunction, a court may grant the equitable relief sought if it concludes that the defendant relied upon an unfair term in resisting the plaintiff's suit.[69]

D. "Public Policy Limitation."[70]

Even where an agreement is enforceable at law with respect to money damages, however, public policy elements may prevent the granting of equitable relief.[71] Where, for example, the granting of specific performance would result in reversing a valid conviction of the defendant for securities fraud and the dismissal of indictments, a court may refuse to grant the relief sought.[72] Specific performance of an alimony agreement was denied where the paramour cohabited with the wife and such activity was considered contrary to public policy.[73] Where a public utility commission approved the construction of a transmission line essential for the public welfare, a court refused to enjoin the breach of an agreement that would have prevented that construction and harmed the public welfare.[74] There is no end to such illustrations since they run the gamut of all of those actions which are bundled beneath the nebulous caption, "public policy." It is, however, important to recognize this additional limitation to the granting of equitable relief.

E. *The Judicial Supervision Limitation — Personal Service Contracts.*

1. General Problems in Judicial Supervision.

If there is no other limitation on the granting of an equitable remedy, a court may still refuse to grant that remedy if the difficulties of supervision are

---

the general rule is that they will not so inquire where the relief sought is the normal remedy of damages. *See* RESTATEMENT 2d § 364(1)(c).

[64] *See* Van Wagner Adv. Corp. v. S & M Enters., 501 N.Y.S.2d 6228, 492 N.E.2d 756 (1986) (disproportionate harm to defendant and benefit to plaintiff).

[65] *See* Concert Radio, Inc. v. GAF Corp., 108 A.D.2d 273, 488 N.Y.S.2d 696 (1985) (defendant mistakenly triggered an option agreement which plaintiff then sought to specifically enforce. Court denied equitable relief because plaintiff took no risks, invested no money, and suffered no losses while defendant would lose large sums simply because of his misinterpretation of contract language).

[66] In questions of equitable relief, courts are particularly conscious of unconscionable conduct. While the court could discover no sharp practice, dishonesty, or overreaching by the plaintiff, it took note that the plaintiff was an attorney and experienced business man while the defendant was a person of limited financial ability and business background.

[67] *See* the exploration of unconscionability at § 96.

[68] *See* RESTATEMENT 2d § 364.

[69] RESTATEMENT 2d § 364(2).

[70] *See* Chapter 8 of RESTATEMENT 2d.

[71] RESTATEMENT 2d § 365.

[72] United States v. McGovern, 822 F.2d 739 (3d Cir. 1987).

[73] Garlinger v. Garlinger, 129 N.J. Super. 37, 322 A.2d 1190 (1974).

[74] Steelwagon v. Pyle, 390 Pa. 17, 133 A.2d 819 (1957).

disproportionate to the benefits of that remedy. If courts are thrust into making judgments about the quality of the performance and/or the supervision of performance will occur over a long period, courts shirk from granting equitable relief.[75] One of the classic examples of these supervisory problems occurs in construction contracts. Typically, breaches of construction contracts can be adequately compensated through the normal remedy of money damages. When asked to specifically enforce the contract of a builder, courts will generally refuse that remedy, partly because damages at law may be adequate, but also because of the difficulty courts would face in attempting to supervise that performance.[76] This is not to suggest that courts will invariably refuse equitable relief in such a contract where such relief was otherwise indicated and supervisory problems are not insuperable.[77] Moreover, what may appear to create almost insuperable supervisory problems may turn out to be a situation which the court can easily supervise.[78] A particular type of contract, however, is particularly troublesome to courts in terms of supervision and other policy constraints. We will now explore the problems in granting equitable relief in personal service contracts.

2. Personal Service Contracts — Injunction.

Notwithstanding some very early lip service paid to the view that "a bird that will not sing will be made to sing," as Professor Corbin has suggested so well, our legal system insists on liberty even at the expense of broken promises.[79] It is clear that personal service promises will not be specifically enforced.[80] While the original resistance to specific enforcement of such promises was based on the difficulties of judicial supervision, the prohibition of involuntary servitude under the Thirteenth Amendment to the Constitution of the United States may also be violated by such an equitable decree.[81] Other statutory prohibitions on servitude may also preclude specific performance.[82] Since specific performance is not available, aggrieved parties may seek injunctions against the defendant's performance elsewhere.

Enjoining the defendant from performing for another is sometimes referred to as "negative enforcement" of the defendant's obligation.[83] In the famous

---

[75] See RESTATEMENT 2d § 366 comment a.

[76] Yonan v. Oak Park Fed. Sav. & Loan Ass'n, 27 Ill. App. 3d 967, 326 N.E.2d 773 (1975).

[77] See O'Neil v. Lipinski, 173 Mont. 332, 567 P.2d 909 (1977).

[78] See Egbert v. Way, 15 Wash. App. 76, 546 P.2d 1246 (1975) (trial court had based its refusal to grant specific performance on mistaken assumptions of supervision and appellate court concluded that it could supervise the clearing of tax liens and inheritance tax on contract for the sale of real property).

[79] See De Rivafinoli v. Corsetti, 4 Paige Ch. 263, 260 (N.Y. Ch. 1833) and A. Corbin, CONTRACTS at § 1204, as quoted in In re Robert A. Noonan, 17 Bankr. 793 (1982).

[80] Motown Record Corp. v. Brockert, 160 Cal. App. 3d 123, 137 (1984) and RESTATEMENT 2d § 367(1). See, however, the enforcement of a contract resulting in compelling the president of a company who acted outrageously to read in person a bargaining order to assembled employees. Conair Corp. v. NLRB, 721 F.2d 1355 (D.C. Cir. 1983), cert. denied, 467 U.S. 1241 (1984).

[81] See Beverly Glen Music, Inc. v. Warner Commun., Inc., 178 Cal. App. 3d 1142, 1144 (1986); American Broadcasting Cos. v. Wolf, 438 N.Y.S.2d 482, 420 N.E.2d 363 (1981).

[82] See, e.g., § 541(a)(6) of the FEDERAL BANKRUPTCY CODE which prohibits creditors from forcing debtors into future servitude for payment of debts. In re James Taylor, 91 Bankr. 302 (D.N.J. 1988).

[83] See American Broadcasting Cos. v. Wolf, supra note 81.

REMEDIES FOR BREACH OF CONTRACT § 127

case of *Lumley v. Wagner*,[84] a Prussian opera singer (Wagner) had agreed to sing exclusively for three months for the plaintiff, who was the proprietor of Her Majesty's Theatre in London. Wagner also stipulated that she would not compete with the employer for the term of the engagement. When she broke her agreement and agreed to sing at another theatre,[85] Lumley sought an injunction to restrain her from performing elsewhere. The injunction was granted with the Chancellor noting that the effect of the injunction may cause her to perform her original promise.[86] Later courts were willing to grant an injunction absent an express stipulation that the employee would not compete during the term of the employment.[87] There are numerous instances of courts granting injunctions against the defendant performing elsewhere if the services of the defendant are unique.[88] Yet, whether the remedy sought is specific performance or an injunction, courts will be loathe to grant it if it will compel the continuance of personal association or will preclude the employee from making a living.[89] Neither will other extraordinary remedies such as mandamus[90] or a temporary restraining order[91] be granted to compel the maintenance of the employer-employee relationship in such cases.[92] Courts may also call upon traditional obstacles to the granting of equitable relief such as the requirement that damages must be inadequate and, when applied to personal services contracts, the court may be willing to discover adequate damages more easily.[93]

Beyond the obstacles of judicial supervision and involuntary servitude, the plaintiff seeking equitable enforcement of a personal service contract must show that the services are unique. While the services of professional athletes or other performers may be presumptively unique,[94] other personal services may be so perfunctory or ministerial that specific enforcement of such contracts would avoid the obstacles normally precluding such relief.[95] Thus, where a realtor sought a writ of mandamus ("We command") ordering respondent to perform her duties as official court reporter by delivering a free statement of facts in a given case, the court granted the relief.[96]

---

[84] 1 DeG. M. & G. 604, 42 Eng. Rep. 687 (Ch. 1852).

[85] She was induced to do so by Frederick Gye who headed the Royal Italian Opera in Covent Garden.

[86] *See* Lumley v. Wagner, *supra* note 84, 42 Eng. Rep. at 693.

[87] Implied covenant recognized in Montague v. Flockton, L.R. 16 Eq. 189 [1873].

[88] *See* Dallas Cowboys Football Club v. Harris, 348 S.W.2d 37 (Tex. App. 1961) (football player); Philadelphia Ball Club v. Lajoie, 202 Pa. 210, 51 A. 973 (1902) (baseball player).

[89] *See* American Broadcasting Cos. v. Wolf., *supra* note 81. *See also* RESTATEMENT 2d § 367(2).

[90] State v. Board of Sch. Comm'rs of Indianapolis, 438 N.E.2d 12 (Ind. App. 1982) (mandamus, like injunctions, will not issue when the result will be specific performance of personal service contracts).

[91] Miller v. Foley, 317 N.W.2d 710 (Minn. 1982).

[92] Though employer's promises generally will not be specifically enforced, it is not uncommon for courts to order reinstatement of discharged employees where the employer has violated anti-discrimination statutes or collective bargaining agreements. *See* RESTATEMENT 2d § 367 comment b.

[93] *See* Radiac Abrasives, Inc. v. Diamond Tech., Inc., 177 Ill. App. 3d 628, 532 N.E.2d 428 (1988).

[94] *See* Nassau Sports v. Peters, 352 F. Supp. 870 (E.D.N.Y. 1972).

[95] *See* RESTATEMENT 2d § 367 comment a suggesting a distinction between personal services for which specific performance or injunctions would not be granted, and other non-delegable duties for which such relief would be granted such as the writing of an autograph or signing of a diploma.

[96] *See* Perez v. McGar, 630 S.W.2d 320 (Tex. App. 1982). It should be noted that the defendant had a statutory duty as a court official to perform this service.

F. *Power of Termination Limitation.*

A contract may expressly provide a party with a power of termination or such a power of avoidance may be provided by law, e.g., to protect an infant from imprudent acts.[97] Courts will properly consider such powers when asked to grant equitable relief against such a party because he may exercise that power and nullify the decree.[98] This is particularly true where the termination would take effect almost immediately. If notice of exercise of the power of termination had to be given some time before the party's performance was discharged, however, a court may grant equitable relief for that period.

Where the party with the power of termination is the party *seeking* equitable relief, there is a problem of assuring the security of the contract for the defendant.[99] If, for example, a court would decree specific performance in such a case and, after the defendant adhered to that order by performing, the plaintiff would exercise his power of termination, the defendant would be irreparably harmed. To avoid that possibility, a court can mold its decree to assure the plaintiff's performance by, for example, extinguishing the power in the plaintiff. There is no preclusion of equitable relief in such cases unless the security of the defendant cannot be assured.[1]

G. *Equitable Relief for Defaulting Plaintiff.*

Where a party seeking specific performance, an injunction, or other equitable relief is, himself, in breach of the contract, whether the court may grant the relief sought may depend upon the nature of the breach. It should be recalled that an uncured material breach will discharge the duties of the other party to the contract. A court could not, therefore, order specific performance (or negative enforcement) of duties that were already discharged. On the other hand, if the defaulting plaintiff's breach was immaterial so that the duties were not discharged, specific performance or an injunction should not be precluded. In a contract for the sale of land, for example, the buyer's delay in making a payment according to the terms of the contract may be a minor breach that should not permit the seller to avoid his or her obligation to convey the property.[2] The FIRST RESTATEMENT permitted specific performance even in the case of a serious breach if that was necessary to avoid an unjust penalty or forfeiture.[3] The RESTATEMENT 2d omits that exception "as unneces-

---

[97] On the power of avoidance by infants and others, *see* §§ 23-27.

[98] *See* ECRI v. McGraw-Hill, Inc., 809 F.2d 223 (3d Cir. 1986) (requirements of preliminary injunctions are more stringent than those for specific performance and court must consider power of termination). *See also* State v. Anacotes Veneer, Inc., 42 Wash. 2d 338, 255 P.2d 338 (1953), and RESTATEMENT 2d § 368(1).

[99] RESTATEMENT 2d § 363 suggests another limitation on the granting of equitable relief, i.e., such relief will be denied if a substantial part of the agreed exchange of the performance to be compelled is unperformed, i.e., the performance of the party seeking relief, and that performance is not secured to the satisfaction of the court.

[1] *See* Stamatiades v. Merit Music Serv., 210 Md. 597, 124 A.2d 829 (1956). *See also* RESTATEMENT 2d § 368(2).

[2] *See* Fleenor v. Church, 681 P.2d 1351 (Alaska 1984). *See also* RESTATEMENT 2d § 369.

[3] FIRST RESTATEMENT § 375(1).

sary in the light of the merger of law and equity and the greater flexibility of legal rules that deal with penalties and forfeitures."[4]

§ 128. Uniform Commercial Code Remedies Survey.

Throughout this chapter on contract remedies, numerous references to the UCC have appeared. On occasion, aspects of UCC remedies have been explored in some detail. These explorations will not be repeated in this section. It is, however, important to consider UCC remedies in an holistic fashion so that these remedies will not be viewed as different from contract remedies in general. In general, UCC remedies for breach of contract for the sale of goods protect the normal expectation interest of the parties by placing the aggrieved party in the position he or she would have occupied had the contract been performed.[5] It is important to view these remedies as facets of a prism protecting that interest. The survey that follows is not intended to be an exhaustive treatment of UCC remedies for breach of contract. Such a treatment is better left to treatises on the UCC.[6]

A. *Prerequisites — Repudiation, Failure of Performance, Rejection, Revocation of Acceptance, Inspection.*

Before a buyer or seller is entitled to a UCC remedy in a contract for the sale of goods, one of four basic events must occur: (1) one of the parties must repudiate the contract[7] (the concept of repudiation was explored earlier);[8] (2) one of the parties must fail to perform, *e.g.,* the seller fails to deliver the goods or the buyer fails to pay for the goods;[9] (3) the buyer must rightfully reject the goods because they are nonconforming (*e.g.,* defective)[10] which provides a cause of action against the seller,[11] or the buyer must wrongfully reject the goods which provides the seller with a cause of action against the buyer;[12] (4) the buyer must revoke his acceptance of the goods upon discovery of a substantial nonconformity[13] which provides him with a cause of action against the seller,[14] or the buyer wrongfully revokes acceptance which provides the seller with a cause of action against the buyer.[15] We have earlier explored the concept of revocation of acceptance.[16]

It should be noted that before a buyer is normally bound to accept or make payment for goods delivered, he has the right to inspect the goods.[17] As is typical throughout Article 2 of the Code, the parties may modify this statutory

---

[4] RESTATEMENT 2d § 369 (Reporter's Note).
[5] *See* UCC § 1-106(1).
[6] *See* J. WHITE & R. SUMMERS, UNIFORM COMMERCIAL CODE chs. 6 and 7 (3d (student) ed. 1988).
[7] *See* UCC § 2-610.
[8] *See* Chapter 8, *supra.*
[9] *See* UCC § 2-301.
[10] *See* UCC § 2-601. As to the requirements of a rightful rejection, *see* UCC § 2-602.
[11] *See* UCC § 2-711.
[12] UCC § 2-703.
[13] UCC § 2-608.
[14] UCC § 2-711.
[15] UCC § 2-703.
[16] *See* Chapter 8, *supra.*
[17] UCC § 2-513.

provision by their contract. If, for example, the parties agree that the shipment is C.O.D. (cash on delivery), they have obviously agreed that payment shall be made at the time of delivery, i.e., prior to inspection.[18] Any similar agreement can eliminate the buyer's prior right to inspection.[19] If such an agreement is made, a nonconformity of the goods does not excuse the duty of payment unless the nonconformity appears without inspection, or unless a justifiable injunction would issue against honor of the documents against which payment is to be made.[20] It should be noted that payment — even a payment which the buyer has agreed to make prior to inspection — does not constitute acceptance of the goods.[21]

B. *Comparison of Seller and Buyer Remedies Under the UCC.*

Two sections of the UCC list the remedies of the seller and the buyer. Section 2-703 lists the seller's remedies, and § 2-711 lists the buyer's remedies. It is useful to compare the counterpart remedies of each of the parties.

1. Resale and Cover — "Lost Volume" Seller.

When the buyer fails to perform, the seller may resell the goods intended for the buyer to a second buyer.[22] The operation of this remedy in the normal case is quite simple. *S* agrees to sell goods to *B* for $1000 and *B* repudiates. Assuming no additional selling or transportation expense, *S* resells the same goods to *B* for $900. To fulfill *S*'s reasonable expectations, he should be awarded damages in the amount of $100 against *B*, i.e., the difference between the contract price and the resale price. The resale must be in good faith and it must be commercially reasonable.[23] It may be either "public," which requires notice of the time and place of resale, or "private," which requires notice to the buyer.[24] The seller must also be able to show that the particular goods delivered to the second buyer were the goods that would have been shipped to the first buyer.[25] While the resale remedy will protect the expectation interest of a seller of a single or unique item, it will not protect that seller if he would have made the second sale in any event, i.e., if he is a "lost volume" seller. We have already explored the remedy for such a seller — the profit he would have made on the breached contract.[26] Since many sellers are "lost volume" sellers, the resale remedy will not provide them with sufficient protection of their expectation

---

[18] UCC § 2-514(3)(a).

[19] If, for example, the parties agree that payment is to be made against documents (*e.g.*, bill of lading), such payment is then due prior to inspection. UCC § 2-513(3)(b).

[20] UCC § 2-512(1).

[21] UCC § 2-512(2).

[22] *See* UCC § 2-706.

[23] *See* Servbest Foods, Inc. v. Emesee Indus., 82 Ill. App. 3d 662, 403 N.E.2d 1 (1980).

[24] In Sprague v. Sumitomo Forestry Co., 104 Wash. 2d 751, 709 P.2d 1200 (1985), the court found that failure to notify the buyer precluded the use of the resale remedy and seller was relegated to damages for buyer's nonacceptance or repudiation under § 2-708(1) (discussed *infra*). The trial court had awarded resale damages which happened to be the same amount that should have been awarded under § 2-708(1). The court, therefore, affirmed.

[25] *See* Hunt-Wesson Foods, Inc. v. Marubeni Alaska Seafoods, Inc., 23 Wash. App. 193, 596 P.2d 666 (1979) (failure to show that the goods delivered to second buyer was caused by first buyer's breach precluded the use of the resale remedy).

[26] *See supra* § 122(D).

interest. The resale remedy, therefore, is only effective where the seller has only one item to sell and can only make one profit thereon.

The buyer's counterpart to the seller's resale remedy is the buyer's remedy of *cover*.[27] The cover remedy allows the buyer to make a reasonable and good faith substitute purchase where the seller fails to supply conforming goods under the contract. Where the buyer makes such a substitute purchase, he may recover the difference between the contract price and the cover price (if any).[28] The substitute goods purchased need not be identical to those under the broken contract. It is sufficient if the cover was reasonable and without unreasonable delay (seasonable).[29] Unlike the seller's resale remedy which we have seen operates effectively only if the seller would not have made the second sale in any event, the buyer's cover remedy is the normal remedy of the buyer who presumably requires the goods the seller failed to supply.

2. Buyer and Seller Remedies for Difference Between Contract Price and Market Price.

The seller need not pursue his resale remedy, and the buyer need not pursue his cover remedy. Absent certain important limitations that will be considered, either party is free to pursue a traditional remedy for the difference between the contract price and market price of the goods. The comparison here, however, is more complicated than the earlier comparison between resale and cover.

a. Cover — Preferred Remedy.

Initially, it is important to understand that the buyer's cover remedy is different from remedies available to him under pre-Code law. If the buyer uses the cover remedy properly, he is entitled to recover the difference between the contract price and his actual cover price, i.e., the price he actually pays for substitute goods. Pre-Code law generally measured the difference between the contract price and the market price, regardless of the buyer's cover purchase.[30] If the buyer paid more than the market price for the substitute goods, he would be relegated to the difference between the contract and market price regardless of his cover price.[31] Cover, therefore, is a more precise measure of the actual damage suffered by the buyer and is clearly the most important remedy for an aggrieved buyer. Notwithstanding the availability of cover, the Code permits the buyer to ignore that remedy.

b. "Hypothetical Cover."

The buyer may choose not to cover and still may recover the difference between the contract price and the market price at the time the buyer

---

[27] UCC § 2-712. For an analysis of this remedy, see Kanzmeier v. McCoppin, 398 N.W.2d 826 (Iowa 1987).

[28] UCC § 2-712(2).

[29] See Meshinsky v. Nicholas Yacht Sales, Inc., 110 N.J. 464, 541 A.2d 1063 (1988).

[30] See McGinnis v. Wentworth Chevrolet Co., 295 Or. 494, 668 P.2d 365 (1982).

[31] Professors White and Summers, supra note 6, at 244 n.5 point out that Professor Honnold found pre-Code case law holding that when the buyer covered for less than the market price, the cover price was the maximum amount on which damages would be permitted.

"learned of the breach."[32] We have already considered a number of problems surrounding the phrase "learned of the breach," particularly with respect to anticipatory repudiation.[33] At this point, it is important to note that, just as the resale remedy for the typical (lost volume) seller is anything but useful, the contract price/market price remedy for the buyer has lost much of its utility in light of the cover remedy. The only significant use of that remedy occurs where the buyer has not covered at all because he changed his mind about the purchase, cannot buy substitute goods, or where he attempted to cover and failed to meet the necessary conditions of a good faith, reasonable cover.[34] Where a buyer chooses not to make a readily available substitute purchase, he may have done so because he has discovered no need for the goods or because he was purchasing the goods for resale and decided that the resale prospects were dim. In either case, the seller has done the buyer a favor by breaching the contract. Should the buyer recover damages even though he chose not to cover? How has the buyer been damaged? The buyer was entitled to certain goods at a certain time at a certain price. Had he received those goods, he would have had goods worth the market price for which he would have paid the contract price. If the contract price is lower than the market price, the buyer has been damaged to the extent of the difference. Though he did not receive the goods and chose not to cover, he has lost the benefit of his bargain to the extent of the contract price/market price differential.[35] The remedy is sometimes referred to as "hypothetical cover,"[36] i.e., if the buyer had covered, presumably he would have paid the market price for substitute goods at the time and place of tender although this may be unrealistic because cover need not and often does not occur at the time and place of tender.[37]

c. Criticism of Uniform Commercial Code Section 2-713 ("Hypothetical Cover").

The remedy has been criticized as contrary to the normal purpose of UCC and contract remedies, because it allegedly fails to place the buyer in the same position he would have been in had the contract been performed. The criticism, however, is less than clear. Although "hypothetical cover" is obviously less precise than actual cover, it remains a decent approximation of damages in the absence of actual cover. It has been called a "statutory liqui-

---

[32] UCC § 2-713(1).

[33] See supra § 122(F) and, in particular, note 71 thereunder.

[34] Where the buyer elects not to cover, his damages are governed by UCC § 2-713. Moridge Mfg. Co. v. Butler, 451 N.E.2d 677 (Ind. App. 1983). See also Dickson v. Delhi Seed Co., 26 Ark. App. 83, 760 S.W.2d 382 (1988) (§§ 2-712 and 2-713 are alternative remedies and § 2-712 is, therefore, available to the buyer unless he did not cover). To the same effect, see State v. Kent Nowlin Constr., Inc., 106 N.M. 539, 746 P.2d 645 (1987).

[35] See Panhandle Agri-Serv. v. Becker, 231 Kan. 291, 644 P.2d 413 (1982) where counsel on either side and the trial court demonstrated a remarkable lack of understanding about this remedy under the UCC. Fortunately, the Supreme Court of Kansas manifested a much better understanding.

[36] Allied Canners & Packers, Inc. v. Victor Packing Co., 162 Cal. App. 3d 905, 209 Cal. Rptr. 60 (1985).

[37] See Dangerfield v. Markel, 278 N.W.2d 364 (N.D. 1979) (reasonable time for cover may go beyond time and place for tender).

dated damages clause"[38] which is a sensible characterization since it suggests a reasonable forecast of direct damages in the event of seller's failure to deliver. The suggestion by Professor White and Professor Summers, however, that § 2-713 bears "no close relation to plaintiff's actual loss"[39] requires analysis.

The authors suggest[40] a hypothetical contract for the sale of overalls at a price of $50,000 which is breached by the seller. The market price at the time the buyer learned of the breach (typically the time of tender) is $55,000 and the buyer decides not to cover. The buyer's measure of damages under § 2-713 is $5000. On these facts, they make different assumptions, each of which they present as support for their view that § 2-713 bears no necessary relation "to the change in the buyer's economic status that the breach causes."[41] They first assume that the buyer decided not to cover because he believes that the overall market is "going cold." That belief turns out to be correct because, had seller delivered, the buyer's gross receipts would have been only $40,000 and he would have lost $10,000. Thus, the § 2-713 measure places him in a better position than if the contract had been performed. The second assumption is that the buyer's choice not to cover is faulty because the supply of overalls turns out to be insufficient and buyer would have earned $20,000 net profit had the contract been performed. Here, the $5000 recovery under § 2-713 places the buyer in a worse position than if the contract had been performed. The authors then suggest that a recent case, *Allied Canners & Packers, Inc. v. Victor Packing Co.,*[42] supports their view that § 2-713 need not bear a close relation to a plaintiff's actual damages.[43] There is, however, a major difference between the holding in that case and the author's hypothetical.

In *Allied,* the seller agreed to sell raisins to the buyer, who had made resale contracts which would net a profit of just under $4,500. The California raisin crop was severely damaged by rain and, because the raisin market is regulated in California, cover could not occur until much later. The diminished supply of raisins resulted in a huge increase in the market price. The buyer did not cover but avoided any liability to its customers. Since the market price had increased more than substantially, the § 2-713 measure of recovery was over $150,000 which the buyer sought to recover (since it had not covered, it sought its alternate remedy in damages for nondelivery), even though it expected to earn a profit of less than $4500 if the contract had been performed. The court was faced with choosing between the "statutory liquidated damages" concept of § 2-713, and the general directive of the Code under § 1-106 that an aggrieved party should be placed in no better position than he would have occupied had the contract been performed. The court chose the latter

---

[38] *See* Allied Canners & Packing, Inc. v. Victor Packing Co., *supra* note 36, which mentions this characterization suggested by Judge (formerly Professor) Peters in her article, *Remedies for Breach of Contract Relating to the Sale of Goods Under the Uniform Commercial Code: A Roadmap for Article Two,* 73 YALE L.J. 199 (1963) and J. White & R. Summers, *supra* note 6, who subscribe to this position in their newest edition at 253.

[39] *See* White & Summers, *supra* note 6, at 253.

[40] *Id.* at 252-53.

[41] *Id.* at 252.

[42] *Supra* note 36.

[43] White & Summers, *supra* note 6, at 253.

view which White and Summers consider support for their position based upon the general view that post-breach behavior should be considered to limit plaintiff's damages. Unlike the White and Summers overall hypothetical, however, the court in *Allied* emphasized the fact that the seller knew the buyer had resale contracts. Where a party is aware of a customer's resale contracts, it can foresee the risk it was assuming at the time of contract formation and that risk should not be enlarged by unforeseeable consequences. There is no suggestion in the overall hypothetical that the gains or losses were foreseeable. In fact, the hypothetical assumes certain market hunches by the purchaser. The *Allied* analysis is the preferable analysis.

d. Seller's Damages for Nonacceptance or Repudiation — "Hypothetical Resale."

Just as the buyer need not cover and may resort to damages for nondelivery under UCC § 2-713, the seller need not resell, and may resort to damages for the buyer's nonacceptance or repudiation under § 2-708.[44] This counterpart to § 2-713 (the buyer's measure of damages) differs in one significant respect. The market is measured under § 2-708(1) at the time and place of tender[45] whereas the buyer's remedy in § 2-713 is measured at the time the buyer "learns of the breach" and it also fixes the market as the market at the place of tender except, where the goods have been rejected or the buyer revokes acceptance of the goods, at the place of arrival.[46] The determination of the market under § 2-713, therefore, is consistent with the concept of "hypothetical cover" since it uses the market where the buyer would probably have covered. If § 2-708(1) may be viewed as the seller's "hypothetical resale" remedy, the determination of the market at the place of tender may be unrealistic with respect to goods that have been delivered to the buyer. In the typical "FOB shipment" contract, the place of tender will be the seller's location where the goods were delivered to a carrier. If, however, the goods have been delivered to the buyer who refuses to accept them even though they are conforming goods, the seller is likely to resell in that market.[47]

Why would a seller choose damages for nonacceptance or repudiation over the resale remedy? Again, the resale remedy is appropriate only if the seller has only one item for sale. If he is a "lost volume" seller,[48] the resale remedy will typically provide nominal damages since he will receive only the difference between the contract price and resale price which prices will often be identical or virtually identical. Where the seller chooses his § 2-708(1) remedy, he will be in the same unfortunate position since that remedy is, in effect,

---

[44] UCC 2-708(1): Subject to subsection (2) and to the provisions of this Article with respect to proof of market price (§ 2-723), the measure of damages for nonacceptance or repudiation by the buyer is the difference between the market price at the time and place for tender and the unpaid contract price together with any incidental damages provided in this Article (2-710), but less expenses saved in consequence of buyer's breach. *See* Allsop Sand & Gravel, Inc. v. Lincoln Sand & Gravel Co., 171 Ill. App. 3d 532, 525 N.E.2d 1185 (1988).

[45] *See* Wendling v. Puls, 227 Kan. 780, 28 U.C.C. Rep. 1362 (1980) (determination of date of tender).

[46] UCC § 2-713(2).

[47] This is the White and Summers view, *supra* note 6, at 308-09, which appears unassailable.

[48] *See supra* text preceding and subsequent to note 24.

a "hypothetical resale" remedy providing the difference between the contract price and market price, which will often be the same.[49] To overcome that injustice to a seller who would have earned profit on the broken contract and all subsequent contracts, § 2-708(2) provides the seller with his lost profit, including reasonable overhead.[50]

B. *Restricting Uniform Commercial Code Remedies to Expectation Interest.*

Throughout the discussion of contract remedies in this entire chapter, we have emphasized the purpose of contract law as the realization of those expectations induced by the making of a promise, which means that the aggrieved party should be placed in the position he would have been in had the contract been performed — no better and no worse.[51] We have also emphasized the adherence of the UCC to this purpose. In § 1-106 of the Code, that purpose is clearly codified: "The remedies provided by this Act shall be liberally administered to the end that the aggrieved party may be put in as good a position as if the other party had fully performed...."[52] There is language in the Code and its comments, however, that can be interpreted to suggest a contradiction of that purpose. For example, in the section listing the seller's remedies, a comment rejects any notion of election of the various remedies of the seller, i.e., such remedies are cumulative.[53] A section of the buyer's cover remedy indicates that the buyer's failure to effect cover "does not bar him from any other remedy."[54] Countervailing comment language is found in the buyer's remedy for nondelivery or repudiation,[55] and, of course, there is the general statement of the purpose of remedies under the Code quoted above.[56] The problem in treating Code remedies as totally available to buyers or sellers under any and all circumstances will necessarily contradict the basic philosophy of Code remedies. Consider, for example, a buyer who decides to cover at a reasonable cover price of $10,000 where the contract price is $7000. The cover measure of damages is $3000. If, however, the relevant market price is $12,000 and the buyer is free to choose his damage for nondelivery or repudiation remedy, he will choose that remedy since it will provide a recovery of $5000. That recovery will, however, overcompensate him to the extent that he is placed in a better position than he would have been in had the contract been performed. Where actual cover has occurred, the buyer should not be able to choose the § 2-713 remedy for the purpose of recovering additional damages.[57] Similarly,

---

[49] For a discussion of why § 2-708(1) is manifestly unjust as applied to the "lost volume" seller, *see* Snyder v. Greenbaum Assocs., 38 Md. App. 144, 380 A.2d 618 (1977).

[50] The analysis of lost profits for the "lost volume" seller appears *supra* Section 122(D).

[51] We have also examined the protection of the reliance and restitution interests which place the aggrieved party in the position he had been in prior to the contract or prior to the unjust enrichment.

[52] UCC § 1-106(1).

[53] UCC § 2-703 comment 1.

[54] UCC § 2-712(3).

[55] UCC § 2-713 comment 5: "The present section provides a remedy which is completely alternative to cover under the preceding section [2-712 — cover] and applies only when and to the extent that the buyer has not covered."

[56] *Supra* text at note 52.

[57] See Sun Maid Raisin Growers v. Victor Packing Co., 146 Cal. App. 3d 787, 792, 194 Cal. Rptr. 612 (1983) which limits damages to an amount that would place the plaintiff in as good a position as if the defendant had performed, consistent with UCC § 1-106.

where a seller who is not a "lost volume" seller has made a reasonable resale of an item, he should be relegated to his resale remedy and recover the difference between the contract and resale price rather than taking advantage of an unanticipated decline in the market price that would produce greater damages under his remedy for nonacceptance or repudiation. We have already seen a court deny the contract price/market price differential to a seller who contemplated profits amounting to less than five percent of that amount,[58] thus effectuating the purpose of UCC remedies. In furtherance of that same purpose, another court denied the seller the use of his "lost volume" measure of damages[59] and awarded damages for the difference between the contract price and market price[60] to protect the seller's reasonable expectation of profits rather than permitting the seller to recover more than three times that amount simply by choosing a different remedy.[61] The statement of the purpose of remedies under the UCC should be given the overriding effect that it has been accorded by the courts to this time.[62]

C. *Damages for Accepted Goods.*

If a buyer receives nonconforming goods, he may reject them[63] if he does so within a reasonable time.[64] If he fails to reject within a reasonable time, he has, in effect, accepted the goods, as he may no longer reject them.[65] Even if the goods are accepted, however, the buyer will be able to revoke his acceptance and return to the status of rejection if the nonconformity in the goods substantially impairs the value of the goods to the buyer, and the nonconformity was not discoverable upon a reasonable inspection or it was discovered and the buyer accepted because the seller gave assurances that he would cure the nonconformity and failed to do so.[66] If the buyer has neither rejected nor revoked his acceptance and the time has passed for the revocation so that he can no longer thrust the goods back on the seller, does he have any claim for nonconformity in the goods which he has accepted?

The buyer may have a cause of action for breach of warranty.[67] Section 2-714(1) of the Code permits the buyer to recover the loss resulting from any

---

[58] *See* Allied Canners & Packers, Inc. v. Victor Packing Co., *supra* note 36.

[59] UCC § 2-708(2).

[60] UCC § 2-708(1).

[61] *See* Nobs Chem., U.S.A., Inc. v. Koppers Co., 616 F.2d 212 (5th Cir. 1980). *See also* Madsen v. Murrey & Sons Co., 743 P.2d 1212 (Utah 1987) (failure to mitigate damages requires damages to be measured by § 2-708(1) rather than by § 2-708(2)).

[62] This is the position of Professors White and Summers, *supra* note 6, as contrasted with the position of Judge (then Professor) Peters, *supra* note 38.

[63] Unless the parties otherwise agree or the contract is an installment contract, the buyer has a right of rejection under UCC § 2-601.

[64] UCC § 2-602 specifies the manner of a rightful rejection.

[65] UCC § 2-606(1)(b) indicates that one instance of accepting goods occurs where the buyer fails to make an effective rejection. The buyer may also accept by signifying to the seller that the goods are conforming (§ 2-606(1)(a)) or doing anything with the goods that is inconsistent with the seller's ownership, i.e., acting as if he accepted the goods (§ 2-606(1)(b)).

[66] UCC § 2-608.

[67] One of the more important sections of Article 2 of the Code is § 2-607(3)(a) which requires the buyer to notify the seller of any nonconformity of accepted goods within a reasonable time after the buyer discovered or should have discovered any breach. Failure to notify bars the buyer from "any remedy."

nonconformity and § 2-714(2) measures that loss as the difference at the time and place of acceptance between the value of the goods accepted and the value they would have had if they had been as warranted.[68] The typical method of measuring this difference in value is the cost of repair.[69] If, for example, the buyer of accepted equipment discovers a defect and the seller refuses to perform its warranty obligation, the buyer may have the equipment repaired by another. The buyer had received equipment that was less valuable than it should have been. The repair, however, restored the equipment to the value it should have had if it had been as warranted. The cost of repair, therefore, is a convenient and reasonably certain measure of the difference in value. The cost of repair, however, is not the exclusive measure. In a contract for the purchase and sale of steel, for example, after receiving the steel from the seller, the buyer expended $2000 in processing before delivering it to its buyer. The steel as originally delivered by the seller had been too soft and could not be used after processing. In addition to recovering the contract price, the buyer also recovered the cost of processing though this recovery protected the reliance rather than the expectation interest.[70] Though the difference in value is the measure of damages set forth in § 2-714(2), the general directive should not be overlooked, i.e., recovery of "the loss resulting...from the seller's breach as determined in any manner which is reasonable."[71]

D. Consequential and Incidental Damages — Seller's Consequences.

In addition to direct or "general" damages recoverable under the UCC remedies already discussed, the UCC permits buyers to recover consequential damages and it also permits buyers or sellers to recover incidental damages.[72] We have seen that consequential damages are defined in terms of the basic foreseeability concept, i.e., "any loss resulting from general or particular requirements and needs of which the seller at the time of contracting had reason to know...."[73] We have also examined the use of the term "consequential" which is often equated with "special" damages though "consequential" damages may be those which any ordinary promisor would foresee at the time the contract is formed.[74] The buyer's incidental damages include a variety of expenses to care for goods which the buyer has rejected, expenses connected with reasonable efforts to cover, or other reasonable expenses caused by the seller's breach.[75] Where the buyer breaches, the seller may encounter various ex-

---

[68] See Michiana Mack, Inc. v. Allendale Rural Fire Protection Dist., 428 N.E.2d 1367 (Ind. App. 1982) (§ 2-714 applies to accepted goods where revocation of acceptance is not possible). See UCC § 2-714 comment 1.

[69] See Continental Sand & Gravel, Inc. v. K & K Sand & Gravel, Inc., 755 F.2d 87 (7th Cir. 1985); Midland Supply Co., Inc. v. Ehret Plumbing & Heating Co., 108 Ill. App. 3d 1120, 440 N.E.2d 153 (1982).

[70] Toyomenka (Am.), Inc. v. Combined Metals Corp., 139 Ill. App. 3d 654, 487 N.E.2d 1172 (1985).

[71] UCC § 2-714(1).

[72] For example, in UCC § 2-712(2) (cover), the buyer is expressly permitted to recover incidental and consequential damages. See also § 2-713(1) and § 2-714(3). The seller is expressly permitted to recover incidental damages in § 2-706(1) (resale). See also § 2-708(1) and § 2-708(2).

[73] UCC § 2-715(2)(a). See supra § 120.

[74] See supra § 120, note 77.

[75] UCC § 2-715(1).

penses in stopping delivery and transportation, as well as care and custody of any conforming goods the buyer has refused to accept.[76] A garden variety case illustrates the differences among general (direct), consequential (special), and incidental damages.

In *Carbo Industries v. Becker Chevrolet, Inc.,*[77] the defendant car dealer sold an auto to the plaintiff, a car leasing firm. The firm leased the car to a commercial client. Mechanical problems required the car to be returned to the dealer on several occasions and the defendant refused to make necessary repairs after the engine seized. The court permitted recovery of the cost of replacing the defective engine, i.e., general or direct damages, to bring the car to the value it would have had without a breach of warranty. Similarly, the damages in the amount of the monthly lease payments were allowed for the period during which the car was unusable since these payments represented "the difference between the car's value if it had functioned as warranted... and its actual value."[78] Towing charges and other expenses incurred in diagnosing the problem with the car were viewed as incidental damages. The plaintiff also presented evidence that, because of the difficulty with this car, its customer had cancelled an order for an additional vehicle. The court characterized these damages as consequential, i.e., they represented lost profit to the plaintiff. Another court permitted the recovery of car insurance expenses as well as the cost of license plates, lost wages, and interest on the purchase price of a defective automobile as incidental damages.[79] Like other courts, however, it would not permit the recovery of attorney's fees as incidental damages.[80]

The UCC sections on Seller's remedies include no provision for consequential damages. It is certainly conceivable that a seller would incur consequential damages after a breach by the purchaser in a given situation.[81] Courts, however, have declined to award "consequential" damages to sellers though it has been suggested that courts can be imaginative in characterizing certain recoverable damages as "incidental" which could have been easily called "consequential."[82] In the usual situation, however, the seller is entitled only to the contract price or any unpaid portion thereof plus incidental damages. This is viewed as complete protection of his expectation interest.

E. *Action for the Price — Specific Performance.*

We have already examined the somewhat expanded availability of specific performance for buyers under the UCC.[83] Specific performance for the seller of

---

[76] UCC § 2-710.

[77] 112 A.D.2d 336, 491 N.Y.S.2d 786 (1985).

[78] 491 N.Y.S.2d at 790.

[79] *See* Devore v. Bostrom, 632 P.2d 832 (Utah 1981).

[80] In addition to the case cited in note 78, *see* Nick's Auto Sales, Inc. v. Radcliffe Auto Sales, Inc., 591 S.W.2d 709 (Ky. App. 1979) (though the UCC definition of incidental damages, like other UCC remedies provisions, is to be liberally administered in accordance with § 1-106, § 2-715(1) does not include attorney's fees). *See also* Murray v. Holiday Rambler, Inc., 83 Wis. 2d 406, 265 N.W.2d 513 (1978).

[81] The buyer may know at the moment of formation that his breach would cause lost profits to the seller well beyond the lost profits on the particular contract with the buyer.

[82] White & Summers, *supra* note 6, at 338-40.

[83] *See* § 127(B)(2)(a).

goods is the buyer's payment of the contract price. The Code expressly permits the seller to bring an action for the price plus any incidental damages under certain circumstances.[84] It may sound like a truism to suggest that where the buyer *accepts* goods delivered by the seller, the buyer should pay for the goods. In prior discussions, we have seen that acceptance of goods under the Code can occur in any one of three essential ways:[85] (1) the buyer's signification that he accepts the goods;[86] (2) the buyer's failure to make an effective rejection of the goods;[87] and (3) the buyer's use of the goods inconsistent with the ownership of the seller.[88] Of these, only (2) causes any analytical difficulty in terms of buyer's acceptance giving rise to the seller's action for the price.

A buyer may effectively reject goods though the rejection is substantively wrongful, i.e., a buyer may comply with all of the necessary requirements for an effective rejection,[89] but may have no substantive basis for that rejection. For example, a buyer may mistakenly believe that the goods are nonconforming and reject them. Even though the rejection is substantively wrongful, it should be clear that the rejection is effective to deny the seller his price remedy, i.e., the buyer has not yet "accepted."[90] Whether a buyer who has accepted but wrongfully revokes his acceptance has still "accepted" so as to allow the seller his action for the price is unclear. The better view is that such a wrongful revocation does not affect the former acceptance so that the action for the price should lie.[91]

Where conforming goods have not been accepted but have been lost or damaged within a commercially reasonable time after their risk of loss has passed to the buyer, the seller may bring his action for the price.[92] For example, risk of loss will pass to the buyer in an FOB "shipment" contract upon delivery of the goods to an independent carrier. If the goods are damaged or destroyed in transit, or misdelivered, the buyer must pay the contract price since the risk of loss was on the buyer.[93]

The last situation which allows the seller to have an action for the price occurs where the goods have been identified[94] to the contract for shipment to the buyer and the seller is, after a reasonable effort, unable to resell them at a

---

[84] UCC § 2-709.

[85] UCC § 2-606.

[86] *See* Lupofresh, Inc. v. Pabst Brewing Co., 505 A.2d 37 (Del. App. 1985) (buyer wrote sellers that it had accepted the goods thereby giving rise to seller's action for the price under § 2-709).

[87] *See* Unlaub Co. v. Sexton, 568 F.2d 72 (8th Cir. 1977) (failure to make effective rejection constituted acceptance permitting seller to recover price). *See also* Akron Brick & Block Co. v. Moniz Eng'g Co., 310 N.E.2d 128 (Mass. 1974) (failure to reject within a reasonable time or to revoke acceptance constituted acceptance permitting seller to recover unpaid portion of contract price).

[88] *See* Dehahn v. Innes, 356 A.2d 711 (Me. 1976) (whether there is an acceptance through acts of the buyer inconsistent with seller's ownership is a question of fact).

[89] UCC § 2-602.

[90] *See* Peters, *supra* note 38 at 241. *See also* White & Summers, *supra* note 6, at 295. *See,* however, Ninth Street East, Ltd. v. Harrison, 5 Conn. Cir. 597, 259 A.2d 772 (1968).

[91] This is the considered view of White & Summers, *supra* note 6, at 296-97. *See* Lupofresh, Inc. v. Pabst Brewing Co., *supra* note 86, where, in note 3, the court opines that goods are no longer accepted where there is a "justified" revocation of acceptance.

[92] UCC § 2-709(2)(b).

[93] *See* Montana Seeds, Inc. v. Holliday, 582 P.2d 1223 (Mont. 1978).

[94] *See* UCC § 2-501. *See also* Great Western Sugar Co. v. Pennant Prods., Inc., 748 P.2d 1359 (Colo. App. 1987) (identification where the goods are fungible).

reasonable price or it is clear that such a resale effort would be fruitless.[95] The typical example occurs with respect to specially manufactured goods that are not resalable to others.

The underlying philosophy of the seller's action for the price is that only the foregoing situations make that remedy necessary. Typically, the seller can resell goods which the buyer refuses to accept and the seller is in a better position than the buyer to resell. To force the sale on the buyer so that he can resell them makes no economic sense since the buyer typically has no experience in selling such goods. The seller's expectation interest can be protected through other UCC remedies. If, however, the buyer has accepted the goods, there is no justification for the buyer's refusal to pay the contract price. Nor is there any justification for refusal to pay the price where the goods were destroyed when the risk was on the buyer because the seller has no goods to resell. If the goods were damaged when the risk was on the buyer, the seller should not be placed in the business of selling damaged goods. If the goods were custom-made for the buyer, the seller should not be asked to resell such goods if others buyers do not want them.

---

[95] UCC § 2-709(1)(b). As to the fruitlessness of resale, see Great Western Sugar Co. v. Pennant Prods., Inc., *supra* note 94 (price of sugar had declined drastically and plaintiff continuously held excess amounts of sugar in its inventory).

Chapter 10

CONTRACT BENEFICIARIES

§ 129. Third Party Beneficiary Contracts.

A. *Nature and History.*

In this chapter we will consider what rights, if any, accrue to a third person who will receive a benefit if the contract is performed, when that person is neither a promisor nor promisee of the contract. The English courts, by an almost unbroken line of decisions, quite consistently adhered to the view that such a person has no enforceable rights.[1] The question is, where *A* makes a

---

[1] *See* Vandepitte v. Preferred Acc. Ins. Corp., A.C. 70 [1933]; Tweedle v. Atkinson, 1. B. & S. 393 [1861]; Bourne v. Mason, 1 Ventirs 6 [1669].

promise induced by *B* that *A* will render a stated performance to *C*, may *C* enforce *A*'s promise?

The reasons which led the English courts to reach the conclusion that such a person has no enforceable rights have been stated in a leading English case as follows:

> My Lords, in the law of England certain principles are fundamental. One is that only a person who is a party to a contract can sue on it. Our law knows nothing of a jus quaesitum tertio arising by way of contract. Such a right may be conferred by way of property, as, for example, under a trust, but it cannot be conferred on a stranger to a contract as a right to enforce the contract in personam. A second principle is that if a person with whom a contract not under seal has been made is to be able to enforce it consideration must have been given by him to the promisor or to some other person at the promisor's request. These two principles are not recognized in the same fashion by the jurisprudence of certain Continental countries or of Scotland, but here they are well established. A third proposition is that a principal not named in the contract may sue upon it if the promisee really contracted as his agent. But again, in order to entitle him to sue, he must have given consideration either personally or through the promisee, acting as his agent giving it.[2]

This view assumes that the third person is not a "party" to the contract. The same thought was often expressed by the statement that the third person was not in "privity" and, therefore, could not have an action on the contract. The term "privity," at least as used in this sense (and probably in any other sense), is meaningless.[3] It suggests that the third person is not one of the parties who "made" the contract, i.e., that such a person is neither promisor nor promisee. Why a person who is neither promisor nor promisee may not be a party to the contract (or be in "privity") is never explained. As typically used, the lack of privity in a third person is merely a conclusion, though it is stated as the reason for refusing to allow the third person to bring an action on the contract. Since they are analytically unsound, it may well be doubted whether the fundamental assumptions of the English common law in this area adequately protect and secure the legitimate interests involved in the transactions whose legal effect is controlled by them. While undoubtedly there are serious difficulties in determining when one should have rights and how they should be sanctioned under a contract to which he is neither promisor nor promisee and for which he may have paid nothing, it seems clear that a mature legal system of law should be able to overcome those difficulties and create a design to react effectively to these problems. Such a design would not only avoid unnecessary litigation, but at the same time would be consistent with the manifest intention of the parties who made the contract with the idea of benefiting the third party.

In general, there are two situations in which the problem arises: (1) those in which *A* makes a promise to *B* for a consideration furnished by *B* to render a

---

[2] Lord Haldane in Dunlop Pneumatic Tyre Co. v. Selfridge & Co., A.C. 847, 853 [1915].

[3] One of the better judicial statements concerning "privity" is that of Justice Stone in La Mourea v. Rhude, 209 Minn. 53, 295 N.W. 304, 307 (1940): "Privity in the law of contracts, is merely the name for a legal relation arising from right and obligation.... To affirm one's right under a contract is therefore to affirm his privity with the party liable to him."

performance to C which is intended to discharge a legal obligation then owing by B to C, and (2) those in which A makes a promise to B for a consideration furnished by B to render a performance to C as a gift to C or which, at any rate, will not operate to discharge any legal obligation then owing by B to C. In the first type of case, C is traditionally called a "creditor" beneficiary because he had a prior legal relationship with B, e.g., B was C's debtor and the debt is satisfied if A performs his promise for the benefit of C.[4] In the second type of case, he is traditionally called a "donee beneficiary" because the performance by A will confer a gift on C.[5] Unless such beneficiaries have rights under the contract, the intentions of the parties will be defeated. This is particularly true in the case of a donee beneficiary. The creditor beneficiary always has an action against the promisee on the obligation owed to him by the promisee, and, if the promisee proves to be execution proof, the beneficiary can presumably subject the right of the promisee against the promisor on the contract between them to the satisfaction of the judgment which he has obtained, in an appropriate creditor's proceedings, subject, however, to the possibility that other creditors of the promisee may intervene and claim a share of the proceeds. On the other hand, if the donee beneficiary has no enforceable right on the contract itself, he has no redress whatever. Moreover, the promisor would escape performance of his promise altogether since the promisee suffers no loss because of his nonperformance. Unless the beneficiary is given a direct right of action on the contract, unnecessary litigation will frequently be the inevitable result. In view of these facts, and taking into account the conclusory rationale for the rule of the English courts, it is not strange that inroads should have been made upon that rule. The rule has been almost universally abandoned in this country, and its effects have been nullified, at least in some cases, in England by a line of decisions purporting to proceed on generally accepted equitable principles. These matters will be discussed in the sections which follow.

Before we consider these and related questions, however, we should distinguish cases where a contract between the parties gives rise to what the law views as a "property right" in a third person, as distinguished from a contract right. It is generally agreed that a third person may become the legal or equitable owner of property as the result of a contract to which he is not a party and for which he furnished no consideration. This occurs when one person, by agreement with another, holds specific property either as bailee or as trustee for a third person. In these cases the right of the third person springs out of the fact that he has acquired ownership, either legal or equitable, of the property in question. Such a right is capable of being vindicated in appropriate proceedings regardless of the law relating to contract beneficiaries. It is only in the cases in which no property right in the third person results from the transaction that the problem becomes acute. In such a case, unless the beneficiary has a right *in personam* on the promise made for his benefit, he may be without redress. It is also well settled that if a contracting party is in fact acting as agent for a principal when he makes an informal

---

[4] *See* FIRST RESTATEMENT § 133(1)(b).
[5] *See* FIRST RESTATEMENT § 133(1)(a).

contract with another, the principal may enforce the promise just as if it had been made directly with him as the promisee. In that situation, the fact of agency must be established before the third person can establish a claim as principal.

B. *English Law.*

While the English courts have consistently held that a mere contract beneficiary has no enforceable rights, they have on occasion mitigated the effects of this rule by the use of a fiction. In some cases where A had made a promise to B to render a performance to C, they have apparently assumed that what the parties had in mind was that A should render the performance to B as trustee for C.[6] On this view of the facts, C becomes the beneficiary of a trust, and as such, does have rights that are indirectly enforceable. B, who is a party to the contract, and who furnished the consideration, can enforce the contract to the full extent, but as a mere trustee of the right, he holds the proceeds of any recovery in trust for C. Moreover, if B should fail to enforce the obligation, C, as the beneficiary of a trust, is entitled to bring a suit to which B will be made a party, to compel A to perform his undertaking. The difficulty with this approach to the problem is that it is unrealistic because it requires a perversion of the facts. As might be expected, the English courts have not always been consistent in the application of this theory but have applied it only in a few of the more urgent cases.[7] A nineteenth century English statute, the Married Women's Property Act,[8] protected a wife, husband, or child named as beneficiary in a policy of life insurance as the party entitled to the proceeds of the policy. Yet, such a beneficiary could not sue for them directly.

C. *American Law.*

Although there were some early cases in Massachusetts[9] based upon dicta found in early English cases which held that a third person might have a direct right of action at law on a contract to which he was not a party and for which he had not furnished any part of the consideration, these cases were overruled when it became clear that English law did not countenance such a view.[10] It remained for New York, in the leading case of *Lawrence v. Fox,*[11] finally to break the tradition and to start a movement which has since spread throughout the country such that it has become the rule in all of the states, that a beneficiary does have rights, in a proper case, which he can enforce directly, just as if he were a promisee.

In that famous case, Holly (A) loaned $300 to Fox (B) and told Fox that Holly owed that amount to Lawrence (C). In repayment of the loan, Fox agreed to pay the $300 to Lawrence. Fox did not perform his promise and

---

[6] *See, e.g.,* Les Affreuteurs Reunia Societe v. Walford, 2 K.B. 498 [1918], X. 801 [1919].

[7] The English cases decided prior to 1930 are collected and discussed in Corbin, *Contracts for the Benefit of Third Persons,* 46 LAW Q. REV. 12 (1930).

[8] 45 & 46 Vict., ch. 75 § 11 [1882]. There are other statutory exceptions in England.

[9] *See* Brewer v. Dyaer, 61 Mass. 97 Cush. 337 (1851).

[10] *See* Marston v. Bigelow, 150 Mass. 45, 22 N.E. 71 (1889); Exchange Bank v. Rice, 107 Mass. 37, 9 Am. Rep. 1 (1871).

[11] 220 N.Y. 268 (1859).

Lawrence brought an action on the contract against Fox. Thus, the court was squarely confronted with the question, where *A* provides consideration to induce *B* to promise to perform for the benefit of *C*, may *C*, though neither promisor nor promisee, recover on the contract? Fox argued that no consideration had moved from Lawrence to Fox and there was no "privity" between Lawrence and Fox, i.e., Lawrence was not a party to the contract. The jury found for Lawrence and Fox appealed to the superior court which affirmed the judgment. An appeal was then taken to the highest court of New York, the New York Court of Appeals, which found a basic principle announced as early as 1806: where one person makes a promise to another for the benefit of a third person, the third person may maintain an action to enforce that promise. The court recognized that much of the precedent announcing this principle had involved trusts where the trustee has a duty to pay the beneficiary of a trust. Two concurring judges[12] insisted the promise to Fox was really the promise of Holly made through the medium of an agent, and the decision could be justified by perverting the facts so that they fit within a familiar doctrinal category.[13] The court, however, insisted that the principle had been applied to trust and other cases not because it was relegated to such cases. Rather, it was a basic principle of law that could be applied to trust cases and other cases including a case such as the one before the court, i.e., a third party beneficiary contract. It was the court's insistence in recognizing the basic principle to be applied regardless of the form in which it arises that has made *Lawrence v. Fox* a landmark opinion.

Lawrence v. Fox was not an immediate success throughout the country due, in no small part, to subsequent New York courts that soon began to limit the application of the broad principle. While *Lawrence v. Fox* involved a creditor beneficiary, the court had made no point of this fact. Again, it simply took the broad view that whenever *A* makes a promise to *B* to render a performance to *C*, the law supplies any "privity" that may be deemed essential and *C* can maintain an action on the promise. Eighteen years later, however, in the case of *Vrooman v. Turner*,[14] a New York court held that the rule of *Lawrence v. Fox* must be limited in its application to its holding. Consequently, a beneficiary could have no right of action unless the promise was made for his benefit and there was a legal duty or obligation of the promisee owed to him which could act as a substitute for the privity deemed necessary to give one a right of action on a contract. So stated, the rule obviously was limited in its application to the protection of creditor beneficiaries exclusively. The New York courts have been struggling to free themselves from this absurd limitation ever since. The first inroad was made by a court taking the position that a moral obligation owed by the promisee to the beneficiary, such as the moral duty owed by a husband-promisee to make provision for his wife, is a substitute for the legal obligation and supplies the connecting link demanded by the holding in *Vrooman v. Turner*.[15] There have been intimations that New York

---

[12]Johnson, C. J., and Denio, J.

[13]As to the law of trusts and agency as they apply to the protection of third parties, *see* RESTATEMENT 2d § 302 comment f.

[14]69 N.Y. 280 (1877).

[15]Buchanan v. Tilden, 1158 N.Y. 109, 52 N.E. 724 (1899). Here, the court relied heavily upon a seventeenth century English case, Dutton v. Poole, 2 Lev. 210 [1677], where the defendant prom-

courts are ready to abandon the shackles of *Vrooman* though more recent retrogressions suggest that New York still awaits the repudiation of that historic limitation.[16]

Largely as a result of this vacillation in New York, cases in other jurisdictions appeared to limit the right of recovery to a creditor beneficiary or one deemed to be in an analogous position.[17] Paradoxically, courts in Pennsylvania had allowed only donee beneficiaries to recover.[18] Except for the confused situation in New York, however, there is no longer any doubt that other jurisdictions will recognize a cause of action in either creditor or donee beneficiaries. Massachusetts had the distinction of refusing to recognize a right in either creditor or donee beneficiaries. Finally, in 1979, Massachusetts overcame more than 125 years of precedent in recognizing the right of a third party beneficiary.[19] Statutes in some jurisdictions recognize such rights.[20]

---

ised his father for a consideration paid by the father to pay the plaintiff, his sister, a sum of money. The court held the sister was entitled to enforce the promise on the ground that her close relationship to the parties to the contract satisfied the requirement of privity to the promise and the consideration. The case, however, was later disapproved in Tweedle v. Atkinson, *supra* note 1.

[16]Encouraging language is found in Seaver v. Ransom, 224 N.Y. 233, 240 120 N.E. 639, 641 (1918): "The doctrine of *Lawrence v. Fox* is progressive not retrograde. The course of the late decisions is to enlarge, not to limit the effect of that case." *See also* Lait v. Leon, 50 Misc. 2d 60, 242 N.Y.S.2d 776 (1963) suggesting that, if there is any requirement of duty from the promisee to the third party (i.e., if there is any requirement that only third party *creditor* beneficiaries may recover), the requirement is nebulous. *See,* however, Scheidl v. Universal Aviation Equip., Inc., 159 N.Y.S.2d 278 (S. Ct. 1957) where the court held that a third party beneficiary could not recover because (1) he had not parted with any consideration in exchange for defendant's promise, and (2) no obligation existed between the promisee and the third party. *See also* Walker v. Phinney, 120 Misc. 2d 513, 466 N.Y.S.2d 227 (1983) suggesting the continued viability of *Vrooman v. Turner.*

[17]*See, e.g.,* West v. Norcross, 190 Ark. 667, 80 S.W.2d 67 (1935) (sharecropper held to be without remedy on a contract made for his benefit between his landlord and the United States). Arkansas, however, has rejected that concept. *See* Coley v. Englis, 235 Ark. 215, 357 S.W.2d 529 (1962). Minnesota long adhered to the view that only creditor beneficiaries could recover. It repudiated that view, however, in La Mourea v. Rhude, 209 Minn. 53, 295 N.W. 304 (1940). Courts of equity arrived at a similar conclusion through the equitable doctrine of subrogation, i.e., where a surety discharges the obligation for which the principal debtor is primarily liable, he has a right to be substituted for the creditor with respect to securities or other obligations that were available to the creditor for collection of his claim. By analogy, this doctrine was extended to give an unpaid creditor a claim against any securities the principal debtor had given his surety for the surety's indemnification. *See* Jennings, *A Creditor's Rights in Securities Held by His Surety,* 22 MINN. L. REV. 316 (1938). Following this analogy to its logical conclusion, equity courts have said that the creditor beneficiary is in the position of such a creditor, i.e., by promising to pay the promisee's debt the promisor has become the principal debtor and the promisee has become a surety. Thus, the argument goes, the doctrine of subrogation gives the creditor beneficiary the right to be substituted for the promisee-surety and he can enforce the promise pursuant to the right of the promisee. *See* Kelley v. Ashford, 133 U.S. 610 (1890). If this is the foundation of the beneficiary's right, it obviously provides no support for a donee beneficiary. Professor Corbin was critical of the view that the doctrine of subrogation is properly applicable to the case of a creditor beneficiary. Corbin, *Contracts for the Benefit of Third Persons,* 27 YALE L.J. 1008, 1015-16 (1918). *See also* Langmaid, *Contracts for the Benefit of Third Persons in California,* 27 CALIF. L. REV. 497, 499 (1939).

[18]*See* Greene County v. Southern Sur. Co., 292 Pa. 304, 141 A. 27 (1927). The Pennsylvania situation was confused for a long time. *See* Corbin, *The Law of Third Party Beneficiaries in Pennsylvania,* 77 U. PA. L. REV. 594 (1928). By 1957, however, it was clear that creditor beneficiaries could recover in Pennsylvania. *See* Burke v. North Huntingdon Twp. Mun. Auth., 390 Pa. 588, 136 A.2d 310, 314 (1957) : "That a third party, not in privity to the original contract, may sue as a creditor beneficiary is now the rule in Pennsylvania [citing cases]."

[19]Choate, Hall & Stewart v. SCA Serv., 378 Mass. 535, 392 N.E.2d 1045 (1979), *on remand,* 22 Mass. App. 522, 495 N.E.2d 562 (1986).

[20]*See, e.g.,* CAL. CIV. CODE § 1559.

§ 130. Protected Versus Incidental Beneficiaries — Restatements.

A. *The Problem of Separating Protected From Unprotected Beneficiaries.*

One of the most troublesome problems courts have encountered is deciding who shall be considered a protected beneficiary. Contracts often benefit third parties who were not consciously considered, much less intended, beneficiaries of those contracts. If parties agree to construct a new shopping mall, nearby business establishments may be benefited by that contract. Consumers would be benefited at least in terms of the convenience of not having to travel to more distant shopping centers. Should all of these "beneficiaries" and numerous others who might benefit from this contract be viewed as "protected" beneficiaries, i.e., parties who have a cause of action if the contract to build the new mall is breached? It is clear that not everyone who would receive a benefit, were the promise performed, should be given rights.[21] So broad a test would open the door far too widely and would often subject a promisor to a liability for which there was no justification. It was imperative to devise appropriate tests to draw the line between "protected" beneficiaries who would have a cause of action and "incidental" beneficiaries who would benefit to some extent from the performance of the contract, but should not be viewed as parties who had a right to enforce that contract. It is important to consider these tests.

B. *The Restatements Compared.*

1. First Restatement — Interdependent Contractors.

The First Restatement of Contracts attempted to deal with the problem by setting forth two categories of protected beneficiaries, i.e., those who had rights under the contract between the promisor and promisee, and one category of unprotected beneficiaries, i.e., those who had no such rights. The first protected category was the "donee" beneficiary,[22] where the purpose of the promisee was to make a gift to the beneficiary or to confer a right upon him against the promisor. The second protected category was the "creditor" beneficiary,[23] where the purpose of the promisee was to satisfy an actual, supposed, or asserted duty of the promisee to the beneficiary. The third and unprotected category, called "incidental" beneficiaries,[24] dealt with all others, i.e., those beneficiaries who simply did not fit within either of the protected categories. Under this First Restatement rubric, therefore, courts only had to consider the purpose of the promisee. If the purpose of the promisee in making the contract was to benefit the third party, either in terms of satisfying an actual or supposed obligation to that party, the third party had a right under the contract as a creditor beneficiary. If the purpose of the promisee was to confer a gift upon the third party, the third party was a protected donee beneficiary.

---

[21] *See* Restatement 2d § 302 ill. 13 where *B* and *A* agree to construct an expensive building on *A*'s land which would benefit *C*, an adjoining landowner. *C* is an incidental beneficiary.

[22] First Restatement § 133(1)(a) and ills. 1-4.

[23] First Restatement § 133(1)(b) and ills. 5-10.

[24] First Restatement § 133(1)(c) and ills. 11 and 12.

If neither purpose was manifested by the promisee, the third party was necessarily an incidental beneficiary. These watertight compartments suggested a high degree of certainty. Unfortunately, their procrustean nature did not allow for cases involving intended beneficiaries who could not be squeezed into either compartment. Consider, for example, a construction project where the owner makes contracts with two prime contractors, each responsible for separate portions of the work. The delay of one contractor causes delays by the second contractor who suffers losses because of these delays. The second contractor brings an action as a third party beneficiary of the contract between the first contractor and the owner under circumstances where all of the parties were aware of the interdependent nature of the work and the second contractor agreed to perform at a contract price on the assumption that the first contractor's work would be completed on time. In such a case, a court held that the second contractor could recover as a third party beneficiary though, had the court applied the FIRST RESTATEMENT analysis, he would not fit easily within either of the protected categories.[25] Other situations can easily be envisioned. The promisor A may be induced to make a promise to B who desires a particular performance to third party C not because B intends to make a gift to C (B may dislike C intensely)[26] or because B has any actual or supposed obligation to C, but because A's performance to C will benefit B with respect to another transaction. C is neither a donee nor creditor beneficiary though B made the contract with A for the express benefit of C. B intended to confer a right upon C against A. Even though B's *motive or purpose* was not to satisfy an actual or supposed obligation to C or to make a gift to C, B *intended* C to be a third party beneficiary of the contract.[27]

2. Intention of Promisee or Both Parties.

Courts were not always ready to accept the FIRST RESTATEMENT concept in other ways. For example, while some courts accepted the view that the intention of the promisee controlled the question of intention to benefit,[28] other courts insisted that *both* parties must intend the benefit to the third party.[29] There would appear to be no justification for insisting that both parties intend to benefit the third party. If B exacts A's promise to perform for the benefit of

---

[25] *See* Moore Constr. Co. v. Clarksville Dep't of Elec., 707 S.W.2d 1 (Tenn. App. 1986) where the court suggests that the FIRST RESTATEMENT categories were too procrustean (citing cases). For another case holding that a second prime contractor can recover as a third party beneficiary, *see* Broadway Main. Corp. v. Rutgers, 90 N.J. 253, 447 A.2d 906, 910 (1982). The *Moore* opinion recognizes a split of authority on this question and cites cases *contra*.

[26] The promisee need not have an altruistic motivation. *See* Vikingstad v. Baggott, 46 Wash. 2d 494, 282 P.2d 824 (1955).

[27] The distinction between motive or purpose and intention in a third party beneficiary context is set forth in Hamill v. Maryland Cas. Co., 209 F.2d 336 (10th Cir. 1954) (party agrees with contractor to advance portions of contract price to contractor to stabilize contractor's financial condition. Issuer of payment bond recovers as third party beneficiary). *See also* Vikingstad v. Baggott, 46 Wash. 2d 494, 282 P.2d 824, 826 (1955) (intent of promisee to confer a benefit upon third party is relevant; promisee's motive is immaterial).

[28] *See* Hamill v. Maryland Cas. Co., *supra* note 27; McCulloch v. Canadian Pac. Ry., 53 F. Supp. 534 (D. Minn. 1943).

[29] *See* Silverman v. Food Fair Stores, Inc., 407 Pa. 507, 180 A.2d 894 (1962); Colonial Discount Co. v. Avon Motors, 137 Conn. 196, 75 A.2d 507 (1950); Ridder v. Blethen, 24 Wash. 2d 552, 166 P.2d 834 (1946).

C, A does not intend to benefit C; he intends to benefit himself through the consideration received from B. The promisee, B, however, intends either to benefit himself or C, the third party. If B intends to benefit the third party, C should be a protected beneficiary.[30]

3. Tests in Lieu of FIRST RESTATEMENT Test — "Direct Obligation," "Direct Benefit" and "Main Purpose" Tests.

Dissatisfaction with the FIRST RESTATEMENT test led courts to create other tests to separate protected and unprotected beneficiaries. If the final test under the FIRST RESTATEMENT was whether a third party was a donee, creditor, or incidental beneficiary, the final test for some courts was whether the parties intended that the promisor assume a *direct obligation* to the third party,[31] or, similarly, whether the promisee intended to confer upon that party a right to enforce the contract against the promisor.[32] The utility of such a test may well be doubted since "direct obligation" is too uncertain. The parties rarely consider the fact that they are creating legal rights and duties. They simply expect their respective promises to be performed.

Another test found in some cases[33] may be called the "direct benefit" test: if the promisor has promised to render a performance directly to or for the third party, it is for his benefit and he may enforce it. If, however, the benefit is indirect, springing from a performance rendered to the promisee, the third party is a mere incidental beneficiary with no rights. This test is very narrow since it excludes third parties who are intended to be the ultimate beneficiaries of the promisor's performance although that performance will be rendered directly to or for the promisee.

Consider, for example, a case where third parties were damaged by the negligence of an attorney in drafting a will. The promisee (testator) intended to benefit certain legatees by entering a contract with his attorney to achieve that goal. The promisor (attorney) failed to perform his duty so as to effectuate

---

[30] The question of whether courts should focus upon the intention of the promisee, alone, rather than the mutual intention of the promisor and promisee in relation to the third party appears to have been resolved. Under the RESTATEMENT 2d formulation to be discussed *infra*, the intention of the promisee is said to be controlling. *See* RESTATEMENT 2d § 302(1)(b)and Midwest Dredging Co. v. Iowa State Dep't of Transp., 424 N.W.2d 216 (Iowa 1988) where the court adopted the RESTATEMENT 2d analysis. Pennsylvania had been a conspicuous dissenter from this view. *See* Spires v. Hanover Fire Ins. Co., 364 Pa. 52, 70 A.2d 828 (1950) and Silverman v. Food Fair Stores, Inc., *supra* note 29. Pennsylvania, however, adopted the RESTATEMENT 2d analysis in Guy v. Liederbach, 501 Pa. 47, 459 A.2d 744 (1983) where the opinion by Hutchinson, J. clearly suggests the analysis set forth herein, i.e., that the promisor does not intend to benefit the third party. Yet, in Commonwealth v. Celli-Flynn & Assoc., 115 Pa. Commw. 494, 540 A.2d 1365 (1988), the court insists that both promisor and promisee must intend to benefit the third party. The court, however, relies upon *Spires* which had been rejected in *Guy* with respect to the requirement that both parties intend to benefit the third party. Again, the RESTATEMENT 2d analysis was adopted in *Guy* which, again, rejects the *Spires* requirement.

[31] Colonial Discount Co. v. Avon Motors, Inc., 137 Conn. 196, 75 A.2d 507 (1950). Robins Dry Dock & Repair Co. v. Flint, 275 U.S. 303 (1927); Montgomery v. Spencer, 15 Utah 495, 50 P. 623 (1897).

[32] Vikingstad v. Baggott, *supra* note 26.

[33] *See* Fidelity & Deposit Co. v. Rainer, 220 Ala. 262, 125 So. 55 (1929). *See also* Carson, Pirie Scott & Co. v. Parrett, 346 Ill. 252, 178 N.E. 498 (1931). This test was prescribed in Mich. Comp. Laws § 600.1405. Discussion is found in Langmaid, *Contracts For the Benefit of Third Persons in California,* 27 CALIF. L. REV. 497, 505 (1939); Note, 6 U. CHI. L. REV. 473 (1939).

that intention at all or in part. The attorney's performance, however, ran directly to or for the promisee though the *main purpose* of the promisee was to benefit the third parties. Under a test that requires the performance to be rendered directly to third parties, these parties would be incidental beneficiaries. In *Lucas v. Hamm*,[34] the court stated, "It is true that under a contract for the benefit of a third person performance is usually to be rendered directly to the beneficiary, but this is not necessary." Rather, where the main purpose of the promisee is to exact the performance from the promisor for the benefit of the third party, the third party has the right to enforce the promisor's duty regardless of whether that performance was to run directly to the third party.[35] Though broad, this test suggests that courts should effectuate the intention of the promisee if it is clear that the promisee's main intention[36] was to benefit the third party, unhampered by the categorization of the beneficiary or by the fact that, in order to effectuate that intention, the promisor's performance may be rendered directly to the promisee. With proper judicial restraint in the interpretation of the promisee's intention, the test appears sound.

4. RESTATEMENT 2d Test — The Radical Change.

To determine whether a party is an intended beneficiary, the RESTATEMENT 2d appears to merge the FIRST RESTATEMENT categories with a Corbin perspective (which is not remarkable since Professor Corbin has had overriding influence in the new RESTATEMENT drafts). Corbin observed that thousands of cases involving third party beneficiary recovery demonstrate "that refusal of remedy would have been out of harmony with generally prevailing ideas of justice and convenience...."[37] Pursuing this thought as well as numerous cases (regardless of the test employed) that suggested intention to benefit as the threshold question, the first condition which must be met by a party who seeks to be included in the RESTATEMENT 2d "intended" and, therefore, protected beneficiary category is that "recognition of a right to performance in the beneficiary is appropriate to effectuate the intention of the parties."[38]

---

[34] 56 Cal. 2d 583, 15 Cal. Rptr. 821, 364 P.2d 685, 688 (1961). Reaffirmed by the California Supreme Court in Heyer v. Glaig, 70 Cal. 2d 223, 74 Cal. Rptr. 225, 449 P.2d 161 (1969).

[35] A number of courts have followed Lucas v. Hamm, *supra* note 34, with respect to intended beneficiaries of wills. *See, e.g.,* Ogle v. Fuiten, 102 Ill. 2d 356, 466 N.E.2d 224, 227 (1984); Auric v. Continental Cas. Co., 111 Wis. 2d 507, 331 N.W.2d 325, 329 (1983); Needham v. Hamilton, 459 A.2d 1060, 1062 (D.C. 1983); Stowe v. Smith, 184 Conn. 194, 441 A.2d 81, 83 (1981); Jaramillo v. Hood, 93 N.M. 433, 601 P.2d 66, 67 (1979); McAbee v. Edwards, 340 So. 2d 1167, 1170 (Fla. App. 1976). Pennsylvania views *Lucas v. Hamm* as stating too broad a rule though it allows a narrow exception for third parties who have been deprived of their legacies through the negligence of attorneys. *See* Guy v. Liederbach, *supra* note 30. Texas recognizes the trend but has recently declined to break from the Texas privity rule. Berry v. Dodson, Nunley & Taylor, P.C., 717 S.W.2d 716 (1986). In general, *see* Annotations, 61 A.L.R.4th 464 (1988) and 61 A.L.R.4th 615 (1988).

[36] The intention need not be the exclusive intention. In a creditor beneficiary situation, for example, it is clear that the promisee intends to benefit himself as well as the third party creditor beneficiary. When the promisor performs, the creditor beneficiary's claim against the promisee will be satisfied, thereby benefiting the promisee. *See* Visintine & Co. v. New York, C. & S.L.R.R., 169 Ohio St. 505, 160 N.E.2d 311 (1959). The beneficiaries' motives may be mixed. Again, the distinction between motive and intent is important. *See supra* note 27.

[37] 4 CORBIN ON CONTRACTS § 772 at 2.

[38] RESTATEMENT 2d § 302(1).

That condition met, either of two additional requirements must be established: (1) performance by the promisor will satisfy an obligation of the promisee to pay money to the beneficiary; or (2) under the circumstances, the promisee intended to give the beneficiary the benefit of the promised performance.[39] Certainly, category (1) is very similar to the old RESTATEMENT "creditor" category and category (2) is very similar to the old RESTATEMENT "donee" category. Yet, the RESTATEMENT 2d insists that the terms "donee" and "creditor" not be used because "they carry overtones of obsolete doctrinal difficulties."[40] Some wondered whether the "new diction" was beneficial.[41]

Considering only the "black letter" of the RESTATEMENT 2d analysis, the changes are disconcerting. As to the "creditor" category, the FIRST RESTATEMENT would include beneficiaries to whom the promisee owed an actual, supposed, or asserted duty.[42] The RESTATEMENT 2d narrows that category by requiring the performance by the promisor to satisfy "an obligation of the promisee to pay money to the beneficiary."[43] A comment explains that, if the promisee's obligation is easily liquidated, it falls within this category, but less liquid obligations would be dealt with under the "gift" category.[44] This is a curious change since a promisee who seeks to benefit a third party as well as himself by discharging an unliquidated obligation to that third party certainly does not intend to make a gift. Apparently, the RESTATEMENT 2d was concerned that only third parties to whom the promisee was under a duty would be included, and to effectuate that purpose, chose to include only manifestations of duty that were clear and certain.[45] Where the duty is actual though unliquidated, the third party will now be classified in the "gift" category. A fortiori, where the duty is only supposed or asserted, or where there is no actual, supposed, or asserted duty, the intended beneficiary will be placed in the "gift" category. The expansion of the "gift" category may be seen as an effort to avoid precise delineation as to where a particular third party should be categorized because the overriding concern is to recognize the right to performance in the third party where that would be *appropriate* to effectuate the intention of the parties.[46]

The lack of clarity in the RESTATEMENT 2d formulation is exacerbated by a comment that suggests a protected category beyond the "creditor" and "gift"

---

[39] A comparison of the two RESTATEMENTS in relation to third party beneficiaries is found in Edward M. Johnson & Assoc. v. Johnson, 845 F.2d 1395 (6th Cir. 1988).

[40] RESTATEMENT 2d, Introductory Note to Chapter 14 (starting at § 302), Contract Beneficiaries.

[41] In a casebook co-authored by the Chief Reporter of the RESTATEMENT 2d after the appearance of the tentative draft on third party beneficiaries, the following statement appears: "It is not altogether clear what is gained by the new diction." E. FARNSWORTH, W. YOUNG & H. JONES, CASES AND MATERIALS ON CONTRACTS 882 (2d ed. 1972). By 1982, however, Professor Farnsworth suggested, "Despite the surprising similarity between these descriptions and the discarded categories of donee and creditor beneficiaries, there are some significant differences." E. FARNSWORTH, CONTRACTS § 10.3 at 717.

[42] FIRST RESTATEMENT § 133(1)(b).

[43] RESTATEMENT 2d § 302(1)(b).

[44] RESTATEMENT 2d § 302 comment b. An example of an easily convertible obligation would be an obligation to deliver commodities or securities actively traded in organized market. A "less liquid" obligation would be a duty that would have to be litigated to determine its value.

[45] RESTATEMENT 2d § 302 comment b suggests that, "there is no suretyship if the promisee has never been under any duty to the beneficiary. Hence, such cases are not covered by § (1)(a).

[46] RESTATEMENT 2d § 302(1).

categories. The comment explains, a promise to pay a debt or make a gift to the beneficiary makes "reliance by the beneficiary both reasonable and probable."[47] "Similar" cases such as "a promise to perform a supposed or asserted duty of the promisee, a promise to discharge a lien on the promisee's property, or a promise to satisfy the duty of a third person" would include the third party within the "protected" category (apparently the "gift" category) because the third party would be reasonable in *relying* on the promise.[48] Presumably, actual reliance would be unnecessary, i.e., the test is whether such reliance by the third party would be reasonable.[49] Where there is doubt as to whether such reliance would be reasonable, courts may consider other policy factors in determining whether recognition of the right in the third party would be "appropriate."[50]

To determine whether a third party is a protected beneficiary by considering whether such a party would have been reasonable in relying upon a promise (again, no actual reliance appears necessary) may be a desirable test. It has already been recognized as a "major factor" under the RESTATEMENT 2d analysis.[51] Again, however, the test appears in a comment with nary a word in the black letter restatement. It appears to be predicated upon the view that "reasonable and probable" reliance by a classical donee or creditor beneficiary is obvious, and such reliance by a third party who would not otherwise fit within the classical categories should also be protected.[52] A straightforward method of "restating" this analysis would have been to articulate the general concept in terms of actual or probable reliance as a broader concept than the traditional categories and to include clear commentary indicating that thrust. Since, however, the American Law Institute sought to restate the extant law on the subject, it would have been difficult to support the new concept with such case law.[53] In summary, the RESTATEMENT 2d has produced a radically different third party beneficiary concept in language that appears very familiar to those who were aware of the traditional categories. There is, however, little that is traditional about them.

---

[47] *See* RESTATEMENT 2d § 302 comment d.

[48] *Id.*

[49] This is consistent with the RESTATEMENT 2d position as the "vesting" of third party beneficiary rights, i.e., the point at which the power of the promisor and promisee to vary the duty to the beneficiary terminates, which can be upon reliance by the third party, but reliance is not necessary since the power also terminates where the third party simply manifests assent to the promise at the request of either the promisor or promisee. RESTATEMENT 2d § 311(3).

[50] RESTATEMENT 2d § 302 comment d. For example, there may be an overriding public policy consideration in a statute that would urge a court to recognize or not recognize the right in the third party. Such a policy could also suggest a third party beneficiary right regardless of the intention of the parties.

[51] *See* Weninegar v. S. S. Steele & Co., 477 So. 2d 949 (Ala. 1985); Beverly v. Macy, 702 F.2d 931 (11th Cir. 1983).

[52] RESTATEMENT 2d § 302 comment d.

[53] The Reporter's note mentions Commercial Ins. Co. v. Pacific-Peru Constr. Corp., 558 F.2d 948 (9th Cir. 1977) concerning reliance, but recognizes that this case was relying upon a tentative draft of the new concept. Other cases are mentioned as including an actual or probable reliance element though "this factor was not discussed." As we have already seen, *supra* text at note 51, other courts have begun to recognize the major importance of the reliance test.

5. Incidental Beneficiaries.

There is no difference between the FIRST RESTATEMENT and RESTATEMENT 2d concerning incidental beneficiaries. The RESTATEMENT 2d suggests the traditional view that an incidental beneficiary is a party who will benefit from the performance of a contract where he is neither promisor nor promisee, but was not intended by the parties as a beneficiary of that contract.[54] From the obvious situation where a contract to improve certain land that will benefit a nearby landowner was not designed to benefit the landowner,[55] it is important to consider other situations that are not so obvious. Where an insurance company contracted with a doctor to care for an injured employee covered by the company's insurance, the employee was not an intended beneficiary of the contract when the doctor allegedly failed to perform effectively.[56] A contract between an owner and an architect did not confer third party beneficiary rights on a commercial lender.[57] Where a bank makes a loan commitment to a home buyer, rights are not created in the home seller though he would benefit from the performance of the contract.[58] An agreement to extend credit to a failing business does not necessarily create rights in creditors of that business even if the creditors are aware of the agreement and prepare to continue to supply the debtor.[59] In a contract for the sale of goods, where the parties know and even name a third party buyer to whom the goods will be resold and delivery will be made directly to the third party, the third party may not be a protected beneficiary.[60] Mere knowledge of resale to a third party is insufficient to create third party beneficiary rights in that party.[61] There is a vast difference between knowing that something will occur and intending to cause that result. These cases illustrate that even though a third party may be identified as having a relationship with the contract, he may be a mere incidental beneficiary.[62] A guide that often proves helpful is to determine the main purpose of the promisee, i.e., not necessarily his sole purpose, but his dominant purpose in exacting the commitment from the promisor.

---

[54] See RESTATEMENT 2d § 302 comment e and § 315 which simply indicates that the incidental beneficiary acquires no right against the promisor or promisee.

[55] See supra text preceding note 21.

[56] Manning v. Aetna Cas. & Sur. Co., 353 Pa. Super. 139, 509 A.2d 374 (1986) (statute of limitations had run on employee's tort action and he brought an action on the contract).

[57] Mears Park Holding Corp. v. Morse/Diesel, Inc., 427 N.W.2d 281 (Minn. 1988).

[58] Khabbaz v. Schwartz, 319 N.W.2d 279, 284-86 (Iowa 1982).

[59] Bratin v. Bankers Trust Co., 60 N.Y.2d 155, 456 N.E.2d 802, 806 (1983).

[60] See Corrugated Paper Prods., Inc. v. Longview Fibre Co., 868 F.2d 908 (7th Cir. 1989) and cases cited therein.

[61] Spiegel v. Sharp Elec. Corp., 125 Ill. App. 3d 897, 903, 446 N.E.2d 1040, 1045 (1984).

[62] See Colonial Discount Co. v. Avon Motors, Inc., 137 Conn. 196, 75 A.2d 507 (1950) (commercial lender named in contract was not an intended beneficiary but was named simply to assure promisee that financing arrangements in promisee's business would be conducted through an established commercial lender).

§ 131. Identification of Beneficiary — "Vesting."

A. *Identification of Beneficiary.*

For some time it has been clear that a beneficiary may have rights under a contract although he is not specifically named in the contract.[63] It is sufficient if he is a member of an identifiable class or group of persons.[64] Nor must the beneficiary be identified when the contract is made though the lack of identification at that time could bear on whether such a beneficiary was intended as a protected beneficiary as well as the question of whether the right created in such a beneficiary is revocable.[65] If the third party is identifiable at the time for performance and is an intended beneficiary, he is entitled to enforce the contract.

B. *When Beneficiary Rights Become Irrevocable — "Vesting."*

A contract between A and B designed to benefit a particular third party, C, may be formed without the knowledge of the third party. For example, A promises $12,000 to B in exchange for B's promise to deliver B's automobile to C (A's daughter) on her twenty-first birthday. A wants the gift to be a surprise and C is unaware of the contract. Absent knowledge of the contract, does C have any rights under it? The analysis may begin by assuming that, prior to the time for delivery of the auto, A becomes disenchanted with C and decides that he does not wish her to have the automobile. If A had promised to give an auto directly to C, absent C's reliance or other validation device, A would not be obligated to perform. Should it make any difference that A's gift promise involves another party in a third party beneficiary context? This requires us to consider whether A and B may modify or rescind the contract without the consent of C who has yet to learn of the contract for her benefit. Another way of putting the question is, when do the rights of a third party beneficiary "vest"?

1. Immediate Vesting.

Over the years, courts have suggested three different responses. A number of older cases took the position that the right vests immediately, i.e., at the moment the contract is formed, though the third party is unaware of the contract.[66] This was the almost universal rule in the case of ordinary life

---

[63]*See, e.g.,* Ables v. United States, 2 Cl. Ct. 494 (1983); Spector v. National Pictures Corp., 201 Cal. App. 2d 217, 224, 20 Cal. Rptr. 307, 311 (1962).

[64]*See* Plantation Pipe Co. v. 3-D Excavators, Inc., 160 Ga. App. 756, 257 S. E.2d 102 (1981); Guardian Depositors Corp. v. Brown, 290 Mich. 433, 287 N.W. 798 (1939).

[65]*See* RESTATEMENT 2d § 308. On the question of revocability, *see* RESTATEMENT 2d § 311 and the discussion of "vesting" of third parties' right, *infra. See also* Levy v. Daniels' U-Drive Auto Renting Co., 108 Conn. 333, 143 A. 163 (1928); R. Connor Co. v. Olson, 136 Wis. 13, 115 N.W. 811 (1908); Whitehead v. Burgess, 61 N.J.L. 75, 38 A. 802 (1897). *Cf.* Control Data Corp. v. International Bus. Mach. Corp., 306 F. Supp. 839 (D. Minn. 1969), *aff'd, per curiam,* 430 F.2d 1277 (8th Cir. 1970), in which an "unborn" beneficiary failed in its ingenious argument that it was a protected beneficiary under an antitrust consent decree between I.B.M. and the United States.

[66]*See* Tweeddale v. Tweeddale, 116 Wis. 517, 93 N.W. 440 (1903) (gift beneficiary); Starbird v. Cranston, 24 Colo. 20, 48 P. 652 (1897) (creditor beneficiary); Bay v. Williams, 112 Ill. 91, 1 N.E. 340 (1884) (creditor beneficiary).

insurance beneficiaries although it was not generally followed with respect to insurance certificates issued by mutual benefit associations.[67] The FIRST RE-STATEMENT was heavily influenced by the insurance cases in suggesting that the rights of *any* donee beneficiary vested immediately unless the power to discharge or modify the contract was reserved by the promisor and promisee.[68] The courts refused to adopt this position except for ordinary life insurance policies.[69] Since insurance companies began inserting standard clauses in such policies to allow for modification or rescission, it is difficult to discover an illustration of immediate and irrevocable vesting. In an insurance contract or any other context, the parties may, of course, agree that the rights of the third party may not be modified without consent.[70] Absent such an agreement, the question remains, at what point will the rights of the third party become irrevocable?

2. Vesting Upon Reliance.

A second view espoused by other cases was that the rights do not vest until the third party relies on the contract made for his benefit.[71] This view is not without justification. If a beneficiary is unaware of the contract, he can have no expectations. Where is the injustice in permitting the promisor and prom-isee to modify or rescind their agreement at this point? It may even be suggested that *after* the beneficiary becomes aware of the contract, absent reliance, there is still no reason to deny the promisor and promisee the power of rescission or modification. This, however, is not the position that has been adopted by our courts.

3. Prevailing View — RESTATEMENT 2d.

The prevailing view which has been set forth in the RESTATEMENT 2d[72] was originally an effort to satisfy the notion of "privity." To make the beneficiary a "party" to the contract, it was necessary that he *assent* to the contract made

---

[67] For a history of the rule applied in life insurance cases, *see* Page, *The Power of the Contracting Parties to Alter a Contract for Rendering Performance to a Third Person,* 12 WIS. L. REV. 141, 167-81 (1936). The rule was not applied to fraternal benefit association life insurance contracts because of statutes as well as charter and by-law provisions. RESTATEMENT 2d § 311 comment c.

[68] FIRST RESTATEMENT § 142. The special rule relating to life insurance policies may be based on the assumption that a third party such as a wife may have sacrificed to pay premiums on such a policy and should, therefore, have an irrevocable right. *See* W. VANCE, LAW OF INSURANCE §§ 107 and 108 (3d ed. 1951).

[69] *See* Comment, *The Third Party Beneficiary Concept: A Proposal,* 57 COLUM. L. REV. 406 (1957). *See,* however, Biggins v. Shore, 585 A.2d 737 (Pa. 1989) where the Pennsylvania Supreme Court, over a vigorous dissent, clings to the FIRST RESTATEMENT position and expressly rejects the adoption of the RESTATEMENT 2d position "merely to align ourselves with the 'weight of authority'."

[70] RESTATEMENT 2d § 311(1).

[71] *See, e.g.,* Sears Roebuck & Co. v. Jardel Co., 421 F.2d 1048 (3d Cir. 1970) (creditor beneficiary); Morstain v. Kircher, 190 Minn. 78, 250 N.W. 727 (1933) (creditor beneficiary); John F. Clark & Co. v. Nelson, 216 Ala. 199, 112 So. 819 (1927) (creditor beneficiary). The FIRST RESTATE-MENT § 143(b) took the position that the rights of the creditor beneficiary vested if he brought suit or otherwise changed his position before he became aware of any modification or rescission of the contract. It also recognized vesting without reliance if the promisee's action would amount to a fraud on creditors.

[72] RESTATEMENT 2d § 311.

for his benefit.[73] More recently, the *assent* rule seemed to be based on an offer and acceptance analogy, i.e., the contract offers the benefit to the third party who may accept it and thereby terminate the power of the promisor and promisee to modify or rescind it.[74] Neither of these rationales is acceptable. While reliance by the beneficiary should certainly prevent any variation of the contract without his consent, reliance may be difficult to prove. Rather than place such a burden on the beneficiary, his manifestation of assent indicates his willingness to accept the benefits of the contract and, because he may begin to rely immediately upon the contract, his rights should be said to vest upon his assent.[75] This possibility of reasonable reliance concept is consistent with the RESTATEMENT 2d view that a test to determine whether a third party is a protected beneficiary is whether such a party would be reasonable in relying on the contract.[76] The RESTATEMENT 2d precludes any modification or rescission of the contract without the third party's consent where (1) the parties have so contracted,[77] or (2) where the third party materially changes his position on the promise or (3) brings suit thereon or manifests assent to it.[78] Such assent must be requested by the promisor or promisee.[79] If the promisor and promisee attempt to modify or rescind the contract after the beneficiary's rights have vested, the beneficiary is not subject to any defenses the promisor may assert against the promisee which affect the rights of the third party.[80]

C. *Disclaimer of Benefit — Infant Beneficiaries.*

While assent will be sufficient to vest the ordinary third party's interest, the third party need not assent. He is like an offeree who may reject an offer, i.e., the third party may disclaim the benefit within a reasonable time after

---

[73] "[U]ntil the third person brings himself into privity with the one who has promised to be his debtor by at least assenting thereto, he has no legal right to the benefit of the promise." Tweeddale v. Tweeddale, *supra* note 66, 93 N.W. at 441.

[74] *See* Copeland v. Beard, 217 Ala. 216, 115 So. 389 (1928).

[75] *See* RESTATEMENT 2d § 311 comment h. *See also* Bridgman v. Curry, 398 N.W.2d 167 (Iowa 1987); Detroit Bank & Trust Co. v. Chicago Flame Hardening Co., 541 F. Supp. (N.D. Ind. 1982).

[76] *See supra* text at notes 47-50.

[77] RESTATEMENT 2d § 311(1).

[78] RESTATEMENT 2d § 311(3). *See* cases cited *supra* note 75. *See also* Supplies for Indus., Inc. v. Christensen, 135 Ariz. 107, 659 P.2d 660 (1983) where a contract between an employer and employee contained a covenant not to compete and the employer attempted to release the employee of his covenant. The court held such a release would have been valid except that it was executed after the employee's contract was assigned to the successor company which was a third party beneficiary of the contract between the company and employee and had vested rights in that contract. *See,* however, Karo v. San Diego Symphony Orchestra Ass'n, 762 F.2d 819 (9th Cir. 1985) and Price v. Pierce, 823 F.2d 1114 (7th Cir. 1987) suggesting that the RESTATEMENT 2d requires reliance by the third party to make his rights irrevocable.

[79] RESTATEMENT 2d § 311(3) states that the power of the promisor and promisee to modify or rescind the contract terminates when the third party "manifests assent to it at the request of the promisor or promisee." This language appears to solidify the offer/acceptance rationale for assent as a vesting concept. *Query:* if the third party learns of the contract through an independent source and notifies the promisor, promisee, or both of his assent to it, has his right vested? Unless an offer is communicated by the offeror or his agent to the offeree, no power of acceptance is created. Yet, there would seem to be no reason to insist that the third party be requested to assent by the promisor or promisee (or their agents).

[80] *See* RESTATEMENT 2d § 309(3).

learning of it.[81] If he first assents and then disclaims, the disclaimer is effective only if it meets the requirements for discharge of a contractual duty.[82] While neither knowledge nor assent is necessary to give the beneficiary a right under the contract, if assent is not given after he learns of the contract, his right would appear to be revoked since he has chosen not to assent. In the case of an infant who lacks capacity, however, this inference is not justified. Some courts have concluded that the assent of an infant is *presumed*.[83] Where, however, a husband and wife orally contracted with an uncle to help the uncle with his farm in exchange for "good wages" and a promise to give the couple's six-year-old son a quarter section of land when the son became twenty-one years old, the promisor and promisees were allowed to modify the contract three years later without concern for the rights of the son. The court recognized that the rights of an infant beneficiary are sometimes presumed, but since the rights under the contract remained executory and the parties apparently did not intend that the son receive a vested interest for performing services for the uncle that any child would perform for a family member, the child's right did not vest when the oral contract was formed.[84]

§ 132. Application of the Standard.

Whether a court applies the FIRST RESTATEMENT or RESTATEMENT 2d analyses or one of the other tests discussed above, it may confront problems in certain types of beneficiary cases. It is important to consider how courts decide upon third party beneficiary status in clusters of cases which manifest some unusual problems.

A. *Government Contracts.*

Where government at the federal, state, or local level makes a contract, the contract is typically made for the benefit of the public.[85] The question arises, should any member of the public or a class of citizens have a cause of action against a promisor who fails to perform where the main or even exclusive purpose of the promisee-government in exacting the promise was to benefit its citizens? Like other third party beneficiaries, beneficiaries of government contracts may face difficulty squeezing into the procrustean donee or creditor beneficiary categories under the FIRST RESTATEMENT analysis.[86] Any of the other tests which may be viewed generically as an "intention to benefit" test, however, would clearly place such beneficiaries within the protected category. Essentially, there is no reason why they should not prevail as third party beneficiaries in terms of meeting extant tests. Yet, they are not treated as protected beneficiaries except in certain cases.

---

[81] RESTATEMENT 2d § 306.

[82] RESTATEMENT 2d § 306 comment b referring to RESTATEMENT 2d § 37.

[83] *See* Plunkett v. Atkins, 371 P.2d 727 (Okla. 1962); Rhodes v. Rhodes, 266 S.W.2d 790 (Ky. 1953).

[84] Lehman v. Stout, 261 Minn. 384, 112 N.W.2d 5640 (1961). *See also* RESTATEMENT 2d § 311 comment d.

[85] *See* Berberich v. United States, 5 Cl. Ct. 652 (1984). There may, of course, be those who subscribe to the cynical view that the contract may benefit certain governmental officials. Such matters must be left for courses in criminal law.

[86] *See* Martinez v. Socoma Cos., 11 Cal. 3d 394, 113 Cal. Rptr. 585, 521 P.2d 841 (1974).

The most famous case is *H.R. Moch v. Rensselaer Water Co.*[87] where Judge Cardozo wrote the opinion for the court denying recovery to a householder who brought an action as a third party beneficiary under a contract between the city and the water company for the latter's failure to maintain sufficient hydrant pressure which allegedly caused the citizen's house to burn down. There are a number of "water company" cases just like *Moch* which have reached identical results.[88] The citizen in such cases is called an incidental beneficiary which is a conclusion reached after deciding that the water company should not be held liable for other reasons. The same water company can be liable to a citizen beneficiary, however, with respect to the company's promise to provide household water at stated rates.[89] The citizen is regarded as a protected beneficiary in this type of case because water rates are charged directly to citizens and where performance runs directly to a party, he should be a protected beneficiary.[90] This rationale, however, is not sufficient. The fact is that the risk of the water company with respect to its promise to maintain rates no higher than stated levels is a risk that does not threaten the water company's existence so as to leave the city with no water.[91] If, however, the water company were subject to consequential damages caused by its failure to maintain hydrant pressure, the water company may not be able to survive.[92] Insufficient water pressure could cause whole neighborhoods to burn. A policy judgment is made in such cases that it is preferable to have the water company survive and continue to serve the public, even in its defective fashion, than to treat a particular citizen as a third party beneficiary, particularly where that citizen can obtain fire insurance. The RESTATEMENT 2d suggests the same thought when it calls a direct action by a third party citizen "inappropriate" where there is a "likelihood of impairment of service" among other factors.[93] In case after case, members of the public are denied third party status under such contracts.[94] It would be ludicrous to permit tens of thou-

---

[87] 247 N.Y. 160, 159 N.E. 896 (1938).

[88] *See, e.g.,* Luis v. Orcutt Town Water Co., 204 Cal. App. 2d 433, 22 Cal. Rptr. 389 (1962); Earl E. Roher Transfer & Storage Co. v. Hutchison Water Co., 182 Kan. 546, 322 P.2d 810 (1958). *Contra* Potter v. Carolina Water Co., 253 N.C. 112, 116 S.E.2d 374 (1960). As to tort liability, *see* Doyle v. South Pittsburgh Water Co., 414 Pa. 199, 199 A.2d 875 (1964).

[89] *See Moch, supra* note 87. *See also* Pond v. New Rochelle Water Co., 183 N.Y. 330, 76 N.E. 211 (1906).

[90] *See* Touchberry v. City of Florence, 295 S.C. 47, 367 S.E.2d 149 (1988) (homeowner was protected beneficiary of contract between county and city to provide owner with water and sewer service since contract was made directly for his benefit).

[91] A cable TV subscriber may also be viewed as a protected beneficiary of the contract between the municipality and the cable company with respect to announced rates. Bush v. Upper Valley Telecable Co., 96 Idaho 83, 524 P.2d 1055 (1974). *Cf.* New York Citizens Committee on Cable TV v. Manhattan Cable TV, Inc., 651 F. Supp. 802 (S.D.N.Y. 1986) (cable subscribers' committee and unaffiliated programmers seek protected beneficiary status under contract between city and cable company concerning refusal of cable company to permit "Showtime" which was not a Time-Life-HBO-Cinemax property, to be included as part of its cable service. *Inter alia,* the court suggested that a party who can show special benefit to himself as contrasted with members of the public at large can be an intended beneficiary of a government contract. There is, however, a contrary suggestion in *Martinez, supra* note 86.

[92] *See* RESTATEMENT 2d § 313(2) stating that a promisor who contracts with a government or governmental agency is not subject to contractual liability to a member of the public for consequential damages, subject to exceptions that will be discussed, *infra.*

[93] RESTATEMENT 2d § 313 comment a.

[94] *See, e.g.,* Angleton v. Pierce, 574 F. Supp. 719 (D. N.J. 1983) (agreement between Department of Housing and Urban Development (HUD) and owner to create condos from rental units did not

sands, if not millions, of direct actions against a utility. Where, for example, a blackout occurred in New York City, the court would not permit direct actions against the power company for every bump, bruise, and inconvenience that allegedly occurred.[95] The RESTATEMENT 2d, therefore, suggests that, the likelihood of impaired service, government control over litigation, the settlement of claims, and excessive financial burden, are factors that must be considered in determining whether a third party should have a direct action against the promisor.[96]

Where there is language in the contract on which the courts might fasten an intention to benefit directly a member of the public, however, courts are generally quick to pounce on that language and declare the citizen a protected beneficiary.[97] Even without such language, a citizen can become a protected beneficiary where the government has a duty to the citizen, the promisor undertakes that duty, and nothing in the contract precludes a direct action by the citizen.[98] Thus, if a city owes a duty to keep streets in repair and contracts with another who promises to maintain the streets but fails to do so, a citizen whose injury occurs because of an unrepaired street will be a protected beneficiary, i.e., he will have a direct action against the promisor.[99] Since the city owes a duty, the recognition of an action by the citizen against the promisor may place the citizen in a traditional creditor beneficiary category,[1] though he would be a "gift" beneficiary under the SECOND RESTATEMENT because of its

---

make tenants of those units third party beneficiaries though the whole purpose of this governmental effort was to benefit parties such as these tenants); Schell v. National Flood Insurer's Ass'n, 520 F. Supp. 159, 157-58 (contract between Federal Government and NFIA did not create duty to inform public at large about flood insurance though existing policyholders may qualify as third party beneficiaries because of reliance — in this connection *see* Beverly v. Macy, 702 F.2d 931 (11th Cir. 1983)); Gallagher v. Continental Ins. Co., 502 F.2d 827, 833 (10th Cir. 1974) (no third party beneficiary status for member of the public to enforce contract between state and contractor); Martinez v. Socoma Cos., *supra* note 86 (failure of defendants (companies) to perform contracts with U.S. Government to provide jobs for hard-core unemployed residents did not confer protected beneficiary status on those who the promisee (U.S.) sought to benefit).

[95] *See* Shubitz v. Consolidated Edison Co., 59 Misc. 2d 732, 301 N.Y.S.2d 926 (1969).

[96] RESTATEMENT 2d § 313 comment a.

[97] *See, e.g.,* Plantation Pipe Co. v. 3-D Excavators, Inc., 160 Ga. App. 756, 287 S.E.2d 102 (1981) where the court found language that it viewed sufficiently similar to the language of RESTATEMENT 2d § 313 ill. 3, to confer protected beneficiary status. The contract language in the illustration has a contractor promising to pay damages directly to any person who may be injured in the construction project. The language which the court felt sufficiently similar was, "Any damage to existing structures . . . shall be repaired or made good by the contractor at no expense to the owner." This language could be viewed as mere indemnity of the owner from any liability the owner would suffer. The court, however, provided a more liberal interpretation, thus creating protected beneficiary status. *See also* La Mourea v. Rhude, 209 Minn. 53, 295 N.W. 304 (1940) (plaintiff's property was injured by contractor's blasting and the contract contained a clause making the contractor liable for damage to public or private property.) *See* RESTATEMENT 2d § 313(2)(a).

[98] *See* RESTATEMENT 2d § 313(2)(b).

[99] *See* Fowler v. Chicago Rys. Co., 285 Ill. 196, 120 N.E. 635 (1918); Cleveland Ry. Co. v. Heller, 15 Ohio App. 346 (1921); Phinney v. Boston Elevated Ry., 201 Mass. 286, 87 N.E. 490 (1909). RESTATEMENT 2d § 313 ill. 5. *See also* Matternes v. City of Winston-Salem, 286 N.C. 1, 209 S.E.2d 481 (1974), distinguishing these cases from its facts where the city contracted with the State Highway System to assist in maintaining certain roads. Plaintiffs alleged the failure of the city to perform its contract and argued as protected beneficiaries. The court held that the road was still a state road, notwithstanding the contract with the city, and, unlike the earlier cases cited, the city had no duty to the citizens to maintain a state road.

[1] *See Matternes, supra* note 99.

expansion of that category and the corresponding narrowing of the "creditor" category.[2]

B. *Suretyship — Payment and Performance Bonds.*

Contractors understand that they must provide assurances of performance on any significant project with the government or a private party. It is common practice for owners to require contractors to obtain surety bonds to provide such assurance to the owner. The owner, therefore, has an additional promisor. The contractor has promised to perform all of the duties under the contract and the bonding company is providing assurances if the contractor defaults. When he does default, he usually has no money and laborers and materialmen on the job are justifiably eager to discover someone to pay them. They would like to be viewed as third party beneficiaries. If the bond assures the owner that the bonding company will ascertain *performance* of the contract if the contractor defaults, such *performance* bonds are designed to benefit the owner. Labor and materialmen will not be protected beneficiaries of such contracts.[3] In addition to performance bonds, however, owners require *payment* bonds. The question is whether payment bonds are designed simply to indemnify the owner against any loss he might suffer, or should be interpreted to create rights in third party labor and material suppliers against the bonding company. The situation has been made clear in government contracts which are exempt from mechanics' liens. Since laborers and materialmen can not obtain such liens against the government, any payment bond can have only one purpose, i.e., the payment of these third parties, since the lien-immune government would have no other reason for insisting upon a payment bond. There are statutes requiring payment bonds in government contracts and some of the statutes make the protected beneficiary status of suppliers of labor and materials clear.[4] In private contracts, the owner can be saddled with mechanic's liens if the contractor fails to pay its labor and material suppliers. If payment bonds are interpreted as only providing indemnity to the owner against such liens, thus saving him harmless for his liability, the laborers and materialmen become incidental beneficiaries.[5] However, it is now clear that courts will interpret the language of payment bonds as providing protected third party beneficiary status to labor and material suppliers even though they have the protection of mechanic's liens.[6]

---

[2]This analysis is explored *supra* § 130(B)(4).

[3]The distinction between performance and payment bonds and third party recovery under either is discussed in Stahlhut v. Sirloin Stockade, Inc., 568 S.W.2d 269 (Mo. App. 1978).

[4]*See* the Miller Act, 40 U.S.C. § 270 a-e, particularly subsection b. *See also* Carolina Bldrs. Corp. v. AAA Dry Wall, Inc., 43 N.C. App. 444, 259 S.E.2d 364 (1979); Robertson Co. v. Globe Indem. Co., 268 Pa. 309, 112 A. 50 (1920).

[5]*See* Fidelity & Deposit Co. v. Rainer, 220 Ala. 262, 125 So. 55, 77 A.L.R. 13 (1929), where the language conditioned the obligation of the bond on the principal's payment of all persons who had contracts directly with the principal for labor and materials and third party beneficiary recoveries were allowed. In Ross v. Imperial Constr. Co., 572 F.2d 518 (5th Cir. 1978), the court distinguished *Fidelity* where the "completion guarantee" did not expressly commit the defendant to pay materialmen or suppliers and held them to be mere incidental beneficiaries.

[6]*See* Ceco Corp. v. Plaza Point, Inc., 573 S.W.2d 92 (Kan. App. 1978), relying upon this proposition in the second edition of this book at 574. *See also* Board of Educ. of Community H.S. Dist. 99 v. Hartford Acc. & Indem. Co., 152 Ill. App. 3d 745, 504 N.E.2d 1000 (1987); Autocon Indus., Inc.

C. The Mortgage Assumption Situation — "Subject to" — "Assuming."

To understand the particular problem of third party beneficiaries in mortgage assumption situations, it is necessary to provide a sketch of the mechanics of assuming a mortgage indebtedness.[7] A mortgage is a security interest in real property which is granted to secure a loan made by a lender to the owner. A prospective buyer of real estate will often seek to finance that purchase through a loan.[8] The lender will typically agree to lend the money only if the owner agrees to repay the loan with interest and, to secure the loan, to execute a mortgage on the property. Normally, the debt secured by the mortgage is significantly less than the value of the property. If the debt is not paid, the lender will attempt to collect from the owner. If the owner cannot pay, the lender will then initiate foreclosure proceedings by having the property sold to satisfy the debt.

Mortgaged real estate is common throughout the United States and it is quite common for an owner of mortgaged property to agree to sell that property. He cannot, however, sell it free of the mortgage which is publicly recorded.[9] When he sells his mortgaged property, what the owner is really selling is his "equity of redemption," i.e., that portion of the value of the property that he owns free of any encumbrance. Thus, e.g., if the mortgagor owns property worth $100,000 which is encumbered by a debt of $50,000, the mortgagor's "equity" in the property is $50,000. With this background sketch, it is possible to understand the operation of the third party beneficiary concept in this context.

First, assume that the owner-mortgagor (R) conveys the property to a grantee (X). There is nothing in the contract concerning the mortgage. The mortgage, however, does not disappear — it is still "attached to the land." If the outstanding mortgage debt is not paid, the mortgagee-bank (E) will foreclose, regardless of the conveyance from R to X. If the foreclosure sale produces sufficient funds to cover the debt and attendant costs of foreclosure, R has no liability. If, however, the land is sold at foreclosure for less than the outstanding debt owed to E,[10] E may recover a deficiency judgment against its debtor, R. X, the grantee, has lost the land. If, however, he did not promise to become liable on the mortgage indebtedness which his grantor (R) owed to the bank-mortgagee (E), X is not personally liable to E. In this situation, we say

---

v. Western States Constr. Co., 728 P.2d 374 (Colo. App. 1986); Barbero v. Equitable Gen. Ins. Co., 607 P.2d 670 (Okla. 1980); Pennsylvania Supply Co. v. National Cas. Co., 152 Pa. Super. 217, 31 A.2d 453 (1943). In Hoiness-Labar Ins. v. Julian Const. Co., 743 P.2d 1262 (Wyo. 1987), the insurer mistakenly failed to issue a payment bond along with the performance bond which was issued and court allowed recovery by third party beneficiary.

[7] The following sketch is based on a similar sketch appearing in MURRAY, CASES AND MATERIALS ON CONTRACTS (3d ed. 1983).

[8] The traditional transaction involved an indebtedness evidenced by a promissory note or bond payable to the lender in the amount of the mortgage loan plus interest.

[9] Where mortgaged property is sold, the typical mortgage loan agreement will contain a "due on sale" clause (acceleration clause) whereby the entire outstanding amount of the mortgage debt will become due under this clause when the mortgaged property is sold. As to the enforceability of such clauses, see Annotation, 61 A.L.R.4th 1070 (1988).

[10] Land values may depreciate and the depreciation may be rapid and substantial as evidenced by the value of farm land in parts of the United States. The farm foreclosures that have occurred in recent years are a strong, albeit sad, illustration of this possibility.

that X took "subject to" the mortgage between R and E. There was no mention of the mortgage debt in the contract between R and X. Again, however, X could not purchase the property free of that mortgage unless the debt had been satisfied. Since it was not satisfied, X took a conveyance of the property "subject to" the mortgage. Another way of stating the situation is that E was not a third party beneficiary of the contract between R and X, again, because X did not promise to become liable on that debt to E.

If we now assume that the conveyance from R to X recited that X "assumes and agrees to pay" the mortgage debt to E, and we further assume that the mortgage debt was not paid in full, E may sue X who has become personally liable for the payment of that debt. E is a third party ("creditor") beneficiary of the contract between R and X because X has agreed to pay R's debt to E. The promisee, has induced X, the promisor, to promise a performance to E and R intends E to be a beneficiary of the contract.[11] If X does not perform by satisfying the debt, E may still bring an action against R who has not been released from his indebtedness to E.[12] R, however, is no longer the principal debtor. X became the principal debtor when he "assumed" the mortgage debt and R became a surety for the payment of that debt. If X does not satisfy the indebtedness to E, E may foreclose on his security, the mortgage, and the property will be sold. If the selling price at the foreclosure sale is sufficient to cover the outstanding debt and attendant foreclosure costs, the debt will be satisfied and neither R nor X would be liable though X, of course, would have lost the property. If the selling price were not sufficient, however, *e.g.*, land values had declined, E would then be entitled to recover the amount of any deficiency from X. If X failed to pay the deficiency, R, the surety, would be liable thereon. If R paid the deficiency, he would be paying an amount that X should have paid and R would stand in the shoes of E as the creditor of X. We say that R, in that situation, is *subrogated* to the rights of E who has been satisfied. If X were incapable of paying E, it is unlikely that R will have much luck in collecting any judgment from X. R, however, is entitled to recover from X the amount R paid to E.

A problem that has caused significant difficulty occurs where R conveys to X who "assumes" the mortgage debt, X conveys to Y who takes "subject to" the mortgage, and Y conveys to Z who "assumes" the debt. There has been a "break in the chain of assumption." E was a creditor beneficiary of the contract between R and X, but he was not a creditor beneficiary of the contract between X and Y since Y failed to assume the indebtedness and was not personally liable to E. When Y sold to Z and Z assumed the indebtedness, the

---

[11] For an example of a third party mortgagee beneficiary contract, *see* Bridgman v. Curry, 398 N.W.2d 167 (Iowa 1987).

[12] If E had agreed to accept X in substitution for R as E's exclusive debtor, R would have been released at the time the contract was formed. At that moment, the only debtor and creditor relationship would have been one between X and E. The consideration to E would be the new duty created in X and the consideration to X would be the property which he owns through the conveyance from R. R would receive consideration in the release from E. Where such a tri-partite contract is formed, where the creditor releases one debtor and takes another in substitution, the contract is called a *novation* which is not a third-party beneficiary contract since, at the moment of formation, only two parties have a legal relationship. Novation is one of several methods of discharging a contractual obligation and will be explored *infra* Chapter 12, dealing with discharge.

question arises, is Z liable to E notwithstanding the break in the chain of assumption?

There is considerable difficulty in understanding the motivation of Y who was not personally liable in asking Z to become personally liable on the mortgage debt to E. Unless Y sought to make a gift to the mortgagee, E, Y's intention to benefit E is questionable. It is unlikely that a private party would be interested in making a gift to a bank. If the mortgagee is a party other than a stranger, it is possible to discover a gratuitous intention.[13] The recorded case law in this area is in conflict. Some courts have allowed the mortgagee to enforce the agreement as written on the footing that the mortgagee is a gift beneficiary.[14] Courts denying recovery have not agreed on the rationale. Some have viewed the right of a beneficiary as necessarily growing out of the doctrine of subrogation which would be applicable only where the beneficiary is a creditor of the promisee.[15] Others have apparently treated the contract as though it had been reformed to call merely for the indemnification of the grantor, and have accordingly reached the conclusion that the mortgagee is a mere incidental beneficiary.[16] Where the language of the contract expresses the intention of the parties, of course, there is every reason for permitting the beneficiary to enforce the promise.[17]

The SECOND RESTATEMENT suggests two possibilities to deal with the "break in the chain of assumption" situation. If the last assuming grantee had agreed to pay the mortgage debt with knowledge of all of the facts, i.e., knowledge of the break in the chain, that grantee is liable to the mortgagee — the mortgagee is a protected beneficiary.[18] If, however, the assuming grantee can show by clear and convincing evidence that the scrivener of the deed inserted the grantee's promise to pay the debt by mistake contrary to the true intention of the grantor and grantee, the equitable remedy of reformation would lie so as to reform the writing to state the true intentions of the parties and the mortgagee would not be a protected beneficiary.[19] The last illustration, however, is conditioned upon the absence of any change in the circumstances making reformation inequitable. It should be recalled that, under the RESTATEMENT 2d as contrasted with the FIRST RESTATEMENT, unless there is an *actual* obli-

[13] *See* Schneider v. Ferrigno, 110 Conn. 86, 147 A. 303 (1929) (promisee intended to benefit brother-in-law).

[14] *See* Corkrell v. Poe, 100 Wash. 625, 171 P. 522, 12 A.L.R. 1524 (1918). Additional cases are collected in Annotation, 12 A.L.R. 1537 (1921). *See also* Schneider v. Ferrigno, *supra* note 13, where at 147 A. 304, the opinion reads, "If the grantor of the equity of redemption who has not assumed the mortgage has no object to protect himself, an intent to confer a right to sue upon the holder of the mortgage would be the most natural motive to assign to him in requiring his grantee to agree to pay it."

[15] *See* Vrooman v. Turner, 69 N.Y. 280, 25 Am. Rep. 195 (1877). It should be recalled that this case limited the landmark case of *Lawrence v. Fox* to its facts, i.e., to creditor beneficiaries. *See supra* § 129(C). Other cases are collected in Annotation, 12 A.L.R. 1531 (1921).

[16] *See, e.g.,* Fry v. Ausman, 29 S.D. 30, 135 N.W. 708 (1921).

[17] *See* Federal Bond & Mtg. Co. v. Shapiro, 219 Mich. 123, 188 N.W. 465 (1922) where a grantor was not liable on the first mortgage but had granted a second mortgage on the land for which he was liable. Thus, he had a real interest in having the first mortgage satisfied since its payment would minimize the possibility of his having to pay any deficiency on the second mortgage. In such a case, the contract should be given effect according to its terms and the beneficiary allowed to enforce it as held by the Michigan court. *See also* FIRST RESTATEMENT § 144 ill. 2.

[18] RESTATEMENT 2d § 312 ill. 3.

[19] RESTATEMENT 2d § 312 ill. 4.

gation owed by the promisee to the third party, the third party cannot be a "creditor" beneficiary. On the other hand, the second category of protected beneficiaries under the RESTATEMENT 2d, albeit labeled "gift" beneficiaries, is much broader than the FIRST RESTATEMENT's donee category.[20] That category would include a third party who "would be reasonable in relying on the promise as manifesting an intention to confer a right on him."[21] As suggested in the earlier analysis of this concept, actual reliance is not necessary, i.e., the test is whether a third party would be reasonable in relying on the promise. If a deed evidenced an assumption of the debt by the grantee notwithstanding a break in the chain, a mortgagee might be reasonable in relying thereon even in the mistake situation. Absent actual reliance, however, reformation may be granted to deprive the mortgagee of protected beneficiary status. The RE-STATEMENT 2d is unclear. Certainly, actual reliance by a third party should be sufficient to protect him as an intended beneficiary. On the other hand, only showing that he would have been reasonable in relying on such a statement in a deed may be insufficient.

D. *Beneficiaries and Statute of Wills.*

Where a contract conditions the right of a beneficiary upon his surviving the promisee, some courts found insuperable difficulty in protecting such a beneficiary. They were concerned that the contract was an attempt to make a testamentary disposition of the property without complying with the Statute of Wills and was, therefore, nugatory. There never was any justification for such a holding which involved a confusion of thought concerning property rights and contract rights. A contract does not purport to dispose of existing rights; rather, it creates a right to performance that did not previously exist. The Statute of Wills, therefore, is not applicable. The fact that a contract right may be contingent on the death of the promisee is immaterial. Moreover, when the testamentary policy behind typical statutes of wills is considered, the matter is even more clear. Cases which had discovered such problems are now viewed as something of an embarrassment.[22]

---

[20] *See* supra § 130 B. 4.

[21] *See* RESTATEMENT 2d § 312 comment a, referring to §§ 302 and 304 and comments to those sections. In § 304 comment e, the reliance factor is separated from others: "In cases of doubt, the question whether such an intention [to benefit the third party] is to be attributed to the promisee may be influenced by the likelihood that recognition of the right will further the legitimate expectations of the promisee, make available a simple and convenient procedure for enforcement, or *protect the beneficiary in his reasonable reliance on the promise.*" (Emphasis added.)

[22] *See, e.g.,* McCarthy v. Pieret, 281 N.Y. 407, 24 N.E.2d 102 (1939) which was strictly limited to its facts in Estate of Hillowitz, 22 N.Y.2d 107, 238 N.E.2d 723 (1968) (in the event of the death of a partner, his share will be transferred to his wife — wife considered protected beneficiary). Decker v. Fowler, 199 Wash. 549, 92 P.2d 254 (1939) was also confused about third party beneficiary contracts and the Wills Statute. In Toulouse v. New York Life Ins. Co., 40 Wash. 2d 538, 245 P.2d 205 (1952) the court announced that the *Decker* view was changed by statute and went on to admit that the overwhelming weight of authority was opposed to *Decker.* There was authority for what has clearly become the prevailing view at the time of *McCarthy* and *Decker. See, e.g.,* Franklin Washington Trust Co. v. Beltram, 133 N.J.Eq. 11, 29 A.2d 854 (1943); *In re* Di Santo's Estate, 142 Ohio St. 223, 51 N.E.2d 639 (1943); Warrent, Ex'x v. United States, 68 Ct. Cl. 634 (1929).

§ 133. Cumulative Rights — Defenses.

A. *Cumulative Rights of Beneficiary.*

A third party "gift" or "donee" beneficiary typically has a cause of action only against the promisor for his failure of performance.[23] Since the promisee owes nothing to a gift beneficiary, the donee beneficiary has no claim against the promisee. A creditor beneficiary, on the other hand, has two sources of satisfaction. The question arises, if the beneficiary chooses to bring an action against the promisor, has he "elected" to surrender any rights he had against the promisee, his original debtor? A few older cases proceeded on the footing that the creditor beneficiary's election to bring an action against the promisor was, in effect, the acceptance of an offer of novation which released the promisee. If he chose to pursue the promisee on the original obligation, he was viewed as rejecting the offer of novation and surrendering his right to enforce the contract made for his benefit.[24] There never was any basis for this approach which apparently arose in still another attempt to find that the third party was in privity which, as we have seen, is a term used as a conclusory label after a court decides that a third party is a protected beneficiary. In the normal third party (creditor) beneficiary situation, there is no thought that the third party is surrendering the promisee as the original obligor. The promisee does become a surety as the promisor becomes the principal debtor.[25] Surety status, however, does not relieve the promisor of his obligation.[26] The third party is not even required to bring an action first against the promisor.[27] If the creditor decides to recover from the promisee and the promisee satisfies the debt, the promisee may then recover from the promisor who, as principal debtor, was supposed to pay the third party. If, however, the beneficiary brings an action against either promisor or promisee and does not achieve satisfaction of the outstanding debt, he may then bring an action against the other party for the balance of the debt.[28] The beneficiary may join the promi-

---

[23] It should be recalled that the promisor and promisee may vary or even rescind the contract without the consent of the beneficiary until the rights of the beneficiary "vest." If the variation or rescission is wrongful and the promisee received consideration for such variation or rescission, the beneficiary may be entitled to that consideration or part thereof to avoid the unjust enrichment of the promisee. *See* RESTATEMENT 2d § 311(4) and comment j thereto.

[24] Wood v. Moriarity, 15 R.I. 518, 9 A. 427 (1887); Bohanan v. Pope, 42 Me. 93 (1856).

[25] This situation was explored with respect to the mortgagee (creditor) beneficiary *supra* § 132(C).

[26] Once the beneficiary is aware of the suretyship, he cannot avoid it since, without his consent, a contract of suretyship has occurred. If, therefore, the beneficiary would simply release the promisor, on the face of it, it would appear that he has also released the promisee-surety. Unless, therefore, the surety has consented to remain liable on the original obligation, or the beneficiary has expressly reserved rights against the promisee, the promisee's duty would be discharged. If the beneficiary decides to modify the duty of the promisor, such a modification could result in augmenting the risk of the promisee. Courts will not impose greater risks upon promisees under these circumstances, i.e., they will enforce the promisee's (surety's) duties only to the extent that they have not been enhanced by modifications of the promisor's duty over which the promisee-surety had no control. *See* RESTATEMENT 2d § 314.

[27] Restatement of Security § 130. Section 131, however, suggests the possibility of great hardship to the promisor which may require the creditor beneficiary to use the promisor's available assets before seeking relief from the surety-promisee.

[28] *See* Erickson v. Grand Ronde Lumber Co., 162 Or. 556, 94 P.2d 139 (1939). *See also* Albert Steinfeld & Co. v. Wing Wong, 14 Ariz. 336, 128 P. 354 (1912); Webster v. Fleming, 178 Ill. 140, 52 N.E. 975 (1899); Davis v. National Bank, 45 Neb. 589, 63 N.W. 852 (1895).

sor and promisee in the same action and obtain a judgment against both though he is entitled to only one satisfaction.[29]

B. *Promisee's Right to Enforce the Promise.*

Third party beneficiaries are usually quite willing to enforce promises made on their behalf. On occasion, a promisee will attempt to enforce the promise. Since the promisee must intend to benefit the third party to enable that party to have an actionable right against the promisor, should the promisee ever be permitted to recover from the promisor?

Where the beneficiary is a "gift" beneficiary, the promisee expects no measurable benefit to himself. He does, however, have a significant interest in ascertaining that the promise for which he has parted with consideration is performed. In the rare case where the third party does not attempt to enforce the promise, the promisee may secure a decree of specific performance of the promise for the third party's benefit since it is clear that the promisee has no adequate remedy at law.[30]

Where the third party is a creditor beneficiary, the promisee's pecuniary interest in the performance of the promise is clear since that performance will satisfy his obligation to the third party. Beyond these obvious damages, the promisee may suffer additional damages because the promisor has failed to perform.[31] The modern view is that the promisee has a cause of action against the promisor.[32] Older cases taking a contrary view were concerned about "privity" and indulged the fallacy that the contract created an offer of novation to the beneficiary. When he "accepted" this offer, he was deemed to be substituted for the promisee so that only an action against the promisor would lie.[33] A more serious concern was the risk of double liability to the promisor. Since the promisee may recover the amount of the debt from the defaulting promisor before the promisee pays the creditor beneficiary (which he may never do),[34] the promisor would still be liable to the creditor beneficiary. There are various solutions to the problem. An action by the promisee could simply

---

[29] *See* Kraus v. Willow Park Pub. Golf Course, 73 Cal. App. 3d 354, 140 Cal. Rptr. 744 (1977) (filing claims in bankruptcy proceeding did not preclude creditor beneficiaries from pursuing their rights against promisor). *See also* RESTATEMENT 2d § 310.

[30] *See* Drewen v. Bank of Manhattan Co., 31 N.J. 110, 155 A.2d 529 (1959) (parents executed divorce agreement which required father to leave a certain portion of his estate to the son. After executing that will in satisfaction of the contract, the father changed the will leaving a much smaller portion of his estate to the son, but including an *in terrorem* clause which would have deprived the son of the smaller legacy should he contest the will. Court granted decedent promisee's representative specific performance of the contract). *See also* Croker v. New York Trust Co., 245 N.Y. 17, 156 N.E. 81 (1927) (promisee permitted to sue for specific performance in a gift-beneficiary case since promisee's remedy at law was inadequate having suffered no damages as a result of the breach). *See* RESTATEMENT 2d § 307.

[31] *See* Miholevich v. Mid-West Mut. Auto Ins. Co., 261 Mich. 495, 246 N.W. 202 (1933) (where insurance company wilfully delayed payment of a judgment against the insured and the insured was imprisoned under a body execution which was permitted at the time of this case).

[32] *See* Buschmann v. Professional Men's Ass'n, 405 F.2d 659 (7th Cir. 1969); Dann v. Studebaker-Packard Corp., 288 F.2d 201 (6th Cir. 1961); Eden v. Miller, 37 F.2d 8 (2d Cir. 1930); RESTATEMENT 2d § 305.

[33] *See* North Ala. Dev. Co. v. Short, 101 Ala. 333, 13 So. 385 (1893) (dictum).

[34] *See* Heins v. Byers, 174 Minn. 350, 219 N.W. 287 (1928). *See also* Jones v. Bates, 241 S.C. 189, 127 S.E.2d 618 (1962).

be barred.[35] There is, however, no justifiable basis for barring the promisee's action. Another solution is to bar the promisee from recovering the amount of the debt from the promisor unless and until he first pays the beneficiary. There is some case law support for this view though courts refusing to permit recovery prior to payment often suggest that the promisee has no right to recover for the promisor's breach, i.e., the promisee may seek reimbursement of payments made since he has become a mere surety for the payment of the debt and is liable on an implied promise to indemnify.[36] This is an unfortunate analysis since, as we have already seen, the promisee may suffer consequential damages resulting from the promisor's failure to perform which should always be recoverable regardless of any prior payment to the beneficiary by the "surety"-promisee. More effective and just solutions are available to modern courts which can infuse equitable notions into the relief granted to avoid double liability to the promisor and simultaneously insure that the promisee has a cause of action where that is necessary. Thus, in an action by the promisee, a modern court could insist that the judgment awarded, at least in terms of the debt owed, must be paid to the creditor beneficiary.[37] When sued by either the third party or the promisee, the promisor could interplead the other party to whom it may also be liable, or simply pay the amount owed into the court and permit the court to determine who should receive it. While a single payment will ordinarily discharge the promisor's duties to both the third party and promisee,[38] again, the possibility of consequential damages to the promisee through the promisor's failure of performance allows a separate, as contrasted with double, recovery.

C. Promisor's Defenses Against Beneficiary.

1. Defenses on the Contract.

The right of a third party beneficiary can exist only when a contract has been made by the promisor and promisee. The rights of a third party, therefore, rise no higher than that of a promisee. Innumerable cases support this proposition by insisting that all defenses that the promisor would have had against the promisee are available to the promisor against the third party beneficiary.[39]

It is important to emphasize, however, that the right of a protected beneficiary is direct and not merely derivative, i.e., any defenses arising out of the

---

[35] Some courts have held that the promisee may not bring an action against the promisor. They do consider the promisee to be a surety, however, and, if he has paid the creditor-beneficiary, the promisee may be reimbursed by the principal debtor-promisor. See John Deere Plow Co. v. Tuinstra, 47 S.D. 555, 200 N.W. 61 1924); Poe v. Dixon, 60 Ohio St. 124, 54 N.E. 86 (1899).

[36] See, e.g., White v. Upton, 255 Ky. 562, 74 S.W.2d 924 (1934); Thomsen v. Kopp, 204 Iowa 1176, 216 N.W. 725 (1927); Lowry v. Hensal's Heirs & Legal Representatives, 281 Pa. St. 572, 127 A. 219 (1924). See Note, Effect of a Suretyship Relation Between Promisor and Promisee in Creditor-Beneficiary Cases, 35 HARV. L. REV. 502 (1925).

[37] See Heins v. Byers, supra note 34.

[38] RESTATEMENT 2d § 305 comment b.

[39] See, e.g., Seaboard Sur. Co. v. Garrison, Webb, & Stanaland, P.A., 823 F.2d 434 (11th Cir. 1987); District Moving & Storage Co. v. Gardiner & Gardiner, Inc., 63 Md. App. 96, 492 A.2d 319 (1985); Martin v. John Hancock Mut. Life Ins. Co., 120 Misc. 2d 776, 466 N.Y.2d 596 (1983); United States v. Industrial Crane & Mfg. Corp., 492 F.2d 772 (5th Cir. 1974). See also RESTATEMENT 2d § 309.

contract which will benefit the third party are available to the promisor, but claims and defenses of the promisee arising out of separate transactions between the promisor and promisee have no effect on the third party.[40] The defenses on the original contract, however, are unlimited. Thus, if there is a lack of mutual assent, consideration, or capacity, the beneficiary is subject to such defenses.[41] Defenses of fraud,[42] breach of express[43] or constructive[44] conditions, mistake,[45] or failure of performance,[46] are also included. If the contract reduced the statute of limitations for the promisee, it is reduced for the beneficiary.[47] If the promisor was entitled to arbitration in any dispute with the promisee, she is entitled to arbitration in any dispute on the same contract with the third party.[48]

2. Breach by Promisee — Setoffs.

Among the defenses available to the promisor we have included failure of performance by the promisee. Whether the promisor may avail himself of setoffs that would have been available against the promisee is a different question. If the promisee's breach is one that does not discharge the promisor's duty, should he be allowed to reduce the beneficiary's recovery through a setoff? The prevailing view is that the setoff will be permitted if it arises from the same transaction.[49]

3. Exceptions.

a. Contract Precludes Defenses.

There are exceptions to the rule that the beneficiary is subject to the defenses the promisor would have been able to assert against the promisee. The obvious exception occurs where the contract expressly provides that the promisor's duty will not be subject to certain defenses. For example, in a fire insurance contract, the loss payable clause usually recites that the mortgagee

---

[40] See RESTATEMENT 2d § 309 comment c.

[41] See Lawhead v. Booth, 115 W. Va. 490, 177 S.E. 283 (1934); Barlow Grain & Stock Exch. v. Nilson, 57 N.D. 624, 223 N.W. 700 (1929); Kuske v. Jevne, 174 Minn. 484, 219 N.W. 766 (1928); Wainwright Trust Co. v. Prudential Life Ins. Co., 80 Ind. App. 37, 134 N.E. 913 (1922).

[42] See Tuttle v. Jockmus, 111 Conn. 269, 149 A. 785 (1930).

[43] Hunt v. Dollar, 224 Wis. 48, 271 N.W. 405 (1937); Sun Indem. Co. v. Dulaney, 264 Ky. 112, 89 S.W.2d 307 (1935). See also Levy v. Glen Falls Indem. Co., 210 Md. 265, 123 A.2d 348 (1956).

[44] Kroening v. Kroening, 223 Wis. 113, 269 N.W. 536 (1936 (dictum); Assets Realization Co. v. Cardon, 72 Utah 597, 272 P. 204 (1928).

[45] Broadbent v. Hutter, 163 Wis. 380, 157 N.W. 1095 (1916); Rogers v. Castle, 51 Minn. 428, 53 N.W. 651 (1892).

[46] Connors v. Van Mulvehill, 679 F. Supp. 1071 (N.D. Ala. 1988); Conrad v. Thompson, 137 Cal. App. 2d 73, 290 P.2d 36 (1955); Duncan v. Nowell, 27 Ariz. 451, 233 P. 582 (1925).

[47] See Barr v. McGraw-Hill, Inc., 710 F. Supp. 95 (S.D.N.Y. 1989); Hercules, Inc. v. Stevens Shipping Co., 629 F.2d 418 (5th Cir. 1981). See also UCC § 2-725(1), permitting parties to agree to reduce statute of limitations period to no less than one year but precluding them from extending it beyond the four-year term.

[48] See District Moving & Storage Co., supra note 39.

[49] See United States v. Industrial Crane & Mfg. Corp., supra note 39, where the court permitted an offset of damages based on the promisee's breach of a covenant not to compete which was not an independent transaction. See also Fulmer v. Goldfarb, 171 Tenn. 218, 101 S.W.2d 1108 (1937). The RESTATEMENT 2d supports this view. See § 309 comment c. Contra, see Commonwealth Life Ins. Co. v. Eline, 274 Ky. 539, 119 S.W.2d 637 (1938).

may recover the insured amount of the loss even though the mortgagor has failed to perform certain conditions.[50]

b. Promisee's Liability or Absolute Promise.

A situation that appears quite similar occurs where the contract requires the promisor to perform a certain duty and there is a question as to whether the promisor must discharge the liability of the promisee, or make a certain payment to the third party regardless of the promisee's liability. What has become a well-known case in this area illustrates the distinction. The promisor assumed payment of $850 for a heating plant as part of the contract to purchase a house. When payment was demanded, the promisor asserted a defense of incorrect installation of the heating plant. The court refused to permit this defense because it interpreted the assumption of the indebtedness in the contract as an absolute obligation regardless of the liability of the promisee. If the contract language had committed the promisor to discharge any liability of the promisee for the heating plant, the defense would have been available to the promisor.[51] Other courts agree, in conformity with Professor Corbin's analysis:

> There is nothing to prevent a promisor from undertaking a larger duty than the duty owed by the promisee to the beneficiary.... If he promises to pay a third party a sum claimed by him against the promisee, irrespective of defenses that the promisee may have, he is bound by his promise in the teeth of those defenses.[52]

c. Employee Benefit Plans — National Labor Policy.

The most significant policy exception involves collective bargaining agreements which require employers to make payments to certain funds for the benefit of employees who are the union members. The members may be in no position to prevent actionable wrongs committed by their union. If the employer were able to raise such defenses, the employee-beneficiaries could be deprived of the fund created for their benefit. As one court recently observed, early in the history of pension and welfare plans, the Supreme Court established that breach by the union would not relieve the employer of its obligation to make pension contributions.[53]

---

[50] *See* Goldstein v. National Liberty Ins. Co. of Am., 256 N.Y. 26, 175 N.E. 359 (1931).

[51] *See* Rouse v. United States, 215 F.2d 872 (D.C. Cir. 1954). *See also* Nu-Way Plumbing, Inc. v. Superior Mech., Inc., 315 So. 2d 556 (1975).

[52] 4 CORBIN, CONTRACTS § 821 at 281, *quoted in* Nu-Way Plumbing, Inc. v. Superior Mech., Inc., 315 So. 2d 556 (Fla. App. 1975). The RESTATEMENT 2d suggests that "a promise to render a performance whether or not there is a pre-existing duty is effective according to its terms. *Prima facie* an unqualified promise to render the performance has the same effect, but mistake as to the existence of the duty may make the contract voidable." RESTATEMENT 2d § 312 comment b. This is, essentially, the same analysis of the mortgage assumption situation where there has been a break in the chain of assumption. *See supra* § 132(C).

[53] Central States, SE & SW Areas Pension Fund v. Gerber Truck Serv., Inc., 870 F.2d 1148 (7th Cir. 1989) referring to Lewis v. Benedict Coal Corp., 361 U.S. 459 (1960). *See also* Goldies, Inc. v. Alaska H & R Emps. H & W Fund, 622 P.2d 979 (1981) and cases cited therein.

§ 134. Third Party Beneficiaries Under the Uniform Commercial Code — Products Liability — Horizontal and Vertical Privity.

In a contract for the sale of goods, the buyer and the seller are the only contracting parties and, under the old terminology, they are in "privity" with each other. If the goods are defective, there is a breach of warranty by the seller. If the goods are not of fair, average, quality, there is a breach of the implied warranty of merchantability.[54] If the buyer has relied on the seller's expertise, skill, and judgment in selecting the goods for a particular purpose, and the goods are not effective for that purpose, there is a breach of the implied warranty of fitness for a particular purpose.[55] The seller may have made certain promises or factual representations about the quality of the goods, or he may have shown the buyer a sample or model of the goods. Even without promises, representations, samples, or models, goods are usually described and the description constitutes statements of fact about them. If the goods do not meet the quality standards established by such descriptions, representations, promises, samples, or models, there is a breach of an express warranty.[56] When a breach of warranty occurs, there has never been any question about the buyer's right to sue his immediate seller with whom the buyer made the contract. Two other questions, however, have created almost interminable litigation over the years: (1) Does the buyer have the right to sue not only his immediate seller but, also, the remote manufacturer of the goods with whom he has not dealt directly and with whom he made no contract? The buyer's immediate seller made a contract with either the manufacturer or a middleman in the distributive chain. May the buyer qualify as a third party beneficiary of that contract? (2) Does anyone other than the buyer, *e.g.*, a member of the buyer's family or household or guest in the home, have any right to sue either the buyer's immediate seller or other suppliers up to the remote manufacturer even though the non-buyer has made no contract with any of them? Should such a party be viewed as a protected beneficiary of the contract between the actual buyer and the seller?

The first question has been popularly characterized as a question of "vertical privity," i.e., may the buyer proceed *up* the channel of distribution not only against his immediate seller but all the way to the remote manufacturer of the goods? Another way of putting this question simply is, "Who can be sued?" The second question is popularly characterized as involving "horizontal privity," i.e., *across* the horizontal line of the buyer, who may stand in the buyer's shoes and sue either the immediate seller or the remote manufacturer. Who may sue?

There have been innumerable law review articles, books, and the like dealing with this problem and thousands of cases spawned by it. For a number of years, the courts have been moving in the direction of abolishing both horizontal and vertical privity as bars to actions by buyers and other contemplated users of goods against immediate and remote sellers.[57] For years, it was a

---

[54] UCC § 2-314.

[55] UCC § 2-315.

[56] UCC § 2-313.

[57] Perhaps the best-known article is Prosser, *The Assault Upon the Citadel (Strict Liability to the Consumer)*, 69 Yale L.J. 1099 (1960).

poorly kept secret that the use of a warranty theory in this area is a device to permit buyers to recover as third party beneficiaries of contracts, particularly for personal injuries, without the need of proving negligence in what was a tort context wrapped in contracts garb. Though the warranty theory originally sounded in tort (*ex delicto*), it took on an *ex contractu* character in the tortured development of the common-law forms of action.

When the UCC was in the drafting stages, the courts had already recognized the warranty theory for personal injuries due to defective products. The father of the Code, Professor Karl Llewellyn, had more than precociously suggested an enterprise liability formula as early as 1941 to be included in the Code. Though the formula was the essence of what became part of the RESTATEMENT 2D OF TORTS more than three decades later, the comprehensive Llewellyn concept was vetoed by the Commissioners on Uniform State Laws as "tort" law that would be an unacceptable inclusion in a "sales" statute.[58] Notwithstanding their rejection of still another Llewellyn idea whose time had not come, the drafters felt compelled to include a provision reflecting the case law development to that time. Since they rejected a comprehensive approach, they included scattered pieces of product liability development[59] which has created some confusion in the courts. For example, they addressed themselves exclusively to the question of horizontal privity, i.e., who can sue.[60] They did not deal with vertical privity in the section language though an interesting comment can be read as manifesting neutrality with respect to judicial abolition of vertical privity and/or extensions of the horizontal privity concepts in the section.[61] The most widely enacted version of this Code section permits a buyer or any member of his family or household, or a household guest, to sue for personal injuries sustained because a product was not as warranted.[62] One alternative draft of the same section goes beyond this extension and permits any "natural user" of the product to sue for breach of warranty when he sustains bodily injury.[63] The most liberal alternative also permits any contemplated user to sue not only for personal injuries but also for any property damage caused by the defective product.[64] Many courts have judicially abolished vertical privity on the footing that they were not precluded by the Code in so doing, i.e., the Code does not speak to vertical priv-

---

[58] *See* Note, *Karl Llewellyn and the Intellectual Foundations of Enterprise Liability Theory,* 97 YALE L.J. 1131 (1988) (suggesting that Llewellyn has not received anything like the credit he deserved for the foundational ideas of enterprise liability which many judges and tort scholars wittingly or unwittingly used in their development of the concept). Llewellyn had included § 16-B in the Uniform Revised Sales Act (later to become the basis for Article 2 of the UCC) as the central products liability section. At a meeting in Indianapolis, the Commissioners on Uniform State Laws rejected this suggestion.

[59] In addition to § 2-318 providing third party beneficiary rights to an injured party, the Code expressly permits recovery of consequential damages for "injury to person or property proximately resulting from any breach of warranty" in § 2-715(2)(b).

[60] UCC § 2-318.

[61] UCC § 2-318 comment 3. The comment is interesting since it suggests that courts should not regard the categories established in the enacted language as frozen. There is an open invitation to judicial extension of the statute.

[62] UCC § 2-318 Alternative A.

[63] Alternative B of § 2-318 extends protection "to any natural person" which would, *e.g.,* include a highly foreseeable user of a product, an employee.

[64] A few jurisdictions enacted Alternative C and some enacted their own version. California and Utah omitted § 2-318.

ity.[65] As to horizontal privity, the most popular version of Code § 2-318 was the more restrictive alternative limiting third party beneficiaries who could sue to members of the family or household or household guests.[66] Many courts have simply accepted the invitation of the comment to that section to extend "horizontal privity" to "beneficiaries" beyond those stated in the section language.[67]

With this unusual judicial-legislative development proceeding apace, the RESTATEMENT 2D OF TORTS has included what is, by now, a well-known provision, § 402A, which allows recovery by any contemplated user for personal injuries or property damage caused by a defective product.[68] This is a mutually exclusive tort theory which is clearly the more forthright and analytically sound means to accomplish the basic end of allocating the risk of injury due to defective products to the party better able to bear such risks. In most cases, that party is the manufacturer of the product though the injured party is not forced to bring the action against that party, i.e., he may sue his immediate seller and the seller will have an action over against the manufacturer.[69] Section 402A has been widely adopted by the courts and, in many states, a liberal Code theory is also available for any plaintiff in such an action. Thus, in the products liability area, a plaintiff with a justifiable claim often has a legal arsenal which can be described as "overkill." Again, this is due to the curious evolution of the warranty theory and the forthright theory of § 402A promulgated as part of the RESTATEMENT 2D OF TORTS in 1964. A comprehensive discussion of products liability is beyond the scope of this book and is normally dealt with in torts and commercial transactions contexts. The presence of § 402A in a given jurisdiction should relegate use of warranty theory to contractual loss, i.e., loss of bargain, rather than personal injury loss for which the UCC is poorly designed.[70] Unfortunately, warranty theory has been

---

[65] See, e.g., Kassab v. Central Soya, 432 Pa. 217, 246 A.2d 848 (1968).
[66] UCC § 2-318 Alternative A.
[67] See, e.g., Salvador v. Atlantic Steel Boiler Co., 457 Pa. 24, 319 A.2d 903 (1974).
[68] RESTATEMENT 2D OF TORTS § 402A provides:

Special Liability of Seller of Product for Physical Harm to User or Consumer.
    (1) One who sells any product in a defective condition unreasonably dangerous to the user or consumer or to his property is subject to liability for physical harm thereby caused to the ultimate user or consumer, or to his property, if
    (a) the seller is engaged in the business of selling such a product, and
    (b) it is expected to and does reach the user or consumer without substantial change in the condition in which it is sold.
    (2) The rule stated in Subsection (1) applies although
    (a) the seller has exercised all possible care in the preparation and sale of his product, and
    (b) the user or consumer has not bought the product or entered into any contractual relation with the seller.

[69] See, e.g., Newmark v. Gimbel's, Inc., 54 N.J. 585, 258 A.2d 697 (1969). The court suggests that the dealer (seller) should implead the manufacturer in the seller's own interest so as to avoid circuity of action.
[70] The UCC, for example, requires notice of breach with respect to accepted goods. Failure to provide such notice within a reasonable time after the buyer discovered or should have discovered such breach bars the buyer from any remedy. UCC § 2-607(3)(a). Notwithstanding comment 5 to this section which suggests some relaxation of the notice requirement for third party beneficiary plaintiffs, the notice requirement remains. Such a requirement for remote purchasers who have sustained bodily injury could work manifest injustice.
One of the better know disagreements between courts and particularly between well-known judges is found in two products liability cases dealing with loss of bargain. Justice Francis wrote

utilized by plaintiffs who have failed to bring their § 402A tort action within the personal injury statute of limitations and have sought relief pursuant to warranty theory solely because the Code features a four-year statute of limitations that could benefit some of these plaintiffs.[71] Because the Code expressly recognizes personal injuries as part of its definition of consequential damages,[72] some courts have felt compelled to permit a plaintiff who is out of time under the appropriate personal injury statute but, through uncommon luck, is able to bring an action within four years from the time the goods were delivered to the buyer,[73] to bring an action under the UCC.[74] This kind of holding is the product of a patchwork products liability concept in the UCC which, again, resulted from the understandable but unfortunate lack of appreciation for the precocious views of Karl Llewellyn in the 1940's. It is also due to the explicable but regrettable failure of courts to pursue the necessary scholarship and reflection to arrive at insightful and cohesive analyses.

---

the opinion for the court in Santor v. A & M Karagheusian, Inc., 44 N.J. 52, 207 A.2d 305 (1965) where a retail purchaser of carpeting that had developed lines brought an action against the manufacturer and the court suggested that § 402A of the RESTATEMENT 2D OF TORTS could be effectively used for this loss of bargain. In Seely v. White Motor Co., 45 Cal. Rptr. 17, 403 P.2d 145 (1965), the court's opinion by Justice Traynor strongly disagreed. The court saw no reason for imposing a strict liability in tort theory in the context of a commercial loss of bargain. Subsequent cases clearly favor the Traynor view even in New Jersey.

[71] See Hahn v. Atlantic Richfield Co., 625 F.2d 1095 (3d Cir. 1980). Unfortunately, the sound analysis in this opinion by Judge Aldisert was not accepted by the Supreme Court of Pennsylvania in Williams v. West Penn Power Co., 502 Pa. 557, 467 A.2d 811 (1983).

[72] UCC § 2-715(2)(b).

[73] The four year UCC statute of limitations begins to run at the time a cause of action accrues and a cause of action accrues when the breach of warranty occurs. The breach of warranty occurs *when tender of delivery is made. See* UCC § 2-725(2). A third party other than the buyer has nothing to do with tender of delivery. If, therefore, a third party is injured, waits beyond the personal injury statutory period, (*e.g.,* two years), and belatedly decides to bring an action against the seller or a remote distributor or manufacturer for his injuries under a warranty (UCC) theory, it is sheer good fortune for him to learn that tender of delivery to the buyer occurred less than four years from the time the third party filed the action. Moreover, it is clear beyond peradventure that § 2-725, the Article 2 UCC statute of limitations, was not designed to have any bearing on personal injury actions. *See* Murray, *Products Liability — Another Word,* 35 U. PITT. L. REV. 255 (1973) which analysis was adopted in *Hahn, supra* note 71.

[74] See Williams, supra note 71. See also Saraniero v. Safeway, Inc., 540 F. Supp. 749 (D. Kan. 1982). Contra see Franzen v. Deere & Co., 334 N.W.2d 730 (Iowa 1983); Witherspoon v. General Motors Corp., 535 F. Supp. 432 (W.D. Mo. 1982).

Chapter 11

THE ASSIGNMENT OF RIGHTS AND DELEGATION OF DUTIES

§ 135. Nature of Assignments.

A. *Concept and Terminology.*

One party to a contract may attempt to transfer his rights and/or duties under it to a third person without the consent of the other party to the contract. This chapter explores questions of to what extent and in what manner the law permits this to be done. At the outset, it is important to become familiar with the terminology courts have developed in discussing these questions. The words "assign" and "delegate" are somewhat unfortunate choices. What is sought to be accomplished is the *transfer* of rights and duties. Rights and duties, however, are subjective in nature and are, therefore, inherently incapable of being transferred. Thus, it is more appropriate to suggest that the subject of the right or duty may have the power, by a purported transfer, to cause a similar right or duty to be created in a third person. The real question to be answered is whether and to what extent an attempted transfer of a contract right or duty has legal significance. Moreover, the problem involved will be quite different depending upon whether it is a right or duty that is the subject matter of the attempted transfer. Consequently, for reasons which will appear in the sections to follow, the term "assignment" is relegated to a transfer of rights and the term "delegation" is used to describe the creation of duties in the third person.

1. Contract Right — "Property."

Where a party assigns his contract right to a third person, it is common to say that he is assigning a property right although the assigned right is to property that is *intangible* or what the common law courts called a "chose in action." A contract right, however, is not property in the usual sense of that term. It is an abstract right against a particular party who has a correlative duty. An owner of land or chattels has property rights in those tangible chattels against any other party, i.e., they may not trespass on his land or take possession of his chattels absent his consent. A house painter who is owed the contract price for his work in painting a house does not have a property right in this sense. Rather, his contract right is the subject matter of property rights. By calling it a "chose in action," the common law courts distinguished it from a "chose in possession."[1] The distinction is seen in a case involving a life insurance policy naming a wife as beneficiary. A decree of divorce was granted under which the former wife was to become the owner of all personal property on the premises which included the life insurance policy. The insured sought the policy to change the beneficiary by naming his second wife which the policy expressly permitted. The first wife refused to surrender the policy and the insured notified the insurer of the change. The insured died and the first wife sought the proceeds of the policy. The court recognized that the policy — the document — was not property, but the contract rights of the insured and the beneficiary were the subject of property rights. The first wife had attempted to interfere with the insured's contract right to change the beneficiary. The court held that she should not profit from her own wrong and held that she had no rights under the policy.[2] While courts may refer to a contract right as a "property right," it is important to remember the special connotation of that phrase as applied to contract rights.

2. Mechanics and Terminology of Assignment and Delegation — Beneficiary Contracts Distinguished.

Prior to this chapter, we spoke essentially in terms of promisors and promisees, adding third party beneficiaries in the last chapter. Where a contract right has been assigned or a contract duty delegated, the contract still involves promisors and promisees but our focus will be on what those parties have done with respect to their rights and duties. A party to a contract who has not yet performed his duty owes an obligation to the other party and, in that sense, he is an *obligor* (*OR*). The party to whom the obligation is owed is called an *obligee* (*OE*) who has a contract right against *OR*. By transferring that contract right, *OE* becomes an *assignor* (*AR*). The third party to whom that right is assigned is an *assignee* (*AE*) who now has the right against *OR* that *AR* had before the assignment. If the duty that *OR* had to *OE/AR* which he now owes to *AE* (because the correlative right has been assigned to *AE*)

---

[1] Professor Corbin explains that the term, "chose" is French expressing the same concept as the Latin "res" or the English, "thing." A chattel such a book or an automobile is a "chose in possession". If I agree to sell my automobile to another, I have a chose in possession until I deliver the car to the buyer. As soon as the contract is formed, I have a "chose in action" against the buyer which is the price he has agreed to pay for the car. Where there is no tangible property involved as in the contract to paint the house, the painter has a chose in action against the owner. This terminology is no longer used. *See* A. CORBIN, 4 CORBIN ON CONTRACTS § 859.

[2] *See* Olinger v. Northwestern Mut. Life Ins. Co., 153 Ind. App. 376, 287 N.E.2d 580 (1972). It should be noted, however, that stock certificates, bonds, and other "commercial specialties" are treated as "property" since the transfer of such a document is considered to be a transfer of property much like the transfer of any chattel. *See* Wolf v. Wolf, 147 Ind. App. 251, 259 N.E.2d 89 (1970) holding that bonds are personal property. The transfer of a negotiable instrument (draft, check, promissory note, or certificate of deposit) is subject to the rules and principles set forth in Articles 3 and 4 of the UCC. It is briefly explored later in this chapter though full discussion is found in treatments of commercial paper.

has been *delegated* to a third party *delegate* (*DE*), *OR* has become a *delegator* (*DR*), though he remains an *OR*, and *DE* owes the duty to *AE* though he would have owed it to *OE* had no assignment of the right occurred.[3] Assignments and delegation involve a third party assignee (*AE*) and/or a third party delegate (*DE*). It is important to distinguish these arrangements from third party beneficiary contracts.

As we saw in the preceding chapter, where a promisee intends to benefit a third party by inducing another (promisor) to make a promise, the performance of which will benefit the third party, a traditional third party beneficiary contract is formed and the third party has rights even before he is aware of the contract made for his benefit.[4] A third party assignee or delegate, on the other hand, becomes a party through the unilateral act of one of the parties to an *existing* contract, i.e., such a third party becomes involved in the contract *after formation.* Upon the delegation of a duty, a new third party beneficiary contract is created. Thus, where the house painter is owed $1000 for his work, the owner (*DR*) may have delegated the duty to pay to another (*DE*) who assumes the duty. The painter (*OE*) is now a third party (creditor) beneficiary of the contract between the owner and the delegate of the owner's duty.[5] The delegator can be viewed as a promisee and the delegate as a promisor who promises to pay the debt to the third party (obligee-painter). Where, however, there is only an assignment of a contract right, the obligor (*OR*) owes the performance of the correlative duty to the assignee (*AE*) who is the exclusive holder of that right since, upon assignment, the right was extinguished in the assignor (*AR*) and a similar right was recreated in the assignee (*AE*). There is no beneficiary contract in this situation since jural relations should exist only between the obligor and assignee.

B. *Evolution of Assignment and Delegation.*

1. Opposition at Early Common Law.

The early common law developed a general rule, subject to a few exceptions which are not important for our present purpose,[6] that an attempted assign-

---

[3] Had no assignment of the right occurred, OE is not AR since he becomes AR only if he assigns. Absent an assignment, AE would not exist.

[4] The rights, however, become "vested" only upon assent or reliance including the bringing of an action.

[5] As will be seen in more detail later in this chapter, the owner (delegator) will remain liable to the painter unless the painter has agreed to accept the delegate in place of the owner thereby forming a contract of novation which discharges the duty of the owner to the painter.

[6] The following exceptions to this rule were recognized from very early times:

(a) Assignments made to or by the Crown were effective and in such cases the assignee could sue at law in his own name. *See* Cardozo, J., in People v. Ladew, 237 N.Y. 413, 143 N.E. 238 at 246 (1924); Holdsworth, *The History of the Treatment of Choses in Action by the Common Law,* 33 Harv. L. Rev. 997 (1920), Selected Readings On Contracts 706, 714 (1931).

(b) Negotiable instruments were assignable by the law merchant, which in time became a part of the common law. The law relating to such instruments has been codified both in England and in the United States. In England it was codified in the Bills Of Exchange Act which was passed in 1882. In the United States it was codified in what is known as the Uniform Negotiable Instruments Law and more recently in Articles 3 and 4 of UCC, which is now the prevailing law. For a good discussion of the difference between negotiable instruments and non-negotiable choses in action *see* Gilmore, *The Commercial Doctrine of Good Faith Purchase,* 63 Yale L.J. 1057, 1063-68 (1954).

ment of a contract right was of no legal effect whatever.[7] This result was apparently reached because of a belief that such a right was too personal to be capable of being placed in hands other than those selected by the obligor. When one considers the severity of the penalties that could be invoked against a defaulting debtor in the early days of the common law, one can understand why the courts were inclined to take the view that he could be made liable only to the person whom he had selected as obligee.[8] It has sometimes been supposed that it was the law against maintenance — encouraging or "stirring up litigation" — that invalidated the assignment of contract rights.[9] However, this could not have been so, since it is clear that the rule prohibiting assignments antedates the law relating to maintenance.[10]

2. Circumvention — Agency — Power of Attorney.

Although contract rights were not assignable, a way of accomplishing much the same result was soon found. It was permissible, even in the early law, for one man to appoint another his agent to receive, in his name and stead, a performance that was due him. This being so, if he gave the other person permission to retain what was received by way of performance of the obligation, the essential objective of an assignment was attained. Consequently, we find that it became customary for a creditor who wished to transfer his claim to appoint the transferee his agent to collect, with a proviso that the agent should retain the proceeds when collected. So common did this practice become, that in the course of time the rule emerged that any attempted assignment, even without an express grant of a power of attorney, by implication conferred upon the assignee such a power to collect in the name of the assignor and to retain the proceeds for his own use.[11] This mode of giving effect to an assignment, however, had distinct disadvantages. Since an assignee acquired merely a power of attorney to enforce the claim in the right of the assignor, if it became necessary to bring an action, that action had to be prosecuted in the name of the assignor. Moreover, this power of attorney was subject to the usual infirmities inherent in such a power, i.e., it might be terminated by the death of the assignor,[12] and it did not survive either his death or his bankruptcy.[13]

(c) Certain covenants in conveyances are said to run with the land; that is, transfer of ownership of the land, in relation to which the covenant was made, carries with it the right or duty, as the case may be, growing out of the covenant. See 3 HOLDSWORTH, HISTORY OF ENGLISH LAW 130-35 (1923).

[7] See Mowse v. Edney, Rolle's Abr., 20 Pl. 12 [1600]; Penson & Higbed's Case, 4 Leon. 99.
See generally Bailey, Assignments of Debts in England from the Twelfth to the Twentieth Century, 47 LAW Q. REV. 516 (1931), 48 LAW Q. REV. 248, 547 (1932).

[8] Id., 48 LAW Q. REV. 547, at 547.

[9] See Lampet's Case, 10 Coke Rep. 48a.

[10] The objection of maintenance did, however, retard the development of the idea of assignability for a long time. See 7 HOLDSWORTH, HISTORY OF ENGLISH LAW 534 (1925); Ames, Disseisin Of Chattels, 3 SELECT ESSAYS IN ANGLO-AMERICAN LEGAL HISTORY 580 (1909).

[11] Apparently at first a power of attorney expressed in terms was essential. See Mallory v. Lane, Cro. Jac. 342.

[12] Potter v. Turner, Winch 7 [1622].

[13] See Backwell v. Litcott, 2 Keble 331 [1669].

3. The Intervention of Equity.

In view of the difficulties which beset the assignee under the common law, it is not strange that he should have appealed to the chancellor. The equity courts seemingly took a different view of the matter from a very early day and soon began to hold that the assignee might bring a suit on the assigned claim in that court in his own name.[14] Moreover, they took the view that the assignee's right was not revocable by the assignor.[15] In fact, they treated the assignee as having a claim in his own right. As a consequence, it came to be said that contract rights were assignable in equity but not at law.[16] Spurred on by this development in equity, the common law courts later re-examined the question and, in the latter part of the 18th century, began to hold that the power of attorney created by an attempted assignment was irrevocable,[17] and that it was not affected by the death or bankruptcy of the assignor.[18] But they did not go further than this. They did not permit the assignee to sue in his own name, in the absence of a statute permitting it, as did the courts of equity.[19]

4. Real Party in Interest Statutes.

Today, there are statutes throughout the country — "real party in interest statutes" — which require an assignee to bring an action in his own name in a court of law. Because of the changed attitude on the part of the law courts, equity courts had renounced the jurisdiction which they once exercised in assignment cases. It is now the general rule that an assignee must seek redress in a law court, in the absence of special circumstances making the remedy in that court inadequate.[20] As a result of these fundamental changes in the law relating to the assignment of contract rights, the nature of the assignee's right had become a prolific source of controversy. The essential dispute was whether the assignee was to be viewed as the legal as well as the equitable owner of the assigned right, or whether he merely held an irrevoca-

---

[14] See Cook, *The Alienability of Choses in Action,* 29 HARV. L. REV. 816 (1916), SELECTED READINGS ON CONTRACTS 738, at 742 (1931).

[15] Peters v. Soame, 2 Vern. 428 [1701]; Fashion v. Atwood, 2 Ch. Cas. 7 [1688].

[16] "That a debt may be assigned in equity there is no doubt, and I should rejoice if the scandal did not exist of there being one rule at law and another in equity." Martin B., in Liversidge v. Broadbent, 4 H. & N. 603 [1859].

[17] Welch v. Mandeville, 14 U.S. (1 Wheat.) 233 (1816) (a dismissal of the suit by the assignor in collusion with the defendant does not bar a later suit by the assignee in the assignor's name); Legh v. Legh, 1 B. & P. 447 [1799] (a release of the debtor by the assignor, when the former had knowledge of the assignment, did not bar a suit by the assignee in the assignor's name).

[18] Winch v. Keeley, 1 Term Rep. 619 [1787] (bankruptcy).

If the assignor dies suit may be brought by the assignee in the name of the assignor's executor or administrator. Foss v. Lowell Five Cents Sav. Bank, 111 Mass. 285 (1873).

[19] See Fed. R. Civ. P. 17 (a). See also Clark & Hutchins, *The Real Party in Interest,* 34 YALE L.J. 259 (1925). For the most recent and detailed compilation of such enactments, see RESTATEMENT 2d Statutory Note to ch. 15.

[20] Hayward v. Andrews, 106 U.S. 672 (1883); Walker v. Brooks, 125 Mass. 241 (1878); Cator v. Burke, 1 Bro. C.C. 434.

But cf. Farmers' Exch. v. Walter M. Lowney Co., 95 Vt. 445, 115 A. 507 (1921), in which it was held that the rights of an assignee, where the assignment is inferred from the assignor's conduct and was not expressed in language, are cognizable only in equity. The soundness of such a holding is open to question.

ble power of attorney to enforce the right with the equitable ownership of the right remaining in the assignor.[21] This dispute is now a matter of antiquarian interest. With the development of "real party in interest" statutes, it is clear that the assignee is the exclusive holder of the contract right without distinguishing between legal and equitable ownership. It is also abundantly clear that, "The force of human convenience and business practice was too strong for the common-law doctrine that choses in action are not assignable."[22]

§ 136. The Uniform Commercial Code — Assignments.

One of the most significant uses of assignments in modern law occurs in the context of commercial financing. Where a retail business sells goods to consumers, more often than not, the sale is on credit, i.e., the buyer promises to pay the price plus interest at some time in the future. The retailer receives a promise from the buyer which can take different forms. Whatever the form, the retailer is interested in converting that promise into money which he may do by assigning his right to a commercial lender such as a bank or other financing institution. The retailer's seller who may be a manufacturer or wholesaler pursues the same process with respect to the retailer's promise to pay for goods sold to the retailer on credit. This is sometimes known as accounts receivable financing, i.e., the buyer is treated as an "account."

The UCC deals with assignment of rights and delegation of duties in Article 2 (concerned only with the sale of goods)[23] and in Article 9 which deals with security interests in personal property.[24] A security interest secures payment or performance of an obligation,[25] i.e., a debtor[26] enters into a security agreement[27] with a creditor which evidences a transfer of a security interest in certain property (collateral)[28] of the debtor to assure the creditor of payment of any outstanding obligation. Once he has such assurance of payment, the creditor is a secured party, i.e., he has a security interest in the property specified in the security agreement.[29] To have an *attached and enforceable*[30]

---

[21] See Cook, *The Alienability of Choses in Action,* 29 HARV. L. REV. 816 (1916), SELECTED READINGS ON CONTRACTS 738 (1931), 30 HARV. L. REV. 449 (1917), SELECTED READINGS ON CONTRACTS 763 (1931); Williston, *Is the Right of an Assignee of a Chose in Action Legal or Equitable?* 30 HARV. L. REV. 97 (1916), SELECTED READINGS ON CONTRACTS 754 (1931), 31 HARV. L. REV. 822 (1918), SELECTED READINGS ON CONTRACTS 790 (1931).

[22] See Union Life Ins. Co. v. Priest, 594 F.2d 1252 (10th Cir. 1982) quoting Professor Corbin at 4 CORBIN ON CONTRACTS § 909 at 643-44.

[23] See UCC § 2-210.

[24] UCC § 9-318. All references to Article 9 of the UCC will be to the 1978 Official Text. The major changes in Article 9 occurred in the 1972 version. In 1977, changes to Article 8 (Investment Securities) required conforming changes in Article 9 and the 1978 version includes all of those changes as well as the major changes in the 1972 version.

[25] UCC § 1-201(37).

[26] UCC § 9-105(1)(d).

[27] UCC § 9-105(1)(l).

[28] UCC § 9-105(1)(c).

[29] UCC § 9-105(1)(m).

[30] The earlier (1968) version of Article 9 dealt with "attached" (§ 9-204) and "enforceable" (§ 9-203) security interests separately. The enforceability of security interests (requiring a writing for non-possessory security interest) is a statute of frauds concept. The 1972 version combines attachment and enforceability in one section (§ 9-203) to avoid the anomaly under the earlier version which allowed a security interest to be attached and even perfected without being enforceable.

security interest, there must be (a) either a security agreement signed by the debtor or the collateral must be in the possession of the secured party pursuant to agreement, (b) the secured party must have given value[31] in exchange for the grant of the security interest, and (c) the debtor must have rights in the collateral.[32] An attached and enforceable security interest will protect the secured party as to his debtor, certain purchasers of the collateral, and unsecured creditors.[33] The secured party, however, needs protection against other secured creditors of the debtor as well as lien creditors.[34] This protection can be obtained through the *perfection* of the security interest in the collateral[35] which occurs typically through filing a financing statement in one or more appropriate state offices,[36] or through possession of the collateral which perfects the security interest without filing.[37] Thus, Article 9 of the UCC establishes a comprehensive structure dealing with security interests in personal property and fixtures[38] which secure payment or performance of obligations. Article 9 is one of the most significant contributions of the Code since it brings uniformity to an aspect of commercial law which had been subjected to highly variable state statutes dealing with such pre-Code security devices as chattel mortgages, conditional sales, trust receipts and factor's liens. All of these devices are now simply called security interests under Article 9 of the Code. While a comprehensive exploration of Article 9 is beyond the scope of this volume, the contracts student must be aware of the Article 9 influence on assignments.

Article 9 may appear to have little to do with assignments since it deals with the transfer of security interests which, again, are property interests designed to assure the repayment of outstanding obligations. The debtor retains rights in the collateral, i.e., he still "owns" the collateral, even though. he has pledged the collateral as security for the loan, just as a mortgagor still owns his real property even though he has granted the bank (mortgagee) a security interest in that property. Granting a security interest in collateral, therefore, is not an assignment of the debtor's rights in the collateral. How, then, does Article 9 affect the law of assignments?

---

[31] UCC § 1-201(44).

[32] UCC § 9-203(1).

[33] UCC § 9-201.

[34] UCC § 9-305.

[35] UCC § 9-303.

[36] UCC §§ 9-302, 9-401, 9-402, 9-403.

[37] UCC § 9-305. While possessory security interests are pragmatic in isolated situations, commercial financing often requires the debtor to retain possession of the collateral which is to be sold or used so as to pay the outstanding indebtedness. Thus, a secured party may take a security interest in a retailer's inventory, i.e., goods held for resale or for lease (§ 9-109(4)). The debtor must have possession of such inventory if he is to earn income so as to, *inter alia*, repay the outstanding debt plus interest which is the secured party's primary goal. When the retailer sells off the inventory, the secured party's security interest is automatically continued in the substitutes for that inventory such as cash, checks, or accounts receivable, i.e., the secured party's interest continues in the *proceeds* received by his debtor (§ 9-306). Another example of the collateral remaining in the possession of the debtor would be the common situation of a security interest in the debtor's equipment (§ 9-109(2)) which the debtor must retain to remain in business and, again, to achieve the primary goal of the secured creditor, i.e., the repayment of the outstanding loan with interest. Thus, possessory security interests are relegated to jewelry, certificates of stock, documents of title, (*e.g.*, bills or lading or warehouse receipts), or other valuables which the debtor can do without during the term of the loan.

[38] UCC § 9-313.

Since commercial financing is filled with the transfer of accounts for the reasons suggested at the beginning of this section,[39] the drafters of Article 9 had to consider whether they were real assignments or whether the debtor was simply granting a security interest in the accounts. Theoretically, Article 9 should apply only to the latter situation since, again, it deals with the creation of security interests in collateral. The reality of commercial financing, however, makes it very difficult to determine precisely whether the debtor has sold (assigned) the accounts or merely granted a security interest in them. Because this distinction is often "blurred,"[40] the drafters decided to include within the coverage of Article 9 the *sale* or assignment of accounts as well as security interests in accounts.[41] If Article 9 applies to the assignment of accounts, the requirements of that Article must be met with respect to any such assignment, i.e., the elements of attachment and enforceability as well as the requirements for perfection must be met.

Essentially, Article 9 will apply to the assignment of accounts in a commercial financing context. A transaction involving the sale of accounts will not be included if it is not designed to finance the business. Thus, for example, the sale of accounts as part of a sale of the business out of which they arose, the assignment of accounts for collection purposes, a transfer of a right to payment under a contract to an assignee who is also to perform under the contract, or the assignment of an account to an assignee in whole or partial satisfaction of a pre-existing debt are not typical commercial financing assignments of accounts. Therefore, Article 9 does not apply to such assignments which means that the requirements of Article 9 need not be met with respect to such assignments.[42] While Article 9 does apply to commercial financing assignments of accounts, if a particular assignment does not transfer a significant part of the outstanding accounts of the assignor (alone or in conjunction with other assignments), there is no need to meet the filing requirements of Article 9 to perfect that assignment and thus provide protection from other secured creditors or lien creditors under Article 9. That type of commercial financing assignment is perfected without filing.[43]

The foregoing sketch of Article 9 as it relates to assignments does not begin to deal with myriad complications that arise in related Article 9 questions. Those questions must be left for the study of commercial law.[44] It is, however, important for the student of contract law to recognize the critical intersection

---

[39] An account is defined as any right to payment for goods sold or leased or for services rendered which is not evidenced by an instrument (*e.g.*, promissory note) or chattel paper (monetary obligation combined with a security agreement (§ 9-105(1)(b)) whether or not it has been earned by performance. § 9-106. Prior to the 1972 version, Article 9 distinguished "accounts" from "contract rights," i.e., where the seller had already performed by delivering goods or rendering services, obligation of the buyer was called an account. Where, however, performance had not occurred on either side, the seller had a mere contract right. In the 1972 version, "contract right" was eliminated as unnecessary and the term "account" applies to a right to payment whether the right is "earned" or "unearned" in the sense that the seller's performance is still executory.

[40] Comment 2 to § 9-102: "Commercial financing on the basis of accounts . . . is often so conducted that the distinction between a security transfer and a sale is blurred. . . ."

[41] UCC § 9-102(1)(b).

[42] UCC § 9-104(f).

[43] UCC § 9-302(1)(e).

[44] *See generally* J. WHITE & R. SUMMERS, UNIFORM COMMERCIAL CODE CHAPTERS 21-25 (1988). As to the applicability of Article 9 to the sale or assignability of accounts, *see* § 21-9 at 955-57.

between the common law of assignments and Article 9 of the UCC since, again, innumerable assignments of this type occur daily.

§ 137. The Form and Revocability of Assignments.

A. *Manifestation of Intention.*

1. Oral — Written — Statute of Frauds — Uniform Commercial Code.

In the absence of a statute or a contract provision to the contrary, there are no prescribed formalities which must be observed to make an effective assignment. It suffices that the assignor has in some way manifested an intention to make a present transfer of his rights to the assignee.[45] This intention may be manifested by words, by conduct, or both.[46] Unless required by statute or the contract itself, the manifested intention to assign need not be evidenced by a writing.[47] Statutes of Frauds, however, apply to assignments. Thus, an assignment of an estate or interest in real property for more than one year requires a writing.[48] An assignment of personal property would require written evidence under the UCC.[49] As suggested in the prior section, an assignment of accounts requires compliance with Article 9 of the Code so that an oral assignment of accounts would not only be unenforceable; it would not even attach.[50] Where, however, an assignor testifies that the assignment occurred, as in other cases of admitting the existence of an oral agreement, the statute of frauds should be satisfied so as to make the oral assignment effective.[51]

2. Present Transfer.

It is abundantly clear that anything other than a manifestation of an intention to make a *present transfer* of a right will not amount to an assignment, whatever else the legal significance of such a manifestation.[52] It should be

---

[45] Zimmerman v. Kyte, 53 Wash. App. 11, 765 P.2d 905 (1988). *See also* Benton v. Alberquerque Nat'l Bank, 103 N.M. 5, 701 P.2d 1025 ("assigned to Bruce Benton" was an unambiguous manifestation of intention to effect an inter vivos assignment). The term "assignment," however, is not essential.

[46] Miller v. Wells Fargo Bank Int'l Corp., 406 F. Supp. 452 (S.D.N.Y. 1975) (may be manifested by conduct, writing, or parol).

[47] *See, e.g.,* Estate of Bryan v. Bryan, 513 Pa. 554, 522 A.2d 40 (1987) (oral assignments are permissible); Kershner v. Hill Truck Line, Inc., 637 S.W.2d 769 (Mo. App. 1982) (oral assignment effective when made and not postponed because of later formal assignment). *See also* Anaconda Alum. Co. v. Sharp, 243 Miss. 9, 136 So. 2d 585 (1962); General Excavator Co. v. Judkins, 128 Ohio St. 160, 190 N.E. 389 (1934); Jewett Lumber Co. v. Anderson Coal Co., 181 Iowa 950, 165 N.W. 211 (1917). RESTATEMENT 2d § 324.

[48] *See, e.g.,* Rosefan Constr. Corp. v. Salazar, 114 Misc. 2d 956, 452 N.Y.S.2d 1016 (1982).

[49] UCC § 2-106. Other sections of the Code deal with the statute of frauds requirements for the sale of goods, investments securities, and security agreements. These provisions prevent enforcement against the assignor, but they do not prevent enforcement against the obligor. RESTATEMENT 2d § 324 comment b referring to § 144. *See also* § 140.

[50] First Nat'l Bank of Gaylord v. Martin, 9 Kan. App. 2d 96, 673 P.2d 448 (1983) (also holding that the assignment of accounts was not excluded under § 9-104(f) as a transfer of a right to payment to an assignee who is also to do the performance under the contract since that exception applies only to situations where the assignor both delegates a duty to perform and assigns the right to payment to the same person).

[51] *See Zimmerman, supra* note 45.

[52] Coca Cola Bottling Co. of Elizabethtown, Inc. v. Coca-Cola Co., 654 F. Supp. 1419 (D. Del. 1987) (owner of right must manifest intention to make present transfer of right without further action).

emphasized that the right may arise from an executory contract, i.e., a house painter may assign his right under a contract to paint the obligor's house before he paints the house.[53] To be effective, an assignment must be a completed transaction between the parties which is intended to vest in the assignee a present right,[54] since assignment extinguishes the right in the assignor and passes all of the assignor's interest to the assignee.[55] Where, for example, a document stated that a party agreed with another that the latter was "entitled" to one half the commission to be earned on the sale of property, the court held that it represented a mere agreement to assign rather than an assignment.[56] A promise to give a party any proceeds recovered from a claim is not an assignment.[57] A promise to make an assignment to a creditor in the future or to collect a sum of money owed the promisor and pay it to the promisee would not constitute an assignment.[58]

3. Order Assignments.

Where money is owed by an obligor (OR) to an obligee (OE), OE may deliver a written instrument to an assignee (AE) which orders OR to pay AE with the intention that AE retain that payment. Such an order constitutes an assignment since the apparent intention of OE is to make a present transfer to AE.[59] If, however, OE simply directs that order to OR, the third party is not an assignee since the intention to transfer to AE is absent.[60] Where a checking account customer (drawer) draws a check on his bank (drawee) which orders the bank to pay to the order of a named party (payee), the payee is not an assignee because the order is directed to the general credit of the bank.[61] If, however, an order is made payable from a particular fund, it is normally held to be an assignment since, by making it payable from a specified fund, there is a manifestation of intention to transfer to the payee presently the drawer's (obligee's) right to the fund or to so much of it as is directed to be paid to the payee.[62]

---

[53] See RESTATEMENT 2d § 320.

[54] Weston v. Dowty, 163 Mich. App. 238, 414 N.W.2d 165 (1987).

[55] In re Musser v. Musser, 24 Bankr. 913 (W.D. Va. 1982). See also Patrons State Bank & Trust Co. v. Shapiro, 215 Kan. 856, 528 P.2d 1198 (1974) (right of assignor is divested).

[56] Donovan v. Middlebrook, 95 App. Div. 365, 88 N.Y.S. 607 (1904).

[57] See Weston v. Dowty, supra note 54.

[58] See State Cent. Sav. Bank v. Hemmy, 77 F.2d 458 (8th Cir. 1935); Lauerman Bros. v. Komp, 156 Wis. 12, 145 N.W. 174 (1914).

[59] RESTATEMENT 2d § 325(1).

[60] Miller v. Wells Fargo Bank Int'l Corp., 406 F. Supp. 452 (S.D.N.Y. 1975); Associated Metals & Minerals Corp. v. Isletmeleri, 6 Ill. App. 2d 548, 128 N.E.2d 595 (1955). If OR pays the third party, however, OR's debt to OE is discharged to that extent. Again, the third party is not an assignee and has no right against OR.

[61] UCC § 3-409(1).

[62] Andrews Elec. Co. v. St. Alphonse Cath. Total Abstinence Soc'y, 233 Mass. 20, 123 N.E. 103 (1919); Fourth Street Nat'l Bank v. Yardley, 165 U.S. 634 (1897); Brill v. Tuttle, 81 N.Y. 454, 37 Am. Dec. 515 (1880). It should be noted that such an instrument would not be a negotiable instrument under the UCC. See UCC § 3-105(1(g) which suggests that an order remain unconditional and, therefore negotiable (if other elements are met) even though payment is limited to a particular fund if the instrument is issued by a government or governmental agency or unit.

B. *Consideration — Gratuitous Assignments.*

1. Gift Assignments — Revocability — History.

There should no longer be any question as to the effectiveness of a gratuitous assignment. The obligor may not defend on the ground that the assignee gave no consideration or that there was no substitute validation device.[63] The problem, however, is that gratuitous assignments are generally said to be revocable. To understand how courts decided that certain gratuitous assignments became irrevocable, it is important to begin with some history.

As we have already seen, historically, an assignment was effective at law only on the theory that it created in the assignee a power of attorney to enforce the claim in the right of the assignor.[64] Such a power, in the course of time, was held to be irrevocable when consideration was paid for it. If it was conferred upon the assignee gratuitously, it continued to be revocable by the assignor and terminable on his death or bankruptcy like any other agency similarly conferred. Moreover, even the court of equity, which seemed to treat the assignee who paid value for his assignment as owner of the claim, was hesitant to take this view in the case of one who had paid no consideration. The oft repeated maxim that "equity will not aid a volunteer" was apparently thought to stand in the way.[65] As time went on, however, courts of law (assisted by legislation) adopted a more favorable attitude toward the assignment of contract rights. They began to deal with the matter by analogizing to the law governing the transfer of tangible chattels.

2. Gift Analogy — Seal — Symbolic Documents — the Contract.

a. Seal.

A gift of a chattel normally occurred through delivery of the chattel with donative intent. Delivery of a deed of gift under seal, however, was also effective.[66] Courts, therefore, were pleased to treat delivered,[67] gratuitous assignments under seal as completed (irrevocable) gifts.[68]

---

[63] *See* Union Life Ins. Co. v. Priest, 694 F.2d 1252 (10th Cir. 1982) quoting Professor Corbin at 4 CORBIN § 909 to the effect that it is no longer necessary to review the learned arguments made for and against the theory that an assignment was ineffective unless it was for value. The cases holding a gift assignment effective are legion. *See* RESTATEMENT 2d § 332.

[64] *See supra* § 135(B).

[65] The early authorities are collected and discussed in Anson, *Assignment of Choses in Action,* 17 LAW Q. REV. 90 (1901); Costigan, *Gifts Inter Vivos of Choses in Action,* 27 LAW Q. REV. 326 (1911); Jenks, *Consideration and the Assignment of Choses in Action,* 16 LAW Q. REV. 241 (1900). It has, of course, always been true that so long as the power of attorney which is implied from the fact of assignment is unrevoked and has not been legally terminated, the assignee has authority to collect the assigned claim. Therefore, want of consideration for the assignment is not, by itself, a defense to the debtor when he is sued by the assignee. Perkes v. Utah Idaho Milk Co., 85 Utah 217, 39 P.2d 308 (1934); Morrison v. Ross, 113 Ind. 186, 14 N.E. 479 (1887); Briscoe v. Eckley, 35 Mich. 112 (1876).

[66] *See* RESTATEMENT 2d § 332 comment b.

[67] The concept of "delivery" is treated the same way for gratuitous assignments as it is for gifts of chattels. For an analysis *see* BROWN, PERSONAL PROPERTY §§ 7.2-7.9 (3d ed. 1975).

[68] Abrain v. Pereira, 336 Mass. 460, 146 N.E.2d 360 (1957); Chase Nat'l Bank v. Sayles, 11 F.2d 948 (1st Cir. 1926); Meyers v. Meyers, 99 N.J. Eq. 560, 134 A. 95 (1926). RESTATEMENT 2d § 332(1)(b).

b. Symbolic Documents.

Certain types of documents are treated as more than mere evidence of a contract right, i.e., the right inheres in the document. They are documents that have to be at least presented or even surrendered to activate the right to performance.[69] The classic example is the savings bank passbook. Delivery of such a passbook with the requisite donative intent creates an irrevocable gratuitous assignment or simply a valid *inter vivos*[70] gift of a chose in action.[71] The same analysis applies to insurance policies[72] and shares of stock.[73]

c. Unsealed, Nonsymbolic, Writings.

With the abolition or substantial weakening of the seal, it is now generally agreed that an assignment in writing, signed and delivered by the assignor to the assignee, or to one on his behalf with an intention to vest the right in the assignee, would constitute an irrevocable gratuitous assignment.[74] The interesting question is whether delivery of such a writing will be effective to transfer rights represented by symbolic documents, i.e., if there are shares of stock or an insurance policy, will the courts insist that the symbolic document be delivered rather than a writing evidencing an intention of the present transfer of that right to the assignee? The cases that have dealt with this question do not require delivery of the symbolic document to effectuate an irrevocable gratuitous assignment.[75]

d. Evidentiary RESTATEMENT 2d Extension.

If there is no symbolic document and no written assignment, may a party assign a contract right by delivery of the "contract" itself, i.e., by delivery of the written evidence of the contract? The case law is scant and divided.[76] The RESTATEMENT 2d suggests that some kinds of writings, albeit not the traditional symbolic document that must be exhibited or surrendered to enforce the right contained therein, are still more than mere written evidence of the contract. The RESTATEMENT 2d calls these writings "evidentiary writings" and

---

[69] Several commercial documents fall into this classification, *e.g.*, a document of title (bill of lading or warehouse receipt), UCC § 1-201(15) or a certificated security, UCC § 8-102.

[70] An *inter vivos* gift (from one living person to another) is a completed gift upon delivery and acceptance by the donee. A *causa mortis* gift (in contemplation of death) is revoked upon the survival of the donor. A gratuitous assignment, *causa mortis*, is subject to the same rule as if it were the gift of a tangible chattel. RESTATEMENT 2d § 332 comment e.

[71] Hileman v. Hulver, 243 Md. 527, 221 A.2d 693 (1965).

[72] *See* Bimestefer v. Bimestefer, 205 Md. 541, 109 A.2d 768 (1954) (insurance policy certificate under a group life plan could be assigned by insured handing the certificate to his son and saying,"I want you to have it. It will be a nest egg for you and will help with David's education. This is yours." Assignment, however, is prevented by effective anti-assignment clause).

[73] Herbert v. Simson, 220 Mass. 480, 108 N.E. 65 (1915). *See* RESTATEMENT 2d § 332(1)(b).

[74] Speelman v. Pascal, 10 N.Y.2d 313, 178 N.E.2d 723 (1961) (applying New York statute); Berl v. Rosenberg, 169 Cal. App. 2d 125, 336 P.2d 975 (1959); Thatcher v. Merriam, 121 Utah 191, 240 P.2d 266 (1952); Petty v. Mutual Benefit Life Ins. Co., 235 Iowa 455, 15 N.W.2d 613 (1944); Steffen v. Davis, 52 S.D. 283, 217 N.W. 221 (1927). RESTATEMENT 2d § 332(1)(a).

[75] *See* Leedham v. Leedham, 218 Iowa 767, 254 N.W. 61 (1934) (rights in shares of stock were effectively assigned by written assignment); Petty v. Mutual Benefit Life Ins. Co., 235 Iowa 455, 15 N.W.2d 613 (1944) (rights under insurance policy effectively assigned by written assignment).

[76] *See, e.g.*, Cook v. Lum, 55 N.J.L. 373, 26 A. 803 (1893) (ineffective assignment); *In re* Huggin's Estate, 204 Pa. 167, 53 A. 746 (1902) (effective assignment).

describes them as the type where the right is "so integrated in the writing" that the parol evidence rule would apply and its delivery is an "appropriate formality" though, again, it is not required.[77] Illustrations of the type of writing contemplated by this extension are a writing evidencing a contract for the sale of land[78] and a bank receipt.[79] We are, however, left with a test that suggests that the "evidentiary writing" must be integrated, presumably it must be both complete and final, so that no evidence of prior contradictory or consistent agreements would be admissible, and it must also be the type of writing making its delivery "an appropriate formality to validate a gift of that right."[80] Presumably, the drafters of this extension felt that they had gone as far as possible in a *restatement* of the law. Unfortunately, the result is a three-tiered analysis. The symbolic tier is reasonably certain; the written assignment tier is equally certain. It is what might be called the middle tier — the nonsymbolic but more than usual written evidence tier — that is filled with ambiguity. It would have been preferable to indulge in an artistic expansion to permit the present transfer of any sufficient writing evidencing the contract to constitute an effective assignment. After all, where there is no writing, there are cases permitting an oral assignment to be effective if the obligor is notified by the assignor.[81]

C. *Revocation of Gratuitous Assignments — Disclaimer.*

Where there is no completed gift, i.e., where there is no delivery of any of the effective writings described above, a gratuitous assignment, like a gift promise, is revocable. If an assignment is supported by consideration, it is not a gratuitous assignment any more than a promise supported by consideration is a gratuitous promise.[82] It must, however, be emphasized that an assignment is not a promise — it is a *present* transfer of a right, i.e., there is nothing *in futuro* about it. An assignment that is not supported by consideration may still have been given for value. The value may have been in total or partial satisfaction of a pre-existing debt or it may have been given as security for such a debt. Value is defined more broadly than consideration[83] and assignment for value is not a gratuitous assignment, i.e., it is irrevocable.

Absent consideration or value, delivery of a symbolic or "evidentiary" writing, or a lesser writing evidencing the assignment, the gratuitous assignment is revocable upon the death or incapacity of the assignor, by his assignment of the right to a subsequent assignee (evidencing his intention to revoke the original assignment), or by a straightforward notice received by the assignee or obligor from the assignor that the assignment is revoked.[84] The power of

---

[77] RESTATEMENT 2d § 332 comment d.

[78] RESTATEMENT 2d § 332 ill. 5 based on *In re* Huggin's Estate, *supra* note 76.

[79] RESTATEMENT 2d § 332 ill. 6 based on Cronin v. Chelsea Sav. Bank, 201 Mass. 146, 87 N.E. 484 (1907).

[80] RESTATEMENT 2d § 332 comment d.

[81] *See, e.g.,* Dinslage v. Stratman, 105 Neb. 274, 180 N.W. 81 (1920).

[82] *See* RESTATEMENT 2d § 332(5)(a).

[83] *See* the definition of "value" in UCC § 1-201(44).

[84] RESTATEMENT 2d § 332(3). Under the Federal Bankruptcy Reform Act (1978), the bankrupt's trustee may exercise the power of revocation of a gratuitous assignment, 11 U.S.C. § 541. If the

revocation, however, can be thwarted before its exercise if the assignee obtains payment or satisfaction of the obligation from the obligor,[85] is awarded a judgment against the obligor on the assigned right,[86] or effects a novation with the obligor,[87] i.e., the assignee agrees to accept a new obligor in substitution for the original obligor who is discharged. Moreover, since consideration or value exchanged for the assigned right will make the assignment irrevocable as a non-gratuitous assignment, it is not remarkable that a gratuitous assignment inducing detrimental reliance by the assignee will be irrevocable to the extent necessary to avoid injustice.[88]

Finally, it should be noted that an assignee may disclaim an assignment made for his benefit,[89] though acceptance of a gratuitous assignment beneficial to the assignee is often said to be presumed.[90]

§ 138. Assignable Rights — Limitations.

We have seen that the assignment of a contract right extinguishes the right in the assignor and causes a similar right to arise in the assignee.[91] Assuming an effective assignment, the legal right which the assignee acquires is not the identical right which the assignor had. Similarly, the correlative duty of the promisor, whose promise was the basis of the assigned right, will necessarily have been changed. Whereas the promisor had owed the duty to the assignor who had the correlative right, the duty is now owed to the assignee who has the right to receive a duplicate performance from the promisor. Whether the law will permit such a change to be made in the obligation of the promisor without his consent will depend upon the circumstances of the particular case. Though the modern view is that contract rights should be freely assignable,[92] there are limitations on the kinds of rights that may be assigned. We will now explore those limitations.

A. *Limitation — Material Change in Duty of Obligor.*

1. The Principle.

The UCC[93] and RESTATEMENT 2d[94] contain virtually identical expressions of this limitation on the assignment of a contract right, i.e., the right can be assigned unless such assignment would materially change the duty of the

---

gratuitous assignment has been irrevocable, the trustee may still be able to set it aside under certain circumstances. 11 U.S.C. § 548.

[85] RESTATEMENT 2d § 332(3)(a).

[86] RESTATEMENT 2d § 332(3)(b).

[87] RESTATEMENT 2d § 332(3)(c).

[88] *See In re* Hazelwood, 43 Bankr. 208 (E.D. Va. 1984), citing the second edition of this book at 601 for this proposition. *See also* RESTATEMENT 2d § 332(4).

[89] RESTATEMENT 2d § 327(2).

[90] Exeter Exploration Co. v. Fitzpatrick, 202 Mont. 209, 661 P.2d 1255 (1983). RESTATEMENT 2d § 327(1) suggests that acceptance is essential to make an assignment effective unless a third party gives consideration for it, or the assignment was irrevocable by delivery of a writing to a third person.

[91] *See supra* § 137(A)(2).

[92] Munchack Corp. v. Cunningham, 457 F.2d 721 (4th Cir. 1972).

[93] UCC § 2-210(2).

[94] RESTATEMENT 2d § 317(2)(a).

obligor, or materially increase the burden of risk imposed on him by his contract, or materially impair his chance of obtaining performance.[95] These classifications are at least overlapping, if not redundant. If forced to choose the more meaningful test, it should be obvious that an obligor should not have to assume a materially greater risk than that which he voluntarily assumed at the time the contract was formed simply because the obligee decides to assign his right. The problem is the determination of whether a change or increase in that risk is material.

2. Payment — Land — Goods — Output and Requirements.

At one extreme, a simple right to be paid money clearly appears to be an assignable right because it has no material effect on the obligor's duty. It should make little difference to the obligor that he must pay a certain sum to the assignee rather than the obligee.[96] The obligee may have been more lenient in permitting the obligor additional time to pay, but this is not a sufficient reason for denying effect to the general rule that money claims are freely assignable.[97] The fact that the assignee can be shown to be *persona non grata* to the obligor, i.e., the obligor would not have contracted with the assignee, is also irrelevant.[98] The right to purchase land[99] or goods[1] may appear freely assignable. Yet, the terms of the contract may leave such discretion in the buyer that a change in buyers could materially increase the risk of the obligor. Where, for example, a small ice cream company agreed to purchase all of its requirements of ice from a particular supplier and the buyer assigned its rights to a larger ice cream company operating in an additional geographic market, the court held the right not assignable because of the increased risk to the obligor-seller.[2] Rights under requirement and output contracts were generally held not assignable prior to the UCC because of the wide personal discretion that buyers and sellers had under such contracts. The UCC, however, substitutes a standard of good faith in such contracts[3] which includes

---

[95] The slight differences in wording between the UCC and Restatement 2d sections are immaterial. This statement represents a collage of both expressions.

[96] In Talmadge v. United States Shipping Bd., Emergency Fleet Corp., 54 F.2d 240, 243 (2d Cir. 1931) Judge Hand writes the opinion for the court which includes the following: "Had the Shipbuilding Company assigned their right in toto, nobody can dispute that the plaintiffs might have sued at law, though the assignment would strictly have varied the defendant's obligation, compelling it to draw cheques to the plaintiff's order, and not as stipulated. So much change in performance is, however, permissible."

[97] Cf. UCC § 9-318(4) making an anti-assignment clause ineffective with respect to accounts in commercial financing transactions. Such clauses are discussed later in this chapter.

[98] See C. H. Little Co. v. Cadwell Transit Co., 197 Mich. 481, 163 N.W. 952 (1917); Fitzroy v. Cave, 2 K.B. 364 [1905].

[99] See Lockhart Co. v. B.F.K. Ltd., 107 Idaho 633, 691 P.2d 1248 (Idaho App. 1984) (sellers obliged under land sale contract to convey title upon payment of all installments and to provide notice of default. Though the assignment added another party to be notified of default, the increased burden was not material). See also Moore v. Gariglietti, 228 Ill. 143, 81 N.E. 826 (1907). See also Smithfield Oil Co. v. Furlonge, 257 N.C. 388, 126 S.E.2d 167 (1962) (assignment of lease and option to purchase).

[1] Rochester Lantern Co. v. Stiles & Parker Press Co., 135 N.Y. 209, 31 N.E. 1018 (1892).

[2] Crane Ice Cream Co. v. Terminal Freezing & Heating Co., 147 Md. 588, 128 A. 280 (1925). See also Kemp v. Baerselman, 2 K.B. 604 [1906]. Contra C. H. Little Co. v. Cadwell Transit Co., 197 Mich. 481, 163 N.W. 952 (1917); Tolhurst v. Associated Portland Cement Co., A.C. 414 [1903].

[3] UCC § 2-306(1).

commercial reasonableness.[4] This objective standard should allow more effective assignments of rights under output and requirements contracts. Where, however, the UCC standard would not preclude a material increase in the obligor's risk, the assignment would be ineffective.[5]

3. Personal Services.

Where the obligor has contracted to perform personal services, the question of assignability of the right to those services can become more difficult. If Helga assigned her right to George to have Andrew Wyeth paint several portraits, it is clear that the right would be nonassignable since a famous artist usually chooses a subject very carefully. The artist, therefore, would be denied the return performance, i.e., the effect he sought to achieve by selecting the original subject.[6] If, however, a boardwalk artist sketches pictures of any subject who sits in the chair and pays the fee, such a right may be assignable.[7] In an employment contract, if no direction or supervision by the assignee is contemplated, the assignment will be effective.[8] A television station's right to the performance of its news anchorperson was held assignable since the performance of the anchor was not based upon a personal relationship or special confidence and was not changed in any material way by the assignment.[9] Similarly, the rights under a contract with a professional athlete should be assignable to new ownership of the team since this is a highly foreseeable event and the player's rights should not be materially affected by such a change.[10] An employee's covenant not to compete with his employer is a right the employer may assign since it involves no personal contact with the successor employer.[11] Where, however, there is a personal relationship or special confidence factor in a personal service contract, an effective assignment without the employee's consent may be precluded.[12]

4. Insurance Policy.

An assignment of the insured's rights under a fire insurance policy has been held ineffective because it may increase the risks of the obligor insurance company.[13] Theoretically, the insurer has issued the policy at least in part on

---

[4] *See* UCC § 2-103(1)(b) defining good faith in the case of a merchant as honesty in fact plus commercial reasonableness.

[5] UCC § 2-210 comment 4.

[6] A famous heart surgeon who has agreed to perform a heart transplant should not be subject to having the correlative right to his duty assigned to another patient since great skill and judgment is demanded of a surgeon in choosing a patient. The same analysis would seem to apply to any doctor/patient or lawyer/client relationship. Query: would a health maintenance organization contract right be assignable to a party who was otherwise qualified, absent contractual prohibitions to the contrary?

[7] More than one boardwalk artist has confessed to the author that the original (paying) subject has said, "Don't draw me; draw my [sister]."

[8] *C. H. Little Co., supra* note 98.

[9] Evening News Ass'n v. Peterson, 477 F. Supp. 77 (D.D.C. 1979).

[10] *See* Munchack Corp. v. Cunningham, *supra* note 92.

[11] *See* Torrington Creamery, Inc. v. Davenport, 126 Conn. 515, 12 A.2d 780 (1940) (employee's covenant not to compete with employer is assignable, even by implication, with sale of business). *See also* Sickles v. Lauman, 185 Iowa 37, 169 N.W. 670 (1918).

[12] Globe & Rutgers Fire Ins. Co. v. Jones, 129 Mich. 664, 89 N.W. 580 (1902).

[13] But the mortgagee of insured property can effectively assign his rights under a fire insurance policy issued to the mortgagor which contains a mortgage clause for the protection of the mortgagee. Central Union Bank v. New York Underwriters' Ins. Co., 52 F.2d 823 (4th Cir. 1931).

the basis of an evaluation of the character of the insured. The duties of the insurer would not change since it would still have the same duty to pay for losses caused by a fire. It is sometimes conclusively presumed that the risk to the insurer would be changed materially.[14] Yet, if the assignee clearly presents a lesser risk to the insurer, there is no basis for invalidating the assignment in light of the general support for the free assignability of contract rights suggested in the RESTATEMENT 2d.[15] If the risk remained essentially as it was or if there was a decrease in the risk to the insurer, the only reason for treating the assignment as ineffective might be the difficulty of measuring the level of risk to the insurer in an assignee. There appears no sound reason why insurers should be excused from this burden since other obligors must shoulder it. The conclusive presumption, therefore, is unwarranted.

5. Material Impairment of Agreed Exchange.

If *AR* agrees to paint a house for *OR* and *AR* assigns his right to *AE* before the house is painted,[16] *AR* may have lost some incentive for performing since he has already transferred the agreed exchange for his performance to another. An assignment will not be ineffective, however, simply because of this possible loss of incentive.[17] Otherwise, only rights which have already been earned by performance could be assigned. There are situations, however, where the executory duties of the assignor are such that it will be difficult to evaluate the sufficiency of their performance. For example, when a patentee licensed another to exercise his patent on a royalty basis and promised to cooperate with the licensee in furthering the exploitation of the patent, an assignment of the right to future royalties was ineffective.[18] Similarly, if a party attempts not only to assign his rights under an executory contract but delegate a substantial part of his duties which are nondelegable, the obligor is entitled to disregard the assignment of the rights as well as the delegation of the duties.[19] The same result follows where the assignor repudiates his liabil-

---

[14] *See* J. CALAMIRI & J. PERILLO, THE LAW OF CONTRACTS, which, in the 1970 edition at § 262, 411, suggests that "courts will not ordinarily inquire into whether the burden of risk is greater or lesser than it was prior to the attempted assignment; rather the inquiry is whether the burden or risk would be *changed* in a material way." In their 1988 edition at § 181-3, 737, the authors suggest that "[T]he insurance company may reject assignment because the risk *may* be different" and even if the assignee were "the most careful person in the world," the assignment would be ineffective. In note 7 to these statements, the authors recognize disagreement in the second edition of this book and concurrence in that analysis in E. FARNSWORTH, CONTRACTS § 11.4, 764 n.21 (1982). However, the authors also point out that their view conforms to the general notion than an insurance contract is deemed to be personal in nature (737 n.8).

[15] *See* RESTATEMENT 2d § 317.

[16] As suggested earlier, rights under an executory contract may be assigned.

[17] *See* Somont Oil Co., Inc. v. Nutter, 44 Mont. Rep. 1685, 743 P.2d 1016 (1987).

[18] Paper Prods. Mach. Co. v. Safepack Mills, 239 Mass. 114, 131 N.E. 288 (1921).

[19] "Where a person contracts with another to do work or perform service, and it can be inferred that the person employed has been selected with reference to his individual skill, competency or other personal qualification, the inability or unwillingness of the party so employed to execute the work or perform the service is a sufficient answer to any demand by a stranger to the original contract of the performance of it by the other party, and entitles the latter to treat the contract as at an end, notwithstanding that the person tendered to take the place of the contracting party may be equally well qualified to do the service." British Waggon Co. v. Lea, 5 Q.B.D. 149 [1880]. *Accord* Folquet v. Woodburn Pub. Schs., 146 Or. 339, 29 P.2d 554 (1934).

ity under the contract.[20] If, however, the assignor substantially performs the duty in spite of the purported assignment, the assignment will be effective if the assignor had a sufficient incentive to perform. Thus, where a party contracted to sell advertising space in a forthcoming magazine (which he was about to publish), assigned the contract with the advertiser to his printer merely as security for the printing bill, and thereafter published the magazine, the assignee had a right to collect the amount promised by the advertiser.[21] Similarly, where partners who had contracted to design and build a machine assigned their rights to a corporation which they had formed to take over the partnership business, the court held the assignment effective since the partners were owners and managers of the corporation and had, therefore, ample incentive to perform the contract.[22]

If a party assigns his right and delegates his duty under a contract calling for the other party to perform before he receives performance from the assignor, there is old authority holding the assignment to be ineffective. For example, it has been said that a right to purchase goods on credit cannot be effectively assigned because the seller is entitled to the credit of the buyer with whom he contracted.[23] The erroneous assumption is that the assignor/delegator succeeds in ridding himself of his duty by way of the assignment and delegation. As will be seen later, this is impossible absent the consent of the obligor. There is no sound reason for denying effect to such an assignment and numerous courts have so held.[24] Under the UCC, however, *any* assignment coupled with a delegation of duty may be treated by the other party as creating reasonable grounds for insecurity,[25] giving rise to a right in the obligor to demand adequate assurances of performance by the assignee/delegate.[26] The term "any" in this Code section suggests certain problems. If, for example, there is an assignment of assignable rights and an attempted delegation of nondelegable duties, there would seem no point in demanding adequate assurances since no assurances would be adequate. Thus, the threshold question should be whether the duties were delegable. If they are not delegable, the attempted assignment should be deemed ineffective without regard for adequate assurances. In the same situation, if the obligor demands adequate assurances (which he need not have done) and accepts such assurances (which he could have rejected since no adequate assurance is possible if the duties are nondelegable), the assignment and delegation should be effective if the assignee/delegate has relied on the obligor's acceptance. Absent such reliance, the obligor should be entitled to withdraw his acceptance of assurances.

---

[20] Western Oil Sales Corp. v. Bliss & Wetherbee, 299 S.W. 637 (Tex. 1927).

[21] American Lithographic Co. v. Ziegler, 216 Mass. 287, 103 N.E. 909 (1914).

[22] Fisher v. Berg, 158 Wash. 176, 290 P. 984 (1930).

[23] *See* Arkansas Valley Smelting Co. v. Belden Mining Co., 127 U.S. 379 (1888).

[24] *See, e.g.,* Voight v. Murphy Heating Co., 164 Mich. 539, 129 N.W. 701 (1911); Minnetonka Oil Co. v. Cleveland Vitrified Brick Co., 27 Okla. 180, 11 P. 326 (1910).

[25] UCC § 2-210(5).

[26] UCC § 2-609(1) permits a party to demand adequate assurance of performance where reasonable grounds for insecurity arise.

6. Assignability of Options.

As every contracts student knows, an offer creates a power of acceptance which may be exercised only by the party to whom it is addressed.[27] An option contract is collateral to an offer and makes the power of acceptance irrevocable.[28] Should the right to the irrevocable power of acceptance under an option contract be assignable even though that would result in a party other than the original offeree exercising that power? While the general rule requiring that only the offeree exercise the power of acceptance is sound, when the power of acceptance is also a contractual right, there is no reason why it should not be assignable like any other contract right, i.e., subject to the same limitations of any other assignment. This is the view that has been generally accepted.[29]

7. Partial Assignments.

If an obligor owes the obligee $10,000, we have seen that there is no obstacle to effectively assigning the right to the payment of money. If, however, the obligee decides to assign $5,000 of that right to an assignee, is the burden on the obligor materially increased so as to make such a partial assignment ineffective?

Historically, the assignment of part of a single claim or cause of action under a contract was not recognized over the objection of the obligor.[30] This rule found its reason in the fact that the common law courts consistently refused to entertain a suit involving more than two parties having adverse interests. If such an assignment were held to be effective, contrary to the will of the debtor, in a law action, the result would be that a creditor could split up his cause of action by making partial assignments, thus subjecting the debtor to a multiplicity of suits.[31] In a court of equity, on the other hand, any number of parties with adverse interests could be brought into a single suit, either as plaintiffs or defendants. As has been well said:

> In equity the interests of all parties can be determined in a single suit. The debtor can bring the entire fund into court, and run no risks as to its proper distribution. If he be in no fault no costs need be imposed upon him, or they may be awarded in his favor. If he be put to extra trouble in keeping separate accounts he can, if it is reasonable, be compensated for it. In many ways a court of equity can, while a court of law, with its present modes cannot, protect the rights and interests of all parties concerned.[32]

---

[27] RESTATEMENT 2d § 29(1).

[28] RESTATEMENT 2d § 25.

[29] See, e.g., Melrose Enters. v. Pawtucket Form Constr. Co., 550 A.2d 300 (R.I. 1988) where the court held the assignment of an option to purchase real estate effective since there was no evidence that the option was dependent upon any trust, confidence or qualification reposed in the original holder of the option. See also RESTATEMENT 2d § 320.

[30] See Mandeville v. Welch, 18 U.S. (5 Wheat.) 277 (1820).

[31] The assignment of the whole of what amounts to a separate and distinct cause of action under a contract, though it is not the whole of what will eventually become due, is not a partial assignment within the rule and is effective at law. Timmons v. Citizens' Bank, 11 Ga. App. 69, 74 S.E. 798 (1912) (assignment of a progress payment under a construction contract).

[32] Exchange Bank v. McLoon, 73 Me. 498, 505, 49 Am. Rep. 388, 389 (1882).

Today, this equity view is generally accepted in actions at law. An assignment of part of a right is effective in the same manner as if the party had been assigned a separate right.[33] If, however, the obligor has not agreed to perform as to the separate part of the right, the obligor may resist any legal proceeding to enforce that separate part unless all parties entitled to the entire promised performance are joined in the proceeding.[34] Modern procedural codes make such joinder possible. If joinder in a given case is not feasible, the action may proceed against the obligor to enforce the separate right only if it is equitable to proceed absent joinder of all the parties.[35] A simple example of the exceptional situation occurs where the obligor owes $1,000 to the assignor who assigns $500 of this claim to the assignee. If the obligor pays the assignor $500, the assignee may maintain an action for the $500 balance against the obligor without joining the assignor.[36]

B. *Limitation — Public Policy.*

A second major limitation on the assignability of rights is the refusal of courts to recognize assignments which are contrary to public policy. Either by statute or judicial decision, certain assignments are considered contrary to public policy for a variety of reasons. The most conspicuous statutory prohibition occurs in relation to attempted assignments of wages.[37] Several different types of statutes restricting the assignment of wages have been enacted throughout the country. The general underlying theory of such statutes is that the wage earner must be protected against his own improvidence as well as against unscrupulous parties who might otherwise take advantage of him. There are also federal statutes which prohibit the assignment of claims against the United States before the issuance of a warranty for payment as well as the assignment of any public contract or order.[38] An exception to these statutes is found in the Assignment of Claims Act of 1940 which permits a single assignment to a financial institution if the contract does not forbid assignment and if written notice is filed with appropriate government officers as well as any surety on a bond relating to the contract.[39] If an assignment is made pursuant to this exception, the assignee is protected against liability to repay the United States and, under certain circumstances, against a setoff of a liability of the assignor to the United States.[40] Many states have statutes

---

[33] *See* J & B Slurry Seal Co. v. Mid-South Aviation, Inc., 88 N.C. App. 1, 362 S.E.2d 812 (1987) (plaintiff assigned to insurer to the extent of insurer's compensation for plaintiff's loss). *See also* RESTATEMENT 2d § 326(1).

[34] *See* Space Coast Credit Union v. Walt Disney World Co., 483 So. 2d 35 (Fla. App. 1986). *See also* RESTATEMENT 2d § 326(2).

[35] The older cases are collected in Annotation, 80 A.L.R. 413-30 (1932). *See also* Phoenix Ins. Co. v. Woosley, 287 F.2d 531 (10th Cir. 1961), where nine partial assignees totaled their respective interests so as to equal the jurisdictional amount.

[36] *See* Staples v. Rush, 99 So. 2d 502 (La. App. 1958).

[37] A useful collection of these statutes and commentary thereon is found in the Statutory Note to Chapter 15 of the RESTATEMENT 2d (prior to § 316) under the caption, "Wage Assignments."

[38] *See* 31 U.S.C. § 203.

[39] *See* Statutory Note in Chapter 15 of the RESTATEMENT 2d under the caption "Government Contracts" prior to § 316.

[40] State statutes may also limit the assignment of public contracts. *See, e.g.,* N.Y. STATE FIN. LAW § 138 and N.Y. GEN. MUN. LAW § 109; N.C. GEN. STAT. § 148-62.

regulating retail installment sales containing provisions affecting assignment by the seller of his rights under a regulated contract.[41] There may be regulations in such statutes regarding the availability of defenses available to a buyer of goods against an assignee. This will be discussed in a subsequent section.[42]

Apart from statutory regulation, other assignments are held to be void under the rules of the common law, because they are deemed to be contrary to public policy.[43] Since the rules applying to the enforceability of contracts generally are applicable to assignments, the determination of whether an assignment is against public policy requires courts to balance public policy interests against the policy of free assignability.[44] If, for example, an assignee took an assignment knowing that it was contrary to a court order, the assignment would be ineffective.[45] It is generally held that the assignment of salary not yet due by a public officer is void, because it tends to impair the efficiency of the public service.[46] Likewise, the assignment of a life insurance policy to one who has no insurable interest in the life of the insured is invalid when the assignment is part of a preconceived plan to evade the rule of law which prohibits the making of wagering contracts.[47] Malpractice claims are not assignable[48] and there is a strong policy against the assignability of unliquidated personal injury claims to preclude champerty and particularly to prevent the unscrupulous from purchasing causes of action dealing in pain and suffering.[49] Where that rationale disappears, however, as where a personal injury claim is reassigned to the original claimant or his estate, there is some authority upholding the assignment.[50]

There is no end to examples of public policy questions. Suffice to say that the public policy concepts discussed earlier in this volume in relation to the enforceability of contracts are applicable to assignments.[51]

---

[41] See Statutory Note in Chapter 15 of the RESTATEMENT 2d under the caption, "Retail Installment Sales" prior to § 316.

[42] See § 138(C).

[43] See Federal Deposit Ins. Corp. v. Barness, 484 F. Supp. 1134, 1151-53 (E.D. Pa. 1980). See also RESTATEMENT 2d § 317(2)(b).

[44] McKnight v. Rice, 678 P.2d 1330 (Alaska 1984). One of the more interesting questions that has arisen recently is whether a purported assignment of an express warranty is effective in a jurisdiction requiring a party to be in privity to enforce such a warranty. The United States Court of Appeals for the Seventh Circuit chose to certify the question to the Illinois Supreme Court. See Collins Co. v. Carboline Co., 837 F.2d 299 (7th Cir. 1988).

[45] Ibid.

[46] Byers v. Comer, 50 Ariz. 8, 68 P.2d 671 (1937), modified, 50 Ariz. 134, 70 P.2d 330 (1937). As to who is a public officer within the meaning of the rule, cf. Kimball v. Ledford, 13 Cal. App. 2d 602, 57 P.2d 163 (1936) (holding that a school teacher is not a public officer) and Schmitt v. Dooling, 145 Ky. 240, 140 S.W. 197 (1911) (holding that a fireman is a public officer).

[47] The cases are collected in Annotation, 30 A.L.R.2d 1310 (1953). A few jurisdictions make the assignment of a life insurance policy to one who has no insurable interest illegal per se. The majority of courts hold otherwise.

[48] Weston v. Dowty, 163 Mich. App. 238, 414 N.W.2d 165 (1987).

[49] Harleysville Mut. Ins. Co. v. Lea, 410 P.2d 495, 498 (Ariz. App. 1966).

[50] See Croxton v. Crowley Maritime Corp., 758 P.2d 97 (Alaska 1988). See also ARIZ. REV. STAT. ANN. § 23-1023. An exculpatory clause in a health club contract whereby the member assumed the risk of physical injury in using health club equipment was effectively assigned when the health club was sold. See Petry v. Cosmopolitan Spa Int'l, Inc., 641 S.W.2d 202 (1982).

[51] See supra Chapter 6, § 98. See also RESTATEMENT 2d Chapter 9.

C. *Limitation — Prohibition of Assignment.*

To what extent the parties to a contract can, by agreement, effectively prohibit or restrict the assignment of rights or duties created by the contract that would otherwise be assignable is a question upon which the courts, over the years, have demonstrated some confusion. On the one hand, it has been asserted that the assignment of money claims,[52] and of rights under contracts for the purchase of land,[53] cannot be prohibited by agreement of the parties, on the ground that such a prohibition is an unlawful restraint on alienation. The theory is that a money claim or a contract right to land is sufficiently like ownership of a tangible chattel or land and should be free from restraints on alienation. On the other hand, it has been asserted categorically that a prohibition or restriction of assignment of any kind of a claim is effective, and may render ineffective the attempt to assign a right or a duty that would otherwise be assignable.[54] The conflict between the policy of freedom of contract and the policy precluding restraints upon alienation is painfully obvious.

More recently we have come to understand that a prohibition of assignment provision in a contract may take any one of at least three distinct forms,[55] and that the form of the provision could very well condition its legal effect: (1) The contract may contain a promise by one or both parties to refrain from assigning. Unless this promise were specifically enforceable, an assignment which violates it would remain effective. The promise creates a duty in the promisor not to assign. It does not deprive the assignor of the *power* to assign and its breach, therefore, would simply subject the promisor to an action for damages while the assignment would be effective.[56] (2) If the contract provides that an assignment will make the *contract* void, the assignment is effective but the nonassigning party may, at his or her election, avoid the contract for breach of condition.[57] (3) The contract may provide that any attempted assignment shall be void. Such a clear stipulation obviously contemplates that the assignment itself shall be deemed ineffective, unless the nonassigning party consents to it.[58] It clearly manifests the intention of the parties to deprive one or both of the *power* to assign rather than merely creating a duty not to assign. Many of the decided cases have not differentiated between these three types of provisions and have assumed that, whatever the form, the stipulation either did or

---

[52] State Street Furniture Co. v. Armour & Co., 345 Ill. 160, 177 N.E. 702 (1932). *See also* the statements of Justice Holmes in Portuguese-American Bank v. Welles, 242 U.S. 7 (1916).

[53] *See* Goddard, *Non-Assignment Provisions in Land Contracts,* 31 MICH. L. REV. 1 (1932).

[54] "Without discussion, it is settled law that parties to a contract can agree that the contract in all its terms shall be non-assignable both at law and in equity, and that the commonwealth in the pending case could refuse to recognize any assignment not within the strict provisions of it." Federal Nat'l Bank v. Commonwealth, 282 Mass. 442, 185 N.E. 9, 12 (1933). *See also* Concrete Form Co. v. W. T. Grange Constr. Co., 320 Pa. 205, 181 A. 589 (1935).

[55] This analysis as it appeared in the second edition of this book was cited with approval in Cedar Point Apts. Ltd. v. Cedar Point Inv. Corp., 693 F.2d 748 (8th Cir. 1982).

[56] *See* The Reuben H. Donnelley Corp. v. McKinnon, 688 S.W.2d 612 (Tex. App. 1985); Hull v. Hostettler, 224 Mich. 365, 194 N.W. 996 (1923); Randal v. Totum, 98 Cal. 390, 33 P. 433 (1893). *See also* RESTATEMENT 2d § 322(2)(b).

[57] *See* Merrill v. New England Mut. Life Ins. Co., 103 Mass. 245, 4 Am. Rep. 548 (1869).

[58] Allhusen v. Caristo Constr. Corp., 303 N.Y. 446, 103 N.E.2d 891, 37 A.L.R.2d 1245 (1952) and Annotation, 37 A.L.R.2d 1251 (1954).

did not invalidate the assignment depending upon the court's view of public policy mentioned previously.[59]

The UCC has effected significant changes in this area. These changes have led to considerable confusion. In Article 2 of the Code (sales and contracts for the sale of goods), there is a presumption of free assignability of rights.[60] However, the subsection indicating such free assignability begins with a familiar Code phrase, "Unless otherwise agreed." Therefore, the parties may agree that all or some of the rights under the contract are not assignable. The last sentence of the same subsection places a restriction on the freedom of the parties to include an enforceable anti-assignment clause. That restriction occurs when one of the parties has breached "the whole contract" or one of the parties has performed "his entire obligation."[61] If either of these events occurs, the right may be assigned regardless of an otherwise effective anti-assignment clause. Thus, even if the contract contains an anti-assignment provision, if a seller of goods tenders conforming (non-defective) goods to a buyer and the buyer wrongfully rejects such tender, the buyer has breached "the whole contract" and the seller's rights may be assigned. Similarly, if the buyer accepts conforming goods from the seller but refuses to pay for them, the seller, having performed "the entire obligation," may assign his rights under the contract notwithstanding an otherwise effective anti-assignment clause. The only other significant Article 2 provision relating to anti-assignment clauses is found in a subsection which simply states a plausible rule of construction: A clause prohibiting assignment of "the contract" is, absent countervailing circumstances, construed as preventing only the delegation of duties rather than the assignment of rights.[62] If these were the only provisions in the Code dealing with anti-assignment clauses, there would be little, if any, confusion. Unfortunately, this is not the case.

As suggested earlier,[63] Article 9 of the Code applies to the sale (assignment) of "accounts" which, under the current version of Article 9 of the Code, includes executory contract rights.[64] This is true though Article 9 is centrally concerned with the transfer of security interests in tangible and intangible collateral. The earlier discussion explained that in modern commercial financing transactions, the line between a security transfer and outright sale of accounts is often blurred. Therefore, the Article 9 draftsmen decided to include such outright sales (assignments). Another provision of Article 9 literally makes anti-assignment provisions totally ineffective when applied to the assignment of accounts.[65] This immediately suggests a contradiction between

---

[59] Many of the cases are discussed in Grismore, *Effect of a Restriction on Assignment in a Contract*, 31 MICH. L. REV. 299 (1933).

[60] UCC § 2-210(2).

[61] *Id.*

[62] UCC § 2-210(3).

[63] *See supra* § 136.

[64] The prior (1968) version of Article 9 included a separate category of "contract rights" to deal with executory contract rights, i.e., rights not yet earned by performance. "Accounts" had been previously relegated to rights earned by performance, i.e., where the contract for the sale or lease of goods or for services had been performed. Under the 1972 version of Article 9, "account" now includes rights to payment whether earned or unearned thus encompassing the former separate classification of "contract rights."

[65] UCC § 9-318(4).

the Article 2 provision just explored and the Article 9 section. The Article 2 provision appears to permit the parties to include an anti-assignment clause subject only to the exceptions noted above. Since that same Article 2 provision refers to all rights of either seller or buyer, the language would literally include "contract rights." There is no difficulty in relation to accounts since the UCC defines "account" as "any right to payment for goods sold or leased or for services rendered."[66] Thus, under the Article 2 provision, the assignment of an account would fall within the restriction which invalidates an anti-assignment clause when the right assigned arises out of the assignor's due performance of his "entire obligation." An account, however, would include a right to performance before it is earned, i.e., before the obligee has performed.[66] Article 2 would seem to permit the parties to agree that such rights are not assignable, while Article 9 suggests that the parties may not prohibit the assignment of such rights. The Code comment to the Article 2 section explains that rights which are no longer executory (such as "accounts" where the seller, lessor, or supplier of services has performed) may be assigned regardless of an anti-assignment clause. It then adds the curious sentence, "The assignment of a 'contract right' as defined in the Article on Secured Transactions (Article 9) is not covered by this subsection."[68] This is confusing since the current version of Article 9 no longer refers to "contract rights" since that term is now subsumed under the broadened term, "account" which would include an executory contract right. The comment to the Article 9 section invalidating anti-assignment clauses relating to accounts (including contract rights) carefully explains the progressive undermining of the original rule of law permitting such anti-assignment clauses and the necessity for this particular aspect of freedom of contract to bow to economic need: the free assignability of accounts and contract rights in modern commercial society.[69] In this explanation, the comment expressly rejects one of the better known cases following the original rule.[70]

It has been suggested that these seemingly conflicting sections in Article 2 and Article 9 *are* conflicting — "they were drafted by different groups for different purposes and were never harmonized."[71] Notwithstanding the failure of the Code drafters of these different Articles to clearly harmonize the sections, there is a possible reconciliation. Another section of Article 9 exempts from the coverage of that Article sales (assignments) of accounts and contract rights which have nothing to do with commercial financing. Section 9-104(f) indicates that the article does not apply to such sales when they form part of a sale of the business out of which they arose, when they are exclusively for the purpose of collection, or when the contract right is assigned to an

---

[66] UCC § 9-106.

[67] UCC § 9-106 defines an "account" as any right to payment for goods sold or leased or for services rendered ... whether or not it has been earned by performance." Thus, if a party had a simple executory contract right under a contract for the sale or lease of goods or where the party was to render services such a painting a house, such a right would be an "account" under Article 9 of the UCC though prior to 1972 it would have been called a "contract right." *Infra* note 64.

[68] UCC § 2-210 comment 3.

[69] UCC § 9-318 comment 4.

[70] It expressly rejects the *Allhusen case, supra* note 58.

[71] R. NORDSTROM, THE LAW OF SALES § 45 at 137 (1970).

assignee who is also to do the performance under the contract. Admittedly, there may be some difficulties in deciding whether the assignment of a contract right falls within this Article 9 exemption provision. If it does, Article 9, including the provision invalidating anti-assignment clauses, does not apply. Of course Article 2 does apply, and the contract rights would be freely assignable "unless otherwise agreed." On the other hand, if the assignment of the contract right is within Article 9 because it does relate to a commercial financing transaction, Article 9 applies and, therefore, any attempt to prohibit the assignment of such contract rights is ineffective regardless of the clarity of the anti-assignment provision. Though this appears to be a plausible reconciliation of the problem created by these seemingly conflicting Code sections, the criticism of the manifest lack of harmony of the provisions is not unsound.

§ 139. The Assignment of "Future Rights."

A. *Meaning of "Future Right."*

There is no question that one can make an effective assignment of an executory right and even a right subject to an express condition under an existing contract.[72] The only question of doubt stems from an attempt to assign a future right which immediately gives rise to semantic difficulties. A "future right" may generally be regarded as one which the assignor does not then have but which he expects to acquire. There are, however, two types of "future rights" which must be distinguished: (1) If the assignor is operating under an *existing contract* and expects to acquire rights in the future under that contract, the rights do not exist. However, they are more than mere hopes since the probabilities are great that they will exist. Thus, if X is employed at a rate of $100 per week under a contract terminable at will, he has no right to future wages since he could be terminated at any time. Yet, absent statutory prohibitions, he may assign his wages for a future period to Y because he is operating under an employment relationship though it is indefinite in duration.[73] (2) Another type of purported assignment of a future right occurs when X has a hope of *entering into a contract* of employment and attempts to assign a right to his first month's wages to Y. Here, there is not only no presently existing right; there is no existing contract from which rights will probably arise. There is simply a hope that one will exist. It is conceivable that a court would recognize the existence of a future right that could be effectively assigned even without an existing contract. Thus, where a party had the exclusive rights to the famous George Bernard Shaw play, Pygmalion, and assigned a portion of the royalties from musical productions of the play for which contracts, much less the productions, did not exist, a court held such an assignment effective.[74] Even here, however, the "future right" assigned was more

---

[72]*See* Bonanza Motors, Inc. v. Webb, 104 Idaho 234, 657 P.2d 1102 (Idaho App. 1983); Rockmore v. Lehman, 129 F.2d 892 (2d Cir. 1942), *cert. denied,* 317 U.S. 700 (1943). *See also* RESTATEMENT 2d § 320.

[73]Citizens Loan Ass'n v. Boston & Maine R.R., 196 Mass. 258, 82 N.E. 696 (1907).

[74]Speelman v. Pascal, 10 N.Y.2d 313, 178 N.E.2d 723 (1961). The musical (stage and screen) productions did follow under the now famous title, "My Fair Lady."

than a mere hope.[75] It is critical to make this basic distinction at the outset of any discussion of the assignment of "future rights."

B. *Earlier Case Law.*

Older decisions took the position that an attempted assignment of any future right, i.e., whether emanating from an existing contract or a mere expectancy, must necessarily fail for the same reason that attempted transfers of after-acquired tangible property were frequently held to fail — simply because one could not transfer a right that did not exist.[76] If it were true that an assignment could operate, if at all, only as a transfer of an existing right, the conclusion stated necessarily followed. However, the rules applied in the case of transfers of tangible property are not necessarily controlling. We know that, historically, an assignment of a chose in action did not operate in the same way in any case. On the contrary, such an attempted transfer was held to vest in the assignee, at most, an irrevocable power of attorney to require performance of the assigned claim and to retain the proceeds thereof.[77] If an assignment be deemed to operate in this way, there is obviously no logical objection to the effectiveness of the assignment of a future right, since it is perfectly possible presently to confer upon another an irrevocable power to require performance of a future obligation. Even on a transfer theory it would be perfectly consistent to say what has sometimes been held in the case of attempted transfers of after-acquired tangible property, namely, that the assignment at least amounts to a contract to assign when the right is acquired, and that equity, which regards that as done which ought to be done, will look upon the assignee as acquiring, the moment the right comes into existence, an equitable title to the claim, or an equitable lien on it, which is good against everyone but a bona fide purchaser for value.

C. *The Modern View — "Equitable" Assignments.*

The semantic difficulties suggested at the beginning of this section must be kept in mind in attempting to understand the modern law in this area. There are many decisions dealing with "future" rights and, often, those decisions do not distinguish between rights arising out of an existing contract (though not presently enforceable) and rights which are mere expectancies where no contract exists. The former are now treated as if they were present, existing rights and are as assignable as any other present right.[78] As to rights expected to arise where no contract yet exists, modern courts treat purported assignments of such rights as they have always been treated in the past, i.e., only as promises to assign such rights when they arise, providing the purported assignee with a power to enforce them. They are often referred to as "equitable assignments," again on the footing that equity will treat such an assignment

---

[75] For an illustration of hope where the court held that the purported assignment was ineffective, *see* Orkow v. Orkow, 133 Cal. App. 50, 23 P.2d 781 (1933).

[76] *See, e.g.,* O'Niel v. Helmke, 124 Wis. 234, 102 N.W. 573 (1905). *See also* Williston, *Transfers of After-Acquired Personal Property,* 19 HARV. L. REV. 557 (1906).

[77] *See supra* § 135(B).

[78] *See Bonanza Motors, supra* note 72. *See also* Loyola Univ. Med. Center v. Med Care HMO, 180 Ill. App. 3d 471, 535 N.E.2d 1125 (1989). RESTATEMENT 2d § 321(1).

as a promise to assign and will normally decree specific performance of that promise when the right comes into existence because "equity looks upon that as done which ought to have been done."[79] Thus, under the modern view, the characterization, "future rights" refers only to those rights which arise from a continuing business or employment relationship and are reasonable expectancies though they are not based upon an existing contract and do not exist at the time of assignment.[80]

If the assignment is characterized as an "equitable assignment," there will normally be little significance to the characterization as between the purported assignor and assignee since, again, when the right comes into existence, specific performance will usually be decreed. Such rights, however, are susceptible to being defeated. Thus, the right of an equitable assignee may be subordinate to an attaching creditor,[81] or an assignee in insolvency or bankruptcy,[82] or the assignor himself and his personal representatives.[83] So long as the assignor of such a future right has not revoked the assignee's power to require performance or it has not been terminated by the death or bankruptcy of the assignor or by the intervention of an attaching creditor, the right (when it comes into existence) may be enforced. In effect, the equitable assignee has a revocable power to enforce the future right, at least to the extent that contractual remedies are available.[84] It is more than likely that such an assignment, while ineffective to transfer the right to the assignee, will be interpreted as a contract to account to the assignee for the proceeds, when they have been obtained by the assignor from a subsequent obligor.[85]

From a commercial financing perspective, the principle that the assignment of non-existent rights would be viewed as an equitable assignment that could be defeated by attaching creditors and good faith purchasers did not provide the necessary security. The only reliable collateral was existing collateral. Long term financing relationships could not exist under these circumstances. The UCC provided a comprehensive solution to this problem.

D. *Uniform Commercial Code — After-Acquired Property.*

The most significant example of the assignment or transfer of "future rights" occurs in commercial financing situations, which are governed by Article 9 of the UCC. In a previous section, the implications of Article 9 in the law of assignments were surveyed.[86] For the student of contract law who has

---

[79] RESTATEMENT 2d § 330 comment c, which also suggests that they may be called "equitable liens." If a party grants a mortgage on real property or a security interest in personalty (a "chattel mortgage") even though he does not own the property, he grants no property interest in his actions. Yet, on the footing that the promise should be enforceable when he acquired rights in the property, the mortgagee acquires an equitable lien.

[80] *See* RESTATEMENT 2d § 321, captioned "Assignment of Future Rights" and comment a which emphasizes that the "Section does not apply to rights in existence at the time of assignment."

[81] O'Niel v. Helmke, 124 Wis. 234, 102 N.W. 573 (1905). Mulhall v. Quinn, 67 Mass. (1 Gray) 105, 61 Am. Dec. 414 (1854).

[82] Taylor v. Barton-Child Co., 228 Mass. 126, 117 N.E. 43 (1917) (book accounts). *Contra In re* United Fuel & Supply Co., 250 Mich. 325, 230 N.W. 164 (1930).

[83] *In* re Nelson's Estate, 211 Iowa 168, 233 N.W. 115, 72 A.L.R. 850 (1930).

[84] *See* RESTATEMENT 2d § 330 comment d.

[85] RESTATEMENT 2d § 330(2).

[86] *See supra* § 136.

not yet explored Article 9, discussions such as the one that follows may be difficult to comprehend. Yet, it is necessary to grasp the fundamental concept of the most significant example of the transfer of "future rights." To assist this process, the exploration will employ a relatively simple example.

Joseph Adams operates the Adams hardware store. To purchase his new inventory, Adams must borrow money from the local bank. The bank and Adams have agreed that from time to time the bank will lend Adams amounts to permit the replenishing of the Adams inventory. Adams will correspondingly repay the outstanding indebtedness on a continuous basis, i.e., as he resells the inventory at a profit, he will repay the amounts to the bank. It is contemplated, therefore, that Adams and the bank will be in a continuous debtor-creditor relationship. The bank, however, will not lend these amounts to Adams on a pure credit basis. The bank, like most creditors, will insist on some security to assure the repayment of the loans. The best security for the bank is the inventory of Adams' store, for that is probably Adams' most valuable asset.[87] When the continuous loan agreement was formed, the bank insisted that Adams sign a security agreement granting the bank as secured creditor a security interest in all of Adams' present inventory.[88] But the bank was also interested in Adams' future inventory, i.e., his after-acquired inventory.[89] In addition, the bank was interested in the proceeds which Adams would obtain in the form of cash, checks, accounts, and the like when he sold the inventory.[90] The bank wants Adams to sell his inventory and make a profit to repay the loan. If, however, the bank has a security interest exclusively in the inventory and not the proceeds, the bank's security disappears as the inventory is sold off. The bank wants a security interest in that which is received by Adams when the inventory is sold (proceeds), and it also wants a way of ascertaining that it will have an automatic, attached, and perfected security interest in the new inventory purchased by Adams. So, the bank takes a security interest not only in the present inventory and proceeds but in all after-acquired inventory and proceeds. Adams granted that security interest (the property right) in such after-acquired inventory and proceeds (future rights) at the time the arrangement was initially consummated.

Conceptually, it is difficult to think of the transfer of nonexistent, future rights in this context and, prior to the Code, it was either impossible or extremely difficult and cumbersome to do so. Article 9 of the Code has removed

---

[87] Inventory is goods "held by a person for sale or lease or to be furnished under contracts of service or if he has so furnished them, or if they are raw materials, work in process or materials used or consumed in a business...." UCC § 9-109(4). The televisions, refrigerators, washers, dryers, and the like in an appliance store are inventory as is the food on the shelves of a super market. Anything held for sale or lease (the autos of a car leasing company) are inventory as are raw materials, packaging, and the like. The office or production machinery used to operate the business is not inventory — it is equipment under § 9-109(2). Goods purchased primarily for personal, family, or household purposes are consumer goods (§ 9-109(1)). Crops, livestock, and their products are farm products (§ 9-109(3)).

[88] UCC § 9-203(1)(a).

[89] *See* UCC § 9-204(1).

[90] UCC § 9-306(1). "Proceeds" includes whatever is received when collateral is sold, exchanged, collected, or otherwise disposed of. Money, checks, and the like are "cash" proceeds. Other proceeds, including accounts, are non-cash proceeds. Proceeds also includes whatever is received from the sale or exchange of proceeds, i.e., the original proceeds may be converted into different proceeds.

the obstacles to this transfer of rights in after-acquired property and, today commercial financing of innumerable establishments occurs on this basis. It is sometimes popularly referred to as a "floating lien" or "floor planning" method of commercial financing.

The question arises: when does the transfer of rights in the after-acquired inventory and proceeds occur? Suppose that Adams must restock certain screwdrivers and orders $5,000 worth of these goods from a supplier. When is the property interest (the security interest) in these particular goods transferred to the bank to partially secure the repayment of Adams' debt to the bank? Assume that Adams ordered the screwdrivers on February 1, 1989, and they were delivered on February 7, 1989. The security agreement granting an interest in such after-acquired property was signed by Adams and the bank on June 1, 1987. On June 2, 1987, the bank filed a financing statement (signed by Adams) in the appropriate public offices.[91] This public notice of the security interest in Adams' inventory and after-acquired property placed all of Adams' creditors on notice that the bank, the Article 9 secured creditor, had a prior claim to the specific collateral described in the publicly filed statement. Should Adams become insolvent and perhaps bankrupt, the bank would have priority over all of the inventory as against all of Adams' other creditors and, if he went bankrupt, even against the trustee in bankruptcy. The public recording of the financing statement is critical to a secured creditor engaged in long term financing arrangements with businesses such as the Adams' hardware store. The UCC does not pretend that a security interest attaches until the debtor (Adams) has rights in the collateral.[92] Adams cannot grant a security interest in property that he does not yet own. The screwdrivers may not have existed anywhere at the time the security agreement was signed or the financing statement was signed or filed. Yet, there is a recognition of the fact that a security interest in that *future* property — after-acquired property — will exist as soon as the debtor obtains rights in that collateral which will occur as soon as the goods are identified for shipment to Adams[93] since the other elements of "attachment" have occurred, i.e., the signed security agreement and the giving of value by the bank.[94] From the moment the financing statement was filed, however, the *priority* security interest, publicly recorded so as not to defraud other potential creditors, was in the bank. This is the reasonable system created by the UCC to facilitate commercial financing. It is sound and workable.

---

[91] The place of filing will depend upon the kind of collateral in which the security interest was taken. *See* UCC § 9-401.

[92] UCC § 9-203(1)(c).

[93] UCC § 2-501.

[94] UCC § 9-203(1)(a) and (b).

§ 140. Delegation of Duties.

A. *Distinguished From Assignment.*

We have said that an effective assignment extinguishes the right in the assignor and creates a similar right in the assignee. A party cannot, however, "assign a duty" in the sense that he can extinguish the duty in himself and create a similar duty in the assignee.[95] If this were permitted, it would be unfair to the other party to the contract since it would enable the assignor unilaterally to discharge his duty to the other party. The discharge of the delegator's duty prior to the performance of that duty can occur only with the consent of the obligee of that duty. If the obligee agrees to accept a delegate in place of the delegator, he has agreed to discharge the assignor by a contract of novation.[96] Though the delegator remains liable absent a novation, he is discharged upon performance of the obligation by the delegate.[97] It must be emphasized that the delegate may or may not have promised to render the performance to the obligee.

B. *Delegable Versus Nondelegable Duties.*

Just as certain rights are not assignable notwithstanding the policy of free assignability, certain duties are not delegable even though delegability of duties is favored. Consequently, unless the duty is a personal one which must be performed by the delegator, or if it is a duty involving personal skill or discretion, the duty may be delegated to another, provided the delegator stands ready to perform in the event the delegate does not perform.[98] In general, unless otherwise agreed, delegation of a duty is considered a normal incident of a contract unless a substantial reason can be shown why the delegated performance would not be as satisfactory as the performance by the delegator.[99] The obligor may have a substantial interest in having a particular person perform. Duties involving artistic skill or unique abilities are not delegable since there is no objective method to determine whether performance by a delegate would be substantially identical with the delegator's performance.[1] The duty to produce entertainment[2] or to create advertising[3]

---

[95] Smith v. Wrede, 199 Neb. 735, 261 N.W.2d 620 (1978); McAlpine v. Magarian, 461 F. Supp. 1232 (E.D. Mich. 1978); Contemporary Mission, Inc. v. Famous Music Corp., 557 F.2d 918 (2d Cir. 1977) (also suggesting that lawyers often inartfully use the term "assignment" to encompass delegation which has a different effect); Davidson v. Madison Corp., 257 N.Y. 120, 177 N.E. 393, 76 A.L.R. 1103 (1931). UCC § 2-210(1). RESTATEMENT 2d § 318(3).

[96] Barton v. Perryman, 265 Ark. 228, 577 S.W.2d 596 (1979). RESTATEMENT 2d § 318 comment d.

[97] Local 205, United Elec. Radio & Mach. Workers of Am. v. Timex Corp., 91 Lab. Cas. (CCH) 12,889 (D. Mass. 1981).

[98] *See* UCC § 2-210(1): "A party may perform his duty through a delegate unless otherwise agreed or unless the other party has a substantial interest in having his original promisor perform or control the acts required by the contract...." *See also* RESTATEMENT 2d § 318(2).

[99] Contemporary Mission, Inc. v. Famous Music Corp., 557 F.2d 918 (2d Cir. 1977) (most obligations can be delegated as long as performance by the delegate will not vary materially from performance by the delegant).

[1] *In re* Compass Van & Storage Corp., 65 Bankr 1007 (E.D.N.Y. 1986) (Trustee in bankruptcy may not assume personal service contract so the issue was whether a franchise agreement for

---

[2] *See* Standard Chautauqua Sys. v. Gift, 120 Kan. 101, 242 P. 145 (1926) (duty to select entertainers, musicians, and other personnel was nondelegable).

[3] Eastern Adv. Co. v. McGaw & Co., 89 Md. 72, 42 A. 923 (1899).

typically involves artistic judgment, creativity, or special skill so as to make
the duty nondelegable. Duties involving unique abilities such as those of an
attorney[4] or a physician[5] are, for the same reasons, nondelegable. Duties of
corporations may be thought to be clearly delegable since the delegator-corpo-
ration itself would not have performed the duties. They would have been
performed by individuals within the corporation. The obligor, however, may
have contracted with the corporation on the basis that certain individuals,
with unique abilities and supervisory skills, would perform the duty. Under
these circumstances, delegation to another entity is ineffective unless the
same individuals will perform the duty.[6] The delegate may be an agent or
franchisee of the obligor and the same principles apply. If there is nothing in
the agency that requires particular skill or judgment, the duty should be
assignable.[7] If, however, the agent's duty involves cooperation in good faith[8]
or the use of "best endeavors" (best efforts),[9] the obligee may have "a substantial interest in having that person perform or control the acts promised."[10]

If the delegated performance is one which does not involve artistic skill,
unique abilities, or the like, delegation is normally permissible. Thus, the
delegation of a duty involving ordinary mechanical repairs or any other duty
which can be objectively measured is normally delegable.[11] Where a duty to
install and maintain vending machines was transferred as part of the sale of
the business, the court held the duty delegable notwithstanding the fact that
the obligee had dealt with the delegate in the past and had chosen the
delegator. The duty was delegable because there was not such a material
difference in the performance of the duty as to justify the obligee in refusing to

---

moving services was such a contract. The court stated that there is a plethora of case authority
dealing with delegable duties under personal service contracts. For example, a contract to paint a
picture; a contract between an author and his publisher; an agreement to sing; and an agreement
to render service as a physician. Just because the contract is one for personal services, however,
does not preclude the delegability of duties. Duties involving judgment, skill, taste, or special
ability may not be delegated. Duties that are not so properly characterized, however, should be
delegable. The court held that there was no special personal relationship, special knowledge, or
unique skill or talent in a distributorship agreement involving the moving and storage business).
In an oft-cited quotation, another court stated, "All painters do not paint portraits like Sir Joshua
Reynolds, nor landscapes like Claude Lorraine, nor do all writers write dramas like Shakespeare
or fiction like Dickens. Rare genius and extraordinary skill are not transferable, and contracts for
their employment are therefore personal, and cannot be assigned. But rare genius and extraordinary skill are not indispensable to the workmanlike digging down of a sand hill or the filling up of
a depression to a given level, or the construction of brick sewers with manholes and covers, and
contracts [duties] for such work are not personal and may be assigned [delegated]." Taylor v.
Palmer, 31 Cal. 240, 247-48 (1866).

[4] See Corson v. Lewis, 77 Neb. 446, 109 N.W. 735 (1906).
[5] See Deaton v. Lawson, 40 Wash. 486, 82 P. 879 (1905).
[6] See In re Milton L. Ehrlich, Inc., 5 N.Y.2d 275, 157 N.E.2d 495 (1959). See also Rossetti v. City
of New Britain, 163 Conn. 283, 303 A.2d 714 (1972) where the court indicated that a duty to
perform architectural services is normally nondelegable, but where the delegate was a new
partnership consisting of two of the three original partners, the duty was delegable since the
obligee was receiving the performance for which it had bargained.
[7] See In re Compass Van & Storage, supra note 1. See also RESTATEMENT 2d § 318 comment b.
[8] See Paper Prods. Mach. Co. v. Safepack Mills, 239 Mass. 114, 131 N.E. 288 (1921).
[9] Wetherell Bros. Co. v. United States Steel Co., 200 F.2d 761 (1st Cir. 1952).
[10] This is the language of RESTATEMENT 2d § 318(2). The same test is found in UCC § 2-210(1).
The test is amorphous. There is no escape from a critical analysis of each situation.
[11] British Waggon Co. v. Lea, 5 Q.B.D. 149 [1880] (ordinary repair of wagons).

recognize the delegation.[12] Again, the amorphous test is whether the obligee has a substantial interest in having the promisor perform or control the duties promised.[13] In the absence of contrary agreement, courts will determine that question on the basis of whether a reasonable party in the position of the obligee has any substantial basis for objecting to the performance of the duty by a delegate.

C. *Contractual Prohibition of Delegation.*

If the performance does not require artistic skill, unique abilities, or the like, the obligor is still entitled to receive performance from the delegator if the parties clearly understood that this was the basis of the bargain. Thus, the performance of an ordinary mechanical repair or the mowing of grass which would normally be delegable becomes nondelegable if the parties clearly understood that only the original promisor would perform such duty, i.e., the parties may agree that an otherwise delegable duty will be nondelegable, just as they may agree that an otherwise nondelegable duty will be delegable.[14]

The parties may include in their contract an ambiguous statement such as, "Assignment of the contract is prohibited." To promote the policy of free transferability of rights as well as the policy of permitting the parties to restrict delegation of duties, both the UCC and the RESTATEMENT 2d construe such clauses as barring only the delegation of duties rather than the assignment of otherwise assignable rights.[15] Absent any agreement by the parties concerning delegation, if the obligor, without objection, permits the delegate to perform the duties and accepts the benefit of that performance, he will thereafter be estopped to raise the question of nondelegability regardless of the delegability of the duty.[16]

D. *Repudiation — Novation — Reservation of Rights — Nondelegable Duty.*

1. Repudiation.

As we have seen, unlike the assignment of a right which extinguishes the right in the assignor and creates a similar right in the assignee, an effective delegation of a contractual duty does not discharge the delegator.[17] If the delegator repudiates his obligation, the obligee is at liberty to refuse performance tendered by the delegate which he would otherwise be obliged to ac-

---

[12] The Macke Co. v. Pizza of Gaithersburg, Inc., 259 Md. 479, 270 A.2d 645 (1970).

[13] RESTATEMENT 2d § 318(2); UCC § 2-210(1). A performance by the delegator may be an express or constructive condition to the duty of the obligee. The delegability of the performance of that condition (whether or not it is a duty of the delegator) is subject to the same RESTATEMENT 2d test as the delegation of duty, i.e., whether the obligor has a substantial interest in having the delegator perform or control the required performance. RESTATEMENT 2d § 319(2). In the delegation of duties or performance of conditions, the delegation would not be effective if contrary to public policy. RESTATEMENT 2d §§ 318(1) and 319(1). Cf. *supra* § 138(B).

[14] RESTATEMENT 2d § 318(2) begins with the phrase, "Unless otherwise agreed...." *See also* comment c to this section. Similarly, UCC § 2-210(1) includes "unless otherwise agreed" in its subsection dealing with delegability of duties.

[15] UCC § 2-210(5) and RESTATEMENT 2d § 322(2).

[16] Griffin v. Oklahoma Nat. Gas Corp., 37 F.2d 545 (10th Cir. 1930); Oak Grove Constr. Co. v. Jefferson Cty., 219 F. 858 (6th Cir. 1915).

[17] *See supra* subsection (A).

cept, and may treat the repudiation as a breach of contract, with its attendant consequences.[18]

2. Novation — Reservation of Rights.

We have seen that the obligee may expressly accept the delegate in substitution for the delegator and discharge the delegator, i.e., the parties may agree upon an express novation.[19] The fact that a duty has been delegated or that the obligee has accepted performance from the delegate, however, does not constitute a novation.[20] If, however, the obligee is aware of a repudiation by the delegator, he is presumed to know that the performance of the delegate is offered as a novation and, if the obligee silently accepts the performance under these circumstances, he has accepted an offer of novation.[21] The obligee, however, is not forced into what may be an oppressive choice between accepting repudiation by the delegator and substitute performance by the delegate. As just noted, his silence will indicate such assent to accept the delegate in substitution, thereby effecting a novation. But if the obligee notifies either the delegator, delegate, or both that he is receiving the performance "without prejudice" or "under protest," or similar language manifesting an intention to reserve his rights against the delegator, the delegator is not discharged.[22]

3. Delegation of Nondelegable Duty.

Where the performance of the delegator is personal and not capable of being delegated, an attempted delegation of such a duty is not a repudiation. Nor is it an implied offer of novation.[23] As we have seen, the obligee need not accept the performance of such a duty from a delegate. If the obligee knows that the work is being performed by the delegate and assents to the substituted performance by failing to object, there is still no novation. The obligor, however, has probably waived his right to demand performance by the delegator though the delegator remains liable in the event of a breach by the delegate.[24]

E. *Liability of Delegate for Nonperformance — Interpretation of General Language of Delegation and Assignment.*

As we have seen, in the absence of a showing that a novation has been agreed upon by the parties, the delegator remains liable to the obligee for

---

[18] Western Oil Sales Corp. v. Bliss & Wetherbee, 299 S.W. 637 (Tex. 1927). *See* RESTATEMENT 2d § 329(1) which states that the legal effect of a repudiation is not affected by the fact that the delegate is a competent party who has promised to perform the duty. *See,* however, Meyer v. Washington Times Co., 76 F.2d 988 (D.C. Cir. 1935), holding that an obligee is not excused from accepting performance from a purchaser at a receiver's sale.

[19] *See Barton v. Perryman, supra* note 96.

[20] *See* Heffelfinger v. Gibson, 290 A. 2d 390 (D.C. App. 1972); Procter & Gamble Distrib. Co. v. Lawrence Am. Field Warehousing, 22 A.D.2d 420, 255 N.Y.2d 788 (1965).

[21] RESTATEMENT 2d § 329(2).

[22] *See* UCC § 1-207; RESTATEMENT 2d § 329(2) and comment c.

[23] *See* Clark v. General Cleaning Co., 345 Mass. 62, 185 N.E.2d 749 (1962).

[24] Seale v. Bates, 145 Colo. 430, 359 P.2d 356 (1961) (attempted delegation of duty to provide dance lessons and obligee took lessons from delegate. Though obligee was bound to continue to take lessons from delegate, the delegator remained liable in the event of a breach by the delegate, i.e., there was no novation).

nonperformance of delegated duties. It should not be assumed that simply because the duties have been delegated, the delegate becomes liable to the obligee. The obligee must accept performance of a delegable duty from a delegate. If, however, the delegate fails to perform, the delegator remains liable but there is no cause of action in the obligee against the delegate unless the delegate has made a binding promise to perform, i.e., unless he assumed the duty.[25] If a delegate does assume the duty, the obligee becomes a third party beneficiary of the contract between the delegator and delegate. The student should recall the example of a sale of real property with a mortgage indebtedness. Where the grantee (delegate) assumes the mortgage indebtedness, the mortgagee (obligee) becomes a third party beneficiary. The grantor becomes a surety and the grantee is the principal debtor. If he fails to pay and the surety pays, the surety has a cause of action against the grantee.[26]

The delegation of duties is often accompanied by an assignment of rights, i.e., a party assigns his rights and delegates his duties to the assignee/delegate. A question of interpretation arises when an "assignment" of duties, or an assignment of both rights and duties, is made in general terms to one who accepts the assignment but does not in so many words make a promise to the assignor to perform the delegated duties. In such a case, will a promise to the assignor to perform these duties be inferred, which the other party to the contract may enforce as a third party beneficiary? In the absence of special circumstances showing a contrary intention, such an implication would seem to be justified in the usual case.[27] Nor is there any valid reason why the right of a beneficiary should not be predicated upon a tacit promise as well as upon an orally expressed promise. This is the position adopted by the UCC[28] and the RESTATEMENT 2d.[29] A large number of cases involving contracts for the sale of land, however, have held that the delegate is not liable in the absence of an expressed-in-language assumption of such a duty.[30] The results in these cases may have been influenced in part by the generally accepted rule that one who takes a conveyance of land subject to a mortgage does not, without more, become obligated to pay off the mortgage. Yet, it is doubtful whether the mortgage cases should be viewed analogously since the grantor in such cases does not purport to transfer to the grantee of the equity of redemption the duties which he owes the mortgagee. Probably, the result reached by the majority of the courts in the land contract cases is also due, in

---

[25] Rochester Lantern Co. v. Stiles & Parker Press Co., 135 N.Y. 209, 31 N.E. 1018 (1892).

[26] See Chapter 10 at § 132(C).

[27] In support of this view, see Grismore, Is the Assignee of a Contract Liable for Non-Performance of Delegated Duties?, 18 MICH. L. REV. 284 (1920).

[28] UCC § 2-210(4): "An assignment of 'the contract' or of 'all my rights under the contract' or an assignment in similar terms is an assignment of rights and unless the language or the circumstances (as in an assignment for security) indicate the contrary, it is a delegation of performance of the duties of the assignor and its acceptance by the assignee constitutes a promise by him to perform those duties. This promise is enforceable by either the assignor or the other party to the original contract."

[29] RESTATEMENT 2d § 328. See Newton v. Merchants & Farmers Bank of Dumas, 11 Ark. App. 167, 668 S.W.2d 51 (1984).

[30] The leading case is Langel v. Betz, 250 N.Y. 159, 164 N.E. 890 (1928) which expressly repudiates FIRST RESTATEMENT § 164. Among numerous other cases so holding, see Henock v. Yemans, 340 F.2d 503, 505 (5th Cir. 1965). One of the very few cases taking an opposite position is Prudential Fed. Sav. & Loan Ass'n v. King, 22 Utah 2d 739, 453 P.2d 697 (1969).

part, to the traditional reluctance of our courts to extend the area of enforceability of promises by beneficiaries. It should also be noted that in a number of cases it has been held that the assignee is under an obligation to reimburse the assignor for damages sustained by the assignor because of the assignee's failure to perform delegated duties, although the assignee had made no expressed-in-words promise to perform those duties.[31]

The RESTATEMENT 2d has taken cognizance of this line of cases by including an explanation of the land contract situation in terms of the mortgage assumption heritage and the doctrinal difficulties that early courts faced with respect to the rights of assignees and third party beneficiaries. Though such doctrinal problems have now been overcome, in the RESTATEMENT 2d the American Law Institute concluded that "the shift in doctrine has not yet produced any definite change in the body of decisions" thereby causing the Institute to express "no opinion on the application of [the general principle] to an assignment by a purchaser under a land contract."[32] The changes may, however, be on the way, as evidenced by the willingness of some courts to permit an inference of the assumption of duties in a land contract by clear and convincing evidence that the parties so intended though, again, the mere acceptance of benefits by the obligee would not be sufficient to establish the assumption of duties.[33]

Notwithstanding the preferred interpretation that an assignment in general terms is both an assignment of rights and a delegation of duties, such an interpretation may be rebutted by evidence of a contrary intention. If the assignment of "all of the rights" under a contract is made to a financial institution as security for an indebtedness, the parties generally do not envision an assumption of duties by the assignee.[34]

F. Authorization of Assignment and Delegation.

As suggested earlier,[35] rights and duties that are otherwise nonassignable and nondelegable may be made assignable and delegable by the authorization of the other party to the contract. So, if the contract contains a provision permitting assignment, such a provision will be given effect according to the apparent intention of the parties.[36] However, the mere fact that the contract specifies that it shall bind or benefit "assigns" will not necessarily be held to accomplish this result, in the absence of some additional evidence that the language was used advisedly for the purpose of conveying that meaning.[37] It is

---

[31] Imperial Ref. Co. v. Kanotex Ref. Co., 29 F.2d 193 (8th Cir. 1928); Corvallis & A.R. R.R. v. Portland E. & E. Ry., 84 Or. 524, 163 P. 1173 (1917); Atlantic & N.C. R.R. v. Atlantic & N.C. Co., 147 N.C. 368, 61 S.E. 185 (1908).

[32] RESTATEMENT 2d § 328 comment c.

[33] Pelz v. Streator Nat'l Bank, 145 Ill. App. 3d 946, 496 N.E. 2d 315 (1986); Harmann v. Davis, 651 S.W.2d 134 (Mo. 1983).

[34] UCC §§ 210(4) and 9-317; RESTATEMENT 2d § 328 comment b.

[35] See supra text at note 14.

[36] Dr. L. M. Saliterman & Assoc., P. A. v. Finney, 361 N.W.2d 175 (Minn. App. 1985). Mail-Well Envelope Co. v. Saley, 262 Or. 143, 497 P.2d 364, 367-68 (1972). D. L. Stern Agency v. Mutual Benefit Health & Acc. Ass'n, 43 F. Supp. 167, 169 (S.D.N.Y. 1941). RESTATEMENT 2d § 323(1).

[37] Standard Chautauqua Sys. v. Gift, 120 Kan. 101, 242 P. 145 (1926); Paige v. Faure, 229 N.Y. 114, 127 N.E. 898 (1920); Swarts v. Narragansett Elec. Lighting Co., 26 R.I. 436, 59 A. 111 (1904). RESTATEMENT 2d § 323 comment b.

not uncommon, in the final clause of a written contract, to use the following or an equivalent expression: "This contract shall bind and benefit the parties, their heirs and assigns." Such a clause is usually a mere formality, and, in the normal case, the probabilities are that the parties in using it did not have in mind the question of assignment at all. Consequently, if this language, standing alone, were always construed to authorize the assignment of what would otherwise be nonassignable, violence would be done too often to the real understanding of the parties.

As we have seen, if a party accepts performance of nondelegable duties from the assignee without objection, he will not thereafter be permitted to say that those duties were nondelegable.[38] If the contract expressly prohibits assignment and delegation, these prohibitions can be waived by the subsequent assent of the parties.[39] Absent consideration, however, the waiver of such a provision may be withdrawn until there is reliance on the waiver.[40]

§ 141. Defenses, Setoffs, Counterclaims, and Equities Available Against the Assignee — Uniform Commercial Code Changes.

A. *General Rule.*

One of the rules of contract law which has been repeated so often that it has become axiomatic is that the assignee "stands in the shoes of the assignor," i.e., he takes rights of the assignor which are no greater in the assignee than they were in the assignor. This suggests that the assignee takes subject to all defenses, setoffs, counterclaims, and other equities which the obligor could have asserted against the assignor.[41] With certain qualifications, this is true. As with many applications of seemingly clear and relatively simple rules, however, there are a number of complex issues involved.

At the inception it must be emphasized that the assignment of a right does not enlarge the duty of the obligor, i.e., the unilateral action of the other party to the contract should not subject the obligor to any greater risk than he or she originally assumed. To achieve this result, the assignee is subject to all of the terms of the contract between the obligor and assignor, and any defense or claim arising from the contract itself is available against the assignee.[42] If the assignor's right is voidable or otherwise unenforceable against the obligor, it is similarly voidable or unenforceable against the obligor when asserted by the assignee.[43] If the assignor is under a duty to perform and fails to perform even after assigning the right and after the obligor receives notice of the assignment, the obligor may recoup damages caused by the breach in an action against him by the assignee.[44] Similarly, if the duty of the obligor is

---

[38] *See supra* text at note 16.

[39] Giles v. Sun Bank, N.A., 450 So. 2d 258 (Fla. App. 1984).

[40] RESTATEMENT 2d § 323 comment c.

[41] *See* Enterprises, Inc. v. Becker, 36 Conn. Supp. 213, 416 A.2d 183 (1980), citing the second edition of this book for this statement. *See also* Business Fin. Servs. v. Butler & Booth Dev. Co., 147 Ariz. 510, 711 P.2d 649 (1985); Olsen Frankman Livestock Mktg. Serv. v. Citizens Nat'l Bank, 605 F.2d 1082 (8th Cir. 1979). RESTATEMENT 2d § 336(1) and (2).

[42] UCC § 9-318(1)(a); RESTATEMENT 2d § 336(1).

[43] RESTATEMENT 2d § 336(1).

[44] *See* American Bridge Co. v. City of Boston, 202 Mass. 374, 88 N.E. 1089 (1909); Cronkelton v. Hastings Theatre & Realty Corp., 13 Neb. 168, 278 N.W. 144 (1938). *See* UCC § 9-318 comment 1.

subject to the occurrence of a condition, the duty is not activated if the condition does not occur, notwithstanding the assignment of the conditional right.[45]

B. *Notification of Assignment.*

The reason for emphasizing the fact that the assignee takes subject to all defenses *arising from the contract itself* is to avoid the misconception that notification of the assignment to the obligor cuts off all defenses. *Notification of the assignment has no effect on the defenses which the obligor can assert if, again, those defenses arise from the terms of the contract itself.*[46] Notification, however, is important in relation to the freedom of the obligor to render performance to the assignor or, as we will see below, to claims or defenses accruing after notification of the assignment.

If the obligor renders performance to the assignor, or secures a discharge of his obligation for consideration, or, for value, acquires any other defense good against the assignor, *before he has knowledge or notice of the assignment,* the assignee's right is subject to such defense.[47] The inherent justice in such a rule is obvious. It would be unfair and inequitable to take a contrary position from the standpoint of the obligor who is entitled to assume that the right continues in the assignor until he is aware of the assignment.[48] As to whether an obligor has received notification or otherwise become aware of the fact of assignment, the definition of notification in the UCC is the preferred, modern view.[49] The Code also indicates the content of the notice, i.e., it must reason-

---

[45] *Cf.* RESTATEMENT 2d § 320.

[46] James Talcott, Inc. v. H. Corenzwit & Co., 76 N.H. 305, 387 A.2d 350 (1978).

[47] Kaw Valley State Bank & Trust v. Commercial Bank of Liberty, 567 S.W.2d 710 (Mo. App. 1978); Farmers Acceptance Corp. v. De Lozier, 178 Colo. 291, 496 P.2d 1016 (1972); Ornbaum v. First Nat'l Bank, 215 Cal. 72, 8 P.2d 470 (1932); Erlandson v. Erskine, 76 Mont. 537, 248 P. 209 (1926); Le Porin v. State Exch. Bank, 113 Kan. 76, 213 P. 650 (1923). UCC § 9-318(1)(b) and comment 1; RESTATEMENT 2d § 336(2).
Failure of performance by the assignor may be shown by way of recoupment though it occurred subsequently to notice of the assignment, since the right to claim damages for breach existed from the time of making the contract. Apple v. Edwards, 92 Mont. 524, 16 P.2d 700, 87 A.L.R. 179 (1932); Annotation, 87 A.L.R. 187 (1933).

[48] It is, however, important to emphasize the fact that the obligor does not become liable to the assignee after receiving notice of the assignment. Van Waters & Rogers, Inc. v. Interchange Resources, Inc., 14 Ariz. App. 414, 484 P.2d 26 (1971).

[49] UCC § 1-201(26) provides: "a person 'notifies' or 'gives' a notice to another by taking such steps as may be reasonably required to inform the other in ordinary course whether or not such other actually comes to know of it. A person 'receives' a notice or notification when (a) it comes to his attention; or (b) it is duly delivered at the place of business through which the contract was made or at any other place held out by him as the place for receipt of such communication."
There is considerable case law concerning notice. *See, e.g.,* Van Dyke's Food Store v. Independent Coal & Coke Co., 84 Utah 95, 34 P.2d 706 (1934) (notice to employee of obligor who was without authority on the premises was insufficient); Bank of Commerce v. Ternes Coal & Lumber Co., 253 Mich. 548, 235 N.W. 249 (1931) (written assignment on face of invoice for goods sold to obligor sent to him by assignor was notice of assignment whether or not debtor saw it); Farmers' Exch. v. Walter M. Lowney, Co., 95 Vt. 445, 115 A. 507 (1921) (fact that assignee billed buyer directly for goods sold was sufficient to charge buyer with notice of assignment. The opinion states, "It is not found that defendant had formal notice of the assignment. But that was not necessary. If it had knowledge of sufficient facts concerning plaintiff's relation to the transaction to put it on inquiry, it must be held to have had notice of all such facts as reasonable diligence in prosecuting its inquiry in the proper direction would have brought to its knowledge." *Id.* at 509. *Cf.* Gibraltar Realty Corp v. Mount Vernon Trust Co., 276 N.Y. 353, 12 N.E.2d 438 (1938), holding that a bank is not to be charged with notice of an assignment of a depositor's account unless the original written evidence of the assignment was presented to it.

ably identify the rights assigned and the obligor may request that the assignee furnish reasonable proof that the assignment has been made.[50]

C. *Uniform Commercial Code — Modification or Substitution.*

The Code changes the common law rule that an assignee acquires no rights under a modified or substituted contract between the obligor and assignor. Under the Code, if the assigned right has not yet been earned by performance, the obligor and assignor may, in good faith and in accordance with reasonable commercial standards, effect a modification or substitution of their contract *notwithstanding notification of the assignment.* The modification or substitution is effective against the assignee, but the assignee acquires rights under the good faith modification or substitution.[51]

D. *Claims and Defenses — Setoffs and Counterclaims.*

1. Rationale for Setoffs and Counterclaims.

Students often become confused concerning the availability of setoffs or counterclaims to an obligor against an assignee. A setoff or counterclaim arises from a collateral transaction between the assignor and obligor, i.e., it does not arise from the contract, the rights of which the assignor has assigned to the assignee. The assignee has nothing to do with such transactions. Yet, it is generally held that the obligor may use them against the assignee. To understand why this is so, take the case of the house painter who has completed his work and is to be paid within thirty days the contract price of $10,000. The obligor sells new and used cars and agrees to sell a used car to the painter for $6,000 on credit. The obligor is not at all concerned about extending $6,000 in credit to a party to whom he owes $10,000. If the painter assigned his right to the $10,000 payment and the obligor was unaware of that fact when he extended the $6,000 credit to the painter, the obligor should not be penalized for making a basic assumption concerning the security for the credit extended to the painter and should be able to offset the $6,000 owed by the painter against the assignee's right to collect $10,000.[52] If, on the other hand, the obligor had been notified of the assignment prior to the extension of credit to the painter, the obligor has assumed the risk knowing that he must pay $10,000 to the assignee and it is, therefore, fair to preclude the use of the setoff against the assignee. Therefore, as to setoffs and counterclaims good against the assignor, i.e., arising from collateral transactions between the obligor and assignor before the obligor is notified of the assignment, it is commonly stated that the obligor may avail himself of such claims.[53]

---

[50] UCC § 9-318(3).

[51] UCC § 9-318(2). *See* Madden Eng'g Corp. v. Major Tube Corp., 568 S.W.2d 614 (Tenn. App. 1978) where, in reaction to the assignee's claim that it had no notice of the modification between the assignor and obligor, the court held the modification effective because it was not only commercially reasonable but assisted the assignor to remain in business as long as it did. *Accord,* RESTATEMENT 2d § 338(2).

[52] *See* Maryland Coop. Milk Producers v. Bell, 206 Md. 168, 110 A.2d 661 (1955).

[53] *See* FED. R. CIV. P. 13. Unless the assignee has assumed the liabilities of the assignor, however, such claims may only be used defensively. The assignee is not liable for any excess. Shepard v. Commercial Credit Corp., 123 Vt. 106, 183 A.2d 525 (1962).

2. Determining Which Setoffs and Counterclaims Are Available — "Matured" — "Accrued."

The right to setoff and counterclaim is largely statutory and, unfortunately, the state statutes were not uniform, resulting in variations in different jurisdictions as to the circumstances under which the obligor could avail himself, as against the assignee, of such claims good against the assignor. There were holdings in some jurisdictions requiring only that the claim have matured at the time of suit, regardless of whether the counterclaim or the assigned claim had matured at the date of the assignment or notice thereof.[54] In other jurisdictions, both the assigned claim and the counterclaim must have matured at the date of the assignment before any counterclaim would be permitted against the assignee.[55] The lack of uniformity in these procedural statutes has been overcome by the UCC, and the RESTATEMENT 2d has followed its normal course in adhering to the Code position.[56] Unfortunately, the uniformity comes at a cost.

Under the RESTATEMENT 2d and the UCC, the rights of an assignee are subject to "any other defense or claim of the account debtor against the assignor which *accrues* before the account debtor receives notification of the assignment."[57] The term "accrues" is unclear. It probably means the point in time when a cause of action exists since it is typically used in relation to statutes of limitation.[58] "Accrued" does not mean "matured" since an "account" under the Code may refer to what used to be called a "contract right," i.e., a right not yet earned by performance or not yet mature.[59] The choice between "mature" and "accrued" has been described as "arbitrary" line drawing to allow some setoffs and counterclaims against the assignee without destabilizing the critically important commercial financing practice of assigning accounts.[60] The result is that the obligor must be able to establish that a setoff or counterclaim accrued before he received notification of the assignment if he wishes to assert such defenses or claims against the assignee.[61]

---

[54]*See* St. Louis Nat'l Bank v. Gay, 101 Cal. 286, 35 P. 876 (1894); First Nat'l Bank v. Bynum, 84 N.C. 24, 37 Am. Rep. 604 (1881).

[55]*See* Koegel v. Michigan Trust Co., 117 Mich. 542, 76 N.W. 74 (1898) (assigned claim not matured at date of the assignment); Fuller v. Steiglitz, 27 Ohio St. 355, 22 Am. Rep. 312 (1875) (both assigned claim and counterclaim unmatured at the date of assignment).

[56]UCC § 9-318(1)(b); RESTATEMENT 2d § 336(2).

[57] UCC § 9-318(1)(b) emphasis added. Farmers Acceptance Corp. v. De Lozier, 178 Colo. 291, 496 P.2d 1016 (1972) holds that a "setoff" is the type of claim contemplated by this section of the UCC.

[58]*See, e.g.,* UCC § 2-725(1) which states that an action for breach of contract (contract for the sale of goods) must be commenced within four years after the cause of action accrues. Subsection (2) then states that, "A cause of action accrues when the breach occurs...." *See also* Seattle-First Nat'l Bank v. Oregon Pac. Indus., 262 Or. 578, 500 P.2d 1033 (1972).

In comparing the FIRST RESTATEMENT analysis which required setoffs and presumably counterclaims to be "based on facts existing at the time of the assignment" with the requirement that such claims have "accrued" before notification to the obligor of the assignment, Professor Gilmore suggests, "It may be admitted that it is no easier to tell when a 'claim' 'accrues' than it is to tell when a 'fact' 'arises.'" Gilmore, *The Assignee of Contract Rights and His Precarious Security,* 74 YALE L. J. 217, 230 (1964).

[59]UCC § 9-106.

[60] *See* Seattle-First Nat'l Bank, *supra* note 58.

[61]*See* Ertel v. Radio Corp. of Am., 261 Ind. 573, 307 N.E.2d 471 (1974); Fall River Trust Co. v. B. G. Browdy, Inc., 346 Mass. 614, 195 N.E.2d 63 (1964).

E. *The Effect of Latent Equities.*

An assignee may innocently take an assignment for value without knowledge that the right of a third party may be involved. Where, for example, the holder of a contract right is induced to assign it through the fraud of the assignee, and that assignee assigns the right to an innocent purchaser for value, should the innocent assignee be able to assert the right regardless of the first assignor's claim of fraud? The issue is often phrased in terms of whether or not the assignee takes subject to latent equities in favor of third persons. It is a question on which the decided cases have not been in agreement. This lack of agreement has apparently resulted from a difference of opinion in regard to the nature of an assignee's ownership. The older cases, which proceeded on the theory that the assignee's ownership is equitable rather than legal, reached the conclusion that the assignee takes subject to the prior equity of a third person.[62] On the other hand, as we have already seen, the present tendency is to deal with transfers of contractual rights according to the same rules that control transfers of tangible property. A court proceeding on this theory is likely to take the view that an assignee for value, without notice of the equity of a third person, takes free from it.[63] This rule has the merit of facilitating the transfer of contract rights, since it is practically impossible for an assignee to learn of the existence of the latent equities of third persons.

F. *Waiver of Defenses Against the Assignee — Holder in Due Course.*

Another question involving defenses against the assignee is whether the obligor and assignor may, at the time their contract is formed, agree that the obligor will not assert defenses against the assignee. To grasp the problem in its most realistic setting requires the student of contract law to become aware of some of the basic elements of the law of commercial paper, sometimes called negotiable instruments, or, in more archaic terms, "bills and notes."[64] Any extensive inquiry into the law of commercial paper is beyond the scope of this

---

[62]Levenbaum v. Hanover Trust Co., 325 Mass. 19, 148 N.E. 227 (1925) (trustee in bankruptcy sought to recover funds paid by the bankrupt in unlawful preference of creditor who deposited the funds in a bank and then assigned his claim against the bank. Trustee prevailed over assignee who paid value and had no notice); Downer v. Royalton, 39 Vt. 25 (1866) (deputy sheriff deposited money which he had collected on an execution in a bank and then wrongfully assigned a judgment recovered by him against the bank to a third person. Held: the execution creditor had a better right to the judgment than the assignee).

[63]*See* McKnight v. McKnight, 678 P.2d 1330 (Alaska 1984) (assignee's service after court order but before notice of the order were in good faith and he is entitled to enforce the right to the extent of the value of services performed before notice was received). *See also* Atkin v. Security Sav. & Trust Co., 157 Or. 172, 68 P.2d 1047, 71 P.2d 321 (1937); Lasser v. Philadelphia Nat'l Bank, 321 Pa. 189, 183 A. 791 (1936); Williams v. Donnelly, 54 Neb. 193, 74 N.W. 601 (1898). *Accord,* RESTATEMENT 2d § 343.

[64]Traditionally, negotiable instruments were classified into two types: (1) promissory notes and (2) bills of exchange. A promissory note represented a promise by the maker or issuer of the instrument to pay a sum of money to another, i.e., the payee. Thus, the transaction involved only two parties (*See* Title III of the Uniform Negotiable Instruments Act). A bill of exchange represented an order by the issuer (drawer) of the instrument to a third party, i.e., the drawee, to pay a sum of money to the payee. Thus, three parties were involved (*See* Title II of the Uniform Negotiable Instruments Act). This terminology is changed under the UCC.

volume.[65] As in some other sections of this work, however, it is necessary to provide some of the basic framework of that branch of law to facilitate comprehension of the problem at hand.

1. A Commercial Paper Primer — Holder in Due Course.

The modern law of commercial paper involving promissory notes and drafts (including checks) is found in Articles 3 and 4 of the UCC. If certain formalities are found in a writing, the writing takes on the unique status of a negotiable instrument.[66] The most popular and easily recognized negotiable instrument is the typical personal or business check. A glance at a typical check reveals that if it is signed by the proper party (drawer) and made payable to a party or to his order (payee) and drawn against a bank which is ordered to pay the "sum certain" set forth in the writing, it meets the basic requirements to attain the status of a negotiable instrument. Such an instrument is often called an "order" instrument or "three-party paper" because it is drawn by the customer of the bank (drawer) against the bank (drawee) and made payable to the party whom the drawer wishes to pay or to his order (payee). The payee is a "holder" of the instrument,[67] and only he can properly transfer that instrument to another. The payee transfers the instrument by "negotiating" it and "negotiates" it by indorsing it, usually by signing his name on the reverse side.[68] He may indorse it to another person, to a bank, or any other entity. Like the payee, the party to whom the payee has "negotiated" the instrument (check) becomes a holder. Moreover, if the transferee (holder) takes the instrument for value, in good faith, and without notice that the instrument is overdue, or has been dishonored or that there is any defense against or claim to it on the part of any person, the transferee is much more than a mere holder — he is a holder in due course.[69]

The holder in due course has a unique status as a transferee as compared with a mere assignee of a contract right. He takes the instrument free from all defenses of any party to the instrument with the exception of certain very basic defenses such as incapacity, duress, "real" or "essential" fraud, and discharge in insolvency proceedings.[70] Except for these so-called "real" defenses, the holder in due course need not worry over more likely defenses (often called "personal" defenses) such as the failure on the part of his transferor (the payee-holder) to perform his promise for the benefit of the drawer.

---

[65] *See generally* J. WHITE & R. SUMMERS, UNIFORM COMMERCIAL CODE CHAPTERS 13-18 (1988).

[66] UCC § 3-104(1) provides: "Any writing to be a negotiable instrument within this Article must
(a) be signed by the maker or drawer; and
(b) contain an unconditional promise or order to pay a sum certain in money and no other promise, order, obligation or power given by the maker or drawer except as authorized by this Article; and
(c) be payable on demand or at a definite time; and
(d) be payable to order or to bearer."

[67] UCC § 1-201(20) defines "holder" as a "person who is in possession of a document of title or an instrument or an investment security drawn, issued or indorsed to him or to his order or to bearer or in blank."

[68] UCC § 3-202.

[69] UCC § 3-302.

[70] Other defenses to which a holder in due course takes subject include infancy, illegality, and any discharge of which he has notice at the time he takes the instrument. UCC § 3-305.

Thus, the holder in due course has better rights than his transferor. *He does not merely stand in the shoes of the transferor — the shoes have become much larger.* The basic reason for this unique status is to permit the holder in due course to negotiate this instrument without fear that it will prove to be a worthless piece of paper. This assures the free transferability of such instruments which are so important to the commercial life of a complex industrialized society.

2. Waiver of Defenses.

This highly simplistic exploration of the transfer of a negotiable instrument is necessary if one is to understand a device known as waiver of defenses by an obligor against an assignee. Another method of accomplishing the same, basic goal of permitting a transferee of a contract right to stand in a *better* position than his transferor is to insert a provision in the original contract between the obligor and assignor whereby the obligor agrees not to assert defenses (which the obligor could have asserted against the assignor) against the assignee, should an assignment occur. Prior to the Code, there was considerable debate about the enforceability of such clauses and, in a number of jurisdictions, they were either unenforceable or enforceable only under certain modified circumstances.[71] The Code drafters included a provision[72] making such agreements enforceable but subject to any statute or judicial decision of the particular jurisdiction involved which established a different rule for buyers or lessees of *consumer* goods.[73] Absent such a different rule, the Code provides that such a clause, waiving the defenses of the obligor against the assignee, is enforceable.[74] To invoke the benefits of this clause, the assignee must have taken the assignment in good faith, for value, and without notice of the same kind of claim or defense which would be effective against a holder of a negotiable instrument who seeks to become a holder in due course. The same "real" defenses available against a holder in due course of a negotiable instrument are available against such an assignee. Therefore, the Code treats the assignee of a contract right under such waiver of defenses clause as identical to a holder in due course.

3. Holder in Due Course, Waiver of Defenses, and the Consumer.

While real holder in due course status or an effective simulation of that status through the use of a waiver of defenses clause has certainly promoted the desirable policy of free transferability of commercial paper, its effect on consumers can be devastating in given cases. Consider the example of a simple purchase of a new television set for which the consumer buyer makes a down payment and then signs a negotiable promissory note for the balance. The note is transferred (negotiated) to a bank or other commercial lender who

---

[71] The cases are collected in Annotations, 31 A.L.R. 876 (1924); 110 A.L.R. 774 (1937).

[72] UCC § 9-206. For a discussion of § 9-206 and its relationship to the usual rule that defenses and claims are available against the assignee pursuant to § 9-318, *see* First New England Fin. Corp. v. Woffard, 421 So. 2d 590 (Fla. App. 1982).

[73] UCC § 9-109(1) defines "consumer goods" as goods "used or bought for use primarily for personal, family or household purposes.

[74] *See* RESTATEMENT 2d § 336 comment f.

buys such "paper" from retailers. If there is no negotiable instrument involved, there is the effective substitute, i.e., a clause waiving defenses, to provide the assignee with the same protection he would have had as a holder in due course of a negotiable instrument. The consumer has the pleasure of watching his television set operate perfectly for three weeks, after which it will no longer operate. The retailer is no longer in business and nowhere to be found. The consumer is notified by the bank that she must continue to make her monthly payments for the now inoperative television set since the bank has nothing to do with the operative fitness of such goods, i.e., warranties of merchantability or other warranties. Defenses such as breach of warranty are not available against either a holder in due course or a transferee of non-negotiable paper that contains the waiver of defenses clause. The consumer has nowhere to turn.

Courts began recognizing this problem by considering the connection between the retailer and the bank or other lender with whom the retailer often dealt on a continuous basis. Often the lender would even supply the printed forms to the retailer for the consumer's signature. Where a commercial lender is so *closely connected* with the retail seller that the lender should not be heard to say that it was an innocent purchaser for value in good faith when it purchased the commercial paper from the retailer, the lender could not be a holder in due course and the normal defenses by an obligor (consumer) against an assignee (lender) are available.[75] Fearing the loss of holder in due course status, a number of lenders began using the waiver of defenses clause in their printed forms to achieve the same protection against the normal defenses of the obligor against the assignee. The waiver of defenses clause is even less obvious in a printed form than the effects of a negotiable instrument about which some consumer may have a myopic but real apprehension in signing. Judicial vigilance in an age of consumer protection penetrated this device and the "too close connection" analysis was applied to waiver of defenses clauses as it had been applied to holder in due course status.[76]

These judicial inroads concerning the necessary protection of deserving consumers gave rise to an enormous statutory effort to protect consumers throughout the country. With respect to the restrictions of holder in due course status which might deprive the consumer of the benefit of her bargain, perhaps the most significant effort was a new regulation from the Federal Trade Commission issued on November 14, 1975, requiring consumer credit contracts to contain conspicuous notices of the fact that any holder of the contract would be subject to all claims and defenses which the debtor could assert against the seller of goods or services.[77] The same concept is found in

---

[75] One of the requirements for holder in due course status is that the holder take the instrument in good faith. If there is a close or intimate connection between the transferor and transferee, the latter may have difficulty showing that he took the instrument in good faith, thus destroying holder in due course status and making the transferee subject to defenses. The seminal case is Mutual Fin. Co. v. Martin, 63 So. 2d 649, 44 A.L.R.2d 1 (Fla. 1953). *See also* Rehurek v. Chrysler Credit Corp., 262 So. 2d 452 (Fla. App. 1972) suggesting the close connection theory which may occur where the financial institution has a close working relationship with the retail seller in a consumer credit transaction.

[76] The seminal case is Unico v. Owen, 50 N.J. 101, 232 A.2d 405 (1967), opinion by Justice Francis.

[77] 16 C.F.R. § 433.2.

state legislation throughout the country.[78] The effect is to negate holder in due course status for purchasers of contract rights in consumer transactions.

§ 142. Priorities — Successive Assignees — Attaching Creditors.

A. *Common Law Priorities — Successive Assignees — "Four Horsemen."*

An assignee who takes an assignment of a claim with notice or knowledge of a prior assignment of the same claim takes subject to the rights of the earlier assignee. Where, however, an assignor has made successive assignments of the same claim to each of two or more assignees, each assignment having been made for a valuable consideration, and the later assignee has no notice or knowledge of the earlier assignment, a difficult question of priority arises, causing conflict in the decisions. One line of decisions took the view that a party receiving his assignment first has the better right in the absence of a superior equity existing in the second assignee.[79] Those courts taking this so-called "New York" or "American" view regarded an assignee as having legal ownership of the claim, i.e., when the assignor makes the first assignment he parts with all his ownership in the assigned right and so has nothing to transfer to the second assignee.[80] Other courts reached the same conclusion proceeding on the theory that an assignee acquires at most an equitable title but applied the equitable maxim, where the equities are equal, the first in point of time prevails.[81] A second line of decisions, based on an early English case,[82] held that the assignee who first notifies the obligor of his assignment is entitled to priority, on the theory that the ownership of the assignee is not complete until he has notified the obligor of his claim.[83] This view was no doubt motivated by the belief that it is good policy to require the assignee to give notice to the obligor for the protection of third persons who may be

---

[78] *See, e.g.,* Uniform Consumer Credit Code, § 3-307 and Iowa Code § 537.3307.

[79] The cases are collected in Annotations, 31 A.L.R. 879-82; 110 A.L.R. 775-78 (1937). In State *ex. rel.* Crane Co. v. Stokke, 65 S.D. 207, 272 N.W. 811 (1937), the court held that, as between a contractor's surety who took an assignment from the principal debtor and a creditor-assignee of the principal debtor who took an assignment to secure the same claim which the surety undertook to secure, the creditor has the stronger equity and is entitled to priority, though he was the second assignee in point of time. *See also* Coon River Coop. Sand Ass'n v. McDougall Constr. Co., 215 Iowa 861, 244 N.W. 847 (1932), holding that a second unconditional assignment to a creditor of a contractor takes priority over an earlier conditional assignment to the contractor's surety.

The United States Supreme Court formerly treated the question as one of general law and applied its own rule holding that "mere priority of notice to the debtor by a second assignee, who lent money to the assignor without making any inquiry of the debtor, is not sufficient to subordinate the first assignment to the second," regardless of the rule adopted in the state in which the case arose. Salem Trust Co. v. Manufacturers' Fin. Co., 264 U.S. 182 (1924). However, since the decision in Erie R.R. v. Tompkins, 304 U.S. 64 (1938), the state rule must be applied in federal courts.

[80] Perhaps the best known illustration of this position is found in Superior Brassiere Co. v. Zimetbaum, 214 App. Div. 525, 212 N.Y.S. 473 (1925) where the plaintiff had manufactured goods for a dealer and took assignments for moneys due from the dealer's customers as payment for the manufactured goods. The dealer made a second assignment to the defendant who proceeded to collect from most of the dealer's customers. The court held that "A subsequent assignee takes nothing by his assignment because the assignor has nothing to give."

[81] *See Salem Trust Co., supra* note 79.

[82] Dearle v. Hall, 3 Russ. 1, 48 [1828].

[83] The cases are collected in Annotations, 31 A.L.R. 876-79 (1924); 110 A.L.R. 774-75 (1937).

induced to deal with the claim in reliance upon information as to its owner-ship obtained from the obligor.[84]

A third position, sometimes referred to as the "four horsemen" rule, sup-ported by both RESTATEMENTS,[85] permits the first assignee (in time) to prevail unless the first assignment is ineffective, revocable, or voidable, or the subse-quent assignment is ineffective, revocable, or voidable, or the subsequent assignee, in good faith, gives value and obtains any of the following: (1) pay-ment or satisfaction of the obligation;[86] (2) judgment against the obligor;[87] (3) a new contract with the obligor (novation),[88] or (4) possession of a symbolic writing.[89] There is judicial support for this compromise between the "Ameri-can" and "English" views. The cases favoring the subsequent assignee in the exceptional situations have usually been justified either on the ground that the subsequent assignee has drawn a "legal title" to his equity and so has the better right,[90] or on the ground of estoppel.[91]

B. *Modern Commercial Financing — Successive Assignees.*

What has been set forth to this point is the prevailing law of priority be-tween successive assignees in relation to wage claims, rights under insurance policies, bank accounts, and certain other types of transactions. However, priority problems involving these types of rights are relatively rare. The most significant problem of priority between successive assignees occurs in relation to the assignment of accounts, and that problem is now covered by Article 9 of the UCC.[92] Prior to the Code, the assignment of accounts was dealt with in accordance with the positions discussed above. It could make a great deal of difference, therefore, whether the particular jurisdiction involved applied the New York (first in time) view, the English (first to notify) view, or the "four horsemen" (sometimes called "Massachusetts") view. The situation was made much more complex because of the Federal Bankruptcy Code.[93] The two basic

---

[84] *See* Jenkinson v. New York Fin. Co., 79 N.J.Eq. 247, 82 A. 36 (1911). *See also* Note, 24 COLUM. L. REV. 501 (1924). For a comparative analysis of the American (New York) and English views, *see* Evans v. Joyner, 195 Va. 851, 77 S.E.2d 420 (1953).

[85] *See* FIRST RESTATEMENT § 173; RESTATEMENT 2d § 342. *See* McKnight v. Rice, 678 P.2d 1330 (Alaska 1984).

[86] *See* Aetna Cas. & Sur. Co. v. Harvard Trust Co., 344 Mass. 160, 181 N.E.2d 673 (1962). Rabinowitz v. Peoples Nat'l Bank, 235 Mass. 102, 126 N.E. 289 (1920); Bridge v. Wheeler, 152 Mass. 343, 25 N.E. 612 (1890).

[87] *See* Judson v. Corcoran, 58 U.S. (17 How. 612 (1855).

[88] *See* Strange v. Houston & T.C. R.R., 53 Tex. 162 (1880); New York & N.H. R.R. v. Schuyler, 34 N.Y. 30 (1865).

[89] *See* Herman v. Connecticut Mut. Life Ins. Co., 218 Mass. 181, 105 N.E. 450 (1914); Washing-ton Twp. v. First Nat'l Bank, 147 Mich. 571, 111 N.W. 349 (1907).

[90] *See* Coffman v. Ligget's Adm'r, 107 Va. 418, 59 S.E. 392 (1907).

[91] *See* the cases cited *supra* note 89.

[92] We have discussed the importance of the assignments of accounts (defined in § 9-106 of the UCC as any right to payment for goods sold or leased or service rendered which is not evidenced by an instrument or chattel paper, whether or not it has been earned by performance) in commer-cial financing in earlier sections of this chapter.

[93] Article 1, section 8, clause 4 of the United States Constitution empowers Congress to "estab-lish uniform laws on the subject of Bankruptcies throughout the United States." Congress used this power to pass four different Bankruptcy Acts during the nineteenth century. The first three had brief lives. The Act of 1800 was repealed in 1803; the Act of 1841 was repealed after only 18 months; the Act of 1867 was repealed in 1878. The fourth, the Bankruptcy Act of 1898, lasted for 81 years. During this period, it was substantially amended and subjected to a great deal of

purposes of the Bankruptcy Act are (1) to permit an insolvent debtor to gain a fresh start by discharging him from his debts (with exceptions), and (2) to assure that the creditors of the bankrupt receive an equitable distribution of the insolvent debtor's assets.[94] In pursuance of the second purpose of equitable distribution among the creditors, the Bankruptcy Act makes certain preferences voidable by the trustee in bankruptcy. For example, if within a certain period prior to bankruptcy,[95] the bankrupt should pay all or virtually all of his remaining assets to one of his many creditors to satisfy antecedent debts, the trustee in bankruptcy could recover this amount from the preferred creditor for the benefit of all the creditors.[96] As to the assignment of accounts receivable, however, such transfers were normally not made on account of an antecedent debt, i.e., they were usually not made to pay an existing (prior) indebtedness. Since only transfers made on account of an antecedent debt were capable of being voidable preferences under the Act, it did not affect the typical accounts receivable transfer which was normally made for a contemporaneous advance ("new value"). However, a 1938 amendment to the Bankruptcy Act provided that a transfer was "deemed" to take effect (in relation to preferences) only when it was "so far perfected" (sufficiently perfected) that it would prevail against bona fide purchasers for value and creditors under the appropriate state law.[97] Under the English view, absent notice to the obligor, an assignment would never become perfected. A practice of "nonnotification" assignments of accounts was prevalent in commercial financing at the time. Under this practice, the assignee would not notify the obligor of the assignment because the assignor did not wish the fact of assignment to be known for pragmatic and good will reasons. If nonnotification assignments were combined with the English (first to notify) rule, no notice to the obligor would ever be given. Therefore, for the purposes of the Bankruptcy Act, the transfer (which was deemed to take effect only when it was secure against creditors and bona fide purchasers) would not be effective when it actually occurred — it would be effective only upon notification to the obligor. Since there was no notification, the transfer was said to take effect immediately prior to bankruptcy which brought the transfer within the four month rule,[98] "for an antecedent debt," at a time when the debtor was insolvent. Therefore, these innu-

---

judicial interpretation. It was replaced by our current Bankruptcy Code (Title 11 of the United States Code), most of which became effective on October 1, 1979. R. Nordstrom, J. Murray & A. Clovis, Problems and Materials on Secured Transactions 259 (1987).

[94] The majority of bankruptcies are liquidation bankruptcies (Chapter 7 of the Bankruptcy Code). The assets of the bankrupt (debtor) are collected by a trustee in bankruptcy and then liquidated. The proceeds are used to pay the expenses of bankruptcy and to provide equitable distribution of the remainder to creditors. Where the bankrupt is an individual, his debts are discharged and he is provided with a "fresh start." If the debtor is a corporation, it will typically be dissolved.

Chapter 11 bankruptcies are rehabilitation bankruptcies (reorganization) though Chapter 13 bankruptcies also have rehabilitation as a goal (adjustment of debts of an individual with regular income). Here, the debtor's obligations are either reduced in amount, deferred in time, or both. By allowing the debtor to continue under these circumstances, creditors will receive more than they would have received had the assets been liquidated and the proceeds therefrom distributed.

[95] The 1950 version of the Bankruptcy Act contained a four month rule. The current (1978) version limits the period to ninety days.

[96] 11 U.S.C. § 547(b).

[97] This was § 60(a)(2) of that version of the Act.

[98] Now the ninety day rule. See supra note 95.

merable assignments of accounts were considered voidable preferences by the United States Supreme Court in the famous *Klauder* case.[99] To avoid the problems created by this interpretation, various state statutes were enacted including "validation" statutes and notice filing statutes.[1] Pennsylvania, the jurisdiction involved in *Klauder,* and two other states passed "book-marking" statutes[2] which were subsequently highly criticized. In 1950, Congress amended the Bankruptcy Act again and removed the "bona fide purchaser test" from the critical subsection. The current version of the Bankruptcy law is the 1978 Bankruptcy Code.[3]

The various state statutes were superseded by the filing provisions of the UCC, which effectively solves the problems in this area. Under the Code, an assignee of an account obtains priority over other assignees, regardless of which assignee was first in time or first notified the obligor, by filing.[4] The first-to-file rule prevails.[5] It is necessary to file a financing statement in the appropriate office.[6] As suggested earlier, however, certain types of accounts are excluded from Article 9,[7] and other types of accounts do not have to be filed in order to be "perfected" for the purposes of priority over other assignees.[8]

C. *Priorities — Assignees Versus Attaching Creditors.*

Almost everyone has creditors who are general creditors, i.e., they have no interest in any particular asset or right of the obligor. A general creditor can, however, procure a specific interest in his debtor's property. He can, for example, become a lien creditor[9] by securing a judgment and having the sheriff "levy" on certain property of the obligor or by securing a writ of attachment and becoming an attaching creditor as to certain accounts of his debtor. If a priority dispute arises between an assignee and a general creditor, the assignee will prevail since he owns the right assigned and the general creditor has no specific interest in that right. When the dispute is between an assignee and an attaching creditor of the assignor, each party has a right in the same

---

[99] Corn Exchange Nat'l Bank v. Klauder, 318 U.S. 434 (1943).

[1] *See, e.g.,* Cal. Stat. 1943 ch. 766, § 1.

[2] 1941 Pa. Laws No. 255. *See also* 1943 Ga. Laws No. 178; 1949 N.D. Laws ch. 113 § 1.

[3] Title 11, U.S.C.

[4] UCC § 9-401 deals with the place of filing which will differ depending upon the type of collateral described in the financing statement, i.e., the statement that is filed. Section 9-402 deals with formal requisites of a financing statement, i.e., what it must contain and the fact that it must be signed by the debtor. The typical financing statement is a prescribed form used throughout the country though filing must occur in respective state offices since the UCC is a state statute. Section 9-403 deals with the effective moment of filing (presentation to the filing officer coupled with the fee) and the duration of the filing statement (five years unless a continuation statement is filed prior to the end of that period).

[5] UCC § 9-312(5) states that the priority is in time of filing, or perfection, whichever is earlier. Perfection as to certain types of collateral can occur through possession or filing. If neither security interest is perfected, the first to attach (§ 9-203) has priority.

[6] *See supra* note 2.

[7] UCC § 9-104(f).

[8] UCC § 9-302(1)(e).

[9] UCC 9-301(3) defines a "lien creditor" as a creditor who has acquired a lien on the property involved by attachment, levy, or the like and includes an assignee for benefit of creditors from the time of assignment and a trustee in bankruptcy from the date of the filing of the petition or a receiver in equity from the time of appointment.

chose in action and it is quite generally held that the one first in point of time has the better right.[10] Since the assignee gave value to the assignor in reliance on the particular claim, whereas the attaching creditor relied upon the general credit of the assignor, it is thought that the assignee has the greater equity, and so should prevail, regardless of whether or not he gave notice to the obligor.[11] This is the rule even in those jurisdictions which, in the case of successive assignees, prefer the one who gives notice to the obligor first. However, if the obligor has paid the attaching creditor before he receives notice of the assignment, he will be protected against further liability.[12] Moreover, a number of courts have held that unless the obligor receives notice of the assignment before the attaching creditor obtains a judgment against him, so that he can defend the action and prevent the entry of judgment, the attaching creditor will prevail.[13] Others have held that the assignee will be entitled to priority even though he gives no notice until after the entry of judgment in the garnishment proceedings, provided such notice be given before the debtor has satisfied the judgment.[14]

As in the discussion of priorities among successive assignees in the previous section, if the assignment is encompassed by Article 9 of the Code, the priority between the assignee and an attaching creditor is easily resolved in the normal case. The Code treats an attaching creditor as a "lien creditor."[15] An Article 9 assignee who has not "perfected" his assigned right is subordinate to such an attaching (lien) creditor.[16] The assignment of many types of collateral under Article 9 may be "perfected" either by filing a financing statement in the appropriate public offices or by taking possession of the collateral. In relation to accounts and general intangibles, however, the only method allowing for "perfection" is filing.[17] There is only one exception in relation to assignment of accounts. When such an assignment does not transfer a significant part of the outstanding accounts of the assignor, the assignment is perfected *without filing*,[18] i.e., the assignment would be perfected upon "attachment."[19] If the assignment is perfected either by filing or by attachment because it is the kind of assignment that comes within the exception, the perfected assignment takes priority over the attaching creditor because the inter-

---

[10] The cases are collected in Annotation 52 A.L.R. 110-17 (1928). In a few states, the assignee's right is subordinated to the claim of the attaching creditor unless he gives notice to the debtor before the creditor causes service of a writ of garnishment. Phelps v. Holden, 107 Vt. 1, 175 A. 250 (1934). Other cases are collected in Annotation, 52 A.L.R. 122-26 (1928).

[11] RESTATEMENT 2d § 341 comment a.

[12] Houtz v. Daniels, 36 Idaho 544, 211 P. 1088 (1922).

[13] Peterson v. Kingman, 59 Neb. 667, 81 N.W. 847 (1900).

[14] McDowell, Pyle & Co. v. Hopfield, 148 Md. 84, 128 A. 742 followed in RESTATEMENT 2d § 341(2) (obligor who does not receive notification of the assignment until after losing the opportunity to assert assignment as a defense in the proceeding in which the judicial lien was obtained is discharged from his duty to the assignee to the extent of his satisfaction of the lien).

[15] *See supra* note 9.

[16] *See* UCC § 9-301(1)(b). *See also* Sun Bank, N.A. v. Parkland Design & Dev. Corp., 466 So. 2d 1089 (Fla. App. 1985) (Under Article 9's priority rules, an unperfected assignee of an account is subordinate to a lien creditor. A garnishing judgment creditor qualifies as a lien creditor under UCC § 9-301(3)).

[17] UCC § 9-305 comment 1.

[18] UCC § 9-302(1)(e).

[19] UCC § 9-203. The concept of attachment was discussed in § 136.

est of a lien creditor is subordinate to the interest of a prior perfected security interest in the same collateral, regardless of how perfection occurred.[20]

---

[20] UCC § 9-301(1)(b) is phrased in the converse, i.e., an *unperfected* security interest is subordinate to the rights of a party who becomes a lien creditor before the security interest is perfected.

Chapter 12

THE DISCHARGE OF CONTRACTS

§ 143. Methods of Discharging a Contractual Duty.

A. *A Survey of Methods.*

The normal method of discharging a contractual duty is by performing it. There are, however, numerous other ways to discharge an obligation, many of which we have seen throughout this volume. If a party commits an uncured material breach, the duty of the other party is discharged. If a duty is subject to a condition, the nonoccurrence of the conditioning event will discharge the duty if the condition can no longer occur. If a performance becomes impossible or impracticable, or if its purpose is frustrated, the performance will be excused and, thereby, discharged. A party lacking capacity can exercise a power of avoidance and effectively discharge his duty in that fashion. A party may be discharged in bankruptcy or an action to enforce his duty may be barred by the statute of limitations, thereby effecting a discharge.

The foregoing is certainly not an exhaustive list of methods of discharge. In this chapter we will consider methods of discharge that we have not, for the most part, explored earlier in this volume though one or more have been mentioned at appropriate points. We begin by considering three methods of discharge that are fundamental: discharge by informal agreement, gift, and rejection of tender.

B. *Discharge by Informal Agreement, Gift, or Rejection of Tender.*

If it is supported by consideration, an agreement to discharge a contractual obligation is as enforceable as any other contract. The only doubt is whether an obligee's informal agreement of discharge is effective in the *absence* of consideration. Rightly or wrongly, our law has generally proceeded on the theory that an informal agreement for the divestment of a right, in the absence of a statute providing otherwise, is not effective without either a consideration or the requisites of an executed gift.[1] Inasmuch as contract rights grow out of promises and are not things that are tangible and deliverable, it is frequently impossible to make an effective gift of such a right by informal transfer, if the normal requisites of the gift transaction are insisted upon, even though the intent to do so exists. However, where the claim is documented, in the sense of being evidenced by a written instrument, which by the terms of the contract or by law or usage is required to be delivered up to the obligor when he performs the obligation, it is generally held that it can be effectively discharged by gift, if the document is delivered or surrendered to the obligor, or to someone on his behalf, with donative intent.[2] Since, in such a case, the right cannot be enforced without accounting for the document, its delivery is regarded as satisfying the delivery requirement of the law relating to gifts.[3] There is, however, a marked tendency on the part of our courts to liberalize the requirement of delivery in this connection, if not to dispense with it altogether, when it is apparent in the particular case that the intent to discharge the right existed. Thus, it has been held that an effective discharge of a claim can be made by delivery of a receipt in full,[4] or even by making an indorsement on a note or mortgage or other instrument in the possession of the obligee, evidencing the claim,[5] if done with donative intent. Since the rules which have been adopted to control the matter of the divestment of rights seem to be largely precautionary in nature, it is difficult to see why any written discharge, if delivered with intent to discharge, should not have been effective. In such a case trustworthy evidence of the intent to divest the right exists.[6] The UCC provides that a written waiver or renunciation signed and delivered by the aggrieved party discharges any claim or right arising out of an alleged breach.[7]

---

[1] On the requisites for the transfer or divestment of rights by way of gift *see generally* BROWN, PERSONAL PROPERTY Chs. 7, 8 (3d ed. 1975).

[2] *See* the discussion of gratuitous assignments *supra* Chapter 11, § 137(B)(1).

[3] *In re* Russell, 385 Pa. 557, 123 A.2d 708 (1956); Vanderbeck v. Vanderbeck, 30 N.J.Eq. 265 (1878); Slade v. Mutrie, 156 Mass. 19, 30 N.E. 168 (1892).

This has not always been so. Apparently in the early law, mere surrender of a specialty to the obligor with intent to discharge it was not effective. Nothing short of a technical release or a cancellation of the document would accomplish the purpose. *See* Ames, *Specialty Contracts and Equitable Defenses,* 9 HARV. L. REV. 49, 54 (1895).

[4] Rye v. Phillips, 203 Minn. 567, 282 N.W. 459 (dictum); Holmes v. Holmes, 129 Mich. 412, 89 N.W. 47 (1902); Gray v. Barton, 55 N.Y. 68, 14 Am. Rep. 181 (1873).

[5] *In re* Lewis' Estate, 139 Pa. 640, 22 A. 635 (1891); Green v. Langdon, 28 Mich. 221 (1873). *Contra* Helmer v. Helmer, 159 Ga. 376, 125 S.E. 849, 37 A.L.R. 1137 (1924).

[6] *See* Marysville Dev. Co. v. Hargis, 41 Idaho 257, 239 P. 522 (1925), which held that delivery of a receipt in full or part payment of a debt extinguished the debt, although no evidence of an intent to make a gift of the balance was offered. *Contra* Schlessinger v. Schlessinger, 39 Colo. 44, 88 P. 970 (1907); St. Louis Ft. S. & W. R.R. v. Davis, 35 Kan. 464, 11 P. 421 (1886).

See generally Ferson, *The Rule in Foakes v. Beer,* 31 YALE L.J. 15 (1921). In a few states it has been provided by statute that a written discharge is effective absent consideration. *See, e.g.,* N.Y. GEN. OBLIG. LAW § 5-1103. A written discharge or renunciation of a negotiable instrument is effective to divest the right subject to the rights of a holder in due course.

[7] UCC § 1-107, which is replicated in RESTATEMENT 2d § 277(1). *See also* UCC § 3-605 which permits the holder of a negotiable instrument without consider to discharge any party to the

Contrary to the general rule, several early English cases held that a voluntary exoneration of the obligor by the obligee, if made before breach of the primary obligation, was effective to bar the later enforcement of the contract, even though it was not supported by consideration.[8] No doubt this holding was motivated by the desire to prevent the injustice which would result if the obligor were to change his position in reliance upon the obligee's affirmation that performance would not be required. However, the rule apparently was not limited to that type of case but was applied generally. While there is little doubt that the same result would be reached by our courts when the elements of a promissory estoppel were present,[9] there is a traditional requirement of consideration to effectuate a discharge of an obligation.[10] A rejection of a good tender of performance will operate to discharge the obligation if the performance promised is of such a kind that it can only be rendered at the time fixed.[11] If the performance is capable of being made at a later date without serious hardship to the obligor, the rejection of tender of an unconditional obligation, while it does not discharge the obligation, does, if the tender is kept good, prevent the obligor from being regarded as in default thereafter, and hence frees him from liability for costs and interest from the date of the tender.[12] One exception, which seems to be quite generally recognized by our courts, is the rule that when an obligee, who is entitled to money payable in installments, as in the case of rent reserved under a lease,[13] or money payable under a separation agreement,[14] agrees to accept less than the amount stipulated, in full satisfaction of his claim, his agreement is effective to discharge the obligor's duty, at least to the extent to which it has been carried out before repudiation by the obligee, although no consideration can be found to support it. Similarly, a promisee who agrees to accept, and does accept, a defective performance of a promise as full satisfaction of the promisor's obligation, cannot thereafter maintain an action for breach of promise because of the defective performance.[15] Of course, if, in such a case, the promisor tenders a performance that is different from that which he was bound to render by the terms of his contract, as a substitute for the performance promised, its accep-

---

instrument, *inter alia,* by renouncing his rights by a signed and delivered writing or by delivery of the instrument to the party to be discharged.

[8] *See* Langdon v. Stokes, 3 Cro. Car. 383, 79 Eng. Rep. 935 [1634]; Edwards v. Weeks, 2 Mod. 260, 86 Eng. Rep. 930 (dictum); Holland & Conier's Case, 2 Leon 214.

[9] Jazlowiecki v. Nicolletti, 34 Conn. Supp. 670, 387 A.2d 1081 (Conn. App. 1977); Fried v. Fisher, 328 Pa. 497, 196 A. 39 (1938); Maryland Steel Co. v. United States, 235 U.S. 451 (1915). *See* RESTATEMENT 2d § 273(c).

[10] Georgeton v. Reynolds, 161 Va. 164, 170 S.E. 741 (1933); Millett v. Temple, 280 Mass. 543, 182 N.E. 921 (1932); Hale v. Dreesen, 76 Minn. 183, 78 N.W. 1045 (1899). RESTATEMENT 2d § 273 comment a.

[11] Under the UCC, a rejection of nonconforming goods (§§ 2-601 and 602) will be final unless "contract time" remains and the seller exercises his right to cure (§ 2-508).

[12] Steckel v. Selix, 198 Iowa 339, 197 N.W. 918 (1924); Forwood v. Magness, 143 Md. 1, 121 A. 855 (1923); Loth Hoffman Clothing Co. v. Schwartz, 74 Okla. 18, 176 P. 916 (1918).

[13] Julian v. Gold, 214 Cal. 74, 3 P.2d 1009 (1931); C. S. Brackett & Co. v. Lofgren, 140 Minn. 52, 167 N.W. 274 (1918).

[14] Vigelius v. Vigelius, 169 Wash. 190, 13 P.2d 425 (1932).

[15] Weisser v. Grand Forks Fed. Sav. & Loan Ass'n, 406 N.W.2d 696 (N.D. 1987); Kangas v. Anthony Trust, 110 Ill. App. 3d 876, 441 N.E.2d 1271 (1982). RESTATEMENT 2d § 277(2). *See also* Lawson & Nelson Sash & Door Co. v. Krauss-Anderson of St. Paul Co., 279 Minn. 218, 156 N.W.2d 208 (1968) (whether acceptance of defective performance occurred is a question of fact).

tance will involve the receipt of a consideration by the promisee which furnishes ample support for the discharge of the original obligation. However, when the promisor in offering the defective performance purports to do only what his contract requires him to do, there is no consideration for the purported discharge, and yet it is frequently held to be effective.[16] In such a case the discharge is said to be accomplished by "waiver." Such decisions have apparently resulted from a confusion of excuse of condition with discharge of liability on a promise. Very often in a bilateral contract a given performance that is promised is at the same time a condition qualifying the duty of the other party to the contract. As we have already seen, the condition may be excused by acceptance of defective performance of it, and from this it seems to be assumed that the obligation growing out of the promise must also necessarily be discharged. This is certainly not a necessary conclusion. It is one thing to say that a duty to pay for a defective performance exists, if that performance is accepted, and quite a different thing to say that liability to render full performance is discharged by acceptance of defective performance.

C. Rescission.

The parties to an executory bilateral contract may decide that they are mutually dissatisfied with their agreement and desire simply to call it off. To accomplish this result, they may form a new contract which has only one purpose, i.e., the discharge of the original contract. Under this contract of discharge known as a rescission,[17] whereby each party surrenders his old rights against the other so that there is ample consideration for such an agreement.[18] As soon as this new contract of rescission is formed it is also discharged by performance,[19] since performance under it is the surrender of existing primary rights under the original contract. Like other contracts, a contract of rescission may be inferred from conduct.[20]

Difficult questions arise when an executory bilateral contract has been partially performed by one or both parties. Whether there is a right to recover for such partial performance depends upon the intention of the parties. If the contract of rescission itself either expressly or impliedly indicates such intent,

---

[16] Frank Japes Co. v. Pagel, 246 Mich. 700, 225 N.W. 521 (1929) (owner who makes payments to contractor without objection for work done after contract time expired cannot recover damages for delay). See also Pressy v. McCornack, 235 Pa. 443, 84 A. 427 (1912).

[17] The term "rescission" should be relegated to a contract to discharge an executory bilateral contract. Unfortunately, it is often used to suggest other meanings. It should be distinguished from "cancellation" and "termination" concerning executory portions of partially executed contracts. As to the executed portions of such contracts, "cancellation" or "termination" preserve any claims for such partial performance. See UCC §§ 2-106 and 2-720.

[18] Eodem modo quo oritur, eodem modo dissolvitur (In the manner in which a thing is created, in that manner it may be dissolved). See Billings v. Gardner, 88 Or. App. 370, 745 P.2d 400 (1987) ("the deal's off" — "everybody acquiesced in that"); Kallenbach v. Lake Publications, 30 Wis. 2d 647, 652, 142 N.W.2d 212, 215 (1966) (where parties decide to call off a contract or declare a contract at an end there is a rescission). See also Lemlich v. Board of Trustees, 282 Me. 495, 385 A.2d 1185 (1978) (Since a rescission is a contract, there must be an offer and acceptance and the offer may be revoked prior to acceptance). See RESTATEMENT 2d § 283.

[19] The contract of rescission is very much like an explosive device, i.e., at the moment of formation, it self-destructs as it destroys the contract to which it is attached. That is its sole purpose.

[20] St. Norbert College Found. v. McCormick, 81 Wis. 2d 423, 435, 260 N.W.2d 776, 782 (1978). See also Mitchell v. Aetna Cas. Co., 579 F.2d 342 (5th Cir. 1978).

there is no problem. Often, however, the contract of rescission does not indicate the intention of the parties in this regard so that the courts are confronted with a difficult question of interpretation. Some courts take the unfortunate position that the very nature of a rescission requires a return to status quo and, therefore, any partial performance by one party must be compensated by the other to preclude the latter from becoming unjustly enriched.[21] This position ignores the fact that a rescission is a contract by which one of the parties who has not performed at all may have agreed to enter into the rescission only if the other party, who has partly performed, agreed to surrender all of his rights against the first party in exchange for the surrender by the first party of his remaining rights. The better view is that taken by most courts which states that there is no presumption that any right to recover for part performance rendered prior to the rescission is intended to be reserved to either party in the absence of affirmative evidence of such intention.[22] These courts emphasize the fact that in each case it is a question of the apparent understanding of the parties at the time of the mutual agreement of rescission.

D. *Renunciation.*

If the contract was originally unilateral, or if it was bilateral and one party had lost all his rights under it through performance or otherwise, a rescission would not be enforceable because it would not be supported by consideration. Yet, when one of the parties has lost all of his rights under a bilateral contract because he has committed an uncured material breach of the contract and the nondefaulting party elects to *renounce* the contract, it has been held that the defaulter's obligation to pay damages or to perform specifically is discharged. He can be held only to make restitution of the performance already rendered by the nondefaulting party in a quasi-contract action.[23] It is frequently suggested that a nondefaulting party has a right to choose between alternative remedies which are inconsistent.[24] Once he has elected to renounce the contract and to seek restitution, he is not permitted to change his mind and to sue on the contract itself. It is easy to see why he should no longer be allowed the remedy of specific performance if the promisor, relying upon the promisee's renunciation, has changed his position in such a way that performance has become more difficult or impossible. However, it is difficult to understand why

---

[21] In Share v. Williams, 204 Or. 664, 277 P.2d 775, 780 (1954), *modified,* 285 P.2d 523 (1955), the court, quoting from a prior Oregon case, states, "'... when the parties voluntarily agree to rescind a contract, there being no express stipulation with reference to payment or payments already made thereunder, the law will imply a promise on the part of the vendor to refund such payment or payments to the purchaser, and the latter may maintain an action to recover back the same.'" In Anderson v. Copeland, 378 P.2d 1006, 1007 (Okla. 1963), the court suggests that the parties rescinded a contract which had the effect of allowing defendant to use plaintiff's tractor without paying for it. Thus, the law implies a contract for defendant to pay the reasonable rental value of the tractor so as to avoid unjust enrichment of the defendant.

[22] McBee Binder Co. v. Fred J. Robinson Lumber Co., 267 Mich. 637, 255 N.W. 329 (1934); Coletti v. Knox Hat Co., 252 N.Y. 468, 169 N.E. 648 (1930); Aderholt v. Wood, 66 Cal. App. 666, 226 P. 950 (1924).

[23] The quasi-contract action would protect the renouncing party's restitution interest.

[24] Walter Wallingford Coal Co. v. A. Himes Coal Co., 223 Mich. 576, 194 N.W. 493 (1923); Thackeray v. Knight, 57 Utah 21, 192 P. 263 (1920).

an election, once made, should preclude the possibility of changing that election, so long as the promisor has not been in any way misled by what had previously been done by the promisee. Discharge of the contract by renunciation under these circumstances is frequently spoken of as "rescission." This is unfortunate, since it leads to the confusion of this kind of discharge, which, while it may cut off the obligee's right to sue for damages or specific performance, does not debar him from seeking restitution, with that type of discharge which results from mutual agreement — in which case the rights of the parties, as already pointed out, must be determined wholly from the terms of the agreement of rescission.

As suggested in the previous section, the UCC permits a party to renounce his rights through a signed waiver without consideration.[25] However, the Code also recognizes that the aggrieved party to a sales contract may announce that he is treating the contract as "cancelled" or even "rescinded." Yet, he may not intend such an expression of cancellation or rescission to amount to a renunciation or discharge of any claim in damages for an antecedent breach. Recognizing this likelihood, the Code safeguards the aggrieved party from such unintentional loss of rights by the unfortunate use of such terms, "unless the contrary intention clearly appears."[26] Put simply, the Code includes a presumption that the term "cancellation" or even "rescission" when used by an aggrieved party does not amount to a renunciation of his remedial rights. Clear evidence of a contrary intention is essential to rebut that presumption.

§ 144. Accord and Satisfaction and Substitute Contract.

A. *Distinguishing Accord and Satisfaction From Substitute Contract.*

Very often the parties to an existing contract, which may or may not have been breached at the time, make a subsequent agreement, which, or the performance of which, they contemplate as a substitution for the obligations under the original contract. The question that arises is when, if at all, does the later agreement or its performance operate to discharge the obligations under the original contract? Unfortunately, the answer to this question has become somewhat complicated by the fact that historic accident caused courts to separate cases involving this question into two distinct categories which differ from each other only superficially. Into one category they have put cases in which the new agreement was not made until after the maturity or breach of the original contract. In this type of case the new agreement is called an *accord* and the acceptance of it, or its performance in discharge of the original contract, is designated a *satisfaction*.[27] On the other hand, if the new agreement is made before the maturity or breach of the original obligation, it is

---

[25] *See* UCC § 1-107 and discussion *supra* note 7.

[26] UCC § 2-720.

[27] "Accord and Satisfaction is the purchase of a release from an obligation whether arising under a contract or tort by means of any valuable consideration, not being the actual performance of the obligation itself." Scrutton, L.J., in British-Russian Gazette, Ltd. v. Associated Newspapers, Ltd., 2 K.B. 616, 643 [1933]. RESTATEMENT 2d § 281(1) defines an accord as a contract under which an obligee promises to accept a stated performance in satisfaction of the existing duty of the obligor, and performance of the accord discharges the original duty.

usually spoken of merely as a substitute contract.[28] While both types of agreements seem to involve essentially the same problems and should be dealt with in the same way, some differences in result are sometimes held to follow from this distinction, as will be pointed out later.

That an accord or a substitute contract which is fully performed will operate to discharge the obligations under the original contract, if it is supported by consideration and if that was the intention of the parties, has never been doubted from the earliest times.[29] The only question of doubt is whether an unperformed accord or substitute contract can have this effect. To understand the modern law on this question one must know something of the way in which that law evolved.

It appears that the question of the discharge of matured obligations by substitute agreement came before the courts a great many times in the days before informal contracts were known to our law.[30] Since an informal promise, even though it was supported by what we now know as consideration, was not legally enforceable at that time, it is easy to understand why the courts would have held that an accord, so long as it was unperformed, could in no event operate to discharge a prior obligation. During the sixteenth or the seventeenth century, however, informal promises supported by consideration did

---

[28] *See* Bandman v. Finn, 185 N.Y. 508, 78 N.E. 175 (1906); Taylor v. Hillary, 1 Cromp. M. & R. 741 [1835]. This distinction was undoubtedly made, in the first instance, in order that the so-called substitute contract could be given effect in accordance with the intentions of the parties without going counter to the established precedents. The rule in relation to the technical accord was well-settled to the effect that such an agreement not only could not be pleaded in bar to the original obligation but was not even an enforceable contract, even though it may have had the usual requisites of an informal contract. Since this rule had very little to commend it other than its antiquity, it is not strange that later courts should have found ways of refusing to apply it further than was required by the facts of earlier decisions.

[29] While mutual assent is necessary to bring about a discharge by "accord and satisfaction," this does not necessarily mean mental assent. Hence, if the creditor accepts and cashes a check or avails himself of some other performance which is tendered as satisfaction, assuming consideration to be present, he cannot show that he did not so accept it, although he may have manifested a refusal at the time.

Perhaps the most significant issue in accord and satisfaction in recent years has been the problems connected with the tender of a check in full satisfaction for the outstanding indebtedness. Assume, for example, a contract for remodeling a house with no price previously agreed upon. Upon completion of the work the remodeler sends his bill for $10,000 to which the owner honestly objects. The owner then sends the contractor a check for $7000 marked "payment in full" or similar phrase. There is no doubt that the cashing of that check by the creditor will accept the offer of an accord and will satisfy the obligor's debt. The problem for the creditor is significant: if he cashes the check he is surrendering any further right against the debtor, but if he doesn't cash the check, he may wait a long time for his money. To avoid this problem, the creditor may write on the check (before indorsing and cashing it) a phrase indicating that he reserves his rights against the debtor. Section 1-207 of the UCC has been used as a basis for arguing that such a reservation of rights preserves the creditor's rights against the debtor even after the creditor cashes the check. There has been considerable litigation in this area which has been explored earlier in this volume. *See supra* Chapter 3, § 64(B).

It is now clear that the courts and most of the authorities have concluded that § 1-207 should not modify the usual rule that a party cashing a check marked "payment in full" has accepted the debtor's offer of accord and the debt is satisfied by the cashing. The cases and authorities are fully explored in the earlier discussion. For a view running counter to the current trend, *see* J. WHITE & R. SUMMERS, UNIFORM COMMERCIAL CODE § 13-24 (1988).

[30] "From time immemorial the acceptance of anything in satisfaction of the damages caused by a tort would bar a subsequent action against the wrong-doer. Accord and satisfaction was, likewise, a bar to an action for damages arising from a breach of covenant." Ames, *Specialty Contracts and Equitable Defenses*, 9 HARV. L. REV. 49, 55 (1895).

become obligatory. There was no longer any reason why an accord, if it was of the type which embodied the essential requisites of an informal contract, should not have been held to be binding and to discharge the prior obligations, if that was the intention of the parties. Nevertheless, the courts were slow to take this step because of the many cases in which it had been said, under the old law, that an unperformed accord not only was not a bar, but was not an enforceable contract.[31] Many courts apparently forgot that the reason why an accord could never operate as a bar in the old law was because it could not be an enforceable contract; and they apparently assumed that the reverse was true; namely, that such a transaction did not result in an enforceable obligation, because it was not a bar. Consequently, we find that for a long time, even after informal contracts came into our law, it was held that if a transaction, although it had all the earmarks of a valid, informal contract, was intended as an accord, then it could not even be given effect as an enforceable obligation, to say nothing of making it a bar to suit on a prior obligation.[32] The old cases were finally overthrown in the nineteenth century. It is now clear that an executory accord, like any other contract, is legally enforceable.[33]

There is confusion in the use of language throughout the topic of discharge of contracts. We have already seen some confusion in the unwieldy use of the term, "rescission," that should be relegated to a contract of discharge. Courts have complained about this confusion[34] and it exists in relation to accord and satisfaction and substitute contracts. An accord can be viewed as a substitute contract in the sense that the parties have agreed upon a contract to substitute for their original obligations. If the parties intend their new executory agreement to discharge their prior obligations the moment it is made and before it is performed, that intention should be effectuated and courts have given such agreements that effect.[35] It is possible to characterize this kind of agreement as one type of accord, i.e., an accord which the parties intend to immediately discharge their prior obligations. It is also possible and quite logical to refer to this type of new agreement as a substitute contract. Where the intention of the parties is to discharge the prior duty only after the new contract is performed, then the old obligation continues to exist along with the new contract.[36] It is possible to characterize this new agreement as a substi-

---

[31] Thus, in Allen v. Harris, 1 Ld. Raym. 122 [1701], in sustaining a demurrer to a plea of accord, the court said, "But upon an accord no remedy lies. And the books are so numerous that an accord ought to be executed that it is not impossible to overthrow all the books." *See* Gold, *Executory Accords,* 21 B.U.L. Rev. 465 (1941).

[32] *See* Hall v. Knapp, 522 S.W.2d 299 (Kan. App. 1977) citing the second edition of this book for this proposition.

[33] The formation and enforceability of an accord is governed by the same rules as those applicable to other contracts. *See* Anderson v. Rosebrook, 737 P.2d 417 (Colo. 1987); McKibbin v. Mohawk Oil Co., Ltd., 667 P.2d 1223 (Alaska 1983). *See also* Flagel v. Southwest Clinical Psychiatrists, 157 Ariz. 196, 755 P.2d 1184 (1988) (there is consideration if only part of the claim is unliquidated). *See* RESTATEMENT 2d § 281 comment a.

[34] *See, e.g.,* Bargale Indus. v. Robert Realty Co., 275 Md. 638, 343 A.2d 529 (1976) where the court suggests confusion between "novation" and other forms of discharge such as accord, substitute contract, and other methods. Some jurisdictions still insist that there are two forms of novation, i.e., two party and three party novation, *see* Dere v. Montgomery Ward & Co., 224 Va. 277, 295 S.E.2d 794 (1982).

[35] Ohlson v. Steinhauser, 218 Or. 532, 346 P.2d 87 (1959); *In re* Kellett Aircraft Corp., 173 F.2d 689. 692 (3d Cir. 1949), *affirming* 77 F. Supp. 959 (E.D. Pa. 1948).

[36] Sherman v. Sidman, 300 Mass. 102, 14 N.E.2d 145 (1938); Reilly v. Barrett, 220 N.Y. 170, 115 N.E. 453 (1917). Professor Corbin suggests that there is "unlimited authority" for this proposition. 6 CORBIN § 1269.

tute contract though it appears more reasonable to view it as an accord which will have to be satisfied (performed) to discharge the original obligation simultaneously with the accord. Since it is deemed unlikely that an obligee would ordinarily wish merely to exchange one cause of action for another, it is generally presumed that the parties intended the old obligation to be discharged only upon the performance of the new contract, in the absence of affirmative evidence of a contrary intention.[37] However one characterizes the new agreement, it is the intention of the parties that should be effectuated. The RESTATEMENT 2d chooses the logical path of calling those agreements which are intended by the parties to discharge the original duty as soon as the new agreement is formed, substitute contracts, and those agreements which are intended to discharge the original obligation only upon performance (satisfaction) of the new agreement, accords.[38] This distinction seems preferable and should remove some of the confusion in this area.[39] There is considerable support for the distinction and we shall maintain that distinction for the remainder of this section.[40]

B. *Obligee's Repudiation of Accord or Substitute Contract.*

Whether an obligee may repudiate an accord and enforce the original duty even though the obligor is not in default under the accord, is a question that caused considerable difficulty for common law courts. When an obligee enters into an accord with an obligor, although he has no intention of discharging the prior duty immediately, it is certainly a fair assumption that he has, by implication, promised to refrain from enforcing the original duty unless and until there has been a breach of the new contract. Moreover, it would seem to be perfectly consistent with generally accepted principles to take the view that this tacit promise should be specifically enforced, if for no other reason than to prevent unnecessary litigation. This result could have been accomplished either by permitting the obligor to plead the new agreement in abatement of a suit founded on the original obligation, thus preventing a suit on it in the absence of a default by the obligor on the new contract, or by permitting a suit in equity for an injunction against enforcement of the original duty,

---

[37] Poggi v. Kates, 115 Ariz. 157, 564 P.2d 380 (1977); *In re Kellett Aircraft Corp., supra* note 35, (Federal District Court opinion); Fricke v. Forbes, 294 Mich. 375, 293 N.W. 686 (1940); Wyatt v. New York O. & W. R.R., 45 F.2d 705 (2d Cir. 1930). RESTATEMENT 2d § 279 comment c is in accord with this view and adds, "It will therefore be less likely to find a substituted contract and more likely to find an accord if the original duty was one to pay money, if it was undisputed, if it was liquidated and if it was matured."

[38] *See* RESTATEMENT 2d § 279 comment c. Substitute contracts are covered in § 279 while accord and satisfaction are dealt with in § 281.

[39] "Accord and satisfaction" have been quite generally used to deal with the kind of case in which the accord is not intended to operate as a discharge until the accord is performed (satisfied). There has been, however, little agreement on the proper term to characterize the new agreement intended to operate as an immediate discharge. Some courts have called such an agreement a "novation," *see* Annotation, 96 A.L.R. 1133 (1935). Some have called it a "compromise and settlement," Moreno v. Russell, 47 Ariz. 38, 53 P.2d 411 (1936).

[40] *See, e.g.,* K-Line Bldrs., Inc. v. First Fed. Sav. & Loan Ass'n, 139 Ariz. 209, 677 P.2d 1317 (1984); Sergeant v. Leonard, 312 N.W.2d 541 (Iowa 1981). *See also* Robison v. Hansen, 594 P.2d 867 (Utah 1978) (substituted agreement may be implied from conduct); Johnson v. Utile, 86 Nev. 593, 472 P.2d 335 (1970) (whether it is an accord or substitute agreement turns on the intention of the parties).

pending performance of the new contract. Unfortunately, the first of these remedies is at war with the unfortunate common law notion that a cause of action once suspended is necessarily barred forever. Paying deference to this mistaken premise,[41] the common law courts logically inferred that an agreement to suspend a cause of action temporarily could have no effect on the original obligation,[42] but merely furnished a basis for a cross-action when the new agreement was violated.[43] At least one definite exception to this rule was found where a negotiable instrument is executed to cover a pre-existing debt.[44] Yet, the antiquated notion had the characteristic of tenacity in many of our older cases[45] and even later cases which have adhered to the rule by holding that the obligee may enforce the original duty at law even though the obligor has tendered performance of the substitute agreement in due time, and even though part performance has already been accepted by the obligee.[46]

Under the modern view, if the obligor has not breached the accord, the original obligation is suspended to provide the obligor with an opportunity to complete the performance of the accord.[47] Once he performs the accord, both his original duty and the duty under the accord are discharged.[48] If the obligee breaches the accord and seeks to recover on the original obligation, the obligor may raise the accord as an affirmative defense[49] and be granted specific performance of the accord and injunctive relief to prevent any action on the accord while the obligor continues to perform the accord in accordance with its terms.[50]

---

[41] See 5 CORBIN § 1251 (1951), and 6 CORBIN § 1274.

[42] To hold otherwise would have done violence to the intention of the parties since the antiquated rule transformed any effort to suspend a cause of action into a completed discharge of the original obligation. It was not the parties' intention to discharge the obligation by the creation of an executory substituted agreement.

[43] Ford v. Beech, 11 Q.B. 852, 116 Eng. Rep. 693 (1848). See, however, Beech v. Ford, 7 Hare 208 [1848], where the appropriate relief was procured in equity.

[44] Walter H. Goodrich & Co. v. Friedman, 92 Conn. 262, 102 A. 607 (1917).

[45] But see Morgan v. Butterfield, 3 Mich. 615 (1855) and Robinson v. Godfrey, 2 Mich. 408 (1852), which hold that an agreement not to sue on a contract for a limited time effects a modification of the original contract and may be pleaded in bar of a suit on it. See generally Shepard, The Executory Accord, 26 ILL. L. REV. 22 (1931), where the cases are collected and discussed.

[46] Taylor v. Central of Georgia Ry., 99 Ga. App. 224, 108 S.E.2d 103 (1959); Reilly v. Barrett, 220 N.Y. 170, 115 N.E. 453 (1917). Other cases are collected in Annotation, 10 A.L.R. 222, 229 (1921). Contra, FIRST RESTATEMENT § 417(a). The New York court apparently applied a different rule in the case of a "substitute contract" holding in that case that the obligee is limited in his recovery to a suit on the new contract when the obligor is not in default thereunder. Bandman v. Finn, 185 N.Y. 508, 78 N.E. 175 (1906). See also N.Y. GEN. OBLIG. LAW § 15-501 which indicates that an executory accord shall not be denied effect as a defense or counter-claim if it is in writing. This is the successor to the same legislative concept found in 1937 N.Y. LAWS 77, amending N.Y. PERS. PROP. LAW § 33. Thus, where the executory accord is in writing, the New York cases are repudiated.

Of course, if the obligee's agreement amounts merely to an offer to discharge in return for the performance of requested acts, he was at liberty to revoke his offer before the acts are done and perhaps even after part of them are done. Kromer v. Heim, 75 N.Y. 574, 31 Am. Rep. 491 (1879), appears to be a case of this kind. See however, N.Y. GEN. OBLIG. LAW § 15-503 indicating that an offer of accord in writing by the obligee followed by tender by the obligor, will be a good defense even though the offeror refuses the tender.

[47] See Spaulding v. Cahill, 146 Vt. 386, 404 A.2d 1186 (1985). See also RESTATEMENT 2d § 281(2).

[48] RESTATEMENT 2d § 281 comment b.

[49] See Bestor v. American Nat'l Stores, Inc., 691 S.W.2d 384 (Mo. App. 1985).

[50] See Dobias v. White, 239 N.C. 409, 80 S.E.2d 23 (1954) (specific performance); Union Central Life Ins. Co. v. Imsland, 91 F.2d 365 (8th Cir. 1937) (accord enforced against attempt to foreclose

The failure of an obligee to perform a substitute contract has no effect on the discharge of the original obligation which the parties intended to be discharged at the moment they formed the substitute contract. Any attempt by the obligor to enforce the original obligation under these circumstances would be met with the affirmative defense that such obligation had been discharged.[51]

C. *Obligor's Failure to Perform Accord or Substitute Contract.*

Where the obligor fails to perform an accord, it is clear that the obligee may elect to enforce either the original duty[52] or the accord.[53] The obligor will, of course, sue on the one which will be more likely to yield the greater recovery. On the other hand, if the parties intended to form a substitute contract to discharge the original duty upon consummation of that contract, and if the obligor failed to perform it, the common law courts found determination of the remedy more difficult. It has frequently been said in such cases that the only redress available to the obligee is to sue on the substitute contract.[54] While there are cases taking the position that the obligee may elect to renounce the substitute contract, thereby reviving the original obligation which can then be enforced,[55] these cases misanalyze the concept of a substitute agreement which has discharged the original obligation. To suggest that a nonexistent obligation can be revived is an extreme fiction. One suggested justification is that this simply permits the obligee to seek his alternative remedy of restitution.[56] It is not necessary to rejuvenate the original obligation to afford such a remedy. If the obligee has conferred a benefit upon the obligor, a quasi-contractual remedy not based upon the original obligation is available to prevent the unjust enrichment of the obligor. This is not an alternative remedy under the original obligation. That obligation is discharged. By reviving the original

---

mortgage); Boston & Maine R.R. v. Union Mut. Fire Ins. Co., 92 Vt. 137, 101 A. 1012 (1917) (accord specifically enforced and action on original claim enjoined); Chicora Fertilizer Co. v. Dunan, 91 Md. 144, 46 A. 347 (1900) (specific enforcement); Cook v. Richardson, 178 Mass. 125, 59 N.E. 675 (1901) (accord specifically enforced and action on original claim enjoined); Very v. Levy, 54 U.S. (13 How.) 345 (1851). *Accord* RESTATEMENT 2d § 281(3) (obligor may specifically enforce accord and also claim any damages for partial breach by obligee). *See also Bestor v. American Nat'l Stores, Inc., supra* note 49, which holds that an accord and satisfaction is an affirmative defense and the defendants did not have to seek specific performance since the breach of the accord was sufficient to release defendants from all claims asserted by the plaintiff.

[51] *See* RESTATEMENT 2d § 279 and, in particular, comment c.

[52] Untermyer v. Bowers, 79 F.2d 9 (2d Cir. 1935); Stanly v. Buser, 105 Kan. 510, 185 P. 39, 10 A.L.R. 218 (1919).

[53] The Hauswald Bakery v. Pantry Pride Enters., 78 Md. App. 495, 553 A.2d 1308 (1989); *Accord* Dissette v. W.J. Cutler Co., 29 Ohio App. 88, 163 N.E. 53 (1928). RESTATEMENT 2d § 281(2).

[54] Jefferson Island Salt Mining Co. v. Empire Box Corp., 41 Del. (2 Terry) 386, 23 A.2d 106 (1941), *aff'd*, 42 Del. (3 Terry) 432, 36 A.2d 40 (1944); Taft v. Valley Oil Co., 126 Conn. 154, 9 A.2d 822 (1939); City of Trinidad v. Trinidad Water Works Co., 67 Colo. 344, 184 P. 368 (1919); Sioux City Stock-Yards Co. v. Sioux City Packing Co., 110 Iowa 396, 81 N.W. 712 (1900); Babcock v. Hawkins, 23 Vt. 561 (1851).

[55] *See* Christensen v. Hamilton Realty Co., 42 Utah 70, 129 P. 412 (1912); Benson v. Larson, 95 Minn. 438, 104 N.W. 307 (1905).

[56] *See, e.g.,* the first edition of this book at 353.

duty, the obligee may be getting more than his restitution interest, to wit, his expectation interest,[57] on a nonexistent contract.

D. Accord and Satisfaction With a Third Person.

The question of whether an obligation is discharged if the obligee accepts something in satisfaction of his claim from a person other than the obligor is one that has been disputed in the cases. Why this should be so is difficult to understand, and the cases fail to illuminate the reasons for the controversy. While it is undoubtedly true that the obligor may refuse to recognize the discharge of his obligation when it is sought to be accomplished without his consent, there seems to be no good reason why it should not be regarded as effective, since it was unfair that the creditor should receive two satisfactions for his claim.[58] However, later cases took the view that it was not effective unless it was obtained by the third person as agent for, and on behalf of, the obligor, and with his prior authorization or later ratification.[59] It is probable that the objection to giving the obligor the benefit of such a transaction, when it was not carried through by one who could be said to be his agent, grew out of the rule of the later common law that one who has furnished no part of the consideration for a contract can have no rights under it.[60] As a matter of fact, it is the generally accepted rule today that such a discharge is effective unless, and until, it is repudiated by the obligor.[61] While it was not uncommon for a court to assert that the discharge was not effective unless accomplished on the obligor's behalf and with his prior authorization or later ratification, the existence of these supposed requirements is usually presumed or found on such slight evidence as to make it clear that they are dealt with as mere fictions.[62] In view of the fact that our courts have abandoned the requirement that one must furnish some part of the consideration to have rights under a contract, there seems no reason whatever for refusing to recognize the effectiveness of a discharge obtained by a third person on sufficient consideration, regardless of the absence of evidence of any agency. Whether a discharge so brought about can be rescinded by the parties to it, without the consent of the obligor, involves the same question that arises in any case in which the parties to a contract, entered into for the benefit of a third person, seek to rescind that

---

[57] This would be the case if the original obligation was contractual.

[58] See Fitzherbert's Abridgement, title Barre, pl. 166. The case is cited with approval in Belshaw v. Bush, 11 C.B. 191 (1851).

[59] See Simpson v. Eggington, 10 Ex. 844 [1855].

[60] See, e.g., Dunlap Pneumatic Tire Co. v. Selfridge & Co., A.C. 847 [1855]; Cottage Street M.E. Church v. Kendall, 121 Mass. 528, 23 Am. Rep. 286 (1877).

[61] See Mayfair Farms Holding Corp. v. Kruvant Enters. Co., 64 N.J. Super. 465, 166 A.2d 585 (1960); Jackson v. Pennsylvania R.R., 66 N.J.L. 319, 49 A. 730 (1901); Gray v. Herman, 75 Wis. 453, 44 N.W. 248 (1890); Hirchand Punamchand v. Temple, 2 K.B. 330 [1911]; and the cases cited in the following notes to this section. Accord RESTATEMENT 2d § 278 comment b.
See Crumlish's Adm'r v. Central Imp. Co. 38 W.Va. 390, 18 S.E. 456 (1893) (perhaps the third person may enforce the obligation in his favor as an equitable assignee in a suit in equity even if its performance is not ratified by the obligor).

[62] See F.I. Somers & Sons v. Le Clerc, 110 Vt. 408, 8 A.2d 663, 124 A.L.R. 1494 (1939); Danzinger v. Hoyt, 120 N.Y. 190, 24 N.E. 294 (1890); Snyder v. Pharo, 25 F. 398 (C.C.D. Del. 1885); Leavitt v. Morrow, 6 Ohio St. 71, 67 Am. Dec. 334 (1856).

contract. That question was explored in the chapter dealing with third party beneficiaries.[63]

§ 145. Other Methods of Discharge.

A. *Account Stated.*

At a very early day there existed a unique device that allowed an obligation to be discharged by an executory agreement. Where parties who had entered into transactions of a monetary character, creating the relationship of debtor and creditor, struck a balance of account, which balance the debtor promised to pay, a court would enforce that agreement. Such an agreement was called an *account stated* and it was binding even though there was no bargain consideration to support the promise. The case seems to have been regarded as within the early rule of the common law that a precedent debt was consideration to support a later promise to pay that debt. It was said in an early case that an account stated operated by way of merger to discharge the original obligation.[64] This was later denied, however, apparently because of its supposed inconsistency with the rule relating to executory accords.[65] Once it came to be the law that an executory agreement could operate to discharge the prior obligation, it was again held to be the rule that an account stated discharged the prior obligation. This came to be the generally accepted view.[66] While it is generally said that to furnish a basis for an account stated, there must be a manifestation of assent to the account submitted,[67] the necessary assent will be inferred when one party submits an account to the other who makes no objection to the account for an unreasonable period of time, or in some other way recognizes its correctness.[68]

It is to be emphasized that an account stated can arise only out of previous transactions of a monetary character which create the relationship of debtor and creditor.[69] The items of the account need not be unliquidated, since the essential requisite is the fixing of the stated sum by way of *computation* rather than by way of compromise.[70] As already indicated, a bargain consideration is not essential to make the promise to pay the amount agreed upon as owed binding.[71] It is, however, said that such a promise does have to be sup-

---

[63] *Supra* Chapter 10, at § 131.

[64] Milward v. Ingram, 2 Mod. 43 [1678].

[65] Atherly v. Evans, Sayre 269 [1756]; May v. King, 12 Mod. 537 [1701].

[66] *See* First Nat'l Bank v. Williamson, 205 Iowa 925, 219 N.W. 32 (1928); Williams v. Casparis Bros., 113 Okla. 51, 238 P. 438 (1925); Griffith v. Hicks, 150 Ark. 297, 233 S.W. 1086 (1921). RESTATEMENT 2d § 282.

[67] *See* Modern Mills, Inc. v. Havens, 112 Idaho 1101, 739 P.2d 400 (Idaho App. 1987).

[68] Argonaut Ins. Cos. v. Tri-West Constr., 107 Idaho 643, 691 P.2d 1258 (Idaho App. 1984); Trimble Cattle Co. v. Henry & Horne, 122 Ariz. 44, 592 P.2d 1311 (1979); Savage v. Currin, 207 N.C. 222, 176 S.E. 569 (1934); Corey v. Jaroch, 229 Mich. 313, 200 N.W. 957 (1924). But failure to object to a statement of account which is obviously inconsistent with the terms of an unambiguous contract does not prevent later objection to its correctness. Nelson v. Chicago Mill & Lumber Corp., 76 F.2d 17 (8th Cir. 1935); Hopwood Plays, Inc. v. Kemper, 264 N.Y. 380, 189 N.E. 461 (1934).

[69] Gordon Stores Co. v. Rubin, 39 N.M. 100, 41 P.2d 276 (1935); Chase v. Chase, 191 Mass. 556, 78 N.E. 115 (1906).

[70] *See* Gerstner v. Lithocraft Studios, Inc., 258 S.W.2d 250 (Mo. App. 1953).

[71] Chrysler Corp. v. Airtemp Corp., 426 A.2d 845 (Del. App. 1980) (consideration for account stated rests solely on pre-existing debt or "past consideration" concept). It is, however, possible to

ported by a pre-existing liability, and it "cannot be made to create a liability per se where none before existed."[72] Moreover, "an account stated may have items on one side only and two items may be sufficient for the purposes of the agreement."[73] An account stated is, of course, subject to attack on the grounds of fraud or mistake,[74] but more than that, courts are very ready to set it aside if there is any evidence of error or overreaching, for the obvious reasons that such an agreement is not designed to create a new liability, but rather to fix the net amount owed under existing obligations.[75] Therefore, the most significant effect of the account stated may be that it constitutes *prima facie* evidence of the correctness of the balance to be paid, casting upon the adverse party the burden of disproving its correctness.[76]

B. *Novation.*

Where the parties make a substituted contract involving a third person who was not a party to the original contract, the new contract is called a novation.[77]

The purpose of a novation is to substitute a new (third) party for the obligor who is discharged at the moment the contract of novation is formed.[78] The question with which we are primarily concerned at this point is whether such a substitute contract is effective to discharge the prior contract, as intended. The early law found difficulty in reaching the conclusion that it was effective, apparently for two reasons. In the first place, to give it effect as a discharge

---

discover a consideration rationale, i.e., the forbearance of the debtor to insist on paying a lesser sum and the discharge of the items in the account.

[72] Pope County State Bank v. U.G.I. Contr'g Co., 265 Ill. App. 420 (1932). *See also Chrysler Corp. supra* note 71.

[73] *In re* Black's Estate, 125 Neb. 75, 249 N.W. 84 (1933).

[74] Estate of Isaacs, 34 Misc. 2d 127, 226 N.Y.S.2d 235 (1962).

[75] In Shell Oil Co. v. Livingston Fertilizer & Chemical Co., 9 Wash. App. 596, 513 P.2d 86 (1973), the court suggests that an account stated is a new obligation, taking the place of previous obligations, and previous defenses on the account are lost. In Perry v. Schwartz, 219 Cal. App. 2d 923, 33 Cal. Rptr. 511, 513 (1963) the court states, "An account stated, by its very nature, normally assumes the consideration of all objections, is usually a compromise, and is a final, conclusive acknowledgment of an exact amount due having in contemplation all credits and offsets. An account stated is an agreed balance of accounts, an account which has been examined and accepted by the parties. It implies an admission that the account is correct, and that the balance struck is due and owing from one party to the other. Its effect is to establish prima facie the accuracy of the items without further proof, and to constitute a new contract on which an action will lie."

[76] Dodson v. Watson, 110 Tex. 355, 320 S.W. 771 (1920).

[77] RESTATEMENT 2d § 280.

[78] *See* Buttonwood Farms, Inc. v. Carson, 329 Pa. Super. 312, 478 A.2d 484 (1984); Metropolitan Trust Co. v. Wolf, 8 Ark. App. 1, 648 S.W.2d 494 (1983).

The word novation originated in the Roman law where it was used to refer to the substitution of a new contract, whether between the same or different parties, for an earlier contract which was thereby discharged. While the common law has borrowed the term, the tendency has been to restrict its use and to apply it only in the type of case described in the text. When the new contract is entered into between the original parties only, the transaction is usually, although not universally, referred to as an accord and satisfaction, a substitute contract, an account stated, a merger, a release, or a rescission, depending upon the particular fact situation. If it is entered into between only one of the parties to the original contract and some third person, it is called an accord and satisfaction with a third person, an assignment, or a beneficiary contract, depending upon the facts of the particular case. We have already discussed these different types of discharge and some judicial tendency to use misnomers.

seemed to run counter to the rule that an executory agreement could not discharge a prior obligation.[79] In the second place, in many of these transactions the person who was intended to receive the new right or be discharged from the old obligation furnished no part of the consideration for the right or discharge and, therefore, was not in a position to avail himself of it because of the old notion that one could not benefit from a contract in which he had parted with no consideration. This was particularly true in the case of what is called a "simple novation." This type of case is illustrated by the situation in which A, who is obligated to B, enters into an agreement with B and C, whereby, in consideration of the discharge of A by B, C promises to do what A was originally obligated to do. While the discharge of A is ample consideration to support the promise of C in such a case, A has furnished no part of it.[80] During the latter part of the nineteenth century, however, these objections were finally ignored. There is no longer any doubt that a contract of novation is effective to discharge the prior contract, regardless of whether the party who was discharged from his old duty or is receiving a right under the new contract furnished any part of the consideration for the new contract.[81]

It is commonly asserted that discharge by novation can take place only upon agreement of all the parties affected by the new contract.[82] While this is true of novation as usually defined, too much emphasis must not be placed upon this fact, since there are analogous kinds of transactions which may accomplish the same result, and which do not require the consent or agreement of all the parties. These are accord and satisfaction with a third person,[83] assignment,[84] and a beneficiary contract,[85] which are discussed elsewhere. It is also frequently said that there must be a valid prior obligation to be displaced before the new agreement can operate as a novation.[86] It is obvious that unless there was a valid prior obligation there was, strictly speaking, nothing to discharge, and hence, novation in the strict sense has not occurred. However, it is to be noted that there is no reason why, in a proper case, the new agreement should not be deemed to be an enforceable contract in spite of this fact, since the discharge of a claim honestly and reasonably believed to be valid

---

[79] See supra Cuxon v. Chadley, 3 B. & C. 591 [1824]. See also Ames, Novation, SELECTED READINGS ON CONTRACTS 1213 (1931).

[80] What is called a compound novation occurs where, in one transaction, two prior obligations are discharged by novation of both obligor and obligee, and another obligation or obligations are substituted therefor. Such a transaction is illustrated by the case in which B, who is both a creditor of A and a debtor of C, discharges A and is discharged by C upon the making of a promise by A to pay B's obligation to C. In this type of transaction, consideration is furnished by each of the parties and no difficulty is encountered on that score.

[81] See, e.g., Greenwood Leflore Hosp. Comm. v. Turner, 213 Miss 200, 56 So. 2d 496, 498 (1952).

[82] See Dick v. Piper, 179 Minn. 408, 229 N.W. 356 (1930); Maine Candy & Prods. Co. v. Turgeon, 124 Me. 411, 130 A. 242 (1925).

The assent of the creditor to discharge the original obligor may be inferred from facts, circumstances, and conduct attending the transaction. See First Presbyterian Church of Pittsburgh v. Oliver-Tyrone Corp., 248 Pa. Super. 470, 375 A.2d 193 (1977).

[83] See supra § 144(D).

[84] See infra Chapter 11.

[85] See infra Chapter 10.

[86] See Buerger Bros. Supply v. El Rey Furn. Co., 43 Ariz. 472, 32 P.2d 1029 (1934); Gillett v. Ivory, 173 Mich. 444, 139 N.W. 53 (1912).

and enforceable is generally held to furnish consideration for a promise.[87] The burden of proving a novation is on the party asserting it.[88]

C. *Release.*

It has been a rule of the common law from a very early day that a purported discharge of a contractual obligation by a sealed and delivered writing is effective for the purpose intended, whether or not it is supported by consideration.[89] In fact, this has been the one generally effective method to terminate any kind of obligation, however created at common law.[90] This method of termination is called a release.[91] It can still take its traditional form where the seal remains effective. Absent the seal or a statute making an unsealed writing evidencing a release effective,[92] a release is effective if it is supported by consideration or detrimental reliance.[93] While the word release, in current usage, is frequently employed in the broad sense of discharge from liability by any method whatsoever, the earlier law used it exclusively in the narrower and technical sense indicated. It is possible to execute a release to take effect upon the happening of some condition not mentioned in the release.[94] It is important to emphasize the requirement that a release must take effect immediately or upon the occurrence of a condition, but it must be clearly distinguished from a promise to release.[95] A promise to discharge an existing duty at some future time is not a release because the parties can discharge the duty made by their contract and the original duty is not released. A release is not a promise. The UCC allows a claim or right to be discharged by a signed and delivered waiver.[96] This provision has the same effect as the release under seal (when the seal was still generally effective) and may be viewed as one of many statutory substitutes for the seal.

D. *Covenant Not to Sue.*

The usual release or agreement of discharge is not promissory in character. It purports to be, and is, an executed transaction. Instead of purporting to discharge the obligor immediately, however, an obligee makes a promise never to sue him on the obligation in question. Such a promise, assuming it is

---

[87] *See* the earlier discussion of the invalid claim in Chapter 3, § 63.

Similarly, when *A* owes *B* and *B* is indebted to *C*, if *A* promises *C* to pay *B*'s debt to *C* in return for the discharge of *A* by *B* and of *B* by *C*, it is not a defense to *A* in a suit on the new promise by *C* that his obligation to *B* was voidable for fraud. Dowling v. Parker, 221 Ala. 63, 127 So. 813 (1930).

Of course, a novation, like any other contract, is voidable for fraud. Husted v. Pogue, 249 Mich. 410, 228 N.W. 737 (1930).

[88] *See* Buttonwood Farms, Inc. v. Carson, *supra* note 78.

[89] *See* Cairo, Truman & S. R.R. v. United States, 267 U.S. 350 (1925); Ingersoll v. Martin, 58 Md. 67, 42 Am. Rep. 322 (1881).

[90] It should be noted that the discharge of an obligation created by a sealed instrument at common law could only occur through the destruction or mutilation of the instrument, or by the delivery of an instrument of "equal sanctity."

[91] RESTATEMENT 2d § 284.

[92] *See supra* Chapter 3, § 53.

[93] RESTATEMENT 2d § 284 comment b.

[94] Stiebel v. Grosberg, 202 N.Y. 266, 95 N.E. 692 (1911). *Accord* RESTATEMENT 2d § 284(1).

[95] *See* Starr v. Nationwide Mut. Ins. Co., 548 A.2d 22 (Del. Ch. 1988) (conditional release).

[96] *See* UCC § 1-107.

accompanied by the essential requirements for the formation of either a formal or an informal contract, is universally given effect as a discharge to prevent circuity of action, whenever the promisee is the only, or a "several" obligor on the obligation in relation to which the promisor has promised to forbear perpetually.[97] As we will see in the next chapter, however, a contract never to sue any fewer than all of a group of joint, or joint and several, debtors does not operate as a discharge, but is enforceable only according to its literal terms.[98]

E. Cancellation and Termination.

Apparently in the early law, one of the normal methods of discharging a contract under seal was by the physical destruction or mutilation of the instrument. The obligation created by the formal contract under seal was in legal contemplation so closely identified with the instrument itself that the mutilation or destruction of the instrument was regarded as necessarily destroying the obligation, regardless of the intention of the parties.[99] The old rule has changed so that, at the present time, intention has become dominant. Thus, a contract under seal or any other written obligation which by its terms, by law, or by usage is unenforceable without delivery of the writing, can be discharged by destruction or mutilation of the instrument by the obligee or by someone authorized by the obligee.[1] Discharge by this method is known as cancellation.[2] *Query:* can such a written obligation be cancelled by its *surrender* to the obligor if the obligee intends to discharge the duty by such surrender? There is ample authority answering this question affirmatively.[3] Any other result would be inconsistent with the view taken by the courts in relation to gratuitous assignments.[4]

The UCC distinguishes "cancellation"[5] from "termination."[6] "Cancellation" occurs when a party puts an end to a contract because of breach by the other, the cancelling party retaining any remedy for breach.[7] "Termination" occurs when a party puts an end to a contract pursuant to a power created by the

---

[97] Flinn v. Carter, 59 Ala. 364 (1877); Ford v. Beech, 11 Q.B. 852, 116 Eng. Rep. 693 [1848]. RESTATEMENT 2d § 285.

[98] *See infra* Chapter 13.

[99] *See* 4 WIGMORE, EVIDENCE § 1177 (3d ed. 1940); Ames, *Specialty Contracts and Equitable Defenses,* 9 HARV. L. REV. 49 (1895).

[1] Wilkins v. Skoglund, 127 Neb. 589, 256 N.W. 31 (1934); McDonald v. Loomis, 233 Mich. 174, 206 N.W. 348 (1925) (note); Rees v. Rees, 11 Rich. Eq. 86 (S.C. 1859); Licey v. Licey, 7 Pa. St. 251, 47 Am. Dec. 513 (1848) (bond).

[2] RESTATEMENT 2d § 274.

[3] Connelly v. Bank of Am. Nat'l Trust & Sav. Ass'n, 138 Cal. App. 2d 303, 291 P.2d 501 (1956); Funston v. Twining, 202 Pa. 88, 51 A. 736 (1902) (creditor delivered bond and mortgage to debtor saying, "Here I give this to you; all you need is to pay the interest at four per cent during my life and then the mortgage is yours." Court held that this was an effective discharge notwithstanding condition of interest payment). *See* RESTATEMENT 2d § 274 and UCC § 3-605(1)(b).

[4] *See supra* Chapter 11 at § 137(B). It should be emphasized that the RESTATEMENT 2d allows for the surrender of an *evidentiary* as well as *symbolic* writing to effecutate cancellation to maintain consistency with its analysis of the surrender of such documents as gratuitous assignments. RESTATEMENT 2d § 332(1)(b). This extension of the usual view was explored in the Chapter 11 section dealing with gratuitous assignments.

[5] *See* UCC § 2-106(4).

[6] *See* UCC § 2-106(3).

[7] *See* UCC § 2-720 and the discussion thereof *supra* § 143(D).

agreement or by law, i.e., where there is no uncured material breach by the other party. All executory obligations are thereby discharged, but any right based upon prior breach or performance survives.

F. *Alteration.*

As suggested in the previous subsection, in the early law "the contract contained in a sealed instrument was bound so indissolubly to the substance of the document that the soul perished with the body when the latter was destroyed or changed in its identity for any cause."[8] In line with this view, the common law courts took the view that, with one exception, any unauthorized alteration made in a sealed contract, whether by the obligee himself or by any third person, with or without the obligee's knowledge or consent, destroyed the obligation.[9] The one exception was the case of an immaterial alteration made by a stranger without the knowledge or consent of the obligee.[10] As time went on there also developed the so-called best evidence rule.[11] As a result of this development, the basis of the rule that the obligation was destroyed by alteration of the instrument became obscured, and some believed that its origins were in the best evidence rule.[12] This misconception seems to have had two effects. In the first place, since the best evidence rule applied to all written contracts, and to memoranda required to satisfy the Statute of Frauds, the result was that the rule in regard to the effect of an alteration was similarly extended.[13] In the second place, since the best evidence rule, as usually applied, prevented proof of the transaction by secondary evidence only when the best evidence had been destroyed with fraudulent intent,[14] the rule in relation to alteration was similarly liberalized by most of our courts. As a consequence, it has come to be the generally accepted view in this country that the alteration of a written contract, made without the authority of the obligor, discharges the contract only if the alteration is material[15] *and* if it is made with fraudulent intent,[16] either by the obligee himself, or by someone else, with the

---

[8]Holmes, J., in Bacon v. Hooker, 177 Mass. 335, 58 N.E. 1078 (1901).

[9]*Id.*

[10]Pigot's Case, 11 Coke 26-b [1615].

[11]*See* McCormick On Evidence ch. 23 (2d ed. 1972).

[12]*See* 4 Wigmore, Evidence § 1198 (Chadbourn rev. 1972); Williston, *Discharge of Contracts by Alteration,* 18 Harv. L. Rev. 105, 165 (1904).

[13] For a collection of cases, *see* Williston, *Discharge of Contracts by Alteration,* 18 Harv. L. Rev. 105, 112 (1904).

[14]4 Wigmore, Evidence § 1198 (Chadbourn rev. 1972).

[15]"A material change in a note is one that causes it to speak a language different in legal effect from that which it originally spoke." Bank of Cedar Bluffs v. Beck, 128 Neb. 244, 258 N.W. 528, 96 A.L.R. 1099 (1935) (memorandum on note showing due date which did not affect the liability of the maker was not material). *See also* Blenkiron Bros. v. Rogers, 87 Neb. 716, 127 N.W. 1062 (1910) (correction of obligee's name not material).

An alteration which changes the apparent legal effect of the instrument is nonetheless material because the change is to the advantage of the obligor. Keller v. State Bank, 292 Ill. 553, 127 N.E. 94, 9 A.L.R. 1082 (1920) (alteration of obligation by reducing amount).

[16]*See* Walker v. Independence Fed. Sav. & Loan Ass'n, 555 A.2d 1018 (D.C. App. 1989). *See also* Hannah v. State Bank, 195 Minn. 54, 261 N.W. 583 (1935) (alteration made in good faith to correct mistake in writing); First Nat'l Bank v. Spalding, 177 Cal. 217, 170 P. 407 (1918). Section 124 of the Uniform Negotiable Instruments Law which, prior to the UCC, was almost universally adopted, took the position that a material but nonfraudulent alteration discharged the instru-

obligee's knowledge or consent.[17] If the alteration is made by a stranger, the obligation is not discharged even if the alteration is material and fraudulent.[18] Of course, before discharge by material alteration can take place, there must have been a contract in existence at the time of the unauthorized alteration. When a writing is altered without proper authority prior to the consummation of the contemplated contract, no obligation is ever created, and the supposed obligor is not liable in any case, whether the alteration be fraudulent or nonfraudulent.[19] This follows, in the case of a proposed informal contract, because in such a situation mutual assent is lacking; in the case of a formal contract, because the writing as altered has never been delivered by the obligor or by someone having the necessary authority.

G. *Merger.*

A discharge by what is called merger occurs whenever an existing obligation in one form is recreated in a different form, and what the law for one reason or another regards as a higher form, between the same parties and without any change in the nature or the extent of the obligation.[20] This recreation may be brought about by the voluntary act of the parties in executing a different form of contract to cover an existing obligation, or by a judgment of a court, or an award of arbitrators which fixes the rights and liabilities of the parties to a contract. Discharge of the prior obligation is said to take place in such cases on the grounds of good policy. The subject of discharge of contract by judgment is outside the scope of this book,[21] and the subject of arbitration and award deserves separate treatment.[22] We content ourselves with a brief discussion of the execution of a contract in a different and "higher" form.

---

ment. Section 3-407(2) of the UCC made a significant change. The Code requires the alteration to be material and fraudulent in order to discharge the instrument involved.

[17] *See* RESTATEMENT 2d § 286.

[18] If the alteration, though material and fraudulent, is made by a stranger without the knowledge or consent, directly or indirectly, of the obligee, the obligation is enforceable according to its original terms. *See* RESTATEMENT 2d § 286 comment a. *See also* Drum v. Drum, 133 Mass. 566 (1882).

This is so although the person making the alteration was, for other purposes, an agent of the obligee. Owosso Sugar Co. v. Arntz, 244 Mich. 351, 221 N.W. 179 (1928); Clyde S.S. Co. v. Whaley, 231 F. 76 (4th Cir. 1916).

Under § 124 of the Uniform Negotiable Instruments Act, a material alteration of a negotiable instrument ("material" was defined in § 125) even though by a stranger, destroyed the obligation. This is changed by the UCC. *See* UCC § 3-407(2) comment 3.

[19] Mayer v. First Nat'l Co. 99 Fla. 173, 125 So. 909 (1930); Wood v. Steele, 73 U.S. (6 Wall.) 80 (1867); Waterman v. Vose, 43 Me. 504 (1857). *See also* Annotation, 44 A.L.R. 1244 (1926).

[20] FIRST RESTATEMENT § 443. The RESTATEMENT 2d omits discharge by merger. *See* Reporter's Note to Chapter 12 at 363.

It is to be observed that the liquidating of a previously unliquidated obligation is not deemed a change in the nature or extent of the obligation for this purpose.

[21] *See* 6 CORBIN § 1318; FIRST RESTATEMENT § 449.

[22] Arbitration awards are freely enforced though early courts were often said to resist being ousted of their jurisdiction when parties decided to submit their dispute to non-judicial persons called arbitrators. Federal and state statutes have been enacted to ascertain the enforcement of arbitration awards. *See, e.g.,* United States Arbitration Act, 9 U.S.C. § 1 *et seq.* Arbitration has been the dispute resolution model in employer-employee relations for many years. Commercial arbitration where parties submit disputes what are typically contracts questions has grown significantly in recent years. The parties may include an arbitration clause in their contract which courts will enforce, or they may agree to submit their cause to arbitration only after the dispute has arisen. Courts are quite willing to transform these awards into judgments and to resist any

As a result of the operation of the parol evidence rule, when parties reduce their agreement to writing under such circumstances as to make it evident that they have intended the writing to be the complete and final expression of their agreement, all prior negotiations are merged in the writing which is called integrated or completely integrated. Thereafter the writing alone is the basis of any obligation that exists because all prior agreements are said to be "merged" in the writing.[23] Any obligation that may have previously existed has been superseded and discharged by the writing ultimately agreed upon. So also when the parties to an informal contract, either oral or written, or to a negotiable instrument, later execute a contract under seal covering the same subject matter, the prior obligation is discharged by the sealed contract, which is deemed to be a contract of a higher nature.[24] It has been said that the reason for the rule that a duty is discharged by merger when a contract under seal is substituted for some other form of obligation is that "to allow a debt to be, at the same time, of different degrees, and recoverable by a multiplicity of inconsistent remedies, would increase litigation, unsettle distinctions and lead to embarrassment in the limitation of actions and the distribution of assets."[25] These reasons obviously had more weight in the days before the abolition of the distinctions between forms of action, although some of them are not without force even today.

Contrary to what might be supposed to be the case, a debt is not merged in a negotiable instrument executed to cover it.[26] In view of the fact that such an instrument is capable of being transferred to a holder for value without notice, free from the equities existing between the debtor and prior holders of the instrument, it is arguable that it should be held to merge and discharge the prior duty in order to protect the debtor from the possibility of liability for double payment. Although our law has not taken this view of the matter,

---

review of awards absent an abuse of discretion by arbitrators. Beyond arbitration, we have entered the alternative dispute resolution era where extra-judicial processes are often viewed as desirable alternatives to the often prolonged and expensive litigation process.

One of the manifestations of the judicial acceptance of arbitration awards is the contrast in the availability of specific performance of such awards at common law and today. Common law courts simply refused to grant specific performance of such awards. Today, if arbitrators grant specific performance, the RESTATEMENT 2d suggests that "a court will be less hesitant in confirming such an award [by the arbitrators] than it would in granting specific performance itself" because of the limited scope of judicial review of arbitration awards. RESTATEMENT 2d § 366 comment a.

[23] For an exploration of the parol evidence process, see supra Chapter 5.

[24] "A simple contract and a contract under seal between the same parties cannot both subsist for the same subject matter or obligation. The contract under seal, being of superior dignity and solemnity in the contemplation of the law, will merge the simple contract ... There will be a merger of the simple contract, whether the parties wish it or not, for the two are incompatible, and except where one is intended to be simply collateral to the other, they cannot subsist together for the same thing and the higher must prevail." Magruder v. Belt, 7 D.C. App. 303, 311 (1895), cert. denied, 169 U.S. 737 (1898).

Costner v. Fisher, 104 N.C. 392, 10 S.E. 526 (1889); Baker v. Baker, 28 N.J.L. 13, 75 Am. Dec. 243 (1859); Howell v. Webb, 2 Ark. 360 (1840). Accord FIRST RESTATEMENT § 446.

The concept, however, takes on an antiquarian perspective in light of the abolition or substantial erosion of the seal.

[25] Jones v. Johnson, 3 W. & S. 276, 277, 38 Am. Dec. 760 (Pa. 1842).

[26] McRae Grocery Co. v. Independence Indem. Co., 33 F.2d 494 (4th Cir. 1929); Segrist v. Crabtree, 131 U.S. 287 (1889).

Moreover, the execution of a renewal note will not ipso facto discharge or merge a prior note. First Nat'l Bank v. Yowell, 155 Tenn. 430, 294 S.W. 1101, 52 A.L.R. 1411 (1927); State Bank v. Mut. Tel. Co., 123 Minn. 314, 143 N.W. 912 (1913).

much the same result has been accomplished by adoption of the rule that the execution and delivery of a negotiable instrument to cover an existing debt suspends the obligation, pending maturity of the negotiable instrument.[27] If the instrument is not paid at maturity, the original obligation is held to revive at the election of the obligee, but, of course, he cannot enforce it without accounting for the dishonored instrument in such a way as to prevent the possibility of double liability.[28] Moreover, it is also generally agreed that a debt is absolutely discharged by *accord* and *satisfaction* upon execution of a negotiable instrument, if that was the intention of the parties.[29] The execution of the instrument is itself regarded as consideration for the discharge of the debt in such cases.[30] But, as in the case of *accord* and *satisfaction* generally, it is also usually held that the execution of the new instrument has this effect only when there is affirmative evidence that it was the intention of the parties that the old obligation should be presently discharged.[31] In the absence of such evidence the negotiable instrument is presumed to have been taken only as conditional payment.

---

[27] *See* UCC § 3-802. *See also* UCC § 2-511(3).

[28] UCC § 3-802(1)(b).

[29] *See* UCC § 3-802(1)(a) which provides: "Unless otherwise agreed where an instrument is taken for an underlying obligation the obligation is pro tanto discharged if a bank is drawer, maker or acceptor of the instrument and there is no recourse on the instrument against the underlying obligor. . . ."

[30] That a note for an amount less than the sum due is consideration for the discharge of the larger amount was held in Bolt v. Dawkins, 16 S.C. 198 (1881).

[31] Holland v. Rongey, 168 Mo. 16, 67 S.W. 568 (1902); Cheltenham Stone & Gravel Co. v. Gates Iron Works, 124 Ill. 623, 16 N.E. 923 (1888); Geib v. Reynolds, 35 Minn. 331, 28 N.W. 923 (1886).

Chapter 13

JOINT AND SEVERAL CONTRACTS

§ 146. Problems of Multiple Promisors and Promisees.

A. *The Complexity of Joint and Several Contracts.*

One of the rubrics of contract law is that two parties are necessary to form a contract. However, it is common for more than two parties to make a contract. When this occurs, complexity may arise. Two or more promisors may contract with two or more promisees. While it is not difficult simply to count the number of promisors and promisees, complications occur when we confront the question: did the multiple promisors promise the same (single) performance or did they each promise a separate performance? If A and B each promise to pay X \$1,000, X is entitled to a total of \$2,000 but he receives that total through the separate performances of A and B. On the other hand, if A and B together promise to pay X a total of \$1,000, X is entitled to only a total of \$1,000 (the same performance) though A and B are each fully responsible for the entire payment. Similarly, A, a sole promisor, may promise to pay \$1,000 to C and \$1,000 to D. Here, C and D are each entitled to a separate performance from A. Or, A may promise C and D together that he will pay both a total of \$1,000 (they are entitled to the same performance). Whether the multiple promises refer to the same performance or to separate performances is a question of interpretation.[1] For the purposes of this chapter, we are dealing exclusively

---

[1] RESTATEMENT 2d § 288 provides:

    (1) Where two or more parties to a contract make a promise or promises to the same promisee, the manifested intention of the parties determines whether they promise that the same performance or separate performance shall be given.

    (2) Unless a contrary intention is manifested, a promise by two or more promisors is a promise that the same performance shall be given.

See also comment b to this section and 4 CORBIN ON CONTRACTS, §§ 925, 926.

with promises of the same performance, i.e., we have already answered the interpretation question by deciding that the same performance was promised by more than one promisor or that more than one promisee is entitled to that performance.

Beyond this basic complication, the contracts student is faced with the superimposed difficulties of terminology and history. The terms "joint" and "several" manifest a significant ambiguity. It is possible to use the term "joint" when referring to two or more promisors who promise the same performance or to two or more promisees who have a right to the same performance. It is possible to use the term "several" to refer to two or more promisors promising separate performances or two or more promisees who are entitled to separate performances. However, this usage of "joint" and "several" is not commonly found in judicial and statutory language. Rather, the terms "joint" and "several" both refer to rights and duties which have been created by promises of the *same* performance.[2] The confusion that may be created by this statement is diminished if not eradicated by the following explanation: the terms "joint" and "several" do not refer to whether the promises call for the same performance or for separate performances. We are always referring to the *same* performance in the use of these terms. Rather, the terms "joint" and "several" refer to whether the *promises* of the same performance *have been made as a unit* or whether the *promises* of the same performance *have been made separately.* If two or more promisors have promised the same performance as a unit, or if two or more promisees are entitled to the same performance as a unit, the obligation is said to be "joint." However, if two or more promises of the same performance have been made to two or more promisees separately, the obligation is said to be "several." With that in mind, we add one further possibility. If there are multiple promisors, promisees, or both, the obligation created may not only be "joint" or "several"; it may be (a) "joint," (b) "several," or, finally, (c) "joint and several."[3] Multiple promisors may promise jointly, or severally, or jointly and severally and promisees may have joint, several, or joint and several rights. These matters are further explored in the sections which follow.

There are two basic questions which must be explored: (1) How is it determined whether the obligation is (a) joint, (b) several, or (c) joint and several, (2) What are the legal consequences of that determination? These questions will be explored in the following sections. Before proceeding to that exploration, the historical perspective must be considered. At common law, once it was determined whether the obligation was joint, several, or joint and several, the legal consequences were governed by rather arbitrary rules which did not always prove workable. Apparently, this was due in no small measure to the fact that, in the early days when courts sought assistance to determine the rights and duties of parties in such cases, they made an analogy to existing rules relating to joint tenancies which seemed, to those courts, to furnish a point of departure for dealing with the problems. Unfortunately, such rules and principles were not particularly well adapted to this task. Common law

---

[2] *See* RESTATEMENT 2d Introductory Note to Chapter 13 at 402.
[3] RESTATEMENT 2d §§ 288-291.

rules relating to joint promisees (supplemented by equity rules) have proved to be reasonably workable. However, there are five common law rules which have proved unsatisfactory in relation to joint promisors: (1) compulsory join-der of joint promisors;[4] (2) requiring a judgment for or against all joint promi-sors;[5] (3) discharging joint promisors by a judgment against co-promisors;[6] (4) the survivorship rule which barred actions against estates of deceased joint promisors whom co-promisors survive;[7] and (5) discharge of some joint promi-sors by release, rescission, and accord and satisfaction discharged all.[8]

According to the compilation of the RESTATEMENT 2d, the first four of the five common law rules just set forth have been substantially eroded in most of the states. In almost half of the states, all five rules have been substantially abolished. There are some states where the common law rules of compulsory joinder, discharge by judgment against co-obligors, survivorship, and the com-mon law rule on releases are still in effect.[9]

B. *Obligors Bound Jointly, Severally, or Jointly and Severally.*

As we have suggested, whether an obligation is joint or several, from the standpoint of the promisors, depends upon whether they have promised as a unit, or separately. Since they may promise both ways, in relation to one and the same performance, the law recognizes three possibilities; namely, that the obligation of the promisors in a given case may be joint, several,[10] or both joint and several, depending upon whether the parties have apparently intended to obligate themselves as a unit, or separately, or both as a unit and separately.[11] Where the multiple promisors promise the same performance to the same promisee, each is bound for the entire performance regardless of whether the duty is joint, several, or joint and several.[12] If the parties have expressed their

---

[4] RESTATEMENT 2d § 190(2) and comment a.

[5] RESTATEMENT 2d § 291 and comment a.

[6] RESTATEMENT 2d § 292.

[7] RESTATEMENT 2d § 296 and comment a.

[8] RESTATEMENT 2d § 294(1) and comment a.

[9] RESTATEMENT 2d Statutory Note to Chapter 13 at 402-06. The statutes often include provisions for guarantors and other sureties. Professor Corbin instructs that the relation of principal and surety exists in cases involving joint promisors and that the equitable doctrine of suretyship may materially affect the common law rules. 4 CORBIN § 924. The suretyship concepts are beyond the purview of this volume. In addition to suretyship, there are two major statutes affecting the concepts explored in this Chapter. Section 15 of the Uniform Partnership Act provides that partners are jointly liable on partnership contracts but jointly and severally liable for claims in tort or breach of trust. As to negotiable instruments, UCC § 3-118(e) provides that, unless the instrument otherwise specifies, two or more parties who sign commercial paper as maker, accep-tor, drawer, or indorser as part of the same transaction are jointly and severally liable.

[10] It is, however, to be noted that when two or more parties have promised only separately, it is possible that they have obligated themselves either for the same performance or for different performances.

[11] RESTATEMENT 2d §§ 288 and 289. It should be emphasized that the sole basis for the distinc-tion between joint and several obligors is that stated in the text. The question as to what has been promised or who, as between the parties, is to render the promised performance, is immaterial in this regard. Therefore, any one of the following contracts may be either joint or several or both joint and several, depending upon whether A, B, and C have promised as a unit or separately: (1) A promise by A, B, and C that each of them will pay $1000 to X; (2) A promise by A, B, and C that A will pay $1000 to X; (3) A promise by A, B, and C that Y will pay $1000 to X; (4) A promise by A, B, and C that they will pay $1000 to X.

[12] RESTATEMENT 2d § 289(1) and comment a. *See* Anderson v. Barnes, 671 P.2d 1327 (Colo. App. 1983); Don L. Tullis & Assoc. v. Gover, 577 S.W.2d 891 (Mo. App. 1979); Shubert v. Ivey, 158 Conn. 583, 264 A.2d 562 (1969).

intentions in clear and unambiguous language, the question of whether the promises are joint, several, or joint and several is easily disposed of since the expressed intention will, of course, control. Unfortunately, it is frequently impossible to determine from the expressions of the parties, or from the surrounding circumstances, what intention, if any, they entertained in regard to this matter.

To deal with this situation, the common law took the position that, "It is a general presumption of law that when two or more persons undertake an obligation they undertake jointly, words of severance being necessary to overcome this primary presumption."[13] However, it may be doubted whether there is, or should be, a hard and fast rule to this effect. In the first place, since the question is fundamentally one of intention, and intention may be expressed by conduct as well as by words, there is no reason for excluding other evidence of intention. Moreover, inasmuch as parties frequently fail to address their minds to this particular aspect of the transaction when the contract is made, an unfair result would often be reached were such an inflexible presumption invariably applied. The fact is that the parties frequently intend merely to obligate themselves each for a separate and different performance, whereas the application of this presumption might render each of them liable for the whole of the promised performance.[14] Consequently, we find that the presumption is applied more as a counsel of caution than as a rule of decision.[15] The modern rule suggests only that the obligation is assumed to be joint unless there is evidence of an intention to be bound severally only, or jointly and severally, or unless the character of the transaction or the surrounding circumstances make it clear that, had the parties directed their minds to this question, they would not, as reasonable parties, have been likely to assume a

---

[13] United States Printing & Lithograph Co. v. Powers, 233 N.Y. 143, 152, 135 N.E. 225 (1922).

The following have been held to be "words of severance": promise of two in general terms followed by statement that the parties "will be personally liable," Yadusky v. Shugars, 301 Pa. 99, 151 A. 785 (1930) (obligation held to be both joint and several); promise in general terms by principal and surety followed by the statement "the payment whereof said principal binds himself ... and said surety binds itself," Morrison v. American Sur. Co., 224 Pa. 41, 73 A. 10 (1909) (obligation held to be both joint and several); promise in general terms followed by the statement "each of the said first parties to be held personally responsible for one-fourth of said fifteen hundred dollars," Larking v. Butterfield, 29 Mich. 254 (1874) (obligation held to be several only).

A written agreement by members of a creditor's committee of an insolvent corporation to "assume responsibility for payment of ... fees ... regardless of any arrangement the Creditor's Committee may have or may obtain for reimbursement" as without words of severance and there was joint liability rather than several liability for a pro rata share. Welch v. Sherwin, 300 F.2d 716 (D.C. Cir. 1962).

See also Hamrick v. Shisladin Fisheries, Inc., 708 P.2d 705 (Alaska 1985) (parties need not pronounce literal "words of severance" to manifest an intention to overcome the presumption of joint liability for joint undertakings.... Given the circumstances surrounding the settlement agreement, and the evidence of custom in negotiating such settlements, we conclude the presumption was overcome in this case.); St. Regis Paper Co. v. Stuart, 214 F.2d 762 (1st Cir. 1954) (The jury could find that a promise to two persons to pay commissions was severable, despite the absence of clear words of severability.).

[14] See, e.g., Davis v. Belford, 70 Mich. 120, 37 N.W. 919 (1888).

[15] "Resort may be had to certain presumptions or to circumstances as aids in cases of doubt, but every other rule yields to the purpose of the parties as disclosed by the words used and by the nature of the understanding disclosed by the instrument. The ultimate and final rule of law in all cases is to discover that purpose." Lovell v. Commonwealth Thread Co., 272 Mass. 138, 172 N.E. 77, 78 (1930).

joint liability.[16] The mere fact that the obligors have agreed among themselves, unknown to the obligee, that each shall be liable only for a ratable portion of the undertaking, does not make the obligation several when it would otherwise be construed to be joint, or joint and several.[17]

There is one type of case in which, by a rule of interpretation that has been universally adopted, an obligation is always held to be joint and several unless such a result is clearly inconsistent with the apparent intentions of the parties. This is the case in which a promise that is expressed in the singular number is signed by more than one obligor.[18] Finally, it should be emphasized that a number of jurisdictions have enacted statutes which direct that joint promises shall have the effect of creating joint and several duties, or that there is a presumption of such an effect.[19] The legal consequences of joint liability have been changed in most states.

C. Obligees — Joint or Several Rights.

Unlike obligors, it was held at a very early time that promisees could not have rights both jointly and severally by the same contract — that their rights might be joint, or they might be several, but could not be both.[20] This conclusion seems to be based on the assumption that it is not possible to have two or more persons separately entitled to the same performance from the same promisor or promisors. It was admitted that they might be entitled jointly to the same or different performances or separately to different performances, but that was all. Otherwise, the court would be in doubt as to which party should receive a judgment, and the promisor would be chargeable more than once for one and the same performance.[21] Though this ancient doctrine found a modicum of support in American case law, it must now be considered repudiated.[22] For a long time, it has been clear that the question is one of interpretation, i.e., courts must consider the interests of the parties and their manifested intentions.[23]

---

[16] See RESTATEMENT 2d § 289(2). See also Pelletier v. Dwyer, 334 A.2d 867 (Me. 1975).

[17] Knowlton v. Parsons, 198 Mass. 439, 84 N.E. 798 (1908).

[18] Continental Ill. Bank & Trust Co. v. Clement, 259 Mich. 167, 242 N.W. 877 (1932); March v. Ward, Peake N. B., 177, 170 Eng. Rep. 120 [1792]. See also UCC § 3-118(e): "Unless the instrument otherwise specifies two or more persons who sign as maker, acceptor or drawer or indorser and as part of the same transaction are jointly and severally liable even though the instrument contains such words as 'I promise to pay.'"

[19] RESTATEMENT 2d § 289 comment d.

[20] Slingsby's Case, 5 Co. Rep. 18-b, 77 Eng. Rep. 77 [1588].

[21] Id.

[22] RESTATEMENT 2d § 297 which is further explained in the text infra note 28.

[23] The guide which has been accepted to determine whether the rights of promisees are joint or several is found in the following excerpt from an old English case:

> The rule that covenants are to be construed according to the interests of the parties, is a rule of construction merely, and it cannot be supposed that such a rule was ever laid down as could prevent parties, whatever words they might use, from covenanting in a different manner. It is impossible to say that parties may not, if they please, use joint words, so as to express a joint covenant, and thereby to exclude a several covenant, and that, because a covenant may relate to several interests, it is therefore necessarily not to be construed as a joint covenant. If there be words capable of two constructions, we must look to the interests of the parties which they intended to protect and construe the words according to that interest.

Keightley v. Watson, 3 Ex. 716, 154 Eng. Rep. 1034 [1849].

The question as to what constitutes a joint, as distinguished from a several, interest, where the nature of the interest of the promisees is deemed to be the controlling factor, is one in regard to which the decided cases are unfortunately not very illuminating. In fact, very little attempt at definition has been made in relation to the matter. The most that can be said is that there is a tendency to emphasize certain commonly recurring factors in making a decision. Thus, if the consideration for the promise has been furnished by the parties acting as a unit, the tendency is to say that the interest, and hence the obligation, is joint, in the absence of countervailing elements.[24] If, however, each of the parties acting separately furnished a part of the consideration, the tendency is to regard the obligation as several.[25] So also, if the promisor has agreed to divide the promised performance among the promisees and to pay a portion to each, the tendency is to say that the interest, and consequently the obligation, is several.[26] If, however, the promise calls for payment to them as a group, or to a part of the group, and it is contemplated that whatever division is to be made will be made by the promisees themselves, the obligation will be held to be joint, because in this case the interest is regarded as joint.[27] The RESTATEMENT 2d treats the question as one of intention and, except where a different intention is manifested or the interests of the obligees in the performance or remedies for breach are distinct, the rights of obligees of the same performance are considered to be joint.[28]

§ 147. Consequences of Liability.

A. *Joint Liability — Compulsory Joinder.*

Inasmuch as the legal conception of a joint duty involves the assumption that two or more have promised as a unit, it is natural that the law should deal with joint obligors just as if they were a single person, insofar as this is practicable. Consequently, we find the general rule at common law that in any action, all of the joint obligors who are alive and not lacking capacity must be joined as defendants.[29] The fact that a joint obligor was insolvent or beyond the jurisdiction was irrelevant. Statutes throughout the country have modified the common law rule by (1) allowing a court, in its discretion, to proceed against those obligors served though all obligors are named as defendants,[30] or (2) permitting the action to proceed against those served as if they

---

[24] Mowry v. Dean, 51 R.I. 156, 152 A. 736 (1931) (husband and wife together furnished care and support); Eveleth v. Sawyer, 96 Me. 227, 52 A. 639 (1902) (tenants in common must join in suit for rent).

[25] L. L. Satler Lumber Co. v. Exler, 239 Pa. 135, 86 A. 793 (1913) (guarantee of notes of two corporate creditors in consideration of renewals).

[26] *See* Anderson v. Nichols, 93 Vt. 262, 207 A. 116 (1910); Curry v. Kansas & C. P. Ry., 58 Kan. 6, 48 P. 579 (1897).

[27] Anderson v. Martindale, 1 East 492, 102 Eng. Rep. 191 [1801] (promise to A and B to pay A an annuity). It is for this reason that persons who, acting independently, have together accepted an offer of reward are to be treated as having a joint right.

[28] RESTATEMENT 2d § 297. *See,* however, comment b to this section which further explains the "distinct interest" exception suggesting that partners, for example, are jointly concerned about the welfare of the partnership and are co-owners of the partnership property. Their interests would be joint, whereas the interests of principal and surety would be separate.

[29] RESTATEMENT 2d § 290 comment a.

[30] Here, the judgment would bind the property of all obligors and the separate property of those served.

were the only obligors though all obligors are named as defendants, or (3) simply permitting an action against any number of joint obligors without naming the others as defendants.[31]

B. *Joint Liability — Judgments.*

1. Joinder of All or Some Joint Obligors.

In the normal case, nothing other than a joint judgment could be rendered in an action against joint promisors under common law rules. "At common law there must be a recovery against all or none of those declared against jointly, unless one defendant has shown a defense personal to himself, not affecting the original joint liability...."[32] This "all-or-nothing" approach has been eliminated through modern procedural reforms and statutes dealing with joint obligations.[33] Joinder of promisors of the same performance is permitted but not required in most states, and judgment against one promisor does not bar an action against his co-obligor, whether the duties are joint, several, or joint and several. The RESTATEMENT 2d sets forth the modern rule that judgment can properly be entered for or against one promisor (whether the duties are joint, several, or both) even though no judgment or a different judgment is entered as to another promisor.[34] There is, however, an exception: it is improper to enter a judgment for one and against another where there has been a determination on the merits and the liability of one promisor cannot exist absent the liability of the other.[35] This exception is simply a statement of the principle of res judicata. While a judgment against one obligor alone is not a bar to an action against another obligor, nevertheless such a judgment is conclusive against the second obligor on the issues determined in the first action.[36] Once a joint judgment has been obtained, the obligee may enforce that judgment in the usual way against any one or all of the joint obligors, and out of their individual assets.[37] If assets owned jointly were alone subject to seizure in satisfaction of the judgment, the obligee would frequently be remediless since joint obligors do not necessarily have joint assets. The net

---

[31] RESTATEMENT 2d § 290 comment b. For a listing of states with one of these three different types of statutes, *see* Reporter's Note to comment b to this section. Partners may also be sued in the firm name. *See, e.g.,* CAL. CIV. PROC. CODE § 3-88.

[32] Harrington v. Bowman, 106 Fla. 86, 143 So. 651, 653 (1932). *Accord,* United States Printing & Lithograph Co. v. Powers, 233 N.Y. 143, 135 N.E. 225 (1922). In Aten v. Brown, 14 Ill. App. 451 (1883), the court stated, "It is a well known universal rule that in actions ex contractu the plaintiff must recover against all the defendants or none unless where a defense is interposed personal to the party who is making it, as infancy, coverture [incapacity of a married woman], lunacy, bankruptcy, and the like." *See* Banking House of A. Castetter v. Rose, 78 Neb. 693, 111 N.W. 590 (1907) (coverture); McCoy v. Jones, 61 Ohio St. 119, 55 N.E. 219 (1899) (surety released by extension of time granted to principal); Belden v. Curtis, 48 Conn. 32 (1880) (bankruptcy); Spalding v. Ludlow Woolen Mill, 36 Vt. 150 (1863) (statute of limitations); Cutts v. Gordon, 13 Me. 474, 29 Am. Dec. 520 (1836) (infancy). *See also* RESTATEMENT 2d § 291 comment a.

[33] RESTATEMENT 2d § 291 comment c.

[34] RESTATEMENT 2d § 291. *See also* Gionfriddo v. Gartenhaus Cafe, 211 Conn. 67, 557 A.2d 540 (1989); United States v. Kohn, 243 F. Supp. 293 (W.D.S.C 1965).

[35] *Id.*

[36] *See* 4 CORBIN § 929 at 722-23.

[37] Miller v. Mynn, 1 El. & El. 1075, 120 Eng. Rep. 1213 [1859]. RESTATEMENT 2d § 289(1). This is so even though, as in the case of partners, the joint debtors have joint property. Boeger & Buchanan v. Hagen, 204 Iowa 435, 215 N.W. 597 (1927).

result is that each joint obligor is, in effect, individually liable for the whole of the joint obligation.

2. Effect of Judgment — Joint Obligors.

The obligation of joint obligors, being single, was also deemed to be indivisible. Consequently, whatever was effective to discharge one of the obligors necessarily discharges all the obligors. This was the rule generally applied, unless the situation was such as to make its application grossly unjust. So we find that a judgment against one joint obligor on the merits, since it merged and so discharged the obligation as to the obligor against whom it was given, prevented a further suit against any other co-obligor who was at the time within the jurisdiction of the court.[38] The same was true of a judgment on the merits in favor of a joint obligor.[39] The modern rule as to joint obligors is that a judgment against one or more does *not* discharge other promisors of the same performance unless joinder of the parties is required because the duty is said to be joint, and the rule has not been changed by statute.[40] The merger doctrine has been changed by various statutes in most states. The most obvious change is that which gives joint promises the effect of joint and several promises.[41]

C. *Joint Liability — Survivorship.*

Largely as a result of the fact that the law relating to joint obligations was patterned after the law of joint tenancy, it was uniformly held that, when one or more of the joint obligors dies, the liability is cast upon the survivor or survivors.[42] If all the obligors died, the representative of the last survivor was alone suable.[43] It is, however, to be observed that the rule of survivorship, as applied to joint obligations, affected merely the right of the obligee to maintain suit. It did not cut off the obligation of the deceased obligor, as between himself and his co-obligors, and so did not necessarily relieve the estate of the deceased from liability. If the survivor or survivors or the representative of the first survivor discharged the obligation, they were entitled to contribution

[38] Mason v. Eldred, 73 U.S. (6 Wall.) 231 (1868) (dictum); King v. Hoare, 13 M. & W. 493 [1844]. This was so even though the plaintiff did not know that the defendant was a joint obligor when he obtained the first judgment. Kendall v. Hamilton, 4 A.C. 504 [1879]. But a co-obligor who was outside the jurisdiction when the prior judgment was secured could be sued separately thereafter. Crehan v. Megargel, 234 N.Y. 67, 136 N.E. 296 (1922); Olcott v. Little, 9 N.H. 259, 32 Am. Dec. 357 (1838).

[39] Cowley v. Patch, 120 Mass. 137 (1876).

[40] RESTATEMENT 2d § 292.

[41] RESTATEMENT 2d § 292 comment b.

[42] RESTATEMENT 2d § 296 comment a. The rule is usually justified on the footing that any other view would require a court either (1) to permit the bringing of separate suits against the survivor and the estate of the deceased contrary to the nature of the contract, or (2) to permit a joinder of the two with the result that a judgment would have to be rendered against defendants in different capacities, which is deemed inexpedient. *See* Ayer v. Wilson, 7 S.C. (2 Mill) 319, 12 Am. Dec. 677 (1818). In Roane's Adm'r v. Drummond's Adm'rs, 6 Rand. 182 at 184 (Va. 1828), it is said, "At the common law, joint obligations and joint judgments could only be enforced against the surviving obligors or defendants."

[43] Ayer v. Wilson, *supra* note 42.

from the estate of any deceased obligor in accordance with the terms of the agreement among the joint obligors, or with the equities of the case.

Statutes in most states have abolished the survivorship rule. Some of these statutes have made joint duties joint and several and therefore have abolished the rule. Others specifically abolish it, and, absent a statutory change, some judicial decisions have negated the rule. Therefore, the RESTATEMENT 2d states the modern rule as follows: "On the death of one or two or more promisors of the same performance in a contract, the estate of the deceased promisor is bound by the contract, whether the duty was joint, several, or joint and several."[44]

D. *Discharge of Joint Obligors.*

At common law, when an obligee voluntarily effectively discharged one of the joint obligors by release, rescission, or accord and satisfaction, all of the obligors were said to be thereby discharged.[45] The unitary character of the obligee's right was the basis for the rule and there was a fear that a contrary rule might allow the obligee to obtain more than his fair compensation or that the expectation of the released obligor would not be met because of the claims of co-obligors for contribution. These arguments do not adequately support the rule and, therefore, the rule has long been considered unjust. One of the early methods of circumventing it was through the covenant not to sue or a reservation of rights in a release which was construed as a covenant not to sue.[46] Recognizing the common law rule, the RESTATEMENT 2d nonetheless suggests that modern decisions have changed the rule from one of defeating intention to one of presumptive intention, i.e., where there is a manifested intention on the part of the obligee that the discharge of one promisor does not release others, the discharge is treated as a covenant not to sue.[47] Statutes also affect the common-law rule. For example, Section 4 of the Model Joint Obligations Act provides that a release of one co-obligor does not discharge others if the obligee expressly reserves his rights.[48] Various state statutes have a similar effect.[49] As to sureties, an analysis differing from the common law rule applies. Since a principal and surety *may* promise as joint promisors, the same rules would seem to apply. However, when a creditor releases a principal knowing of the suretyship relationship, the surety is released absent a reser-

---

[44] RESTATEMENT 2d § 296.

[45] Pacific S.W. Trust & Sav. Bank v. Mayer, 138 Wash. 85, 244 P. 248 (1926) (accord and satisfaction); Brooks v. Neal, 223 Mass. 467, 112 N.E. 78 (1916) (release). *See also* Annotation, 53 A.L.R. 1420 (1928).

[46] *See* RESTATEMENT 2d § 295 (1) and (2).

[47] RESTATEMENT 2d § 294 comment a.

[48] Section 5 of the same Act deals with a release in the absence of a reservation of rights. In this situation, the claim of the obligee is satisfied to the extent that the obligee knows or has reason to know that the released obligor did not pay as much of the claim as he was bound to pay under his agreement or because of his relationship with the co-obligor. Thus, if *A*, *B*, and *C* are jointly obligated to *X* in the amount of $200,000 and they have agreed among themselves that *A* shall be liable for 1/4, *B* for 1/4, and *C* for 1/2, when *X* (who knows or has reason to know of this agreement among the co-obligors) releases *C*, then *A* and *B* are liable for only $100,000. *Cf.* UCC § 3-306 as to commercial paper.

[49] *See* RESTATEMENT 2d Statutory Note to Chapter 13.

vation of rights.[50] Similarly, the discharge of a surety does not discharge the principal obligor.[51]

E. *Several Liability — Consequences.*

Since several obligors are deemed to have promised separately, the law requires them to be dealt with separately. Hence, several obligors cannot be joined in a single suit at the common law. Each must be sued separately,[52] and, if each has promised the same performance, a judgment for the same amount can be had against each of them in separate suits for failure to render the same performance.[53] However, in this case the satisfaction of one judgment, in whole or in part, will satisfy all the judgments *pro tanto.*[54] On the other hand, if each has separately promised a different performance, as is often the case, then the judgment against each will necessarily be for a different nonperformance, and satisfaction of one judgment, in whole or in part, will have no effect on the right to satisfaction of the rest of the judgments.[55] Moreover, in the case of several obligors, the rule of survivorship is not applicable, and consequently the death of a several obligor has no effect on the rights of the obligee. He may sue the representative of the deceased in a separate action just as he would have been able to sue the deceased, had he survived.[56] Except when the principles of the law of suretyship require a different result, it has never been asserted that the voluntary discharge of a several debtor discharges the other several debtors.[57] It is also clear that a judgment in favor of a several obligor, even for the same performance, is not a bar to later suits against the other obligors unless the judgment is secured on a defense, such as payment, which goes to the merits of the obligations of all the obligors.[58] Modern procedural reforms often allow several obligors to be joined as defendants.

F. *Joint and Several Liability — Consequences.*

Where the obligation is both joint and several, at common law the obligee could elect to proceed either way, i.e., he could sue the obligors all jointly or each of them separately, but he could not do both.[59] Neither could he sue part of the obligors jointly, when there were more than two, if they were all alive, any more than he could in the case of joint liability alone.[60] Of course, the rule of survivorship had applied to the joint liability, and if some of the joint and

---

[50] RESTATEMENT 2d § 294 comment b.

[51] RESTATEMENT 2d § 294 comment g.

[52] Mintz v. Tri-Cty. Nat. Gas Co., 259 Pa. 477, 103 A. 285 (1918) (dictum); Davis v. Belford, 70 Mich. 120, 37 N.W. 919 (1888).

[53] Simonds v. Center, 6 Mass. 18 (1809).

[54] Cox v. Smith, 10 Or. 418 (1882).

[55] *See, e.g.,* Davis v. Belford, *supra* note 52.

[56] First Nat'l Bank v. Dodd, 118 Or. 1, 245 P. 503 (1926).

[57] For the applicable principles of the law of suretyship, *see* 10 WILLISTON § 1220.

[58] *See* Armour & Co. v. Justice Dairy, 311 S.W.2d 555 (Ky. 1958); United States v. Ames, 99 U.S. 35 (1879).

[59] Adams v. McNutt, 83 Ind. App. 694, 149 N.E. 735 (1925); Sessions v. Johnson, 95 U.S. 347 (1877); Clinton Bank v. Hart, 5 Ohio St. 33 (1855).

[60] State v. Chandler, 79 Me. 172, 8 A. 553 (1887); Bangor Bank v. Treat, 6 Greenl. 207, 19 Am. Dec. 210 (Me. 1829).

several obligors had died, the obligee could sue the survivors jointly,[61] but could not join the estate of the deceased.[62] In the normal case, a judgment for or against one of two or more joint and several obligors on his several liability was not a bar to an action against the other or others separately, although, of course, it is a bar to a later joint judgment.[63] Whether a joint judgment against two or more, but fewer than all of the obligors, obtained without objection being made, or a judgment against survivors jointly, precludes suits against the other obligors, or the estate of a deceased obligor, on the several liability, seems to be open to question.[64] There does not seem to be any very good reason why it should. To permit such suits would serve the very useful purpose of tending to reduce the amount of litigation.

Strangely enough, it was held at a very early day that a technical release of a joint and several obligor discharged all the obligors, not only as to their joint liability, but also as to all liability.[65] The reason for this holding also is not apparent, but the rule has become well established, and in many jurisdictions it has been extended to any case of the discharge of a joint and several obligor by the voluntary at of the obligee.[66] The statutes and judicial decisions explored in earlier sections dealing with joint obligations have also changed the common law rules of joint and several obligations.

§ 148. Co-obligees — Joint — Several Rights.

Just as multiple promisors may have joint, several, or joint and several duties, multiple promisees may have joint, several, or joint and several rights. As in the case of multiple promisors, the problems explored here do not occur when different performances are promised to multiple promisees but only when the same performance is promised to multiple promisees.

As to whether the rights of multiple promisees are joint, several, or joint and several, the modern view is that the question is one of intention.[67] Where the intention is unclear, the rights of multiple promisees to the same performance are joint except to the extent that the interests of the promisees in the performance or the remedies for breach are distinct.[68] All of the circumstances surrounding the transaction must be considered to make this determination. If X promises to pay $10,000 to A and B for a certain performance, the rights of A and B would be joint if they were partners or engaged in a joint venture.[69] This is because the parties have a joint interest in the performance of the promise made to them and they reasonably expect the partnership or joint

---

[61] Stevens v. Catlin, 152 Ill. 56, 37 N.E. 1023 (1894).

[62] Eggleston v. Buck, 31 Ill. 254 (1863).

[63] See cases cited supra note 58.

[64] In Olcott v. Little, 9 N.H. 259, 32 Am. Dec. 357, at 358 (1838), the court stated, "It is said that when three contract jointly and separately, and the plaintiff sues two, without objection to judgment, he cannot afterwards sue the other, having elected to consider the agreement a joint one. . . ." See also Shoenterprise Corp. v. Willingham, 258 N.C. 36, 127 S.E.2d 767 (1962).

[65] See Hammon v. Roll, March (N.C.) 202, 82 Eng. Rep. 475 [1642].

[66] See North Pac. Mortgage Co. v. Krewson, 129 Wash. 239, 224 P. 566 (1924). This was also true at common law in relation to joint tort feasors. See Dwy v. Connecticut Co., 89 Conn. 74, 92 A. 883 (1915).

[67] RESTATEMENT 2d § 297(1).

[68] RESTATEMENT 2d § 297(2).

[69] RESTATEMENT 2d § 297 comment b and ill. 1.

venture to receive the payment from X. On the other hand, if A and B were employees[70] or separate land owners,[71] they have no community of interest and the rights are several.

At common law, when two or more persons have a joint right under a contract, all of them who are alive must join in the prosecution of any suit that is brought for the enforcement of the right.[72] It is not an excuse for failure to join a co-promisee that this promise is outside the jurisdiction of the court or does not wish to participate in the action. The relationship of joint promisees is deemed to be such that those who wish to sue have implied authority to join the others who may not wish to participate, provided indemnity against liability be given to the unwilling party or parties.[73] Modern statutes and judicial rules follow the more liberalized procedures formerly prevailing only in courts of equity. While joint promisees are still required to join as plaintiffs or be joined as defendants, joinder is more easily permitted and misjoinder or nonjoinder may be cured by adding or dropping parties. Moreover, partial or conditional relief can be granted.[74]

As in the case of joint obligors, the rule of survivorship applies, and consequently, the representative of a deceased joint obligee not only need not join in the suit, but will not be permitted to do so. The right, so far as its enforcement is concerned, vests in the survivor or survivors or the representative of the last survivor.[75] However, it does not follow that the survivor is necessarily entitled to retain all the avails of the suit. In fact, it is difficult to see why the rule of survivorship should apply to anything more than the remedy. There may be some practical advantage in giving the survivor the sole right and the power to enforce the claim, but there seems to be little reason for permitting her to retain the avails of the suit, unless that appears to have been the intention of the parties. While the cases are by no means harmonious in their approach to the problem, they appear to suggest that the survivor must account to the estate of the deceased for what would have been the deceased's share, had he lived, in the absence of some evidence that the parties had a contrary intention.[76] The handling of the matter frequently has been complicated by the unfortunate assumption that the problem involved is one of joint tenancy in personal property, and it frequently has been dealt with on that basis.[77] The right of joint promisees under a contract is not sufficiently analo-

---

[70] See 4 CORBIN § 939 at 789.

[71] See RESTATEMENT 2d § 297 ill. 2.

[72] In re Nitka's Will, 208 Wis. 181, 242 N.W. 504 (1932); Thomas v. Benson, 264 Mass. 555, 163 N.E. 181 (1928). RESTATEMENT 2d § 298(1).

[73] Ingham Lumber Co. v. Ingersoll & Co., 93 Ark. 447, 125 S.W. 139 (1910); Darling v. Simpson, 15 Me. 175 (1838). RESTATEMENT 2d § 298(2).

[74] See, e.g., FED. R. CIV. P. 19-21.

[75] Ehrlich v. Mulligan, 104 N.J.L. 375, 140 A. 463 (1928); Israel v. Jones, 97 W. Va. 173, 124 S.E. 665 (1924).

[76] Park v. Parker, 217 Mass. 405, 103 N.E. 936 (1914) (tenants in common taking a joint note for purchase price of land); Semper v. Coates, 93 Minn. 76, 100 N.W. 662 (1904) (husband and wife joint promisees in a note). See also Uniform Partnership Act §§ 37 and 38. RESTATEMENT 2d § 301 comment a suggests that, whether the estate of a joint obligee succeeds to the deceased obligee's beneficial interest depends upon the agreement or law governing the relationship among the obligees. Survivors have the right to receive performance or they may settle the claim. They may, however, have a duty to account to those beneficially interested.

[77] See Lober v. Dorgan, 215 Mich. 62, 183 N.W. 942 (1921).

gous to the right of joint owners of tangible personal property to call for identical treatment in this connection.

Just as the discharge of one joint obligor discharges all the obligors, so a discharge given to the obligor by a joint promisee cuts off the right as to all the promisees, since it destroys the joint right, and there is no other.[78] Also, a payment made to one joint promisee is a satisfaction of the obligation as to all the joint promisees.[79] But an indebtedness due from one of the promisees cannot be set off against the joint right.[80] There are two exceptions which must be noted. The first involves negotiable instruments and is beyond the purview of this volume. The second relates to the agreement or relation among the promisees. Usually, each promisee has a beneficial interest but one or more may be a nominal party or mere agent. When a promisor discharges a promisee in violation of that promisee's duty to a co-promisee of the same performance, the discharge is voidable to the extent necessary to protect the co-promisee's interest in the performance. This exception is qualified to the extent that the promisor has given value or suffered detrimental reliance absent knowledge or reason to know of the discharged promisee's violation to his co-promisee.[81] When the promisees have several rights, each of them must sue separately for his portion of the promised performance,[82] and, of course, a judgment in favor of a several promisee will not bar suits by the other promisees, nor will a discharge given by one of several promisee cut off the rights of other promisees.

§ 149. Statutory Changes.

As suggested at the beginning of this chapter and discussed throughout, the rather arbitrary rules developed by the common law in relation to joint and several contracts have spawned considerable legislative and judicial change. The most complete analysis of the statutory changes is found in the RESTATEMENT 2d which surveys the extensive statutory modification.[83] The RESTATEMENT 2d, however, is careful to state the common law rule before indicating the statutory change. This is desirable since an understanding of the common law rule is essential before the effect of particular statutory changes can be appraised. The statutes have been concerned with the five unsatisfactory common law rules listed at the outset of this chapter and discussed at appropriate points herein: (1) compulsory joinder of joint promisors; (2) the requirement of a judgment for or against all joint promisors; (3) the discharge of joint promisors by a judgment entered against their co-promisors; (4) the survivorship rule, and (5) the discharge of some joint promisors results in the discharge of all. One of the most basic statutory changes effectively modified the first four of these antiquated common law rule prescriptions, i.e., changing the funda-

---

[78] Freedman v. Montague Assocs. 18 Misc. 2d 1, 187 N.Y.S.2d 636 (1959) *rev'd on other grounds,* 9 App. Div. 2d 936, 195 N.Y.S.2d 392 (1959); Osborn v. Martha's Vineyard R.R., 140 Mass. 549, 5 N.E. 486 (1886) (accord and satisfaction with two out of three joint promisees).

[79] *See In re Nitka's Will, supra* note 72; Lake v. Wilson, 183 Ark. 180, 38 S.W.2d 25 (1931); Allen v. South Penn Oil Co., 72 W. Va. 155, 77 S.E. 905 (1913).

[80] *In re Nitka's Will, supra* note 72.

[81] *See* RESTATEMENT 2d § 300(2).

[82] Anderson v. Nichols, 93 Vt. 262, 107 A. 116 (1919).

[83] RESTATEMENT 2d Statutory Note to Chapter 13.

mental nature of the joint obligation by converting it to a joint and several obligation in all cases. The fifth common law rule (discharge) has been specifically dealt with by other statutes including the Model Joint Obligations Act. Seldom has any statutory change been made in the common law rules relating to joint and several rights.

Chapter 14

UNITED NATIONS CONVENTION ON CONTRACTS FOR THE INTERNATIONAL SALE OF GOODS: A PRIMER

§ 150. Introduction.

A. *A Uniform Law for International Sale-of-Goods Contracts.*

Just as the UCC provides uniformity for *domestic* contracts for the sale of goods, the economic interdependence of States (countries) throughout the world demonstrates a need for uniformity with respect to *international* contracts for the sale of goods. Even prior to 1930, efforts were made to construct such a code that would bind all of the major trading nations in the world.[1] The United States, however, did not participate in this effort until the eve of the 1964 Diplomatic Conference at the Hague which produced two conventions on international sales, the ULF (contract formation) and the ULIS (rights and duties under international contracts). Though these two conventions became effective in a few countries in Western Europe, the common law world, including the United States, did not participate. It is often suggested that the failure of the 1964 Hague Conventions was due to the lack of participation by the United States and other nations in the formulation of the Conventions which did not assimilate common law concepts.

Notwithstanding this failure, the expansion of international trade demanded an effective reaction in terms of a uniform sales law for international transactions. The reaction came in the form of the United Nations Commission on International Trade (UNCITRAL) which overcame the fundamental defect of the Hague Conventions by ascertaining that its thirty-six members represented all parts of the world from the commencement of its efforts. UNCITRAL produced Arbitration Rules in 1976 which are used throughout the world. In 1985 it also produced a Model Arbitration Law which promises to be widely enacted. The most significant achievement of UNCITRAL, however, was the creation of a *Convention on Contracts for the International Sale of Goods* (hereinafter CISG).[2] A draft of this Convention was submitted to a Diplomatic Conference in Vienna in 1980 where sixty-two nations were represented as well as international organizations such as the European Economic Community (EEC). The Conference lasted for five weeks and resulted in unanimous approval. The slow ratification process then began.

The Convention was approved by the United States Senate on October 9, 1986, and the ratifications of eleven nations, including the United States,[3] were deposited on December 11, 1986. The Convention became effective in the

---

[1] Commercial law experts throughout Western Europe were assembled under the auspices of the International Institute for the Unification of Private Law (UNIDROIT) with headquarters in Rome. *See* J. HONNOLD, UNIFORM LAW FOR INTERNATIONAL SALES UNDER THE 1980 SALES CONVENTION 49-56 (1982) (hereinafter cited as Honnold).

[2] *See* Appendix 2. Among the other publications of the Convention *see* U.N. Conference on Contracts for the International Sale of Goods, Final Act (April 10, 1980), U.N. Doc. A/Conf. 97/18, *reprinted in* S. Treaty Doc. 98-9, 98th Cong., 1st Sess., 52 Fed. Reg. 6262-6280 (Mar. 2, 1987), and 19 I.L.M. 668 (1980). The text of the Convention may also be found in the Uniform Commercial Code Reporting Service, Current Materials (Callaghan). Finally the text of CISG is reprinted in 8 J.L. & Com. 213-243 (1988) as part of a symposium on CISG in that issue of the Journal.

[3] Ratifications by ten nations were required to give effect to the Convention. "This Convention enters into force, subject to the provisions of paragraph (6) of this article, on the first day of the month following the expiration of twelve months after the date of deposit of the tenth instrument of ratification...." Art. 99(1).

United States on January 1, 1988. At the time of this writing, twenty-six nations have ratified the Convention.[4]

B. *Source Materials.*

In addition to the text of the 101 Articles in CISG,[5] there is limited commentary on CISG, though its scope and complexity augur a plethora of future commentary. The basic work is that of Professor John Honnold,[6] the leading American legal scholar in this area. Professor Honnold has spent a considerable portion of his illustrious career in the study of international trade law and has represented the United States very effectively.[7] The literature includes discussions of specific Articles of the Convention[8] and helpful symposia treatment.[9] As to source material, the commentators are essentially limited to the language of the Convention and certain documents that may be viewed as a kind of legislative history.[10]

It would be premature to attempt a comprehensive treatment of CISG for many reasons, not the least of which is the necessity to observe its future application by courts throughout the world.[11] Yet, when the trading nations of the world enact a uniform law on contracts for the sale of goods, any student of contract law should be aware of its existence and its broad outline. This chapter deals, essentially, with fundamental contract doctrines and contract remedies as set forth in CISG and compares certain CISG formulations and American contract law, particularly the contract law of the UCC. Differences

---

[4]Argentina, Australia, Austria, Byelorussian Soviet Socialist Republic, Chile, China, Czechoslovakia, Denmark, Egypt, Federal Republic of Germany, Finland, France, German Democratic Republic, Hungary, Iraq, Italy, Lesotho, Mexico, Norway, Sweden, Switzerland, Syria, Ukranian Soviet Socialist Republic, United States, Yugoslavia, and Zambia. Information on more recent additions can be obtained through the United Nations, Treaty Section, New York N. Y. at (212) 963-7985/5048.

[5]*See* supra note 2.

[6]*See* Honnold, *supra* note 1.

[7]Another American legal scholar who deserves much credit for CISG is Professor Alan Farnsworth.

[8]*See, e.g.,* Kastely, *The Right to Require Performance in International Sales: Towards an International Interpretation of the Vienna Convention,* 63 WASH. L. REV. 607 (1988); Comment, *Measuring Damages Under the United Nations Convention on the International Sale of Goods,* 50 OHIO ST. L.J. 737 (1989); Note, *The United Nations Convention on Contracts for the International Sale of Goods: Contract Formation and the Battle of the Forms,* 21 COLUM. J. TRANSNAT'L L. 529 (1983).

[9]*See, e.g.,* the Symposium on CISG at the University of Pittsburgh School of Law and the papers therefrom, published in 8 J.L & Com. 1-244 (1988). *See also* International Sales: The United Nations Convention on Contracts for the International Sale of Goods (1984).

[10]The United Nations Conference on Contracts for the International Sale of Goods — Official Records, U.N. Doc. A/Conf. 97/19 (1981). This collection of documents, characterized as "Official Records," includes previous drafts of CISG and commentary by various governments and organizations as well as commentary by the U.N. Secretary General on the penultimate draft. Those who have been intimately involved in the process leading to the creation of CISG (such as Professors Honnold and Farnsworth) may also bring their personal recollections of the legislative debate in their writings about CISG for the benefit of other scholars.

[11]At the time of this writing, there are only two recorded cases from courts in the United States which mention the Convention. In commenting on the problems existing in international trade, one court opines that progress may be found in CISG. Promaulayko v. Amtorg Trading Corp., 224 N.J. Super. 391, 540 A.2d 893 (1988). The United States Court of International Trade has recently held that the UCC would not apply to a particular transaction for several reasons including the fact that, in the transaction before the court, the Code had been displaced by CISG. Orbisphere Corp. v. United States, 1989 Ct. Int'l Trade, LEXIS 326 (1989).

between CISG and the UCC are emphasized as are differences between CISG and the common law of contracts, which is found, in its modern form, in the RESTATEMENT 2d.

§ 151. Essential Scope of CISG.

A. *Applicability.*

CISG applies to contracts *for the sale of goods* between parties *whose places of business are in different States* where the States *are Contracting States* (i.e., they have ratified or approved CISG) *or* where *only one of the States is a Contracting State and the rules of private international law lead to the application of the law of the Contracting State.*[12] Rather than attempt to decide whether the goods would be shipped from one State to another, since the buyer typically does not care where the seller procured the goods and the seller does not care where the buyer will take the goods, the critical application question was deemed to be whether the contracting parties had their places of business in different States. Where the parties have their places of business in different States and both States are Contracting States, the general rule is that CISG preempts the internal contract law of either State. If a party has places of business in more than one State, the relevant State is the one with the closest relationship to the contract and its performance.[13] Where only one of the parties has a place of business in a Contracting State (again, a State that has ratified CISG), the application of CISG would depend upon normal rules of private international law that choose the appropriate law according to conflict-of-laws principles, *e.g.,* the most significant contacts rule. If, therefore, the contract manifested the most significant contacts with the Contracting State, CISG would apply; otherwise, the law of the non-Contracting State would apply.[14]

B. *Exclusions.*

CISG applies only to contracts for the sale of goods, but it does not apply to every contract for the sale of goods between parties from different Contracting States. Goods to be manufactured[15] are covered by CISG unless the buyer agreed to supply a substantial part of the materials essential to manufacture or production.[16] The Convention does not apply where the "preponderant" performance of the seller is the supply of labor or other services.[17] Beyond these exclusions, there are a number of others which were designed to avoid not only endless discussion but the failure of the entire process. Article 2 of

---

[12] CISG Art. 1(1)(a) and (b).

[13] CISG Art. 10(a). If a party has no place of business, reference is to be made to his habitual residence under Art. 10(b).

[14] CISG Art. 1(b). Controversy over this principle led to the creation of Article 95 which permits any ratifying state to declare that it will not be bound by Art. 1(b). The United States made this declaration. *See* Senate Treaty Doc. No. 98-9 at 21-22 where the Message of the President transmitting the Convention announces the rationale for this declaration.

[15] Such goods would be called "future" goods under the UCC. UCC § 2-105(2).

[16] CISG Art. 3(1).

[17] CISG Art. 3(2).

the Convention lists these exclusions: (a) consumer goods;[18] (b) auction sales; (c) execution sales or other sales by authority of law; (d) stocks, shares, investment securities, negotiable instruments or money; (e) ships, vessels, hovercraft or aircraft, and; (f) electricity. Another important exclusion is the entire doctrine of products liability, which is not affected by the Convention.[19] Since the Convention deals only with the *formation* of sale-of-goods contracts *and the rights and obligations of the parties to such contracts,* it is expressly *not* concerned with the *validity* of the contract.[20] Thus, the Convention would not displace domestic law with respect to such issues as fraud, duress, illegality, mistake, or unconscionability.[21] Moreover, the Convention is not concerned with the effect of the contract on the "property in the goods sold," i.e., with issues of the rights of creditors in the goods or insolvency proceedings.[22]

The most important provision relating to exclusion is found in Article 6 of CISG. To foster freedom of the parties to make their own contracts and to avoid the dogmatic assertions of their predecessors under the Hague Conventions, the drafters of CISG included a *provision permitting the parties to exclude the application of the Convention entirely, derogate from it, or vary the effect of any of its provisions.*[23] This freedom may be particularly important in negotiating and drafting the terms of a contract to which CISG would normally apply.

§ 152. Contract Formation and Agreement Terms Under CISG.

A. *Formation Questions.*[24]

1. Offer.

Part II (Articles 14 through 24) of CISG deals with contract formation and the first section defines "offer" in a fashion that should be familiar to American lawyers: "A proposal for concluding a contract addressed to one or more specific persons constitutes an offer if it is sufficiently definite and indicates the intention of the offeror to be bound in case of acceptance."[25] How is the intention of the offeror "indicated"? Another Article provides the interpretation guide, i.e., statements and conduct "are to be interpreted according to the

---

[18] These are defined in CISG as goods bought for personal, family, or household use. Art. 2(a) then adds phraseology that will undoubtedly cause interpretation questions: "...unless the seller, at any time before or at the conclusion of the contract, neither knew nor ought to have known that the goods were bought for any such use."

[19] CISG Art. 5 states that the Convention does not apply to the liability of the seller for death or personal injury caused by the goods to any person.

[20] CISG Art. 4(a).

[21] *See* Winship, *The Scope of the Vienna Convention on International Sales Contracts* in International Sales: The United Nations Convention on Contracts for the International Sale of Goods § 1.02[6] at 1-37 (1984). Other examples of "validity" not governed by CISG would include a provision such as UCC § 2-718 refusing enforceability to "penalty" clauses. Whether UCC § 2-719(2) dealing with "failure of essential purpose" is a rule of "validity" is questionable since the circumstances giving rise to "failure of essential purpose" arise after the contract is formed.

[22] CISG Art. 4(b).

[23] CISG Art. 6.

[24] This discussion is based on Murray, *An Essay on the Formation of Contracts and Related Matters Under the United Nations Convention on Contracts for the International Sale of Goods,* 8 J.L. & COM. 11 (1988).

[25] CISG Art. 14(1).

understanding that a reasonable person of the same kind as the other party would have had in the same circumstances."[26] The RESTATEMENT 2d suggests that an offer is a manifestation of a willingness to enter a bargain made in such a fashion as to justify an understanding by the offeree that his assent will conclude a bargain. The "indication" in CISG is equivalent to the "manifestation" in the RESTATEMENT 2d and the test in both formulations is indistinguishable.

2. "Sufficiently Definite" — Price Term Omitted.

The CISG requirement that the offer be "sufficiently definite" may appear similar if not identical to a common law requirement. The CISG definition of "sufficiently definite," however, is troublesome: "A proposal is sufficiently definite if it indicates the goods and expressly or implicitly makes provision for determining the quantity and price."[27] Neither the requirement that the proposal "indicate the goods" nor the requirement that the quantity term be sufficiently definite (expressly or implicitly) should trouble the American lawyer who is familiar with these requirements. If, however, the *price* is not sufficiently set forth, how may the price be "implicitly" determined? Under the UCC, a manifestation that the parties intend to be bound to a contract with a sufficient description of the goods and sufficiently definite quantity term would result in an enforceable contract even if the price could not be implicitly determined because the Code permits a court to insert a reasonable price under such circumstances.[28] Under CISG, if the parties had a prior course of dealing that would permit the implication of a price, a contract could be discovered since CISG expressly allows for trade usage and prior course of performance as does the Code.[29] Absent such "relevant circumstances,"[30] however, there would appear to be no basis for discovering an *implicit* price under CISG. Unlike the UCC,[31] Article 14(1) of CISG, on its face, does not permit the judicial insertion of a reasonable price. Moreover, earlier efforts by CISG delegates to resolve the question through the insertion of other language were unsuccessful.[32] There is a dispute among the scholars as to whether Article 55 of the Convention solves the problem. Article 55 appears in Part III of CISG and deals with the obligations of the buyer under a sales contract where the price is not explicitly or implicitly fixed. The price is then said to be that which is "generally charged at the time of the conclusion of the contract."[33] That Article, however, begins with the phrase, "Where a contract has been validly concluded...."[34] One scholar interprets Article 55 as allowing a con-

---

[26] CISG Art. 8(2).

[27] CISG Art. 14(1).

[28] *See* UCC §§ 2-204(3) and 2-305(1)(a).

[29] CISG Art. 8(3). UCC §§ 1-205(1) and (2).

[30] CISG Art. 8(3).

[31] UCC § 2-305(1)(a).

[32] Professor Honnold suggests that the issue arose in relation to the corresponding Article of the 1978 Draft Convention (Art. 51) which provided that the buyer must pay the price generally charged by the seller. Fearing that the seller's price might be abused, some delegates suggested language that would permit the price "generally charged." *See* Honnold, *supra* note 1, at 163.

[33] CISG Art. 55.

[34] *Id.*

tract to be "validly concluded" absent any express or implicit fixing of the price.[35] Another scholar discovers no solution in Article 55 since that Article becomes operative only *after* a contract is "validly concluded". Moreover, consistent opposition by American delegates to the requirement that a proposal would not be sufficiently definite to constitute an offer unless the price were explicitly or implicitly determined met with consistent opposition.[36] This scholar joins others in asserting that Article 55, in Part III of CISG dealing with the obligations of the parties to an existing contract, was designed for use only where a Contracting State made a declaration under Article 92(1) that it will not be bound by Part II of the Convention.[37] If the non-CISG law of that State found a contract to have been "validly concluded" but litigation ensued concerning the obligations of the parties under the contract to which Part III of CISG, ratified by the Contract State, would apply, Article 55 of Part III would permit a court to insert the "price generally charged" in such a "validly concluded" contract.[38] There is support for this view in the legislative history of CISG.[39]

3. Offer Versus Invitation.

American courts often struggle with the factual question of whether a statement constitutes an offer or a mere invitation to negotiate. An Article of CISG suggests that "A proposal, other than one addressed to one or more specific persons, is to be considered merely as an invitation to make offers, unless the contrary is clearly indicated".[40] Many factors are often considered in distinguishing mere invitations from offers and one of the more unreliable guides is whether the proposal is addressed to a specific person or persons. Public proposals, *e.g.,* rewards, are typically offers though they are not addressed to a specific person at the time the offer is made. Innumerable proposals addressed to specific persons are clearly not offers (*e.g.,* advertisements, trade circulars and the like). Thus, the CISG directive to distinguish invitations from offers is unreliable and confusing. It has been suggested that advertisements and the like addressed to specific persons may be viewed as mere invitations under another CISG requirement that requires an indication that the offeror intended to be bound.[41] The "intention to be bound" requirement, however, is hardly a test. A common law lawyer may infer no intention to be bound in sending an advertisement to a specific person because that lawyer's common law tradition compels the lawyer to believe that the typical advertisement or the like is not an offer. CISG, however, does not emanate from the common law and the "specific person" concept is a test that may be viewed as the controlling test. Thus, an American seller may be well advised to state con-

---

[35] Honnold, *supra* note 1, at 163-64.

[36] Farnsworth, *Formation of Contract,* in INTERNATIONAL SALES: THE UNITED NATIONS CONVENTION ON CONTRACTS FOR THE INTERNATIONAL SALE OF GOODS § 3.04 at 3-8 (1984).

[37] Article 92(1) permits a Contract State to declare, at the time of signature, ratification, acceptance, approval or accession, that it will not be bound by Part II of the Convention, or that it will not be bound by Part III of the Convention.

[38] *See* Note, *supra* note 8, at 537-38.

[39] *See* "Official Records," *supra* note 10, at 44.

[40] CISG Art. 14(2).

[41] Honnold, *supra* note 1, n.22 at 162, relying on CISG Art. 14(1).

spicuously in any advertisement, trade circular, catalogue, or the like, which is addressed to specific persons where CISG may control, that the statements in such publications are not offers. Similarly, if the proposer would like to make an offer notwithstanding the lack of a specific addressee, the proposal should indicate that it is an offer.

4. Duration of Offers.

One of the fundamental concepts of the agreement process is that a party cannot be an offeree until he or she learns of the offer.[42] CISG, however, states that an offer becomes effective when it reaches the offeree and it *reaches* the offeree when it is delivered to his or her place of business or mailing address.[43] Thus, a party could be an offeree before learning of the offer because CISG promotes the notion that he or she has a power of acceptance before reading the offer or otherwise knowing of it. Common law adherents may find this troubling because it is antithetical to their learning. Moreover, additional problems are found in other Articles of CISG relating to this concept.

Assume an offer is dispatched on June 1 which provides that the offeree has twenty days in which to accept. Classical common law analysis suggests that the twenty-day period begins to run at the time the offer is received.[44] CISG rejects this analysis by interpreting the offer as commencing the twenty-day period from the time it is dispatched in the case of a telegram, or, in the case of a letter, from the date shown on the letter, or in the absence of a date on the letter, the date on the envelope.[45] The only exceptions occur where the offer expressly indicates that the period will commence to run only when the offer reaches the offeree[46] or where instantaneous communications such as telephone, telex, or the like are used and the twenty days would begin to run when the offer *reaches* the offeree, i.e., the general rule.[47] It is interesting to combine these CISG directives in the case posed, assuming the communication is a letter, telegram, or other non-instantaneous medium. The offer stated in the letter would become effective only when it *reaches* the offeree, i.e., when it is delivered to the appropriate mailing address. Yet, the twenty days began to run the moment the offeror dispatched the letter. Thus, before the offeree became an offeree, the twenty days he was to have to consider accepting is already shortened by the time required for the letter to reach his address.

If we add still another CISG directive, the situation becomes even more onerous. As will be seen later in this chapter, CISG adheres to the civil law tradition in rejecting the common law "dispatch" or "mailbox" rule that makes an acceptance effective when sent. CISG states that an acceptance is

---

[42] *See, e.g.,* RESTATEMENT 2d § 23 comment c.

[43] CISG Art. 15(1).

[44] The classic case is Caldwell v. Cline, 109 W. Va. 553, 156 S.E. 55 (1930).

[45] CISG Art. 20(1).

[46] CISG Art. 18(2) permits the offeror to "fix" the time for acceptance. Presumably, therefore, CISG recognizes the common law view that the offeror is master of the offer and if the offeror expressly states that the period in the offer begins to run from the time the offer reaches the offeree, that manifested intention will be enforced. *See* Honnold, *supra* note 1, at 197.

[47] *Id.*

effective if it reaches the offeror within the time fixed in the offer.[48] Again, assume the mailed offer states that the offeree has twenty days in which to accept. By the time the letter is received, a certain number of the twenty days have expired. Assume that a date on the letter is five days before the letter reached the offeree. If the offeree reads the letter as soon as it reaches him, the twenty days he had to consider the offer is reduced to no more than fifteen days as soon as he learned of the offer. Assuming the offeree is to mail his acceptance, he must now deduct the time required for the postal process to ascertain that the acceptance reaches the offeror within the time fixed in the offer. The twenty days has now been reduced to ten and, to be safe, it may be necessary to reduce it further. While the offeree in this hypothetical retained up to ten days to consider whether to exercise his power of acceptance, a reduction of days in the original offer to a smaller number (e.g., five) would preclude any acceptance, at least by return mail. If the offer took five days to reach the offeree, he would be out of time before becoming an offeree. It may be suggested that such an absurd result should preclude the application of the CISG Article which directs that the time fixed in the offer begins to run from the time of dispatch of the offer on the footing that the Article[49] is merely an interpretation guide and should be excised because of the time required for a mailed acceptance to reach the offeror.[50] A solution that requires a portion of a statute to be avoided where it literally applies, however, is not an easy solution though it may be appropriate. The Convention should have avoided this circuitous route to an effective solution.

5. Revocable and Irrevocable Offers — "Firm" Offers.

The common law treats offers as revocable unless the parties have made a separate contract, an option contract, to make the offer irrevocable. Such option contracts, however, require *consideration,* a common law concept which is not found in CISG. Statutory devices such as the UCC firm offer section[51] or judicial devices in limited situations (*e.g.,* the bid of a subcontractor to permit the general contractor to assemble a final bid[52]) can also make offers irrevocable. The general rule under CISG duplicates the common law rule that offers may be revoked if the revocation reaches the offeree before the offeree dispatches an acceptance.[53] The exceptions to this rule, however, are markedly different from the common law or American law traditions.

The UCC firm offer section[54] superficially appears to be duplicated in CISG,[55] but there are differences. Under the Code, there is an express limitation on the duration of a firm offer, i.e., three months, regardless of the statement of duration in the firm offer. No such limitation is found in CISG.[56] Beyond this minor difference, there is a major difference in the interpretation

---

[48] CISG Art. 18(1).
[49] CISG Art. 20(1).
[50] *See* Honnold, *supra* note 1, at 197-98.
[51] UCC § 2-205.
[52] *See, e.g.,* the classic case of Drennan v. Star Paving Co., 51 Cal. 2d 409, 333 P.2d 757 (1958).
[53] CISG Art. 16(1).
[54] UCC § 2-205.
[55] CISG Art. 16(1).
[56] *Id.*

of language making an offer irrevocable or "firm." For an offer to be "firm" under the UCC, the terms of the offer must "give assurance that it will be held open...." While there is no UCC elaboration of this requirement, it is clear that courts will insist upon sufficient evidence of such an "assurance."[57] An offer that merely states the duration of the offer is *not* a firm (irrevocable) offer. This rubric of the common law is not shared by civil law systems.[58] While CISG Article 16 begins with the general directive that offers may be revoked,[59] it quickly moves from that common law influence to a civil law posture: "However, an offer cannot be revoked: (a) if it indicates whether by stating a fixed time or otherwise, that it is irrevocable...."[60] This language requires any offer stating a time for acceptance to be an irrevocable offer because the subsection partakes of the civil law tradition.[61] Thus, if an offer simply states that the offeree has a certain time in which to accept the offer, the common law would treat the offer as having lapsed at the end of the duration stated in the offer but the offer would be revocable during that period.[62] CISG, however, would treat that offer as irrevocable during the stated period. Even an offer stating that the offer will lapse after a certain period may create an irrevocable offer under CISG. Thus, an American offeror who desires to establish a lapse date but does not wish to be bound to an irrevocable offer during the period established for acceptance would be well advised to state clearly that the offer remains revocable during the period fixed for acceptance.

Like American law, CISG also permits an offer to become irrevocable through the offeree's reasonable reliance.[63] Again, however, there may be a major difference. The CISG provision is so broadly drafted ("an offer cannot be revoked ... if it was reasonable for the offeree to rely on the offer as being irrevocable and the offeree has acted in reliance on the offer") that it may be interpreted to apply to situations beyond any currently recognized in American case law. Thus, mere preparation to accept an offer, absent substantial expense, substantial commitments, or foregoing alternatives, would not constitute justifiable reliance under the American view.[64] Certain CISG commentary, however, suggests that "[e]xtensive *investigation* to determine whether [one] should accept an offer" may constitute justifiable reliance to make an offer irrevocable.[65] Moreover, the civil law proclivity toward making offers irrevocable in general could induce a much wider use of reliance to achieve irrevocability. The suggestion that this provision of CISG will prove to be

---

[57] *See, e.g.,* Frieman v. Sommer, 63 N.Y.2d 788, 471 N.E.2d 246 (1984); E.A. Coronis Assocs. v. M. Gordon Constr. Co., 90 N.J. Super. 69, 216 A.2d 246 (1966); Ivey's Plumbing & Elec. Co. v. Petrochem Maint., Inc., 463 F. Supp. 543 (N.D. Miss. 1978).

[58] *See* FORMATION OF CONTRACTS: A STUDY OF THE COMMON CORE OF LEGAL SYSTEMS 780-83 (R. Schlesinger ed. 1968).

[59] CISG Art. 16(1).

[60] CISG Art. 16(2)(a).

[61] *See supra* note 57.

[62] The classic case is Dickinson v. Dodds, 2 Ch. D. 463 (1876).

[63] CISG Art. 16(2)(b).

[64] RESTATEMENT 2d § 87(2) comment e.

[65] Official Records, *supra* note 10, at 22 (emphasis added).

"substantially the same" as the RESTATEMENT 2d provision[66] may be premature.

Finally, it should be noted that an otherwise revocable offer will become irrevocable through the dispatch of an acceptance under CISG[67] though the acceptance will not become effective until it reaches the offeror.[68] This phenomenon will be explored later in the discussion of when the acceptance becomes effective.

6. Acceptance.

The general concept of acceptance under CISG should be very familiar to an American lawyer. It requires an "indication" of "assent" if an offer is said to be accepted and the "indication" may occur through language or conduct.[69] Another familiar caveat appears in this Article: "Silence or inactivity does not in itself amount to acceptance."[70] This familiar context, however, quickly changes to the unfamiliar with respect to the time when acceptance becomes effective.

7. "Mailbox" Rule Rejected.

The "dispatch" ("mailbox" or "post box") rule of the common law which makes a properly dispatched acceptance through an impliedly authorized medium effective upon dispatch, absent a reservation in the offer that it shall not become effective until received by the offeror,[71] is rejected by CISG. CISG adheres to the civil law tradition in requiring an acceptance to "reach" the offeror within the time fixed in the offer or, if no time is fixed, within a reasonable time.[72] As suggested earlier,[73] the principal problem with this approach is the change in the risk of transmission or delay in the acceptance. The offeree must be concerned that the acceptance reaches the offeror and that it arrives within the time fixed in the offer. Moreover, the offeree must be able to prove that the acceptance reached the offeror within the controlling time frame. Though CISG requires no written evidence of contracts for the sale of goods (there is no Statute of Frauds requirement in CISG), a careful offeree will arrange for a medium of acceptance that will provide evidence that the acceptance reached the offeror in timely fashion.

8. Ramifications of CISG Acceptance and Revocation Rules.

If CISG requires that, to be effective, an acceptance must reach the offeror, it may seem that the offeror could revoke the offer after the offeree has mailed the acceptance but before it is received by the offeror. To avoid that problem for the offeree, CISG allows offers to be revoked *if the revocation reaches the*

---

[66] *See* Farnsworth, *supra* note 36, § 3.04 at 3-12.
[67] CISG Art. 16(1).
[68] CISG Art. 18(1).
[69] CISG Art. 18(1).
[70] *Id.*
[71] RESTATEMENT 2d § 63(a).
[72] CISG Art. 18(2).
[73] *See* the discussion of the Duration of Offers, *supra* subsection 4.

offeree before the offeree has dispatched an acceptance.[74] The effect of this rule is not to make acceptances effective upon dispatch since that would violate the general rule that they become effective only upon reaching the offeror. Rather, the effect is to make the offer irrevocable once the offeree has dispatched acceptance. Consequently, there is a "mailbox" rule of sorts under CISG to protect the offeree. Complications arise when this rule is activated with other CISG rules.

Another CISG provision permits an acceptance to be withdrawn if the withdrawal reaches the offeror before or at the same time as the acceptance would have become effective (i.e., when it reaches the offeror).[75] This provision is the counterpart to another CISG Article that permits even an irrevocable offer to be withdrawn by the offeror if the withdrawal reaches the offeree before or at the same time as the offer.[76] All of these three provisions, i.e., (1) making an offer irrevocable after dispatch of acceptance, (2) permitting an offer to be withdrawn if the withdrawal reaches the offeree before or at the same time as the offer, and (3) permitting an acceptance to be withdrawn if the withdrawal reaches the offeror before or at the same time as the acceptance, are defensible and even desirable provisions. Their combined effect, however, may prove harmful to the offeror.

Assume an offer is received by the offeree who dispatches an acceptance in timely fashion. When that offer was received by the offeree, absent a prior or simultaneous withdrawal, it became an irrevocable offer.[77] The power of revocation in the offeror is extinguished upon the offeree's dispatch of the acceptance.[78] The irrevocable power of acceptance in the offeree can be withdrawn by the offeree until the acceptance reaches the offeror.[79] Thus, assume an acceptance was dispatched on June 1, that it will not arrive until June 5, and June 5 is within the time fixed in the offer for an effective acceptance. From June 1, the offer is irrevocable and the offeree may unilaterally withdraw. This withdrawal could be accomplished by telephone. The offeree may, therefore, speculate at the expense of the offeror between June 1 and June 5. Under American contract law, the RESTATEMENT 2d wars against this possibility even where the acceptance arrives in a timely fashion because such speculation is a manifestation of bad faith.[80] While CISG expressly sets forth a standard of "good faith in international trade" as one of its purposes,[81] its procrustean rules, perhaps unwittingly, promote the possibility of such speculation by the offeree in this situation. This problem is sometimes not addressed by the premier commentators on CISG,[82] and when it is addressed, it may be treated as "a minor problem."[83] This reaction is disconcerting.

---

[74] CISG Art. 16(1).

[75] CISG Art. 22.

[76] CISG Art. 15(2).

[77] CISG Art. 15(2).

[78] CISG Art. 16(1).

[79] CISG Art. 22.

[80] *See* RESTATEMENT 2d § 41, particularly ill. 8.

[81] CISG Art. 7.

[82] Professor Honnold does not address these questions in his otherwise splendid effort. *See* Honnold, *supra* note 1.

[83] *See* Farnsworth, *supra* note 36, § 3.03 at 3-13.

9. Acceptance by Conduct.

CISG permits an acceptance by conduct as well as language[84] and further states the general rule that either type of acceptance becomes effective when that indication of assent reaches the offeror.[85] Another provision, however, suggests that, in certain situations, the offeree may indicate assent by performing an act *without notice to the offeror,* i.e., it suggests that acceptance becomes effective upon the performance of the act before notice of the performance of the act reaches the offeror.[86] This exception to the general rule is activated first, in the obvious situation where the offer expressly permits such an acceptance, and second, in other situations where trade usage or prior course of dealing indicates assent by performing an act such as shipping the goods or paying the price.[87] American lawyers understand the problem of a conduct acceptance and the question of whether notice of the performance of the act constituting acceptance must occur. The UCC contains a confusing provision concerning the notice requirement, i.e., it may be read literally to suggest that notice is part of the acceptance where performance rather than a promise is a reasonable manner of acceptance.[88] It is, however, clear that notice is not part of the acceptance. It is a condition to the duty of the former offeror in situations where that party would not promptly become aware of the performance constituting the act of acceptance of the offer.[89] CISG suggests a similar concept. There is, however, some confusion in the CISG commentary concerning it.[90]

10. Effect of Late Acceptance.

Under the common law, if an offeree attempts to exercise his or her power of acceptance after an offer has lapsed, the attempt is a nullity. It will be recalled that CISG requires an acceptance to reach the offeror within the time fixed in the offer or within a reasonable time absent a fixed time in the offer.[91] An acceptance arriving after this time is ineffective. Another CISG provision, however, *permits the offeror to treat a late acceptance as effective* where the tardiness of the offeree is the cause of the late acceptance. If the offeror chooses to treat the late acceptance as effective, he or she need only orally notify the offeree of the intention or dispatch a notice to this effect.[92] The offeree who sends a late acceptance may not, therefore, rely upon the late acceptance as ineffective since the offeror may decide to treat it as effective. If an offeree decides to withdraw the late acceptance, it must be withdrawn

---

[84] CISG Art. 18(1).

[85] CISG Art. 18(2).

[86] CISG Art. 18(3).

[87] CISG Art. 18(3).

[88] *See* UCC § 2-206(2). For an analysis on this an related contract formation sections of the Code, *see* Murray, *A New Design for the Agreement Process,* 53 CORNELL L. REV. 785 (1968).

[89] This concept is found in the classic case of Bishop v. Eaton, 161 Mass. 496, 37 N.E. 665 (1894). For further elaboration *see* Murray, *supra* note 88. RESTATEMENT 2d § 54 also provides some assistance in the characterization of notice as a condition rather than as part of the acceptance.

[90] *See* the discussion of Professor Honnold's analysis of this concept in Murray, *supra* note 24, at 30-33.

[91] CISG Art. 18(2).

[92] CISG Art. 21(1).

before the offeror orally informs the offeree that the late acceptance will be treated as effective, or before the offeror *dispatches* a notice to this effect. It is particularly interesting to note that there is no CISG requirement that the *dispatch* of a notice informing the offeree that the late acceptance is effective must be received by the offeree, i.e., a "dispatch" or "mailbox" rule applies in this situation.[93]

In the situation just described, the offeror is protected because the late acceptance was due to the tardiness of the offeree. Thus, the offeror is given the choice as to whether to treat the late acceptance as effective. The offeree is not treated harshly in this situation since he chose to dispatch a late acceptance. The CISG drafters then turned their attention to the situation where the offeree is not at fault, i.e., he dispatched a timely acceptance but it was delayed through the intermediary and did not reach the offeror within the time fixed in the offer. Moreover, the offeror was or should have been reasonably aware of the timely dispatch and delay without the fault of the offeree. To protect the diligent offeree under these circumstances, CISG permits the late acceptance to be effective unless the offeror orally notifies the offeree that the offeror considers the offer as having lapsed, or dispatches a notice to that effect.[94] In this situation, therefore, the offeror will be bound to a contract unless he takes positive steps to avoid that liability. The offeror is permitted to preclude an enforceable contract because he may have changed his position when the acceptance did not reach him in a timely fashion. Thus, the rule protects a diligent offeree and, by permitting an offeror to notify the offeree that he treats the offer as having lapsed, it protects an offeror who may have changed his position after not receiving an acceptance within the time fixed in his offer.[95]

11. Different or Additional Terms in the Acceptance — The "Battle of the Forms" Under CISG.

One of the most controversial modifications of the common law of contracts in the UCC is the section that recognizes an acceptance of an offer as effective even though the acceptance contains terms that are different from or addi-

---

[93] This situation should be distinguished from the situation permitting "dispatch" of an acceptance by the offeree to make the offer irrevocable under Art. 16(1). Though the "dispatch" has that effect in 16(1), the acceptance must still reach the offeror to be effective.

[94] CISG Art. 21(2).

[95] The CISG treatment of a late acceptance from a diligent offeree may suggest injustice to the offeree in certain circumstances. For example, assume a diligent offeree dispatches a timely acceptance but, through the fault of the intermediary, it is quite late in arriving. During the delay, the market price for the goods has plummeted so that the offeror is delighted to sell the goods at the contract price to the offeree. The offeror will not, under these circumstances, notify the offeree that the offeror chooses to treat the offer as having lapsed. This seeming injustice to the offeree is, however, fallacious. The situation would be particularly rare in that it must assume no communication between the parties during the delay in transmission. If the offeree were aware of the delay in transmission, he could withdraw the acceptance before it reaches the offeror (Art. 22). If he were not aware of the delay in transmission, he would presumably assume that he was bound to a contract that has become undesirable because of market changes. In that situation, it does not appear any more undesirable to hold an offeree to such a contract than to hold any party to a bargain that has become less desirable because of market changes. Professor Honnold presents a confusing analysis of this situation which is discussed in Murray, *supra* note 24, at 36-38.

tional to the terms of the offer.[96] The purpose of that section was to avoid the mechanical application of common law offer and acceptance rules. The sacred rule of the common law was that any change in the response to an offer mandated the characterization of that response as a counter offer, i.e., to constitute an acceptance, the response had to exactly match the terms of the offer — the "matching acceptance" or "mirror image" rule. In the typical case of a buyer sending a purchase order (offer) the response exactly matched the offer with respect to "dickered" terms, i.e., terms that the parties had or may have consciously considered or would consider as important. However, the response also included printed form clauses such as warranty disclaimers or exclusions of consequential damages which typically differed from the terms of the offer. Neither buyer nor seller read or understood their own printed forms, much less the other's printed form. They intended to form a contract. If the goods were shipped, accepted, and used without difficulty, the parties assumed that they had performed a contract which they had originally made through their exchange of printed forms. If, however, the goods were unmerchantable and particularly if the defect in the goods led to a buyer's claim for consequential damages, the seller's attorneys would re-examine the exchanged forms and would emphasize the "matching acceptance" rule. With unassailable logic, the seller would point to the different terms in seller's response to the buyer's offer which necessarily made that response a counter offer. Normally, counter offers reject offers under the common law rubric. Thus, the buyer's offer (including express or implied warranty and remedy protection) would have been annihilated by the counter offer, leaving the seller's terms as the only operative terms. When the buyer accepted the shipped goods, the buyer would be said to have accepted the counter offer, including all of seller's terms. Thus, the contract would be said to have contained no implied warranty of merchantability or right to recover provable consequential damages. The seller would prevail in the "battle of the forms" simply because the seller fired the "last shot" in the battle, i.e., the seller would use the common law offer-acceptance — counter-offer rules of the common law in mechanical fashion to avoid meeting the reasonable expectations of the buyer.

Section 2-207 of the UCC was designed to avoid this mechanical and often unjust analysis. Recognizing the fact that reasonable buyers and sellers do not read or understand printed clauses in exchanged forms, § 2-207 sought to effectuate the real bargain of the parties, the "bargain-in-fact." Thus, where a response to an offer could be reasonably viewed as a "definite and seasonable expression of acceptance," it was considered to be an operative acceptance even though it contained terms different from or additional to the terms of the offer.

Unfortunately, courts did not appreciate the underlying philosophy of § 2-207. They glimpsed its radical implications but proceeded to undermine its effectiveness by applying it mechanically, which lead to absurd and contradictory results.[97] It is patently clear that only a modification of the Code section

---

[96] UCC § 2-207.

[97] The entire "battle of the forms" problem is analyzed earlier in this volume. *See* Chapter 2, § 50. *See also* Murray, *The Chaos of the Battle of the Forms*, 39 VAND. L. REV. 1307 (1986).

will promote a workable analysis. Under these circumstances, it is anything but remarkable that the drafters of CISG chose to avoid the UCC solution.[98] The CISG response, however, failed to consider the noble purpose of § 2-207. Notwithstanding the imperfections of § 2-207 and, particularly, the misanalysis of that section by the courts, the purpose of § 2-207 cannot be faulted, i.e., to overcome the manifest injustice of a mechanistic common law approach to the "battle of the forms." That noble purpose was either unseen, deliberately ignored, or thought impossible to attain and, therefore, deliberately ignored by CISG delegates. The "matching acceptance" rule was again raised to sacred status[99] in a section which returns to the basic common law prescription:

"A reply to an offer which purports to be an acceptance but contains additions, limitations or other modifications is a rejection of the offer and constitutes a counter-offer."[1]

While condoning the basic common law rule, the CISG provision worsens that rule in an interesting fashion. The provision goes on to direct that, if the reply to the offer contains different or additional terms that do not *materially* alter the terms of the offer, the reply constitutes an acceptance *unless* the offeror promptly objects by orally informing the offeree or dispatching a notice to that effect.[2] Permitting a contract to be formed notwithstanding immaterial variations of the offer may appear to constitute some recognition that an acceptance, and therefore, a contract, should not be destroyed for mechanical reasons. To assist the determination of materiality, the CISG provision contains another subsection listing, in non-exhaustive fashion, those terms that would be material.[3] Allowing a contract to stand notwithstanding immaterial alterations in the acceptance, however, is hardly worth the candle under these circumstances. It is difficult, for example, for Professor Farnsworth "to imagine variations that would not be material."[4]

Assuming a situation where the alterations in the reply to the offer were immaterial, CISG creates an anomaly by permitting the offeror to destroy the acceptance by objecting to the immaterial terms. To emphasize the potential injustice of this design, consider an offeror who would like to revoke the offer but is precluded from revocation because the offeree has already dispatched an acceptance.[5] The acceptance will not be effective until it reaches the offeror and it does reach the offeror within the time fixed in the offer. Upon receipt of

---

[98] *See* Farnsworth, *supra* note 36, § 3.04 at 3-17: "[G]iven the controversy and uncertainty provoked by the Code provision, the Convention solution may be a sound, if conservative one." *See also* Honnold, *supra* note 1: "[L]egal science has not yet found a satisfactory way to decide what the parties have 'agreed' when they have consummated a transaction on the basis of the routine exchange of inconsistent forms" (at 189); "The framers of the 1964 and 1980 Conventions were well advised not to follow this feature of the Uniform Commercial Code" [Section 2-207] (at 193).

[99] *See* Official Records, *supra* note 10, at 24.

[1] CISG Art. 19(1).

[2] CISG Art. 19(2).

[3] "Additional or different terms relating, among other things, to the price, payment quality and quantity of the goods, place and time of delivery, extent of one party's liability to the other or the settlement of disputes are considered to alter the terms of the offer materially." CISG Art. 19(3).

[4] *See* Farnsworth, *supra* note 24, § 3.04 at 3-16. Professor Honnold agrees. *See* Honnold, *supra* note 1, at 193.

[5] CISG Art. 16(1).

the acceptance, the offeror could examine it closely to discover immaterial alterations. If he discovers one, he may exercise his power to object to the alteration and destroy the reply as an acceptance.[6] Surely it would have been preferable to borrow a concept from § 2-207 of the UCC which permits the offeror to eliminate immaterial alterations from the terms of the contract[7] but treats the acceptance without such immaterial alterations as effective to form a contract. The offeror should not have to live with even immaterial alterations, but that effect can be achieved without destroying the contract to the possible injustice to the offeree.

It may have been oversanguine to expect CISG delegates to deal effectively with the difficult problem of the "battle of the forms." Their solution, however, does not address the problems leading to the ill-fated § 2-207 of the UCC. Those problems will remain under CISG, and there is ample evidence in the pre-Code law of the United States that those problems will not be dealt with effectively under a "matching acceptance" provision.

B. *No Statute of Frauds.*

Article 11 of CISG states, "A contract of sale need not be concluded in or evidenced by writing and is not subject to any other requirement as to form. It may be proved by any means, including witnesses." It is not remarkable that the Statute of Frauds, a product of England, which has since repudiated it, and lives in the United States with considerable doubt as to its desirability, should not have become part of CISG. There are, however, two other articles that have an important bearing on this general provision. Article 12 of CISG emphasizes the power of a Contracting State whose legislation requires a contract of sale to be evidenced by a writing to utilize Article 96 which permits that State, at any time, to make a declaration that any provision of CISG that permits contracts, modifications, terminations, or any other event to be operative without a writing does not apply where any party has a place of business in that Contracting State.

C. *Consideration — Contract Modification.*

An American lawyer should not expect to discover the common law doctrine of consideration in CISG and he or she will not be disappointed. For example, CISG permits the parties to modify or terminate their contract by "mere agreement"[8] which is a reflection of the civil law.[9] With respect to modifications in contracts for the sale of goods, the UCC had removed the consideration requirement as an unnecessary technical bar to good faith modifications.[10] Thus, with respect to modifications and the consideration requirement, CISG and the UCC are identical.

---

[6] It should be remembered that CISG Art. 19(2) states that a reply containing immaterial alterations constitutes an acceptance unless the offeror objects.

[7] *See* UCC §§ 2-207(2)(a) and (2)(c).

[8] CISG Art. 29(1).

[9] *See* Official Records, *supra* note 10, n.31 at 28. The civil law permits a modification if there was sufficient *cause* regardless of consideration.

[10] UCC § 2-209(1).

The same section of the UCC proceeds to deal with the requirements of a writing for modifications, either because the parties have inserted a "no oral modification" clause (the "private" statute of frauds),[11] or because the contract, as modified, itself falls within the "public" statute of frauds.[12] Two additional provisions deal with "waiver" and reinstatement of the writing requirement in a fashion that has proven more than confusing to American courts and lawyers.[13] Since CISG has no Statute of Frauds requirement,[14] it can deal with these problems in a much less complicated fashion.

Since there is no "public" Statute of Frauds under CISG, absent a declaration from a Contracting State,[15] CISG delegates had only to consider a possible "private" statute of frauds, i.e., whether to allow the parties to insert a "no oral modification" clause in their contract. CISG permits such a clause with respect to either modifications or terminations.[16] The delegates then had to consider whether an oral modification in breach of such a clause could still be enforced on the basis of the reliance of a party to the contract. They chose to allow such enforcement, i.e., to prevent the non-relying party from asserting the "no oral modification" clause where the other party has relied.[17] In general, CISG provides a more effective and easily assimilated design for dealing with the enforceability of contract modifications and "no oral modification" clauses. This is due, in large part, to the absence of a "public" Statute of Frauds and, perhaps, to the American experience with those portions of UCC § 2-209 that have caused consternation.

D. *Interpretation and the Parol Evidence Rule.*

1. Interpretation — "Subjective" Standard — "Reasonable Person."

The American lawyer seeking a standard of interpretation under CISG may be puzzled by an Article of CISG directing that statements and other conduct of a party "are to be interpreted according to his intent."[18] On its face, it appears to be and, indeed, has been characterized as a "subjective" standard.[19] There is, however, a critically important qualification of that standard, i.e., the intent of the party will be the standard of interpretation *only* "where the other party knew or could not have been unaware of what that intent was."[20] The second section of the same article states the standard of interpretation where the first standard is not applicable: statements and conduct of a party "are to be interpreted according to the understanding that a reasonable person of the same kind as the other party would have had in the same circum-

---

[11] UCC § 2-209(2).
[12] UCC § 2-209(3).
[13] UCC §§ 2-209(4) and (5). For an elaboration of these problems, *see* the earlier discussion of UCC § 2-209 in this volume. *See also* Murray, *The Modification Mystery: Section 2-209 of the Uniform Commercial Code,* 32 VILL. L. REV. 1 (1987).
[14] *See supra* subsection B.
[15] *See* subsection (B), *supra.*
[16] CISG Art. 29(2).
[17] CISG, *id.*
[18] CISG Art. 8(1).
[19] *See* Honnold, *supra* note 1, at 137-38.
[20] CISG Art. 8(1).

stances."[21] This is the familiar "reasonable person" standard — the "objective" test to which the common law and American contract law have adhered.

While the "reasonable person" standard applies only where the "intent of the party" standard is inapplicable, there can be no doubt that the latter standard will be applicable only in those isolated situations where the other party knew or could not have been unaware of what that intent was. American lawyers are familiar with those situations. If, for example, an offer contains a mistake of which the other party has reason to know, the offeree may not "snap up" the offer.[22] If the offeror misspeaks and, by that slip of the tongue, makes an offer that the other party must have understood as a mistake because the other party knew the true intention of the offeror, there is no power of acceptance for that which the offeree knew to be mistaken.[23] Another isolated situation to which the CISG "intent of the party" standard would appear to apply is the famous latent ambiguity situation illustrated most often by the well-known case of *Raffles v. Wichelhaus*.[24] The parties agreed to buy and sell cotton to be transported by a ship named Peerless. Unknown to either party, there were two ships named Peerless. From that case, the familiar incantation emerged: Where neither or both parties are aware of the latent ambiguity, there is no contract — there is no *objective* basis for choosing one interpretation over the other. Where, however, one party knows of a different meaning attached by the other and the other party is unaware of any different meaning, there is a contract according to the intention of the unknowing, innocent party.[25] Each of these situations would come within the CISG standard that it is the intent of the party that controls where the other party knew or could not have been unaware of what that intent was.[26] Again, however, these situations are rare. The typical situation, therefore, is controlled by the "reasonable person" standard[27] and CISG leaves no doubt that the "reasonable person" standard includes "relevant circumstances" that are very familiar to American lawyers.

2. Trade Usage, Prior Course of Dealing, Course of Performance.

The UCC emphasizes the importance of trade usage,[28] prior course of dealing,[29] and course of performance[30] in the interpretation or construction of the agreement of the parties.[31] CISG directs that "due consideration is to be given

---

[21] CISG Art. 8(2).

[22] *See* RESTATEMENT 2d § 153(b).

[23] Both the FIRST RESTATEMENT and RESTATEMENT 2d contain the illustration of an offer to sell a horse where the offeree knows that the offeror intended to sell a cow, i.e., "horse" was a slip of the tongue. Neither Restatement finds a contract for the sale of the horse, though the RESTATEMENT 2d would find a contract for the sale of the cow. FIRST RESTATEMENT § 71 ill. 2; RESTATEMENT 2d § 20 ill. 5.

[24] 2 H. & C. 906 (1864). *See supra* Chapter 5, § 91.

[25] RESTATEMENT 2d § 20.

[26] CISG Art. 8(1).

[27] CISG Art. 8(2).

[28] UCC § 1-205(2).

[29] UCC § 1-205(1).

[30] UCC § 2-208(1).

[31] The Code is particularly emphatic in its definition of "agreement" as the "bargain in fact" of the parties which expressly includes trade usage, prior course of dealing and course of performance. UCC § 1-201(3).

to all relevant circumstances of the case including ... any practices which the parties have established between themselves [prior dealings], usages [trade usage], and subsequent conduct of the parties [course of performance]."[32] Again, the standards are very familiar.

3. The Parol Evidence Rule — "Merger" ("Integration") Clauses.

CISG does not recognize the parol evidence rule, which is a very clear part of the UCC.[33] CISG expressly permits evidence of *negotiations* prior to the formation of the contract to be considered as a relevant circumstance along with trade usage, prior course of dealing, and course of performance.[34] The absence of the parol evidence rule in CISG comes as no surprise since the civil law has often managed without it,[35] or has applied it sparingly.[36] Moreover, the rule is not without its critics in this country.[37] While the UCC has retained the rule, it has liberalized it by permitting more evidence of prior negotiations to be admitted than the traditional common law rule.[38]

Though the parol evidence rule is not part of CISG, it must not be forgotten that CISG permits the parties to exclude the application of CISG or to derogate or vary the effect of any of its provisions.[39] American lawyers who seek the protection of the parol evidence rule often attempt to secure that protection beyond any doubt through the inclusion of a "merger" clause (sometimes called an "integration" or "zipper" clause) in the contract. The clause recites the intention of the parties to treat the writing evidencing the contract as final and complete, i.e., the exclusive repository of their agreement. The question arises, will the inclusion of the typical merger clause serve to vary the terms of CISG, i.e., to permit the application of the parol evidence process in a CISG contract? Professor Honnold suggests that such a clause may have this effect.[40] There is, however, doubt about the *implied* derogation or variance of CISG since the enabling Article does not suggest the possibility of that effect through implication.[41]

4. Drafting Suggestions — Specific and General.

A much safer course for the American draftsman would be to supplement the normal merger clause to the effect that, pursuant to Article 6 (the en-

---

[32] CISG Art. 8(3).

[33] UCC § 2-202. An analysis of the parol evidence process is found earlier in this volume. For a critical analysis of the RESTATEMENT 2d parol evidence process, *see* Murray, *The Parol Evidence Process and Standardized Agreements Under the Restatement, Second, Contracts,* 123 U. PA. L. REV. 1342 (1975).

[34] CISG Art. 8(3).

[35] There is no parol evidence rule in German Law.

[36] In France, the parol evidence rule does not apply to commercial contracts.

[37] For criticisms of the rule, particularly those of Professor Corbin, *see* Murray, *supra* note 33.

[38] The pre-Code test was typically the "Williston" test: would parties, situated as were the parties to this contract, naturally and normally include such extrinsic matter in the writing evidencing the contract. The UCC test modifies this standard: would such parties *certainly* have included such extrinsic matter in the writing. UCC § 2-202 comment 3. For a judicial recognition of this change, *see* the opinion by Justice Traynor in Masterson v. Sine, 65 Cal. Rptr. 545, 436 P.2d 561 (1968).

[39] CISG Art. 6.

[40] *See* Honnold, *supra* note 1, at 142.

[41] CISG Art. 6.

abling section), the parties expressly agree to derogate from that portion of Article 8(3), (permitting prior negotiations to be admitted into evidence as a relevant circumstance) and intend the contract to be subject to the parol evidence rule as found in UCC § 2-202. Though we have been addressing the specific problem of merger clauses in contracts governed by CISG, in *any* derogation from or variance of CISG, it is always wise to include a specific reference to Article 6 as an express indication of the parties' intention to avoid the application of CISG. There is also a reason to include a specific reference to the UCC (as in the merger clause example) or other relevant United States law. With respect to any variance or derogation from CISG, to refer generally to "American" or "United States" law could create confusion since United States law now includes CISG.

E. *Warranties and Disclaimers.*

1. Warranties.

The comparison of the warranty Article of CISG and sections of the UCC dealing with warranties of quality is particularly interesting. The CISG treatment begins with the general principle requiring the seller to "deliver goods which are of the quantity, quality and description required by the contract and which are contained or packaged in the manner required by the contract."[42] The contract might say nothing about the quality of the goods as such. Certainly, it contains a description of the goods and, as seen in the quoted language, CISG requires the goods to meet that description. This directive is the equivalent of the UCC section dealing with express warranties by description.[43]

The UCC also finds express warranties through affirmations or representations of fact relating to the goods which become part of the basis of the bargain.[44] Though there is no specific CISG reference to such statements by the seller, presumably they would be included in the general principle that the goods must meet "the quantity, quality and description required by the contract."[45] Since there is no parol evidence bar under CISG, statements by the seller would be admissible as part of the contract, whereas under the UCC, the parol evidence rule can operate to preclude evidence of such statements that may otherwise be express warranties.[46]

Another category of express warranties under the Code are express warranties created by sample or model.[47] This category of UCC express warranties is found in a subsection of the CISG which UCC lawyers would view as a provision amalgamating express and implied warranty standards.[48] The same subsection contains the central concept of the implied warranty of merchantabil-

---

[42] CISG Art. 35(1).
[43] UCC § 2-313(1)(b).
[44] UCC § 2-313(1)(a).
[45] CISG Art. 35(1).
[46] UCC § 2-316(1).
[47] UCC § 2-313(1)(c).
[48] CISG Art. 35(2)(c) indicates that the "goods do not conform with the contract unless they...Possessed the qualities of goods which the seller has held out to the buyer as a sample or model; ..."

ity,[49] and a statement of another type of implied warranty that is indistinguishable from the UCC implied warranty of fitness for a particular purpose.[50] Finally, the subsection expressly requires the goods to be properly contained and packaged just as the UCC requires proper containers and packaging if the goods are to be merchantable.[51]

The comparison between the warranty article of CISG and the sections of the UCC reveals the frugality of the CISG treatment. While the UCC contains six subsections describing the implied warranty of merchantability,[52] only two of those subsections are replicated in CISG.[53] Again, these standards are commingled in the same provision with an express warranty standard and the standard for the implied warranty of fitness for a particular purpose. CISG does not distinguish among express warranties, implied warranties of merchantability, and implied warranties of fitness for a particular purpose. Since it is an open secret that these warranty categories under the UCC are not watertight, i.e., they overlap in certain situations and cause confusion to courts in their application, the CISG treatment may be more effective in its unified concept of warranty.

2. Disclaimers.

If the CISG description of the warranty standard is frugal, its treatment of warranty disclaimers in comparison with the UCC is astonishingly frugal. The UCC contains a rather elaborate treatment of types of warranty disclaimers and requirements for their effectiveness.[54] Requirements such as the use of particular term[55] or the appearance of the disclaimer[56] attend an exhaustive list of the ways in which implied warranties may be disclaimed. Because the UCC distinguishes types of implied warranties,[57] these differences must be considered in the disclaimer provisions.[58] The absence of warranty categories under CISG allows for a much simpler disclaimer device.

---

[49] CISG Art. 35(2)(a): to conform to the contract, the goods must be "fit for the purposes for which goods of the same description would ordinarily be used" — comparable to the central standard for implied warranties under the UCC in § 2-314(2)(c) stating that the goods, to be "merchantable" must be "fit for the ordinary purposes for which such goods are used...."

[50] CISG Art. 35(2)(b) — the goods must be "fit for any particular purpose expressly or impliedly made known to the seller at the time of the conclusion of the contract, except where the circumstances show that the buyer did not rely, or that it was unreasonable for him to rely, on the seller's skill and judgment...." The comparable UCC section is 2-315.

[51] CISG Art. 35(2)(d); UCC § 2-314(2)(e).

[52] UCC §§ 2-314(2)(a) through (f).

[53] CISG Art. 35(2)(a) and (d).

[54] UCC § 2-316(2).

[55] In § 2-316(2), for example, the term "merchantability" must appear for a particular kind of disclaimer of the implied warranty of merchantability.

[56] See, e.g., the requirement of conspicuousness in UCC § 2-316(2).

[57] Notwithstanding the angular language of UCC § 2-316(1), it is clear that express warranties may not be disclaimed, i.e., they either exist or they do not exist. Section 2-316(1), however, does preclude the admission of parol evidence to prove an express warranty. Such preclusion, however, does not amount to a disclaimer of an express warranty.

[58] An implied warranty of merchantability must, if in writing, be conspicuous and mention "merchantability," but a disclaimer of the implied warranty of fitness for a particular purpose need only be conspicuous, i.e., it need not be set forth in any particular language. UCC § 2-316(2). Curiously, § 2-316(2) allows for an oral disclaimer of the warranty of merchantability but insists that any disclaimer of the fitness warranty must be in writing.

CISG also eschews any particular requirements such as a writing, conspicuousness, or certain language to make a disclaimer effective. Essentially, the CISG disclaimer is found in a simple proviso introducing the warranty standards: "Except where the parties have agreed otherwise...."[59] Except where the parties have otherwise agreed, the goods must meet the standards that follow. If the parties *have* otherwise agreed, they need not meet such standards. This powerful proviso disclaimer is supplemented in a subsection that excludes warranties where "the buyer knew or could not have been unaware" of the lack of conformity of the goods to CISG warranty standards at the time the contract was formed.[60] Thus, even where the parties could not be said to have "agreed otherwise" as to warranty standards, if the buyer knew or should have known that the goods did not conform to warranty standards, the standards never became part of the contract. This concept is totally consistent with a CISG standard of interpretation considered earlier.[61] It is also consistent with specific methods of disclaiming implied warranties under the UCC, i.e., disclaimer by inspection and disclaimer by course of performance, course of dealing, or usage of trade.[62]

Whether the warranty and disclaimer Article of CISG will prove to be too frugal in application remains to be seen. Its avoidance of unnecessary complications found in the UCC, however, augurs successful application by courts throughout the world.

F. *Risk of Loss.*

The risk of loss Articles of CISG[63] will come as no shock to the American lawyer. The buyer has the obligation to pay the price for goods lost or damaged if the loss or damage occurred after risk of loss had passed to the buyer unless the seller was responsible for such loss or damage.[64] If the seller is not bound to "hand over" the goods at a particular place, the risk passes to the buyer when the goods are "handed over" to the first carrier[65] — comparable to the UCC allocation of risk where the contract does not require the seller to deliver the goods to a particular place and shipment is by an independent carrier.[66] Where the seller must hand over the goods to a carrier in a particular place, the risk does not pass to the buyer until that event occurs,[67] and the risk with respect to goods sold in transit passes to the buyer at the time the contract is formed, absent countervailing circumstances.[68] In cases that do not fall within these Articles, the general residual CISG rule is that the risk

---

[59] CISG Art. 35(2).

[60] CISG Art. 35(3).

[61] *See* CISG Art. 8(1) discussed *supra* subsection (D)(1).

[62] UCC § 2-316(3)(b) and (c).

[63] CISG Articles 66-70.

[64] CISG Art. 66. *See* UCC § 2-709(1)(a) requiring the buyer to pay the contract price for conforming goods lost or damaged within a commercially reasonable time after risk of their loss has passed to the buyer.

[65] CISG Art. 67(1).

[66] UCC § 2-509(1)(a). This would be an F.O.B. "shipment" contract as defined in UCC § 2-319(1)(a).

[67] CISG Art. 67(1).

[68] CISG Art. 68.

passes to the buyer "when he takes over the goods."[69] There is a pervasive requirement that the risk does not pass to the buyer until the goods are clearly *identified* to the contract, i.e., by markings on the goods, shipping documents, or notice to the buyer.[70]

§ 153. Remedies Under CISG.[71]

A. *The Uniform Commercial Code Remedial Structure.*

The underlying philosophy of UCC remedies is to place the aggrieved party[72] in as good a position as if the other party had fully performed the contract, i.e., to protect the aggrieved party's expectation interest.[73] Where the buyer has breached the contract, this purpose is accomplished by providing appropriate remedies to the seller under the particular circumstances of the breach. If the buyer has *accepted* the goods[74] and has no right to revoke acceptance, the seller is entitled to the full performance promised by the buyer, i.e., the price of the goods.[75] The seller is also entitled to the price where the goods have suffered casualty after risk of loss has passed to the buyer.[76] If the goods have been identified to the contract and the seller is unable to resell them at a reasonable price, the seller is entitled to the price. The price remedy is, in effect, a specific performance remedy for the seller.

The buyer may not have accepted the goods. He may have rejected them wrongfully or he may have repudiated the contract prior to the seller's shipment of the goods. If the seller has retained the goods, he may resell them and collect the difference between the contract price and the lower resale price.[77] The resale remedy, however, may not place the seller in the position he would have been in had the contract been performed by the purchaser. The seller may, for example, have been able to make the second or many successive sales in any event because he has an almost inexhaustible supply of such goods. This "lost volume" seller may then recover his profit, including a reasonable overhead, for the lost sale with the breaching buyer.[78] If a seller chooses not to

---

[69] CISG Art. 69(1). If, however, the buyer does not take over the goods in due time, the risk passes when the goods are placed at his disposal. Similarly, if he is bound to take over the goods at a place other than the seller's place of business, the risk passes when delivery is due and the buyer is aware of the fact that the goods are placed at his disposal at that place.

[70] CISG Art. 67(2). *See also* CISG Art. 69(3). For the UCC concept of identification, *see* UCC § 2-501.

[71] For a very helpful exploration of remedies under CISG, *see* Flechtner, *Remedies Under the New International Sales Convention: The Perspective from Article 2 of the U. C. C.,* 8 J.L. & COM. 53 (1988).

[72] "Aggrieved party" is defined in the UCC as a party entitled to resort to a remedy. UCC § 1-201(2).

[73] UCC § 1-106(1).

[74] Acceptance of the goods is not the mere receipt of the goods by the purchaser. Acceptance is defined in UCC § 2-606 as occurring where (a) the buyer signifies to the seller that the buyer will take or retain the goods regardless of their conformity to the terms of the contract; (b) the buyer fails to make an effective rejection under § 2-602. In either of these situations, a reasonable opportunity to inspect the goods must precede the act constituting acceptance. (c) Where the buyer does any act inconsistent with the seller's ownership, the buyer has accepted the goods.

[75] UCC § 2-709(1)(a).

[76] UCC § 2-709(1)(a).

[77] UCC § 2-706.

[78] UCC § 2-708(2).

resell, he may recover the difference between the contract price and the lower market price to overcome his lost bargain.[79] Under very limited circumstances, the seller may also reclaim delivered goods where the buyer is insolvent.[80]

Where the seller breaches, the buyer is typically interested in making a substitute purchase, i.e., a "cover" purchase. He may *reject* the goods[81] or he may *revoke his acceptance of the goods,*[82] proceed to make a reasonable cover purchase, and recover the difference between the lower contract price and the cover price.[83] The buyer need not cover — he may recover the difference between the contract price and the market price at the time he learned of the breach.[84] Even if the buyer has accepted the goods and chooses to retain them, he may bring an action for the difference between the value of the goods received and the value the goods would have had if they had been as warranted.[85] The buyer may, in limited cases, sue for specific performance of the contract[86] or bring a successful replevin action if the goods were identified to the contract and the buyer is unable to cover.[87] Notwithstanding some liberalization of the specific performance remedy under the UCC, that remedy retains its common law nature as an extraordinary remedy, i.e., the normal remedy under the Code is still a remedy for money damages. Finally, the buyer may have a right to identified goods upon the seller's insolvency.[88] The buyer is also entitled to recover reasonable incidental damages[89] and consequential damages where such damages were foreseeable at the time the contract was made.[90]

B. *The CISG Remedial Structure.*

1. Overview.

American lawyers use the term "avoidance" to characterize the end of a contractual obligation without liability. Thus, for example, where the parties agree to buy and sell identified goods and the goods are destroyed, without the fault of the seller, before the risk of their loss passes to the buyer, the contractual obligation is avoided.[91] At common law, an infant or a mentally ill person may have a power of avoidance based upon his or her incapacity. Under CISG, *avoidance* has a different meaning. Where a breach occurs under CISG, the aggrieved party may *avoid* the contract if a substantial breach, called a *fundamental breach,* has occurred. A fundamental breach is one which causes sub-

---

[79] UCC § 2-708(1).
[80] UCC § 2-702(2).
[81] UCC § 2-601 provides the buyer with the right to reject for any defect subject to certain constraints such as a contrary agreement of the parties and installment contracts (§ 2-612).
[82] UCC § 2-608.
[83] UCC § 2-712.
[84] UCC § 2-713.
[85] UCC § 2-714.
[86] UCC § 2-716(1).
[87] UCC § 2-716(3).
[88] UCC § 2-502(1).
[89] UCC § 2-715(1).
[90] UCC § 2-715(2).
[91] UCC § 2-613(a).

stantial deprivation to the aggrieved party in terms of *reasonable expectations* where the breaching party or a reasonable person in his or her position would have foreseen the result.[92] If a fundamental breach occurs, thereby permitting the aggrieved party to avoid the contract, the contractual obligation is at an end but the aggrieved party is entitled to recover damages much like the damages recoverable by buyers and sellers under the UCC.[93] The common law concept of foreseeability, codified in the UCC,[94] is also an overriding limitation under CISG.[95] With only one exception,[96] where the breach is not a fundamental breach, the aggrieved party cannot avoid the contract. In this *nonavoidance* situation, the contract will be performed but damages will be awarded much like UCC damages.[97] A nonavoiding buyer may, however, have certain advantages. It is also important to note that, even where a fundamental breach has occurred, the aggrieved party may choose the nonavoidance route, i.e., the Convention does not require the aggrieved party to avoid the contract simply because the other party has committed a fundamental breach.[98] By choosing the *nonavoidance* route, the aggrieved party activates the set of remedies available where there is no fundamental breach, some of which go beyond anything available to an American buyer under the UCC. For example, CISG permits a buyer choosing nonavoidance to demand substitute goods if the lack of conformity of the goods constitutes a fundamental breach.[99] If not unreasonable under the circumstances, a buyer may demand that the seller repair any nonconformity in the goods even though the nonconformity did not amount to a fundamental breach.[1] Neither of these remedies is available to an American buyer under the UCC. The UCC permits the *seller* to cure any defects if he can do so within contract time,[2] but it does not permit the buyer to demand replacement goods or repair. The nonavoiding buyer is also entitled to "reduce the price in the same proportion as the value that the goods actually delivered had at the time of delivery bears to the value that conforming goods would have had at that time."[3]

---

[92] A breach is *fundamental* "if it results in such detriment to the other party as substantially to deprive him of what he is entitled to expect under the contract, unless the party in breach did not foresee, and a reasonable person of the same kind in the same circumstances would not have foreseen, such a result." CISG Art. 25.

[93] CISG Art. 75 combines the buyer's remedy of replacement purchase (UCC "cover") and the seller's resale remedy. CISG Art. 76 permits an aggrieved buyer or seller to recover the difference between the contract and market prices.

[94] UCC § 2-715(2).

[95] CISG Art. 74.

[96] The exception is known as *Nachfrist* and will be discussed, *infra*.

[97] For example, the seller has an action for the price of the accepted goods under CISG Art. 62 and Art. 74 provides damages for losses including lost profit.

[98] CISG Articles 49(1)(a) and 64(1)(a) insist that the aggrieved party *may* avoid the contract where the other party commits a fundamental breach.

[99] CISG Art. 46(2).

[1] CISG Art. 46(3).

[2] UCC § 2-508(1). Section 2-508(2) will provide the seller with additional time to cure if he had reason to believe such time would be available.

[3] CISG Art. 50. This concept differs from the UCC § 2-717 deduction of damages resulting from *any* breach from the price. The measure in Article 50, however, is very similar to the measure found in UCC § 2-714(2) ("The measure of damages for breach of warranty is the difference at the time and place of acceptance between the value of the goods accepted and the value they would have had if they had been as warranted ...") though the latter is a measure of damages rather

By far, the most significant difference between the remedial structures of the UCC (or common law) and CISG is the *availability of the specific performance remedy*. In furtherance of the civil law tradition, that remedy is generally available under CISG[4] though, as we will see, it is subject to certain limitations, some of which can be severe.

2. Fundamental Breach.

Before considering particular CISG remedies in more detail, it is important to consider the fundamental CISG concept known as fundamental breach which, as we have just seen, with only one exception to be discussed below, is a necessary condition to activate the avoidance path for an aggrieved party. The definition of fundamental breach[5] which requires the aggrieved party to be *substantially deprived of what he is entitled to expect* sounds very much like the UCC standard of substantial impairment of value,[6] which is typically regarded as a material breach standard.[7] Should the standard of fundamental breach be equated with the familiar standard of material breach in the contract law of the United States?

Language in two other sections of the Convention is sometimes used to suggest that the standards are different, i.e., that a fundamental breach requires more than a material breach. Article 71 permits a party to suspend performance if it becomes apparent that the other party will not perform a *substantial part* of his or her obligations.[8] Article 72 permits the aggrieved party to declare the contract avoided if it is clear that the other party will commit a *fundamental breach*.[9] This distinction suggests that "[A] breach may be 'substantial' without being 'fundamental'."[10] The Article 71 standard, however, is more than reminiscent of the familiar right to suspend performance upon reasonable grounds for insecurity and the attendant right to demand adequate assurances[11] because, under the CISG language, it is only *apparent* that the other party will not perform a substantial part of his contractual obligation — the evidence is insufficient to find what American lawyers would call an anticipatory repudiation.[12] The Article 72 standard, on the other hand, is invoked only when "it is *clear* that one of the parties will commit a fundamental breach," i.e., it is *clear* that at the time for performance he will not perform. American lawyers will remember the requirement

---

than a price reduction measure and the time of "delivery" (CISG) differs from the time of "acceptance" (UCC).

[4] CISG Articles 46(1) and 62.

[5] CISG Art. 25. *See supra* note 92.

[6] *See* this standard in §§ 2-608(1) and 2-612(2) and (3) of the UCC.

[7] It should be noted, however, that the UCC § 2-608(1) phraseology is substantial impairment of the value "to him," i.e., the buyer, a subjective standard. *See* comment 2 to UCC § 2-608.

[8] CISG Art. 71(1).

[9] CISG Art. 72(1).

[10] *See* Flechtner, *supra* note 71, at 75.

[11] UCC § 2-609. This is not to suggest, however, that Article 71 of CISG and § 2-609 of the UCC are identical. They are quite similar.

[12] Article 71 also suggests two situations which sound very much like reasonable grounds for insecurity, "A serious deficiency in his ability to perform or in his creditworthiness" (71(a)), or "His conduct in preparing to perform or in performing the contract" (71(b)).

that a repudiation must be clear and unequivocal.[13] Since the argument based on Articles 71 and 72 can be overcome in this fashion or in other ways,[14] it seems appropriate to avoid unnecessary confusion in the comparison of fundamental breach with material breach. Moreover, the definition of fundamental breach in CISG suggests no such distinction.

Another problem in the definition of fundamental breach is more serious. The definition requires that the substantial deprivation of the aggrieved party must have been foreseeable.[15] It does not, however, suggest whether the substantial deprivation had to be foreseeable at the time of contract formation or only later, at the time of breach. The question has produced scholarly debate.[16] The first CISG Article in the section on damages directs that foreseeability must be measured at the time of contract formation.[17] It is difficult to quarrel with this familiar common law standard and its express inclusion in CISG may appear to resolve the dispute. That would, however, be an unfortunate analysis since foreseeability as to damages (which should be measured as of the time of contracting) has nothing to do with foreseeability of substantial deprivation. Though it may be difficult for a lawyer from the common law tradition to think of foreseeability in these terms, CISG does not view a breach as fundamental with its consequences of avoidance unless the breaching party knew or should have known that the breach would cause substantial deprivation, i.e., substantial deprivation, per se, is insufficient to constitute a fundamental breach. Absent that kind of foreseeability, CISG prefers the contract to be continued though some compensable loss may be suffered. While the UCC modified certain technical or draconian common law views with an eye to fostering performance of the contract, CISG is even more committed to the view of completion of the exchange as evidenced, *inter alia*, by the civil law tradition of the relatively liberal allowance of the remedy of specific performance, which will be discussed below.

3. Nachfrist Procedure.

There is just one exception to the requirement of fundamental breach if a party chooses to avoid the completion of the contract. CISG permits an aggrieved party to avoid the contract, absent a fundamental breach, only if the *Nachfrist* procedure is followed. The concept of *Nachfrist* is taken from German Law and permits an aggrieved party to fix an additional reasonable period for performance by the other party.[18] If, for example, a seller has failed

---

[13] While there are parallels between CISG Art. 72 and UCC § 2-610 (anticipatory repudiation), there are differences. For example, Article 72(2) permits the aggrieved party to avoid the contract only if (time permitting) he provides reasonable notice to permit the other party to provide adequate assurance of performance. There is no similar provision in UCC § 2-610.

[14] *See, e.g.,* Flechtner, *supra* note 71, at n. 101 (last par.) 75.

[15] CISG Art. 25.

[16] *See* Ziegel, *The Remedial Provisions in the Vienna Sales Convention: Some Common Law Perspectives,* INTERNATIONAL SALES: THE UNITED NATIONS CONVENTION ON CONTRACTS FOR THE INTERNATIONAL SALE OF GOODS § 9.03 at 9-19 (1984) (suggesting that foreseeability should be measured at the time of contracting) and Flechtner, *supra* note 71, at 75-78 (suggesting that, for the purposes of avoidance as contrasted with damage liability, foreseeability should be measured at the time of the breach).

[17] CISG Art. 74.

[18] CISG Articles 47 and 63.

to deliver goods on time, the buyer may be uncertain as to whether the seller's delay amounts to a fundamental breach which would permit the buyer to choose avoidance of the contract. To eliminate that uncertainty, the buyer may fix the additional reasonable time for performance by the seller.[19] If the seller does not deliver the goods within this time frame, or declares that he will not perform within that period, the buyer may declare the contract avoided.[20] The seller may pursue the same procedure with respect to a buyer who fails to perform an obligation to pay the price or take delivery of the goods[21] with the same avoidance result if the buyer does not perform within the additional period or declares that he will not perform within that period.[22] While the *Nachfrist* concept is not devoid of all ambiguity,[23] it is a workable and desirable concept.

4. Nonavoidance Procedure — Specific Performance.

To foster completion of the contract, notwithstanding the possibility of compensable losses, CISG provides a liberal remedy of specific performance to the buyer[24] and the seller[25] unless either party has chosen the inconsistent avoidance process. There are, however, limitations on this otherwise liberal remedy. The most severe limitation is found in a provision which states that a court is not bound to enter a judgment for specific performance unless it would do so under its own law with respect to similar contracts of sale not governed by CISG.[26] While this provision does not compel a court to be governed by its own law of specific performance, it permits the court to disavow the liberality of the CISG remedy. A United States court could, therefore, apply a UCC standard of specific performance without violating CISG. Other limitations may prove to be severe. Since CISG does not deal with rights of third parties,[27] domestic law may permit such parties to have rights in the goods that would frustrate the nonavoidance/specific performance choice. The duties of a seller to take reasonable steps to preserve goods where the buyer delays in taking them or paying for them may interfere with the specific performance remedy.[28] Similarly, where the goods are of such a nature as to deteriorate, they

---

[19] CISG Art. 47(1).

[20] CISG Art. 49(1)(b).

[21] CISG Art. 63(1).

[22] CISG Art. 64(1)(b).

[23] Professor Flechtner points to the failure of the drafters to distinguish material from immaterial failures of performance during the *Nachfrist* period. Assuming, for example, a party completes all but a trivial portion of his performance during that period, should such a failure amount to a fundamental breach leading to avoidance? Professor Flechtner suggests that Articles 49(1)(b) and 64(1)(b) should be construed to permit avoidance only where there has been a *material* failure of performance during the *Nachfrist* period. He bases this suggestion on Article 7(2) which directs questions to be settled in accordance with general principles of CISG and one of those principles is that avoidance should be permitted only upon a serious breach. He also suggests the policy in article 7(1), i.e., that the Convention be interpreted to promote good faith in international trade. Flechtner, *supra* note 71, at 71-73.

[24] CISG Art. 46(1).

[25] CISG Art. 62.

[26] CISG Art. 28.

[27] CISG Art. 4.

[28] CISG Art. 85.

may have to be sold to another.[29] Notwithstanding these limitations, the CISG remedy of specific performance is generally available and is not subject to the inherent limitations found in the UCC or common law remedy of specific performance.[30]

5. Securing the Nonavoidance Route.

We have seen that a fundamental breach or the use of the *Nachfrist* procedure allows a party to avoid the contract. We have also seen that such a party may choose to pursue the completion of the contract and still recover damages for any losses. To secure this nonavoidance path, the aggrieved party must follow a certain procedure. Where the seller breaches by shipping nonconforming goods, the aggrieved buyer must provide notice to the seller specifying the nature of the nonconformity[31] and this notice must be given within a reasonable time after the buyer discovered or should have discovered the defect, or two years from the date of delivery to the buyer, whichever is shorter.[32]

If a seller chooses the nonavoidance route, the seller must take reasonable steps to preserve the goods in her control though she can be reimbursed for any expenses in performing that duty.[33] Where the seller is performing that duty and the buyer delays unreasonably in taking the goods, the seller is *permitted* to resell them after notifying the buyer of that intention.[34] If the goods are subject to rapid deterioration, the seller *must* make a reasonable effort to resell them after providing notice to the buyer to the extent possible under the circumstances.[35]

The basic remedy of the nonavoiding buyer is the right to specific performance.[36] Similarly, an aggrieved seller has a right to specific performance, i.e., a right to demand that the buyer take delivery of the goods and pay the price.[37] We have already explored the limitations of this remedy under CISG.[38]

---

[29] CISG Art. 88(2).

[30] UCC § 2-716(1) restricts the right to specific performance where the goods are unique (the common law restriction dealing with an inadequate remedy at law) "or in other proper circumstances." The latter situation, though originally touted to expand the remedy significantly, has been limited essentially to situations where the buyer was unable to cover, i.e., make a substitute purchase. In effect, where cover is not available, the goods have taken on a "unique" quality, i.e., their immediate scarcity makes them, in effect, unique.

[31] CISG Art. 39.

[32] CISG Art. 39(2). Both Articles 39 and 43 of CISG insist that a notice specifying the breach be given as a condition to an aggrieved buyer pursuing either the avoidance or nonavoidance routes. UCC § 2-607(3)(a) is a general notice provision requiring a buyer who has accepted the goods to give notice of the breach within a reasonable time after the buyer discovered or should have discovered the breach. While there has been some controversy concerning the content of the notice based upon different interpretations of the second paragraph of comment 4 to § 2-607. *See, e.g.,* Eastern Airlines, Inc. v. McDonnell-Douglas Corp., 532 F.2d 957 (5th Cir. 1976), there is no UCC requirement that the notice be particularized. Where, however, the buyer fails to state a particular defect in the notice which defect was ascertainable by reasonable inspection, and this failure interferes with the seller's right to cure the defect under § 2-508, the buyer may not rely on the unstated defect to justify rejection or establish breach. UCC § 2-605.

[33] CISG Art. 85.

[34] CISG Art. 88(1).

[35] CISG Art. 88(2). If the proceeds exceed the reasonable expense of preserving and reselling, the seller must account to the buyer for such excess proceeds under Art. 88(3).

[36] CISG Art. 46(1).

[37] CISG Art. 62.

[38] *See* text at note 24 *et seq.*

Additional remedies include the right of the buyer to demand substitute goods where the breach was fundamental (though the buyer chose the nonavoidance route),[39] and the buyer's right to demand repair of the nonconformity if that is not unreasonable under the circumstances.[40] The buyer may also reduce the price in proportion to the loss in value of the delivered goods.[41] All of these remedies may not, however, fully protect the reasonable expectations of an aggrieved party. CISG, therefore, provides further relief to compensate for losses, including lost profit, suffered as a consequence of the breach.[42]

6. Securing the Avoidance Route.

As noted, the commission of a fundamental breach allows the aggrieved party to avoid the contract. It is important to emphasize the effect of avoidance: both the aggrieved party and the breaching party are relieved from their obligations under the contract, but the breaching party remains subject to any damages caused by the breach.[43] Notice of avoidance must be given by the aggrieved party[44] and if that party attempted to communicate the notice by appropriate means, the notice will be effective if it contains errors, if it is delayed, or even if it is not received by the other party.[45] There is a curiosity in CISG, however, regarding the *time* for notice. Where the goods have arrived late, the buyer must exercise the right to avoid within a reasonable time after the delivery was made.[46] Where the goods have arrived on time but are nonconforming, avoidance must occur within a reasonable time after the buyer knew or ought to have known of the breach.[47] Where there has been no delivery of goods to the buyer, CISG does not suggest any time for notice of avoidance. Where the buyer breaches through lateness in taking delivery or paying the price, the seller must avoid the contract before becoming aware that performance has been rendered.[48] If the buyer's breach is other than lateness, such as refusal to accept conforming goods, the seller must avoid within a reasonable time after it knew or should have known of the breach.[49] Where the buyer has not paid the price, there is no CISG indication of the time in which notice of avoidance must be given. Thus, with respect to unpaid sellers or buyers who have not received delivery, CISG does not indicate when notice of avoidance must be given. The absence of such a provision is said to relieve an aggrieved party from the often difficult task of estimating when a delay in performance amounts to a fundamental breach.[50]

CISG permits a buyer to *partially avoid* the contract by treating any nonconforming or missing goods as if they were the subject matter of a severable

---

[39] CISG Art. 46(2).
[40] CISG Art. 46(3).
[41] CISG Art. 50.
[42] CISG Art. 74.
[43] CISG Art. 81(1). The parties' rights and obligations "consequent upon the avoidance of the contract" are also preserved under this Article.
[44] CISG Art. 26.
[45] CISG Art. 27.
[46] CISG Art. 49(2)(a).
[47] CISG Art. 49 (2)(b)(i). *Cf.* UCC § 2-607(3)(a).
[48] CISG Art. 64(2).
[49] CISG Art. 64(2)(b)(i).
[50] *See* Honnold, *supra* note 1, at 320, 363-64.

contract. Partial avoidance, however, is possible only if the breach as to part of the goods was a fundamental breach or if the seller has not delivered within the time fixed in a *Nachfrist* notice.[51] If the breach is fundamental, the buyer may reject the nonconforming goods or withhold payment for them, though the buyer will also be able to exercise nonavoidance rights with respect to such goods.[52] CISG also provides that an aggrieved party can avoid an installment of an installment contract if the other party has committed a fundamental breach with respect to that installment.[53] Moreover, where a breach as to any installment permits the aggrieved party to conclude (with "good grounds") that a fundamental breach may occur with respect to future installments, he may declare the contract avoided for the future.[54]

Where the contract is avoided, CISG requires restitution from both parties. If the seller has supplied goods or if the buyer has made payments under the contract, each party has a duty to make restitution of whatever has been supplied or paid.[55]

The aggrieved party who avoids the contract may claim damages that are generally measured in a fashion familiar to American lawyers, i.e., the difference between the contract price and the price in a reasonable substitute contract.[56] Moreover, an aggrieved party may also recover consequential and incidental damages.[57] For an aggrieved seller who has not resold or an aggrieved buyer who has not entered into a substitute transaction (i.e., the buyer has not "covered"), CISG measures damages by the difference between the contract price and the current market price[58] which are familiar standards for the UCC lawyer.[59] Both CISG and the UCC follow the same general

---

[51] CISG Art. 51(1).

[52] For example, the buyer can require the seller to repair (Art. 46(3)) or the buyer can pursue its claim for damages (Art. 45(1)(b)).

[53] CISG Art. 73(1). While this provision may appear to be a replication of UCC § 2-612(2), the purposes of these two provisions are different. Generally, the UCC permits rejection for any defect (the "perfect tender" rule). With respect to installment contracts, however, the UCC applies a material breach standard, i.e., substantial impairment of the value. To avoid the interruption of an installment contract through a defect in one installment, UCC § 2-612(2) insists that an installment can be rejected only if the nonconformity substantially impairs the value of that installment and cannot be cured. The purpose of Article 73(1), however, is to permit each installment to be treated as if it were a severable contract.

[54] CISG Art. 73(2). The similarity between this Article and UCC § 2-612(3) should not obscure the major difference in the purposes of these provisions. The UCC provision is designed to avoid the "perfect tender" rule by requiring a material breach (substantial impairment of value). Since CISG requires a fundamental breach for any avoidance, there is no need for CISG to emulate the UCC in this regard. Article 73(2) essentially permits the aggrieved party to utilize what American lawyers would call anticipatory repudiation for future deliveries under the installment contract.

[55] CISG Art. 81(2). Problems may arise where the buyer has received goods and made payment, the seller commits a fundamental breach, and the buyer seeks restitution of his part payment but the seller refuses. The buyer may then retain the goods and eventually sell the goods for the account of the seller under Article 88(1).

[56] CISG Art. 75. *See* UCC §§ 2-706 (seller's resale damages) and 2-712 (buyer's cover damages) which are very similar though CISG imposes no duty upon the seller concerning notice of resale.

[57] CISG Art. 74.

[58] CISG Art. 76(1).

[59] UCC § 2-708(1) and § 2-713 use the contract price/market price differential. CISG Art. 76, however, measures market price at the time of avoidance or, if avoidance occurs after the buyer has taken over the goods, at the time the goods are taken over. The UCC seller's damages are measured by the market price at the time of tender and the buyer's damages are measured by the market price at the time the buyer learned of the breach. In anticipatory repudiation situations,

standard as to which market should control for measuring market price, i.e., the market price at the place of tender.[60] Where the goods have arrived and the buyer rejects or revokes acceptance pursuant to the UCC, however, the market for measurement is the place of arrival under the Code.[61] The UCC provision to deal with a "lost volume" seller[62] is reflected very simply in CISG in an article allowing the recovery of lost profits where supplementary damages are required.[63]

C. Summary.

Notwithstanding differences between the remedial structures of CISG and the UCC, the Convention and the Code are designed, essentially, to protect the expectation interests of the parties.[64] The frugal language of the remedial structure of CISG will require considerable interpretation and construction. The American lawyer, however, is not placed in a position of being forced to become conversant with a system that is totally unfamiliar.

§ 154. Conclusion.

It would be a mistake for an American lawyer to view CISG provisions exclusively through a UCC lens. The symmetry and the differences between the Convention and the Code can help the American lawyer understand CISG. It is essential, however, to recognize the Civil Law antecedents to CISG. Unlike prior efforts at a uniform trade law, CISG clearly reflects the American contract law and UCC influence. The frugality of the entire Convention will require much adumbration. Some of its provisions have been justifiably criticized. In general, however, CISG represents a vast improvement over the confusion of the past and presents hope for a cohesive system of international contracts for the sale of goods. The interdependence of the world could not be more obvious and CISG is a critically important component of the necessary process to facilitate that interdependence. Though there may be legitimate scholarly disagreement concerning certain provisions of CISG with Professor Honnold, Professor Farnsworth, and others who facilitated the successful ratification of CISG, we are particularly indebted to them for their dedication and scholarship in this achievement.

---

where the case comes to trial prior to the time for performance, the measure is the market price at the time of repudiation under UCC § 2-723.

[60] CISG Art. 76(2). UCC §§ 2-708(1) and 2-713(2).

[61] UCC § 2-713(2).

[62] For a lost volume seller, i.e., one who sells standardized goods and has a theoretically inexhaustible supply, the resale remedy or contract price/market price differential will theoretically yield no damages. The lost volume seller would have made the additional sale in any event and has, therefore, lost the profit (plus reasonable overhead) on the contract that the buyer has breached. UCC § 2-708(2) permits such a seller to recover lost profit on that sale plus reasonable overhead.

[63] CISG Art. 74.

[64] See Official Records, *supra* note 10, at 59, indicating the basic philosophy to place the aggrieved party in the same economic position he or she would have been in had the contract been performed.

APPENDIX 1

UNIFORM COMMERCIAL CODE

Articles 1, 3, 7, and 9

ARTICLE 1

GENERAL PROVISIONS

§ 1-101. Short Title

This Act shall be known and may be cited as Uniform Commercial Code.

§ 1-102. Purposes; Rules of Construction; Variation by Agreement

(1) This Act shall be liberally construed and applied to promote its underlying purposes and policies.

(2) Underlying purposes and policies of this Act are

    (a) to simplify, clarify and modernize the law governing commercial transactions;

    (b) to permit the continued expansion of commercial practices through custom, usage and agreement of the parties;

    (c) to make uniform the law among the various jurisdictions.

(3) The effect of provisions of this Act may be varied by agreement, except as otherwise provided in this Act and except that the obligations of good faith, diligence, reasonableness and care prescribed by this Act may not be disclaimed by agreement but the parties may by agreement determine the standards by which the performance of such obligations is to be measured if such standards are not manifestly unreasonable.

(4) The presence in certain provisions of this Act of the words "unless otherwise agreed" or words of similar import does not imply that the effect of other provisions may not be varied by agreement under subsection (3).

(5) In this Act unless the context otherwise requires

    (a) words in the singular number include the plural, and in the plural include the singular;

    (b) words of the masculine gender include the feminine and the neuter, and when the sense so indicates words of the neuter gender may refer to any gender.

§ 1-103. Supplementary General Principles of Law Applicable

Unless displaced by the particular provisions of this Act, the principles of law and equity, including the law merchant and the law relative to capacity to contract, principal and agent, estoppel, fraud, misrepresentation, duress, coercion, mistake, bankruptcy, or other validating or invalidating cause shall supplement its provisions.

§ 1-104. Construction Against Implicit Repeal

This Act being a general act intended as a unified coverage of its subject matter, no part of it shall be deemed to be impliedly repealed by subsequent legislation if such construction can reasonably be avoided.

§ 1-105. Territorial Application of the Act; Parties' Power to Choose Applicable Law

(1) Except as provided hereafter in this section, when a transaction bears a reasonable relation to this state and also to another state or nation the parties may agree that the law either of this state or of such other state or nation shall govern their rights and duties. Failing such agreement this Act applies to transactions bearing an appropriate relation to this state.

(2) Where one of the following provisions of this Act specifies the applicable law, that provision governs and a contrary agreement is effective only to the extent permitted by the law (including the conflict of laws rules) so specified:

Rights of creditors against sold goods. Section 2-402.

Applicability of the Article on Leases. Sections 2A-105 and 2A-106.

Applicability of the Article on Bank Deposits and Collections. Section 4-102.

Bulk transfers subject to the Article on Bulk Transfers. Section 6-102.

Applicability of the Article on Investment Securities. Section 8-106.

Perfection provisions of the Article on Secured Transactions. Section 9-103.

As amended 1972 and 1987.

§ 1-106. Remedies to Be Liberally Administered

(1) The remedies provided by this Act shall be liberally administered to the end that the aggrieved party may be put in as good a position as if the other party had fully performed but neither consequential or special nor penal damages may be had except as specifically provided in this Act or by other rule of law.

(2) Any right or obligation declared by this Act is enforceable by action unless the provision declaring it specifies a different and limited effect.

§ 1-107. Waiver or Renunciation of Claim or Right After Breach

Any claim or right arising out of an alleged breach can be discharged in whole or in part without consideration by a written waiver or renunciation signed and delivered by the aggrieved party.

§ 1-108. Severability

If any provision or clause of this Act or application thereof to any person or circumstances is held invalid, such invalidity shall not affect other provisions or applications of the Act which can be given effect without the invalid provision or application, and to this end the provisions of this Act are declared to be severable.

§ 1-109. Section Captions

Section captions are parts of this Act.

§ 1-201. General Definitions

Subject to additional definitions contained in the subsequent Articles of this Act which are applicable to specific Articles or Parts thereof, and unless the context otherwise requires, in this Act:

(1) "Action" in the sense of a judicial proceeding includes recoupment, counterclaim, set-off, suit in equity and any other proceedings in which rights are determined.

(2) "Aggrieved party" means a party entitled to resort to a remedy.

(3) "Agreement" means the bargain of the parties in fact as found in their language or by implication from other circumstances including course of dealing or usage of trade or course of performance as provided in this Act (Sections 1-205 and 2-208). Whether an agreement has legal consequences is determined by the provisions of this Act, if applicable; otherwise by the law of contracts (Section 1-103). (Compare "Contract".)

(4) "Bank" means any person engaged in the business of banking.

(5) "Bearer" means the person in possession of an instrument, document of title, or certificated security payable to bearer or indorsed in blank.

(6) "Bill of lading" means a document evidencing the receipt of goods for shipment issued by a person engaged in the business of transporting or forwarding goods, and includes an airbill. "Airbill" means a document serving for air transportation as a bill of lading does for marine or rail transportation, and includes an air consignment note or air waybill.

(7) "Branch" includes a separately incorporated foreign branch of a bank.

(8) "Burden of establishing" a fact means the burden of persuading the triers of fact that the existence of the fact is more probable than its nonexistence.

(9) "Buyer in ordinary course of business" means a person who in good faith and without knowledge that the sale to him is in violation of the ownership rights or security interest of a third party in the goods buys in ordinary course from a person in the business of selling goods of that kind but does not include a pawnbroker. All persons who sell minerals or the like (including oil and gas) at wellhead or minehead shall be deemed to be persons in the business of selling goods of that kind. "Buying" may be for cash or by exchange of other property or on secured or unsecured credit and includes receiving goods or documents of title under a pre-existing contract for sale but does not include a transfer in bulk or as security for or in total or partial satisfaction of a money debt.

(10) "Conspicuous": A term or clause is conspicuous when it is so written that a reasonable person against whom it is to operate ought to have noticed it. A printed heading in capitals (as: NON-NEGOTIABLE BILL OF LADING) is conspicuous. Language in the body of a form is "conspicuous" if it is in larger or other contrasting type or color. But in a telegram any stated term is "conspicuous". Whether a term or clause is "conspicuous" or not is for decision by the court.

(11) "Contract" means the total legal obligation which results from the parties' agreement as affected by this Act and any other applicable rules of law. (Compare "Agreement".)

(12) "Creditor" includes a general creditor, a secured creditor, a lien creditor and any representative of creditors, including an assignee for the benefit of creditors, a trustee in bankruptcy, a receiver in equity and an executor or administrator of an insolvent debtor's or assignor's estate.

(13) "Defendant" includes a person in the position of defendant in a cross-action or counterclaim.

(14) "Delivery" with respect to instruments, documents of title, chattel paper, or certificated securities means voluntary transfer of possession.

(15) "Document of title" includes bill of lading, dock warrant, dock receipt, warehouse receipt or order for the delivery of goods, and also any other document which in the regular course of business or financing is treated as adequately evidencing that the person in possession of it is entitled to receive, hold and dispose of the document and the goods it covers. To be a document of title a document must purport to be issued by or addressed to a bailee and purport to cover goods in the bailee's possession which are either identified or are fungible portions of an identified mass.

(16) "Fault" means wrongful act, omission or breach.

(17) "Fungible" with respect to goods or securities means goods or securities of which any unit is, by nature or usage of trade, the equivalent of any other like unit. Goods which are not fungible shall be deemed fungible for the purposes of this Act to the extent that under a particular agreement or document unlike units are treated as equivalents.

(18) "Genuine" means free of forgery or counterfeiting.

(19) "Good faith" means honesty in fact in the conduct or transaction concerned.

(20) "Holder" means a person who is in possession of a document of title or an instrument or a certificated investment security drawn, issued, or indorsed to him or his order or to bearer or in blank.

(21) To "honor" is to pay or to accept and pay, or where a credit so engages to purchase or discount a draft complying with the terms of the credit.

(22) "Insolvency proceedings" includes any assignment for the benefit of creditors or other proceedings intended to liquidate or rehabilitate the estate of the person involved.

(23) A person is "insolvent" who either has ceased to pay his debts in the ordinary course of business or cannot pay his debts as they become due or is insolvent within the meaning of the federal bankruptcy law.

(24) "Money" means a medium of exchange authorized or adopted by a domestic or foreign government as a part of its currency.

(25) A person has "notice" of a fact when

    (a) he has actual knowledge of it; or

    (b) he has received a notice or notification of it; or

    (c) from all the facts and circumstances known to him at the time in question he has reason to know that it exists.

A person "knows" or has "knowledge" of a fact when he has actual knowledge of it. "Discover" or "learn" or a word or phrase of similar import refers to knowledge rather than to reason to know. The time and circumstances under which a notice or notification may cease to be effective are not determined by this Act.

(26) A person "notifies" or "gives" a notice or notification to another by taking such steps as may be reasonably required to inform the other in ordinary course whether or not such other actually comes to know of it. A person "receives" a notice or notification when

    (a) it comes to his attention; or

    (b) it is duly delivered at the place of business through which the contract was made or at any other place held out by him as the place for receipt of such communications.

(27) Notice, knowledge or a notice or notification received by an organization is effective for a particular transaction from the time when it is brought to the attention of the individual conducting that transaction, and in any event from the time when it would have been brought to his attention if the organization had exercised due diligence. An organization exercises due diligence if it maintains reasonable routines for communicating significant information to the person conducting the transaction and there is reasonable compliance with the routines. Due diligence does not require an individual acting for the organization to communicate information unless such communication is part of his regular duties or unless he has reason to know of the transaction and that the transaction would be materially affected by the information.

(28) "Organization" includes a corporation, government or governmental subdivision or agency, business trust, estate, trust, partnership or association, two or more persons having a joint or common interest, or any other legal or commercial entity.

(29) "Party", as distinct from "third party", means a person who has engaged in a transaction or made an agreement within this Act.

(30) "Person" includes an individual or an organization (See Section 1-102).

(31) "Presumption" or "presumed" means that the trier of fact must find the existence of the fact presumed unless and until evidence is introduced which would support a finding of its non-existence.

(32) "Purchase" includes taking by sale, discount, negotiation, mortgage, pledge, lien, issue or re-issue, gift or any other voluntary transaction creating an interest in property.

(33) "Purchaser" means a person who takes by purchase.

(34) "Remedy" means any remedial right to which an aggrieved party is entitled with or without resort to a tribunal.

(35) "Representative" includes an agent, an officer of a corporation or association, and a trustee, executor or administrator of an estate, or any other person empowered to act for another.

(36) "Rights" includes remedies.

(37) "Security interest" means an interest in personal property or fixtures which secures payment or performance of an obligation. The retention or reservation of title by a seller of goods notwithstanding shipment or delivery to the buyer (Section 2-401) is limited in effect to a reservation of a "security interest". The term also includes any interest of a buyer of accounts or chattel paper which is subject to Article 9. The special property interest of a buyer of goods on identification of such goods to a contract for sale under Section 2-401 is not a "security interest", but a buyer may also acquire a "security interest" by complying with Article 9. Unless a lease or consignment is intended as security, reservation of title thereunder is not a "security interest" but a consignment is in any event subject to the provisions on consignment sales (Section 2-326).

Whether a transaction creates a lease or security interest is determined by the facts of each case; however, a transaction creates a security interest if the consideration the lessee is to pay the lessor for the right to possession and use of the goods is an obligation for the term of the lease not subject to termination by the lessee, and

(a) the original term of the lease is equal to or greater than the remaining economic life of the goods,

(b) the lessee is bound to renew the lease for the remaining economic life of the goods or is bound to become the owner of the goods,

(c) the lessee has an option to renew the lease for the remaining economic life of the goods for no additional consideration or nominal additional consideration upon compliance with the lease agreement, or

(d) the lessee has an option to become the owner of the goods for no additional consideration or nominal additional consideration upon compliance with the lease agreement.

A transaction does not create a security interest merely because it provides that

(a) the present value of the consideration the lessee is obligated to pay the lessor for the right to possession and use of the goods is substantially equal to or is greater than the fair market value of the goods at the time the lease is entered into,

(b) the lessee assumes risk of loss of the goods, or agrees to pay taxes, insurance, filing, recording, or registration fees, or service or maintenance costs with respect to the goods,

(c) the lessee has an option to renew the lease or to become the owner of the goods,

(d) the lessee has an option to renew the lease for a fixed rent that is equal to or greater than the reasonably predictable fair market rent for the use of the goods for the term of the renewal at the time the option is to be performed, or

(e) the lessee has an option to become the owner of the goods for a fixed price that is equal to or greater than the reasonably predictable fair market value of the goods at the time the option is to be performed.

For purposes of this subsection (37):

(x) Additional consideration is not nominal if (i) when the option to renew the lease is granted to the lessee the rent is stated to be the fair market rent for the use of the goods for the term of the renewal determined at the time the option is to be performed, or (ii) when the option to become the owner of the goods is granted to the lessee the price is stated to be the fair market value of the goods determined at the time the option is to be performed. Additional consideration is nominal if it is less than the lessee's reasonably predictable cost of performing under the lease agreement if the option is not exercised;

(y) "Reasonably predictable" and "remaining economic life of the goods" are to be determined with reference to the facts and circumstances at the time the transaction is entered into; and

(z) "Present value" means the amount as of a date certain of one or more sums payable in the future, discounted to the date certain. The discount is determined by the interest rate specified by the parties if the rate is not manifestly unreasonable at the time the transaction is entered into; otherwise, the discount is determined by a commercially reasonable rate that takes into account the facts and circumstances of each case at the time the transaction was entered into.

(38) "Send" in connection with any writing or notice means to deposit in the mail or deliver for transmission by any other usual means of communication with postage or cost of transmission provided for and properly addressed and in the case of an instrument to an address specified thereon or otherwise agreed, or if there be none to any address reasonable under the circumstances. The receipt of any writing or notice within the time at which it would have arrived if properly sent has the effect of a proper sending.

(39) "Signed" includes any symbol executed or adopted by a party with present intention to authenticate a writing.

(40) "Surety" includes guarantor.

(41) "Telegram" includes a message transmitted by radio, teletype, cable, any mechanical method of transmission, or the like.

(42) "Term" means that portion of an agreement which relates to a particular matter.

(43) "Unauthorized" signature or indorsement means one made without actual, implied or apparent authority and includes a forgery.

(44) "Value". Except as otherwise provided with respect to negotiable instruments and bank collections (Sections 3-303, 4-208 and 4-209) a person gives "value" for rights if he acquires them

(a) in return for a binding commitment to extend credit or for the extension of immediately available credit whether or not drawn upon and whether or not a charge-back is provided for in the event of difficulties in collection; or

(b) as security for or in total or partial satisfaction of a pre-existing claim; or

(c) by accepting delivery pursuant to a pre-existing contract for purchase; or

(d) generally, in return for any consideration sufficient to support a simple contract.

(45) "Warehouse receipt" means a receipt issued by a person engaged in the business of storing goods for hire.

(46) "Written" or "writing" includes printing, typewriting or any other intentional reduction to tangible form. As amended in 1962, 1972 and 1977.

§ 1-202. Prima Facie Evidence by Third Party Documents

A document in due form purporting to be a bill of lading, policy or certificate of insurance, official weigher's or inspector's certificate, consular invoice, or any other document authorized or required by the contract to be issued by a third party shall be prima facie evidence of its own authenticity and genuineness and of the facts stated in the document by the third party.

§ 1-203. Obligation of Good Faith

Every contract or duty within this Act imposes an obligation of good faith in its performance or enforcement.

§ 1-204. Time; Reasonable Time; "Seasonably"

(1) Whenever this Act requires any action to be taken within a reasonable time, any time which is not manifestly unreasonable may be fixed by agreement.

(2) What is a reasonable time for taking any action depends on the nature, purpose and circumstances of such action.

(3) An action is taken "seasonably" when it is taken at or within the time agreed or if no time is agreed at or within a reasonable time.

§ 1-205. Course of Dealing and Usage of Trade

(1) A course of dealing is a sequence of previous conduct between the parties to a particular transaction which is fairly to be regarded as establishing a common basis of understanding for interpreting their expressions and other conduct.

(2) A usage of trade is any practice or method of dealing having such regularity of observance in a place, vocation or trade as to justify an expectation that it will be observed with respect to the transaction in question. The existence and scope of such a usage are to be proved as facts. If it is established that such a usage is embodied in a written trade code or similar writing the interpretation of the writing is for the court.

(3) A course of dealing between parties and any usage of trade in the vocation or trade in which they are engaged or of which they are or should be aware give particular meaning to and supplement or qualify terms of an agreement.

(4) The express terms of an agreement and an applicable course of dealing or usage of trade shall be construed wherever reasonable as consistent with each other; but when such construction is unreasonable express terms control both course of dealing and usage of trade and course of dealing controls usage of trade.

(5) An applicable usage of trade in the place where any part of performance is to occur shall be used in interpreting the agreement as to that part of the performance.

(6) Evidence of a relevant usage of trade offered by one party is not admissible unless and until he has given the other party such notice as the court finds sufficient to prevent unfair surprise to the latter.

§ 1-206. Statute of Frauds for Kinds of Personal Property Not Otherwise Covered

(1) Except in the cases described in subsection (2) of this section a contract for the sale of personal property is not enforceable by way of action or defense beyond five thousand dollars in amount or value of remedy unless there is some writing which indicates that a contract for sale has been made between the parties at a defined or stated price, reasonably identifies the subject matter, and is signed by the party against whom enforcement is sought or by his authorized agent.

(2) Subsection (1) of this section does not apply to contracts for the sale of goods (Section 2-201) nor of securities (Section 8-319) nor to security agreements (Section 9-203).

§ 1-207. Performances or Acceptance Under Reservation of Rights

A party who with explicit reservation of rights performs or promises performance or assents to performance in a manner demanded or offered by the other party does not thereby prejudice the rights reserved. Such words as "without prejudice", "under protest" or the like are sufficient.

§ 1-208. Option to Accelerate at Will

A term providing that one party or his successor in interest may accelerate payment or performance or require collateral or additional collateral "at will" or "when he deems himself insecure" or in words of similar import shall be construed to mean that he shall have power to do so only if he in good faith believes that the prospect of payment or performance is impaired. The burden of establishing lack of good faith is on the party against whom the power has been exercised.

§ 1-209. Subordinated Obligations

An obligation may be issued as subordinated to payment of another obligation of the person obligated, or a creditor may subordinate his right to payment of an obligation by agreement with either the person obligated or another creditor of the person obligated. Such a subordination does not create a security interest as against either the common debtor or a subordinated creditor. This section shall be construed as declaring the law as it existed prior to the enactment of this section and not as modifying it. Added 1966.

Note: *This new section is proposed as an optional provision to make it clear that a subordination agreement does not create a security interest unless so intended.*

ARTICLE 2

SALES

§ 2-101. Short Title

This Article shall be known and may be cited as Uniform Commercial Code — Sales.

§ 2-102. Scope; Certain Security and Other Transactions Exclude From This Article

Unless the context otherwise requires, this Article applies to transactions in goods; it does not apply to any transaction which although in the form of an unconditional contract to sell or present sale is intended to operate only as a security transaction nor does this Article impair or repeal any statute regulating sales to consumers, farmers or other specified classes of buyers.

§ 2-103. Definitions and Index of Definitions

(1) In this Article unless the context otherwise requires
  (a) "Buyer" means a person who buys or contracts to buy goods.
  (b) "Good faith" in the case of a merchant means honesty in fact and the observance of reasonable commercial standards of fair dealing in the trade.
  (c) "Receipt" of goods means taking physical possession of them.
  (d) "Seller" means a person who sells or contracts to sell goods.

(2) Other definitions applying to this Article or to specified Parts thereof, and the sections in which they appear are:
  "Acceptance". Section 2-606.
  "Banker's credit". Section 2-325.
  "Between merchants". Section 2-104.
  "Cancellation". Section 2-106(4).
  "Commercial unit". Section 2-105.
  "Confirmed credit". Section 2-325.
  "Conforming to contract". Section 2-106.
  "Contract for sale". Section 2-106.
  "Cover". Section 2-712.
  "Entrusting". Section 2-403.
  "Financing agency". Section 2-104.
  "Future goods". Section 2-105.
  "Goods". Section 2-105.
  "Identification". Section 2-501.
  "Installment contract". Section 2-612.
  "Letter of Credit". Section 2-325.
  "Lot". Section 2-105.
  "Merchant". Section 2-104.
  "Overseas". Section 2-323.
  "Person in position of seller". Section 2-707.

"Present sale". Section 2-106.
"Sale". Section 2-106.
"Sale on approval". Section 2-326.
"Sale or return". Section 2-326.
"Termination". Section 2-106.
  (3) The following definitions in other Articles apply to this Article:
"Check". Section 3-104.
"Consignee". Section 7-102.
"Consignor". Section 7-102.
"Consumer goods". Section 9-109.
"Dishonor". Section 3-507.
"Draft". Section 3-104.
  (4) In addition Article 1 contains general definitions and principles of construction and interpretation applicable throughout this Article.

§ 2-104. Definitions: "Merchant"; "Between Merchants"; "Financing Agency"

  (1) "Merchant" means a person who deals in goods of the kind or otherwise by his occupation holds himself out as having knowledge or skill peculiar to the practices or goods involved in the transaction or to whom such knowledge or skill may be attributed by his employment of an agent or broker or other intermediary who by his occupation holds himself out as having such knowledge or skill.

  (2) "Financing agency" means a bank, finance company or other person who in the ordinary course of business makes advances against goods or documents of title or who by arrangement with either the seller or the buyer intervenes in ordinary course to make or collect payment due or claimed under the contract for sale, as by purchasing or paying the seller's draft or making advances against it or by merely taking it for collection whether or not documents of title accompany the draft. "Financing agency" includes also a bank or other person who similarly intervenes between persons who are in the position of seller and buyer in respect to the goods (Section 2-707).

  (3) "Between merchants" means in any transaction with respect to which both parties are chargeable with the knowledge or skill of merchants.

§ 2-105. Definitions: Transferability; "Goods"; "Future" Goods; "Lot"; "Commercial Unit"

  (1) "Goods" means all things (including specially manufactured goods) which are movable at the time of identification to the contract for sale other than the money in which the price is to be paid, investment securities (Article 8) and things in action. "Goods" also includes the unborn young of animals and growing crops and other identified things attached to realty as described in the section on goods to be severed from realty (Section 2-107).

  (2) Goods must be both existing and identified before any interest in them can pass. Goods which are not both existing and identified are "future" goods. A purported present sale of future goods or of any interest therein operates as a contract to sell.

(3) There may be a sale of a part interest in existing identified goods.

(4) An undivided share in an identified bulk of fungible goods is sufficiently identified to be sold although the quantity of the bulk is not determined. Any agreed proportion of such a bulk or any quantity thereof agreed upon by number, weight or other measure may to the extent of the seller's interest in the bulk be sold to the buyer who then becomes an owner in common.

(5) "Lot" means a parcel or a single article which is the subject matter of a separate sale or delivery, whether or not it is sufficient to perform the contract.

(6) "Commercial unit" means such a unit of goods as by commercial usage is a single whole for purposes of sale and division of which materially impairs its character or value on the market or in use. A commercial unit may be a single article (as a machine) or a set of articles (as a suite of furniture or an assortment of sizes) or a quantity (as a bale, gross, or carload) or any other unit treated in use or in the relevant market as a single whole.

§ 2-106. Definitions: "Contract"; "Agreement"; "Contract for Sale"; "Sale"; "Present Sale"; "Conforming" to Contract; "Termination"; "Cancellation"

(1) In this Article unless the context otherwise requires "contract" and "agreement" are limited to those relating to the present or future sale of goods. "Contract for sale" includes both a present sale of goods and a contract to sell goods at a future time. A "sale" consists in the passing of title from the seller to the buyer for a price (Section 2-401). A "present sale" means a sale which is accomplished by the making of the contract.

(2) Goods or conduct including any part of a performance are "conforming" or conform to the contract when they are in accordance with the obligations under the contract.

(3) "Termination" occurs when either party pursuant to a power created by agreement or law puts an end to the contract otherwise than for its breach. On "termination" all obligations which are still executory on both sides are discharged but any right based on prior breach or performance survives.

(4) "Cancellation" occurs when either party puts an end to the contract for breach by the other and its effect is the same as that of "termination" except that the cancelling party also retains any remedy for breach of the whole contract or any unperformed balance.

§ 2-107. Goods to Be Severed From Realty: Recording

(1) A contract for the sale of minerals or the like (including oil and gas) or a structure or its materials to be removed from realty is a contract for the sale of goods within this Article if they are to be severed by the seller but until severance a purported present sale thereof which is not effective as a transfer of an interest in land is effective only as a contract to sell.

(2) A contract for the sale apart from the land of growing crops or other things attached to realty and capable of severance without material harm thereto but not described in subsection (1) or of timber to be cut is a contract for the sale of goods within this Article whether the subject matter is to be

severed by the buyer or by the seller even though it forms part of the realty at the time of contracting, and the parties can by identification effect a present sale before severance.

(3) The provisions of this section are subject to any third party rights provided by the law relating to realty records, and the contract for sale may be executed and recorded as a document transferring an interest in land and shall then constitute notice to third parties of the buyer's rights under the contract for sale.

As amended in 1972.

§ 2-201. Formal Requirements; Statute of Frauds

(1) Except as otherwise provided in this section a contract for the sale of goods for the price of $500 or more is not enforceable by way of action or defense unless there is some writing sufficient to indicate that a contract for sale has been made between the parties and signed by the party against whom enforcement is sought or by his authorized agent or broker. A writing is not insufficient because it omits or incorrectly states a term agreed upon but the contract is not enforceable under this paragraph beyond the quantity of goods shown in such writing.

(2) Between merchants if within a reasonable time a writing in confirmation of the contract and sufficient against the sender is received and the party receiving it has reason to know its contents, it satisfies the requirements of subsection (1) against such party unless written notice of objection to its contents is given within 10 days after it is received.

(3) A contract which does not satisfy the requirements of subsection (1) but which is valid in other respects is enforceable

  (a) if the goods are to be specially manufactured for the buyer and are not suitable for sale to others in the ordinary course of the seller's business and the seller, before notice of repudiation is received and under circumstances which reasonably indicate that the goods are for the buyer, has made either a substantial beginning of their manufacture or commitments for their procurement; or

  (b) if the party against whom enforcement is sought admits in his pleading, testimony or otherwise in court that a contract for sale was made, but the contract is not enforceable under this provision beyond the quantity of goods admitted; or

  (c) with respect to goods for which payment has been made and accepted or which have been received and accepted (Sec. 2-606).

§ 2-202. Final Written Expression: Parol or Extrinsic Evidence

Terms with respect to which the confirmatory memoranda of the parties agree or which are otherwise set forth in a writing intended by the parties as a final expression of their agreement with respect to such terms as are included therein may not be contradicted by evidence of any prior agreement or of a contemporaneous oral agreement but may be explained or supplemented

  (a) by course of dealing or usage of trade (Section 1-205) or by course of performance (Section 2-208); and

(b) by evidence of consistent additional terms unless the court finds the writing to have been intended also as a complete and exclusive statement of the terms of the agreement.

§ 2-203. Seals Inoperative

The affixing of a seal to a writing evidencing a contract for sale or an offer to buy or sell goods does not constitute the writing a sealed instrument and the law with respect to sealed instruments does not apply to such a contract or offer.

§ 2-204. Formation in General

(1) A contract for sale of goods may be made in any manner sufficient to show agreement, including conduct by both parties which recognizes the existence of such a contract.

(2) An agreement sufficient to constitute a contract for sale may be found even though the moment of its making is undetermined.

(3) Even though one or more terms are left open a contract for sale does not fail for indefiniteness if the parties have intended to make a contract and there is a reasonably certain basis for giving an appropriate remedy.

§ 2-205. Firm Offers

An offer by a merchant to buy or sell goods in a signed writing which by its terms gives assurance that it will be held open is not revocable, for lack of consideration, during the time stated or if no time is stated for a reasonable time, but in no event may such period of irrevocability exceed three months; but any such term of assurance on a form supplied by the offeree must be separately signed by the offeror.

§ 2-206. Offer and Acceptance in Formation of Contract

(1) Unless otherwise unambiguously indicated by the language or circumstances

(a) an offer to make a contract shall be construed as inviting acceptance in any manner and by any medium reasonable in the circumstances;

(b) an order or other offer to buy goods for prompt or current shipment shall be construed as inviting acceptance either by a prompt promise to ship or by the prompt or current shipment of conforming or non-conforming goods, but such a shipment of non-conforming goods does not constitute an acceptance if the seller seasonably notifies the buyer that the shipment is offered only as an accommodation to the buyer.

(2) Where the beginning of a requested performance is a reasonable mode of acceptance an offeror who is not notified of acceptance within a reasonable time may treat the offer as having lapsed before acceptance.

§ 2-207. Additional Terms in Acceptance or Confirmation

(1) A definite and seasonable expression of acceptance or a written confirmation which is sent within a reasonable time operates as an acceptance even though it states terms additional to or different from those offered or agreed upon, unless acceptance is expressly made conditional on assent to the additional different terms.

(2) The additional terms are to be construed as proposals for addition to the contract. Between merchants such terms become part of the contract unless:

    (a) the offer expressly limits acceptance to the terms of the offer;

    (b) they materially alter it; or

    (c) notification of objection to them has already been given or is given within a reasonable time after notice of them is received.

(3) Conduct by both parties which recognizes the existence of a contract is sufficient to establish a contract for sale although the writings of the parties do not otherwise establish a contract. In such case the terms of the particular contract consist of those terms on which the writings of the parties agree, together with any supplementary terms incorporated under any other provisions of this Act.

§ 2-208. Course of Performance or Practical Construction

(1) Where the contract for sale involves repeated occasions for performance by either party with knowledge of the nature of the performance and opportunity for objection to it by the other, any course of performance accepted or acquiesced in without objection shall be relevant to determine the meaning of the agreement.

(2) The express terms of the agreement and any such course of performance, as well as any course of dealing and usage of trade, shall be construed whenever reasonable as consistent with each other; but when such construction is unreasonable, express terms shall control course of performance and course of performance shall control both course of dealing and usage of trade (Section 1-205).

(3) Subject to the provisions of the next section on modification and waiver, such course of performance shall be relevant to show a waiver or modification of any term inconsistent with such course of performance.

§ 2-209. Modification, Rescission and Waiver

(1) An agreement modifying a contract within this Article needs no consideration to be binding.

(2) A signed agreement which excludes modification or rescission except by a signed writing cannot be otherwise modified or rescinded, but except as between merchants such a requirement on a form supplied by the merchant must be separately signed by the other party.

(3) The requirements of the statute of frauds section of this Article (Section 2-201) must be satisfied if the contract as modified is within its provisions.

(4) Although an attempt at modification or rescission does not satisfy the requirements of subsection (2) or (3) it can operate as a waiver.

(5) A party who has made a waiver affecting an executory portion of the contract may retract the waiver by reasonable notification received by the other party that strict performance will be required of any term waived, unless the retraction would be unjust in view of a material change of position in reliance on the waiver.

§ 2-210. Delegation of Performance; Assignment of Rights

(1) A party may perform his duty through a delegate unless otherwise agreed or unless the other party has a substantial interest in having his original promisor perform or control the acts required by the contract. No delegation of performance relieves the party delegating of any duty to perform or any liability for breach.

(2) Unless otherwise agreed all rights of either seller or buyer can be assigned except where the assignment would materially change the duty of the other party, or increase materially the burden or risk imposed on him by his contract, or impair materially his chance of obtaining return performance. A right to damages for breach of the whole contract or a right arising out of the assignor's due performance of his entire obligation can be assigned despite agreement otherwise.

(3) Unless the circumstances indicate the contrary a prohibition of assignment of "the contract" is to be construed as barring only the delegation to the assignee of the assignor's performance.

(4) An assignment of "the contract" or of "all my rights under the contract" or an assignment in similar general terms is an assignment of rights and unless the language or the circumstances (as in an assignment for security) indicate the contrary, it is a delegation of performance of the duties of the assignor and its acceptance by the assignee constitutes a promise by him to perform those duties. This promise is enforceable by either the assignor or the other party to the original contract.

(5) The other party may treat any assignment which delegates performance as creating reasonable grounds for insecurity and may without prejudice to his rights against the assignor demand assurances from the assignee (Section 2-609).

§ 2-301. General Obligations of Parties

The obligation of the seller is to transfer and deliver and that of the buyer is to accept and pay in accordance with the contract.

§ 2-302. Unconscionable Contract or Clause

(1) If the court as a matter of law finds the contract or any clause of the contract to have been unconscionable at the time it was made the court may refuse to enforce the contract, or it may enforce the remainder of the contract without the unconscionable clause, or it may so limit the application of any unconscionable clause as to avoid any unconscionable result.

(2) When it is claimed or appears to the court that the contract or any clause thereof may be unconscionable the parties shall be afforded a reason-

able opportunity to present evidence as to its commercial setting, purpose and effect to aid the court in making the determination.

§ 2-303. Allocation or Division of Risks

Where this Article allocates a risk or a burden as between the parties "unless otherwise agreed", the agreement may not only shift the allocation but may also divide the risk or burden.

§ 2-304. Price Payable in Money, Goods, Realty, or Otherwise

(1) The price can be made payable in money or otherwise. If it is payable in whole or in part in goods each party is a seller of the goods which he is to transfer.

(2) Even though all or part of the price is payable in an interest in realty the transfer of the goods and the seller's obligations with reference to them are subject to this Article, but not the transfer of the interest in realty or the transferor's obligations in connection therewith.

§ 2-305. Open Price Term

(1) The parties if they so intend can conclude a contract for sale even though the price is not settled. In such a case the price is a reasonable price at the time for delivery if

    (a) nothing is said as to price; or

    (b) the price is left to be agreed by the parties and they fail to agree; or

    (c) the price is to be fixed in terms of some agreed market or other standard as set or recorded by a third person or agency and it is not so set or recorded.

(2) A price to be fixed by the seller or by the buyer means a price for him to fix in good faith.

(3) When a price left to be fixed otherwise than by agreement of the parties fails to be fixed through fault of one party the other may at his option treat the contract as cancelled or himself fix a reasonable price.

(4) Where, however, the parties intend not to be bound unless the price be fixed or agreed and it is not fixed or agreed there is no contract. In such a case the buyer must return any goods already received or if unable so to do must pay their reasonable value at the time of delivery and the seller must return any portion of the price paid on account.

§ 2-306. Output, Requirements and Exclusive Dealings

(1) A term which measures the quantity by the output of the seller or the requirements of the buyer means such actual output or requirements as may occur in good faith, except that no quantity unreasonably disproportionate to any stated estimate or in the absence of a stated estimate to any normal or otherwise comparable prior output or requirements may be tendered or demanded.

(2) A lawful agreement by either the seller or the buyer for exclusive dealing in the kind of goods concerned imposes unless otherwise agreed an obliga-

tion by the seller to use best efforts to supply the goods and by the buyer to use best efforts to promote their sale.

§ 2-307. Delivery in Single Lot or Several Lots

Unless otherwise agreed all goods called for by a contract for sale must be tendered in a single delivery and payment is due only on such tender but where the circumstances give either party the right to make or demand delivery in lots the price if it can be apportioned may be demanded for each lot.

§ 2-308. Absence of Specified Place for Delivery

Unless otherwise agreed
- (a) the place for delivery of goods is the seller's place of business or if he has none his residence; but
- (b) in a contract for sale of identified goods which to the knowledge of the parties at the time of contracting are in some other place, that place is the place for their delivery; and
- (c) documents of title may be delivered through customary banking channels.

§ 2-309. Absence of Specific Time Provisions; Notice of Termination

(1) The time for shipment or delivery or any other action under a contract if not provided in this Article or agreed upon shall be a reasonable time.

(2) Where the contract provides for successive performances but is indefinite in duration it is valid for a reasonable time but unless otherwise agreed may be terminated at any time by either party.

(3) Termination of a contract by one party except on the happening of an agreed event requires that reasonable notification be received by the other party and an agreement dispensing with notification is invalid if its operation would be unconscionable.

§ 2-310. Open Time for Payment or Running of Credit; Authority to Ship Under Reservation

Unless otherwise agreed
- (a) payment is due at the time and place at which the buyer is to receive the goods even though the place of shipment is the place of delivery; and
- (b) if the seller is authorized to send the goods he may ship them under reservation, and may tender the documents of title, but the buyer may inspect the goods after their arrival before payment is due unless such inspection is inconsistent with the terms of the contract (Section 2-513); and
- (c) if delivery is authorized and made by way of documents of title otherwise than by subsection (b) then payment is due at the time and place at which the buyer is to receive the documents regardless of where the goods are to be received; and
- (d) where the seller is required or authorized to ship the goods on credit the credit period runs from the time of shipment but post-dating the

invoice or delaying its dispatch will correspondingly delay the starting of the credit period.

§ 2-311. Options and Cooperation Respecting Performance

(1) An agreement for sale which is otherwise sufficiently definite (subsection (3) of Section 2-204) to be a contract is not made invalid by the fact that it leaves particulars of performance to be specified by one of the parties. Any such specification must be made in good faith and within limits set by commercial reasonableness.

(2) Unless otherwise agreed specifications relating to assortment of the goods are at the buyer's option and except as otherwise provided in subsections (1) (c) and (3) of Section 2-319 specifications or arrangements relating to shipment are at the seller's option.

(3) Where such specification would materially affect the other party's performance but is not seasonably made or where one party's cooperation is necessary to the agreed performance of the other but is not seasonably forthcoming, the other party in addition to all other remedies

    (a) is excused for any resulting delay in his own performance; and

    (b) may also either proceed to perform in any reasonable manner or after the time for a material part of his own performance treat the failure to specify or to cooperate as a breach by failure to deliver or accept the goods.

§ 2-312. Warranty of Title and Against Infringement; Buyer's Obligation Against Infringement

(1) Subject to subsection (2) there is in a contract for sale a warranty by the seller that

    (a) the title conveyed shall be good, and its transfer rightful; and

    (b) the goods shall be delivered free from any security interest or other lien or encumbrance of which the buyer at the time of contracting has no knowledge.

(2) A warranty under subsection (1) will be excluded or modified only by specific language or by circumstances which give the buyer reason to know that the person selling does not claim title in himself or that he is purporting to sell only such right or title as he or a third person may have.

(3) Unless otherwise agreed a seller who is a merchant regularly dealing in goods of the kind warrants that the goods shall be delivered free of the rightful claim of any third person by way of infringement or the like but a buyer who furnishes specifications to the seller must hold the seller harmless against any such claim which arises out of compliance with the specifications.

§ 2-313. Express Warranties by Affirmation, Promise, Description, Sample

(1) Express warranties by the seller are created as follows:

(a) Any affirmation of fact or promise made by the seller to the buyer which relates to the goods and becomes part of the basis of the bargain creates an express warranty that the goods shall conform to the affirmation or promise.

(b) Any description of the goods which is made part of the basis of the bargain creates an express warranty that the goods shall conform to the description.

(c) Any sample or model which is made part of the basis of the bargain creates an express warranty that the whole of the goods shall conform to the sample or model.

(2) It is not necessary to the creation of an express warranty that the seller use formal words such as "warrant" or "guarantee" or that he have a specific intention to make a warranty, but an affirmation merely of the value of the goods or a statement purporting to be merely the seller's opinion or commendation of the goods does not create a warranty.

§ 2-314. Replied Warranty: Merchantability; Usage of Trade

(1) Unless excluded or modified (Section 2-316), a warranty that the goods shall be merchantable is implied in a contract for their sale if the seller is a merchant with respect to goods of that kind. Under this section the serving for value of food or drink to be consumed either on the premises or elsewhere is a sale.

(2) Goods to be merchantable must be at least such as

(a) pass without objection in the trade under the contract description; and

(b) in the case of fungible goods, are of fair average quality within the description; and

(c) are fit for the ordinary purposes for which such goods are used; and

(d) run, within the variations permitted by the agreement, of even kind, quality and quantity within each unit and among all units involved; and

(e) are adequately contained, packaged, and labeled as the agreement may require; and

(f) conform to the promises or affirmations of fact made on the container or label if any.

(3) Unless excluded or modified (Section 2-316) other implied warranties may arise from course of dealing or usage of trade.

§ 2-315. Implied Warranty: Fitness for Particular Purpose

Where the seller at the time of contracting has reason to know any particular purpose for which the goods are required and that the buyer is relying on the seller's skill or judgment to select or furnish suitable goods, there is unless excluded or modified under the next section an implied warranty that the goods shall be fit for such purpose.

§ 2-316. Exclusion or Modification of Warranties

(1) Words or conduct relevant to the creation of an express warranty and words or conduct tending to negate or limit warranty shall be construed wherever reasonable as consistent with each other; but subject to the provisions of this Article on parol or extrinsic evidence (Section 2-202) negation or limitation is inoperative to the extent that such construction is unreasonable.

(2) Subject to subsection (3), to exclude or modify the implied warranty of merchantability or any part of it the language must mention merchantability and in case of a writing must be conspicuous, and to exclude or modify any implied warranty of fitness the exclusion must be by a writing and conspicuous. Language to exclude all implied warranties of fitness is sufficient if it states, for example, that "There are no warranties which extend beyond the description on the face hereof."

(3) Notwithstanding subsection (2)

   (a) unless the circumstances indicate otherwise, all implied warranties are excluded by expressions like "as is", "with all faults" or other language which in common understanding calls the buyer's attention to the exclusion of warranties and makes plain that there is no implied warranty; and

   (b) when the buyer before entering into the contract has examined the goods or the sample or model as fully as he desired or has refused to examine the goods there is no implied warranty with regard to defects which an examination ought in the circumstances to have revealed to him; and

   (c) an implied warranty can also be excluded or modified by course of dealing or course of performance or usage of trade.

(4) Remedies for breach of warranty can be limited in accordance with the provisions of this Article on liquidation or limitation of damages and on contractual modification of remedy (Sections 2-718 and 2-719).

§ 2-317. Cumulation and Conflict of Warranties Express or Implied

Warranties whether express or implied shall be construed as consistent with each other and as cumulative, but if such construction is unreasonable the intention of the parties shall determine which warranty is dominant. In ascertaining that intention the following rules apply:

   (a) Exact or technical specifications displace an inconsistent sample or model or general language of description.

   (b) A sample from an existing bulk displaces inconsistent general language of description.

(c) Express warranties displace inconsistent implied warranties other than an implied warranty of fitness for a particular purpose.

§ 2-318. Third Party Beneficiaries of Warranties Express or Implied

Note: *If this Act is introduced in the Congress of the United States this section should be omitted.*

(States to select one alternative.)

Alternative A

A seller's warranty whether express or implied extends to any natural person who is in the family or household of his buyer or who is a guest in his home if it is reasonable to expect that such person may use, consume or be affected by the goods and who is injured in person by breach of the warranty. A seller may not exclude or limit the operation of this section.

Alternative B

A seller's warranty whether express or implied extends to any natural person who may reasonably be expected to use, consume or be affected by the goods and who is injured in person by breach of the warranty. A seller may not exclude or limit the operation of this section.

Alternative C

A seller's warranty whether express or implied extends to any person who may reasonably be expected to use, consume or be affected by the goods and who is injured by breach of the warranty. A seller may not exclude or limit the operation of this section with respect to injury to the person of an individual to whom the warranty extends.
As amended in 1966.

§ 2-319. F.O.B. and F.A.S. Terms

(1) Unless otherwise agreed the term F.O.B. (which means "free on board") at a named place, even though used only in connection with the stated price, is a delivery term under which
  (a) when the term is F.O.B. the place of shipment, the seller must at that place ship the goods in the manner provided in this Article (Section 2-504) and bear the expense and risk of putting them into the possession of the carrier; or
  (b) when the term is F.O.B. the place of destination, the seller must at his own expense and risk transport the goods to that place and there tender delivery of them in the manner provided in this Article (Section 2-503);
  (c) when under either (a) or (b) the term is also F.O.B. vessel, car or other vehicle, the seller must in addition at his own expense and risk load the goods on board. If the term is F.O.B. vessel the buyer must name the vessel and in an appropriate case the seller must comply with the provisions of this Article on the form of bill of lading (Section 2-323).

(2) Unless otherwise agreed the term F.A.S. vessel (which means "free alongside") at a named port, even though used only in connection with the stated price, is a delivery term under which the seller must

    (a) at his own expense and risk deliver the goods alongside the vessel in the manner usual in that port or on a dock designated and provided by the buyer; and

    (b) obtain and tender a receipt for the goods in exchange for which the carrier is under a duty to issue a bill of lading.

(3) Unless otherwise agreed in any case falling within subsection (1) (a) or (c) or subsection (2) the buyer must seasonably give any needed instructions for making delivery, including when the term is F.A.S. or F.O.B. the loading berth of the vessel and in an appropriate case its name and sailing date. The seller may treat the failure of needed instructions as a failure of cooperation under this Article (Section 2-311). He may also at his option move the goods in any reasonable manner preparatory to delivery or shipment.

(4) Under the term F.O.B. vessel or F.A.S. unless otherwise agreed the buyer must make payment against tender of the required documents and the seller may not tender nor the buyer demand delivery of the goods in substitution for the documents.

§ 2-320. C.I.F. and C. & F. Terms

(1) The term C.I.F. means that the price includes in a lump sum the cost of the goods and the insurance and freight to the named destination. The term C. & F. or C.F. means that the price so includes cost and freight to the named destination.

(2) Unless otherwise agreed and even though used only in connection with the stated price and destination, the term C.I.F. destination or its equivalent requires the seller at his own expense and risk to

    (a) put the goods into the possession of a carrier at the port for shipment and obtain a negotiable bill or bills of lading covering the entire transportation to the named destination; and

    (b) load the goods and obtain a receipt from the carrier (which may be contained in the bill of lading) showing that the freight has been paid or provided for; and

    (c) obtain a policy or certificate of insurance, including any war risk insurance, of a kind and on terms then current at the port of shipment in the usual amount, in the currency of the contract, shown to cover the same goods covered by the bill of lading and providing for payment of loss to the order of the buyer or for the account of whom it may concern; but the seller may add to the price the amount of the premium for any such war risk insurance; and

    (d) prepare an invoice of the goods and procure any other documents required to effect shipment or to comply with the contract; and

    (e) forward and tender with commercial promptness all the documents in due form and with any indorsement necessary to perfect the buyer's rights.

(3) Unless otherwise agreed the term C. & F. or its equivalent has the same effect and imposes upon the seller the same obligations and risks as a C.I.F. term except the obligation as to insurance.

(4) Under the term C.I.F. or C. & F. unless otherwise agreed the buyer must make payment against tender of the required documents and the seller may not tender nor the buyer demand delivery of the goods in substitution for the documents.

§ 2-321. C.I.F. or C. & F.: "Net Landed Weights"; "Payment on Arrival"; Warranty of Condition on Arrival

Under a contract containing a term C.I.F. or C. & F.

(1) Where the price is based on or is to be adjusted according to "net landed weights", "delivered weights", "out turn" quantity or quality or the like, unless otherwise agreed the seller must reasonably estimate the price. The payment due on tender of the documents called for by the contract is the amount so estimated, but after final adjustment of the price a settlement must be made with commercial promptness.

(2) An agreement described in subsection (1) or any warranty of quality or condition of the goods on arrival places upon the seller the risk of ordinary deterioration, shrinkage and the like in transportation but has no effect on the place or time of identification to the contract for sale or delivery or on the passing of the risk of loss.

(3) Unless otherwise agreed where the contract provides for payment on or after arrival of the goods the seller must before payment allow such preliminary inspection as is feasible; but if the goods are lost delivery of the documents and payment are due when the goods should have arrived.

§ 2-322. Delivery "Ex-Ship"

(1) Unless otherwise agreed a term for delivery of goods "ex-ship" (which means from the carrying vessel) or in equivalent language is not restricted to a particular ship and requires delivery from a ship which has reached a place at the named port of destination where goods of the kind are usually discharged.

(2) Under such a term unless otherwise agreed
  (a) the seller must discharge all liens arising out of the carriage and furnish the buyer with a direction which puts the carrier under a duty to deliver the goods; and
  (b) the risk of loss does not pass to the buyer until the goods leave the ship's tackle or are otherwise properly unloaded.

§ 2-323. Form of Bill of Lading Required in Overseas Shipment; "Overseas"

(1) Where the contract contemplates overseas shipment and contains a term C.I.F. or C. & F. or F.O.B. vessel, the seller unless otherwise agreed must obtain a negotiable bill of lading stating that the goods have been loaded on board or, in the case of a term C.I.F. or C. & F., received for shipment.

(2) Where in a case within subsection (1) a bill of lading has been issued in a set of parts, unless otherwise agreed if the documents are not to be sent from abroad the buyer may demand tender of the full set; otherwise only one part of the bill of lading need be tendered. Even if the agreement expressly requires a full set

    (a) due tender of a single part is acceptable within the provisions of this Article on cure of improper delivery (subsection (1) of Section 2-508); and

    (b) even though the full set is demanded, if the documents are sent from abroad the person tendering an incomplete set may nevertheless require payment upon furnishing an indemnity which the buyer in good faith deems adequate.

(3) A shipment by water or by air or a contract contemplating such shipment is "overseas" insofar as by usage of trade or agreement it is subject to the commercial, financing or shipping practices characteristic of international deep water commerce.

§ 2-324. "No Arrival, No Sale" Term

Under a term "no arrival, no sale" or terms of like meaning, unless otherwise agreed,

    (a) the seller must properly ship conforming goods and if they arrive by any means he must tender them on arrival but he assumes no obligation that the goods will arrive unless he has caused the non-arrival; and

    (b) where without fault of the seller the goods are in part lost or have so deteriorated as no longer to conform to the contract or arrive after the contract time, the buyer may proceed as if there had been casualty to identified goods (Section 2-613).

§ 2-325. "Letter of Credit" Term; "Confirmed Credit"

(1) Failure of the buyer seasonably to furnish an agreed letter of credit is a breach of the contract for sale.

(2) The delivery to seller of a proper letter of credit suspends the buyer's obligation to pay. If the letter of credit is dishonored, the seller may on seasonable notification to the buyer require payment directly from him.

(3) Unless otherwise agreed the term "letter of credit" or "banker's credit" in a contract for sale means an irrevocable credit issued by a financing agency of good repute and, where the shipment is overseas, of good international repute. The term "confirmed credit" means that the credit must also carry the direct obligation of such an agency which does business in the seller's financial market.

§ 2-326. Sale on Approval and Sale or Return; Consignment Sales and Rights of Creditors

(1) Unless otherwise agreed, if delivered goods may be returned by the buyer even though they conform to the contract, the transaction is

(a) a "sale on approval" if the goods are delivered primarily for use, and

(b) a "sale or return" if the goods are delivered primarily for resale.

(2) Except as provided in subsection (3), goods held on approval are not subject to the claims of the buyer's creditors until acceptance; goods held on sale or return are subject to such claims while in the buyer's possession.

(3) Where goods are delivered to a person for sale and such person maintains a place of business at which he deals in goods of the kind involved, under a name other than the name of the person making delivery, then with respect to claims of creditors of the person conducting the business the goods are deemed to be on sale or return. The provisions of this subsection are applicable even though an agreement purports to reserve title to the person making delivery until payment or resale or uses such words as "on consignment" or "on memorandum". However, this subsection is not applicable if the person making delivery

(a) complies with an applicable law providing for a consignor's interest or the like to be evidenced by a sign, or

(b) establishes that the person conducting the business is generally known by his creditors to be substantially engaged in selling the goods of others, or

(c) complies with the filing provisions of the Article on Secured Transactions (Article 9).

(4) Any "or return" term of a contract for sale is to be treated as a separate contract for sale within the statute of frauds section of this Article (Section 2-201) and as contradicting the sale aspect of the contract within the provisions of this Article on parol or extrinsic evidence (Section 2-202).

§ 2-327. Special Incidents of Sale on Approval and Sale or Return

(1) Under a sale on approval unless otherwise agreed

(a) although the goods are identified to the contract the risk of loss and the title do not pass to the buyer until acceptance; and

(b) use of the goods consistent with the purpose of trial is not acceptance but failure seasonably to notify the seller of election to return the goods is acceptance, and if the goods conform to the contract acceptance of any part is acceptance of the whole; and

(c) after due notification of election to return, the return is at the seller's risk and expense but a merchant buyer must follow any reasonable instructions.

(2) Under a sale or return unless otherwise agreed

(a) the option to return extends to the whole or any commercial unit of the goods while in substantially their original condition, but must be exercised seasonably; and

(b) the return is at the buyer's risk and expense.

§ 2-328. Sale by Auction

(1) In a sale by auction if goods are put up in lots each lot is the subject of a separate sale.

(2) A sale by auction is complete when the auctioneer so announces by the fall of the hammer or in other customary manner. Where a bid is made while the hammer is falling in acceptance of a prior bid the auctioneer may in his discretion reopen the bidding or declare the goods sold under the bid on which the hammer was falling.

(3) Such a sale is with reserve unless the goods are in explicit terms put up without reserve. In an auction with reserve the auctioneer may withdraw the goods at any time until he announces completion of the sale. In an auction without reserve, after the auctioneer calls for bids on an article or lot, that article or lot cannot be withdrawn unless no bid is made within a reasonable time. In either case a bidder may retract his bid until the auctioneer's announcement of completion of the sale, but a bidder's retraction does not revive any previous bid.

(4) If the auctioneer knowingly receives a bid on the seller's behalf or the seller makes or procures such a bid, and notice has not been given that liberty for such bidding is reserved, the buyer may at his option avoid the sale or take the goods at the price of the last good faith bid prior to the completion of the sale. This subsection shall not apply to any bid at a forced sale.

§ 2-401. Passing of Title; Reservation for Security; Limited Application of This Section

Each provision of this Article with regard to the rights, obligations and remedies of the seller, the buyer, purchasers or other third parties applies irrespective of title to the goods except where the provision refers to such title. Insofar as situations are not covered by the other provisions of this Article and matters concerning title become material the following rules apply:

(1) Title to goods cannot pass under a contract for sale prior to their identification to the contract (Section 2-501), and unless otherwise explicitly agreed the buyer acquires by their identification a special property as limited by this Act. Any retention or reservation by the seller of the title (property) in goods shipped or delivered to the buyer is limited in effect to a reservation of a security interest. Subject to these provisions and to the provisions of the Article on Secured Transactions (Article 9), title to goods passes from the seller to the buyer in any manner and on any conditions explicitly agreed on by the parties.

(2) Unless otherwise explicitly agreed title passes to the buyer at the time and place at which the seller completes his performance with reference to the physical delivery of the goods, despite any reservation of a security interest and even though a document of title is to be delivered at a different time or place; and in particular and despite any reservation of a security interest by the bill of lading

    (a) if the contract requires or authorizes the seller to send the goods to the buyer but does not require him to deliver them at destination, title passes to the buyer at the time and place of shipment; but

(b) if the contract requires delivery at destination, title passes on tender there.

(3) Unless otherwise explicitly agreed where delivery is to be made without moving the goods,

(a) if the seller is to deliver a document of title, title passes at the time when and the place where he delivers such documents; or

(b) if the goods are at the time of contracting already identified and no documents are to be delivered, title passes at the time and place of contracting.

(4) A rejection or other refusal by the buyer to receive or retain the goods, whether or not justified, or a justified revocation of acceptance revests title to the goods in the seller. Such revesting occurs by operation of law and is not a "sale".

§ 2-402. Rights of Seller's Creditors Against Sold Goods

(1) Except as provided in subsections (2) and (3), rights of unsecured creditors of the seller with respect to goods which have been identified to a contract for sale are subject to the buyer's rights to recover the goods under this Article (Sections 2-502 and 2-716).

(2) A creditor of the seller may treat a sale or an identification of goods to a contract for sale as void if as against him a retention of possession by the seller is fraudulent under any rule of law of the state where the goods are situated, except that retention of possession in good faith and current course of trade by a merchant-seller for a commercially reasonable time after a sale or identification is not fraudulent.

(3) Nothing in this Article shall be deemed to impair the rights of creditors of the seller

(a) under the provisions of the Article on Secured Transactions (Article 9); or

(b) where identification to the contract or delivery is made not in current course of trade but in satisfaction of or as security for a pre-existing claim for money, security or the like and is made under circumstances which under any rule of law of the state where the goods are situated would apart from this Article constitute the transaction a fraudulent transfer or voidable preference.

§ 2-403. Power to Transfer; Good Faith Purchase of Goods; "Entrusting"

(1) A purchaser of goods acquires all title which his transferor had or had power to transfer except that a purchaser of a limited interest acquires rights only to the extent of the interest purchased. A person with voidable title has power to transfer a good title to a good faith purchaser for value. When goods have been delivered under a transaction of purchase the purchaser has such power even though

(a) the transferor was deceived as to the identity of the purchaser, or

(b) the delivery was in exchange for a check which is later dishonored, or

(c) it was agreed that the transaction was to be a "cash sale", or

(d) the delivery was procured through fraud punishable as larcenous under the criminal law.

(2) Any entrusting of possession of goods to a merchant who deals in goods of that kind gives him power to transfer all rights of the entruster to a buyer in ordinary course of business.

(3) "Entrusting" includes any delivery and any acquiescence in retention of possession regardless of any condition expressed between the parties to the delivery or acquiescence and regardless of whether the procurement of the entrusting or the possessor's disposition of the goods have been such as to be larcenous under the criminal law.

(4) The rights of other purchasers of goods and of lien creditors are governed by the Articles on Secured Transactions (Article 9), Bulk Transfers (Article 6) and Documents of Title (Article 7).

§ 2-501. Insurable Interest in Goods; Manner of Identification of Goods

(1) The buyer obtains a special property and an insurable interest in goods by identification of existing goods as goods to which the contract refers even though the goods so identified are non-conforming and he has an option to return or reject them. Such identification can be made at any time and in any manner explicitly agreed to by the parties. In the absence of explicit agreement identification occurs

(a) when the contract is made if it is for the sale of goods already existing and identified;

(b) if the contract is for the sale of future goods other than those described in paragraph (c), when goods are shipped, marked or otherwise designated by the seller as goods to which the contract refers;

(c) when the crops are planted or otherwise become growing crops or the young are conceived if the contract is for the sale of unborn young to be born within twelve months after contracting or for the sale of crops to be harvested within twelve months or the next normal harvest season after contracting whichever is longer.

(2) The seller retains an insurable interest in goods so long as title to or any security interest in the goods remains in him and where the identification is by the seller alone he may until default or insolvency or notification to the buyer that the identification is final substitute other goods for those identified.

(3) Nothing in this section impairs any insurable interest recognized under any other statute or rule of law.

§ 2-502. Buyer's Right to Goods on Seller's Insolvency

(1) Subject to subsection (2) and even though the goods have not been shipped a buyer who has paid a part or all of the price of goods in which he has a special property under the provisions of the immediately preceding section may on making and keeping good a tender of any unpaid portion of their price recover them from the seller if the seller becomes insolvent within ten days after receipt of the first installment on their price.

(2) If the identification creating his special property has been made by the buyer he acquires the right to recover the goods only if they conform to the contract for sale.

§ 2-503. Manner of Seller's Tender of Delivery

(1) Tender of delivery requires that the seller put and hold conforming goods at the buyer's disposition and give the buyer any notification reasonably necessary to enable him to take delivery. The manner, time and place for tender are determined by the agreement and this Article, and in particular

    (a) tender must be at a reasonable hour, and if it is of goods they must be kept available for the period reasonably necessary to enable the buyer to take possession; but

    (b) unless otherwise agreed the buyer must furnish facilities reasonably suited to the receipt of the goods.

(2) Where the case is within the next section respecting shipment tender requires that the seller comply with its provisions.

(3) Where the seller is required to deliver at a particular destination tender requires that he comply with subsection (1) and also in any appropriate case tender documents as described in subsections (4) and (5) of this section.

(4) Where goods are in the possession of a bailee and are to be delivered without being moved

    (a) tender requires that the seller either tender a negotiable document of title covering such goods or procure acknowledgment by the bailee of the buyer's right to possession of the goods; but

    (b) tender to the buyer of a non-negotiable document of title or of a written direction to the bailee to deliver is sufficient tender unless the buyer seasonably objects, and receipt by the bailee of notification of the buyer's rights fixes those rights as against the bailee and all third persons; but risk of loss of the goods and of any failure by the bailee to honor the non-negotiable document of title or to obey the direction remains on the seller until the buyer has had a reasonable time to present the document or direction, and a refusal by the bailee to honor the document or to obey the direction defeats the tender.

(5) Where the contract requires the seller to deliver documents

    (a) he must tender all such documents in correct form, except as provided in this Article with respect to bills of lading in a set (subsection (2) of Section 2-323); and

    (b) tender through customary banking channels is sufficient and dishonor of a draft accompanying the documents constitutes non-acceptance or rejection.

§ 2-504. Shipment by Seller

Where the seller is required or authorized to send the goods to the buyer and the contract does not require him to deliver them at a particular destination, then unless otherwise agreed he must
  (a) put the goods in the possession of such a carrier and make such a contract for their transportation as may be reasonable having regard to the nature of the goods and other circumstances of the case; and
  (b) obtain and promptly deliver or tender in due form any document necessary to enable the buyer to obtain possession of the goods or otherwise required by the agreement or by usage of trade; and
  (c) promptly notify the buyer of the shipment.
Failure to notify the buyer under paragraph (c) or to make a proper contract under paragraph (a) is a ground for rejection only if material delay or loss ensues.

§ 2-505. Seller's Shipment Under Reservation

(1) Where the seller has identified goods to the contract by or before shipment:
  (a) his procurement of a negotiable bill of lading to his own order or otherwise reserves in him a security interest in the goods. His procurement of the bill to the order of a financing agency or of the buyer indicates in addition only the seller's expectation of transferring that interest to the person named.
  (b) a non-negotiable bill of lading to himself or his nominee reserves possession of the goods as security but except in a case of conditional delivery (subsection (2) of Section 2-507) a non-negotiable bill of lading naming the buyer as consignee reserves no security interest even though the seller retains possession of the bill of lading.
(2) When shipment by the seller with reservation of a security interest is in violation of the contract for sale it constitutes an improper contract for transportation within the preceding section but impairs neither the rights given to the buyer by shipment and identification of the goods to the contract nor the seller's powers as a holder of a negotiable document.

§ 2-506. Rights of Financing Agency

(1) A financing agency by paying or purchasing for value a draft which relates to a shipment of goods acquires to the extent of the payment or purchase and in addition to its own rights under the draft and any document of title securing it any rights of the shipper in the goods including the right to stop delivery and the shipper's right to have the draft honored by the buyer.

(2) The right to reimbursement of a financing agency which has in good faith honored or purchased the draft under commitment to or authority from the buyer is not impaired by subsequent discovery of defects with reference to any relevant document which was apparently regular on its face.

§ 2-507. Effect of Seller's Tender; Delivery on Condition

(1) Tender of delivery is a condition to the buyer's duty to accept the goods and, unless otherwise agreed, to his duty to pay for them. Tender entitles the seller to acceptance of the goods and to payment according to the contract.

(2) Where payment is due and demanded on the delivery to the buyer of goods or documents of title, his right as against the seller to retain or dispose of them is conditional upon his making the payment due.

§ 2-508. Cure by Seller of Improper Tender or Delivery; Replacement

(1) Where any tender or delivery by the seller is rejected because non-conforming and the time for performance has not yet expired, the seller may seasonably notify the buyer of his intention to cure and may then within the contract time make a conforming delivery.

(2) Where the buyer rejects a non-conforming tender which the seller had reasonable grounds to believe would be acceptable with or without money allowance the seller may if he seasonably notifies the buyer have a further reasonable time to substitute a conforming tender.

§ 2-509. Risk of Loss in the Absence of Breach

(1) Where the contract requires or authorizes the seller to ship the goods by carrier
   (a) if it does not require him to deliver them at a particular destination, the risk of loss passes to the buyer when the goods are duly delivered to the carrier even though the shipment is under reservation (Section 2-505); but
   (b) if it does require him to deliver them at a particular destination and the goods are there duly tendered while in the possession of the carrier, the risk of loss passes to the buyer when the goods are there duly so tendered as to enable the buyer to take delivery.

(2) Where the goods are held by a bailee to be delivered without being moved, the risk of loss passes to the buyer
   (a) on his receipt of a negotiable document of title covering the goods; or
   (b) on acknowledgment by the bailee of the buyer's right to possession of the goods; or
   (c) after his receipt of a non-negotiable document of title or other written direction to deliver, as provided in subsection (4) (b) of Section 2-503.

(3) In any case not within subsection (1) or (2), the risk of loss passes to the buyer on his receipt of the goods if the seller is a merchant; otherwise the risk passes to the buyer on tender of delivery.

(4) The provisions of this section are subject to contrary agreement of the parties and to the provisions of this Article on sale on approval (Section 2-327) and on effect of breach on risk of loss (Section 2-510).

§ 2-510. Effect of Breach on Risk of Loss

(1) Where a tender or delivery of goods so fails to conform to the contract as to give a right of rejection the risk of their loss remains on the seller until cure or acceptance.

(2) Where the buyer rightfully revokes acceptance he may to the extent of any deficiency in his effective insurance coverage treat the risk of loss as having rested on the seller from the beginning.

(3) Where the buyer as to conforming goods already identified to the contract for sale repudiates or is otherwise in breach before risk of their loss has passed to him, the seller may to the extent of any deficiency in his effective insurance coverage treat the risk of loss as resting on the buyer for a commercially reasonable time.

§ 2-511. Tender of Payment by Buyer; Payment by Check

(1) Unless otherwise agreed tender of payment is a condition to the seller's duty to tender and complete any delivery.

(2) Tender of payment is sufficient when made by any means or in any manner current in the ordinary course of business unless the seller demands payment in legal tender and gives any extension of time reasonably necessary to procure it.

(3) Subject to the provisions of this Act on the effect of an instrument on an obligation (Section 3-802), payment by check is conditional and is defeated as between the parties by dishonor of the check on due presentment.

§ 2-512. Payment by Buyer Before Inspection

(1) Where the contract requires payment before inspection non-conformity of the goods does not excuse the buyer from so making payment unless
   (a) the non-conformity appears without inspection; or
   (b) despite tender of the required documents the circumstances would justify injunction against honor under the provisions of this Act (Section 5-114).

(2) Payment pursuant to subsection (1) does not constitute an acceptance of goods or impair the buyer's right to inspect or any of his remedies.

§ 2-513. Buyer's Right to Inspection of Goods

(1) Unless otherwise agreed and subject to subsection (3), where goods are tendered or delivered or identified to the contract for sale, the buyer has a right before payment or acceptance to inspect them at any reasonable place and time and in any reasonable manner. When the seller is required or authorized to send the goods to the buyer, the inspection may be after their arrival.

(2) Expenses of inspection must be borne by the buyer but may be recovered from the seller if the goods do not conform and are rejected.

(3) Unless otherwise agreed and subject to the provisions of this Article on C.I.F. contracts (subsection (3) of Section 2-321), the buyer is not entitled to inspect the goods before payment of the price when the contract provides
   (a) for delivery "C.O.D." or on other like terms; or

(b) for payment against documents of title, except where such payment is due only after the goods are to become available for inspection.

(4) A place or method of inspection fixed by the parties is presumed to be exclusive but unless otherwise expressly agreed it does not postpone identification or shift the place for delivery or for passing the risk of loss. If compliance becomes impossible, inspection shall be as provided in this section unless the place or method fixed was clearly intended as an indispensable condition failure of which avoids the contract.

§ 2-514. When Documents Deliverable on Acceptance; When on Payment

Unless otherwise agreed documents against which a draft is drawn are to be delivered to the drawee on acceptance of the draft if it is payable more than three days after presentment; otherwise, only on payment.

§ 2-515. Preserving Evidence of Goods in Dispute

In furtherance of the adjustment of any claim or dispute
   (a) either party on reasonable notification to the other and for the purpose of ascertaining the facts and preserving evidence has the right to inspect, test and sample the goods including such of them as may be in the possession or control of the other; and
   (b) the parties may agree to a third party inspection or survey to determine the conformity or condition of the goods and may agree that the findings shall be binding upon them in any subsequent litigation or adjustment.

§ 2-601. Buyer's Rights on Improper Delivery

Subject to the provisions of this Article on breach in installment contracts (Section 2-612) and unless otherwise agreed under the sections on contractual limitations of remedy (Sections 2-718 and 2-719), if the goods or the tender of delivery fail in any respect to conform to the contract, the buyer may
   (a) reject the whole; or
   (b) accept the whole; or
   (c) accept any commercial unit or units and reject the rest.

§ 2-602. Manner and Effect of Rightful Rejection

(1) Rejection of goods must be within a reasonable time after their delivery or tender. It is ineffective unless the buyer seasonably notifies the seller.

(2) Subject to the provisions of the two following sections on rejected goods (Sections 2-603 and 2-604),
   (a) after rejection any exercise of ownership by the buyer with respect to any commercial unit is wrongful as against the seller; and
   (b) if the buyer has before rejection taken physical possession of goods in which he does not have a security interest under the provisions of this Article (subsection (3) of Section 2-711), he is under a duty after rejec-

tion to hold them with reasonable care at the seller's disposition for a
time sufficient to permit the seller to remove them; but

(c) the buyer has no further obligations with regard to goods rightfully
rejected.

(3) The seller's rights with respect to goods wrongfully rejected are governed by the provisions of this Article on Seller's remedies in general (Section 2-703).

§ 2-603. Merchant Buyer's Duties as to Rightfully Rejected Goods

(1) Subject to any security interest in the buyer (subsection (3) of Section 2-711), when the seller has no agent or place of business at the market of rejection a merchant buyer is under a duty after rejection of goods in his possession or control to follow any reasonable instructions received from the seller with respect to the goods and in the absence of such instructions to make reasonable efforts to sell them for the seller's account if they are perishable or threaten to decline in value speedily. Instructions are not reasonable if on demand indemnity for expenses is not forthcoming.

(2) When the buyer sells goods under subsection (1), he is entitled to reimbursement from the seller or out of the proceeds for reasonable expenses of caring for and selling them, and if the expenses include no selling commission then to such commission as is usual in the trade or if there is none to a reasonable sum not exceeding ten per cent on the gross proceeds.

(3) In complying with this section the buyer is held only to good faith and good faith conduct hereunder is neither acceptance nor conversion nor the basis of an action for damages.

§ 2-604. Buyer's Options as to Salvage of Rightfully Rejected Goods

Subject to the provisions of the immediately preceding section on perishables if the seller gives no instructions within a reasonable time after notification of rejection the buyer may store the rejected goods for the seller's account or reship them to him or resell them for the seller's account with reimbursement as provided in the preceding section. Such action is not acceptance or conversion.

§ 2-605. Waiver of Buyer's Objections by Failure to Particularize

(1) The buyer's failure to state in connection with rejection a particular defect which is ascertainable by reasonable inspection precludes him from relying on the unstated defect to justify rejection or to establish breach

(a) where the seller could have cured it if stated seasonably; or

(b) between merchants when the seller has after rejection made a request in writing for a full and final written statement of all defects on which the buyer proposes to rely.

(2) Payment against documents made without reservation of rights precludes recovery of the payment for defects apparent on the face of the documents.

§ 2-606. What Constitutes Acceptance of Goods

(1) Acceptance of goods occurs when the buyer
   (a) after a reasonable opportunity to inspect the goods signifies to the seller that the goods are conforming or that he will take or retain them in spite of their non-conformity; or
   (b) fails to make an effective rejection (subsection (1) of Section 2-602), but such acceptance does not occur until the buyer has had a reasonable opportunity to inspect them; or
   (c) does any act inconsistent with the seller's ownership; but if such act is wrongful as against the seller it is an acceptance only if ratified by him.

(2) Acceptance of a part of any commercial unit is acceptance of that entire unit.

§ 2-607. Effect of Acceptance; Notice of Breach; Burden of Establishing Breach After Acceptance; Notice of Claim or Litigation to Person Answerable Over

(1) The buyer must pay at the contract rate for any goods accepted.

(2) Acceptance of goods by the buyer precludes rejection of the goods accepted and if made with knowledge of a non-conformity cannot be revoked because of it unless the acceptance was on the reasonable assumption that the non-conformity would be seasonably cured but acceptance does not of itself impair any other remedy provided by this Article for non-conformity.

(3) Where a tender has been accepted
   (a) the buyer must within a reasonable time after he discovers or should have discovered any breach notify the seller of breach or be barred from any remedy; and
   (b) if the claim is one for infringement or the like (subsection (3) of Section 2-312) and the buyer is sued as a result of such a breach he must so notify the seller within a reasonable time after he receives notice of the litigation or be barred from any remedy over for liability established by the litigation.

(4) The burden is on the buyer to establish any breach with respect to the goods accepted.

(5) Where the buyer is sued for breach of a warranty or other obligation for which his seller is answerable over
   (a) he may give his seller written notice of the litigation. If the notice states that the seller may come in and defend and that if the seller does not do so he will be bound in any action against him by his buyer by any determination of fact common to the two litigations, then unless the seller after seasonable receipt of the notice does come in and defend he is so bound.
   (b) if the claim is one for infringement or the like (subsection (3) of Section 2-312) the original seller may demand in writing that his buyer turn over to him control of the litigation including settlement or else be barred from any remedy over and if he also agrees to bear all expense and to satisfy any adverse judgment, then unless the buyer

after seasonable receipt of the demand does turn over control the buyer is so barred.

(6) The provisions of subsections (3), (4) and (5) apply to any obligation of a buyer to hold the seller harmless against infringement or the like (subsection (3) of Section 2-312).

§ 2-608. Revocation of Acceptance in Whole or in Part

(1) The buyer may revoke his acceptance of a lot or commercial unit whose non-conformity substantially impairs its value to him if he has accepted it
  (a) on the reasonable assumption that its non-conformity would be cured and it has not been seasonably cured; or
  (b) without discovery of such non-conformity if his acceptance was reasonably induced either by the difficulty of discovery before acceptance or by the seller's assurances.

(2) Revocation of acceptance must occur within a reasonable time after the buyer discovers or should have discovered the ground for it and before any substantial change in condition of the goods which is not caused by their own defects. It is not effective until the buyer notifies the seller of it.

(3) A buyer who so revokes has the same rights and duties with regard to the goods involved as if he had rejected them.

§ 2-609. Right to Adequate Assurance of Performance

(1) A contract for sale imposes an obligation on each party that the other's expectation of receiving due performance will not be impaired. When reasonable grounds for insecurity arise with respect to the performance of either party the other may in writing demand adequate assurance of due performance and until he receives such assurance may if commercially reasonable suspend any performance for which he has not already received the agreed return.

(2) Between merchants the reasonableness of grounds for insecurity and the adequacy of any assurance offered shall be determined according to commercial standards.

(3) Acceptance of any improper delivery or payment does not prejudice the aggrieved party's right to demand adequate assurance of future performance.

(3) After receipt of a justified demand failure to provide within a reasonable time not exceeding thirty days such assurance of due performance as is adequate under the circumstances of the particular case is a repudiation of the contract.

§ 2-610. Anticipatory Repudiation

When either party repudiates the contract with respect to a performance not yet due the loss of which will substantially impair the value of the contract to the other, the aggrieved party may
  (a) for a commercially reasonable time await performance by the repudiating party; or

(b) resort to any remedy for breach (Section 2-703 or Section 2-711), even though he has notified the repudiating party that he would await the latter's performance and has urged retraction; and

(c) in either case suspend his own performance or proceed in accordance with the provisions of this Article on the seller's right to identify goods to the contract notwithstanding breach or to salvage unfinished goods (Section 2-704).

§ 2-611. Retraction of Anticipatory Repudiation

(1) Until the repudiating party's next performance is due he can retract his repudiation unless the aggrieved party has since the repudiation cancelled or materially changed his position or otherwise indicated that he considers the repudiation final.

(2) Retraction may be by any method which clearly indicates to the aggrieved party that the repudiating party intends to perform, but must include any assurance justifiably demanded under the provisions of this Article (Section 2-609).

(3) Retraction reinstates the repudiating party's rights under the contract with due excuse and allowance to the aggrieved party for any delay occasioned by the repudiation.

§ 2-612. "Installment Contract"; Breach

(1) An "installment contract" is one which requires or authorizes the delivery of goods in separate lots to be separately accepted, even though the contract contains a clause "each delivery is a separate contract" or its equivalent.

(2) The buyer may reject any installment which is non-conforming if the non-conformity substantially impairs the value of that installment and cannot be cured or if the non-conformity is a defect in the required documents; but if the non-conformity does not fall within subsection (3) and the seller gives adequate assurance of its cure the buyer must accept that installment.

(3) Whenever non-conformity or default with respect to one or more installments substantially impairs the value of the whole contract there is a breach of the whole. But the aggrieved party reinstates the contract if he accepts a non-conforming installment without seasonably notifying of cancellation or if he brings an action with respect only to past installments or demands performance as to future installments.

§ 2-613. Casualty to Identified Goods

Where the contract requires for its performance goods identified when the contract is made, and the goods suffer casualty without fault of either party before the risk of loss passes to the buyer, or in a proper case under a "no arrival, no sale" term (Section 2-324) then

(a) if the loss is total the contract is avoided; and

(b) if the loss is partial or the goods have so deteriorated as no longer to conform to the contract the buyer may nevertheless demand inspection and at his option either treat the contract as avoided or accept the goods with due allowance from the contract price for the deterioration or the deficiency in quantity but without further right against the seller.

§ 2-614. Substituted Performance

(1) Where without fault of either party the agreed berthing, loading, or unloading facilities fail or an agreed type of carrier becomes unavailable or the agreed manner of delivery otherwise becomes commercially impracticable but a commercially reasonable substitute is available, such substitute performance must be tendered and accepted.

(2) If the agreed means or manner of payment fails because of domestic or foreign governmental regulation, the seller may withhold or stop delivery unless the buyer provides a means or manner of payment which is commercially a substantial equivalent. If delivery has already been taken, payment by the means or in the manner provided by the regulation discharges the buyer's obligation unless the regulation is discriminatory, oppressive or predatory.

§ 2-615. Excuse by Failure of Presupposed Conditions

Except so far as a seller may have assumed a greater obligation and subject to the preceding section on substituted performance:
  (a) Delay in delivery or non-delivery in whole or in part by a seller who complies with paragraphs (b) and (c) is not a breach of his duty under a contract for sale if performance as agreed has been made impracticable by the occurrence of a contingency the non-occurrence of which was a basic assumption on which the contract was made or by compliance in good faith with any applicable foreign or domestic governmental regulation or order whether or not it later proves to be invalid.
  (b) Where the causes mentioned in paragraph (a) affect only a part of the seller's capacity to perform, he must allocate production and deliveries among his customers but may at his option include regular customers not then under contract as well as his own requirements for further manufacture. He may so allocate in any manner which is fair and reasonable.
  (c) The seller must notify the buyer seasonably that there will be delay or non-delivery and, when allocation is required under paragraph (b), of the estimated quota thus made available for the buyer.

§ 2-616. Procedure on Notice Claiming Excuse

(1) Where the buyer receives notification of a material or indefinite delay or an allocation justified under the preceding section he may by written notification to the seller as to any delivery concerned, and where the prospective deficiency substantially impairs the value of the whole contract under the provisions of this Article relating to breach of installment contracts (Section 2-612), then also as to the whole,
  (a) terminate and thereby discharge any unexecuted portion of the contract; or

(b) modify the contract by agreeing to take his available quota in substitution.

(2) If after receipt of such notification from the seller the buyer fails so to modify the contract within a reasonable time not exceeding thirty days the contract lapses with respect to any deliveries affected.

(3) The provisions of this section may not be negated by agreement except in so far as the seller has assumed a greater obligation under the preceding section.

§ 2-701. Remedies for Breach of Collateral Contracts Not Impaired

Remedies for breach of any obligation or promise collateral or ancillary to a contract for sale are not impaired by the provisions of this Article.

§ 2-702. Seller's Remedies on Discovery of Buyer's Insolvency

(1) Where the seller discovers the buyer to be insolvent he may refuse delivery except for cash including payment for all goods theretofore delivered under the contract, and stop delivery under this Article (Section 2-705).

(2) Where the seller discovers that the buyer has received goods on credit while insolvent he may reclaim the goods upon demand made within ten days after the receipt, but if misrepresentation of solvency has been made to the particular seller in writing within three months before delivery the ten day limitation does not apply. Except as provided in this subsection the seller may not base a right to reclaim goods on the buyer's fraudulent or innocent misrepresentation of solvency or of intent to pay.

(3) The seller's right to reclaim under subsection (2) is subject to the rights of a buyer in ordinary course or other good faith purchaser under this Article (Section 2-403). Successful reclamation of goods excludes all other remedies with respect to them.
As amended in 1966.

§ 2-703. Seller's Remedies in General

Where the buyer wrongfully rejects or revokes acceptance of goods or fails to make a payment due on or before delivery or repudiates with respect to a part or the whole, then with respect to any goods directly affected and, if the breach is of the whole contract (Section 2-612), then also with respect to the whole undelivered balance, the aggrieved seller may

    (a) withhold delivery of such goods;

    (b) stop delivery by any bailee as hereafter provided (Section 2-705);

    (c) proceed under the next section respecting goods still unidentified to the contract;

    (d) resell and recover damages as hereafter provided (Section 2-706);

    (e) recover damages for non-acceptance (Section 2-708) or in a proper case the price (Section 2-709);

    (f) cancel.

§ 2-704. Seller's Right to Identify Goods to the Contract Notwithstanding Breach or to Salvage Unfinished Goods

(1) An aggrieved seller under the preceding section may
    (a) identify to the contract conforming goods not already identified if at the time he learned of the breach they are in his possession or control;
    (b) treat as the subject of resale goods which have demonstrably been intended for the particular contract even though those goods are unfinished.

(2) Where the goods are unfinished an aggrieved seller may in the exercise of reasonable commercial judgment for the purposes of avoiding loss and of effective realization either complete the manufacture and wholly identify the goods to the contract or cease manufacture and resell for scrap or salvage value or proceed in any other reasonable manner.

§ 2-705. Seller's Stoppage of Delivery in Transit or Otherwise

(1) The seller may stop delivery of goods in the possession of a carrier or other bailee when he discovers the buyer to be insolvent (Section 2-702) and may stop delivery of carload, truckload, planeload or larger shipments of express or freight when the buyer repudiates or fails to make a payment due before delivery or if for any other reason the seller has a right to withhold or reclaim the goods.

(2) As against such buyer the seller may stop delivery until
    (a) receipt of the goods by the buyer; or
    (b) acknowledgment to the buyer by any bailee of the goods except a carrier that the bailee holds the goods for the buyer; or
    (c) such acknowledgment to the buyer by a carrier by reshipment or as warehouseman; or
    (d) negotiation to the buyer of any negotiable document of title covering the goods.

(3) (a) To stop delivery the seller must so notify as to enable the bailee by reasonable diligence to prevent delivery of the goods.
    (b) After such notification the bailee must hold and deliver the goods according to the directions of the seller but the seller is liable to the bailee for any ensuing charges or damages.
    (c) If a negotiable document of title has been issued for goods the bailee is not obliged to obey a notification to stop until surrender of the document.
    (d) A carrier who has issued a non-negotiable bill of lading is not obliged to obey a notification to stop received from a person other than the consignor.

§ 2-706. Seller's Resale Including Contract for Resale

(1) Under the conditions stated in Section 2-703 on seller's remedies, the seller may resell the goods concerned or the undelivered balance thereof. Where the resale is made in good faith and in a commercially reasonable manner the seller may recover the difference between the resale price and the contract price together with any incidental damages allowed under the provisions of this Article (Section 2-710), but less expenses saved in consequence of the buyer's breach.

(2) Except as otherwise provided in subsection (3) or unless otherwise agreed resale may be at public or private sale including sale by way of one or more contracts to sell or of identification to an existing contract of the seller. Sale may be as a unit or in parcels and at any time and place and on any terms but every aspect of the sale including the method, manner, time, place and terms must be commercially reasonable. The resale must be reasonably identified as referring to the broken contract, but it is not necessary that the goods be in existence or that any or all of them have been identified to the contract before the breach.

(3) Where the resale is at private sale the seller must give the buyer reasonable notification of his intention to resell.

(4) Where the resale is at public sale

   (a) only identified goods can be sold except where there is a recognized market for a public sale of futures in goods of the kind; and

   (b) it must be made at a usual place or market for public sale if one is reasonably available and except in the case of goods which are perishable or threaten to decline in value speedily the seller must give the buyer reasonable notice of the time and place of the resale; and

   (c) if the goods are not to be within the view of those attending the sale the notification of sale must state the place where the goods are located and provide for their reasonable inspection by prospective bidders; and

   (d) the seller may buy.

(5) A purchaser who buys in good faith at a resale takes the goods free of any rights of the original buyer even though the seller fails to comply with one or more of the requirements of this section.

(6) The seller is not accountable to the buyer for any profit made on any resale. A person in the position of a seller (Section 2-707) or a buyer who has rightfully rejected or justifiably revoked acceptance must account for any excess over the amount of his security interest, as hereinafter defined (subsection (3) of Section 2-711).

§ 2-707. "Person in the Position of a Seller"

(1) A "person in the position of a seller" includes as against a principal an agent who has paid or become responsible for the price of goods on behalf of his principal or anyone who otherwise holds a security interest or other right in goods similar to that of a seller.

(2) A person in the position of a seller may as provided in this Article withhold or stop delivery (Section 2-705) and resell (Section 2-706) and recover incidental damages (Section 2-710).

§ 2-708. Seller's Damages for Non-acceptance or Repudiation

(1) Subject to subsection (2) and to the provisions of this Article with respect to proof of market price (Section 2-723), the measure of damages for non-acceptance or repudiation by the buyer is the difference between the market price at the time and place for tender and the unpaid contract price together with any incidental damages provided in this Article (Section 2-710), but less expenses saved in consequence of the buyer's breach.

(2) If the measure of damages provided in subsection (1) is inadequate to put the seller in as good a position as performance would have done then the measure of damages is the profit (including reasonable overhead) which the seller would have made from full performance by the buyer, together with any incidental damages provided in this Article (Section 2-710), due allowance for costs reasonably incurred and due credit for payments or proceeds of resale.

§ 2-709. Action for the Price

(1) When the buyer fails to pay the price as it becomes due the seller may recover, together with any incidental damages under the next section, the price

(a) of goods accepted or of conforming goods lost or damaged within a commercially reasonably time after risk of their loss has passed to the buyer; and

(b) of goods identified to the contract if the seller is unable after reasonable effort to resell them at a reasonable price or the circumstances reasonably indicate that such effort will be unavailing.

(2) Where the seller sues for the price he must hold for the buyer any goods which have been identified to the contract and are still in his control except that if resale becomes possible he may resell them at any time prior to the collection of the judgment. The net proceeds of any such resale must be credited to the buyer and payment of the judgment entitles him to any goods not resold.

(3) After the buyer has wrongfully rejected or revoked acceptance of the goods or has failed to make a payment due or has repudiated (Section 2-610), a seller who is held not entitled to the price under this section shall nevertheless be awarded damages for non-acceptance under the preceding section.

§ 2-710. Seller's Incidental Damages

Incidental damages to an aggrieved seller include any commercially reasonable charges, expenses or commissions incurred in stopping delivery, in the transportation, care and custody of goods after the buyer's breach, in connection with return or resale of the goods or otherwise resulting from the breach.

§ 2-711. Buyer's Remedies in General; Buyer's Security Interest in Rejected Goods

(1) Where the seller fails to make delivery or repudiates or the buyer rightfully rejects or justifiably revokes acceptance then with respect to any goods involved, and with respect to the whole if the breach goes to the whole contract (Section 2-612), the buyer may cancel and whether or not he has done so may in addition to recovering so much of the price as has been paid

    (a) "cover" and have damages under the next section as to all the goods affected whether or not they have been identified to the contract; or

    (b) recover damages for non-delivery as provided in this Article (Section 2-713).

(2) Where the seller fails to deliver or repudiates the buyer may also

    (a) if the goods have been identified recover them as provided in this Article (Section 2-502); or

    (b) in a proper case obtain specific performance or replevy the goods as provided in this Article (Section 2-716).

(3) On rightful rejection or justifiable revocation of acceptance a buyer has a security interest in goods in his possession or control for any payments made on their price and any expenses reasonably incurred in their inspection, receipt, transportation, care and custody and may hold such goods and resell them in like manner as an aggrieved seller (Section 2-706).

§ 2-712. "Cover"; Buyer's Procurement of Substitute Goods

(1) After a breach within the preceding section the buyer may "cover" by making in good faith and without unreasonable delay any reasonable purchase of or contract to purchase goods in substitution for those due from the seller.

(2) The buyer may recover from the seller as damages the difference between the cost of cover and the contract price together with any incidental or consequential damages as hereinafter defined (Section 2-715), but less expenses saved in consequence of the seller's breach.

(3) Failure of the buyer to effect cover within this section does not bar him from any other remedy.

§ 2-713. Buyer's Damages for Non-Delivery or Repudiation

(1) Subject to the provisions of this Article with respect to proof of market price (Section 2-723), the measure of damages for non-delivery or repudiation by the seller is the difference between the market price at the time when the buyer learned of the breach and the contract price together with any incidental and consequential damages provided in this Article (Section 2-715), but less expenses saved in consequence of the seller's breach.

(2) Market price is to be determined as of the place for tender or, in cases of rejection after arrival or revocation of acceptance, as of the place of arrival.

§ 2-714. Buyer's Damages for Breach in Regard to Accepted Goods

(1) Where the buyer has accepted goods and given notification (subsection (3) of Section 2-607) he may recover as damages for any non-conformity of tender the loss resulting in the ordinary course of events from the seller's breach as determined in any manner which is reasonable.

(2) The measure of damages for breach of warranty is the difference at the time and place of acceptance between the value of the goods accepted and the value they would have had if they had been as warranted, unless special circumstances show proximate damages of a different amount.

(3) In a proper case any incidental and consequential damages under the next section may also be recovered.

§ 2-715. Buyer's Incidental and Consequential Damages

(1) Incidental damages resulting from the seller's breach include expenses reasonably incurred in inspection, receipt, transportation and care and custody of goods rightfully rejected, any commercially reasonable charges, expenses or commissions in connection with effecting cover and any other reasonable expense incident to the delay or other breach.

(2) Consequential damages resulting from the seller's breach include
  (a) any loss resulting from general or particular requirements and needs of which the seller at the time of contracting had reason to know and which could not reasonably be prevented by cover or otherwise; and
  (b) injury to person or property proximately resulting from any breach of warranty.

§ 2-716. Buyer's Right to Specific Performance or Replevin

(1) Specific performance may be decreed where the goods are unique or in other proper circumstances.

(2) The decree for specific performance may include such terms and conditions as to payment of the price, damages, or other relief as the court may deem just.

(3) The buyer has a right of replevin for goods identified to the contract if after reasonable effort he is unable to effect cover for such goods or the circumstances reasonably indicate that such effort will be unavailing or if the goods have been shipped under reservation and satisfaction of the security interest in them has been made or tendered.

§ 2-717. Deduction of Damages From the Price

The buyer on notifying the seller of his intention to do so may deduct all or any part of the damages resulting from any breach of the contract from any part of the price still due under the same contract.

§ 2-718. Liquidation or Limitation of Damages; Deposits

(1) Damages for breach by either party may be liquidated in the agreement but only at an amount which is reasonable in the light of the anticipated or actual harm caused by the breach, the difficulties of proof of loss, and the inconvenience or nonfeasibility of otherwise obtaining an adequate remedy. A term fixing unreasonably large liquidated damages is void as a penalty.

(2) Where the seller justifiably withholds delivery of goods because of the buyer's breach, the buyer is entitled to restitution of any amount by which the sum of his payments exceeds

    (a) the amount to which the seller is entitled by virtue of terms liquidating the seller's damages in accordance with subsection (1), or

    (b) in the absence of such terms, twenty per cent of the value of the total performance for which the buyer is obligated under the contract or $500, whichever is smaller.

(3) The buyer's right to restitution under subsection (2) is subject to offset to the extent that the seller establishes

    (a) a right to recover damages under the provisions of this Article other than subsection (1), and

    (b) the amount or value of any benefits received by the buyer directly or indirectly by reason of the contract.

(4) Where a seller has received payment in goods their reasonable value or the proceeds of their resale shall be treated as payments for the purpose of subsection (2), but if the seller has notice of the buyer's breach before reselling goods received in part performance, his resale is subject to the conditions laid down in this Article on resale by an aggrieved seller (Section 2-706).

§ 2-719. Contractual Modification or Limitation of Remedy

(1) Subject to the provisions of subsections (2) and (3) of this section and of the preceding section on liquidation and limitation of damages,

    (a) the agreement may provide for remedies in addition to or in substitution for those provided in this Article and may limit or alter the measure of damages recoverable under this Article, as by limiting the buyer's remedies to return of the goods and repayment of the price or to repair and replacement of non-conforming goods or parts; and

    (b) resort to a remedy as provided is optional unless the remedy is expressly agreed to be exclusive, in which case it is the sole remedy.

(2) Where circumstances cause an exclusive or limited remedy to fail of its essential purpose, remedy may be had as provided in this Act.

(3) Consequential damages may be limited or excluded unless the limitation or exclusion is unconscionable. Limitation of consequential damages for injury to the person in the case of consumer goods is prima facie unconscionable but limitation of damages where the loss is commercial is not.

§ 2-720. Effect of "Cancellation" or "Rescission" on Claims for Antecedent Breach

Unless the contrary intention clearly appears, expressions of "cancellation" or "recission" of the contract or the like shall not be construed as a renunciation or discharge of any claim in damages for an antecedent breach.

§ 2-721. Remedies for Fraud

Remedies for material misrepresentation or fraud include all remedies available under this Article for non-fraudulent breach. Neither rescission or a claim for rescission of the contract for sale nor rejection or return of the goods shall bar or be deemed inconsistent with a claim for damages or other remedy.

§ 2-722. Who Can Sue Third Parties for Injury to Goods

Where a third party so deals with goods which have been identified to a contract for sale as to cause actionable injury to a party to that contract
  (a) a right of action against the third party is in either party to the contract for sale who has title to or a security interest or a special property or an insurable interest in the goods; and if the goods have been destroyed or converted a right of action is also in the party who either bore the risk of loss under the contract for sale or has since the injury assumed that risk as against the other;
  (b) if at the time of the injury the party plaintiff did not bear the risk of loss as against the other party to the contract for sale and there is no arrangement between them for disposition of the recovery, his suit or settlement is, subject to his own interest, as a fiduciary for the other party to the contract;
  (c) either party may with the consent of the other sue for the benefit of whom it may concern.

§ 2-723. Proof of Market Price: Time and Place

(1) If an action based on anticipatory repudiation comes to trial before the time for performance with respect to some or all of the goods, any damages based on market price (Section 2-708 or Section 2-713) shall be determined according to the price of such goods prevailing at the time when the aggrieved party learned of the repudiation.

(2) If evidence of a price prevailing at the times or places described in this Article is not readily available the price prevailing within any reasonable time before or after the time described or at any other place which in commercial judgment or under usage of trade would serve as a reasonable substitute for the one described may be used, making any proper allowance for the cost of transporting the goods to or from such other place.

(3) Evidence of a relevant price prevailing at a time or place other than the one described in this Article offered by one party is not admissible unless and until he has given the other party such notice as the court finds sufficient to prevent unfair surprise.

§ 2-724. Admissibility of Market Quotations

Whenever the prevailing price or value of any goods regularly bought and sold in any established commodity market is in issue, reports in official publications or trade journals or in newspapers or periodicals of general circulation published as the reports of such market shall be admissible in evidence. The circumstances of the preparation of such a report may be shown to affect its weight but not its admissibility.

§ 2-725. Statute of Limitations in Contracts for Sale

(1) An action for breach of any contract for sale must be commenced within four years after the cause of action has accrued. By the original agreement the parties may reduce the period of limitation to not less than one year but may not extend it.

(2) A cause of action accrues when the breach occurs, regardless of the aggrieved party's lack of knowledge of the breach. A breach of warranty occurs when tender of delivery is made, except that where a warranty explicitly extends to future performance of the goods and discovery of the breach must await the time of such performance the cause of action accrues when the breach is or should have been discovered.

(3) Where an action commenced within the time limited by subsection (1) is so terminated as to leave available a remedy by another action for the same breach such other action may be commenced after the expiration of the time limited and within six months after the termination of the first action unless the termination resulted from voluntary discontinuance or from dismissal for failure or neglect to prosecute.

(4) This section does not alter the law on tolling of the statute of limitations nor does it apply to causes of action which have accrued before this Act becomes effective.

ARTICLE 3

COMMERCIAL PAPER

§ 3-101. Short Title

This Article shall be known and may be cited as Uniform Commercial Code — Commercial Paper.

§ 3-102. Definitions and Index of Definitions

(1) In this Article unless the context otherwise requires
    (a) "Issue" means the first delivery of an instrument to a holder or a remitter.
    (b) An "order" is a direction to pay and must be more than an authorization or request. It must identify the person to pay with reasonable certainty. It may be addressed to one or more such persons jointly or in the alternative but not in succession.

(c) A "promise" is an undertaking to pay and must be more than an acknowledgment of an obligation.

(d) "Secondary party" means a drawer or endorser.

(e) "Instrument" means a negotiable instrument.

(2) Other definitions applying to this Article and the sections in which they appear are:

"Acceptance". Section 3-410.

"Accommodation party". Section 3-415.

"Alteration". Section 3-407.

"Certificate of deposit". Section 3-104.

"Certification". Section 3-411.

"Check". Section 3-104.

"Definite time". Section 3-109.

"Dishonor". Section 3-507.

"Draft". Section 3-104.

"Holder in due course". Section 3-302.

"Negotiation". Section 3-202.

"Note". Section 3-104.

"Notice of dishonor". Section 3-508.

"On demand". Section 3-108.

"Presentment". Section 3-504.

"Protest". Section 3-509.

"Restrictive Indorsement". Section 3-205.

"Signature". Section 3-401.

(3) The following definitions in other Articles apply to this Article:

"Account". Section 4-104.

"Banking Day". Section 4-104.

"Clearing house". Section 4-104.

"Collecting bank". Section 4-105.

"Customer". Section 4-104.

"Depositary Bank". Section 4-105.

"Documentary Draft". Section 4-104.

"Intermediary Bank". Section 4-105.

"Item". Section 4-104.

"Midnight deadline". Section 4-104.

"Payor bank". Section 4-105.

(4) In addition Article 1 contains general definitions and principles of construction and interpretation applicable throughout this Article.

§ 3-103. Limitations on Scope of Article

(1) This Article does not apply to money, documents of title or investment securities.

(2) The provisions of this Article are subject to the provisions of the Article on Bank Deposits and Collections (Article 4) and Secured Transactions (Article 9).

§ 3-104. Form of Negotiable Instruments; "Draft"; "Check"; "Certificate of Deposit"; "Note"

(1) Any writing to be a negotiable instrument within this Article must
  (a) be signed by the maker or drawer; and
  (b) contain an unconditional promise or order to pay a sum certain in money and no other promise, order, obligation or power given by the maker or drawer except as authorized by this Article; and
  (c) be payable on demand or at a definite time; and
  (d) be payable to order or to bearer.

(2) A writing which complies with the requirements of this section is
  (a) a "draft" ("bill of exchange") if it is an order;
  (b) a "check" if it is a draft drawn on a bank and payable on demand;
  (c) a "certificate of deposit" if it is an acknowledgment by a bank of receipt of money with an engagement to repay it;
  (d) a "note" if it is a promise other than a certificate of deposit.

(3) As used in other Articles of this Act, and as the context may require, the terms "draft", "check", "certificate of deposit" and "note" may refer to instruments which are not negotiable within this Article as well as to instruments which are so negotiable.

§ 3-105. When Promise or Order Unconditional

(1) A promise or order otherwise unconditional is not made conditional by the fact that the instrument
  (a) is subject to implied or constructive conditions; or
  (b) states its consideration, whether performed or promised, or the transaction which gave rise to the instrument, or that the promise or order is made or the instrument matures in accordance with or "as per" such transaction; or
  (c) refers to or states that it arises out of a separate agreement or refers to a separate agreement for rights as to prepayment or acceleration; or
  (d) states that it is drawn under a letter of credit; or
  (e) states that it is secured, whether by mortgage, reservation of title or otherwise; or
  (f) indicates a particular account to be debited or any other fund or source from which reimbursement is expected; or
  (g) is limited to payment out of a particular fund or the proceeds of a particular source, if the instrument is issued by a government or governmental agency or unit; or
  (h) is limited to payment out of the entire assets of a partnership, unincorporated association, trust or estate by or on behalf of which the instrument is issued.

(2) A promise or order is not unconditional if the instrument
  (a) states that it is subject to or governed by any other agreement; or
  (b) states that it is to be paid only out of a particular fund or source except as provided in this section.

As amended in 1962.

§ 3-106. Sum Certain

(1) The sum payable is a sum certain even though it is to be paid

    (a) with stated interest or by stated installments; or

    (b) with stated different rates of interest before and after default or a specified date; or

    (c) with a stated discount or addition if paid before or after the date fixed for payment; or

    (d) with exchange or less exchange, whether at a fixed rate or at the current rate; or

    (e) with costs of collection or an attorney's fee or both upon default.

(2) Nothing in this section shall validate any term which is otherwise illegal.

§ 3-107. Money

(1) An instrument is payable in money if the medium of exchange in which it is payable is money at the time the instrument is made. An instrument payable in "currency" or "current funds" is payable in money.

(2) A promise or order to pay a sum stated in a foreign currency is for a sum certain in money and, unless a different medium of payment is specified in the instrument, may be satisfied by payment of that number of dollars which the stated foreign currency will purchase at the buying sight rate for that currency on the day on which the instrument is payable or, if payable on demand, on the day of demand. If such an instrument specifies a foreign currency as the medium of payment the instrument is payable in that currency.

§ 3-108. Payable on Demand

Instruments payable on demand include those payable at sight or on presentation and those in which no time for payment is stated.

§ 3-109. Definite Time

(1) An instrument is payable at a definite time if by its terms it is payable

    (a) on or before a stated date or at a fixed period after a stated date; or

    (b) at a fixed period after sight; or

    (c) at a definite time subject to any acceleration; or

    (d) at a definite time subject to extension at the option of the holder, or to extension to a further definite time at the option of the maker or acceptor or automatically upon or after a specified act or event.

(2) An instrument which by its terms is otherwise payable only upon an act or event uncertain as to time of occurrence is not payable at a definite time even though the act or event has occurred.

§ 3-110. Payable to Order

(1) An instrument is payable to order when by its terms it is payable to the order or assigns of any person therein specified with reasonable certainty, or to him or his order, or when it is conspicuously designated on its face as "exchange" or the like and names a payee. It may be payable to the order of

(a) the maker or drawer; or

(b) the drawee; or

(c) a payee who is not maker, drawer or drawee; or

(d) two or more payees together or in the alternative; or

(e) an estate, trust or fund, in which case it is payable to the order of the representative of such estate, trust or fund or his successors; or

(f) an office, or an officer by his title as such in which case it is payable to the principal but the incumbent of the office or his successors may act as if he or they were the holder; or

(g) a partnership or unincorporated association, in which case it is payable to the partnership or association and may be indorsed or transferred by any person thereto authorized.

(2) An instrument not payable to order is not made so payable by such words as "payable upon return of this instrument properly indorsed."

(3) An instrument made payable both to order and to bearer is payable to order unless the bearer words are handwritten or typewritten.

§ 3-111. Payable to Bearer

An instrument is payable to bearer when by its terms it is payable to

(a) bearer or the order of bearer; or

(b) a specified person or bearer; or

(c) "cash" or the order of "cash", or any other indication which does not purport to designate a specific payee.

§ 3-112. Terms and Omissions Not Affecting Negotiability

(1) The negotiability of an instrument is not affected by

(a) the omission of a statement of any consideration or of the place where the instrument is drawn or payable; or

(b) a statement that collateral his been given to secure obligations either on the instrument or otherwise of an obligor on the instrument or that in case of default on those obligations the holder may realize on or dispose of the collateral; or

(c) a promise or power to maintain or protect collateral or to give additional collateral; or

(d) a term authorizing a confession of judgment on the instrument if it is not paid when due; or

(e) a term purporting to waive the benefit of any law intended for the advantage or protection of any obligor; or

(f) a term in a draft providing that the payee by indorsing or cashing it acknowledges full satisfaction of an obligation of the drawer; or

(g) A statement in a draft drawn in a set of parts (Section 3-801) to the effect that the order is effective only if no other part has been honored.

(2) Nothing in this section shall validate any term which is otherwise illegal.
As amended in 1962.

§ 3-113. Seal

An instrument otherwise negotiable is within this Article even though it is under a seal.

§ 3-114. Date, Antedating, Postdating

(1) The negotiability of an instrument is not affected by the fact that it is undated, antedated or postdated.

(2) Where an instrument is antedated or postdated the time when it is payable is determined by the stated date if the instrument is payable on demand or at a fixed period after date.

(3) Where the instrument or any signature thereon is dated, the date is presumed to be correct.

§ 3-115. Incomplete Instruments

(1) When a paper whose contents at the time of signing show that it is intended to become an instrument is signed while still incomplete in any necessary respect it cannot be enforced until completed, but when it is completed in accordance with authority given it is effective as completed.

(2) If the completion is unauthorized the rules as to material alteration apply (Section 3-407), even though the paper was not delivered by the maker or drawer; but the burden of establishing that any completion is unauthorized is on the party so asserting.

§ 3-116. Instruments Payable to Two or More Persons

An instrument payable to the order of two or more persons
    (a) if in the alternative is payable to any one of them and may be negotiated, discharged or enforced by any of them who has possession of it;
    (b) if not in the alternative is payable to all of them and may be negotiated, discharged or enforced only by all of them.

§ 3-117. Instruments Payable With Words of Description

An instrument made payable to a named person with the addition of words describing him
    (a) as agent or officer of a specified person is payable to his principal but the agent or officer may act as if he were the holder;
    (b) as any other fiduciary for a specified person or purpose is payable to the payee and may be negotiated, discharged or enforced by him;
    (c) in any other manner is payable to the payee unconditionally and the additional words are without effect on subsequent parties.

§ 3-118. Ambiguous Terms and Rules of Construction

The following rules apply to every instrument:

   (a) Where there is doubt whether the instrument is a draft or a note the holder may treat it as either. A draft drawn on the drawer is effective as a note.

   (b) Handwritten terms control typewritten and printed terms, and typewritten control printed.

   (c) Words control figures except that if the words are ambiguous figures control.

   (d) Unless otherwise specified a provision for interest means interest at the judgment rate at the place of payment from the date of the instrument, or if it is undated from the date of issue.

   (e) Unless the instrument otherwise specifies two or more persons who sign as maker, acceptor or drawer or indorser and as a part of the same transaction are jointly and severally liable even though the instrument contains such words as "I promise to pay."

   (f) Unless otherwise specified consent to extension authorizes a single extension for not longer than the original period. A consent to extension, expressed in the instrument, is binding on secondary parties and accommodation makers. A holder may not exercise his option to extend an instrument over the objection of a maker or acceptor or other party who in accordance with Section 3-604 tenders full payment when the instrument is due.

§ 3-119. Other Writings Affecting Instrument

(1) As between the obligor and his immediate obligee or any transferee the terms of an instrument may be modified or affected by any other written agreement executed as a part of the same transaction, except that a holder in due course is not affected by any limitation of his rights arising out of the separate written agreement if he had no notice of the limitation when he took the instrument.

(2) A separate agreement does not affect the negotiability of an instrument.

§ 3-120. Instruments "Payable Through" Bank

An instrument which states that it is "payable through" a bank or the like designates that bank as a collecting bank to make presentment but does not of itself authorize the bank to pay the instrument.

§ 3-121. Instruments Payable at Bank

Note: *If this Act is introduced in the Congress of the United States this section should be omitted.*

(States to select either alternative)

Alternative A—

A note or acceptance which states that it is payable at a bank is the equivalent of a draft drawn on the bank payable when it falls due out of any funds of the maker or acceptor in current account or otherwise available for such payment.

Alternative B—

A note or acceptance which states that it is payable at a bank is not of itself an order or authorization to the bank to pay it.

§ 3-122. Accrual of Cause of Action

(1) A cause of action against a maker or an acceptor accrues
  (a) in the case of a time instrument on the day after maturity;
  (b) in the case of a demand instrument upon its date or, if no date is stated, on the date of issue.

(2) A cause of action against the obligor of a demand or time certificate of deposit accrues upon demand, but demand on a time certificate may not be made until on or after the date of maturity.

(3) A cause of action against a drawer of a draft or an indorser of any instrument accrues upon demand following dishonor of the instrument. Notice of dishonor is a demand.

(4) Unless an instrument provides otherwise, interest runs at the rate provided by law for a judgment
  (a) in the case of a maker, acceptor or other primary obligor of a demand instrument, from the date of demand;
  (b) in all other cases from the date of accrual of the cause of action.
As amended in 1962.

§ 3-201. Transfer: Right to Indorsement

(1) Transfer of an instrument vests in the transferee such rights as the transferor has therein, except that a transferee who has himself been a party to any fraud or illegality affecting the instrument or who as a prior holder had notice of a defense or claim against it cannot improve his position by taking from a later holder in due course.

(2) A transfer of a security interest in an instrument vests the foregoing rights in the transferee to the extent of the interest transferred.

(3) Unless otherwise agreed any transfer for value of an instrument not then payable to bearer gives the transferee the specifically enforceable right to have the unqualified indorsement of the transferor. Negotiation takes effect only when the indorsement is made and until that time there is no presumption that the transferee is the owner.

§ 3-202. Negotiation

(1) Negotiation is the transfer of an instrument in such form that the transferee becomes a holder. If the instrument is payable to order it is negotiated by delivery with any necessary indorsement; if payable to bearer it is negotiated by delivery.

(2) An indorsement must be written by or on behalf of the holder and on the instrument or on a paper so firmly affixed thereto as to become a part thereof.

(3) An indorsement is effective for negotiation only when it conveys the entire instrument or any unpaid residue. If it purports to be of less it operates only as a partial assignment.

(4) Words of assignment, condition, waiver, guaranty, limitation or disclaimer of liability and the like accompanying an indorsement do not affect its character as an indorsement.

§ 3-203. Wrong or Misspelled Name

Where an instrument is made payable to a person under a misspelled name or one other than his own he may indorse in that name or his own or both; but signature in both names may be required by a person paying or giving value for the instrument.

§ 3-204. Special Indorsement; Blank Indorsement

(1) A special indorsement specifies the person to whom or to whose order it makes the instrument payable. Any instrument specially indorsed becomes payable to the order of the special indorsee and may be further negotiated only by his indorsement.

(2) An indorsement in blank specifies no particular indorsee and may consist of a mere signature. An instrument payable to order and indorsed in blank becomes payable to bearer and may be negotiated by delivery alone until specially indorsed.

(3) The holder may convert a blank indorsement into a special indorsement by writing over the signature of the indorser in blank any contract consistent with the character of the indorsement.

§ 3-205. Restrictive Indorsements

An indorsement is restrictive which either
   (a) is conditional; or
   (b) purports to prohibit further transfer of the instrument; or
   (c) includes the words "for collection", "for deposit", "pay any bank", or like terms signifying a purpose of deposit or collection; or
   (d) otherwise states that it is for the benefit or use of the indorser or of another person.

§ 3-206. Effect of Restrictive Indorsement

(1) No restrictive indorsement prevents further transfer or negotiation of the instrument.

(2) An intermediary bank, or a payor bank which is not the depositary bank, is neither given notice nor otherwise affected by a restrictive indorsement of any person except the bank's immediate transferor or the person presenting for payment.

(3) Except for an intermediary bank, any transferee under an indorsement which is conditional or includes the words "for collection", "for deposit", "pay any bank", or like terms (subparagraphs (a) and (c) of Section 3-205) must pay or apply any value given by him for or on the security of the instrument consistently with the indorsement and to the extent that he does so he becomes a holder for value. In addition such transferee is a holder in due course if he otherwise complies with the requirements of Section 3-302 on what constitutes a holder in due course.

(4) The first taker under an indorsement for the benefit of the indorser or another person (subparagraph (d) of Section 3-205) must pay or apply any value given by him for or on the security of the instrument consistently with the indorsement and to the extent that he does so he becomes a holder for value. In addition such taker is a holder in due course if he otherwise complies with the requirements of Section 3-302 on what constitutes a holder in due course. A later holder for value is neither given notice nor otherwise affected by such restrictive indorsement unless he has knowledge that a fiduciary or other person has negotiated the instrument in any transaction for his own benefit or otherwise in breach of duty (subsection (2) of Section 3-304).

§ 3-207. Negotiation Effective Although It May Be Rescinded

(1) Negotiation is effective to transfer the instrument although the negotiation is
   (a) made by an infant, a corporation exceeding its powers, or any other person without capacity; or
   (b) obtained by fraud, duress or mistake of any kind; or
   (c) part of an illegal transaction; or
   (d) made in breach of duty.

(2) Except as against a subsequent holder in due course such negotiation is in an appropriate case subject to rescission, the declaration of a constructive trust or any other remedy permitted by law.

§ 3-208. Reacquisition

Where an instrument is returned to or reacquired by a prior party he may cancel any indorsement which is not necessary to his title and reissue or further negotiate the instrument, but any intervening party is discharged as against the reacquiring party and subsequent holders not in due course and if his indorsement has been cancelled is discharged as against subsequent holders in due course as well.

§ 3-301. Rights of a Holder

The holder of an instrument whether or not he is the owner may transfer or negotiate it and, except as otherwise provided in Section 3-603 on payment or satisfaction, discharge it or enforce payment in his own name.

§ 3-302. Holder in Due Course

(1) A holder in due course is a holder who takes the instrument
    (a) for value; and
    (b) in good faith; and
    (c) without notice that it is overdue or has been dishonored or of any defense against or claim to it on the part of any person.

(2) A payee may be a holder in due course.

(3) A holder does not become a holder in due course of an instrument:
    (a) by purchase of it at judicial sale or by taking it under legal process; or
    (b) by acquiring it in taking over an estate; or
    (c) by purchasing it as part of a bulk transaction not in regular course of business of the transferor.

(4) A purchaser of a limited interest can be a holder in due course only to the extent of the interest purchased.

§ 3-303. Taking for Value

A holder takes the instrument for value
    (a) to the extent that the agreed consideration has been performed or that he acquires a security interest in or a lien on the instrument otherwise than by legal process; or
    (b) when he takes the instrument in payment of or as security for an antecedent claim against any person whether or not the claim is due; or
    (c) when he gives a negotiable instrument for it or makes an irrevocable commitment to a third person.

§ 3-304. Notice to Purchaser

(1) The purchaser has notice of a claim or defense if
    (a) the instrument is so incomplete, bears such visible evidence of forgery or alteration, or is otherwise so irregular as to call into question its validity, terms or ownership or to create an ambiguity as to the party to pay; or
    (b) the purchaser has notice that the obligation of any party is voidable in whole or in part, or that all parties have been discharged.

(2) The purchaser has notice of a claim against the instrument when he has knowledge that a fiduciary has negotiated the instrument in payment of or as security for his own debt or in any transaction for his own benefit or otherwise in breach of duty.

(3) The purchaser has notice that an instrument is overdue if he has reason to know

    (a) that any part of the principal amount is overdue or that there is an uncured default in payment of another instrument of the same series; or

    (b) that acceleration of the instrument has been made; or

    (c) that he is taking a demand instrument after demand has been made or more than a reasonable length of time after its issue. A reasonable time for a check drawn and payable within the states and territories of the United States and the District of Columbia is presumed to be thirty days.

(4) Knowledge of the following facts does not of itself give the purchaser notice of a defense or claim

    (a) that the instrument is antedated or postdated;

    (b) that it was issued or negotiated in return for an executory promise or accompanied by a separate agreement, unless the purchaser has notice that a defense or claim has arisen from the terms thereof;

    (c) that any party has signed for accommodation;

    (d) that an incomplete instrument has been completed, unless the purchaser has notice of any improper completion;

    (e) that any person negotiating the instrument is or was a fiduciary;

    (f) that there has been default in payment of interest on the instrument or in payment of any other instrument, except one of the same series.

(5) The filing or recording of a document does not of itself constitute notice within the provisions of this Article to a person who would otherwise be a holder in due course.

(6) To be effective notice must be received at such time and in such manner as to give a reasonable opportunity to act on it.

§ 3-305. Rights of a Holder in Due Course

To the extent that a holder is a holder in due course he takes the instrument free from

(1) all claims to it on the part of any person; and

(2) all defenses of any party to the instrument with whom the holder has not dealt except

    (a) infancy, to the extent that it is a defense to a simple contract; and

    (b) such other incapacity, or duress, or illegality of the transaction, as renders the obligation of the party a nullity; and

    (c) such misrepresentation as has induced the party to sign the instrument with neither knowledge nor reasonable opportunity to obtain knowledge of its character or its essential terms; and

    (d) discharge in insolvency proceedings; and

    (e) any other discharge of which the holder has notice when he takes the instrument.

§ 3-306. Rights of One Not Holder in Due Course

Unless he has the rights of a holder in due course any person takes the instrument subject to
  (a) all valid claims to it on the part of any person; and
  (b) all defenses of any party which would be available in an action on a simple contract; and
  (c) the defenses of want or failure of consideration, non-performance of any condition precedent, non-delivery, or delivery for a special purpose (Section 3-408); and
  (d) the defense that he or a person through whom he holds the instrument acquired it by theft, or that payment or satisfaction to such holder would be inconsistent with the terms of a restrictive indorsement. The claim of any third person to the instrument is not otherwise available as a defense to any party liable thereon unless the third person himself defends the action for such party.

§ 3-307. Burden of Establishing Signatures, Defenses and Due Course

(1) Unless specifically denied in the pleadings each signature on an instrument is admitted. When the effectiveness of a signature is put in issue
  (a) the burden of establishing it is on the party claiming under the signature; but
  (b) the signature is presumed to be genuine or authorized except where the action is to enforce the obligation of a purported signer who has died or become incompetent before proof is required.

(2) When signatures are admitted or established, production of the instrument entitles a holder to recover on it unless the defendant establishes a defense.

(3) After it is shown that a defense exists a person claiming the rights of a holder in due course has the burden of establishing that he or some person under whom he claims is in all respects a holder in due course.

§ 3-401. Signature

(1) No person is liable on an instrument unless his signature appears thereon.

(2) A signature is made by use of any name, including any trade or assumed name, upon an instrument, or by any word or mark used in lieu of a written signature.

§ 3-402. Signature in Ambiguous Capacity

Unless the instrument clearly indicates that a signature is made in some other capacity it is an indorsement.

§ 3-403. Signature by Authorized Representative

(1) A signature may be made by an agent or other representative, and his authority to make it may be established as in other cases of representation. No particular form of appointment is necessary to establish such authority.

(2) An authorized representative who signs his own name to an instrument

    (a) is personally obligated if the instrument neither names the person represented nor shows that the representative signed in a representative capacity;

    (b) except as otherwise established between the immediate parties, is personally obligated if the instrument names the person represented but does not show that the representative signed in a representative capacity, or if the instrument does not name the person represented but does show that the representative signed in a representative capacity.

(3) Except as otherwise established the name of an organization preceded or followed by the name and office of an authorized individual is a signature made in a representative capacity.

§ 3-404. Unauthorized Signatures

(1) Any unauthorized signature is wholly inoperative as that of the person whose name is signed unless he ratifies it or is precluded from denying it; but it operates as the signature of the unauthorized signer in favor of any person who in good faith pays the instrument or takes it for value.

(2) Any unauthorized signature may be ratified for all purposes of this Article. Such ratification does not of itself affect any rights of the person ratifying against the actual signer.

§ 3-405. Impostors; Signature in Name of Payee

(1) An indorsement by any person in the name of a named payee is effective if

    (a) an impostor by use of the mails or otherwise has induced the maker or drawer to issue the instrument to him or his confederate in the name of the payee; or

    (b) a person signing as or on behalf of a maker or drawer intends the payee to have no interest in the instrument; or

    (c) an agent or employee of the maker or drawer has supplied him with the name of the payee intending the latter to have no such interest.

(2) Nothing in this section shall affect the criminal or civil liability of the person so indorsing.

§ 3-406. Negligence Contributing to Alteration or Unauthorized Signature

Any person who by his negligence substantially contributes to a material alteration of the instrument or to the making of an unauthorized signature is precluded from asserting the alteration or lack of authority against a holder in due course or against a drawee or other payor who pays the instrument in good faith and in accordance with the reasonable commercial standards of the drawee's or payor's business.

§ 3-407. Alteration

(1) Any alteration of an instrument is material which changes the contract of any party thereto in any respect, including any such change in
   (a) the number or relations of the parties; or
   (b) an incomplete instrument, by completing it otherwise than as authorized; or
   (c) the writing as signed, by adding to it or by removing any part of it.
(2) As against any person other than a subsequent holder in due course.
   (a) alteration by the holder which is both fraudulent and material discharges any party whose contract is thereby changed unless that party assents or is precluded from asserting the defense;
   (b) no other alteration discharges any party and the instrument may be enforced according to its original tenor, or as to incomplete instruments according to the authority given.
(3) A subsequent holder in due course may in all cases enforce the instrument according to its original tenor, and when an incomplete instrument has been completed, he may enforce it as completed.

§ 3-408. Consideration

Want or failure of consideration is a defense as against any person not having the rights of a holder in due course (Section 3-305), except that no consideration is necessary for an instrument or obligation thereon given in payment of or as security for an antecedent obligation of any kind. Nothing in this section shall be taken to displace any statute outside this Act under which a promise is enforceable notwithstanding lack or failure of consideration. Partial failure of consideration is a defense pro tanto whether or not the failure is in an ascertained or liquidated amount.

§ 3-409. Draft Not an Assignment

(1) A check or other draft does not of itself operate as an assignment of any funds in the hands of the drawee available for its payment, and the drawee is not liable on the instrument until he accepts it.
(2) Nothing in this section shall affect any liability in contract, tort or otherwise arising from any letter of credit or other obligation or representation which is not an acceptance.

§ 3-410. Definition and Operation of Acceptance

(1) Acceptance is the drawee's signed engagement to honor the draft as presented. It must be written on the draft, and may consist of his signature alone. It becomes operative when completed by delivery or notification.

(2) A draft may be accepted although it has not been signed by the drawer or is otherwise incomplete or is overdue or has been dishonored.

(3) Where the draft is payable at a fixed period after sight and the acceptor fails to date his acceptance the holder may complete it by supplying a date in good faith.

§ 3-411. Certification of a Check

(1) Certification of a check is acceptance. Where a holder procures certification the drawer and all prior indorsers are discharged.

(2) Unless otherwise agreed a bank has no obligation to certify a check.

(3) A bank may certify a check before returning it for lack of proper indorsement. If it does so the drawer is discharged.

§ 3-412. Acceptance Varying Draft

(1) Where the drawee's proffered acceptance in any manner varies the draft as presented the holder may refuse the acceptance and treat the draft as dishonored in which case the drawee is entitled to have his acceptance cancelled.

(2) The terms of the draft are not varied by an acceptance to pay at any particular bank or place in the United States, unless the acceptance states that the draft is to be paid only at such bank or place.

(3) Where the holder assents to an acceptance varying the terms of the draft each drawer and indorser who does not affirmatively assent is discharged.
As amended in 1962.

§ 3-413. Contract of Maker, Drawer and Acceptor

(1) The maker or acceptor engages that he will pay the instrument according to its tenor at the time of his engagement or as completed pursuant to Section 3-115 on incomplete instruments.

(2) The drawer engages that upon dishonor of the draft and any necessary notice of dishonor or protest he will pay the amount of the draft to the holder or to any indorser who takes it up. The drawer may disclaim this liability by drawing without recourse.

(3) By making, drawing or accepting the party admits as against all subsequent parties including the drawee the existence of the payee and his then capacity to indorse.

§ 3-414. Contract of Indorser; Order of Liability

(1) Unless the indorsement otherwise specifies (as by such words as "without recourse") every indorser engages that upon dishonor and any necessary notice of dishonor and protest he will pay the instrument according to its tenor at the time of his indorsement to the holder or to any subsequent indorser who takes it up, even though the indorser who takes it up was not obligated to do so.

(2) Unless they otherwise agree indorsers are liable to one another in the order in which they indorse, which is presumed to be the order in which their signatures appear on the instrument.

§ 3-415. Contract of Accommodation Party

(1) An accommodation party is one who signs the instrument in any capacity for the purpose of lending his name to another party to it.

(2) When the instrument has been taken for value before it is due the accommodation party is liable in the capacity in which he has signed even though the taker knows of the accommodation.

(3) As against a holder in due course and without notice of the accommodation oral proof of the accommodation is not admissible to give the accommodation party the benefit of discharges dependent on his character as such. In other cases the accommodation character may be shown by oral proof.

(4) An indorsement which shows that it is not in the chain of title is notice of its accommodation character.

(5) An accommodation party is not liable to the party accommodated, and if he pays the instrument has a right of recourse on the instrument against such party.

§ 3-416. Contract of Guarantor

(1) "Payment guaranteed" or equivalent words added to a signature mean that the signer engages that if the instrument is not paid when due he will pay it according to its tenor without resort by the holder to any other party.

(2) "Collection guaranteed" or equivalent words added to a signature mean that the signer engages that if the instrument is not paid when due he will pay it according to its tenor, but only after the holder has reduced his claim against the maker or acceptor to judgment and execution has been returned unsatisfied, or after the maker or acceptor has become insolvent or it is otherwise apparent that it is useless to proceed against him.

(3) Words of guaranty which do not otherwise specify guarantee payment.

(4) No words of guaranty added to the signature of a sole maker or acceptor affect his liability on the instrument. Such words added to the signature of one of two or more makers or acceptors create a presumption that the signature is for the accommodation of the others.

(5) When words of guaranty are used presentment, notice of dishonor and protest are not necessary to charge the user.

(6) Any guaranty written on the instrument is enforcible notwithstanding any statute of frauds.

§ 3-417. Warranties on Presentment and Transfer

(1) Any person who obtains payment or acceptance and any prior transferor warrants to a person who in good faith pays or accepts that

    (a) he has a good title to the instrument or is authorized to obtain payment or acceptance on behalf of one who has a good title; and

    (b) he has no knowledge that the signature of the maker or drawer is unauthorized, except that this warranty is not given by a holder in due course acting in good faith

        (i) to a maker with respect to the maker's own signature; or

        (ii) to a drawer with respect to the drawer's own signature, whether or not the drawer is also the drawee; or

        (iii) to an acceptor of a draft if the holder in due course took the draft after the acceptance or obtained the acceptance without knowledge that the drawer's signature was unauthorized; and

    (c) the instrument has not been materially altered, except that this warranty is not given by a holder in due course acting in good faith

        (i) to the maker of a note; or

        (ii) to the drawer of a draft whether or not the drawer is also the drawee; or

        (iii) to the acceptor of a draft with respect to an alteration made prior to the acceptance if the holder in due course took the draft after the acceptance, even though the acceptance provided "payable as originally drawn" or equivalent terms; or

        (iv) to the acceptor of a draft with respect to an alteration made after the acceptance.

(2) Any person who transfers an instrument and receives consideration warrants to his transferee and if the transfer is by indorsement to any subsequent holder who takes the instrument in good faith that

    (a) he has a good title to the instrument or is authorized to obtain payment or acceptance on behalf of one who has a good title and the transfer is otherwise rightful; and

    (b) all signatures are genuine or authorized; and

    (c) the instrument has not been materially altered; and

    (d) no defense of any party is good against him; and

    (e) he has no knowledge of any insolvency proceeding instituted with respect to the maker or acceptor or the drawer of an unaccepted instrument.

(3) By transferring "without recourse" the transferor limits the obligation stated in subsection (2)(d) to a warranty that he has no knowledge of such a defense.

(4) A selling agent or broker who does not disclose the fact that he is acting only as such gives the warranties provided in this section, but if he makes such disclosure warrants only his good faith and authority.

§ 3-418. Finality of Payment or Acceptance

Except for recovery of bank payments as provided in the Article on Bank Deposits and Collections (Article 4) and except for liability for breach of warranty on presentment under the preceding section, payment or acceptance of any instrument is final in favor of a holder in due course, or a person who has in good faith changed his position in reliance on the payment.

§ 3-419. Conversion of Instrument; Innocent Representative

(1) An instrument is converted when
   (a) a drawee to whom it is delivered for acceptance refuses to return it on demand; or
   (b) any person to whom it is delivered for payment refuses on demand either to pay or to return it; or
   (c) it is paid on a forged indorsement.

(2) In an action against a drawee under subsection (1) the measure of the drawee's liability is the face amount of the instrument. In any other action under subsection (1) the measure of liability is presumed to be the face amount of the instrument.

(3) Subject to the provisions of this Act concerning restrictive indorsements a representative, including a depositary or collecting bank, who has in good faith and in accordance with the reasonable commercial standards applicable to the business of such representative dealt with an instrument or its proceeds on behalf of one who was not the true owner is not liable in conversion or otherwise to the true owner beyond the amount of any proceeds remaining in his hands.

(4) An intermediary bank or payor bank which is not a depositary bank is not liable in conversion solely by reason of the fact that proceeds of an item indorsed restrictively (Sections 3-205 and 3-206) are not paid or applied consistently with the restrictive indorsement of an indorser other than its immediate transferor.

§ 3-501. When Presentment, Notice of Dishonor, and Protest Necessary or Permissible

(1) Unless excused (Section 3-511) presentment is necessary to charge secondary parties as follows:
   (a) presentment for acceptance is necessary to charge the drawer and indorsers of a draft where the draft so provides, or is payable elsewhere than at the residence or place of business of the drawee, or its date of payment depends upon such presentment. The holder may at his option present for acceptance any other draft payable at a stated date;
   (b) presentment for payment is necessary to charge any indorser;
   (c) in the case of any drawer, the acceptor of a draft payable at a bank or the maker of a note payable at a bank, presentment for payment is necessary, but failure to make presentment discharges such drawer, acceptor or maker only as stated in Section 3-502(1)(b).

(2) Unless excused (Section 3-511)

    (a) notice of any dishonor is necessary to charge any indorser;

    (b) in the case of any drawer, the acceptor of a draft payable at a bank or the maker of a note payable at a bank, notice of any dishonor is necessary, but failure to give such notice discharges such drawer, acceptor or maker only as stated in Section 3-502(1)(b).

(3) Unless excused (Section 3-511) protest of any dishonor is necessary to charge the drawer and indorsers of any draft which on its face appears to be drawn or payable outside of the states, territories, dependencies and possessions of the United States, the District of Columbia and the Commonwealth of Puerto Rico. The holder may at his option make protest of any dishonor of any other instrument and in the case of a foreign draft may on insolvency of the acceptor before maturity make protest for better security.

(4) Notwithstanding any provision of this section, neither presentment nor notice of dishonor nor protest is necessary to charge an indorser who has indorsed an instrument after maturity.

As amended in 1966.

§ 3-502. Unexcused Delay; Discharge

(1) Where without excuse any necessary presentment or notice of dishonor is delayed beyond the time when it is due

    (a) any indorser is discharged; and

    (b) any drawer or the acceptor of a draft payable at a bank or the maker of a note payable at a bank who because the drawee or payor bank becomes insolvent during the delay is deprived of funds maintained with the drawee or payor bank to cover the instrument may discharge his liability by written assignment to the holder of his rights against the drawee or payor bank in respect of such funds, but such drawer, acceptor or maker is not otherwise discharged.

(2) Where without excuse a necessary protest is delayed beyond the time when it is due any drawer or indorser is discharged.

§ 3-503. Time of Presentment

(1) Unless a different time is expressed in the instrument the time for any presentment is determined as follows:

    (a) where an instrument is payable at or a fixed period after a stated date any presentment for acceptance must be made on or before the date it is payable;

    (b) where an instrument is payable after sight it must either be presented for acceptance or negotiated within a reasonable time after date or issue whichever is later;

    (c) where an instrument shows the date on which it is payable presentment for payment is due on that date;

    (d) where an instrument is accelerated presentment for payment is due within a reasonable time after the acceleration;

    (e) with respect to the liability of any secondary party presentment for acceptance or payment of any other instrument is due within a reasonable time after such party becomes liable thereon.

(2) A reasonable time for presentment is determined by the nature of the instrument, any usage of banking or trade and the facts of the particular case. In the case of an uncertified check which is drawn and payable within the United States and which is not a draft drawn by a bank the following are presumed to be reasonable periods within which to present for payment or to initiate bank collection:

    (a) with respect to the liability of the drawer, thirty days after date or issue whichever is later; and

    (b) with respect to the liability of an indorser, seven days after his indorsement.

(3) Where any presentment is due on a day which is not a full business day for either the person making presentment or the party to pay or accept, presentment is due on the next following day which is a full business day for both parties.

(4) Presentment to be sufficient must be made at a reasonable hour, and if at a bank during its banking day.

§ 3-504. How Presentment Made

(1) Presentment is a demand for acceptance or payment made upon the maker, acceptor, drawee or other payor by or on behalf of the holder.

(2) Presentment may be made

    (a) by mail, in which event the time of presentment is determined by the time of receipt of the mail; or

    (b) through a clearing house; or

    (c) at the place of acceptance or payment specified in the instrument or if there be none at the place of business or residence of the party to accept or pay. If neither the party to accept or pay nor anyone authorized to act for him is present or accessible at such place presentment is excused.

(3) It may be made

    (a) to any one of two or more makers, acceptors, drawees or other payors; or

    (b) to any person who has authority to make or refuse the acceptance or payment.

(4) A draft accepted or a note made payable at a bank in the United States must be presented at such bank.

(5) In the cases described in Section 4-210 presentment may be made in the manner and with the result stated in that section.

As amended in 1962.

§ 3-505. Rights of Party to Whom Presentment Is Made

(1) The party to whom presentment is made may without dishonor require
   (a) exhibition of the instrument; and
   (b) reasonable identification of the person making presentment and evidence of his authority to make it if made for another; and
   (c) that the instrument be produced for acceptance or payment at a place specified in it, or if there be none at any place reasonable in the circumstances; and
   (d) a signed receipt on the instrument for any partial or full payment and its surrender upon full payment.

(2) Failure to comply with any such requirement invalidates the presentment but the person presenting has a reasonable time in which to comply and the time for acceptance or payment runs from the time of compliance.

§ 3-506. Time Allowed for Acceptance or Payment

(1) Acceptance may be deferred without dishonor until the close of the next business day following presentment. The holder may also in a good faith effort to obtain acceptance and without either dishonor of the instrument or discharge of secondary parties allow postponement of acceptance for an additional business day.

(2) Except as a longer time is allowed in the case of documentary drafts drawn under a letter of credit, and unless an earlier time is agreed to by the party to pay, payment of an instrument may be deferred without dishonor pending reasonable examination to determine whether it is properly payable, but payment must be made in any event before the close of business on the day of presentment.

§ 3-507. Dishonor; Holder's Right of Recourse; Term Allowing Re-Presentment

(1) An instrument is dishonored when
   (a) a necessary or optional presentment is duly made and due acceptance or payment is refused or cannot be obtained within the prescribed time or in case of bank collections the instrument is seasonably returned by the midnight deadline (Section 4-301); or
   (b) presentment is excused and the instrument is not duly accepted or paid.

(2) Subject to any necessary notice of dishonor and protest, the holder has upon dishonor an immediate right of recourse against the drawers and indorsers.

(3) Return of an instrument for lack of proper indorsement is not dishonor.

(4) A term in a draft or an indorsement thereof allowing a stated time for re-presentment in the event of any dishonor of the draft by nonacceptance if a time draft or by nonpayment if a sight draft gives the holder as against any secondary party bound by the term an option to waive the dishonor without affecting the liability of the secondary party and he may present again up to the end of the stated time.

§ 3-508. Notice of Dishonor

(1) Notice of dishonor may be given to any person who may be liable on the instrument by or on behalf of the holder or any party who has himself received notice, or any other party who can be compelled to pay the instrument. In addition an agent or bank in whose hands the instrument is dishonored may give notice to his principal or customer or to another agent or bank from which the instrument was received.

(2) Any necessary notice must be given by a bank before its midnight deadline and by any other person before midnight of the third business day after dishonor or receipt of notice of dishonor.

(3) Notice may be given in any reasonable manner. It may be oral or written and in any terms which identify the instrument and state that it has been dishonored. A misdescription which does not mislead the party notified does not vitiate the notice. Sending the instrument bearing a stamp, ticket or writing stating that acceptance or payment has been refused or sending a notice of debit with respect to the instrument is sufficient.

(4) Written notice is given when sent although it is not received.

(5) Notice to one partner is notice to each although the firm has been dissolved.

(6) When any party is in insolvency proceedings instituted after the issue of the instrument notice may be given either to the party or to the representative of his estate.

(7) When any party is dead or incompetent notice may be sent to his last known address or given to his personal representative.

(8) Notice operates for the benefit of all parties who have rights on the instrument against the party notified.

§ 3-509. Protest; Noting for Protest

(1) A protest is a certificate of dishonor made under the hand and seal of a United States consul or vice consul or a notary public or other person authorized to certify dishonor by the law of the place where dishonor occurs. It may be made upon information satisfactory to such person.

(2) The protest must identify the instrument and certify either that due presentment has been made or the reason why it is excused and that the instrument has been dishonored by non-acceptance or nonpayment.

(3) The protest may also certify that notice of dishonor has been given to all parties or to specified parties.

(4) Subject to subsection (5) any necessary protest is due by the time that notice of dishonor is due.

(5) If, before protest is due, an instrument has been noted for protest by the officer to make protest, the protest may be made at any time thereafter as of the date of the noting.

§ 3-510. Evidence of Dishonor and Notice of Dishonor

The following are admissible as evidence and create a presumption of dishonor and of any notice of dishonor therein shown:

(a) a document regular in form as provided in the preceding section which purports to be a protest;

(b) the purported stamp or writing of the drawee, payor bank or presenting bank on the instrument or accompanying it stating that acceptance or payment has been refused for reasons consistent with dishonor;

(c) any book or record of the drawee, payor bank, or any collecting bank kept in the usual course of business which shows dishonor, even though there is no evidence of who made the entry.

§ 3-511. Waived or Excused Presentment, Protest or Notice of Dishonor or Delay Therein

(1) Delay in presentment, protest or notice of dishonor is excused when the party is without notice that it is due or when the delay is caused by circumstances beyond his control and he exercises reasonable diligence after the cause of the delay ceases to operate.

(2) Presentment or notice or protest as the case may be is entirely excused when

(a) the party to be charged has waived it expressly or by implication either before or after it is due; or

(b) such party has himself dishonored the instrument or has countermanded payment or otherwise has no reason to expect or right to require that the instrument be accepted or paid; or

(c) by reasonable diligence the presentment or protest cannot be made or the notice given.

(3) Presentment is also entirely excused when

(a) the maker, acceptor or drawee of any instrument except a documentary draft is dead or in insolvency proceedings instituted after the issue of the instrument; or

(b) acceptance or payment is refused but not for want of proper presentment.

(4) Where a draft has been dishonored by nonacceptance a later presentment for payment and any notice of dishonor and protest for nonpayment are excused unless in the meantime the instrument has been accepted.

(5) A waiver of protest is also a waiver of presentment and of notice of dishonor even though protest is not required.

(6) Where a waiver of presentment or notice or protest is embodied in the instrument itself it is binding upon all parties; but where it is written above the signature of an indorser it binds him only.

§ 3-601. Discharge of Parties

(1) The extent of the discharge of any party from liability on an instrument is governed by the sections on
- (a) payment or satisfaction (Section 3-603); or
- (b) tender of payment (Section 3-604); or
- (c) cancellation or renunciation (Section 3-605); or
- (d) impairment of right of recourse or of collateral (Section 3-606); or
- (e) reacquisition of the instrument by a prior party (Section 3-208); or
- (f) fraudulent and material alteration (Section 3-407); or
- (g) certification of a check (Section 3-411); or
- (h) acceptance varying a draft (Section 3-412); or
- (i) unexcused delay in presentment or notice of dishonor or protest (Section 3-502).

(2) Any party is also discharged from his liability on an instrument to another party by any other act or agreement with such party which would discharge his simple contract for the payment of money.

(3) The liability of all parties is discharged when any party who has himself no right of action or recourse on the instrument
- (a) reacquires the instrument in his own right; or
- (b) is discharged under any provision of this Article, except as otherwise provided with respect to discharge for impairment of recourse or of collateral (Section 3-606).

§ 3-602. Effect of Discharge Against Holder in Due Course

No discharge of any party provided by this Article is effective against a subsequent holder in due course unless he has notice thereof when he takes the instrument.

§ 3-603. Payment or Satisfaction

(1) The liability of any party is discharged to the extent of his payment or satisfaction to the holder even though it is made with knowledge of a claim of another person to the instrument unless prior to such payment or satisfaction the person making the claim either supplies indemnity deemed adequate by the party seeking the discharge or enjoins payment or satisfaction by order of a court of competent jurisdiction in an action in which the adverse claimant and the holder are parties. This subsection does not, however, result in the discharge of the liability
- (a) of a party who in bad faith pays or satisfies a holder who acquired the instrument by theft or who (unless having the rights of a holder in due course) holds through one who so acquired it; or
- (b) of a party (other than an intermediary bank or a payor bank which is not a depositary bank) who pays or satisfies the holder of an instrument which has been restrictively indorsed in a manner not consistent with the terms of such restrictive indorsement.

(2) Payment or satisfaction may be made with the consent of the holder by any person including a stranger to the instrument. Surrender of the instrument to such a person gives him the rights of a transferee (Section 3-201).

§ 3-604. Tender of Payment

(1) Any party making tender of full payment to a holder when or after it is due is discharged to the extent of all subsequent liability for interest, costs and attorney's fees.

(2) The holder's refusal of such tender wholly discharges any party who has a right of recourse against the party making the tender.

(3) Where the maker or acceptor of an instrument payable otherwise than on demand is able and ready to pay at every place of payment specified in the instrument when it is due, it is equivalent to tender.

§ 3-605. Cancellation and Renunciation

(1) The holder of an instrument may even without consideration discharge any party

  (a) in any manner apparent on the face of the instrument or the indorsement, as by intentionally cancelling the instrument or the party's signature by destruction or mutilation, or by striking out the party's signature; or

  (b) by renouncing his rights by a writing signed and delivered or by surrender of the instrument to the party to be discharged.

(2) Neither cancellation nor renunciation without surrender of the instrument affects the title thereto.

§ 3-606. Impairment of Recourse or of Collateral

(1) The holder discharges any party to the instrument to the extent that without such party's consent the holder

  (a) without express reservation of rights releases or agrees not to sue any person against whom the party has to the knowledge of the holder a right of recourse or agrees to suspend the right to enforce against such person the instrument or collateral or otherwise discharges such person, except that failure or delay in effecting any required presentment, protest or notice of dishonor with respect to any such person does not discharge any party as to whom presentment, protest or notice of dishonor is effective or unnecessary; or

  (b) unjustifiably impairs any collateral for the instrument given by or on behalf of the party or any person against whom he has a right of recourse.

(2) By express reservation of rights against a party with a right of recourse the holder preserves

  (a) all his rights against such party as of the time when the instrument was originally due; and

  (b) the right of the party to pay the instrument as of that time; and

  (c) all rights of such party to recourse against others.

§ 3-701. Letter of Advice of International Sight Draft

(1) A "letter of advice" is a drawer's communication to the drawee that a described draft has been drawn.

(2) Unless otherwise agreed when a bank receives from another bank a letter of advice of an international sight draft the drawee bank may immediately debit the drawer's account and stop the running of interest pro tanto. Such a debit and any resulting credit to any account covering outstanding drafts leaves in the drawer full power to stop payment or otherwise dispose of the amount and creates no trust or interest in favor of the holder.

(3) Unless otherwise agreed and except where a draft is drawn under a credit issued by the drawee, the drawee of an international sight draft owes the drawer no duty to pay an unadvised draft but if it does so and the draft is genuine, may appropriately debit the drawer's account.

§ 3-801. Drafts in a Set

(1) Where a draft is drawn in a set of parts, each of which is numbered and expressed to be an order only if no other part has been honored, the whole of the parts constitutes one draft but a taker of any part may become a holder in due course of the draft.

(2) Any person who negotiates, indorses or accepts a single part of a draft drawn in a set thereby becomes liable to any holder in due course of that part as if it were the whole set, but as between different holders in due course to whom different parts have been negotiated the holder whose title first accrues has all rights to the draft and its proceeds.

(3) As against the drawee the first presented part of a draft drawn in a set is the part entitled to payment, or if a time draft to acceptance and payment. Acceptance of any subsequently presented part renders the drawee liable thereon under subsection (2). With respect both to a holder and to the drawer payment of a subsequently presented part of a draft payable at sight has the same effect as payment of a check notwithstanding an effective stop order (Section 4-407).

(4) Except as otherwise provided in this section, where any part of a draft in a set is discharged by payment or otherwise the whole draft is discharged.

§ 3-802. Effect of Instrument on Obligation for Which It Is Given

(1) Unless otherwise agreed where an instrument is taken for an underlying obligation

  (a) the obligation is pro tanto discharged if a bank is drawer, maker or acceptor of the instrument and there is no recourse on the instrument against the underlying obligor; and

  (b) in any other case the obligation is suspended pro tanto until the instrument is due or if it is payable on demand until its presentment. If the instrument is dishonored action may be maintained on either the instrument or the obligation; discharge of the underlying obligor on the instrument also discharges him on the obligation.

(2) The taking in good faith of a check which is not post-dated does not of itself so extend the time on the original obligation as to discharge a surety.

§ 3-803. Notice to Third Party

Where a defendant is sued for breach of an obligation for which a third person is answerable over under this Article he may give the third person written notice of the litigation, and the person notified may then give similar notice to any other person who is answerable over to him under this Article. If the notice states that the person notified may come in and defend and that if the person notified does not do so he will in any action against him by the person giving the notice be bound by any determination of fact common to the two litigations, then unless after seasonable receipt of the notice the person notified does come in and defend he is so bound.

§ 3-804. Lost, Destroyed or Stolen Instruments

The owner of an instrument which is lost, whether by destruction, theft or otherwise, may maintain an action in his own name and recover from any party liable thereon upon due proof of his ownership, the facts which prevent his production of the instrument and its terms. The court may require security indemnifying the defendant against loss by reason of further claims on the instrument.

§ 3-805. Instruments Not Payable to Order or to Bearer

This Article applies to any instrument whose terms do not preclude transfer and which is otherwise negotiable within this Article but which is not payable to order or to bearer, except that there can be no holder in due course of such an instrument.

ARTICLE 9

Secured Transactions; Sales of Accounts and Chattel Paper

§ 9-101. Short Title

This Article shall be known and may be cited as Uniform Commercial Code — Secured Transactions.

§ 9-102. Policy and Subject Matter of Article

(1) Except as otherwise provided in Section 9-104 on excluded transactions, this Article applies
  (a) to any transaction (regardless of its form) which is intended to create a security interest in personal property or fixtures including goods, documents, instruments, general intangibles, chattel paper or accounts; and also
  (b) to any sale of accounts or chattel paper.
(2) This Article applies to security interests created by contract including pledge, assignment, chattel mortgage, chattel trust, trust deed, factor's lien, equipment trust, conditional sale, trust receipt, other lien or title retention

contract and lease or consignment intended as security. This Article does not apply to statutory liens except as provided in Section 9-310.

(3) The application of this Article to a security interest in a secured obligation is not affected by the fact that the obligation is itself secured by a transaction or interest to which this Article does not apply.

As amended in 1972.

§ 9-103. Perfection of Security Interest in Multiple State Transactions

(1) Documents, instruments and ordinary goods.

  (a) This subsection applies to documents and instruments and to goods other than those covered by a certificate of title described in subsection (2), mobile goods described in subsection (3), and minerals described in subsection (5).

  (b) Except as otherwise provided in this subsection, perfection and the effect of perfection or non-perfection of a security interest in collateral are governed by the law of the jurisdiction where the collateral is when the last event occurs on which is based the assertion that the security interest is perfected or unperfected.

  (c) If the parties to a transaction creating a purchase money security interest in goods in one jurisdiction understand at the time that the security interest attaches that the goods will be kept in another jurisdiction, then the law of the other jurisdiction governs the perfection and the effect of perfection or non-perfection of the security interest from the time it attaches until thirty days after the debtor receives possession of the goods and thereafter if the goods are taken to the other jurisdiction before the end of the thirty-day period.

  (d) When collateral is brought into and kept in this state while subject to a security interest perfected under the law of the jurisdiction from which the collateral was removed, the security interest remains perfected, but if action is required by Part 3 of this Article to perfect the security interest,

      (i) if the action is not taken before the expiration of the period of perfection in the other jurisdiction or the end of four months after the collateral is brought into this state, whichever period first expires, the security interest becomes unperfected at the end of that period and is thereafter deemed to have been unperfected as against a person who became a purchaser after removal;

      (ii) if the action is taken before the expiration of the period specified in subparagraph (i), the security interest continues perfected thereafter;

      (iii) for the purpose of priority over a buyer of consumer goods (subsection (2) of Section 9-307), the period of the effectiveness of a filing in the jurisdiction from which the collateral is removed is governed by the rules with respect to perfection in subparagraphs (i) and (ii).

(2) Certificate of title.

  (a) This subsection applies to goods covered by a certificate of title issued under a statute of this state or of another jurisdiction under the law of which indication of a security interest on the certificate is required as a condition of perfection.

  (b) Except as otherwise provided in this subsection, perfection and the effect of perfection or non-perfection of the security interest are governed by the law (including the conflict of laws rules) of the jurisdiction issuing the certificate until four months after the goods are removed from that jurisdiction and thereafter until the goods are registered in another jurisdiction, but in any event not beyond surrender of the certificate. After the expiration of that period, the goods are not covered by the certificate of title within the meaning of this section.

  (c) Except with respect to the rights of a buyer described in the next paragraph, a security interest, perfected in another jurisdiction otherwise than by notation on a certificate of title, in goods brought into this state and thereafter covered by a certificate of title issued by this state is subject to the rules stated in paragraph (d) of subsection (1).

  (d) If goods are brought into this state while a security interest therein is perfected in any manner under the law of the jurisdiction from which the goods are removed and a certificate of title is issued by this state and the certificate does not show that the goods are subject to the security interest or that they may be subject to security interests not shown on the certificate, the security interest is subordinate to the rights of a buyer of the goods who is not in the business of selling goods of that kind to the extent that he gives value and receives delivery of the goods after issuance of the certificate and without knowledge of the security interest.

(3) Accounts, general intangibles and mobile goods.

  (a) This subsection applies to accounts (other than an account described in subsection (5) on minerals) and general intangibles (other than uncertificated securities) and to goods which are mobile and which are of a type normally used in more than one jurisdiction, such as motor vehicles, trailers, rolling stock, airplanes, shipping containers, road building and construction machinery and commercial harvesting machinery and the like, if the goods are equipment or are inventory leased or held for lease by the debtor to others, and are not covered by a certificate of title described in subsection (2).

  (b) The law (including the conflict of laws rules) of the jurisdiction in which the debtor is located governs the perfection and the effect of perfection or non-perfection of the security interest.

  (c) If, however, the debtor is located in a jurisdiction which is not a part of the United States, and which does not provide for perfection of the security interest by filing or recording in that jurisdiction, the law of the jurisdiction in the United States in which the debtor has its major executive office in the United States governs the perfection and the effect of perfection or non-perfection of the security interest through filing. In the alternative, if the debtor is located in a jurisdiction which is not a part of the United States or Canada and the collateral is accounts or general intangibles for money due or to become due, the security interest may be perfected by notification to the account debtor. As used in this paragraph, "United States" includes its territories and possessions and the Commonwealth of Puerto Rico.

(d) A debtor shall be deemed located at his place of business if he has one, at his chief executive office if he has more than one place of business, otherwise at his residence. If, however, the debtor is a foreign air carrier under the Federal Aviation Act of 1958, as amended, it shall be deemed located at the designated office of the agent upon whom service of process may be made on behalf of the foreign air carrier.

(e) A security interest perfected under the law of the jurisdiction of the location of the debtor is perfected until the expiration of four months after a change of the debtor's location to another jurisdiction, or until perfection would have ceased by the law of the first jurisdiction, whichever period first expires. Unless perfected in the new jurisdiction before the end of that period, it becomes unperfected thereafter and is deemed to have been unperfected as against a person who became a purchaser after the change.

(4) Chattel paper.

The rules stated for goods in subsection (1) apply to a possessory security interest in chattel paper. The rules stated for accounts in subsection (3) apply to a non-possessory security interest in chattel paper, but the security interest may not be perfected by notification to the account debtor.

(5) Minerals.

Perfection and the effect of perfection or non-perfection of a security interest which is created by a debtor who has an interest in minerals or the like (including oil and gas) before extraction and which attaches thereto as extracted, or which attaches to an account resulting from the sale thereof at the wellhead or minehead are governed by the law (including the conflict of laws rules) of the jurisdiction wherein the wellhead or minehead is located.

(6) Uncertificated securities.

The law (including the conflict of laws rules) of the jurisdiction of organization of the issuer governs the perfection and the effect of perfection or non-perfection of a security interest in uncertificated securities.

As amended in 1972 and 1977.

§ 9-104. Transactions Excluded From Article

This Article does not apply

(a) to a security interest subject to any statute of the United States, to the extent that such statute governs the rights of parties to and third parties affected by transactions in particular types of property; or

(b) to a landlord's lien; or

(c) to a lien given by statute or other rule of law for services or materials except as provided in Section 9-310 on priority of such liens; or

(d) to a transfer of a claim for wages, salary or other compensation of an employee; or

(e) to a transfer by a government or governmental subdivision or agency; or

(f) to a sale of accounts or chattel paper as part of a sale of the business out of which they arose, or an assignment of accounts or chattel paper which is for the purpose of collection only, or a transfer of a right to payment under a contract to an assignee who is also to do the performance under the contract or a transfer of a single account to an assignee in whole or partial satisfaction of a preexisting indebtedness; or

(g) to a transfer of an interest in or claim in or under any policy of insurance, except as provided with respect to proceeds (Section 9-306) and priorities in proceeds (Section 9-312); or

(h) to a right represented by a judgment (other than a judgment taken on a right to payment which was collateral); or

(i) to any right of set-off; or

(j) except to the extent that provision is made for fixtures in Section 9-313, to the creation or transfer of an interest in or lien on real estate, including a lease or rents thereunder; or

(k) to a transfer in whole or in part of any claim arising out of tort; or

(*l*) to a transfer of an interest in any deposit account (subsection (1) of Section 9-105), except as provided with respect to proceeds (Section 9-306) and priorities in proceeds (Section 9-312).

As amended in 1972.

§ 9-105. Definitions and Index of Definitions

(1) In this Article unless the context otherwise requires:

(a) "Account debtor" means the person who is obligated on an account, chattel paper or general intangible;

(b) "Chattel paper" means a writing or writings which evidence both a monetary obligation and a security interest in or a lease of specific goods, but a charter or other contract involving the use or hire of a vessel is not chattel paper. When a transaction is evidenced both by such a security agreement or a lease and by an instrument or a series of instruments, the group of writings taken together constitutes chattel paper;

(c) "Collateral" means the property subject to a security interest, and includes accounts and chattel paper which have been sold;

(d) "Debtor" means the person who owes payment or other performance of the obligation secured, whether or not he owns or has rights in the collateral, and includes the seller of accounts or chattel paper. Where the debtor and the owner of the collateral are not the same person, the term "debtor" means the owner of the collateral in any provision of the Article dealing with the collateral, the obligor in any provision dealing with the obligation, and may include both where the context so requires;

(e) "Deposit account" means a demand, time, savings, passbook or like account maintained with a bank, savings and loan association, credit union or like organization, other than an account evidenced by a certificate of deposit;

(f) "Document" means document of title as defined in the general definitions of Article 1 (Section 1-201), and a receipt of the kind described in subsection (2) of Section 7-201;

(g) "Encumbrance" includes real estate mortgages and other liens on real estate and all other rights in real estate that are not ownership interests;

(h) "Goods" includes all things which are movable at the time the security interest attaches or which are fixtures (Section 9-313), but does not include money, documents, instruments, accounts, chattel paper, general intangibles, or minerals or the like (including oil and gas) before extraction. "Goods" also includes standing timber which is to be cut and removed under a conveyance or contract for sale, the unborn young of animals, and growing crops;

(i) "Instrument" means a negotiable instrument (defined in Section 3-104), or a certificated security (defined in Section 8-102) or any other writing which evidences a right to the payment of money and is not itself a security agreement or lease and is of a type which is in ordinary course of business transferred by delivery with any necessary indorsement or assignment;

(j) "Mortgage" means a consensual interest created by a real estate mortgage, a trust deed on real estate, or the like;

(k) An advance is made "pursuant to commitment" if the secured party has bound himself to make it, whether or not a subsequent event of default or other event not within his control has relieved or may relieve him from his obligation;

(l) "Security agreement" means an agreement which creates or provides for a security interest;

(m) "Secured party" means a lender, seller or other person in whose favor there is a security interest, including a person to whom accounts or chattel paper have been sold. When the holders of obligations issued under an indenture of trust, equipment trust agreement or the like are represented by a trustee or other person, the representative is the secured party;

(n) "Transmitting utility" means any person primarily engaged in the railroad, street railway or trolley bus business, the electric or electronics communications transmission business, the transmission of goods by pipeline, or the transmission or the production and transmission of electricity, steam, gas or water, or the provision of sewer service.

(2) Other definitions applying to this Article and the sections in which they appear are:

"Account".	Section 9-106.
"Attach".	Section 9-203.
"Construction mortgage".	Section 9-313(1).
"Consumer goods".	Section 9-109(1).
"Equipment".	Section 9-109(2).
"Farm products".	Section 9-109(3).
"Fixture".	Section 9-313(1).

"Fixture filing".	Section 9-313(1).
"General intangibles".	Section 9-106.
"Inventory".	Section 9-109(4).
"Lien creditor".	Section 9-301(3).
"Proceeds".	Section 9-306(1).
"Purchase money security interest".	Section 9-107.
"United States".	Section 9-103.

(3) The following definitions in other Articles apply to this Article:

"Check".	Section 3-104.
"Contract for sale".	Section 2-106.
"Holder in due course".	Section 3-302.
"Note".	Section 3-104.
"Sale".	Section 2-106.

(4) In addition Article 1 contains general definitions and principles of construction and interpretation applicable throughout this Article.

As amended in 1966, 1972 and 1977.

§ 9-106. Definitions: "Account"; "General Intangibles"

"Account" means any right to payment for goods sold or leased or for services rendered which is not evidenced by an instrument or chattel paper, whether or not it has been earned by performance. "General intangibles" means any personal property (including things in action) other than goods, accounts, chattel paper, documents, instruments, and money. All rights to payment earned or unearned under a charter or other contract involving the use or hire of a vessel and all rights incident to the charter or contract are accounts.

As amended in 1966 and 1972.

§ 9-107. Definitions: "Purchase Money Security Interest"

A security interest is a "purchase money security interest" to the extent that it is

(a) taken or retained by the seller of the collateral to secure all or part of its price; or

(b) taken by a person who by making advances or incurring an obligation gives value to enable the debtor to acquire rights in or the use of collateral if such value is in fact so used.

§ 9-108. When After-Acquired Collateral Not Security for Antecedent Debt

Where a secured party makes an advance, incurs an obligation, releases a perfected security interest, or otherwise gives new value which is to be secured in whole or in part by after-acquired property his security interest in the after-acquired collateral shall be deemed to be taken for new value and not as security for an antecedent debt if the debtor acquires his rights in such collateral either in the ordinary course of his business or under a contract of purchase made pursuant to the security agreement within a reasonable time after new value is given.

§ 9-109. Classification of Goods: "Consumer Goods"; "Equipment"; "Farm Products"; "Inventory"

Goods are

(1) "consumer goods" if they are used or bought for use primarily for personal, family or household purposes;

(2) "equipment" if they are used or bought for use primarily in business (including farming or a profession) or by a debtor who is a non-profit organization or a governmental subdivision or agency or if the goods are not included in the definitions of inventory, farm products or consumer goods;

(3) "farm products" if they are crops or livestock or supplies used or produced in farming operations or if they are products of crops or livestock in their unmanufactured states (such as ginned cotton, wool-clip, maple syrup, milk and eggs), and if they are in the possession of a debtor engaged in raising, fattening, grazing or other farming operations. If goods are farm products they are neither equipment nor inventory;

(4) "inventory" if they are held by a person who holds them for sale or lease or to be furnished under contracts of service or if he has so furnished them, or if they are raw materials, work in process or materials used or consumed in a business. Inventory of a person is not to be classified as his equipment.

§ 9-110. Sufficiency of Description

For the purposes of this Article any description of personal property or real estate is sufficient whether or not it is specific if it reasonably identifies what is described.

§ 9-111. Applicability of Bulk Transfer Laws

The creation of a security interest is not a bulk transfer under Article 6 (see Section 6-103).

§ 9-112. Where Collateral Is Not Owned by Debtor

Unless otherwise agreed, when a secured party knows that collateral is owned by a person who is not the debtor, the owner of the collateral is entitled to receive from the secured party any surplus under Section 9-502(2) or under Section 9-504(1), and is not liable for the debt or for any deficiency after resale, and he has the same right as the debtor

    (a) to receive statements under Section 9-208;

    (b) to receive notice of and to object to a secured party's proposal to retain the collateral in satisfaction of the indebtedness under Section 9-505;

    (c) to redeem the collateral under Section 9-506;

    (d) to obtain injunctive or other relief under Section 9-507(1); and

    (e) to recover losses caused to him under Section 9-208(2).

§ 9-113. Security Interests Arising Under Article on Sales or Under Article on Leases

A security interest arising solely under the Article on Sales (Article 2) or the Article on Leases (Article 2A) is subject to the provisions of this Article except that to the extent that and so long as the debtor does not have or does not lawfully obtain possession of the goods

(a) no security agreement is necessary to make the security interest enforceable; and

(b) no filing is required to perfect the security interest; and

(c) the rights of the secured party on default by the debtor are governed (i) by the Article on Sales (Article 2) in the case of a security interest arising solely under such Article or (ii) by the Article on Leases (Article 2A) in the case of a security interest arising solely under such article.

As amended in 1987.

§ 9-114. Consignment

(1) A person who delivers goods under a consignment which is not a security interest and who would be required to file under this Article by paragraph (3)(c) of Section 2-326 has priority over a secured party who is or becomes a creditor of the consignee and who would have a perfected security interest in the goods if they were the property of the consignee, and also has priority with respect to identifiable cash proceeds received on or before delivery of the goods to a buyer, if

(a) the consignor complies with the filing provision of the Article on Sales with respect to consignments (paragraph (3) (c) of Section 2-326) before the consignee receives possession of the goods; and

(b) the consignor gives notification in writing to the holder of the security interest if the holder has filed a financing statement covering the same types of goods before the date of the filing made by the consignor; and

(c) the holder of the security interest receives the notification within five years before the consignee receives possession of the goods; and

(d) the notification states that the consignor expects to deliver goods on consignment to the consignee, describing the goods by item or type.

(2) In the case of a consignment which is not a security interest and in which the requirements of the preceding subsection have not been met, a person who delivers goods to another is subordinate to a person who would have a perfected security interest in the goods if they were the property of the debtor.

As added in 1972.

§ 9-201. General Validity of Security Agreement

Except as otherwise provided by this Act a security agreement is effective according to its terms between the parties, against purchasers of the collateral and against creditors. Nothing in this Article validates any charge or practice illegal under any statute or regulation thereunder governing usury, small loans, retail installment sales, or the like, or extends the application of any such statute or regulation to any transaction not otherwise subject thereto.

§ 9-202. Title to Collateral Immaterial

Each provision of this Article with regard to rights, obligations and remedies applies whether title to collateral is in the secured party or in the debtor.

§ 9-203. Attachment and Enforceability of Security Interest; Proceeds; Formal Requisites

(1) Subject to the provisions of Section 4-208 on the security interest of a collecting bank, Section 8-321 on security interests in securities and Section 9-113 on a security interest arising under the Article on Sales, a security interest is not enforceable against the debtor or third parties with respect to the collateral and does not attach unless:

    (a) the collateral is in the possession of the secured party pursuant to agreement, or the debtor has signed a security agreement which contains a description of the collateral and in addition, when the security interest covers crops growing or to be grown or timber to be cut, a description of the land concerned;

    (b) value has been given; and

    (c) the debtor has rights in the collateral.

(2) A security interest attaches when it becomes enforceable against the debtor with respect to the collateral. Attachment occurs as soon as all of the events specified in subsection (1) have taken place unless explicit agreement postpones the time of attaching.

(3) Unless otherwise agreed a security agreement gives the secured party the rights to proceeds provided by Section 9-306.

(4) A transaction, although subject to this Article, is also subject to ....*, and in the case of conflict between the provisions of this Article and any such statute, the provisions of such statute control. Failure to comply with any applicable statute has only the effect which is specified therein. As amended in 1972 and 1977.

Note: *At * in subsection (4) insert reference to any local statute regulating small loans, retail installment sales and the like....*

§ 9-204. After-Acquired Property; Future Advances

(1) Except as provided in subsection (2), a security agreement may provide that any or all obligations covered by the security agreement are to be secured by after-acquired collateral.

(2) No security interest attaches under an after-acquired property clause to consumer goods other than accessions (Section 9-314) when given as additional security unless the debtor acquires rights in them within ten days after the secured party gives value.

(3) Obligations covered by a security agreement may include future advances or other value whether or not the advances or value are given pursuant to commitment (subsection (1) of Section 9-105). Amended in 1972.

§ 9-205. Use or Disposition of Collateral Without Accounting Permissible

A security interest is not invalid or fraudulent against creditors by reason of liberty in the debtor to use, commingle or dispose of all or part of the collateral (including returned or repossessed goods) or to collect or compromise accounts or chattel paper, or to accept the return of goods or make repossessions, or to use, commingle or dispose of proceeds, or by reason of the failure of the secured party to require the debtor to account for proceeds or replace collateral. This section does not relax the requirements of possession where perfection of a security interest depends upon possession of the collateral by the secured party or by a bailee.
As amended in 1972.

§ 9-206. Agreement Not to Assert Defenses Against Assignee; Modification of Sales Warranties Where Security Agreement Exists

(1) Subject to any statute or decision which establishes a different rule for buyers or lessees of consumer goods, an agreement by a buyer or lessee that he will not assert against an assignee any claim or defense which he may have against the seller or lessor is enforceable by an assignee who takes his assignment for value, in good faith and without notice of a claim or defense, except as to defenses of a type which may be asserted against a holder in due course of a negotiable instrument under the Article on Commercial Paper (Article 3). A buyer who as part of one transaction signs both a negotiable instrument and a security agreement makes such an agreement.

(2) When a seller retains a purchase money security interest in goods the Article on Sales (Article 2) governs the sale and any disclaimer, limitation or modification of the seller's warranties.
As amended in 1962.

§ 9-207. Rights and Duties When Collateral is in Secured Party's Possession

(1) A secured party must use reasonable care in the custody and preservation of collateral in his possession. In the case of an instrument or chattel paper reasonable care includes taking necessary steps to preserve rights against prior parties unless otherwise agreed.

(2) Unless otherwise agreed, when collateral is in the secured party's possession

   (a) reasonable expenses (including the cost of any insurance and payment of taxes or other charges) incurred in the custody, preservation, use or operation of the collateral are chargeable to the debtor and are secured by the collateral;

   (b) the risk of accidental loss or damage is on the debtor to the extent of any deficiency in any effective insurance coverage;

   (c) the secured party may hold as additional security any increase or profits (except money) received from the collateral, but money so received, unless remitted to the debtor, shall be applied in reduction of the secured obligation;

   (d) the secured party must keep the collateral identifiable but fungible collateral may be commingled;

   (e) the secured party may repledge the collateral upon terms which do not impair the debtor's right to redeem it.

(3) A secured party is liable for any loss caused by his failure to meet any obligation imposed by the preceding subsections but does not lose his security interest.

(4) A secured party may use or operate the collateral for the purpose of preserving the collateral or its value or pursuant to the order of a court of appropriate jurisdiction or, except in the case of consumer goods, in the manner and to the extent provided in the security agreement.

§ 9-208. Request for Statement of Account or List of Collateral

(1) A debtor may sign a statement indicating what he believes to be the aggregate amount of unpaid indebtedness as of a specified date and may send it to the secured party with a request that the statement be approved or corrected and returned to the debtor. When the security agreement or any other record kept by the secured party identifies the collateral a debtor may similarly request the secured party to approve or correct a list of the collateral.

(2) The secured party must comply with such a request within two weeks after receipt by sending a written correction or approval. If the secured party claims a security interest in all of a particular type of collateral owned by the debtor he may indicate that fact in his reply and need not approve or correct an itemized list of such collateral. If the secured party without reasonable excuse fails to comply he is liable for any loss caused to the debtor thereby; and if the debtor has properly included in his request a good faith statement of the obligation or a list of the collateral or both the secured party may claim a security interest only as shown in the statement against persons misled by his

failure to comply. If he no longer has an interest in the obligation or collateral at the time the request is received he must disclose the name and address of any successor in interest known to him and he is liable for any loss caused to the debtor as a result of failure to disclose. A successor in interest is not subject to this section until a request is received by him.

(3) A debtor is entitled to such a statement once every six months without charge. The secured party may require payment of a charge not exceeding $10 for each additional statement furnished.

§ 9-301. Persons Who Take Priority Over Unperfected Security Interests; Rights of "Lien Creditor"

(1) Except as otherwise provided in subsection (2), an unperfected security interest is subordinate to the rights of
  (a) persons entitled to priority under Section 9-312;
  (b) a person who becomes a lien creditor before the security interest is perfected;
  (c) in the case of goods, instruments, documents, and chattel paper, a person who is not a secured party and who is a transferee in bulk or other buyer not in ordinary course of business or is a buyer of farm products in ordinary course of business, to the extent that he gives value and receives delivery of the collateral without knowledge of the security interest and before it is perfected;
  (d) in the case of accounts and general intangibles, a person who is not a secured party and who is a transferee to the extent that he gives value without knowledge of the security interest and before it is perfected.

(2) If the secured party files with respect to a purchase money security interest before or within ten days after the debtor receives possession of the collateral, he takes priority over the rights of a transferee in bulk or of a lien creditor which arise between the time the security interest attaches and the time of filing.

(3) A "lien creditor" means a creditor who has acquired a lien on the property involved by attachment, levy or the like and includes an assignee for benefit of creditors from the time of assignment, and a trustee in bankruptcy from the date of the filing of the petition or a receiver in equity from the time of appointment.

(4) A person who becomes a lien creditor while a security interest is perfected takes subject to the security interest only to the extent that it secures advances made before he becomes a lien creditor or within 45 day's thereafter or made without knowledge of the lien or pursuant to a commitment entered into without knowledge of the lien. Amended in 1972.

§ 9-302. When Filing Is Required to Perfect Security Interest; Security Interests to Which Filing Provisions of This Article Do Not Apply

(1) A financing statement must be filed to perfect all security interests except the following:

(a) a security interest in collateral in possession of the secured party under Section 9-305;

(b) a security interest temporarily perfected in instruments or documents without delivery under Section 9-304 or in proceeds for a 10 day period under Section 9-306;

(c) a security interest created by an assignment of a beneficial interest in a trust or a decedent's estate;

(d) a purchase money security interest in consumer goods; but filing is required for a motor vehicle required to be registered; and fixture filing is required for priority over conflicting interests in fixtures to the extent provided in Section 9-313;

(e) an assignment of accounts which does not alone or in conjunction with other assignments to the same assignee transfer a significant part of the outstanding accounts of the assignor;

(f) a security interest of a collecting bank (Section 4-208) or in securities (Section 8-321) or arising under the Article on Sales (see Section 9-113) or covered in subsection (3) of this section;

(g) an assignment for the benefit of all the creditors of the transferor, and subsequent transfers by the assignee thereunder.

(2) If a secured party assigns a perfected security interest, no filing under this Article is required in order to continue the perfected status of the security interest against creditors of and transferees from the original debtor.

(3) The filing of a financing statement otherwise required by this Article is not necessary or effective to perfect a security interest in property subject to

(a) a statute or treaty of the United States which provides for a national or international registration or a national or international certificate of title or which specifies a place of filing different from that specified in this Article for filing of the security interest; or

(b) the following statutes of this state; [list any certificate of title statute covering automobiles, trailers, mobile homes, boats, farm tractors, or the like, and any central filing statute *.]; but during any period in which collateral is inventory held for sale by a person who is in the business of selling goods of that kind, the filing provisions of this Article (Part 4) apply to a security interest in that collateral created by him as debtor; or

(c) a certificate of title statute of another jurisdiction under the law of which indication of a security interest on the certificate is required as a condition of perfection (subsection (2) of Section 9-103).

(4) Compliance with a statute or treaty described in subsection (3) is equivalent to the filing of a financing statement under this Article, and a security interest in property subject to the statute or treaty can be perfected only by compliance therewith except as provided in Section 9-103 on multiple state

transactions. Duration and renewal of perfection of a security interest perfected by compliance with the statute or treaty are governed by the provisions of the statute or treaty; in other respects the security interest is subject to this Article.
As amended in 1972 and 1977.

§ 9-303. When Security Interest Is Perfected; Continuity of Perfection

(1) A security interest is perfected when it has attached and when all of the applicable steps required for perfection have been taken. Such steps are specified in Sections 9-302, 9-304, 9-305 and 9-306. If such steps are taken before the security interest attaches, it is perfected at the time when it attaches.

(2) If a security interest is originally perfected in any way permitted under this Article and is subsequently perfected in some other way under this Article, without an intermediate period when it was unperfected, the security interest shall be deemed to be perfected continuously for the purposes of this Article.

§ 9-304. Perfection of Security Interest in Instruments, Documents, and Goods Covered by Documents; Perfection by Permissive Filing; Temporary Perfection Without Filing or Transfer of Possession

(1) A security interest in chattel paper or negotiable documents may be perfected by filing. A security interest in money or instruments (other than certificated securities or instruments which constitute part of chattel paper) can be perfected only by the secured party's taking possession, except as provided in subsections (4) and (5) of this section and subsections (2) and (3) of Section 9-306 on proceeds.

(2) During the period that goods are in the possession of the issuer of a negotiable document therefor, a security interest in the goods is perfected by perfecting a security interest in the document, and any security interest in the goods otherwise perfected during such period is subject thereto.

(3) A security interest in goods in the possession of a bailee other than one who has issued a negotiable document therefor is perfected by issuance of a document in the name of the secured party or by the bailee's receipt of notification of the secured party's interest or by filing as to the goods.

(4) A security interest in instruments (other than certificated securities) or negotiable documents is perfected without filing or the taking of possession for a period of 21 days from the time it attaches to the extent that it arises for new value given under a written security agreement.

(5) A security interest remains perfected for a period of 21 days without filing where a secured party having a perfected security interest in an instrument (other than a certificated security), a negotiable document or goods in possession of a bailee other than one who has issued a negotiable document therefor

    (a) makes available to the debtor the goods or documents representing the goods for the purpose of ultimate sale or exchange or for the purpose of loading, unloading, storing, shipping, transshipping, manufacturing, processing or otherwise dealing with them in a manner preliminary to their sale or exchange, but priority between conflicting security interests in the goods is subject to subsection (3) of Section 9-312; or

(b) delivers the instrument to the debtor for the purpose of ultimate sale or exchange or of presentation, collection, renewal or registration of transfer.

(6) After the 21 day period in subsections (4) and (5) perfection depends upon compliance with applicable provisions of *this Article.*
As amended in 1972 and 1977.

§ 9-305. When Possession by Secured Party Perfects Security Interest Without Filing

A security interest in letters of credit and advices of credit (subsection (2) (a) of Section 5-116), goods, instruments (other than certificated securities), money, negotiable documents, or chattel paper may be perfected by the secured party's taking possession of the collateral. If such collateral other than goods covered by a negotiable document is held by a bailee, the secured party is deemed to have possession from the time the bailee receives notification of the secured party's interest. A security interest is perfected by possession from the time possession is taken without a relation back and continues only so long as possession is retained, unless otherwise specified in this Article. The security interest may be otherwise perfected as provided in this Article before or after the period of possession by the secured party.
As amended in 1972 and 1977.

§ 9-306. "Proceeds"; Secured Party's Rights on Disposition of Collateral

(1) "Proceeds" includes whatever is received upon the sale, exchange, collection or other disposition of collateral or proceeds. Insurance payable by reason of loss or damage to the collateral is proceeds, except to the extent that it is payable to a person other than a party to the security agreement. Money, checks, deposit accounts, and the like are "cash proceeds". All other proceeds are "non-cash proceeds".

(2) Except where this Article otherwise provides, a security interest continues in collateral notwithstanding sale, exchange or other disposition thereof unless the disposition was authorized by the secured party in the security agreement or otherwise, and also continues in any identifiable proceeds including collections received by the debtor.

(3) The security interest in proceeds is a continuously perfected security interest if the interest in the original collateral was perfected but it ceases to be a perfected security interest and becomes unperfected ten days after receipt of the proceeds by the debtor unless

(a) a filed financing statement covers the original collateral and the proceeds are collateral in which a security interest may be perfected by filing in the office or offices where the financing statement has been filed and, if the proceeds are acquired with cash proceeds, the description of collateral in the financing statement indicates the types of property constituting the proceeds; or

(b) a filed financing statement covers the original collateral and the proceeds are identifiable cash proceeds; or

(c) the security interest in the proceeds is perfected before the expiration of the ten day period.

Except as provided in this section, a security interest in proceeds can be perfected only by the methods or under the circumstances permitted in this Article for original collateral of the same type.

(4) In the event of insolvency proceedings instituted by or against a debtor, a secured party with a perfected security interest in proceeds has a perfected security interest only in the following proceeds:

(a) in identifiable non-cash proceeds and in separate deposit accounts containing only proceeds;

(b) in identifiable cash proceeds in the form of money which is neither commingled with other money nor deposited in a deposit account prior to the insolvency proceedings;

(c) in identifiable cash proceeds in the form of checks and the like which are not deposited in a deposit account prior to the insolvency proceedings; and

(d) in all cash and deposit accounts of the debtor in which proceeds have been commingled with other funds, but the perfected security interest under this paragraph (d) is

(i) subject to any right to setoff; and

(ii) limited to an amount not greater than the amount of any cash proceeds received by the debtor within ten days before the institution of the insolvency proceedings less the sum of (I) the payments to the secured party on account of cash proceeds received by the debtor during such period and (II) the cash proceeds received by the debtor during such period to which the secured party is entitled under paragraphs (a) through (c) of this subsection (4).

(5) If a sale of goods results in an account or chattel paper which is transferred by the seller to a secured party, and if the goods are returned to or are repossessed by the seller or the secured party, the following rules determine priorities:

(a) If the goods were collateral at the time of sale, for an indebtedness of the seller which is still unpaid, the original security interest attaches again to the goods and continues as a perfected security interest if it was perfected at the time when the goods were sold. If the security interest was originally perfected by a filing which is still effective, nothing further is required to continue the perfected status; in any other case, the secured party must take possession of the returned or repossessed goods or must file.

(b) An unpaid transferee of the chattel paper has a security interest in the goods against the transferor. Such security interest is prior to a security interest asserted under paragraph (a) to the extent that the transferee of the chattel paper was entitled to priority under Section 9-308.

(c) An unpaid transferee of the account has a security interest in the goods against the transferor. Such security interest is subordinate to a security interest asserted under paragraph (a).

(d) A security interest of an unpaid transferee asserted under paragraph (b) or (c) must be perfected for protection against creditors of the transferor and purchasers of the returned or repossessed goods.

As amended in 1972.

§ 9-307. Protection of Buyers of Goods

(1) A buyer in ordinary course of business (subsection (9) of Section 1-201) other than a person buying farm products from a person engaged in farming operations takes free of a security interest created by his seller even though the security interest is perfected and even though the buyer knows of its existence.

(2) In the case of consumer goods, a buyer takes free of a security interest even though perfected if he buys without knowledge of the security interest, for value and for his own personal, family or household purposes unless prior to the purchase the secured party has filed a financing statement covering such goods.

(3) A buyer other than a buyer in ordinary course of business (subsection (1) of this section) takes free of a security interest to the extent that it secures future advances made after the secured party acquires knowledge of the purchase, or more than 45 days after the purchase, whichever first occurs, unless made pursuant to a commitment entered into without knowledge of the purchase and before the expiration of the 45 day period.

As amended in 1972.

§ 9-308. Purchase of Chattel Paper and Instruments

A purchaser of chattel paper or an instrument who gives new value and takes possession of it in the ordinary course of his business has priority over a security interest in the chattel paper or instrument

(a) which is perfected under Section 9-304 (permissive filing and temporary perfection) or under Section 9-306 (perfection as to proceeds) if he acts without knowledge that the specific paper or instrument is subject to a security interest; or

(b) which is claimed merely as proceeds of inventory subject to a security interest (Section 9-306) even though he knows that the specific paper or instrument is subject to the security interest.

As amended in 1972.

§ 9-309. Protection of Purchasers of Instruments, Documents and Securities

Nothing in this Article limits the rights of a holder in due course of a negotiable instrument (Section 3-302) or a holder to whom a negotiable document of title has been duly negotiated (Section 7-501) or a bona fide purchaser of a security (Section 8-302) and the holders or purchasers take priority over an earlier security interest even though perfected. Filing under this Article does not constitute notice of the security interest to such holders or purchasers.
As amended in 1977.

§ 9-310. Priority of Certain Liens Arising by Operation of Law

When a person in the ordinary course of his business furnishes services or materials with respect to goods subject to a security interest, a lien upon goods in the possession of such person given by statute or rule of law for such materials or services takes priority over a perfected security interest unless the lien is statutory and the statute expressly provides otherwise.

§ 9-311. Alienability of Debtor's Rights: Judicial Process

The debtor's rights in collateral may be voluntarily or involuntarily transferred (by way of sale, creation of a security interest, attachment, levy, garnishment or other judicial process) notwithstanding a provision in the security agreement prohibiting any transfer or making the transfer constitute a default.

§ 9-312. Priorities Among Conflicting Security Interests in the Same Collateral

(1) The rules of priority stated in other sections of this Part and in the following sections shall govern when applicable: Section 4-208 with respect to the security interests of collecting banks in items being collected, accompanying documents and proceeds; Section 9-103 on security interests related to other jurisdictions; Section 9-114 on consignments.

(2) A perfected security interest in crops for new value given to enable the debtor to produce the crops during the production season and given not more than three months before the crops become growing crops by planting or otherwise takes priority over an earlier perfected security interest to the extent that such earlier interest secures obligations due more than six months before the crops become growing crops by planting or otherwise, even though the person giving new value had knowledge of the earlier security interest.

(3) A perfected purchase money security interest in inventory has priority over a conflicting security interest in the same inventory and also has priority in identifiable cash proceeds received on or before the delivery of the inventory to a buyer if

    (a) the purchase money security interest is perfected at the time the debtor receives possession of the inventory; and

    (b) the purchase money secured party gives notification in writing to the holder of the conflicting security interest if the holder had filed a financing statement covering the same types of inventory (i) before the date of the filing made by the purchase money secured party, or (ii) before the beginning of the 21 day period where the purchase money security interest is temporarily perfected without filing or possession (subsection (5) of Section 9-304); and

(c) the holder of the conflicting security interest receives the notification within five years before the debtor receives possession of the inventory; and

(d) the notification states that the person giving the notice has or expects to acquire a purchase money security interest in inventory of the debtor, describing such inventory by item or type.

(4) A purchase money security interest in collateral other than inventory has priority over a conflicting security interest in the same collateral or its proceeds if the purchase money security interest is perfected at the time the debtor receives possession of the collateral or within ten days thereafter.

(5) In all cases not governed by other rules stated in this section (including cases of purchase money security interests which do not qualify for the special priorities set forth in subsections (3) and (4) of this section), priority between conflicting security interests in the same collateral shall be determined according to the following rules:

(a) Conflicting security interests rank according to priority in time of filing or perfection. Priority dates from the time a filing is first made covering the collateral or the time the security interest is first perfected, whichever is earlier, provided that there is no period thereafter when there is neither filing nor perfection.

(b) So long as conflicting security interests are unperfected, the first to attach has priority.

(6) For the purposes of subsection (5) a date of filing or perfection as to collateral is also a date of filing or perfection as to proceeds.

(7) If future advances are made while a security interest is perfected by filing, the taking of possession, or under Section 8-321 on securities, the security interest has the same priority for the purposes of subsection (5) with respect to the future advances as it does with respect to the first advance. If a commitment is made before or while the security interest is so perfected, the security interest has the same priority with respect to advances made pursuant thereto. In other cases a perfected security interest has priority from the date the advance is made.

As amended in 1972 and 1977.

§ 9-313. Priority of Security Interests in Fixtures

(1) In this section and in the provisions of Part 4 of this Article referring to fixture filing, unless the context otherwise requires

(a) goods are "fixtures" when they become so related to particular real estate that an interest in them arises under real estate law

(b) a "fixture filing" is the filing in the office where a mortgage on the real estate would be filed or recorded of a financing statement covering goods which are or are to become fixtures and conforming to the requirements of subsection (5) of Section 9-402

(c) a mortgage is a "construction mortgage" to the extent that it secures an obligation incurred for the construction of an improvement on land including the acquisition cost of the land, if the recorded writing so indicates.

(2) A security interest under this Article may be created in goods which are fixtures or may continue in goods which become fixtures, but no security interest exists under this Article in ordinary building materials incorporated into an improvement on land.

(3) This Article does not prevent creation of an encumbrance upon fixtures pursuant to real estate law.

(4) A perfected security interest in fixtures has priority over the conflicting interest of an encumbrancer or owner of the real estate where

(a) the security interest is a purchase money security interest, the interest of the encumbrancer or owner arises before the goods become fixtures, the security interest is perfected by a fixture filing before the goods become fixtures or within ten days thereafter, and the debtor has an interest of record in the real estate or is in possession of the real estate; or

(b) the security interest is perfected by a fixture filing before the interest of the encumbrancer or owner is of record, the security interest has priority over any conflicting interest of a predecessor in title of the encumbrancer or owner, and the debtor has an interest of record in the real estate or is in possession of the real estate; or

(c) the fixtures are readily removable factory or office machines or readily removable replacements of domestic appliances which are consumer goods, and before the goods become fixtures the security interest is perfected by any method permitted by this Article; or

(d) the conflicting interest is a lien on the real estate obtained by legal or equitable proceedings after the security interest was perfected by any method permitted by this Article.

(5) A security interest in fixtures, whether or not perfected, has priority over the conflicting interest of an encumbrancer or owner of the real estate where

(a) the encumbrancer or owner has consented in writing to the security interest or has disclaimed an interest in the goods as fixtures; or

(b) the debtor has a right to remove the goods as against the encumbrancer or owner. If the debtor's right terminates, the priority of the security interest continues for a reasonable time.

(6) Notwithstanding paragraph (a) of subsection (4) but otherwise subject to subsections (4) and (5), a security interest in fixtures is subordinate to a construction mortgage recorded before the goods become fixtures if the goods become fixtures before the completion of the construction. To the extent that it is given to refinance a construction mortgage, a mortgage has this priority to the same extent as the construction mortgage.

(7) In cases not within the preceding subsections, a security interest in fixtures is subordinate to the conflicting interest of an encumbrancer or owner of the related real estate who is not the debtor.

(8) When the secured party has priority over all owners and encumbrancers of the real estate, he may, on default, subject to the provisions of Part 5, remove his collateral from the real estate but he must reimburse any encumbrancer or owner of the real estate who is not the debtor and who has not otherwise agreed for the cost of repair of any physical injury, but not for any diminution in value of the real estate caused by the absence of the goods removed or by any necessity of replacing them. A person entitled to reimbursement may refuse permission to remove until the secured party gives adequate security for the performance of this obligation.
As amended in 1972.

§ 9-314. Accessions

(1) A security interest in goods which attaches before they are installed in or affixed to other goods takes priority as to the goods installed or affixed (called in this section "accessions") over the claims of all persons to the whole except as stated in subsection (3) and subject to Section 9-315(1).

(2) A security interest which attaches to goods after they become part of a whole is valid against all persons subsequently acquiring interests in the whole except as stated in subsection (3) but is invalid against any person with an interest in the whole at the time the security interest attaches to the goods who has not in writing consented to the security interest or disclaimed an interest in the goods as part of the whole.

(3) The security interests described in subsections (1) and (2) do not take priority over

    (a) a subsequent purchaser for value of any interest in the whole; or

    (b) a creditor with a lien on the whole subsequently obtained by judicial proceedings; or

    (c) a creditor with a prior perfected security interest in the whole to the extent that he makes subsequent advances

if the subsequent purchase is made, the lien by judicial proceedings obtained or the subsequent advance under the prior perfected security interest is made or contracted for without knowledge of the security interest and before it is perfected. A purchaser of the whole at a foreclosure sale other than the holder of a perfected security interest purchasing at his own foreclosure sale is a subsequent purchaser within this section.

(4) When under subsections (1) or (2) and (3) a secured party has an interest in accessions which has priority over the claims of all persons who have interests in the whole, he may on default subject to the provisions of Part 5 remove his collateral from the whole but he must reimburse any encumbrancer or owner of the whole who is not the debtor and who has not otherwise agreed for the cost of repair of any physical injury but not for any diminution in value of the whole caused by the absence of the goods removed or by any necessity for replacing them. A person entitled to reimbursement may refuse permission to remove until the secured party gives adequate security for the performance of this obligation.

§ 9-315. Priority When Goods Are Commingled or Processed

(1) If a security interest in goods was perfected and subsequently the goods or a part thereof have become part of a product or mass, the security interest continues in the product or mass if
  - (a) the goods are so manufactured, processed, assembled or commingled that their identity is lost in the product or mass; or
  - (b) a financing statement covering the original goods also covers the product into which the goods have been manufactured, processed or assembled.

In a case to which paragraph (b) applies, no separate security interest in that part of the original goods which has been manufactured, processed or assembled into the product may be claimed under Section 9-314.

(2) When under subsection (1) more than one security interest attaches to the product or mass, they rank equally according to the ratio that the cost of the goods to which each interest originally attached bears to the cost of the total product or mass.

§ 9-316. Priority Subject to Subordination

Nothing in this Article prevents subordination by agreement by any person entitled to priority.

§ 9-317. Secured Party Not Obligated on Contract of Debtor

The mere existence of a security interest or authority given to the debtor to dispose of or use collateral does not impose contract or tort liability upon the secured party for the debtor's acts or omissions.

§ 9-318. Defenses Against Assignee; Modification of Contract After Notification of Assignment; Term Prohibiting Assignment Ineffective; Identification and Proof of Assignment

(1) Unless an account debtor has made an enforceable agreement not to assert defenses or claims arising out of a sale as provided in Section 9-206 the rights of an assignee are subject to
  - (a) all the terms of the contract between the account debtor and assignor and any defense or claim arising therefrom; and
  - (b) any other defense or claim of the account debtor against the assignor which accrues before the account debtor receives notification of the assignment.

(2) So far as the right to payment or a part thereof under an assigned contract has not been fully earned by performance, and notwithstanding notification of the assignment, any modification of or substitution for the contract made in good faith and in accordance with reasonable commercial standards is effective against an assignee unless the account debtor has otherwise agreed but the assignee acquires corresponding rights under the modified or substituted contract. The assignment may provide that such modification or substitution is a breach by the assignor.

(3) The account debtor is authorized to pay the assignor until the account debtor receives notification that the amount due or to become due has been

assigned and that payment is to be made to the assignee. A notification which does not reasonably identify the rights assigned is ineffective. If requested by the account debtor, the assignee must seasonably furnish reasonable proof that the assignment has been made and unless he does so the account debtor may pay the assignor.

(4) A term in any contract between an account debtor and an assignor is ineffective if it prohibits assignment of an account or prohibits creation of a security interest in a general intangible for money due or to become due or requires the account debtor's consent to such assignment or security interest. As amended in 1972.

§ 9-401. Place of Filing; Erroneous Filing; Removal of Collateral

First Alternative Subsection (1)

(1) The proper place to file in order to perfect a security interest is as follows:

(a) when the collateral is timber to be cut or is minerals or the like (including oil and gas) or accounts subject to subsection (5) of Section 9-103, or when the financing statement is filed as a fixture filing (Section 9-313) and the collateral is goods which are or are to become fixtures, then in the office where a mortgage on the real estate would be filed or recorded;

(b) in all other cases, in the office of the [Secretary of State].

Second Alternative Subsection (1)

(1) The proper place to file in order to perfect a security interest is as follows:

(a) when the collateral is equipment used in farming operations, or farm products, or accounts or general intangibles arising from or relating to the sale of farm products by a farmer, or consumer goods, then in the office of the .... in the county of the debtor's residence or if the debtor is not a resident of this state then in the office of the .... in the county where the goods are kept, and in addition when the collateral is crops growing or to be grown in the office of the .... in the county where the land is located;

(b) when the collateral is timber to be cut or is minerals or the like (including oil and gas) or accounts subject to subsection (5) of Section 9-103, or when the financing statement is filed as a fixture filing (Section 9-313) and the collateral is goods which are or are to become fixtures, then in the office where a mortgage on the real estate would be filed or recorded;

(c) in all other cases, in the office of the [Secretary of State].

Third Alternative Subsection (1)

(1) The proper place to file in order to perfect a security interest is as follows:

(a) when the collateral is equipment used in farming operations, or farm products, or accounts or general intangibles arising from or relating to the sale of farm products by a farmer, or consumer goods, then in the office of the ...... in the county of the debtor's residence or if the debtor is not a resident of this state then in the office of the .... in the county where the goods are kept, and in addition when the collateral is crops growing or to be grown in the office of the ...... in the county where the land is located;

(b) when the collateral is timber to be cut or is minerals or the like (including oil and gas) or accounts subject to subsection (5) of Section 9-103, or when the financing statement is filed as a fixture filing (Section 9-313) and the collateral is goods which are or are to become fixtures, then in the office where a mortgage on the real estate would be filed or recorded;

(c) in all other cases, in the office of the [Secretary of State] and in addition, if the debtor has a place of business in only one county of this state, also in the office of ...... of such county, or, if the debtor has no place of business in this state, but resides in the state, also in the office of ...... of the county in which he resides.

Note: *One of the three alternatives should be selected as subsection (1).*

(2) A filing which is made in good faith in an improper place or not in all of the places required by this section is nevertheless effective with regard to any collateral as to which the filing complied with the requirements of this Article and is also effective with regard to collateral covered by the financing statement against any person who has knowledge of the contents of such financing statement.

(3) A filing which is made in the proper place in this state continues effective even though the debtor's residence or place of business or the location of the collateral or its use, whichever controlled the original filing, is thereafter changed.

Alternative Subsection (3)

[(3) A filing which is made in the proper county continues effective for four months after a change to another county of the debtor's residence or place of business or the location of the collateral, whichever controlled the original filing. It becomes ineffective thereafter unless a copy of the financing statement signed by the secured party is filed in the new county within said period. The security interest may also be perfected in the new county after the expiration of the four-month period; in such case perfection dates from the time of perfection in the new county. A change in the use of the collateral does not impair the effectiveness of the original filing.]

(4) The rules stated in Section 9-103 determine whether filing is necessary in this state.

(5) Notwithstanding the preceding subsections, and subject to subsection (3) of Section 9-302, the proper place to file in order to perfect a security interest in collateral, including fixtures, of a transmitting utility is the office

of the [Secretary of State]. This filing constitutes a fixture filing (Section 9-313) as to the collateral described therein which is or is to become fixtures.

(6) For the purposes of this section, the residence of an organization is its place of business if it has one or its chief executive office if it has more than one place of business.

As amended in 1962 and 1972.

> *See Appendix II for changes made in former text and the reasons for change.*

> **Note:** *Subsection (6) should be used only if the state chooses the Second or Third Alternative Subsection (1).*

§ 9-402. Formal Requisites of Financing Statement; Amendments; Mortgage as Financing Statement

(1) A financing statement is sufficient if it gives the names of the debtor and the secured party, is signed by the debtor, gives an address of the secured party from which information concerning the security interest may be obtained, gives a mailing address of the debtor and contains a statement indicating the types, or describing the items, of collateral. A financing statement may be filed before a security agreement is made or a security interest otherwise attaches. When the financing statement covers crops growing or to be grown, the statement must also contain a description of the real estate concerned. When the financing statement covers timber to be cut or covers minerals or the like (including oil and gas) or accounts subject to subsection (5) of Section 9-103, or when the financing statement is filed as a fixture filing (Section 9-313) and the collateral is goods which are or are to become fixtures, the statement must also comply with subsection (5). A copy of the security agreement is sufficient as a financing statement if it contains the above information and is signed by the debtor. A carbon, photographic or other reproduction of a security agreement or a financing statement is sufficient as a financing statement if the security agreement so provides or if the original has been filed in this state.

(2) A financing statement which otherwise complies with subsection (1) is sufficient when it is signed by the secured party instead of the debtor if it is filed to perfect a security interest in

    (a) collateral already subject to a security interest in another jurisdiction when it is brought into this state, or when the debtor's location is changed to this state. Such a financing statement must state that the collateral was brought into this state or that the debtor's location was changed to this state under such circumstances; or

    (b) proceeds under Section 9-306 if the security interest in the original collateral was perfected. Such a financing statement must describe the original collateral; or

    (c) collateral as to which the filing has lapsed; or

    (d) collateral acquired after a change of name, identity or corporate structure of the debtor (subsection (7)).

(3) A form substantially as follows is sufficient to comply with subsection (1):

Name of debtor (or assignor) ....

Address ....

Name of secured party (or assignee) ....

Address ....

1. This financing statement covers the following types (or items) of property:

   (Describe) ....

2. (If collateral is crops) The above described crops are growing or are to be grown on:

   (Describe Real Estate) ....

3. (If applicable) The above goods are to become fixtures on*

   (Describe Real Estate) .... and this financing statement is to be filed [for record] in the real estate records. (If the debtor does not have an interest of record) The name of a record owner is ....

4. (If products of collateral are claimed) Products of the collateral are also covered.

(use whichever is applicable) } ....
Signature of Debtor (or Assignor)
....
Signature of Secured Party (or Assignee)

(4) A financing statement may be amended by filing a writing signed by both the debtor and the secured party. An amendment does not extend the period of effectiveness of a financing statement. If any amendment adds collateral, it is effective as to the added collateral only from the filing date of the amendment. In this Article, unless the context otherwise requires, the term "financing statement" means the original financing statement and any amendments.

(5) A financing statement covering timber to be cut or covering minerals or the like (including oil and gas) or accounts subject to subsection (5) of Section 9-103, or a financing statement filed as a fixture filing (Section 9-313) where the debtor is not a transmitting utility, must show that it covers this type of collateral, must recite that it is to be filed [for record] in the real estate records, and the financing statement must contain a description of the real estate [sufficient if it were contained in a mortgage of the real estate to give constructive notice of the mortgage under the law of this state]. If the debtor does not have an interest of record in the real estate, the financing statement must show the name of a record owner.

(6) A mortgage is effective as a financing statement filed as a fixture filing from the date of its recording if

(a) the goods are described in the mortgage by item or type; and

---

*Where appropriate substitute either "The above timber is standing on ...." or "The above minerals or the like (including oil and gas) or accounts will be financed at the wellhead or minehead of the well or mine located on ...."

(b) the goods are or are to become fixtures related to the real estate described in the mortgage; and

(c) the mortgage complies with the requirements for a financing statement in this section other than a recital that it is to be filed in the real estate records; and

(d) the mortgage is duly recorded. No fee with reference to the financing statement is required other than the regular recording and satisfaction fees with respect to the mortgage.

(7) A financing statement sufficiently shows the name of the debtor if it gives the individual, partnership or corporate name of the debtor, whether or not it adds other trade names or names of partners. Where the debtor so changes his name or in the case of an organization its name, identity or corporate structure that a filed financing statement becomes seriously misleading, the filing is not effective to perfect a security interest in collateral acquired by the debtor more than four months after the change, unless a new appropriate financing statement is filed before the expiration of that time. A filed financing statement remains effective with respect to collateral transferred by the debtor even though the secured party knows of or consents to the transfer.

(8) A financing statement substantially complying with the requirements of this section is effective even though it contains minor errors which are not seriously misleading.

As amended in 1972.

§ 9-403. What Constitutes Filing; Duration of Filing; Effect of Lapsed Filing; Duties of Filing Officer

(1) Presentation for filing of a financing statement and tender of the filing fee or acceptance of the statement by the filing officer constitutes filing under this Article.

(2) Except as provided in subsection (6) a filed financing statement is effective for a period of five years from the date of filing. The effectiveness of a filed financing statement lapses on the expiration of the five year period unless a continuation statement is filed prior to the lapse. If a security interest perfected by filing exists at the time insolvency proceedings are commenced by or against the debtor, the security interest remains perfected until termination of the insolvency proceedings and thereafter for a period of sixty days or until expiration of the five year period, whichever occurs later. Upon lapse the security interest becomes unperfected, unless it is perfected without filing. If the security interest becomes unperfected upon lapse, it is deemed to have been unperfected as against a person who became a purchaser or lien creditor before lapse.

(3) A continuation statement may be filed by the secured party within six months prior to the expiration of the five year period specified in subsection (2). Any such continuation statement must be signed by the secured party, identify the original statement by file number and state that the original statement is still effective. A continuation statement signed by a person other

than the secured party of record must be accompanied by a separate written statement of assignment signed by the secured party of record and complying with subsection (2) of Section 9-405, including payment of the required fee. Upon timely filing of the continuation statement, the effectiveness of the original statement is continued for five years after the last date to which the filing was effective whereupon it lapses in the same manner as provided in subsection (2) unless another continuation statement is filed prior to such lapse. Succeeding continuation statements may be filed in the same manner to continue the effectiveness of the original statement. Unless a statute on disposition of public records provides otherwise, the filing officer may remove a lapsed statement from the files and destroy it immediately if he has retained a microfilm or other photographic record, or in other cases after one year after the lapse. The filing officer shall so arrange matters by physical annexation of financing statements to continuation statements or other related filings, or by other means, that if he physically destroys the financing statements of a period more than five years past, those which have been continued by a continuation statement or which are still effective under subsection (6) shall be retained.

(4) Except as provided in subsection (7) a filing officer shall mark each statement with a file number and with the date and hour of filing and shall hold the statement or a microfilm or other photographic copy thereof for public inspection. In addition the filing officer shall index the statement according to the name of the debtor and shall note in the index the file number and the address of the debtor given in the statement.

(5) The uniform fee for filing and indexing and for stamping a copy furnished by the secured party to show the date and place of filing for an original financing statement or for a continuation statement shall be $.......... if the statement is in the standard form prescribed by the [Secretary of State] and otherwise shall be $.........., plus in each case, if the financing statement is subject to subsection (5) of Section 9-402, $....... The uniform fee for each name more than one required to be indexed shall be $.......... The secured party may at his option show a trade name for any person and an extra uniform indexing fee of $.......... shall be paid with respect thereto.

(6) If the debtor is a transmitting utility (subsection (5) of Section 9-401) and a filed financing statement so states, it is effective until a termination statement is filed. A real estate mortgage which is effective as a fixture filing under subsection (6) of Section 9-402 remains effective as a fixture filing until the mortgage is released or satisfied of record or its effectiveness otherwise terminates as to the real estate.

(7) When a financing statement covers timber to be cut or covers minerals or the like (including oil and gas) or accounts subject to subsection (5) of Section 9-103, or is filed as a fixture filing, [it shall be filed for record and] the filing officer shall index it under the names of the debtor and any owner of record shown on the financing statement in the same fashion as if they were the mortgagors in a mortgage of the real estate described, and, to the extent that the law of this state provides for indexing of mortgages under the name of the mortgagee, under the name of the secured party as if he were the mort-

gagee thereunder, or where indexing is by description in the same fashion as if the financing statement were a mortgage of the real estate described. As amended in 1972.

§ 9-404. Termination Statement

(1) If a financing statement covering consumer goods is filed on or after ...., then within one month or within ten days following written demand by the debtor after there is no outstanding secured obligation and no commitment to make advances, incur obligations or otherwise give value, the secured party must file with each filing officer with whom the financing statement was filed, a termination statement to the effect that he no longer claims a security interest under the financing statement, which shall be identified by file number. In other cases whenever there is no outstanding secured obligation and no commitment to make advances, incur obligations or otherwise give value, the secured party must on written demand by the debtor send the debtor, for each filing officer with whom the financing statement was filed, a termination statement to the effect that he no longer claims a security interest under the financing statement, which shall be identified by file number. A termination statement signed by a person other than the secured party of record must be accompanied by a separate written statement of assignment signed by the secured party of record complying with subsection (2) of Section 9-405, including payment of the required fee. If the affected secured party fails to file such a termination statement as required by this subsection, or to send such a termination statement within ten days after proper demand therefor, he shall be liable to the debtor for one hundred dollars, and in addition for any loss caused to the debtor by such failure.

(2) On presentation to the filing officer of such a termination statement he must note it in the index. If he has received the termination statement in duplicate, he shall return one copy of the termination statement to the secured party stamped to show the time of receipt thereof. If the filing officer has a microfilm or other photographic record of the financing statement, and of any related continuation statement, statement of assignment and statement of release, he may remove the originals from the files at any time after receipt of the termination statement, or if he has no such record, he may remove them from the files at any time after one year after receipt of the termination statement.

(3) If the termination statement is in the standard form prescribed by the [Secretary of State], the uniform fee for filing and indexing the termination statement shall be $......, and otherwise shall be $......, plus in each case an additional fee of $...... for each name more than one against which the termination statement is required to be indexed.
As amended in 1972.

§ 9-405. Assignment of Security Interest; Duties of Filing Officer; Fees

(1) A financing statement may disclose in assignment of a security interest in the collateral described in the financing statement by indication in the financing statement of the name and address of the assignee or by an assignment itself or a copy thereof on the face or back of the statement. On presentation to the filing officer of such a financing statement the filing officer shall mark the same as provided in Section 9-403(4). The uniform fee for filing, indexing and furnishing filing data for a financing statement so indicating an assignment shall be $...... if the statement is in the standard form prescribed by the [Secretary of State] and otherwise shall be $......, plus in each case an additional fee of $...... for each name more than one against which the financing statement is required to be indexed.

(2) A secured party may assign of record all or part of his rights under a financing statement by the filing in the place where the original financing statement was filed of a separate written statement of assignment signed by the secured party of record and setting forth the name of the secured party of record and the debtor, the file number and the date of filing of the financing statement and the name and address of the assignee and containing a description of the collateral assigned. A copy of the assignment is sufficient as a separate statement if it complies with the preceding sentence. On presentation to the filing officer of such a separate statement, the filing officer shall mark such separate statement with the date and hour of the filing. He shall note the assignment on the index of the financing statement, or in the case of a fixture filing, or a filing covering timber to be cut, or covering minerals or the like (including oil and gas) or accounts subject to subsection (5) of Section 9-103, he shall index the assignment under the name of the assignor as grantor and, to the extent that the law of this state provides for indexing the assignment of a mortgage under the name of the assignee, he shall index the assignment of the financing statement under the name of the assignee. The uniform fee for filing, indexing and furnishing filing data about such a separate statement of assignment shall be $...... if the statement is in the standard form prescribed by the [Secretary of State] and otherwise shall be $......, plus in each case an additional fee of $...... for each name more than one against which the statement of assignment is required to be indexed. Notwithstanding the provisions of this subsection, an assignment of record of a security interest in a fixture contained in a mortgage effective as a fixture filing (subsection (6) of Section 9-402) may be made only by an assignment of the mortgage in the manner provided by the law of this state other than this Act.

(3) After the disclosure or filing of an assignment under this section, the assignee is the secured party of record.
As amended in 1972.

§ 9-406. Release of Collateral; Duties of Filing Officer; Fees

A secured party of record may by his signed statement release all or a part of any collateral described in a filed financing statement. The statement of release is sufficient if it contains a description of the collateral being released, the name and address of the debtor, the name and address of the secured party, and the file number of the financing statement. A statement of release signed by a person other than the secured party of record must be accompanied by a separate written statement of assignment signed by the secured party of record and complying with subsection (2) of Section 9-405, including payment of the required fee. Upon presentation of such a statement of release to the filing officer he shall mark the statement with the hour and date of filing and shall note the same upon the margin of the index of the filing of the financing statement. The uniform fee for filing and noting such a statement of release shall be $...... if the statement is in the standard form prescribed by the [Secretary of State] and otherwise shall be $......, plus in each case an additional fee of $...... for each name more than one against which the statement of release is required to be indexed.

As amended in 1972.

[§ 9-407. Information From Filing Officer]

[(1) If the person filing any financing statement, termination statement, statement of assignment, or statement of release, furnishes the filing officer a copy thereof, the filing officer shall upon request note upon the copy the file number and date and hour of the filing of the original and deliver or send the copy to such person.]

[(2) Upon request of any person, the filing officer shall issue his certificate showing whether there is on file on the date and hour stated therein, any presently effective financing statement naming a particular debtor and any statement of assignment thereof and if there is, giving the date and hour of filing of each such statement and the names and addresses of each secured party therein. The uniform fee for such a certificate shall be $...... if the request for the certificate is in the standard form prescribed by the [Secretary of State] and otherwise shall be $....... Upon request the filing officer shall furnish a copy of any filed financing statement or statement of assignment for a uniform fee of $...... per page.]

As amended in 1972.

§ 9-408. Financing Statements Covering Consigned or Leased Goods

A consignor or lessor of goods may file a financing statement using the terms "consignor," "consignee," "lessor," "lessee" or the like instead of the terms specified in Section 9-402. The provisions of this Part shall apply as appropriate to such a financing statement but its filing shall not of itself be a factor in determining whether or not the consignment or lease is intended as security (Section 1-201 (37)). However, if it is determined for other reasons that the consignment or lease is so intended, a security interest of the consignor or lessor which attaches to the consigned or leased goods is perfected by such filing.

Added in 1972.

§ 9-501. Default; Procedure When Security Agreement Covers Both Real and Personal Property

(1) When a debtor is in default under a security agreement, a secured party has the rights and remedies provided in this Part and except as limited by subsection (3) those provided in the security agreement. He may reduce his claim to judgment, foreclose or otherwise enforce the security interest by any available judicial procedure. If the collateral is documents the secured party may proceed either as to the documents or as to the goods covered thereby. A secured party in possession has the rights, remedies and duties provided in Section 9-207. The rights and remedies referred to in this subsection are cumulative.

(2) After default, the debtor has the rights and remedies provided in this Part, those provided in the security agreement and those provided in Section 9-207.

(3) To the extent that they give rights to the debtor and impose duties on the secured party, the rules stated in the subsections referred to below may not be waived or varied except as provided with respect to compulsory disposition of collateral (subsection (3) of Section 9-504 and Section 9-505) and with respect to redemption of collateral (Section 9-506) but the parties may by agreement determine the standards by which the fulfillment of these rights and duties is to be measured if such standards are not manifestly unreasonable:

  (a) subsection (2) of Section 9-502 and subsection (2) of Section 9-504 insofar as they require accounting for surplus proceeds of collateral;
  (b) subsection (3) of Section 9-504 and subsection (1) of Section 9-505 which deal with disposition of collateral;
  (c) subsection (2) of Section 9-505 which deals with acceptance of collateral as discharge of obligation;
  (d) Section 9-506 which deals with redemption of collateral; and
  (e) subsection (1) of Section 9-507 which deals with the secured party's liability for failure to comply with this Part.

(4) If the security agreement covers both real and personal property, the secured party may proceed under this Part as to the personal property or he may proceed as to both the real and the personal property in accordance with his rights and remedies in respect of the real property in which case the provisions of this Part do not apply.

(5) When a secured party has reduced his claim to judgment the lien of any levy which may be made upon his collateral by virtue of any execution based upon the judgment shall relate back to the date of the perfection of the security interest in such collateral. A judicial sale, pursuant to such execution, is a foreclosure of the security interest by judicial procedure within the meaning of this section, and the secured party may purchase at the sale and thereafter hold the collateral free of any other requirements of this Article.
As amended in 1972.

§ 9-502. Collection Rights of Secured Party

(1) When so agreed and in any event on default the secured party is entitled to notify an account debtor or the obligor on an instrument to make payment to him whether or not the assignor was theretofore making collections on the collateral, and also to take control of any proceeds to which he is entitled under Section 9-306.

(2) A secured party who by agreement is entitled to charge back uncollected collateral or otherwise to full or limited recourse against the debtor and who undertakes to collect from the account debtors or obligors must proceed in a commercially reasonable manner and may deduct his reasonable expenses of realization from the collections. If the security agreement secures an indebtedness, the secured party must account to the debtor for any surplus, and unless otherwise agreed, the debtor is liable for any deficiency. But, if the underlying transaction was a sale of accounts or chattel paper, the debtor is entitled to any surplus or is liable for any deficiency only if the security agreement so provides.

As amended in 1972.

§ 9-503. Secured Party's Right to Take Possession After Default

Unless otherwise agreed a secured party has on default the right to take possession of the collateral. In taking possession a secured party may proceed without judicial process if this can be done without breach of the peace or may proceed by action. If the security agreement so provides the secured party may require the debtor to assemble the collateral and make it available to the secured party at a place to be designated by the secured party which is reasonably convenient to both parties. Without removal a secured party may render equipment unusable, and may dispose of collateral on the debtor's premises under Section 9-504.

§ 9-504. Secured Party's Right to Dispose of Collateral After Default; Effect of Disposition

(1) A secured party after default may sell, lease or otherwise dispose of any or all of the collateral in its then condition or following any commercially reasonable preparation or processing. Any sale of goods is subject to the Article on Sales (Article 2). The proceeds of disposition shall be applied in the order following to

   (a) the reasonable expenses of retaking, holding, preparing for sale or lease, selling, leasing and the like and, to the extent provided for in the agreement and not prohibited by law, the reasonable attorneys' fees and legal expenses incurred by the secured party;

   (b) the satisfaction of indebtedness secured by the security interest under which the disposition is made;

   (c) the satisfaction of indebtedness secured by any subordinate security interest in the collateral if written notification of demand therefor is received before distribution of the proceeds is completed. If requested by the secured party, the holder of a subordinate security interest must seasonably furnish reasonable proof of his interest, and unless he does so, the secured party need not comply with his demand.

(2) If the security interest secures an indebtedness, the secured party must account to the debtor for any surplus, and, unless otherwise agreed, the debtor is liable for any deficiency. But if the underlying transaction was a sale of accounts or chattel paper, the debtor is entitled to any surplus or is liable for any deficiency only if the security agreement so provides.

(3) Disposition of the collateral may be by public or private proceedings and may be made by way of one or more contracts. Sale or other disposition may be as a unit or in parcels and at any time and place and on any terms but every aspect of the disposition including the method, manner, time, place and terms must be commercially reasonable. Unless collateral is perishable or threatens to decline speedily in value or is of a type customarily sold on a recognized market, reasonable notification of the time and place of any public sale or reasonable notification of the time after which any private sale or other intended disposition is to be made shall be sent by the secured party to the debtor, if he has not signed after default a statement renouncing or modifying his right to notification of sale. In the case of consumer goods no other notification need be sent. In other cases notification shall be sent to any other secured party from whom the secured party has received (before sending his notification to the debtor or before the debtor's renunciation of his rights) written notice of a claim of an interest in the collateral. The secured party may buy at any public sale and if the collateral is of a type customarily sold in a recognized market or is of a type which is the subject of widely distributed standard price quotations he may buy at private sale.

(4) When collateral is disposed of by a secured party after default, the disposition transfers to a purchaser for value all of the debtor's rights therein, discharges the security interest under which it is made and any security interest or lien subordinate thereto. The purchaser takes free of all such rights and interests even though the secured party fails to comply with the requirements of this Part or of any judicial proceedings

    (a) in the case of a public sale, if the purchaser has no knowledge of any defects in the sale and if he does not buy in collusion with the secured party, other bidders or the person conducting the sale; or

    (b) in any other case, if the purchaser acts in good faith.

(5) A person who is liable to a secured party under a guaranty, indorsement, repurchase agreement or the like and who receives a transfer of collateral from the secured party or is subrogated to his rights has thereafter the rights and duties of the secured party. Such a transfer of collateral is not a sale or disposition of the collateral under this Article.

As amended in 1972.

§ 9-505. Compulsory Disposition of Collateral; Acceptance of the Collateral as Discharge of Obligation

(1) If the debtor has paid sixty per cent of the cash price in the case of a purchase money security interest in consumer goods or sixty per cent of the loan in the case of another security interest in consumer goods, and has not signed after default a statement renouncing or modifying his rights under this Part a secured party who has taken possession of collateral must dispose of it under Section 9-504 and if he fails to do so within ninety days after he takes possession the debtor at his option may recover in conversion or under Section 9-507(1) on secured party's liability.

(2) In any other case involving consumer goods or any other collateral a secured party in possession may, after default, propose to retain the collateral in satisfaction of the obligation. Written notice of such proposal shall be sent to the debtor if he has not signed after default a statement renouncing or modifying his rights under this subsection. In the case of consumer goods no other notice need be given. In other cases notice shall be sent to any other secured party from whom the secured party has received before sending his notice to the debtor or before the debtor's renunciation of his rights) written notice of a claim of an interest in the collateral. If the secured party receives objection in writing from a person entitled to receive notification within twenty-one days after the notice was sent, the secured party must dispose of the collateral under Section 9-504. In the absence of such written objection the secured party may retain the collateral in satisfaction of the debtor's obligation.

As amended in 1972.

§ 9-506. Debtor's Right to Redeem Collateral

At any time before the secured party has disposed of collateral or entered into a contract for its disposition under Section 9-504 or before the obligation has been discharged under Section 9-505(2) the debtor or any other secured party may unless otherwise agreed in writing after default redeem the collateral by tendering fulfillment of all obligations secured by the collateral as well as the expenses reasonably incurred by the secured party in retaking, holding and preparing the collateral for disposition, in arranging for the sale, and to the extent provided in the agreement and not prohibited by law, his reasonable attorneys' fees and legal expenses.

§ 9-507. Secured Party's Liability for Failure to Comply With This Part

(1) If it is established that the secured party is not proceeding in accordance with the provisions of this Part disposition may be ordered or restrained on appropriate terms and conditions. If the disposition has occurred the debtor or any person entitled to notification or whose security interest has been made known to the secured party prior to the disposition has a right to recover from the secured party any loss caused by a failure to comply with the provisions of this Part. If the collateral is consumer goods, the debtor has a right to recover in any event an amount not less than the credit service charge plus ten per

cent of the principal amount of the debt or the time price differential plus 10 per cent of the cash price.

(2) The fact that a better price could have been obtained by a sale at a different time or in a different method from that selected by the secured party is not of itself sufficient to establish that the sale was not made in a commercially reasonable manner. If the secured party either sells the collateral in the usual manner in any recognized market therefor or if he sells at the price current in such market at the time of his sale or if he has otherwise sold in conformity with reasonable commercial practices among dealers in the type of property sold he has sold in a commercially reasonable manner. The principles stated in the two preceding sentences with respect to sales also apply as may be appropriate to other types of disposition. A disposition which has been approved in any judicial proceeding or by any bona fide creditors' committee or representative of creditors shall conclusively be deemed to be commercially reasonable, but this sentence does not indicate that any such approval must be obtained in any case nor does it indicate that any disposition not so approved is not commercially reasonable.

UNITED NATIONS CONVENTION ON CONTRACTS FOR THE INTERNATIONAL SALE OF GOODS

THE STATES PARTIES TO THIS CONVENTION,

BEARING IN MIND the broad objectives in the resolutions adopted by the sixth special session of the General Assembly of the United Nations on the establishment of a New International Economic Order,

CONSIDERING that the development of international trade on the basis of equality and mutual benefit is an important element in promoting friendly relations among States,

BEING OF THE OPINION that the adoption of uniform rules which govern contracts for the international sale of goods and take into account the different social, economic and legal systems would contribute to the removal of legal barriers in international trade and promote the development of international trade,

HAVE AGREED as follows:

PART I. SPHERE OF APPLICATION AND GENERAL PROVISIONS

Chapter I. SPHERE OF APPLICATION

Article 1

(1) This Convention applies to contracts of sale of goods between parties whose places of business are in different States:

(a) when the States are Contracting States; or

(b) when the rules of private international law lead to the application of the law of a Contracting State.

(2) The fact that the parties have their places of business in different States is to be disregarded whenever this fact does not appear either from the contract or from any dealings between, or from information disclosed by, the parties at any time before or at the conclusion of the contract.

(3) Neither the nationality of the parties nor the civil or commercial character of the parties or of the contract is to be taken into consideration in determining the application of this Convention.

Article 2

This Convention does not apply to sales:

(a) of goods bought for personal, family or household use, unless the seller, at any time before or at the conclusion of the contract, neither knew nor ought to have known that the goods were bought for any such use;

(b) by auction;

(c) on execution or otherwise by authority of law;

(d) of stocks, shares, investment securities, negotiable instruments or money;

(e) of ships, vessels, hovercraft or aircraft;

(f) of electricity.

Article 3

(1) Contracts for the supply of goods to be manufactured or produced are to be considered sales unless the party who orders the goods undertakes to supply a substantial part of the materials necessary for such manufacture or production.

(2) This Convention does not apply to contracts in which the preponderant part of the obligations of the party who furnishes the goods consists in the supply of labour or other services.

Article 4

This Convention governs only the formation of the contract of sale and the rights and obligations of the seller and the buyer arising from such a contract. In particular, except as otherwise expressly provided in this Convention, it is not concerned with:

(a) the validity of the contract or of any of its provisions or of any usage;

(b) the effect which the contract may have on the property in the goods sold.

Article 5

This Convention does not apply to the liability of the seller for death or personal injury caused by the goods to any person.

Article 6

The parties may exclude the application of this Convention or, subject to article 12, derogate from or vary the effect of any of its provisions.

Chapter II. GENERAL PROVISIONS

Article 7

(1) In the interpretation of this Convention, regard is to be had to its international character and to the need to promote uniformity in its application and the observance of good faith in international trade.

(2) Questions concerning matters governed by this Convention which are not expressly settled in it are to be settled in conformity with the general principles on which it is based or, in the absence of such principles, in conformity with the law applicable by virtue of the rules of private international law.

Article 8

(1) For the purposes of this Convention statements made by and other conduct of a party are to be interpreted according to his intent where the other party knew or could not have been unaware what that intent was.

(2) If the preceding paragraph is not applicable, statements made by and other conduct of a party are to be interpreted according to the understanding

that a reasonable person of the same kind as the other party would have had in the same circumstances.

(3) In determining the intent of a party or the understanding a reasonable person would have had, due consideration is to be given to all relevant circumstances of the case including the negotiations, any practices which the parties have established between themselves, usages and any subsequent conduct of the parties.

Article 9

(1) The parties are bound by any usage to which they have agreed and by any practices which they have established between themselves.

(2) The parties are considered, unless otherwise agreed, to have impliedly made applicable to their contract or its formation a usage of which the parties knew or ought to have known and which in international trade is widely known to, and regularly observed by, parties to contracts of the type involved in the particular trade concerned.

Article 10

For the purposes of this Convention:
(a) if a party has more than one place of business, the place of business is that which has the closest relationship to the contract and its performance, having regard to the circumstances known to or contemplated by the parties at any time before or at the conclusion of the contract;
(b) if a party does not have a place of business, reference is to be made to his habitual residence.

Article 11

A contract of sale need not be concluded in or evidenced by writing and is not subject to any other requirement as to form. It may be proved by any means, including witnesses.

Article 12

Any provision of article 11, article 29 or Part II of this Convention that allows a contract of sale or its modification or termination by agreement or any offer, acceptance or other indication of intention to be made in any form other than in writing does not apply where any party has his place of business in a Contracting State which has made a declaration under article 96 of this Convention. The parties may not derogate from or vary the effect of this article.

Article 13

For the purposes of this Convention "writing" includes telegram and telex.

PART II.   FORMATION OF THE CONTRACT

Article 14

(1) A proposal for concluding a contract addressed to one or more specific persons constitutes an offer if it is sufficiently definite and indicates the inten-

tion of the offeror to be bound in case of acceptance. A proposal is sufficiently definite if it indicates the goods and expressly or implicitly fixes or makes provision for determining the quantity and the price.

(2) A proposal other than one addressed to one or more specific persons is to be considered merely as an invitation to make offers, unless the contrary is clearly indicated by the person making the proposal.

Article 15

(1) An offer becomes effective when it reaches the offeree.

(2) An offer, even if it is irrevocable, may be withdrawn if the withdrawal reaches the offeree before or at the same time as the offer.

Article 16

(1) Until a contract is concluded an offer may be revoked if the revocation reaches the offeree before he has dispatched an acceptance.

(2) However, an offer cannot be revoked:

(a) if it indicates, whether by stating a fixed time for acceptance or otherwise, that it is irrevocable; or

(b) if it was reasonable for the offeree to rely on the offer as being irrevocable and the offeree has acted in reliance on the offer.

Article 17

An offer, even if it is irrevocable, is terminated when a rejection reaches the offeror.

Article 18

(1) A statement made by or other conduct of the offeree indicating assent to an offer is an acceptance. Silence or inactivity does not in itself amount to acceptance.

(2) An acceptance of an offer becomes effective at the moment the indication of assent reaches the offeror. An acceptance is not effective if the indication of assent does not reach the offeror within the time he has fixed or, if no time is fixed, within a reasonable time, due account being taken of the circumstances of the transaction, including the rapidity of the means of communication employed by the offeror. An oral offer must be accepted immediately unless the circumstances indicate otherwise.

(3) However, if, by virtue of the offer or as a result of practices which the parties have established between themselves or of usage, the offeree may indicate assent by performing an act, such as one relating to the dispatch of the goods or payment of the price, without notice to the offeror, the acceptance is effective at the moment the act is performed, provided that the act is performed within the period of time laid down in the preceding paragraph.

Article 19

(1) A reply to an offer which purports to be an acceptance but contains additions, limitations or other modifications is a rejection of the offer and constitutes a counter-offer.

(2) However, a reply to an offer which purports to be an acceptance but contains additional or different terms which do not materially alter the terms of the offer constitutes an acceptance, unless the offeror, without undue delay, objects orally to the discrepancy or dispatches a notice to that effect. If he does not so object, the terms of the contract are the terms of the offer with the modifications contained in the acceptance.

(3) Additional or different terms relating, among other things, to the price, payment, quality and quantity of the goods, place and time of delivery, extent of one party's liability to the other or the settlement of disputes are considered to alter the terms of the offer materially.

Article 20

(1) A period of time for acceptance fixed by the offeror in a telegram or a letter begins to run from the moment the telegram is handed in for dispatch or from the date shown on the letter or, if no such date is shown, from the date shown on the envelope. A period of time for acceptance fixed by the offeror by telephone, telex or other means of instantaneous communication, begins to run from the moment that the offer reaches the offeree.

(2) Official holidays or non-business days occurring during the period for acceptance are included in calculating the period. However, if a notice of acceptance cannot be delivered at the address of the offeror on the last day of the period because that day falls on an official holiday or a non-business day at the place of business of the offeror, the period is extended until the first business day which follows.

Article 21

(1) A late acceptance is nevertheless effective as an acceptance if without delay the offeror orally so informs the offeree or dispatches a notice to that effect.

(2) If a letter or other writing containing a late acceptance shows that it has been sent in such circumstances that if its transmission had been normal it would have reached the offeror in due time, the late acceptance is effective as an acceptance unless, without delay, the offeror orally informs the offeree that he considers his offer as having lapsed or dispatches a notice to that effect.

Article 22

An acceptance may be withdrawn if the withdrawal reaches the offeror before or at the same time as the acceptance would have become effective.

Article 23

A contract is concluded at the moment when an acceptance of an offer becomes effective in accordance with the provisions of this Convention.

Article 24

For the purposes of this Part of the Convention, an offer, declaration of acceptance or any other indication of intention "reaches" the addressee when it is made orally to him or delivered by any other means to him personally, to his place of business or mailing address or, if he does not have a place of business or mailing address, to his habitual residence.

PART III.   SALE OF GOODS

Chapter I.   GENERAL PROVISIONS

Article 25

A breach of contract committed by one of the parties is fundamental if it results in such detriment to the other party as substantially to deprive him of what he is entitled to expect under the contract, unless the party in breach did not foresee and a reasonable person of the same kind in the same circumstances would not have foreseen such a result.

Article 26

A declaration of avoidance of the contract is effective only if made by notice to the other party.

Article 27

Unless otherwise expressly provided in this Part of the Convention, if any notice, request or other communication is given or made by a party in accordance with this Part and by means appropriate in the circumstances, a delay or error in the transmission of the communication or its failure to arrive does not deprive that party of the right to rely on the communication.

Article 28

If, in accordance with the provisions of this Convention, one party is entitled to require performance of any obligation by the other party, a court is not bound to enter a judgement for specific performance unless the court would do so under its own law in respect of similar contracts of sale not governed by this Convention.

Article 29

(1) A contract may be modified or terminated by the mere agreement of the parties.

(2) A contract in writing which contains a provision requiring any modification or termination by agreement to be in writing may not be otherwise modified or terminated by agreement. However, a party may be precluded by his conduct from asserting such a provision to the extent that the other party has relied on that conduct.

Chapter II.   OBLIGATIONS OF THE SELLER

Article 30

The seller must deliver the goods, hand over any documents relating to them and transfer the property in the goods, as required by the contract and this Convention.

Section I. <u>Delivery of the goods and handing over of documents</u>

Article 31

If the seller is not bound to deliver the goods at any other particular place, his obligation to deliver consists:

(a) if the contract of sale involves carriage of the goods — in handing the goods over to the first carrier for transmission to the buyer;

(b) if, in cases not within the preceding subparagraph, the contract relates to specific goods, or unidentified goods to be drawn from a specific stock or to be manufactured or produced, and at the time of the conclusion of the contract the parties knew that the goods were at, or were to be manufactured or produced at, a particular place — in placing the goods at the buyer's disposal at that place;

(c) in other cases — in placing the goods at the buyer's disposal at the place where the seller had his place of business at the time of the conclusion of the contract.

Article 32

(1) If the seller, in accordance with the contract or this Convention, hands the goods over to a carrier and if the goods are not clearly identified to the contract by markings on the goods, by shipping documents or otherwise, the seller must give the buyer notice of the consignment specifying the goods.

(2) If the seller is bound to arrange for carriage of the goods, he must make such contracts as are necessary for carriage to the place fixed by means of transportation appropriate in the circumstances and according to the usual terms for such transportation.

(3) If the seller is not bound to effect insurance in respect of the carriage of the goods, he must, at the buyer's request, provide him with all available information necessary to enable him to effect such insurance.

Article 33

The seller must deliver the goods:

(a) if a date is fixed by or determinable from the contract, on that date;

(b) if a period of time is fixed by or determinable from the contract, at any time within that period unless circumstances indicate that the buyer is to choose a date; or

(c) in any other case, within a reasonable time after the conclusion of the contract.

Article 34

If the seller is bound to hand over documents relating to the goods, he must hand them over at the time and place and in the form required by the contract. If the seller has handed over documents before that time, he may, up to that time, cure any lack of conformity in the documents, if the exercise of this right does not cause the buyer unreasonable inconvenience or unreasonable expense. However, the buyer retains any right to claim damages as provided for in this Convention.

Section II. <u>Conformity of the goods and third party claims</u>

Article 35

(1) The seller must deliver goods which are of the quantity, quality and description required by the contract and which are contained or packaged in the manner required by the contract.

(2) Except where the parties have agreed otherwise, the goods do not conform with the contract unless they:

(a) are fit for the purposes for which goods of the same description would ordinarily be used;

(b) are fit for any particular purpose expressly or impliedly made known to the seller at the time of the conclusion of the contract, except where the circumstances show that the buyer did not rely, or that it was unreasonable for him to rely, on the seller's skill and judgement;

(c) possess the qualities of goods which the seller has held out to the buyer as a sample or model;

(d) are contained or packaged in the manner usual for such goods or, where there is no such manner, in a manner adequate to preserve and protect the goods.

(3) The seller is not liable under subparagraphs (a) to (d) of the preceding paragraph for any lack of conformity of the goods if at the time of the conclusion of the contract the buyer knew or could not have been unaware of such lack of conformity.

Article 36

(1) The seller is liable in accordance with the contract and this Convention for any lack of conformity which exists at the time when the risk passes to the buyer, even though the lack of conformity becomes apparent only after that time.

(2) The seller is also liable for any lack of conformity which occurs after the time indicated in the preceding paragraph and which is due to a breach of any of his obligations, including a breach of any guarantee that for a period of time the goods will remain fit for their ordinary purpose or for some particular purpose or will retain specified qualities or characteristics.

Article 37

If the seller has delivered goods before the date for delivery, he may, up to that date, deliver any missing part or make up any deficiency in the quantity of the goods delivered, or deliver goods in replacement of any non-conforming goods delivered or remedy any lack of conformity in the goods delivered, provided that the exercise of this right does not cause the buyer unreasonable inconvenience or unreasonable expense. However, the buyer retains any right to claim damages as provided for in this Convention.

Article 38

(1) The buyer must examine the goods, or cause them to be examined, within as short a period as is practicable in the circumstances.

(2) If the contract involves carriage of the goods, examination may be deferred until after the goods have arrived at their destination.

(3) If the goods are redirected in transit or redispatched by the buyer without a reasonable opportunity for examination by him and at the time of the conclusion of the contract the seller knew or ought to have known of the possibility of such redirection or redispatch, examination may be deferred until after the goods have arrived at the new destination.

Article 39

(1) The buyer loses the right to rely on a lack of conformity of the goods if he does not give notice to the seller specifying the nature of the lack of conformity within a reasonable time after he has discovered it or ought to have discovered it.

(2) In any event, the buyer loses the right to rely on a lack of conformity of the goods if he does not give the seller notice thereof at the latest within a period of two years from the date on which the goods were actually handed over to the buyer, unless this time-limit is inconsistent with a contractual period of guarantee.

Article 40

The seller is not entitled to rely on the provisions of articles 38 and 39 if the lack of conformity relates to facts of which he knew or could not have been unaware and which he did not disclose to the buyer.

Article 41

The seller must deliver goods which are free from any right or claim of a third party, unless the buyer agreed to take the goods subject to that right or claim. However, if such right or claim is based on industrial property or other intellectual property, the seller's obligation is governed by article 42.

Article 42

(1) The seller must deliver goods which are free from any right or claim of a third party based on industrial property or other intellectual property, of which at the time of the conclusion of the contract the seller knew or could not have been unaware, provided that the right or claim is based on industrial property or other intellectual property:
  (a) under the law of the State where the goods will be resold or otherwise used, if it was contemplated by the parties at the time of the conclusion of the contract that the goods would be resold or otherwise used in that State; or
  (b) in any other case, under the law of the State where the buyer has his place of business.

(2) The obligation of the seller under the preceding paragraph does not extend to cases where:
  (a) at the time of the conclusion of the contract the buyer knew or could not have been unaware of the right or claim; or

(b) the right or claim results from the seller's compliance with technical drawings, designs, formulae or other such specifications furnished by the buyer.

Article 43

(1) The buyer loses the right to rely on the provisions of article 41 or article 42 if he does not give notice to the seller specifying the nature of the right or claim of the third party within a reasonable time after he has become aware or ought to have become aware of the right or claim.

(2) The seller is not entitled to rely on the provisions of the preceding paragraph if he knew of the right or claim of the third party and the nature of it.

Article 44

Notwithstanding the provisions of paragraph (1) of article 39 and paragraph (1) of article 43, the buyer may reduce the price in accordance with article 50 or claim damages, except for loss of profit, if he has a reasonable excuse for his failure to give the required notice.

Section III. Remedies for breach of contract by the seller

Article 45

(1) If the seller fails to perform any of his obligations under the contract or this Convention, the buyer may:

(a) exercise the rights provided in articles 46 to 52;

(b) claim damages as provided in articles 74 to 77.

(2) The buyer is not deprived of any right he may have to claim damages by exercising his right to other remedies.

(3) No period of grace may be granted to the seller by a court or arbitral tribunal when the buyer resorts to a remedy for breach of contract.

Article 46

(1) The buyer may require performance by the seller of his obligations unless the buyer has resorted to a remedy which is inconsistent with this requirement.

(2) If the goods do not conform with the contract, the buyer may require delivery of substitute goods only if the lack of conformity constitutes a fundamental breach of contract and a request for substitute goods is made either in conjunction with notice given under article 39 or within a reasonable time thereafter.

(3) If the goods do not conform with the contract, the buyer may require the seller to remedy the lack of conformity by repair, unless this is unreasonable having regard to all the circumstances. A request for repair must be made either in conjunction with notice given under article 39 or within a reasonable time thereafter.

Article 47

(1) The buyer may fix an additional period of time of reasonable length for performance by the seller of his obligations.

(2) Unless the buyer has received notice from the seller that he will not perform within the period so fixed, the buyer may not, during that period, resort to any remedy for breach of contract. However, the buyer is not deprived thereby of any right he may have to claim damages for delay in performance.

Article 48

(1) Subject to article 49, the seller may, even after the date for delivery, remedy at his own expense any failure to perform his obligations, if he can do so without unreasonable delay and without causing the buyer unreasonable inconvenience or uncertainty of reimbursement by the seller of expenses advanced by the buyer. However, the buyer retains any right to claim damages as provided for in this Convention.

(2) If the seller requests the buyer to make known whether he will accept performance and the buyer does not comply with the request within a reasonable time, the seller may perform within the time indicated in his request. The buyer may not, during that period of time, resort to any remedy which is inconsistent with performance by the seller.

(3) A notice by the seller that he will perform within a specified period of time is assumed to include a request, under the preceding paragraph, that the buyer make known his decision.

(4) A request or notice by the seller under paragraph (2) or (3) of this article is not effective unless received by the buyer.

Article 49

(1) The buyer may declare the contract avoided:
(a) if the failure by the seller to perform any of his obligations under the contract or this Convention amounts to a fundamental breach of contract; or
(b) in case of non-delivery, if the seller does not deliver the goods within the additional period of time fixed by the buyer in accordance with paragraph (1) of article 47 or declares that he will not deliver within the period so fixed.

(2) However, in cases where the seller has delivered the goods, the buyer loses the right to declare the contract avoided unless he does so:
(a) in respect of late delivery, within a reasonable time after he has become aware that delivery has been made;
(b) in respect of any breach other than late delivery, within a reasonable time:
(i) after he knew or ought to have known of the breach;
(ii) after the expiration of any additional period of time fixed by the buyer in accordance with paragraph (1) of article 47, or after the seller has declared that he will not perform his obligations within such an additional period; or

(iii) after the expiration of any additional period of time indicated by the seller in accordance with paragraph (2) of article 48, or after the buyer has declared that he will not accept performance.

Article 50

If the goods do not conform with the contract and whether or not the price has already been paid, the buyer may reduce the price in the same proportion as the value that the goods actually delivered had at the time of the delivery bears to the value that conforming goods would have had at that time. However, if the seller remedies any failure to perform his obligations in accordance with article 37 or article 48 or if the buyer refuses to accept performance by the seller in accordance with those articles, the buyer may not reduce the price.

Article 51

(1) If the seller delivers only a part of the goods or if only a part of the goods delivered is in conformity with the contract, articles 46 to 50 apply in respect of the part which is missing or which does not conform.

(2) The buyer may declare the contract avoided in its entirety only if the failure to make delivery completely or in conformity with the contract amounts to a fundamental breach of the contract.

Article 52

(1) If the seller delivers the goods before the date fixed, the buyer may take delivery or refuse to take delivery.

(2) If the seller delivers a quantity of goods greater than that provided for in the contract, the buyer may take delivery or refuse to take delivery of the excess quantity. If the buyer takes delivery of all or part of the excess quantity, he must pay for it at the contract rate.

Chapter III. OBLIGATIONS OF THE BUYER

Article 53

The buyer must pay the price for the goods and take delivery of them as required by the contract and this Convention.

Section I. Payment of the price

Article 54

The buyer's obligation to pay the price includes taking such steps and complying with such formalities as may be required under the contract or any laws and regulations to enable payment to be made.

Article 55

Where a contract has been validly concluded but does not expressly or implicitly fix or make provision for determining the price, the parties are considered, in the absence of any indication to the contrary, to have impliedly made reference to the price generally charged at the time of the conclusion of the contract for such goods sold under comparable circumstances in the trade concerned.

Article 56

If the price is fixed according to the weight of the goods, in case of doubt it is to be determined by the net weight.

Article 57

(1) If the buyer is not bound to pay the price at any other particular place, he must pay it to the seller:
(a) at the seller's place of business; or
(b) if the payment is to be made against the handing over of the goods or of documents, at the place where the handing over takes place.

(2) The seller must bear any increase in the expenses incidental to payment which is caused by a change in his place of business subsequent to the conclusion of the contract.

Article 58

(1) If the buyer is not bound to pay the price at any other specific time, he must pay it when the seller places either the goods or documents controlling their disposition at the buyer's disposal in accordance with the contract and this Convention. The seller may make such payment a condition for handing over the goods or documents.

(2) If the contract involves carriage of the goods, the seller may dispatch the goods on terms whereby the goods, or documents controlling their disposition, will not be handed over to the buyer except against payment of the price.

(3) The buyer is not bound to pay the price until he has had an opportunity to examine the goods, unless the procedures for delivery or payment agreed upon by the parties are inconsistent with his having such an opportunity.

Article 59

The buyer must pay the price on the date fixed by or determinable from the contract and this Convention without the need for any request or compliance with any formality on the part of the seller.

Section II. Taking delivery

Article 60

The buyer's obligation to take delivery consists:
(a) in doing all the acts which could reasonably be expected of him in order to enable the seller to make delivery; and
(b) in taking over the goods.

Section III. Remedies for breach of contract by the buyer

Article 61

(1) If the buyer fails to perform any of his obligations under the contract or this Convention, the seller may:
(a) exercise the rights provided in articles 62 to 65;

(b) claim damages as provided in articles 74 to 77.

(2) The seller is not deprived of any right he may have to claim damages by exercising his right to other remedies.

(3) No period of grace may be granted to the buyer by a court or arbitral tribunal when the seller resorts to a remedy for breach of contract.

Article 62

The seller may require the buyer to pay the price, take delivery or perform his other obligations, unless the seller has resorted to a remedy which is inconsistent with this requirement.

Article 63

(1) The seller may fix an additional period of time of reasonable length for performance by the buyer of his obligations.

(2) Unless the seller has received notice from the buyer that he will not perform within the period so fixed, the seller may not, during that period, resort to any remedy for breach of contract. However, the seller is not deprived thereby of any right he may have to claim damages for delay in performance.

Article 64

(1) The seller may declare the contract avoided:

(a) if the failure by the buyer to perform any of his obligations under the contract or this Convention amounts to a fundamental breach of contract; or

(b) if the buyer does not, within the additional period of time fixed by the seller in accordance with paragraph (1) of article 63, perform his obligation to pay the price or take delivery of the goods, or declares that he will not do so within the period so fixed.

(2) However, in cases where the buyer has paid the price, the seller loses the right to declare the contract avoided unless he does so:

(a) in respect of late performance by the buyer, before the seller has become aware that performance has been rendered; or

(b) in respect of any breach other than late performance by the buyer, within a reasonable time:

    (i)   after the seller knew or ought to have known of the breach; or

    (ii) after the expiration of any additional period of time fixed by the seller in accordance with paragraph (1) of article 63, or after the buyer has declared that he will not perform his obligations within such an additional period.

Article 65

(1) If under the contract the buyer is to specify the form, measurement or other features of the goods and he fails to make such specification either on the date agreed upon or within a reasonable time after receipt of a request from the seller, the seller may, without prejudice to any other rights he may

have, make the specification himself in accordance with the requirements of the buyer that may be known to him.

(2) If the seller makes the specification himself, he must inform the buyer of the details thereof and must fix a reasonable time within which the buyer may make a different specification. If, after receipt of such a communication, the buyer fails to do so within the time so fixed, the specification made by the seller is binding.

Chapter IV. PASSING OF RISK

Article 66

Loss of or damage to the goods after the risk has passed to the buyer does not discharge him from his obligation to pay the price, unless the loss or damage is due to an act or omission of the seller.

Article 67

(1) If the contract of sale involves carriage of the goods and the seller is not bound to hand them over at a particular place, the risk passes to the buyer when the goods are handed over to the first carrier for transmission to the buyer in accordance with the contract of sale. If the seller is bound to hand the goods over to a carrier at a particular place, the risk does not pass to the buyer until the goods are handed over to the carrier at that place. The fact that the seller is authorized to retain documents controlling the disposition of the goods does not affect the passage of the risk.

(2) Nevertheless, the risk does not pass to the buyer until the goods are clearly identified to the contract, whether by markings on the goods, by shipping documents, by notice given to the buyer or otherwise.

Article 68

The risk in respect of goods sold in transit passes to the buyer from the time of the conclusion of the contract. However, if the circumstances so indicate, the risk is assumed by the buyer from the time the goods were handed over to the carrier who issued the documents embodying the contract of carriage. Nevertheless, if at the time of the conclusion of the contract of sale the seller knew or ought to have known that the goods had been lost or damaged and did not disclose this to the buyer, the loss or damage is at the risk of the seller.

Article 69

(1) In cases not within articles 67 and 68, the risk passes to the buyer when he takes over the goods or, if he does not do so in due time, from the time when the goods are placed at his disposal and he commits a breach of contract by failing to take delivery.

(2) However, if the buyer is bound to take over the goods at a place other than a place of business of the seller, the risk passes when delivery is due and the buyer is aware of the fact that the goods are placed at his disposal at that place.

(3) If the contract relates to goods not then identified, the goods are considered not to be placed at the disposal of the buyer until they are clearly identified to the contract.

Article 70

If the seller has committed a fundamental breach of contract, articles 67, 68 and 69 do not impair the remedies available to the buyer on account of the breach.

Chapter V. PROVISIONS COMMON TO THE OBLIGATIONS OF THE SELLER AND OF THE BUYER

Section I. Anticipatory breach and instalment contracts

Article 71

(1) A party may suspend the performance of his obligations if, after the conclusion of the contract, it becomes apparent that the other party will not perform a substantial part of his obligations as a result of:
  (a) a serious deficiency in his ability to perform or in his creditworthiness; or
  (b) his conduct in preparing to perform or in performing the contract.

(2) If the seller has already dispatched the goods before the grounds described in the preceding paragraph become evident, he may prevent the handing over of the goods to the buyer even though the buyer holds a document which entitles him to obtain them. The present paragraph relates only to the rights in the goods as between the buyer and the seller.

(3) A party suspending performance, whether before or after dispatch of the goods, must immediately give notice of the suspension to the other party and must continue with performance if the other party provides adequate assurance of his performance.

Article 72

(1) If prior to the date for performance of the contract it is clear that one of the parties will commit a fundamental breach of contract, the other party may declare the contract avoided.

(2) If time allows, the party intending to declare the contract avoided must give reasonable notice to the other party in order to permit him to provide adequate assurance of his performance.

(3) The requirements of the preceding paragraph do not apply if the other party has declared that he will not perform his obligations.

Article 73

(1) In the case of a contract for delivery of goods by instalments, if the failure of one party to perform any of his obligations in respect of any instalment constitutes a fundamental breach of contract with respect to that instalment, the other party may declare the contract avoided with respect to that instalment.

(2) If one party's failure to perform any of his obligations in respect of any instalment gives the other party good grounds to conclude that a fundamental breach of contract will occur with respect to future instalments, he may declare the contract avoided for the future, provided that he does so within a reasonable time.

(3) A buyer who declares the contract avoided in respect of any delivery may, at the same time, declare it avoided in respect of deliveries already made or of future deliveries if, by reason of their interdependence, those deliveries could not be used for the purpose contemplated by the parties at the time of the conclusion of the contract.

Section II. Damages

Article 74

Damages for breach of contract by one party consist of a sum equal to the loss, including loss of profit, suffered by the other party as a consequence of the breach. Such damages may not exceed the loss which the party in breach foresaw or ought to have forseen at the time of the conclusion of the contract, in the light of the facts and matters of which he then knew or ought to have known, as a possible consequence of the breach of contract.

Article 75

If the contract is avoided and if, in a reasonable manner and within a reasonable time after avoidance, the buyer has bought goods in replacement or the seller has resold the goods, the party claiming damages may recover the difference between the contract price and the price in the substitute transaction as well as any further damages recoverable under article 74.

Article 76

(1) If the contract is avoided and there is a current price for the goods, the party claiming damages may, if he has not made a purchase or resale under article 75, recover the difference between the price fixed by the contract and the current price at the time of avoidance as well as any further damages recoverable under article 74. If, however, the party claiming damages has avoided the contract after taking over the goods, the current price at the time of such taking over shall be applied instead of the current price at the time of avoidance.

(2) For the purposes of the preceding paragraph, the current price is the price prevailing at the place where delivery of the goods should have been made or, if there is no current price at that place, the price at such other place as serves as a reasonable substitute, making due allowance for differences in the cost of transporting the goods.

Article 77

A party who relies on a breach of contract must take such measures as are reasonable in the circumstances to mitigate the loss, including loss of profit, resulting from the breach. If he fails to take such measures, the party in breach may claim a reduction in the damages in the amount by which the loss should have been mitigated.

Section III. Interest

Article 78

If a party fails to pay the price or any other sum that is in arrears, the other party is entitled to interest on it, without prejudice to any claim for damages recoverable under article 74.

Section IV. Exemptions

Article 79

(1) A party is not liable for a failure to perform any of his obligations if he proves that the failure was due to an impediment beyond his control and that he could not reasonably be expected to have taken the impediment into account at the time of the conclusion of the contract or to have avoided or overcome it or its consequences.

(2) If the party's failure is due to the failure by a third person whom he has engaged to perform the whole or a part of the contract, that party is exempt from liability only if:

(a) he is exempt under the preceding paragraph; and

(b) the person whom he has so engaged would be so exempt if the provisions of that paragraph were applied to him.

(3) The exemption provided by this article has effect for the period during which the impediment exists.

(4) The party who fails to perform must give notice to the other party of the impediment and its effect on his ability to perform. If the notice is not received by the other party within a reasonable time after the party who fails to perform knew or ought to have known of the impediment, he is liable for damages resulting from such non-receipt.

(5) Nothing in this article prevents either party from exercising any right other than to claim damages under this Convention.

Article 80

A party may not rely on a failure of the other party to perform, to the extent that such failure was caused by the first party's act or omission.

Section V. Effects of avoidance

Article 81

(1) Avoidance of the contract releases both parties from their obligations under it, subject to any damages which may be due. Avoidance does not affect any provision of the contract for the settlement of disputes or any other provision of the contract governing the rights and obligations of the parties consequent upon the avoidance of the contract.

(2) A party who has performed the contract either wholly or in part may claim restitution from the other party of whatever the first party has supplied or paid under the contract. If both parties are bound to make restitution, they must do so concurrently.

Article 82

(1) The buyer loses the right to declare the contract avoided or to require the seller to deliver substitute goods if it is impossible for him to make restitution of the goods substantially in the condition in which he received them.

(2) The preceding paragraph does not apply:

(a) if the impossibility of making restitution of the goods or of making restitution of the goods substantially in the condition in which the buyer received them is not due to his act or omission;

(b) if the goods or part of the goods have perished or deteriorated as a result of the examination provided for in article 38; or

(c) if the goods or part of the goods have been sold in the normal course of business or have been consumed or transformed by the buyer in the course of normal use before he discovered or ought to have discovered the lack of conformity.

Article 83

A buyer who has lost the right to declare the contract avoided or to require the seller to deliver substitute goods in accordance with article 82 retains all other remedies under the contract and this Convention.

Article 84

(1) If the seller is bound to refund the price, he must also pay interest on it, from the date on which the price was paid.

(2) The buyer must account to the seller for all benefits which he has derived from the goods or part of them:

(a) if he must make restitution of the goods or part of them; or

(b) if it is impossible for him to make restitution of all or part of the goods or to make restitution of all or part of the goods substantially in the condition in which he received them, but he has nevertheless declared the contract avoided or required the seller to deliver substitute goods.

Section VI. Preservation of the goods

Article 85

If the buyer is in delay in taking delivery of the goods or, where payment of the price and delivery of the goods are to be made concurrently, if he fails to pay the price, and the seller is either in possession of the goods or otherwise able to control their disposition, the seller must take such steps as are reasonable in the circumstances to preserve them. He is entitled to retain them until he has been reimbursed his reasonable expenses by the buyer.

Article 86

(1) If the buyer has received the goods and intends to exercise any right under the contract or this Convention to reject them, he must take such steps to preserve them as are reasonable in the circumstances. He is entitled to retain them until he has been reimbursed his reasonable expenses by the seller.

(2) If goods dispatched to the buyer have been placed at his disposal at their destination and he exercises the right to reject them, he must take possession of them on behalf of the seller, provided that this can be done without payment of the price and without unreasonable inconvenience or unreasonable expense. This provision does not apply if the seller or a person authorized to take charge of the goods on his behalf is present at the destination. If the buyer takes possession of the goods under this paragraph, his rights and obligations are governed by the preceding paragraph.

Article 87

A party who is bound to take steps to preserve the goods may deposit them in a warehouse of a third person at the expense of the other party provided that the expense incurred is not unreasonable.

Article 88

(1) A party who is bound to preserve the goods in accordance with article 85 or 86 may sell them by any appropriate means if there has been an unreasonable delay by the other party in taking possession of the goods or in taking them back or in paying the price or the cost of preservation, provided that reasonable notice of the intention to sell has been given to the other party.

(2) If the goods are subject to rapid deterioration or their preservation would involve unreasonable expense, a party who is bound to preserve the goods in accordance with article 85 or 86 must take reasonable measures to sell them. To the extent possible he must give notice to the other party of his intention to sell.

(3) A party selling the goods has the right to retain out of the proceeds of sale an amount equal to the reasonable expenses of preserving the goods and of selling them. He must account to the other party for the balance.

PART IV.   FINAL PROVISIONS

Article 89

The Secretary-General of the United Nations is hereby designated as the depositary for this Convention.

Article 90

This Convention does not prevail over any international agreement which has already been or may be entered into and which contains provisions concerning the matters governed by this Convention, provided that the parties have their places of business in States parties to such agreement.

Article 91

(1) This Convention is open for signature at the concluding meeting of the United Nations Conference on Contracts for the International Sale of Goods and will remain open for signature by all States at the Headquarters of the United Nations, New York until 30 September 1981.

(2) This Convention is subject to ratification, acceptance or approval by the signatory States.

(3) This Convention is open for accession by all States which are not signatory States as from the date it is open for signature.

(4) Instruments of ratification, acceptance, approval and accession are to be deposited with the Secretary-General of the United Nations.

Article 92

(1) A Contracting State may declare at the time of signature, ratification, acceptance, approval or accession that it will not be bound by Part II of this Convention or that it will not be bound by Part III of this Convention.

(2) A Contracting State which makes a declaration in accordance with the preceding paragraph in respect of Part II or Part III of this Convention is not to be considered a Contracting State within paragraph (1) of article 1 of this Convention in respect of matters governed by the Part to which the declaration applies.

Article 93

(1) If a Contracting State has two or more territorial units in which, according to its constitution, different systems of law are applicable in relation to the matters dealt with in this Convention, it may, at the time of signature, ratification, acceptance, approval or accession, declare that this Convention is to extend to all its territorial units or only to one or more of them, and may amend its declaration by submitting another declaration at any time.

(2) These declarations are to be notified to the depositary and are to state expressly the territorial units to which the Convention extends.

(3) If, by virtue of a declaration under this article, this Convention extends to one or more but not all of the territorial units of a Contracting State, and if the place of business of a party is located in that State, this place of business, for the purposes of this Convention, is considered not to be in a Contracting State, unless it is in a territorial unit to which the Convention extends.

(4) If a Contracting State makes no declaration under paragraph (1) of this article, the Convention is to extend to all territorial units of that State.

Article 94

(1) Two or more Contracting States which have the same or closely related legal rules on matters governed by this Convention may at any time declare that the Convention is not to apply to contracts of sale or to their formation where the parties have their places of business in those States. Such declarations may be made jointly or by reciprocal unilateral declarations.

(2) A Contracting State which has the same or closely related legal rules on matters governed by this Convention as one or more non-Contracting States

may at any time declare that the Convention is not to apply to contracts of sale or to their formation where the parties have their places of business in those States.

(3) If a State which is the object of a declaration under the preceding paragraph subsequently becomes a Contracting State, the declaration made will, as from the date on which the Convention enters into force in respect of the new Contracting State, have the effect of a declaration made under paragraph (1), provided that the new Contracting State joins in such declaration or makes a reciprocal unilateral declaration.

Article 95

Any State may declare at the time of the deposit of its instrument of ratification, acceptance, approval or accession that it will not be bound by subparagraph (1)(b) of article 1 of this Convention.

Article 96

A Contracting State whose legislation requires contracts of sale to be concluded in or evidenced by writing may at any time make a declaration in accordance with article 12 that any provision of article 11, article 29, or Part II of this Convention, that allows a contract of sale or its modification or termination by agreement or any offer, acceptance, or other indication of intention to be made in any form other than in writing, does not apply where any party has his place of business in that State.

Article 97

(1) Declarations made under this Convention at the time of signature are subject to confirmation upon ratification, acceptance or approval.

(2) Declarations and confirmations of declarations are to be in writing and be formally notified to the depositary.

(3) A declaration takes effect simultaneously with the entry into force of this Convention in respect of the State concerned. However, a declaration of which the depositary receives formal notification after such entry into force takes effect on the first day of the month following the expiration of six months after the date of its receipt by the depositary. Reciprocal unilateral declarations under article 94 take effect on the first day of the month following the expiration of six months after the receipt of the latest declaration by the depositary.

(4) Any State which makes a declaration under this Convention may withdraw it at any time by a formal notification in writing addressed to the depositary. Such withdrawal is to take effect on the first day of the month following the expiration of six months after the date of the receipt of the notification by the depositary.

(5) A withdrawal of a declaration made under article 94 renders inoperative, as from the date on which the withdrawal takes effect, any reciprocal declaration made by another State under that article.

Article 98

No reservations are permitted except those expressly authorized in this Convention.

Article 99

(1) This Convention enters into force, subject to the provisions of paragraph (6) of this article, on the first day of the month following the expiration of twelve months after the date of deposit of the tenth instrument of ratification, acceptance, approval or accession, including an instrument which contains a declaration made under article 92.

(2) When a State ratifies, accepts, approves or accedes to this Convention after the deposit of the tenth instrument of ratification, acceptance, approval or accession, this Convention, with the exception of the Part excluded, enters into force in respect of that State, subject to the provisions of paragraph (6) of this article, on the first day of the month following the expiration of twelve months after the date of the deposit of its instrument of ratification, acceptance, approval or accession.

(3) A State which ratifies, accepts, approves or accedes to this Convention and is a party to either or both the Convention relating to a Uniform Law on the Formation of Contracts for the International Sale of Goods done at The Hague on 1 July 1964 (1964 Hague Formation Convention) and the Convention relating to a Uniform Law on the International Sale of Goods done at The Hague on 1 July 1964 (1964 Hague Sales Convention) shall at the same time denounce, as the case may be, either or both the 1964 Hague Sales Convention and the 1964 Hague Formation Convention by notifying the Government of the Netherlands to that effect.

(4) A State party to the 1964 Hague Sales Convention which ratifies, accepts, approves or accedes to the present Convention and declares or has declared under article 92 that it will not be bound by Part II of this Convention shall at the time of ratification, acceptance, approval or accession denounce the 1964 Hague Sales Convention by notifying the Government of the Netherlands to that effect.

(5) A State party to the 1964 Hague Formation Convention which ratifies, accepts, approves or accedes to the present Convention and declares or has declared under article 92 that it will not be bound by Part III of this Convention shall at the time of ratification, acceptance, approval or accession denounce the 1964 Hague Formation Convention by notifying the Government of the Netherlands to that effect.

(6) For the purpose of this article, ratifications, acceptances, approvals and accessions in respect of this Convention by States parties to the 1964 Hague Formation Convention or to the 1964 Hague Sales Convention shall not be effective until such denunciations as may be required on the part of those States in respect of the latter two Conventions have themselves become effective. The depositary of this Convention shall consult with the Government of the Netherlands, as the depositary of the 1964 Conventions, so as to ensure necessary co-ordination in this respect.

Article 100

(1) This Convention applies to the formation of a contract only when the proposal for concluding the contract is made on or after the date when the Convention enters into force in respect of the Contracting States referred to in

subparagraph (1)(a) or the Contracting State referred to in subparagraph (1)(b) of article 1.

(2) This Convention applies only to contracts concluded on or after the date when the Convention enters into force in respect of the Contracting States referred to in subparagraph (1)(a) or the Contracting State referred to in subparagraph (1)(b) of article 1.

Article 101

(1) A Contracting State may denounce this Convention, or Part II or Part III of the Convention, by a formal notification in writing addressed to the depositary.

(2) The denunciation takes effect on the first day of the month following the expiration of twelve months after the notification is received by the depositary. Where a longer period for the denunciation to take effect is specified in the notification, the denunciation takes effect upon the expiration of such longer period after the notification is received by the depositary.

DONE at Vienna, this eleventh day of April, one thousand nine hundred and eighty, in a single original, of which the Arabic, Chinese, English, French, Russian and Spanish texts are equally authentic.

IN WITNESS WHEREOF the undersigned plenipotentiaries, being duly authorized by their respective Governments, have signed this Convention.

TABLE OF UNIFORM COMMERCIAL CODE CITATIONS

References are to Sections and Notes

TABLE OF ORIGINAL RESTATEMENT OF CONTRACTS CITATIONS

References are to Sections and Notes

TABLE OF RESTATEMENT (SECOND) OF CONTRACTS CITATIONS

References are to Sections and Notes

TABLE OF CASES

References are to Sections and Notes

A

B

C

O

Index

A

ABUSE OF BARGAIN.
Duress.
Generally, §93.
Illegal bargain.
Generally, §98.
Introduction, §92.
Misrepresentation.
Generally, §95.
Public policy.
Contracts against.
Generally, §98.
Unconscionability.
Generally, §96.
Undue influence.
Generally, §94.

ACCEPTANCE.
Auctions.
When acceptance of offer occurs, §36(A).
Battle of the forms.
See BATTLE OF THE FORMS.
Benefits.
Retention, §51(B).
Bilateral contracts.
Manner of acceptance, §45(B).
Notice, §46(A).
Capacity to contract.
Incapacity.
Termination of power of acceptance, §42(E).
Captions and headings on documents.
Effect as offers, §35.
Common law.
Manner of acceptance, §45(B).
Computation of period of acceptance.
Offers with specified time limit, §41(B).
Conditional acceptance, §48(B).
Conduct.
Assent through conduct, §37.
Convention on contracts for international sale of goods, §152(A)(9).
Continuing power of acceptance.
Offers without specified time limit.
Continuation of power for reasonable time, §41(C).
Acceptance beyond reasonable time effective, §41(C)(1).

ACCEPTANCE—Cont'd
Counter offers.
Battle of the forms.
Section 2-207 of the uniform commercial code.
Solutions, §50(B).
Termination of power of acceptance, §42(D)
Cross offers.
Offers without specified time limit.
Acceptance beyond reasonable time limit.
Cross offers distinguished, §41(C)(1).
Death.
Termination of power of acceptance, §42(E).
Determining whether offer made.
Tests, §34.
Detrimental reliance.
Irrevocable power of acceptance.
Irrevocability through reliance.
Promissory estoppel, §43(E).
Dispatch rule.
Generally, §47(A).
Implied authorization, §47(D).
Interference with normal operation of rule, §47(H).
Modern rationale, §47(B).
Normal operation of rule.
Interference with, §47(H).
Option contracts.
Non-application, §45(C).
Proving acceptance dispatched, §47(F).
Reasonable medium, §47(E).
Proper address and payment of charges, §47(E).
Telephone, teletype or other instantaneous media.
Application of rule to, §47(G).
Breaks in communication, §47(G)(1).
Doubtful offers.
Manner of acceptance, §45(C).
Duration of power of acceptance, §41(A).
Effect of offers, §33.
Equivocal acceptance, §48(C).
Essence of acceptance, §44(A).
Exercise of domain as acceptance, §51(B).
Exercising power of acceptance, §33.
Existence of offer.
Acceptance without knowledge, §44(B).

CAPACITY TO CONTRACT—Cont'd
Voidable contracts.
Infants.
Power of disaffirmance, §23.
Mentally incompetent persons, §25.
Partial lack of capacity, §21.

CHAMPERTY.
Contracts against public policy.
Contracts adversely affecting
administration of justice, §98(H).

CHARITABLE SUBSCRIPTION
AGREEMENTS.
Consideration, §62.
Detrimental reliance, §66(A)(4).

CLASSIFICATION OF CONTRACTS, §14.
Bilateral contracts, §14.
Enforceable contracts, §14.
Express contracts, §19.
Formal contracts, §14.
Implied contracts, §19.
Informal contracts, §14.
Unenforceable contracts, §14.
Unilateral contracts, §14.
Voidable contracts, §14.

COGNITIVE TEST.
Mentally ill persons.
Test of contractual mental competency,
§25.

COHABITANTS.
Contracts against public policy, §98(J).
Intent to contract.
No manifestation of intention about legal
consequences, §31(D).

COMMERCIAL CODE.
General provisions.
See UNIFORM COMMERCIAL CODE.

COMMERCIAL PAPER.
Assignments.
Holders in due course, §141(F)(1).
Waiver of defenses, §141(F)(3).
Uniform commercial code.
Overview of article 3, §11.

COMMON COUNTS.
Enforcement of promises, §3.

COMMON LAW.
Acceptance.
Manner of acceptance, §45(B).
Assignments.
Opposition at early common law,
§135(B)(1).
Circumvention of opposition,
§135(B)(2).
Intervention of equity, §135(B)(3).
Priorities, §142(A).
Assumpsit.
Enforcement of promises, §3.
Implied-in-law contracts, §19.

COMMON LAW—Cont'd
Breach of contract.
Equitable remedies and common law,
§127(A).
Flexible equitable relief, §127(A)(1).
Liquidated damage clauses.
Tests to distinguish from penalties.
Traditional test, §125(B)(1).
Capacity to contract.
Infants, §23.
Married women, §22.
Common counts.
Enforcement of promises, §3.
Covenant.
Enforcement of promises, §2.
Debt.
Enforcement of promises, §2.
Detinue.
Enforcement of promises, §2.
Duress.
Improper threats, §93(B).
Enforcement of promises.
Assumpsit, §3.
Common counts, §3.
Covenant, §2.
Debt, §2.
Detinue, §2.
History, §2.
Slades case, §3.
Implied-in-law contracts.
Assumpsit, §19.
Infants.
Capacity to contract, §23.
Joint and several contracts.
Consequences of liability, §147(A).
Obligors bound jointly, severally, or
jointly and severally, §146(B).
Married women.
Capacity to contract, §22.
Minors.
Capacity to contract, §23.
Mutual assent.
Simultaneous mutual assent, §30.
Offers.
Revocability of offers, §43(A).
Slade's case.
Enforcement of promises, §3.
Sources of law of contracts, §9.
Third party beneficiaries.
Nature and history of contracts, §129(A).

COMMON USAGE.
Conditions, §99(A).

COMPUTERS.
Statutes of frauds.
Electronic files.
Form of memorandum, §74(A)(2).

CONCEPT OF CONTRACT, §1.

CONDITIONS.
Acceptance.
Conditional acceptance, §48(B).

F

FAILURE OF PERFORMANCE.
General provisions.
See PERFORMANCE.
Risk allocation.
Impossibility and impracticability of
performance.
See RISK ALLOCATION.

FAMILY.
Detrimental reliance.
Promises within family, §66(A)(1).

FINAL WRITING.
Contemplated by parties, §32.

FIRM OFFERS.
Convention on contracts for
international sale of goods,
§152(A)(5).
Irrevocable power of acceptance,
§43(C).

FITNESS FOR A PARTICULAR
PURPOSE.
Implied warranties, §100(D).

FORBEARANCE FROM SUIT.
Consideration, §63.
Invalid claims, §63.

FORFEITURES.
Conditions.
Form of expression.
Avoidance of forfeitures.
Interpretation of conditions, §102(B).
Interpretation of conditions.
Avoidance of forfeitures, §102(A).

FORMAL CONTRACTS.
Classification, §14.
Generally, §15.
Letters of credit, §15.
Negotiable instruments, §15.
Recognizance, §15.
Seals.
Contracts under seal, §15.

FORMS.
Battle of the forms.
Bound by what signed, §49.
Convention on contracts for international
sale of goods, §152(A)(11).
Uniform commercial code.
Section 2-207.
Solutions, §50.
Standardized agreements (printed
forms).
Basic problems, §97(A).
Reasonable expectation tests, §97(B).
Restatement of contracts.
Approach, §97(A).

FRANCHISE CONTRACTS.
Illusory contracts.
Notice of termination and good faith,
§57(D)(2).

FRAUD.
Infants.
Misrepresentation of age.
Disallowing power of affirmance, §24.
Misrepresentation.
General provisions.
See MISREPRESENTATION.
Voidable contracts.
Power of avoidance or disaffirmance, §17.

FRAUDS, STATUTE OF.
General provisions.
See STATUTES OF FRAUDS.

FRUSTRATION OF PURPOSE.
Risk allocation.
General provisions.
See RISK ALLOCATION.

FUTURE EXCHANGES.
Contract law and economics.
Economic exchange, §5.

FUTURES.
Contracts against public policy, §98(G).

G

GAMBLING CONTRACTS.
Contracts against public policy, §98(G).

GENTLEMENS' AGREEMENTS.
Intent to contract.
Expression of intention not to be legally
bound, §31(B).

GIFTS.
Consideration.
Bargain and gift motivations combined,
§61(B).
Discharge of contracts.
Methods of discharging, §143(B).
Gratuitous assignments.
Delivery of contract.
Restatement of contracts.
Evidentiary extension, §137(B)(2)(d).
Disclaimer, §137(C).
Generally, §137(B)(1).
History, §137(B)(1).
Revocability, §137(B)(1).
Seals, §137(B)(2)(a).
Symbolic documents, §137(B)(2)(b).
Unsealed nonsymbolic writings,
§137(B)(2)(c).

GOOD FAITH.
Abuse of bargain.
Introduction, §92.
Conditions.
Excuse of condition, §111(D).
Satisfaction of performance.
Good faith standard, §103(B).
Duress.
Threat of civil process, §93(F).
Threat of criminal prosecution, §93(E).